THE SPORTSPAGES
ALMANAC 1992

THE SPORTSPAGES
ALMANAC 1992

THE COMPLETE SPORTING FACTBOOK

Matthew Engel and Ian Morrison

SPORTS PAGES
SIMON & SCHUSTER

A SPORTSPAGES BOOK

First published in Great Britain by
Simon and Schuster Ltd in 1991

Copyright © Matthew Engel and Ian Morrison 1991

SPORTSPAGES
The Specialist Sports Bookshop
Caxton Way
94-96 Charing Cross Road
London WC2H 0JG

Simon & Schuster Ltd
West Garden Place
Kendal Street
London W2 2AQ

Simon & Schuster of Australia Pty Ltd
Sydney

British Library Cataloguing-in-Publication Data available
ISBN 0-671-71080-X

Typeset by Learning Curve, Watford
Printed and bound in Great Britain
by Billing & Sons, Worcester

CONTENTS

INTRODUCTION

Welcome to the third edition of *The Sportspages Almanac*. The first two appear to have attained what is known as cult status: i.e. everyone who bought the book tells the authors how much they love it, but we don't seem to be making any money.

For those unfamiliar with the book, the *Almanac* provides all the trivial information about sport which anyone could possibly need - all the major fixtures for 1992, full details of events in 1991 and the answer to all the obvious questions about sporting history: Who won the Derby in 18—? Who won the FA Cup? Who won the Open golf?

However, it also contains really important sporting information as well: the latest news of shove ha'penny, ear pulling and bog snorkelling. It also reveals the answers to such mysteries as The Case of the Psychiatrist Referee and The Scottish Sprinter and the Packet of Crisps. And it names the most erotic water-jump in Britain.

For those familiar with the book, there is one important change. Since 1992 is Olympic year, all the Olympic champions are listed, for ease of access, in the chapters headed Olympic Games or Winter Olympics instead of under the individual sports. There is also a full schedule for the Games at both Barcelona and Albertville.

The words are again mine, the statistics almost all compiled by the amazing Ian Morrison. Despite his best efforts, the *Almanac* is not yet totally infallible, especially on fixtures: dates and times can obviously be changed, so please double-check. If there are any mistakes that can be eliminated for future editions, please let us know, though not too gleefully. My thanks to those who have written to us this year, particularly our far-flung correspondents who have sent us cuttings, quotes and oddities from the newspapers. More please, especially from foreign and local papers.

Our most special thanks go to our wives, Hilary and Ann, for all their love and help; how they tolerate us, and this book in particular, remains one of life's most enchanting mysteries. Special thanks also to Jo Beerts and her magnificent team at Learning Curve, to Fenella Smart, Richard Wigmore and everyone at Simon & Schuster, to John Gaustad and his staff at Sportspages, to all the helpful sporting officials who patiently answered queries and, for assistance above and beyond the call of duty, to Jeremy Alexander, Steph Fincham, Tony Harper, Richard Lockwood and John Trachim.

We would also like to thank Mike Averis, Peter Bartholomew, Jill Beagley, John Behan, Scyld Berry, Hugh Clark, Roy Collins, Roger Cowe, K Crowley, Dai Davies, Nigel Davies, Peter Donald, Robert Eastaway, Paul Fitzpatrick, Mike Getty, Trevor Grant, Dave Hadert, Colin Hart, Alan Henry, David Irvine, Stephen Jackson, Roger Knox, Tim Lamb, Bryan McAllister, Ceci Magee, Sean Magee, Mark Mansfield, Nick Mason, Bill Matthews, Andrew Nickolds, David Northwood, Steve Perkin, Giles Phillips, Bob Pryce, Andrew Radd, Catherine Reed, Jack Richmond, John Rodda, John Samuel, Mike Selvey, Peter Smith, Sarah Smith, Steve Thorpe, Chris Wallsgrove and Sam Wolfe.

We would like them to share in any credit that might be going. We take the blame, but I expect we will try and palm it off somehow.

Matthew Engel, October 1991
c/o Simon & Schuster Ltd., West Garden Place, Kendal Street, London W2 2AQ

ABBREVIATIONS

List of abbreviations for countries commonly used in this book.

Alb	Albania
Alg	Algeria
Arg	Argentina
Aus	Australia
Aut	Austria
Bah	Bahamas
Bar	Barbados
Bel	Belgium
Ber	Bermuda
Boh	Bohemia
Bol	Bolivia
Bra	Brazil
Bul	Bulgaria
Bur	Burma
Cam	Cameroon
Can	Canada
Chi	Chile
Chn	China
Col	Colombia
Cub	Cuba
Cyp	Cyprus
Cze	Czechoslovakia
Den	Denmark
Dji	Djibouti
Dom	Dominican Republic
Ecu	Ecuador
Egy	Egypt
Eng	England
Est	Estonia
Eth	Ethiopia
Fij	Fiji
Fin	Finland
Fra	France
FRG	West Germany
GB	Great Britain
GDR	East Germany
Ger	Germany
Gha	Ghana
Gre	Greece
Gue	Guernsey
Guy	Guyana
Hai	Haiti
Haw	Hawaii
HK	Hong Kong
Hol	The Netherlands
Hun	Hungary
Ice	Iceland
Ina	Indonesia
Ind	India
IOM	Isle of Man
Ire	Republic of Ireland
Irn	Iran
Irq	Iraq
Isr	Israel
Ita	Italy
Jam	Jamaica
Jap	Japan

Jer	Jersey
Ken	Kenya
Kuw	Kuwait
Lie	Liechtenstein
Lux	Luxembourg
Mal	Malta
Mex	Mexico
Mon	Mongolia
Mor	Morocco
NI	Northern Ireland
Nic	Nicaragua
Nig	Nigeria
NKo	North Korea
Nor	Norway
NRo	Northern Rhodesia
NZ	New Zealand
Pak	Pakistan
Pan	Panama
Par	Paraguay
Per	Peru
Phi	Philippines
Pol	Poland
Por	Portugal
PR	Puerto Rico
Rho	Rhodesia
Rom	Romania
SAf	South Africa
Sco	Scotland
Sen	Senegal
Sin	Singapore
SKo	South Korea
Som	Somalia
Spa	Spain
Sri	Sri Lanka
SRo	Southern Rhodesia
Sud	Sudan
Sur	Surinam
SVi	St Vincent
Swe	Sweden
Swi	Switzerland
Syr	Syria
Tai	Taiwan
Tan	Tanzania
Tha	Thailand
Tri	Trinidad & Tobago
Tun	Tunisia
Tur	Turkey
UAR	United Arab Emirates
Uga	Uganda
Uru	Uruguay
US	United States
USSR	Soviet Union
Ven	Venezuela
VI	Virgin Islands
Wal	Wales
Yug	Yugoslavia
Zai	Zaire
Zam	Zambia
Zim	Zimbabwe

SPORTS ROUND-UP

ANGLING

The North West Association of Sea Angling Clubs advised members not to eat anything they might catch in the Mersey, because of rising mercury levels in the fish. A 150-pound Atlantic bluefin tuna, hooked 80 miles off the New Jersey coast, was found to contain: an elastic ponytail holder, a fishing line, fragments of pens, plastic bags, drinking straws and balloons, several bands used to bind newspapers and two cocaine inhalation straws.

It was reported that the test required to get a licence to fish in Germany was harder than most countries' driving tests. Applicants must answer 45 out of 60 questions correctly and then perform a practical exam.

BEAGLING

Eton boys were barred from exercising the school's beagles without the kennel huntsman after a local woman and her pet mongrel were terrified by 20 dogs. It was considered the worst incident involving the pack since it was unleashed on a Liberal supporter during an election.

BOG SNORKELLING

Sian Evans from Cheltenham took a second off her own record to win the annual bog snorkelling championship at Llanwrtyd Wells in mid-Wales in two minutes 14 seconds. Fourteen competitors completed the 60-yard course cut through a peat bog; a large number of frogs hitched rides on their backs. The field was way below the 50 who took part in 1990; Evans said she did not enjoy it much herself.

BRIDGE

Leading bridge players were reported to be using international tournaments as a cover for smuggling caviar into France, avoiding hundreds of thousands of pounds in import duties.

BUFFALO RACING

Harvey Wallbanger, a 2,000 pound bison from Wyoming, travelled round America taking on horses in 110-yard sprint races. Harvey was reported to do seven seconds from a running start. He won 79 races out of 92.

CHARIOT RACING

Anne Haeckl, an archaelogist digging the ruins of the Roman circus at Carthage, said fans at chariot races inscribed curses against riders they wanted to lose on lead tablets and nailed them near the starting gate.

COCKROACH RACING

Citizens of Omsk, Siberia, have revived the old pastime of coackroach racing in the subways under the roads with five-rouble stakes.

CONKERS

Ivan Potter was disqualified from a pub contest at Castle Donington, Leicestershire for baking his conker in a microwave.

EAR PULLING

One of the events held at the World Eskimo-Indian Olympics at Fairbanks, Alaska. "Strong ears and strong neck, that's what you need," said the champion Joshua Okpik. Other contests at the Games included greased-pole walking and muktuk-eating, in which competitors race each other to finish eating a piece of whale skin.

ELEVATOR SURFING

Edwin Ortiz, 12, became the 14th youth to die in New York over the past seven years by riding on the top of lifts in high-rise blocks and jumping from one to the other. It was reported that a similar craze was popular in Brazil where dozens of kids do similar stunts on the top of commuter trains.

ENTHUSIASM

During Britain's February blizzards, Tim Garner, 20, travelled for six hours from his college at Loughborough to Essex to play an away second division national league squash match for Lingfield. It took him a further 11 hours to get home. He lost in 40 minutes.

FOX HUNTING

Mrs Oney Goschen, senior master of the Hampshire-based Mr Goschen's Hounds, founded by her husband, announced the closure of the hunt because of the spread of suburbia. "We can never have a proper gallop and jump now," she said, "and I'm always worried about the hounds when we get close to a main road."

GAY HAND BAG THROWING

This contest was the highlight of a Gay and Lesbian weekend held at Butlins, Skegness. Undercover reporters from tabloid newspapers came first, third and fourth.

GOOSE FIGHTING

Reported to be newly-popular as a betting sport in Southern Russia. Two ganders hiss and peck at each other but refuse to go for the kill. One surrenders after about 30 minutes. Both of them then usually turn on the crowd and try to grab people by the trousers.

HANG GLIDING

Dr John R Tongue, an American orthopaedic surgeon, said 20 to 30 per cent of people killed hang gliding had intoxicating levels of alcohol in their blood.

HELI-SKIING

Nine skiers were killed in an avalanche in British Columbia, bringing the total to 40 in the last 12 years. Heli-skiers reach remote areas by helicopter and are forced by tour operators to sign waivers of liability.

HUSKEY RACING

Dee Dee Jonrowe lost her chance of victory in the 500-mile Beargrease Sled Dog Marathon across Minnesota when two of her 16 huskies took advantage of a brief stop to start making love to each other.

HOOVERBALL

Hooverball, a cross between volleyball and caber-tossing using a heavy medicine ball, was revived in Washington DC after almost 58 years. The game was pioneered by US President Herbert Hoover (1929-33) who played it at 7am with a 4lb ball most mornings on the South Lawn of the White House. The modern version uses a 6lb ball and has been compared to catching your luggage. "It exercises every major muscle group of the body," said the organiser Tom Walsh, "except the portion of the brain that controls common sense."

JACKAL HUNTING

It was reported that jackals were still protected on the Wenlock Downs, Southern India under a charter of 1900 so they can be hunted in traditional foxy fashion by members of the club at the hill station of Ootacamund ("Snooty Ooty"). However, the jackal is not killed - the hounds are called off at the last moment.

JAI ALAI

Professionals in Florida returned to the courts after a 2-year strike, believed to be the longest in professional sport.

KITE FLYING

A two-day festival in Pakistan left four people dead and 100 injured, through falls, fights or electrocution.

LE MOT JUSTE

A ministerial commission on sporting terminology set up by the French Government recommended new French words to replace anglophone phrases traditionally used in sport in an attempt to preserve the language. A tie-break became *un jeu décisif*; a let *un filet* and to break service *faire la brèache*. In soccer, a corner became *un tir d'angle*.

MARBLES

The Black Dog Boozers of Crawley lost the world title they had held since 1985 to the Moonshiners from Charlwood, Surrey.

MARTIAL ARTS

A crowd invaded the garden of a resident's home at Chigwell, Essex to threaten him and accuse him of pouring acid over their cars after he complained about the noise from their party. Unfortunately, the resident was David "Ticky" Donovan, the British and European karate champion. He broke one partygoer's jaw, sent another flying six feet through the air and knocked another's teeth out. He was acquitted of causing actual bodily harm at Chelmsford Crown Court on the grounds that he had acted in self-defence.

MONOPOLY

Parker Brothers, which has sold 100 million US Monopoly sets since it bought the game from its inventor Charles Darrow in 1935, sued a Californian firm marketing an alleged rip-off game called Cityopoly. "They should go directly to jail," said Arthur Greenbaum, a Parker lawyer.

PORCUPINE RACING

The annual porcupine race at the Baker City miners' jubilee has been banned by the state of Oregon after years of protests by animal welfare activists. A "jockey" trailed each porcupine over a 50-foot course, encouraging it by swatting the ground with a broom. The record stood at 10.5 seconds.

PROFESSIONAL WRESTLING

Promoters claimed a surge in attendance, especially from young people, three years after ITV dropped the pastime from its Saturday schedules because of plummeting ratings. American wrestling, featuring stars like Hulk Hogan, Lex Luger and Ric Flair, gained some of satellite TV's highest ratings. Danny Boy Collins, the 22-year-old British champion, won his 1,634th fight.

RAT OLYMPICS

The US Olympic Committee ordered Kalamazoo College, Michigan to change the name of its annual Rat Olympics. The rats jump hurdles and walk tightropes for the benefit of psychology students learning about conditioning. "It's not the kind of image we want to convey," said an Olympic official.

SCHOOL SPORTS

Fathers in Jordan were barred from watching their daughters take part in sports at school. Abdullah Akaileh, minister of Education and a Muslim fundamentalist, said the ban "would allow girls total freedom to display their skills without embarrassment". "What kind of people does he think we are?" asked an angry father.

A 13-year-old boy ordered home for misbehaviour from a school sports day in Coffs Harbour, Australia came back with a .22 rifle and shot two teachers, critically wounding one, and a girl.

SHEEP RACING

Sheep racing with knitted-wool jockeys was arranged at a theme park in Devon. Contestants included Red Ram, Alderknitti and Sheargar. However, lamb racing, planned to raise money to buy playground equipment at a local school, was stopped in Swindon after the local Animal Welfare Trust called it degrading. "It would only have entailed the lambs running a short distance in little jackets," said the headmistress Fiona Dally. "The shepherd rattles his food bucket just like he does when he calls them into their pen."

SHOVE HA'PENNY

Hurricane Hugo, which devastated large parts of the West Indies, also managed to wreck shove ha'penny leagues in the West of England. The hurricane ruined the arrowroot crop, which meant the arrowroot powder used to make the coins skid across the table had to be imported instead from Thailand. The new Thai arrowroot was a disaster.

"Suddenly coins are sticking and we can't play. It's causing havoc," said Bob Goodman, treasurer of the Radstock and District League. "We've tried everything from snuff and talc to custard powder," said Barrington Whale, landlord of the Apple Tree at Shoscombe near Bath, "but nothing compares. We're all very concerned because it could mean the end of a great old pub game."

SKY-DIVING

The new craze in Tokyo was reported to be indoor sky-diving. For £9 a time people can leap off a narrow ledge into something like a lift shaft and be suspended in midair without a parachute, held aloft by an 80-mile blast of wind from a fan at the bottom.
The American edition of the book *Easy Sky Diving* appeared with the following apology inserted: Page 8 line 7 delete "state zip code" and insert "pull rip cord".

SOLAR POWERED CAR RACING

The start of a Trans-Australia race for solar-powered cars was delayed when it rained in the Northern Territory for the first time in six months. Although several major car makers were entered, the race was won by "Spirit of Biel", a machine shaped like a cockroach and built by Swiss engineering students.

SPORT AND WAR

Gamblers in Haifa, Israel, deprived of their usual football pools because of the Gulf War, grouped together and printed a form in which punters had to predict when Iraq would next fire a Scud, whether it would be aimed at Haifa or Tel Aviv and whether it would be intercepted or not.
The publishers of the magazine *Boxing Illustrated* offered to send copies to the troops in Saudi Arabia; the US army told them the Saudis found pictures of men in shorts obscene. US soldiers were, however, sent portable desert golf courses by James Brown, a New Jersey engineer. The kits included two watering cans to mix oil with sand to make greens. And the 24th Infantry Division founded the Burning Sands Golf and Country Club using empty water bottles in the sand, bamboo tent poles as flags and one wedge.
British Army rugby players in the Gulf had to practise with American footballs because of a shortage of proper balls. The British expats of the Bahrain Rugby Football Club had their team picture taken with everyone wearing gasmasks.
Before an NBA basketball game in Milwaukee, both teams and thousands of fans all joined hands to symbolise unity. Before a college game in Montana, anti-war protesters lay down on the court to delay the start and were pelted with potatoes. An Italian pacifist left Seton Hall University and went back home after being booed off the basketball court for not wearing a US flag on his uniform. A parent complained that a wrestler from Fordson High School in Dearborn, Michigan was wearing Hussein on a warm-up jacket. "She didn't think it was appropriate," said the school's athletic director, "Well, that's the kid's name."
Patty Johnson, a trainer in Iowa, named her new-born filly Bomb Saddam. A US Jockey Club official said about every fifth name requested for a new horse in February and March was Desert Storm, Patriot Missile, Scud Buster or Stormin' Norman.
The 1992 Gulf Cup soccer tournament, due to take place in February, was postponed until September while organisers tried to recover the trophy, won by Kuwait in 1990 and believed stolen by Iraq. The trophy was recovered, not in Baghdad, but in a shop in Ely, Cambridgeshire. The Royal Engineers were believed responsible.

SPORTS ROUND-UP

SUBBUTEO

The junior championship for the south-west of England was won by a 13-year-old Bristol schoolboy called Richard Flicker (*Sun* Nov 22)

SUMO

Chiyonofuji "The Wolf" concluded his illustrious career after a record 1,045 wins and, in accordance with tradition, then ritually cut off his top-knot. Hawaiian-born Ozeki Konishiki became the heaviest-ever sumo when he weighed in for the autumn tournament at Tokyo at 253.5 kilograms (39 stone 11 lbs). Konishiki, who had just got engaged to a 26-year-old Japanese model, said he had drunk too much water during the summer practice tour.

There were reported to be 25 sumo wrestlers active in Britain. According to Syd Hoare, founder of the British Sumo Wrestling Association, they all have trouble with the "mawashi", the fighting belt sumo wrestlers wear. "It takes some getting used to," said Hoare. "As a sumo trainer, you have to put up with spending most of your time with your hands around your fighter's backside."

SURFING

Cornish-based surfers, angry at the state of the sea, formed Surfers Against Sewage and were reported to be gaining 100 new members a week. "It's taking up so much time," said one of the founders Gareth Kent, "it's interfering with our surfing." A Derbyshire-based hairnet firm said its exports to Australia were rising fast, largely because surfers were using them when they came off the beach and used their blow dryers.

TEN PIN BOWLING

John Venturello of Sunrise, Florida rolled a three-game 537 series, an impressive score at any age, shortly after his 102nd birthday. Venturello was reported to be bowling in three leagues a week and averaging more than 140 a game. He rolled a maximum 300 in 1906 then gave up the sport until he retired to Florida 60 years later.

Amanda Guild, 30, was named Bowler of the Week by the Saginaw News, Michigan. Her smiling picture in the paper was seen by a law enforcement official who recognised her as the woman who had fled Tennessee seven months earlier after being indicted on drug-dealing charges. She was arrested at the bowling alley as she stepped up to play her next league game.

TROTTING

Tenor de Baune won his 30th successive race at Vincennes, France, equalling the world record. His attempt to beat it failed when he was beaten in race no 31 by Ultra Ducal.

VELCRO JUMPING

Organised by Jerry Bayliss the landlord of the Criterion Hotel, Napier, New Zealand for the benefit of well-fortified customers, it involves dressing up in a Velcro suit, getting on to a trampoline, leaping as high as possible up a Velcro wall and staying there. The record was 15 feet and Mr Bayliss claimed that no one had rebounded and hurt themselves: "In most cases they stick so well we have to peel them off."

WEIGHT PULLING

Hundreds of Staffordshire bull terriers in Britain were being specially trained to be harnessed to trolleys laden with concrete blocks and obliged to pull up to 50 times their own weight. Lenny, owned by Anthony Keogh, a fork-lift truck driver, won the grand championship in Bootle by pulling 2,016 lb (almost a ton) 15 feet in a minute. Vets said the sport was not illegal nor necessarily harmful though the RSPCA feared connections with dogfighting.

WHIPPET RACING

A whippet called Clever Boy was banned from racing in north-east England because he insisted on turning round and running away from the hare.

WINDSURFING

The Professional Boardsailors Association held a $100,000 championship in an 80 x 30-metre indoor pool at Bercy, near Paris. The competitors had to contend with 25-knot winds produced by turbines lining the pool and a ramp which projected the sailors 12 feet in the air. "The jump ramp's destroying our equipment," said Robby Naish from Hawaii. "We've done $10,000 worth of damage."

AMERICAN FOOTBALL

SOMBRE BUT SENSATIONAL

Superbowl XXV - "the Sombre Bowl" - took place against the background of the air war in the Gulf and thus for once the event had a slightly less exaggerated sense of its own importance. Talk of cancelling the game was finally stopped by Jack Kemp, the former star quarterback and President Bush's Housing Secretary: "I don't believe we should allow a rattlesnake like Saddam to disrupt life," he said.

So soldiers in desert encampments and foxholes 5,000 miles away listened to the showdown in Tampa, creating a moving sense of American unity; even Iraq was sufficiently awestruck not to launch any Scuds for the duration. America forgot its troubles and got one of the great games: the New York Giants beat the Buffalo Bills 20-19 after Scott Norwood missed a field goal for the Bills in the closing seconds.

Though it was the closest Superbowl ever, it was a tactical triumph for the Giants who controlled the ball for 40 minutes 33 seconds, a Superbowl record, and succeeded in their aim in keeping the all-action, no-huddle Bills defending and the opposing quarterback Jim Kelly off the field. The Giants were powered by Jeff Hostetler, a patient understudy to Phil Simms for six years until Simms was injured in mid-season. Hostetler was the first back-up quarterback ever to win a Superbowl.

But the city of Buffalo, where sporting glory comes infrequently, greeted their team like winners. Tens of thousands turned up to see the Bills come home and chanted "We love Scott!" to cheer up Norwood. The Giants were met by only a few hundred and were denied a ticker-tape parade through Manhattan because New York was broke; the club said they did not want to celebrate anyway because of the war. Less than four months after his triumph the winning coach, Bill Parcells, resigned.

The Superbowl itself had been kept lower-key than usual. The traditional 2,000-guest blow-out was scrapped; security arrangements included a ban on the TV blimp; and the scoreboard cartoons were revised, apparently to avoid references to the long, high passes known as 'bombs'.

The San Francisco 49ers had been hot favourites to win an unprecedented third successive Superbowl. Their chance vanished with the last kick of the NFC Championship Game when the Giants' Matt Barr scored his fifth field goal with four seconds left. The 49ers' quarterback Joe Montana - who was still named the League's Player of the Year - finished the game with a broken finger in his right hand. In contrast, the Bills had romped to a 51-3 victory over the Los Angeles Raiders to win their Conference, the AFC. Their ultimate failure emphasised the NFC's current dominance: its teams have now won seven successive Superbowls. The Giants and 49ers dominated the regular season as well. Both won their first ten games and San Francisco equalled the NFL record of 18 consecutive wins.

The scandal-ette of the season occurred in the New England Patriots locker room where several naked players made lewd suggestions to a woman reporter, Lisa Olson. She accused the players of "mind-rape" and the League slapped heavy fines on the players and the club, which was also ordered to pay a further $25,000 for "instructional material on responsible dealings with the media". The Patriots' real punishment was internal confusion and 14 successive defeats. Victor Kiam, the shaver magnate and the club's owner, refused to be appropriately contrite and was forced to apologise yet again when he repeated the Gulf War joke: "What has Lisa Olson got in common with the Iraqis? They've both seen Patriot missiles up close." The National Organisation for Women called him "sexist and inhumane" and Olson sued the Patriots, claiming violation of her civil rights.

The game's genuine scandals, as ever, received less attention. Lyle Alzado, one of the great Oakland Raiders, said he had inoperable brain cancer caused by taking steroids while trying to make a comeback aged 41 in 1990. The cocaine addict Dexter Manley was reinstated and played for the Phoenix Cardinals a year after being banned for life for failing three drugs tests. The star quarterback at the University of Southern California, Todd Marinovich, was arrested for possessing cocaine while other players at USC were said to be buying clean urine to pass drugs tests.

The top college player of the year, Raghib "Rocket" Ismail, actually turned down the NFL and signed a four-year contract worth $25 million with the Toronto Argonauts of the Canadian Football League. The NFL owners announced plans to add two teams in 1994. In the spring, the World League of American football began pitting three European teams against seven from America, using up-and-coming players and paying basic wages of only £10,000. TV ratings in the US were poor but there was an overwhelming response in Europe, and especially in London, where crowds larger than First Division soccer gates regularly turned up at Wembley to watch the Crown Jewels cheerleaders, a great deal of related hoop-la and possibly the football. More than 60,000 went there to see the Monarchs beat the Barcelona Dragons in the inaugural World Bowl and Stan Gelbaugh, their quarterback, lifted the trophy Cup Final style. The loudspeaker played both the team's theme song,"All Right Now", and "Land of Hope and Glory".

For the first time in 60 years, no one in the US died from a football-related injury in 1990; this compares to a total of 69 in the 80's and 154 in the six years 1967-72. The decline was attributed to coaches no longer advising players to tackle by putting their faces in ball-carriers' chests and to better helmets and medical care.

Schools in Denver banned Los Angeles Raiders' silver-and-black colours because they had become associated with gang warfare. Arne Riepe, an exchange student from Germany who had not even seen a game before the season began, kicked a record 85 extra points for Haynesville High School in New Orleans. Claude Dawson Jones, 32, was charged with robbing 24 banks in Sacramento, California, all to finance trips to watch, appropriately enough, the Raiders. A woman in Channelview, Texas was convicted of plotting to kill the mother of a girl who was a rival to her daughter for a place on the high school cheerleading squad. A spectator, Mike Pierce, won a free pizza for all 58,000 people at an Indianapolis Colts game by successfully kicking three field goals during the interval.

——— 1990-91 ———

NATIONAL FOOTBALL LEAGUE (NFL)
FINAL NFL STANDING
American Conference (AFC)

EAST	W	L	T	F	A
1 (1) Buffalo Bills	13	3	0	428	263
2 (2) Miami Dolphins (*)	12	4	0	336	242
3 (3) Indianapolis Colts	7	9	0	282	353
4 (5) New York Jets	6	10	0	295	345
5 (4) New England Patriots	1	15	0	181	446
CENTRAL					
1 (4) Cincinnati Bengals	9	7	0	360	352
2 (2) Houston Oilers (*)	9	7	0	405	307
3 (3) Pittsburgh Steelers	9	7	0	292	240
4 (1) Cleveland Browns	3	13	0	228	462
WEST					
1 (2) Los Angeles Raiders	12	4	0	337	268
2 (3) Kansas City Royals (*)	11	5	0	369	257
3 (4) Seattle Seahawks	9	7	0	306	286
4 (5) San Diego Chargers	6	10	0	315	281
5 (1) Denver Broncos	5	11	0	331	374

National Conference (NFC)

EAST	W	L	T	F	A
1 (1) New York Giants	13	3	0	335	211
2 (2) Philadelphia Eagles (*)	10	6	0	396	299
3 (3) Washington Redskins (*)	10	6	0	381	301
4 (5) Dallas Cowboys	7	9	0	244	308
5 (4) Phoenix Cardinals	5	11	0	258	396
CENTRAL					
1 (4) Chicago Bears	11	5	0	348	280
2 (5) Tampa Bay Buccaneers	6	10	0	264	367
3 (2) Green Bay Packers	6	10	0	271	247
4 (3) Detroit Lions	6	10	0	373	413
5 (1) Minnesota Vikings	6	10	0	351	426
WEST					
1 (1) San Francisco 49ers	14	2	0	353	239
2 (3) New Orleans Saints (*)	8	8	0	274	275
3 (4) Atlanta Falcons	5	11	0	348	365
4 (2) Los Angeles Rams	5	11	0	345	413

Last season's positions in brackets. (*) indicates wild-card berth in play-offs

Play-offs

AFC
First Round
CINCINNATI 41 Houston 14; MIAMI 17 Kansas City 16
Semi-finals
BUFFALO 44 Miami 34; LOS ANGELES RAIDERS 20
Cincinnati 10
Championship Game
BUFFALO 51 Los Angeles Raiders 3

NFC
First Round
WASHINGTON 20 Philadelphia 6; CHICAGO 16 New
Orleans 6
Semi-finals
SAN FRANCISCO 28 Washington 10; NEW YORK
GIANTS 31 Chicago 3
Championship Game
NEW YORK GIANTS 15 San Francisco 13

How the teams reached the Superbowl
NEW YORK GIANTS

Home		Away	
27-20	Philadelphia	28-7	Dallas
20-3	Miami	24-20	Washington
31-17	Dallas	24-7	Indianapolis
20-19	Phoenix	31-7	LA Rams
21-10	Washington	13-31	Philadelphia
20-0	Detroit	3-7	San Francisco
23-15	Minnesota	24-21	Phoenix
13-17	Buffalo	13-10	New England

BUFFALO BILLS

Home		Away	
26-10	Indianapolis	7-30	Miami
29-28	Denver	30-7	NY Jets
38-24	LA Raiders	27-10	New England
30-27	NY Jets	42-0	Cleveland
45-14	Phoenix	24-27	Houston
14-0	New England	31-7	Indianapolis
30-23	Philadelphia	17-13	N Giants
24-14	Miami	14-29	Washington

SUPERBOWL XXV
Tampa, Jan 27

New York Giants   3   7   7   3   -   20
Touchdowns: Baker, Anderson
Points after: Bahr 2
Field Goals: Bahr 2

Buffalo Bills   3   9   0   7   -   19
Touchdowns: D Smith, Thomas
Points after: Norwood 2
Field Goal: Norwood
Safety: B Smith
Attendance: 73,813
Most Valuable Player: Ottis Anderson (Giants)
Anderson is third oldest winner of MVP

SUPERBOWL RECORDS SET IN 1991
1. **Longest time in posession**: 40min 33sec, by New York Giants
2. **Longest touchdown drive:** Giants 14-play, 75-yard drive for Anderson's touchdown lasted 9min 29sec
3. **Narrowest margin of victory**: One point
4. **Fewest turnovers (both teams)**: none

SAN FRANCISCO'S WINNING STREAK
When the 49ers lost to the Los Angeles Rams on Nov 25, 1990 it was their first defeat since Nov 19, 1989 and ended a run of 18 games without defeat, which equalled the all-time NFL record

Most Consecutive Wins
18 Miami Dolphins 1972
18 San Francisco 49ers 1989-90
17 Oakland Raiders 1976
14 Washington Redskins 1942

XXV AND COUNTING

❝My favourite word that I learned from Coach Levy? It was 'pontificate'. He pontificated for 15 minutes on how he was not going to pontificate.❞
Ray Bentley, Buffalo Bill Linebacker

"This isn't a game for well-adjusted people."
Bill Parcells, Giants coach

"I'm sure I will never get to the point in my life where I'll forget what happened tonight."
Scott Norwood after the Super Bowl

"I've never felt more loved than this."
Scott Norwood after returning to Buffalo

"If these guys get to the Super Bowl, I'll push a peanut down Main Street with my nose."
Bob Roberts, Hornell Evening Tribune, on the Bills' chances pre-season

"I didn't scrape my nose too bad."
Roberts, after he kept his promise

"It's not a dream come true. I always knew I was good enough."
Jeff Hostetler

"I can't take this another year.❞
Dolly Hostetler, Jeff's mom

21st AFC-NFC PRO BOWL
Honolulu, Feb 3

AFC   3   0   3   17   -   23
Touchdowns: Reed, Givins
Points after: Lowery 2
Field Goals: Lowery 3

NFC   0   7   7   7   -   21
Touchdowns: Johnson 2, Sanders
Points after: Andersen 3
Attendance: 50,345

1990-91 BOWL GAMES
Raisin Bowl SAN JOSE STATE 48 Cent.Michigan 24 (25,431); *Independence Bowl* LOUISIANA TECH 34 MARYLAND 34 (Tie) (48,325); *Aloha Bowl* SYRACUSE 28 Arizona 0 (14,185); *Liberty Bowl* AIR FORCE 23 Ohio State 11 (13,144); *All American Bowl* NORTH CAROLINA STATE 31 Southern Missouri 27 (44,000);

Blockbuster Bowl FLORIDA STATE 24 Penn State 17 (74,021); *Peach Bowl* AUBURN 27 Indiana 23 (38,912); *Freedom Bowl* COLORADO STATE 32 Oregon 31 (41,450); *Holiday Bowl* TEXAS A & M 65 Brigham Young 14 (61,441); *John Hancock Bowl* MICHIGAN STATE 17 University of Southern California (50,562); *Copper Bowl* CALIFORNIA 17 Wyoming 15 (36,340); *Gator Bowl* MICHIGAN 35 Mississippi 3 (68,927); *Hall of Fame Bowl* CLEMSON 30 Illinois 0 (63,154); *Citrus Bowl* GEORGIA TECH 45 Nebraska 21 (72,328); *Cotton Bowl* MIAMI 46 Texas 3 (73,521); *Fiesta Bowl* LOUISVILLE 34 Alabama 7 (69,098); *Rose Bowl* WASHINGTON 46 Iowa 34 (101,273); *Orange Bowl* COLORADO 10 Notre Dame 9 (77,062); *Sugar Bowl* TENNESSEE 23 Virginia 22 (75,132)

Figures in brackets indicate attendances

Washington collected $6 million for winning the Rose Bowl

Colorado won the College Football National Championship, decided by a poll of journalists

WORLD LEAGUE OF AMERICAN FOOTBALL
Final standings
European Division

	W	L	T	Pct	PF	PA
London Monarchs	9	1	0	.900	310	121
Barcelona Dragons	8	2	0	.800	206	126
Frankfurt Galaxy	7	3	0	.700	155	139

North American East Division

N Y/New Jersey Knights	5	5	0	.500	257	155
Orlando Thunder	5	5	0	.500	242	286
Montreal Machine	4	6	0	.400	145	244
Raleigh-Durham Skyhawks	0	10	0	.000	123	300

North American West Division

Birmingham Fire	5	5	0	.500	140	140
San Antonio Raiders	4	6	0	.400	176	196
Sacramento Surge	3	7	0	.300	179	226

Semi-finals
New York/New Jersey Knights 26 LONDON MONARCHS 42; Birmingham Fire 3 BARCELONA DRAGONS 10

Final
Wembley Stadium, Jun 9

LONDON MONARCHS	7	14	0	0	-	21

Touchdowns: Horton, Crossman, Garrett
Points after: P Alexander 3

Barcelona Dragons	0	0	0	0	-	0

Attendance: 61,108

MVP: Dan Crossman (Monarchs)

THE MONARCHS' REGULAR SEASON MATCHES

Date	Opponents	Result		Attendance
Mar 23	Frankfurt (a)	won	24-11	23,169
Mar 31	NY/New Jersey(h)	won	22-18	46,952
Apr 7	Orlando (h)	won	35-12	35.327
Apr 16	Birmingham (a)	won	27-0	18,500
Apr 20	Montreal (h)	won	45-7	35,294
Apr 28	Raleigh-Durham (h)	won	35-10	33,997
May 6	San Antonio (a)	won	38-15	12,328
May 12	NY/New Jersey (a)	won	22-7	41,219
May 19	Sacramento (a)	won	45-21	21,409
May 27	Barcelona (h)	lost	17-20	50,835

In their game with New York/New Jersey Knights on May 12 the Monarchs registered 14 sacks, beating the old pro football record of 12

Monarchs' scorers (All games)
Touchdowns: 11 John Horton; 10 Jeff Alexander; 7 David Smith; 5 Andre Riley; 4 Tony Sargent; 3 Dana Brinson, Judd Garrett; 2 Dan Crossman, Dedrick Dodge; 1 Victor Ebubedike, Danny Lockett, Pat Davis
Points After: 46 Phil Alexander
Field Goals: 9 Phil Alexander
Leading scorers: 73 Phil Alexander; 66 John Horton; 60 Jeff Alexander; 42 David Smith

TOMORROW THE WORLD . . .

❝We hope our broadcast partners are as patient as we are and are in it for the long-term."
   Mike Lynn, World League president

"This is ridiculous for the money paid. We could get better ratings spending much less money on other things."
   Gordon Beck of the USA cable network

"This league makes sense. They're actually paying the coaches more than the players."
   Larry Kennan, London Monarchs head coach

"We've got great uniforms"
   Marvin Hargrove of the Raleigh-Durham Skyhawks, who lost every game

"Sex, Dragons and Rock n' Roll"
   Banner at Barcelona game

"We're getting paid to play football and see the world. How can you beat that?❞
   Mike Ruth, Barcelona noseguard

WORLD LEAGUE OF AMERICAN FOOTBALL

EUROPEAN CLUBS

Team	Ground	Team
BARCELONA DRAGONS	Montjuic Stadium	Jack Bicknell
FRANKFURT GALAXY	Waldstadion	Jack Elway
LONDON MONARCHS	Wembley Stadium	Larry Kennan

US CLUBS

Team	Ground	Team
BIRMINGHAM FIRE	Legion Field	Chan Gailey
MONTREAL MACHINE	Olympic Stadium	Jacques Dussault
NEW YORK-NEW JERSEY KNIGHTS	Giants Stadium	Mouse Davis
ORLANDO THUNDER	Citrus Bowl	Don Matthews
RALEIGH-DURHAM SKYHAWKS	Carter-Finley Stadium	Roman Gabriel
SACRAMENTO SURGE	Hughes Stadium	Kay Stephenson
SAN ANTONIO RIDERS	Alamo Stadium	Mike Riley

——— CHAMPIONS ———

The National Football League (NFL) has been constituted as follows:
1921-32 One League only; 1933-49 Two divisions (Eastern and Western); 1950-52 Two Divisions and National Conferences; 1953-59 Two Divisions (Eastern and Western Conferences); 1960-69 Two Leagues (American Football League (AFL) and National Football League (NFL); 1970- Two (American Football Conference (AFC) and National Football Conference (NFC)
Play-offs introduced in 1933

Champions:

1921	Chicago Staleys
1922	Canton Bulldogs (Ohio)
1923	Canton Bulldogs (Ohio)
1924	Cleveland Bulldogs
1925	Chicago Cardinals
1926	Frankford Yellowjackets (Philadelphia)
1927	New York Giants
1928	Providence Streamroller
1929	Green Bay Packers
1930	Green Bay Packers
1931	Green Bay Packers
1932	Chicago Bears

NFL Play-off

1933	Chicago Bears	23-21	New York Giants
1934	New York Giants	30-13	Chicago Bears
1935	Detroit Lions	26-7	New York Giants
1936	Green Bay Packers	21-6	Boston Redskins
1937	Washington Redskins	28-21	Chicago Bears
1938	New York Giants	23-17	Green Bay Packers
1939	Green Bay Packers	27-0	New York Giants
1940	Chicago Bears	73-0	Washington Reds
1941	Chicago Bears	37-9	New York Giants
1942	Washington Redskins	14-6	Chicago Bears
1943	Chicago Bears	41-21	Washington Reds
1944	Green Bay Packers	14-7	New York Giants
1945	Cleveland Rams	15-14	Washington Reds
1946	Chicago Bears	24-14	New York Giants
1947	Chicago Cardinals	28-21	Philadelphia Eagles
1948	Philadelphia Eagles	7-0	Chicago Cardinals
1949	Philadelphia Eagles	14-0	Los Angeles Rams
1950	Cleveland Browns	30-28	Los Angeles Rams
1951	Los Angeles Rams	24-17	Cleveland Browns
1952	Detroit Lions	17-7	Cleveland Browns
1953	Detroit Lions	17-16	Cleveland Browns
1954	Cleveland Browns	56-10	Detroit Lions
1955	Cleveland Browns	38-14	Los Angeles Rams
1956	New York Giants	47-7	Chicago Bears
1957	Detroit Lions	59-14	Cleveland Browns
1958	Baltimore Colts	23-17	New York Giants
1959	Baltimore Colts	31-16	New York Giants

AFL/AFC Championship

1960	Houston Oilers	24-16	LA Chargers
1961	Houston Oilers	10-3	S.Diego Chargers
1962	Dallas Texans	20-17	Houston Oilers
1963	San Diego Chargers	51-10	Boston Patriots
1964	Buffalo Bills	20-7	S.Diego Chargers
1965	Buffalo Bills	23-0	S.Diego Chargers
1966	Kansas City Chiefs	31-7	Buffalo Bills
1967	Oakland Raiders	40-7	Houston Oilers
1968	New York Jets	27-23	Oakland Raiders
1969	Kansas City Chiefs	17-7	Oakland Raiders
1970	Baltimore Colts	27-17	Oakland Raiders
1971	Miami Dolphins	21-0	Baltimore Colts
1972	Miami Dolphins	21-17	Pitt. Steelers
1973	Miami Dolphins	27-10	Oakland Raiders
1974	Pittsburgh Steelers	24-13	Oakland Raiders
1975	Pittsburgh Steelers	16-10	Oakland Raiders
1976	Oakland Raiders	24-7	Pitt. Steelers
1977	Denver Broncos	20-17	Oakland Raiders
1978	Pittsburgh Steelers	34-5	Houston Oilers
1979	Pittsburgh Steelers	27-13	Houston Oilers
1980	Oakland Raiders	34-27	S.Diego Chargers
1981	Cincinnati Bengals	27-7	S.Diego Chargers
1982	Miami Dolphins	14-0	New York Jets
1983	Los Angeles Raiders	30-14	Seattle Seahawks
1984	Miami Dolphins	45-28	Pitt. Steelers
1985	New England Pats	31-14	Miami Dolphins
1986	Denver Broncos	23-20	Cleveland Browns
1987	Denver Broncos	38-33	Cleveland Browns
1988	Cincinnati Bengals	21-10	Buffalo Bills
1989	Denver Broncos	37-21	Cleveland Browns
1990	Buffalo Bills	51-3	LA Raiders

NFL/NFC Championship

1960	Philadelphia Eagles	17-13	Green Bay Packers
1961	Green Bay Packers	37-0	New York Giants
1962	Green Bay Packers	16-7	New York Giants
1963	Chicago Bears	14-10	New York Giants
1964	Cleveland Browns	27-0	Baltimore Colts
1965	Green Bay Packers	23-12	Cleveland Browns
1966	Green Bay Packers	34-27	Dallas Cowboys
1967	Green Bay Packers	21-17	Dallas Cowboys
1968	Baltimore Colts	34-0	Cleveland Browns
1969	Minnesota Vikings	27-7	Cleveland Browns
1970	Dallas Cowboys	17-10	San Fran 49ers
1971	Dallas Cowboys	14-3	San Fran 49ers
1972	Washington Redskins	26-3	Dallas Cowboys
1973	Minnesota Vikings	27-10	Dallas Cowboys
1974	Minnesota Vikings	14-10	Los Angeles Rams
1975	Dallas Cowboys	37-7	Los Angeles Rams
1976	Minnesota Vikings	24-13	Los Angeles Rams
1977	Dallas Cowboys	23-6	Minnesota Vikings
1978	Dallas Cowboys	28-0	Los Angeles Rams
1979	Los Angeles Rams	9-0	Tampa Bay Buccs
1980	Philadelphia Eagles	20-7	Dallas Cowboys

1981	San Francisco 49ers	28-27	Dallas Cowboys
1982	Washington Redskins	31-17	Dallas Cowboys
1983	Washington Redskins	24-21	San Fran 49ers
1984	San Francisco 49ers	23-0	Chicago Bears
1985	Chicago Bears	24-0	Los Angeles Rams
1986	New York Giants	17-0	Washington Reds
1987	Washington Redskins	17-10	Minnesota Vikings
1988	San Francisco 49ers	28-3	Chicago Bears
1989	San Francisco 49ers	30-3	Los Angeles Rams
1990	New York Giants	15-13	San Francisco 49ers

Superbowl

1967	Green Bay Packers	35-10	Kansas City Chiefs
	Memorial Coliseum, Los Angeles		
1968	Green Bay Packers	33-14	Oakland Raiders
	Orange Bowl, Miami		
1969	New York Jets	16-7	Baltimore Colts
	Orange Bowl, Miami		
1970	Kansas City Chiefs	23-7	Minnesota Vikings
	Tulane Stadium, New Orleans		
1971	Baltimore Colts	16-13	Dallas Cowboys
	Orange Bowl, Miami		
1972	Dallas Cowboys	24-3	Miami Dolphins
	Tulane Stadium, New Orleans		
1973	Miami Dolphins	14-7	Washington Redskins
	Memorial Coliseum, Los Angeles		
1974	Miami Dolphins	24-7	Minnesota Vikings
	Rice Stadium, Houston		
1975	Pittsburgh Steelers	16-6	Minnesota Vikings
	Tulane Stadium, New Orleans		
1976	Pittsburgh Steelers	21-17	Dallas Cowboys
	Orange Bowl, Miami		
1977	Oakland Raiders	32-14	Minnesota Vikings
	Rose Bowl, Pasadena		
1978	Dallas Cowboys	27-10	Denver Broncos
	Louisiana Superdome, New Orleans		
1979	Pittsburgh Steelers	35-31	Dallas Cowboys
	Orange Bowl, Miami		
1980	Pittsburgh Steelers	31-19	Los Angeles Rams
	Rose Bowl, Pasadena		
1981	Oakland Raiders	27-10	Philadelphia Eagles
	Louisiana Superdome, New Orleans		
1982	San Francisco 49ers	26-21	Cincinnati Bengals
	Pontiac Silverdome, Pontiac		
1983	Washington Redskins	27-17	Miami Dolphins
	Rose Bowl, Pasadena		
1984	Los Angeles Raiders	38-9	Washington Redskins
	Tampa Stadium, Tampa		
1985	San Francisco 49ers	38-16	Miami Dolphins
	Stanford Stadium, Stanford		
1986	Chicago Bears	46-10	New England Patriots
	Louisiana Superdome, New Orleans		
1987	New York Giants	39-20	Denver Broncos
	Rose Bowl, Pasadena		
1988	Washington Redskins	42-10	Denver Broncos
	Jack Murphy Stadium, San Diego		
1989	San Francisco 49ers	20-16	Cincinnati Bengals
	John Robbie Stadium, Miami		
1990	San Francisco 49ers	55-10	Denver Broncos
	Louisiana Superdome, New Orleans		
1991	New York Giants	20-19	Buffalo Bills
	Tampa Stadium, Tampa		

Wins: **4** Pittsburgh Steelers, San Francisco 49ers; **3** Oakland/LA Raiders; **2** Green Bay Packers, Washington Redskins, Dallas Cowboys, Miami Dolphins, New York

Giants; **1** Chicago Bears, Kansas City Chiefs, Baltimore Colts.

Appearances: **5** Dallas Cowboys, Miami Dolphins; **4** Minnesota Vikings; Oakland/LA Raiders, Pittsburgh Steelers San Francisco 49ers Washington Redskins; **3** Denver Broncos; **2** Baltimore Colts, Green Bay Packers, Kansas City Chiefs, Cincinnati Bengals, New York Giants; **1** Chicago Bears, Los Angeles Rams, New Patriots, New York Jets, Philadelphia Eagles, Buffalo Bills.

Note: all Superbowls are played in the calendar year after the season they refer to. Thus the 1988 champions played the 1989 Superbowl.

ROSE BOWL

First played in 1902, and regularly since 1916. *All games played at the Rose Bowl, Pasadena, except 1942 at Durham, N. Carolina.*

Results since 1982:

1982	Washington	28-0	Iowa
1983	UCLA	24-14	Michigan
1984	UCLA	45-9	Illinois
1985	USC	20-17	Ohio State
1986	UCLA	45-28	Iowa
1987	Arizona State	22-15	Michigan
1988	Michigan	20-17	So. California
1989	Michigan	22-14	So. California
1990	So. California	17-10	Michigan
1991	Washington	46-34	Iowa

AMERICAN BOWL

All Played at Wembley Stadium

1983	Minnesota Vikings	28-10	St Louis Cardinals
1986	Chicago Bears	17-6	Dallas Cowboys
1987	Los Angeles Rams	28-27	Denver Broncos
1988	Miami Dolphins	27-21	San Francisco 49ers
1989	Philadelphia Eagles	17-3	Cleveland Browns
1990	New Orleans Saints	17-10	Los Angeles Raiders
1991	Buffalo Bills	17-13	Philadelphia Eagles

COCA-COLA BOWL (formerly Budweiser Bowl)

1986	London Ravens	20-12	Streatham Olympians
1987	London Ravens	40-23	Manchester All Stars
1988	Birmingham Bulls	30-6	London Olympians
1989	Manchester Spartans	21-14	Birmingham Bulls
1990	Manchester Spartans	27-25	Northampton Storm
1991	Birmingham Bulls	39-38	London Olympians

EUROPEAN CHAMPIONSHIPS

1983	Italy	18-6	Finland
1985	Finland	13-2	Italy
1987	Italy	24-22	West Germany
1989	Great Britain	26-0	Finland
1991	Great Britain	14-3	Finland

——— 1992 ———

Jan 4-5 AFC/NFC play-offs; Jan 12 AFC/NFC championship games; Jan 26 SUPERBOWL XXVI (Minneapolis)

ANGLING

WORLD FRESHWATER CHAMPIONSHIPS
Szegad, Hungary, Aug 31

Individual
1 Bob Nudd (Eng)
2 Kevin Ashurst (Eng)
3 Jan van Schendel (Hol)

Team
1 England 44 pts
2 France 48 pts
3 Italy 51 pts

NATIONAL LEAGUE FIRST DIVISION CHAMPIONSHIPS
Trent & Mersey Canal, Sep 28

Individual
1 Pete Hargreaves (Alrewas)
2 Ivan Capsey (Telford)
3 Pete Wade (Leicester)

Team
1 Izaak Walton, Preston 823 pts
2 Birmingham Starlets 802 pts
3 Southport 802 pts

OCTOPLUS UK CHAMPIONSHIP
Worsborough Reservoir, Barnsley, Aug 8

Individual
1 Alan Scotthorne 42 pts
2 Tony Trough 39 pts
3 Bob Nudd 38 pts

CHAMPIONS

WORLD FRESHWATER CHAMPIONS
(First held 1957. Winners since 1982)

	Individual	Team
1982	Kevin Ashurst (Eng)	Holland
1983	Wolf-Rudiger Kremkus (FRG)	Belgium
1984	Bobby Smithers (Ire)	Luxembourg
1985	Dave Roper (Eng)	England
1986	Lud Wever (Hol)	Italy
1987	Clive Branson (Wal)	England
1988	Jean-Pierre Fouquet (Fra)	England
1989	Tom Pickering (Eng)	France
1990	Bob Nudd (Eng)	France
1991	Bob Nudd (Eng)	England

Most wins - *Individual:* 3 Robert Tesse (Fra) 1959-60, 1965. *Team:* 12 France

ARCHERY

WORLD TARGET CHAMPIONSHIPS
Krakow, Poland, Aug 20-24
Men - Individual
1 Simon Fairweather (Aus)
2 W Szikareyev (USSR)
3 Chung Jae-Hun (SKo)
Men - Team
1 South Korea 998 pts
2 Finland 989 pts
3 Australia 989 pts
Women - Individual
1 Soo Nyung-Kim (SKo)
2 Lee Eyun-Kyung (SKo)
3 Z Okten (Tur)
Women - Team
1 South Korea 1,030 pts
2 Soviet Union 999 pts
3 United States 995 pts

WORLD INDOOR CHAMPIONSHIPS
(Inaugurated 1991)
Oula, Finland, Mar 12-16
Men
Freestyle: Sebastian Flute (Fra)
Compound Bow: Joe Asay (US)
Women
Freestyle: Natalya Valeeva (USSR)
Compound Bow: Lucia Panico (Ita)

BRITISH TARGET CHAMPIONSHIPS
Lichfield, Aug 10-11
Men: Steve Hallard (Dunlop)
Women: Jo Edens (Royal Leamington Spa)

CHAMPIONS

WORLD CHAMPIONS
(First staged 1931. Winners since 1983)
Men

	Individual	Team
1983	Richard McKinney (US)	United States
1985	Richard McKinney (US)	South Korea
1987	Vladimir Yesheyev (USSR)	South Korea
1989	Stanislav Zabrodsky (USSR)	USSR
1991	Simon Fairweather (Aus)	South Korea

Most wins - *Individual:* 4 Hans Deutgen (Swe) (1947-50); *Team:* 12 United States

Women

	Individual	Team
1983	Kim Jin-Ho (SKo)	South Korea
1985	Irina Soldatova (USSR)	USSR
1987	Ma Xiagjun (Chn)	USSR
1989	Soo Nyung-Kim (SKo)	South Korea
1991	Soo Nyung-Kim (SKo)	South Korea

Most wins - *Individual:* 7 Janina Spychajowa-Kurkowska (Pol) (1931-34, 36, 39, 47); *Team:* 9 United States

OF GUNNERS AND GAZZA

Two men emerged from the 1990 World Cup in Italy as the most charismatic characters in world soccer. One was Paul Gascoigne of England; the other was Diego Maradona of Argentina. A year later both found the world was on their backs rather than at their feet.

One moment of lunacy in the FA Cup final meant that Gascoigne ended the season in plaster with his career in doubt. One positive drug test on Maradona allowed everyone to peer into his sleazewrapped life. He ended the season with his freedom in doubt. Their fate somehow summed up the 1990-91 season, a time when soccer tried hard to build on the popularity of Italia '90 but kept falling back. It also emphasised that, whatever the papers might say, soccer is still a team game.

In Britain, the news was dominated by Gazzamania. Gascoigne's successes and failures – which were equally extreme and dramatic – were paraded across the nation's papers and TV screens until Gazza the footballer was almost buried beneath Gazza the media celebrity. He became famous for being famous. And just when the fuss might have died down there came the saga of his on-off-on-off-on-off-on move to Lazio (re-scheduled for 1992) and his brief, catastrophic Cup Final, all set against the background of Tottenham's horrendous financial problems.

It was salutary amid all this that the dominant team on the field was actually Arsenal, thriving on a system rather than stars, who went quietly through the season losing only one match and steadily stretching clear of the field to win the First Division, seven points ahead of Liverpool. The gap would have been bigger had not the FA, to the fury of supporters, taken two points off Arsenal after a mass punch-up with Manchester United in October. The club fined the manager, George Graham, two weeks' wages (about £10,000) as well as the players and for a moment Graham's job might have been endangered.

Only for a moment, though. Many people never seemed to notice that Arsenal were successful. "Arsenal's day of crisis" said the *Mail on Sunday* headline after they had lost 2-1 at Chelsea in February, which happened to be their only League defeat. There was less attention given to their record than to that of their captain Tony Adams who was given four months' jail for reckless driving. He was unable to play for the Chelmsford prison team because of Arsenal's insurance policy.

But everyone else's crises were worse. Liverpool began the season in even more striking fashion than usual: they won their first eight games (three short of the record set by Tottenham in 1960-61) and were unbeaten until Arsenal beat them 3-0 at Highbury on December 2, which proved to be the turning point of the season. Something cracked: it was Kenny Dalglish. On February 22, with Liverpool still top of the table, and only two days after a 4-4 draw with Everton in the FA Cup which enthralled everyone else, he dramatically announced his resignation, saying he could not stand the pressure. The news might have been described as a bombshell had the recapture of Kuwait not begun the previous day.

In the best Liverpool tradition, the coach Ronnie Moran was given first crack at the job. But Moran never had a chance. Liverpool lost the lead when they went down at Luton the day after Dalglish went. Everton knocked them out of the Cup after that, Arsenal came to Anfield and won 1-0 the following week and Alan Hansen, the Liverpool captain, said he was quitting the game. It was not all one-way traffic: Liverpool relieved their frustrations by winning 7-1 at Derby, their biggest away win since 1896. But two defeats over Easter sealed their fate and Moran's. Graeme Souness, a distinguished old boy but still the first manager to come in from outside since Bill Shankly, was lured from Rangers to replace Dalglish at a reported salary of £350,000, more even than most chairmen of privatised industries. And Arsenal celebrated with a huge procession from Highbury down to Islington Town Hall where the civic dignitaries were regaled with chants of "Gazza is a nobhead" among the more traditional shanties.

KING KENNY'S ABDICATION

❝I felt I had gone far enough and I could not delay it any longer. The biggest problem was pressure that I was putting myself under because of the desire to be successful.❞
Kenny Dalglish, resigning from Liverpool

"He is the moaningest Minnie I've ever known."
John Bond, Shrewsbury manager

"It is important to all of us to have control over our fate, and this is just what a football manager does not have. His fate is in the hands of 11 (at least) other people."
Dr William Davies, consultant psychologist

"If Kenny Dalglish has resigned because of pressures, the rest of us have no chance."
Howard Wilkinson, Leeds manager

"Resignations are for Prime Ministers and Cabinet Ministers caught with their trousers down, not for football managers in work."
Brian Clough, Nottingham Forest manager

"He'll be back. What else is he going to do: play golf the rest of his life?"
Ronnie Moran, Liverpool coach

"He has of course one terrific advantage as a prose stylist. He will never have to interview the monosyllabic and antagonistic bane of a journalist's life, Kenny Dalglish.❞
Sue Mott, Sunday Times, on Kenny Dalglish's appointment as soccer columnist of the Sunday Scot

One way or another, everything seemed to involve Gazza. His tears in the World Cup semi-final had moved people who were quite untouched by his football skills and he became perhaps the biggest British cultural phenomenon since the Beatles. After the World Cup he went on the Wogan chat show to tell everyone he wanted to be left alone. Thereafter he made Madame Tussaud's, was photographed cuddling Mrs Thatcher at Downing Street (fat lot of good the publicity did her – it was almost her last cuddle as Prime Minister), made a hit record, switched on the Regent Street Christmas lights, was voted BBC Sports Personality of the Year, was sent off for swearing in a televised match against Manchester United, questioned by police about allegedly thumping photographers and charged with assault after a punch-up in Newcastle. His business advisers said they were turning down 100 requests for personal appearances every week. There were Gazza games, calendars and duvet covers.

Naturally there was a reaction. Mr Justice Harman enquired (unconvincingly) who he was and refused to grant an injunction stopping the publication of a book called *Gazza*, saying that the Duke of Wellington had failed in a similar attempt after the Battle of Waterloo. Dennis Skinner MP pointed out that Gascoigne was valued at £8 million, £1.5 million more than Britain's total aid to Bangladesh. Readers of the *Record Mirror* voted Gazza less likeable than Saddam Hussein. A Paul Gascoigne lookalike contest in South Shields was won by a black teenage girl dressed as a fairy.

Somehow he found time to play football, some of it quite brilliant, most especially in the FA Cup. Gascoigne turned Spurs' fifth and sixth round ties, against Portsmouth and Notts County. Then he went into hospital for a groin operation. Less than five weeks later he beat Arsenal in the FA Cup semi-final (the first ever staged at Wembley) with what Terry Venables, the Spurs manager, called the "best free-kick in the history of the FA Cup". Gascoigne only stayed on for an hour but in that time scored one goal, made another and gave the half-time pep-talk. "I couldn't get a word in," said Venables.

All the while, it was becoming increasingly probable that Spurs were going to have to sell their most famous asset to pay for the directors' catastrophic dabbling in non-soccer matters. Tottenham Hotspur plc, the first club to turn itself into a public company, was £20 million in debt and Lazio of Italy were willing to pay almost half of that to get Gazza. But first the FA Cup Final was to be Tottenham v Nottingham Forest, or in keeping with the prevailing cult of the individual, Gascoigne v Brian Clough, who was anxious to cap his managerial career with the one major trophy that had eluded him.

ALL GAS AND GAZZA

❝The most bare-faced piece of catchpenny hype since the hula-hoop."
David Lacey, The Guardian, on Gazzamania

Michael Silverleaf, counsel for the plaintiff: "Paul Gascoigne is a very well-known footballer..."
Mr Justice Harman: "Rugby or association football?"
Exchange in court

"There are plenty of reasons why he won't last and the main one, sad to say, is he's just not good enough."
George Best on Gascoigne

"I don't want to end up like him."
Gascoigne on Best

"He is getting away with things that would land other players in trouble. If Vinny Jones had behaved like Gazza, he would have been on News at Ten and Prime Minister's Question Time."
Dave Bassett, Sheffield United manager

"I gave her a hug. It wasn't bad, she was nice and cuddly like."
Gazza on meeting Margaret Thatcher

"He's a traitor, a puppet, an idiot."
Roy Boulter, guitarist with The Farm

"I love it when he smells the referee's armpit."
Franco Zeffirelli, film director

"If my kids behaved like him they would get a smack and be sent to their room."
Dave Bassett

"People should realise they will never take the smile off my face. Never. It's in my blood to enjoy myself."
Gascoigne

"Do you want this bag in your face?"
To photographer at Heathrow

"I don't think I swore. If I did, it was not at the referee. It was just me swearing."
Gascoigne, after being sent off

"When Gazzamania dies, we must make sure Paul Gascoigne the footballer is still alive."
Graham Taylor

"Whoever we are, we're human. And we need normal everyday relationships to keep us in the real world. So it is a good thing Gazza's England manager isn't afraid of dropping him."
Editorial in the Salvation Army paper, War Cry

"The poor young man's a talented enough footballer but is in danger of becoming nothing more than the fairy on top of the Christmas tree".
Tommy Docherty

"I love football but sometimes I think I am playing in the wrong era."
Gascoigne

"In 20 years time the same journalists queueing up to knock him down will be asking why British football can't produce the likes of Gazza any more."
The Independent

"I don't want him to be a singing star, just a better player."
Taylor

"I would like to sign him for 40 years."
Giancarlo Calleri, president of Lazio

"Sue, the tea-lady here, makes such a good lasagne that there's no need to go all the way to Europe."
Gascoigne, in his book, rejecting the idea of a move

"Coping with the language shouldn't be a problem. I can't speak English yet."
Gascoigne, starting to change his mind

"Yes, I was guilty. I didn't stick to the laws, but I just couldn't bring myself to do it."
Roger Milford, Cup Final referee, on why Gazza was not sent off before he was carried off.

"God alone knows what went through my mind, because I don't.. it was my own stupid fault."
Gascoigne, after the Cup Final

"Happy birthday Gazza, the next with us."
Lazio fans' banner a week later

"It describes how he couldn't be without us, relies on us for everything and how we'll never let him down. And we won't, because he's family."
Mel Stein, Gascoigne's business adviser, after Gazza wrote a poem from hospital to Stein and his partner Len Lazarus.

"He behaved really well when he was here, a true gentleman. When he's in England I don't know what happens to him."
Giancarlo Calleri

"I have every faith in the sublime talents of Gascoigne – but I fear for Gazza. ❞
Simon Barnes, The Times

Gascoigne, however, began the final with two interventions: a flying drop-kick on Gary Parker and a scissors tackle on Gary Charles–either of which might have got him sent off. Instead, after the second, he was carried off. His anterior cruciate ligament, which helps keep the tibia fixed to the femur, had gone; and nothing had kept his brain attached to his body either. It was a moment of awful drama.

But nor was it Clough's day either. His performance was almost as bizarre as Gascoigne's. He sat throughout the game as though mummified and declined to speak to his players between full-time and extra-time. Meanwhile, Venables rallied his troops like Henry V and Spurs, who on top of everything had had a Gary Lineker goal wrongly disallowed and a penalty saved, came back to win in extra time.

Venables won the more important battle in extra time too. After a long struggle, the consortium he put together, backed by the electronics tycoon Alan Sugar, won control of Tottenham, beating off the attentions of the fidgety newspaper proprietor Robert Maxwell. Venables was installed as managing director and had the satisfaction of reversing normal soccer precedent and sacking his chairman, Irving Scholar. Gascoigne was supposed to arrive at Lazio the following Sunday, his 24th birthday. Fifty thousand fans still turned out to greet him though he was lying prone in hospital, reduced to writing verses, including one to his business advisers. The clubs who had turned themselves into public companies in the capitalist euphoria of the late 80's all suffered. Millwall lost money and Manchester United's share offer was under-subscribed. Every footballer was uneasy about the future too. After the season ended, the First Division clubs linked up with the Football Association and announced plans, the best-laid of many such schemes over the years, to break away, form a Superleague and keep more of the TV and sponsorship revenues for themselves rather than the clubs beneath them. This League would supposedly contain only 18 clubs. But at the start of 1991-92 the First Division had actually reverted to 22 clubs–so the rebels included such glamorous names as Oldham, who had won promotion after a 68-year absence, Notts County, who won the Second Division play-offs, Sheffield United, who did not win a game until December 22 before recovering spectacularly, Luton, who avoided relegation on the final day yet again, and Wimbledon, whose gates remained humiliating–but not Sunderland or Derby (who were both relegated), Newcastle or Wolves. On the eve of the new season, all 22 formally resigned from the League.

RETURN TO EUROPE

The successful teams in English soccer had something else in view again too: Aston Villa and Manchester United were the first English clubs allowed to compete in Europe since the Heysel tragedy. Villa had the bad luck to meet Inter Milan, the eventual winners, early in the UEFA Cup but United made it a triumphant return by winning the Cup-Winners Cup with an unexpected 2-1 win over Barcelona in the same Rotterdam stadium in which Everton had won England's last Euro-title six years earlier.

Mark Hughes, who scored six goals in two miserable years playing for Barcelona, scored two against them in seven minutes. It was the 23rd European honour for English clubs, and the sixth Cup-Winners' Cup. Only five United supporters were arrested on the whole trip. Indeed, there were growing signs all over that England was no longer the world's major producer of hooliganism. Amid the new spirit of cautious optimism about English fans, the extra ban on Liverpool was also lifted and they were allowed to compete in the 1991-92 UEFA Cup. The bizarre belief that England might stage the 1998 World Cup was not sustainable, however, and the FA withdrew in the hope of getting the 1996 European Championship instead.

United far outshone the winners of Europe's senior trophy. Red Star Belgrade won the European Cup for the fast-fragmenting state of Yugoslavia but did so only after a terrible final against Marseille and a penalty shoot-out; they cheerfully admitted that they had played for a draw all along and had practised the penalty kicks beforehand.

The England team had a good year too. Graham Taylor, who had replaced Bobby Robson as manager after the World Cup, went through his first 12 matches without defeat, beating Don Revie's record of nine. Not all these performances were distinguished and the last four were cheap wins with a weakened team on tour in Australasia and Asia. The important stuff was the European Championship in which there were two draws with Jack Charlton's Republic of Ireland (maintaining the tradition of dreadful matches between these teams), a good home win over Poland and a narrow one in Turkey, where the travelling fans chanted "There's only one Bobby Robson". However, Ireland failed to beat Poland the same day and so England finished the season as likely qualifiers for the finals in Sweden in 1992.

They were better placed than the obvious favourites for the Championship, Germany and Italy, who were both in trouble in their groups. Germany, the world champions, were beaten 1-0 in Cardiff by an Ian Rush goal which gave Wales perhaps their greatest-ever win. Italy were in a fearful mess after losing in Norway. The Scots were their usual exasperating selves, dropping a crucial point when Bulgaria equalised in the last minute, and struggling to beat San Marino. "We've been playing an hour," said Ian Archer on Radio Scotland, "and it's just occurred to me that we're drawing 0-0 with a mountain top."

The heroes of the Championship were the other micro-nation newly allowed in to the competition: the Faroe Islands stunned the continent when they won their first match, beating Austria 1-0. The Faroes had to play in Sweden because they did not even have a suitable pitch. Jens Martin Knudsen, goalkeeper and lorry driver, became an instant hero, along with his lucky bobble hat. It was not a complete fluke: the Faroes later drew 1-1 in Belfast. There were reports that Laponia, covering Lapp people in four countries, wanted to play in the next Championships.

ALL CHANGE

Back in the frozen wastes of the Football League, the average manager was finding that Venables's success did not extend to them. Nearly half the League managers departed over the course of 12 months. Some bettered themselves: Howard Kendall moved back to Everton from Manchester City and bitter Maine Road fans carried a banner accusing him of doing the burglary at the home of Derek and Mavis Riley, the Coronation Street characters. Most did not. Even Southampton, who had never sacked a manager, joined the herd: Chris Nicholl was removed after six years. Jim Ryan was fired by Luton two days after the club avoided relegation. Aston Villa's imaginative appointment of the Czechoslovak intellectual Dr Jo Venglos to succeed Graham Taylor was recognised as a failure and he left by mutual consent all round. Some thought he had not been decisive enough. Ron Atkinson agreed to replace him, changed his mind and then agreed again. The *Birmingham Evening Mail* ran a 28–page supplement to greet him.

Atkinson had taken Wednesday back to the First Division at the first attempt and to a surprise win in the League Cup final over Manchester United. This tournament is now sponsored by Rumbelows. Instead of the usual minor royal, they got their Employee of the Year, Tracey Bateman, to present the cup to the winning captain Nigel Pearson. It was an appropriately homely touch: Wednesday were the first Second Division team to win the cup in 16 years.

United's progress to the final had included a 6-2 win at Highbury, by far Arsenal's worst result of the season. The game had been chosen by two Arsenal fans, Dr George Carey and Rabbi Jonathan Sacks, the newly-appointed Archbishop of Canterbury and Chief Rabbi, for their first official meeting. "It was a catastrophe," said Dr Sacks. "We were trying to work out the theological implications. Does it mean our prayers were not heard, that the players were relying on us or that God is a Manchester United fan?"

West Ham also returned to the First Division. West Bromwich Albion were relegated to the Third for the first time. One of the team, Graham Roberts, became the first player in England to fail an initial dope test; he was cleared as the drug involved, diethylpropion, an appetite-depressant which can make users more aggressive, had been prescribed. Portsmouth's video of the season's highlights, sold to supporters, turned out to contain Port Vale games. Watford experimented with canned cheering over the Tannoy against Newcastle; they lost 2-1. Bristol Rovers sacked their Tannoy-man Keith Valle after he announced, when Bristol City sent their substitute on in the local derby: "Here comes Junior Bent. I bet he is."

Cambridge, Southend and Grimsby – all fresh up from the Fourth – were promoted to the Second. Cambridge also reached the sixth round of the FA Cup for the second year running. Their victims included Wolves, about whom their assistant manager Gary Johnson gained information by ringing the Wolves Clubcall line. "It was 44p very well spent," he said. Tranmere also returned to the Second Division, after 52 years, beating Bolton in extra time of the play-off final at Wembley, having finished five points behind them in the League. Tommy Hutchison reappeared for Swansea against Birmingham, aged 43 years 171 days, making him the fourth oldest postwar League player.

TRANMERE AT WEMBLEY
Since 1987 Tranmere have played seven matches at Wembley, a figure equalled only by Nottingham Forest in the same period

YEAR OPPONENTS	COMPETITION	RESULT	
1987 v Wimbledon	League Centenary	won	1-0
1987 v Newcastle United	League Centenary	won	2-0
1987 v Nottingham Forest	League Centenary	drew	2-2
(Lost 1-0 on pens)			
1990 v Bristol Rovers	Leyland Daf Cup	won	2-1
1990 v Notts County	Div 3 Play-off	lost	0-2
1991 v Birmingham City	Leyland Daf Cup	lost	2-3
1991 v Bolton Wanderers	Div 3 Play-off	won	1-0

Torquay won the Fourth Division play-off on penalties. Blackpool missed promotion, although they were second on the final morning. Hartlepool also went into the Third Division after 22 years as a byword for bottom-division incompetence. Reg Weston, who was named as Stockport County's top fan, left his pregnant wife to run off with the promotions girl who organised the contest. "Running off with the promotions girl," a pal was quoted as saying, "is the nearest he can get to sleeping with County." Kevin Francis, Stockport's striker, proposed to his girlfriend Sharon via the club's programme. She said yes through more usual channels. The *Grantham Journal* published a classified ad offering: "11 Lincoln Red heifers for sale"; the phone number given was that of Lincoln City. Scarborough v Wrexham on the cold, wet Friday night of December 7 had the lowest crowd in Fourth Division history: 625; the previous low was 811 for Workington v Southport in March 1977.

Tranmere's play-off win was actually their seventh appearance at Wembley in three years and Liverpool were jealous. They also reached the final of the ludicrous Leyland Daf Cup, for the two lower divisions. The draw for the second round of this event produced the following: Burnley or Stockport v Crewe, Burnley or Stockport. One group, nicknamed the Group of Death, produced nothing but 1-1 draws and had to be entirely replayed. Stand tickets for the Leyland Daf game between Birmingham and Lincoln, held on a frozen November night, carried the instruction: "Please be seated one hour before kick-off".

Irons and Steel scored for Tranmere against Huddersfield. Bamber played against Gascoigne in the Blackpool v Spurs cup-tie. Bryant and May played together for Bristol

City, but not as strikers. Gillingham's fanzine, Brian Moore's Head Looks Uncannily Like The London Planetarium, was named Fanzine of the Year.

BEYOND THE BORDER

The Scottish season was rescued from boredom after Souness's departure southwards when Rangers, having led the Premier Division unchallenged for months, were almost unhorsed by a late surge from Aberdeen. By happy chance everything rested on a showdown between the clubs on the last day of the season with Aberdeen needing to draw at Ibrox to be champions. There were rumours of black-market tickets going for £1000 and the game was even regarded as match of the day in England. But then most of the Rangers team were English. Rangers' decisive goals both came from the Sassenach Mark Hateley. There had not been a last-ditcher like it since 1965 when Kilmarnock took the championship by beating Hearts at Tynecastle.

The Scottish Cup final was just as dramatic. Motherwell, managed by Tommy McLean, won it for the first time in 39 years beating Dundee United, managed by his brother Jim, 4-3. Their father, Thomas snr. died, aged 78, four days before the final. The Motherwell goalkeeper spent most of the match in agony after being charged by United defender John Clark but still managed an almost miraculous extra-time save. United's Jim McInally threw a boot at the referee after the game. It was United's sixth successive Cup Final defeat, going back to 1974, and ended their unbroken 15-year run of qualifying for Europe. To add insult to everything, United's neighbours Dundee then tried to take them over. The saddest team of all were Celtic, who had a dismal season by their standards (i.e. they were third) and fired the manager Billy McNeill, who had spent 30 years out of the last 34 at Parkhead as player and manager. He was replaced by Liam Brady, who was, unprecedentedly, neither a former Celtic player nor a Scotsman.

The most exciting title race of all took place at the top of the English non-League system where Barnet eventually emerged at the top of a four-club pile-up to get admittance to the Football League. Altrincham would already have been dreaming of thrilling derby games with Rochdale after a run of 28 games without defeat had put them in pole position with games in hand. But they suddenly collapsed and Barnet, having been runners-up three years out of four, finally got lucky. Under the League's restructuring no one was booted out and the "ticket-broker" Stan Flashman became the 93rd League chairman. Barnet's sponsor, the Levitt Group, went spectacularly bust in mid-season and its boss was arrested.

The best individual performance from a non-League club came from Woking of the Vauxhall League, who won 4-2 at West Bromwich in the third round of the FA Cup with a hat-trick in 15 minutes from Tim Buzaglo, a computer operator who plays cricket for Gibraltar. Drawn at home to Everton in the next round, Woking unromantically put cash before glory and switched the tie to Goodison, losing only 1-0. Two days later Woking had to play Walton and Hersham in the Surrey Demolition and Excavation Cup. Gretna Town, from over the Scottish border, had their second shock win in the FA Trophy in three years, beating Macclesfield, the 1989 finalists. Chengez Khan, Stafford Rangers' 19-year-old full-back, was reported to have developed a new throw-in based on turning a full somersault and then sending the ball 50 yards. The throw is legal but at Stafford can only be used near the halfway line where he can use the tunnel as his run-up.

Wycombe Wanderers were barred from using a parody of the ancient Dion hit, The Wanderer, by Michael Jackson who owns the rights to the music; no one that famous had ever cared what the club did before. Albert Lambie, 83, was team mascot for Slough Town in their home Conference game against Gateshead; he had done the same job for South Shields as a four-year-old in 1911.

Nympsfield accidentally fielded 12 men in the Stroud League Fifth Division match against Price Walker. They were losing 3-0 before the referee realised and sent someone off. The game ended 3-3. Kashim Abdul, 15, offered to wash the kit for his team-mates of the Bangladeshi Northern Eagles at Hyde, Manchester but picked up curry powder instead of washing powder and turned the green strip yellow. The village club of Freshford United near Bath split because the reserve team won two cups, grew as strong as the first team and then started refusing to provide it with players; the reserves were banned from the pitch. Cyril Hart, 36, of Stockton-on-Tees scored his first goal in 24 years of playing in the last minute of his last game. Paul Homer, the goalkeeper for Long Sutton in Somerset, suffered his 25th broken bone in seven years - the left arm for the sixth time.

It was a bad year, too, for far more distinguished names. Indeed, almost everyone who had starred in the World Cup seemed to find their reputation flaking at the edges. When Cameroon came to play a celebratory game at Wembley, the former super-sub Roger Milla refused to play because the FA would not give him a £5,000 appearance fee. Cameroon's World Cup manager Valeri Nepomniachi resigned because he had not been paid and the season there had to be postponed because rioting pop fans had smashed up the stadium in Douala. Undergraduates at Magdalen College, Oxford acquired the M'bouh M'bouh reading room in honour of the Cameroon international, which may have been some compensation. Salvatore Schillaci, Italy's goalscoring hero in the World Cup, failed to score at all between November and April, had a trial separation from his wife and children and was suspended for threatening to shoot a rival player.

FALLEN IDOL

However, no one since Lucifer has fallen quite so far or so fast as Diego Maradona. At first, he seemed invulnerable. When an Italian court official first said that Maradona was under investigation for handling drugs, a letter-writer to *The Guardian* said someone should tell the court he never gets convicted of handling anything. But then traces of cocaine were found in a drugs test after a Napoli match in March and he promptly fled back to Argentina, where he was arrested the following month and charged with using and supplying the drug. The local paper *El Grafico* said an undercover policewoman infiltrated Maradona's social circle, that he was arrested naked in his bedroom and was one of the last people in the area to know: 200 people were in the street. Maradona failed to appear at the start of his trial in Naples; his lawyer produced an Argentine doctor's certificate saying he was suffering from stress.

The love affair between Maradona and Naples was over anyway; the club were suing him for breach of contract. Italian newspaper readers voted him the most unpopular man in the world, just ahead of Saddam Hussein. He also beat off the same opposition in a traditional vote by villagers in Murieta, Spain to find a scapegoat to be burned in effigy for "The May" to ward off bad weather. Previous winners include Margaret Thatcher. It was a bad year for the whole family: Maradona's younger brother Hugo was voted Flop of the Year in Austria by the newspaper *Kurier*. He played 94 minutes for Rapid Vienna all season at a salary of £4000 a week.

The decline of hooliganism in Britain was not matched elsewhere. In Orkney, South Africa, 42 fans were trampled to death when fights broke out after a goal was scored during a friendly game between two top teams, Kaizer Chiefs and Orlando Pirates. Fans fleeing the fighting crushed others against a security fence. "The tragedy was caused by human conduct and reaction," said Cyril Kobus, chief executive of the National Soccer League. Alcohol was subsequently barred from South African grounds. Ten people were killed and 128 injured in Santiago when fans celebrated Colo Colo's victory that made them the first Chilean club to be South American champions. At African Nations Cup ties two people were killed after a stampede in

Kenya and one in a riot in Gabon. There were familiar problems in Holland, where a court cancelled Feyenoord's win in the Dutch cup final because of pitch invasions, and unfamiliar ones in the old East Germany: a post-unification commemorative match between East and West was cancelled by Leipzig city officials afraid of violence. There was regular trouble throughout the autumn at matches in the east and a man died in Leipzig when police fired on rioting fans.

THE TROUBLES OF DIEGO

❝I've had enough. I'm tired of struggling. I'm retiring for good.❞
Maradona

"He is 30 going on 50, a man satiated with riches and battered toward submission...he would pose no problem to a psychiatrist: classic schizophrenia brought on by a lifetime of being passed from boot to boot of opponents, from palm to palm by employers."
Rob Hughes, International Herald Tribune, on Maradona

"Since he gave himself to his game, he simply stopped growing. My client has the mind of a 15-year-old."
Vincenzo Siniscalchi, Maradona's lawyer

"It's as if they'd disqualified the sport of soccer."
Gianfranco Zola, Maradona's team-mate at Napoli, on his ban

"He is a sick lad and, as such, has to be helped to drop this vice which is destroying him morally and physically."
President Menem of Argentina

"Naples has said a silent goodbye to seven years of screams, sighs and overwhelming emotion."
Mario Orfeo, La Repubblica

"Diego, facci ancora sognere" ("Diego, make us dream again)❞
Graffito in Naples

On the field, too, Britain's disciplinary problems seemed comparatively easy. Fifteen players were sent off in the League in one weekend (December 22/23), beating the previous record of 13 set in 1985. But officials were interpreting the FIFA edict on professional fouls strictly. And this was small beer: in Ghaziabad, India, Vijendra Singh, the Iqram Institute goalkeeper, was killed when a fight erupted after a semi-final against the Times Institute. In Swaziland, five players were charged with murder after clubbing an opponent to death during a game. British troubles were more gently eccentric. Mark Gibbs of Holyhead Mountain Rangers in the Anglesey League was banned for seven weeks after giving his name to the referee as James Bond. Richard Evans, ten, was banned for three weeks by the North East Wales FA after being sent off by his father for punching an opponent – "Rules are rules," said Wilton Evans. Terry Powell, a 33-year-old building worker, knocked out the 15-year-old referee of an under-10's match in Maes-y-Cymer, Glamorgan, after his nine-year old son had been felled by a high tackle. "I'm no hooligan," said Powell, "I only did what any parent would do to protect their child. This ref was diabolical." Dr John Gayford, a psychiatrist, booked all 22 players while refereeing a reserve team game between Croydon Municipal Officers and Merton Officers. "Dr Gayford should get help," said Croydon secretary Tony Osborn.

Parents of pupils at St John's Prep School were asked not to cheer so hard by the headmaster after rivals Witham Hall protested. They were urged not to use offensive phrases like 'rush forward', 'clear the ball' and 'tackle'. One head even thought soccer could set an example: Colin Smith, headmaster of a middle school in Blyth, Northumberland, introduced a system of red and yellow cards for naughty pupils. Further afield, Ruben Olivera, playing for Santo in the Uruguayan First Division, was sent off for kissing an opponent who had missed an easy goal. The referee of the game between Toledo Imperial and Gamonal in Spain sent off the entire Gamonal team, one by one. "I was insulted gravely," he said.

Professional soccer in Iraq, which did not exist until 1989, was reported to be an oasis of happiness with good-humoured and well-behaved players and fans. However, the game was struggling in Brazil: the local derby between Flamengo and Fuminense, which used to get huge crowds, attracted only 8,597 and the Maracana stadium was closed temporarily as a dangerous structure. Brazil lost their grip on the South American Championship, won by Argentina – without Maradona – for the first time in 32 years. The Albanian national team went to play France with a 16-man squad and returned with nine; the rest defected. Fifteen Ethiopian youth players had to be dragged off a bus and on to a plane in Cairo after being refused political asylum.

In New Zealand Nelson United's plans to be sponsored by an antismoking group and call themselves "Lifespan Nelson" or "SmokeFree Nelson" were rejected by the national soccer association, which was getting £350,000 a year from tobacco sponsorship. In the Israeli Third Division, Hapoel Kiryat, 15 goals behind their promotion rivals on goal difference, won a game against strugglers Hapoel Shtullm 25-0. The Israeli FA criticised the referee for not mentioning in his report that there was something unusual; he said that after writing down the goalscorers there was no room on the page. Burma was reported to have 1,840 referees but only 1,231 players. In comparison, the game's problems elsewhere in the world seem entirely soluble.

1990 - 91

ENGLAND'S INTERNATIONAL MATCHES

Wembley, Sep 12, Friendly
England (1) 1 **Hungary** (0) 0
Lineker 44
Attendance: 51,459
Woods; Dixon, Parker, M Wright, Walker, Pearce (Dorigo), Platt, Gascoigne, Barnes, Bull (Waddle), Lineker
Graham Taylor's first match as manager. Gary Lineker was made captain, having led Leicestershire Schools at cricket but never a football team.

Wembley, Oct 17, European Champs qualifier
England (1) 2 **Poland** (0) 0
Lineker 39 (pen)
Beardsley 89
Attendance: 77,040
Woods; Dixon, Parker, M Wright, Walker, Pearce, Platt, Gascoigne, Barnes, Bull (Waddle), Lineker (Beardsley)
Lineker went off with a cut head that required eight stitches

Dublin, Nov 14, European Champs qualifier
Rep.of Ireland (0) 1 **England** (0) 1
Cascarino 79 Platt 67
Attendance: 46,000
Woods; Dixon, Pearce, Adams, Walker, M Wright, Platt, Cowans, Beardsley, Lineker, McMahon
Taylor controversially omitted Gascoigne, saying it was not his sort of game. "This was the usual load of old rubbish masquerading as international football between these teams" –Colin Malam, Daily Telegraph.

Wembley, Feb 6, Friendly
England (1) 2 **Cameroon** (0) 0
Lineker 20 (pen), 61
Attendance: 61,075
Seaman; Dixon, Pearce, Steven, Walker, M Wright, Robson (Pallister), Gascoigne (Hodge), I Wright, Lineker, Barnes
Bryan Robson returned as captain. Ian Wright (Crystal

Palace) made debut. *"Everything about the Cameroon performance was unpleasant and unattractive"–Colin Gibson,* Daily Telegraph.

Wembley, Mar 27, European Champs qualifier
England (1) 1 **Rep.of Ireland** (1) 1
Dixon 9 Quinn 27
Attendance: 77,753
Seaman; Dixon, Pearce, Adams (Sharpe), Walker, M Wright, Robson, Platt, Beardsley, Lineker (I Wright), Barnes
Lee Sharpe (Manchester United), 19, made his debut as substitute after half-time to be the youngest England player since Peter Barnes in 1977-78. He replaced Adams who, it was remarked, had seemed happier in jail.

Izmir, May 1, European Champs qualifier
Turkey (0) 0 **England** (1) 1
Wise 32
Attendance 25,000
Seaman; Dixon, Pearce, Wise, Walker, Pallister, Platt, Thomas (Hodge), Smith, Lineker, Barnes
Gascoigne unavailable through injury. Debut: Geoff Thomas (Crystal Palace). England largely outplayed but went top of the group because Ireland failed to beat Poland.

Wembley, May 21, Friendly
England (2) 3 **Soviet Union** (1) 1
Platt 44 (pen), 89 M Wright (og) 9
Smith 16
Attendance: 23,789
Woods; Stevens, Dorigo, Wise (Batty), Parker, M Wright, Platt, Thomas, Smith, I Wright (Beardsley), Barnes
Only two survivors from the World Cup semi-final team in the starting line-up: Mark Wright and Platt. Debut: David Batty (Leeds).

Wembley May 25, Friendly
England (1) 2 **Argentina** (0) 2
Lineker 15 Garcia 66
Platt 51 Franco 72

Attendance 44,497
Seaman; Dixon, Pearce, Batty, Walker, M Wright, Platt, Thomas, Smith, Lineker, Barnes (Clough)
This result ensured that England won the "England Challenge Cup", a three team variation on the Rous Cup. Argentina and the Soviet Union had drawn 1-1 at Old Trafford.

Sydney, Jun 1, Friendly

| **Australia** (0) 0 | **England** (1) 1 |
| | Gray (og) 40 |

Attendance: 35,472
Woods; Parker, Pearce, Batty, Walker, M Wright, Platt, Thomas, Clough, Lineker (Wise), Hirst (Salako)
Debuts: David Hirst (Sheffield Wednesday), John Salako (Crystal Palace). England were jet-lagged, having flown out only three days earlier. Taylor said he had inherited the itinerary and never liked it.

ENGLAND'S LEADING SCORERS

49	**Bobby Charlton**
45	**GARY LINEKER**
44	**Jimmy Greaves**
30	**Tom Finney**
29	**Viv Woodward**
28	**Steve Bloomer**
26	**Bryan Robson**
23	**Stan Mortensen**
23	**Own Goals**
21	**Mick Channon**

Correct at start of 1991-92 Season

> **"... NEXT!"**
> **I like the look of Graham Taylor as England manager. In many ways he reminds me of me."**
> *Sir Alf Ramsey*

Graham Taylor: "Told you I'd make it, Barnsey"
John Barnes: "What kept you?"
Exchange at Taylor's first England training session

> **"If we are talking about getting things wrong, I will get things wrong my way."**
> *Taylor*

> **"**** off Taylor"**
> *Sun headline*

> **"If you go back all the way to Walter Winterbottom, I think on the whole we're pretty decent fellows, yet the position of England manager is kicked around like nobody's business."**
> *Taylor*

> **"Anyone who is criticised by Emlyn Hughes, Kevin Keegan and the Sun leader column must be doing something right."**
> *Pat Collins, Mail on Sunday*

> **"In football the manager gets the blame not the captain."**
> *Gary Lineker, England captain*

> **"Gary Lineker should be designated a national asset and confined to a strongroom between international matches. Lineker played his multi-role as captain, hit man, superstar, diplomat, chief smiler and focal interviewee to something near perfection."**
> *Bryon Butler, The Observer, on England' summer tour*

Auckland, Jun 3, Friendly

| **New Zealand** (0) 0 | **England** (0) 1 |
| | Lineker 93 |

Attendance: 17,520
Woods; Parker, Pearce, Batty (Deane), Walker, Barrett, Platt, Thomas, Wise, Lineker, Walters (Salako)
The 10th unbeaten game under Taylor, beating Revie's starting record. Debuts: Earl Barrett (Oldham), Mark Walters (Rangers), Brian Deane (Sheffield United).

Wellington, Jun 8, Friendly

New Zealand (0) 0	**England** (1) 2
	Pearce 14
	Hirst 50

Attendance: 12,000
Woods; Charles, Pearce, Wise, Walker, M Wright, Platt, Thomas, Deane (Hirst), I Wright, Salako
Pearce captain for the first time. Debut: Gary Charles (Nottingham Forest).

Kuala Lumpur, Jun 12, Friendly

| **Malaysia** (0) 2 | **England** (3) 4 |
| Matlan 53, 76 | Lineker 1, 23, 30, 70 |

Attendance: 45,000
Woods; Charles, Pearce, Batty, Walker, M Wright, Platt, Thomas, Clough, Lineker, Salako
Lineker's goals gave him 45 for England, one more than Jimmy Greaves and four behind Bobby Charlton's record.

ENGLAND PLAYERS 1990-91

	Appearances		Goals	
	1990-91	Career	1990-91	Career
Tony ADAMS	2	19	-	4
John BARNES	7	65	-	10
Earl BARRETT	1	1	-	-
David BATTY	5	5	-	-
Peter BEARDSLEY	4	49	1	8
Steve BULL	2	13	-	4
Gary CHARLES	2	2	-	-
Nigel CLOUGH	3	4	-	-
Gordon COWANS	1	10	-	2
Brian DEANE	2	2	-	-
Lee DIXON	7	8	1	1
Tony DORIGO	2	6	-	-
Paul GASCOIGNE	3	20	-	2
David HIRST	2	2	1	1
Steve HODGE	2	24	-	-
Gary LINEKER	10	68	10	45
Steve McMAHON	1	17	-	-
Gary PALLISTER	2	4	-	-
Paul PARKER	5	16	-	-
Stuart PEARCE	11	41	1	2
David PLATT	11	22	4	7
Bryan ROBSON	2	89	-	26
John SALAKO	4	4	-	-
David SEAMAN	4	7	-	-
Lee SHARPE	1	1	-	-
Alan SMITH	3	7	1	1
Trevor STEVEN	1	30	-	-
Gary STEVENS	1	42	-	-
Geoff THOMAS	7	7	-	-
Chris WADDLE	2	61	-	6
Des WALKER	11	35	-	-
Mark WALTERS	1	1	-	-
Dennis WISE	5	6	1	1
Chris WOODS	8	24	-	-
Ian WRIGHT	4	4	-	-
Mark WRIGHT	10	40	-	1

NORTHERN IRELAND 1990-91

12 Sep v YUGOSLAVIA (h)	Euro Champs Qualifier	lost 0-2	
17 Oct v DENMARK (h)	Euro Champs Qualifier	drew 1-1	Clarke

Stephen McBride, a prison PE officer playing part-time with Glenavon, was brought on as substitute

14 Nov v AUSTRIA (a)	Euro Champs Qualifier	drew 0-0	

Crowd only 7,000

5 Feb v POLAND (h)	Friendly	won 3-1	Taggart 2, Magilton
27 Mar v YUGOSLAVIA (a)	Euro Champs Qualifier	lost 1-4	Hill
1 May v FAROE ISLANDS (h)	Euro Champs Qualifier	drew 1-1	Clarke

Kari Reynheim, an electrician, equalised for the Faroes in the 65th minute

SCOTLAND 1990-91

12 Sep v ROMANIA (h)	Euro Champs Qualifier	won 2-1	Robertson, McCoist

Only 12,801 at Hampden due to live TV

17 Oct v SWITZERLAND	Euro Champs Qualifier	won 2-1	Robertson (pen), McAllister

Three penalties: one scored for each side, one missed for Scotland by McCoist

14 Nov v BULGARIA (a)	Euro Champs Qualifier	drew 1-1	McCoist

Scotland led from the 9th to 70th minute. Six men booked. Bulgarian manager Ivan Voutsev ordered from the dug-out by the referee

6 Feb v SOVIET UNION (h)	Friendly	Lost 0-1	

First international at Ibrox for 52 years

27 Mar v BULGARIA (h)	Euro Champs Qualifier	drew 1-1	Collins

Bulgaria equalised in the last minute

1 May v SAN MARINO (a)	Euro Champs Qualifier	won 2-0	Strachan pen, Durie

WALES 1990-91

11 Sep v DENMARK (a)	Friendly	lost 0-1	
17 Oct v BELGIUM (h)	Euro Champs Qualifier	won 3-1	Rush, Saunders, Hughes

Wales's first win in a competitive fixture since 1987

14 Nov v LUXEMBOURG (a)	Euro Champs Qualifier	won 1-0	Rush

Clayton Blackmore became the first Welsh player to be sent of in an international since Byron Stevenson in 1979.

6 Feb v REP. OF IRELAND (h)	Friendly	lost 0-3	
27 Mar v BELGIUM (a)	Euro Champs Qualifier	drew 1-1	Saunders

Referee refused to call game off on frozen Wrexham pitch despite pleas from both managers

1 May v ICELAND (h)	Friendly	won 1-0	Bodin (pen)
29 May v POLAND (a)	Friendly	drew 0-0	
5 Jun v GERMANY (h)	Euro Champs Qualifier	won 1-0	Rush

Rush scored after 69 minutes to break 16-match German unbeaten run

REPUBLIC OF IRELAND 1990-91

12 Sep v MOROCCO (h)	Friendly	won 1-0	D Kelly
17 Oct v TURKEY (h)	Euro Champs Qualifier	won 5-0	Aldridge 3, O'Leary, Quinn
14 Nov v ENGLAND (h)	Euro Champs Qualifier	drew 1-1	Cascarino
6 Feb v WALES (a)	Friendly	won 3-0	Quinn 2, Byrne
27 Mar v ENGLAND(a)	Euro Champs Qualifier	drew 1-1	Quinn
1 May v POLAND (h)	Euro Champs Qualifier	drew 0-0	
22 May v CHILE (h)	Friendly	drew 1-1	D Kelly

Charlton's 50th game as manager

2 Jun v UNITED STATES (a)	Friendly	drew 1-1	Cascarino

EUROPEAN CHAMPIONSHIP

GROUP ONE

ICELAND 2 Albania 0; Iceland 1 FRANCE 2; CZECHOSLOVAKIA 1 Iceland 0; SPAIN 2 Iceland 1; FRANCE 2 Czechoslovakia 1; CZECHOSLOVAKIA 3 Spain 2; Albania 0 FRANCE 1; SPAIN 9 Albania 0; FRANCE 3 Spain 1; FRANCE 5 Albania 0; Albania 0 CZECHOSLOVAKIA 2; ALBANIA 1 Iceland 0; Iceland 0 CZECHOSLOVAKIA 1; Czechoslovakia 1 FRANCE 2; ICELAND 2 Spain 0; Spain v. France, Oct 12; Czechoslovakia v. Albania, Oct 16; Spain v. Czechoslovakia, Nov 13; France v. Iceland, Nov 13 or 20; Albania v. Spain, Dec 18.

GROUP TWO

SWITZERLAND 2 Bulgaria 0; SCOTLAND 2 Romania 1; Romania 0 BULGARIA 3; SCOTLAND 2 Switzerland 1; Bulgaria 1 Scotland 1; San Marino 0 SWITZERLAND 4; ROMANIA 6 San Marino 0; Scotland 1 Bulgaria 1; San Marino 1 ROMANIA 3; Switzerland 0 Romania 0; Bulgaria 2 SWITZERLAND 3; San Marino 0 SCOTLAND 2; San Marino 0 BULGARIA 3; SWITZERLAND 7 San Marino 0; Switzerland 2 Scotland 2; Bulgaria v. San Marino, Oct 16; Romania v. Scotland, Oct 16; Scotland v. San Marino, Nov 13; Romania v. Switzerland, Nov 13; Bulgaria v. Romania, Nov 20.

GROUP THREE

SOVIET UNION 2 Norway 0; Norway 0 Hungary 0; Hungary 1 Italy 1; HUNGARY 4 Cyprus 2; Italy 0 Soviet Union 0; Cyprus 0 NORWAY 3; Cyprus 0 ITALY 4; Cyprus 0 HUNGARY 2; Hungary 0 SOVIET UNION 1; ITALY 3 Hungary 1; NORWAY 3 Cyprus 0; SOVIET UNION 4 Cyprus 0; NORWAY 2 Italy 1; Soviet Union 2 Hungary 2; Soviet Union v. Italy, Oct 12; Hungary v. Norway, Oct 30; Italy v. Norway, Nov 13; Cyprus v. Soviet Union, Nov 13; Italy v. Cyprus, Dec 21.

GROUP FOUR

Northern Ireland 0 YUGOSLAVIA 2; FAROE ISLANDS 1 Austria 0; DENMARK 4 Faroe Islands 1; Northern Ireland 1 Denmark 1; YUGOSLAVIA 4 Austria 1; Denmark 0 YUGOSLAVIA 2; Austria 0 Northern Ireland 0; YUGOSLAVIA 4 Northern Ireland 1; Yugoslavia 1 DENMARK 2; Northern Ireland 1 Faroe Islands1; YUGOSLAVIA 7 Faroe Islands 0; AUSTRIA 3 Faroe Islands 1; DENMARK 2 Austria 1; Faroe Islands 0 NORTHERN IRELAND 5; Faroe Islands 0 DENMARK 4; Austria v. Denmark, Oct 9; Faroe Islands v. Yugoslavia, Oct 16; Northern Ireland v. Austria, Oct 16; Denmark v. Northern Ireland, Nov 13; Austria v. Yugoslavia, Nov 13.

GROUP FIVE

East Germany withdrew
WALES 3 Belgium 1; Luxembourg 2 GERMANY 3; Luxembourg 0 WALES 1; BELGIUM 3 Luxembourg 0; Belgium 1 Wales 1; Germany 1 Belgium 1; WALES 1 Germany 0; Luxembourg 0 BELGIUM 2; Germany v. Wales, Oct 16; Wales v. Luxembourg, Nov 13; Belgium v. Germany, Nov 20; Germany v. Luxembourg, Dec 17.

GROUP SIX

Finland 0 Portugal 0; Portugal 0 Holland 0; GREECE 4 Malta 0; HOLLAND 2 Greece 0; Malta 1 Finland 1; Malta 0 HOLLAND 8; GREECE 3 Portugal 2; Malta 0 PORTUGAL 1; PORTUGAL 5 Malta 0; HOLLAND 1 Malta 0; HOLLAND 2 Finland 0; FINLAND 2 Malta 0; Finland 1 Holland 1; PORTUGAL 1 Finland 0; Finland v. Greece, Oct 9; Holland v. Portugal, Oct 16; Greece v. Finland, Oct 30; Portugal v. Greece, Nov 20; Greece v. Holland, Dec 4; Malta v. Greece, Dec 22
Marco Van Basten scored 5 goals in Holland's 8-0 win over Malta

GROUP SEVEN

ENGLAND 2 Poland 0; REPUBLIC OF IRELAND 5 Turkey 0; Republic of Ireland 1 England 1; Turkey 0 POLAND 1; England 1 Republic of Ireland 1; POLAND 3 Turkey 0; Turkey 0 ENGLAND 1; Republic of Ireland 0 Poland, 0; Poland v. Republic of Ireland, Oct 16; England v. Turkey, Oct 16; Turkey v. Republic of Ireland, Nov 13; Poland v. England, Nov 13

COPA AMERICA

SOUTH AMERICAN CHAMPIONSHIP

Chile, July 6-21

Group A

Chile 2 Venezuela 0; Paraguay 1 Peru 0; Argentina 3 Venezuela 0; Paraguay 5 Venezuela 0; Argentina 1 Chile 0; Peru 5 Venezuela 1; Argentina 4 Paraguay 1; Argentina 3 Peru 2; Chile 4 Paraguay 0

Final Table	P	W	D	L	F	A	Pts
Argentina	4	4	0	0	11	3	8
Chile	4	3	0	1	10	3	6
Paraguay	4	2	0	2	7	8	4
Peru	4	1	0	3	9	9	2
Venezuela	4	0	0	4	1	15	0

Group B

Columbia 1 Ecuador 0; Bolivia 1 Uruguay 1; Ecuador 1 Uruguay 1; Brazil 2 Bolivia 1; Bolivia 0 Columbia 0; Brazil 1 Uruguay 1; Ecuador 4 Bolivia 0; Columbia 2 Brazil 0; Uruguay 1 Columbia 0; Brazil 3 Ecuador 1
Brazil's 3rd goal against Ecuador came in the very last minute and had they won by only 2-1 they would not have qualified for the final phase

Final Table	P	W	D	L	F	A	Pts
Columbia	4	2	1	1	3	1	5
Brazil	4	2	1	1	6	5	5
Uruguay	4	1	3	0	4	3	3
Ecuador	4	1	1	2	6	5	3
Bolivia	4	0	2	2	2	7	2

Final Phase

Argentina 3 Brazil 2; Chile 1 Columbia 1; Brazil 2 Columbia 0; Argentina 0 Chile 0; Brazil 2 Chile 0; Argentina 2 Columbia 1;

Final Standings

	P	W	D	L	F	A	Pts
ARGENTINA	3	2	1	0	5	3	5
Brazil	3	2	0	1	6	3	4
Chile	3	0	2	1	1	3	2
Columbia	3	0	1	2	2	5	1

ENGLISH SOCCER 1990-91

FOOTBALL LEAGUE
(1989-90 positions in brackets. Promoted clubs in **bold**. Relegated clubs in *italics*)

FIRST DIVISION

In Div. Since				P	HOME W	D	L	F	A	AWAY W	D	L	F	A	Pts	Average Home Gate	Sent Off
1919	1	(4)	**ARSENAL**	38	15	4	0	51	10	9	9	1	23	8	83	36,907	1
1962	2	(1)	Liverpool	38	14	3	2	42	13	9	4	6	35	27	76	35,938	0
1989	3	(15)	Crystal Palace	38	11	6	2	26	17	9	3	7	24	24	69	19,521	1
1990	4	(P)	Leeds United	38	12	2	5	46	23	7	5	7	19	24	64	28,961	1
1989	5	(14)	Manchester C	38	12	3	4	35	25	5	8	6	29	28	62	27,862	2
1975	6	(13)	Manchester U	38	11	4	4	34	17	5	8	6	24	28	59	43,084	1
1986	7	(8)	Wimbledon	38	8	6	5	28	22	6	8	5	25	24	56	7,140	3
1977	8	(9)	Nottingham F	38	11	4	4	42	21	3	8	8	23	29	54	22,137	0
1954	9	(6)	Everton	38	9	5	5	26	15	4	7	8	24	31	51	25,127	1
1978	10	(3)	Tottenham H	38	8	9	2	35	22	3	7	9	16	28	49	30,632	3
1989	11	(P)	Chelsea	38	10	6	3	33	25	3	4	12	25	44	49	20,940	4
1983	12	(11)	QPR	38	8	5	6	27	22	4	5	10	17	31	46	13,504	1
1990	13	(P)	Sheffield Utd	38	9	3	7	23	23	4	4	11	13	32	46	21,451	3
1978	14	(7)	Southampton	38	9	6	4	33	22	3	3	13	25	47	45	16,925	0
1986	15	(10)	Norwich City	38	9	3	7	27	32	4	3	12	14	32	45	15,552	0
1967	16	(12)	Coventry City	38	10	6	3	30	16	1	5	13	12	33	44	13,880	1
1988	17	(2)	Aston Villa	38	7	9	3	29	25	2	5	12	17	33	41	25,552	1
1982	18	(17)	Luton Town	38	7	5	7	22	18	3	2	14	20	43	37	10,275	2
1990	19	(P)	*Sunderland*	38	6	6	7	15	16	2	4	13	23	44	34	22,358	4
1987	20	(16)	*Derby County*	38	3	8	8	25	36	2	1	16	12	39	24	16,380	0

Arsenal 2pts deducted, Manchester U 1pt deducted

Highest Attendance: 47,485 Manchester U v Aston Villa, Dec 29, 1990

Lowest Attendance: 3,981 Wimbledon v Coventry C, Feb 2, 1991

TOP SCORERS
League Only
22 Alan Smith (Arsenal)
21 Lee Chapman (Leeds)
20 John Fashanu (Wimbledon)
20 Niall Quinn (Manchester C)
19 Matthew le Tissier (Southampton)
19 David Platt (Aston Villa)

League & Cup
31 Lee Chapman
27 Alan Smith
26 Ian Rush (Liverpool)
25 Ian Wright (Crystal P)
24 David Platt
24 Tony Cottee (Everton)

FIRST DIVISION HAT-TRICKS (13)
Paul Gascoigne, Tottenham v Derby, Sep 8; Peter Beardsley, Liverpool v Manchester U, Sep 16; Lars Elstrup, Luton v Norwich, Sep 29; Paul Walsh, Tottenham H v Sheffield U, Oct 20; Dean Saunders, Derby v Sunderland, Mar 2; David Platt, Aston Villa v Tottenham, Mar 16; Niall Quinn, Manchester C v Crystal P, Apr 1; Lee Chapman, Leeds v Liverpool, Apr 12; David White (4 goals), Manchester C v Aston Villa, Apr 23; Paul Williams, Derby v Southampton, May 4; Ian Wright, Crystal P v Wimbledon, May 4; Alan Smith, Arsenal v Manchester U, May 6; Anders Limpar, Arsenal v Coventry, May 11.

HOW THE LEAD CHANGED HANDS
Aug 29 Arsenal; Sep 1 Liverpool; Jan 19 Arsenal; Feb 9 Liverpool; Feb 23 Arsenal; Mar 16 Liverpool; Mar 17 Arsenal; Mar 23 Liverpool; Mar 30 ARSENAL.

FIRST DIVISION NOTES
Total goals 1,046, average 2.76 per game; 89 came from penalties–Manchester City (10) and Liverpool (9) scored the most; Norwich and Wimbledon (0), Everton and Sheffield United (1) the least. In the 380 games the most popular score was 2-1 (48 times). All nine of the crowds above 45,000 were at Manchester United; the four crowds under 5,000 were at Wimbledon

YELLOW CARDS
Most (players): Chris Whyte (Leeds) 8; Marvin Johnson (Luton) 6+1 red; Vinny Jones (Sheffield United) 6+1 red; David Burrows (Liverpool) 7; Neil Ruddock (Southampton) 7. Kevin Ball (Sunderland) had 4 yellow cards and 2 reds.

Most (teams): Sunderland 36, Luton 33, Sheffield United 31

Fewest (teams): Aston Villa 11, Nottingham Forest 12, Norwich 13

LONGEST UNBEATEN RUNS FROM THE START OF THE SEASON

Matches	Club	Div	Season
29	Leeds	1	1973-74
29	Liverpool	1	1987-88
28*	Liverpool	2	1893-94
23	Arsenal	1	1990-91
22*	Preston	1	1888-89
22	Sheffield U	1	1899-1900

*Indicates complete season

SECOND DIVISION

In Div Since				P	HOME W	D	L	F	A	AWAY W	D	L	F	A	Pts	Average Home Gate	Sent Off
1974	1	(8)	OLDHAM	46	17	5	1	55	21	8	8	7	28	32	88	13,232	2
1989	2	(7)	West Ham United	46	15	6	2	41	18	9	9	5	19	16	87	22,565	1
1990	3	(R)	Sheffield Wednesday	46	12	10	1	43	23	10	6	7	37	28	82	26,282	2
1990	4	(P)	Notts County	46	14	4	5	45	28	9	7	7	31	27	80	8,391	2
1990	5	(R)	Millwall	46	11	6	6	43	28	9	7	7	27	23	73	11,024	1
1988	6	(18)	Brighton	46	12	4	7	37	31	9	3	11	26	38	70	8,306	1
1989	7	(21)	Middlesbrough	46	12	4	7	36	17	8	5	10	30	30	69	17,042	0
1981	8	(19)	Barnsley	46	13	7	3	39	16	6	5	12	24	32	69	8,895	3
1990	9	(P)	Bristol City	46	14	5	4	44	28	6	2	15	24	43	67	13,382	2
1988	10	(17)	Oxford United	46	10	9	4	41	29	4	10	9	28	37	61	5,656	2
1989	11	(3)	Newcastle United	46	8	10	5	24	22	6	7	10	25	34	59	16,887	3
1989	12	(10)	Wolverhampton	46	11	6	6	45	35	2	13	8	18	28	58	15,842	2
1990	13	(P)	Bristol Rovers	46	11	7	5	29	20	4	6	13	27	39	58	5,921	2
1986	14	(9)	Ipswich Town	46	9	8	6	32	28	4	10	9	28	40	57	11,813	2
1989	15	(11)	Port Vale	46	10	4	9	32	24	5	8	10	24	40	57	7,995	2
1990	16	(R)	Charlton Athletic	46	8	7	8	27	25	5	10	8	30	36	56	6,592	1
1988	17	(12)	Portsmouth	46	10	6	7	34	27	4	5	14	24	43	53	9,583	3
1986	18	(16)	Plymouth Argyle	46	10	10	3	36	20	2	7	14	18	48	53	6,850	1
1980	19	(5)	Blackburn Rovers	46	8	6	9	26	27	6	4	13	25	39	52	8,114	3
1988	20	(15)	Watford	46	5	8	10	24	32	7	7	9	21	27	51	9,573	5
1987	21	(4)	Swindon Town	46	8	6	9	31	30	4	8	11	34	43	50	9,436	2
1987	22	(13)	Leicester City	46	12	4	7	41	33	2	4	17	19	50	50	11,545	3
1986	23	(20)	West Bromwich	46	7	11	5	26	21	3	7	13	26	40	48	11,804	3
1985	24	(14)	Hull City	46	6	10	7	35	32	4	5	14	22	53	45	6,164	0

Play-offs
SEMI-FINALS: BRIGHTON 4 2 Millwall 1 1;
Middlesbrough 1 0 NOTTS COUNTY 1 1
FINAL: *Wembley, June 2*
NOTTS COUNTY 3 Brighton 1 *Attendance 59,940*

Highest Attendance: 34,845 Sheffield W v Oldham, Nov 3, 1990
Lowest Attendance: 3,175 Hull v Plymouth, May 4, 1991

TOP SCORERS
League Only
33 Teddy Sheringham (Millwall)
26 Steve Bull (Wolves)
25 Andy Payton (Hull)
24 David Hirst (Sheff Wed)
22 Darren Beckford (Port Vale)
22 Steve Butler (Watford)
22 Duncan Shearer (Swindon)

League & Cup
38 Teddy Sheringham
32 David Hirst
27 Steve Bull
26 Steve Butler
25 Andy Payton

SECOND DIVISION HAT-TRICKS (21)
Ian Marshall, Oldham v Wolves, Aug 25; David Hirst (4 goals), Sheffield W v Hull, Sep 1; Teddy Sheringham, Millwall v West Brom, Oct 6; Steve Bull, Wolves v Bristol C, Oct 6; Paul Simpson, Oxford v Brighton, Oct 20; Bernie Slaven, Middlesbrough v Brighton, Oct 27; Frank Stapleton, Blackburn v Wolves, Oct 27; Ian Baird, Middlesbrough v Oxford Nov 25; David Kelly, Leicester v Newcastle, Dec 1; Mick Quinn, Newcastle v Leicester, Dec 1; Bryan Wade (4 goals), Brighton v Newcastle, Jan 16; Teddy Sheringham (4 goals), Millwall v Plymouth, Feb 16; Jason Beckford, Port Vale v Blackburn, Mar 9; Steve Bull, Wolves v Oxford Mar 16; Tommy Johnson, Notts C v Blackburn, Mar 30; Colin Clarke, Portsmouth v Bristol C, Mar 30; Teddy Sheringham, Millwall v Charlton, Apr 10; Paul Wilkinson, Watford v Wolves, Apr 13; Teddy Sheringham, Millwall v Bristol C, Apr 27; David Regis, Notts C v Plymouth, Apr 27; Steve Foley, Swindon v Leicester, Apr 27.

HOW THE LEAD CHANGED HANDS
Sep 1 Oldham; Oct 13 Sheffield Wednesday; Oct 20 Oldham; Nov 24 West Ham; Dec 21 Oldham; Dec 26 West Ham; Dec 21 Oldham; Dec 26 West Ham; Mar 9 Oldham; Apr 6 West Ham; Apr 16 Oldham; Apr 17 West Ham; May 7 Oldham; May 8 West Ham; May 11 OLDHAM.

SECOND DIVISION NOTES
Total goals 1,480, average 2.68 per game; 93 came from penalties–Portsmouth (10) scored the most, Watford and Wolves (1) the least. In the 552 games the most popular score was 1-1 (81 times). The biggest victory was Oldham's 6-1 home win over Brighton. The most goals were in Leicester's 5-4 home win over Newcastle. All seven crowds above 30,000 were at Sheffield Wednesday; of the 22 under 5,000 eight were at Oxford

OLDEST POST-WAR FOOTBALL LEAGUE PLAYERS
Age
51y 120d	NEIL McBAIN (New Brighton)	1946-47
50y 5d	STANLEY MATTHEWS (Stoke City)	1964-65
43y 199d	ALF WOOD (Coventry)	1958-59
43y 171d	TOMMY HUTCHINSON (Swansea)	1990-91
43y 121d	MICHAEL BURNS (Ipswich)	1951-52
43y 103d	ALEX FERGUSON (Swindon)	1047-48

THIRD DIVISION

In Div Since				P	HOME W	D	L	F	A	AWAY W	D	L	F	A	Pts	Average Sent Home Gate Off
1990	1	(P)	CAMBRIDGE U	46	14	5	4	42	22	11	6	6	33	23	86	5,497	2
1990	2	(P)	Southend United	46	13	6	4	34	23	13	1	9	33	28	85	6,177	4
1990	3	(P)	Grimsby Town	46	16	3	4	42	13	8	8	7	24	21	83	7,252	0
1988	4	(6)	Bolton Wanderers	46	14	5	4	33	18	10	6	7	31	32	83	7,254	2
1989	5	(4)	Tranmere Rovers	46	13	5	5	38	21	10	4	9	26	25	78	6,798	3
1978	6	(13)	Brentford	46	12	4	7	30	22	9	9	5	29	25	76	6,145	5
1985	7	(5)	Bury	46	13	6	4	39	26	7	7	9	28	30	73	3,571	5
1990	8	(R)	Bradford City	46	13	3	7	36	22	7	7	9	26	32	70	6,643	3
1990	9	(R)	Bournemouth	46	14	6	3	37	20	5	7	11	21	38	70	6,059	1
1982	10	(18)	Wigan Athletic	46	14	3	6	40	20	6	6	11	31	34	69	2,871	3
1988	11	(8)	Huddersfield Town	46	13	3	7	37	23	5	10	8	20	28	67	5,351	3
1989	12	(7)	Birmingham City	46	8	9	6	21	21	8	8	7	24	28	65	7,030	0
1989	13	(14)	Leyton Orient	46	15	2	6	35	19	3	8	12	20	39	64	4,175	0
1990	14	(R)	Stoke City	46	9	7	7	36	29	7	5	11	19	30	60	11,272	2
1988	15	(10)	Reading	46	11	5	7	34	28	6	3	14	19	38	59	4,072	4
1990	16	(P)	Exeter City	46	12	6	5	35	16	4	3	16	23	36	57	4,248	5
1987	17	(19)	Preston North End	46	11	5	7	33	29	4	6	13	21	38	56	5,210	2
1989	18	(11)	Shrewsbury Town	46	8	7	8	29	22	6	3	14	32	46	52	3,437	2
1986	19	(16)	Chester City	46	10	3	10	27	27	4	6	13	19	31	51	1,622	3
1988	20	(17)	Swansea City	46	8	6	9	31	33	5	3	15	18	39	48	3,661	2
1986	21	(20)	Fulham	46	8	8	7	27	22	2	8	13	14	34	46	4,055	0
1989	22	(12)	Crewe Alexandra	46	6	9	8	35	35	5	2	16	27	45	44	3,756	2
1989	23	(9)	Rotherham United	46	5	10	8	31	38	5	2	16	19	49	42	4,595	3
1986	24	(15)	Mansfield Town	46	5	8	10	23	27	3	6	14	19	36	38	2,771	4

Play-offs

SEMI-FINALS: Brentford 2 0 TRANMERE 2 1; Bury 1 0 BOLTON 1 1
FINAL: *Wembley, Jun 1*: TRANMERE 1 Bolton 0
Attendance 30,217

Highest Attendance: 16,135 Stoke v Birmingham, Sep 8, 1990

Lowest Attendance: 631 Chester v Reading, Mar 5, 1991

TOP SCORERS

League Only	*League & Cup*
19 Luther Blissett (Bournemouth)	26 Brett Angell
19 Tony Philliskirk (Bolton)	26 Tony Philliskirk
17 Dion Dublin (Cambridge)	23 Dion Dublin
16 Jimmy Gilligan (Swansea)	21 Luther Blissett
15 Brett Angell (Southend)	21 Ian Muir (Tranmere)
15 David Lee (Bury)	
15 Trevor Senior (Reading)	

THIRD DIVISION HAT-TRICKS (11)

Keith Edwards, Huddersfield v Bolton, Sep 8; Ernie Bishop, Tranmere v Mansfield Oct 22; Wayne Clarke, Shrewsbury v Birmingham, Oct 27; Luther Blissett, Bournemouth v Bradford, Nov 10; Gary Shaw, Shrewsbury v Bradford, Dec 22; Jimmy Gilligan, Swansea v Wigan, Dec 29; Steve Neville, Exeter v Swansea, Feb 26; John McGinley, Bury v Bolton, Mar 19; David Lee, Bury v Cambridge, Mar 23; Craig Hignett, Crewe v Rotherham, Apr 30; Tony Kelly, Shrewsbury v Reading, May 7.

HOW THE LEAD CHANGED HANDS

Sep 1 Grimsby; Sep 9 Southend; Sep 22 Grimsby; Sep 29 Southend; Oct 13 Grimsby; Oct 23 Southend; Jan 26 Grimsby; Feb 2 Southend; Mar 30 Grimsby; Apr 12 Southend; May 11 CAMBRIDGE.

THIRD DIVISION NOTES

Total goals 1,381, average 2.5 per game. Of these 596 were in the first half and 785 in the second half; 91 came from penalties—Bolton, Bournemouth and Huddersfield scored the most (8) and Mansfield and Shrewsbury (0) and Reading and Stoke (1) the least. 78 of the 552 games were 1-0 to the home team. The biggest wins were Wigan's 6-1 win away to Swansea and Grimsby's 5-0 win against Bournemouth. Tranmere won 6-2 at home to Mansfield. Stoke City had 17 of the 28 crowds above 10,000; Chester had the only one under 1,000.

West Bromwich's relegation to the third Division leaves 11 League clubs that have never been out of the top two Divisions: Southend's promotion leaves 13 clubs that have never been in the top two Divisions.

Never Out
Arsenal, Chelsea, Everton, Leeds United, Leicester City, Liverpool, Manchester City, Manchester United, Newcastle, Tottenham, West Ham.
Everton now last founder members never to have been in Third Division.

Never In
Aldershot, Barnet, Chester, Exeter, Gillingham, Halifax, Hartlepool, Maidstone, Peterborough, Rochdale, Scarborough, Torquay, Wigan.

FOURTH DIVISION

In Div Since			P	HOME					AWAY					Pts	Average Home Gate	Sent Off
				W	D	L	F	A	W	D	L	F	A			
1990	1	(P)	**DARLINGTON**	46	13	8	2	36	14	9	9	5	32	24	83	3,959	3
1970	2	(4)	**Stockport County**	46	16	6	1	54	19	7	7	9	30	28	82	3,565	2
1969	3	(19)	**Hartlepool United**	46	15	5	3	35	15	9	5	9	32	33	82	3,166	1
1979	4	(9)	**Peterborough**	46	13	9	1	38	15	8	8	7	29	30	80	5,164	1
1990	5	(R)	**Blackpool**	46	17	3	3	55	17	6	7	10	23	30	79	4,058	4
1985	6	(16)	**Burnley**	46	17	5	1	46	16	6	5	12	24	35	79	7,871	3
1972	7	(15)	**Torquay United**	46	14	7	2	37	13	4	11	8	27	34	72	2,965	3
1984	8	(11)	**Scunthorpe United**	46	17	4	2	51	20	3	7	13	20	42	71	3,114	2
1987	9	(18)	**Scarborough**	46	13	5	5	36	21	6	7	10	23	35	69	1,593	0
1990	10	(R)	**Northampton Town**	46	14	5	4	34	21	4	8	11	23	37	67	3,693	4
1988	11	(20)	**Doncaster Rovers**	46	12	5	6	36	22	5	9	9	20	24	65	2,734	6
1974	12	(12)	**Rochdale**	46	10	9	4	29	22	5	8	10	21	31	62	2,253	0
1990	13	(R)	**Cardiff City**	46	10	6	7	26	23	5	9	9	17	31	60	2,991	2
1988	14	(10)	**Lincoln City**	46	10	7	6	32	27	4	10	9	18	34	59	2,941	5
1989	15	(14)	**Gillingham**	46	9	9	5	35	27	3	9	11	22	33	54	3,506	3
1990	16	(R)	**Walsall**	46	7	12	4	25	17	5	5	13	23	34	53	4,078	1
1978	17	(17)	**Hereford United**	46	9	10	4	32	19	4	4	15	21	39	53	2,521	0
1989	18	(7)	**Chesterfield**	46	8	12	3	33	26	5	2	16	14	36	53	3,725	1
1989	19	(5)	**Maidstone United**	46	9	5	9	42	34	4	7	12	24	37	51	1,920	9
1987	20	(8)	**Carlisle United**	46	12	3	8	30	30	1	6	16	17	59	48	3,005	4
1988	21	(13)	**York City**	46	8	6	9	21	23	3	7	13	24	34	46	2,438	4
1976	22	(23)	**Halifax Town**	46	9	6	8	34	29	3	4	16	25	50	46	1,700	2
1989	23	(22)	**Aldershot**	46	8	7	8	38	43	2	4	17	23	58	41	2,207	4
1983	24	(21)	**Wrexham**	46	8	7	8	33	34	2	3	18	15	40	40	2,019	2

Play-offs

SEMI-FINALS: Scunthorpe 1 1 BLACKPOOL 1 2; TORQUAY 2 0 Burnley 0 1

FINAL: *Wembley, May 31*: TORQUAY 2 Blackpool 2 (Torquay won 5-4 on pens) *Attendance: 21,615*

Highest Attendance: 18,395 Burnley v Blackpool, Apr 23, 1991

Lowest Attendance 625 Scarborough v Wrexham, Dec 7, 1990

TOP SCORERS

League Only	*League & Cup*
32 Steve Norris (Halifax)	35 Joe Allon
28 Joe Allon (Hartlepool)	35 Steve Norris
23 Andy Flounders (Scunthorpe)	27 Andy Flounders
21 David Puckett (Aldershot)	26 David Puckett
19 Steve Lovell (Gillingham)	21 Steve Lovell

FOURTH DIVISION HAT-TRICKS (12) Jon Narbett, Hereford v Carlisle, Sep 15; Ken Charlery, Maidstone v Lincoln, Sep 29; Stewart Phillips, Hereford v Halifax, Oct 23; Lee Turnbull, Doncaster v Aldershot, Dec 1; David Crown, Gillingham v Burnley, Dec 15; Ian Blackstone, York v Wrexham, Dec 29; Andy Flounders, Scunthorpe v Aldershot, Jan 12; Steve Butler, Maidstone v York, Jan 19; Mark Gall, Maidstone v Halifax, Feb 27; Steve Norris, Halifax v Walsall, Mar 2; Paul Dalton Hartlepool v Aldershot Mar 12 Dean Edwards, Torquay v Northampton, Apr 15; Tony Lormor (4 goals), Lincoln v Carlisle, May 11.

BOB AND TERRY, THE LIKELY LADS

❝ The mismanagement committee are bungling, bumbling idiots. They couldn't pump up a football between them.❞
Robert Maxwell

"Regrettably, Robert Maxwell mirrors one of the unfortunate traits of the modern game - he can afford the entrance fee but he doesn't seem to appreciate the values of decorum."
Andy Williamson, Football League spokesman

"I can't keep records of such petty cash."
Robert Maxwell, asked if Spurs had repaid a £1.1m loan

"One of the further conditions to the proposal to subscribe is that a key player,

P Gascoigne Esq, will not be transferred."
Statement by Terry Venables

"I'm working round the clock to save the club and it has been murder. I'm past the Kenny Dalglish stage. I've gone potty."
Venables

"Bob's Yer Uncle!"
Daily Mirror *headline, June 18, predicting that Maxwell would take over Spurs.*

"...to which Venables can retort with some feeling 'Yeah, and Fanny's Yer Aunt.'❞❞
David Lacey, The Guardian, June 21, after Maxwell failed

HOW THE LEAD CHANGED HANDS

Sep 1 Doncaster; Sep 29 Torquay; Dec 1 Northampton; Dec 26 Doncaster; Jan 5 Darlington; Jan 12 Stockport; Jan 25 Doncaster; Jan 26 Northampton; Feb 5 Darlington; Feb 15 Northampton; Feb 19 DARLINGTON

FOURTH DIVISION NOTES

Total goals 1,415, average 2.56 per game. Of these 627 were in the first half and 788 in the second half; 125 came from penalties. Scarborough (9) scored the most, six clubs had the least (3). The most common score was 1-1 (67 times). The biggest victory was Blackpool's 6-0 home win against Carlisle. Maidstone (6-1 v Scunthorpe), Lincoln (6-2 v Carlisle) and Scunthorpe (6-2 v Aldershot) also scored six, all at home. The biggest away win was by Hereford, 4-0 at Halifax. There were 23 crowds above 7,000, 11 of them at Burnley and two under 1,000, both at Scarborough.

Main source for Notes: *The Observer.*

FA CUP

FIRST ROUND

ALDERSHOT 6 Tiverton 2; Altrincham 1 HUDDERSFIELD 2; ATHERSTONE 3 Fleetwood 1; Aylesbury 0 WALSALL 1; BARNET 2 2 Chelmsford 2 0; BIRMINGHAM 1 Cheltenham 0; Bishop Auckland 0 BARROW 1; BLACKPOOL 2 Grimsby 0; Boston 1 0 WYCOMBE 1 4; BOURNEMOUTH 2 Gillingham 1; Bradford 0 1 SHREWSBURY 0 2; BRENTFORD 5 Yeovil 0; Cardiff 0 0 HAYES 0 1; CHESTER 2 2 Doncaster 2 1; CHESTERFIELD 3 Spennymoor 2; CHORLEY 2 Bury 1; COLCHESTER 2 Reading 1; Darlington 1 0 YORK 1 1; Exeter 1 4 CAMBRIDGE U 2; FULHAM 2 Farnborough 1; Halesowen 1 TRANMERE 2; HALIFAX 3 Wrexham 2; Hereford 1 1 PETERBOROUGH 1 2; LEYTON ORIENT 3 Southend 2; Lincoln 1 CREWE 4; Littlehampton 0 NORTHAMPTON 4; MAIDSTONE 4 Torquay 1; MERTHYR 1 1 Sutton 1 0; Preston 0 MANSFIELD 1; Rochdale 1 SCUNTHORPE 1 2; ROTHERHAM 1 Stockport 0; Runcorn 0 HARTLEPOOL 3; Scarborough 0 LEEK 2; Stafford 1 BURNLEY 3; SWANSEA 5 Welling 2; Tamworth 4 WHITLEY BAY 6; Telford 0 0 STOKE 0 1; WIGAN 5 Carlisle 0; Witton 1 BOLTON 2; WOKING 0 1 2 Kidderminster 0 1 1

SECOND ROUND

Fulham 0 1 CAMBRIDGE 0 2; ALDERSHOT 2 Maidstone 1; BARNET 0 1 Northampton 0 0; BOURNEMOUTH 1 Hayes 0; SCUNTHORPE 3 Tranmere 1; SWANSEA 2 Walsall 1; WIGAN 2 Hartlepool 0; WOKING 5 Merthyr 1; Chesterfield 3 BOLTON 4; SHREWSBURY 1 Chorley 0; Birmingham 1 BRENTFORD 3; BURNLEY 2 Stoke 0; CREWE 1 Atherstone 0; Whitley Bay 0 BARROW 1; MANSFIELD 2 York 1; Wycombe 1 0 PETERBOROUGH 1 2; ROTHERHAM 1 2 Halifax 1 1; Colchester 0 1 LEYTON ORIENT 0 4; Leek 1 0 CHESTER 1 4; Huddersfield 0 BLACKPOOL 2

THIRD ROUND

Aldershot 0 1 WEST HAM 0 6; ARSENAL 2 Sunderland 1; Aston Villa 1 0 WIMBLEDON 1 1; Barnet 0 PORTSMOUTH 5; Barnsley 1 0 LEEDS 1 4; Blackburn 1 0 LIVERPOOL 1 3; Blackpool 0 TOTTENHAM 1; BOLTON 1 Barrow 0; BRIGHTON 3 Scunthorpe 2; Bristol Rovers 0 CREWE 2; Burnley 0 MANCHESTER C 1; Charlton 1 EVERTON 0; Chelsea 1 OXFORD 1; Chester 2 BOURNEMOUTH 3; COVENTRY 1 1 Wigan 1 0; Crystal Palace 0 2 0 NOTTINGHAM FOREST 0 2 3; Hull 1 0 NOTTS COUNTY 5; Leyton Orient 1 SWINDON 1 1; MANCHESTER UNITED 2 QPR 1; Mansfield 0 SHEFFIELD WEDNESDAY 2; MIDDLESBROUGH 0 2 Plymouth 0 1; MILLWALL 2 Leicester 1; NEWCASTLE 2 Derby 0; NORWICH 2

Bristol City 1; OLDHAM 3 Brentford 1; PORT VALE 2 Peterborough 1; Sheffield United 1 LUTON 3; SHREWSBURY 4 Watford 1; SOUTHAMPTON 3 Ipswich 2; Swansea 0 0 ROTHERHAM 0 4; West Bromwich Albion 2 WOKING 4; Wolves 0 CAMBRIDGE 1

FOURTH ROUND

ARSENAL 0 1 0 2 Leeds 0 1 0 1; CAMBRIDGE 2 Middlesbrough 0; Coventry 1 0 SOUTHAMPTON 1 2; CREWE 1 Rotherham 0; LIVERPOOL 2 3 Brighton 2 2; Luton 1 0 WEST HAM 0 5; MANCHESTER U 1 Bolton 0; Millwall 4 0 SHEFFIELD WEDNESDAY 4 2; Newcastle 2 0 NOTTINGHAM FOREST 2 3; NORWICH 3 Swindon 1; NOTTS COUNTY 2 Oldham 0; PORTSMOUTH 5 Bournemouth 1; Port Vale 1 MANCHESTER CITY 2; SHREWSBURY 1 Wimbledon 0; TOTTENHAM 4 Oxford 2; Woking 0 EVERTON 1 (played at Goodison Park);

NON-LEAGUE TEAMS IN FOURTH ROUND OF THE FA CUP SINCE 1980-81

1980-81 Enfield (lost 0-3 to Barnsley, after 1-1)
1983-84 Telford (lost 2-3 to Derby)
1984-85 Telford (lost 0-3 to Everton in fifth round)
1985-86 Altrincham (lost 0-2 to York)
1988-89 Kettering (lost 1-2 to Charlton)
1988-89 Sutton (lost 0-8 to Norwich)
1990-91 Woking (lost 0-1 to Everton)

FIFTH ROUND

CAMBRIDGE 4 Sheffield Wednesday 0; Liverpool 0 4 0 EVERTON 0 4 1; NORWICH 2 Manchester U 1; NOTTS COUNTY 1 Manchester C 0; Portsmouth 1 TOTTENHAM 2; Shrewsbury 0 ARSENAL 1; Southampton 1 1 NOTTINGHAM FOREST 1 3; WEST HAM 1 Crewe 0

This was Crewe's first appearance in the fifth round since 1888

SIXTH ROUND

ARSENAL 2 Cambridge 1; Norwich 0 NOTTINGHAM FOREST 1; TOTTENHAM 2 Notts County 1; WEST HAM 2 Everton 1

SEMI-FINALS

(at Wembley)
TOTTENHAM 3 Arsenal 1
(at Villa Park)
NOTTINGHAM FOREST 4 West Ham 0
The Tottenham-Arsenal game was the first semi-final staged at Wembley. No other London ground was considered adequate.

FINAL

Wembley, May 18
TOTTENHAM HOTSPUR 2 Nottingham Forest 1
(after extra time)
Stewart 55, Walker (og) 94   Pearce 15
Tottenham Hotspur: Thorstvedt; Edinburgh, van den Hauwe, Sedgley, Howells, Mabbutt, Stewart, Gascoigne (Nayim), Samways (Walsh), Lineker, Allen.

Nottingham Forest: Crossley; Charles, Pearce, Walker, Chettle, Keane, Crosby, Parker, Clough, Glover (Laws), Woan (Hodge).
Referee: Roger Milford (Bristol)
Attendance: 80,000
Receipts: £2,016,000 (record)

Teams underlined beat opposition from a higher division

A WORD FROM THE MANAGEMENT

❝If players are not going to die for this club then I don't want them."
Alex Miller, Hibs manager

"This is a language more appropriate to a war zone than a sporting occasion."
Jim Farry, Scottish FA secretary

"Players here learn to mark their man before they learn to dribble. The Brazilian thinks of scoring but the Italian objective is to stop the other team."
Sebatiao Lazaroni, Fiorentina's Brazilian manager

"Sport is not entertainment. It's an activity for the benefit of the participants. If you run away from that you risk having the wrong pipers calling the tune."
Howard Wilkinson, Leeds manager

"Welcome to Bath who've found the opening part of the season I'm sure one to learn from but like everyone else there's no need for panics after only a hand full of games which also means we've got to be on our toes. Good luck. PS.If this doesn't make any sense it's because I'm not very well.".
Programme notes by Dave Cusack, Boston United manager

"How ironic this should happen on the anniversary of the Coventry blitz. When I received the phone call from the chairman

it felt like my house had just been bombed."
John Sillett, on being sacked by Coventry

"We haven't had a penalty all season. You have to rape our players to give away a penalty."
Dave Bassett, Sheffield United manager

"The defeat at Carshalton wasn't as bad as it sounds. But we let in five bad goals."
Joe Boon, Worthing manager, after losing 13-0

"Now it's all come good, it's a lovely feeling. See you all next season."
Jim Ryan, Luton manager, after his team avoided relegation, May 11

"This is what I get for keeping the team up."
Jim Ryan, after being sacked, May 13

"Ask Bob Stokoe what it means to win the Cup. Ask John Sillett. Ask Tommy Docherty. And then go and ask Kenny Dalglish. That lot won the Cup. And where are they now? They're out of work."
*Brian Clough
Nottingham Forest manager*

"Not long ago a manager had three years to get results. Now it's more like three weeks or you're out.❞
Gerry Francis, QPR manager

RUMBELOWS LEAGUE CUP

FIRST ROUND

Birmingham 0 1 BOURNEMOUTH 1 1; BRADFORD CITY 2 2 Bury 0 3; BRENTFORD 2 0 Hereford 0 1; Brighton 0 1 NORTHAMPTON 2 1; Bristol R 1 1 TORQUAY 2 1; CARLISLE 1 1 Scunthorpe 0 1; Chesterfield 1 2 HARTLEPOOL 2 2; DARLINGTON 0 1 Blackpool 0 1 (Darlington won on away goals); Doncaster 2 1 ROTHERHAM 6 2; Exeter 1 0 NOTTS COUNTY 1 1; Fulham 1 0 PETERBOROUGH 2 2; Gillingham 1 0 SHREWSBURY 0 2; Grimsby 2 0 CREWE 1 1 (Crewe won on away goals); HALIFAX 2 0 Lincoln 0 1; Huddersfield 1 1 BOLTON 3 2; Maidstone 2 1 LEYTON ORIENT 2 4; Mansfield 1 0 CARDIFF 1 3; MIDDLESBROUGH 1 2 Tranmere 1 1; Preston 2 1 CHESTER 0 5; Reading 1 1 OXFORD 1 2; ROCHDALE 4 3 Scarborough 0 3; SOUTHEND 2 2 Aldershot 1 2; Stockport 0 1 BURNLEY 2 0; STOKE 0 1 Swansea 0 0; WALSALL 4 1 Cambridge 2 2; West Brom 2 0 BRISTOL CITY 2 1; Wigan 0 1 BARNSLEY 1 0 (Barnsley won 4-3

on pens); York 0 0 WREXHAM 1 2

SECOND ROUND

ASTON VILLA 1 1 Barnsley 0 0; Bournemouth 0 1 MILLWALL 0 2; Cardiff 1 1 PORTSMOUTH 1 3; Carlisle 1 0 DERBY 1 1; Charlton 2 0 LEYTON ORIENT 2 1; Chester 0 0 ARSENAL 1 5; COVENTRY 4 3 Bolton 2 2; CRYSTAL PALACE 8 2 Southend 0 1; Darlington 3 0 SWINDON 0 4; Halifax 1 1 MANCHESTER UNITED 3 2; HULL 0 1 Wolverhampton 0 1 (Hull won on away goals); Leicester 1 0 LEEDS 0 3; LIVERPOOL 5 4 Crewe 1 1; Luton 1 1 BRADFORD CITY 1 1 (Bradford won 5-4 on pens); MIDDLESBROUGH 2 0 Newcastle 0 1; Northampton 0 1 SHEFFIELD UNITED 1 2; NORWICH 2 3 Watford 0 0; NOTTINGHAM F 4 1 Burnley 1 0; Notts C 1 2 OLDHAM 0 5; PLYMOUTH 1 2 Wimbledon 0 0; Port Vale 0 0 OXFORD 2 0; QPR 3 1 Peterborough 1 1; Rochdale 0 0 SOUTHAMPTON 5 3; Rotherham 1 0 BLACKBURN 1 1; SHEFFIELD WEDNESDAY 2 2 Brentford 1 1; Shrewsbury 1 0 IPSWICH 1 3; SUNDERLAND 0 6 Bristol C 1 1; Torquay 0 0 MANCHESTER CITY 4 0; TOTTENHAM 5 2

Hartlepool 0 1; Walsall 0 1 CHELSEA 5 4; WEST HAM 3 2 Stoke 0 1; Wrexham 0 0 EVERTON 5 6

THIRD ROUND

ASTON VILLA 2 Millwall 0; CHELSEA 0 3 Portsmouth 0 2; COVENTRY 3 Hull 0; CRYSTAL PALACE 0 1 Leyton Orient 0 0; DERBY 6 Sunderland 0; Ipswich 0 SOUTHAMPTON 2; LEEDS 2 Oldham 0; Manchester City 1 ARSENAL 2; MANCHESTER UNITED 3 Liverpool 1; MIDDLESBROUGH 2 Norwich 0; OXFORD 2 West Ham 1; Plymouth 1 NOTTINGHAM FOREST 2; QPR 2 Blackburn 1; SHEFFIELD United 2 Everton 1; SHEFFIELD WEDNESDAY 0 1 Swindon 0 0; TOTTENHAM 2 Bradford C 1

FOURTH ROUND

Arsenal 2 MANCHESTER UNITED 6; ASTON VILLA 3 Middlesbrough 2; COVENTRY 5 Nottingham F 4; SHEFFIELD WEDNESDAY 1 2 Derby 1 1; Oxford 1 CHELSEA 2; Queen's Park Rangers 0 LEEDS 3; Sheffield United 0 TOTTENHAM 2; SOUTHAMPTON 2 Crystal Palace 0

FIFTH ROUND

LEEDS 4 Aston Villa 1; Coventry 0 SHEFFIELD WEDNESDAY 1; CHELSEA 0 3 Tottenham 0 0; Southampton 1 2 MANCHESTER UNITED 1 3

SEMI-FINALS

MANCHESTER UNITED 2 1 Leeds 1 0
Chelsea 0 1 SHEFFIELD WEDNESDAY 2 3

FINAL

Wembley, Apr 21
SHEFFIELD WED (1)1 Manchester United (0) 0
Sheridan 37
Sheffield Wednesday: Turner; Nilsson, King, Harkes (Madden), Shirtliff, Pearson, Wilson, Sheridan, Hirst, Williams, Worthington
Manchester United: Sealey; Irwin, Blackmore, Bruce, Webb (Phelan), Pallister, Robson, Ince, McClair, Hughes, Sharpe
Referee: R Lewis (Gt.Bookham)
Attendance: 80,000
Teams underlined beat opponents from a higher division

SCOTTISH SOCCER

SCOTTISH LEAGUE

Promoted clubs in bold. Relegated clubs in italics.
1989-90 positions in brackets.

PREMIER DIVISION

				HOME					AWAY						Average
			P	W	D	L	F	A	W	D	L	F	A	Pts	Home Gate
1	(1)	**RANGERS**	36	14	3	1	40	8	10	4	4	22	15	55	35,969
2	(2)	Aberdeen	36	12	5	1	30	7	10	4	4	32	20	53	15,273
3	(5)	Celtic	36	10	4	4	30	14	7	3	8	22	24	41	29,012
4	(4)	Dundee United	36	11	3	4	28	16	6	4	8	13	13	41	10,089
5	(3)	Hearts	36	10	3	5	28	22	4	4	10	20	33	35	13,232
6	(6)	Motherwell	36	9	5	4	28	18	3	4	11	23	32	33	7,787
7	(P)	St Johnstone	36	6	4	8	23	25	5	5	8	18	29	31	7,755
8	(8)	Dunfermline A	36	5	7	6	23	26	3	4	11	15	35	27	8,257
9	(7)	Hibernian	36	6	5	7	17	25	0	8	10	7	26	25	9,257
10	(9)	St Mirren	36	5	5	9	14	25	1	4	13	14	34	19	7,612

No clubs relegated: Premier Division increasing to 12 teams in 1991-92

HOW THE LEAD CHANGED HANDS

Sep 1 Aberdeen; Sep 8 Dundee United; Oct 6 Rangers; Oct 10 Dundee United; Nov 24 Aberdeen; Nov 25 Rangers; May 4 Aberdeen; May 11 RANGERS.

FIRST DIVISION

				HOME					AWAY						Average
			P	W	D	L	F	A	W	D	L	F	A	Pts	Home Gate
1	(4)	**FALKIRK**	39	12	4	4	40	18	9	8	2	30	17	54	4,505
2	(2)	**Airdrieonians**	39	9	5	5	32	21	12	6	2	37	22	53	3,183
3	(R)	Dundee	39	12	3	4	33	15	10	5	5	26	18	52	3,636
4	(8)	Partick Thistle	39	7	6	6	25	24	9	7	4	31	29	45	3,700
5	(P)	Kilmarnock	39	10	6	3	32	21	5	7	8	26	27	43	4,904
6	(6)	Hamilton Academical	39	8	6	6	25	20	8	4	7	25	21	42	1,779
7	(5)	Raith Rovers	39	7	5	8	22	26	7	4	8	32	38	37	1,841
8	(1)	Clydebank	39	6	6	8	40	39	7	4	8	25	31	36	1,410
9	(11)	Morton	39	6	7	6	25	22	5	6	9	23	33	35	1,886
10	(12)	Forfar Athletic	39	6	9	5	32	28	3	6	10	18	29	33	1,018
11	(7)	Meadowbank Thistle	39	4	7	8	25	33	6	6	8	31	35	33	763
12	(10)	Ayr United	39	7	7	6	32	24	3	5	11	15	35	32	2,766
13	(9)	*Clyde*	39	6	4	10	24	32	3	5	11	17	28	27	1,127
14	(P)	*Brechin City*	39	3	4	12	19	37	4	6	10	24	43	24	768

HOW THE LEAD CHANGED HANDS

Sep 1 Airdrie; Dec 1 Dundee; Dec 8 Airdrie; Dec 11 Hamilton; Dec 15 Falkirk; Mar 5 Dundee; Mar 20 Falkirk; May 4 Airdrie; May 8 FALKIRK.

SECOND DIVISION

			HOME					AWAY						Average
			P	W	D	L	F	A	W	D	L	F	A	Pts	Home Gate
1	(3)	**STIRLING ALBION**	39	12	3	4	39	11	8	11	1	23	13	54	793
2	(13)	**Montrose**	39	11	2	7	30	18	9	4	6	24	16	46	457
3	(7)	Cowdenbeath	39	9	4	7	31	26	9	5	5	33	24	45	295
4	(4)	Stenhousemuir	39	11	4	5	32	20	5	8	6	24	22	44	482
5	(11)	Queen's Park	39	11	6	2	27	12	6	2	12	21	30	42	602
6	(8)	Stranraer	39	8	3	8	30	30	10	9	1	31	30	40	588
7	(6)	Dumbarton	39	8	8	4	23	20	7	2	10	26	29	40	502
8	(5)	Berwick Rangers	39	9	6	4	27	18	6	4	10	24	39	40	429
9	(R)	Alloa	39	8	4	7	27	22	5	7	8	24	24	37	458
10	(9)	East Fife	39	7	7	6	30	31	7	2	10	27	34	37	662
11	(R)	Albion Rovers	39	8	5	6	31	30	3	8	9	17	33	35	321
12	(10)	Queen of the South	39	7	6	7	31	29	2	6	11	15	33	30	619
13	(14)	East Stirlingshire	39	5	7	7	22	31	4	4	12	14	40	29	256
14	(12)	Arbroath	39	5	5	10	22	24	3	6	10	19	35	27	395

HOW THE LEAD CHANGED HANDS

Sep 1 Montrose; Sep 8 Stirling Albion; Sep 15 Montrose; Sep 22 East Fife; Oct 23 STIRLING ALBION.

SCOTLAND'S LEADING SCORERS

League Games Only

32 Ken Eadie (Clydebank)
25 Gordon Dalziel (Raith)
20 Owen Coyle (Airdrie)
20 David MacCabe (Morton)
19 Keith Wright (Dundee)
The Premier Division's top scorer was Tommy Coyne
(Celtic) with 18

TENNENTS SCOTTISH CUP

FIRST ROUND

East Stirling 1 QUEEN OF THE SOUTH 3;
FRASERBURGH 3 Vale of Leithen 1; Threave 1
SPARTANS 2; Whitehill 0 EAST FIFE 4; ROSS
COUNTY 1 3 Alloa 1 1; MONTROSE 0. 4 Dumbarton 0
1;

SECOND ROUND

BERWICK 1 Albion 0; Fraserburgh 1 COVE RANGERS
4; Inverness Thistle 1 0 EAST FIFE 1 1; Montrose 0
ARBROATH 2; Queen's Park 1 STRANRAER 2; ROSS
COUNTY 2 6 Queen of the South 2 2; Spartans 0 0
COWDENBEATH 0 2; STIRLING 2 Stenhousemuir 0;

THIRD ROUND

Aberdeen 0 MOTHERWELL 1; AIRDRIE 2 Hearts 1;
Clyde 0 HIBERNIAN 2; Clydebank 0 AYR 1; Cove
Rangers 1 COWDENBEATH 2; DUNDEE 1 Brechin 0;
East Fife 1 1 DUNDEE UNITED 1 2; Forfar 0 CELTIC 2;
KILMARNOCK 3 Arbroath 2; Partick 0 3 FALKIRK 0 4;
Raith 0 HAMILTON 1; RANGERS 2 Dunfermline 0;
Ross County 1 MEADOWBANK 6; ST JOHNSTONE 0 4
Berwick 0 3; Stirling 0 MORTON 1; Stranraer 1 ST
MIRREN 5
*This was the first time in 33 matches, stretching back to
March 1990, that Hibernian had scored more than one
goal in a game*

FOURTH ROUND

AYR 0 3 Hamilton 0 2; CELTIC 3 St Mirren 0; DUNDEE
2 Kilmarnock 0; DUNDEE UNITED 2 Airdrie 0;
MORTON 3 Meadowbank 1; MOTHERWELL 4 Falkirk
2; RANGERS 5 Cowdenbeath 0; ST JOHNSTONE 2
Hibernian 1

FIFTH ROUND

CELTIC 2 Rangers 0; DUNDEE UNITED 3 Dundee 1;
MOTHERWELL 0 1 Morton 0 1 (Motherwell won on
pens); ST JOHNSTONE 5 Ayr 2

SEMI-FINALS

Celtic 0 2 MOTHERWELL 0 4; DUNDEE UNITED 2 St
Johnstone 1

FINAL

Hampden Park, May 18
MOTHERWELL (1)4 Dundee United (0) 3
(after extra time: 90 mins 3-3)
Ferguson 32   Bowman 55
O'Donnell 60   O'Neill 67,
Angus 65   Jackson 90
Kirk 94
Motherwell: Maxwell; Nijholt, Boyd, Griffin, Paterson,
McCart, Arnott, Angus, I Ferguson (Kirk), O'Donnell,
Cooper (O'Neill).
Dundee Utd: Main; Clark, Malpas, McInally, Krivokapic,
Bowman, Van der Hoorn, McKinnon (McKinley), French,
D Ferguson (O'Neill), Jackson.
Referee: David Syme (Rutherglen)
Attendance: 57,319
*Opposing managers were Jim (Dundee United) and
Tommy McLean (Motherwell). It was the first time since
1912, when the Mailey brothers opposed each other, that
brothers have managed Scottish FA Cup final teams
Teams underlined beat opponents from a higher division*

SCOTTISH LEAGUE (SKOL) CUP

SEMI-FINALS

CELTIC 2 Dundee U 0; RANGERS 1 Aberdeen 0

FINAL

Hampden Park, Oct 28
RANGERS (0)2   Celtic   (0)
1 act
Walters 65, Gough 105   Elliott 52
RANGERS: Woods, Stevens, Munroe, Gough, Spackman,
Brown, Steven, Hurlock (Huistra), McCoist (Ferguson).
Hateley, Walters.
Celtic: Bonner, Grant, Wdowczyk, Fulton (Hewitt),
Elliott, Rogan, Miller (Morris), McStay, Dziekanowski,
Creaney, Collins.
Referee: J McCluskey (Stewarton)
Attendance: 62,817

NON-LEAGUE SOCCER
GM VAUXHALL CONFERENCE

			P	HOME W	D	L	F	A	AWAY W	D	L	F	A	Pts	Average Home Gate
1	(2)	**BARNET**	42	13	4	4	50	23	13	5	3	53	29	87	2,918
2	(R)	Colchester United	42	16	4	1	41	13	9	6	6	27	22	85	3,003
3	(16)	Altrincham	42	12	6	3	48	22	11	7	3	39	24	82	1,385
4	(5)	Kettering Town	42	12	6	3	38	19	11	5	5	29	26	80	2,563
5	(10)	Wycombe Wanderers	42	15	3	3	46	17	6	8	7	29	29	74	2,794
6	(12)	Telford United	42	11	3	7	30	21	9	4	8	32	31	67	1,186
7	(4)	Macclesfield	42	11	4	6	38	22	6	8	7	25	30	63	1,001
8	(3)	Runcorn	42	12	4	5	44	29	4	6	11	25	38	58	729
9	(9)	Merthyr Tydfil	42	9	5	7	37	24	7	4	10	25	37	57	824
10	(14)	Barrow	42	10	8	3	34	24	5	4	12	25	41	57	1,427
11	(6)	Welling United	42	7	10	4	33	27	6	5	10	22	30	54	985
12	(15)	Northwich Victoria	42	8	7	6	33	30	5	6	10	32	45	52	748
13	(13)	Kidderminster H	42	8	5	8	33	30	6	5	10	23	37	52	1,197
14	(7)	Yeovil Town	42	9	5	7	38	29	4	6	11	20	29	50	2,634
15	(17)	Stafford Rangers	42	7	9	5	30	26	5	5	11	18	25	50	1,174
16	(11)	Cheltenham Town	42	8	6	7	29	25	4	6	11	25	47	48	1,029
17	(P)	Gateshead	42	10	3	8	32	38	4	3	14	20	54	48	586
18	(18)	Boston United	42	9	4	8	40	31	3	7	11	15	38	47	1,372
19	(P)	Slough Town	42	9	4	8	31	29	4	2	15	20	51	45	1,168
20	(P)	Bath City	42	9	4	8	39	27	1	8	12	16	34	42	883
21	(8)	*Sutton United*	42	6	6	9	29	33	4	3	14	33	49	39	874
22	(19)	*Fisher Athletic*	42	3	9	9	22	30	2	6	13	16	49	30	651

Highest GM Vauxhall Attendances 1990-91
7,221 Colchester v Altrincham
5,105 Barnet v Colchester
5,048 Colchester v Kettering
5,020 Kettering v Colchester

HOW THE LEAD CHANGED HANDS
Aug 25 Barnet; Aug 27 Kettering; Mar 2 Barnet; Mar 16 Kettering; Mar 23 Altrincham; Apr 9 Colchester; Apr 13 Kettering; Apr 16 Altrincham; Apr 17 Colchester; Apr 19 Barnet; Apr 20 Colchester; Apr 22 Altrincham; Apr 27 BARNET.

OTHER CHAMPIONS
BEAZER HOMES LEAGUE
Premier Division: FARNBOROUGH TOWN
Midland Division: STOURBRIDGE
Southern Division: BUCKINGHAM TOWN

VAUXHALL LEAGUE
Premier Division: REDBRIDGE FOREST
First Division : CHESHAM

HFS LOANS LEAGUE
Premier Division: WITTON ALBION
First Division : WHITLEY BAY

FA TROPHY FINAL
Wembley, May 11
WYCOMBE WANDERERS 2 Kidderminster Harriers 1
Scott 16 Hadley 60
West 64
Attendance: 34,842 (record)

OTHER MATCHES
REPRESENTATIVE MATCH
Naples, Jan 16
ITALIAN LEAGUE 3 Football League 0
Van Basten
Careca
Simeone
Attendance: 10,000

FA CHARITY SHIELD
Wembley, Aug 18
Liverpool (0) 1 MANCHESTER UTD. (1) 1
Barnes (pen) 50
Blackmore 44
Attendance: 66,558

ZENITH DATA SYSTEMS CUP
Wembley, Apr 7
CRYSTAL PALACE (0) 4 Everton (0) 1
Thomas 67 Warzycha 69
Wright 101, 115
Salako 113
Attendance: 52,460

LEYLAND DAF CUP
Wembley, May 26
BIRMINGHAM CITY (2) 3 Tranmere Rovers (0) 2
Sturridge 21 Cooper 61
Gayle 40, 85 Steel 69

Attendance: 58,756
The previous day only 44,497 watched England play Argentina at Wembley

FA VASE FINAL
Wembley, May 4
Gresley Rovers 4 Guiseley 4 (aet)
Attendance: 11,000
Replay, *Bramall Lane, Sheffield, May 7*
GUISELEY 3 Gresley Rovers 1
Attendance: 7,585

UNIVERSITY MATCH
Craven Cottage, Fulham, Mar 30
Cambridge University 0 Oxford University 0
Attendance: 1,099
The game was played on the morning of the Boat Race in an attempt to improve the gate.

FA YOUTH CUP FINAL

1st Leg, May 4

| Sheffield Wednesday | 0 | MILLWALL | 3 |

2nd Leg, May 7

| Millwall | 0 | Sheffield Wednesday 0 |

WELSH CUP FINAL

Cardiff, May 12

| SWANSEA CITY | 2 | WREXHAM | 0 |

Penny (pen) 62
Raynor 78
Attendance: 5,000

WOMEN'S FA CUP

Semi-finals

| MILLWALL | 2 | Arsenal | 1 |
| DONCASTER | 8 | Leasowe Pacific | 1 |

Final

Prenton Park, Tranmere, Apr 27

| MILLWALL LIONESSES | 1 | Doncaster Belles | 0 |

Attendance: 4,000

Millwall's winning goal was scored by Yvonne Baldeo, who scored twice for Howbury Grange when they won, also against Doncaster, in 1984.

EUROPEAN SUPER CUP

First Leg, Oct 10

| Sampdoria | (1) 1 | AC Milan | (1) 1 |

Mikhailichenko 31   Evani 39
Attendance: 25,000

Second Leg, Nov 29

| AC MILAN | (1) 2 | Sampdoria | (0) 0 |

Gullit 44
Rijkaard 76
Attendance: 25,000

EUROPEAN CUP

FIRST ROUND

Valetta (Mal) 0 0 RANGERS (Sco) 4 6; PORTO (Por) 5 8 Portadown (NI) 0 1; DINAMO BUCHAREST (Rom) 4 1 St Patricks (Ire) 0 1; MARSEILLE (Fra) 5 0 Dinamo Tirana (Alb) 1 0; Sparta Prague (Cze) 0 0 SPARTAK MOSCOW (USSR) 2 2; FC TIROL (Aut) 5 2 Kuusysi Lahti (Fin) 0 1; NAPOLI (Ita) 3 2 Ujpest Dozsa (Hun) 0 0; LECH POZNAN (Pol) 3 2 Panathinaikos (Gre) 0 1; MALMO (Swe) 3 2 Besiktas (Tur) 2 2; Akureyri (Ice) 1 0 CSKA SOFIA (Bul) 0 3; Lillestrom (Nor) 1 0 FC BRUGES (Bel) 1 2; RED STAR BELGRADE (Yug) 1 4 Grasshoppers (Swi) 1 1; Union Luxembourg (Lux) 1 0 DYNAMO DRESDEN (GDR) 3 3; Odense BK (Den) 2 0 REAL MADRID (Spa) 4 6; Apoel Nicosia (Cyp) 2 0 BAYERN MUNICH (FRG) 3 4 AC MILAN, bye

SECOND ROUND

BAYERN MUNICH 4 3 CSKA Sofia 0 0; RED STAR BELGRADE 3 1 Rangers 0 1; DYNAMO DRESDEN 1 1 Malmo 1 1 (Dresden won 5-4 on pens); REAL MADRID 9 1 FC Tirol 1 2; Lech Poznan 3 1 MARSEILLE 2 6; Napoli 0 0 SPARTAK MOSCOW 0 0 (Spartak won 5-3 on pens); AC MILAN 0 1 FC Bruges 0 0; Dinamo Bucharest 0 0 PORTO 0 4

QUARTER-FINALS

AC Milan 1 0 MARSEILLE 1 1; BAYERN MUNICH 1 2 FC Porto 1 0; RED STAR BELGRADE 3 Dinamo Dresden 0; SPARTAK MOSCOW 0 3 Real Madrid 0 1

AC Milan refused to complete the second game after floodlight failure. Marseille were declared the 3-0 winners (which meant Waddle's goal for them was cancelled and Milan were banned for a year. Red Star were leading Dresden 2-1 in the second leg when the tie was abandoned

because of crowd trouble; Red Star awarded victory.

SEMI-FINALS

Bayern Munich 1 2 RED STAR BELGRADE 2 2; Spartak Moscow 1 1 MARSEILLE 3 2

FINAL

Bari, May 29

| RED STAR BELGRADE | (0) 0 | Olympique Marseille | (0) 0 |

(after extra time: Red Star won 5-3 on penalties)

Red Star: Stojanovic; Jugovic, Marovic, Sabandzovic, Belodedic, Najdoski, Prosinecki, Mihailovic, Pancev, Savicevic (Stosic), Binic

Marseille: Olmeta; Amoros, Di Meco (Stojkovic), Boli, Mozer, Germain, Casoni, Waddle, Papin, Pele, Fournier (Vercruysse)

Referee: T Lanese (Italy)
Attendance: 50,000

EUROPEAN CUP-WINNERS' CUP

PRELIMINARY ROUND

Bray Wanderers (Ire)   1 0   TRABZONSPOR (Tur) 1 2

FIRST ROUND

Salamina Famagusta (Cyp) 0 0 ABERDEEN (Sco) 2 3; WREXHAM (Wal) 0 1 Lyngby (Den) 0 0; MANCHESTER U (Eng) 2 1 Pecsi Mukas (Hun) 0 0; Glentoran (NI) 1 0 STEAUA BUCHAREST (Rom) 1 5; Sliema W (Mal) 1 0 DUKLA PRAGUE (Cze) 2 2; OLYMPIAKOS (Gre) 3 2 Flamurtari Vlora (Alb) 1 0; Kuopion Palloseura (Fin) 2 0 DINAMO KIEV (USSR) 2 4; FRAM REYKJAVIK (Ice) 3 1 Djurgaarden (Swe) 0 1; LEGIA WARSAW (Pol) 3 3 Swift Hesperange (Lux) 0 0; Schwerin (GDR) 0 0 AUSTRIA VIENNA (Aut) 2 0; PSV Eindhoven (Hol) 0 0 MONTPELLIER (Fra) 1 0; Viking Stavanger (Nor) 0 0 LIEGE (Bel) 2 3; Sliven (Bul) 0 1 JUVENTUS (Ita) 2 6; Trabzonspor (Tur) 1 1 BARCELONA (Spa) 0 7; ESTRELA DE AMADORA (Por) 1 1 Neuchatel Xamax (Swi) 1 1 (Estrela won 4-3 on pens); Kaiserslautern (FRG) 1 0 SAMPDORIA (Ita) 0 2

SECOND ROUND

Aberdeen 0 0 LEGIA WARSAW 0 1; MANCHESTER U 3 2 Wrexham 0 0; Dynamo Kiev 1 2 DUKLA PRAGUE 0 2; Olympiakos 0 1 SAMPDORIA 1 3; Fram Reykjavik 1 0 BARCELONA 2 3; MONTPELLIER 5 3 Steaua Bucharest 0 0; Austria Vienna 0 0 JUVENTUS 4 4; LIEGE 2 0 Estrela de Amadora 0 1

QUARTER-FINALS

Dynamo Kiev 2 1 BARCELONA 3 1; Liege 1 0 JUVENTUS 3 3; LEGIA WARSAW 1 2 Sampdoria 0 2; MANCHESTER UNITED 1 2 Montpellier 1 0

SEMI-FINALS

BARCELONA 3 0 Juventus 1 1; Legia Warsaw 1 1 MANCHESTER UNITED 3 1

FINAL

Rotterdam, May 15

| MANCHESTER UNITED | (0) 2 | Barcelona | (0) 1 |

Hughes 67, 74   Koeman 78

Manchester United: Sealey; Irwin, Blackmore, Bruce, Phelan, Pallister, Robson, Ince, McClair, Hughes, Sharpe

Barcelona: Busquets; Nando, Alexanco, Koeman, Ferrer, Bakero, Goicoechea, Eusebio, Salinas, Laudrup, Beguiristain

Referee: B Karlsson (Sweden)
Attendance: 44,000

UEFA CUP FINAL

FIRST ROUND

Glenavon (NI) 0 0 BORDEAUX (Fra) 0 2; Derry C (Ire) 0 0 VIT ARNHEM (Hol) 1 1; BORUSSIA DORTMUND (FRG) 2 2 Chemnitzer (GDR) 0 0; Lausanne (Swi) 3 0 REAL SOCIEDAD (Spa) 2 1 (Real won on away goals); Vejle (Den) 0 0 ADMIRA WACKER (Aut) 1 3; MTK Budapest (Hun) 1 1 LUCERNE (Swi) 1 2; ASTON VILLA (Eng) 3 2 Banik Ostrava (Cze) 1 1; Hafnfjarder (Ice) ! 2 DUNDEE U (Sco) 3 2; Dnepropetsk (USSR) 1 1 HEARTS (Sco) 1 3; Partizan Tirana (Alb) 0 0 UNIVERSITATAE CRAIOVA (Rom) 1 1; ANDERLECHT (Bel) 2 2 Petrolul Ploiesti (Rom) 0 0; MAGDEBURG (GDR) 3 3; Rovanieman Palloseura (Fin) 0 0; Avenir Beggen (Lux) 2 0 INTER BRATISLAVA (Cze) 1 5; Antwerp (Bel) 0 1 FERENCVAROS (Hun) 0 3; GKS KATOWICE (Pol) 3 1 Turun Palloseura (Fin) 0 0; IFK Norrkopping (Swe) 0 1 COLOGNE (FRG) 0 3; TORPEDO MOSCOW (USSR) 4 1 GAIS Gothenburg (Swe) 1 1; Hibernians (Mal) 0 0 PARTIZAN BELGRADE (Yug) 3 2; ATALANTA (Ita) 0 1 Dinamo Zagreb (Yug) 0 1 (Atalanta won on away goals); SV Roda (Hol) 1 1 MONACO (Fra) 3 3; POLITECHNICA TIMISOARA (Rom) 2 0 Atletico Madrid (Spa) 0 1; Slavia Sofia (Bul) 2 2 OMONIA NICOSIA (Cyp) 1 4; BAYER LEVERKUSEN (FRG) 1 1 Twente Enschede (Hol) 0 1; BRONDBY (Den) 5 1 Eintracht Frankfurt (FRG) 0 4; SEVILLE (Spa) 0 0 PAOK Salonika (Gre) 0 0 (Seville won 4-3 on pens); SPORTING LISBON (Por) 1 2 Mechelen (Bel) 0 2; Zaglebie Lubin (Pol) 0 0 BOLOGNA (Ita) 1 1; CHERNOMORETZ ODESSA (USSR) 3 1 Rosenborg BK (Nor) 1 2; Rapid Vienna (Aut) 2 1 INTER MILAN (Ita) 1 3; AS ROMA (Ita) 1 1 Benfica (Por) 0 0; FENERBAHCE (Tur) 3 3 Vitorio Guimaraes (Por) 0 2; Iraklis Salonika (Gre) 0 0 VALENCIA (Spa) 0 2

SECOND ROUND

Magdeburg 0 0 BORDEAUX 1 1; COLOGNE 0 2 Inter Bratislava 1 0; Universitatae Craiova 0 0 BORUSSIA DORTMUND 3 1; Hearts 3 0 BOLOGNA 1 3; VITESSE ARNHEM 1 4 Dundee United 0 0; Aston Villa 2 0 INTER MILAN 0 3; BRONDBY 3 1 Ferencvaros 0 0; Lucerne 0 1 ADMIRA WACKER 1 1; GKS Katowice 1 0 BAYER LEVERKUSEN 2 4; Fenerbahce 0 1 ATALANTA 1 4; SPORTING LISBON 7 0 Politechnica Timisoara 0 2; Valencia 1 1 AS ROMA 1 2; Chernomoretz Odessa 0 0

MONACO 0 1; Omonia Nicosia 1 0 ANDERLECHT 1 3; TORPEDO MOSCOW 3 1 Seville 1 2; Real Sociedad 1 0 PARTIZAN BELGRADE 0 1 (Partizan won 5-4 on pens)

THIRD ROUND

Admira Wacker 3 0 BOLOGNA 0 3 (Bologna won on pens 6-5); ANDERLECHT 1 1 Borussia Dortmund 0 2 (Anderlecht won on away goals); BRONDBY 3 0 Bayer Leverkusen 0 0; Cologne 1 0 ATALANTA 1 1; INTER MILAN 3 1 Partizan Belgrade 0 1; AS ROMA 5 2 Bordeaux 0 0; TORPEDO MOSCOW 2 2 Monaco 1 1; Vitesse Arnhem 0 1 SPORTING LISBON 2 2

QUARTER-FINALS

Atalanta 0 0 INTER MILAN 0 2; Bologna 1 0 SPORTING LISBON 1 2; BRONDBY 1 0 Torpedo Moscow 0 1 (Brondby won 4-2 on pens); ROMA 3 3 Anderlecht 0 2

SEMI-FINALS

Brondby 0 1 AS ROMA 0 2; Sporting Lisbon 0 0 INTER MILAN 0 2

FINAL

First Leg, Milan, May 8

INTER MILAN (0) 2   AS Roma (0) 0
Matthäus (pen) 55
Berti 65

Inter Milan: Zenga; Bergomi, Brehme, Battistini, Ferri, Paganin (Baresi), Bianchi, Berti, Klinsmann, Matthäus, Serena (Pizzi)
AS Roma: Cervone; Tempestilli, Neala (Carboni), Berthold, Aldair, Comi, Gerolin, (Salsano), Di Mauro, Voller, Giannini, Rizzitelli
Referee: I Spirin (USSR)
Attendance: 68,887

2nd Leg, Rome, May 22

AS ROMA (0) 1   Inter Milan (0) 0
Rizzitelli 80

AS Roma: Cervone; Tempestilli (Salsano), Gerolin, Berthold, Aldair, Neala, Desideri (Muzzi), Di Mauro, Voller, Giannini, Rizzitelli
Inter Milan: Zenga; Bergomi, Brehme, Battistini, Ferri, Paganin, Bianchi, Berti, Klinsmann, Matthäus, Pizzi (Mandorlini)
Referee: J Quiniou (Fra)
Attendance: 71,000
INTER MILAN won 2-1 on aggregate

BRITISH ISLES CLUBS IN EUROPE

EUROPEAN CUP

			Attendance
RANGERS			
First Round	1st Leg	Valetta (a) 4-0 (Johnston 2, McCoist, Hateley)	4,000
	2nd Leg	Valetta (h) 6-0 (Johnston 3, Dodds, Spencer, McCoist)	20,627
Second Round	1st Leg	Red Star Belgrade (a) 0-3	89,000
	2nd Leg	Red Star Belgrade (h) 1-1 (McCoist)	23,821
PORTADOWN			
First Round	1st Leg	Porto (a) 0-5	5,000
	2nd Leg	Porto (h) 1-8 (Fraser)	5,000
ST PATRICKS			
First Round	1st Leg	Dinamo Bucharest (a) 0-4	13,000
	2nd Leg	Dinamo Bucharest (h) 1-1 (Fenlon)	1,500

CUP-WINNERS' CUP

ABERDEEN			
First Round	1st Leg	Famagusta (a) 2-0 (Mason, Gillhaus)	7,000
	2nd Leg	Famagusta (h) 3-0 (C Robertson, Gillhaus, Jess)	11,000
Second Round	1st Leg	Legia Warsaw (h) 0-0	16,000
	2nd Leg	Legia Warsaw (a) 0-1	5,665

BRAY WANDERERS

Prelim.Round	1st Leg	Trabzonspor (h) 1-1 (Nugent)	3,000
	2nd Leg	Trabzonspor (a) 0-2	10,000

GLENTORAN

First Round	1st Leg	Steaua Bucharest (h) 1-1 (Douglas)	8,000
	2nd Leg	Steaua Bucharest (a) 0-5	5,000

MANCHESTER UNITED

First Round	1st Leg	Pecsi Munkas (h) 2-0 (Blackmore, Webb)	28,411
	2nd Leg	Pecsi Munkas (a) 1-0 (McClair)	16,000
Second Round	1st Leg	Wrexham (h) 3-0 (McClair, Bruce, Pallister)	29,405
	2nd Leg	Wrexham (a) 2-0 (Robins, Bruce)	13.327
Quarter-final	1st Leg	Montpellier (h) 1-1 (McClair)	41,942
	2nd Leg	Montpellier (a) 2-0 (Blackmore, Bruce)	18,000
Semi-final	1st Leg	Legia Warsaw (a) 3-1 (McClair, Hughes, Bruce)	20,000
	2nd Leg	Legia Warsaw (h) 1-1 (Sharpe)	44,269
Final		Barcelona 2-1 (Hughes 2)	44,000
(Played at Rotterdam)			

WREXHAM

First Round	1st Leg	Lyngby (h) 0-0	3,417
	2nd Leg	Lyngby (a) 1-0 (Armstrong)	1,548
Second Round	1st Leg	Manchester U (a) 0-3	29,405
	2nd Leg	Manchester U (h) 0-2	13,327

UEFA CUP

ASTON VILLA

First Round	1st Leg	Banik Ostrava (h) 3-1 (Platt, Mountfield, Olney)	27,137
	2nd Leg	Banik Ostrava (a) 2-1 (Mountfield, Stas og)	20,000
Second Round	1st Leg	Inter Milan (h) 2-0 (Nielsen, Platt)	36,461
	2nd Leg	Inter Milan (a) 0-3	80,000

DERRY CITY

First Round	1st Leg	Vitesse Arnhem (h) 0-1	3,500
	2nd Leg	Vitesse Arnhem (a) 0-1	7,000

DUNDEE UNITED

First Round	1st Leg	Hafnfjardar (a) 3-1 (Cleland 2, Jackson)	213
	2nd Leg	Hafnfjardar (h) 2-2 (Connolly, Himarsson og)	5,475
Second Round	1st Leg	Vitesse Arnhem (a) 0-1	9,000
	2nd Leg	Vitesse Arnhem (h) 0-4	10,261

GLENAVON

First Round	1st Leg	Bordeaux (h) 0-0	4,000
	2nd Leg	Bordeaux (a) 0-2	11,000

HEARTS

First Round	1st Leg	Dnepr (a) 1-1 (Robertson)	15,500
	2nd Leg	Dnepr (h) 3-1 (Robertson 2, McKinlay)	18,760
Second Round	1st Leg	Bologna (h) 3-1 (Foster 2, Ferguson)	11,155
	2nd Leg	Bologna (a) 0-3	12,224

BRITAIN'S MOST SUCCESSFUL CLUBS IN EUROPE

Wins	EC	ECWC	UEFA
6 Liverpool	4	-	2
3 Tottenham Hotspur	-	1	2
2 Nottingham Forest	2	-	-
2 Manchester United	1	1	-
2 Rangers	-	2	-
2 Leeds United	-	-	2
1 Celtic	1	-	-
1 Aston Villa	1	-	-
1 West Ham United	-	1	-
1 Manchester City	-	1	-
1 Chelsea	-	1	-
1 Aberdeen	-	1	-
1 Everton	-	1	-
1 Newcastle United	-	-	1
1 Arsenal	-	-	1
1 Ipswich Town	-	-	1

ACROSS EUROPE
All the Champions 1990-91

Country	League Champions	Cup Winners
Albania	Flamurtari Viora	Partizan Tirana
Austria	Austria Vienna	Stockerau
Belgium	Anderlecht	F C Bruges
Bulgaria	Etar Tarnova	Levski Sofia
Cyprus	Apollon Limassol	Omonia
Czechoslovakia	Sparta Prague	Banik Ostrava
Denmark	Brondby	Lyngby
Faroe Islands	HB	KI
Finland	JK Helsinki	Lives Tampere
France	Olympique Marseille	Monaco
Germany, West	Kaiserslautern	Kaiserslautern
Germany, East	Hansa Rostock	Hansa Rostock
Greece	Panathinaikos	Panathinaikos
Holland	PSV Eindhoven	Feyenoord
Hungary	Honved	Perencvaros
Iceland	Fram Reykjavik	Valur
Ireland, Northern	Portadown	Portadown
Ireland, Republic of	Dundalk	Galway United
Italy	Sampdoria	Roma
Luxembourg	Union Sportive	Union
Malta	Hamrun Spartans	Valletta
Norway	Rosenborg	Rosenborg
Poland	Zaglebie Lubin	Katowice
Portugal	Benfica	Oporto
Romania	Uni Craiova	Uni Craiova
Soviet Union	Dinamo Kiev	Dinamo Kiev
Spain	Barcelona	Atletico
Sweden	Gothenburg	Norrköping
Switzerland	Grasshoppers	Sion
Turkey	Besiktas	Galatasaray
Wales	–	Swansea City
Yugoslavia	Red Star Belgrade	Hadjuk Split

AWARDS 1991

PFA Player of the Year
1 Mark Hughes (Manchester U)
2 Gordon Strachan (Leeds U)
3 Paul Gascoigne (Tottenham H)
Hughes became the first person to win the award twice.
PFA Young Player of the Year
1 Lee Sharpe (Manchester U)
2 David Batty (Leeds U)
3 Roy Keane (Nottingham F)
PFA Merit Award
Tommy Hutchison
Football Writers' Player of the Year
1 Gordon Strachan (Leeds United)
2 Stuart Pearce (Nottingham Forest)
3 Paul Gascoigne (Tottenham Hotspur)

SCOTTISH AWARDS

Scottish FWA Player of the Year
Maurice Malpas (Dundee United)
Scotish PFA Player of the Year
Paul Elliott (Celtic)
Scottish PFA Young Player of the Year
Eion Jess (Aberdeen)
Manager of the Year
George Graham (Arsenal)

CHAMPIONS

WORLD CUP

Year	Winners		Runners-up	Venue
1930	Uruguay	4-2	Argentina	Montevideo
1934	Italy	2-1†	Czechoslovakia	Rome
1938	Italy	4-2	Hungary	Paris
1950	Uruguay	2-1*	Brazil	Rio de Janeiro
1954	W Ger	3-2	Hungary	Berne
1958	Brazil	5-2	Sweden	Stockholm
1962	Brazil	3-1	Czechoslovakia	Santiago
1966	England	4-2†	West Germany	London
1970	Brazil	4-1	Italy	Mexico City
1974	W Ger	2-1	Holland	Munich
1978	Argentina	3-1†	Holland	Buenos Aires
1982	Italy	3-1	West Germany	Madrid
1986	Argentina	3-2	West Germany	Mexico City
1990	W Ger	1-0	Argentina	Rome

† After extra time
* Last four teams engaged in a final pool, Uruguay played Brazil in the deciding match, Sweden finished in third place

EUROPEAN CHAMPIONSHIP

Year	Winners		Runners-up	Venue
1960	USSR	2-1†	Yugoslavia	Paris
1964	Spain	2-1	USSR	Madrid
1968	Italy	2-0	Yugoslavia	Rome
	(after 1-1 draw)			
1972	W. Germany	3-0	USSR	Brussels
1976	Czechoslovakia	2-2†	W. Germany	Belgrade
	(Czechoslovakia won 5-3 on penalties)			
1980	West Germany	2-1	Belgium	Rome
1984	France	2-0	Spain	Paris
1988	Holland	2-0	USSR	Munich

EUROPEAN CUP

Year	Winners		Runners-up
1956	Real Madrid	4-3	Rheims
1957	Real Madrid	2-0	Fiorentina
1958	Real Madrid	3-2†	AC Milan
1959	Real Madrid	2-0	Rheims
1960	Real Madrid	7-3	Eintracht Frankfurt
1961	Benfica	3-2	Barcelona
1962	Benfica	5-3	Real Madrid
1963	AC Milan	2-1	Benfica
1964	Inter-Milan	3-1	Real Madrid
1965	Inter-Milan	1-0	Benfica
1966	Real Madrid	2-1	Partizan Belgrade
1967	Celtic	2-1	Inter-Milan
1968	Man Utd.	4-1†	Benfica
1969	AC Milan	4-1	Ajax
1970	Feyenoord	2-1†	Celtic
1971	Ajax	2-0	Panathinaikos
1972	Ajax	2-0	Inter-Milan
1973	Ajax	1-0	Juventus
1974	Bayern Munich	4-0	Atletico Madrid
	(after 1-1 draw)		
1975	Bayern Munich	2-0	Leeds United
1976	Bayern Munich	1-0	St. Etienne
1977	Liverpool	3-1	B.M/gladbach
1978	Liverpool	1-0	FC Bruges
1979	Nottingham F	1-0	Malmo
1980	Nottingham F	1-0	SV Hamburg
1981	Liverpool	1-0	Real Madrid
1982	Aston Villa	1-0	Bayern Munich
1983	SV Hamburg	1-0	Juventus
1984	Liverpool	1-1†	AS Roma
	(Liverpool won 4-2 on penalties)		
1985	Juventus	1-0	Liverpool

WORLD RECORD TRANSFERS

PLAYER	FROM	TO	YEAR	FEE (£ MILL.)
Roberto Baggio	Fiorentina	Juventus	1990	£7.7
Diego Maradona	Barcelona	Napoli	1984	£6.9
Ruud Gullit	PSV Eindhoven	AC Milan	1987	£5.5
Karl-Heinz Reidle	Werder Bremen	Lazio	1990	£5.5
David Platt	Aston Villa	Bari	1991	£5.5
Paul Gascoigne	Tottenham Hotspur	Lazio	1991	£5.5
Thomas Hässler	Cologne	Juventus	1990	£5.0
Trevor Steven	Rangers	Marseille	1991	£5.0

1986   Steaua Bucharest 0-0†   Barcelona
    (Steaua won 2-0 on penalties)
1987   FC Porto   2-1   Bayern Munich
1988   PSV Eindhoven   0-0† Benfica
    (Eindhoven won 6-5 on penalties)
1989   AC Milan   4-0   Steaua Bucharest
1990   AC Milan   1-0   Benfica
1991   Red Star Belgrade 0-0 Olympique Marseille
    (Red Star won 5-3 on penalties)

Winning Countries: England 8; Italy 7; Spain 6; Holland 5; West Germany 4; Portugal 3; Romania, Scotland, Yugoslavia 1

EUROPEAN CUP-WINNERS' CUP

Year	Winners		Runners-up
1961	Rangers	0-2	Fiorentina
	Fiorentina	2-1	Rangers
	(Fiorentina won 4-1 on aggregate)		
1962	At. Madrid	3-0	Fiorentina
	(after 1-1 draw)		
1963	Tottenham H	5-1	Atletico Madrid
1964	Sporting Lisbon	1-0	MTK Budapest
	(after 3-3 draw)		
1965	West Ham U	2-0	Munich 1860
1966	B. Dortmund	2-1†	Liverpool
1967	Bayern Munich	1-0†	Rangers
1968	AC Milan	2-0	SV Hamburg
1969	Slovan Brat.	3-2	Barcelona
1970	Man City	2-1	Gornik Zabrze
1971	Chelsea	2-1	Real Madrid
	(after 1-1 draw)		
1972	Rangers	3-2	Moscow Dynamo
1973	AC Milan	1-0	Leeds United
1974	FC Magdeburg	2-0	AC Milan
1975	Dynamo Kiev	3-0	Ferencvaros
1976	Anderlecht	4-2	West Ham United
1977	SV Hamburg	2-0	Anderlecht
1978	Anderlecht	4-0	Austria/WAC
1979	Barcelona	4-3†	Fortuna Dusseldorf
1980	Valencia	0-0†	Arsenal
	(Valencia won 5-4 on penalties)		
1981	Dynamo Tbilisi	2-1	Carl Zeiss Jena
1982	Barcelona	2-1	Standard Liège
1983	Aberdeen	2-1	Real Madrid
1984	Juventus	2-1	FC Porto
1985	Everton	3-1	R. Vienna
1986	Dynamo Kiev	3-0	Atletico Madrid
1987	Ajax	1-0	Lokomotiv Leipzig
1988	Mechelen	1-0	Ajax
1989	Barcelona	2-0	Sampdoria
1990	Sampdoria	2-0	Anderlecht
1991	Manchester United	2-1	Barcelona

Winning Countries: England 6; Spain, Italy 5; Belgium, Soviet Union, West Germany 3; Scotland 2; Czechoslovakia, East Germany, Holland, Portugal 1.

† after extra time

UEFA CUP
Known as the International Industries Fairs
Inter-Cities Cup 1958-65 and European Fairs Cup 1966-70

Year	Winners			Runners-up
1958	Barcelona	6-0	2-2†	London
1960	Barcelona	4-1	0-0	Birmingham City
1961	AS Roma	2-0	2-2	Birmingham City
1962	Valencia	6-2	1-1	Barcelona
1963	Valencia	2-1	2-0	Dynamo Zagreb
1964	Real Zaragoza	2-1		Valencia
1965	Ferencvaros	1-0		Juventus
1966	Barcelona	4-2	0-1	Real Zaragoza
1967	Dynamo Zagreb	2-0	0-0	Leeds United
1968	Leeds United	1-0	0-0	Ferencvaros
1969	Newcastle Utd.	3-0	3-2	Ujpest Dozsa
1970	Arsenal	3-0	1-3	Anderlecht
1971	Leeds United	1-1	2-2*	Juventus
1972	Tottenham H	2-1	1-1	Wolverhampton W
1973	Liverpool	3-0	0-2	B.M/gladbach
1974	Feyenoord	2-0	2-2	Tottenham H
1975	B.M/gladbach	5-1	0-0	Twente Enschede
1976	Liverpool	3-2	1-1	FC Bruges
1977	Juventus	1-0	1-2*	Ath. Bilbao
1978	PSV Eindhoven	3-0	0-0	Bastia
1979	B.M/gladbach	1-0	1-1	Red Star B'grade
1980	Eintracht F/furt	1-0	2-3*	B.M/gladbach
1981	Ipswich Town	3-0	2-4	AZ 67 Alkmaar
1982	IFK Gothenburg	1-0	3-0	SV Hamburg
1983	Anderlecht	1-0	1-1	Benfica
1984	Tottenham H	1-1	1-1§	Anderlecht
1985	Real Madrid	3-0	0-1	Videoton
1986	Real Madrid	5-1	0-2	Cologne
1987	IFK Gothenburg	1-0	1-1	Dundee United
1988	Bayer Leverkusen	0-3	3-0§	Espanol
1989	Napoli	2-1	3-3	VFB Stuttgart
1990	Juventus	3-1	0-0	Fiorentina
1991	Inter-Milan	2-0	0-1	AS Roma

Winning Countries: England 9; Spain 8; Italy 5; West Germany 4; Holland, Sweden 2; Belgium, Hungary, Yugoslavia 1.

* Won on away goals rule
§ Won on penalties
† Contested between cities, not clubs

EUROPE'S MOST SUCCESSFUL TEAMS

Wins	Total	EC	ECWC	UEFA
Real Madrid	8	6	-	2
Liverpool	6	4	-	2
Barcelona	6	-	3	3
AC Milan	6	4	2	-
Ajax	4	3	1	-
Bayern Munich	4	3	1	-
Juventus	4	1	1	2
Anderlecht	3	-	2	1
Inter-Milan	3	2	-	1
Tottenham Hotspur	3	-	1	2
Valencia	3	-	1	2

EUROPE'S MOST SUCCESSFUL NATIONS

Wins	Total	EC	ECWC	UEFA
England	23	8	6	9
Spain	19	6	5	8
Italy	17	7	5	5
West Germany	11	4	3	4
Holland	8	5	1	2
Portugal	4	3	1	-
Belgium	4	-	3	1
Scotland	3	1	2	-
USSR	3	-	3	-
Sweden	2	-	-	2
Yugoslavia	2	1	-	1

The following countries have each produced one winner:
Romania, Czechoslovakia, East Germany, Hungary.

EUROPEAN SUPER CUP

Winners (aggregate scores)

1973	Ajax	6-3	Rangers
1974	Ajax	6-1	AC Milan
1975	Dynamo Kiev	3-0	Bayern Munich
1976	Anderlecht	5-3	Bayern Munich
1977	Liverpool	7-1	SV Hamburg
1978	Anderlecht	4-3	Liverpool
1979	Nottingham F	2-1	Barcelona
1980	Valencia	2-2	Nottingham F
	(Valencia won on away goals)		
1981	Not held		
1982	Aston Villa	3-1	Barcelona
1983	Aberdeen	2-0	SV Hamburg
1984	Juventus	2-0	Liverpool
	(one game; played in Turin)		
1985	Not held		
1986	Steaua Bucharest	1-0	Dynamo Kiev
	(one game; played in Monaco)		
1987	FC Porto	2-0	Ajax
1988	Mechelen	3-1	PSV Eindhoven
1989	AC Milan	2-1	Barcelona
1990	AC Milan	2-0	Sampdoria

WORLD CLUB CHAMPIONSHIP

(1960-79 played over two games (except 1973). Not held 1975 and 1978. Scores are aggregates. Since 1980 a single game played in Tokyo for the Toyota Cup.)

Year	Winners		Runners-up
1960	Real Madrid (Spa)	5-1	Penarol (Uru)
1961	Penarol (Uru)	7-2*	Benfica (Por)
1962	Santos (Bra)	8-4	Benfica (Por)
1963	Santos (Bra)	7-6*	AC Milan (Ita)
1964	Inter Milan (Ita)	3-1*	Independiente (Arg)
1965	Inter Milan (Ita)	3-0	Independiente (Arg)
1966	Penarol (Uru)	4-0	Real Madrid (Spa)
1967	Racing Club (Arg)	3-2*	Celtic (Sco)
1968	Estudiantes (Arg)	2-1	Man Utd (Eng)
1969	AC Milan (Ita)	4-2	Estudiantes (Arg)
1970	Feyenoord (Hol)	3-2	Estudiantes (Arg)
1971	Nacional (Uru)	3-2	Panathinaikos (Gre)
1972	Ajax (Hol)	4-1	Independiente (Arg)
1973	Independiente (Arg)	1-0	Juventus (Ita)
1974	At. Madrid (Spa)	2-1	Independiente (Arg)
1976	Bayern Munich (FRG)	2-0	Cruzeiro (Bra)
1977	Boca Juniors (Arg)	5-2	B. M/gladbach (FRG)
1979	Olimpia (Par)	3-1	Malmo (Swe)
1980	Nacional (Uru)	1-0	Nottingham F (Eng)
1981	Flamengo (Bra)	3-0	Liverpool (Eng)
1982	Penarol (Uru)	2-0	Aston Villa (Eng)
1983	Gremio (Bra)	2-1	SV Hamburg (FRG)
1984	Independiente (Arg)	1-0	Liverpool (Eng)
1985	Juventus (Ita)	2-2	Argentinos Jr (Arg)
	(Juventus won 4-2 on penalties)		
1986	River Plate (Arg)	1-0	Steaua Buch. (Rom)
1987	FC Porto (Por)	2-1	Penarol (Uru)
1988	Nacional (Uru)	2-2	PSV Eindhoven (Hol)
	(Nacional won 7-6 on penalties)		
1989	AC Milan (Ita)	1-0	Atletico Nacional (Col)
1990	AC Milan (Ita)	3-0	Olimpia (Par)

* Including a play-off match

Most Wins *Clubs:* 3 Penarol, Nacional, AC Milan
Countries: 6 Argentina, Italy, Uruguay;
Continents: 17 South America; 12 Europe

FOOTBALL LEAGUE

Double Winners in capitals

	Winners	Pts	Runners-up	Pts
1871-72	-			
1872-73	-			
1873-74	-			
1874-75	-			
1875-76	-			
1876-77	-			
1877-78	-			
1878-79	-			
1879-80	-			
1880-81	-			
1881-82	-			
1882-83	-			
1883-84	-			
1884-85	-			
1885-86	-			
1886-87	-			
1887-88	-			
1888-89	PRESTON NE	40	Aston Villa	29
1889-90	Preston NE	33	Everton	31
1890-91	Everton	29	Preston NE	27
1891-92	Sunderland	42	Preston NE	37
1892-93	Sunderland	48	Preston NE	37
1893-94	Aston Villa	44	Sunderland	38
1894-95	Sunderland	47	Everton	42

FA CUP

Winners	Score	Runners-up
Wanderers	1-0	Royal Engineers
Wanderers	2-0	Oxford University
Oxford Univ	2-0	Royal Engineers
Royal Engineers	1-1 2-0	Old Etonians
Wanderers	1-1 3-0	Old Etonians
Wanderers	2-1	Oxford University
Wanderers	3-1	Royal Engineers
Old Etonians	1-0	Clapham Rovers
Clapham Rovers	1-0	Oxford University
Old Carthusians	3-0	Old Etonians
Old Etonians	1-0	Blackburn Rovers
Blackburn Olympic	2-1	Old Etonians
Blackburn Rovers	2-1	Queen's Park
Blackburn Rovers	2-0	Queen's Park
Blackburn Rovers	0-0 2-0	West Bromwich A
Aston Villa	2-0	West Bromwich A
West Bromwich A	2-1	Preston NE
PRESTON NE	3-0	Wolverhampton W
Blackburn R	6-1	Sheffield W
Blackburn R	3-1	Notts County
West Bromwich A	3-0	Aston Villa
Wolverhampton W	1-0	Everton
Notts County	4-1	Bolton County
Aston Villa	1-0	West Bromwich A

FOOTBALL LEAGUE

This is how membership of the Football League has changed over the years.

Year	Total Clubs	1	2	3S	3N	3	4
1888	12	-	-	-	-	-	-
1891	14	-	-	-	-	-	-
1892	28	16	12	-	-	-	-
1893	31	16	15	-	-	-	-
1894	32	16	16	-	-	-	-
1898	36	18	18	-	-	-	-
1905	40	20	20	-	-	-	-
1919	44	22	22	-	-	-	-
1920	66	22	22	-	-	22	-
1921	86	22	22	22	20	-	-
1923	88	22	22	22	22	-	-
1950	92	22	22	24	24	-	-
1958	92	22	22	-	-	24	24
1987	92	21	23	-	-	24	24
1988	92	20	24	-	-	24	24
1991	93	22	24	-	-	24	23
Proposed							
1992	94	22*	24	-	-	24	24

* Or none, if the First Division clubs resign

THE FOLLOWING CLUBS HAVE JOINED AND LEFT THE FOOTBALL LEAGUE SINCE 1923

Year	Joined	Left
1923	Bournemouth	Stalybridge Celtic
	Doncaster Rovers	
	New Brighton	
1927	Torquay United	Aberdare Athletic
1928	Carlisle United	Durham City
1929	York City	Ashington
1930	Thames	Merthyr Tydfil
1931	Mansfield Town	Newport County
	Chester	Nelson
1932	Aldershot	Thames
	Newport County	Wigan Borough
1938	Ipswich Town	Gillingham
1950	Colchester United	-
	Gillingham	
	Scunthorpe United	
	Shrewsbury Town	
1951	Workington	New Brighton
1960	Peterborough United	Gateshead
1962	Oxford United	Accrington Stanley
1970	Cambridge United	Bradford PA
1972	Hereford United	Barrow
1977	Wimbledon	Workington
1978	Wigan Athletic	Southport
1987	Scarborough	Lincoln City
1988	Lincoln City	Newport County
1989	Maidstone United	Darlington
1990	Darlington	Colchester United
1991	Barnet	-

FOOTBALL LEAGUE				FA CUP		
Winners	Pts	Runners-up	Pts	Winners	Score	Runners-up
1895-96 Aston Villa	45	Derby C	41	Sheffield W	2-1	W'hampton
1896-97 ASTON VILLA	47	Sheffield U	36	ASTON VILLA	3-2	Everton
1897-98 Sheffield U	42	Sunderland	37	Nottingham Forest	3-1	Derby County
1898-99 Aston Villa	45	Liverpool	43	Sheffield U	4-1	Derby County
1899-00 Aston Villa	50	Sheffield U	48	Bury	4-0	Southampton
1900-01 Liverpool	45	Sunderland	43	Tottenham H	2-2 3-1	Sheffield U
1901-02 Sunderland	44	Everton	41	Sheffield U	1-1 2-1	Southampton
1902-03 Sheffield W	42	Aston Villa	41	Bury	6-0	Derby County
1903-04 Sheffield W	47	Man City	44	Man City	1-0	Bolton Wanderers
1904-05 Newcastle U	48	Everton	47	Aston Villa	2-0	Newcastle U
1905-06 Liverpool	51	Preston NE	47	Everton	1-0	Newcastle U
1906-07 Newcastle U	51	Bristol C	48	Sheffield W	2-1	Everton
1907-08 Man Utd	52	Aston Villa	43	Wolverhampton	3-1	Newcastle U
1908-09 Newcastle U	53	Everton	46	Man Utd	1-0	Bristol City
1909-10 Aston Villa	53	Liverpool	48	Newcastle U	1-1 2-0	Barnsley
1910-11 Man Utd	52	Aston Villa	51	Bradford City	0-0 1-0	Newcastle
1911-12 Blackburn R	49	Everton	46	Barnsley	0-0 1-0	West Bromwich A
1912-13 Sunderland	54	Aston Villa	50	Aston Villa	1-0	Sunderland
1913-14 Blackburn R	51	Aston Villa	44	Burnley	1-0	Liverpool
1914-15 Everton	46	Oldham A	45	SheffieldUnited	3-0	Chelsea
1919-20 West Brom. A	60	Burnley	51	Aston Villa	1-0	Huddersfield Town
1920-21 Burnley	59	Man City	54	Tottenham H	1-0	W'hampton
1921-22 Liverpool	57	Tottenham	51	Huddersfield Town	1-0	Preston NE
1922-23 Liverpool	60	Sunderland	54	Bolton Wanderers	2-0	West Ham U
1923-24 Huddersfield T	57	Cardiff C	57	Newcastle United	2-0	Aston Villa
1924-25 Huddersfield T	58	West Brom. A	56	Sheffield United	1-0	Cardiff City
1925-26 Huddersfield T	57	Arsenal	52	Bolton Wanderers	1-0	Man City
1926-27 Newcastle U	56	Huddersfield T	51	Cardiff City	1-0	Arsenal
1927-28 Everton	53	Huddersfield T	51	Blackburn R	3-1	Huddersfield Town
1928-29 Sheffield W	52	Leicester City	51	Bolton Wanderers	2-0	Portsmouth
1929-30 Sheffield W	60	Derby County	50	Arsenal	2-0	Huddersfield Town
1930-31 Arsenal	66	Aston Villa	59	West Bromwich A	2-1	Birmingham
1931-32 Everton	56	Arsenal	54	Newcastle United	2-1	Arsenal
1932-33 Arsenal	58	Aston Villa	54	Everton	3-0	Man City
1933-34 Arsenal	59	Huddersfield T	56	Man City	2-1	Portsmouth
1934-35 Arsenal	58	Sunderland	54	Sheffield W	4-2	West Bromwich A
1935-36 Sunderland	56	Derby County	48	Arsenal	1-0	Sheffield United
1936-37 Man City	57	Charlton A	54	Sunderland	3-1	Preston NE
1937-38 Arsenal	52	W'hampton	51	Preston NE	1-0	Huddersfield Town
1938-39 Everton	59	W'hampton	55	Portsmouth	4-1	W'hampton
1945-46 -				Derby County	4-1	Charlton Athletic
1946-47 Liverpool	57	Man Utd	56	Charlton Athletic	1-0	Burnley
1947-48 Arsenal	59	Man Utd	52	Man Utd	4-2	Blackpool
1948-49 Portsmouth	58	Man Utd	53	Wolverhampton	3-1	Leicester City
1949-50 Portsmouth	53	W'hampton	53	Arsenal	2-0	Liverpool
1950-51 Tottenham H	60	Man Utd	56	Newcastle United	2-0	Blackpool
1951-52 Man Utd	57	Tottenham H	53	Newcastle United	1-0	Arsenal
1952-53 Arsenal	54	Preston NE	54	Blackpool	4-3	Bolton Wanderers
1953-54 W'hampton	57	West Brom. A	53	West Bromwich A	3-2	Preston NE
1954-55 Chelsea	52	W'hampton	48	Newcastle United	3-1	Man City
1955-56 Man Utd	60	Blackpool	49	Man City	3-1	Birmingham C
1956-57 Man Utd	64	Tottenham	56	Aston Villa	2-1	Man Utd
1957-58 W'hampton	64	Preston NE	59	Bolton W	2-0	Man Utd
1958-59 W'hampton	61	Man Utd	55	Nottingham Forest	2-1	Luton Town
1959-60 Burnley	55	W'hampton	54	W'hampton	3-0	Blackburn R
1960-61 TOTTENHAM H	66	Sheffield W	58	TOTTENHAM H	2-0	Leicester City
1961-62 Ipswich Town	56	Burnley	53	Tottenham Hotspur	3-1	Burnley
1962-63 Everton	61	Tottenham	55	Man Utd	3-1	Leicester City
1963-64 Liverpool	57	Man Utd	53	West Ham U	3-2	Preston NE
1964-65 Man Utd	61	Leeds United	61	Liverpool	2-1	Leeds United
1965-66 Liverpool	61	Leeds United	55	Everton	3-2	Sheffield W
1966-67 Man Utd	60	Nottingham F	56	Tottenham Hotspur	2-1	Chelsea
1967-68 Man City	58	Man Utd	56	West Bromwich A	1-0	Everton
1968-69 Leeds United	67	Liverpool	61	Man City	1-0	Leicester City
1969-70 Everton	66	Leeds United	57	Chelsea	2-2 2-1	Leeds United
1970-71 ARSENAL	65	Leeds United	64	ARSENAL	2-1	Liverpool
1971-72 Derby County	58	Leeds United	57	Leeds United	1-0	Arsenal
1972-73 Liverpool	60	Arsenal	57	Sunderland	1-0	Leeds United
1973-74 Leeds United	62	Liverpool	57	Liverpool	3-0	Newcastle United

FOOTBALL LEAGUE

1974-75	Derby County	53	Liverpool	51
1975-76	Liverpool	60	QPR	59
1976-77	Liverpool	57	Man City	56
1977-78	Nottingham F	64	Liverpool	57
1978-79	Liverpool	68	Nottingham F	60
1979-80	Liverpool	60	Man Utd	58
1980-81	Aston Villa	60	Ipswich Town	56
1981-82	Liverpool	87	Ipswich Town	83
1982-83	Liverpool	82	Watford	71
1983-84	Liverpool	80	Southampton	77
1984-85	Everton	90	Liverpool	77
1985-86	LIVERPOOL	88	Everton	86
1986-87	Everton	86	Liverpool	77
1987-88	Liverpool	90	Man Utd	81
1988-89	Arsenal	76	Liverpool	76
1989-90	Liverpool	79	Aston Villa	70
1990-91	Arsenal	83	Liverpool	76

FOOTBALL LEAGUE

Most titles

Div 1: 18 Liverpool; 10 Arsenal, 9 Everton; 7 Manchester United, Aston Villa; 6 Sunderland

Div 2: 6 Leicester, Man City; 5 Sheffield Wednesday; 4 Derby, Liverpool, Birmingham; 3 Notts County, Preston NE, Middlesbrough, Leeds United

Div 3: 2 Portsmouth, Oxford United

Div 4: 2 Chesterfield, Doncaster , Peterborough

Div 3(S): 3 Bristol City; 2 Charlton, Ipswich, Millwall, Notts County, Plymouth , Swansea

Div 3(N): 3 Barnsley, Doncaster , Lincoln ; 2 Chesterfield, Grimsby , Hull , Port Vale, Stockport

FA CUP

Venues (Excluding replays)

63 times Wembley 1923-39, 1946-91; 20 Kennington Oval 1872, 1874-92, Crystal Palace 1895-1914; 3 Stamford Bridge 1920-22; 1 Lillie Bridge 1873, Fallowfield 1893, Goodison Park 1894, Old Trafford 1915

Replay Venues

Kennington Oval 1875, 1876;
Derby 1886;
Burnden Park 1901;
Crystal Palace 1902;
Goodison Park 1910;
Old Trafford 1911, 1970;
Bramall Lane 1912;
Wembley 1981, 1982, 1983, 1990.

THE TOP TEAMS: FA CUP

	Wins	Finals	SF
Tottenham Hotspur	8	9	13
Manchester United	7	11	18
Aston Villa	7	9	17
Newcastle United	6	11	13
Blackburn Rovers	6	8	16
Arsenal	5	11	17
West Bromwich Albion	5	10	19
The Wanderers	5	5	5
Everton	4	11	22
Liverpool	4	9	18
Wolverhampton Wanderers	4	8	13
Manchester City	4	8	10
Bolton Wanderers	4	7	12
Sheffield United	4	6	10
Sheffield Wednesday	3	5	15
West Ham United	3	4	6
Preston North End	2	7	10
Old Etonians	2	6	6
Sunderland	2	3	10
Nottingham Forest	2	3	11
Bury	2	2	2

F A CUP

West Ham U	2-0		Fulham
Southampton	1-0		Man Utd
Man Utd	2-1		Liverpool
Ipswich Town	1-0		Arsenal
Arsenal	3-2		Man Utd
West Ham U	1-0		Arsenal
Tottenham Hotspur	1-1	3-2	Man City
Tottenham Hotspur	1-1	1-0	Queen's Park R
Man Utd	2-2	4-0	Brighton & Hove A
Everton	2-0		Watford
Man Utd	1-0		Everton
LIVERPOOL	3-1		Everton
Coventry City	3-2		Tottenham Hotspur
Wimbledon	1-0		Liverpool
Liverpool	3-2		Everton
Man Utd	3-3-	1-0	Crystal Palace
Tottenham Hotspur	2-1		Nottingham Forest

Most wins at Wembley

6 Tottenham; 5 Arsenal, Newcastle; 4 Bolton, Liverpool, Manchester United; 3 Everton, Manchester City, West Bromwich, West Ham

Most appearances at Wembley

11 Arsenal; 10 Manchester United; 8 Liverpool; 7 Everton, Manchester City, Tottenham.

FOOTBALL LEAGUE CUP

Known as the Milk Cup 1982-85, Littlewoods Cup 1986-90, Rumbelows League Cup 1991. All finals 1961-66 were over two legs; since then they have been single games at Wembley.

Finals

1961	Aston Villa	3-0† 0-2	Rotherham U
1962	Norwich City	3-0 1-0	Rochdale
1963	Birmingham City	3-1 0-0	Aston Villa
1964	Leicester City	1-1 3-2	Stoke City
1965	Chelsea	3-2 0-0	Leicester City
1966	West Bromwich A	1-2 4-1	West Ham U
1967	Queen's Park R	3-2	West Brom. A
1968	Leeds United	1-0	Arsenal
1969	Swindon Town	3-1	Arsenal
1970	Man City	2-1	West Brom. A
1971	Tottenham Hotspur	2-0	Aston Villa
1972	Stoke City	2-1	Chelsea
1973	Tottenham Hotspur	1-0	Norwich City
1974	Wolverhampton W	2-1	Man City
1975	Aston Villa	1-0	Norwich City
1976	Man City	2-1	Newcastle U
1977	Aston Villa	0-0, 1-1† 3-2	Everton
1978	Nottingham Forest	0-0† 1-0	Liverpool
1979	Nottingham Forest	3-2	Southampton
1980	Wolverhampton W	1-0	Nottingham F
1981	Liverpool	1-1† 2-1	West Ham U
1982	Liverpool	3-1†	Tottenham H
1983	Liverpool	2-1†	Manchester Utd
1984	Liverpool	0-0† 1-0	Everton
1985	Norwich City	1-0	Sunderland
1986	Oxford United	3-0	QPR
1987	Arsenal	2-1	Liverpool
1988	Luton Town	3-2	Arsenal
1989	Nottingham Forest	3-1	Luton Town
1990	Nottingham Forest	1-0	Oldham Athletic
1991	Sheffield Wednesday	1-0	Manchester Utd

† after extra time

Most wins:
4 Liverpool, Nottingham Forest; 3 Aston Villa

Most finals:
6 Liverpool; 5 Aston Villa, Nottingham Forest; 4 Arsenal, Norwich C; 3 Manchester C, Tottenham H

LIVERPOOL'S POST-WAR MANAGERS

Manager	League	FA Cup	League Cup	European Cup	UEFA Cup
George Kay (1936-51)	1	-	-	-	-
Don Welsh (1951-56)	-	-	-	-	-
Phil Taylor (1956-59)	-	-	-	-	-
Bill Shankly (1959-74)	3	2	-	-	1
Bob Paisley (1974-83)	6	-	3	3	1
Joe Fagan (1983-85)	1	-	1	1	-
Kenny Dalglish (1985-91)	3	2	-	-	-

KENNY DALGLISH'S RECORD

1968 Joined Celtic. 324 appearances, 167 goals: Honours: 4 League titles, 4 Scottish Cups, 1 League Cup

1971 Played first international. Went on to win 102 caps and score 30 goals

1977 Joined Liverpool for British record £440,000. Played in 515 games and scored 173 goals

As player: 3 European Cups, 5 League titles, 4 League Cups, 2 FWA Player of the Year awards, 1 PFA Player of the Year award.

As manager: 3 League titles, 2 FA Cups, 3 Manager of the Year awards

MOST SUCCESSFUL ENGLISH CLUBS
(All Major Tournaments)

Total		FL	FAC	FLC	Eur.
32	Liverpool	18	4	4	6
18	Aston Villa	7	7	3	1
17	Arsenal	10	5	1	1
16	Manchester United	7	7	-	2
15	Tottenham Hotspur	2	8	2	3
14	Everton	9	4	-	1
11	Newcastle United	4	6	-	1
9	Wolverhampton W	3	4	2	-
9	Manchester City	2	4	2	1
9	Nottingham Forest	1	2	4	2
8	Sunderland	6	2	-	-
8	Blackburn Rovers	2	6	-	-
8	Sheffield Wednesday	4	3	1	-
7	West Bromwich Albion	1	5	1	-
6	Leeds United	2	1	1	2

SCOTLAND

	LEAGUE				CUP		
	Winners	Pts	Runners-up	Pts	Winners	Score	Runners-up
1873-74	-				Queen's Park	2-0	Clydesdale
1874-75	-				Queen's Park	3-0	Renton
1875-76	-				Queen's Park	1-1 2-0	Third Lanark
1876-77	-				Vale of Leven	1-1 1-1 3-2	Rangers
1877-78	-				Vale of Leven	1-0	Third Lanark
1878-79	-				(a)		
1879-80	-				Queen's Park	3-0	Thornlibank
1880-81	-				Queen's Park	3-1	Dumbarton
1881-82	-				Queen's Park	2-2 4-1	Dumbarton
1882-83	-				Dumbarton	2-2 2-1	Vale of Leven
1883-84	-				(b)		
1884-85	-				Renton	0-0 3-1	Vale of Leven
1885-86	-				Queen's Park	3-1	Renton
1886-87	-				Hibernian	2-1	Dumbarton
1887-88	-				Renton	6-1	Cambuslang
1888-89	-				Third Lanark	2-1	Celtic
1889-90	-				Queen's Park	1-1 2-1	Vale of Leven
1890-91	Dumbarton/ Rangers	29	-		Hearts	1-0	Dumbarton
1891-92	Dumbarton	37	Celtic	35	Celtic	5-1	Queen's Park
1892-93	Celtic	29	Rangers	28	Queen's Park	2-1	Celtic
	Division I						
1893-94	Celtic	29	Hearts	26	Rangers	3-1	Celtic

	LEAGUE				CUP		
	Winners	Pts	Runners-up	Pts	Winners	Score	Runners-up
1894-95	Hearts	31	Celtic	26	St. Bernard's	2-1	Renton
1895-96	Celtic	30	Rangers	26	Hearts	3-1	Hibernian
1896-97	Hearts	28	Hibernian	26	Rangers	5-1	Dumbarton
1897-98	Celtic	33	Rangers	29	Rangers	2-0	Kilmarnock
1898-99	Rangers	36	Hearts	26	Celtic	2-0	Rangers
1899-00	Rangers	32	Celtic	25	Celtic	4-3	Queen's Park
1900-01	Rangers	35	Celtic	29	Hearts	4-3	Celtic
1901-02	Rangers	28	Celtic	26	Hibernian	1-0	Celtic
1902-03	Hibernian	37	Dundee	31	Rangers	1-1 0-0 2-0	Hearts
1903-04	Third Lanark	43	Hearts	39	Celtic	3-2	Rangers
1904-05	Celtic	41	Rangers	41	Third Lanark	0-0 3-1	Rangers
1905-06	Celtic	49	Hearts	43	Hearts	1-0	Third Lanark
1906-07	Celtic	55	Dundee	48	Celtic	3-0	Hearts
1907-08	Celtic	55	Falkirk	51	Celtic	5-1	St. Mirren
1908-09	Celtic	51	Dundee	50	(c)		
1909-10	Celtic	54	Falkirk	52	Dundee	2-2 0-0 2-1	Clyde
1910-11	Rangers	52	Aberdeen	48	Celtic	0-0 2-0	Hamilton A
1911-12	Rangers	51	Celtic	45	Celtic	2-0	Clyde
1912-13	Rangers	53	Celtic	49	Falkirk	2-0	Raith R
1913-14	Celtic	65	Rangers	59	Celtic	0-0 4-1	Hibernian
1914-15	Celtic	65	Hearts	61	-		
1915-16	Celtic	67	Rangers	56	-		
1917-18	Rangers	56	Celtic	55	-		
1919-20	Rangers	71	Celtic	68	Kilmarnock	3-2	Albion R
1920-21	Rangers	76	Celtic	66	Partick Thistle	1-0	Rangers
1921-22	Celtic	67	Rangers	66	Morton	1-0	Rangers
1922-23	Rangers	55	Airdrieonians	50	Celtic	1-0	Hibernian
1923-24	Rangers	59	Airdrieonians	50	Airdrieonians	2-0	Hibernian
1924-25	Rangers	60	Airdrieonians	57	Celtic	2-1	Dundee
1925-26	Celtic	58	Airdrieonians	50	St. Mirren	2-0	Celtic
1926-27	Rangers	56	Motherwell	51	Celtic	3-1	East Fife
1927-28	Rangers	60	Celtic	55	Rangers	4-0	Celtic
1928-29	Rangers	67	Celtic	51	Kilmarnock	2-0	Rangers
1929-30	Rangers	60	Motherwell	55	Rangers	0-0 2-1	Partick T
1930-31	Rangers	60	Celtic	58	Celtic	2-2 4-2	Motherwell
1931-32	Motherwell	66	Rangers	61	Rangers	1-1 3-0	Kilmarnock
1932-33	Rangers	62	Motherwell	59	Celtic	1-0	Motherwell
1933-34	Rangers	66	Motherwell	62	Rangers	5-0	St. Mirren
1934-35	Rangers	55	Celtic	52	Rangers	2-1	Hamilton A
1935-36	Celtic	66	Rangers	61	Rangers	1-0	Third Lanark
1936-37	Rangers	61	Aberdeen	54	Celtic	2-1	Aberdeen
1937-38	Celtic	61	Hearts	58	East Fife	1-1 4-2	Kilmarnock
1938-39	Rangers	59	Celtic	48	Clyde	4-0	Motherwell
1946-47	Rangers	46	Hibernian	44	Aberdeen	2-1	Hibernian
1947-48	Hibernian	48	Rangers	46	Rangers	1-1 1-0	Morton
1948-49	Rangers	46	Dundee	45	Rangers	4-1	Clyde
1949-50	Rangers	50	Hibernian	49	Rangers	3-0	East Fife
1950-51	Hibernian	48	Rangers	38	Celtic	1-0	Motherwell
1951-52	Hibernian	45	Rangers	41	Motherwell	4-0	Dundee
1952-53	Rangers	43	Hibernian	43	Rangers	1-1 1-0	Aberdeen
1953-54	Celtic	43	Hearts	38	Celtic	2-1	Aberdeen
1954-55	Aberdeen	49	Celtic	46	Clyde	1-1 1-0	Celtic
1955-56	Rangers	52	Aberdeen	46	Hearts	3-1	Celtic
1956-57	Rangers	55	Hearts	53	Falkirk	1-1 2-1	Kilmarnock
1957-58	Hearts	62	Rangers	49	Clyde	1-0	Hibernian
1958-59	Rangers	50	Hearts	48	St. Mirren	3-1	Aberdeen
1959-60	Hearts	54	Kilmarnock	50	Rangers	2-0	Kilmarnock
1960-61	Rangers	51	Kilmarnock	50	Dunfermline A	0-0 2-0	Celtic
1961-62	Dundee	54	Rangers	51	Rangers	2-0	St. Mirren
1962-63	Rangers	57	Kilmarnock	48	Rangers	1-1 3-0	Celtic
1963-64	Rangers	55	Kilmarnock	49	Rangers	3-1	Dundee
1964-65	Kilmarnock	50	Hearts	50	Celtic	3-2	Dunfermline A
1965-66	Celtic	57	Rangers	55	Rangers	0-0 1-0	Celtic
1966-67	Celtic	58	Rangers	55	Celtic	2-0	Aberdeen
1967-68	Celtic	63	Rangers	61	Dunfermline A	3-1	Hearts
1968-69	Celtic	54	Rangers	49	Celtic	4-0	Rangers
1969-70	Celtic	57	Rangers	45	Aberdeen	3-1	Celtic
1970-71	Celtic	56	Aberdeen	54	Celtic	1-1 2-1	Rangers
1971-72	Celtic	60	Aberdeen	50	Celtic	6-1	Hibernian
1972-73	Celtic	57	Rangers	56	Rangers	3-2	Celtic
1973-74	Celtic	53	Hibernian	49	Celtic	3-0	Dundee United
1974-75	Rangers	56	Hibernian	49	Celtic	3-1	Airdrieonians

LEAGUE
Premier Division

Season	Champion	Pts	Runner-up	Pts
1975-76	Rangers	54	Celtic	48
1976-77	Celtic	55	Rangers	46
1977-78	Rangers	55	Aberdeen	53
1978-79	Celtic	48	Rangers	45
1979-80	Aberdeen	48	Celtic	47
1980-81	Celtic	56	Aberdeen	49
1981-82	Celtic	55	Aberdeen	53
1982-83	Dundee U	56	Celtic	55
1983-84	Aberdeen	57	Celtic	50
1984-85	Aberdeen	59	Celtic	52
1985-86	Celtic	50	Hearts	50
1986-87	Rangers	69	Celtic	63
1987-88	Celtic	72	Hearts	62
1988-89	Rangers	56	Aberdeen	50
1989-90	Rangers	51	Aberdeen	44
1990-91	Rangers	55	Aberdeen	53

CUP

Winner	Score	Runner-up
Rangers	3-1	Hearts
Celtic	1-0	Rangers
Rangers	2-1	Aberdeen
Rangers	0-0 0-0 3-2	Hibernian
Celtic	1-0	Rangers
Rangers	0-0 4-1	Dundee United
Aberdeen	4-1	Rangers
Aberdeen	1-0	Rangers
Aberdeen	2-1	Celtic
Celtic	2-1	Dundee United
Aberdeen	3-0	Hearts
St. Mirren	1-0	Dundee United
Celtic	2-1	Dundee United
Celtic	1-0	Rangers
Aberdeen	0-0 (d)	Celtic
Motherwell	4-3	Dundee United

(a) Cup awarded to Vale of Leven, Rangers failed to appear for replay after 1-1 draw
(b) Cup awarded to Queen's Park, Vale of Leven failed to appear for the final
(c) After two drawn games (2-2 and 1-1) between Celtic and Rangers, the Cup was withdrawn following a riot
(d) Aberdeen won 9-8 on penalties.

LEAGUE

Most titles:
Premier/1st Division:
41 Rangers; **35** Celtic; **4** Aberdeen, Hearts, Hibernian;
1st/2nd Division:
6 Ayr United, Morton; **5** Clyde, St Johnstone; **4** Falkirk, Hibernian, Motherwell, Partick Thistle, Raith Rovers, Stirling Albion
(New) 2nd Division: **2** Clyde, Brechin City, Stirling Albion

CUP

Most wins:
29 Celtic; **24** Rangers; **10** Queen's Park; **7** Aberdeen; **5** Hearts; **3** Clyde, St. Mirren, Vale of Leven

Most finals:
46 Celtic; **40** Rangers; **13** Aberdeen, Queen's Park; **10** Hearts, Hibernian; **7** Kilmarnock, Vale of Leven; **6** Clyde, Dumbarton, Dundee United, Motherwell, St. Mirren, Third Lanark

Venues (excluding replays)
Matches played at various Glasgow venues until 1924, except Logie Green, Edinburgh 1896. Current Hampden Park first used 1904 and every year since 1925. All replays have been in Glasgow and at Hampden Park regularly since 1930

SCOTTISH LEAGUE CUP
Skol Cup since 1984-85

Season	Winner	Score	Runner-up
1946-47	Rangers	4-0	Aberdeen
1947-48	East Fife	1-1 4-1	Falkirk
1948-49	Rangers	2-0	Raith Rovers
1949-50	East Fife	3-0	Dunfermline
1950-51	Motherwell	3-0	Hibernian
1951-52	Dundee	3-2	Rangers
1952-53	Dundee	2-0	Kilmarnock
1953-54	East Fife	3-2	Partick Thistle
1954-55	Hearts	4-2	Motherwell
1955-56	Aberdeen	2-1	St. Mirren
1956-57	Celtic	0-0 3-0	Partick Thistle
1957-58	Celtic	7-1	Rangers
1958-59	Hearts	5-1	Partick Thistle
1959-60	Hearts	2-1	Third Lanark
1960-61	Rangers	2-0	Kilmarnock
1961-62	Rangers	1-1 3-1	Hearts
1962-63	Hearts	1-0	Kilmarnock
1963-64	Rangers	5-0	Morton
1964-65	Rangers	2-1	Celtic
1965-66	Celtic	2-1	Rangers
1966-67	Celtic	1-0	Rangers
1967-68	Celtic	5-3	Dundee
1968-69	Celtic	6-2	Hibernian
1969-70	Celtic	1-0	St. Johnstone
1970-71	Rangers	1-0	Celtic
1971-72	Partick Thistle	4-1	Celtic
1972-73	Hibernian	2-1	Celtic
1973-74	Dundee United	1-0	Celtic
1974-75	Celtic	6-3	Hibernian
1975-76	Rangers	1-0	Celtic
1976-77	Aberdeen	2-1	Celtic
1977-78	Rangers	2-1	Celtic
1978-79	Rangers	2-1	Aberdeen
1979-80	Dundee United	0-0 3-0	Aberdeen
1980-81	Dundee United	3-0	Dundee
1981-82	Rangers	2-1	Dundee United
1982-83	Celtic	2-1	Rangers
1983-84	Rangers	3-2	Celtic
1984-85	Rangers	1-0	Dundee United
1985-86	Aberdeen	3-0	Hibernian
1986-87	Rangers	2-1	Celtic
1987-88	Rangers	3-3	Aberdeen
	(Rangers won 5-3 on penalties)		
1988-89	Rangers	3-2	Aberdeen
1989-90	Aberdeen	2-1	Rangers
1990-91	Rangers	2-1	Celtic

Venues:
All finals and replays at Hampden Park except 1980 replay and 1981 final, which were played at Dens Park, Dundee

Most wins:
17 Rangers; **9** Celtic; **4** Hearts, Aberdeen, **3** Dundee, East Fife

Most finals:
23 Rangers; **20** Celtic; **9** Aberdeen; **5** Dundee, Hearts, Hibernian; **4** Dundee U, Partick T

ENGLISH HONOURS BOARD - QUICK REFERENCE GUIDE

	Football League	FA Cup	Football League Cup
Arsenal	1931, 1933, 1934, 1935, 1938, 1948, 1953, 1971, 1989, 1991	1930, 1936, 1950, 1971, 1979	1987
Aston Villa	1894, 1896, 1897, 1899, 1900, 1910, 1981	1887, 1895, 1897, 1905, 1913, 1920, 1957	1961, 1975, 1977
Barnsley		1912	
Birmingham City			1963
Blackburn Olympic		1883	
Blackburn Rovers	1912, 1914	1884, 1885, 1886, 1890, 1891, 1928	
Blackpool		1953	
Bolton Wanderers		1923, 1926, 1929, 1958	
Bradford City		1911	
Burnley	1921, 1960	1914	
Bury		1900, 1903	
Cardiff City		1927	
Charlton Athletic		1947	
Chelsea	1955	1970	1965
Clapham Rovers		1880	
Coventry City		1987	
Derby County	1972, 1975	1946	
Everton	1891, 1915, 1928, 1932, 1939, 1963, 1970, 1985, 1987	1906, 1933, 1966, 1984	
Huddersfield Town	1924, 1925, 1926	1922	
Ipswich Town	1962	1978	
Leeds United	1969, 1974	1972	1968
Leicester City			1964
Liverpool	1901, 1906, 1922, 1923, 1947, 1964, 1966, 1973, 1976, 1977, 1979, 1980, 1982, 1983, 1984, 1986, 1988, 1990	1965, 1974, 1986, 1989	1981, 1982, 1983, 1984
Luton Town			1988
Manchester City	1937, 1968	1904, 1934, 1956, 1969	1970, 1976
Manchester United	1908, 1911, 1952, 1956, 1957, 1965, 1967	1909, 1948, 1963, 1977, 1983, 1985, 1990	
Newcastle United	1905, 1907, 1909, 1927	1910, 1924, 1932, 1951, 1952, 1955	
Norwich City			1962, 1985
Nottingham Forest	1978	1898, 1959	1978, 1979, 1989, 1990
Notts County		1894	
Old Carthusians		1881	
Old Etonians		1879, 1882	
Oxford United			1986
Oxford University		1874	
Portsmouth	1949, 1950	1939	
Preston North End	1889, 1890	1889, 1938	
Queen's Park Rangers			1967
Royal Engineers		1875	
Sheffield United	1898	1899, 1902, 1915, 1925	
Sheffield Wednesday	1903, 1904, 1929, 1930	1896, 1907, 1935	1991
Southampton		1976	
Stoke City			1972
Sunderland	1892, 1893, 1895, 1902, 1913, 1936	1937, 1973	
Swindon Town			1969
Tottenham Hotspur	1951, 1961	1901, 1921, 1961, 1962, 1967, 1981, 1982, 1991	1971, 1973
Wanderers		1872, 1873, 1876, 1877, 1878	
West Bromwich A	1920	1888, 1892, 1931, 1954, 1968	1966
West Ham United		1964, 1975, 1980	
Wimbledon		1988	
Wolverhampton W	1954, 1958, 1959	1893, 1908, 1949, 1960	1974, 1980

TEN-YEAR LEAGUE TABLE

Football League standings for the ten years 1981/82 - 1990/91 based on awarding points for each position: 92 for the League champions down to one for the bottom team in the Fourth Division - (e.g. the Fourth Division champions receive 24 and the bottom team in the Third 25)

1	Liverpool	916	65	Leyton Orient	288
2	Arsenal	879	66	Bury	286
3	Everton	877	67	Southend United	275
4	Manchester United	869	68	Blackpool	251
5	Tottenham Hotspur	866	69	Chesterfield	246
6	Nottingham Forest	862	70	Chester City	242
7	Southampton	832	71	Doncaster Rovers	234
8	Aston Villa	796	72	Burnley	229
9	Queen's Park Rangers	790	73	Lincoln City*	223
10	Coventry City	788	74	Mansfield Town	221
11=	Norwich City	786	75	York City	218
11=	West Ham United	786	76	Newport County*	201
13	Luton Town	784	77	Tranmere Rovers	188
14	Sheffield Wednesday	759	78	Exeter City	180
15	Chelsea	752	79	Northampton Town	177
16=	Manchester City	742	80	Scunthorpe United	167
16=	Watford	742	81	Wrexham	157
18=	Newcastle	723	82	Peterborough United	154
18=	Ipswich	723	83	Darlington*	152
20	Leeds	674	84	Crewe Alexandra	142
21	Leicester	662	85	Aldershot	135
22	West Bromwich Albion	661	86	Colchester United*	132
23	Sunderland	658	87=	Hereford United	106
24	Crystal Palace	656	87=	Stockport County	106
25	Charlton Athletic	653	89	Torquay United	102
26	Wimbledon	651	90	Hartlepool United	90
27	Derby County	638	91	Rochdale	68
28	Stoke City	630	92	Halifax Town	59
29=	Blackburn Rovers	620	93	Scarborough*	56
29=	Oldham Athletic	620	94	Maidstone United*	26
31	Brighton	610			
32	Barnsley	605			
33	Oxford United	603			
34	Birmingham City	601			
35	Middlesbrough	591			
36	Portsmouth	586			
37	Millwall	571			
38	Notts County	562			
39	Sheffield United	536			
40	Shrewsbury Town	522			
41	Wolverhampton	504			
42	Plymouth Argyle	478			
43	Bradford City	477			
44	Hull City	470			
45	Huddersfield Town	467			
46	Fulham	457			
47	Grimsby Town	451			
48	Bristol Rovers	419			
49	Bournemouth	416			
50	Swansea City	393			
51=	Reading	387			
51=	Swindon Town	387			
53	Brentford	381			
54	Bolton Wanderers	380			
55	Bristol City	378			
56	Rotherham United	371			
57	Walsall	362			
58	Wigan Athletic	354			
59	Port Vale	341			
60	Cardiff City	339			
61	Carlisle United	338			
62	Gillingham	336			
63	Cambridge United	301			
64	Preston North End	290			

* Teams played for less than the full 10 seasons: Colchester, Darlington and Lincoln 9, Newport 7, Scarborough 4, Maidstone 2

NON-LEAGUE
(since 1970)

Northern Premier		Southern League		FA Challenge Trophy			
1969-70	Macclesfield Town	Cambridge United		Macclesfield Town	2-0		Telford United
1970-71	Wigan Athletic	Yeovil Town		Telford United	3-2		Hillingdon Borough
1971-72	Stafford Rangers	Chelmsford City		Stafford Rangers	3-0		Barnet
1972-73	Boston United	Kettering Town		Scarborough	2-1†		Wigan Athletic
1973-74	Boston United	Dartford		Morecambe	2-1		Dartford
1974-75	Wigan Athletic	Wimbledon		Matlock Town	4-0		Scarborough
1975-76	Runcorn	Wimbledon		Scarborough	3-2†		Stafford Rangers
1976-77	Boston United	Wimbledon		Scarborough	2-1		Dagenham
1977-78	Boston United	Bath City		Altrincham	3-1		Leatherhead
1978-79	Mossley	Worcester City		Stafford Rangers	2-0		Kettering Town

Alliance Premier League							
1979-80	Altrincham	56	Weymouth	54	Dagenham	2-1		Mossley
1980-81	Altrincham	54	Kettering Town	51	Bishop's Stortford	1-0		Sutton United
1981-82	Runcorn	93	Enfield	86	Enfield	1-0†		Altrincham
1982-83	Enfield	84	Maidstone United	83	Telford United	2-1		Northwich Vic
1983-84	Maidstone Utd	70	Nuneaton Borough	69	Northwich Victoria	1-1† 2-1		Bangor City
1984-85	Wealdstone	62	Nuneaton Borough	58	Wealdstone	2-1		Boston United
1985-86	Enfield	76	Frickley Athletic	69	Altrincham	1-0		Runcorn
1986-87	Scarborough	91	Barnet	85	Kidderminster Harriers	0-0† 2-1		Burton Albion
1987-88	Lincoln City	82	Barnet	80	Enfield	0-0† 3-2		Telford United
1988-89	Maidstone Utd	84	Kettering Town	76	Telford United	1-0†		Macclesfield
1989-90	Darlington	87	Barnet	85	Barrow	3-0		Leek Town
1990-91	Barnet	87	Colchester United	85	Wycombe Wanderers	2-1		Kidderminster Harriers

† after extra time

Alliance Premier League 1979-83, Gola League 1984-85,
GM Vauxhall Conference 1986-

RECORDS
(to end of 1990-91 season)

APPEARANCES
Football League

PLAYERS WITH 760 OR MORE APPEARANCES:
930 Peter Shilton (Leicester C, Stoke C, Nottingham F, Southampton, Derby C) 1966-
824 Terry Paine (Southampton and Hereford U) 1957-77
790 Tommy Hutchison (Blackpool, Coventry, Manchester City, Burnley, Swansea) 1968-
777 Alan Oakes (Manchester C, Chester, Port Vale) 1959-84
770 John Trollope (Swindon T) 1960-80
764 Jimmy Dickinson (Portsmouth) 1946-65
762 Roy Sproson (Port Vale) 1950-72
Trollope's 770 games for Swindon are a record for one club.
The most appearances in the Scottish League:
626 by Bob Ferrier (Motherwell) 1918-37

International Matches
BRITISH ISLES PLAYERS WITH OVER 100 CAPS:
125 Peter Shilton (England) 1970-90
119 Pat Jennings (Northern Ireland) 1964-86
108 Bobby Moore (England) 1962-73
106 Bobby Charlton (England) 1958-70
105 Billy Wright (England) 1946-59
102 Kenny Dalglish (Scotland) 1971-86
The most caps won by the other two nations:
Most for Wales: 72 Joey Jones 1972-86; Peter Nicholas 1979-91
Most for Republic of Ireland: 72 Liam Brady 1974-90

OTHER LEADING CAPPED PLAYERS:
120 Rivelino (Brazil) 1968-79
115 Bjorn Nordqvist (Sweden) 1963-78
112 Dino Zoff (Italy) 1968-83
111 Pele (Brazil) 1957-71
111 Hector Chumpitaz (Peru) 1963-82
Chumpitaz's figure, previously given as 150, has been revised after FIFA issued a list ruling that 39 of his caps were not in official internationals.

ROBERT MAXWELL'S MOVES

Jan 1982	Buys OXFORD UNITED. Orders players to be in Second Division by 1984. They were.
Apr 1983	Tries to buy READING to merge them with Oxford as "Thames Valley Royals". Deal off a month later.
Feb 1984	Buys DERBY COUNTY, then fighting relegation to Third Division. Five years later back in the First
Nov 1987	His company BPCC tries to buy Watford - prevented by new League rules. Had deal gone ahead the family would have had the control of three League clubs
Jul 1990	Tries to merge Israeli clubs into "JERUSALEM UNITED". Fails.
Aug 1990	Lends money to TOTTENHAM HOTSPUR
Jun 1991	Fails in his attempt to buy Tottenham.
Jul 1991	Sells Derby

Main Source: When Saturday Comes

ATTENDANCES
Record Attendances

World Cup: 199,854 Brazil v Uruguay 1950, Maracana Stadium, Rio de Janeiro

European Championship: 103,000 USSR v Hungary 1968, Moscow

International (Britain): 149,547 Scotland v England, 1937 Hampden Park

Club match (World): 177,656 Flamengo v Fuminense, 1963 (Brazilian League) Maracana Stadium, Rio de Janeiro

Club match (Europe): 146,433 Celtic v Aberdeen 1937, (Scottish Cup Final), Hampden Park

European Cup: 136,505 Celtic v Leeds U, 1970, Hampden Park

FA Cup Final: 126,047 Bolton W v West Ham U, 1923, Wembley Stadium

FA Cup (other than final): 84,569 Manchester C v Stoke C, 1934 (6th Round), Maine Road

League Cup (other than final): 63,418 Manchester U v Manchester C, 1969 (Semi-final), Old Trafford

Football League:

Div 1: 83,260 Man Utd v Arsenal, 1948, Maine Road

Div 2: 68,029 Aston Villa v Coventry C, 1937, Villa Park

Div 3: 49,309 Sheffield W v Sheffield U, 1979, Hillsborough

Div 4: 37,774 Crystal P v Millwall, 1961, Selhurst Park

Div 3 (S): 51,621 Cardiff C v Bristol C, 1947, Ninian Park

Div 3 (N): 49,655 Hull C v Rotherham U, 1948, Boothferry Park

Highest Post-War Average: 57,552 Manchester U 1967-68

Scottish League

Div 1/Premier: 118,567 Rangers v Celtic, 1939, Ibrox Stadium

Lower Divisions: 27,205 Queen's Park v Kilmarnock, Div 2, 1950, Hampden Park

Scottish FA Cup: 146,433 Celtic v Aberdeen (as above)

Scottish League Cup: 107,647 Celtic v Rangers, 1965, Hampden Park

GM Vauxhall Conference: 7,522 Lincoln C v Boston U, 1988, Sincil Bank

Lowest attendances
(Excluding matches played behind closed doors)

Football League: 13 Stockport C v Leicester C (Div 2), 1921, Old Trafford (*); 450 Rochdale v Cambridge U (Div 3), 1974, Scotland

Football League Div 1: 3,618 Wimbledon v Luton Town, 1990, Plough Lane

Scottish League: 80 Meadowbank T v Stenhousemuir (Div 2), 1979 Meadowbank Stadium

Major European Cup match: 483 Rapid Vienna v Juventus, (UEFA Cup), 1971

Home International: 2,315 Wales v Northern Ireland, 1982, Wrexham

England International at Wembley: 15,628 v Chile, 1989

(*)Disputed. Up to 2,000 believed present despite official figure

WINS
Most in a season
33(42) Doncaster R, Div 3(N), 1946-47
Div 1 record: 31(42) Tottenham H, 1960-61
Scottish record: 35(42) Rangers, 1920-21

Fewest in a season
1(34) Loughborough T, Div 2, 1899-1900
Div 1 record: 3(38) Woolwich Arsenal, 1912-13; 3(42) Stoke City, 1984-85
Scottish record: 0(22) Vale of Leven, 1891-92; post-war 1(34) Ayr U, Div 1, 1966-67

DEFEATS
Most in a season
33(40) Rochdale, Div 3(N), 1931-32
33(46) Cambridge U, Div 3, 1984-85
33(46) Newport C, Div 4, 1987-88
Div 1 record: 31(42) Stoke C, 1984-85
Scottish record: 31(42) St Mirren, Div 1, 1920-21

Fewest in a season
0(22) Preston NE, Football League, 1888-89
0(28) Liverpool, Div 2, 1893-94
0(18) Celtic, Scottish Div 1, 1897-98
0(18) Rangers, Scottish Div 1, 1898-99
0(18) Kilmarnock, Scottish Div 2 1898-99
Post-war record: 1(38) Arsenal, Div 1, 1990-91; 2(42) Leeds U, Div 1, 1968-69; 2(40) Liverpool, Div 1, 1987-88; 2(39) St Mirren, Scottish Div 1, 1976-77; 2(38) Morton, Scottish Div 2, 1966-67
Figures in brackets indicate matches played

DRAWS
Most in a season
Football League
23(42) Norwich C, Div 1, 1978-79
23(46) Exeter C, Div 4, 1986-87

Scottish record: 21(44) East Fife, Div 1, 1986-87
Figures in brackets indicate matches played

MOVES SINCE THE WAR

Club	From	To
1946 HULL CITY	Anlaby Road	Boothferry Park
1946 NEW BRIGHTON	Rake Lane	Tower Ground
1950 PORT VALE	Old Recreation Ground	Vale Park
1955 SOUTHEND UNITED	Southend Stadium	Roots Hall
1962 QUEEN'S PARK RANGERS	Loftus Road	White City
1963 QUEEN'S PARK RANGERS	White City	Loftus Road
1985 CHARLTON ATHLETIC	The Valley	Selhurst Park
1986 BRISTOL ROVERS	Eastville	Twerton Park, Bath
1988 SCUNTHORPE UNITED	Old Show Ground	Glanford Park
1990 WALSALL	Fellows Park	Bescot Stadium
1990 CHESTER	Sealand Road	Moss Rose, Macclesfield
1991 WIMBLEDON	Plough Lane	Selhurst Park
1991 CHARLTON ATHLETIC	Selhurst Park	The Valley

POINTS

Most points in a season

(Points available in brackets)

Football League (2pts for a win): 74(92) Lincoln C, Div 4, 1975-76

Div 1: 68(84) Liverpool, 1978-79

Football League (3 pts for a win): 102(138) Swindon T, Div 4, 1985-86

Div 1: 90(120) Liverpool, 1987-88; 90(126) Everton, 1984-85

Scottish League (2pts for a win): 76(84) Rangers, Div 1, 1920-21

Premier Division: 72(88) Celtic, 1987-88

Fewest points in a season

(Since expansion in 1898)

Football League: 8(68) Loughborough Town, Div 2, 1899-1900; Doncaster R, Div 2, 1904-05

Div 1: 17(126) Stoke C, 1984-85 (since expansion in 1905)

Scottish League: 6(60) Stirling A, Div 1, 1954-55

Premier Division: 11(72) St Johnstone, 1975-76

In 1896-97 Abercorn collected just 3 points in the Scottish 1st Division from their 18 games, an all-time low for a British League side.

GOALSCORING

Fast Scoring

Fastest Football League Goals

(From kick-off): all 6 secs: Albert Mundy, Aldershot v Hartlepool U, 1958, Div 4; Barrie Jones, Notts C v Torquay U, 1962, Div 3; Keith Smith, Crystal Palace v Derby C, 1964, Div 2; Tommy Langley, Queen's Park R v Bolton W, 1980, Div 2

Fastest FA Cup Goal:

8 secs: Vic Lambden, Bristol R v Aldershot, 1951, 3rd Round

Fastest Goal for England:

27 secs; Bryan Robson, v France, 1982 World Cup

Fastest hat-trick:

2½ mins: Jimmy Scarth, Gillingham v Leyton O, 1952, Div 3(S)

Fastest International hat-trick:

3½ mins: Willie Hall, England v Ireland, 1938

Fastest own goal:

6 secs: Pat Kruse, Torquay U v Cambridge U, 1977, Div 4

Individual Scoring Records

Most Goals in a Single Game:

First Class Match: 16 Stephan Stanis, Racing Club Lens v Aubry-Asturies, (French Cup) 1942

Internationals: 10 Sofus Nielsen, Denmark v France, 1908 Olympics; 10 Gottfried Fuchs, Germany v Russia, 1912 Olympics

British International Football: 6 Joe Bambrick, N. Ireland v Wales, 1930

The record for England is: 5 Oliver Vaughton, v Ireland, 1882, 5 Steve Bloomer, v Wales, 1896; 5 Gilbert Smith, v Ireland, 1899; 5 Willie Hall, v Ireland, 1938; 5 Malcolm Macdonald, v Cyprus, 1975

European Club Competition: 6 Lothar Emmerich, Borussia Dortmund v Floriana, Cup-winners' Cup, 1965

British Record in Europe: 5 Ray Crawford, Ipswich T v Floriana (European Cup), 1962; 5 Peter Osgood, Chelsea v Jeunesse Hautcharage (Cup-winners' Cup), 1971

Football League: 10 Joe Payne, Luton T v Bristol R, Div 3(S), 1936

Div 1 record: 7 Jimmy Ross, Preston NE v Stoke, 1888; 7 Ted Drake, Arsenal v Aston Villa, 1935

FA Cup: *Preliminary competition:* 10 Chris Marron, South Shields v Radcliffe Borough, 1947

Competition proper: 9 Ted MacDougall, Bournemouth v Margate, 1st round, 1971

Scottish League: 8 Owen McNally, Arthurlie v Armadale, Div 2, 1927; 8 Jimmy McGrory, Celtic v Dumfermline A, Div 1, 1928; 8 Jim Dyet, King's Park v Forfar A, Div 2, 1930; 8 John Calder, Morton v Raith R, Div 2, 1936; 8 Norman Haywood, Raith R v Brechin C, Div 2, 20 Aug 1937

Scottish Cup: 13 John Petrie, Arbroath v Bon Accord, 1885

Most Goals in a season

World Record: 127 Pele (Santos, Brazil) 1959

European Cup: 14 Jose Altafini (AC Milan) 1962-63

European Cup-winners' Cup: 14 Lothar Emmerich (Borussia Dortmund) 1965-66

Football League:

60 Dixie Dean (Everton), Div 1, 1927-28

The leading scorers in the other divisions have been: Div 2: 59 George Camsell (Middlesbrough), 1927-28; Div 3: 39 Derek Reeves (Southampton), 1959-60; Div 4: 52 Terry Bly (Peterborough U), 1960-61; Div 3(S): 55 Joe Payne (Luton T), 1936-37; Div 3(N): 55 Ted Harston (Mansfield R), 1936-37

Scottish League: 66 Jim Smith (Ayr U), Div 2, 1927-28

FA Cup: 15 Albert Brown (Tottenham H), 1900-01

Football League Cup: 12 Clive Allen (Tottenham H), 1986-87

Most Goals in a Career

World Record: 1329 Artur Friedenreich (Germanio, CA Ipiranga, Americano, CA Paulistano, Sao Paulo, Flamengo, Brazil) 1909-35

Two other players have scored more than 1000 first-class goals: 1280 Pele 1956-77; 1006 Franz Binder 1930-50

Internationals: 97 Pele (Brazil), 1957-70

British Internationals: 49 Bobby Charlton (England); 45 Gary Lineker (England); 44 Jimmy Greaves (England); 30 Tom Finney (England), Nat Lofthouse (England), Denis Law (Scotland), Kenny Dalglish (Scotland); 29 Vivian Woodward (England); 26 Steve Bloomer (England)

The records for the other countries are: *Northern Ireland:* 12 Joe Bambrick, Billy Gillespie, Gerry Armstrong; *Wales:* 23 Ivor Allchurch, Trevor Ford; *Republic of Ireland:* 20 Frank Stapleton

European Cup: 49 Alfredo di Stefano (Real Madrid) 1955-64

British Record: 30 Peter Lorimer (Leeds U), 1965-77

Football League: 434 Arthur Rowley (West Bromwich A, Fulham, Leicester C, Shrewsbury T), 1946-65

Scottish League: 410 Jimmy McGrory (Celtic, Clydebank), 1922-38

FA Cup: 41 Denis Law (Huddersfield T, Man City, Man Utd)

Hat Tricks

Football League

Most in a career: 37 Dixie Dean (Tranmere R, Everton, Notts C), 1923-37

Most in one season: 9 George Camsell (Middlesbrough), Div 2, 1926-27

Hat tricks in FA Cup finals: William Townley, Blackburn R v Sheffield W, 1890; Jimmy Logan, Notts C v Bolton W, 1894; Stanley Mortensen, Blackpool v Bolton W, 1953

Team Records

Most goals scored in a season

Football League: 134 Peterborough U, Div 4, 1960-61
Div 1 record: 128 Aston Villa, 1930-31

Scottish League: 142 Raith R, Div 2, 1937-38
Div 1/Premier Division record: 132 Hearts, Div 1, 1957-58

Fewest goals scored in a season

Football League *(since expansion in 1905):*
24 Watford, Div 2, 1971-72; 24 Stoke C, Div 1, 1984-85

Scottish League: 18 Stirling A, Div 1, 1980-81

Most goals conceded in a season

Football League: 141 Darwen, Div 2, 1898-99
Div 1 record: 125 Blackpool, 1930-31

Scottish League: 146 Edinburgh C, Div 2 1931-32
Div 1/Premier Division record: 137 Leith Athletic, Div 1, 1931-32

Fewest goals conceded in a season
(since expansion in 1905)

Football League: 16 Liverpool, Div 1, 1978-79

Scottish League: 14 Celtic, Div 1, 1913-14

Record Scores

Football League:

13-0 Stockport C v Halifax T, Div 3(N), 1933-34; 13-0 Newcastle U v Newport C 1946-47; 13-4 Tranmere R v Oldham A, Div 3(N), 1935-36;

Div 1 record: 12-0 West Bromwich v Darwen, 1891-92; 12-0 Nottingham F v Leicester Fosse, 1908-09

Record Away Win: 10-0 Sheffield U at Burslem Port Vale, Div 2, 1892-93

Scottish League:

15-1 Airdrieonians v Dundee Wanderers, Div 2, 1894-95
Div 1/Premier Division: 11-0 Celtic v Dundee, 1895-95

1992

GENERAL FIXTURES

Jan 4 FA Cup third round, Scottish Cup second round; Jan 8 League Cup fifth round; Jan 25 FA Cup fourth round, Scottish Cup third round.

Feb 12 League Cup semi-final first-leg; Feb 15 FA Cup fifth round, Scottish Cup fourth round; Feb 19 England v France (Wembley).

Mar 4 European club competitions quarter-finals, first leg; Mar 7 FA Cup sixth round, Scottish Cup fifth round; Mar 15 League Cup semi-final, second leg; Mar 18 European club competitions quarter-finals, second leg; Mar 25 Czechoslovakia v England.

Apr 1 European club competitions semi-finals, first leg; Apr 4 Scottish cup semi-finals; Apr 5 FA Cup semi-finals; Apr 15 European club competitions semi-finals, second leg; Apr 25 FA Vase final (Wembley); Apr 29 USSR v England; UEFA Cup final, first leg; May 6 European Cup Winners' Cup final; May 9 FA CUP FINAL (Wembley); SCOTTISH CUP FINAL (Hampden); May 10 FA Trophy final (Wembley); May 13 UEFA Cup final, second leg; May 20 European Cup final; Jun 3 Finland v England; Jun 10-26 European Championship finals (Sweden).

EUROPEAN CHAMPIONSHIP

Jun 10	Group 1	Stockholm	19.15
Jun 11	Group 1	Malmö	19.15
Jun 12	Group 2	Gothenburg	16.15
Jun 12	Group 2	Norrköping	19.15
Jun 14	Group 1	Stockholm	19.15
Jun 14	Group 1	Malmö	16.15
Jun 15	Group 2	Gothenburg	19.15
Jun 15	Group 2	Norrköping	16.15
Jun 17	Group 1	Stockholm	19.15
Jun 17	Group 1	Malmö	19.15
Jun 18	Group 2	Gothenburg	19.15
Jun 18	Group 2	Norrköping	19.15

Jun 21	Semi-final	Winner Group 1 v Runner-up Group 2 Stockholm 19.15
Jun 22	Semi-final	Winner Group 2 v Runner-up Group 1 Gothenburg 19.15
Jun 26	FINAL	Gothenburg 19.15

All times are BST

FIRST DIVISION FIXTURES 1991-92

Home Team \ Away Team	Arsenal	Aston V	Chelsea	Coventry	Crystal P	Everton	Leeds	Liverpool	Luton T	Man C	Man U	Norwich	Nottm F	Notts C	Oldham	QPR	Sheff U	Sheff W	Soton	Tottenham	West Ham	Wimbledon
Arsenal	–	Jan 11	Oct 5	Sep 7	Apr 11	Dec 21	Mar 21	Apr 20	Aug 27	Aug 31	Feb 1	Dec 14	Feb 29	Oct 26	Mar 10	Aug 17	Sep 21	Feb 15	May 2	Nov 30	Nov 2	Jan 1
Aston V	Aug 24	–	Apr 20	May 2	Sep 4	Feb 1	Nov 23	Apr 11	Oct 5	Dec 7	Aug 21	Mar 28	Sep 21	Nov 16	Feb 22	Mar 14	Mar 7	Jan 18	Dec 28	Sep 7	Dec 26	Oct 26
Chelsea	Apr 25	Sep 18	–	Mar 14	Feb 8	Sep 28	Sep 14	Oct 19	Aug 31	Jan 1	Dec 14	Nov 16	Sep 21	Aug 28	Dec 21	Apr 18	Mar 7	Feb 29	Feb 15	Jan 11	Apr 4	Aug 17
Coventry	Apr 4	Sep 28	Nov 2	–	Oct 19	Apr 18	Sep 18	Feb 8	Aug 21	Aug 17	Feb 29	Feb 15	Mar 11	Sep 14	Mar 21	Jan 11	Mar 21	Dec 14	Nov 30	Jan 1	Apr 25	Aug 31
Crystal P	Sep 14	Mar 21	Oct 26	Feb 1	–	Apr 4	Aug 17	Nov 2	Dec 15	Aug 24	Nov 30	Feb 29	Mar 11	Jan 1	Apr 18	Sep 28	Aug 31	Apr 25	Nov 16	Dec 22	Sep 17	Aug 27
Everton	Aug 20	Oct 19	May 2	Sep 17	Sep 7	–	Feb 22	Dec 28	Mar 14	Apr 20	Aug 24	Sep 3	Nov 23	Feb 1	Mar 7	Feb 8	Apr 11	Dec 26	Mar 28	Oct 5	Dec 7	Nov 16
Leeds	Sep 3	Feb 15	Apr 11	Sep 21	Jan 18	Aug 31	–	Sep 21	Feb 29	Dec 7	Mar 7	Sep 3	Jan 18	Feb 1	Aug 17	Dec 21	Oct 5	Aug 24	Mar 28	Dec 14	Mar 28	Nov 2
Liverpool	Jan 28	Sep 14	Feb 1	Apr 21	Nov 2	Dec 28	Sep 21	–	Aug 24	Aug 21	Apr 18	Feb 22	Mar 7	Sep 7	Jan 18	Dec 26	Mar 28	May 2	Dec 7	Mar 28	Nov 16	Nov 23
Luton T	Dec 26	Apr 25	Dec 28	Sep 7	Mar 7	Sep 17	Dec 7	Aug 24	–	Jan 11	Sep 21	Oct 26	Jan 1	May 2	Apr 11	Apr 20	Nov 30	Feb 1	Mar 21	Nov 16	Aug 17	Sep 7
Man C	Dec 28	Feb 29	Mar 28	Jan 18	Aug 24	Jan 11	Dec 7	Aug 21	Jan 11	–	Apr 18	Dec 14	Sep 28	Aug 28	Aug 17	Aug 28	Nov 2	Feb 8	Oct 5	Feb 1	Aug 20	Nov 30
Man U	Oct 19	Dec 21	Mar 7	Sep 3	Feb 22	Mar 21	Mar 7	Apr 18	Sep 21	Apr 18	–	Sep 7	Apr 20	Aug 17	Apr 25	Jan 1	Nov 2	Sep 18	Apr 11	May 2	Sep 4	Mar 21
Norwich	Mar 7	Jan 1	Mar 1	Aug 24	Dec 7	Aug 17	May 2	Feb 22	Oct 26	Dec 14	Sep 7	–	Nov 2	Mar 14	Jan 11	Dec 21	Nov 23	Feb 8	Aug 31	Mar 14	Sep 14	Apr 11
Nottm F	Dec 7	Apr 18	Feb 22	Apr 11	Nov 23	Feb 15	Dec 22	Mar 7	Jan 1	Aug 31	Jan 29	Mar 14	–	Jan 11	Aug 31	Dec 21	Apr 4	Sep 18	Sep 14	Aug 31	Sep 28	Dec 14
Notts C	Feb 8	Mar 10	Dec 26	Mar 28	Mar 28	Feb 1	Oct 19	Sep 7	May 2	Sep 28	Jan 18	Sep 21	Feb 22	–	Nov 23	Apr 25	Feb 1	Apr 4	Sep 3	Aug 28	Dec 28	Feb 29
Oldham	Nov 16	Feb 22	Dec 21	Dec 7	Sep 21	Oct 26	Feb 8	Jan 18	Apr 11	Aug 17	Dec 26	Nov 2	Mar 14	Nov 23	–	Feb 15	Sep 7	Nov 17	Aug 24	Feb 29	Oct 19	Feb 1
QPR	Jan 18	Nov 2	Sep 21	Mar 11	Dec 28	Feb 8	Dec 21	Dec 26	Apr 20	Aug 28	Jan 1	Dec 21	Feb 29	Apr 4	Feb 15	–	Sep 7	Dec 28	Sep 7	Apr 11	Sep 4	Sep 28
Sheff U	Apr 18	Dec 14	Apr 11	Sep 21	May 2	Apr 11	Oct 5	Mar 28	Nov 30	Nov 2	Oct 26	Apr 20	Apr 4	Feb 1	Apr 4	Aug 31	–	Nov 17	Aug 24	Feb 15	Aug 20	Sep 28
Sheff W	Nov 23	Aug 17	Nov 23	Feb 22	Dec 7	Feb 15	Aug 24	May 2	Feb 1	Aug 31	Sep 14	Oct 19	Sep 7	Dec 21	Nov 17	Mar 11	Apr 18	–	Sep 21	Nov 2	Feb 22	Dec 21
Soton	Feb 22	Aug 31	Sep 7	Dec 7	Mar 11	Dec 14	Mar 7	Dec 7	Jan 18	Apr 25	Sep 28	Dec 28	Feb 8	Dec 7	Jan 28	Jan 11	Nov 23	Apr 18	–	Aug 17	Mar 7	Apr 18
Tottenham	Mar 14	Dec 14	Sep 3	Mar 7	Apr 20	Feb 29	Jan 1	Nov 16	Aug 17	Feb 15	Feb 15	Apr 11	Mar 7	Nov 30	Dec 14	May 2	May 2	Mar 14	Dec 14	–	Feb 8	Apr 20
West Ham	Mar 14	Aug 28	Apr 4	Apr 4	Feb 29	Dec 7	Mar 7	Nov 16	Aug 17	Aug 20	Feb 15	May 2	Aug 31	Mar 7	Dec 7	Sep 4	May 2	Nov 30	Dec 14	Feb 8	–	Jan 11
Wimbledon	Mar 28	Feb 8	Jan 18	Dec 28	Dec 26	Mar 10	Nov 2	Nov 23	Sep 7	Nov 30	Mar 21	Apr 11	Dec 14	Feb 29	Feb 1	Oct 19	Dec 21	Aug 20	Apr 20	Sep 21	Aug 24	–

DIRECTORY

Managers as at start 1991-92 season. Changes in 1990-91 indicated with an asterisk.

FIRST DIVISION

Team	Ground	Manager
ARSENAL (Gunners)	Highbury	George Graham
ASTON VILLA (Villa)	Villa Park	Ron Atkinson*
CHELSEA (Blues)	Stamford Bridge	Ian Porterfield*
COVENTRY CITY (Sky Blues)	Highfield Road	Terry Butcher
CRYSTAL PALACE (Eagles)	Selhurst Park	Steve Coppell
EVERTON (Toffeemen)	Goodison Park	Howard Kendall*
LEEDS UNITED	Elland Road	Howard Wilkinson
LIVERPOOL (Reds)	Anfield	Graeme Souness*
LUTON TOWN (Hatters)	Kenilworth Road	David Pleat*
MANCHESTER CITY (Blues)	Maine Road	Peter Reid
MANCHESTER UNITED (Reds)	Old Trafford	Alex Ferguson
NORWICH CITY (Canaries)	Carrow Road	Dave Stringer
NOTTINGHAM FOREST (Reds)	City Ground	Brian Clough
NOTTS COUNTY (Magpies)	Meadow Lane	Neil Warnock
OLDHAM ATHLETIC (Latics)	Boundary Park	Joe Royle
QUEEN'S PARK RANGERS (R's)	Loftus Road	Gerry Francis*
SHEFFIELD UNITED (Blades)	Bramall Lane	Dave Bassett
SHEFFIELD WEDNESDAY (Owls)	Hillsborough	Trevor Francis*
SOUTHAMPTON (Saints)	The Dell	Ian Branfoot*
TOTTENHAM HOTSPUR (Spurs)	White Hart Lane	Peter Shreeves*
WEST HAM UNITED (Hammers)	Upton Park	Billy Bonds
WIMBLEDON (Dons)	Selhurst Park	Ray Harford

Ground changes: Wimbledon left Plough Lane to share with Crystal Palace.

MANAGERIAL CHANGES 1990-91

November: Colin Harvey sacked by Everton; Howard Kendall resigned from Manchester City to replace Harvey; John Sillett released early from Coventry after announcing plans to retire. February: Kenny Dalglish resigned from Liverpool. May: Bobby Campbell resigned at Chelsea to be Ken Bates's assistant; Jim Ryan sacked by Luton two days after the club avoided relegation; Don Howe sacked by QPR; Chris Nicholl sacked from Southampton after six years; Dr Josef Venglos left Aston Villa by "mutual consent"; June: Ron Atkinson resigned from Sheffield Wednesday to replace Venglos; Terry Venables became managing director of Tottenham.

SECOND DIVISION

Team	Ground	Manager
BARNSLEY	Oakwell	Mel Machin
BLACKBURN ROVERS	Ewood Park	Don Mackay†
BRIGHTON & HOVE ALBION (Seagulls)	Goldstone Ground	Barry Lloyd
BRISTOL CITY (Robins)	Ashton Gate	Jimmy Lumsden*
BRISTOL ROVERS (Pirates)	Twerton Park	Martin Dobson*
CHARLTON ATHLETIC (Valiants)	The Valley	Steve Gritt/ Alan Curbishley*
DERBY COUNTY (Rams)	Baseball Ground	Arthur Cox
GRIMSBY TOWN (Mariners)	Blundell Park	Alan Buckley
MIDDLESBROUGH (Boro)	Ayresome Park	Lennie Lawrence*
MILLWALL (Lions)	The Den	Bruce Rioch
IPSWICH TOWN	Portman Road	John Lyall
LEICESTER CITY	Filbert Street	Brian Little*
NEWCASTLE UNITED (Magpies)	St James' Park	Osvaldo Ardiles*
PLYMOUTH ARGYLE (Pilgrims)	Home Park	David Kemp
PORTSMOUTH (Pompey)	Fratton Park	Jim Smith*
PORT VALE	Vale Park	John Rudge
SOUTHEND UNITED (Shrimpers)	Roots Hall	David Webb
SUNDERLAND	Roker Park	Denis Smith
SWINDON TOWN (Robins)	County Ground	Glenn Hoddle*
TRANMERE ROVERS	Prenton Park	John King
WATFORD (Hornets)	Vicarage Road	Steve Perryman*
WOLVERHAMPTON WANDERERS (Wolves)	Molineux	Graham Turner

Ground changes 1991: Charlton Athletic left Selhurst Park to play at Upton Park pending a return to The Valley

MANAGERIAL CHANGES 1990-91

September: Joe Jordan resigned from Bristol City to manage Hearts; November: Colin Lee sacked by Watford; January: David Pleat sacked by Leicester; March: Jim Smith resigned from Newcastle; Osvaldo Ardiles resigned from Swindon to replace him; Frank Burrows left Portsmouth "mutual consent"; May: Gerry Francis resigned from Bristol Rovers to manage QPR; June: Colin Todd resigned from Middlesbrough; July: Lennie Lawrence resigned from Charlton to replace Todd.

†*Sacked Sep 2 1991*

THIRD DIVISION

Team	Ground	Manager
BIRMINGHAM CITY (Blues)	St Andrews	Terry Cooper*
BOLTON WANDERERS (Trotters)	Burnden Park	Phil Neal
BOURNEMOUTH (Cherries)	Dean Court	Harry Redknapp
BRADFORD CITY (Bantams)	Valley Parade	John Docherty
BRENTFORD (Bees)	Griffin Park	Phil Holder
BURY (Shakers)	Gigg Lane	*
CHESTER CITY	Moss Rose	Harry McNally
DARLINGTON (Quakers)	Feethams	Frank Gray*
EXETER CITY (Grecians)	St James Park	Alan Ball
FULHAM (Cottagers)	Craven Cottage	Alan Dicks
HARTLEPOOL UNITED (Pool)	Victoria Ground	Alan Murray*
HUDDERSFIELD TOWN (Terriers)	Leeds Road	Eoin Hand
HULL CITY (Tigers)	Boothferry Park	Terry Dolan*
LEYTON ORIENT (O's)	Brisbane Road	Peter Eustace*
PETERBOROUGH UNITED (Posh)	London Road	Chris Turner*
PRESTON NORTH END (Lillywhites)	Deepdale	Les Chapman
READING (Royals)	Elm Park	Mark McGhee*
SHREWSBURY TOWN (Shrews)	Gay Meadow	John Bond*
STOCKPORT COUNTY	Edgeley Park	Danny Bergara
STOKE CITY (Potters)	Victoria Ground	Lou Macari
SWANSEA CITY (Swans)	Vetch Field	Frank Burrows*
TORQUAY UNITED (Gulls)	Plainmoor	John Impey*
WEST BROMWICH ALBION (Baggies)	The Hawthorns	Bobby Gould*
WIGAN ATHLETIC (Latics)	Springfield Park	Bryan Hamilton

MANAGERIAL CHANGES 1990-91

November: Mark Lawrenson resigned from Peterborough; January: Stan Ternent sacked by Hull; Brian Talbot sacked by WBA; Dave Booth sacked by Peterborough; Asa Hartford sacked by Shrewsbury; Dave Mackay resigned from Birmingham after receiving vote of confidence; February: Alan Ball resigned from Stoke; March: Terry Yorath left Swansea ("resigned" - the board, "sacked" - Yorath). April: Dave Smith resigned from Torquay; Ian Porterfield sacked by Reading. June: Brian Little resigned from Darlington to manage Leicester; Cyril Knowles sacked by Hartlepool because of illness; July: Frank Clark made managing director of Leyton Orient; August: Lou Macari resigned from Birmingham to replace Ball; Terry Cooper resigned from Exeter to replace Macari.

FOURTH DIVISION

Team	Ground	Manager
ALDERSHOT (Shots)	Recreation Ground	Brian Talbot*
BARNET	Underhill	Barry Fry
BLACKPOOL (Tangerines)	Bloomfield Road	Billy Ayre*
BURNLEY (Clarets)	Turf Moor	Frank Casper
CARDIFF CITY (Bluebirds)	Ninian Park	*
CARLISLE UNITED	Brunton Park	Aidan McCaffery*
CHESTERFIELD (Spireites)	Saltergate	Chris McMenemy*
CREWE ALEXANDRA (Railwaymen)	Gresty Road	Dario Gradi
DONCASTER ROVERS	Belle Vue	Billy Bremner
GILLINGHAM (Gills)	Priestfield	Damien Richardson
HALIFAX TOWN (Shaymen)	The Shay	Jim McCalliog§
HEREFORD UNITED	Edgar Street	John Sillett*
LINCOLN CITY (Imps)	Sincil Bank	Steve Thompson*
MAIDSTONE UNITED (Stones)	Watling Street	Graham Carr*†
MANSFIELD TOWN (Stags)	Field Mill	George Foster
NORTHAMPTON TOWN (Cobblers)	County Ground	Theo Foley
ROCHDALE	Spotland	Dave Sutton*
ROTHERHAM UNITED (Millers)	Millmoor	Phil Henson*
SCARBOROUGH	Seamer Road	Ray McHale
SCUNTHORPE UNITED (Irons)	Glanford Park	Bill Green*
WALSALL (Saddlers)	Bescot Stadium	Kenny Hibbitt
WREXHAM (Robins)	Racecourse Ground	Brian Flynn
YORK CITY	Bootham Crescent	John Bird

MANAGERIAL CHANGES 1990-91

November: Graham Carr sacked by Blackpool; Allan Clarke sacked by Lincoln; January: Paul Hart sacked by Chesterfield; Keith Peacock sacked by Maidstone; Billy McEwan resigned from Rotherham; Terry Dolan resigned from Rochdale to manage Hull; Mick Buxton left Scunthorpe by "mutual consent", March: Clive Middlemass sacked by Carlisle; April: Len Walker made Aldershot general manager; May: Len Ashurst sacked by Cardiff; Colin Addison resigned from Hereford.

§ Sacked Oct 2 1991
† Resigned Sep 2 1991

ATHLETICS

ONE GIANT LEAP FOR MANKIND

Twice in Tokyo the earth shook. On the second night of the third World Championship, Carl Lewis led the field in the fastest 100 metres in history, smashing the world record, establishing himself indisputably as the fastest man on earth and consigning the name Ben Johnson to the dustbin of history.

Five days later Lewis himself was vanquished: the longest-standing, most resonant and most famous record in athletics, Bob Beamon's 23-year-old long jump of 8.90 metres, was finally beaten - not, as everyone anticipated, by Lewis but by his young rival Mike Powell.

With his fifth leap, Powell came nearer than any man in history to flying, landing 8.95 metres (29 ft 4 ½ in) into the pit. Powell was so thrilled he embraced the first man in sight, who happened to be a bemused Japanese official. It was Lewis's first defeat in 10 years and 66 long jump competitions. He reacted sourly, noting that he had put together a more consistent set of jumps.

This was a far cry from the jollity after the sprint when Lewis beat his friend and training partner Leroy Burrell to set a world record of 9.86 seconds, .04 of a second faster than the record Burrell had set in the American trials. It was a race of such

THE GREAT RACE...

❝You ran your best race in the semis in the LA Olympics. You ran your best race in the Rome World Championships in the semis. You ran your best race in the Seoul Olympics in the semis. I will not have you run your best race in the damn semis here."
Tom Tellez, Carl Lewis's coach, before the 100 metres final

"I felt great at 60 metres and I was still about fifth. At 60 metres I said 'Hey, I have a shot.'At 80 metres I felt very good. I said 'Hey, I have a great shot.' And then at 90, when I'd cleared everyone except Leroy, I thought 'Hey, I can win this.' I felt I was really rolling."
Lewis, after the final

"He's probably the greatest track athlete that's ever graced the planet and he's proved it tonight."
Mitchell on Lewis

"I'm just proud to be part of the greatest race of all time...We needed to wipe out everything Ben Johnson ever did."
Leroy Burrell, runner-up

...THE GREAT JUMP

"Even my neighbours didn't know I was in track."
Mike Powell

"I knew it was inevitable that someone would break my record. But like everyone else, I assumed it would be Carl Lewis."
Bob Beamon

"I was talking to my therapist and she said it was kinda like a heavyweight fight. If you're going to fight the champion, you can't beat him with a split decision, you've got to knock him out."
Powell

"Mike had the one great jump. He may never do it again. I could have gone farther on my last jump. But I didn't. That is something I have to accept."
Lewis

"If Carl wants to say negative things about me, it's only going to fuel my motivation."
Powell

"Lewis is a jumper. My man's a leaper.❞
Randy Huntington, Powell's coach

grandeur no one seemed to mind who won and lost: the first six did a once-unthinkable 9.96 or better. It took 24 hours for any doubts to creep in: then it became known that Dennis Mitchell, the bronze medallist, had, by an infinitesimal fraction of a second, made a false start, something the starter would have realised except that, mysteriously, he did not have his headphones on at the time.

There was only one other world record in the 43 events at the championship: by the US team in the 4 x 100 relay. Records were possible in the explosive events because of the extra-fast polyurethane track. In most other competitions, performances were well down and no one minded: it provided further evidence that constant random drug testing was having its effect.

Ben Johnson, the world's most famous steroid-user, made a hugely-publicised comeback in January after his two-year ban. But he was a shadow of his old self (in his physique too) and his presence on the circuit soon became an embarrassing joke; the richest track race in history, his grudge-match with Lewis in Lille, was in fact won by Mitchell, supposedly one of the spear-carriers. Johnson's time of 10.46 would only have tied for victory in the British junior title the previous day and he was obliged to give back 25 per cent of his $150,000 fee. He failed to qualify for the world championships except in the Canadian relay team.

THE 100 METRES

Lane			Previous best	Reaction time	Finish	
Lane	1	Bruny Surin (Can)	10.07	0.148s	10.14	8th
Lane	2	Ray Stewart (Jam)	9.97	0.114s	9.96	6th
Lane	3	Leroy Burrell (US)	9.90	0.120s	9.88	2nd
Lane	4	Linford Christie (GB)	9.97	0.126s	9.92	4th
Lane	5	Carl Lewis (US)	9.92	0.140s	9.86	1st
Lane	6	Dennis Mitchell (US)	10.00	0.090s*	9.91	3rd
Lane	7	Frank Fredericks (Nam)	10.02	0.151s	9.95	5th
Lane	8	Robson da Silva (Bra)	10.00	0.172s	10.12	7th

* Technical false start

TIMES FOR EACH 10 METRES

	10	20	30	40	50	60	70	80	90	100
Lewis	1.88	2.96	3.88	4.77	5.61	6.46	7.30	8.13	9.00	9.86
Burrell	1.83	2.89	3.79	4.68	5.55	6.41	7.28	8.12	9.01	9.88
Mitchell	1.80	2.87	3.80	4.68	5.55	6.42	7.28	8.14	9.01	9.91

The Tokyo fiesta was the biggest and best athletics event ever staged: 168 nations competed including such improbable entrants as the Northern Mariana Islands; their sole female competitor, Tehani Kirby, competed in the 100 metres the week after her 14th birthday but, alas, finished almost four seconds behind the winner of her heat. But more and more countries, from Africa especially, demanded to be taken seriously. Kenya won not only its customary collection of men's track medals but its first-ever women's medal; Algeria became the first country to provide the winner of both the men's and women's 1500 metres at this level; and a Zambian, Samuel Matete, spectacularly won the 400 metres hurdles.

The only significant absentees were South Africa. They were invited after their re-admission to the Olympic movement but then withdrew when their new black sporting officials said they were not ready - to the disgust of the International Amateur Athletic Federation which threatened dire but meaningless retribution. The IAAF decided to hold future championships every two years instead of every four, against the opposition of many athletes who said they were being overworked. The Federation also voted not to drop the word "amateur" from its title, which might fool someone.

Germany won five gold medals, half the total won by East Germany alone in the 1987 championships. Further hair-raising revelations about the dead nation's pharmaceutical policies kept seeping out: the College of Physical Culture in Leipzig closed in January after 40 years and the magazine *Stern* listed 280 top athletes who took part in the doping programme there. Documents obtained by the *Washington Post* named seven Olympic gold medallists and several current athletes from old East Germany who were enrolled

THE LONGEST JUMP

Jump	1	2	3	4	5	6
Powell	7.85	8.54	8.29	x	8.95	x
Lewis	8.68	x	8.83w	8.91w	8.87	8.84
Myricks	x	8.20	x	8.41	8.42	x

x = no jump   w=wind assisted

Powell's speed in the six metres before take-off for his record jump was recorded as 10.94 metres per second; his big toe was three centimetres behind the take-off board

in long-term government-sponsored steroid programmes. A letter was also found from the 1980 gold medallist Marita Koch complaining that her team-mate Barbel Wockel was getting larger doses because she had a relative at the drug firm.

The Americans Randy Barnes and Butch Reynolds, world record holders in the shot and 400 metres, were banned for two years for using steroids. Subsequently, the IAAF increased the sentence for future drug-users to four years. A Swedish newspaper found an advert dated 1931 in which Paavo Nurmi, the Flying Finn, recommended a cure-all called Rejuven, which contained anabolic steroids.

Britain started the World Championships with boundless optimism but finished with seven medals - exactly the same number as at the two previous Championships - two of them gold. The week started disastrously with a succession of hoped-for winners going out in a blaze of ignominy: Peter Elliott withdrew from the 1500 metres through injury; Steve Backley in the javelin and Tom McKean in the 800 metres failed even to qualify for the final. Yvonne Murray faded into 10th place in the 3,000 metres, having already had T-shirts printed saying "This one's for Scotland". Another Scot, Liz McColgan, came good in the 10,000 metres but no one outside Britain noticed because her win came moments after Powell's long jump. Then, far more dramatically, Kriss Akabusi barrelled his way in front of Antonio Pettigrew, the individual 400 metres champion, to give Britain gold in the 4 x 400 metres relay, the final event before the closing ceremony.

OUT OF THE BOX

The other highlight of the British athletic year came when the men's team thought they had won the European Cup for the second time running. But the sprint relay team was disqualified, getting no points instead of eight, when Marcus Adam fumbled a changeover and Linford Christie stepped out of the box. The Soviet Union were evidently the winners. Then Britain appeared to have won a second time: the Soviet lead-off runner in the 4 x 400 relay, Dmitri Golovastov, was disqualified for stepping out of his lane. So the Soviet Union were disqualified and the British team celebrated exuberantly on the track. However, the jury of appeal reversed the result. The British were convinced this was a political ploy to ensure the Soviets qualified for the World Cup, due to be held in Cuba in 1992. The Soviets then lost the women's European Cup to Germany when Yelena Rodina tested positive after winning the high jump. The AAA and WAAA were abolished and replaced by a British Athletics Federation. British indoor athletics finally moved out of his aircraft hangar at Cosford after 23 years and into a proper arena at Birmingham.

The record breaker of the year was Sergey Bubka of the Soviet Union, who broke his 27th world record (indoors and out) on August 5 in Malmo when he took his outdoor mark to 6.10 metres - 20 feet exactly. Bubka was maintaining a policy of increasing his record by a centimetre a time for any promoter who paid him the standard fee: believed to be about £30,000. Steve Backley lost his world javelin record to the Finn Seppo Räty, who then threw 96.96 metres, adding almost five metres to his own mark, thus alarming officials as throws slightly further than this endanger other users of the stadium. There were also fears that the event was turning into an competition between rival manufacturers rather than athletes: Räty himself called for the javelin to be modified yet again. Many leading athletes, less charismatic than Lewis or Bubka, found the combination of recession and their own exorbitant demands were making it harder for them to get big pay-days.

CHEATING HARVE

At other levels, the sport's enthusiasts remained unbowed. Johnny Kelley, 83, running in his 60th Boston marathon, finished in 5hrs 42 mins and collided with his wife at the finish. Both fell over but Kelley pronounced himself fit for his 61st in 1992; he won in 1935 and 1945 and has finished 56 times. Vietnam announced plans for the Ho Chi Minh Marathon (generous prizes) in February 1992. The organisation of the London Marathon was investigated by the Fraud Squad. A 62-year-old American runner was jailed for 90 days for cheating in a 10km road race; Harvey Sanders claimed the $100 prize for being the fastest man over 60 but no one saw him pass any of the checkpoints. "If he cheated in the race, I'll bet he's been cheating on me for years," said his wife.

British indoor athletics finally moved out of his aircraft hangar at Cosford after 23 years and into a proper arena at Birmingham. The AAA and WAAA were abolished and replaced by a British Athletics Federation. Willie McBrinn of Glasgow, magician and British over-60s marathon champion, was trying to combine his two skills by pulling a rabbit out of a hat on the run for photographers: he fell over a fence and was injured. The British 10,000 metres runner, Carl Thackery, was injured training in New Mexico when he fell into a cactus. Euan Clarke, the Scottish sprinter, cut his eyeball wiping his forehead with a crisp packet.

A tombstone was finally erected on the unmarked grave of Eric Liddell, the Chariots of Fire athlete and missionary who died in Wei-Fang, China in 1945. The inscription said: "They shall mount up with wings as eagles, they shall run and not be weary." The makers of a film about the 1930's New Zealand runner Jack Lovelock were forced to recast after local objections to the part being played by an Australian. Abel Kiviat, 99, who won the silver medal in the 1500 metres at the 1912 Olympics, said he was looking for a wife: "She doesn't have to have teeth," he said. "She just has to have a driver's licence."

Johan Landsman of Stellensbosch University won the first underground mile, held in a 6x3 metres shaft 100 metres down a coal mine at Secunda, South Africa. Landsman beat a field of 18 in 4:01.14. The 240 million Americans reportedly bought 393 million pairs of running shoes in 1990 at an average price of $30 a pair. A study of US army trainees showed that flat feet, traditionally an excuse to escape military service, were an advantage to runners compared to high arches, which lack shock resistance. In the United States, the Clydesdale Runners Association began to frame races segregated by weight, thus, as *The Times* noted, eliminating the sport's ancient prejudice in favour of fit people.

1990

3RD IAAF WORLD CHAMPIONSHIPS
Tokyo, Aug 24-Sep 1
Men
100 Metres
1 Carl Lewis (US) 9.86 (WR)
2 Leroy Burrell (US) 9.88s
3 Dennis Mitchell (US) 9.91s

FASTEST LEGAL 100 METRES

Lewis	9.86	Tokyo 1991
Burrell	9.88	Tokyo 1991
Burrell	9.90	New York 1991
Mitchell	9.91	Tokyo 1991
Lewis	9.92	Seoul 1988
Christie	9.92	Tokyo 1991

200 Metres
1 Michael Johnson (US) 20.01s
2 Frankie Fredericks (Nam) 20.34s
3 Atlee Mahorn (Can) 20.49s
400 Metres
1 Antonio Pettigrew (US) 44.57s
2 Roger Black (GB) 44.62s
3 Danny Everett (US) 44.63s
800 Metres
1 Billy Konchellah (Ken) 1m 43.99s
2 José Luiz Barbosa (Bra) 1m 44.24s
3 Mark Everett (US) 1m 44.67s
1500 Metres
1 Noureddine Morceli (Alg) 3m 32.84s
2 Wilfred Kirochi (Ken) 3m 34.84s
3 Hauke Fuhlbrugge (Ger) 3m 35.28s
5000 Metres
1 Yobes Ondieki (Ken) 13m 14.45s
2 Fita Bayesi (Eth) 13m 16.64s
3 Brahim Boutayeb (Mor) 13m 22.70s
10,000 Metres
1 Moses Tanui (Ken) 27m 38.74s
2 Richard Chelimo (Ken) 27m 39.41s
3 Khalid Skah (Mor) 27m 41.74s
Marathon
1 Hiromi Taniguchi (Jap) 2h 14m 57s
2 Ahmed Salah (Dji) 2h 15m 26s
3 Steve Spence (US) 2h 15m 36s
110 Metres Hurdles
1 Greg Foster (US) 13.06s
2 Jack Pierce (US) 13.06s
3 Tony Jarrett (GB) 13.25s
400 Metres Hurdles
1 Samuel Matete (Zam) 47.64s
2 Winthrop Graham (Jam) 47.74s
3 Kriss Akabusi (GB) 47.86s
3000 Metres Steeplechase
1 Moses Kiptanui (Ken) 8m 12.59s
2 Patrick Sang (Ken) 8m 13.44s
3 Azzedine Brahmi (Alg) 8m 15.44s
Kiptanui, 19, was the youngest-ever world champion. He had run his first steeplechase two months earlier.

20km Walk
1 Maurizio Damilano (Ita) 1h 19m 37s
2 Mikhail Schennikov (USSR) 1h 19m 46s
3 Yevgeny Misyula (USSR) 1h 20m 22s
50km Walk
1 Alexandr Potashov (USSR) 3h 53m 09s
2 Andrei Perlov (USSR) 3m 53.09s
3 Hartwig Gauder (Ger) 3m 55.14s
4 x 100 Metres Relay
1 United States 37.50s (WR)
2 France 37.87s
3 Great Britain 38.09s
This was the fourth world record in this event inside 12 months.
4 x 400 Metres Relay
1 Great Britain 2m 57.53s
2 United States 2m 57.57s
3 Jamaica 3m 00.10s
High Jump
1 Charles Austin (US) 2.38m
2 Javier Sotomayor (Cub) 2.36m
3 Hollis Conway (US) 2.36m
Sotomayor withdrew through injury without attempting to equal Austin.
Long Jump
1 Mike Powell (US) 8.95m (WR)
2 Carl Lewis (US) 8.91m
3 Larry Myricks (US) 8.42m
Pole Vault
1 Sergey Bubka (USSR) 5.95m
2 Istvan Bagyula (Hun) 5.90m
3 Maksim Tarasov (USSR) 5.85m
Triple Jump
1 Kenny Harrison (US) 17.78m
2 Leonid Voloshin (USSR) 17.75m
3 Mike Conley (US) 17.62m
Shot
1 Werner Gunthor (Swi) 21.67m
2 George Andersen (Nor) 20.81m
3 Lars-Arvid Nilsen (Nor) 20.75m
Discus
1 Lars Riedel (Ger) 66.20m
2 Erik De Bruin (Hol) 65.82m
3 Attila Horvath (Hun) 65.32m
Javelin
1 Kimmo Kinnunen (Fin) 90.82m
2 Seppo Raty (Fin) 88.12m
3 Vladimir Sasimovich (USSR) 87.08m
Hammer
1 Yuriy Sedykh (USSR) 81.70m
2 Igor Astapkovich (USSR) 80.94m
3 Heinz Weiss (Ger) 80.44m
Decathlon
1 Dan O'Brien (US) 8,812 pts
2 Mike Smith (Can) 8,549 pts
3 Christian Schenk (Ger) 8,394 pts

Women
100 Metres
1 Katrin Krabbe (Ger) 10.99s
2 Gwen Torrence (US) 11.03s
3 Merlene Ottey (Jam) 1.06s
Ottey's first defeat in 56 races at this distance

200 Metres
1 Katrin Krabbe (Ger) 22.09s
2 Gwen Torence (US) 22.16s
3 Merlene Ottey (Jam) 22.21s

400 Metres
1 Marie-Jose Perec (Fra) 49.13s
2 Grit Breuer (Ger) 49.42s
3 Sandra Myers (Spa) 49.78s

800 Metres
1 Lilia Nurutdinova (USSR) 1m 57.50s
2 Ana Quirot (Cub) 1m 57.55s
3 Ella Kovacs (Rom) 1m 57.58s

1500 Metres
1 Hassiba Boulmerka (Alg) 4m 02.21s
2 Tatyana Dorovskikh (USSR) 4m 02.58s
3 Lyudmila Rogacheva (USSR) 4m 02.72s

3000 Metres
1 Tatyana Dorovskikh (USSR) 8m 35.82
2 Elena Romanova (USSR) 8m 36.06s
3 Susan Sirma (Ken) 8m 39.41s
Sirma's medal was the first by a Kenyan woman

10,000 Metres
1 Liz McColgan (GB) 31m 14.31s
2 Zhong Huandi (Chn) 31m 35.08s
3 Wang Xiuting (Chn) 31m 35.99s

Marathon
1 Wanda Panfil (Pol) 2h 29m 53s
2 Sachiko Yamashita (Jap) 2h 29m 57s
3 Katrin Dorre (Ger) 2h 30m 10s

100 Metres Hurdles
1 Lyudmila Narozhilenko (USSR) 12.59s
2 Gail Devers-Roberts (US) 12.63s
3 Natalya Grigoryeva (USSR) 12.69s

400 Metres Hurdles
1 Tatyana Ledovskaya (USSR) 53.11s
2 Sally Gunnell (GB) 53.16s
3 Janeene Vickers (US) 53.47s

10km Walk
1 Alina Ivanova (USSR) 42m 57s
2 Madeleine Svensson (Swe) 43m 13s
3 Sari Essayah (Fin) 43m 13s

4 x 100 Metres Relay
1 Jamaica 41.94s
2 Soviet Union 42.20s
3 Germany 42.33s

4 x 400 Metres Relay
1 Soviet Union 3m 18.43s
2 United States 3m 20.15s
3 Germany 3m 21.25s

High Jump
1 Heike Henkel (Ger) 2.05m
2 Yelena Yelesina (USSR) 1.98m
3 Inga Babakova (USSR) 1.96m

Long Jump
1 Jackie Joyner-Kersee (US) 7.32m
2 Heike Drechsler (Ger) 7.29m
3 Larisa Berezhnaya (USSR) 7.11m

NOT SO BIG BEN

I don't call it cheating. Cheating is doing something nobody else is doing."
Charlie Francis, Ben Johnson's coach,

"The truth doesn't necessarily set you free. Sometimes it sets you adrift.... I'm done with hypocrisy. This is because I failed to maintain the conspiracy of silence."
Francis, after being banned for life

"In barring Francis for life, Athletics Canada has stumbled to a new level of hypocrisy...he is being vilified for speaking the truth."
Jim O'Leary, Toronto Sun

"Charlie Francis a martyr? A victim of rampant hypocrisy? A fount of credible opinions? Excuse me while I upchuck."
Jim Proudfoot, Toronto Star

"Every move he made was cheered hysterically...Some remarked that the welcome revealed noble qualities of forgiveness. Others believe that they are so pleased that a Canadian should be famous for anything, even drug-abuse, that forgiveness is automatic; he may be a cheat but he's a famous Canadian cheat."
Patrick Collins, Mail on Sunday, on Johnson's comeback race

"I still like Ben. He's like the mobster when he shoots you in the kneecap: nothing personal, only business."
Francis

"He's a decent sprinter but he doesn't know what to do with a non-super body. It must be like you were once a stud horse and now you're a gelding."
Tom Tellez, Carl Lewis's coach, on Johnson

"You can become well-known through good performances but with a negative deed you can become really famous."
Herbert Bohr, German promoter, on paying Johnson £15,000

"The laughing stock of the European track circuit."
Nick Davies, Athletics Today, on Johnson

"If I am 35 and running times like Johnson I sure wouldn't hang around to become an embarrassment."
Carl Lewis

"The council also deplored the reported statement of the IAAF president, Primo Nebiolo, in saying that he welcomed back Ben Johnson. The council would not agree with that statement, just as people would not say that they welcome back the Kray twins.
Tony Ward, British athletics spokesman

Shot
1 Huang Zhihong (Chn) 20.83m
2 Natalya Lisovskaya (USSR) 20.29m
3 Svetlana Krivelyova (USSR) 20.16m

Discus
1 Tsvetanka Khristova (Bul) 71.02m
2 Ilke Wyludda (Ger) 69.12m
3 Larisa Mikhalchenko (USSR) 68.26m
Wyludda's first defeat since 1988

Javelin
1 Xu Demei (Chn) 68.78m
2 Petra Felke-Meyer Ger) 68.68m
3 Silke Renk (Ger) 66.80m

Heptathlon
1 Sabine Braun (Ger) 6,672 pts
2 Liliana Nastase (Rom) 6,493 pts
3 Irena Byelova (USSR) 6,448 pts
Jackie Joyner-Kersee strained a hamstring in the 200 metres, the fourth event. She was 165 points ahead of Braun and considered certain to win.

Medal Table

	G	S	B	Total
Soviet Union	9	9	10	28
United States	10	8	8	26
Germany	5	4	8	17
Kenya	4	3	1	8
Great Britain	2	2	3	7
Jamaica	1	1	3	5
China	2	1	1	4
Algeria	2	0	1	3
Finland	1	1	1	3
France	1	1	0	2
Japan	1	1	0	2
Cuba	0	2	0	2
Canada	0	1	1	2
Hungary	0	1	1	2
Norway	0	1	1	2
Romania	0	1	1	2
Morocco	0	0	2	2
Bulgaria	1	0	0	1
Italy	1	0	0	1
Poland	1	0	0	1
Switzerland	1	0	0	1
Zambia	1	0	0	1
Brazil	0	1	0	1
Djibouti	0	1	0	1
Ethiopia	0	1	0	1
Holland	0	1	0	1
Namibia	0	1	0	1
Sweden	0	1	0	1
Spain	0	0	1	1

MOBIL GRAND PRIX
Final Standings
Men
1 Sergy Bubka (USSR) 69 pts
2 Jan Zelezny (Cze) 63 pts
3 Michael Johnson (US) 63 pts
Women
1 Heike Henkel (Ger) 63 pts
2 Merlene Ottey (Jam) 63 pts
3 Natalya Artymova (USSR) 63 pts

Individual Event Winners
Men
200 metres: Michael Johnson (US) 54 pts
400 metres: Roger Black (US) 54 pts
1500 metres: Noureddine Morceli (Alg) 63 pts
5000 metres: Brahim Boutayeb (Mor) 51 pts

110 metres hurdles: Tony Dees (US) 61 pts
3000m steeplechase: Moses Kiptanui (Ken) 57 pts
Long jump: Lee Starks (US) 59 pts
Pole vault : Sergy Bubka (USSR) 69 pts
Javelin: Jan Zelezny (Cze) 63 pts
Discus: Romas Ubartas (USSR) 55 pts

Women
100 metres: Merlene Ottey (Jam) 63 pts
800 metres: Ana Quirot (Cub) 59 pts
Mile: Natalya Artymova (USSR) 63 pts
3000 metres: Susan Sirma (Ken) 48 pts
400 metres hurdles: Sandra Farmer-Patrick (US) 63 pts
High jump: Heike Henkel (Ger) 63 pts
Shot: Huang Zhihong (Chn) 61 pts

EUROPEAN CUP FINAL
Frankfurt, Jun 29-30
Men

100 metres	Linford Christie (GB) 10.18s
200 metres	Jean-Charles Trouabal (Fra) 20.60s
400 metres	Roger Black (GB) 44.91s
800 metres	Tom McKean (GB) 1m 45.6s
1500 metres	Peter Elliot (GB 3m 43.39s
5000 metres	Salvatore Antibo (Ita) 13m 21.68s
10,000 metres	Eamonn Martin (GB) 28m 00.53s
110 metres hurdles	Colin Jackson (GB) 13.31s
400 metres hurdles	Kriss Akabusi (GB) 48.39s
3000m S/chase	Alessandro Lambruschini (Ita) 8m 29.62s
4 x 100m relay	France 38.67s
4 x 400m relay	Great Britain 3m 00.58s
High jump	Dalton Grant (GB) 2.30m
Long jump	Dietmar Haaf (Ger) 8.30m
Triple jump	Ralf Jaros (Ger) 17.66m
Pole vault	Grigoriy Yegorov (USSR) 5.67m
Javelin	Jan Zelezny (Cze) 2.84m
Shot	Ulf Timmermann (Ger) 20.26m
Discus	Attila Horvath (Hun) 65.24m
Hammer	Igor Astopkovich (USSR) 81.60m

Final Standings
1 Soviet Union 114pts
2 Great Britain 110.5pts
3 Germany 108pts
4 Italy 106pts
5 France 98.5pts
6 Czechoslovakia 66.5pts
7 Hungary 52pts
8 Bulgaria 52.5pts

Women

100 metres	Irena Segeyeva (USSR) 11.29s
200 metres	Irena Segeyeva (USSR) 22.48s
400 metres	Maria-Jose Perec (Fra) 49.32s
800 metres	Ella Kovacs (Rom) 1m 59.01s
1500 metres	Doina Melinte (Rom) 4m 00,83s
3000 metres	Margareta Keszeg (Rom) 8m 44.47s
10000 metres	Kathrin Ullrich (Ger) 31m 03.62s
100 metres hurdles	Lyudmila Narozhilenko (USSR) 12.55s
400 metres hurdles	Margarita Ponomareva (USSR) 54.42s
4 x 100m Relay	Soviet Union 42.51s
4 x 100m Relay	Soviet Union 3m 21.77s
High Jump	Elena Rodina (USSR) 1.98m
Long Jump	Heike Dreschler (Ger) 7.20m
Javelin	Tessa Sanderson (GB) 65.18m
Shot	Natalya Lisovskaya (USSR) 21.12m
Discus	Ilke Wyluda (Ger) 68.82m

Final Standings
1 Soviet Union 113pts
2 Germany 109pts

3	Great Britain	81pts
4	Romania	70pts
5	France	61pts
7	Bulgaria	45pts
8	Hungary	43pts

AAA/WAAA CHAMPIONSHIPS
Birmingham, Jul 26-27

Men

100 metres	Linford Christie (Chalford Hundred) 10.14s
200 metres	Jon Drummond (US) 20.61s
400 metres	Derek Redmond (Birchfield) 46.07s
800 metres	Tom McKean (Belshill) 1m 45.67s
1500 metres	Matthew Yates (Newham) 3m 40.88s
3000 metres	Tom Hanlon (Reebok) 8m 02.11s
5000 metres	Eamonn Martin 13m 22.99s
110 metres hurdles	David Nelson (Wolverhampton) 13.55s
400 metres hurdles	Max Robertson (Wolverhampton) 49.98s
3000m S/chase	Colin Walker (Gateshead) 8m 38.02s
10,000 metres walk	Ian McCombie (Cambridge) 41m 24.69s
High jump	Hollis Conway (US) 2.31m
Long jump	Barrington Williams (Cannock) 7.94m
Triple jump	Willie Banks (US) 16.60m
Pole vault	Tim Bright (US) 5.50m
Shot	Paul Edwards (Belgrave) 18.92m
Discus	Werner Reiterer (Aus) 59.56m
Javelin	Mick Hill (Chalford Hundred) 84.54m
Hammer	Sean Carlin (Aus) 72.58m

Women

100 metres	Evelyn Ashford (USA) 11.15s
200 metres	Stephanie Douglas (Milton Keynes) 23.37s
400 metres	Maicel Malone (USA) 50.89s
800 metres	Paula Fryer (Sale) 2m 02.19s
1500 metres	Ann Williams (Sale) 4m 08.93s
3000 metres	Yvonne Murray (Claford Hundred) 8m 46.47s
100 metres hurdles	Sally Gunnell (Chalford Hundred) 13.02s
400 metres hurdles	Gowry Retchakan (Thurrock) 5.67s
5000 metres walk	Betty Sworowski (Sheffield) 22m 29.04s
High jump	Debbie Marti (Bromley) 1.88m
Long jump	Fiona May (Derby) 6.58m
Triple jump	Evette Finikan (Shaftesbury) 13.46m
Shot	Judy Oakes (Croydon) 18.24m
Discus	Jacqueline McKernan (Lisburn) 57.76m
Javelin	Sharon Gibson (Notts) 57.34m

PEARL ASSURANCE UK CHAMPIONSHIPS
Cardiff, Jun 8-9

Men

100m	Linford Christie (Thames Valley) 10.39s
200m	John Regis (Belgrave) 21.24s
400m	Paul Sanders (Team Solent) 47.69s
800m	David Sharpe (Jarrow) 1m 50.31s
1500m	Simon Fairbrother (Haringey) 3m48.59s

3000m	Peter Elliott (Rotherham) 8m 07.51s
5000m	Ian Hamer (Swansea) 13m 49.86s
10,000m(*)	Carl Thackery (Hallamshire) 28m 37.52s
110m hurdles	David Nelson (Wolverhampton) 13.88s
400m hurdles	Max Robertson (Wolverhampton) 50.33s
3000m S/chase	Peter McColgan Dundee) 8m 49.54s
10,000m Walk	Steve Partington (Boundary) 42m 26.28s
High jump	Dalton Grant (Haringey) 2.20m
Long jump	Mark Forsythe (Balymena) 7.81m
Triple jump	Vernon Samuels (Wolverhampton) 16.19m
Pole vault	Andy Ashurst (Sale) 5.15m
Shot	Paul Edwards (Walton) 16,86m
Hammer	Paul Head (Newham) 73.64m
Discus	Paul Mardle (Wolverhampton) 54.66m
Javelin	Gary Jenson (Haringey) 76.90m

Invitation Pole Vault

| | Dean Mellor (Rotherham) 5.10m |

(*) For the AAA championship

Women

100m	Bev Kinch (Hounslow) 11.63s
200m	Linda Keough (Basingstoke) 24.25s
400m	Sandra Leigh (Stevenage) 53.55s
800m	Paula Fryer (Sale) 2m 05.43s
1500m	Alison Wyeth (Parkside) 4m 14.98s
3000m	Liz McColgan (Dundee) 8m 59.39s
100m hurdles	Lesley-Ann Skeete (Swindon) 13.66s
400m hurdles	Jacqui Parker (Essex) 57.64s
5000m walk	Vicky Lupton (Sheffield) 22m 51.38s
High jump	Lea Haggett (Croydon) 1.85m
Long jump	Fiona May (Derby) 6.74m
Triple jump	Evette Finikin (Shaftesbury Barnet) 13.23m
Shot	Judy Oakes (Croydon) 18.37m
Discus	Jacqueline McKernan (Lisburn) 53.14m
Javelin	Sharon Gibson (Notts) 60.14m

Invitation Hammer

| | Fiona Whitehead (Havant) 45.94m |

IAAF WORLD CROSS COUNTRY CHAMPIONSHIPS
Antwerp, Mar 23

Men - Individual
1 Khalid Skah (Mor) 33m 53s
2 Moses Tanui (Ken) 33m 54s
3 Simon Karori (Ken) 33m 54s

Men - Team
1 Kenya 38 pts
2 Ethiopia 104 pts
3 Spain 198 pts

Women - Individual
1 Lynn Jennings (US) 20m 24s
2 Tulu Derartu (Eth) 20m 27s
3 Liz McColgan (GB) 20m 28s

Women - Team
1= Ethiopia 36 pts
1= Kenya 36 pts
3 Soviet Union 48 pts

GRE BRITISH MEN'S LEAGUE
Division One
1	Haringey	30pts
2	Belgrave Harriers	28pts
3	Thames Valley Harriers	19pts

Division Two
| 1 | Caledon Park | 22 ½ pts |
| 2 | Old Gaytonians | 17 ½ pts |

3 Blackheath 16 pts

Division Three
1 Leeds City 21 ½ pts
2 Sale 20 pts
3 Swansea 18 ½ pts

Division Four
1 Crawley 22 pts
2 Windsor, Slough and Eton 22 pts
3 Morpeth 13 pts

Division Five
1 Havering 24 pts
2 Liverpool Harriers 18 pts
3 Cannock and Stafford 15 pts

DAILY TELEGRAPH UK WOMEN'S LEAGUE

Division One
1 Sale 21 pts
2 Essex Ladies 21 pts
3 Glasgow 16 pts

Division Two
1 Coventry 16 pts
2 Birchfield Harriers 15 pts
3 City of Hull 12 pts

Division Three
1 Hounslow 17 pts
2 Notts AC 13 pts
3 Cardiff 12 ½ pts

Division Four
1 Cannock & Stafford 17 pts
2 Peterborough 15 pts
3 Bournemouth 12 pts

GRE GOLD CUP
Gateshead, Aug 10
1 Belgrave 121 pts
2 Haringey 118 pts
3 Birchfield 107 pts
4 Shaftesbury 106 ½ pts
5 Wolverhampton 79 pts
6 Thames Valley 77 ½ pts
7 Woodford Green 70 pts
8 Newham 56 pts

GRE JUBILEE CUP FINAL
Gateshead , Aug 10
1 Essex 107 ½ pts
2 Birchfield 90 pts
3 Stretford 71 pts
4 Sale 63 pts
5 Croydon 62 pts
6 Coventry 61 ½ pts
7 Hounslow 59 pts
8 Glasgow 40 pts

BOSTON MARATHON
Apr 14
Men
1 Ibrahim Hussein (Ken) 2h 11m 06s
2 Abebe Mekonnen (Eth) 2h 11m 22s
3 Andy Ronan (Ire) 2h 11m 26s
Women
1 Wanda Panfil (Pol) 2h 24m 18s
2 Kim Jones (US) 2h 26m 05s
3 Uta Pippig (Ger) 2h 26m 52s

" East German athletes clearly did use drugs, fastidiously. But the true secret of their success was less that athletes were doped by the state, more that the state doped itself with athletes."
The Economist

"In the past, the rumour mill was out of control. You always heard 'What's this person using? What's that person using?' This time, you heard very little of that, and I think it's been really good for the sport."
Dave Rodda, US women's coach, after the World Championships

"They are interested only in those people who excite commercial interest. The real social commitment of a run for London is being swept aside and it suddenly stopped being a people's race."
Illtyd Harrington resigning from the London Marathon governing board

"My national pride is no longer so strong. I am from the East, that's the way I feel and always will."
Katrin Krabbe, German sprinter

"Oh, we are on the verge of everything, so far as I can see. Everything. It is time to go. Enough has happened, it is time, it is time. My God, how I hope it is time."
Matthew Motshwarateu, South Africa's 10,000-metre champion

"I still go down to the track in the morning but instead of eight hours a day it's five. I get the same things done. I just talk less."
Daley Thompson, former decathlon champion

"I can tell the difference between a man and a woman just by seeing them in their kit on television."
Dr Malcolm Brown, British team doctor, refusing to carry out sex tests

"You like to hear the music of the event and I couldn't hear anything."
Steve Backley, after failing to qualify for the javelin final in Tokyo

"Every time I win she expects me to buy another cow for the farm. Now she thinks it's time I found myself a wife to help her. **"**
Billy Konchellah, world 800 metres champion

ADT LONDON MARATHON/IAAF WORLD CUP
Apr 21

Men - Individual
1 Iakov Tolstikov (USSR) 2h 09m 17s
2 Manuel Matias (Por) 2h 10m 21s
3 Jan Huruk (Pol) 2h 10m 21s

Men - Team
1 Great Britain 6h 35m 01s
2 Portugal 6h 35m 55s
3 Poland 6h 36m 12s

Women - Individual
1 Rosa Mota (Por) 2h 26m 14s
2 Francie Larrieu Smith (US) 2h 27m 35s
3 Valentina Yegorova (USSR) 2h 28m 18s

Women - Team
1 USSR 7h 30m 33s
2 Italy 7h 36m 37s
3 United States 7h 40m 05s

Wheelchair - Men
Farid Amarouche (Fra) 1h 52m 52s

Wheelchair - Women
Connie Hansen (Den) 2h 04m 40s

EMSLEY CARR MILE
Sheffield, Sep 15
1 Peter Elliott (GB) 3m 52.10s
2 Steve Cram (GB) 3m 52.79s
3 Jans-Peter Herold (Ger) 3m 53.64s

WORLD INDOOR CHAMPIONSHIPS
Seville, Mar 8-10

Men
60 metres	Andre Cason (US) 6.54s
200 metres	Nikolay Antonov (Bul) 20.67s
400 metres	Devon Morris (Jam) 46.17s
800 metres	Paul Ereng (Ken) 1m 47.08s
1500 metres	Noureddine Morceli (Alg) 3m 41.57s
3,000 metres	Frank O'Mara (Ire) 7m 41.14s
60m hurdles	Greg Foster (US) 7.45s
5km walk	Mikhail Schennikov (USSR) 18m 23.55s
4 x 400m relay	Germany 3m 03.05s
High jump	Hollis Conway (US) 2.40m
Long jump	Dietmar Haaf (Ger) 8.15m
Triple jump	Igor Lapshin (USSR) 17.31m
Pole vault	Sergey Bubka (USSR) 6.00m
Shot	Werner Gunthor (Swi) 21.17m

Women
60 metres	Irina Sergeyeva (USSR) 7.02s
200 metres	Merlene Ottey (Jam) 22.24s
400 metre:	Diane Dixon (US) 50.64s
800 metres	Christine Wachtel (Ger) 2m 01.51s
1500 metres	Lyudmila Rogachova (USSR) 4m 05.09s
3000 metres	Marie Pierre Duros (Fra) 8m 50.69s
60m hurdles	Lyudmila Narozhilenko (USSR) 7.88s
3km walk	Beate Anders (Ger) 11m 50.90s
4 x 400m relay	Germany 3m 27.22s
High jump	Heike Henkel (Ger) 2.00m
Long jump	Larissa Berezhnaya (USSR) 6.84m
Shot	Sui Xinmei (Chn) 20.54m

British Medallists: Silver (2): Linford Christie (Men's 60 metres and 200 metres); **Bronze** (2): Ade Mafe (Men's 200 metres); Rob Denmark (Men's 3000 metres)

SERGEY BUBKA'S WORLD RECORDS

Outdoor
5.85m	19' 2¼"	Bratislava	May 26 1984
5.88m	19' 3½"	St Denis, France	Jun 2 1984
5.90m	19' 4¼"	London	Jul 13 1984
5.94m	19' 5¾"	Rome	Aug 31 1984
6.00m	19' 8¼"	Paris	JulY 13 1985
6.01m	19' 8½"	Moscow	Jul 8 1986
6.03m	19' 9¼"	Prague	Jun 23 1987
6.05m	19' 10¼"	Bratislava	Jun 9 1988
6.06m	19' 10½"	Nice	Jul 10 1988
6.07m	19' 11"	Shuzuoka, Japan	May 6 1991
6.08m	19' 11¼"	Moscow	Jun 9 1991
6.09m	19' 11¾"	Formia, Italy	Jul 8 1991
6.10m	20' 0¼"	Malmo, Sweden	Aug 6 1991

Indoors
5.81m	19' 0¾"	Vilnius, USSR	Jan 15 1984
5.82m	19' 1"	Milan	Feb 1 1984
5.83m	19' 1½"	Inglewood, California	Feb 10 1984
5.92m	19' 5"	Moscow	Feb 8 1986
5.94m	19' 5¾"	Inglewood	Feb 21 1986
5.95m	19' 6¼"	New York	Feb 28 1986
5.96m	19' 6"	Osaka, Japan	Jan 15 1987
5.97m	19' 7"	Turin	Mar 17 1987
6.03m	19' 9¼"	Osaka	Feb 11 1989
6.05m	19' 10¼"	Donetsk, USSR	Mar 17 1990
6.08m	19' 11¼"	Volgograd, USSR	Feb 9 1991
6.10m	20' 0¼"	San Sebastian, Spain	Mar 15 1991
6.11m	20' 0½"	Donetsk	Mar 19 1991
6.12m	20' 1"	Grenoble, France	Mar 23 1991

POLE VAULT
THE CLIMB TOWARDS 20 FEET
Milestone	Achieved by:
11ft	Edwin Woodburn (GB) 1876
12ft	Norman Dale (US) 1904
13ft	Robert Gardner (US) 1912
14ft	Sabin Carr (US) 1927
15ft	Cornelius Warmerdam (US) 1941
16ft	John Uelses (US) 1962
17ft	John Pennel (US) 1963
18ft	Christos Papanikolau (Gre) 1970
19ft	Thierry Vigneron (Fra) 1981
20ft	Sergey Bubka (USSR) 1991

CHAMPIONS

Olympic champions in Olympic Games section.

WORLD CHAMPIONSHIPS
Inaugurated at Helsinki in 1983. The second championships were in Rome in 1987 and the third in Tokyo in 1991.

Men

100 Metres
1983 Carl Lewis (US) 10.07s
1987 Ben Johnson (Can) 9.83s
1991 Carl Lewis (US) 9.86

200 Metres
1983 Calvin Smith (US) 20.14s
1987 Calvin Smith (US) 20.16s
1991 Michael Johnson (US) 20.01s

400 Metres
1983 Bert Cameron (Jam) 45.05s
1987 Thomas Schoenlebe (GDR) 44.33s
1991 Antonio Pettigrew (US) 44.57s

800 Metres
1983 Willi Wullbeck (FRG) 1m 43.65s
1987 Billy Konchellah (Ken) 1m 43.06s
1991 Billy Konchellah (Ken) 1m 43.99s

1500 Metres
1983 Steve Cram (GB) 3m 41.59s
1987 Abdi Bile (Som) 3m 36.80s
1991 Noureddine Morceli (Alg) 3m 32.84s

5000 Metres
1983 Eamonn Coghlan (Ire) 13m 28.53s
1987 Said Aouita (Mor) 13m 26.44s
1991 Yobes Ondieki (Ken) 13m 14.45s

10,000 Metres
1983 Alberto Cova (Ita) 28m 01.04s
1987 Paul Kipkoech (Ken) 27m 38.63s
1991 Moses Tanui (Ken) 27m 38.74s

Marathon
1983 Rob de Castella (Aus) 2h 10m 03s
1987 Douglas Wakiihuri (Ken) 2h 11m 48s
1991 Hiromi Taniguchi (Jap) 2h 14m 57s

110 Metres Hurdles
1983 Greg Foster (US) 13.42s
1987 Greg Foster (US) 13.21s
1991 Greg Foster (US) 13.06s

400 Metres Hurdles
1983 Edwin Moses (US) 47.50s
1987 Edwin Moses (US) 47.46s
1991 Samuel Matete (Zam) 47.64s

3000 Metres Steeplechase
1983 Patriz Ilg (FRG) 8m 15.06s
1987 Francesco Panetta (Ita) 8m 08.57s
1991 Moses Kiptanui (Ken) 8m 12.59s

20km Walk
1983 Ernesto Canto (Mex) 1h 20m 49s
1987 Maurizio Damilano (Ita) 1h 20m 45s
1991 Maurizio Damilano (Ita) 1h 19m 37s

50km Walk
1983 Ronald Weigel (GDR) 3h 43m 08s
1987 Hartwig Gauder (GDR) 3h 40m 53s
1991 Alexandr Potashov (USSR) 3h 53m 09s

4 x 100 Metres Relay
1983 United States 37.86s
1987 United States 37.90s
1991 United States 37.50s (WR)

4 x 400 Metres Relay
1983 Soviet Union 3m 00.79s
1987 United States 2m 57.29s

1991 Great Britain 2m 57.53s

High Jump
1983 Gennadiy Avdeyenko (USSR) 2.32m
1987 Patrik Sjöberg (Swe) 2.38m
1991 Charles Austin (US) 2.38m

Long Jump
1983 Carl Lewis 8.55m
1987 Carl Lewis 8.67m
1991 Mike Powell (US) 8.95m

Pole Vault
1983 Sergey Bubka (USSR) 5.70m
1987 Sergey Bubka (USSR) 5.85m
1991 Sergey Bubka (USSR) 5.95m

Triple Jump
1983 Zdislaw Hoffmann (Pol) 17.42m
1987 Khristo Markov (Bul) 17.92m
1991 Kenny Harrison (US) 17.78m

Shot
1983 Edward Sarul (Pol) 21.39m
1987 Werner Gunthor (Swi) 22.23m
1991 Werner Gunthor (Swi) 21.67m

Discus
1983 Imrich Bugar (Cze) 67.72m
1987 Jurgen Schult (GDR) 68.74m
1991 Lars Riedel (Ger) 66.20m

Javelin
1983 Detlef Michel (GDR) 89.48m
1987 Seppo Räty (Fin) 83.54m
1991 Kimmo Kinnunen (Fin) 90.82m

Hammer
1983 Sergey Litvinov (USSR) 82.68m
1987 Sergey Litvinov (USSR) 83.06m
1991 Yuriy Sedykh (USSR) 81.70m

Decathlon
1983 Daley Thompson (GB) 8,714 pts
1987 Torsten Voss (GDR) 8,680 pts
1991 Dan O'Brien (US) 8,812 pts

Women

100 Metres
1983 Marlies Gohr (GDR) 10.97s
1987 Silke Gladisch (GDR) 10.90s
1991 Katrin Krabbe (Ger) 10.99s

200 Metres
1983 Marita Koch (GDR) 22.13s
1987 Silke Gladisch (GDR) 21.74s
1991 Katrin Krabbe (Ger) 2.09s

400 Metres
1983 Jarmila Kratochvilova (Cze) 47.99s
1987 Olga Bryzgina (USSR) 49.38s
1991 Marie-Jose Perec (Fra) 49.13s

800 Metres
1983 Jarmila Kratochvilova (Cze) 1m 54.68s
1987 Sigrun Wodars (GDR) 1m 55.26s
1991 Lilia Nurutdinova (USSR) 1m 57.50s

1500 Metres
1983 Mary Decker (US) 4m 00.90s
1987 Tatyana Samolenko USSR) 3m 58.56s
1991 Hassiba Boulmerka (Alg) 4m 02.21s

3000 Metres
1983 Mary Decker (US) 8m 34.62s
1987 Tatyana Samolenko (USSR) 8m 38.73s
1991 Tatyana Dorovskikh (née Samolenko) (USSR) 8m 35.82

10,000 Metres
1987 Ingrid Kristiansen (Nor) 31m 05.85s
1991 Liz McColgan (GB) 31m 14.31s

Marathon
1983 Grete Waitz (Nor) 2h 28m 09s
1987 Rosa Mota (Por) 2h 25m 17s
1991 Wanda Panfil (Pol) 2h 29m 53s

100 Metres Hurdles
1983 Bettina Jahn (GDR) 12.35s
1987 Ginka Zagorcheva (Bul) 12.34s
1991 Lyudmila Narozhilenko (USSR) 12.59s

400 Metres Hurdles
1983 Ekaterina Fesenko (USSR) 54.14s
1987 Sabine Busche (GDR) 53.62s
1991 Tatyana Ledovskaya (USSR) 53.11s

10km Walk
1987 Irina Strakhoba (USSR)44m 12s
1991 Alina Ivanova (USSR) 42m 57s

4 x 100 Metres Relay
1983 East Germany 41.76s
1987 United States 41.58s
1991 Jamaica 41.94s

4 x 400 Metres Relay
1983 East Germany 3m 19.73s
1987 East Germany 3m 18.63s
1991 Soviet Union 3m 18.43s

High Jump
1983 Tamara Bykova (USSR) 2.01m
1987 Stefka Kostadinova (Bul) 2.09m
1991 Heike Henkel (Ger) 2.05m

Long Jump
1983 Heike Daute (GDR) 7.27m
1987 Jackie Joyner-Kersee (US) 7.36m
1991 Jackie Joyner-Kersee (US) 7.32m

Shot
1983 Helen Fibingerova (Cze) 21.05m
1987 Natalya Lisovskaya (USSR) 21.24m
1991 Huang Zhihong (Chn) 20.83m

Discus
1983 Martina Opitz (GDR) 68.94m
1987 Martina Hellman (née Opitz) (GDR) 71.62m
1991 Tsvetanka Khristova (Bul) 71.02m

Javelin
1983 Tiina Lillak (Fin) 70.82m
1987 Fatima Whitbread (GB) 76.64m
1991 Xu Demei (Chn) 68.78m

Heptathlon
1983 Ramona Neubert (GDR) 6,770 pts
1987 Jackie Joyner-Kersee (US) 7,128 pts
1991 Sabine Braun (Ger) 6,672 pts

Leading Medal-winning Nations
A total of 40 nations (including the two Germanys) have won medals at the championships. The following are the leading nations:

	G	S	B	Total
Germany	27	28	26	81
East Germany	20	18	15	53
West Germany	2	6	3	11
Soviet Union	22	27	27	76
United States	27	22	20	69
Great Britain	5	7	9	21
Jamaica	2	2	8	12
Kenya	7	3	1	11
Czechoslovakia	4	4	3	11
Italy	4	3	3	10

WORLD CUP

Men		Women	
1977 Düsseldorf			
1 East Germany	127pts	Europe	107pts
2 United States	120pts	East Germany	102pts
3 West Germany	112pts	USSR	89pts
1979 Montreal			
1 United States	119pts	East Germany	106pts
2 Europe	112pts	USSR	98pts
3 East Germany	108pts	Europe	88pts
1981 Rome			
1 Europe	147pts	East Germany	120.5pts
2 East Germany	130pts	Europe	110pts
3 United States	127pts	USSR	98pts
1985 Canberra			
1 United States	123pts	East Germany	121pts
2 USSR	115pts	USSR	105.5pts
3 East Germany	114pts	Europe	86pts
1989 Barcelona			
1 United States	133pts	East Germany	124pts
2 Europe	127pts	USSR	106pts
3 Great Britain	119pts	Americas	94pts

EUROPEAN CUP
Winners

	Men	Women
1965	USSR	USSR
1967	USSR	USSR
1970	East Germany	East Germany
1973	USSR	East Germany
1975	East Germany	East Germany
1977	East Germany	East Germany
1979	East Germany	East Germany
1981	East Germany	East Germany
1983	East Germany	East Germany
1985	USSR	USSR
1987	USSR	East Germany
1989	Great Britain	East Germany
1991	USSR	Germany

IAAF/MOBIL GRAND PRIX

	Men	Women
1985	Doug Padilla (US)	Mary Slaney (US)
1986	Said Aouita (Mor)	Yordanka Donkova (Bul)
1987	Tonie Campbell (US)	Merlene Ottey (Jam)
1988	Said Aouita (Mor)	Paula Ivan (Rom)
1989	Said Aouita (Mor)	Paula Ivan (Rom)
1990	Leroy Burrell (US)	Merlene Ottey (Jam)
1991	Sergy Bubka (USSR)	Heike Henkel (Ger)

MARATHON WORLD CUP
Inaugurated 1985
Men

	Individual	Team
1985	Ahmed Salah (Dji)	Djibouti
1987	Ahmed Salah (Dji)	Italy
1989	Keleke Metafeira (Eth)	Ethiopia
1991	Iakov Tolstikov (USSR)	Great Britain

Women

	Individual	Team
1985	Katrine Dorre (GDR)	Italy
1987	Zoya Ivanova (USSR)	USSR
1989	Sue Marchiano (US)	USSR
1991	Rosa Mota (Por)	USSR

LONDON MARATHON
Men

1981	Dick Beardsley (US) &	
	Inge Simonsen (Nor)	2h 11m 48s
1982	Hugh Jones (GB)	2h 09m 24s
1983	Mike Gratton (GB)	2h 09m 43s
1984	Charlie Spedding (GB)	2h 09m 57s
1985	Steve Jones (GB)	2h 08m 16s
1986	Toshihiko Seko (Jap)	2h 10m 02s
1987	Hiromi Taniguchi (Jap)	2h 09m 50s
1988	Henryk Jorgensen (Den)	2h 10m 20s
1989	Douglas Wakiihuri (Ken)	2h 09m 03s
1990	Allister Hutton (GB)	2h 10m 10s
1991	Iakov Tolstikov (USSR)	2h 09m 17s

Women

1981	Joyce Smith (GB)	2h 29m 57s
1982	Joyce Smith (GB)	2h 29m 43s
1983	Grete Waitz (Nor)	2h 25m 29s
1984	Ingrid Kristiansen (Nor)	2h 24m 26s

1985	Ingrid Kristiansen (Nor)	2h 21m 06s
1986	Grete Waitz (Nor)	2h 24m 54s
1987	Ingrid Kristiansen (Nor)	2h 22m 48s
1988	Ingrid Kristiansen (Nor)	2h 25m 41s
1989	Veronique Marot (GB)	2h 25m 56s
1990	Wanda Panfil (Pol)	2h 26m 31s
1991	Rosa Mota (Por)	2h 26m 14s

WORLD CROSS COUNTRY CHAMPIONSHIPS
Winners since 1982
Men

	Individual	Team
1982	Mohamed Kedir (Eth)	Ethiopia
1983	Bekele Debele (Eth)	Ethiopia
1984	Carlos Lopes (Por)	Ethiopia
1985	Carlos Lopes (Por)	Ethiopia
1986	John Ngugi (Ken)	Kenya
1987	John Ngugi (Ken)	Kenya
1988	John Ngugi (Ken)	Kenya
1989	John Ngugi (Ken)	Kenya
1990	Khalid Skah (Mor)	Kenya
1991	Khalid Skah (Mor)	Kenya

Women

1982	Maricica Puica (Rom)	USSR
1983	Greta Waitz (Nor)	United States
1984	Maricica Puica (Rom)	United States
1985	Zola Budd (Eng)	United States
1986	Zola Budd (Eng)	England
1987	Annette Sergent (Fra)	United States
1988	Ingrid Kristiansen (Nor)	USSR
1989	Annette Sergent (Fra)	USSR
1990	Lynn Jennings (US)	USSR
1991	Lynn Jennings (US)	Ethiopia/Kenya

RECORDS

WORLD OUTDOOR RECORDS
(September 1991)
Men

100m:	9.86s Carl Lewis (US); Tokyo, Aug 25 1991
200m:	19.72s Pietro Mennea (Ita); Mexico City Sep 12, 1979
400m:	43.29s Butch Reynolds (US); Zurich, Aug 17 1988
800m:	1m 41.73s Sebastian Coe (GB); Florence, Jun 10 1981
1,000m:	2m 12.18s Sebastian Coe (GB); Oslo, Jul 11 1981
1500m:	3m 29.46s Said Aouita (Mor); Berlin, Aug 23 1985
Mile:	3m 46.32s Steve Cram (GB); Oslo, Jul 27 1985
2,000m:	4m 50.81s Said Aouita (Mor); Paris, Jul 16 1987
3,000m:	7m 29.45s Said Aouita (Mor); Cologne, Aug 20 1989
5,000m:	12m 58.39s Said Aouita (Mor); Rome, Jul 27 1987
10,000m:	27m 08.23s Arturo Barrios (Mex); Berlin, Aug 18 1989
20,000m:	56m 55.6s Arturo Barrios (Mex); La Flèche, France, Mar 30 1991
1 Hour:	21,101m Arturo Barrios (Mex); La Flèche, France, Mar 30 1991
25,000m:	1h 13m 55.8s Toshihiko Seko (Jap); Christchurch, NZ, Mar 22 1981
30,000m:	1h 29m 18.8s Toshihiko Seko (Jap); Christchurch, NZ, Mar 22 1981
110m Hurdles:	12.92s Roger Kingdom (US); Zurich, Aug 16 1989
400m Hurdles:	47.02s Edwin Moses (US); Koblenz, Aug 31 1983
3,000m S/chase:	8m 05.35s Peter Koech (Ken); Stockholm, Jul 3 1989
4 x 100m Relay:	37.50s United States; Tokyo, Sep 1 1991
4 x 400m Relay:	2m 56.16s United States; Mexico City, Oct 20 1968
	2m 56.16s United States; Seoul, Oct 1 1988
4x800m Relay:	7m 03.89s Great Britain; London, Aug 30 1982
4x1500m Relay:	14m 38.8s West Germany; Cologne, Aug 17 1977
High Jump:	2.44 Javier Sotomayor (Cub); San Juan, Puerto Rico, Jul 30 1989
Pole Vault:	6.10m Sergey Bubka (USSR); Nice, Jul 10 1988
Long Jump:	8.95 Mike Powell (US); Tokyo, Aug 30 1990
Triple Jump:	17.79m Willie Banks (US); Indianapolis, Jun 16 1985

Shot:	23.12m Randy Barnes (US); Los Angeles, May 20 1990
Discus:	74.08m Jurgen Schult (GDR); Neubrandenburg, GDR, Jun 6 1986
Hammer:	86.74m Yuriy Sedykh (USSR); Stuttgart, Aug 30 1986
Javelin:	96.96m Seppo Räty (Fin); Punkalaidun, Finland, Jun 2 1991
Decathlon:	8847 pts Daley Thompson (GB); Los Angeles, Aug 8/9 1984
Marathon (†):	2h 06m 50s Belayneh Dinsamo (Eth); Rotterdam, Apr 17 1988

Women

100m:	10.49s Florence Griffith-Joyner (US); Indianapolis, Jul 16 1988
200m:	21.34s Florence Griffith-Joyner (US); Seoul, Sep 29 1988
400m:	47.60s Marita Koch (GDR); Canberra, Oct 6 1985
800m:	1m 53.28s Jarmila Kratochvilov (Cze); Munich, Jul 26 1983
1500m:	3m 52.47s Tatyana Kazankini (USSR); Zurich, Aug 13 1980
Mile:	4m 15.61s Paula Ivan (Rom); Nice, Jul 10 1989
2,000m:	5m 28.69s Maricica Puica (Rom); London, Jul 11 1986
3,000m:	8m 22.62s Tatyana Kazankini (USSR); Leningrad, Aug 26 1984
5,000m:	14m 37.33s Ingrid Kristiansen (Nor); Stockholm, Aug 5 1986
10,000m:	30m 13.74s Ingrid Kristiansen (Nor); Oslo, Jul 5 1986
20,000m:	1h 29m 29.2s Karolina Szabo (Hun); Budapest, Apr 22 1988
30,000m:	1h 49m 05.6s Karolina Szabo (Hun); Budapest, Apr 22 1988
100m Hurdles:	12.21 Yordanka Donkova (Bul); Stara Zagora, Bul, Aug 20 1988
400m Hurdles:	52.94s Marina Stepanova (USSR); Tashkent, Sep 17 1986
4x100m Relay:	41.37s East Germany; Canberra, Oct 6 1985
4x200m Relay:	1m 28.15s East Germany; Jena, GDR, Aug 9 1980
4x400m Relay:	3m 15.17s USSR; Seoul, Oct 1 1988
4x800m Relay:	7m 50.17s USSR; Moscow, Aug 5 1984
High Jump:	2.09m Stefka Kostadinova (Bul); Rome, Aug 30 1987
Long Jump:	7.52m Galina Chistyakova (USSR); Leningrad, Jun 11 1988
Shot:	22.63m Natalya Lisovskaya (USSR); Moscow, Jun 7 1987
Discus:	76.80m Gabriele Reinsch (GDR); Neubrandenburg, GDR, Jul 9 1988
Javelin:	80.00m Petra Felke (GDR); Potsdam, GDR, Sep 9 1988
Heptathlon:	7,291 pts Jackie Joyner-Kersee (US); Seoul, Sep 23/24 1988
Marathon (†):	2h 21m 06s Ingrid Kristiansen (Nor); London, Apr 21 1985

† World records not recognised for the Marathon, only best time

1992

RECORDS SET IN 1991

Men

Mar 30 20,000 metres: 56m 55.6s Arturo Barrios (Mex) La Flèche

Mar 30 One Hour: 21,101m Arturo Barrios (Mex) La Flèche

May 6 Javelin: 91.98m Seppo Räty (Fin), Shizuoka, Japan

May 6 Pole Vault: 6.07m Sergey Bubka (USSR), Shizuoka, Japan

Jun 2 Javelin: 96.96m Seppo Räty (Fin), Punkalaidun, Finland

Jun 9 Pole Vault: 6.08m Sergey Bubka (USSR), Moscow

Jun 14 100 metres: 9.90 Leroy Burrell (US), New York

Jul 8 Pole Vault: 6.09m Sergey Bubka (USSR), Formia, Italy

Aug 3, 4 x 100 metres relay: 37.79s Santa Monica Track Club, Monte Carlo

Aug 5, Pole Vault: 6.10m Sergey Bubka (USSR) Malmo, Sweeden

First 20ft jump outdoors

Aug 7 4x100 metres relay: 37.67s United States, Zurich

Aug 25 100 metres: 9.86s Carl Lewis (US), Tokyo

Aug 30 Long Jump: 8.95m Mike Powell (US), Tokyo

Sep 1 4 x 100 metres relay: 37.50 United States, Tokyo

Women

None set

Feb 15-16 National Indoor Championships (National Indoor Arena, Birmingham); Mar 21 Cross-Country Championships (Boston, Massachusetts); April 12 London Marathon; July 10 ParcelForce Games (Crystal Palace); Sep 1 Grand Prix finals; Sep 25-27 World Cup (Havana).

AUSTRALIAN RULES FOOTBALL

1991

AUSTRALIAN FOOTBALL LEAGUE

			P	W	L	D	Pts
1	(3)	WEST COAST	22	19	3	0	76
2	(5)	Hawthorn	22	16	6	0	64
3	(10)	Geelong	22	16	6	0	64
4	(9)	St Kilda	22	14	7	1	58
5	(4)	Melbourne	22	13	9	0	52
6	(1)	Essendon	22	13	9	0	52
7	(2)	Collingwood	22	12	9	1	50
8	(6)	N Melbourne	22	12	10	0	48
9	(-)	Adelaide	22	10	12	0	40
10	(7)	Footscray	22	9	12	1	38
11	(8)	Carlton	22	8	14	0	32
12	(13)	Sydney	22	7	14	1	30
13	(11)	Richmond	22	7	15	0	28
14	(12)	Fitzroy	22	4	18	0	16
15	(14)	Brisbane	22	3	19	0	12

Elimination Finals
MELBOURNE 17.11 (113) Essendon 11.9 (75);
GEELONG 15.14 (104) St Kilda 14.13 (97)
Qualifying Final
HAWTHORN 18.16 (124) West Coast 15.11 (101)
Semi-finals
WEST COAST 17.15 (115) Melbourne 12.7 (79);
HAWTHORN 13.17 (95) Geelong 13.15 (93)
Preliminary Final
WEST COAST 11.13 (79) Geelong 8.16 (64)
Grand Final
VFL Park, Sep 28
HAWTHORN 20.19 (139) West Coast 13.8 (86)

BROWNLOW MEDAL
Jim Stynes (Melbourne)
Stynes is a former Gaelic footballer, recruited by Melbourne from Dublin. The medal is the sport's premier individual award.

BRITISH GRAND FINAL
Hendon Rugby Club, Aug 25
EARL'S COURT 123 Wandsworth 87

1935	Collingwood
1936	Collingwood
1937	Geelong
1938	Carlton
1939	Melbourne
1940	Melbourne
1941	Melbourne
1942	Essendon
1943	Richmond
1944	Fitzroy
1945	Carlton
1946	Essendon
1947	Carlton
1948	Melbourne
1949	Essendon
1950	Essendon
1951	Geelong
1952	Geelong
1953	Collingwood
1954	Footscray
1955	Melbourne
1956	Melbourne
1957	Melbourne
1958	Collingwood
1959	Melbourne
1960	Melbourne
1961	Hawthorn
1962	Essendon
1963	Geelong
1964	Melbourne
1965	Essendon
1966	St Kilda
1967	Richmond
1968	Carlton
1969	Richmond
1970	Carlton
1971	Hawthorn
1972	Carlton
1973	Richmond
1974	Richmond
1975	North Melbourne
1976	Hawthorn
1977	North Melbourne
1978	Hawthorn
1979	Carlton
1980	Richmond
1981	Carlton
1982	Carlton
1983	Hawthorn
1984	Essendon
1985	Essendon
1986	Hawthorn
1987	Carlton
1988	Hawthorn
1989	Hawthorn
1990	Collingwood
1991	Hawthorn

Most Wins:
15 Carlton; 14 Essendon; 13 Collingwood; 12 Melbourne

CHAMPIONS

GRAND FINAL WINNERS
(Victorian Football League 1897-1989; Australian Football League 1990-)

1897	Essendon	1916	Fitzroy
1898	Fitzroy	1917	Collingwood
1899	Fitzroy	1918	South Melbourne
1900	Melbourne	1919	Collingwood
1901	Essendon	1920	Richmond
1902	Collingwood	1921	Richmond
1903	Collingwood	1922	Fitzroy
1904	Fitzroy	1923	Essendon
1905	Fitzroy	1924	Essendon
1906	Charlton	1925	Geelong
1907	Charlton	1926	Melbourne
1908	Charlton	1927	Collingwood
1909	South Melbourne	1928	Collingwood
1910	Collingwood	1929	Collingwood
1911	Essendon	1930	Collingwood
1912	Essendon	1931	Geelong
1913	Fitzroy	1932	Richmond
1914	Carlton	1933	South Melbourne
1915	Carlton	1934	Richmond

BADMINTON

1991

WORLD CHAMPIONSHIPS
Copenhagen, Apr 29-May 12

Team (Sudirman Cup)
SEMI-FINALS
SOUTH KOREA 3 China 2; INDONESIA 3 Denmark 2
FINAL
SOUTH KOREA 3 Indonesia 2

Men's Singles
SEMI-FINALS
ZHAO JIANHUA (Chn) beat Ardy Wiranata (Ina) 15-2,
10-15,15-6; ALLAN BUDI KUSUMA (Ina) beat Liu Jun
(Chn) 15-11,15-11
FINAL
ZHAO JIANHUA beat Budi Kusuma 18-13,15-4
*Morten Frost, four times All-England champion and
probably the greatest player of the 80s, announced his
retirement from top-level play after losing the first round
before his home crowd.*

Women's Singles
SEMI-FINALS
TANG JIUHONG (Chn) beat Susi Susanti (Ina) 11-4,11-1;
SARWENDAH KUSUMAWARDHANI (Ina) beat Lee
Heng Soon (SKo) 2-11,11-7,11-6
FINAL
TANG JIUHONG beat Kusumawardhani 11-6,11-1

Men's Doubles
FINAL
PARK JOO BONG & KIM MOON SOO (SKo) beat
Thomas Lund & John Holst-Christiansen (Den) 15-4,15-6

Women's Doubles
FINAL
GUAN WEIZHEN & NONG QUNHUA (Chn) beat Maria
Bengtsson & Christine Magnusson (Swe) 15-7,15-4

Mixed Doubles
FINAL
PARK JOO BONG & CHUNG MYUNG HEE (SKo) beat
Thomas Lund & Pernille Dupont (Den) 15-5,15-17,15-9

YONEX ALL-ENGLAND CHAMPIONSHIPS
Wembley Arena, Mar 13-16

Men's Singles
SEMI-FINALS
ARDI WIRANATA (Ina) beat Wu Wenkai (Chn) 8-15,17-
16,15-5; FOO KOK KEONG (Mal) beat Zhao Jianhua
(Chn) 15-11, 15-7
FINAL
WIRANATA beat Foo Kok Keong 15-12,15-10

Women's Singles
SEMI-FINALS
SUSI SUSANTI (Ina) beat Huang Hua (Chn) 11-4, 12-10;
Sarwendah KUSUMAWARDHANI (Ina) beat Tang
Jiuhong (Chn) 11-5, 10-12, 11-8
FINAL
SUSANTI beat Kusumawardhani 0-11,11-2,11-6

Men's Doubles
FINAL
LI YONGBO & TIAN BINGYI (Chn) beat Park Joo Bong
& Kim Moon Soo (SKo) 12-15,15-7,15-8

Women's Doubles
FINAL
CHUNG SO YOUNG & HWANG HYE YOUNG (SKo)
beat Kimiko Jinnai & Hisakio Mori (Jap) 15-5,15-3

Mixed Doubles
FINAL
PARK JOO BONG & CHUNG MYUNG HEE (SKo) beat
Thomas Lund & Pernille Dupont (Den) 15-10, 10-15, 15-4

HI-TEC ENGLISH NATIONAL CHAMPIONSHIPS
Torbay, Feb 22-24

Men's Singles
DARREN HALL beat Anders Nielsen 17-14,15-3

Women's Singles
JULIE BRADBURY beat Felicity Gallup 11-7,7-11,11-1

1990

WORLD CUP
Jakarta, Nov 18

Men's Singles
WU WENKAI (Chn) beat Zhao Jianhua (Chn) 15-6,15-7

Women's Singles
SARWENDAH KUSUMAWARDHANI (Ina) beat Susi
Susanti (Ina) 11-5,1-11,12-11

Men's Doubles
RASHID & JALANI SIDEK (Mal) beat Eddie Hartono &
Rudy Gunawan (Ina) 14-17,15-8,15-7

Women's Doubles
YAO FEN & LAI CAIQIN (Chn) beat Rosiania Tendean
& Erma Sulistianingsih (Ina) 3-15,15-10,15-4

Mixed Doubles
RUDY GUNAWAN & ROSIANIA TENDEAN (Ina) beat
Jan Paulsen (Den) & Gillian Gowers (GB) 11-15,15-9,15-3

CHAMPIONS

THOMAS CUP
(Men's World Team Championship)

1949	Malaya
1952	Malaya
1955	Malaya
1958	Indonesia
1961	Indonesia
1964	Indonesia
1967	Malaysia
1970	Indonesia
1973	Indonesia
1976	Indonesia
1979	Indonesia
1982	China
1984	Indonesia
1986	China
1988	China
1990	China
Most wins: 8 Indonesia	

UBER CUP
(Women's World Team Championship)

1957	United States
1960	United States

1963	United States
1966	Japan
1969	Japan
1972	Japan
1975	Indonesia
1978	Japan
1981	Japan
1984	China
1986	China
1988	China
1990	China

Most wins: 5 Japan

WORLD CHAMPIONSHIPS
Men's Singles
1977	Flemming Delfs (Den)
1980	Rudy Hartono (Ina)
1983	Icuk Sugiarto (Ina)
1985	Han Jian (Chn)
1987	Yang Yang (Chn)
1989	Yang Yang (Chn)
1991	Zhao Jianhua (Chn)

Women's Singles
1977	Lene Koppen (Den)
1980	Wiharjo Verawaty (Ina)
1983	Li Lingwei (Chn)
1985	Han Aiping (Chn)
1987	Han Aiping (Chn)
1989	Li Lingwei (Chn)
1991	Tang Jiuhong (Chn)

Men's Doubles
1977	Tjun Tjun & Johan Wahjudi (Ina)
1980	Ade Chandra & Hadinata Christian (Ina)
1983	Steen Fladberg & Jesper Helledie (Den)
1985	Park Joo Bong & Kim Moon Soo (SKo)
1987	Tian Bingyi & Li Yongbo (Chn)
1989	Tian Bingyi & Li Yongbo (Chn)
1991	Park Joo Bong & Kim Moon Soo (SKo)

Women's Doubles
1977	Etsuko Tuganoo & Emiko Vero (Jap)
1980	Nora Perry & Jane Webster (GB)
1983	Wu Dixi & Lin Ying (Chn)
1985	Han Aiping & Li Lingwei (Chn)
1987	Guan Weizhen & Lin Ying (Chn)
1989	Guan Weizhen & Lin Ying (Chn)
1991	Guan Weizhen & Nong Qunhua (Chn)

Mixed Doubles
1977	Steen Stovgaard & Lene Koppen (Den)
1980	Hadinata Christian & Imelda Wigoeno (Ina)
1983	Thomas Kihlstrom (Swe) & Nora Perry (GB)
1985	Park Joo Bong & Yoo Sang Hee (SKo)
1987	Wang Pengrin & Shi Fangjing (Chn)
1989	Park Joo Bong & Chung Myung Hee (SKo)
1991	Park Joo Bong & Chung Myung Hee (SKo)

ALL-ENGLAND CHAMPIONSHIPS
Inaugurated 1899 for doubles only. Singles first held 1900.
Post-war winners
Men's Singles
1947	Conny Jepsen (Swe)
1948	Jörn Skaarup (Den)
1949	Dave Freeman (US)
1950	Wong Peng Soon (Mal)
1951	Wong Peng Soon (Mal)
1952	Wong Peng Soon (Mal)
1953	Eddie Choong (Mal)

1954	Eddie Choong (Mal)
1955	Wong Peng Soon (Mal)
1956	Eddie Choong (Mal)
1957	Eddie Choong (Mal)
1958	Erland Kops (Den)
1959	Tan Joe Hok (Ina)
1960	Erland Kops (Den)
1961	Erland Kops (Den)
1962	Erland Kops (Den)
1963	Erland Kops (Den)
1964	Knud Nielsen (Den)
1965	Erland Kops (Den)
1966	Tan Aik Huang (Mal)
1967	Erland Kops (Den)
1968	Rudy Hartono (Ina)
1969	Rudy Hartono (Ina)
1970	Rudy Hartono (Ina)
1971	Rudy Hartono (Ina)
1972	Rudy Hartono (Ina)
1973	Rudy Hartono (Ina)
1974	Rudy Hartono (Ina)
1975	Sven Pri (Den)
1976	Rudy Hartono (Ina)
1977	Flemming Delfs (Den)
1978	Liem Swie King (Ina)
1979	Liem Swie King (Ina)
1980	Prakash Padukone (Ind)
1981	Liem Swie King (Ina)
1982	Morten Frost (Den)
1983	Luan Jin (Chn)
1984	Morten Frost (Den)
1985	Zhao Jianhua (Chn)
1986	Morten Frost (Den)
1987	Morten Frost (Den)
1988	Ib Frederiksen (Den)
1989	Yang Yang (Chn)
1990	Zhao Jianhua (Chn)
1991	Ardi Wiranata (Ina)

Most wins:
8 Rudy Hartono; 6 Frank Devlin (Ire) 1925-29, 1931, Erland Kops; 5 Ralph Nicholls (Eng) 1932, 1934, 1936-38; 4 George Thomas (Eng) 1920-23, Wong Peng Soon, Eddie Choong, Morten Frost

Women's Singles
1947	Marie Ussing (Den)
1948	Kirsten Thorndahl (Den)
1949	Aase Jacobsen (Den)
1950	Tonny Olsen-Ahm (Den)
1951	Aase Jacobsen (Den)
1952	Tonny Olsen-Ahm (Den)
1953	Marie Ussing (Den)
1954	Judy Devlin (US)
1955	Margaret Varner (US)
1956	Margaret Varner (US)
1957	Judy Devlin (US)
1958	Judy Devlin (US)
1959	Heather Ward (Eng)
1960	Judy Devlin (US)
1961	Judy Hashman (née Devlin) (US)
1962	Judy Hashman (US)
1963	Judy Hashman (US)
1964	Judy Hashman (US)
1965	Ursula Smith (Eng)
1966	Judy Hashman (US)
1967	Judy Hashman (US)
1968	Eva Twedberg (Swe)
1969	Hiroe Yuki (Jap)
1970	Etsuko Takenaka (Jap)

1971	Eva Twedberg (Swe)
1972	Noriko Nakayama (Jap)
1973	Margaret Beck (Eng)
1974	Hiroe Yuki (Jap)
1975	Hiroe Yuki (Jap)
1976	Gillian Gilks (Eng)
1977	Hiroe Yuki (Jap)
1978	Gillian Gilks (Eng)
1979	Lene Köppen (Den)
1980	Lene Köppen (Den)
1981	Sun Ai Hwang (SKo)
1982	Zang Ailing (Chn)
1983	Zang Ailing (Chn)
1984	Li Lingwei (Chn)
1985	Han Aiping (Chn)
1986	Kim Yun Ja (SKo)
1987	Kirsten Larsen (Den)
1988	Gu Jiaming (Chn)
1989	Li Lingwei (Chn)
1990	Susi Susanti (Ina)
1991	Susi Susanti (Ina)

Most wins:
10 Judy Hashman (née Devlin); 6 Meriel Lucas (Eng) 1902, 1905, 1907-10; 5 Ethel Thomson (Eng) 1900-01, 1903-04, 1906, Marjorie Barrett (Eng) 1926-27, 1929-31; **4** Kitty McKane (Eng) 1920-22, 1924.

Men's Doubles
Winners since 1987

1987	Li Yongbo & Tian Bingyi (Chn)
1988	Li Yongbo & Tian Bingyi (Chn)
1989	Lee Sang Bok & Park Joo Bong (SKo)
1990	Kim Moon Soo & Park Joo Bong (SKo)
1991	Li Yongbo & Tian Bingyi (Chn)

Women's Doubles

1987	Chung Myung Hee & Hwang Hye Young (SKo)
1988	Chung So Young & Kim Yun Ja (SKo)
1989	Chung Myung Hee & Chung So Young (SKo)
1990	Chung Myung Hee & Hwang Hye Young (SKo)
1991	Chung So Young & Hwang Hye Young (SKo)

Mixed Doubles

1987	Lee Deuk-Choon & Chung Myung-Hee (SKo)
1988	Wang Pengrin & Shi Fangjing (Chn)
1989	Park Joo Bong & Chung Myung Hee (SKo)
1990	Park Joo Bong & Chung Myung Hee (SKo)
1991	Park Joo Bong & Chung Myung Hee (SKo)

Most Overall All-England Titles:
21 George Thomas 1903-28; **18** Frank Devlin 1922-31; **17** Meriel Lucas 1899-1910, Judy Hashman (née Devlin) 1954-67

1992

Mar 11-14 All-England championships (Wembley); Apr 12-18 European championships (Glasgow)

BASEBALL

For the first time in baseball history, the Biblical principle of the last being first was proved right, not just once but twice. The Minnesota Twins and the Atlanta Braves won their divisions after finishing bottom in 1990 and went into the play-offs. The Twins met the Toronto Blue Jays to decide the American League championship while the Braves met the Pittsburgh Pirates to settle the National League championships.

The tightest race was in the National League West where the Braves overhauled the fancied Los Angeles Dodgers on the final weekend after years of failure, despite the loss of the League's leading base-stealer, Otis Nixon, who was suspended for 60 days after testing positive for cocaine.

The Oakland Athletics, American League champions three times running, faded from the race early. The Cincinnati Reds, who beat Oakland in the 1990 World Series, broke up their team of relief pitchers known as the "Nasty Boys" and also struggled. The club's decline was exemplified by the death of the mascot Schottzie, the St Bernard belonging to the owner Marge Schott; players had often complained that Schottzie was treated better than they were.

Denis Martinez of the Montreal Expos pitched the 15th perfect game (in which no batter reaches base) in baseball history against the Dodgers on July 28. When he flew back to his home in Nicaragua, his arrival relegated the coup in Moscow to the bottom half of the front pages. Nolan Ryan, the 44-year-old Texas Rangers pitcher, broke his own record by throwing the seventh no-hitter of his career, three more than anyone else. Wilson Alvarez, a more obscure player, also threw one: it was in his second major league game and his first for the Chicago White Sox - even his team-mates hardly knew who he was. Rickey Henderson of the Oakland Athletics broke Lou Brock's record of 938 stolen bases; it took Henderson 12 years against Brock's 19.

Denver and Miami were awarded expansion franchises by the National League: the Colorado Rockies and the Florida Marlins will begin playing in 1993. The average salary on opening day for the 708 rostered players was $890,800, a 53 per cent increase on the 1990 figure of $580,000. The Boston Pitcher Roger Clemens became the first $5 million-a-year man. A letter-writer to the *New York Times* suggested players needed a bonus system on top of their salaries to give them an incentive to win. The Toronto Blue Jays became the first club to pull in four million spectators in a season. The Headwear Institute of America announced that baseball caps account for 70 per cent of all hats sold in the US. Mickey Mantle's 1952 baseball card was reported to be selling for $8,000, $3,000 more than his salary at the time. The Topps Company, which has traditionally included a card of a player in its packets of bubble gum, decided to stop selling the gum and just included the card.

Smoking was banned at Oakland games. The San Francisco Giants held a Gay and Lesbian Day. Los Angeles became the first club to employ a full-time psychiatrist. Domingo Carrasquel, manager of the Cardenales de Lara in Venezuela, was fined $1,000 for trying to bite an umpire. The Queen watched two innings of the Baltimore Orioles v Oakland game with President Bush during her visit to America. Jon Miller, the Orioles' radio announcer, inserted various British Monarchy Moments into his commentary: "I was just trying to get her to come on the air with me," said Miller. "I was hoping she'd come up and read the Esskay Meats out-of-town scoreboard."

─────── **1991** ───────

MAJOR LEAGUES
FINAL STANDINGS
American League - East

			W	L	%	GB
1	(2)	Toronto Blue Jays	91	71	.562	-
2	(1)	Boston Red Sox	84	78	.519	7
3	(3)	Detroit Tigers	84	78	.519	7
4	(6)	Milwaukee Brewers	83	79	.512	8
5	(7)	New York Yankees	71	91	.438	20
6	(5)	Baltimore Orioles	67	95	.414	24
7	(4)	Cleveland Indians	57	105	.352	34

American League - West

			W	L	%	GB
1	(7)	Minnesota Twins	95	67	.586	-
2	(2)	Chicago White Sox	87	75	.537	8
3	(3)	Texas Rangers	85	77	.525	10
4	(1)	Oakland Athletics	84	78	.519	11
5	(5)	Seattle Mariners	83	79	.512	12
6	(6)	Kansas City Royals	82	80	.506	13
7	(4)	California Angels	81	81	.500	14

Batting Title: Julio Franco (Texas) .341. **Most Home Runs:** Jose Canseco (Oakland), Cecil Fielder (Detroit) 44

National League - East

			W	L	%	GB
1	(1)	Pittsburgh Pirates	98	64	.605	-
2	(6)	St Louis Cardinals	84	78	.519	14
3	(5)	Philadelphia Phillies	78	84	.481	20
4	(4)	Chicago Cubs	77	83	.481	20
5	(2)	New York Mets	77	84	.475	20 ½
6	(3)	Montreal Expos	71	90	.441	26 ½

National League - West

			W	L	%	GB
1	(6)	Atlanta Braves	94	68	.580	-
2	(2)	Los Angeles Dodgers	93	69	.574	1
3	(5)	San Diego Padres	84	78	.519	10
4	(3)	San Francisco Giants	75	87	.463	19
5	(1)	Cincinnati Reds	74	88	.457	20
6	(4)	Houston Astros	65	97	.401	29

Batting Title: Terry Pendleton (Atlanta) .319. **Most Home Runs:** Howard Johnson (New York) 38

Last season's positions in brackets. GB = games behind leader

Minnesota Twins' winning streak ended at 15 games on June 17. It was the longest streak since the Kansas City Royals went 16 consecutive in 1977. The AL record is 19 by the Chicago White Sox in 1906 and by the Yankees in 1947

62nd ALL STAR GAME
Toronto, Jul 9
AMERICAN LEAGUE 0 0 3　0 0 0　1 0 x - 4
Runs: R Henderson, Carter, Boggs, Ripken
National league　　1 0 0　1 0 0　0 0 0 - 2
Runs: Gwynn, Dawson
Attendance: 52,383

Xth INTERCONTINENTAL CUP
Barcelona, Jul 14
Third Place Play-off
NICARAGUA 4 Taiwan 3
Final
CUBA 5 Japan 4

─────── **1990** ───────

WORLD SERIES
Game 1 Oct 16 CINCINNATI REDS 7 Oakland Athletics 0
Attendance: 55,830
Game 2 Oct 17 CINCINNATI REDS 5 Oakland Athletics 4
Attendance: 55,832
Game 3 Oct 19 Oakland Athletics 3 CINCINNATI REDS 8
Attendance: 48,269
Game 4 Oct 20 Oakland Athletics 1 CINCINNATI REDS 2
Attendance: 48,613

HIGHEST WORLD SERIES AVERAGES
(Minimum 10 at-bats)
.750 BILLY HATCHER, Cincinnati 1990
.625 Babe Ruth, New York Yankees 1928
.563 Chris Sabo, Cincinnati 1990
.545 Hank Gowdy, Boston Braves 1914
.545 Lou Gehrig, New York Yankees 1928

─────── **CHAMPIONS** ───────

WORLD SERIES

1903	Boston Red Sox (AL)	5
	Pittsburgh Pirates (NL)	3
1904	Not held	
1905	New York Giants (NL)	4
	Philadelphia Athletics (AL)	1
1906	Chicago White Sox (AL)	4
	Chicago Cubs (NL)	2
1907	Chicago Cubs (NL)	4(*)
	Detroit Tigers (AL)	0
1908	Chicago Cubs (NL)	4
	Detroit Tigers (AL)	1
1909	Pittsburgh Pirates (NL)	4
	Detroit Tigers (AL)	3
1910	Philadelphia Athletics (AL)	4
	Chicago Cubs (NL)	1
1911	Philadelphia Athletics (AL)	4
	New York Giants (NL)	2
1912	Boston Red Sox (AL)	4
	New York Giants (NL)	3(*)
1913	Philadelphia Athletics (AL)	4
	New York Giants (NL)	1
1914	Boston Braves (NL)	4
	Philadelphia Athletics (AL)	0
1915	Boston Red Sox (AL)	4
	Philadelphia Phillies (NL)	1
1916	Boston Red Sox (AL)	4
	Brooklyn Dodgers (NL)	1
1917	Chicago White Sox (AL)	4
	New York Giants (NL)	1
1918	Boston Red Sox (AL)	4
	Chicago Cubs (NL)	2
1919	Cincinnati Reds (NL)	5
	Chicago White Sox (AL)	3

Year	Team	Wins
1920	Cleveland Indians (AL)	5
	Brooklyn Dodgers (NL)	2
1921	New York Giants (NL)	4
	New York Yankees (AL)	3
1922	New York Giants (NL)	4
	New York Yankees (AL)	0(*)
1923	New York Yankees (AL)	4
	New York Giants (NL)	2
1924	Washington Senators (AL)	4
	New York Giants (NL)	3
1925	Pittsburgh Pirates (NL)	4
	Washington Senators (AL)	3
1926	St Louis Cardinals (NL)	4
	New York Yankees (AL)	3
1927	New York Yankees (AL)	4
	Pittsburgh Pirates (NL)	0
1928	New York Yankees (AL)	4
	St Louis Cardinals (NL)	0
1929	Philadelphia Athletics (AL)	4
	Chicago Cubs (NL)	1
1930	Philadelphia Athletics (AL)	4
	St Louis Cardinals (NL)	2
1931	St Louis Cardinals (NL)	4
	Philadelphia Athletics (AL)	3
1932	New York Yankees (AL)	4
	Chicago Cubs (NL)	0
1933	New York Giants (NL)	4
	Washington Senators (AL)	1
1934	St Louis Cardinals (NL)	4
	Detroit Tigers (AL)	3
1935	Detroit Tigers (AL)	4
	Chicago Cubs (NL)	2
1936	New York Yankees (AL)	4
	New York Giants (NL)	2
1937	New York Yankees (AL)	4
	New York Giants (NL)	1
1938	New York Yankees (AL)	4
	Chicago Cubs (NL)	0
1939	New York Yankees (AL)	4
	Cincinnati Reds (NL)	0
1940	Cincinnati Reds (NL)	4
	Detroit Tigers (AL)	3
1941	New York Yankees (AL)	4
	Brooklyn Dodgers (NL)	1
1942	St Louis Cardinals (NL)	4
	New York Yankees (AL)	1
1943	New York Yankees (AL)	4
	St Louis Cardinals (NL)	1
1944	St Louis Cardinals (NL)	4
	St Louis Browns (AL)	2
1945	Detroit Tigers (AL)	4
	Chicago Cubs (NL)	3
1946	St Louis Cardinals (NL)	4
	Boston Red Sox (AL)	3
1947	New York Yankees (AL)	4
	Brooklyn Dodgers (NL)	3
1948	Cleveland Indians (AL)	4
	Boston Braves (NL)	2
1949	New York Yankees (AL)	4
	Brooklyn Dodgers (NL)	1
1950	New York Yankees (AL)	4
	Philadelphia Phillies (NL)	0
1951	New York Yankees (AL)	4
	New York Giants (NL)	2
1952	New York Yankees (AL)	4
	Brooklyn Dodgers (NL)	3
1953	New York Yankees (AL)	4
	Brooklyn Dodgers (NL)	2
1954	New York Giants (NL)	4
	Cleveland Indians (AL)	0
1955	Brooklyn Dodgers (NL)	4
	New York Yankees (AL)	3
1956	New York Yankees (AL)	4
	Brooklyn Dodgers (NL)	3
1957	Milwaukee Braves (NL)	4
	New York Yankees (AL)	3
1958	New York Yankees (AL)	4
	Milwaukee Braves (NL)	3
1959	Los Angeles Dodgers (NL)	4
	Chicago White Sox (AL)	2
1960	Pittsburgh Pirates (NL)	4
	New York Yankees (AL)	3
1961	New York Yankees (AL)	4
	Cincinnati Reds (NL)	1
1962	New York Yankees (AL)	4
	San Francisco Giants (NL)	3
1963	Los Angeles Dodgers (NL)	4
	New York Yankees (AL)	0
1964	St Louis Cardinals (NL)	4
	New York Yankees (AL)	3
1965	Los Angeles Dodgers (NL)	4
	Minnesota Twins (AL)	3
1966	Baltimore Orioles (AL)	4
	Los Angeles Dodgers (NL)	0
1967	St Louis Cardinals (NL)	4
	Boston Red Sox (AL)	3
1968	Detroit Tigers (AL)	4
	St Louis Cardinals (NL)	3
1969	New York Mets(NL)	4
	Baltimore Orioles (AL)	1
1970	Baltimore Orioles (AL)	4
	Cincinnati Reds (NL)	1
1971	Pittsburgh Pirates (NL)	4
	Baltimore Orioles (AL)	3
1972	Oakland A's (AL)	4
	Cincinnati Reds (NL)	3
1973	Oakland A's (AL)	4
	New York Mets (NL)	3
1974	Oakland A's (AL)	4
	Los Angeles Dodgers (NL)	1
1975	Cincinnati Reds (NL)	4
	Boston Red Sox (AL)	3
1976	Cincinnati Reds (NL)	4
	New York Yankees (AL)	0
1977	New York Yankees (AL)	4
	Los Angeles Dodgers (NL)	3
1978	New York Yankees (AL)	4
	Los Angeles Dodgers (NL)	2
1979	Pittsburgh Pirates (NL)	4
	Baltimore Orioles (AL)	3
1980	Philadelphia Phillies (NL)	4
	Kansas City Royals (AL)	2
1981	Los Angeles Dodgers (NL)	4
	New York Yankees (AL)	2
1982	St Louis Cardinals (NL)	4
	Milwaukee Brewers (AL)	3
1983	Baltimore Orioles (AL)	4
	Philadelphia Phillies (NL)	1
1984	Detroit Tigers (AL)	4
	San Diego Padres (NL)	1
1985	Kansas City Royals (AL)	4
	St Louis Cardinals (NL)	3
1986	New York Mets (NL)	4
	Boston Red Sox (AL)	3
1987	Minnesota Twins (AL)	4
	St Louis Cardinals (NL)	3
1988	Los Angeles Dodgers (NL)	4
	Oakland Athletics (AL)	1
1989	Oakland Athletics (AL)	4
	San Francisco Giants (NL)	0
1990	Cincinnati Reds (NL)	4
	Oakland Athletics (AL)	0

(*) Included one tied game
(AL) American League (NL) National Leauge

Most Wins
22 New York Yankees; **9** St Louis Cardinals; **5** Boston Red Sox, Cincinnati Reds, Pittsburgh Pirates, Philadelphia Athletics, Los Angeles Dodgers, New York Giants; **4** Detroit Tigers, Oakland Athletics

PLAY-OFFS (Since 1981)
(Between winners of East division and West division)

American League

1981	Kansas City (W) beat New York (E)	3-0
1982	Milwaukee (E) beat California (W)	3-2
1983	Baltimore (E) beat Chicago (W)	3-1
1984	Detroit (E) beat Kansas City (W)	3-0
1985	Kansas City (W) beat Toronto (E)	4-3
1986	Boston (E) beat California (W)	4-3
1987	Minnesota (W) beat Detroit (E)	4-1
1988	Oakland (W) beat Boston (E)	4-0
1989	Oakland (W) beat Toronto (E)	4-1
1990	Oakland (W) beat Boston (E)	4-0

National League

1981	Los Angeles (W) beat Montreal (E)	3-2
1982	St Louis (E) beat Atlanta (W)	3-0
1983	Philadelphia (E) beat Los Angeles (W)	3-1
1984	San Diego (W) beat Chicago (E)	3-2
1985	St Louis (E) beat Los Angeles (W)	4-2
1986	New York (E) beat Houston (W)	4-2
1987	St Louis (E) beat San Francisco (W)	4-3
1988	Los Angeles (W) beat New York (E)	4-3
1989	San Francisco (W) beat Chicago (E)	4-1
1990	Cincinnati (W) beat Pittsburgh (E)	4-2

RECORDS

MOST HITS
4256 Pete Rose
4191 Ty Cobb
3771 Hank Aaron
3630 Stan Musial
3515 Tris Speaker

MOST HOME RUNS
755 Hank Aaron
714 Babe Ruth
660 Willie Mays
586 Frank Robinson
573 Harmon Killibrew
563 Reggie Jackson

MOST NO-HITTERS
7 Nolan Ryan
4 Sandy Koufax
3 Cy Young
  Bob Feller

BASKETBALL

BULL'S-EYE FOR JORDAN

Michael Jordan, the man who has transcended his sport and become America's leading black role model, collected the one honour he had previously missed when he led his team, the Chicago Bulls, to their first NBA Championship. The Bulls beat the Los Angeles Lakers by four games to one, having lost the opener dramatically when a straightforward jump shot from Jordan spun out of the basket with seconds to go.

From then on, though, it was a rout. And when the Bulls won Game Five to clinch the title Jordan kissed the floor and his team-mates poured champagne over his head. Then they all said the Lord's Prayer. Jordan, who in the past has been prone to describe his team-mates as "my supporting cast", paid them handsome tribute and said the win should remove the stigma that the Bulls were a one-man team. The effect on America was akin to that of the 1953 Stanley Matthews Cup Final in Britain. The focus, however, was on Jordan. He completely outplayed his rival Magic Johnson of the Lakers, who averaged 18.6 points against Jordan's 31.2. The conservative columnist George Will said Jordan's face should appear on banknotes.

Chicago had stormed through the play-offs, winning 15 games out of 17 and crushing the 1989 and 1990 champions the Detroit Pistons, who many people thought played unsportingly as well as badly. To ensure anonymity the Pistons booked into their hotel under such names as Mickey Mouse and Kim Basinger. Subsequently, Isiah Thomas, the Pistons' guard, was controversially left off the all-professional US squad for the 1992 Olympics, reputedly at Jordan's instigation.

Muggsy Bogues of the Charlotte Hornets (5ft 3 in) became the smallest-ever player in the NBA; the average height in the league is 6ft 7in. Charles Barkley of the Philadelphia 76ers said after a narrow win that his wife would be delighted because he would not have to go home and beat her up; women's groups forced him to issue a public apology. Shawn Bradley (19 and 7ft 6in) turned down rumoured offers of $3 million to play pro basketball by becoming a Mormon missionary in Australia for two years. The actress Dyan Cannon and her husband Stan Fimberg agreed to split their Lakers tickets as part of their divorce settlement. JC Rogers of Florence, South Carolina ran back into his blazing house to save his tickets for a local college game. The leading scorers for Lincoln University, Pennsylvania in the game against West Chester University were called Don King and Mike Tyson.

Yugoslavia won the European Championship as the country broke up. The team's Slovene guard Jurij Zdovic had to withdraw from the semi-finals and final after he received calls saying he would be considered a traitor if he played. Al Powell, a forward on the Jacksonville University team, quit the college complaining about the disciplinarian methods of the coach Matt Kilcullen; he joined the Air Force instead.

1991

NBA FINAL STANDINGS
Eastern Conference

ATLANTIC

			W	L	%
1	(2)	Boston Celtics	56	26	.683
2	(1)	Philadelphia 76ers	44	38	.537
3	(3)	New York Knicks	39	43	.476
4	(4)	Washington Bullets	30	52	.366
5	(6)	New Jersey Nets	26	56	.317
6	(5)	Miami Heat	24	58	.293

CENTRAL

			W	L	%
1	(2)	Chicago Bulls	61	21	.744
2	(1)	Detroit Pistons	50	32	.610
3	(3)	Milwaukee Bucks	48	34	.585
4	(6)	Atlanta Hawks	43	39	.524
5	(5)	Indiana Pacers	41	41	.500
6	(4)	Cleveland Cavaliers	33	49	.402
7	(7)	Charlotte Hornets*	26	56	.317

(*) 7th in Western Conference (Mid West) in 1990

Western Conference

MID WEST

			W	L	%
1	(1)	San Antonio Spurs	55	27	.671
2	(2)	Utah Jazz	54	28	.659
3	(5)	Houston Rockets	52	30	.634
4	(7)	Orlando Magic*	31	51	.378
5	(6)	Minnesota Timberwolves	29	53	.354
6	(3)	Dallas Mavericks	28	54	.341
7	(4)	Denver Nuggets	20	62	.244

(*) 7th in the Eastern Conference (Central) in 1990

		PACIFIC	W	L	%
1	(2)	Portland Trail Blazers	63	19	.768
2	(1)	Los Angeles Lakers	58	24	.707
3	(3)	Phoenix Suns	55	27	.671
4	(5)	Golden State Warriors	44	38	.537
5	(4)	Seattle SuperSonics	41	41	.500
6	(6)	Los Angeles Clippers	31	51	.378
7	(7)	Sacramento Kings	25	57	.305

Last year's positions in brackets

PLAY-OFFS
Eastern Conference
SEMI-FINALS
CHICAGO 4 Philadelphia 1; DETROIT 4 Boston 2
CONFERENCE FINAL
CHICAGO 4 Detroit 0

Western Conference
SEMI-FINALS
LOS ANGELES LAKERS 4 Golden State 1; PORTLAND 4 Utah 1

CONFERENCE FINAL
LOS ANGELES LAKERS 4 Portland 2

NBA CHAMPIONSHIP
Game 1: Chicago 91 LOS ANGELES LAKERS 93
Game 2: CHICAGO 107 Los Angeles Lakers 86
Game 3: Los Angeles Lakers 96 CHICAGO 104 (OT)
Game 4: Los Angeles Lakers 82 CHICAGO 97
Game 5: Los Angeles Lakers 101 CHICAGO 108
CHICAGO won best-of-seven series 4-1
MVP in Play-offs: Michael Jordan (Chicago)

ENGLISH BASKETBALL ASSOCIATION
Carlsberg National League
FIRST DIVISION

		P	W	L	F	A	Pts
1(1)	Kingston	24	23	1	2356	1992	46
2(3)	Sunderland Saints	24	18	6	2424	2198	36
3(-)	Thames Valley Tigers	24	14	10	2325	2149	28
4(6)	Leicester Raiders	24	14	10	2303	2235	28
5(5)	Derby Rams	24	12	12	2269	2351	24
6(2)	Manchester Giants	24	12	12	2246	2129	24
7(-)	Worthing Bears	24	10	14	2330	2339	20
8(-)	Hemel Hemp. Royals	24	4	20	2115	2492	8
9(8)	London Docklands	24	1	23	1943	2426	2

Last year's positions in brackets
Player of the Year: Alton Byrd (Kingston)

SECOND DIVISION

		P	W	L	F	A	Pts
1	Cheshire Jets	22	17	5	2146	1929	34
2	Bury Lobos	22	16	6	1865	1669	32
3	Broxbourne	22	16	6	2105	1914	32
4	Watford Rebels	22	14	8	2252	2088	28
5	Oldham Celtics	22	13	9	1839	1736	26
6	Doncaster Eagles	22	11	11	1982	1888	22
7	Middlesbro Mohawks	22	11	11	1949	2022	22
8	Birmingham Bullets	22	10	12	1857	1798	20
9	Brixton Topcats	22	10	12	1875	1847	20
10	Coventry Flyers	22	6	16	1852	1999	12
11	Manchester 'B'	22	4	18	1751	2181	8
12	Plymouth Raiders	22	4	18	1808	2210	8

WOMEN'S DIVISION ONE

		P	W	L	F	A	Pts
1	Sheffield Hatters	20	18	2	1541	1067	36
2	London C. YMCA	20	15	5	1386	1182	30
3	Northampton Roos	20	15	5	1430	1131	30
4	Crystal Palace	20	15	5	1320	1140	30
5	Nottingham Wildcats	20	14	6	1228	1046	28
6	Rhondda	20	8	12	1211	1314	16
7	Ipswich	20	8	12	1220	1372	16
8	Brixton Lady Topcats	20	7	13	1126	1379	14
9	Tyneside	20	5	15	1083	1336	10
10	London Jets	20	4	16	1134	1299	8
11	Manchester Giants	20	1	19	1033	1446	2

CARLSBERG CHAMPIONSHIP PLAY-OFFS
NEC, Birmingham, Apr 12-13
Semi-finals
SUNDERLAND 99 Thames Valley Tigers 89; KINGSTON 85 Leicester 62
Final
KINGSTON 94 Sunderland 72

Division Two Final
BIRMINGHAM 61 Bury 58

Women's Division One Final
CRYSTAL PALACE 56 Northampton 52

COCA-COLA NATIONAL CUP
London Arena, Mar 2-3
Men
Semi-finals
LEICESTER 94 Thames Valley Tigers 91 (overtime); SUNDERLAND 86 Kingston 81
Final
SUNDERLAND 88 Leicester 81

Women
Semi-finals
Crystal Palace 53 SHEFFIELD 65; NOTTINGHAM 56 Northampton 48
Final
SHEFFIELD 79 Nottingham 46

MEN'S EUROPEAN CHAMPIONSHIP
Rome, Jun 25-30
Third Place Play-off
SPAIN 101 France 83
Final
YUGOSLAVIA 88 Italy 73

WOMEN'S EUROPEAN CHAMPIONSHIP
Tel Aviv, Jun 12-17
Third Place Play-off
HUNGARY 65 Bulgaria 61
Final
SOVIET UNION 97 Yugoslavia 84

EUROPEAN CUP-WINNERS' CUP FINAL
Geneva, Mar 26
PAOK SALONIKA (Greece) 76 CAI Zaragoza (Spain) 72

EUROPEAN KORAC CUP FINAL
1st Leg, Mar 20
Real Madrid (Spain) 71 CANTU (Italy) 73
2nd Leg, Mar 27
CANTU 95 Real Madrid 93 (OT)
Cantu won on aggregate 168-164

EUROPEAN RONCHETTI CUP FINAL
1st Leg, Mar 20
GEMAEZ CUSIN MILAN (Italy) 94 Como (Italy) 76
2nd Leg, Mar 27
COMO 69 Gemaez Cusin Milan 58
Milan won on aggregate 152-145

MEN'S EUROPEAN CHAMPIONS' CUP FINAL
Paris, Apr 18
POP 84 SPLIT (Yug) 70 FC Barcelona (Spa) 65

WOMEN'S EUROPEAN CHAMPIONS' CUP FINAL
Barcelona, Apr 11
CESENA (Italy) 84 Arvika (Sweden) 66

─────── CHAMPIONS ───────

WORLD CHAMPIONSHIPS

Men		*Women*	
1950	Argentina	1953	United States
1954	United States	1957	United States
1959	Brazil	1959	USSR
1963	Brazil	1964	USSR
1967	USSR	1967	USSR
1970	Yugoslavia	1971	USSR
1974	USSR	1975	USSR
1978	Yugoslavia	1979	United States
1982	USSR	1983	USSR
1986	United States	1987	United States
1990	Yugoslavia	1990	United States

EUROPEAN CHAMPIONSHIPS

Men		*Women*	
1935	Latvia		
1937	Lithuania	1938	Italy
1939	Lithuania		
1946	Czechoslovakia		
1947	USSR		
1949	Egypt	1950	USSR
1951	USSR	1952	USSR
1953	USSR	1954	USSR
1955	Hungary	1956	USSR
1957	USSR	1958	Bulgaria
1959	USSR	1960	USSR
1961	USSR	1962	USSR
1963	USSR	1964	USSR
1965	USSR	1966	USSR
1967	USSR	1968	USSR
1969	USSR	1970	USSR
1971	USSR	1972	USSR
1973	Yugoslavia	1974	USSR
1975	Yugoslavia	1976	USSR
1977	Yugoslavia	1978	USSR
1979	USSR	1980	USSR
1981	USSR	1981	USSR
1983	Italy	1983	USSR
1985	USSR	1985	USSR
1987	Greece	1987	USSR
1989	Yugoslavia	1989	USSR
1991	Yugoslavia	1991	USSR

NBA

1947	Philadelphia Warriors
1948	Baltimore Bullets
1949	Minneapolis Lakers
1950	Minneapolis Lakers
1951	Rochester Royals
1952	Minneapolis Lakers
1953	Minneapolis Lakers
1954	Minneapolis Lakers
1955	Syracuse Nationals
1956	Philadelphia Warriors
1957	Boston Celtics
1958	St Louis Hawks
1959	Boston Celtics
1960	Boston Celtics
1961	Boston Celtics
1962	Boston Celtics
1963	Boston Celtics
1964	Boston Celtics
1965	Boston Celtics
1966	Boston Celtics
1967	Philadelphia 76ers
1968	Boston Celtics
1969	Boston Celtics
1970	New York Knicks
1971	Milwaukee Bucks
1972	Los Angeles Lakers
1973	New York Knicks
1974	Boston Celtics
1975	Golden State Warriors
1976	Boston Celtics
1977	Portland Trail Blazers
1978	Washington Bullets
1979	Seattle Supersonics
1980	Los Angeles Lakers
1981	Boston Celtics
1982	Los Angeles Lakers
1983	Philadelphia 76ers
1984	Boston Celtics
1985	Los Angeles Lakers
1986	Boston Celtics
1987	Los Angeles Lakers
1988	Los Angeles Lakers
1989	Detroit Pistons
1990	Detroit Pistons
1991	Chicago Bulls

❝He's so thin the 76ers don't bother to take him on the road; they just fax him from town to town.❞
Woody Allen on Manute Bole, 7ft 7in.

ENGLISH BASKETBALL ASSOCIATION
National Champions
Since 1982

Men

1982	Crystal Palace
1983	Sunderland
1984	Solent
1985	Manchester Untied
1986	Kingston
1987	BCP London
1988	Murray Livingston
1989	Glasgow Rangers
1990	Kingston
1991	Kingston

Women

1982	Southgate
1983	Southgate
1984	A.C. Northampton
1985	A.C. Northampton
1986	Crystal Palace
1987	A.C. Northampton
1988	Stockport
1989	Northampton
1990	Northampton
1991	Crystal Palace

BILLIARDS

STRACHAN UK PROFESIONAL CHAMPIONSHIP

Sheffield, Feb 28-Mar 3

QUARTER-FINALS
MIKE RUSSELL (Eng) bea Robby Foldvari (Aus) 806-389; PETER GILCHRIST (Eng) beat Bob Close (Eng) 728-505; IAN WILLIAMSON (Eng) beat John Murphy (Eng) 622-303; GEET SETHI (Ind) beat David Edwards (Wal) 1065-406

SEMI-FINALS
RUSSELL beat Gilchrist (2058-1054; SETHI beat *Williamson 2065-811*

FINAL
RUSSELL beat Sethi 1839-1538

BRITISH OPEN CHAMPIONSHIP

Barbican Centre, London, Jan 26-27

SEMI-FINALS
IAN WILLIAMSON (Eng) beat Peter Gilchrist (Eng) 4-1; NORMAN DAGLEY (Eng) beat Geet Sethi (Ind) 4-3
Final
DAGLEY beat Williamson 7-5

WORLD MATCH-PLAY CHAMPIONSHIP

Moscow, Oct 5

SEMI-FINALS
GEET SETHI (Ind) beat Ian Williamson (Eng) 4-0; MIKE RUSSELL (Eng) beat Robby Foldvari (Aus) 4-2

FINAL
RUSSELL beat Sethi 7-6

WORLD AMATEUR CHAMPIONSHIP

Bangalore, India, Aug 14-25

SEMI-FINALS
MANOJ KOTHARI (Ind) beat Nalin Patel (Ind) 1654-1571; ASHOK SHANDILYA (Ind) beat Subash Agrawal (Ind) 2111-2041

FINAL
KOTAHRI beat Shandilya 2890-2422

MYSORE LAMPS WORLD PROFESSIONAL CHAMPIONSHIP

New Delhi, Jul 25-29

FIRST ROUND
HUGH NIMMO (GB) beat Michael Ferreira (Ind) 1463-742; MIKE RUSSELL (GB) bea David Edwards (GB) 2003-846; ROBBY FOLDVARI (Aus) beat Ray Edmonds (GB) 1263-687; CLIVE EVERTON (GB) beat Eddie Charlton (Aus) won outright; NORMAN DAGLEY (GB) beat Des Heald (GB) 1572-726; IAN WILLIAMSON (GB) beat Mark Wildman (GB) 1136-582; GEET SETHI (Ind) bat Bob Close (GB) 1228-1213; PETER GILCHRIST (GB) beat John Murphy (GB) 1704-978

QUARTER-FINALS
RUSSELL beat Everton 1693-723; GILCHRIST beat Nimmo 1423-1127; FOLDVARI beat Williamson 850-757; SETHI beat Dagley 1389-1194

SEMI-FINALS
RUSSELL beat Gilchrist 1907-1021; FOLDVARI beat Sethi 946-899

FINAL
RUSSELL beat Foldvari 1352-876

CHAMPIONS

WORLD PROFESSIONAL CHAMPIONSHIP

1870–1909 operated on a challenge system and again 1951-71. Since 1980 it has been held on a knockout basis All winners British unless otherwise stated

1870	William Cook
1870	John Roberts, Jnr
1870	Joseph Bennett
1871	John Roberts, Jnr
1871	William Cook
1875	John Roberts, Jnr
1880	Joseph Bennett
1885	John Roberts, Jnr
1889	Charles Dawson
1901	H. W. Stevenson
1901	Charles Dawson
1901	H. W. Stevenson
1903	Charles Dawson
1908	Melbourne Inman
1909	H. W. Stevenson
1910	H. W. Stevenson
1911	H. W. Stevenson
1912	Melbourne Inman
1913	Melbourne Inman
1914	Melbourne Inman
1919	Melbourne Inman
1920	Willie Smith
1921	Tom Newman
1922	Tom Newman
1923	Willie Smith
1924	Tom Newman
1925	Tom Newman
1926	Tom Newman
1927	Tom Newman
1928	Joe Davis
1929	Joe Davis
1930	Joe Davis
1931	Not held
1932	Joe Davis
1933	Walter Lindrum (Aus)
1934	Walter Lindrum (Aus)
1951	Clark McConachy (NZ)
1968	Rex Williams
1971	Leslie Driffield
1971	Rex Williams
1980	Fred Davis
1982	Rex Williams
1983	Rex Williams
1984	Mark Wildman
1985	Ray Edmonds
1986	Robby Foldvari (Aus)
1987	Norman Dagley
1988	Norman Dagley
1989	Mike Russell
1991	Mike Russell

RECORDS

Highest break: 499,135 Tom Reece Jun 3 – Jul 6 1907 (this incorporated the cradle cannon which is no longer allowed)

Highest break since introduction of 25-hazard rule (1926): 4,137 Walter Lindrum 1932

Highest break under current 'two pot' rule: 962 (unfinished) Michael Ferreira 29 Apr 1986

BOWLS

avid Bryant, 60, the man whose name has become synonymous with bowls, was left out of the England team for the 1992 World Championship for the first time since the event began in 1966. The 11-man selection committee said the decision was unanimous. Tony Allcock was chosen for the singles and for the pairs, along with John Ottaway. The rest of the team will comprise Roy Cutts, Andy Thomson and John Bell.

Allcock immediately proved his worth by retaining the EBA singles championship (the event that is open to every bowler in the country), beating David Hobbis 21-3. The only other person to retain the Championship since it began in 1905 was Bryant, between 1971 and 1973. John Bell skipped Wigton of Cumbria, who won the pairs and triples; his no. 2 in the triples was Andrew Baxter, whose father Ron and late grandfather Josie won the title with Bell 15 years ago.

Edna Bessell, 43, from Yeovil, qualified for all four events of the English women's championships; she reached the finals of the fours, triples and singles but lost them all. Helen Charlton, 10, became the youngest player to compete in a major bowls championship when she played in the junior singles at the English Bowling Federation championship at Skegness. The record was once held by her uncle Robert when he was 14. The bowling green in Kariba, Zimbabwe was trampled by elephants, driven into the town by drought. Bowlers in Goomalling, Western Australia dyed their green red to stop plagues of locusts eating the turf.

1991

MEN - OUTDOOR
WOOLWICH EBA NATIONAL CHAMPIONSHIPS
Worthing, Aug 11-23
Singles
Semi-finals
TONY ALLCOCK ((Cheltenham) beat Jim Hobday (West Backwell, Somerset) 21-12; DAVID HOBBIS (Stratford-upon-Avon) beat Malcolm Struthers (Thetford, Norfolk) 21-9
Final
ALLCOCK beat Hobbis 21-3
Pairs
Semi-finals
RON GASS & JOHN BELL (Wigton, Cumbria) 19 David Lockhart & Gordon Niven (Bolton) 17; JIM MARSH & DAVID HALL (National Physical Lab, Middlesex) 21 Steve Sanders & Alan Aspey (Bristol) 13
Final
GASS & BELL 29 Marsh & Hall 16
Triples
Semi-finals
SUMMERTOWN (Oxon) 25 Mansfield Colliery (Notts) 8; WIGTON (Cumbria) 25 Stenalees (Cornwall) 7
Final
WIGTON 16 Summertown 15
Fours
Semi-finals
WOKINGHAM (Berks) 25 Liberty of Havering (Essex) 15; SPENCER MELKSHAM (Wilts) 17 Cleethorpes (Lincs) 16
Final
WOKINGHAM 21 Spencer Melksham 20

NATWEST BRITISH ISLES CHAMPIONSHIPS
Ebbw Vale, Jul 1-5
International Series
1 ENGLAND; 2 Scotland; 3 Ireland; 4 Wales

Singles
WILL THOMAS (Wales) beat Steve Adamson (Ireland) 25-16
Pairs
SCOTLAND (Ian Emslie & Alastair Will) 17 Wales (Terry Sullivan & Stephen Rees) 16
Triples
WALES 21 Ireland 20
Fours
IRELAND 18 England 18

NATWEST MIDDLETON CUP
Quarter-finals
DURHAM 132 Northants 117; NORFOLK 132 Notts 110; KENT 146 Gloucs 92; DEVON 110 Surrey 104
Semi-finals
KENT 130 Durham 101; DEVON 105 Norfolk 103
Final
Worthing, Aug 24
KENT 123 Devon 107
Kent won for the third time in five years

EBA CHAMPION OF CHAMPIONS
Bath, Sep 1
TONY ALLCOCK (Cheltenham) beat John Kelly (Devon) 21-11

MEN - INDOOR
MIDLAND BANK WORLD CHAMPIONSHIPS
Preston Guildhall, Feb 13-24
Singles
Quarter-finals
RICHARD CORSIE (Sco) beat Rob Perrella (Aus) 7-1 7-0 7-4; TONY ALLCOCK (Eng) beat Gary Smith (Eng) 7-6 7-5 7-0; MARK McMAHON (HK) beat John Evans (Eng) 7-0 7-6 7-6; IAN SCHUBACK (Aus) beat Willie Wood (Sco) 7-3 7-4 0-7 0-7 7-1
Semi-finals
SCHUBACK beat Allcock 7-3 7-4 0-7 0-7 7-1; CORSIE beat McMahon 7-2 7-4 7-5

Final
CORSIE beat Schuback 6-7 7-2 7-6 7-5
This was Corsie's second title in three years. He collected the sport's biggest first prize, £22,500

Pairs
Final
TONY ALLCOCK & DAVID BRYANT (Eng) beat Richard Corsie & Willie Wood (Sco) 2-7 7-6 4-7 7-4 7-5

HAVEN/COMMERCIAL UNION NATIONAL CLUB CHAMPIONSHIP
Bedford, Mar 2-3
Semi-finals
ELY 80 Bristol 71; CAMBRIDGE PARK 104 Hartlepool 58
Final
CAMBRIDGE PARK 87 Ely 60

BRITISH ISLES CHAMPIONSHIPS
Aberdeen, Mar 18-22
Singles
ANDY THOMSON (Eng) beat Graham Robertson (Sco) 21-20
Pairs
SCOTLAND (Adam & Graham Robertson) 20 England (Terry Scott & David Webb) 9
Triples
ENGLAND 19 Scotland 13
Fours
ENGLAND 15 Scotland 13
Home International Series
1 SCOTLAND; 2 England; 3 Ireland; 4 Wales

ALL-ENGLAND CHAMPION OF CHAMPIONS
Wellingborough, Mar 25
Semi-finals
JOHN OTTAWAY (Wymondham Dell) beat Peter Hobday (Victory, Portsmouth) 21-5; IAN PEACOCK (Consett) beat David Holt (Blackpool Borough) 21-14
Final
OTTAWAY beat Peacock 21-17

ENGLISH NATIONAL CHAMPIONSHIPS
Melton Mowbray, Apr 6-13
Singles
ANDY THOMSON (Cyphers, Beckenham) beat Mel Biggs (Thamesdown, Swindon) 21-12
Pairs
CYPHERS, Beckenham (Andy Thomson & Gary Smith) 29 Dolphin (Chris Martin & Adam Tidby) 7
Triples
CUMBRIA 21 Haverhill 11
Fours
NOTTINGHAM 24 Ipswich 15
Liberty Trophy
DURHAM 120 Middlesex 118

UNITED KINGDOM CHAMPIONSHIP
Carlisle, Apr 24-26
Semi-finals
TONY ALLCOCK (Eng) beat Alex Marshall (Sco) 7-5 0-7 7-5 7-6; ANDY THOMSON (Eng) beat Angus Blair (Sco) 6-7 7-2 7-4 7-3
Final
THOMSON beat Allcock 6-7 4-7 7-5 7-2 7-1

WOMEN - OUTDOOR
BRITISH CHAMPIONSHIPS
Belfast, Jun 26-28
Home International Championship
1 SCOTLAND; 2 England; 3 Wales; 4 Ireland
Singles
BARBARA TILL (Eng) beat Eileen Thomas (Wal) 25-18
Pairs
WALES (M Burn & M Marquiss) 20 IRELAND (B McKeag & M Martin) 17
Triples
WALES 28 England 9
Fours
WALES 27 England 18

COUNTY CHAMPIONSHIP
Leamington Spa, Jul 30
Semi-finals
NORFOLK 51 Middlesex 27; HAMPSHIRE 51 Cumbria 34
Final
NORFOLK 37 Hampshire 32

LIVERPOOL VICTORIA ENGLISH NATIONAL CHAMPIONSHIPS
Leamington Spa, Jul 31-Aug 10
Singles
JEAN EVANS (Perkins, Peterborough) beat Edna Bessell (Yeovil) 21-15
Pairs
TONBRIDGE (Dora Farman & Joan Campbell) 27 Carlton Conway (Jackie Turner & Brenda Atherton) 13
Triples
OXFORD CITY & COUNTY 23 Yeovil 17
Fours
EDMONTON 22 Yeovil 19

WOMEN - INDOOR
WORLD CHAMPIONSHIP
Guernsey, Apr 21
Semi-finals
MARY PRICE (Eng) beat Margaret Letham (Sco) 7-2 4-7 3-7 7-4 7-6; MARGARET JOHNSTON (Ire) beat Jenny Nicolle (Gue) 7-6 1-7 7-3 3-7 7-3
Final
PRICE beat Johnston 6-7 7-4 0-7 7-4 7-2

PEDIGREE FILMS ENGLISH CHAMPIONSHIPS
Lawson Park, Bedford, Mar 4-11
Singles
MARY PRICE (Desborough, Maidenhead) beat Eileen Vigor (Croydon) 21-18
Pairs
NORWICH (Madelaine Ward & Elizabeth Shorter) 21 Cumbria (Margaret Norris & Eleanor Trotter) 12
Triples
NOTTINGHAM 16 Paddington 10
Fours
EGHAM 19 Rugby Thornfield 12
Yetton Trophy
ST NEOTS 88 King George Field 62

Champion of Champions
LYNN FELWELL (Handy Cross) beat Sharon Rickman (King George Field) 21-14

BRITISH ISLES CHAMPIONSHIPS
Prestwick, Mar 18-21
Singles
MARGARET LETHAM (Blantyre) beat Rita Jones (Merthyr Tydfil) 21-17
Pairs
ALICE ELLIOTT & JOYCE MULHOLLAND (Ballymoney) beat Mary Reid & Georgie Blane (Ayr) 28-13
Triples
BOSTON 18 Arbroath 13
Fours
COUNTY ANTRIM 17 Torfaen 16
Home International Series
1 ENGLAND; 2 Scotland; 3 Wales; 4 Ireland

MIXED
MACKESON ALL-ENGLAND INDOOR PAIRS
Scarborough, Mar 30-31
RIVERAIN (Pam Garside & Arthur Hemmings) 18 Christie Miller (Joan Tugwell & Steve Remington) 17

MACKESON ALL-ENGLAND INDOOR FOURS
Maidstone, Apr 20-21
ELY 21 Ashfield 13

LIVERPOOL VICTORIA NATIONAL OUTDOOR FOURS
Nottingham, Sep 17-18
First team LIBERTY OF HAVERING 15 North Walsham 13
CROWN GREEN BOWLS
WATERLOO HANDICAP
Blackpool, Sep 14-18
Quarter-finals
MICK LEACH (Warton) beat Andrew Cairns (Rossendale) 21-14; SIMON COUPE (Houghton, Preston) beat Kevin Graham (Reddish) 21-15; JOHN ECCLES (Heywood) beat Peter Lawrenson (Blackpool) 21-16; JOHN GURNEY (Northwich) beat John Sparks (Mold) 21-9
Semi-finals
COUPE beat Leach 21-17; ECCLES beat Gurney 21-15
Final
ECCLES beat Coupe 21-20
Eccles won with the last bowl of the match
Women's Final
JOYCE FOXCROFT (Hale, Cumbria) beat Lorna Pimblott (Southport) 21-15

——— CHAMPIONS ———

WORLD CHAMPIONSHIPS
Men-Outdoors
Singles
1966 David Bryant (Eng)

1972 Malwyn Evans (Wal)
1976 Doug Watson (SAf)
1980 David Bryant (Eng)
1984 Peter Belliss (NZ)
1988 David Bryant (Eng)
Pairs
1966 Geoff Kelly & Bert Palm (Aus)
1972 Clementi Delgado & Eric Liddell (HK)
1976 Doug Watson & William Moseley (SAf)
1980 Alf Sandercock & Peter Rheuben (Aus)
1984 George Adrain (Sco) & Skippy Arculli (US)
1988 Rowan Brassey & Peter Belliss (NZ)

Triples		Fours	
1966	Australia	1966	New Zealand
1972	United States	1972	England
1976	South Africa	1976	South Africa
1980	England	1980	Hong Kong
1984	Ireland	1984	England
1988	New Zealand	1988	Ireland

Team
(Leonard Trophy)
1966 Australia
1972 Scotland
1976 South Africa
1980 England
1984 England
1988 England

Men-Indoors
Singles
1979 David Bryant (Eng)
1980 David Bryant (Eng)
1981 David Bryant (Eng)
1982 John Watson (Sco)
1983 Bob Sutherland (Sco)
1984 Jim Baker (Ire)
1985 Terry Sullivan (Wal)
1986 Tony Allcock (Eng)
1987 Tony Allcock (Eng)
1988 Hugh Duff (Sco)
1989 Richard Corsie (Sco)
1990 John Price (Wal)
1991 Richard Corsie (Sco)

Women-Outdoors
Singles
1969 Gladys Doyle (PNG)
1973 Elsie Wilke (NZ)
1977 Elsie Wilke (NZ)
1981 Norma Shaw (Eng)
1985 Merle Richardson (Aus)
1988 Janet Ackland (Wal)
Pairs
1969 E McDonald & M Cridlan (SAf)
1973 Lorna Lucas & Dot Jenkinson (Aus)
1977 Helen Wong & Elvie Chok (HK)
1981 Eileen Bell & Nan Allely (Ire)
1985 Merle Richardson & Fay Craig (Aus)
1988 Margaret Johnston & Phyllis Nolan (Ire)

Triples		Fours	
1969	South Africa	1969	South Africa
1973	New Zealand	1973	New Zealand
1977	Wales	1977	Australia
1981	Hong Kong	1981	England
1985	Australia	1985	Scotland
1988	Australia	1988	Australia

Team
1969 South Africa
1973 New Zealand
1977 Australia
1981 England
1985 Australia
1988 England

Women-Indoors
Singles
1988 Margaret Johnston (Ire)
1989 Margaret Johnston (Ire)
1991 Mary Price (Eng)

EBA CHAMPIONSHIPS
Inaugurated 1905. Winners since 1982
Singles
1982 Chris Ward, Norfolk
1983 John Bell, Cumbria
1984 Wynne Richards, Surrey
1985 Roy Keating, Devon
1986 Wynne Richards, Surrey
1987 David Holt, Lancs
1988 Richard Bray, Cornwall
1989 John Ottaway, Norfolk
1990 Tony Allcock, Cheltenham
1991 Tony Allcock, Cheltenham

Pairs
1982 Bedford Borough
1983 Eldon Grove, Durham
1984 Lenham, Kent
1985 Haxby Road, Yorks
1986 Owton Lodge, Durham
1987 Bolton, Lancs
1988 Leicester
1989 Essex County
1990 Wymondham Dell, Norfolk
1991 Wigton, Cumbria

Triples
1982 Lenham, Kent
1983 Marlborough, Suffolk
1984 Clevedon, Somerset
1985 Clevedon, Somerset
1986 Poole Park, Dorset
1987 Worcester County
1988 Belgrave, Leicester
1989 Southbourne, Sussex
1990 Cheltenham
1991 Wigton, Cumbria

Fours
1982 Castle, Nottinghamshire
1983 Bolton, Lancs
1984 Boscombe Cliff, Hampshire
1985 Aldershot, Essex
1986 Stony Stratford, Bucks
1987 Aylesbury Town, Bucks
1988 Summertown, Oxon
1989 Blackheath & Greenwich, Kent
1990 Bath
1991 Wokingham, Berks

MIDDLETON CUP
Inaugurated 1911. Winners since 1982
1982 Berkshire
1983 Surrey
1984 Somerset
1985 Northumberland
1986 Wiltshire
1987 Kent
1988 Northumberland
1989 Kent
1990 Yorkshire
1991 Kent

CROWN GREEN BOWLS

WATERLOO CUP
Inaugurated 1907. Played at Waterloo Hotel, Blackpool.
Winners since 1982
Men
1982 Dennis Mercer
1983 Stan Frith
1984 Steve Ellis
1985 Tommy Johnstone
1986 Brian Duncan
1987 Brian Duncan
1988 Ingham Gregory
1989 Brian Duncan
1990 John Bancroft
1991 John Eccles
Most wins: 4 Brian Duncan

Women
Inaugurated 1988
1988 Barbara Rawcliffe
1989 Diane Hunt
1990 Jane Jones
1991 Joyce Foxcroft

—————— 1992 ——————

Aug 8-23 World Bowls (Beach House Park, Worthing)

BOXING

ST. GEORGE'S DAY

On an April night in Atlantic City, Evander Holyfield - a champion at least as charismatic as Tony Tubbs or Bonecrusher Smith - was officially confirmed as the greatest heavyweight boxer on earth, for the time being. But the Rev. George Foreman, the man he beat, was confirmed as one of the heroes of the age and one of the most lovable and noble losers of all time.

It was a fight that defied all predictions. Some experts expected Foreman to fell Holyfield with one enormous punch; others said the fight was a farce and a con perpetrated by 42-year-old George. No one anticipated the way it did go: Holyfield - scientific and super-fit - hit Foreman again and again and old George stood there and took it for 12 rounds without flinching or even apparently noticing, as though his head as well as his constitution were made of steel.

Foreman, preaching Christianity, looking like Buddha and sounding like an old vaudeville hand, was unrecognisable as the surly brute who was champion in the 70s. His string of one-line gags, and a deal with pay-TV, helped make the fight the biggest grosser in the sport's history. But he was a throwback. His conqueror, with an ex-ballerina as a fitness coach and a whole entourage of hi-tech-minded advisers, looked like the forerunner of a new generation of boxing athletes.

However, Holyfield remained a grey figure. He had won the title seven months earlier in Las Vegas when James "Buster" Douglas, whose shock win over Mike Tyson in Tokyo convulsed the boxing world, took his money and collapsed in a heap. Holyfield knocked him out in the third round and Douglas made no attempt to get up. Holyfield

BUSTER...

"When fighting is brave and dedicated, no reward - even in these days of mountains of dollar bills - can be too great, but Douglas's offering verged upon the fraudulent."

John Rodda, The Guardian

"I thought Douglas was disgraceful: the fact that he allowed himself to get into that condition for a heavyweight championship fight. This is the greatest prize in sport and he treated it with disdain."

Eddie Futch, veteran trainer

"Delivery men were risking hernias - and sauce burns - by carrying pizza pies six at a time to Douglas's suite at The Mirage."

Steve Farhood, The Ring

...AND GEORGE

"Evander has a nutritionist. I have room service."

George Foreman

"Some say George is as fit as a fiddle but I think he looks more like a cello."

Lou Duva, Holyfield's manager

"If you don't dream you might as well be dead."

Foreman

"The only thing the elephant is afraid of is a mouse. The elephant can't find a mouse."

George Benton, Holyfield's trainer

"Ironic, isn't it? The purists of boxing, thin-lipped and stiff-necked and small-minded in their righteous indignation, said the old man was making a mockery of the game. And yet in the end he saved it from their pettiness and short-sightedness and sourness. They said he would be the ruination of boxing. Instead, he turned out to be its salvation."

Bill Lyon, Philadelphia Inquirer

"I promise to refrain from spending any more of my bosses' money watching an ancient lummox stagger around throwing sofa pillows...Lord knows we love you, George. You're sweet. You're funny. You can take a lick. So can a mahogany tree, but I'm not about about to freeze on the Boardwalk again to watch it."

Edwin Pope, Miami Herald

"I think it should be mandatory for all fighters to retire at 65."

Foreman

"My greatest desire in my previous career was that I would kill someone and that all boxers would fear me."

Foreman

was 38lb lighter than the champion but most of the difference was Douglas's flab, put on in his eight improbable months as champion.

Meanwhile, Tyson brooded over the fight scene like Margaret Thatcher, awaiting his chance for a comeback. He beat British-born Alex Stewart in just 147 seconds and then beat Razor Ruddock twice - winning the first time controversially when the fight was stopped in the seventh with Ruddock apparently unhurt. The referee Richard Steele happened to be an employee of the Mirage casino, who had the contract for Tyson's next fight; there was a small riot in the ring after this decision and Murad Muhammad, Ruddock's promoter, was suspended for a year. Tyson outpointed Ruddock in the rematch but looked ponderous in the process. Everything was building up to a Tyson-Holyfield showdown, which Tyson might well win, but much of the old sharpness seemed to have vanished.

A CHAMP IN EXILE

❝I didn't stop the fight too soon. I saved a life.❞
Richard Steele, referee who controversially stopped the Tyson-Ruddock fight

"What?"
Ruddock to Steele on being stopped

"Tyson's attacks were ploddingly unimaginative, almost devoid of that foot, body and head movement which conveyed such an electric sense of vitality and destructive variety."
Hugh McIlvannney, The Observer, on Tyson-Ruddock I

"It was a sight to make Buster Douglas cancel his lastest room-service order and hurry back to the gym...Tyson had to be grateful he was dealing with someone as fundamentally limited and patently ill-tutored as Ruddock."
Hugh McIlvannney, The Observer, on Tyson-Ruddock II

"Mike's the real champ. The belt is only symbolic."
Don King, ditto

"Being a champion is a frame of mind."
Tyson

"This is a man who goes around the country doing this to women and he brags about it to the press...This is a civil rights case, in case you haven't figured this out yet."
Irving Pinsky, Rosie Jones's lawyer, suing Tyson for $100 million for putting his hands on her buttocks

"...Of course, it is clearly a civil rights case. When Martin Luther King marched in Selma, it was for the express purpose of preventing Mike Tyson putting his hand on Jones's buttocks."
Mike Royko, Chicago Tribune

"When they wrote about the old-time champions who had girls lining the dressing room walls they called them heroes. When they say the same about me I'm supposed to be a perverted sex-crazed psychopath."
Tyson

Foreman: "It's been my experience that fighters are all basically good guys."
Question: "Mike Tyson included?"
Foreman: "Well, yeah. there's good in Tyson deep down - deep, deep, DEEP, down, deep, deep, DEEP, down.❞

The bullying nature remained, especially out of the ring. Tyson was charged with raping a contestant in the Miss Black America competition. And Miss Black America 1990, Rosie Jones, filed a $100 million lawsuit against Tyson, alleging he had grabbed her buttocks; Jones's suit described Tyson as "a serial buttocks-fondler of black women and a perpetrator of lewd and disrespectful acts". Those whom the gods wish to destroy they first put in the hands of American lawyers. A woman who made the same allegation in 1990 and sued for $2.5 million was awarded $100.

Tyson was also at odds with his promoter Don King, who was shut out of Foreman-Holyfield - the first Kingless heavyweight title fight since 1978. Tyson reportedly hurled a toaster at him when King refused to meet demands that included provision of a white bus with a gold-plated toilet.

Foreman's success encouraged all kinds of improbable imitators. The former champion Larry Holmes returned, aged 41, with four wins in the ring and a fifth in the street after his comeback fight against Tim "Doc" Anderson. Holmes was taunted by his former opponent Trevor Berbick; he responded by leaping on to two parked cars and landing with both feet on Berbick. The former New York Jets player Mark Gastineau began a heavyweight career, aged 34 and weighing 18st 6lb. The ageing juvenile film actor Mickey Rourke entered the ring wearing orange satin shorts with shamrocks against Steve Powell and beat him; Powell, *Sports Illustrated* remarked, had been ranked among Boston's top 20 auto mechanics.

Slightly more legitimately, Thomas Hearns, 32, won his sixth title at a fifth different weight when he beat the previously unbeaten Virgil Hill for the WBA light-heavyweight championship. Sugar Ray Leonard's 14-year career, including titles in five divisions, ended - if any boxing career ever ends - when he was knocked down twice and lost heavily on points to Terry Norris. Michael Nunn, supposedly the best of the younger boxers, lost his IBF middleweight title and a 36-fight unbeaten record with a stunning defeat against James Toney, the biggest upset since Tyson-Douglas. Hector "Macho" Camacho, lost his 40-fight unbeaten record and his WBO junior welterweight title on a split decision to Greg Haugen; the point he lost for throwing sucker punches instead of obeying an order to touch gloves at the start of the final round was decisive.

In Britain, the absurdity of boxing was overtaken by its horror. After losing a ferocious contest for the WBO middleweight title against Chris Eubank, Michael Watson slumped in his corner, almost unnoticed in the general post-fight bedlam. He had serious brain damage and lay in a coma near death. On the same night, by grotesque coincidence, Fernie Morales needed brain surgery after being outpointed by Orlando Canizales in California for the IBF bantamweight title. The arguments of the ban-boxing lobby grew louder; those of its defenders more convoluted.

The WBO had been conducting its middleweight division purely for British consumption. The loudmouth Eubank had won the title off Nigel Benn and promptly proposed to his girlfriend Karron on TV. His first defence against Watson had ended controversially with almost everyone except three American judges believing Watson had won.

Dennis Andries (age 37-40 "depending on his mood") lost the WBC light-heavyweight title to the Australian Jeff Harding, leaving two Britons, apart from Eubank, holding on to titles. Dave McAuley from Larne stopped Jake Matlala from Soweto in September, thus successfully defending the IBF flyweight title for the fifth time and beating Jim Watt's record for any post-war British champion. Duke McKenzie easily outpointed Gaby Canizales at the Elephant and Castle to win the WBO

HEAVY, MAN...

The highest weights in heavyweight title fights

1	Primo Carnera	19st 4lb	beat Tommy Loughran, pts	1934
2	Primo Carnera	18st 11 ¼ lb	lost to Max Baer, rsf 11	1934
3	Primo Carnera	18st 8 ½ lb	beat Jack Sharkey, ko 6	1933
4	Primo Carnera	18st 7 ½ lb	beat Paolino Uzcudun, pts	1933
5	GEORGE FOREMAN	18ST 5LB	LOST TO EVANDER HOLYFIELD, PTS	1991
6	Abe Simon	18st 3 ½ lb	lost to Joe Louis, ko 6	1942

The highest weight totals in heavyweight title fights:

1	Carnera and Uzcudun	34st 12 ¾ lb	1933
2	Carnera and Baer	33st 10 ¾ lb	1934
3	Tim Witherspoon and Tony Tubbs	33st 9lb	1986
4	Greg Page and Tony Tubbs	33st 6 ½ lb	1985
5	Larry Holmes and Leroy Jones	33st 3 ½ lb	1980
6	FOREMAN and HOLYFIELD	33st 3lb	1991

Source: Associated Press

bantamweight title and become the first British-based boxer to win world titles at different weights.

Lennox Lewis added the British heavyweight title to his European one when he beat Gary Mason in the seventh; Mason was later forced to retire on the advice of eye specialists. The pantomime star Frank Bruno signed with Mickey Duff to make a comeback in the ring, 2½ years after his last fight, against Tyson. Screaming Lord Sutch promised to make Bruno Minister of Education in a Loony party government.

The British lightweight champion Carl Crook from Chorley set a record for winning a Lonsdale Belt: 161 days, beating the 203 days by Robert Dickie in 1986. Light-heavyweight John Ellis, 30, was knocked out by Nicky Piper after 12 seconds, including the count, of a televised bout in Norwich. Two seconds into the contest, he was hit by a right and was out cold for two minutes. A junior-middleweight bout in Brisbane, Australia, was stopped after five seconds when Charlie Hansen complained of double vision after being hit. The British welterweight Kirkland Laing announced that he was training on cow's feet boiled for five hours; he said this also had aphrodisiac properties. He promptly lost his European welterweight title to Patrizio Oliva of Italy. Mike Morrison, a welterweight from Pembroke, retired in July after his 30th defeat in 31 fights. The British Boxing Board of Control reported that there were 984 licensed professional boxers in Britain in April 1991, compared to 650 in the rest of Europe.

CRIME AND PUNISHMENT

One former British world champion, Terry Marsh, was acquitted of attempting to murder the promoter Frank Warren. Another, Maurice Hope, was awarded £50,000 damages and £20,000 costs against the Metropolitan Police for false arrest and wrongful imprisonment on a drugs charge. Asked if he thought his arrest had been racially motivated Hope replied: "Not what I think, what I know." Ambrose Mendy, Nigel Benn's manager, was jailed for 2½ years for fraud; the judge said he had been at the heart of swindles involving more than £1m. The Glasgow promoter Alex Morrison staged a promotion inside Shotts maximum security prison. Paul Sykes, who fought John L Gardner for the British heavyweight title but had spent 21 of the past 26 years in prison for a succession of violent offences, was reported to be running a boys' club in Wakefield, Yorkshire. Boxing was not among its activities: "I hate to see young lads beating hell out of each other," said Sykes.

Tocker Pudwill, 19, fought on the same bill in Mandan, North Dakota as his father

---

INSIDE AND OUT

❝I am taken to the canteen where I am told I have the princely sum of £1.50 - my wages for the week - to spend on anything I want. It's like being a kid again, asking the price of everything. I end up buying teabags, powdered milk, a bar of chocolate. It costs £1.46. You are not allowed change, so they give me four one-penny Black Jack sweets. I remember that for my last fight, one evening's work, I netted £78,000. Funny old world, isn't it?"

Terry Marsh, in his jail diary

"On the first day one inmate told me that if I bought him cigarettes every week I wouldn't get hurt. So I slapped him across the face, jammed his head against the cell bars and threw him around for a while. We became good friends after that."

Chuck Wepner, former boxer and inmate

"The Justice Department has charged me with every known crime and misdemeanor - kickbacks, racketeering, ticket scalping, skimming, fixing fights, preordaining them, vitiating officials and laundering money. The only thing they missed was kidnapping the Lindbergh baby."

Don King

"Being in jail is really great. I know everybody here.**❞**

Dan Elbaum, former boxing promoter jailed for tax evasion

Terry and his uncle Mark. The American cruiserweight Walli Muhammed denied biting an opponent despite videotape evidence. "I'm a vegetarian," he said. Police in Titograd, Yugoslavia intervened to save a referee from being hanged: after a controversial decision against a local fighter, Miodrag Bozjak was dragged out of the hall and a noose tied round his neck. Albania legalised boxing, which was banned in 1963 by the late dictator Enver Hoxha, reportedly after his two sons come home from workouts with cuts and bruises; boxers who protested against the ban were jailed, one for more than 20 years.

Muhammad Ali flew to Baghdad to secure the release of 17 hostages, but failed to fly to London to attend a dinner with Henry Cooper, celebrating the 25th anniversary of their world title fight. Three months after his fight against Holyfield, George Foreman's wife gave birth to his ninth child, to be known as George V. His three other sons are also called George. Had it been a girl, Foreman said, her first name would have been Judy and her middle name George.

════ 1990-91 ════

WORLD TITLE FIGHTS
new champions underlined

Heavyweight
Champions as at Aug 20, 1990: WBC/WBA/IBF James 'Buster' Douglas (US) WBO Francesco Damiani (Ita)
WBC/WBA/IBF Las Vegas, Oct 25: Evander Holyfield (US) beat James 'Buster' Douglas ko 3rd
WBO Atlantic City, Jan 11: Ray Mercer (US) beat Francesco Damiani ko 9th
WBC/WBA/IBF Atlantic City, Apr 20: Evander Holyfield beat George Foreman (US) pts

PUNCH CHART

	HOLYFIELD	FOREMAN
Total punches	584	444
Connected	355	188
Jabs thrown	237	200
Connected	130	108
Power punches thrown	347	244
Connected	225	80

Source: CompuBox Inc.

Cruiserweight
Champions as at Aug 20, 1990: WBC Massimilio Duran (Ita) WBA Robert Daniels (US) IBF Jeff Lampkin (US) WBO Magne Havnaa (Nor)
WBA Madrid, Nov 22: Robert Daniels and Taoufik Belbouli (Fra) drew *(Daniels retained title)*
WBC Ferrara, Italy, Dec 8: Massimilio Duran beat Anaclet Wamba (Fra) disq.12th
WBO Aalborg, Denmark, Dec 8: Magne Havnaa beat Daniel Eduardo Neto (Arg) pts
WBO Randers, Denmark, Feb 15: Magne Havnaa beat Tyrone Booze (US) pts
WBA Atlantic City, Mar 9: Bobby Czyz (US) beat Robert Daniels pts
WBC Palermo, Italy, Jul 20: Anaclet Wamba (Fra) beat Massimilio Duran rsf 11th
WBA Atlantic City, Aug 9: Bobby Czyz beat Bashiru Alli (US) pts

Light-Heavyweight
Champions as at Aug 20, 1990: WBC Dennis Andries (GB) WBA Virgil Hill (US) IBF Prince Charles Williams (US) WBO Michael Moorer (US)
WBC London, Oct 10: Dennis Andries beat Sergio

Merani (Arg) rtd 4th
WBO Pittsburgh, Dec 15: Michael Moorer beat Danny Lindstrom (Can) ko 8th
WBA Bismarck, North Dakota, Jan 6: Virgil Hill beat Mike Peak (US) pts
IBF St Vincent, Italy, Jan 12: Prince Charles Williams beat Mwehu Beya (Ita) pts
WBC Adelaide, Jan 19: Dennis Andries beat Guy Waters (Aus) pts
IBF Atlantic City, Apr 20: Prince Charles Williams beat James Kinchen (US) rsf 2nd
WBO Leeds, May 9: Leeonzer Barber (US) beat Tom Collins (GB) rtd 5th
For vacant title after Moorer opted to fight at heavyweight
WBA Las Vegas, Jun 3: Thomas Hearns (US) beat Virgil Hill pts
Hearns won an unprecedented sixth world title
IBF San Remo, Jul 20: Prince Charles Williams beat Vince Boulware (US) ko 3rd

Super-Middleweight
Champions as at Aug 20, 1990: WBC Vacant WBA Christophe Tiozzo (Fra) IBF Lindell Holmes (US) WBO Thomas Hearns (US)
WBA Cergy Pontoise, France, Nov 23: Christophe Tiozzo beat Danny Morgan (US) rsf 2nd
WBC Monaco, Dec 15: Mauro Galvano (Ita) beat Dario Matteoni (Arg) pts
IBF Marino, Italy, Dec 16: Lindell Holmes beat Sugar Boy Malinga (SAf) pts
IBF Madrid, Mar 7: Lindell Holmes beat Antoine Byrd (US) pts
WBA Marseille, Apr 5: Victor Cordoba (Pan) beat Christophe Tiozzo rsf 9th
IBF Verbania, Italy, May 18: Darrin van Horn (US) beat Lindell Holmes rsf 11th
WBC Capo d'Orlando, Italy, Jul 27: Mauro Galvano beat Ron Essett (US) pts

Middleweight
Champions as at Aug 20, 1990: WBC Vacant WBA Mike McCallum (Jam) IBF Michael Nunn (US) WBO Nigel Benn (GB)
IBF Paris, Oct 18: Michael Nunn beat Don Curry (US) rsf 10th
WBO Birmingham, England, Nov 18: Chris Eubank (GB) beat Nigel Benn rsf 9th
WBC Benalmadena, Spain, Nov 24: Julian Jackson (VI) beat Herol Graham (GB) ko 4th

WBO Brighton, Feb 23: Chris Eubank beat Dan Sherry (Can) pts

WBA Monte Carlo, Apr 1: Mike McCallum beat Sumbu Kalambay (Ita) pts

WBO Kensington, London, Apr 18 Chris Eubank beat Gary Stretch (GB) rsf 6th

IBF Devonport, Iowa, May 10: James Toney (US) beat Michael Nunn rsf 11th

Biggest upset since Tyson defeat by Douglas

WBO Earl's Court, London, Jun 22: Chris Eubank beat Michael Watson (GB) pts

First boxing at Earl's Court since the Joe Frazier-Joe Bugner fight in 1973

IBF Las Vegas, Jun 29: James Toney beat Reggie Johnson (US) pts

Junior-Middleweight/Super-Welterweight

Champions as at Aug 20, 1990: WBC Terry Norris (US) WBA Julian Jackson (VI) IBF Gianfranco Rosi (Ita) WBO John David Jackson (US)

WBO Leicester, Oct 23: John David Jackson beat Chris Pyatt (GB) pts

IBF Marsala, Italy, Nov 30: Gianfranco Rosi beat Rene Jacquot (Fra) pts

WBC New York, Feb 9: Terry Norris (US) beat Sugar Ray Leonard (US) pts

WBA Pointe-a-Pitre, Guadeloupe, Feb 23: Gilbert Dele (Fra) beat Carlos Elliott (US) rsf 7th

For vacant title

IBF St Vincent, Italy, Mar 16: Gianfranco Rosi beat Ron Amundsen (US) pts

WBA Paris, May 5: Gilbert Dele beat Hwang Jun-Suk (SKo) pts

WBC Palm Springs, Jun 1: Terry Norris beat Don Curry (US) ko 8th

IBF Avezzano, Italy, Jul 13: Gianfranco Rosi beat Glenn Wolfe (US) pts

WBO McKee City, New Jersey, Jul 20: John David Jackson beat Tyrone Trice (US) pts

WBC San Diego, California, Aug 16: Terry Norris beat Brett Lally (US) rsf 1st

Welterweight

Champions as at Aug 20, 1990: WBC Maurice Blocker (US) WBA Aaron Davis (US) IBF Simon Brown (Jam) WBO Manning Galloway

WBO Lewiston, Maine, Aug 25: Manning Galloway beat Nika Khumalo (SAf) pts

WBA Atlantic City, Jan 19: Meldrick Taylor (US) beat Aaron Davis pts

WBO Randers, Denmark, Feb 15: Manning Galloway beat Gert Bo Jacobsen (Den) rtd 8th

WBC/IBF Las Vegas, Mar 18: Simon Brown beat Meldrick Taylor rsf 11th

Simon Brown vacated IBF title in May citing "frustrations" and the IBF's decision to sanction fights in South Africa

WBO Copenhagen, May 17: Manning Galloway beat Racheed Lawal (Den) rtd 7th

WBA Palm Springs, Jun 1: Meldrick Taylor beat Luis Garcia (Ven) pts

Junior-Welterweight/Super-Lightweight

Champions as at Aug 20, 1990: WBC/IBF Julio Cesar Chavez (Mex) WBA Loreto Garza (US) WBO Hector Camacho (PR)

WBA Sacramento, Dec 1: Loreto Garza beat Vinny Pazienza (US) disq 11th

WBC/IBF Atlantic City, Dec 8: Julio Cesar Chavez beat Ahn Kyung-Duk (SKo) rsf 3rd

WBO Las Vegas, Feb 23: Greg Haugen (US) beat Hector Camacho pts

Haugen stripped of title by WBO for failing a post-fight drugs test. Result still stands as Camacho's first defeat in 41 fights although title vacant following WBO's decision.

WBC/IBF Las Vegas, Mar 18: Julio Cesar Chavez beat Johnny Duplessis (US) rsf 4th

Chavez relinquished title Apr 23 rather than accept challenge from Raphael Pineda (Mex)

WBO Reno, Nevada, May 18: Hector Camacho (US) beat Greg Haugen (US) pts

Even though he failed a drugs test after the first fight, the WBO still allowed Haugen to fight for the vacant title

WBA Sacramento, Jun 14: Edwin Rosario (PR) beat

THE CAREER OF SUGAR RAY LEONARD

After losing to Terry Norris at the Madison Square Garden on February 9, Sugar Ray Leonard retired.

Career Record

Fights	Won	Drew	Lost
39	36	1	2

25 of his wins were inside the distance; Norris and Roberto Duran (1980) were the only men to beat him; the draw was against Tommy Hearns in 1989

World Title Fights

1979	**Wilfred Benitez**	**WBC welter**	**Las Vegas**	Won rsf 15th
1980	**Dave 'Boy' Green**	**WBC welter**	**Landover, Maryland**	Won ko 4th
1980	**Roberto Duran**	**WBC welter**	**Montreal**	Lost pts
1980	**Roberto Duran**	**WBC welter**	**New Orleans**	Won rsf 8th
1981	**Larry Bonds**	**WBC welter**	**Syracuse**	Won rsf 10th
1981	**Ayub Kalule**	**WBA junior-middle**	**Houston**	Won ko 9th
1981	**Tommy Hearns**	**Undisputed welter**	**Las Vegas**	Won rsf 14th
1982	**Bruce Finch**	**WBC welter**	**Reno, Necada**	Won rsf 3rd
1987	**Marvin Hagler**	**WBC middle**	**Las Vegas**	Won pts
1988	**Donny Lalonde**	**WBC light-heavy & WBC super-middle**	**Las Vegas**	Won rsf 9th
1989	**Tommy Hearns**	**WBC super-middle**	**Las Vegas**	Drew
1989	**Roberto Duran**	**WBC super-middle**	**Las Vegas**	Won pts
1991	**Terry Norris**	**WBC junior-middle & super-welter**	**New York**	Lost pts

Leonard was inactive in 1983 and again 1985-86

GOODNIGHT, SUGAR

❝No one else will decide when I quit. I'm greedy. I want the Nineties as well.❞
Sugar Ray Leonard, January 31

"This is my last fight. Thank you for coming."
Sugar Ray Leonard, February 9, after losing to Terry Norris

"He met the enemy...and it was youth and quickness."
Tony Kornheiser, Washington Post

"It's a sad victory. He's my idol and I beat him badly. I didn't want it to be that way. He's still my idol."
Norris

"Now I am going to learn how to play golf.❞❞
Leonard

Loreto Garza (US) ko 3rd

Lightweight
Champions as at Aug 20, 1990: WBC/WBA/IBF Pernell Whitaker (US) WBO Mauricio Aceves (Mex)
WBO Brownsville, Texas, Sep 22: <u>Dingaan Thobela (SAf)</u> beat Mauricio Aceves pts
WBC/WBA/IBF Las Vegas, Feb 23: Pernell Whitaker beat Anthony Jones (US) pts
WBO San Jose, California, Mar 2: Dingaan Thobela beat Mario Martinez (Mex) pts
WBA/WBC/IBF Norfolk, Virginia, Jul 27: Pernell Whitaker beat Policarpo Diaz (Spa) pts

Junior-Lightweight/Super-Featherweight
Champions as at Aug 20, 1990: WBC Azumah Nelson (Gha) WBA Brian Mitchell (SAf) IBF Tony Lopez (US) WBO Kamel Bou Ali (Tun)
IBF Sacramento, Sep 22: Tony Lopez beat Jorge Paez (Mex) pts
WBA Aosta, Italy, Sep 29: Brian Mitchell beat Frankie Mitchell (US) pts
WBC Sydney, Oct 13: Azumah Nelson beat Juan Laporte (PR) pts
WBO Cesena, Italy, Oct 20: Kamel Bou Ali beat Pedro Florindo Villegas (Arg) No contest
WBA/IBF Sacramento, Mar 15: Brian Mitchell and Tony Lopez drew
Brian Mitchell vacated WBA title April.
WBO Ragusa, Sicily, Jun 1: Kamel Bou Ali beat Joey Jacobs (GB) ko 3rd
WBA Lewiston, Maine, Jun 28: Joey Gamache (US) beat Jerry Ngobeni (SAf) rsf 10th
First fight at Lewiston since Muhammad Ali beat Sonny Liston to retain his world heavyweight title in May 1965
WBC Las Vegas, Jun 28: Azumah Nelson (Gha) and Jeff Fenech (Aus) drew
Nelson retained his world title and Fenech narrowly missed winning his fourth world title. The decision caused a furore in Australia.

Featherweight
Champions as at Aug 20, 1990: WBC Marcos Villasana (Mex) WBA Antonio Esparragoza (Ven) IBF/WBO Jorge Paez (Mex)
WBC Mexico City, Sep 30: Marcos Villasana beat Javier Marquez (Mex) rsf 8th
WBO Sassari, Sardinia, Jan 26: <u>Maurizio Stecca (Ita)</u> beat Armando Reves (Dom) rsf 5th

For vacant title after Jorge Paez quit the division to fight as a lightweight
WBA Seoul, S.Korea, Mar 30: <u>Park Yung-Kyun (SKo)</u> beat Antonio Esparragoza pts
Esparragoza had been champion since March 1987
WBC Mexico City, Apr 11: Marcos Villasana beat Rafael Zuniga (Col) rsf 6th
IBF Las Vegas, Jun 3: <u>Troy Dorsey (US)</u> beat Alfred Rangel (US) ko 1st
WBA Seoul, Jun 15: Park Yung-Kyun beat Masuaki Takeda (Jap) rsf th
WBO Montichiari, Italy, Jun 15: Maurizio Stecca beat Fernando Ramos Salas (Mex) pts
IBF Inglewood, California, Aug 12: <u>Manuel Medina (Mex)</u> beat Troy Dorsey pts
WBC Marbella, Spain, Aug 16: Marcos Villasana beat Ricardo Cepeda (PR) pts

Junior-Featherweight/Super-Bantamweight
Champions as at Aug 20, 1990: WBC Paul Banke (US) WBA Vacant IBF Welcome Ncita (SAf) WBO Orlando Fernandez (PR)
WBA Miami, Sep 11: <u>Luis Mendoza (Col)</u> beat Ruben Palacios (Col) rsf 3rd
IBF Aosta, Italy, Sep 29: Welcome Ncita beat Gerardo Lopez (Pan) rsf 8th
WBA Paris, Oct 18: Luis Mendoza beat Fabrice Benichou (Fra) pts
WBC Inglewood, California, Nov 5: <u>Pedro Decima (Arg)</u> beat Paul Banke rsf 4th
WBA Bangkok, Jan 19: Luis Mendoza beat Noree Jockegym (Tha) tko 8th
WBC Nagoya, Japan, Feb 3: <u>Kiyoshi Hatanaka (Jap)</u> beat Pedro Decima rsf 8th
IBF St Vincent, Italy, Feb 28: Welcome Ncita beat Jose Rojas (Col) pts
WBA Cartagena, Colombia, Apr 21 Luis Mendoza beat Carlos Uribe (Chi) pts
WBO Corpus Christi, Texas, May 24: <u>Jesse Benevides (US)</u> beat Orlando Fernandez pts
WBA Madrid, May 30: Luis Mendoza beat Joao Cardosa de Oliveira (Bra) ko 7th
WBC Tokyo, Jun 14: <u>Daniel Zaragoza (Mex)</u> beat Kiyoshi Hatanaka pts
Zaragoza's third world title
IBF San Antonio, Texas, Jun 15: Welcome Ncita beat Hurley Snead (US) pts

Bantamweight
Champions as at Aug 20, 1990: WBC Raul Perez (Mex) WBA Luisito Espinosa (PR) IBF Orlando Canizales (US) WBO Israel Contreras (Ven)
WBO Nassau, Bahamas, Sep 2: Israel Contreras beat Ray Minus, jnr (Bah) rsf 9th
WBC Culiacán, Mexico, Sep 14: Raul Perez drew with Jose Valdez (Mex)
Perez retained his title
WBA Manila, Philippines, Oct 12: Luisito Espinosa beat Chun Yong-Man (SKo) ko 1st
WBA Bangkok, Nov 29: Luisito Espinosa beat Thalerngak Sitbonbeh (Tha) pts
WBC Tijuana, Mexico, Dec 17: Raul Perez beat Candelario Carmona (Mex) ko 8th
WBC Inglewood, California, Feb 26 <u>Greg Richardson (US)</u> beat Raul Perez pts
WBO Auburn Hills, Michigan, Mar 12: <u>Gaby Canizales (US)</u> beat Miguel Lora (Col) ko 2nd
For vacant title
IBF Laredo, Texas, May 4: <u>Orlando Canizales</u> beat Billy Hardy (GB) rsf 8th

WBC Inglewood, California, May 20: Greg Richardson beat Victor Rabanales (Mex) pts
WBO, Southwark, London, Jun 30: Duke McKenzie (GB) beat Gaby Canizales pts
McKenzie became the first British-based boxer to win world titles at different weights

Super Flyweight/Junior Bantamweight

Champions as at Aug 20, 1990: WBC Moon Sung-Kil (SKo) WBA Kaosai Galaxy (Tha) IBF Robert Quiroga (US) WBO Jose Ruiz (PR)
WBA Suphan Buri, Thailand, Sep 29: Kaosai Galaxy beat Kim Yong-Kan (SKo) ko 6th
IBF Pagliara, Italy, Oct 6: Robert Quiroga beat Vuyani Nene (SAf) rtd 3
WBC Seoul, Oct 20: Moon Sung-Kil beat Kenji Matsumura (Jap) pts
WBO Acapulco, Mexico, Nov 3: Jose Ruiz beat Armando Velasco (Mex) pts
WBA Petchabun, Thailand, Dec 9: Kaosai Galaxy beat Ernesto Ford (Pan) ko 6th
IBF Capo D'Orlando, Italy, Jan 26: Robert Quiroga beat Vincenzo Nelcato (Ita) pts
WBC Zaragoza, Spain, Mar 16: Moon Sung-Kil beat Nana Yaw Konadu (Gha) rsf 4th
WBA Bangkok, Apr 6: Kaosai Galaxy beat Park Jae-Sup (SKo) rsf 5th
IBF San Antonio, Texas, Jun 15: Robert Quiroga beat Akeem Anifowoshe (Nig) pts
WBA Bangkok, Jul 20: Kaosai Galaxy beat David Griman Mendez (Ven) rsf 5th
Galaxy's 18th successful defence
WBC Seoul, Jul 20: Moon Sung-Kil beat Ernesto Ford (Pan) ko 5th

Flyweight

Champions as at Aug 20, 1990: WBC Sot Chitalada (Tha) WBA Leopard Tamakuma (Jap) IBF Dave McAuley (GB) WBO Isidro Perez (Mex)
WBC Kingston, Jamaica, Sep 9: Sot Chitalada beat Richard Clarke (Jam) ko 11th
IBF Belfast, Sep 15: Dave McAuley beat Rodolfo Blanco (Col) pts
WBO Acapulco, Mexico, Nov 3: Isidro Perez beat Alli Galvez (Chi) pts
WBC Seoul, Nov 24: Sot Chitalada beat Chang Jung-Koo (SKo) pts
WBA Aomori, Japan, Dec 6: Leopard Tamakuma beat Jesus Rojas (Ven) pts
WBC Ayuthaya, Thailand, Feb 15: Muangchai Kittikasem (Tha) beat Sot Chitalada (Tha) rsf 6th
WBA Tokyo, Mar 14: Elvis Alvarez (Col) beat Leopard Tamakuma pts
IBF Belfast, May 11: Dave McAuley (GB) beat Pedro Feliciano (PR) pts
WBC Seoul, South Korea, May 18: Muangchai Kittikasem (Tha) beat Chang Jung-Koo (SKo) rsf 12th
WBA Seoul, Jun 1: Kim Yong-Kang (SKo) beat Elvis Alvarez pts
WBO Santiago, Chile, Aug 10: Isidro Perez beat Alli Galvez (Chi) pts

Junior-Flyweight

Champions as at Aug 20, 1990: WBC Humberto Gonzalez (Mex) WBA Yuh Myung-Woo (SKo) IBF Michael Carbajal (US) WBO Jose De Jesus (PR)
WBC, Cancun, Mexico, Aug 26: Humberto Gonzalez beat Jorge Rivera (Mex) ko 8th
WBA Seoul, Nov 10: Yuh Myung-Woo beat Leo Gamez (Ven) pts
WBO Medan, Indonesia, Nov 10: Jose De Jesus beat Abdi

Pohan (Ina) rsf 7th
IBF Scottsdale, Arizona, Dec 8: Michael Carbajal beat Leon Salazar (Pan) ko 4th
WBC Inglewood, California, Dec 19: Rolando Pascua (Phi) beat Humberto Gonzalez ko 6th
IBF Las Vegas, Feb 17: Michael Carbajal beat Macario Santos (Mex) ko 2nd
IBF Las Vegas, Mar 17: Michael Carbajal beat Javier Varguez (Mex) pts
Varguez was a substitute for a substitute
WBC Inglewood, California, Mar 25: Melchor Cob Castro (Mex) beat Rolando Pascua rtd 10th
WBA Musan, South Korea, Apr 28: Yuh Myung-Woo beat Kajkong Danphoothai (Tha) rsf 10th
IBF Devonport, Iowa, May 10: Michael Carbajal beat Hector Luis Tatri (Arg) pts
WBC Las Vegas Jun 3: Humberto Gonzalez (Mex) beat Melchor Cob Castro pts

Straw-weight

Champions as at Aug 20, 1990: WBC Hideyuki Ohashi (Jap) WBA Kim Bong-Jun (SKo) IBF Fahlan Lookmingkwan (Tha) WBO Rafael Torres (DR)
WBC Tokyo, Oct 25: Ricardo Lopez (Mex) beat Hideyuki Ohashi ko 5th
WBA, Taegu, South Korea, Nov 3: Kim Bong-Jun beat Silverio Barcenas (Pan) pts
IBF Bangkok, Dec 20: Fhalan Lookmingkwan drew with Domingo Lucas (Phi)
Lookmingkwan retained his title
WBA Pujan, South Korea, Feb 2: Choi Hi-Yong (SKo) beat Kim Bong-Jun (SKo) pts
WBC Shizuoka, Japan May 18: Ricardo Lopez beat Kimio Hirano (Jap) rsf 8th
WBA Seoul, Jun 15: Choi Hi-Yong beat Sugar Ray Mike (Phi) pts
IBF Bangkok, Jun 25: Fhalan Lookmingkwan beat Abdy Pohan (Ina) pts

BRITISH TITLE FIGHTS 1990-91

Heavyweight

Champion as at Aug 20, 1990: Gary Mason (Wandsworth)
Mar 7, Wembley Arena: Lennox Lewis (Crayford) beat Gary Mason rsf 7th
Also for European title

Cruiserweight

Champion as at Aug 20, 1990: Johnny Nelson (Sheffield)
Feb 13, Wembley: Derek Angol (Gravesend) beat Dave Garside (Hartlepool) rsf 2nd
For vacant title after Nelson relinquished crown to fight for European title. Angol also won Commonwealth title
May 8, Royal Albert Hall: Derek Angol beat Tee Jay (Nottingham) rsf 3rd
Also for Commonwealth title

Light-Heavyweight

Champion as at Aug 20, 1990: Vacant
Oct 25, Battersea: Steve McCarthy (Southampton) beat Serge Fame (Paddington) pts
McCarthy stripped of title Jun 12 when he walked out at the weigh-in before scheduled defence against Roy Skeldon after finding out he was receiving only a £1,500 live television fee
Jul 25, Dudley: Crawford Ashley (Leeds) beat Roy Skeldon (Tipton) rsf 7th
Skeldon, at 38, was hoping to become the oldest British champion since Nel Tarleton in 1947

Super-Middleweight
Champion as at Aug 20, 1990: Sam Storey (Belfast)
Oct 30, Belfast: <u>James Cook (Peckham)</u> beat Sam Storey rsf 10th

Middleweight
Champion as at Aug 20, 1990: Herol Graham (Sheffield)
No Fights

Light-Middleweight
Champion as at Aug 20, 1990: Gary Stretch (St Helens)
Mar 19, Birmingham : <u>Wally Swift (Birmingham)</u> beat Ensley Bingham (Manchester) ko 4th
For title vacated by Stretch, Sep 1990
Jul 3, Reading: Wally Swift beat Tony Collins (Yateley) pts

Welterweight
Champion as at Aug 20, 1990: Kirkland Laing (Hackney)
Jan 16, London: <u>Delroy Bryan (Nottingham)</u> beat Kirkland Laing pts

Light-Welterweight
Champion as at Aug 20, 1990: Pat Barrett (Manchester)
Sep 26, Manchester: <u>Tony Ekubia (Manchester)</u> beat Alex Dickson (Larkhall) ko 11th
For vacant title
Jun 20, Liverpool: <u>Andy Holligan (Liverpool)</u> beat Tony Ekubia (Manchester) pts
Also for the Commonwealth title

Lightweight
Champion as at Aug 20, 1990: Steve Boyle (Glasgow)
Nov 14, Sheffield: <u>Carl Crook (Chorley)</u> beat Tony Richards (Nottingham) pts
For vacant title
Dec 19, Preston: Carl Crook beat Ian Honeywood (Peterborough) rsf 4th

Apr 24, Preston: Carl Crook beat Najib Daho (Manchester) rsf 10th
Also for Commonwealth title
Crook won Lonsdale Belt outright in record time: 161 days beating the 203 days set by Robert Dickie between Apr 9 and Oct 29 in 1986
Jun 22, Earl's Court, London: Carl Crook beat Brian Roche (Bacup) ko 10th
Also for Commonwealth title

Super-Featherweight
Champion as at Aug 20, 1990: Joey Jacobs (Oldham)
Sep 18, Wolverhampton: <u>Hugh Forde (Birmingham)</u> beat Joey Jacobs rsf 11th
Oct 24, Dudley: <u>Kevin Pritchard (Liverpool)</u> beat Hugh Forde ko 4th
Mar 6, Cardiff: <u>Robert Dickie (Swansea)</u> beat Kevin Pritchard rsf 8th
Apr 30, Stockport: <u>Sugar Gibiliru (Liverpool)</u> beat Robert Dickie rsf 9th

Featherweight
Champion as at Aug 20, 1990: Sean Murphy (St Albans)
Sep 25, Millwall: Sean Murphy beat Johnny B Good (Croydon) ko 2nd
Mar 6, London Arena: <u>Gary De Roux (Peterborough)</u> beat Sean Murphy ko 5th
May 22, London Arena: <u>Colin McMillan (Barking)</u> beat Gary De Roux rsf 7th

Bantamweight
Champion as at Aug 20, 1990: Billy Hardy (Sunderland)
Nov 29, Sunderland: Billy Hardy beat Ronnie Carroll (Glasgow) rsf 8th

Flyweight
Champion as at Aug 20, 1990: Vacant

COMMONWEALTH CHAMPIONS 1990-91

Weight	Champions as at Aug 20, 1990	Champions since then
HEAVYWEIGHT	Derek Williams (Eng)	None
CRUISERWEIGHT	Derek Angol (Eng)	None
LIGHT-HEAVYWEIGHT	Guy Waters (Aus)	None
SUPER-MIDDLEWEIGHT	Lou Cafaro (Aus)	Henry Wharton (Eng)
MIDDLEWEIGHT	Michael Watson (Eng)	None
LIGHT-MIDDLEWEIGHT	Troy Waters (Aus)	None
WELTERWEIGHT	Donovan Boucher (Can)	None
LIGHT-WELTERWEIGHT	Tony Ekubia (Eng)	Andy Holligan (Eng)
LIGHTWEIGHT	Carl Crook (Eng)	None
SUPER-FEATHERWEIGHT	Mark Reefer (Eng)	Thunder Aryeh (Gha)
FEATHERWEIGHT	Modest Napunyi (Ken)	Barrington Francis (Can)
BANTAMWEIGHT	Ray Minus jnr (Bah)	None
FLYWEIGHT	Alfred Khotey (Gha)	None

EUROPEAN CHAMPIONS 1990-91

Weight	Champions as at Aug 20, 1990	Champions since then
HEAVYWEIGHT	Jean-Maurice Chanet (Fra)	Lennox Lewis (GB)
CRUISERWEIGHT	Vacant	Johnny Nelson (GB)
LIGHT-HEAVYWEIGHT	Tom Collins (GB)	Graciano Rocchigiani (Ger)
SUPER-MIDDLEWEIGHT	Mauro Galvano (Ita)	James Cook (GB)
MIDDLEWEIGHT	Sumbu Kalambay (Ita)	None
LIGHT-MIDDLEWEIGHT	Gilbert Dele (Fra)	Said Skouma (GB)
		Mourad Louati (Hol)
		Jean-Claude Fontana (Fra)
WELTERWEIGHT	Kirkland Laing (GB)	Patrizio Oliva (Ita)
LIGHT-WELTERWEIGHT	Efrem Calamati (Ita)	Pat Barrett (GB)
LIGHTWEIGHT	Policarpo Diaz (Spa)	Antonio Renzo (Ita)
SUPER-FEATHERWEIGHT	Daniel Londas (Fra)	None
FEATHERWEIGHT	Paul Hodkinson (GB)	Fabrice Benichou (Fra)
BANTAMWEIGHT	Vacant	Thierry Jacob (Fra)
FLYWEIGHT	Pat Clinton (GB)	Salvatore Fanni (Ita)

AMATEUR
ABA FINALS

Royal Albert Hall, May 7

Super-heavyweight Kevin McCormack (Coed-Eva) beat Gareth Edwards (Leith Victoria) pts

Heavyweight Paul Lawson (Newco-Repton) beat David Roberts (Willaston) pts

Light-heavyweight Anthony Todd (Darlington) beat Geoff Donaldson (Basingstoke) pts

Middleweight Mark Edwards (Royal Navy) beat Eric Noi (Moss Side) ko 1st

Light-middleweight Tim Taylor (Newco-Repton) beat Lee Ferrie (Triumph) pts

Welterweight Joe Calzache (Newbridge) beat Trevor French (Royal Navy) pts

Light-welterweight Jason Matthews (Abergoed) beat George Smith (Canvey Island) pts

Lightweight Paul Ramsey (Small Heath) Patrick Gallagher (Angel) did not contest final

Featherweight John Irwin (Tom Hill) beat Mark Bowers (Pinewood Star) pts

Bantamweight David Hardie (Gallowgate) beat Michael Gibbons (South Bank) pts

Flyweight Paul Ingle (Scarborough) beat Micky Horobin (St Pancras) pts

Light-flyweight Peter Culshaw (Huyton) beat Allan Mooney (Sydney Street) rsf 2nd

---

"I was ordered to clean shoes, make beds and even steal sweets from shops. No one should suffer from bullying."
Frank Bruno on his schooldays

"People may think I am mad to fight again, but it's in my blood."
Bruno

"He should come back. All Americans love beating up on poor old Frank."
Mike Tyson

"Whenever people ask me where Harry is I say he's in bed bonking. That soon shuts them up."
Bruno

"Once I got started it was always going to be a one-horse race. Ours is such a strong operation that it was always difficult to see the old school living with us. Now it will be impossible....The way I promote fights gives everyone a better deal. The fans see the fights they want, the boxers get paid better and I make a profit. Everyone is happy."
Barry Hearn after the Eubank-Benn fight

"He seems to think boxing is like snooker, that even if your man is hammered 17 frames to nil one day, he can go out the next day and do it all over again. He just chucks money around. I'm not doubting his honesty but in boxing terms he's a complete prat."
Frank Warren on Hearn

"He's a good promoter, a good publicist. But he interferes with other people's fighters. He approaches them direct and I have complained repeatedly to the board about this."
Mickey Duff on Hearn

THE HEAVYWEIGHT CHAMPIONS

Record of all world heavyweight champions in fights for the title

	Bouts	Won	Lost
James J Corbett	5	2	3
Bob Fitzsimmons	3	1	2
James J Jeffries	9	8	1
Marvin Hart	2	1	1
Tommy Burns (a)	13	11	1
Jack Johnson (a) (b)	11	5	1
Jess Willard (b)	3	1	1
Jack Dempsey	8	6	2
Gene Tunney	3	3	0
Max Schmeling	4	2	2
Jack Sharkey	3	1	2
Primo Carnera	4	3	1
Max Baer	2	1	1
James J Braddock	2	1	1
Joe Louis	27	26	1
Ezzard Charles	13	9	4
Jersey Joe Walcott	7	2	5
Rocky Marciano	7	7	0
Floyd Patterson	13	8	5
Ingemar Johansson	3	1	2
Sonny Liston	4	2	2
Muhammad Ali	25	22	3
Ernie Terrell	4	3	1
Joe Frazier	12	10	2
Jimmy Ellis	3	2	1
George Foreman	5	3	2
Leon Spinks	3	1	2
Ken Norton (c)	3	0	3
Larry Holmes	24	21	3
John Tate	2	1	1
Mike Weaver (a)	7	3	3
Mike Dokes (b)	3	1	1
Gerrie Coetzee	4	1	3
Tim Witherspoon	6	3	3
Pinklon Thomas	4	2	2
Greg Page	3	1	2
Tony Tubbs	3	1	2
Michael Spinks	4	3	1
Trevor Berbick	3	1	2
Mike Tyson	11	10	1
James Smith	3	1	2
Tony Tucker	2	1	1
Francesco Damiani (d)	3	2	1
James Douglas	2	1	1
Evander Holyfield	2	2	0
Ray Mercer (d)	1	1	0

(a) The records of Burns, Johnson, Weaver and Dokes include one draw

(b) The record of Johnson includes four "no-decisions" or "no-contests" and Willard's includes one

(c) Norton never won the world title; he was declared champion by the WBC in March 1978

(d) Recognised only by the World Boxing Organisation

WORLD CHAMPIONS

Heavyweight

1882	John L. Sullivan (US)	
1892	James J. Corbett (US)	
1897	Bob Fitzsimmons (GB)	
1899	James J. Jefferies (US)	
1905	Marvin Hart (US)	
1906	Tommy Burns (Can)	
1908	Jack Johnson (US)	
1915	Jess Willard (US)	
1919	Jack Dempsey (US)	
1926	Gene Tunney (US)	
1930	Max Schmeling (Ger)	
1932	Jack Sharkey (US)	
1933	Primo Carnera (Ita)	
1934	Max Baer (US)	
1935	James J. Braddock (US)	
1937	Joe Louis (US)	
1949	Ezzard Charles (US)	
1951	Jersey Joe Walcott (US)	
1952	Rocky Marciano (US)	
1956	Floyd Patterson (US)	
1959	Ingemar Johansson (Swe)	
1960	Floyd Patterson (US)	
1962	Sonny Liston (US)	
1964	Cassius Clay (US)	
1965	Ernie Terrell (US)	(WBA)
1968	Jimmy Ellis (US)	(WBA)
1970	Joe Frazier (US)	
1973	George Foreman (US)	
1974	Muhammad Ali (US)	
1978	Leon Spinks (US)	
1978	Ken Norton (US)	(WBC)
1978	Muhammad Ali (US)	(WBA)
1978	Larry Holmes (US)	(WBC)
1979	John Tate (US)	(WBA)
1980	Mike Weaver (US)	(WBA)
1982	Mike Dokes (US)	(WBA)
1983	Gerrie Coetzee (SA)	(WBA)
1984	Larry Holmes (US)	(IBF)

Cruiserweight

1979	Marvin Camel (US)	(WBC)
1980	Carlos de Leon (PR)	(WBC)
1982	Ossie Ocasio (PR)	(WBA)
1982	S.T. Gordon (US)	(WBC)
1983	Carlos de Leon (PR)	(WBC)
1983	Marvin Camel (US)	(IBF)
1984	Lee Roy Murphy (US)	(IBF)
1984	Piet Crous (SA)	(WBA)
1985	Alfonso Ratliff (US)	(WBC)
1985	Dwight Muhammad Qawi (US)	(WBA)
1985	Bernard Benton (US)	(WBC)
1986	Carlos de Leon (PR)	(WBC)
1986	Evander Holyfield (US)	(WBA)
1986	Rickey Parkey (US)	(IBF)
1987	Francesco Damiani (Ita)	(WBA)
1987	Evander Holyfield (US)	(IBF)
1988	Evander Holyfield (US)	
1989	Taoufik Belbouli (Fra)	(WBA)
1989	Carlos de Leon (PR)	(WBC)
1989	Glenn McCrory (GB)	(IBF)
1990	Jeff Lampkin (US)	(IBF)
1990	Magne Havnaa (Nor)	(WBO)
1990	Massimilio Duran (Ita)	(WBC)
1991	Bobby Czyz (US)	(WBA)
1991	Anaclet Wamba (Fra)	(WBC)

Light-Heavyweight

1903	Jack Root (Aut)	
1903	George Gardner (Ire)	
1903	Bob Fitzsimmons (GB)	
1905	Jack O'Brien (US)	
1912	Jack Dillon (US)	
1916	Battling Levinsky (US)	
1920	Georges Carpentier (Fra)	
1922	Battling Siki (Sen)	
1923	Mike McTigue (Ire)	
1925	Paul Berlenbach (US)	
1926	Jack Delaney (Can)	
1927	Jim Slattery (US)	

BOXING'S HIGHEST GUARANTEED PURSES

	Fighters	Year	Total Purse $ millions
1	Evander Holyfield (30) v Mike Tyson (15)	1991	$45
2	Mike Tyson (20) v Michael Spinks (13.5)	1988	$33.5
3	Evander Holyfield (20) v George Foreman (12)	1991	$32
4	James 'Buster' Douglas (19.5) v Evander Holyfield (8)	1990	$27.5
5	Sugar Ray Leonard (13) v Tommy Hearns (11)	1989 *	$24
6	Marvin Hagler (12) v Sugar Ray Leonard (11)	1987	$23

Figures in brackets indicate amount each boxer received in $ millions
* Re-match

1984	Tim Witherspoon (US)	(WBC)	1927	Tommy Loughran (US)	
1984	Pinklon Thomas (US)	(WBC)	1930	Jim Slattery (US)	
1984	Greg Page (US)	(WBA)	1930	Maxie Rosenbloom (US)	
1985	Michael Spinks (US)	(IBF)	1934	Bob Olin (US)	
1985	Tony Tubbs (US)	(WBA)	1935	John Henry Lewis (US)	
1986	Tim Witherspoon (US)	(WBA)	1939	Melio Bettina (US)	
1986	Trevor Berbick (Jam)	(WBC)	1939	Billy Conn (US)	
1986	James Smith (US)	(WBA)	1941	Anton Christoforidis (Gre)	
1987	Mike Tyson (US)	(WBA/WBC)	1941	Gus Lesnevich (US)	
1987	Tony Tucker (US)	(IBF)	1948	Freddie Mills (GB)	
1987	Mike Tyson (US)		1950	Joey Maxim (US)	
1989	Francesco Damiani (Ita)	(WBO)	1952	Archie Moore (US)	
1989	Mike Tyson (US)	(WBA/WBC/IBF)	1962	Harold Johnson (US)	
1990	James Douglas (US)	(WBAWBC/IBF)	1963	Willie Pastrano (US)	
1990	Evander Holyfield (US)	(WBC/WBA/IBF)	1965	Jose Torres (PR)	
1991	Ray Mercer (US)	(WBO)	1966	Dick Tiger (Nig)	

1968	Bob Foster (US)					
1971	Vicente Rondon (Ven)	(WBA)	1912	Billy Papke (US)		
1974	John Conteh (GB)	(WBC)	1913	Frank Klaus (US)		
1974	Victor Galindez (Arg)	(WBA)	1913	George Chip (US)		
1977	Miguel Cuello (Arg)	(WBC)	1914	Al McCoy (US)		
1978	Mate Parlov (Yug)	(WBC)	1917	Mike O'Dowd (US)		
1978	Mike Rossman (US)	(WBA)	1920	Johnny Wilson (US)		
1978	Marvin Johnson (US)	(WBC)	1923	Harry Greb (US)		
1979	Victor Galindez (Arg)	(WBA)	1926	Tiger Flowers (US)		
1979	Matthew Saad Muhammad (US)	(WBC)	1926	Mickey Walker (US)		
1979	Marvin Johnson (US)	(WBA)	1931	Gorilla Jones (US)		
1980	Eddie Mustafa Muhammad (US)	(WBA)	1932	Marcel Thil (Fra)		
1981	Michael Spinks (US)	(WBA)	1937	Fred Apostoli (US)		
1981	Dwight Muhammah Qawi (US)	(WBC)	1939	Ceferino Garcia (Phi)		
1983	Michael Spinks (US)		1940	Ken Overlin (US)		
1985	J.B. Williamson (US)	(WBC)	1941	Billy Soose (US)		
1985	Slobodan Kacar (Yug)	(IBF)	1941	Tony Zale (US)		
1986	Marvin Johnson (US)	(WBA)	1947	Rocky Graziano (US)		
1986	Dennis Andries (GB)	(WBC)	1948	Tony Zale (US)		

TOMMY HEARNS' SIX WORLD TITLES

Date	Opponent	Title
Aug 2 1980	Pipino Cuevas (Mex)	WBA welterweight
Dec 3 1982	Wilfred Benitez (US)	WBC Junior-middleweight
Mar 7 1987	Dennis Andries (GB)	WBC Light-heavyweight
Oct 29 1987	Juan Roldan (Arg)	WBC Middleweight
Nov 4 1988	James Kinchen (US)	WBO Super-middleweight
Jun 3 1991	Virgil Hill (US)	WBA Light-heavyweight

1986	Bobby Czyz (US)	(IBF)	1948	Marcel Cerdan (Alg)	
1987	Thomas Hearns (US)	(WBC)	1949	Jake la Motta (US)	
1987	Leslie Stewart (Jam)	(WBA)	1951	Sugar Ray Robinson (US)	
1987	Virgil Hill (US)	(WBA)	1951	Randolph Turpin (GB)	
1987	Prince Charles Williams (US)	(IBF)	1951	Sugar Ray Robinson (US)	
1988	Donny Lalonde (Can)	(WBC)	1953	Carl Bobo Olsen (Haw)	
1988	Sugar Ray Leonard (US)	(WBC)	1955	Sugar Ray Robinson (US)	
1988	Michael Moorer (US)	(WBO)	1957	Gene Fullmer (US)	
1989	Dennis Andries (GB)	(WBC)	1957	Sugar Ray Robinson (US)	
1989	Jeff Harding (Aus)	(WBC)	1957	Carmen Basilio (US)	
1990	Dennis Andries (GB)	(WBC)	1958	Sugar Ray Robinson (US)	
1991	Leeonzer Barber (US)	(WBO)	1960	Paul Pender (US)	
1991	Thomas Hearns (US)	(WBA)	1961	Terry Downes (GB)	

Super-Middleweight

1984	Murray Sutherland (Can)	(IBF)	1962	Paul Pender (US)	
1984	Chong-Pal Park (SKo)	(WBA)	1962	Dick Tiger (Nig)	
1988	Graciano Rocchigniani (FRG)	(IBF)	1963	Joey Giardello (US)	
1988	Fulgencio Obelmejias (Ven)	(WBA)	1965	Dick Tiger (Nig)	
1988	Sugar Ray Leonard (US)	(WBC)	1966	Emile Griffith (VI)	
1988	Thomas Hearns (US)	(WBO)	1968	Nino Benvenuti (Ita)	
1989	In-Chul Baek (SKo)	(WBA)	1970	Carlos Monzon (Arg)	
1990	Lindell Holmes (US)	(IBF)	1974	Rodrigo Valdez (Col)	(WBC)
1990	Christophe Tiozzo (Fra)	(WBA)	1976	Carlos Monzon (Arg)	
1990	Mauro Galvano (Ita)	(WBC)	1977	Rodrigo Valdez (Col)	
1991	Victor Cordoba (Pan)	(WBA)	1978	Hugo Corro (Arg)	
1991	Darrin van Horn (US)	(IBF)	1979	Vito Antuofermo (Ita)	

Middleweight

			1980	Alan Minter (GB)	
1891	Nonpareil Jack Dempsey (Ire)		1980	Marvin Hagler (US)	
1891	Bob Fitzsimmons (GB)		1987	Sugar Ray Leonard (US)	(WBC)
1897	Kid McCoy (US)		1987	Frank Tate (US)	(IBF)
1898	Tommy Ryan (US)		1987	Sumbu Kalambay (Zai)	(WBA)
1908	Stanley Ketchel (US)		1987	Thomas Hearns (US)	(WBC)
1908	Billy Papke (US)		1988	Iran Barkley (US)	(WBC)
1908	Stanley Ketchel (US)		1988	Michael Nunn (US)	(IBF)
1910	Billy Papke (US)		1989	Roberto Duran (Pan)	(WBC)
1911	Cyclone Thompson (US)		1989	Mike McCallum (US)	(WBA)
1911	Billy Papke (US)		1990	Nigel Benn (GB)	(WBO)
1912	Frank Mantell (US)		1990	Chris Eubank (GB)	(WBO)
			1990	Julian Jackson (VI)	(WBC)
			1991	James Toney (US)	(IBF)

Junior-Middleweight

1962	Denny Moyer (US)	
1963	Ralph Dupas (US)	
1963	Sandro Mazzinghi (Ita)	
1965	Nino Benvenuti (Ita)	
1966	Ki-Soo Kim (SKo)	
1968	Sandro Mazzinghi (Ita)	
1969	Freddie Little (US)	
1970	Carmelo Bossi (Ita)	
1971	Koichi Wajima (Jap)	
1974	Oscar Albarado (US)	
1975	Koichi Wajima (Jap)	
1975	Miguel de Oliviera (Bra)	(WBC)
1975	Jae-Do Yuh (SKo)	(WBA)
1975	Elisha Obed (Bah)	(WBC)
1976	Koichi Wajima (Jap)	(WBA)
1976	Jose Duran (Spa)	(WBA)
1976	Eckhard Dagge (FRG)	(WBC)
1976	Angel Castellini (Arg)	(WBA)
1977	Eddie Gazo (Nic)	(WBA)
1977	Rocky Mattioli (Ita)	(WBC)
1978	Masashi Kudo (Jap)	(WBA)
1979	Maurice Hope (GB)	(WBC)
1979	Ayube Kalule (Uga)	(WBA)
1981	Wilfred Benitez (US)	(WBC)
1981	Sugar Ray Leonard (US)	(WBA)
1981	Tadashi Mihara (Jap)	(WBA)
1982	Davey Moore (US)	(WBA)
1982	Thomas Hearns (US)	(WBC)
1983	Roberto Duran (Pan)	(WBA)
1984	Mark Medal (US)	(IBF)
1984	Mike McCallum (Jam)	(WBA)
1984	Carlos Santos (PR)	(IBF)
1986	Buster Drayton (US)	(IBF)
1986	Duane Thomas (US)	(WBC)
1987	Matthew Hilton (Can)	(IBF)
1987	Lupe Aquino (Mex)	(WBC)
1988	Gianfranco Rosi (Ita)	(WBC)
1988	Don Curry (US)	(WBC)
1988	Julian Jackson (VI)	(WBA)
1988	Robert Hines (US)	(IBF)
1988	John David Jackson (US)	(WBO)
1989	Darrin van Horn (US)	(IBF)
1989	René Jacquot (Fra)	(WBC)
1989	John Mugabi (Uga)	(WBC)
1989	Gianfranco Rosi (Ita)	(IBF)
1990	Terry Norris (US)	(WBC)
1991	Gilbert Dele (Fra)	(WBA)

Welterweight

1892	Billy Smith (US)	
1894	Tommy Ryan (US)	
1898	Billy Smith (US)	
1900	Rube Ferns (US)	
1900	Matty Matthews (US)	
1901	Rube Ferns (US)	
1901	Joe Walcott (Bar)	
1904	Dixie Kid (US)	
1905	Joe Walcott (Bar)	
1906	Honey Mellody (US)	
1907	Mike Sullivan (US)	
1908	Harry Lewis (US)	
1914	Waldemar Holberg (Den)	
1914	Tom McCormick (Ire)	
1914	Matt Wells (GB)	
1915	Mike Glover (US)	
1915	Jack Britton (US)	
1915	Ted Kid Lewis (GB)	
1916	Jack Britton (US)	
1917	Ted Kid Lewis (GB)	
1919	Jack Britton (US)	

1922	Mickey Walker (US)	
1926	Pete Latzo (US)	
1927	Joe Dundee (Ita)	
1928	Jack Thompson (US)	
1929	Jackie Fields (US)	
1930	Jack Thompson (US)	
1930	Tommy Freeman (US)	
1931	Jack Thompson (US)	
1931	Lou Brouillard (Can)	
1932	Jackie Fields (US)	
1933	Young Corbett III (US)	
1933	Jimmy McLarnin (Ire)	
1934	Barney Ross (US)	
1934	Jimmy McLarnin (Ire)	
1935	Barney Ross (US)	
1938	Henry Armstrong (US)	
1940	Fritzie Zivic (US)	
1941	Red Cochrane (US)	
1946	Marty Servo (US)	
1946	Sugar Ray Robinson (US)	
1951	Johnny Bratton (US)	
1951	Kid Gavilan (Cub)	
1954	Johnny Saxton (US)	
1955	Tony de Marco (US)	
1955	Carmen Basilio (US)	
1956	Johnny Saxton (US)	
1956	Carmen Basilio (US)	
1958	Virgil Atkins (US)	
1958	Don Jordon (Dom)	
1960	Benny Kid Paret (Cub)	
1961	Emile Griffith (VI)	
1961	Benny Kid Paret (Cub)	
1962	Emile Griffith (VI)	
1963	Louis Rodriguez (Cub)	
1963	Emile Griffith (VI)	
1966	Curtis Cokes (US)	
1969	Jose Napoles (Cub)	
1970	Billy Backus (US)	
1971	Jose Napoles (Cub)	
1975	Angel Espada (PR)	(WBA)
1975	John H. Stracey (GB)	(WBC)
1976	Carlos Palomino (Mex)	(WBC)
1976	Pipino Cuevas (Mex)	(WBA)
1979	Wilfred Benitez (US)	(WBC)
1979	Sugar Ray Leonard (US)	(WBC)
1980	Roberto Duran (Pan)	(WBC)
1980	Thomas Hearns (US)	(WBA)
1980	Sugar Ray Leonard (US)	(WBC)
1981	Sugar Ray Leonard (US)	
1983	Don Curry (US)	(WBA)
1983	Milton McCrory (US)	(WBC)
1984	Don Curry (US)	(IBF)
1985	Don Curry (US)	
1986	Lloyd Honeyghan (GB)	
1987	Mark Breland (US)	(WBA)
1987	Lloyd Honeyghan (GB)	(WBC/IBF)
1987	Marlon Starling (US)	(WBA)
1987	Jorge Vaca (Mex)	(WBC)
1988	Simon Brown (Jam)	(IBF)
1988	Tomas Molinares (Col)	(WBA)
1988	Lloyd Honeyghan (GB)	(WBC)
1989	Mark Breland (US)	(WBA)
1989	Marlon Starling (US)	(WBC)
1989	Genaro Leon (Mex)	(WBO)
1990	Aaron Davis (US)	(WBA)
1990	Maurice Blocker (US)	(WBC)
1991	Meldrick Taylor (US)	(WBA)

Junior-Welterweight

1922	Pinky Mitchell (US)	
1926	Mushy Callahan (US)	

1930	Jackie Kid Berg (GB)	
1931	Tony Canzoneri (US)	
1932	Johnny Jaddick (US)	
1933	Battling Shaw (Mex)	
1933	Tony Canzoneri (US)	
1933	Barney Ross (US)	
1946	Tippy Larkin (US)	
1959	Carlos Ortiz (PR)	
1969	Duilio Loi (Ita)	
1962	Eddie Perkins (US)	
1962	Duilio Loi (Ita)	
1963	Roberto Cruz (Phi)	
1963	Eddie Perkins (US)	
1965	Carlos Hernandez (Ven)	
1966	Sandro Lopoplo (Ita)	
1967	Paul Fujii (Haw)	
1968	Nicolino Loche (Arg)	(WBA)
1968	Pedro Adigue (Phi)	(WBC)
1970	Bruno Acari (Ita)	(WBC)
1972	Alfonso Frazer (Pan)	(WBA)
1972	Antonio Cervantes (Col)	(WBA)
1974	Perico Fernandez (Spa)	(WBC)
1975	Saensak Muangsurin (Tha)	(WBC)
1976	Wilfred Benitez (US)	(WBA)
1976	Miguel Velasquez (Spa)	(WBC)
1976	Saensak Muangsurin (Tha)	(WBC)
1977	Antonio Cervantes (Col)	(WBA)
1978	Sang-Hyun Kim (SKo)	(WBC)
1980	Saoul Mamby (US)	(WBC)
1980	Aaron Pryor (US)	(WBA)
1982	Leroy Haley (US)	(WBC)
1983	Aaron Pryor (US)	(IBF)
1983	Bruce Curry (US)	(WBC)
1984	Johnny Bumphus (US)	(WBA)
1984	Billy Costello (US)	(WBC)
1984	Gene Hatcher (US)	(WBA)
1985	Ubaldo Sacco (Arg)	(WBA)
1985	Lonnie Smith (US)	(WBC)
1986	Patrizio Oliva (Ita)	(WBA)
1986	Gary Hinton (US)	(IBF)
1986	René Arredondo (Mex)	(WBC)
1986	Tsuyoshi Hamada (Jap)	(WBC)
1986	Joe Louis Manley (US)	(IBF)
1987	Terry Marsh (GB)	(IBF)
1987	Juan Martin Coggi (Arg)	(WBA)
1987	René Arredondo (Mex)	(WBC)
1988	James Buddy McGirt (US)	(IBF)
1988	Roger Mayweather (US)	(WBC)
1988	Meldrick Taylor (US)	(IBF)
1989	Hector Camacho (PR)	(WBO)
1989	Julio Cesar Chavez (Mex)	(WBC)
1990	Loreto Garza (US)	(WBA)
1991	Greg Haugen (US)	(WBO)
1991	Hector Camacho (US)	(WBO)
1991	Edwin Rosario (PR)	(WBA)

Lightweight

1896	George Lavigne (US)	
1899	Frank Erne (Swi)	
1902	Joe Gans (US)	
1908	Battling Nelson (Den)	
1910	Ad Wolgast (US)	
1912	Willie Ritchie (US)	
1914	Freddie Welsh (GB)	
1917	Benny Leonard (US)	
1925	Jimmy Goodrich (US)	
1925	Rocky Kansas (US)	
1926	Sammy Mandell (US)	
1930	Al Singer (US)	
1930	Tony Canzoneri (US)	
1933	Barney Ross (US)	
1935	Tony Canzoneri (US)	

1936	Lou Ambers (US)	
1938	Henry Armstrong (US)	
1939	Lou Ambers (US)	
1940	Lew Jenkins (US)	
1941	Sammy Angott (US)	
1942	Beau Jack (US)	
1943	Bob Montgomery (US)	
1943	Sammy Angott (US)	
1944	Juan Zurita (Mex)	
1945	Ike Williams (US)	
1951	Jimmy Carter (US)	
1952	Lauro Salas (Mex)	
1952	Jimmy Carter (US)	
1954	Paddy de Marco (US)	
1954	Jimmy Carter (US)	
1955	Wallace Bud Smith (US)	
1956	Joe Brown (US)	
1962	Carlos Ortiz (PR)	
1965	Ismael Laguna (Pan)	
1965	Carlos Ortiz (PR)	
1968	Carlos Teo Cruz (Dom)	
1969	Mando Ramos (US)	
1970	Ismael Laguna (Pan)	
1970	Ken Buchanan (GB)	(WBA)
1971	Pedro Carrasco (Spa)	(WBC)
1972	Mando Ramos (US)	(WBC)
1972	Roberto Duran (Pan)	(WBA)
1972	Chango Carmona (Mex)	(WBC)
1972	Rodolfo Gonzalez (Mex)	(WBC)
1974	Guts Ishimatsu (Jap)	(WBC)
1976	Esteban de Jesus (PR)	(WBC)
1978	Roberto Duran (Pan)	
1979	Jim Watt (GB)	(WBC)
1979	Ernesto Espana (Ven)	(WBA)
1980	Hilmer Kenty (US)	(WBA)
1981	Sean O'Grady (US)	(WBA)
1981	Alexis Arguello (Nic)	(WBC)
1981	Claude Noel (Tri)	(WBA)
1981	Arturo Frias (US)	(WBA)
1982	Ray Mancini (US)	(WBA)
1983	Edwin Rosario (PR)	(WBC)
1984	Charlie Brown (US)	(IBF)
1984	Livingstone Bramble (US)	(WBA)
1984	Harry Arroyo (US)	(IBF)
1984	Jose Luis Ramirez (Mex)	(WBC)
1985	Jimmy Paul (US)	(IBF)
1985	Hector Camacho (PR)	(WBC)
1986	Edwin Rosario (PR)	(WBA)
1986	Greg Haugen (US)	(IBF)
1987	Vinny Pazienza (US)	(IBF)
1987	Jose Luis Ramirez (Mex)	(WBC)
1987	Julio Cesar Chavez (Mex)	(WBA)
1988	Greg Haugen (US)	(IBF)
1988	Julio Cesar Chavez (Mex)	(WBC/WBA)
1989	Amancio Castro (Col)	(WBO)
1989	Pernell Whitaker (US)	(IBF)
1989	Mauricio Aceves (PR)	(WBO)
1989	Edwin Rosario (PR)	(WBA)
1990	Juan Nazario (PR)	(WBA)
1990	Pernell Whitaker (US)	(WBC/WBA/IBF)
1990	Dingaan Thobela (SAf)	(WBO)

Super-Featherweight

1921	Johnny Dundee (Ita)	
1923	Jack Bernstein (US)	
1923	Johnny Dundee (Ita)	
1924	Kid Sullivan (US)	
1925	Mike Ballerino (US)	
1925	Tod Morgan (US)	
1929	Benny Bass (US)	
1931	Kid Chocolate (Cub)	
1933	Frankie Klick (US)	

Year	Boxer	Org
1959	Harold Gomes (US)	
1960	Flash Elorde (Phi)	
1967	Yoshiaki Numata (Jap)	
1967	Hiroshi Kobayashi (Jap)	
1969	Rene Barrientos (Phi)	(WBC)
1970	Yoshiaki Numata (Jap)	(WBC)
1971	Alfredo Marcano (Ven)	(WBA)
1971	Ricardo Aredondo (Mex)	(WBC)
1972	Ben Villaflor (Phi)	(WBA)
1973	Kuniaki Shibata (Jap)	(WBA)
1973	Ben Villaflor (Phi)	(WBA)
1974	Kuniaki Shibata (Jap)	(WBC)
1975	Alfredo Escalera (PR)	(WBC)
1976	Sam Serrano (PR)	(WBA)
1978	Alexis Arguello (Nic)	(WBC)
1980	Yasutsune Vehare (Jap)	(WBA)
1980	Rafael Limon (Mex)	(WBC)
1981	Cornelius Boza Edwards (Uga)	(WBC)
1981	Sam Serrano (PR)	(WBA)
1981	Rolando Navarette (Phi)	(WBC)
1982	Rafael Limon (Mex)	(WBC)
1982	Bobby Chacon (US)	(WBC)
1983	Roger Mayweather (US)	(WBA)
1983	Hector Camacho (PR)	(WBC)
1984	Rocky Lockridge (US)	(WBA)
1984	Hwan-Kil Yuh (SKo)	(IBF)
1984	Julio Cesar Chavez (Mex)	(WBC)
1985	Lester Ellis (Aus)	(IBF)
1985	Wilfredo Gomez (PR)	(WBA)
1985	Barry Michael (Aus)	(IBF)
1986	Alfredo Layne (Pan)	(WBA)
1986	Brian Mitchell (SA)	(WBA)
1987	Julio Cesar Chavez (Mex)	(WBC)
1987	Rocky Lockridge (US)	(IBF)
1988	Azumah Nelson (Gha)	(WBC)
1988	Tony Lopez (US)	(IBF)
1989	Juan Molina (PR)	(WBO)
1990	Tony Lopez (US)	(IBF)
1991	Joey Gamache (US)	(WBA)

Featherweight

Year	Boxer	Org
1891	Young Griffo (Aus)	
1892	George Dixon (Can)	
1897	Solly Smith (US)	
1898	Dave Sullivan (Ire)	
1898	George Dixon (Can)	
1900	Terry McGovern (US)	
1901	Young Corbett II (US)	
1904	Jimmy Britt (US)	
1904	Tommy Sullivan (US)	
1906	Abe Attell (US)	
1912	Johnny Kilbane (US)	
1923	Eugene Criqui (Fra)	
1923	Johnny Dundee (Ita)	
1925	Kid Kaplan (US)	
1927	Benny Bass (US)	
1928	Tony Canzoneri (US)	
1928	André Routis (Fra)	
1929	Battling Battalino (US)	
1932	Kid Chocolate (Cub)	
1933	Freddie Miller (US)	
1936	Petey Sarron (US)	
1937	Henry Armstrong (US)	
1938	Joey Archibald (US)	
1940	Harry Jeffra (US)	
1941	Joey Archibald (US)	
1941	Chalky Wright (Mex)	
1942	Willie Pep (US)	
1948	Sandy Saddler (US)	
1949	Willie Pep (US)	
1950	Sandy Saddler (US)	

Year	Boxer	Org
1957	Hogan Kid Bassey (Nig)	
1959	Davey Moore (US)	
1963	Sugar Ramos (Cub)	
1964	Vicente Saldivar (Mex)	
1968	Howard Winstone (GB)	(WBC)
1968	Raul Rojas (US)	(WBA)
1968	Jose Legra (Cub)	(WBC)
1968	Shozo Saijyo (Jap)	(WBA)
1969	Johnny Famechon (Fra)	(WBC)
1970	Vicente Saldivar (Mex)	(WBC)
1970	Kuniaki Shibata (Jap)	(WBC)
1971	Antonio Gomez (Ven)	(WBA)
1972	Clemente Sanchez (Mex)	(WBC)
1972	Ernesto Marcel (Pan)	(WBA)
1972	Jose Legra (Cub)	(WBC)
1973	Eder Jofre (Bra)	(WBC)
1974	Ruben Olivares (Mex)	(WBA)
1974	Bobby Chacon (US)	(WBC)
1974	Alexis Arguello (Nic)	(WBA)
1975	Ruben Olivares (Mex)	(WBC)
1975	David Kotey (Gha)	(WBC)
1976	Danny Lopez (US)	(WBC)
1977	Rafael Ortega (Pan)	(WBA)
1977	Cecilio Lastra (Spa)	(WBA)
1978	Eusebio Pedroza (Pan)	(WBA)
1980	Salvador Sanchez (Mex)	(WBC)
1982	Juan Laporte (PR)	(WBC)
1984	Min-Keum Oh (SKo)	(IBF)
1984	Wilfredo Gomez (PR)	(WBC)
1984	Azumah Nelson (Gha)	(WBC)
1985	Barry McGuigan (Ire)	(WBA)
1985	Ki-Young Chung (SKo)	(IBF)
1986	Steve Cruz (US)	(WBA)
1986	Antonio Rivera (PR)	(IBF)
1987	Antonio Esparragoza (Ven)	(WBA)
1988	Calvin Grove (US)	(IBF)
1988	Jeff Fenech (Aus)	(WBC)
1988	Jorge Paez (Mex)	(IBF)
1989	Maurizio Stecca (Ita)	(WBO)
1990	Marcos Villasana (Mex)	(WBC)
1990	Jorge Paez	(IBF/WBO)
1991	Maurizio Stecca (Ita)	(WBO)
1991	Pak Yung-Kyun (SKo)	(WBA)
1991	Troy Dorsey (US)	(IBF)
1991	Manuel Medina (Mex)	(IBF)

Junior-Featherweight

Year	Boxer	Org
1922	Jack Kid Wolfe (US)	
1923	Carl Duane (US)	
1976	Rigoberto Riasca (Pan)	(WBC)
1976	Royal Kobayashi (Jap)	(WBC)
1976	Dong-Kyun Yum (SKo)	(WBC)
1977	Wilfredo Gomez (PR)	(WBC)
1977	Soo-Hwan Hong (SKo)	(WBA)
1978	Ricardo Cardona (Col)	(WBA)
1980	Leo Randolph (US)	(WBA)
1980	Sergio Palma (Arg)	(WBA)
1982	Leo Cruz (Dom)	(WBA)
1983	Jaime Garza (US)	(WBC)
1983	Bobby Berna (Phi)	(IBF)
1984	Loris Stecca (Ita)	(WBA)
1984	Seung-Il Suh (SKo)	(IBF)
1984	Victor Callejas (PR)	(WBA)
1984	Juan Meza (Mex)	(WBC)
1985	Ji-Won Kim (SKo)	(IBF)
1985	Lupe Pintot (Mex)	(WBC)
1986	Samart Payakarun (Tha)	(WBC)
1987	Louis Espinoza (US)	(WBA)
1987	Seung-Hoon Lee (SKo)	(IBF)
1987	Jeff Fenech (Aus)	(WBC)
1987	Julio Gervacio (Dom)	(WBA)

1988	Bernardo Pinango (Ven)	(WBA)
1988	Daniel Zaragoza (Mex)	(WBC)
1988	Jose Sanabria (Ven)	(IBF)
1988	Juan Jose Estrada (Mex)	(WBA)
1989	Fabrice Benichou (Fra)	(IBF)
1989	Kenny Mitchell (US)	(WBO)
1990	Welcome Ncita (SAf)	(IBF)
1990	Paul Banke (US)	(WBC)
1990	Orlando Fernandez (PR)	(WBO)
1990	Luis Mendoza (Col)	(WBA)
1990	Pedro Decima (Arg)	(WBC)
1991	Kiyoshi Hatanaka (Jap)	(WBC)
1991	Jesse Benevides (US)	(WBO)
1991	Daniel Zaragoza (Mex)	(WBC)

Bantamweight

1891	George Dixon (Can)	
1892	Billy Plimmer (GB)	
1895	Pedlar Palmer (GB)	
1899	Terry McGovern (US)	
1901	Harry Forbes (US)	
1903	Frankie Neil (US)	
1904	Joe Bowker (GB)	
1905	Jimmy Walsh (US)	
1907	Owen Moran (GB)	
1908	Johnny Coulon (Can)	
1914	Kid Williams (Den)	
1917	Pete Herman (US)	
1920	Joe Lynch (US)	
1921	Pete Herman (US)	
1921	Johnny Buff (US)	
1922	Joe Lynch (US)	
1924	Abe Goldstein (US)	
1924	Eddie Martin (US)	
1925	Charlie Rosenberg (US)	
1927	Bud Taylor (US)	
1928	Bushy Graham (Ita)	
1929	Al Brown (Pan)	
1935	Baltazar Sangchilli (Spa)	
1936	Tony Marino (US)	
1936	Sixto Escobar (Spa)	
1937	Harry Jeffra (US)	
1938	Sixto Escobar (Spa)	

1940	Lou Salica (US)	
1942	Manuel Ortiz (US)	
1947	Harold Dade (US)	
1947	Manuel Ortiz (US)	
1950	Vic Toweel (SA)	
1952	Jimmy Carruthers (Aus)	
1954	Robert Cohen (Alg)	
1956	Mario D'Agata (Ita)	
1957	Alphonse Halimi (Alg)	
1959	Joe Becerra (Mex)	
1960	Eder Jofre (Bra)	
1965	Fighting Harada (Jap)	
1968	Lionel Rose (Aus)	
1969	Ruben Olivares (Mex)	
1970	Chucho Castillo (Mex)	
1971	Ruben Olivares (Mex)	
1972	Rafael Herrera (Mex)	
1972	Enrique Pinder (Pan)	
1973	Romeo Anaya (Mex)	(WBA)
1973	Rafael Herrera (Mex)	(WBC)
1973	Arnold Taylor (SA)	(WBA)
1974	Soo-Hwan Hong (SKo)	(WBA)
1974	Rudolfo Martinez (Mex)	(WBC)
1975	Alfonso Zamora (Mex)	(WBA)
1976	Carlos Zarate (Mex)	(WBC)
1977	Jorge Lujan (Pan)	(WBA)
1979	Lupe Pintor (Mex)	(WBC)
1980	Julian Solis (PR)	(WBA)
1980	Jeff Changler (US)	(WBA)
1983	Alberto Davila (US)	(WBC)
1984	Richard Sandoval (US)	(WBA)
1984	Satoshi Shingaki (Jap)	(IBF)
1985	Jeff Fenech (Aus)	(IBF)
1985	Daniel Zaragoza (Mex)	(WBC)
1985	Miguel Lora (Col)	(WBC)
1986	Gaby Canizales (US)	(WBA)
1986	Bernardo Pinanago (Ven)	(WBA)
1987	Takuya Muguruma (Jap)	(WBA)
1987	Kelvin Seabrooks (US)	(IBF)
1987	Chang-Young Park (SKo)	(WBA)
1987	Wilfredo Vasquez (PR)	(WBA)
1988	Kaokor Galaxy (Tha)	(WBA)
1988	Orlando Canizales (US)	(IBF)

---

ff **Statistics compiled by Michigan State University and the Michigan Rural Safety Council show at least 24 people died in accidents on Michigan farms in 1988. In addition, it is estimated that 8,000 people were injured in farm accidents for the same period. No wonder Jess Willard came off the farm to fight Jack Johnson. It was far safer."**
Bert Randolph Sugar, Boxing Illustrated

"He's asked that I speak freely and completely, so I'll tell you my diagnosis that it was a post-traumatic Parkinsonism due to injuries from fighting...My assumption is that his physical condition resulted from repeated blows to the head over time."
Dr Stanley Fahn, neurologist, who examined Muhammad Ali in 1984

"For me, boxing is therapy. I'd rather do this than sit on a shrink's couch and talk for hours."
Mickey Rourke, actor, on his pro debut

"Boxing's corrupt, life's corrupt, everything's corrupt."
Jeff Fenech, Australian boxer, after controversially failing to win world title

"I never liked you the first time I saw you."
Najib Daho on his opponent Carl Crook

"I actually think he's a likeable guy."
Crook on Daho

"TV is responsible for having four champions at every weight. It might look good to bill a fight as a championship of the world, but I think it's disgusting and bad for boxing. All they've done is devalue a world title."
Barry McGuigan, former WBA featherweight champion

"He's like the old-fashioned waltz. He's coming round again."
Mickey Duff on Lloyd Honeyghan

"Only wimps worry about getting hit. Me, I'm a winner, I'm a warrior, I'm a trojan." **JJ**
Honeyghan

1988	Sung-Kil Moon (SKo)	(WBA)
1988	Raul Perez (Mex)	(WBC)
1989	Israel Contreras (Ven)	(WBO)
1989	Kaokor Galaxy (Tha)	(WBA)
1990	Luisito Espinosa (Phi)	(WBA)
1991	Greg Richardson (US)	(WBC)
1991	Gaby Canizales (US)	(WBO)
1991	Duke McKenzie (GB)	(WBO)

Super-Flyweight

1980	Rafael Orono (Ven)	(WBC)
1981	Chul-Ho Kim (SKo)	(WBC)
1981	Gustavo Ballas (Arg)	(WBA)
1981	Rafael Pedroza (Pan)	(WBA)
1982	Jiro Watanabe (Jap)	(WBA)
1982	Rafael Orono (Ven)	(WBC)
1983	Payao Poontarat (Tha)	(WBC)
1983	Joo-Do Chun (SKo)	(IBF)
1984	Jiro Watanabe (Jap)	(WBC)
1984	Kaosai Galaxy (Tha)	(WBA)
1985	Ellyas Pical (Ina)	(IBF)
1986	Cesar Polanco (Dom)	(IBF)
1986	Gilberto Roman (Mex)	(WBC)
1986	Tae-Il Chang (SKo)	(IBF)
1986	Ellyas Pical (Ina)	(IBF)
1987	Santos Laciar (Arg)	(WBC)
1987	Jesus Rojas (Col)	(WBC)
1988	Gilberto Roman (Mex)	(WBC)
1989	Jose Ruiz (PR)	(WBO)
1990	Moon Sung-Kil (SKo)	(WBC)
1990	Roberto Quiroga (US)	(IBF)

Flyweight

1913	Sid Smith (GB)	
1913	Bill Ladbury (GB)	
1914	Percy Jones (GB)	
1915	Joe Symonds (GB)	
1916	Jimmy Wilde (GB)	
1923	Pancho Villa (Phi)	
1925	Fidel la Barba (US)	
1928	Frankie Genaro (US)	
1929	Emile Pladner (Fra)	
1929	Frankie Genaro (US)	
1931	Young Perez (Tun)	
1932	Jackie Brown (GB)	
1935	Benny Lynch (GB)	
1938	Peter Kane (GB)	
1943	Jackie Paterson (GB)	
1948	Rinty Monaghan (GB)	
1950	Terry Allen (GB)	
1950	Dado Marino (Haw)	
1952	Yoshio Shirai (Jap)	
1954	Pascual Perez (Arg)	
1960	Pone Kingpetch (Tha)	
1960	Fighting Harada (Jap)	
1963	Pone Kingpetch (Tha)	
1963	Hiroyuki Ebihara (Jap)	
1964	Pone Kingpetch (Tha)	
1965	Salvatore Burruni (Ita)	
1966	Horacio Accavallo (Arg)	(WBA)
1966	Walter McGowan (GB)	(WBC)
1966	Chartchai Chionoi (Tha)	(WBC)
1969	Efren Torres (Mex)	(WBC)
1969	Hiroyuki Ebihara (Jap)	(WBA)
1969	Bernabe Villacampo (Phi)	(WBA)
1970	Chartchai Chionoi (Tha)	(WBC)
1970	Berkrerk Chartvanchai (Tha)	(WBA)
1970	Masao Ohba (Jap)	(WBA)
1970	Erbito Salavarria (Phi)	(WBC)
1972	Venice Borkorsor (Tha)	(WBC)
1973	Chartchai Chionoi (Tha)	(WBA)
1973	Betulio Gonzalez (Ven)	(WBC)

1974	Shoji Oguma (Jap)	(WBC)
1974	Susumu Hanagata (Jap)	(WBA)
1975	Miguel Canto (Mex)	(WBC)
1975	Erbito Salavarria (Phi)	(WBA)
1976	Alfonso Lopez (Pan)	(WBA)
1976	Guty Espadas (Mex)	(WBA)
1978	Betulio Gonzalez (Ven)	(WBA)
1979	Chan-Hee Park (SKo)	(WBC)
1979	Luis Ibarra (Pan)	(WBA)
1980	Tae-Shik Kim (SKo)	(WBA)
1980	Shoji Oguma (Jap)	(WBA)
1980	Peter Mathebula (SA)	(WBA)
1981	Santos Laciar (Arg)	(WBA)
1981	Antonio Avelar (Mex)	(WBC)
1981	Luis Ibarra (Pan)	(WBA)
1981	Juan Herrera (Mex)	(WBA)
1982	Prudencio Cardona (Col)	(WBC)
1982	Santos Laciar (Arg)	(WBA)
1982	Freddie Castillo (Mex)	(WBC)
1982	Eleoncio Mercedes (Dom)	(WBC)
1983	Charlie Magri (GB)	(WBC)
1983	Frank Cedeno (Phi)	(WBC)
1983	Soon-Chun Kwon (SKo)	(IBF)
1984	Koji Kobayashi (Jap)	(WBC)
1984	Gabriel Bernal (Mex)	(WBC)
1984	Sot Chitalada (Tha)	(WBC)
1985	Hilario Zapata (Pan)	(WBA)
1985	Chong-Kwan Chung (SKo)	(IBF)
1986	Bi-Won Chung (SKo)	(IBF)
1986	Hi-Sup Shin (SKo)	(IBF)
1987	Fidel Bassa (Col)	(WBA)
1987	Dodie Penalosa (Phi)	(IBF)
1987	Chang-Ho Choi (SKo)	(IBF)
1988	Rolando Bohol (Phi)	(IBF)
1988	Yung-Kang Kim (SKo)	(WBC)
1988	Duke McKenzie (GB)	(IBF)
1989	Elvis Alvarez (Col)	(WBO)
1989	Sot Chitalada (Tha)	(WBC)
1989	Dave McAuley (GB)	(IBF)
1990	Lee Yul-Woo (SKo)	(WBA)
1990	Leonard Tamakuma (Jap)	(WBA)
1990	Isidiro Perez (Mex)	(WBO)
1991	Muangchai Kittikasem (Tha)	(WBC)
1991	Elvis Alvarez (Col)	(WBA)
1991	Kim Yong-kang (SKo)	(WBA)

Junior-Flyweight

1975	Franco Udella (Ita)	(WBC)
1975	Jaime Rios (Pan)	(WBA)
1975	Luis Estaba (Ven)	(WBC)
1976	Juan Jose Guzman (Dom)	(WBA)
1976	Yoko Gushiken (Jap)	(WBA)
1978	Freddie Castillo (Mex)	(WBC)
1978	Netrnoi Vorasingh (Tha)	(WBC)
1978	Sung-Jun Kim (SKo)	(WBC)
1980	Shigeo Nakajima (Jap)	(WBC)
1980	Hilario Zapata (Pan)	(WBC)
1981	Pedro Flores (Mex)	(WBA)
1981	Hwan-Jin Kim (SKo)	(WBA)
1981	Katsuo Takashiki (Jap)	(WBA)
1982	Amado Ursua (Mex)	(WBC)
1982	Tadashi Tomori (Jap)	(WBC)
1982	Hilario Zapata (Pan)	(WBC)
1983	Jung-Koo Chang (Kor)	(WBC)
1983	Lupe Madera (Mex)	(WBA)
1983	Dodie Penalosa (Phi)	(IBF)
1984	Francisco Quiroz (Dom)	(WBA)
1985	Joey Olivo (US)	(WBA)
1985	Yuh Myung-Woo (SKo)	(WBA)
1986	Chong-Hwan Choi (SKo)	(IBF)
1988	Tacy Macalos (Phi)	(IBF)

1988	German Torres (Mex)	(WBC)
1989	Yol-Woo Lee (SKo)	(WBC)
1989	Muangchai Kittikasem (Tha)	(IBF)
1989	Jose de Jesus (PR)	(WBO)
1989	Humberto Gonzalez (Mex)	(WBC)
1990	Michael Carbajal (US)	(IBF)
1990	Rolando Pascua (Phi)	(WBC)
1991	Melchor Cob Castro (Mex)	(WBC)
1991	Humberto Gonzalez (Mex)	(WBC)

Straw-weight

1987	Kyung-Yung Lee (SKo)	(WBC)
1988	Leo Gomez (Dom)	(WBA)
1988	Hiroki Ioka (Jap)	(WBC)
1988	Samuth Sithnaruepol (Tha)	(IBF)
1988	Napa Kiatwanchai (Tha)	(WBC)
1989	Kim Bong-Jun (SKo)	(WBA)
1989	Nico Thomas (Ina)	(IBF)
1990	Hideyuki Ohastii (Jap)	(WBC)
1990	Falan Lookmingkwan (Tha)	(IBF)
1990	Ricardo Lopez (Mex)	(WBC)
1991	Choi-Hi Yong (SKo)	(WBA)

━━ RECORDS ━━

MOST WORLD TITLES
(at different weights)
6 Thomas Hearns; 5 Sugar Ray Leonard; 4 Roberto Duran; 3 Terry McGovern; Bob Fitzsimmons; Stanley Ketchel; Tony Canzoneri; Barney Ross; Henry Armstrong; Emile Griffiths; Wilfred Benitez; Alexis Arguello; Wilfredo Gomez; Hector Camacho; Julio Cesar Chavez; Jeff Fenech

UNDEFEATED WORLD CHAMPIONS
Jimmy Barry (70 bouts); Jack McAuliffe (53 bouts); Rocky Marciano (49 bouts).

LONGEST REIGNING WORLD CHAMPION
11 years 252 days Joe Louis (heavyweight) 22 June 1937 to 1 March 1949.

MOST SUCCESSFUL WORLD TITLE DEFENCES
25 Joe Louis (heavyweight) 1937-48

MOST WORLD TITLE FIGHTS
27 Joe Louis (heavyweight) 1937-50

SHORTEST WORLD TITLE FIGHTS
45 seconds Al McCoy (US) v George Chip (US), middleweight 1914
45 seconds Lloyd Honeyghan (GB) v Gene Hatcher (US) welterweight 1987.

MOST KNOCKDOWNS IN WORLD TITLE FIGHT
14 – Vic Toweel (SA) knocked down Danny O'Sullivan (GB) 14 times during their bantamweight contest in 1950.

OLDEST WORLD CHAMPION
48 yr 59 dy Archie Moore (light-heavyweight). Moore may have been only 45. Either way, he is still the oldest world champion.

HEAVIEST WORLD CHAMPION
270 lb Primo Carnera (heavyweight)

CANOEING

1991

WORLD CHAMPIONSHIPS
Paris, Aug 19-25

Men

KAYAK

500m	Singles	R Critchlow (Can) 1m 42.14s
500m	Pairs	Juan José Roman & Juan Manuel Sanchez (Spa) 1m 31.70s
500m	Fours	Germany 1m 23.25s
1,000m	Singles	Knut Holmann (Nor) 3m 35.19s
1,000m	Pairs	Kay Bluhm & Torsten Gutsche (Ger) 3m 15.16s
1,000m	Fours	Hungary 2m 58.15s
10,000m	Singles	Greg Barton (US) 41m 54.73s
10,000m	Pairs	Philippe Boccara & Pascal Boucherit (Fra) 38m 58.69s
10,000m	Fours	Germany 35m 37.98s

CANADIAN

500m	Singles	Mikhail Slivinsky (USSR) 1m 52.28s
500m	Pairs	Attila Palizs & Attila Szabo (Hun) 1m 42.00s
500m	Fours	Soviet Union 1m 32.42s
1,000m	Singles	Ivan Klementiev (USSR) 4m 2.61s
1,000m	Pairs	Ulriche Papke & Ingo Spelly (Ger) 3m 43.42s
1,000m	Fours	USSR 3m 19.50s
10,000m	Singles	Zsolt Bohacs (Hun) 46m 57.58s
10,000m	Pairs	Istvan Gyulay & Pal Petervari (Hun) 42m 58.20s

Women

KAYAK

500m	Singles	Katrin Borchert (Ger) 1m 53.59s
500m	Pairs	Ramona Portwick & Anke von Seck (Ger) 1m 43.21s
500m	Fours	Germany 1m 36.58s
5,000m	Singles	Josefa Idem (Ita) 22m 30.70s
5,000m	Pairs	Ramona Portwick & Anke von Seck (Ger) 20m 43.92s

CHAMPIONS

WORLD CHAMPIONSHIPS
Inaugurated 1938. Not held in Olympic years
Winners since 1987

Men

500 Metres Kayak Singles
1987	Peter MacDonald (NZ)
1989	Martin Hunter (Aus)
1990	Sergey Kalesnik (USSR)
1991	Ron Critchlow (Can)

1,000 Metres Kayak Singles
1987	Greg Barton (US)
1989	Zsolt Gyulay (Hun)
1990	Knut Holmann (Nor)
1991	Knut Holmann (Nor)

10,000 Metres Kayak Singles
1987	Greg Barton (US)
1989	Attila Szabo (Cze)
1990	Philippe Boccara (Fra)
1991	Greg Barton (US)

500 Metres Kayak Pairs
1987	Hungary
1989	East Germany
1990	USSR
1991	Spain

1,000 Metres Kayak Pairs
1987	New Zealand
1989	East Germany
1990	East Germany
1991	Hungary

10,000 Metres Kayak Pairs
1987	France
1989	Hungary
1990	Great Britain
1991	France

500 Metres Kayak Fours
1987	USSR
1989	USSR
1990	USSR
1991	Germany

1,000 Metres Kayak Fours
1987	Hungary
1989	Hungary
1990	East Germany
1991	Hungary

10,000 Metres Kayak Fours
1987	Norway
1989	USSR
1990	USSR
1991	Germany

500 Metres Canadian Singles
1987	Olaf Heokrodt (GDR)
1989	Mikhail Slivinsky (USSR)
1990	Mikhail Slivinsky (USSR)
1991	Mikhail Slivinsky (USSR)

1,000 Metres Canadian Singles
1987	Olaf Heokrodt (GDR)
1989	Ivan Klementiev (USSR)
1990	Ivan Klementiev (USSR)
1991	Ivan Klementiev (USSR)

10,000 Metres Canadian Singles
1987	Ivan Sabjan (Yug)
1989	Ivan Klementiev (USSR)
1990	Zsolt Bohacs (Hun)
1991	Zsolt Bohacs (Hun)

500 Metres Canadian Pairs
1987	Poland
1989	USSR
1990	USSR
1991	Hungary

1,000 Metres Canadian Pairs
1987	USSR
1989	Denmark
1990	USSR
1991	Germany

10,000 Metres Canadian Pairs
1987	Denmark
1989	Denmark
1990	Denmark
1991	Hungary

500 Metres Canadian Fours
First held 1989
1989	USSR

1990　USSR
1991　USSR

1,000 Metres Canadian Fours
First held 1989
1989　USSR
1990　USSR
1991　USSR

Women

500 Metres Kayak Singles
1987　Birgit Schmidt (GDR)
1989　Katrin Borchert (GDR)
1990　Josefa Idem (Ita)
1991　Katrin Borchert (Ger)

5,000 Metres Kayak Singles
First held 1989
1989　Katrin Borchert (GDR)
1991　Josefa Idem (Ita)

500 Metres Kayak Pairs
1987　East Germany
1989　East Germany
1990　East Germany
1991　Germany

5,000 Metres Kayak Pairs
First held 1989
1989　East Germany
1991　Germany

500 Metres Kayak Fours
1987　East Germany
1989　East Germany
1990　East Germany
1991　Germany

CRICKET

WOEFUL WINTER, SPLENDID SUMMER

On a Monday afternoon, with an extraordinarily large last-day crowd packing The Oval, Ian Botham marched to the crease just in time to hit the winning four for England against the West Indies. Even for Botham, this was a bit theatrical.

England had forced West Indies to follow-on for the first time in 22 years. And Botham (whose part in the overall success had been pretty marginal) gave England a five-wicket victory and a 2-2 draw in the series. Beating the West Indies was less of a novelty after the triumph at Kingston in 1990. But the opening win at Headingley was remarkable nonetheless: it was entirely contrived by Gooch, who carried his bat for 154 not out in the second innings. It was England's first home win against the West Indies since July 15 1969, six days before Neil Armstrong walked on the moon. Mark Ramprakash, whose dogged batting and brilliant fielding were a major part of England's success, was not even born and about half the others had not yet arrived in England. Even after that, it was assumed, not least by Viv Richards, that it could not last.

Indeed, with easy victories at Trent Bridge and Edgbaston, West Indies took their accustomed lead in the series. Defeat on the bland pitch at The Oval seemed unthinkable. However, on a bizarre Saturday, the pride of West Indian batting collapsed to the Middlesex spinner Phil Tufnell, who had been kept out of the earlier Tests in the series because of an "attitude problem".

When West Indies batted again, Tufnell followed his six for 25 with one for 150. And, needing 143 to win, England tottered nervily at 80 for four. But they kept their nerve and won. After years of easy triumph, Richards finished his last Test as captain with defeat. The match enthralled Britain. *The Times* at once proclaimed 1991 "a golden summer". In the euphoria of victory it was able to forget all the tarnish including a rain-sodden May, June and July, the decline of the County Championship into near-farce and, before summer began, one of the most humiliating of all Ashes tours which ended in a 3-0 win for Australia.

Graham Gooch missed the opening Test of that series and it was only his presence that made England look even a quarter of a team. He did not score quite as phenomenally in 1991 as in 1990 but by the end of summer - which also included an easy win over Sri Lanka - his reputation as batsman and leader remained unassailable. Gooch was among seven players given a £20,000 annual contract to discourage them from being disloyal; the other six proved a less reliable investment. Robin Smith fought back after injury. But Mike Atherton had a disappointing summer and required a back operation; Angus Fraser's hip injury was bad enough for him to fear for his cricketing future; Allan Lamb and Devon Malcolm were both dropped from the Test team and even Jack Russell became unsure of his place. Lamb and Gooch had a blazing row behind locked doors in the Lord's pavilion, during which Gooch told Lamb he wanted to sack him as vice-captain; unfortunately for the England team's general policy of secretiveness, the door that was locked was the balcony door and they were on the outside, in full view of the press box. The biggest flop of all, however, was the ex-Zimbabwean Graeme Hick who finally became officially English at the beginning of summer and entered the team amid great fanfares: he published an autobiography entitled *My Early Life*, a title previously used by Churchill, and departed very quietly, four Tests later, the technique that had proved so devastating in county cricket having been found quite inadequate to face really insistent fast bowling. For once, however, the West Indies were the team worse affected by injuries: to their opener Gordon Greenidge - whose replacement Phil Simmons was not up to the job - and the fast bowler Ian Bishop. With Richards talking of a future in politics - an improbable departure for such an unyielding man - they seemed a little less ravenous for victory than before. The position as top dogs in world cricket remained theirs, almost by default: in the spring, they beat Australia 2-1 in an ill-tempered series in the Caribbean. Even their traditional supporters seemed to care less: the immigrants who had traditionally flocked to see them in England were almost entirely absent from the Tests, for reasons no one could quite fathom.

Botham had returned to the centre of English cricket after 21 months' absence in the opening one-day international at Edgbaston, when he took a wicket second ball. Next day, he tore a hamstring and missed huge chunks of the summer. Nonetheless, he was so much back in favour with the selectors that he was allowed to arrive on the 1991-92 winter tour almost a month late after finishing his run as The King in *Jack and the Beanstalk* at Bournemouth. It was generally held, though, that his instinct for dramatic timing on the cricket field did not really translate to the stage.

In contrast, his contemporary David Gower remained in outer darkness. Gower scored two Test centuries in Australia and finished the series only 33 short of Geoff Boycott's record total of 8114 runs for England. However, to the new tote-that-barge, lift-that-bale regime of Gooch and the manager Micky Stewart, Gower's outward flipness was anathema. The night before England's final collapse at Brisbane, he was seen in a casino with Lamb, the acting captain; it was presumed they were betting on zero. In the Adelaide Test, Gower offended Gooch by getting out to a lax shot. And, during the last state game of the tour, against Queensland, Gower and the Derbyshire batsman John Morris took a joyride in a Tiger Moth which buzzed the ground at Carrara. The pilot was fined £250 by the Australian aviation authorities for contravening air regulations; Gower and Morris were fined £1000 by the tour management; a letter-writer to *The Times* noted that both players were born on April Fools Day.

HIGHEST SHARE OF A TEST INNINGS

					Score	Total	%
1	Charles Bannerman	A v E	Melbourne	1876-77	165*	245	67.34
2	Gordon Greenidge	WI v E	Old Trafford	1976	134	211	63.50
3	John Reid	NZ v E	Christchurch	1962-63	100	159	62.89
4	Seymour Nurse	WI v NZ	Christchurch	1968-69	258	417	61.87
5	Mohinder Amarnath	I v WI	Kingston	1975-76	60	97	61.85
(five players absent hurt)							
6=	GRAHAM GOOCH	E v WI	HEADINGLEY	1991	154*	252	61.11
6=	Graham Yallop	A v E	Sydney	1978-79	121	198	61.11

The roulette wheel kept spinning during that Brisbane Test. England collapsed then Australia collapsed then England collapsed again. But Australia made their target of 157 without losing a wicket. On the same weekend England were humiliated by Australia at rugby league, netball and hockey, though the Royal Portland Arms in Dorset played a long-distance darts match against the league in Portland, Victoria and won 8-5. "All is not doom and gloom," said one of the organisers. After the cricket finished, Atherton was spotted reading Nabokov's *Invitation to a Beheading*.

With Gooch back, England lost again in Melbourne, this time to Bruce Reid who took 13 wickets. The New Year Honours, containing Gooch's OBE, were announced immediately after the game. It stands for "Overwhelmingly Beaten Englishman" said an Aussie commentator.

England won only one first-class match on tour (their last), failed to make the final of the three-team World Series Cup and lost the one-day series in New Zealand as well. The only discernible difference between England in the summer and on tour was that they had appointed the Rev. Andrew Wingfield Digby as team chaplain.

The effect of all this was to create a thoroughly confused set of signals for the World Cup in 1992. But then even the line-up for the competition was confused. Twenty-one years after their last Test match, South Africa were re-admitted to international cricket but there was much dithering about whether to allow them into the tournament. The Test match bans on 31 English cricketers - 16 who toured South Africa on Mike Gatting's absurd tour in 1990 and 15 others who defied the boycott to coach there - remained in force.

USUAL SORT OF WINTER...

"The worst touring team ever?
Sunday Age, *Melbourne, on England before the First Test*

"I wasn't there."
Lamb, after being seen at a casino the night before England lost the Test

"How could he honestly expect not to get noticed when he walked in with Kerry Packer, Tony Greig and David Gower? Allan, they may be a bit slow in Queensland but they're not completely dim-witted."
Sunday Age, *Melbourne*

"The England players enjoyed an unearned day off yesterday while manager Micky Stewart told all-smirking Australia that their first Test defeat was 'just one of those things'. Napoleon probably attempted a similar PR job after Waterloo."
Peter Johnson, *Daily Mail*

"They finally surrendered the Ashes, their pride, their dignity and their marbles...decided to stamp their feet, suck their thumbs and have a bloody good sulk instead."
Peter Hayter, *Mail on Sunday, on the Third Test*

"You just don't do that kind of thing if you are an England player. Just imagine the fuss if it happened at Lord's."
Peter Lush, *England manager, on Gower's aerial joyride at Carrara*

"I am not ecstatic about paying a thousand pounds for 20 minutes in the air. It is more than commercial rates and in these days of deregulation it is a scandal."
Gower

"England now fold so readily that they could be popped in a Jiffy Bag and posted home."
Mike Selvey, *The Guardian*

Tony Greig: Bad luck
Graham Gooch: Luck had nothing to do with it.
TV interview

"The only difference between Gooch's tour and what happened on the Bounty was that Captain Bligh got that bit more support."
Greg Chappell, *Melbourne Herald-Sun*

"It's the worst fielding I've ever seen. Anywhere."
Gooch on the tour

"I know we've copped some flak at home during this tour, but the bottom line is that we've deserved all of it."
Gooch

"Gooch might appear more the guardian of this grandest game if he chose to stand a quarter-inch closer to his razor each morning, and not to utter his comments in a rather querulous whine."
Don Cameron, *New Zealand Herald*

...UNEXPECTED SUMMER

"Another invasion is upon us by a West Indies team which is the most fearsome, the most successful and the most unpopular in the world. Their game is founded on vengeance and violence and is fringed by arrogance. The only mercy is that they're not bringing their umpires with them."
David Frith, *Wisden Cricket Monthly*

"What we are looking for is a nice, peaceful tour."
Viv Richards, arriving in England

"We love you, Del Boy, we do."
The Headingley crowd to Derek Pringle

"Oh 'twas a famous victory for Gooch and his men
We shall never see its like again.
And everyone in England felt astonishingly proud
Especially the seven wet spectators who were in the crowd."
Private Eye, *after William McGonagall*

"Their performance during the last few years does not suggest that the selectors of the English Test team, still less the managers, are particularly well-endowed mentally. Even so, it should surely occur to them that when England has at the most three batsmen of world class it is
not exactly sensible to make a point of leaving out one of them."
Letter to The Guardian *from Sir Ian Gilmour, Conservative MP*

"He has been hit so many times it's frightening...Test cricket is not the place to iron out technical faults."
Tom Graveney on Graeme Hick

"A lot of people said I was finished and that Malcolm Marshall was past it but that just gave us the confidence to go and prove them wrong."
Richards, *after the Third Test*

"I would have liked the most Test runs, and the most Test centuries, but I am satisfied."
Viv Richards, on retirement

"While others in and around the England dressing room were drinking and, in Philip Tufnell's case, spraying the victory champagne, Gooch went in search of a cup of tea."
Alan Lee, *The Times*

"He deserves it not least for making this the happiest and most sporting of tours I can remember."
Lance Gibbs, making Gooch man of the series

English county cricket also gained a team. Durham became the first side elected to first-class status for 71 years; they signed the Australian batsman Dean Jones as their overseas player and then acquired Botham, who announced (less rancorously than when he quit Somerset) that he was leaving Worcestershire. Unfortunately, Durham were joining the Championship just when it had reached an appallingly low ebb. County cricket in 1991 was not quite as one-sided as in 1990, when the bat dominated the ball more than at any time in the game's history. But the 17 counties were mostly playing three-day cricket on pitches designed to last four or five days with the effect that it was almost impossible to achieve results except by mutually arranged declarations. Gower was so disgusted by it all that he retired, hurt only inside, before a declaration against Essex.

Miraculously, the strongest team, Essex, did win the Championship - for the fifth time in 13 seasons - but only after an unexpectedly strong challenge from Warwickshire, whose powerful seam attack, spearheaded by the South African Allan Donald, was exceptionally effective on some, er, sporting Edgbaston pitches. Warwickshire led for most of the summer but Essex bowled out Middlesex for 51 on the first morning of their last game; since Gooch made a double-century before the day was out no one tried to blame the pitch. The bowler of the year, however, was Surrey's Pakistani, Waqar Younis, allegedly only 19 years old, who became the first bowler for three years to take 100 wickets and consistently put the wind up opposing batsmen in a manner not seen since Malcolm Marshall's younger days.

SELLING THEIR BIRTHRIGHT

Yorkshire finished fourth from bottom. More important, they finished a century of tradition by deciding to sign players born outside the county, ending the presumed practice of exiled fathers rushing their heavily pregnant wives northward so their new-born males might be eligible for county cricket. At first, it was agreed only that players with strong local connections would be qualified: Michael Vaughan, a 16-year-old schoolboy, raised in Sheffield but born in Manchester, was the first beneficiary. After the first breach, though, the walls came tumbling down. In midsummer, with Yorkshire struggling again, the committee voted to abolish all restrictions and on July 19 Craig McDermott signed to become Yorkshire's first overseas player. Chris Hassell, the new chief executive, said two days later that two members had resigned and 13 people had applied to join; Hassell was previously secretary of Lancashire. A letter-writer to the *Yorkshire Post* said, that if the county was getting rid of its traditions, it should remove the "ludicrous mis-formed daisy" designed by Lord Hawke from its badge and get a proper white rose instead.

Middlesex, the 1990 champions, fell away horribly and finished below even Yorkshire. Worcestershire and Lancashire contested the Benson and Hedges final for the second year running but this time managed a different result: Worcestershire won, their first victory in a Lord's final after six failures (Glamorgan were left as the only county, pending Durham's entry, without a Cup victory). However, there were suggestions of bickering in both dressing rooms. The Lancashire captain, 44-year-old David Hughes, dropped himself from what would have been his tenth one-day final, after rumours of dissent in the dressing room, and retired into team management. The winning captain, Phil Neale, lost the job a few weeks later after ten years. Graeme Hick, after his dreadful run for England, won the game for Worcestershire with 88. The match, for the first time, finished on the Sunday.

All three one-day competitions had new winners. Hampshire took the NatWest Trophy after a tense struggle against Surrey. The trophy was lifted, most improbably, by David Gower after the regular captain, Mark Nicholas, had had his finger broken by Waqar in a county match two days earlier. Hampshire lost only 12 wickets in their five matches and their win meant that for the sixth time in a row and the 15th year out of 18, the side batting second won the final. On this occasion, on one of the most glorious days of a glorious late summer, the result was more due to Surrey's failure to force the pace than the September dew. Adrian Aymes, the Hampshire wicket-keeper, completed a unique double: he had also played in the national village final, for Hursley Park in 1984. Douglas Bruce streaked across the pitch carrying a sign saying "Zara, I love you". He told the court later that it was an attempt to stop his wife divorcing him. "Have you tried a bunch of red roses?" said the magistrate. On Cup Final morning an Inter-City express was held up at Wakefield for 10 minutes to allow Dickie Bird to find his ticket. Before the game, Yvonne Cleminson, landlady of the Cherry Tree Inn at Rowledge, where the Surrey-Hampshire border runs through the bar, painted a white line to keep opposing supporters in their own county.

The most lunatic moment of the NatWest came in the first round. To fit in with the new practice of starting county games on Tuesdays and Fridays the TCCB gambled on leaving only two days for matches. Naturally, it was the wettest June in memory. Two games had to be settled by getting the bowlers to hit an undefended wicket: Surrey beat Oxfordshire by three hits out of ten to two; Hertfordshire beat Derbyshire two-one. It was the eighth win by a Minor County over a major one, but even David Surridge, the winning captain, thought it was a hollow victory. There was general consternation at Derbyshire's bowling. John Snow said they should go to the opticians. Pat Pocock, 44, came out of retirement to prove the point in a newspaper stunt and hit six times out of ten.

Nottinghamshire won the Sunday League after Lancashire blew an apparently unassailable position. Refuge Assurance ended their sponsorship of the League, citing the collapse in the TV audience since it was shifted to a satellite channel: viewing figures were said to be down to 47,000. The TCCB scuppered a plan by Sky TV to wire Mike Gatting for sound so he could explain his tactics; wise guys said Gatting had never been able to explain them before.

RECORDS AND RETIREMENTS

Alan Butcher, the Glamorgan captain, played against his son Mark of Surrey, an unprecedented conjunction in county cricket. Steve Marsh of Kent, playing against Middlesex at Lord's, equalled the world record of eight catches in an innings held by Wally Grout and David East. Chris Smith and Kevan James both scored centuries against Derbyshire at Chesterfield but Hampshire were bowled out for 254, the lowest first-class total ever to contain two centuries (beating Lancashire's 271 against Northants in 1947). On his 20th birthday, Dominic Cork of Derbyshire took eight wickets before lunch against Essex. Simon Hinks of Kent walked out to bat without his bat at Canterbury against Leicestershire. The Dog Inn at Over, Gloucestershire was re-opened, after a facelift, by Jack Russell. Graham Cowdrey of Kent went to his 93rd Van Morrison concert. The Middlesex batsmen at Canterbury complained that they were being dazzled by the whiteness of umpire Basharat Hassan's coat. The Hampshire batsman Chris Smith, 32, missed the NatWest final after deciding to retire in mid-season to become marketing manager of West Australian cricket; he had been the first batsman to reach 1000 runs in the Championship and only days before his decision, some newspapers were suggesting he should be recalled by England. The former England wicket-keeper Paul Downton, 34, was forced to retire in mid-season because of a damaged eye. Arnold Sidebottom, 37, and Peter Roebuck, 35, retired; Chris Cowdrey, 33, the one-time England captain, was sacked by Kent.

Margaret Thatcher fell from power after an artillery barrage of cricketing metaphors. She was succeeded by the candidate best-informed on cricket, John Major, who became almost as familiar on the Test match grounds as in the Commons and was admitted to membership of the MCC 18 years ahead of schedule. Research by Coopers Deloitte suggested there was a correlation between improved performances by England cricketers and an upturn in the economy. Unfortunately for the Government they also found a two-year timelag.

It was a bad time for pushy women: MCC voted to formalise their unofficial ban on female members after Rachael Heyhoe-Flint, a more distinguished cricketer than 99% of the membership, applied to join. This continued several traditions, mainly the one whereby MCC members consistently make prats of themselves. An attempt to allow honorary women members gained a majority but not a sufficient one. Mrs Flint said women should boycott pavilion tea-making duties in protest. The editor of *Wisden,* Graeme Wright, agreed to include Roedean's record in the 1992 edition. Wrekin College's girls team, captained by Claire Taylor (daughter of Bob) beat Ellesmere College, captained by Melissa Lloyd (daughter of Clive). Jacqui Hawker, 10, was made captain of Plympton under-11s team to the disgust of her team-mates: "We are not going to be told how to play by a girl," said one boy. "They'll soon see I'm not be messed with," said Jacqui.

A survey in schools in Kent and south-east London, supposedly a hotbed of cricket, showed that 167 sides and 1,680 fixtures had vanished in the past 10 years: Willesden High School, which produced two 1991 England players, DeFreitas and Lewis, was said to be playing only Gaelic football. Leicestershire were obliged to forfeit their Second XI game against Sussex because half the team went down with food poisoning. Play was stopped in a second XI match between Yorkshire and Middlesex at Headingley when a thief was spotted in the dressing room. Detective-Constable Brian Arkle, playing for Gateshead Fell against Durham City, actually arrested a dressing-room thief, then went out and scored his maiden century. Vaughan Walsh, a 26-year-old plumber from Antigua who was reputed to be the world's fastest bowler, took nine for four including four wickets in successive balls for his club Leicester Nomads. The last man refused to bat against him. Walsh was offered a game for Somerset against Sri Lanka but dropped out at the last minute. Bill Nimmo took all ten wickets for 20 for Scalebor Park against Leeds Police without the aid of a fielder: eight were bowled, two went to return catches.

CAUGHT MAJOR, BOWLED HOWE

"The bowling's going to get hit all round the ground, that's my style."
Margaret Thatcher, Nov 12

"...I hope there is no monopoly of cricketing metaphors. It's rather like sending your opening batsmen to the crease only to find the moment the first balls are bowled that their bats have been broken before the game by the team captain."
Sir Geoffrey Howe in his resignation speech, Nov 13

"I think that's what you would call 'bowling a googly'."
President Bush on being asked a difficult question during Mr Major's first visit

"No man who likes cricket can be all bad."
Alan Watkins, The Spectator, on John Major

"There have been more cricketers inside no. 10 since last November than there have been in the dressing room at Lord's."
Anonymous civil servant

"I think the whole question of cricket was more important to him than sanctions."
Nelson Mandela on John Major

"Like our new Prime Minister, he had a passion for cricket and believed sufficiently in its civilising qualities to attempt to introduce it to the Russians while he sat on the Moscow Soviet. I have often wondered what might have happened if he'd succeeded. Alas, a forerunner of the KGB was so suspicious of the bats, balls and pads he had ordered from London that they slit them open to see what was inside."**
Ian Aitken, The Guardian, on his Communist father

Mr Gerald Howarth (Conservative, Cannock and Burntwood): "It would not be right to proceed with the important legislation we are discussing without acknowledging the tremendous English success in the Test match...It would be appropriate for the House to convey to the England team, to my hon. Friend the Minister of Sport and to my right hon. Friend the Prime Minister its enormous thanks to the efforts of our team and the inspiration of our Ministers."

Mr Speaker: "I am not certain whether there is any Government responsibility for that."

Mr Win Griffiths (Labour, Bridgend): "...It was not an English cricket team, but a British cricket team. The principal bowler is from Glamorgan."

Mr Speaker: That is very good news. "
Hansard, June 10

Malcolm Eustace, captain of Moseley in the Birmingham League, declared at 16 for nine against Old Hill to make the score look better in the record books; Eustace was one of seven players out for a duck. In the Yorkshire League, Harrogate's captain Austin Jelfs insisted on a prompt start even though eight Cleethorpes players had not yet arrived; Cleethorpes were forced to declare at 11 for 2 and Harrogate had 12 points deducted for not playing "in the proper spirit of the game". "If I'd been really unsporting," said Jelfs, "I would have batted first."

Neil Taylor, playing for Swardeston, Norfolk, conceded six sixes and a wide in an over to Chris Harrison of Fakenham. Jed Bowers, the wicket-keeper for Trevone (Cornwall), completed probably the slowest hat-trick ever. He took two wickets with his last two balls on his last bowl in 1989 and another when he was finally put on again in 1991. Near Bath, Ellis Lyppiatt, playing for South Stoke against Priston, needed to hit four to win but had his shot blocked by a duck waddling across the edge of the outfield. Terry Sutherland, 52, batting at Dunston, Norfolk, was struck on the trouser pocket and the ball ignited a box of matches he was carrying. Jack Hyams, 71, a retired pet shop owner from Hertfordshire, made what was reported to be his 169th century, playing in an over-35s match for Cockfosters against Winchmore Hill. Brian Tancock, 66, took eight wickets in the opening game of his 53rd season for Ashill, Somerset. The Herald Cricket Club of Milton Keynes, having finished bottom of its league for three seasons, found itself with funds of £70 and a bill for pitch hire of £350. It stuck the entire kitty on a horse called Buddy Holly, which won at Plumpton at 6-1. Coldharbour Cricket Club of Surrey hired The Oval for a special match to celebrate 62-year-old Reg Comber's 50 years in the team. The game near Bath between the Compton Dando village team and the Compton pub was abandoned after Bob Horler, the village team captain, ejected one of the opposing players, Nigel Hyde, from the pavilion. Three years earlier, Hyde had named Horler as co-respondent when he divorced his wife.

HEROICS DOWN UNDER

The ICC voted to restrict bowlers to one bouncer per batsman per over; the West Indians protested vigorously. Sir Richard Hadlee had a five-hour open-heart operation exactly a year after he played his final Test. The twins Mark and Steve Waugh put on 464 for the fifth wicket for New South Wales against Western Australia in Perth, a world record for the fifth wicket, an Australian record for any wicket and the 11th highest stand ever. It was certainly the highest by brothers, never mind twins. Colin Miller of South Australia took six wickets in ten balls against New South Wales; Tasmania's wicket-keeper Joe Holyman, 20, took seven catches in an innings on his first-class debut against Western Australia; Tim Nielsen of South Australia became the fourth wicket-keeper in history to take 11 catches in a match (after Long, Marsh and Bairstow). Peter Leroy, curator of the Sydney Cricket Ground, went prospecting in the New South Wales countryside to find the legendary Bulli soil, base of the SCG wicket for 97 years.

The Leeward Islands fast bowler Winston Benjamin was slightly injured when he was larking about with a gun, along with a team-mate, and it went off. The Leewards ended their ban on cricketers with dreadlocks. The Indian Test bowler Rashid Patel was banned for a year after he attacked two opposition batsmen with a stump during the five-day inter-zonal Duleep Trophy final in Jamshedpur. He had been angered by an accusation of deliberate intimidation, and possibly by the scores (North Zone 729-9 dec and 59-0. West Zone 561).

South Africa introduced "substitution cricket" into the limited-overs game, permitting up to six changes at any time, including the replacement of a bogged-down batsman. Fred Goodall, the former New Zealand Test umpire, married Di Malthus, a woman he met when she was playing and he gave her out. Fred Trueman's daughter Rebecca married Raquel Welch's son Damon and had her union blessed at Bolton Abbey, Yorkshire, on the eve of the Headingley Test. Ms Welch upstaged the bride and upset her father by arriving 10 minutes late and underclothed. "I think she left half her dress behind," said Trueman.

Cricket returned to Iran for the first time since the Revolution when a five-a-side tournament was held in the British Embassy garden; a ball out of the grounds was deemed to be out rather than six because of a shortage of balls and the need not to upset the Iranians. The annual match between the Royal Southern Yacht Club and the Island Sailing Club of Cowes on the Brambles Bank in the middle of the Solent was restricted to seven overs a side before the sandbank was covered with water again. The Royal Navy nuclear submarine HMS Tireless and the American sub USS Pargo broke through the ice in the Antarctic so the crews could play each other; unfortunately, the Americans failed to grasp the rules and lost by 187 runs to eight homers. The vessels were conducting a survey on global warming. Australian troops beat the British in a Test played by occupying forces in Northern Iraq; after the game the equipment was given to

COOPERS DELOITTE RATINGS

Computer rankings of Test cricketers - September 1991
(September 1990 in brackets)

BATTING

1	(3)	Graham Gooch (Eng)	894
2	(5)	Robin Smith (Eng)	872
3	(6)	Richie Richardson (WI)	829
4	(24)	Shoaib Mohammad (Pak)	773
5	(1)	Mark Taylor (Aus)	742
6	(10)	Imran Khan (Pak)	740
7	(18)	Salim Malik (Pak)	739
8	(4)	Desmond Haynes (WI)	722
9	(15)	Martin Crowe (NZ)	721
10	(8)	Mohammed Azharuddin (Ind)	710

BOWLING

1	(2)	Malcolm Marshall (WI)	877
2	(50)	Waqar Younis (Pak)	852
3	(7)	Curtly Ambrose (WI)	764
4	(5)	Imran Khan (Pak)	761
5	(3)	Ian Bishop (WI)	749
6	(8)	Wasim Akram (Pak)	747
7	(-)	Craig McDermott (Aus)	727
8	(-)	Bruce Reid (Aus)	686
9	(4)	Angus Fraser (Eng)	676
10	(9)	Merv Hughes (Aus)	658

Javed Miandad, second in September 1990, was 13th

The leading bowler in September 1990 was Sir Richard Hadlee, who then retired

bewildered local Kurds. The Laws of Cricket were translated into both Chinese and Japanese. Belgium and Germany became affiliated to the ICC. In the home of the game, the country governed by a cricket fanatic with a team good enough to hold the West Indies, ball-by-ball Test Match coverage appeared to be on the edge of abolition because the BBC no longer had a suitable wavelength.

1991

ENGLAND v WEST INDIES
First Test
Headingley, Jun 6-10

Compared to England's last Test team in Australia four months earlier, Hick, Ramprakash, Watkin (all debuts), Pringle and Russell replaced Gower, Stewart, Newport, Small and Tufnell. Lewis (injured) and Illingworth were in the original 12 but left out; Watkin was a late addition, originally as cover for Pringle. West Indies won toss.

ENGLAND
First Innings
G A Gooch c Dujon b Marshall 34
M A Atherton b Patterson 2
G A Hick c Dujon b Walsh 6
A J Lamb c Hooper b Marshall 11
M R Ramprakash c Hooper b Marshall 27
R A Smith run out 54
R C Russell lbw Patterson 5
D R Pringle c Logie b Patterson 16
P A J DeFreitas c Simmons b Ambrose 15
S L Watkin b Ambrose 2
D E Malcolm not out 5
Extras (lb5, w2, nb14) 21
Total (79.2 overs) **198**
Fall of wickets: 1-13, 2-45, 3-45, 4-64, 5-129, 6-149, 7-154, 8-177, 9-181
Bowling: Ambrose 26-8-49-2; Patterson 26.2-8-67-3; Walsh 14-7-31-1; Marshall 13-4-46-3

WEST INDIES
First Innings
P V Simmons c Ramprakash b DeFreitas 38
D L Haynes c Russell b Watkin 7
R B Richardson run out 29
C L Hooper run out 0
I V A Richards c Lamb b Pringle 73
A L Logie c Lamb b DeFreitas 6
P J Dujon c Ramprakash b Watkin 6
M D Marshall c Hick b Pringle 0
C E L Ambrose c Hick b DeFreitas 0
C A Walsh c Gooch b DeFreitas 3
B P Patterson not out 5
Extras (lb1, nb5) 6
Total (54.1 overs) **173**
Fall of wickets: 1-36, 2-54, 3-58, 4-102, 5-139, 6-156, 7-160, 8-165, 9-167
Bowling: Malcolm 14-0-69-0; DeFreitas 17.1-5-34-4; Watkin 14-2-55-2; Pringle 9-3-14-2

ENGLAND
Second Innings
G A Gooch not out 154
M A Atherton c Dujon b Ambrose 6
G A Hick b Ambrose 6
A J Lamb c Dujon b Ambrose 0
M R Ramprakash c Dujon b Ambrose 27
R A Smith lbw Ambrose 0
R C Russell c Dujon b Ambrose 4
D R Pringle c Dujon b Marshall 27
P A J DeFreitas lbw Walsh 3
S L Watkin c Hooper b Marshall 0
D E Malcolm b Marshall 4
Extras (b4, lb9, w1, nb7) 21
Total (106 overs) **252**
Fall of wickets: 1-22, 2-38, 3-38, 4-116, 5-116, 6-124, 7-222, 8-236, 9-238
Bowling: Ambrose 28-6-52-6; Patterson 15-1-52-0; Marshall 25-4-58-3; Walsh 30-5-61-1; Hooper 4-1-11-0; Richards 4-1-5-0
Graham Gooch became only the fifth Englishman to carry his bat through a Test innings

WEST INDIES
Second Innings
P V Simmons b DeFreitas..0
D L Haynes c Smith b Pringle 19
R B Richardson c Lamb b DeFreitas 68
C L Hooper c Lamb b Watkin 5
I V A Richards c Gooch b Watkin 3
A L Logie c Gooch b Watkin 3
P J Dujon lbw DeFreitas 33
M D Marshall lbw Pringle 1
C E L Ambrose c Pringle b DeFreitas 14
C A Walsh c Atherton b Malcolm......................................9
B P Patterson not out 0
Extras (lb1 b6) 7
Total (56.4 overs) **162**
Fall of wickets: 1-0; 2-61, 3-77, 4-85, 5-88, 6-136, 7-137, 8-139, 9-162
Bowling: DeFreitas 21-4-59-4; Malcolm 6.4-0-26-1; Pringle 22-6-38-2; Watkin 7-0-38-3
ENGLAND WON BY 115 RUNS
England's first home win against the West Indies since 1969 when Ray Illingworth led the side.
Man of the Match: Graham Gooch

Second Test
Lord's, Jun 20- 24
England unchanged. Illingworth and Lawrence were left out of a squad of 13. West Indies brought in Allen (debut) for Patterson (injured). West Indies won toss.

WEST INDIES
First Innings
P V Simmons c Lamb b Hick 33
D L Haynes c Russell b Pringle 60
R B Richardson c DeFreitas b Hick 57
C L Hooper c Lamb b Pringle 111
I V A Richards lbw DeFreitas 63
A L Logie b DeFreitas 5
P J L Dujon c Lamb b Pringle 20
M D Marshall lbw Pringle 25
C E L Ambrose c & b Malcolm 5
C A Walsh c Atherton b Pringle 10
I B A Allen not out 1
Extras (b3, lb7, nb19) 29
Total (120.1 overs) **419**
Fall of wickets: 1-90, 2-102, 3-198, 4-322, 5-332, 6-366, 7-382, 8-402, 9-410
Haynes scored his 50th Test 50 in his 99th Test.
Bowling: DeFreitas 31-6-93-2; Malcolm 19-3-76-1; Watkin 15-2-60-0; Pringle 35.1-6-100-5; Hick 18-4-77-2; Gooch 2-0-3-0
ENGLAND
First Innings
G A Gooch b Walsh 37
M A Atherton b Ambrose 5
G A Hick c Richardson b Ambrose 0
A J Lamb c Haynes b Marshall 1
M R Ramprakash c Richards b Allen 24
R A Smith not out 148
R C Russell c Dujon b Hooper 46
D R Pringle c Simmons b Allen 35
P A J DeFreitas c Dujon b Marshall 29
S L Watkin b Ambrose 6
D E Malcolm b Ambrose 0
Extras (lb1, nb22) 23
Total (118 overs) **354**
Fall of wickets: 1-5; 2-6, 3-16, 4-60, 5-84, 6180, 7-269, 8-316, 9-353
Bowling: Ambrose 34-10-87-4; Marshall 30-4-78-2; Walsh 26-4-90-1; Allen 23-2-88-2; Hooper 5-2-10-1

WEST INDIES
Second Innings
P V Simmons lbw DeFreitas...2
D L Haynes not out..4
R B Richardson c Hick b Malcolm 1
C L Hooper not out..1
Extras (lb2, nb2) 4
Total (2 wkts, 5.5 overs)...**12**
Fall of wickets: 1-9, 2-10
Bowling: DeFreitas 3-2-1-1; Malcolm 2.5-0-9-1
MATCH DRAWN
Sunday's play, the first scheduled in a Lord's Test since 1982, was entirely washed out costing the TCCB, which had decided not to insure, £400,000, 10 per cent of the season's projected Test match profit. Only 25 minutes play was possible on Monday, the final day.
Man of the match: *Smith*

Third Test
Trent Bridge, Jul 4-9
Morris, Reeve and Malcolm left out of England 14. Illingworth made debut. England won toss.
ENGLAND
First Innings
G A Gooch lbw Marshall..68
M A Atherton lbw Ambrose 32
G A Hick c Dujon b Ambrose 43
A J Lamb lbw Ambrose...13
M R Ramprakash b Ambrose 13
R A Smith not out...64
R C Russell c Logie b Allen 3
D R Pringle c sub (Lambert) b Allen 0
P A J DeFreitas b Walsh 8
R K Illingworth c Hooper b Ambrose 13
D V Lawrence c Allen b Marshall 4
Extras (lb17, w1, nb21) 39
Total (103.5 overs)...**300**
Fall of wickets: 1-108, 2-113, 3-138, 4-186, 5-192, 6-212, 7-217, 8-228, 9-270
Bowling: Ambrose 34-7-74-5; Marshall 21.5-6-54-2; Walsh 24-4-75-1; Allen 17-0-69-2; Hooper 6-4-10-0; Richards 1-0-1-0
WEST INDIES
First Innings
P V Simmons b Illingworth 12
D L Haynes c Smith b Lawrence 18
R B Richardson b Lawrence 43
C L Hooper c Russell b DeFreitas 11
I V A Richards b Illingworth 80
A L Logie c Ramprakash b DeFreitas 78
P J L Dujon c Hick b Pringle 19
M D Marshall c Illingworth b DeFreitas 67
C E L Ambrose b Illingworth 17
C A Walsh lbw Pringle 12
I B A Allen not out...4
Extras (b2, lb13, w1, nb20) 36
Total (118.1 overs)..**397**
Fall of wickets: 1-32, 2-32, 3-45, 4-118, 5-239, 6-272, 7-324, 8-358, 9-392
Bowling: DeFreitas 31.1-9-67-3; Lawrence 24-2-116-2; Illingworth 33-8-110-3; Pringle 25-6-71-2; Hick 5-0-18-0
Illingworth bowled Simmons to become the 11th man to take a wicket with his first ball in Test cricket. TV replays suggested Richards was stumped off Jack Russell's pad but the bowler's end umpire John Hampshire gave him out first.

ENGLAND
Second Innings
G A Gooch b Ambrose 13
M A Atherton b Marshall..4
G A Hick c Dujon b Ambrose 0
A J Lamb lbw Marshall 29
M R Ramprakash c Dujon b Ambrose 21
R A Smith c Richards b Walsh 15

R C Russell b Walsh 3
D R Pringle c Simmons b Walsh.....................................3
P A J DeFreitas not out 55
R K Illingworth c Simmons b Walsh 13
D V Lawrence c Hooper b Allen 34
Extras (lb14, w3, nb4) 21
Total (79 overs)..**211**
Fall of wickets: 1-4, 2-8, 3-25, 4-67, 5-100, 6-106, 7-106, 8-115, 9-153
Bowling: Ambrose 27-2-61-3; Marshall 21-6-49-2; Allen 7-2-23-1; Walsh 24-7-64-4
WEST INDIES
Second Innings
P V Simmons c Russell b Lawrence 1
D L Haynes not out...57
R B Richardson not out 52
Extras (nb5) 5
Total (1 wicket, 32.2 overs) **115**
Fall of wicket: 1-1
Bowling: DeFreitas 11-3-29-0; Lawrence 12.2-0-61-1; Pringle 7-2-20-0; Illingworth 2-0-5-0
WEST INDIES WON BY 9 WICKETS
West Indies won before lunch on the fifth day.
Man of the Match: *Ambrose*

Fourth Test
Edgbaston, Jul 25-29
Morris (debut) and Lewis replaced Smith (injured) and Lawrence in final 11, even though Morris had been out for nought to Ambrose twice at Swansea in the previous game. Lewis and DeFreitas of Willesden High School became the first players from the same school to play together for England since Chris Cowdrey and Richard Ellison (Tonbridge) in India in 1984-85. West Indies won toss.
ENGLAND
First Innings
G A Gooch b Marshall..45
H Morris c Dujon b Patterson 3
M A Atherton lbw Walsh..16
G A Hick c Richards b Ambrose 19
A J Lamb lbw Marshall 9
M R Ramprakash c Logie b Walsh 29
R C Russell c Richardson b Ambrose.............................12
D R Pringle b Ambrose 2
P A J DeFreitas c Richardson b Marshall 10
C C Lewis lbw Marshall 13
R K Illingworth not out..0
Extras (b4, lb3, nb23) 30
Total (70.4 overs)..**188**
Fall of wickets: 1-6, 2-53, 3-88, 4-108, 5-129, 6-159, 7-163, 8-163, 9-184
Bowling: Ambrose 23-6-64-3; Patterson 11-2-39-1; Walsh 21-6-43-2; Marshall 12.4-1-33-4; Hooper 3-2-2-0
WEST INDIES
First Innings
P V Simmons c Hick b Lewis...28
D L Haynes c Russell b DeFreitas 32
R B Richardson lbw Lewis 104
C L Hooper b Illingworth 31
I V A Richards c Lewis b Pringle 22
A L Logie c Atherton b Lewis 28
P J Dujon lbw DeFreitas 6
M D Marshall not out 6
C E L Ambrose c Hick b Lewis.......................................1
C A Walsh c & b Lewis 18
B P Patterson b Lewis 3
Extras (lb7 nb6) 13
Total (107.3 overs)..**292**
Fall of wickets: 1-52, 2-93, 3-148, 4-194, 5-257, 6-258, 7-26, 8-267, 9-285
Bowling: DeFreitas 25.3-9-40-2; Lewis 35-10-111-6; Pringle 23-9-48-1; Illingworth 17-2-75-1; Gooch 4-1-11-0; Hick 1-1-0-0

ENGLAND
Second Innings

G A Gooch b Patterson 40
H Morris lbw Patterson 1
M A Atherton c Hooper b Patterson 1
G A Hick b Ambrose 1
A J Lamb c Dujon b Walsh 25
M R Ramprakash c Dujon b Marshall 25
R C Russell c Dujon b Patterson 0
D R Pringle c Logie b Marshall 45
P A J DeFreitas b Patterson 7
C C Lewis b Ambrose 65
R K Illingworth not out 5
Extras (b5, lb21, nb14) 40
Total (105.4 overs) **255**
Fall of wickets: 1-2, 2-4, 3-5, 4-71, 5-94, 6-96, 7-127, 8-144, 9-236
Bowling: Ambrose 33-16-42-2; Patterson 31-6-81-5; Marshall 19.4-3-53-2; Walsh 7-1-20-1; Simmons 3-0-7-0; Hooper 12-3-26-0

WEST INDIES
Second Innings

P V Simmons lbw DeFreitas 16
D L Haynes c Hick b DeFreitas 8
R B Richardson c Hick b DeFreitas 0
C L Hooper not out 55
I V A Richards not out 73
Extras (lb4, nb1) 5
Total (3 wkts, 40.4 overs) **157**
Fall of wickets: 1-23, 2-23, 3-24
Bowling: DeFreitas 13-2-54-3; Lewis 16-7-45-0; Pringle 7-1-31-0; Illingworth 4.4-0-23-0

WEST INDIES WON BY 7 WICKETS
Jeffrey Dujon moved above Alan Knott into 2nd place in the all-time list of Test wicket-keeping dismissals. Richie Richardson scored his first Test century in England. Richards won the game with a six off Illingworth.
Man of the Match: Richardson

Fifth Test
The Oval, Aug 8-12
Lamb, Hick, Russell and Illingworth dropped. Pringle withdrew through flu. Botham, Lawrence, Tufnell, Stewart, Smith in. West Indies: Clayton Lambert (debut) replaced Gus Logie (knee injury). England won toss.

ENGLAND
First Innings

G A Gooch lbw Ambrose 60
H Morris c Lambert b Ambrose 44
M A Atherton c Hooper b Walsh 0
R A Smith lbw Marshall 109
M R Ramprakash c Lambert b Hooper 25
A J Stewart c Richardson b Patterson 31
I T Botham hit wkt b Ambrose 31
C C Lewis not out 47
P A J DeFreitas c Dujon b Walsh 7
D V Lawrence c Richards b Walsh 9
P C R Tufnell c Haynes b Patterson 2
Extras (b8, lb10, w1, nb35) 54
Total (151.1 overs) **419**
Fall of wickets: 1-112, 2-114, 3-120, 4-188, 5-263, 6-336, 7-351, 8-386, 9-411
Bowling: Ambrose 36-8-83-3; Patterson 25.1-3-87-2; Walsh 32-5-91-3; Marshall 24-5-62-1; Hooper 34-1-78-1
England passed 400 against the West Indies for the first time in 33 Tests, since The Oval 1976.

WEST INDIES
First Innings

P V Simmons lbw Lawrence 15
D L Haynes not out 75
R B Richardson c Stewart b Botham 20
C L Hooper c Stewart b DeFreitas 3
C B Lambert c Ramprakash b Tufnell 39
P J L Dujon lbw Lawrence 0
M D Marshall c Botham b Tufnell 0
I V A Richards c Stewart b Tufnell 2
C E L Ambrose c Botham b Tufnell 0
C A Walsh c Gooch b Tufnell 0
B P Patterson c Botham b Tufnell 2
Extras (lb9, nb11) 20
Total (57.3 overs) **176**
Fall of wickets: 1-52, 2-95, 3-98, 4-158, 5-160, 6-161, 7-172, 8-172, 9-172
Bowling: DeFreitas 13-6-38-1; Lawrence 16-1-67-2; Tufnell 14.3-3-25-6; Botham 11-4-27-1; Lewis 3-1-10-0
West Indies forced to follow on by England for the first time since Old Trafford 1969. Haynes became the second West Indian (after Sir Frank Worrell) to carry his bat against England.

WEST INDIES
Second Innings

P V Simmons c Lewis b Botham 36
D L Haynes lbw Lawrence 43
C B Lambert lbw Botham 14
R B Richardson c Gooch b Lawrence 121
C L Hooper c Gooch b Tufnell 54
I V A Richards c Morris b Lawrence 60
P J L Dujon c Stewart b Lawrence 5
M D Marshall b DeFreitas 17
C E L Ambrose b DeFreitas 0
C A Walsh lbw Lawrence 14
B P Patterson not out 1
Extras (b7, lb5, w2, nb6) 20
Total (132.5 overs) **385**
Fall of wickets: 1-53; 2-71; 3-125; 4-208; 5-305; 6-311; 7-356, 8-356, 9-378
Bowling: DeFreitas 20-9-42-2; Lawrence 25.5-4-106-5; Lewis 25-12-35-0; Tufnell 46-6-150-1; Botham 16-4-40-2

ENGLAND
Second Innings

G A Gooch lbw Marshall 29
H Morris c Dujon b Patterson 2
M A Atherton c Hooper b Patterson 13
R A Smith c Patterson b Walsh 26
M R Ramprakash lbw Lambert 19
A J Stewart not out 38
I T Botham not out 4
Extras (b4, w1, nb10) 15
Total (5 wkts) (31.4 overs) **146**
Fall of wickets: 1-3, 2-40, 3-80, 4-80, 5-142
Bowling: Ambrose 8-0-48-0; Patterson 9-0-63-2; Marshall 5-3-9-1; Walsh 9-3-18-1; Lambert 0.4-0-4-1

ENGLAND WON BY 5 WICKETS

Man of the Match: Smith

Men of the Series:
England: Graham Gooch, *West Indies:* Curtly Ambrose

Leading Batting Averages

	M	I	NO	Runs	HS	Avge
1 Robin Smith (E)	4	7	2	416	148*	83.20
2 Alec Stewart (E)	1	2	1	69	38*	69.00
3 Chris Lewis (E)	2	3	1	125	65	62.50
4 Graham Gooch (E)	5	9	1	480	154*	60.00
5 Richie Richardson (WI)	5	10	1	495	121	55.00
6 Viv Richards (WI)	5	8	1	376	80	53.71

Leading Bowling Averages

	M	Balls	Runs	Wkts	Avge	Best
1 Clayton Lambert (WI)	1	4	4	1	4.00	1-4
2 Curtly Ambrose (WI)	5	1494	560	28	20.00	6-52
3 Phil DeFreitas (E)	5	1115	457	22	20.77	4-34
4 Malcolm Marshall (WI)	5	1033	442	20	22.10	4-33
5 Ian Botham (E)	1	162	67	3	22.33	2-40
6 Phillip Tufnell (E)	1	363	175	7	25.00	6-25

VIVIAN RICHARDS-Test match record

	M	I	NO	R	HS	Ave	Wkts	Ave
v England	36	50	4	2869	291	63.19	6	76.50
v India	28	41	3	1927	192*	50.71	5	70.60
v Australia	34	54	3	2266	208	44.43	7	99.14
v New Zealand	7	10	1	387	105	43.00	3	78.67
v Pakistan	16	27	1	1091	123	41.96	11	20.18
Total	**121**	**182**	**12**	**8540**	**291**	**50.23**	**32**	**61.38**

ENGLAND v SRI LANKA

Only Test

Lord's, Aug 22-27
Russell replaced Atherton (injured). England won the toss.
Debut: Wijegunawardene (SL)

ENGLAND
First Innings

G A Gooch c & b Ramanayake	38
H Morris lbw Ratnayake	42
A J Stewart not out	113
R A Smith c Tillekeratne b Ratnayake	4
M R Ramprakash c Mahanama b Hathurusinghe	0
I T Botham c Mahanama b Ramanayake	22
C C Lewis c de Silva b Anurasiri	11
R C Russell b Anurasiri	17
P A J DeFreitas b Ratnayake	1
D V Lawrence c & b Ratnayake	3
P C R Tufnell lbw Ratnayake	0
Extras (b9, lb8, nb14)	31
Total (95 overs)	**282**

Fall of wickets: 1-70, 2-114, 3-119, 4-120, 5-160, 6-183, 7-246, 8-258, 9-276

Bowling: Ratnayake 27-4-69-5; Ramanayake 24-5-75-2; Wijegunawardene 10-1-36-0; Hathurusinghe 17-6-40-1; Anurasiri 17-4-45-2

SRI LANKA
First Innings

D S B P Kuruppu b DeFreitas	5
U C Hathurusinghe c Tufnell b DeFreitas	66
A P Gurusinha b DeFreitas	4
P A de Silva c Lewis b DeFreitas	42
R S Mahanama c Russell b Botham	2
S T Jayasuriya c Smith b DeFreitas	11
H P Tillekeratne c Morris b Lawrence	20
R J Ratnayake b DeFreitas	52
C P Ramanayake lbw DeFreitas	0
K I W Wijegunawardene not out	6
S D Anurasiri b Lawrence	1
Extras (lb15)	15
Total (68.1 overs)	**224**

Fall of wickets: 1-12, 2-22, 3-75, 4-86, 5-105, 6-139, 7-213, 8-213, 9-220

Bowling: DeFreitas 26-8-70-7; Lawrence 15.1-3-61-2; Lewis 10-5-29-0; Botham 10-3-26-1; Tufnell 7-2-23-0

ENGLAND
Second Innings

G A Gooch b Anurasiri	174
H Morris c Mahanama b Anurasiri	23
A J Stewart c de Silva b Anurasiri	43
R A Smith not out	63
R C Russell not out	12
Extras (b15, lb23, w1, nb10)	49
Total (3 wkts, 85.1 overs)	**364**

Fall of wickets: 1-78, 2-217, 3-322

Bowling: Ratnayake ;26-4-91-0; Ramanayake 20-2-86-0; Wijegunawardene 2-0-13-0; Anurasiri 36.1-8-135-3; Jayasuriya 1-0-1-0

SRI LANKA
Second Innings

D S B P Kuruppu lbw Lewis	21
U C Hathurusinghe c Morris b Tufnell	25
A P Gurusinha b Tufnell	34
P A de Silva c Russell b Lawrence	18
R S Mahanama c Botham b Tufnell	15
S T Jayasuriya c Russell b Lewis	66
H P Tillekeratne b Tufnell	16
R J Ratnayake c sub (Salisbury) b Lawrence	17
C P Ramanayake not out	34
K I W Wijegunawardene c Botham b DeFreitas	4
S D Anurasiri lbw Tufnell	16
Extras (b1, lb16, nb2)	19
Total (103.3 overs)	**285**

Fall of wickets: 1-50, 2-50, 3-111, 4-119, 5-159, 6-212, 7-212, 8-241, 9-253

Bowling: DeFreitas 22-8-45-1; Lawrence 23-7-83-2; Botham 6-2-15-0; Lewis 18-4-31-2; Tufnell 34.3-14-94-5

ENGLAND WON BY 137 RUNS
Men of the Match: Ratnayake and Stewart

ENGLAND'S TESTS 1990-91

Australia v England

Brisbane, Nov 25	AUSTRALIA won by 10 wickets
Melbourne, Dec 30	AUSTRALIA won by 8 wickets
Sydney, Jan 8	Drawn
Adelaide, Jan 29	Drawn
Perth, Feb 5	AUSTRALIA won by 9 wickets

England v West Indies

Headingley, Jun 10	ENGLAND won by 115 runs
Lord's, Jun 24	Drawn
Trent Bridge, Jul 9	WEST INDIES won by 9 wickets
Edgbaston, Jul 29	WEST INDIES won by 7 wickets
The Oval, Aug 13	ENGLAND won by 5 wickets

England v Sri Lanka

Lord's, Aug 27	ENGLAND won by 137 runs

ENGLISHMEN WHO HAVE CARRIED THEIR BAT THROUGH A TEST INNINGS

Bobby Abel v Australia (Sydney) 1891-92
Pelham Warner v South Africa (Johannesburg) 1898-99
Len Hutton v West Indies (The Oval) 1950
Len Hutton v Australia (Adelaide) 1950-51
Geoff Boycott v Australia (Perth) 1979-80
Graham Gooch West Indies (Headingley) 1991

A WICKET FIRST BALL IN TESTS

Arthur Coningham	Australia	1894-95
Walter Bradley	England	1899
Ted Arnold	England	1903-04
George Macaulay	England	1922-23
Maurice Tate	England	1924
Matthew Henderson	New Zealand	1929-30
Horace Smith	New Zealand	1932-33
Tyrel Johnson	West Indies	1939
Dick Howorth	England	1947
Intikhab Alam	Pakistan	1959-60
Richard Illingworth	England	1991

OFF THE AIR

❝...Atherton's looking pretty comfortable out there. And if you want to be comfortable when you're visiting the north-west, why not stay at the Mottram Hall Hotel in Cheshire?"
Bob Willis, commentating on Sky TV

"Would it be too much to ask my old television colleague, Geoffrey Boycott, whose knowledge of cricket is so profound and whose comments are so often illuminating, to pause for breath now and again and ease up on his tutorial?"
Letter to The Times from Peter West

"...Such a shambles of personal indiscipline that the programme has sounded somewhere between Gussie Fink-Nottle's speech day address and the Monty Python Twit of the Year contest."
Don Mosey on Test Match Special

"I have never had a quarrel nor heard one in the box."
Brian Johnston,

"It cannot be compared with any other kind of commentary. Longer, freer, yet with its own conventions and characteristics, it is an instant poem for six voices, fabricated daily, unique in the world. It could not have happened on any other than public service radio. It is an instituion which I believe should be preserved."
Gillian Reynolds, Daily Telegraph, on Test Match Special

"He couldn't get his leg over.❞
Jonathan Agnew explaining Botham's dismissal at The Oval

1990-91

ENGLAND'S TOUR OF AUSTRALIA

Gooch injured his finger in practice at Perth Oct 23. This became infected and he was forced to have emergency operation Nov 11. Hugh Morris called in as temporary cover for Gooch. Dec 10: Phil DeFreitas called into touring party as cover for Gladstone Small. Dec 27: Chris Lewis to fly home because of back trouble. Jan 27: Phil Newport flown out as emergency general cover

First Test

Brisbane, Nov 23-25
England players were banned from giving interviews, a policy criticised by the Australian Board. The banned Mike Gatting was briefly called in to help at net practice, a decision described by the ICC secretary Colonel John Stephenson as "rather insensitive". Compared to

England's previous Test team against India, Larkins, Stewart, Lewis and Small replaced Gooch (injured), Williams (not selected for tour), Morris and Hemmings. Australia won toss.

ENGLAND
First Innings

M A Atherton lbw Reid	13
W Larkins c Healy b Hughes	12
D I Gower c Healy b Reid	61
A J Lamb c Hughes b Matthews	32
R A Smith b Reid	7
A J Stewart lbw Reid	4
R C Russell c & b Alderman	16
C C Lewis c Border b Hughes	20
G C Small not out	12
A R C Fraser c Healy b Alderman	1
D E Malcolm c Waugh b Hughes	5
Extras (b1, lb7, nb3)	11

Total (78 overs) **194**
Fall of wickets: 1-23 2-43 3-117 4-123 5-134 6-135 7-167 8-181 9-187
Bowling: Alderman 18-5-44-2; Reid 18-3-53-4; Hughes 19-5-39-3; Waugh 7-2-20-0; Matthews 16-8-30-1
England's lowest first innings total against Australia since Edgbaston 1981
AUSTRALIA
First Innings
G R Marsh lbw Fraser 9
M A Taylor c Lewis b Fraser 10
D C Boon lbw Small...18
A R Border c Atherton b Small 9
D M Jones c Small b Lewis. 17
S R Waugh c Smith b Small..1
G R J Matthews c Small b Malcolm 35
I A Healy c Atherton b Lewis.....................................22
M G Hughes c Russell b Fraser 9
B A Reid b Lewis..0
T M Alderman not out 0
Extras (b1 lb10 nb11) 22
Total (63 overs)..**152**
Fall of wickets: 1-22 2-35 3-49 4-60 5-64 6-89 7-135 8-150 9-150
Bowling: Malcolm 17-2-45-1; Fraser 21-6-33-3; Small 16-4-34-3; Lewis 9-0-29-3
ENGLAND
Second Innings
M A Atherton b Alderman...15
W Larkins lbw Reid..0
D I Gower b Hughes..27
A J Lamb lbw Alderman...14
R C Russell lbw Waugh...15
R A Smith c Taylor b Alderman.....................................1
A J Stewart c Sub (Cantrell) b Alderman 6
C C Lewis lbw Alderman..14
G C Small c Alderman b Hughes.....................................15
A R C Fraser c Sub (Cantrell) b Alderman 0
D E Malcolm not out...0
Extras (lb3, nb4) 7
Total (53.1 overs)..**114**
Fall of wickets 1-0 2-42 3-46 4-60 5-78 6-84 7-93 8-112 9-114
Bowling: Alderman 22-7-47-6; Reid 14-3-40-1; Hughes 12.1-5-17-2; Matthews 1-1-0-0; Waugh 4-2-7-1
England's lowest total on the ground and lowest against Australia since the 95 in the Centenary Test of 1976-77
AUSTRALIA
Second Innings
M A Taylor not out..67
G R Marsh not out...72
Extras (b3, lb2, w3, nb10) 18
Total (0 wkts, 46 overs)......................................**157**
Bowling: Fraser 14-2-49-0; Small 15-2-36-0; Malcolm 9-5-22-0; Lewis 6-0-29-0; Atherton 2-0-16-0
AUSTRALIA WON BY 10 WICKETS
Match finished at 5.56 pm on third day. England's first three-day defeat against Australia since Headingley 1938. Lamb's third defeat out of three as captain.
Man of the Match: Alderman

Second Test
Melbourne, Dec 26-30
Gooch, DeFreitas and Tufnell (debut) for Lamb, Small, and Lewis (all injured). England won toss.
ENGLAND
First Innings
G A Gooch lbw Alderman 20
M A Atherton c Boon b Reid..0
W Larkins c Healy b Reid..64
R A Smith c Healy b Hughes..30
D I Gower c & b Reid...100
A J Stewart c Healy b Reid..79
R C Russell c Healy b Hughes......................................15
P A J DeFreitas c Healy b Reid.....................................3

A R C Fraser c Jones b Alderman...................................24
D E Malcolm c Taylor b Reid..6
P C R Tufnell not out..0
Extras (lb2 nb9) 11
Total (131.4 overs)...**352**
Fall of wickets: 1-12 2-30 3-109 4-152 5-274 6-303 7-307 8-324 9-344
Bowling: Alderman 30.4.-7-86-2; Reid 39-8-97-6; Hughes 29-7-83-2; Matthews 27-8-65-0; Waugh 6-2-19-0
Gower followed Hobbs and Bradman in scoring 3000 runs in England-Australia Tests
AUSTRALIA
First Innings
G R Marsh c Russell b DeFreitas...................................36
M A Taylor c Russell b DeFreitas..................................61
D C Boon c Russell b Malcolm......................................28
A R Border c Russell b Fraser.....................................62
D M Jones c Russell b Fraser......................................44
S R Waugh b Fraser..19
G R J Matthews lbw Fraser...12
I A Healy c Russell b Fraser.......................................5
M G Hughes lbw Malcolm...4
T M Alderman b Fraser..0
B A Reid not out...3
Extras (b4, lb2, nb16)..32
Total (112.5 overs)...**306**
Fall of wickets: 1-63 2-133 3-149 4-224 5-564 6-281 7-289 8-298 9-302
Bowling: Malcolm 25.5-4-74-2; Fraser 39-10-82-6; Tufnell 21-5-62-0; DeFreitas 25-5-69-2; Atherton 2-1-3-0
Russell equalled Marsh's Ashes record of six catches in an innings

ENGLAND
Second Innings
G A Gooch c Alderman b Reid.......................................58
M A Atherton c Healy b Reid..4
W Larkins c Healy b Reid..54
R A Smith c Taylor b Reid..8
D I Gower c Border b Matthews......................................0
A J Stewart c Marsh b Reid...8
R C Russell c Jones b Matthews.....................................1
P A J DeFreitas lbw Reid...0
A R C Fraser c Taylor b Reid.......................................0
D E Malcolm lbw Matthews...1
P C R Tufnell not out..0
Extras (b7, lb3, nb6)...16
Total (73 overs)..**150**
Fall of wickets 1-17, 2-103, 3-115, 4-122, 5-147, 6-148, 7-148, 8-148, 9-150
Bowling: Alderman 10-2-19-0; Reid 22-12-51-7; Hughes 9-4-26-0; Matthews 25-9-3-40; 7-6-4-0
Gower's first 0 for 120 Test innings. England lost six wickets for three runs in twelve overs. Reid's match figures of 13 for 148 were Australia's fifth-best in Ashes history
AUSTRALIA
Second Innings
M A Taylor c Atherton b Malcolm....................................5
G R Marsh not out...79
I A Healy c Atherton ɓ Fraser......................................1
D C Boon not out..94
Extras (b4, lb12, nb2)..18
Total (2 wkts, 86 overs)......................................**197**
Fall of wickets: 1-9 2-10
Bowling: Malcolm 23-7-52-1; Fraser 20-4-33-1; Tufnell 24-12-36-0; DeFreitas 16-3-46-0; Atherton 3-0-14-0
AUSTRALIA WON BY 8 WICKETS
Man of the Match: Reid

Third Test
Sydney, Jan 4-8
Hemmings and Small for Fraser (injured) and DeFreitas. England won toss
AUSTRALIA
First Innings

G R Marsh c Larkins b Malcolm 13
M A Taylor c Russell b Malcolm 11
D C Boon c Atherton b Gooch....................97
A R Border b Hemmings 78
D M Jones st Russell b Small 60
S R Waugh c Stewart b Malcolm 48
G R J Matthews c Hemmings b Tufnell.......128
I A Healy c Small b Hemmings 35
G C Rackemann b Hemmings 1
T M Alderman not out 26
B A Reid c Smith b Malcolm......................0
Extras (b5, lb8, nb8) **21**
Total (157 overs) **518**
Fall of wickets 1-21 2-38 3-185 4-226 5-292 6-347 7-442
8-457 9-512
Bowling: Malcolm 45-12-128-4; Small 35-5-103-1;
Hemmings 32-7-105-3; Tufnell 30-6-95-1; Gooch 14-3-
46-1; Atherton 5-0-28-0

ENGLAND
First Innings
G A Gooch c Healy b Reid 59
M A Atherton c Boon b Matthews.............105
W Larkins run out 11
R A Smith c Healy b Reid 18
D I Gower c Marsh b Reid.......................123
A J Stewart lbw Alderman 91
R C Russell not out 30
G C Small lbw Alderman 10
E E Hemmings b Alderman 0
P C R Tufnell not out 5
Extras (b1, lb8, nb8) **17**
Total (8 wkts dec, 172.1 overs) **469**
Did not bat: D E Malcolm
Fall of wickets 1-95 2-116 3-156 4-295 5-394 6-426 7-
444 8-444
Bowling: Alderman 20.1-4-62-3; Reid 35.1-9-79-3;
Rackemann 25.5-5-89-0; Matthews 58-16-145-1; Border
19-5-45-0; Waugh 14-3-40-0
*Atherton scored the slowest century in an England-
Australia Test, 424 minutes, 13 minutes longer than
Randall at Sydney in 1978-79*

AUSTRALIA
Second Innings
M A Taylor lbw Hemmings 19
G R Marsh c Stewart b Malcolm 4
I A Healy c Smith b Tufnell.......................9
D C Boon c Gooch b Tufnell......................29
A R Border c Gooch b Tufnell....................20
D M Jones c & b Tufnell............................0
S R Waugh c Russell b Hemmings 14
G R J Matthews b Hemmings 19
C G Rackemann b Malcolm.........................9
T M Alderman c Gower b Tufnell 1
B A Reid not out 5
Extras (lb16) **16**
Total (89 overs) **205**
Fall of wickets 1-21 2-29 3-81 4-129 5-129 6-166 7-166
8-9-192
Bowling: Malcolm 6-1-19-2; Small 2-1-6-0; Hemmings
41-9-94-3; Atherton 3-1-9-0; Tufnell 37-18-61-5
*Rackemann was scoreless for 72 minutes, an Australian
Test record*

ENGLAND
Second Innings
G A Gooch c Border b Matthews 54
D I Gower c Taylor b Matthews 36
W Larkins lbw Border 0
A J Stewart run out 7
R A Smith not out 10
M A Atherton not out.............................3
Extras (lb1, nb2)................................**3**
Total (4 wkts, 25 overs) **113**
Fall of wickets:: 1-84 2-84 3-100 4-100

Bowling: Alderman 4-0-29-0; Rackemann 3-0-20-0;
Matthews 9-2-26-2; Border 9-1-37-1
MATCH DRAWN
Man of the Match: Atherton

Fourth Test
Adelaide, Jan 25-29
*Fraser and Lamb replaced Russell and Larkins. Stewart
kept wicket. Australia dropped Steve Waugh after 42
consecutive Tests and replaced him with his twin Mark,
making the Waughs the first twins to play Test cricket.
Australia won toss.*

AUSTRALIA
First Innings
G R Marsh c Gooch b Small......................37
M A Taylor run out..................................5
D C Boon c Fraser b Malcolm 49
A R Border b DeFreitas 12
D M Jones lbw DeFreitas...........................0
M E Waugh b Malcolm............................138
G R J Matthews c Stewart b Gooch............65
I A Healy c Stewart b DeFreitas 1
C J McDermott not out 42
M G Hughes lbw Small 1
B A Reid c Lamb b DeFreitas......................2
Extras (b2, lb23, nb4, w2)......................**31**
Total (135.2 overs).............................**386**
Fall of wickets 1-11 2-62 3-104 4-104 5-124 6-295 7-298
8-358 9-373
Bowling: Malcolm 38-7-104-2; Fraser 23-6-48-0; Small
34-10-92-2; DeFreitas 26.2-6-56-4; Tufnell 5-0-38-0;
Gooch 9-2-23-1

ENGLAND
First Innings
G A Gooch c Healy b Reid 87
M A Atherton lbw McDermott 0
A J Lamb c Healy b McDermott 0
R A Smith c & b Hughes 53
D I Gower c Hughes b McDermott 11
A J Stewart c Healy b Reid 11
P A J DeFreitas c Matthews b McDermott 45
G C Small b McDermott.............................1
A R C Fraser c Healy b Reid 2
D E Malcolm c Healy b Reid 2
P C R Tufnell not out 0
Extras (b1, lb3, nb13).........................**17**
Total (81.3 overs) **229**
Fall of wickets: 1-10 2-11 3-137 4-160 5-176 6-179 7-
198 8-215 9-219
Bowling: Reid 29-9-53-4; McDermott 26.3-3-97-5;
Hughes 22-4-62-1; Waugh 4-1-13-0

AUSTRALIA
Second Innings
M A Taylor run out.................................4
G R Marsh c Gooch b Small 0
D C Boon b Tufnell................................21
D M Jones lbw DeFreitas...........................8
M E Waugh b Malcolm.............................23
M G Hughes c Gooch b Fraser 30
A R Border not out................................83
G R J Matthews not out 34
Extras (b1, lb7, w1, nb2).......................**11**
Total (6 wkts, 104 overs).....................**314**
Fall of wickets 1-1 2-8 3-25 4-64 5-130 6-240
Bowling: Malcolm 21-0-87-1; Small 18-3-64-1; DeFreitas
23-6-61-1; Fraser 26-3-66-1; Tufnell 16-3-28-1

ENGLAND
Second Innings
G A Gooch c Marsh b Reid......................117
M A Atherton c Waugh b Reid 87
A J Lamb c McDermott 53
D I Gower lbw Hughes 16
R A Smith not out 10

A J Stewart c Jones b McDermott 9
P A J DeFreitas not out..19
Extras (b5, lb9, w1, nb9) 24
Total (5 wkts, 96 overs)..**335**
Fall of wickets 1-203 2-246 3-287 4-287 5-297
Bowling: Reid 23-5-59-2; McDermott 27-5-106-2;
Matthews 31-7-100-0; Hughes 14-3-52-1; Waugh 1-0-4-0
MATCH DRAWN
Man of the Match: Waugh

Fifth Test
Perth, Feb 1-6
*Newport replaced Fraser (unfit). Gower equalled Colin
Cowdrey's English record of 114 Test appearances.
England won toss.*
ENGLAND
First Innings
G A Gooch c Healy b McDermott 13
M A Atherton c Healy b McDermott...............................27
A J Lamb c Border b McDermott 91
R A Smith c Taylor b McDermott...................................58
D I Gower not out 28
A J Stewart lbw McDermott 2
P A J DeFreitas c Marsh b McDermott.............................5
P J Newport c Healy b McDermott...................................0
G C Small c Boon b Hughes...0
P C R Tufnell c Healy b Hughes.......................................0
D E Malcolm c Marsh b McDermott 7
Extras (b1, lb6, w1, nb5) 13
Total (66.4 overs)...**244**
Fall of wickets: 1-27 2-50 3-191 4-212 5-220 6-226 7-
226 8-227 9-227
Bowling: Alderman 22-5-66-0; McDermott 24.4-2- 97-
8; Hughes 17-3-49-2; Waugh 1-0-9-0; Matthews 2-0-16-0
*McDermott took the first seven wickets. England were 212
for 3 at tea*
AUSTRALIA
First Innings
G R Marsh c Stewart b Small 1
M A Taylor c Stewart b Malcolm 12
D C Boon c Stewart b Malcolm......................................64
A R Border lbw DeFreitas 17
D M Jones b Newport 34
M E Waugh c Small b Malcolm 26
G R J Matthews not out 60
I A Healy c Lamb b Small 42
C J McDermott b Tufnell 25
M G Hughes c Gooch b Tufnell..0
T M Alderman lbw DeFreitas 7
Extras (b2, lb8, w1, nb8) 19
Total (90.5 overs)...**307**
Fall of wickets: 1-1 2-44 3-90 4-113 5-161 6-168 7-230
8-281 9-283
Bowling: Malcolm 30-4-94-3; Small 23-3-65-2; DeFreitas
16.5-2-57-2; Newport 14-0-56-1; Tufnell 7-1-25-2

ENGLAND
Second Innings
G A Gooch c Alderman b Hughes 18
M A Atherton c Boon b Hughes 25
A J Lamb lbw McDermott 5
R A Smith lbw Alderman 43
D I Gower c Taylor b Alderman 5
A J Stewart c Healy b McDermott....................................7
P A J DeFreitas c Healy b Alderman.................................5
P J Newport not out 40
G C Small c Taylor b Hughes...4
P C R Tufnell c Healy b Hughes.......................................8
D E Malcolm c Jones b McDermott 6
Extras (b5, lb5, nb6) 16
Total (61.3 overs)...**182**
Fall of wickets 1-41 2-49 3-75 4-80 5-114 6-118 7-125 8-
134 9-144
Bowling: McDermott 19.3-2-60-3; Alderman 22-3- 75-3;

Hughes 20-7-37-4
AUSTRALIA
Second Innings
M A Taylor c Stewart b DeFreitas 19
G R Marsh not out...63
D C Boon not out..30
Extras (lb5, w2, nb1) 8
Total (1 w kt, 31.2 overs) **120**
Fall of wicket: 1-39
Bowling: Malcolm 9-0-40-0; Small 10-5-24-0; DeFreitas
6.2-0-29-1; Newport 6-0-2-0
AUSTRALIA WON BY 9 WICKETS
Man of the Match: McDermott

OTHER FIRST-CLASS MATCHES
Western Australia v England XI
Perth, Nov 2-5
Match drawn
WESTERN AUSTRALIA 289 (G M Wood 108) & 329-4
(G R Marsh 151); ENGLAND 246 (C D Matthews 5-66)
& 222-9

South Australia v England XI
Adelaide, Nov 9-12
South Australia won by six wickets
SOUTH AUSTRALIA 431-6dec (G A Bishop 154, P C
Nobes 131) & 112-4; ENGLAND 217 & 325 (Hickey 5-
83)

Australian XI v England XI
Hobart, Nov 16-19
Match Drawn
ENGLAND 340 (A J Lamb 154, C D Matthews 6-71) &
192-4 dec (A J Lamb 105); AUSTRALIA 192 (D E
Malcolm 7-74) & 214-6 (D C Boon 108)

Victoria v England XI
Ballarat, Dec 20-23
Match Drawn
VICTORIA 441-7 dec (W G Ayres 139, D M Jones 110)
& 215-7 dec; ENGLAND 353-6 dec (A J Lamb 143) &
204-7

New South Wales v England XI
Albury, Jan 14-16
New South Wales won by 6 wickets
ENGLAND 164 & 235 (M A Atherton 114); NEW
SOUTH WALES 321 (G S Milliken 107) & 79-4

Queensland v England XI
Carrara, Jan 19-22
England won by 10 wickets
QUEENSLAND 286 (P C R Tufnell 5-108) & 175;
ENGLAND 430 (J E Morris 132, R A Smith 108) & 32-0
*Had England not won this game, they would have become
the first England team that had toured Australia without
winning a first-class match*

ENGLAND TOUR RECORD

	D	W	L	D
Test Matches	5	0	3	2
Other 1st Class Matches	6	1	1	4
One Day Internationals	8	2	6	0
Other One Day matches	8	5	3	0
Total	27	8	13	6

Leading Test Batting Averages

		M	I	NO	RUNS	HS	AVGE
1	D C Boon (A)	5	9	2	530	121	75.71
2	G R Matthews (A)	5	7	2	353	128	70.60
3	C J McDermott (A)	2	2	1	67	42*	67.00
4	M E Waugh (A)	2	3	0	187	138	62.33
5	G A Gooch (E)	4	8	0	426	117	53.25

Leading Test Bowling Averages

		M	BALLS	RUNS	WKTS	AVGE	BEST
1	B A Reid (A)	4	1081	432	27	16.00	7-51
2	C C Lewis (E)	1	90	58	3	19.33	3-29
3	C J McDermott (A)	2	486	360	18	20.00	8-97
4	M G Hughes (A)	4	853	365	15	24.33	4-37
5	T M Alderman (A)	4	993	428	16	26.75	6-47

ENGLAND TEST AVERAGES 1990-91

(Composite figures from the three series)

Batting

	M	I	NO	RUNS	BEST	AVGE	*Updated Career Figures* M	I	NO	RUNS	BEST	AVGE
Graham Gooch	10	19	1	1120	174	62.22	91	166	6	7028	333	43.92
Robin Smith	10	19	5	721	148*	51.50	28	53	13	2118	148*	52.95
David Gower	5	10	1	407	123	45.22	114	199	16	8081	215	44.15
Philip Newport	1	2	1	40	40*	40.00	3	5	1	110	40*	27.50
Alec Stewart	7	14	2	449	113*	37.42	14	27	3	766	113*	31.91
Chris Lewis	4	6	1	170	65	34.00	7	9	1	206	65	25.75
Ian Botham	2	3	1	57	31	28.50	99	157	6	5176	208	34.27
Wayne Larkins	3	6	0	141	64	23.50	13	25	1	493	64	20.54
Allan Lamb	7	13	0	283	91	21.77	74	131	10	4264	139	35.23
Mark Ramprakash	6	10	0	210	29	21.00	6	10	0	210	29	21.00
Michael Atherton	10	19	1	358	105	19.89	18	34	1	1166	151	35.33
Hugh Morris	3	6	0	115	44	19.17	3	6	0	115	44	19.17
Derek Pringle	4	7	0	128	45	18.29	25	43	3	640	63	16.00
Phil DeFreitas	9	15	2	212	55*	16.31	26	40	3	513	55*	13.86
Richard Illingworth	2	4	2	31	13	15.50	2	4	2	31	13	15.50
Jack Russell	8	14	2	179	46	14.92	25	40	7	869	128*	26.33
David Lawrence	3	4	0	50	34	12.50	4	5	0	54	34	10.80
Graeme Hick	4	7	0	75	43	10.71	4	7	0	75	43	10.71
Gladstone Small	4	6	1	42	15	8.40	17	24	7	263	59	15.47
Angus Fraser	3	5	0	27	24	5.40	11	14	1	88	29	6.76
Devon Malcolm	7	10	2	36	7	4.50	18	24	8	99	15*	6.19
Phil Tufnell	6	8	4	15	8	3.75	6	8	4	15	8	3.75
Steve Watkin	2	3	0	8	6	2.67	2	3	0	8	6	2.67
Eddie Hemmings	1	1	0	0	0	-	16	21	4	383	95	22.52

Bowling

	BALLS	RUNS	WKTS	BEST	AVGE	*Updated Career Figures* BALLS	RUNS	WKTS	BEST	AVGE
Phil DeFreitas	2084	890	40	7-70	22.25	5634	2603	78	7-70	33.37
Derek Pringle	769	322	12	5-100	25.83	4519	2129	60	5-95	35.48
Ian Botham	258	108	4	2-40	27.00	21539	10741	380	8-34	28.26
Angus Fraser	858	311	11	6-82	28.27	3106	1255	47	6-82	26.70
Chris Lewis	732	319	11	6-111	29.00	1368	727	20	6-111	36.35
Phil Tufnell	1452	637	21	6-25	30.33	1452	637	21	6-25	30.33
Steve Watkin	216	153	5	3-38	30.60	216	153	5	3-38	30.60
Eddie Hemmings	438	199	6	3-94	33.17	4437	1825	43	6-58	42.44
David Lawrence	698	494	14	5-106	35.29	914	605	17	5-106	35.59
Graham Gooch	186	83	2	1-23	41.50	1989	800	17	2-12	47.05
Devon Malcolm	1598	845	19	4-128	44.47	4204	2293	61	6-77	37.59
Gladstone Small	894	424	9	3-34	47.11	3927	1871	55	5-48	34.01
Graeme Hick	144	95	2	2-77	47.50	144	95	2	2-77	47.50
Richard Illingworth	340	213	4	3-110	53.25	340	213	4	3-110	53.25
Phil Newport	120	78	1	1-56	78.00	669	417	10	4-87	41.70
Michael Atherton	90	70	0	-	-	366	282	1	1-60	282.00
Allan Lamb	-	-	-	-	-	30	23	1	1-6	23.00
David Gower	-	-	-	-	-	36	20	1	1-1	20.00

ENGLAND'S ONE DAY INTERNATIONALS WORLD SERIES CUP

Adelaide, Dec 1
New Zealand won by 7 runs
NEW ZEALAND 199-6 (40 overs) (J G Wright 67, K R Rutherford 50); ENGLAND 192-9 (40 overs) (J E Morris 63*)

Perth, Dec 7
England won by 4 wickets
NEW ZEALAND 158 (49.2 overs); ENGLAND 161-6 (43.5 overs)
England's second win in 13 one-day internationals

Perth, Dec 8
Australia won by 6 wickets
ENGLAND 192-9 (50 overs) (S P O'Donnell 4-45); AUSTRALIA 193-4 (41 overs) (D M Jones 63)

Sydney, Dec 14
England won by 33 runs
ENGLAND 194 (46.4 overs) (A J Lamb 72, C Pringle 4-35); NEW ZEALAND 161 (48.1 overs) (M D Crowe 76, C C Lewis 4-35)

Brisbane, Dec 15
New Zealand won by 8 wickets
ENGLAND 203-6 (50 overs) ; NEW ZEALAND 204-2 (45 overs) M D Crowe 78, J G Wright 54)

Brisbane, Dec 16
Australia won by 37 runs
AUSTRALIA 283-5 (50 overs) D M Jones 145, G M Marsh 82); ENGLAND 246-7 (50 overs)

Sydney, Jan 1
Australia won by 68 runs
AUSTRALIA 221-7 (50 overs) (M E Waugh 62, S P O'Donnell 72*; ENGLAND 153 (45.5 overs)

Melbourne, Jan 10
Australia won by 3 runs
AUSTRALIA 222-6 (50 overs) (S R Waugh 65*, I A Healy 50*); ENGLAND 219-9 (50 overs) (A J Stewart 55)
England failed to reach the final when Tufnell was unable to hit a four off the last ball

Final Table

	P	W	L	Pts	Run Rate
Australia	8	7	1	14	4.77
New Zealand	8	3	5	6	4.06
England	8	2	6	4	4.06

Australia won the final 2-0

NEW ZEALAND v ENGLAND 1990-91

Christchurch, Feb 9
England won by 14 runs

ENGLAND 230-7 (50 overs) (A J Lamb 61, R A Smith 65); NEW ZEALAND 216-8 (50 overs) (K R Rutherford 77, C Z Harris 56)

Wellington, Feb 13
New Zealand won by 9 runs
NEW ZEALAND 196-8 (49 overs) (A H Jones 64); ENGLAND 187 (48 overs)
England were 147 for 3 at one stage

Auckland, Feb 16
New Zealand won by 7 runs
NEW ZEALAND 224-7 (50 overs) (A H Jones 64, I D S Smith 51*); ENGLAND 217 (49.5 overs) (Cairns 4-55)
England were 171 for 3 at one stage

TEXACO TROPHY

Edgbaston, May 23-24
England won by 1 wkt
WEST INDIES 173-8 (55 overs) (I T Botham 4-45); ENGLAND 175-9 (49.4 overs) (M A Atherton 69*)

Old Trafford May 25
England won by 9 runs
ENGLAND 270-4 (55 overs) (M A Atherton 74, A J Lamb 62, G A Gooch 54); WEST INDIES 261-8 (55 overs) (I V A Richards 78)

Lord's, May 27
England won by 7 wkts
WEST INDIES 264-9 (55 overs) (A L Logie 82, D V Lawrence 4-67); ENGLAND 265-3 (46.1 overs) (N H Fairbrother 113, G A Hick 86*)

England Man of the Series: Mike Atherton
West Indies Man of the Series Viv Richards

ENGLAND IN ONE DAY INTERNATIONALS

Opponents	P	W	L	Tied	NR
Australia	51	24	25	1	1
West Indies	42	17	23	-	2
New Zealand	36	17	16	-	3
Pakistan	29	19	10	-	-
India	22	12	10	-	-
Sri Lanka	8	7	1	-	-
Canada	1	1	-	-	-
East Africa	1	1	-	-	-
Totals	**190**	**98**	**85**	**1**	**6**

> **❝ I designed a programme for them specifically focused on inter-personal communications. It features sequences of practical role-playing in handling potential difficulties and conflicts.**
> *Barry Watson, of the "charm school" hired to coach Lord's gatemen*

> **"Oi, you! Aht!"**
> *Lord's steward to photographer, first day of Test*

> **"Once I put on that costume, that's it, I am the King."**
> *Ian Botham, on his role in Jack and the Beanstalk*

> **"The expressionless Botham is the only wooden thing on stage apart from the beanstalk - and even that projects itself better."**
> *Maureen Paton, Daily Express, ditto*

> **"I asked someone at Lord's what I'd done wrong to this man who, after all, didn't even know me. He said: 'You must remember how brave Keith was in World War Two.' I just said: 'Do you think I wouldn't have been?' and walked away."**
> *Ian Botham on being criticised by Keith Miller*

ENGLAND 'A' TOUR OF PAKISTAN & SRI LANKA

Venue, Date	*Opponents*	*Result*
Karachi, Jan 11	Karachi City Cricket Association	Lost by 29 runs
Lahore, Jan 12	Hyderabad	Won by 3 runs
Lahore, Jan 14-16	Combined Universities	Drew

Pakistan tour cancelled Jan 17 after start of Gulf War and re-scheduled tour to Sri Lanka arranged.

Colombo, Jan 26-27	Mercantile Cricket Association XI	Drew
Matara, Jan 29-31	Matara District Association XI	Won by 171 runs
Kandy, Feb 2	Sri Lanka 'A' (*)	Lost by 4 wkts
Kurunegala, Feb 4	Sri Lanka 'A' (*)	Lost by 40 runs
Kandy, Feb 8-12	Sri Lanka 'A' (+)	Drew
Colombo, Feb 15-20	Sri Lanka 'A' (+)	Drew
Colombo, Feb 23	Sri Lanka 'A' (*)	Lost by 8 wkts
Colombo, Feb 24	Sri Lanka 'A' (*)	Lost by 1 run
Katunayake, Feb 26-27	Gampaha Districts XI	Drew
Colombo, Mar 1-5	Sri Lanka 'A' (+)	Drew
Colombo, Mar 8	Sri Lanka 'A' (*)	Won by 51 runs

* One-day international + "Test Match"

OTHER TEST MATCHES 1990-91

PAKISTAN v NEW ZEALAND

New Zealand were without six leading players from their England tour: two had retired and four were unavailable. The Pakistan captain Imran Khan declined to play, saying he had no motivation to take part in a mismatch.

First Test
Karachi, Oct 11-16
Pakistan won by an innings and 43 runs
NEW ZEALAND 196 & 194; PAKISTAN 433-6 dec (Shoaib Mohammad 203*)
Eight New Zealand batsmen were lbw, one Pakistani; Martin Crowe, the NZ captain, repeated his call for neutral umpires.

Second Test
Lahore, Oct 18-23
Pakistan won by 9 wickets
NEW ZEALAND 160 & 287 (M D Crowe 108*, Waqar Younis 7-86); PAKISTAN 373-9 dec (Shoaib Mohammed 105, W Watson 6-78) & 77-1
Waqar Younis had match figures of 10 for 106

Third Test
Faisalabad, Oct 26-31
Pakistan won by 65 runs
PAKISTAN 102 (C Pringle 7-52) & 357 (Shoaib Mohammad 142); NEW ZEALAND 217 (Waqar Younis 7-76) & 177 (Waqar Younis 5-54)
Pringle had match figures of 11 for 152; Waqar Younis had match figures of 12 for 130
Pakistan won series 3-0

PAKISTAN v WEST INDIES

First Test
Karachi, Nov 15-20
Pakistan won by 8 wickets
WEST INDIES 261 (D L Haynes 117, Waqar Younis 5-76) & 181; PAKISTAN 345 (Salim Malik 102) & 98-2

Second Test
Faisalabad, Nov 20-24
West Indies won by 7 wickets
PAKISTAN 170 & 154; WEST INDIES 195 (Waqar Younis 5-43) & 130-3
West Indies won in three days. Pakistan lost their last six second-innings wickets for 10.

Third Test
Lahore, Dec 7-12
Match Drawn
WEST INDIES 294 (C L Hooper 134) & 173 (Wasim Akram 5-28); PAKISTAN 122 (C E L Ambrose 5-35, I R

Bishop 5-41) & 242-6
Wasim Akram became the third player after Maurice Allom and Chris Old (both England) to take four wickets in five balls in a Test.
Series drawn 1-1

INDIA v SRI LANKA

Chandigarh, Nov 22-27
India won by an innings and 8 runs
INDIA 288; SRI LANKA 82 (V Raju 6-12) & 198
The Sector 16 Stadium became the 63rd Test ground. Kapil Dev joined Ian Botham on 376 wickets, behind only Hadlee. Sri Lanka's lowest Test score

NEW ZEALAND v SRI LANKA

First Test
Wellington, Jan 31-Feb 4
Match Drawn
NEW ZEALAND 174 & 671-4 (A H Jones 186, M D Crowe 299); SRI LANKA 497-9 dec (Aravinda De Silva 267, Morrison 5-153)
Martin Crowe and Andrew Jones put on 467, the highest stand in the history of Test cricket. Crowe was out for 299 to the last ball of the day. Sri Lanka's highest Test score.

Second Test
Hamilton, Feb 22-26
Match drawn
NEW ZEALAND 296 (A H Jones 122, R J Ratnayake 5-77) & 374-6 dec (J G Wright 101, A H Jones 100*): SRI LANKA 253 (A P Gurusinha 119) & 344-6 (A P Gurusinha 102)
Gurusinha and Jones scored centuries in both innings, only the second time two different men have scored centuries in both innings of the same Test (Ian & Greg Chappell versus New Zealand, 1973-74) and the only time the two have been from opposing sides. Seddon Park became 64th Test venue. Ian Smith equalled Test wicket-keeping record of seven dismissals in an innings.

Third Test
Auckland, Mar 1-5
Match drawn
SRI LANKA 380 & 319) P A De Silva 123, C L Cairns 5-75); NEW ZEALAND 317 & 261-5
Series drawn 0-0

WEST INDIES v AUSTRALIA

First Test
Kingston, Jamaica, Feb 28-Mar 5
Match drawn
WEST INDIES 264 (C J McDermott 5-80) & 283-3;

AUSTRALIA 371 (D C Boon 109*, B P Patterson 5-83)
Richards passed Sobers' total of 8032 to become West Indies' highest Test scorer

Second Test
Georgetown, Guyana, Mar 22-27
West Indies won by 10 wickets
AUSTRALIA 348 & 248; WEST INDIES 569 (R B Richardson 182, D L Haynes 111, A R Border 5-68) & 31-0
Dean Jones was given run out by umpire Clyde Duncan after he was bowled by a no-ball and was walking to the pavilion thinking he was out. West Indies' first win on the ground for 26 years.

Third Test
Port of Spain, Apr 5-10
Match drawn
AUSTRALIA 294 and 123-3 dec; WEST INDIES 227
Waughs became 35th pair of brothers to play together in the same Test team, but the first twins.

Fourth Test
Bridgetown, Apr 19-24
West Indies won by 343 runs
WEST INDIES 149 & 536-9 dec (C G Greenidge 226); AUSTRALIA 134 & 208
West Indies' 10th consecutive win in a Bridgetown Test

Fifth Test
St John's, Antigua, Apr 27-May 2
Australia won by 157 runs
AUSTRALIA 403 (M E Waugh 139*) & 265 (M A Taylor 144); WEST INDIES 214 & 297
Richards out for nought and two in his last Antigua Test, equalling his worst performance in 116 Tests
West Indies won series 2-1

ENGLISH CRICKET 1991

BRITANNIC ASSURANCE CHAMPIONSHIP

		P	W	L	D	Tie	Bonus Bat	Bowl	Pts	Top Batsman		Top Bowler	
1 (2)	**ESSEX**	22	11	5	6	0	69	67	312	Salim Malik	1891	Neil Foster	91
2 (5)	Warwickshire	22	11	4	7	0	58	65	299	Dominic Ostler	1284	Allan Donald	83
3 (12)	Derbyshire	22	9	5	8	0	46	68	258	Azharuddin	1773	Ole Mortensen	58
4 (13)	Notts	22	7	5	10	0	64	69	245	Chris Broad	1739	Franklyn Stephenson	78
5 (9)	Surrey	22	8	6	8	0	47	66	241	Darren Bicknell	1762	Waqar Younis	113
6 (4)	Worcestershire	22	6	4	12	0	54	59	209	Tom Moody	1770	Phil Newport	54
7 (16)	Kent	22	6	3	12	1	50	55	209	Neil Taylor	1647	Tony Merrick	58
8 (6)	Lancashire	22	6	9	7	0	60	49	205	Gehan Mendis	1223	Wasim Akram	56
9 (3)	Hampshire	22	5	7	10	0	57	56	193	Chris Smith	1353	Aqib Javed	53
10 (11)	Northants	22	5	6	11	0	55	54	189	Alan Fordham	1725	Eldine Baptiste	49
11 (17)	Sussex	22	4	3	14	1	57	60	189	Alan Wells	1777	Adrian Jones	53
12 (8)	Glamorgan	22	5	5	12	0	50	57	187	Matthew Maynard	1766	Steve Watkin	66
13 (13)	Gloucestershire	22	5	10	7	0	42	53	175	Tony Wright	1477	David Lawrence	60
14 (10)	Yorkshire	22	4	6	12	0	58	37	159	Martyn Moxon	1669	Phil Carrick	61
15 (1)	Middlesex	22	3	9	10	0	48	63	159	Mike Gatting	2044	Phil Tufnell	70
16 (7)	Leicestershire	22	3	8	11	0	46	53	147	Nigel Briers	1358	John Maguire	69
17 (15)	Somerset	22	2	5	15	0	66	45	143	Jimmy Cook	2370	David Graveney	53

1990 positions in brackets

First-Class Averages
1990 positions in brackets

Batting		Runs	Avge
1	(-) Carl Hooper	1501	93.81
2	(7) Jimmy Cook	2755	81.02
3	(31) Mike Gatting	2057	73.46
4	(-) Salim Malik	1972	73.03
5	(1) Graham Gooch	1911	70.77
6	(-) Richie Richardson	1403	66.81
7	(22) Chris Smith	1553	64.70
8	(194) David Leatherdale	379	63.16
9	(3) Tom Moody	1887	62.90
10	(126) Derek Randall	1567	62.68
11	(86) Matthew Maynard	1803	60.10
12	(91) Alan Wells	1784	59.46
13	(4) Mohammad Azharuddin	2016	59.29
14	(20) Viv Richards	817	58.35
15	(199) Graeme Turner	349	58.16

Others with 1500 runs

16	(89) Tim Robinson	1673	57.69
17	(21) Neil Taylor	1806	56.43
21	(25) Chris Tavare	1601	53.36
22	(34) Hugh Morris	1803	53.02
24	(37) Chris Broad	1739	49.68
30	(12) Darren Bicknell	1888	47.20
32	(85) Alan Fordham	1840	47.17
36	(59) Martyn Moxon	1669	46.36
38	(192) Tony Wright	1596	45.60
39	(24) Alan Butcher	1677	45.32
40	(43) Bill Athey	1522	44.76
41	(32) Tim Curtis	1653	44.67
43	(176) David Byas	1557	44.48
68	(107) Mike Roseberry	1511	37.77

Bowling

1	(7) Waqar Younis	113	14.65
2	(6) Curtly Ambrose	51	17.03
3	(78) Paul Jarvis	12	19.58
4	(76) Allan Donald	83	19.68
5	(-) Mark Ealham	17	20.82
6	(11) Neil Foster	102	20.96
7	(22) Dermot Reeve	45	21.26
8	(11) Neil Kendrick	12	21.83
9	(49) Graham Dilley	37	22.24
10	(96) Wasim Akram	56	22.33
11	(-) Chris Tolley	18	22.94
12	(35) Neil Mallender	42	23.07
13	(-) Ravi Shastri	31	23.35
14	(-) John Stephenson	17	23.47
15	(133) Jonathan Ayling	25	23.80

Others with 70 wickets

17	(51) David Lawrence	74	24.18
18	(63) Phil DeFreitas	73	24.38
23	(58) Phil Tufnell	88	25.21
26	(25) Tim Munton	73	25.52
28	(86) Franklyn Stephenson	78	25.76
47	(92) Steve Watkin	74	29.39
62	(-) John Maguire	77	31.64

WICKET-KEEPERS:

1	Colin Metson	76	(73 ct, 3 st)
2	Steve Marsh	70	(66ct, 4 st)
3	Bruce French	62	(54 ct, 8 st)
4	Mike Garnham	62	(62 ct)
5	Peter Moores	62	(56 ct, 6 st)
6	Steve Rhodes	62	(54 ct, 8 st)

FIELDERS

1	Nasser Hussain	38
2	Tom Moody	37
3	Rajesh Maru	31

Highest Totals

621	Essex v Leics	(Leicester)
575-8d	Worcs v Somerset	(Worcester)
572-7d	Derbys v Notts	(Derby)
566-6d	Essex v Middlesex	(Chelmsford)
544	Essex v Kent	(Folkestone)
543-8d	Essex v Derbys	(Chelmsford)
514-9d	Glamorgan v Gloucs	(Abergavenny)
504	Glamorgan v Hampshire	(Southampton)
501-6d	Yorkshire v Lancashire	(Scarborough)

Lowest Totals

51	Middlesex v Essex	(Chelmsford)
68	Northants v Notts	(Wellingborough)
83	Somerset v Worcs	(Worcester)
83	Warwicks v Kent	(Tunbridge Wells)
96	Middlesex v Kent	(Canterbury)
97	Sri Lanka v Gloucs	(Bristol)
99	Cambridge U v Glamorgan	(Fenner's)

Highest Individual Scores

259	Graham Gooch	Essex v Middlesex (Chelmsford)
257	Mark Benson	Kent v Hampshire (Southampton)
253*	Alan Wells	Sussex v Yorkshire (Middlesbrough)
248	Tim Curtis	Worcs v Somerset (Worcester)
243	Matthew Maynard	Glamorgan v Hampshire (Southampton)
237	Damian D'Oliveira	Worcs v Oxford U (The Parks)
235*	Trevor Ward	Kent v Middlesex (Canterbury)
217	Kim Barnett	Derbys v Notts (Derby)
215*	Mike Gatting	Middlesex v Derbys (Lord's)
215	Salim Malik	Essex v Leics (Ilford)

Best Innings Bowling

9-37	David Millns	Leics v Derbys (Derby)
8-53	Dominic Cork	Derbys v Essex (Derby)
8-55	Dave Gilbert	Gloucs v Kent (Canterbury)
8-89	Tim Munton	Warwicks v Middlesex (Edgbaston)
8-99	Neil Foster	Essex v Lancashire (Old Trafford)
7-33	Richard Ellison	Kent v Warwicks (Tunbridge Wells)
7-42	Colin Wells	Sussex v Derbys (Derby)
7-43	Neal Radford	Worcs v Somerset (Worcester)
7-52	Martin Bicknell	Surrey v Sussex (The Oval)
7-54	Ian Botham	Worcs v Warwicks (Worcester)

Best Match Bowling

12-91	David Millns	Leics v Derbys (Derby)
12-92	Waqar Younis	Surrey v Hampshire (The Oval)
11-122	Waqar Younis	Surrey v Lancashire (The Oval)
11-127	Tim Munton	Warwicks v Middlesex (Edgbaston)
11-129	David Lawrence	Gloucs v Hampshire (Bristol)
11-129	Wasim Akram	Lancashire v Middlesex (Uxbridge)

Most First-Class Centuries

11	Jimmy Cook (Somerset)
8	Mike Gatting (Middlesex)
7	Matthew Maynard (Glamorgan)
7	Neil Taylor (Kent)
7	Alan Wells (Sussex)
7	Mohammad Azharuddin (Derbys)
6	Graham Gooch (Essex)
6	Tom Moody (Worcs)
6	Chris Smith (Hampshire)
6	Richie Richardson (West Indies)
6	Salim Malik (Essex)

Most One-Day Centuries

6	Tom Moody (Worcs)
4	Chris Smith (Hampshire)
3	Chris Broad (Notts)
3	Martyn Moxon (Yorkshire)

Fastest First-Class Century

61 balls   Ian Austin   Lancashire v Yorkshire (Scarborough)

Most First-Class Five Wickets in an Innings

13	Waqar Younis (Surrey)
8	Allan Donald (Warwicks)
7	Neil Foster (Essex)
7	Wasim Akram (Lancashire)
7	Phil Tufnell (Middlesex)

Most runs in all matches

3570	Jimmy Cook (Somesret)
3274	Tom Moody (Worcs)
2901	Mike Gatting (Middlesex)
2875	Martyn Moxon (Yorkshire)
2820	Alan Fordham (Northants)
2803	Salim Malik (Essex)
2760	Graham Gooch (Essex)
2666	Tim Curtis (Worcs)
2664	Derek Randall (Notts)
2624	Chris Broad (Notts)

Most wickets in all matches

151	Waqar Younis (Surrey)
119	Neil Foster (Essex)
119	Franklyn Stephenson (Notts)
110	David Lawrence (Gloucs)
109	John Emburey (Middlesex)
108	Allan Donald (Warwicks)
101	John Maguire (Leics)
99	Tim Munton (Warwicks)
99	Steve Watkin (Glamorgan)

"It's like climbing Everest and pulling a hamstring in the last stride."
Martin Crowe, on being out for 299

Worcestershire player, doing crossword: "Sherlock Holmes's partner?"
Graeme Hick: "We didn't do Shakespeare in Zimbabwe."
Alleged dressing-room exchange

"Cricketers need to recognise their own negative thoughts and replace them with a thought-stoppage technique."
Darryl Foster, Kent manager

"When things go wrong, it is amazing how complicated the game appears."
David Gower

"I talk to the umpires, explain the angle, how the ball would have hit the wicket, but it makes no difference. And then some seamer comes up from the outside edge, hits the pad and up goes the finger. Wouldn't have hit another set."
Jack Simmons, 50, retiring from League cricket after getting one lbw decision in two years

"I find it ridiculous, but quite typical of the people in charge of international cricket."
Viv Richards on the new restriction on bouncers

"Those who fear that fast bowlers will all be turned into eunuchs and that the hook-shot will become obsolete seem to have overlooked the reality that the legal potential ration is still 180 bouncers a day. And that is still far too many."
David Frith, Wisden Cricket Monthly

"It is high time the umpires signalled the onset of declaration bowling by waving red flags, at which point the first-class averages would be suspended while shame-faced full tosses were delivered and fielders made no attempt to field the ball. At least then the proper cricket would resume sooner and the paying public would receive the respect they deserve."
David Hopps, The Guardian

"Cricket has wholly changed over the last two years. What we now have in the championship is a dreary collection of facts and figures over the first two days, followed by a dreadful artificial orgy of runs. It's dreary, cynical stuff, eventually erupting into life in a way that isn't to my taste."
Peter Roebuck, on retiring

"Cricket's demise in schools appears to be accelerating, and this is a poor prospect for the future of our national game."
Anthony Swainson, director of the Lord's Taverners

"The stands have apparently won the Concrete Society Award for 1991. Next year's will surely go to the men on the north gate, whose attitude is as rigid as ever."
Mike Selvey, The Guardian, on Lord's

"Just because Devon didn't bowl well in one Test, Stewart comes rushing up the M1 from London. We don't need the England manager coming here like Mighty Jove from Mount Olympus."
Chris Middleton, Derbyshire chairman, who was fined £750 for saying so

"Safe alternatives to sex should be sought. A strong possibility is cricket. Cricket-playing nations are capable of only limited amounts of sexual activity."
Letter to the Bangkok Post

NATWEST TROPHY
First Round
Canterbury KENT beat Cambridgeshire by 6 wkts; *Exmouth* ESSEX beat Devon by 8 wkts; *Stone* NORTHAMPTONSHIRE beat Staffordshire by 152 runs; *Edinburgh* SUSSEX beat Scotland by 72 runs; Leicester LEICESTERSHIRE beat Shropshire by 7 wkts; *Bournemouth* LANCASHIRE beat Dorset by 5 wkts; *Darlington* GLAMORGAN beat Durham by 40 runs; *Edgbaston* WARWICKSHIRE beat Yorkshire by 7 wkts; *Bath* SOMERSET beat Buckinghamshire by 6 wkts; *Bedford* WORCESTERSHIRE beat Bedfordshire by 8 wkts; *Trent Bridge* NOTTINGHAMSHIRE beat Lincolnshire by 134 runs; *Reading* HAMPSHIRE beat Berkshire by 10 wkts; *Bristol* GLOUCESTERSHIRE beat Norfolk by 153 runs; *Dublin* MIDDLESEX beat Ireland by 45 runs; *The Oval* SURREY beat Oxfordshire 3-2 in a 'bowl-out' after match abandoned; *Bishop's Stortford* HERTFORDSHIRE beat Derbyshire 2-1 in 'bowl-out' after match abandoned

Second Round
Hove ESSEX beat Sussex by 4 wkts; *Northampton* NORTHAMPTONSHIRE beat Leicestershire by 9 wkts; *The Oval* SURREY beat Kent by 7 wkts; *Edgbaston* WARWICKSHIRE beat Hertfordshire by 10 wkts; *Southampton* HAMPSHIRE beat Lancashire by 8 wkts; *Worcester* GLAMORGAN beat Worcestershire by 7 wkts; *Bristol* NOTTINGHAMSHIRE beat Gloucestershire by 3 wkts; *Taunton* SOMERSET beat Middlesex by 10 runs

Quarter-finals
The Oval SURREY beat Essex by 31 runs; *Edgbaston* WARWICKSHIRE beat Somerset by 5 runs; *Southampton* HAMPSHIRE beat Nottinghamshire by 7 wkts; *Northampton* NORTHAMPTONSHIRE beat Glamorgan by 26 runs

Semi-finals
Edgbaston HAMPSHIRE beat Warwickshire by 9 wkts; *The Oval* SURREY beat Northamptonshire by 7 runs

Final
Lord's, Sep 7
Surrey

D J Bicknell b Ayling		13
J D Robinson not out		3
A J Stewart b Ayling		61
G B Thorpe c James b Connor		93
D M Ward c Maru b Connor		43
M A Lynch c Ayling b Connor		10
I A Greig not out		7
Extras (b2, lb4, w3, nb1)		10
Total (5 wkts, 60 overs)		**240**

Fall of Wickets 1-25, 2-139, 3-203, 4-222, 5-233
Did not bat M P Bicknell, J Boiling, Waqar Younis, A J Murphy
Bowling Aqib 12-2-54-0; Connor 12-4-39-3; Ayling 12-0-39-2; James 9-3-33-0; Maru 6-0-23-0; Udal 9-0-46-0

Hampshire

V P Terry run out		32
T C Middleton b Murphy		78
R A Smith run out		78
D I Gower lbw Waqar Younis		9
K D James c Stewart b M P Bicknell		0
J R Ayling not out		18
A N Aymes run out		2
R J Maru not out		1
Extras (lb17, w5, nb3)		25
Total (6 wkts, 59.4 overs)		**243**

Fall of wickets 1-90, 2-160, 3-192, 4-193, 5-231, 6-238
Did not bat S D Udal, C A Connor, Aqib Javed
Bowling Waqar Younis 12-0-43-1; M P Bicknell 11.4-1-32-1; Murphy 12-0-56-1; Robinson 12-0-43-0; Boiling 12-1-52-0

HAMPSHIRE WON BY 4 WICKETS
Man of the Match: Robin Smith (Hants)

Best Performances
Batting - Team
354-2 (60 overs) Glamorgan v Durham, Jun 26; **306-4** (60 overs) Notts v Lincs, Jun 26; **305-9** (60 overs) Durham v Glamorgan, Jun 26
Batting - Individual
151* M P Maynard, Glamorgan v Durham, Jun 26; **145** R J Bailey, Northants v Staffs, Jun 26; **132*** A Fordham, Northants v Leics, Jul 11
Bowling
7-19 N V Radford, Worcs v Beds, Jun 26; **5-40** Waqar Younis, Surrey v Northants, Aug 15; **5-60** A N Hayhurst, Somerset v Warwicks, Jul 31

BENSON & HEDGES CUP

Group A
Derby NORTHAMPTONSHIRE beat Derbyshire by 66 runs; *Bristol* GLOUCESTERSHIRE beat Combined Universities by 66 runs; *The Parks* DERBYSHIRE beat Combined Universities by 206 runs; *Worcester* WORCESTERSHIRE beat Gloucestershire by 6 wkts; *Fenner's* WORCESTERSHIRE beat Combined Universities by 6 wkts; *Bristol* GLOUCESTERSHIRE beat Northamptonshire by 7 wkts; *Worcester* WORCESTERSHIRE beat Derbyshire by 7 wkts; *Northampton* NORTHAMPTONSHIRE beat Combined Universities by 6 wkts; *Derby* DERBYSHIRE beat Gloucestershire lost fewer wkts; *Northampton* NORTHAMPTONSHIRE beat Worcestershire by 75 runs
WORCESTERSHIRE & NORTHAMPTONSHIRE qualified

Group B
Taunton MIDDLESEX beat Somerset by 8 wkts; *The Oval* ESSEX beat Surrey by 53 runs; *Lord's* SURREY beat Middlesex by 75 runs; *Edgbaston:* ESSEX beat Warwickshire by 12 runs; *Edgbaston* WARWICKSHIRE beat Somerset by 33 runs; *Chelmsford* ESSEX beat Middlesex by 3 wkts; *Lord's* WARWICKSHIRE beat Middlesex by 39 runs; *Taunton* SOMERSET beat Surrey by 4 wkts; *Chelmsford* ESSEX beat Somerset by 8 wkts; *The Oval* WARWICKSHIRE beat Surrey by 1 run
ESSEX & WARWICKSHIRE qualified

Group C
Forfar LANCASHIRE beat Scotland by 7 wkts; *Canterbury* KENT beat Leicestershire by 74 runs; *Old Trafford:* LANCASHIRE beat Kent by 6 wkts; *Hove* SUSSEX beat Leicestershire by 72 runs; *Canterbury* KENT beat Sussex by 4 wkts; *Leicester* LEICESTERSHIRE beat Scotland by 45 runs; *Leicester* LANCASHIRE beat Leicestershire by 7 wkts; *Hove* SUSSEX beat Scotland by 4 runs; *Old Trafford* LANCASHIRE beat Sussex by 123 runs; *Glasgow* KENT beat Scotland by 130 runs
LANCASHIRE & KENT qualified

GROUP D
Southampton HAMPSHIRE beat Nottinghamshire by 4 runs; *Trowbridge* GLAMORGAN beat Minor Counties by 17 runs; *Trent Bridge:* NOTTINGHAMSHIRE beat Yorkshire by 7 wkts; *Trowbridge* HAMPSHIRE beat Minor Counties by 8 wkts; *Headingley* YORKSHIRE beat Minor Counties by 7 wkts; *Southampton* HAMPSHIRE beat Glamorgan by 59 runs; *Headingley* YORKSHIRE beat Hampshire by 189 runs; *Cardiff* GLAMORGAN beat Nottinghamshire by 1 run; *Trent Bridge* NOTTINGHAMSHIRE beat Minor Counties by 51 runs; *Cardiff* YORKSHIRE beat Glamorgan by 8 wkts
HAMPSHIRE & YORKSHIRE qualified

QUARTER-FINALS

Worcester WORCESTERSHIRE beat Kent by 27 runs; *Headingley* YORKSHIRE beat Warwickshire by 122 runs; *Chelmsford* ESSEX beat Hampshire by 32 runs; *Old Trafford* LANCASHIRE beat Northamptonshire by 7 wkts

SEMI-FINALS

Old Trafford LANCASHIRE beat Yorkshire by 68 runs; *Chelmsford* WORCESTERSHIRE beat Essex by 9 wkts

FINAL

Lord's, Jul 13

WORCESTERSHIRE

T S Curtis b DeFreitas	4
T M Moody b Allott	12
GA Hick c & b Allott	88
D B D'Oliveira c DeFreitas b Akram	25
I T Botham c Fowler b Watkinson	19
P A Neale c Watkinson b Austin	4
S J Rhodes c Allott b Akram	13
R K Illingworth not out	17
P J Newport c DeFreitas b Akram	2
N V Radford not out	25
Extras (lb8, w15, nb4)	27
Total (8 wkts, 55 overs)	236

Did not bat: G R Dilley

Fall of wickets: 1-4, 2-38, 3-97, 4-166, 5-172, 6-175, 7-195, 8-203

Bowling: DeFreitas 11-1-38-1; Allott 11-3-26-2; Watkinson 11-0-54-1; Wasim Akram 11-1-58-3; Austin 11-0-52-1

LANCASHIRE

G D Mendis b Radford	14
G Fowler c Hick b Radford	54
M A Atherton c Rhodes b Radford	5
N H Fairbrother run out	1
G D Lloyd c Hick b Botham	10
M Watkinson c Hick b Dilley	13
Wasim Akram run out	14
P A J DeFreitas c Neale b Newport	19
W K Hegg not out	13
I D Austin c Illingworth b Newport	7
P J W Alltt c Neale b Dilley	10
Extras (lb5, w4, nb2)	11
Total (47.2 overs)	171

Fall of wickets: 1-24, 2-31, 3-32, 4-64, 5-92, 6-111, 7-134, 8-140, 9-158

Bowling: Dilley 8.2-2-19-2; Radford 9-1-48-3; Botham 8-1-23-1; Newport 11-1-38-2; Illingworth 11-0-38-0

WORCESTERSHIRE WON BY 65 RUNS

Gold Award: Graeme Hick

Best Performances

Batting-Team

366-4 (55 overs) Derbyshire v Combined Universities; **330-4** (55 overs) Lancashire v Sussex; **319-8** (55 overs) Kent v Scotland

Batting-Individual

142 J P Stephenson Essex v Warwickshire, C L Smith Hampshire v Glamorgan; **141*** M D Moxon Yorkshire v Glamorgan

Bowling

6-20 D V Lawrence Gloucestershire v Combined Universities;
6-36 R H Macdonald Combined Universities v Gloucestershire;
5-29 J G Thomas Northamptonshire v Derbyshire

CRY, THE BELOVED COUNTY

❝In England even politics moves on, but Yorkshire cricket does not. We are still living in the dark ages.❞
Paul Jarvis, complaining that Yorkshire's original plan to allow in some outsiders was not enough

"It's a bloody disgrace. Anybody who was not born in this great county - no matter who they are - should not be allowed to take the field for Yorkshire."
Fred Trueman, complaining that it was far too much

"I have, for instance, advised people like Lord Whitelaw, Leon Brittan and Douglas Hurd on various problems such as the coalminers' strike, and perhaps it was felt I could help guide Yorkshire."
Sir Lawrence Byford, explaining how he came to be Yorkshire president

"He doesn't understand cricket, but it doesn't matter. We'll put him on one of the committees."
Fred Trueman on his son-in-law Damon Welch

"As I told a member of the Polish government bewailing the difficulties of governing the Poles in 1988, 'try running Yorkshire County Cricket Club'."
Sir Bernard Ingham

"We just have to enjoy the day out."
Martyn Moxon, when Yorkshire were drawn to play Lancashire in a cup-tie

"...the first Roses captain to talk about the contest in terms more suited to a trip to Alton Towers."
David Hopps, The Guardian

"You don't have to be a mathematician to see that if the present trend continues, this great club will be bankrupt."
Sir Lawrence Byford, announcing the end of all restrictions on non-Yorkshiremen

"I was the prophet who first called for change."
Geoff Boycott

"I think we are taking a short cut to success but if that's what everyone wants I'll go along with it."
Brian Close

"It is my beloved Yorkshire that I am concerned about. We have a proud tradition and I feel a little part of me has been destroyed.❞
Roland Boyes MP, tabling a Commons motion deploring the decision

REFUGE ASSURANCE LEAGUE FINAL TABLE

		P	W	L	T	NR	Pts	Run Rate	Top Batsman		Top Bowler	
1(4)	Notts	16	13	3	0	0	52	83.47	Derek Randall	673	Franklyn Stephenson	30
2(2)	Lancashire	16	12	3	0	1	50	89.78	Graeme Fowler	521	Ian Austin	28
3(17)	Northants	16	10	4	0	2	44	86.26	Alan Fordham	455	David Capel	16
4(10)	Worcestershire	16	9	4	1	2	42	95.16	Tom Moody	917	Neal Radford	20
5(14)	Warwickshire	16	8	4	1	3	40	82.53	Andy Moles	385	Paul Smith	21
6(12)	Essex	16	7	4	1	4	38	84.41	Salim Malik	451	Don Topley	20
7(6)	Yorkshire	16	9	7	0	0	36	86.38	Martyn Moxon	561	Phil Carrick	19
8(7)	Surrey	16	7	7	0	2	32	81.94	Monte Lynch	433	Waqar Younis	21
9(8)	Somerset	16	7	7	0	2	32	80.85	Jimmy Cook	546	Roland Lefebvre	15
10(11)	Kent	16	6	8	1	1	28	87.46	Neil Taylor	467	Alan Igglesden	23
11(3)	Middlesex	16	6	9	0	1	26	79.15	Mike Gatting	525	John Emburey	28
12(9)	Gloucestershire	16	5	9	0	2	24	77.68	Tony Wright	414	Mark Smith	15
13(13)	Sussex	16	5	9	0	2	24	81.42	Keith Greenfield	341	Tony Pigott	27
14(16)	Leicestershire	16	5	10	0	1	22	78.29	James Whitaker	550	John Maguire	21
15(1)	Derbyshire	16	5	11	0	0	20	84.38	Peter Bowler	396	Simon Base	18
16(15)	Glamorgan	16	4	10	0	2	20	82.61	Matthew Maynard	458	Steve Watkin	16
17(5)	Hampshire	16	3	12	0	1	14	79.24	Mark Nicholas	462	Cardigan Connor	18

Best Performances

Batting Team
283-4 (40 overs) Worcestershire v Kent; **281-2** (40 overs) Gloucestershire v Hampshire; **280-4** (36 overs) Northamptonshire v Hampshire,

Batting Individual
160 T M Moody (Worcestershire v Kent) Apr 21; **130*** R J Blakey (Yorkshire v Kent) Jun 16; **129*** M D Moxon (Yorks v Surrey) Jul 21, S J Cook (Somerset v Worcestershire) Aug 18

Bowling
6-9 N G Cowans (Middlesex v Lancashire); **5-22** P Carrick (Yorkshire v Glamorgan); **5-23** J E Emburey (Middlesex v Somerset)

REFUGE ASSURANCE CUP

Semi-finals
WORCESTERSHIRE beat Nottinghamshire by 14 runs; LANCASHIRE beat Northamptonshire by 4 wkts

Final
Old Trafford, Sep 15
WORCESTERSHIRE 235-5 (40 overs) (S J Rhodes 105); LANCASHIRE 228 (40 overs) (G Fowler 51, N V Radford 5-42)
Worcestershire won by 7 runs
Man of the Match: Steve Rhodes (Worcestershire)

MINOR COUNTIES CHAMPIONSHIP

Wardown Park, Luton, Sep 8
OXFORDSHIRE 215-8 (55 overs) (P J Garner 75); STAFFORDSHIRE 216-0 (37.5 overs) (S J Dean 117*, D Cartledge 83*)
Staffordshire won by 10 wickets
Staffordshire's first title since 1927

——— OVERSEAS CRICKET———

AUSTRALIA
Sheffield Shield

Final placings	P	W	D	L	Pts
1 Victoria	10	4	4	2	29.8
2 New South Wales	10	3	5	2	24
3 Queensland	10	3	4	3	22
4 Western Australia	10	2	5	3	18
5 South Australia	10	2	7	1	16
6 Tasmania	10	1	5	4	7.9

Victoria deducted 0.2 of a point and Tasmania 0.1 for slow over rates

FINAL
Melbourne, Mar 22-26
NEW SOUTH WALES 223 & 134 (A I C Dodemaide 5-25); VICTORIA 119 (W J Holdsworth 5-55) & 239-2 (J D Siddons 124*)
Victoria won by 8 wickets

WEST INDIES
Red Stripe Cup

Final table	P	W	L	D	Pts
Barbados	5	4	0	1	72
Trinidad & Tobago	5	1	1	3	37
Leeward Island	5	1	1	3	36
Guyana	5	1	1	3	36
Jamaica	5	0	2	3	20
Windward Islands	5	0	2	3	12

PEACE IN OUR TIME

❝Ali, you know 12 months ago I wanted to bomb this place.❞
Mlulecki George, anti-apartheid leader, making peace with Ali Bacher

"This has got to be the happiest day of my life."
Ali Bacher, on South Africa's return

"We did what we felt was right, at the time, to maintain our quality of cricket. But I would be man enough to say that, whilst I cannot have regrets because I was part of the system, I am desperately sorry for any inconvenience caused."
Geoff Dakin, president of South Africa's new non-racial board, on rebel tours

"We are delighted to be back in an atmosphere of desire and I would even say love."
Dakin

"An awful lot of money was involved. I shouldn't imagine they'd be very interested in handing it back.❞
Robert Bailey, non-rebel, on Gatting and co's hopes of a reprieve

CHAMPIONS

WORLD CUP

1975	West Indies beat Australia by 17 runs
1979	West Indies beat England by 92 runs
1983	India beat West Indies by 43 runs
1987	Australia beat England by 7 runs

COUNTY CHAMPIONS

1864	Surrey	1906	Kent	1957	Surrey
1865	Nottinghamshire	1907	Nottinghamshire	1958	Surrey
1866	Middlesex	1908	Yorkshire	1959	Yorkshire
1867	Yorkshire	1909	Kent	1960	Yorkshire
1868	Nottinghamshire	1910	Kent	1961	Hampshire
1869	Notts & Yorks (shared)	1911	Warwickshire	1962	Yorkshire
1870	Yorkshire	1912	Yorkshire	1963	Yorkshire
1871	Notts	1913	Kent	1964	Worcestershire
1872	Notts	1914	Surrey	1965	Worcestershire
1873	Gloucs & Notts (shared)	1915-18	Not held	1966	Yorkshire
1874	Gloucestershire	1919	Yorkshire	1967	Yorkshire
1875	Nottinghamshire	1920	Middlesex	1968	Yorkshire
1876	Gloucestershire	1921	Middlesex	1969	Glamorgan
1877	Gloucestershire	1922	Yorkshire	1970	Kent
1878	Undecided	1923	Yorkshire	1971	Surrey
1879	Lancs & Notts (shared)	1924	Yorkshire	1972	Warwickshire
1880	Nottinghamshire	1925	Yorkshire	1973	Hampshire
1881	Lancashire	1926	Lancashire	1974	Worcestershire
1882	Lancs & Notts (shared)	1927	Lancashire	1975	Leicestershire
1883	Nottinghamshire	1928	Lancashire	1976	Middlesex
1884	Nottinghamshire	1929	Nottinghamshire	1977	Kent & Middx (shared)
1885	Nottinghamshire	1930	Lancashire	1978	Kent
1886	Nottinghamshire	1931	Yorkshire	1979	Essex
1887	Surrey	1932	Yorkshire	1980	Middlesex
1888	Surrey	1933	Yorkshire	1981	Nottinghamshire
1889	Lancs, Notts & Surrey	1934	Lancashire	1982	Middlesex
	(shared)	1935	Yorkshire	1983	Essex
1890	Surrey	1936	Derbyshire	1984	Essex
1891	Surrey	1937	Yorkshire	1985	Middlesex
1892	Surrey	1938	Yorkshire	1986	Essex
1893	Yorkshire	1939	Yorkshire	1987	Nottinghamshire
1894	Surrey	1940-45	Not held	1988	Worcestershire
1895	Surrey	1946	Yorkshire	1989	Worcestershire
1896	Yorkshire	1947	Middlesex	1990	Middlesex
1897	Lancashire	1948	Glamorgan	1991	Essex
1898	Yorkshire	1949	Middx & Yorks (shared)		
1899	Surrey	1950	Lancs & Surrey (shared)		
1900	Yorkshire	1951	Warwickshire		
1901	Yorkshire	1952	Surrey		
1902	Yorkshire	1953	Surrey		
1903	Middlesex	1954	Surrey		
1904	Lancashire	1955	Surrey		
1905	Yorkshire	1956	Surrey		

Most outright wins
31 Yorkshire; **18** Surrey; **14** Nottinghamshire; **10** Middlesex; **8** Lancashire; **6** Kent; **5** Essex, Worcestershire.

THE COUNTY CHAMPIONSHIP 1921-91

The 17-county era. A chart showing the performances of all counties based on 17 points for winning title, 16 points for finishing second down to one point for finishing 17th.

1	Yorkshire	812
2	Surrey	785
3	Middlesex	743
4	Lancashire	673
5	Kent	656
6	Essex	618
7	Gloucestershire	590
8=	Derbyshire	557
8=	Warwickshire	557
10=	Hampshire	555
10=	Nottinghamshire	555
12	Sussex	544
13	Worcestershire	516
14	Somerset	482
15	Leicestershire	474
16	Northamptonshire	460
17	Glamorgan	399

NATWEST BANK TROPHY
(Gillette Cup 1963-80)

1963 Sussex beat Worcestershire by 14 runs
1964 Sussex beat Warwickshire by 8 wickets
1965 Yorkshire beat Surrey by 175 runs
1966 Warwickshire beat Worcs by 5 wickets
1967 Kent beat Somerset by 32 runs
1968 Warwickshire beat Sussex by 4 wickets
1969 Yorkshire beat Derbyshire by 69 runs
1970 Lancashire beat Sussex by 6 wickets
1971 Lancashire beat Kent by 24 runs
1972 Lancashire beat Warwickshire by 4 wickets
1973 Gloucestershire beat Sussex by 40 runs
1974 Kent beat Lancashire by 4 wickets
1975 Lancashire beat Middlesex by 7 wickets
1976 Northants beat Lancashire by 4 wickets
1977 Middlesex beat Glamorgan by 5 wickets
1978 Sussex beat Somerset by 5 wickets

REFUGE ASSURANCE LEAGUE
(John Player League 1969-86)

		Pts
1969	Lancashire	49
1970	Lancashire	53
1971	Worcestershire	44
1972	Kent	45
1973	Kent	50
1974	Leicestershire	54
1975	Hampshire	52
1976	Kent	40
1977	Leicestershire	52
1978	Hampshire	48
1979	Somerset	50
1980	Warwickshire	46
1981	Essex	50
1982	Sussex	58
1983	Yorkshire	46
1984	Essex	50
1985	Essex	44
1986	Hampshire	50
1987	Worcestershire	46
1988	Worcestershire	50
1989	Lancashire	52
1990	Derbyshire	50
1991	Nottinghamshire	52

Most wins
3 Essex, Kent, Hampshire, Worcestershire, Lancashire

1979 Somerset beat Northants by 45 runs
1980 Middlesex beat Surrey by 7 wickets
1981 Derbyshire beat Northants fewer wickets lost (scores level)
1982 Surrey beat Warwickshire by 9 wickets
1983 Somerset beat Kent by 24 runs
1984 Middlesex beat Kent by 4 wickets
1985 Essex beat Nottinghamshire by 1 run
1986 Sussex beat Lancashire by 7 wickets
1987 Nottinghamshire beat Northants by 3 wickets
1988 Middlesex beat Worcestershire by 3 wickets
1989 Warwickshire beat Middlesex by 4 wickets
1990 Lancashire beat Northants by 7 wickets
1991 Hampshire beat Surrey by 4 wickets
Most wins
5 Lancashire, **4** Sussex, Middlesex

BENSON & HEDGES CUP
1972 Leicestershire beat Yorkshire by 5 wickets
1973 Kent beat Worcestershire by 39 runs
1974 Surrey beat Leicestershire by 27 runs
1975 Leicestershire beat Middlesex by 5 wickets
1976 Kent beat Worcestershire by 43 runs
1977 Gloucestershire beat Kent by 64 runs
1978 Kent beat Derbyshire by 6 wickets
1979 Essex beat Surrey by 35 runs
1980 Northants beat Essex by 6 runs
1981 Somerset beat Surrey by 7 wickets
1982 Somerset beat Nottinghamshire by 9 wickets
1983 Middlesex beat Essex by 4 runs
1984 Lancashire beat Warwickshire by 6 wickets
1985 Leicestershire beat Essex by 5 wickets
1986 Middlesex beat Kent by 2 runs
1987 Yorkshire beat Northants fewer wickets lost (scores level)
1988 Hampshire beat Derbyshire by 7 wickets
1989 Nottinghamshire beat Essex by 3 wickets
1990 Lancashire beat Worcestershire by 69 runs
1991 Worcestershire beat Lancashire by 65 runs
Most wins
3 Leicestershire, Kent

ENGLAND AGAINST OTHER COUNTRIES
v Australia

	A	E	D
1876-77	1	1	0
1878-79	0	1	0
1880	1	0	0
1881-82	0	2	2
1882	0	1	0
1882-83	2	2	0
1884	1	0	2
1884-85	3	2	0
1886	3	0	0
1886-87	2	0	0
1887-88	1	0	0
1888	2	1	0
1890	2	0	0
1891-92	1	2	0
1893	1	0	2
1894-95	3	2	0
1896	2	1	0
1897-98	1	4	0
1899	0	1	4
1901-02	1	4	0
1902	1	2	2
1903-04	3	2	0
1905	2	0	3
1907-08	1	4	0
1909	1	2	2
1911-12	4	1	0
1912	1	0	2
1920-21	0	5	0
1921	0	3	2
1924-25	1	4	0
1926	1	0	4
1928-29	4	1	0
1930	1	2	2
1932-33	4	1	0
1934	1	2	2
1936-37	2	3	0
1938	1	1	2
1946-47	0	3	2
1948	0	4	1
1950-51	1	4	0
1953	1	0	4
1954-55	3	1	1
1956	2	1	2
1958-59	0	4	1
1961	1	2	2
1962-63	1	1	3
1964	0	1	4
1965-66	1	1	3
1968	1	1	3
1970-71	2	0	4
1972	2	2	1

1974-75	1	4	1
1975	0	1	3
1976-77	0	1	0
1977	3	0	2
1978-79	5	1	0
1979-80	0	3	0
1980	0	0	1
1981	3	1	2
1982-83	1	2	2
1985	3	1	2
1986-87	2	1	2
1987-88	0	0	1
1989	0	4	2
1990-91	0	3	2
Total	88	104	82

v South Africa

	E	SA	D
1888-89	2	0	0
1891-92	1	0	0
1895-96	3	0	0
1898-99	2	0	0
1905-06	1	4	0
1907	1	0	2
1909-10	2	3	0
1912	3	0	0
1913-14	4	0	1
1922-23	2	1	2
1924	3	0	2
1927-28	2	2	1
1929	2	0	3
1930-31	0	1	4
1935	0	1	4
1938-39	1	0	4
1947	3	0	2
1948-49	2	0	3
1951	3	1	1
1955	3	2	0
1956-57	2	2	1
1960	3	0	2
1964-65	1	0	4
1965	0	1	2
Total	46	18	38

v West Indies

	E	WI	D
1928	3	0	0
1929-30	1	1	2
1933	2	0	1
1934-35	1	2	1
1939	1	0	2
1947-48	0	2	2
1950	1	3	0
1953-54	2	2	1
1957	3	0	2
1959-60	1	0	4
1963	1	3	1
1966	1	3	1
1967-68	1	0	4
1969	2	0	1
1973	0	2	1
1973-74	1	1	3
1976	0	3	2
1980	0	1	4
1980-81	0	2	2
1984	0	5	0
1985-86	0	5	0
1988	0	4	1
1989-90	1	2	1
1991	2	2	1
Total	24	43	37

v New Zealand

	E	NZ	D
1929-30	1	0	3
1931	1	0	2
1932-33	0	0	2

1937	1	0	2
1946-47	0	0	1
1949	0	0	4
1950-51	1	0	1
1954-55	2	0	0
1958	4	0	1
1958-59	1	0	1
1962-63	3	0	0
1965	3	0	0
1965-66	0	0	3
1969	2	0	1
1970-71	1	0	1
1973	2	0	1
1974-75	1	0	1
1977-78	1	1	1
1978	3	0	0
1983	3	1	0
1983-84	0	1	2
1986	0	1	2
1987-88	0	0	3
1990	1	0	2
Total	31	4	34

v India

	E	I	D
1932	1	0	0
1933-34	2	0	1
1936	2	0	1
1946	1	0	2
1951-52	1	1	3
1952	3	0	1
1959	5	0	0
1961-62	0	2	3
1963-64	0	0	5
1967	3	0	0
1971	0	1	2
1972-73	1	2	2
1974	3	0	0
1976-77	3	1	1
1979	1	0	3
1979-80	1	0	0
1981-82	0	1	5
1982	1	0	2
1984-85	2	1	2
1986	0	2	1
1990	1	0	2
Total	31	11	36

v Pakistan

	E	P	D
1954	1	1	2
1961-62	1	0	2
1962	4	0	1
1967	2	0	1
1968-69	0	0	3
1971	1	0	2
1972-73	0	0	3
1974	0	0	3
1977-78	0	0	3
1978	2	0	1
1982	2	1	0
1983-84	0	1	2
1987	0	1	4
1987-88	0	1	2
Total	13	5	29

v Sri Lanka

	E	SL	D
1981-82	1	0	0
1984	0	0	1
1988	1	0	0
1991	1	0	0
Total	3	0	1

RECORDS

BATTING RECORDS

Most Runs in a Career
61,237 J.B. Hobbs; 58,969 F.E. Woolley; 57,611 E.H. Hendren; 55,061 C.P. Mead; 54,896 W.G. Grace; 50,551 W.R. Hammond; 50,138 H. Sutcliffe

Highest Individual Scores
499 Hanif Mohammad, Karachi v Bahawalpur (Karachi) 1958-59; 452* D.G. Bradman NSW v Queensland (Sydney) 1929-30; 443* B.B. Nimbalkar, Maharashtra v Kathiawar (Poona) 1948-49

Most Runs in an Over
77: L. K. Germon and R. M. Ford off R H Vance, Canterbury v Wellington (Christchurch) 1989-90; Off a six-ball over −36: G.S. Sobers off M.A. Nash, Nottinghamshire v Glamorgan (Swansea) 1968; R.J. Shastri off Tilak Raj, Bombay v Baroda (Bombay) 1984-85

Most Sixes
In an innings: 15 J.R. Reid, Wellington v Northern Districts (Wellington) 1962-63

In a match: 17 W.J. Stewart, Warwickshire v Lancashire (Blackpool) 1959

In a season: 80 I.T. Botham, Somerset 1985

Separate Hundreds in a Match
Eight times: Zaheer Abbas; seven times: W.R. Hammond; six times: J.B. Hobbs, G.M. Turner

Most Consecutive Hundreds
Six: C.B. Fry 1901; D.G. Bradman 1938-39; M.J. Procter 1970-71. Five E.D. Weekes 1955-56

Most Hundreds in a Season
18 D.C.S. Compton 1947. 16 J.B. Hobbs 1925. 15 W.R. Hammond 1938. 14 H. Sutcliffe 1932

Most Runs in a Season
3816 D.C.S. Compton 1947; 3539 W.J. Edrich 1947; 3518 T.W. Hayward 1906

Most Hundreds in a Career
197 J.B.Hobbs; 170 E.H. Hendren; 167 W.R. Hammond; 153 C.P. Mead; 151 G. Boycott

Highest Average in an English Season
115.66 D.G. Bradman 1938; 102.53 G. Boycott 1979; 102.00 W.A. Johnston 1953; 101.70 G. A. Gooch 1990; 100.12 G. Boycott 1971

Fastest Fifty
Eight minutes: C.C. Inman (57), Leicestershire v Nottinghamshire (Nottingham) 1965

Fastest Hundred
26 minutes T. Moody, Warwicks v Glamorgan (Swansea),1990; 35 minutes P. G. H. Fender (113*), Surrey v Northamptonshire (Northampton), 1920; 35 minutes S. J. O'Shaughnessy (105), Lancashire v Leicestershire (Manchester), 1983

Highest Partnerships
577: V.S. Hazare (288) and Gul Mahomed (319), fourth wicket, Baroda v Holkar (Baroda) 1946-47; 574*: F.M. Worrell (255*) and C.L. Walcott (314*), fourth wicket, Barbados v Trinidad (Port of Spain) 1945-46; 561: Waheed Mirza (324) and Mansoor Akhtar (224*), first wicket, Karachi Whites v Quetta (Karachi) 1976-77

1,000 Runs before June
1,000 in May: W.G. Grace 1895; W.R. Hammond 1927; C. Hallows 1928

1,000 before June: T.W. Hayward 1900; D.G. Bradman 1930, 1938; W.J. Edrich 1938; G.M. Turner 1973; G.A. Hick 1988

BOWLING RECORDS

Most Wickets in a Career
4,187 W. Rhodes, 1898-1930; 3,776 A.P. Freeman, 1914-36; 3,278 C.W.L. Parker, 1903-35; 3,061 J.T. Hearne, 1888-1923

Most Wickets in a Match
19-90 J.C. Laker, England v Australia (Manchester) 1956

Most Wickets in a Day
17-48 C. Blythe, Kent v Northamptonshire (Northampton) 1907; 17-91 H. Verity, Yorkshire v Essex (Leyton) 1933; 17-106 T.W. Goddard, Gloucestershire v Kent (Bristol) 1939

Most Hat-Tricks in a Career
Seven: D.V.P. Wright; six: T.W. Goddard, C.W.L. Parker; five: S. Haigh, V.W.C. Jupp, A.E.G. Rhodes, F.A. Tarrant

Most Wickets in a Season
304 A.P. Freeman 1928; 298 A.P. Freeman 1933; 290 T. Richardson 1895

100 Wickets in a Season Most Times
23 W. Rhodes; 20 D. Shackleton (in successive seasons 1949-68); 17 A.P. Freeman

The Double: 1,000 Runs and 100 Wickets in a Season
16 W. Rhodes; 14 G.H. Hirst; 10 V.W.C. Jupp

WICKETKEEPING RECORDS

Most Dismissals in an Innings
Eight (all ct): A.T.W. Grout, Queensland v Western Australia (Brisbane) 1959-60; D.E. East, Essex v Somerset (Taunton) 1985; S.A. Marsh Kent v Middlesex (Lord's) 1991

Most Dismissals in a Match
12: (8ct 4st) E. Pooley, Surrey v Sussex (The Oval) 1868; (9ct 3st) D. Tallon, Queensland v New South Wales (Sydney) 1938-39; (9ct 3st) H.B. Taber, New South Wales v South Australia (Adelaide) 1968-69

Most Dismissals in a Season
128 (79ct 49st) L.E.G. Ames 1929; 122 (70ct 52st) L.E.G. Ames 1928; 110 (63ct 47st) H. Yarnold 1949

Most Dismissals in a Career
1,648 R.W. Taylor 1960-86; 1,527 J.T. Murray 1952-75; 1,497 H. Strudwick 1902-27; 1,344 A.P.E. Knott 1964-85; 1,310 F.H. Huish 1895-1914

FIELDING RECORDS

Most Catches in an Innings
Seven: M.J. Stewart, Surrey v Northamptonshire (Northampton) 1957; A.S. Brown, Gloucestershire v Nottinghamshire (Nottingham) 1966

Most Catches in a Match
Ten: W.R. Hammond, Gloucestershire v Surrey (Cheltenham) 1928

Most Catches in a Season
78 W.R. Hammond 1928; 77 M.J. Stewart 1957; 73 P.M. Walker 1961; 71 P.J. Sharpe 1962

Most Catches in a Career
1,018 F.E. Woolley 1906-38; 887 W.G. Grace 1865-1908; 831 G.A.R. Lock 1946-70; 819 W.R. Hammond 1920-51; 813 D.B. Close 1949-86

TEAM RECORDS

Highest Totals
1,107: Victoria v New South Wales (Melbourne) 1926-27; 1,059: Victoria v Tasmania (Melbourne) 1922-23
County Championship 887: Yorkshire v Warwickshire (Birmingham) 1896; 863 Lancashire v Surrey (The Oval) 1990

Lowest Totals
12: Oxford University v MCC and Ground (Oxford) 1877, Northamptonshire v Gloucestershire (Gloucester) 1907

Largest Victories
Inns and 851 runs: Railways (910-6 dec) v Dera Ismail Khan (Lahore) 1964-65; Inns and 666 runs: Victoria (1,059) v Tasmania (Melbourne) 1922-23; Inns and 656 runs: Victoria (1,107) v New South Wales (Melbourne) 1926-27

TEST MATCH RECORDS
BATTING
Most Runs in a Career
10,122 S.M. Gavaskar 1971-87; 9257 A.R. Border 1974-91; 8540 I.V.A. Richards 1974-91; 8114 G. Boycott 1964-82; 8081 D.I. Gower 1978-91; 8064 Javed Miandad 1976-91; 8032 G.S. Sobers 1954-74; 7624 M.C. Cowdrey 1954-75; 7558 C.G. Greenidge 1974-91

Highest Individual Innings
365* G.S. Sobers, West Indies v Pakistan (Kingston) 1957-58; 364 L. Hutton, England v Australia (The Oval) 1938; 337 Hanif Mohammad, Pakistan v West Indies (Bridgetown) 1957-58; 336* W.R. Hammond, England v New Zealand (Auckland) 1932-33; 334 D.G. Bradman, Australia v England (Leeds) 1930; 333 G. A.Gooch, England v India (Lord's) 1990

Most Runs in a Series
974 D.G. Bradman 1930; 905 W.R. Hammond 1928-29; 839 M.A. Taylor 1989

Highest Career Averages
99.94 D.G. Bradman; 60.97 R.G. Pollock; 60.83 G.A. Headley; 60.73 H. Sutcliffe

Most Hundreds
34 S.M. Gavaskar; 29 D.G. Bradman; 26 G.S. Sobers; 24 G.S. Chappell, I.V.A. Richards; 23 A.R. Border

---

RECORD TEST STANDS

467	**Martin Crowe & Andrew Jones (3rd wkt), New Zealand v Sri Lanka 1990-91**
451	**Don Bradman & Bill Ponsford (2nd wkt), Australia v England 1934**
451	**Mudassar Nazar & Javed Miandad (3rd wkt), Pakistan v India 1982-83**
446	**Conrad Hunte & Gary Sobers (2nd wkt), West Indies v Pakistan 1957-58**
413	**Vinoo Mankad & Pankaj Roy (1st wkt), India v New Zealand 1955-56**
411	**Peter May & Colin Cowdrey (4th wkt), England v West Indies 1957**
405	**Sidney Barnes & Don Bradman (5th wkt), Australia v England 1946-47**

BOWLING
Most Wickets in a Career
431 R.J. Hadlee 1973-90; 380 I.T. Botham 1977--91; 376 Kapil Dev 1978-91; 376 M.D. Marshall 1978-91; 362 Imran Khan 1971-90; 355 D.K. Lillee 1971-84; 325 R.G.D. Willis 1971-84; 309 L.R. Gibbs 1958-76; 307 F.S. Trueman 1952-65

Most Wickets in an Innings
10-53 J.C. Laker, England v Australia (Manchester) 1956

Most Wickets in a Match
19-90 J.C. Laker, England v Australia (Manchester) 1956;

17-159 S.F. Barnes, England v South Africa (Johannesburg) 1913-14

Most Wickets in a Series
49 S.F. Barnes 1913-14; 46 J.C. Laker 1956; 44 C.V. Grimmett 1935-36; 42 T.M.Alderman 1981

ENGLAND'S TOP RUN-MAKERS

Geoffrey Boycott	**8,114**
David Gower	**8,081**
Colin Cowdrey	**7,624**
Walter Hammond	**7,249**
Graham Gooch	**7,028**
Sir Leonard Hutton	**6,971**

WICKETKEEPING
Most Dismissals in a Career
355 R.W. Marsh; 272 P J Dujon; 269 A.P.E. Knott; 228 Wasim Bari; 219 T.G. Evans

Most Dismissals in One Test
10 R.W. Taylor, England v India (Bombay) 1979-80

Most Dismissals in an Innings
7: Wasim Bari, Pakistan v New Zealand (Auckland) 1978-79, R.W. Taylor, England v India (Bombay) 1979-80

FIELDING
Most Catches in an Innings
5: V.Y. Richardson, Australia v South Africa (Durban) 1935-36; Yajurvindra Singh, India v England (Bangalore) 1976-77; Mohammed Azharuddin, India v Pakistan (Karachi) 1989-90

Most Catches in a Career
130 A. R. Border 1978-91; 122 G.S. Chappell 1970-84; 122 M.C. Cowdrey1954, Richards1974-91; 117 I.T. Botham 1977-91; 110 R.B. Simpson 1957-78; 110 W.R. Hammond 1927-47

TEAM RECORDS
Highest Team Totals
903-7 dec England v Australia (The Oval) 1938; 849 England v West Indies (Kingston) 1929-30; 790-3 dec West Indies v Pakistan (Kingston) 1957-58; 758-8 dec Australia v West Indies (Kingston) 1954-55

Lowest Team Totals
26: New Zealand v England (Auckland) 1954-55; 30: South Africa v England (Port Elizabeth) 1895-96; South Africa v England (Birmingham) 1924; 35: South Africa v ngland (Cape Town) 1898-99

--- **1991-92** ---

ENGLAND TOURING TEAM

To New Zealand and the World Cup:

Graham Gooch (Essex, capt), Michael Atherton (Lancashire), Ian Botham* (Durham), Phil DeFreitas (Lancashire), Neil Fairbrother (Lancashire), Angus Fraser (Middlesex or Dermot Reeve (Warwickshire), Graeme Hick (Worcestershire), Richard Illingworth (Worcestershire), Alan Lamb (Northamptonshire), David Lawrence (Gloucestershire), Chris Lewis (Leicestershire), Derek Pringle (Essex), Mark Ramprakash (Middlesex), Jack Russell (Gloucestershire), Robin Smith (Hampshire), Alec Stewart (Surrey), Phil Tufnell (Middlesex). Manager:

Bob Bennett (Lancashire). Team Manager: Micky Stewart. Physio: Laurie Brown (Lancashire).

Botham will join the party after Jack and the Beanstalk finishes its run in Bournemouth, before the Second Test

ITINERARY IN NEW ZEALAND

Dec 27 Depart UK; Jan 2 Auckland (Auckland, 1-day); Jan 4 NZ Emerging Players (Hamilton, 3 days); Jan 8 NZ U-Bix XI (Napier, 3 days); Jan 11 New Zealand (one-day international, Auckland); Jan 14 NZ XI (Nelson, 3 days); Jan 20 FIRST TEST (Christchurch); Jan 25 Central Districts (New Plymouth, 3 days); Jan 31 SECOND TEST (Auckland); Feb 6 THIRD TEST (Wellington); Feb 12 New Zealand (second one-day international, Dunedin); Feb 15 New Zealand (third one-day international, Christchurch)

WORLD CUP SCHEDULE

The fifth cricket World Cup will take place in Australia and New Zealand between February 22 and March 25. The seven Test-playing nations plus Zimbabwe will play each other in a round-robin format with the top four qualifying for the semi-finals. This schedule would be completely revised if South Africa were allowed to participate as well.

FEBRUARY

22	Perth	England v Sri Lanka (D/N)
	Auckland	New Zealand v Australia
23	Melbourne	Pakistan v India
25	Hamilton	New Zealand v Zimbabwe
26	Sydney	Australia v West Indies (D/N)
28	New Plymouth	Sri Lanka v Zimbabwe
29	Brisbane	West Indies v Pakistan

MARCH

1	Adelaide	Australia v India
	Wellington	New Zealand v England
3	Mackay	Pakistan v Sri Lanka
4	Sydney	England v West Indies (D/N)
7	Hobart	Australia v Zimbabwe
	Christchurch	New Zealand v India
	Adelaide	West Indies v Sri Lanka
8	Melbourne	England v Pakistan
10	Wellington	West Indies v India
11	Perth	Australia v Pakistan (D/N)
12	Christchurch	New Zealand v Sri Lanka
14	Sydney	England v India
15	Brisbane	Australia v Sri Lanka
	Auckland	New Zealand v West Indies
18	Melbourne	Australia v England (D/N)
	Dunedin	New Zealand v Pakistan
	Berri	India v Sri Lanka
21	Auckland	SEMI-FINAL
22	Sydney	SEMI-FINAL
25	Melbourne	FINAL (D/N)

One reserve day has been set aside for each semi-final and two for the final. D/N: Day-Night game

WORLD CUP RECORDS 1975-1987
League Table

	P	W	L	NR	Winners	Finalists	S-F
West Indies	24	18	5	1	2	1	-
England	24	17	7	-	-	2	2
Australia	22	13	9	-	1	1	-
India	21	12	9	-	1	-	1
Pakistan	21	11	10	-	-	-	3
New Zealand	20	9	11	-	-	-	2
Sri Lanka	20	2	15	1	-	-	-
Zimbabwe	12	1	11	-	-	-	-
East Africa	3	-	3	-	-	-	-
Canada	3	-	3	-	-	-	-

England are the only team to have qualified for the semi-finals in each competition

Played in most matches

23	Viv Richards (West Indies)
20	Imran Khan (Pakistan)
19	Sunil Gavaskar (India)
19	Javed Miandad (Pakistan)

Leading run-makers

1013	Viv Richards (West Indies)
681	Graham Gooch (England)
612	Glenn Turner (New Zealand)
603	Desmond Haynes (West Indies)

Leading wicket-takers

27	Imran Khan (Pakistan)
27	Abdul Qadir (Pakistan)
26	Andy Roberts (West Indies)

Played in all four World Cups

Sunil Gavaskar (India)
Imran Khan (Pakistan)
Javed Miandad (Pakistan)
Duleep Mendis (Sri Lanka)
Viv Richards (West Indies)

ENGLAND A TEAM
To Bermuda and West Indies:

Martyn Moxon (Yorkshire, capt), Michael Atherton (Lancashire) or Mark Ramprakash (Middlesex), Darren Bicknell (Surrey), Martin Bicknell (Surrey), Dominic Cork (Derbyshire), Robert Croft (Glamorgan), Warren Hegg (Lancashire), Nasser Hussain (Essex), Paul Johnson (Nottinghamshire), Devon Malcolm (Derbyshire), Hugh Morris (Glamorgan), Andy Pick (Nottinghamshire), Dermot Reeve (Warwickshire) or Tim Munton (Warwickshire), Ian Salisbury (Sussex), Graham Thorpe (Surrey). Standby: Steve Rhodes (Worcestershire). Manager: Steve Coverdale (Northamptonshire); Team manager: Keith Fletcher (Essex); Physio: Dave Roberts (Worcestershire)

A TEAM ITINERARY

Feb 18: Bermuda (2 days); Feb 25 Bermuda (1 day); Feb 27 Bermuda (1 day); Mar 4 Barbados (1 day); Mar 6 Windward Islands (Grenada or St Vincent, 3 days); Mar 10 Trinidad (Pointe-a-Pierre, 3 days); Mar 14 West Indies A (Port of Spain, 4 days); Mar 21 West Indies A (St Vincent or Grenada, 4 days); Mar 28 West Indies A (Barbados, 4 days)

1992

THE ENGLISH SEASON

After 71 years in which the membership of the County
Championship has remained unchanged, Durham will be
elevated to first-class status in 1992 as the 18th county.
Their first competitive match will be at Duham University
against Lancashire on April 19 with the opening first-class
match on the same ground against Leicestershire six days
later. Other Durham home venues will be Stockton,
Darlington, Chester-le-Street, Jesmond, Gateshead Fell and
Scarborough where they will play Yorkshire on a
traditional Yorkshire ground.

England's opponents in 1992 are Pakistan who will play
five Test matches (there is no game at Trent Bridge) and,
for the first time in England, five one-day internationals.

Duration of Matches

Cornhill Insurance Test Matches	5 days
Britannic Assurance Championship	5 days unless stated
Tourist Matches (Tetley Bitter Challenge)	3 days
Other Tourist Matches	As stated
Universities v Counties	3 days
Texaco Trophy One Day Internationals	1 day
Benson and Hedges Cup	1 day
NatWest Bank Trophy	1 day
Sunday League	1 day
Other Matches	As stated

* includes Sunday play

Date	Venue	Match
April		
13	Lord's	England 'A' v Britannic Assurance Champions *(Four days)*
14	Fenner's	Cambridge University v Leicestershire
	The Parks	Oxford University v Durham
17	Fenner's	Cambridge University v Middlesex
	The Parks	Oxford University v Worcestershire
19		**Sunday League**
	Derby	Derbyshire v Essex
	Durham Uni.	Durham v Lancashire
	Southampton	Hampshire v Gloucestershire
	Canterbury	Kent v Somerset
	Leicester	Leicestershire v Middlesex
	Trent Bridge	Nottinghamshire v Sussex
	The Oval	Surrey v Northamptonshire
	Edgbaston	Warwickshire v Glamorgan
	Worcester	Worcestershire v Yorkshire
21		**Benson and Hedges Cup**
	Durham Uni.	Durham v Glamorgan
	Chelmsford	Essex v Lancashire
	Cheltenham ±	Gloucestershire v Leicestershire
	Canterbury	Kent v Somerset
	Lord's	Middlesex v Minor Counties
	Forfar	Scotland v Northamptonshire
	Hove	Sussex v Surrey
	Edgbaston	Warwickshire v Yorkshire
	Worcester	Worcestershire v Derbyshire
23		**Benson and Hedges Cup**
	Derby	Derbyshire v Glamorgan
	Cheltenham±	Gloucestershire v Minor Counties
	Southampton	Hampshire v Essex
	Old Trafford	Lancashire v Scotland
	Leicester	Leicestershire v Sussex
	Trent Bridge	Nottinghamshire v Kent
	Taunton	Somerset v Yorkshire
	The Oval	Surrey v Middlesex
	The Parks	Combined Universities v Worcestershire
25		**Britannic Assurance Championship** *(4 days)*
	Durham Uni.	Durham v Leicestershire
	Southampton	Hampshire v Sussex

	Old Trafford	*Lancashire v Kent
	Lord's	Middlesex v Glamorgan
	Trent Bridge	* Nottinghamshire v Warwickshire
	Taunton	* Somerset v Gloucestershire
	The Oval	Surrey v Yorkshire
	Worcester	Worcestershire v Northamptonshire
		Other Matches
	Fenner's	Cambridge University v Essex
26		**Sunday League**
	Durham Uni.	Durham v Leicestershire
	Chelmsford	Essex v Surrey
	Lord's	Middlesex v Glamorgan
	Hove	Sussex v Yorkshire
	Worcester	Worcestershire v Northamptonshire
30		**Benson and Hedges Cup**
	Derby	Derbyshire v Combined Universities
	Chelmsford	Essex v Scotland
	Southampton	Hampshire v Northamptonshire
	Leicester	Leicestershire v Surrey
	Lord's	Middlesex v Gloucestershire
	Marlow	Minor Counties v Sussex
	Edgbaston	Warwickshire v Nottinghamshire
	Worcester	Worcestershire v Durham
	Headingley	Yorkshire v Kent

± *Dowty Arle Court Ground (provisional)*

May		
2		**Benson and Hedges Cup**
	Fenner's	Combined Universities v Durham
	Cardiff	Glamorgan v Worcestershire
	Old Trafford	Lancashire v Hampshire
	Leicester	Leicestershire v Middlesex
	Northampton	Northamptonshire v Essex
	Taunton	Somerset v Warwickshire
	The Oval	Surrey v Minor Counties
	Hove	Sussex v Gloucestershire
	Headingley	Yorkshire v Nottinghamshire
3		**Sunday League**
	Cardiff	Glamorgan v Worcestershire
	Old Trafford	Lancashire v Hampshire
	Leicester	Leicestershire v Essex
	Lord's	Middlesex v Gloucestershire
	Northampton	Northamptonshire v Kent
	Taunton	Somerset v Warwickshire
	Headingley	Yorkshire v Nottinghamshire
		Tourist Match
	Arundel	Lavinia, Duchess of Norfolk's XI v Pakistan (1 day)
4		**Tourist Match**
	Canterbury	Kent v Pakistan (1 day)
5		**Benson and Hedges Cup**
	Jesmond	Durham v Derbyshire
	Cardiff	Glamorgan v Combined Universities
	Glasgow	Scotland v Hampshire
	Canterbury	Kent v Warwickshire
	Stone	Minor Counties v Leicestershire
	Northampton	Northamptonshire v Lancashire
	Trent Bridge	Nottinghamshire v Somerset
	The Oval	Surrey v Gloucestershire
	Hove	Sussex v Middlesex
6		**Tetley Bitter Challenge**
	Worcester	Worcestershire v Pakistan
7		**Britannic Assurance Championship** *(4 days)*
	Chelmsford	Essex v Leicestershire
	Canterbury	Kent v Durham
	Lord's	* Middlesex v Lancashire
	Northampton	Northamptonshire v Surrey
	Hove	Sussex v Somerset
	Edgbaston	Warwickshire v Derbyshire
	Headingley	Yorkshire v Hampshire
		Other Match
	The Parks	Oxford University v Nottinghamshire
9		**Tetley Bitter Challenge**
	Cardiff	* Glamorgan v Pakistan
10		**Sunday League**

Derby	Derbyshire v Gloucestershire
Chelmsford	Essex v Northamptonshire
Canterbury	Kent v Durham
Trent Bridge	Nottinghamshire v Surrey
Hove	Sussex v Somerset
Worcester	Worcestershire v Warwickshire
12 Fenner's	Cambridge University v Warwickshire
The Parks	Oxford University v Middlesex
13	**Tetley Bitter Challenge**
Taunton	Somerset v Pakistan
14	**Britannic Assurance Championship**
	(4 days)
Derby	Derbyshire v Worcestershire
Chelmsford	Essex v Kent
Cardiff	* Glamorgan v Durham
Leicester	Leicestershire v Lancashire
Northampton	Northamptonshire v Nottinghamshire
Headingley	* Yorkshire v Gloucestershire
15 Fenner's	Cambridge University v Surrey
The Parks	Oxford University v Hampshire
16	**Tourist Match**
Hove	Sussex v Pakistan (1 day)
17	**Sunday League**
Derby	Derbyshire v Worcestershire
Northampton	Northamptonshire v Lancashire
Trent Bridge	Nottinghamshire v Middlesex
Taunton	Somerset v Hampshire
The Oval	Surrey v Kent
Edgbaston	Warwickshire v Leicestershire
	Tourist Match
Hove	Sussex v Pakistan
19	**Britannic Assurance Championship**
	(4 days)
Gloucester	Gloucestershire v Worcestershire
Southampton	Hampshire v Surrey
Leicester	Leicestershire v Middlesex
20	**Texaco Trophy**
Lord's	ENGLAND v PAKISTAN
	(First One-Day International)
	Britannic Assurance Championship
Swansea	Glamorgan v Warwickshire
Canterbury	Kent v Yorkshire
Blackpool	Lancashire v Derbyshire
Trent Bridge	Nottinghamshire v Sussex
Taunton	Somerset v Essex
22	**Texaco Trophy**
The Oval	ENGLAND v PAKISTAN
	(Second One-Day International)
23	**Britannic Assurance Championship**
Derby	Derbyshire v Nottinghamshire
Stockton	Durham v Northamptonshire
Gloucester	Gloucestershire v Somerset
Old Trafford	Lancashire v Hampshire
Lord's	Middlesex v Surrey
Hove	Sussex v Kent
Edgbaston	Warwickshire v Worcestershire
	Tetley Bitter Challenge
Leicester	* Leicestershire v Pakistan
24	**Sunday League**
Derby	Derbyshire v Nottinghamshire
Stockton	Durham v Nottinghamshire
Chelmsford	Essex v Glamorgan
Gloucester	Gloucestershire v Somerset
Canterbury	Kent v Middlesex
The Oval	Surrey v Sussex
Edgbaston	Warwickshire v Lancashire
Headingley	Yorkshire v Hampshire
27	**Benson and Hedges Cup**
	Quarter Finals
	Tourist Match
	England Amateur XI v Pakistan
	(2 days)
29	**Britannic Assurance Cup**
Swansea	Glamorgan v Leicestershire
Southampton	Hampshire v Durham

Old Trafford	Lancashire v Somerset
Northampton	Northamptonshire v Derbyshire
The Oval	Surrey v Sussex
Worcester	Worcestershire v Gloucestershire
	Other Match
The Parks	Oxford University v Yorkshire
30	**Tetley Bitter Challenge**
Lord's	* Middlesex v Pakistan
31	**Sunday League**
Swansea	Glamorgan v Leicestershire
Southampton	Hampshire v Durham
Canterbury	Kent v Yorkshire
Old Trafford	Lancashire v Somerset
Northampton	Northamptonshire v Derbyshire
Trent Bridge	Nottinghamshire v Gloucestershire
Hove	Sussex v Warwickshire
Worcester	Worcestershire v Essex
June	
2	**Britannic Assurance Cup**
Darlington	Durham v Somerset
Chelmsford	Essex v Glamorgan
Basingstoke	Hampshire v Yorkshire
Tunbridge W	Kent v Worcestershire
Northampton	Northamptonshire v Leicestershire
Trent Bridge	Nottinghamshire v Middlesex
The Oval	Surrey v Derbyshire
Hove	Sussex v Warwickshire
	Other Match
The Parks	Oxford University v Lancashire
	Cornhill Insurance Test Match
Edgbaston	* ENGLAND v PAKISTAN
	(First Test Match)
5	**Britannic Assurance Championship**
Chesterfield	Derbyshire v Durham
Tunbridge W	Kent v Essex
Old Trafford	Lancashire v Gloucestershire
Lord's	Middlesex v Leicestershire
Middlesbrough	Yorkshire v Somerset
7	**Sunday League**
Chesterfield	Derbyshire v Durham
Chelmsford	Essex v Kent
Basingstoke	Hampshire v Surrey
Old Trafford	Lancashire v Gloucestershire
Lord's	Middlesex v Warwickshire
Hove	Sussex v Glamorgan
Middlesbrough	Yorkshire v Somerset
9 Harrogate	**Tilcon Trophy** *(3 days)*
10	**Benson and Hedges Cup**
	Semi Finals
	Tetley Bitter Challenge
Northampton	* Northamptonshire v Pakistan
14	**Sunday League**
Hartlepool	Durham v Essex
Colwyn Bay	Glamorgan v Lancashire
Swindon	Gloucestershire v Kent
Leicester	Leicestershire v Sussex
Bath	Somerset v Nottinghamshire
The Oval	Surrey v Worcestershire
Edgbaston	Warwickshire v Hampshire
Headingley	Yorkshire v Derbyshire
16	**Britannic Assurance Championship**
Bristol	Gloucestershire v Kent
Hinckley	Leicestershire v Hampshire
Trent Bridge	Nottinghamshire v Lancashire
Bath	Somerset v Northamptonshire
Coventry	Warwickshire v Middlesex
Worcester	Worcestershire v Glamorgan
Headingley	Yorkshire v Essex
	Other Match
Fenner's	Cambridge University v Derbyshire
	Cornhill Insurance Test Match
18 Lord's	* ENGLAND v PAKISTAN
	(Second Test Match)
19	**Britannic Assurance Championship**
Bristol	Gloucestershire v Warwickshire

Bournemouth	Hampshire v Essex
Old Trafford	Lancashire v Middlesex
Trent Bridge	Nottinghamshire v Northamptonshire
Bath	Somerset v Surrey
Horsham	Sussex v Durham
Worcester	Worcestershire v Yorkshire
	Other Match
Fenner's	Cambridge University v Derbyshire
The Parks	Oxford University v Glamorgan

21   **Sunday League**

Derby	Derbyshire v Middlesex
Ebbw Vale	Glamorgan v Yorkshire
Bristol	Gloucestershire v Warwickshire
Bournemouth	Hampshire v Essex
Old Trafford	Lancashire v Leicestershire
Trent Bridge	Nottinghamshire v Northamptonshire
Bath	Somerset v Surrey
Horsham	Sussex v Durham

24   **NatWest Bank Trophy** *(First Round)*

	Buckinghamshire v Sussex
Derby	Derbyshire v Berkshire
Chelmsford	Essex v Cumberland
Swansea	Glamorgan v Surrey
Bristol	Gloucestershire v Cheshire
Southampton	Hampshire v Dorset
	Ireland v Durham
Canterbury	Kent v Devon
Leicester	Leicestershire v Norfolk
Northampton	Northamptonshire v Cambridgeshire
Trent Bridge	Nottinghamshire v Worcestershire
	Shropshire v Middlesex
	Oxfordshire v Lancashire
Taunton	Somerset v Scotland
Edgbaston	Warwickshire v Staffordshire
Headingley	Yorkshire v Northumberland
	Tourist Match
Fenner's	Oxbridge v Pakistan (3 days)

26   **Britannic Assurance Championship**

Derby	Derbyshire v Warwickshire
Gateshead	* Durham v Kent
Ilford	Essex v Lancashire
Bristol	Gloucestershire v Surrey
Lord's	Middlesex v Somerset
Luton	Northamptonshire v Glamorgan
Worcester	Worcestershire v Sussex

27

Southampton	Tetley Bitter Challenge
Southampton	Hampshire v Pakistan
	Other Match
Trent Bridge	* Nottinghamshire v Cambridge Uni.

28   **Sunday League**

Derby	Derbyshire v Leicestershire
Ilford	Essex v Lancashire
Bristol	Gloucestershire v Surrey
Lord's	Middlesex v Somerset
Worcester	Worcestershire v Sussex
Scarborough	Yorkshire v Warwickshire

30   **Britannic Assurance Championship**

Derby	Derbyshire v Gloucestershire
Ilford	Essex v Middlesex
Maidstone	Kent v Nottinghamshire
Leicester	Leicestershire v Worcestershire
The Oval	Surrey v Northamptonshire
Arundel	Sussex v Hampshire
	Other Match
Lord's	Oxford Uni. v Cambridge Uni.
	(Varsity Match)

July

2   **Cornhill Insurance Test Match**

Old Trafford	ENGLAND v PAKISTAN
	(Third Test Match)

3   **Britannic Assurance Championship**

Stockton	Durham v Gloucestershire
Neath	Glamorgan v Surrey
Southampton	Hampshire v Nottinghamshire
Maidstone	Kent v Lancashire

Northampton	Northamptonshire v Sussex
Taunton	Somerset v Derbyshire
Edgbaston	Warwickshire v Essex
Sheffield	Yorkshire v Leicestershire

5   **Sunday League**

Stockton	Durham v Gloucestershire
Llanelli	Glamorgan v Surrey
Southampton	Hampshire v Nottinghamshire
Maidstone	Kent v Lancashire
Lord's	Middlesex v Worcestershire
Tring	Northamptonshire v Sussex
Taunton	Somerset v Derbyshire
Edgbaston	Warwickshire v Essex
Sheffield	Yorkshire v Leicestershire

9   **NatWest Bank Trophy**

	Second Round
	Tourist Match
	League Cricket Conference v Pakistan
	(1 day)

11 Lord's   **BENSON AND HEDGES CUP FINAL**

	Tourist Match
Glasgow	Scotland v Pakistan *(One day)*

12   **Sunday League**

Moreton	Gloucestershire v Northamptonshire
Canterbury	Kent v Nottinghamshire
Old Trafford	Lancashire v Middlesex
Leicester	Leicestershire v Worcestershire
Taunton	Somerset v Durham
The Oval	Surrey v Derbyshire
Hove	Sussex v Hampshire
Scarborough	Yorkshire v Essex

(Matches involving B & H finalists to be arranged)

	Tourist Match
	Scotland v Pakistan (One day)

14   **Britannic Assurance Championship**

Southend	Essex v Gloucestershire
Portsmouth	Hampshire v Derbyshire
Southport	Lancashire v Leicestershire
Uxbridge	Middlesex v Northamptonshire
Trent Bridge	Nottinghamshire v Worcestershire
Guildford	Surrey v Kent
Sheffield	Yorkshire v Warwickshire
	Tetley Bitter Challenge
Chester-le-Street	Durham v Pakistan

17   **Britannic Assurance Championship**

Southend	Essex v Sussex
Cheltenham	Gloucestershire v Yorkshire
Portsmouth	Hampshire v Glamorgan
Leicester	Leicestershire v Somerset
Uxbridge	Middlesex v Worcestershire
Northampton	Northamptonshire v Lancashire
Trent Bridge	Nottinghamshire v Durham
Guildford	Surrey v Warwickshire

18   **Tetley Bitter Challenge**

Derby	Derbyshire v Pakistan

19   **Sunday League**

Southend	Essex v Sussex
Cheltenham	Gloucestershire v Yorkshire
Portsmouth	Hampshire v Glamorgan
Canterbury	Kent v Worcestershire
Leicester	Leicestershire v Somerset
Northampton	Northamptonshire v Middlesex
Trent Bridge	Nottinghamshire v Durham
The Oval	Surrey v Warwickshire

21   **Britannic Assurance Championship**

Derby	Derbyshire v Middlesex
Cardiff	Glamorgan v Yorkshire
Cheltenham	Gloucestershire v Hampshire
Canterbury	Kent v Somerset
Hinckley	Leicestershire v Durham
Northampton	Northamptonshire v Warwickshire
The Oval	Surrey v Nottinghamshire
Hove	Sussex v Lancashire

	Kidderminster	Worcestershire v Essex	Edgbaston	Warwickshire v Durham
23		**Cornhill Insurance Test Match**	12	**NatWest Bank Trophy**
	Headingley	ENGLAND v PAKISTAN		Semi Finals
		(Fourth Test Match)		**Tourist Match**
24		**Britannic Assurance Championship**	Edgbaston	Warwickshire v Pakistan (1 day)
	Abergavenny	Glamorgan v Somerset	13	**Tourist Match**
	Cheltenham	Gloucestershire v Sussex	Edgbaston	Warwickshire v Pakistan (1 day)
	Leicester	Leicestershire v Essex		(or another county if Warwickshire
	Lord's	Middlesex v Durham		in semi finals)
	Edgbaston	Warwickshire v Nottinghamshire	14	**Britannic Assurance Championship**
	Worcester	Worcestershire v Derbyshire	Chesterfield	Derbyshire v Kent
26		Sunday League	Hartlepool	Durham v Glamorgan
	Pontypridd	Glamorgan v Derbyshire	Colchester	Essex v Nottinghamshire
	Cheltenham	Gloucestershire v Sussex	Bournemouth	Hampshire v Northamptonshire
	Old Trafford	Lancashire v Surrey	Uxbridge	Middlesex v Yorkshire
	Leicester	Leicestershire v Kent	The Oval	Surrey v Leicestershire
	Lord's	Middlesex v Durham	15	**Tetley Bitter Challenge**
	Taunton	Somerset v Northamptonshire	Bristol	* Gloucestershire v Pakistan
	Edgbaston	Warwickshire v Nottinghamshire	16	**Sunday League**
	Worcester	Worcestershire v Hampshire	Chesterfield	Derbyshire v Kent
29		**NatWest Bank Trophy**	Hartlepool	Durham v Glamorgan
		Quarter Finals	Colchester	Essex v Nottinghamshire
		Tourist Match	Bournemouth	Hampshire v Northamptonshire
	Marlow	Minor Counties v Pakistan (Two days)	Uxbridge	Middlesex v Yorkshire
		Other Match	Taunton	Somerset v Worcestershire
30	Jesmond	England XI v Rest of the World XI	The Oval	Surrey v Leicestershire
		(One day)	Hove	Sussex v Lancashire
		(Heritage Homes Festival)	18	**Britannic Assurance Championship**
31		**Britannic Assurance Championship**	Chesterfield	Derbyshire v Glamorgan
	Durham Uni	Durham v Surrey	Colchester	Essex v Surrey
	Swansea	Glamorgan v Kent	Bristol	Gloucestershire v Northamptonshire
	Taunton	Somerset v Sussex	Bournemouth	Hampshire v Middlesex
	Edgbaston	Warwickshire v Leicestershire	Leicester	Leicestershire v Kent
	Headingley	Yorkshire v Lancashire	Weston	Somerset v Worcestershire
August			Edgbaston	Warwickshire v Lancashire
1		**Tetley Bitter Challenge**	Scarborough	Yorkshire v Nottinghamshire
	Chelmsford	Essex v Pakistan	20	**Texaco Trophy**
2		**Sunday League**	Trent Bridge	ENGLAND v PAKISTAN
	Leek	Derbyshire v Warwickshire		*(Third One-day International)*
	Durham Uni.	Durham v Surrey	21	**Britannic Assurance Championship**
	Swansea	Glamorgan v Kent	Swansea	Glamorgan v Gloucestershire
	Southampton	Hampshire v Middlesex	Leicester	Leicestershire v Nottinghamshire
	Trent Bridge	Nottinghamshire v Leicestershire	Northampton	Northamptonshire v Kent
	Worcester	Worcestershire v Gloucestershire	Weston	Somerset v Hampshire
	Headingley	Yorkshire v Lancashire	Hove	Sussex v Middlesex
4		**Britannic Assurance Championship**	Worcester	Worcestershire v Durham
	Derby	Derbyshire v Leicestershire	Scarborough	Yorkshire v Surrey
	Durham Uni.	Durham v Yorkshire	22	**Texaco Trophy**
	Chelmsford	Essex v Northamptonshire	Lord's	ENGLAND v PAKISTAN
	Canterbury	Kent v Middlesex		*(Fourth One-day International)*
	Lytham	Lancashire v Surrey	23	**Sunday League**
	Worksop	Nottinghamshire v Gloucestershire	Bristol	Gloucestershire v Glamorgan
	Taunton	Somerset v Warwickshire	Southampton	Hampshire v Derbyshire
	Eastbourne	Sussex v Glamorgan	Leicester	Leicestershire v Northamptonshire
	Worcester	Worcestershire v Hampshire	Trent Bridge	Nottinghamshire v Lancashire
6		**Cornhill Insurance Test Match**	Weston	Somerset v Essex
	The Oval	* ENGLAND v PAKISTAN	Hove	Sussex v Middlesex
		(Fifth Test Match)	Edgbaston	Warwickshire v Kent
7		**Britannic Assurance Championship**	Worcester	Worcestershire v Durham
	Canterbury	Kent v Hampshire	Scarborough	Yorkshire v Surrey
	Old Trafford	Lancashire v Worcestershire	24	**Texaco Trophy**
	Lord's	Middlesex v Gloucestershire	Old Trafford	ENGLAND v PAKISTAN
	Northampton	Northamptonshire v Yorkshire		*(Fifth One-day International)*
	Trent Bridge	Nottinghamshire v Glamorgan	26	**Britannic Assurance Championship**
	Eastbourne	Sussex v Derbyshire		*(4 days)*
	Edgbaston	Warwickshire v Durham	Derby	Derbyshire v Somerset
9		**Sunday League**	Darlington	Durham v Hampshire
	Bristol	Gloucestershire v Leicestershire	Canterbury	Kent v Gloucestershire
	Canterbury	Kent v Hampshire	Old Trafford	Lancashire v Yorkshire
	Old Trafford	Lancashire v Worcestershire	Northampton	Northamptonshire v Middlesex
	Lord's	Middlesex v Essex	Hove	Sussex v Essex
	Northampton	Northamptonshire v Yorkshire	Edgbaston	Warwickshire v Glamorgan
	Trent Bridge	Nottinghamshire v Glamorgan	Worcester	Worcestershire v Nottinghamshire
	Eastbourne	Sussex v Derbyshire		

31		**Britannic Assurance Championship** *(4 days)*	8		**Britannic Assurance Championship** *(4 days)*

31   **Britannic Assurance Championship**
                        (4 days)

Chelmsford   Essex v Hampshire
Cardiff   Glamorgan v Sussex
Bristol   Gloucestershire v Leicestershire
Trent Bridge   Nottinghamshire v Derbyshire
The Oval   Surrey v Somerset
Worcester   Worcestershire v Warwickshire
Scarborough   Yorkshire v Northamptonshire

September
5   Lord's   **NATWEST BANK TROPHY FINAL**
7   **Britannic Assurance Championship**
                        (4 days)

Derby   Derbyshire v Essex
Canterbury   Kent v Glamorgan
Old Trafford   Lancashire v Sussex
Trent Bridge   Nottinghamshire v Surrey
Taunton   Somerset v Durham

(Matches involving Trophy finalists to be put back one day)

8   **Britannic Assurance Championship**
                        (4 days)
Lord's   Middlesex v Warwickshire
12   **Britannic Assurance Championship**
                        (4 days)
Gateshead   * Durham v Lancashire
Cardiff   * Glamorgan v Derbyshire
Bristol   * Gloucestershire v Essex
Southampton   * Hampshire v Worcestershire
Leicester   * Leicestershire v Northamptonshire
Taunton   * Somerset v Nottinghamshire
The Oval   * Surrey v Middlesex
Hove   * Sussex v Yorkshire
Edgbaston   * Warwickshire v Kent

CROQUET

WORLD CHAMPIONSHIPS
Hurlingham, Sep 8-15

SEMI-FINALS
JOHN WALTERS (GB) beat Robert Fulford (GB) 2-0;
DAVID OPENSHAW (GB) beat Chris Clarke (GB) 2-1

FINAL
WALTERS beat Openshaw 2-0

SOLOMON TROPHY
Palm Beach, Florida, Apr 13-16
GREAT BRITAIN 12 United States 5

BRITISH CHAMPIONSHIPS
Cheltenham, May 29-Jun 3

Men's
DAVID OPENSHAW beat Chris Haslam 3-2

Women's
GAIL CURRY beat Pat Hague 2-0

Mixed Doubles
FRANCES & RAY SANSOM beat Pamela Fellows & Peter Dorke 1-0

HOME INTERNATIONAL CHAMPIONSHIP
Glasgow, Jun 15-16
1 ENGLAND; 2 Wales; 3 Ireland; 4 Scotland

ATCO BRITISH OPEN
Hurlingham, Jul 27-28
Singles
ROBERT FULFORD beat Chris Clarke 3-1
Doubles
ROBERT FULFORD & CHRIS CLARKE beat Stephen Mulliner & Mark Saurin 2-0

━━━━━━━ CHAMPIONS ━━━━━━━

WORLD CHAMPIONSHIPS
Inaugurated 1989

1989	Joe Hogan (NZ)
1990	Robert Fulford (GB)
1991	John Walters (GB)

BRITISH CHAMPIONSHIPS
Inaugurated 1867
Winners since 1982 (British unless stated)

1982	Nigel Aspinall
1983	Nigel Aspinall
1984	Nigel Aspinall
1985	David Openshaw
1986	Joe Hogan (NZ)
1987	Mark Avery
1988	Steve Mulliner
1989	Joe Hogan (NZ)
1990	Robert Fulford
1991	David Openshaw

Most wins
10 John Solomon 1953, 1956, 1959, 1961, 1963-68; **8** Nigel Aspinall 1969, 1974-76, 1978, 1982-84; **7** Humphrey Hicks 1932, 1939, 1947-50, 1952; **5** Cyril Corbally 1902-03, 1906, 1908, 1913

CURLING

WORLD CHAMPIONSHIP
Winnipeg, Canada, Mar 23- 31

Men
Final Round Robin standings

		Won	Lost
1	Canada	9	0
2	Scotland	7	2
3	United States	6	3
4	Norway	6	3
5	Switzerland	5	4
6	Sweden	4	5
7	Germany	3	6
8	Denmark	2	7
9	France	2	7
10	Finland	1	8

SEMI-FINALS
SCOTLAND 4 United States 2; CANADA 5 Norway 3
FINAL
SCOTLAND 7 Canada 2
Winning Skip: David Smith

Women
Final Round Robin standings

		Won	Lost
1	Norway	8	1
2	Sweden	7	2
3	Canada	7	2
4	Scotland	6	3
5	Germany	5	4
6	Denmark	4	5
7	Switzerland	4	5
8	France	2	7
9	Austria	1	8
10	United States	1	8

SEMI-FINALS
CANADA 6 Sweden 4; NORWAY 8 Scotland 4
FINAL
NORWAY 4 Canada 3
Winning Skip: Dordi Nordby

━━━━━━━ CHAMPIONS ━━━━━━━

WORLD CHAMPIONS

	Men	Women
1959-64	Canada	-
1965	United States	-
1966	Canada	-
1967	Scotland	-
1968-72	Canada	-
1973	Sweden	-
1974	United States	-
1975	Switzerland	-
1976	United States	-
1977	Sweden	-
1978	United States	-
1979	Norway	Switzerland
1980	Canada	Canada
1981	Switzerland	Sweden
1982	Canada	Denmark
1983	Canada	Switzerland
1984	Norway	Canada
1985	Canada	Canada
1986	Canada	Canada
1987	Canada	Canada
1988	Norway	West Germany
1989	Canada	Canada
1990	Canada	Norway
1991	Scotland	Norway
Most wins		**Most wins**
Canada **21**		Canada **6**

CYCLING

SINGING INDURAIN

Miguel Indurain of Spain, a farm boy from just outside Pamplona, became the fourth Spaniard to win the Tour de France. He took the yellow jersey in the Pyrenees when Greg LeMond, hot favourite to win for the third successive year, began to fade in pain. In the Alps Indurain effectively clinched victory.

The new champion dominated the race but not the occasion. In seven previous tours Indurain had never finished higher than tenth and was accustomed to doing the donkey work for his team leader, Pedro Delgado. Journalists had trouble finding anything interesting to say about him: he does not speak French and it was said he nodded in response to questions during radio interviews.

Even his moment of victory was overshadowed by a crash on the Champs Elysées when the Soviet rider Djamol Abdoujaparov fell and broke a collarbone. Abdoujaparov, the first Muslim to ride the tour, kept the green jersey as points winner because of a special dispensation covering the last kilometre.

It was a tour full of small disasters. LeMond could only finish seventh. Sean Kelly's 13th and - he said - last Tour ended when the entire PDM team was forced to withdraw after 10 stages because of mass food poisoning. As ever on the Tour, there were darker rumours about the nature of the poison: the team later admitted it injected its riders with "liquid food". Stephen Roche, the 1987 winner, was eliminated on the second day because he missed the start of a time trial by seven minutes; he said he was sick in the toilet. Rolf Sorensen broke his collar-bone near the end of the fifth stage and finished in agony; on his way to hospital he was told he still had the yellow jersey, but he was unable to start the next morning. Reynel Montoya from Colombia became the first rider to fail a drugs test since 1988.

France's sequence of not providing a winner stretched to six years but at least in 1991 the French had four riders in the top 10, a major improvement over 1990. Belgium, however, which has provided 18 of the 78 winners, had no one in the top 30.

Riders were fined a total of £85,000 for taking off their helmets. This followed a new rule making helmets compulsory and a mass boycott by riders earlier in the season after a French competitor, Francis Moreau, was disqualified in the Paris-Nice race for removing his during a hot mountain climb.

A drug created for people suffering from kidney failure, recombinant erythropietin (EPO) was suspected of being implicated in the deaths of 18 European cyclists in the past four years. Carey Hall and Stephen Pate of Australia, who finished first and third in the professional sprint at the World Track Championships in Stuttgart, were both disqualified after positive tests. The British cyclist Malcolm Elliott lifted his arms in triumph before the finish line of a race in Spain, allowing two riders to go past him.

1991

TOUR DE FRANCE
Started Lyon Jul 6, finished Paris Jul 28.
Total distance 3,942 km

Stage Winners

	Stage Details	Stage Winner	Yellow Jersey
Prologue:	Lyon (5.4km)	Thierry Marie (Fra/Castorama)	Marie
Stage 1:	Lyon - Lyon (114.5km)	Djamol Abdoljaparov (USSR/Carrera)	Greg LeMond (US/Z)
Stage 2:	Bron - Eurexpo (36.5km) (*)	Ariostea	Rolf Sorensen (Den/Ariostea)
Stage 3:	Villeurbane - Dijon (210.5km)	Etienne De Wilde (Bel/Histor)	Sorensen
Stage 4:	Dijon - Reims (286km)	Abdoujaparov	Sorensen
Stage 5:	Reims - Valenciennes (149.5km)	Jelle Nijdam (Hol/Bucker)	Sorensen

Sorensen crashed three miles from the finish and broke his collar-bone

Stage 6:	Arras - Le Havre (259km)	Marie	Marie
Stage 7:	Le Havre - Argentan (165 km)	John Paul Von Poppel (Hol/PDM)	Marie
Stage 8:	Argentan - Alençon (73km)	Miguel Indurain (Spa/Banesto)	LeMond
Stage 9:	Alençon - Rennes (161 km)	Mauro Ribeiro (Bra/RMO)	LeMond

Ribeiro was the first Brazilian to win a stage in the Tour de France

Stage 10:	Rennes - Quimper (207.5km)	Phil Anderson (Aus/Motorola)	LeMond
Stage 11:	Quimper - St-Herblain (246km)	Charly Mottet (Fra/RMO)	LeMond
Stage 12:	Pau - Jaca (Spain) (192km)	Mottet	Luc Leblanc (Fra/Helvetia)
Stage 13:	Jaca - Vallouron (232km)	Claudio Chiappucci (Ita/Carrera)	Indurain

LeMond fell more than seven minutes behind the leader

Stage 14:	St-Gaudens - Castres (172.5km)	Bruno Cenghialta (Ita/Ariostea)	Indurain
Stage 15:	Albi - Ales (235km)	Moreno Argentin (Ita/Ariostea)	Indurain
Stage 16:	Ales - Gap (215km)	Marco Lietti (Ita/Ariostea)	Indurain
Stage 17:	Gap - L'Alpe d'Huez (125km)	Gianni Bugno (Ita/Gatorade) 3h 25m 48s	Indurain
Stage 18:	Bourg d'Oisons - Morzine (255km)	Thierry Claveyrolat (Fra/RMO) 7h 26m 47s	Indurain
Stage 19:	Morzine - Aix-Les-Bains (177km)	Dimitri Konyshev (USSR/TVM) 4h 19m 28s	Indurain
Stage 20:	Aix-Les-Bains - Macon (160km)	Viacheslav Ekimov (USSR/Panasonic)	Indurain
Stage 21:	Lugny- Macon (57km)	Indurain	Indurain
Stage 22:	Melun - Paris (178km)	Konyshev	Indurain

(*) Indicates team time-trial

Overall

1 Miguel Indurain (Spa/Banesto) 101h 1m 20s
2 Gianni Bugno (Ita/Gatorade) at 3m 36s
3 Claudio Chiappucci (Ita/Carrera) at 5m 56s
4 Charly Mottet (Fra/RMO) at 7m 37s
5 Luc Leblanc (Fra/Castorama) at 10m 10s
6 Laurent Fignon Fra/Castorama) at 11m 27s
7 Greg LeMond (US/Z) at 13m 13s
8 Andy Hampsten (US/Motorola) at 13m 40s
9 Pedro Delgado (Spa/Banesto) at 20m 13s
10 Gerard Rue (Fra/Helvetia) at 20m 20s
11 Eduardo Chozas (Spa/ONCE) at 21m 00s
12 Abelardo Rondon (Col/Banesto) at 26m 47s
13 Gert-Jan Theunisse (Hol/TVM) at 27m 10s
14 Jean-Francois Bernard (Fra/Banesto) at 28m 57s
15 Maurizio Fondriest (Ita/Panasonic) at 30m 09s
British Isles riders:
72 Robert Millar (Z) at 1h 3m06s
153 Laurence Roche (Tonton Tapis), at 2h 59m 25s

Team

1 Banesto 303h 28m 50s
2 Castorama at 25m 44s
3 RMO at 27m 29s

Points Winner

1 Djamo Abdoujaparov (USSR/Carrera) 316 pts
2 Laurent Jalabert (Fra/Toshiba) 263 pts
3 Olaf Ludwig (Ger/Panasonic) 263 pts

King of the Mountains

1 Claudio Chiappucci (Ita/Carrera) 312 pts
2 Thierry Claveyrolat (Fra/RMO) 277 pts
3 Luc Leblanc (Fra/Castorama) 164 pts

❝❝Bonking: Completely running out of energy.

From the glossary of cycling terms in the Motorola team manual at the Tour de France

"I think we're adults and would have liked to have freedom of choice."
Greg Le Mond, on being forced to wear a helmethelmet

"LeMond is involved in a heavy responsibility. If there is a mortal accident, the rider's widow can discuss with LeMond why he is against wearing a helmet. If LeMond can accept that kind of responsibility, good luck to him."
Hein Verbrugen, head of the International Federation of Professional Cycling

"They are a curious physical breed: slender yet imposing. The muscles of calf and thigh are dramatically defined. Faces and forearms are baked a deep brown, with stark white lines at brow and bicep where the sun has been repelled by cap and jersey. Imagine a breed of toasted whippets, and you have the general picture."
Pat Collins, Mail on Sunday, at the Tour de France

"To be honest, I didn't have to go deep into my physical reserves to win."
Miguel Indurain, Tour de France winner

"I've learned that when you push yourself and win, it's much easier than when you push yourself and lose."
Greg LeMond

"The future has a name: Indurain.❞❞
Marca, Spanish sports daily

TOUR OF SPAIN
Apr 29-May 19
1 Melchor Mauri (Spa) 82h 48m 07s
2 Miguel Indurain (Spa) at 2m 52s
3 Marino Lejaretta (Spa) at 3m 11s
4 Federico Echave (Spa) at 3m 54s
5 Fabio Parra (Col) at 5m 38s
6 Peio Ruiz Cabestany (Spa) at 6m 50s

TOUR OF ITALY
(Giro d'Italia)
May 26-Jun 16
1 Franco Chioccioli (Ita) 99h 35m 43s
2 Claudio Chiappucchi (Ita) at 3m 48s
3 Massimiliano Lelli (Ita) at 6m 56s
4 Gianni Bugno (Ita) at 7m 49s
5 Marino Lajarreta (Spa) at 10m 23s
6 Eric Boyer (Fra) at 11m 09s

WORLD TRACK CHAMPIONSHIPS
Stuttgart, Aug 13-20
Men - Professional
Sprint
1 Carey Hall (Aus) won 2-0
2 Fabrice Colas (Fra)
3 Stephen Pate (Aus)
*Hall and Pate subsequently stripped of their medals
following a positive drug test*
Individual Pursuit
1 Francis Moreau (Fra) 5m 34.44s
2 Shaun Wallace (GB) 5m 39.59s
3 Colin Sturgess (GB)
Kierin
1 Michael Huebner (Ger) 10.79s
2 Claudio Golinelli (Ita)
3 Fabrice Colas (Fra)
Motor Paced
1 Danny Clark (Aus) 59m 28.97s
2 Peter Steiger (Swi) at one lap
3 Arno Küttel (Swi) at one lap
*Clark, at 39years 353days, became the oldest ever world
champion. The previous oldest was Jan Derksen (Den)
aged 39yrs 6mths in 1957*
Points Race
1 Viacheslav Ekimov (USSR) 47 pts
2 Francis Moreau (Fra) 44 pts
3 Peter Pieters (Hol) 44 pts
Men - Amateur
1km Individual Time Trial
1 José Moreno (Spa) 1m 03.827s
2 Jens Gluecklich (Ger) 1m 04.379s
3 Gene Samuel (Tri) 1m 04.797s
4000 Metres Individual Pursuit
1 Jens Lehmann (Ger) 4m 25.775s
2 Michael Gloeckner (Ger) 4m 31.465s
3 Jan-Bo Petersen (Den)
4000 Metres Team Pursuit
1 Germany 4m 07.003s
2 Soviet Union 4m 12.259s
3 Australia
Sprint
1 Jens Fiedler (Ger) won 2-0
2 Bill Huck (Ger)
3 Gary Neiwand (Aus)
Points Race
1 Bruno Risi (Swi) 55pts
2 Stephen McGlede (Aus) 40 pts

3 Jan-Bo Petersen (Den) 31 pts
Tandem
1 Eyk Pokórny & Emanuel Raasch (Ger) won 2-0
2 Pavel Buran & Lubomir Hargas (Cze)
3 Frederic Lancien & Denis Lemyre (Fra)
50km Motor Paced
1 Roland Königshofer (Aut) 42m 46.69s
2 David Solari (Ita) at 2 laps
3 Carsten Podlesch (Ger) at 4 laps

Women
Sprint
1 Ingrid Haringa (Hol) won 2-0
2 Annette Neumann (Ger)
3 Connie Paraskevin-Young (US)
Individual Pursuit
1 Petra Rossner (Ger) 3m 39.88s
2 Janie Eickhoff (US) 3m 40.37s
3 Marion Clignet (Fra)
Points Race
1 Ingrid Haringa (Hol) 40 pts
2 Kristel Merckx (Bel) 37 pts
3 Janie Eickhoff (US) 37 pts
Leading Medal Winners

	G	S	B	Total
Germany	6	4	1	11
France	1	2	2	5
Austria	2	0	2	4
Holland	2	0	1	3
Switzerland	1	1	1	3
United States	0	1	2	3
Great Britain	0	1	1	2

WORLD ROAD RACE CHAMPIONSHIPS
Stuttgart, Aug 21-25
Men - Professional
1 Gianni Bugno (Ita) 6h 20m 23s
2 Steven Rooks (Hol) same time
3 Miguel Indurain ((Spa) same time
Men - Amateur
1 Viktor Rjakskinski (USSR) 4h 28m 04s
2 Davide Rebellin (Ita) same time
3 Beat Zberg (Swi) same time
Men-100km Team Time Trial (Amateur)
1 Italy 1h 54m 48s
2 Germany 1h 57m 21s
3 Norway 1h 57m 39s
Women
1 Leontien van Moorsel (Hol) 2h 09m 47s
2 Inga Thompson (US) at 1m 54s
3 Alison Sydor (Can) at 2m 46s
Women-50km Team Time Trial
1 France 1h 02m 14.1s
2 Holland 1h 02m 41.5s
3 Soviet Union 1h 02m 51.1s

WORLD CUP
Milan San-Remo
Mar 23
1 Claudio Chiappucci (Ita) 6h 56m 36s
2 Rolf Sorensen (Den) at 45s
3 Eric Vanderaerden (Bel) at 57s
Tour Of Flanders
Apr 7
1 Edwin Van Hooydonck (Bel) 7h 02m 00s
2 Johann Musseuw (Bel) at 45s
3 Rolf Sorensen (Den) same time

Paris-Roubaix
Apr 14
1 Marc Madiot (Fra) 7h 08m 19s
2 Jean-Claude Colotti (Fra) at 1m 07s
3 Carlo Bomans (Bel) at 1m 41s

Liège-Bastogne-Liège
Apr 21
1 Moreno Argentin (Ita) 7h 15m 00s
2 Claude Criquiellion (Bel) same time
3 Rolf Sorensen (Den) same time

Amstel Gold Race
Heerlem to Maastricht, Holland, Apr 28
1 Frans Maassen (Hol) 6h 04m 46s
2 Maurizio Fondriest (Ita) same time
3 Dirk de Woold (Bel) same time

Wincanton Classic
Brighton, Aug 5
1 Eric Van Lancker (Bel) 6h 16m 5s
2 Rolf Golz (Ger) at 29s
3 Jan Goessens (Bel) at 44s

San Sebastian Classic
San Sebastian, Aug 10
1 Gianni Bugno (Ita) 6h 04m 28s
2 Pedro Delgado (Spa) at 55s
3 Maurizio Fondriest (Ita) at 1m 17s

Championship Of Zurich
Zurich, Aug 18
1 Johann Museuw (Bel) 6h 28m 13s
2 Laurent Jalabert (Fra) same time
3 Maximillian Sciandri (Ita) same time

Grand Prix De La Liberation
(Team time trial)
Eindhoven, Holland, Sep 15
1 Buckler (Hol) 1h 37m 15s
2 ONCE (Spa) at 18s
3 Panasonic (Hol) at 42s

OTHER MAJOR OVERSEAS RACES

Het Volk
Ghent, Belgium, Mar 2
1 Andreas Kappes (Ger) 4h 46m 30s
2 Carlo Bomans (Bel) same time
3 Edwin Van Hooydonck (Bel) same time

Fleche Wallone
Spa-Huy, Apr 17
1 Moreno Argentin (Ita) 5h 13m 14s
2 Claude Criquiellion (Bel) at 2m 20s
3 Claudio Chiappucci (Ita) at 2m 31s

Paris-Nice
Mar 10-17
1 Tony Rominger (Swi) 24h 09m 09s
2 Laurent Jalabert (Fra) at 1m 55s
3 Martial Gayant (Fra) at 2m 27s

Paris-Brussels
Sep 18
1 B Holm (Den) 6h 3m 10s
2 Olaf Ludwig (Ger) at 7s
3 Johan Musseuw (Bel) at 7s

MAJOR BRITISH RACES
MILK RACE
Bridlington-Liverpool, May 26-Jun 8
1 Chris Walker (Banana-Falcon/GB) 45h 33m 21s
2 Simeon Hempsall (England Amateurs) at 22s
3 Keith Reynolds (Banana-Falcon/GB) at 25s
4 Harry Lodge (Colstrop-Isoglass/GB) at 51s
5 Rob Holden (Banana-Falcon/GB) at 56s
6 Paul Curran (England Amateurs) at 1m 02s
Team
1 Banana-Falcon 136h 31m 44s
2 England Amateurs at 1m 52s
3 Colstrop-Isoglass at 4m 21s

KELLOGG'S TOUR OF BRITAIN
Windsor - Leeds, Aug 6-10
Final Standings
1 Phil Anderson (Aus/Panasonic) 24h 59m 57s
2 Rudy Verdonck (Bel/Weinmann) at 1s
3 Heinz Imboden (Swi/Helvetia) at 1s
Team: Panasonic

SCOTTISH PROVIDENT LEAGUE
CITY CENTRE SERIES
Leeds, May 2 Jon Clay
(Banana-Falcon)

Sheffield, May 10	Keith Reynolds (Banana-Falcon)
Bradford, May 17	John Walshaw (AMS-Nigel Dean)
Bristol, May 20	Dave Rayner (Buckler)
Portsmouth, May 22	Chris Walker (Banana-Falcon)
Newcastle, Jun 10	Chris Walker (Banana-Falcon)

Walker's win came just two days after he won the Milk Race

Cambridge, Jun 20	Chris Lillywhite (Banana-Falcon)
Belfast, Jun 27	Jon Clay (Banana-Falcon)
Glasgow, Aug 21	Chris Lillywhite (Banana-Falcon)
Edinburgh, Aug 25	Chris Walker (Banana-Falcon)

Final Standings
1 Jon Clay (Banana-Falcon) 233 pts
2 Chris Walker (Banana-Falcon) 220 pts
3 Ben Luckwell (Townsend Cycles) 178 pts

BRITISH PROFESSIONAL ROAD RACE
CHAMPIONSHIP
Newport, Shropshire, Jun 30
1 Brian Smith (Banana-Falcon) 5h 01m 20s
2 Keith Reynolds (Banana-Falcon) at 1m 10s
3 Dave Rayner (Buckler) same time

WORLD CYCLO CROSS CHAMPIONSHIPS
Gieten, Holland Feb 2-3
Professional
1 Radomir Simunek (Cze) 1h 04m 22s
2 Adri van der Poel (Hol) same time
3 Bruno le Bras (Fra) at 6s
Simunek became the first Eastern European to win the professional title. He also became the first man to win all three main titles; junior, amateur and professional
Amateur
1 Thomas Frischknecht (Swi) 50m 19s
2 Henrik Djernies (Den) at 22s
3 Daniele Pontoni (Ita) at 23s

———————— **1990** ————————
WORLD CUP
Final Standings
1 Gianni Bugno (Ita) 133 pts
2 Rudy Dhaemens (Bel) 99 pts
3 Sean Kelly (Ire) 94 pts
4 Franco Ballerini (Ita) 89 pts
5 Gilles Delion (Fra) 82 pts
6 Claudio Chiappucci (Ita) 78 pts

CHAMPIONS

TOUR DE FRANCE

1903	Maurice Garin (Fra)	1914	Philippe Thys (Bel)	1929	Maurice de Waele (Bel)
1904	Henri Cornet (Fra)	1919	Firmin Lambot (Bel)	1930	André Leducq (Fra)
1905	Louis Trousselier (Fra)	1920	Philippe Thys (Bel)	1931	Antonin Magne (Fra)
1906	René Pottier (Fra)	1921	Leon Scieur (Bel)	1932	Andre Leducq (Fra)
1907	Lucien Petit-Breton (Fra)	1922	Firmin Lambot (Bel)	1933	Georges Speicher (Fra)
1908	Lucien Petit-Breton (Fra)	1923	Henri Pelissier (Fra)	1934	Antonin Magne (Fra)
1909	François Faber (Lux)	1924	Ottavio Bottecchia (Ita)	1935	Romain Maes (Bel)
1910	Octave Lapize (Fra)	1925	Ottavio Bottecchia (Ita)	1936	Sylvère Maes (Bel)
1911	Gustave Garrigou (Fra)	1926	Lucien Buysse (Bel)	1937	Roger Lapebie (Fra)
1912	Odile Defraye (Bel)	1927	Nicholas Frantz (Lux)	1938	Gino Bartali (Ita)
1913	Philippe Thys (Bel)	1928	Nicholas Frantz (Lux)	1939	Sylvère Maes (Bel)

POST-WAR WINNERS OF THE THREE MAJOR TOURS

	Tour de France	Tour of Italy	Tour of Spain
1947	Jean Robic (Fra)	Fausto Coppi (Ita)	Edourd Van Dyck (Bel)
1948	Gino Bartali (Ita)	Fiorenzo Magni (Ita)	Bernardo Ruiz (Spa)
1949	Fausto Coppi (Ita)	Fausto Coppi (Ita)	–
1950	Ferdinand Kebler (Swi)	Hugo Koblet (Swi)	Emilio Rodriquez (Spa)
1951	Hugo Koblet (Swi)	Fiorenzo Magni (Ita)	–
1952	Fausto Coppi (Ita)	Fausto Coppi (Ita)	–
1953	Louison Bobet (Fra)	Fausto Coppi (Ita)	–
1954	Louison Bobet (Fra)	Carlo Clerici (Swi)	–
1955	Louison Bobet (Fra)	Fiorenzo Magni (Ita)	J Dotto (Fra)
1956	Roger Walkowiak (Fra)	Charly Gaul (Lux)	A Contero (Ita)
1957	Jacques Anquetil (Fra)	Gastone Nencini (Ita)	Jesus Lorono (Spa)
1958	Charly Gaul (Lux)	Ercole Baldini (Ita)	Jean Stablinski (Fra)
1959	Federico Bahamontès (Spa)	Charly Gaul (Lux)	Antonio Suarez (Spa)
1960	Gastone Nencini (Ita)	Jacques Anquetil (Fra)	F de Mulder (Bel)
1961	Jacques Anquetil (Fra)	Arn Pambianco (Ita)	Angelino Soler (Spa)
1962	Jacques Anquetil (Fra)	Franco Balmamion (Ita)	Rudi Altig (FRG)
1963	Jacques Anquetil (Fra)	Franco Balmamion (Ita)	Jacques Anquetil (Fra)
1964	Jacques Anquetil (Fra)	Jacques Anquetil (Fra)	Raymond Poulidor (Fra)
1965	Felice Gimondi (Ita)	Vittorio Ardoni (Ita)	Rolf Wolfshohl (FRG)
1966	Lucien Aimar (Fra)	Gianni Motta (Ita)	Francisco Gabicagogeascoa (Spa)
1967	Roger Pingeon (Fra)	Felice Gimondi (Ita)	Jan Janssen (Hol)
1968	Jan Janssen (Hol)	Eddy Merckx (Bel)	Felice Gimondi (Ita)
1969	Eddy Merckx (Bel)	Felice Gimondi (Ita)	Roger Pingeon (Fra)
1970	Eddy Merckx (Bel)	Eddy Merckx (Bel)	Luis Ocana (Spa)
1971	Eddy Merckx (Bel)	Gosta Petterson (Swe)	F Bracke (Bel)
1972	Eddy Merckx (Bel)	Eddy Merckx (Bel)	José-Manuel Fuente (Spa)
1973	Luis Ocana (Spa)	Eddy Merckx (Bel)	Eddy Merckx (Bel)
1974	Eddy Merckx (Bel)	Eddy Merckx (Bel)	José-Manuel Fuente (Spa)
1975	Bernard Thevenet (Fra)	F Bertoglio (Ita)	G Tamames (Spa)
1976	Lucien van Impe (Bel)	Felice Gimondi (Ita)	J Pesarrodona (Spa)
1977	Bernard Thevenet (Fra)	Michel Pollentier (Bel)	Freddy Maertens (Bel)
1978	Bernard Hinault (Fra)	Johan De Muynck (Bel)	Bernard Hinault (Fra)
1979	Bernard Hinault (Fra)	Giuseppe Saronni (Ita)	Joop Zoetemelk (Hol)
1980	Joop Zoetemelk (Hol)	Bernard Hinault (Fra)	Faustino Ruperez (Spa)
1981	Bernard Hinault (Fra)	Giovanni Bartaglin (Ita)	Giovanni Bartaglin (Ita)
1982	Bernard Hinault (Fra)	Bernard Hinault (Fra)	Marino Lejaretta (Spa)
1983	Laurent Fignon (Fra)	Giuseppe Saronni (Ita)	Bernard Hinault (Fra)
1984	Laurent Fignon (Fra)	Francesco Moser (Ita)	Eric Caritoux (Fra)
1985	Bernard Hinault (Fra)	Bernard Hinault (Fra)	Pedro Delgado (Spa)
1986	Greg LeMond (US)	Roberto Visentini (Ita)	Alvaro Pino (Spa)
1987	Stephen Roche (Ire)	Stephen Roche (Ire)	Luis Herrera (Col)
1988	Pedro Delgado (Spa)	Andy Hampsten (US)	Sean Kelly (Ire)
1989	Greg LeMond (US)	Laurent Fignon (Fra)	Pedro Delgado (Spa)
1990	Greg LeMond (US)	Gianni Bugno (Ita)	Marco Giovanetti (Ita)
1991	Miguel Indurain (Spa)	Franco Chioccioli (Ita)	Melchor Mauri (Spa)

Most Wins

Tour de France: 5 Jacques Anquetil, Eddy Merckx, Bernard Hinault

Tour of Italy: 5 Alfredo Binda (Ita) 1925, 1927-29, 1933;
Fausto Coppi 1940, 1947, 1949, 1952-53; Eddy Merckx

Tour of Spain: 2 Gustave Deloor (Bel) 1935-36; Julio Barrendero (Spa) 1941-42; José-Manuel Fuente; Bernard
Hinault; Pedro Delgado.

WORLD PROFESSIONAL ROAD RACE CHAMPIONSHIP
(Post-war winners)

1946	Hans Knecht (Swi)
1947	Theo Middelkamp (Hol)
1948	Alberic Scotte (Bel)
1949	Rik van Steenbergen (Bel)
1950	Alberic Schotts (Bel)
1951	Ferdi Kubler (Swi)
1952	Heinz Muller (Ger)
1953	Fausto Coppi (Ita)
1954	Louison Bobet (Fra)
1955	Stan Ockers (Bel)
1956	Rik van Steenbergen (Bel)
1957	Rik van Steenbergen (Bel)
1958	Ercole Baldini (Ita)
1959	André Darrigade (Fra)
1960	Rik van Looy (Bel)
1961	Rik van Looy (Bel)
1962	Jean Stablinski (Fra)
1963	Renoni Beheyt (Bel)
1964	Jan Janssen (Hol)
1965	Tom Simpson (GB)
1966	Rudi Altig (FRG)
1967	Eddy Merckx (Bel)
1968	Vittorio Adorni (Ita)
1969	Harm Ottenbros (Hol)
1970	Jean-Pierre Monsère (Bel)
1971	Eddy Merckx (Bel)
1972	Marino Basso (Ita)
1973	Felice Gimondi (Ita)
1974	Eddy Merckx (Bel)
1975	Hennie Kuiper (Hol)
1976	Freddy Maertens (Bel)
1977	Francesco Moser (Ita)
1978	Gerrie Knetemann (Hol)
1979	Jan Raas (Hol)
1980	Bernard Hinault (Fra)
1981	Freddy Maertens (Bel)
1982	Giuseppe Saronni (Ita)
1983	Greg LeMond (US)
1984	Claude Criquiellion (Bel)
1985	Joop Zoetemelk (Hol)
1986	Moreno Argentin (Ita)
1987	Stephen Roche (Ire)
1988	Maurizio Fondriest (Ita)
1989	Greg LeMond (US)
1990	Rudy Dhaemens (Bel)
1991	Gianni Bugno (Ita)

Most Wins
3 Alfredo Binda (Ita) 1927, 1930, 1932;
   Rik van Steenbergen, Eddy Merckx

TOUR OF BRITAIN (Milk Race)

1951	Ian Steel (GB)
1952	Ken Russell (GB)
1953	Gordon Thomas (GB)
1954	Eugène Tamburlini (Fra)
1955	Anthony Hewson (GB)
1958	Richard Durlacher (Aut)
1959	Bill Bradley (GB)
1960	Bill Bradley (GB)
1961	Billy Holmes (GB)
1962	Eugen Pokorny (Pol)
1963	Peter Chisman (GB)
1964	Arthur Metcalfe (GB)
1965	Les West (GB)
1966	Josef Gawliczek (Pol)
1967	Les West (GB)
1968	Gosta Pettersson (Swe)
1969	Fedor Den Hertog (Hol)

1970	Jiri Mainus (Cze)
1971	Fedor Den Hertog (Hol)
1972	Hennie Kuiper (Hol)
1973	Piet van Katwijk (Hol)
1974	Roy Schuiten (Hol)
1975	Bernt Johansson (Swe)
1976	Bill Nickson (GB)
1977	Said Gusseinov (USSR)
1978	Jan Brzezny (Pol)
1979	Yuriy Kashirin (USSR)
1980	Ivan Mitchtenko (USSR)
1981	Sergey Krivocheyev (USSR)
1982	Yuriy Kashirin (USSR)
1983	Matt Eaton (US)
1984	Oleg Czougeda (USSR)
1985	Eric van Lancker (Bel)
1986	Joey McLoughlin (GB)
1987	Malcolm Elliott (GB)
1988	Vasiliy Zhdanov (USSR)
1989	Brian Walton (Can)
1990	Shane Sutton (Aus)
1991	Chris Walker (GB)

KELLOGG'S TOUR OF BRITAIN
(Inaugurated 1987)

1987	Joey McLoughlin (GB)
1988	Malcolm Elliott (GB)
1989	Robert Millar (GB)
1990	Michel Dernies (Bel)
1991	Phil Anderson (Aus)

WORLD CHAMPIONS
(Since 1982)
(In Olympic years, if an event is included at the Games;
then it is not contested at the World Championships)
Men – Professional
Sprint

1982	Koichi Nakano (Jap)
1983	Koichi Nakano (Jap)
1984	Koichi Nakano (Jap)
1985	Koichi Nakano (Jap)
1986	Koichi Nakano (Jap)
1987	Nabuyuki Tawara (Jap)
1988	Stephen Pate (Aus)
1989	Claudio Golinelli (Ita)
1990	Michael Huebner (GDR)
1991	Fabrice Colas (Fra)

Individual Pursuit

1982	Alain Bondue (Fra)
1983	Steele Bishop (Aus)
1984	Hans-Henrik Oersted (Den)
1985	Hans-Henrik Oersted (Den)
1986	Tony Doyle (GB)
1987	Hans-Henrik Oersted (Den)
1988	Lech Piasecki (Pol)
1989	Colin Sturgess (GB)
1990	Viacheslav Ekimov (USSR)
1991	Francis Moreau (Fra)

Kierin

1982	Gordon Singleton (Can)
1983	Urs Freuler (Swi)
1984	Robert Dill-Bundi (Swi)
1985	Urs Freuler (Swi)
1986	Michel Vaarten (Bel)
1987	Hazuni Honda (Jap)
1988	Claudio Golinelli (Ita)
1989	Claudio Golinelli (Ita)
1990	Michael Huebner (GDR)
1991	Michael Huebner (Ger)

Motor Paced

1982   Martin Venix (Hol)
1983   Bruno Vicini (Ita)
1984   Horst Schutz (FRG)
1985   Bruno Vicini (Ita)
1986   Bruno Vicini (Ita)
1987   Max Hurzeler (Swi)
1988   Danny Clark (Aus)
1989   Giovanni Renosto (Ita)
1990   Walter Brugna (Ita)
1991   Danny Clark (Aus)

Points Race

1982   Urs Freuler (Swi)
1983   Urs Freuler (Swi)
1984   Urs Freuler (Swi)
1985   Urs Freuler (Swi)
1986   Urs Freuler (Swi)
1987   Urs Freuler (Swi)
1988   Daniel Wyder (Swi)
1989   Urs Freuler (Swi)
1990   Laurent Biondi (Fra)
1991   Viacheslav Ekimov (USSR)

Men – Amateur

1 km Individual Time Trial

1982   Fredy Schmidteke (FRG)
1983   Sergey Kopylov (USSR)
1985   Jens Glücklich (GDR)
1986   Maik Malchow (GDR)
1987   Martin Vinnicombe (Aus)
1989   Jens Glücklich (GDR)
1990   Alexsandr Kirichenko (USSR)
1991   Jose Moreno (Spa)

Individual Pursuit

1982   Detlef Macha (GDR)
1983   Viktor Kupovets (USSR)
1985   Viacheslav Ekimov (USSR)
1986   Viacheslav Ekimov (USSR)
1987   Guintautas Umaros (USSR)
1989   Viacheslav Ekimov (USSR)
1990   Evgeni Berzin (USSR)
1991   Jans Lehmann (Ger)

Team Pursuit

1982   USSR
1983   West Germany
1985   Italy
1986   Czechoslovakia
1987   USSR
1989   East Germany
1990   USSR
1991   Germany

Sprint

1982   Sergey Kopylov (USSR)
1983   Lutz Hesslich (GDR)
1985   Lutz Hesslich (GDR)
1986   Michael Hubner (GDR)
1987   Lutz Hesslich (GDR)
1989   Bill Huck (GDR)
1990   Bill Huck (GDR)
1991   Jens Fiedler (Ger)

Points Race

1982   Hans-Jaochim Pohl (GDR)
1983   Michael Marcussen (Den)
1985   Martin Penc (Cze)
1986   Dan Frost (Den)
1987   Marat Ganeev (USSR)
1989   Marat Satybaliev (USSR)
1990   Stephen McGlede (Aus)
1991   Bruno Risi (Swi)

Tandem

1982   Ivan Kucirek & Pavel Martinek (Cze)
1983   Philippe Vernet & Frank Depine (Fra)
1984   Jürgen Greil & Frank Weber (FRG)
1985   Vitezlav Voboril & Roman Rekhousek (Cze)
1986   Vitezlav Voboril & Roman Rekhousek (Cze)
1987   Fabrice Colas & Frédéric Magne (Fra)
1988   Fabrice Colas & Frédéric Magne (Fra)
1989   Fabrice Colas & Frédéric Magne (Fra)
1990   Gianluca Capitano & Federico Paris (Ita)
1991   Eyk Pokorny & Emanuel Raasch (Ger)

Motor Paced

1982   Gaby Minneboo (Hol)
1983   Rainer Podlesch (GDR)
1984   Jan de Nijs (Hol)
1985   Roberto Dotti (Ita)
1986   Mario Gentilo (Ita)
1987   Mario Gentilo (Ita)
1988   Vincenzo Colamartino (Ita)
1989   Roland Königshofer (Aut)
1990   Roland Königshofer (Aut)
1991   Roland Königshofer (Aut)

Road Team Time Trial

1982   Netherlands
1983   USSR
1985   USSR
1986   Netherlands
1987   Italy
1989   East Germany
1990   USSR
1991   Italy

Road Race

1982   Bernd Drogan (GDR)
1983   Uwe Raab (GDR)
1985   Lech Piasecki (Pol)
1986   Uwe Ampler (GDR)
1987   Richard Vivean (Fra)
1989   Joachim Halupczok (Pol)
1990   Mirko Gualdi (Ita)
1991   Viktor Rjakskinski (USSR)

Women

Sprint

1982   Connie Paraskevin (US)
1983   Connie Paraskevin (US)
1984   Connie Paraskevin (US)
1985   Isabelle Nicoloso (Fra)
1986   Christa Rothenburger (GDR)
1987   Erika Salumiae (USSR)
1989   Erika Salumiae (USSR)
1990   Connie Young (US)
1991   Ingrid Haringa (Hol)

Individual Pursuit

1982   Rebecca Twigg (US)
1983   Connie Carpenter (US)
1984   Rebecca Twigg (US)
1985   Rebecca Twigg (US)
1986   Jeannie Longo (Fra)
1987   Rebecca Twigg-Whitehead (US)
1988   Jeannie Longo (Fra)
1989   Jeannie Longo (Fra)
1990   Leontien van Moorsel (Hol)
1991   Petra Rossner (Ger)

Points Race

1988   Sally Hodge (GB)
1989   Jeannie Longo (Fra)
1990   Karen Holliday (NZ)
1991   Ingrid Haringa (Hol)

Road Team Time Trial

1987   USSR
1988   Italy
1989   USSR
1990   Holland
1991   France

Road Race
1982   Mandy Jones (GB)
1983   Marianne Berglund (Swe)
1985   Jeannie Longo (Fra)
1986   Jeannie Longo (Fra)
1987   Jeannie Longo (Fra)
1989   Jeannie Longo (Fra)
1990   Catherine Marsal (Fra)
1991   Leontien van Moorsel (Hol)

CYCLO CROSS
WORLD CHAMPIONS
(Since 1982)
Professional
1982   Roland Liboton (Bel)
1983   Roland Liboton (Bel)
1984   Roland Liboton (Bel)
1985   Klaus-Peter Thaler (FRG)
1986   Albert Zweifel (Swi)
1987   Klaus-Peter Thaler (FRG)
1988   Pascal Richard (Swi)
1989   Danny De Bie (Bel)
1990   Henk Baars (Hol)
1991   Radomir Simunek (Cze)

Most Wins:
7 Eric de Vlaeminck (Bel) 1966, 1968-73

Amateur
1982   Milos Fisera (Cze)
1983   Radomir Simunek (Cze)
1984   Radomir Simunek (Cze)
1985   Mike Kluge (FRG)
1986   Vito di Tano (Ita)
1987   Mike Kluge (FRG)
1988   K Camrda (Cze)
1989   Ondrej Glajza (Cze)
1990   Andreas Buesser (Swi)
1991   Thomas Frischknecht (Swi)

Most Wins:
5 Robert Vermiere (Bel) 1970-71, 1974-75, 1977

1992

Apr 27-May 17 Tour of Spain; *May 24-Jun 6* Milk Race;
May 24-Jun 14 Tour of Italy; *Jul 4-26* TOUR DE
FRANCE (start San Sebastian, finish Paris); *Aug 10-14*
Kellogg's Tour of Britain; *Aug 16* Wincanton Classic

DARTS

THE HIGH PRIEST

Dennis Priestley, a 40-year-old Yorkshire coal merchant, shocked Eric Bristow, the five-times champion, in the final of the World Championship at Frimley Green. Priestley won 6-0, taking 18 legs to four, having beaten three other seeded players on the way including two previous champions, Bob Anderson and Phil Taylor. It was the fourth year out of five that Bristow had lost the final: "It's getting boring," he said.

Priestley was unseeded and an 80-1 chance at the start of the championships. He said he intended to sell the coal business and turn pro: "Anyone wanna buy a coal lorry and skip?" he asked. The following day he was back playing in the Yorkshire Superleague for nothing at the Balby Bridge Working Men's Club, Doncaster. Priestley began playing darts in the mid-70s when the Mexborough Power Station team were a man short; he bought his first arrows aged 25 with part-proceeds of a £6 bet on Grundy in the 1975 Derby. He said his main ambition was to meet the Barnsley FC players.

The *News of the World* Championship, which dates back to 1928, was scrapped after the paper withdrew its support. In San Diego, California, Danny Ledcke opened a non-alcoholic darts hall; other teams refused to play there and accused Ledcke of turning darts matches into "cake and ice cream socials". Princess Diana proved her skill by hitting three playing cards at a fair in Tetbury, Gloucestershire. She won three goldfish.

1990-91

WINMAU WORLD MASTERS
Kensington, Dec 9
Men
PHIL TAYLOR (Staffs) beat Jocky Wilson (Scotland) 3-2
Women
RHIAN SPEED (Wales) beat Deta Hedman (Essex) 3-1

WEBSTER'S YORKSHIRE BITTER BRITISH OPEN
Horticultural Hall, London, Dec 27-29
Men
MIKE GREGORY beat John Lowe 2-1
Women
PAULINE DYER beat Frances Hoenlsaar (Hol) 3-1

EMBASSY WORLD PROFESSIONAL CHAMPIONSHIP
Frimley Green, Surrey, Jan 4-12
Second Round
BOB ANDERSON (Eng) beat Russell Stewart (Aus) 3-2;
PHIL TAYLOR (Eng) beat Tony Payne (US) 3-1;
DENNIS PRIESTLEY (Eng) beat Bob Sinneave (Can) 3-0;
ALAN WARRINER (Eng) beat Keith Sullivan (Aus) 3-2;
KEVIN KENNY (Eng) beat Peter Evison (Eng) 3-1;
JOCKY WILSON (Sco) beat Ronnie Baxter (Eng) 3-1;
DAVE WHITCOMBE (Eng) beat Cliff Lazarenko (Eng) 3-1; ERIC BRISTOW (Eng) beat Mike Gregory (Eng) 3-0

Quarter-finals
PRIESTLEY beat Taylor 4-3; ANDERSON beat Warriner 4-3; KENNY beat Wilson 4-3; BRISTOW beat Whitcombe 4-3
Semi-finals
PRIESTLEY beat Anderson 5-2; BRISTOW beat Kenny 5-2

Final
PRIESTLEY beat Bristow 6-0
Priestley threw a championship record 25 maximums

> **❝I do all right. I earn about a grand a week. I'm not complaining, but if I'd been at the top five years ago, I'd be earning a grand a day, easily.❞**
> *Phil Taylor, 1990 world champion*

CHAMPIONS
(All winners British)
EMBASSY WORLD PROFESSIONAL CHAMPIONSHIP
Venues: 1978 Heart of the Midlands Night Club, Nottingham; 1979-85 Jollees, Longton, Stoke-on-Trent; 1986 Lakeside Country Club, Frimley Green, Surrey.

Year	Winner	Runner-up
1978	Leighton Rees	John Lowe
1979	John Lowe	Leighton Rees
1980	Eric Bristow	Bobby George
1981	Eric Bristow	John Lowe
1982	Jocky Wilson	John Lowe
1983	Keith Deller	Eric Bristow
1984	Eric Bristow	Dave Whitcombe
1985	Eric Bristow	John Lowe
1986	Eric Bristow	Dave Whitcombe
1987	John Lowe	Eric Bristow
1988	Bob Anderson	John Lowe
1989	Jocky Wilson	Eric Bristow
1990	Phil Taylor	Eric Bristow
1991	Dennis Priestley	Eric Bristow

1992
Jan 3-11 World Championship (Frimley Green)

1991

SHOW JUMPING
Volvo World Cup Final
Gothenburg, Apr 10-14
1 John Whitaker (GB) on *Henderson Milton*
2 Nelson Pessoa (Bra) on *Special Envoy*
3 Roger-Yves Bost (Fra) on *Norton de Rhuys*

Royal International Horse Show
NEC, Birmingham, Jun 13-16

King George V Gold Cup
1 David Broome on *Lannegan*
2 Nick Skelton on *Alanpaul Major Wager*
3 John Whitaker on *Henderson Gammon*

Queen Elizabeth II Cup
1 Janet Hunter on *Everest Lisnamarrow*
2 Jane Ware on *Tarzan Van Bellet*
3 Marie Edgar on *Everest Sure Thing*

European Championship
La Baule, France, Jul 21
Individual
1 Eric Navet (Fra) on *Waiti Quito de Baussy*
2 Frank Sloothaak (Ger) on *Optiebeurs Wazerkoenig*
3 Jos Lansink (Hol) on *Optiebeurs Egano*

Team
1 Holland
2 Great Britain
3 Switzerland

Silk Cut Derby
Hickstead, Aug 4
1 Michael Whitaker (GB) on *Henderson Monsanta*
2 Tina Cassan (GB) on *Treffer*
3 Ludger Beerbaum (Ger) on *Almox Athletico*

Nations Cup
1 Great Britain
2 France
3 Holland

Nations Cup Final
Lanaken, Belgium, Sep 19-22
1 United States
2 Germany
3 Great Britain
This was a competition for the top six teams in the Nations Cup

THREE-DAY EVENTING
Badminton Horse Trials (Whitbread Trophy)
Badminton, May 2-5
1 Rodney Powell (GB) on *The Irishman II*
2 Ian Stark (GB) on *Murphy Himself*
3 Helen Bell (GB) on *Troubleshooter*
This was the last time the Whitbread Trophy was contested: the company withdrew its sponsorship after 30 years.

European Championship
Punchestown, Sep 6-9
1 Ian Stark (GB) on *Glenburnie*
2 Richard Walker (GB) on *Jacana*
3 Karen Straker (GB) on *Get Smart*

Team
1 Great Britain
2 Ireland
3 France

Burghley Horse Trials
Burghley House, Sep 12-15
1 Mark Todd (NZ) on *Welton Greylag*
2 Greg Watson (Aus) on *Chaka*
3 Karen Lende (US) on *Mr Maxwell*

DRESSAGE
European Championships
Donaueschingen, Germany, Sep 12-15
1 Isabell Werth (Ger) on *Gigolo*
2 Nicole Uphoff (Ger) on *Rembrandt Borbet*
3 Margrit Otto-Crepin (Fra) on *Corlandus*

CARRIAGE DRIVING
World Pairs Championship
Salzburg, Sep 4-8
1 United States 355.8 pts
2 Germany 357.4 pts
3 Poland 362.2 pts

> **Carl Shimmin, gateman at the Royal Windsor Horse Show: "Sorry, love, you can't come in without a sticker."**
> **Queen Elizabeth II: "My husband is taking part. I think if you check, I will be allowed to come in and watch him."**
> *Reported conversation*

> "I thought at first it was just some old dear who'd got lost.
> *Shimmin, later*

CHAMPIONS

WORLD CHAMPIONSHIPS
Show Jumping
Individual

	Rider	Horse
1953	Francisco Goyoago (Spa)	Quorum
1954	Hans-Günter Winkler (FRG)	Halla
1955	Hans-Günter Winkler (FRG)	Halla
1956	Raimondo d'Inzeo (Ita)	Merano
1960	Raimondo d'Inzeo (Ita)	Gowran Girl
1966	Pierre d'Oriola (Fra)	Pomone
1970	David Broome (GB)	Beethoven
1974	Hartwig Steenken (FRG)	Simona
1978	Gerd Wiltfang (FRG)	Roman
1982	Norbert Koof (FRG)	Fire II
1986	Gail Greenhough (Can)	Mr T
1990	Eric Navet (Fra)	Malesan Quito de Baussy

Women

	Rider	Horse
1965	Marion Coakes (GB)	Stroller
1970	Janou Lefèbvre (Fra)	Rocket
1974	Janou Tissot (née Lefèbvre) (Fra)	Rocket

Team
| 1978 | Britain |

1982	France
1986	United States
1990	France

Three-Day Event
Individual

	Rider	Horse
1966	Carlos Moratorio (Arg)	Chalon
1970	Mary Gordon-Watson (GB)	Cornishman V
1974	Bruce Davidson (US)	Irish Cap
1978	Bruce Davidson (US)	Might Tango
1982	Lucinda Green (GB)	Regal Realm
1986	Virginia Leng (GB)	Priceless
1990	Blyth Tait (NZ)	Messiah

Team
1966	Ireland
1970	Great Britain
1974	United States
1978	Canada
1982	Great Britain
1986	Great Britain
1990	New Zealand

Dressage
Individual

	Rider	Horse
1966	Josef Neckermann (FRG)	Mariano
1970	Yelena Petouchkova (USSR)	Pepel
1974	Reiner Klimke (FRG)	Mehmed
1978	Christine Stuckelberger (Swi)	Granat
1982	Reiner Klimke (FRG)	Ahlerich
1986	Anne Grethe Jensen (Den)	Marzog
1990	Nicole Uphoff (FRG)	Rembrandt

Team
1966	West Germany
1970	USSR
1974	West Germany
1978	West Germany
1982	West Germany
1986	West Germany
1990	West Germany

Carriage Driving
Individual

		Team
1972	Auguste Dubey (Swi)	Great Britain
1974	Sandor Fulop (Hun)	Great Britain
1976	Imre Abonyi (Hun)	Hungary
1978	Gyorgy Bardos (Hun)	Hungary
1980	Gyorgy Bardos (Hun)	Great Britain
1982	Tjeerd Velstra (Hol)	Holland
1984	Laszlo Juhasz (Hun)	Hungary
1986	Tjeerd Velstra (Hol)	Holland
1988	Ijsbrand Chardon (Hol)	Holland
1990	Ad Aarts (Hol)	Holland

Endurance
Individual

	Rider	Horse
1986	Cassandra Schuler (US)	Skikos Omar
1988	Becky Hart (US)	RO Grand Sultan
1990	Becky Hart (US)	RO GrandSultan

Team
1986	Great Britain
1988	United States
1990	Great Britain

Vaulting
Men's Individual
1986	Dietmar Ott (FRG)
1988	Christopher Pensing (FRG)
1990	Michael Lehner (FRG)

Women's Individual
1986	Silke Bernhard (FRG)
1988	Silke Bernhard (FRG)
1990	Silke Bernhard (FRG)

Team
1986	West Germany
1988	West Germany
1990	Switzerland

EUROPEAN CHAMPIONSHIPS
Show Jumping
Individual

	Rider	Horse
1957	Hans-Günter Winkler (FRG)	Sonnenglanz
1958	Fritz Thiedemann (FRG)	Meteor
1959	Piero d'Inzeo (Ita)	Uruguay
1961	David Broome (GB)	Sunsalve
1962	David Barker (GB)	Mister Softee
1963	Graziano Mancinelli (Ita)	Rockette
1965	Hermann Schridde (FRG)	Dozent
1966	Nelson Pessoa (Bra)	Gran Geste
1967	David Broome (GB)	Mister Softee
1969	David Broome (GB)	Mister Softee
1971	Hartwig Steenken (FRG)	Simona
1973	Paddy McMahon (GB)	Penwood
		Forge Mill
1975	Alwin Schockemohle (FRG)	Warwick
1977	Johan Heins (Hol)	Seven Valleys
1979	Gerd Wiltfang (FRG)	Roman
1981	Paul Schockemohle (FRG)	Deister
1983	Paul Schockemohle (FRG)	Deister
1985	Paul Schockemohle (FRG)	Deister
1987	Pierre Durand (Fra)	Jappeloup
1989	John Whitaker (GB)	Next Milton
1991	Erik Navet (Fra)	Waiti Quito
		de Baussy

Women

	Rider	Horse
1957	Pat Smythe (GB)	Flanagan
1958	Giulia Serventi (Ita)	Doly
1959	Ann Townsend (GB)	Bandit
1960	Susan Cohen (GB)	Clare Castle
1961	Pat Smythe (GB)	Flanagan
1962	Pat Smythe (GB)	Flanagan
1963	Pat Smythe (GB)	Flanagan
1966	Janou Lefèbvre (Fra)	Kenavo
1967	Kathy Kusner (US)	Untouchable
1968	Anneli Drummond-Hay (GB)	Merely-a-Monarch
1969	Iris Kellett (Ire)	Morning Light
1971	Ann Moore (GB)	Psalm
1973	Ann Moore (GB)	Psalm

Team
1975	West Germany	1985	Britain
1977	Holland	1987	Britain
1979	Britain	1989	Britain
1981	West Germany	1991	Holland
1983	Switzerland		

Three-Day Event
Individual

	Rider	Horse
1953	Lawrence Rook (GB)	Starlight
1954	Albert Hill (GB)	Crispin
1955	Frank Weldon (GB)	Kilbarry
1957	Sheila Willcox (GB)	High and Mighty
1959	Hans Schwarzenbach (Swi)	Burn Trout
1962	James Templar (GB)	M'Lord Connolly
1965	Marian Babirecki (Pol)	Volt
1967	Eddie Boylan (Ire)	Durlas Eile
1969	Mary Gordon-Watson (GB)	Cornishman V
1971	HRH Princess Anne (GB)	Doublet
1973	Aleksandr Yevdokimov (USSR)	Jeger
1975	Lucinda Prior-Palmer (GB)	Be Fair

1977	Lucinda Prior-Palmer (GB)	George
1979	Nils Haagensen (Den)	Monaco
1981	Hansueli Schmutz (Swi)	Oran
1983	Rachel Bayliss (GB)	Mystic
		Minstrel
1985	Virginia Holgate (GB)	Priceless
1987	Virginia Leng (née Holgate) (GB)	Night Cap
1989	Virginia Leng (GB)	Master
		Craftsman
1991	Ian Stark (GB)	Glenburnie

Team

1953	Britain	1973	West Germany
1954	Britain	1975	USSR
1955	Britain	1977	Britain
1957	Britain	1979	Ireland
1959	West Germany	1981	Britain
1962	USSR	1983	Sweden
1965	USSR	1985	Britain
1967	Britain	1987	Britain
1969	Britain	1989	Britain
1971	Britain	1991	Britain

Dressage
Individual

	Rider	Horse
1963	Henri Chammartin (Swi)	Wolfdietrich
1965	Henri Chammartin (Swi)	Wolfdietrich
1967	Reiner Klimke (FRG)	Dux
1969	Liselott Linsenhoff (FRG)	Piaff
1971	Liselott Linsenhoff (FRG)	Piaff
1973	Reiner Klimke (FRG)	Mehmed
1975	Christine Stuckelberger (Swi)	Granat
1977	Christine Stuckelberger (Swi)	Granat
1979	Elisabeth Theurer (Aut)	Mon Chérie
1981	Uwe Schulten-Baumer (FRG)	Madras
1983	Anne Grethe Jensen (Den)	Marzog
1985	Reiner Klimke (FRG)	Ahlerich
1987	Margrit Otto-Crepin (Fra)	Corlandus
1989	Nicole Uphoff (FRG)	Rembrandt
1991	Isabell Werth (Ger)	Gigolo

Team

| 1963 | Britain |
| 1965-91 | West Germany |

OTHER MAJOR SHOW JUMPING COMPETITIONS
British Derby
Hickstead

1961	Seamus Hayes (Ire)	Goodbye III
1962	Pat Smythe (GB)	Flanagan
1963	Nelson Pessoa (Bra)	Gran Geste
1964	Seamus Hayes (Ire)	Goodbye III
1965	Nelson Pessoa (Bra)	Gran Geste
1966	David Broome (GB)	Mister Softee
1967	Marion Coakes (GB)	Stroller
1968	Alison Westwood (GB)	The Maverick VII
1969	Anneli Drummond-Hay (GB)	Xanthos
1970	Harvey Smith (GB)	Mattie Brown
1971	Harvey Smith (GB)	Mattie Brown
1972	Hendrick Snoek (FRG)	Shirokko
1973	Alison Dawes (née Westwood) (GB)	Mr Banbury
1974	Harvey Smith (GB)	Salvador
1975	Paul Darragh (Ire)	Pele
1976	Eddie Macken (Ire)	Boomerang
1977	Eddie Macken (Ire)	Boomerang
1978	Eddie Macken (Ire)	Boomerang
1979	Eddie Macken (Ire)	Boomerang
1980	Michael Whitaker (GB)	Owen Gregory
1981	Harvey Smith (GB)	Sanyo Video
1982	Paul Schockemohle (FRG)	Deister

1983	John Whitaker (GB)	Ryan's Son
1984	John Ledingham (Ire)	Gabhram
1985	Paul Schockemohle (FRG)	Lorenzo
1986	Paul Schockemohle (FRG)	Next Deister
1987	Nick Skelton (GB)	Raffles
1988	Nick Skelton (GB)	Apollo
1989	Nick Skelton (GB)	Burmah Apollo
1990	Joe Turi (GB)	Vital
1991	Michael Whitaker (GB)	Henderson Monsanta

King George V Gold Cup
First held 1911. Winners since 1982

1982	Michael Whitaker (GB)	Disney Way
1983	Paul Schockemohle (FRG)	Deister
1984	Nick Skelton (GB)	St James
1985	Malcolm Pyrah (GB)	Towerlands Anglezark
1986	John Whitaker (GB)	Next Ryan's Son
1987	Malcolm Pyrah (GB)	Towerlands Anglezark
1988	Robert Smith (GB)	Brook Street Boysie
1989	Michael Whitaker (GB)	Next Didi
1990	Michael Whitaker (GB)	Henderson Milton
1991	David Broome (GB)	Lannegan

Most wins
6 David Broome 1960, 1966, 1972, 1977, 1981, 1991

Queen Elizabeth II Cup
First held 1949. Winners since 1982

1982	Liz Edgar (GB)	Everest Forever
1983	Jean Germany (GB)	Mandingo
1984	Veronique Whitaker (GB)	Next's Jingo
1985	Sue Pountain (GB)	Ned Kelly
1986	Liz Edgar (GB)	Everest Rapier
1987	Gillian Greenwood (GB)	Monsanta
1988	Janet Hunter (GB)	Everest Lisnamarrow
1989	Janet Hunter (GB)	Everest Lisnamarrow
1990	Emma-Jane Mac (GB)	Everest Oyster
1991	Janet Hunter (GB)	Everest Lisnamarrow

Most wins
5 Liz Edgar 1977, 1979, 1981-82, 1986

Volvo World Cup
Inaugurated 1979

1979	Hugo Simon (Aut)	Gladstone
1980	Conrad Homfeld (US)	Balbuco
1981	Mike Matz (US)	Jet Run
1982	Melanie Smith (US)	Calypso
1983	Norman Dello Joio (US)	I Love You
1984	Mario Deslauriers (Can)	Aramis
1985	Conrad Homfeld (US)	Abdullah
1986	Leslie Burr-Lenehan (US)	McLain
1987	Katherine Burdsall (US)	The Natural
1988	Ian Miller (Can)	Big Ben
1989	Ian Miller (Can)	Big Ben
1990	John Whitaker (GB)	Henderson Milton
1991	John Whitaker (GB)	Henderson Milton

Nations Cup
Inaugurated 1947. Winners since 1981

1981	West Germany
1982	West Germany
1983	Britain
1984	West Germany
1985	Britain
1986	Britain
1987	France
1988	France
1989	Britain
1990	France
1991	Britain

THREE-DAY EVENT
Badminton Horse Trials
(1956 event at Windsor)

1949	John Shedden (GB)	Golden Willow
1950	Tony Collings (GB)	Remus
1951	Hans Schwarzenbach (Swi)	Vae Victus
1952	Mark Darley (Ire)	Emily Little
1953	Lawrence Rook (GB)	Starlight
1954	Margaret Hough (GB)	Bambi
1955	Frank Weldon (GB)	Kilbarry
1956	Frank Weldon (GB)	Kilbarry
1957	Sheila Willcox (GB)	High and Mighty
1958	Sheila Willcox (GB)	High and Mighty
1959	Sheila Waddington (née Willcox) (GB)	Airs and Graces
1960	Bill Roycroft (Aus)	Our Solo
1961	Lawrence Morgan (Aus)	Salad Days
1962	Anneli Drummond-Hay (GB)	Merely-a-Monarch
1963	Susan Fleet (GB)	Gladiator#
1964	James Templar (GB)	M'Lord Connolly
1965	Eddie Boylan (Ire)	Durlas Eile
1966	Not held	
1967	Celia Ross-Taylor (GB)	Jonathan
1968	Jane Bullen (GB)	Our Nobby
1969	Richard Walker (GB)	Pasha
1970	Richard Meade (GB)	The Poacher
1971	Mark Phillips (GB)	Great Ovation
1972	Mark Phillips (GB)	Great Ovation
1973	Lucinda Prior-Palmer (GB)	Be Fair
1974	Mark Phillips (GB)	Columbus
1975	Cancelled after dressage	
1976	Lucinda Prior-Palmer (GB)	Wideawake
1977	Lucinda Prior-Palmer (GB)	George
1978	Jane Holderness-Roddam (née Bullen) (GB)	Warrior
1979	Lucinda Prior-Palmer (GB)	Killaire
1980	Mark Todd (NZ)	Southern Comfort
1981	Mark Phillips (GB)	Lincoln
1982	Richard Meade (GB)	Speculator III
1983	Lucinda Green (née Prior-Palmer) (GB)	Regal Realm
1984	Lucinda Green (GB)	Beagle Bay
1985	Virginia Holgate (GB)	Priceless
1986	Ian Stark (GB)	Sir Wattie
1987	cancelled	
1988	Ian Stark (GB)	Sir Wattie
1989	Virginia Leng (GB)	Master Craftsman
1990	Nicola McIrvine (GB)	Middle Road
1991	Rodney Powell (GB)	The Irishman II

 # reduced to a One-Day Event because of the weather

Burghley Horse Trials

1961	Anneli Drummond-Hay (GB)	Merely-a-Monarch
1962	European Championship	
1963	Harry Freeman-Jackson (Ire)	St Finbar
1964	Richard Meade (GB)	Barberry
1965	Jeremy Beale (GB)	Victoria Bridge
1966	World Championship	
1967	Lorna Sutherland (GB)	Popadom
1968	Sheila Willcox (GB)	Fair and Square
1969	Gillian Watson (GB)	Shaitan
1970	Judy Bradwell (GB)	Don Camillo
1971	European Championship	
1972	Janet Hodgson (GB)	Larkspur
1973	Mark Phillips (GB)	Maid Marion
1974	World Championship	
1975	Aly Pattinson (GB)	Carawich
1976	Jane Holderness-Roddam (GB)	Warrior
1977	Lucinda Prior-Palmer (GB)	George

1978	Lorna Clarke (née Sutherland) (GB)	Greco
1979	Andrew Hoy (Aus)	Davy
1980	Richard Walker (GB)	John of Gaunt
1981	Lucinda Prior-Palmer (GB)	Beagle Bay
1982	Richard Walker (GB)	Ryan's Cross
1983	Virginia Holgate (GB)	Priceless
1984	Virginia Holgate (GB)	Night Cap
1985	European Championship	
1986	Virginia Leng (née Holgate) (GB)	Murphy Himself
1987	Mark Todd (NZ)	Wilton Fair
1988	Jane Thelwall (GB)	Kings Jester
1989	European Championship	
1990	Mark Todd (NZ)	Face the Music
1991	Mark Todd (NZ)	Welton Greylag

1992

May 7-10 Badminton Horse Trials; May 13-17 Royal Windsor Horse Show; Jun 11-14 Royal International Horse Show (NEC, Birmingham); Aug 22-23 British Open Horse Trials (Gatcombe Park); Sep 10-13 Burghley Horse Trials; Oct 6-11 Horse of the Year Show (Wembley)

FENCING

============ 1991 ============

WORLD CHAMPIONSHIPS
Budapest, Jun 11-17

Men
FOIL
Individual	*Team*
1 Ingo Weissenborn (Ger)	1 Cuba
2 Thorsten Weidner (Ger)	2 Germany
3 Yossef Hocin (Fra) &	3 France
Laurent Bel (Fra)	

EPEE
Individual	*Team*
1 Andrei Chouvalov (USSR)	1 USSR
2 Robert Felisiak (Ger)	2 France
3 Sergey Kostarev (USSR) &	3 Germany
Ivan Kovacs (Hun)	

SABRE
Individual	*Team*
1 Grigoriy Kirienko (USSR)	1 Hungary
2 Peter Abay (Hun)	2 USSR
3 Gyorgy Nebald (Hun) &	3 Germany
Vadim Goutzeit (USSR)	

Women
FOIL
Individual	*Team*
1 Giovann Trillini (Ita)	1 Italy
2 Culad Grigorescu (Rom)	2 USSR
3 Tatyana Sadaovskaya (USSR) &	3 Germany
Sabine Bau (Ger)	

EPEE
Individual	*Team*
1 Mariann Horvath (Hun)	1 Hungary
2 Eva Maria Ittne (Ger)	2 France
3 Marina Vartonyi (Hun) &	3 USSR
Oksana Ermakova (USSR)	

BRITISH NATIONAL CHAMPIONSHIPS
Men
FOIL
Sheffield, May 11-12
1 Bill Gosbee (Salle Boston)
2 Donnie McKenzie (Meadowbank)
3 Johnny Davis (Salle Boston)

EPEE
London, Jan 26
1 John Llewellyn (Reading)
2 Stephen Paul (Salle Paul)
3 Richard Phelps (MPAGP)

SABRE
Stalybridge, Mar 9-10
1 Ian Williams (London Thames)
2 Nick Fletcher (Bristol University)
3 Richard Cohen (Polytechnic)

Women
FOIL
Sheffield, May 11-12
1 Fiona McIntosh (Salle Paul)
2 Amanda Ferguson (Salle Ashton)
3 Jane Hanlon (Stockport)

EPEE
Colchester, Feb 3
1 Georgina Usher (Meadowbank)
2 Valerie Cramb (Meadowbank)
3 Sheila Pearce (Stockport)

SABRE
Stalybridge, Mar 9-10
1 Sue Benny (Glastonbury)
2 Sally Claxton (London Thames)
3 Penny Turner (Harlequins)

============ CHAMPIONS ============

WORLD CHAMPIONSHIPS
(since 1982)
Olympic champions are automatic world champions

Men
FOIL
	Individual	*Team*
1982	Aleksandr Romankov (USSR)	USSR
1983	Aleksandr Romankov (USSR)	W Germany
1985	Mauro Numa (Ita)	Italy
1986	Andrea Borella (Ita)	USSR
1987	Mathias Gey (FRG)	USSR
1989	Alexander Koch (FRG)	USSR
1990	Philippe Omnes (Fra)	Italy
1991	Ingo Weissenborn (Ger)	Cuba

EPEE
1982	Jeno Pap (Hun)	France
1983	Ellmar Bormann (FRG)	France
1985	Phillippe Boisse (Fra)	W Germany
1986	Phillippe Riboud (Fra)	W Germany
1987	Volker Fisher (FRG)	W Germany
1989	Manuel Pereira (Spa)	Italy
1990	Thomas Gerull (FRG)	Italy
1991	Andrei Chouvalov (USSR)	USSR

SABRE
1982	Viktor Krovopuskov (USSR)	Hungary
1983	Vasiliy Etropolski (Pol)	USSR
1985	Gyorgy Nebald (Hun)	USSR
1986	Sergey Mindirgassov (USSR)	USSR
1987	Jean-François Lamour (Fra)	USSR
1989	Grigoriy Kirienko (USSR)	USSR
1990	Gyorgy Nebald (Hun)	USSR
1991	Grigoriy Kirienko (USSR)	Hungary

Women
FOIL
1982	Nalia Galiazova (USSR)	Italy
1983	Dorina Vaccoroni	Italy
1985	Cornelia Hanisch (FRG)	W Germany
1986	Anja Fichtel (FRG)	USSR
1987	Elisabeta Tufan (Rom)	Hungary
1989	Olga Velitchko (USSR)	W Germany
1990	Anja Fichtel (FRG)	Italy
1991	Giovann Trillini (Ita)	Italy

EPEE
1989	Anja Straub (Swi)	Hungary
1990	Taime Chappe (Cub)	W Germany
1991	Mariann Horvath (Hun)	Hungary

GAELIC SPORTS

━━━━ 1991 ━━━━

ALL-IRELAND HURLING FINAL
Croke Park, Dublin, Sep 1
TIPPERARY 1-16   Kilkenny 0-15

ALL-IRELAND GAELIC FOOTBALL CHAMPIONSHIP
Croke Park, Dublin, Sep 16
DOWN 1-16 (19)   Meath 1-14 (17)

━━━━ CHAMPIONS ━━━━

	Hurling	Football
1887	Tipperary	Limerick
1888	Not held	
1889	Dublin	Tipperary
1890	Cork	Cork
1891	Kerry	Dublin
1892	Cork	Dublin
1893	Cork	Wexford
1894	Cork	Dublin
1895	Tipperary	Tipperary
1896	Tipperary	Limerick
1897	Limerick	Dublin
1898	Tipperary	Dublin
1899	Tipperary	Dublin
1900	Tipperary	Tipperary
1901	London Irish	Dublin
1902	Cork	Dublin
1903	Cork	Kerry
1904	Kilkenny	Kerry
1905	Kilkenny	Kildare
1906	Tipperary	Dublin
1907	Kilkenny	Dublin
1908	Tipperary	Dublin
1909	Kilkenny	Kerry
1910	Wexford	Louth
1911	Kilkenny	Cork
1912	Kilkenny	Louth
1913	Kilkenny	Kerry
1914	Clare	Kerry
1915	Laois	Wexford
1916	Tipperary	Wexford
1917	Dublin	Wexford
1918	Limerick	Wexford
1919	Cork	Kildare
1920	Dublin	Tipperary
1921	Limerick	Dublin
1922	Kilkenny	Dublin
1923	Galway	Dublin
1924	Dublin	Kerry
1925	Tipperary	Galway
1926	Cork	Kerry
1927	Dublin	Kildare
1928	Cork	Kildare
1929	Cork	Kerry
1930	Tipperary	Kerry
1931	Cork	Kerry
1932	Kilkenny	Kerry
1933	Kilkenny	Cavan
1934	Limerick	Galway
1935	Kilkenny	Cavan
1936	Limerick	Mayo
1937	Tipperary	Kerry
1938	Dublin	Galway
1939	Kilkenny	Kerry
1940	Limerick	Kerry
1941	Cork	Kerry
1942	Cork	Dublin
1943	Cork	Roscommon
1944	Cork	Roscommon
1945	Tipperary	Cork
1946	Cork	Kerry
1947	Kilkenny	Cavan
1948	Waterford	Cavan
1949	Tipperary	Meath
1950	Tipperary	Mayo
1951	Tipperary	Mayo
1952	Cork	Cavan
1953	Cork	Kerry
1954	Cork	Meath
1955	Wexford	Kerry
1956	Wexford	Galway
1957	Kilkenny	Louth
1958	Tipperary	Dublin
1959	Waterford	Kerry
1960	Wexford	Down
1961	Tipperary	Down
1962	Tipperary	Kerry
1963	Kilkenny	Dublin
1964	Tipperary	Galway
1965	Tipperary	Galway
1966	Cork	Galway
1967	Kilkenny	Meath
1968	Wexford	Down
1969	Kilkenny	Kerry
1970	Cork	Kerry
1971	Tipperary	Offaly
1972	Kilkenny	Offaly
1973	Limerick	Cork
1974	Kilkenny	Dublin
1975	Kilkenny	Kerry
1976	Cork	Dublin
1977	Cork	Dublin
1978	Cork	Kerry
1979	Kilkenny	Kerry
1980	Galway	Kerry
1981	Offaly	Kerry
1982	Kilkenny	Offaly
1983	Kilkenny	Dublin
1984	Cork	Kerry
1985	Offaly	Kerry
1986	Cork	Kerry
1987	Galway	Meath
1988	Galway	Meath
1989	Tipperary	Cork
1990	Cork	Cork
1991	Tipperary	Down

Teams underlined completed Hurling/Football 'double'

Wins (Hurling):
27 Cork (Corcaigh); 24 Tipperary (Tiobrad Arann); Kilkenny (Cill Chainnigh); 7 Limerick (Luimneach); 6 Dublin (Ath Cliath); 5 Wexford (Loch Garman); 4 Galway (Gaillimh); 2 Waterford (Port Lairge), Offaly (Uibh Fhrili); 1 Kerry (Ciarraidhe), London Irish (Lonndain), Clare (An Clar), Laois (Laois)

Wins (Football):
30 Kerry (Ciarraidhe); 21 Dublin (Ath Cliath); 7 Galway (Gaillimh); 6 Cork (Corcaigh); 5 Wexford (Loch Garman), Cavan (Cabhan), Meath (An Mhidhe); 4 Down (An Dun), Tipperary (Tiobrad Arann), Kildare (Cill Dara); 3 Louth (Lughbhaidh), Mayo (Muigheo), Offaly (Uibh Fhrili); 2 Limerick (Luimneach), Roscommon (Ros Comain)

GOLF

ALAS, POOR BERNHARD

Bernhard Langer stepped on to the 18th green at Kiawah Island to try and sink a four-footer that must be regarded as the most important putt in the history of golf. The putt slid right and the Ryder Cup slid away from Europe, after six years, and back to its traditional home in the United States.

The US won the 29th Cup by a solitary point, 14½ - 13½ , after three days of utterly enthralling golf. The centimetre of Langer's miss enabled Americans to claim that the balance of power in world golf had shifted back to the US. Paul Azinger compared the win to the victory over the Iraqis. Everyone agreed that the pressure on Langer and everyone else was infinitely greater than anything that normally obtains in golf when the mere matter of millions of dollars is at stake. Along with several of his team-mates, Langer was reported to be in tears after the defeat. But there was no sign of psychological damage: Langer won the German Masters the following week.

It was a small miracle that Europe were even able to stay in the competition until the last putt. After the Saturday morning foursomes, the Americans led by three points and there were fears of a rout. The traditional pairing of Nick Faldo and Ian Woosnam had to be broken up after a disastrous day when they were evidently not on speaking terms either with their putters or each other. The Europeans were kept in contention only by the brilliance of the Spaniards, Severiano Ballesteros and José-Maria Olazabal. Ballesteros was personally responsible for 4½ of Europe's points.

The American network NBC was so enraptured by the contest that it overran for 90 minutes on the second day without showing an advert. Hundreds of fans, mainly British, climbed on to tables and a replica Statue of Liberty in the course bar after the defeat and consoled themselves by singing football songs. The victorious US team threw their captain, Dave Stockton, into the Atlantic. Most of the alligators who normally inhabit the island's lagoons and swamps were removed for the duration; so no one was sacrificed to them, not even Langer.

WOOSNAM'S WIN

Europe's one great success of the year had come early when, as has now become traditional, a British golfer won the Masters. The tall, intense and almost psychotically dedicated Faldo was replaced by the small, outgoing, booze-and-fags Woosnam. A three-way battle between Woosnam, Olazabal and Tom Watson looked certain to provide yet another shoot-out in the Augusta dusk but on the 18th Olazabal drove into the fairway

OPEN STATISTICS
Most birdies: Mark Mouland 19; Ian Baker-Finch 17 birdies, 1 eagle.
Hardest hole: 6th (par four) No eagles, 18 birdies, 235 pars, 243 bogeys, 41 double bogeys or worse.
Easiest hole: 17th (par five) 38 eagles, 357 birdies, 128 pars, 11 bogeys, two double bogeys or worse.

	ST ANDREWS 1990	ROYAL BIRKDALE 1991
Eagles	23	43
Birdies	1490	1409
Pars	5343	5852
Bogeys	1220	2077
Double bogeys or worse	132	274
Average score	71.95 (par 72)	72.20 (par 70)

Source: Unisys

bunker and Watson into the trees, leaving Woosnam the winner by a shot. Olazabal was second, giving Europeans the first two places for the first time; the first three all had British caddies. Woosnam's playing partner Watson reassured him when he was mildly heckled by telling him how Don January would just tip his cap and mutter pleasantries at his tormentors. Woosnam could afford to be pleasant: the win took his prize money close to Jack Nicklaus's career total and afterwards he lashed out on an eight-seat Cessna.

The win confirmed Woosnam's position as no 1 on the computer rankings. But it was not a precedent. There was no pattern to the major championships in 1991. The Open at Royal Birkdale was so shapeless that before the last day almost half the field had a realistic chance - or they might have done had not the Australian Ian Baker-Finch produced a brilliant display of front-running to win his first major.

Baker-Finch ("tall, dark and hyphenated") went out last on the final round for the third time in eight years and, having been called Baker-Flinch in the past, this time had the maturity to stay there. Indeed, his last two rounds of 64 and 66 matched Watson's 65-65 finish at Turnberry in 1977. In theory, Baker-Finch was the most unexpected winner for at least a decade; but he had been heavily backed at 50-1 and the bookmakers took big losses. He was a graceful winner, his charm being outdone only by his two-year-old daughter Hayley who tried to rush on while he was chipping to the last green and successfully grabbed her daddy's leg during his acceptance speech. The previous day, she had mistaken the BBC microphone for an ice lolly and licked it. Baker-Finch's compatriot Mike Harwood was second, the first time Australians have finished1-2. The crowd's assault on the 18th fairway at the end was worse than ever and Mark O'Meara, Baker-Finch's partner, was knocked over in the rush. Jim Payne from Cleethorpes won

---

THE DALY SUCCESS

❝This is the greatest story in the world."
John Daly

"Goodness, gracious. What a coil, what an unleashing of power. Unbelievable power."
Jack Nicklaus, on first seeing John Daly

"He's longer than Fred Couples, he's longer than Greg Norman, he's even longer than War and Peace."
Bob Verdi, Chicago Tribune

"I watched him hit a few shots on Saturday and went home with a bad back."
Ray Floyd

"Not since Arnold Palmer burst upon the scene in the 1950s has a newcomer inspired such euphoria and hero worship with his personal style both on and off the fairways.❞
Michael McDonnell, Daily Mail

---

the amateur medal, playing with Nicklaus on the final day and beating him. "He's going to win a lot of things in the future," said Nicklaus. On the opening day, Sherrie Beavan, 16, streaked down the first fairway in pursuit of Olazabal. Before the tournament began, Payne Stewart was refused permission to play Muirfield, site of the 1992 Open.

Stewart had just won the US Open, which for the third time in four years went to a play-off that the organisers there still insist on playing over the full 18 holes. It was not an especially distinguished win: Stewart scored 75 over the extra 18, the highest winning score in an Open play-off since 1927. However, his opponent Scott Simpson was even more determined to lose - he blew a a two-stroke lead on the closing holes three days running. Stewart said afterwards he considered the British Open more important. Halfway through the second round, Ronan Rafferty told his playing partner Craig Parry he was going to the toilet. Instead, he went to the airport and flew home.

The most sensational result came in the championship where nothing much usually happens: John Daly from Arkansas, the ninth reserve, the final entrant and a tour rookie, caused almost certainly the biggest upset in major tournament history by winning the US PGA title. Daly only came in because Nick Price withdrew when his wife started giving birth. Daly jumped into his car and drove the 7 ½ hours from Memphis to Indiana; it was his longest drive, but not by much. On each tee, his caddie Squeaky would say "Kill" and he did. He averaged 303.6 yards and was said to be going through a dozen balls a round, turning them oval or oblong; he had not even seen the course before he teed off in the first round. Daly was already the longest hitter on the tour (286 yards through the season) but only 185th in driving accuracy and the win was compared with Francis Ouimet's emergence from the caddie shack to beat Harry Vardon and Ted Ray in the 1913 US Open.

At both the US Open and the PGA a spectator died when hit by lightning. William Fadell, 27, was hit when he sheltered under a willow tree at Hazeltine; Thomas Weaver, 39, was killed in the car park at Crooked Stick, the PGA course; Daly gave $30,000 of his $230,000 first prize to a scholarship fund for Weaver's daughters.

Other unfamiliar names were winners too: Phil Mickelson became the first amateur in 5 ½ years to win a tour event, getting nothing for victory in the $1 million Tucson Open except a lot of speculation that he was going to be the game's next great star. Billy Andrade won two successive victories on the US golf circuit, the Kemper Open and Buick Classic, but was ineligible for Ryder Cup points because he had never filled out his PGA membership form. Tom Purtzer had his swing voted best on the tour by his fellow-pros in a poll by *Golf Digest*; 33 out of 100 voted for Purtzer, 18 for Payne Stewart and nine for Steve Elkington. Asked why Purtzer does not win much else, one of his colleagues explained: "He's also got the worst putting stroke." Some of the losers were, however, all too familiar. Greg Norman blew a five-stroke lead with eight holes to go in the Western Open in Illinois and lost three shots over the last four holes to throw away the Australian Masters.

Others were far less predictable: Ballesteros started the season disastrously, then hit form with an amazing run from the start of May, finishing third, first (both in Japan), second (losing a seven-hole play-off to Eduardo Romero in the Spanish Open), first and first (in the British PGA and Masters) and winning £300,000 in just over a month. Faldo was criticised for playing too little in the spring, then won the Irish Open. Neither produced his best form in the majors and Faldo's putting touch was far less sure than in 1990.

Steven Richardson emerged as a potential star by winning two of the first five European tournaments. Fred Couples broke the European Tour record by returning 12 birdies in a 61 in the Scandinavian Masters at Drottningholm. The former Open champion Kel Nagle, 69, fired a 67 in the New Zealand Open to become the first person to beat his age in a professional tournament since Sam Snead in 1965.

FAIR PLAY ON THE FAIRWAY

❝We have no discrimination clauses in our by-laws but we have no black members.”
Spokesman for the Cypress Point club, California

“We have no restrictions at the R and A except that it's a male club.”
Michael Bonallack, R and A secretary

“No discrimination exists at this club as we do not have any women members.”
Statement by Royal Dublin Golf Club

“I see nothing wrong with private clubs, be they for men, women, Jews, blacks, Catholics, Hispanics, Asians, whomever. Just let them own up to it, not hide it.”
Tom Watson

“Ladies wearing trousers are requested to remove them before entering the clubhouse.❞
Sign at Royal St George's, Sandwich

QUEUEING TO QUEUE

The golf boom went on relentlessly. By May, 1,420 planning applications for golf courses were being considered by local councils in Britain. According to English Heritage, about 80 of them affected sites of historic interest, including the stately homes of Mentmore, Castle Howard and Warwick Castle. Golfers at Leigh-on-Sea, Essex were reported to be sleeping in their cars until the booking office opened and then queueing to book a game eight days ahead. It was even more hopeless elsewhere: it was revealed that the cost of membership in the Peking Golf Club (membership 95% Japanese) was £27,000, which the average Chinese worker would earn in 90 years.

Elsewhere, technology was springing to the rescue of helpless addicts. A nine-hole indoor course on natural grass, the Wintergreens GC, featuring trees up to 25 feet, opened in Flint, Michigan. A Japanese building firm unveiled plans for a nine-hole course with only three fairways: computer-controlled golf carts would force the players to maintain pace and video cameras would be used to prevent accidents. The Glenmore Country Club in Sydney installed a new system using ultra-violet lamps specifically designed for night golf. Roger Ahlgrim, owner of a Chicago funeral home, opened a nine-hole crazy golf course in the basement of his mortuary; the features included mock skulls and headstones. Some enthusiasts hardly knew when to stop: at Newport, Isle of Wight someone stole a newly-laid putting green. Ronald Kantner, a chiropractor from Wapakoneta, Ohio, played 366 holes in 24 hours, beating the previous record by two. He played 2134 strokes and was helped by a crew of 36. However, he was beaten for the title Golf Nut of the Year by one David Earl; the bad news for Earl was that his wife left him in disgust.

In the year after the Shoal Creek controversy over discrimination, nine clubs gave up tour events rather than admit a black member; several others, including Augusta, elected just one. The Chicago Golf Club withdrew from staging the 1993 Walker Cup because it could not meet new anti-discrimination guidelines. A black boy, Dondre Green, was barred from a school game on a private course in Columbia, Louisiana. Tom Watson resigned from the Kansas City Country Club to protest against the blackballing of a Jewish applicant. Claire Bidwell, a farmer's wife from Congresbury, near Bristol, announced plans to open a course open only to women who, she said, "feel intimidated by the prevailing chauvinism at most clubs".

AN APPLE FOR TEE

Paul Malkinson, a Canadian hacker, invented a tree iron, a plastic replica club which could be safely wrapped round trees. The parents of Casey Golden, 12, of Evergreen, Colorado formed a company to market the biodegradable golf tees he invented using a recipe based on apple sauce. The Lawrence Livermore Laboratory in California, which helped produce the H-bomb, was considering the possibility of using a ceramic metal which it invented for armour plating to make golf clubs instead.

The best-publicised holes in one of 1991 came from Matthias Herrstrom, a 12-year-old Swedish schoolboy who received worldwide publicity for achieving four in four weeks, one of them at a 309-yard par-four. Herrstrom then admitted fibbing about that one, creating considerable doubts about the other three. Better authenticated hole-in-one achievers included:

Marcus Barrett, 12, who bought fizzy pop for his friends in the clubhouse at Norwich.

Rick Allen, 26, on his first round of golf ever, at Chipping Norton, Oxfordshire.

Clem Bolam, after 50 years of trying and a frantic search for his apparently lost ball, at Yeovil, Somerset.

Elaine Flaxman and her husband Robert, within two days of each other, at Cirencester, Gloucestershire.

Frank Copsey and his wife Sylvia, within a week of each other and both from the third tee at Dereham, Norfolk.

Alan Winstone, three times in the first four months of 1991, at Wokingham, Berks.

Dick Downey and Les Gallagher, playing together at Oakmont, Pennsylvania. Gallagher won the hole on handicap.

The American pro Jay Don Blake, at a pro-am in Potomac, Maryland, having just been asked by a marshal about his chances of repeating his ace at the same hole (3rd, 208 yards) the year before. "Why not?" said Blake, and did it.

Lee Trevino, at the 14th at Royal Birkdale in practice for the Open: "I was aiming for the bunker and pulled it," he explained.

Mitchell Hollis, aged 2 years 11 months, on the 50-yard 8th at the Eagles pitch-and-putt course in Norfolk.

And the resourceful British punters who fooled bookmakers into offering absurdly long odds against holes in one at professional tournaments.

The Auchterlonie collection of 23 ancient golf clubs belonging to Open champions between 1860 and 1930 was sold by Sotheby's at Chester for £617,000. A collection of old clubs and balls, in a cabinet in the members' bar at Fortrose and Rosemarkie, turned out to be worth £250,000. The gun used by Clifford Roberts, co-founder of Augusta National, to commit suicide, turned up in a New Jersey dealer's catalogue of golf collectibles.

Bryan Rozier of Orlando, Florida won his fourth major tournament aged five, having started by winning the International Pee Wee Championship aged three; Golf Magazine chose him to be PGA Golfer of the Year in 2010. George Sehlbach of Crystal River, Florida, played nine holes in 46, aged 104; he was born two years before the first American golf club was founded. Ben, a labrador belonging to the former Scottish football international, Tony Green, was taken sick with a stomach upset; the vet found 11 golf balls inside.

Adrian Atkinson, a bank executive from Kent, won an unfair dismissal case after his employers sacked him for winning the company's golf tournament when he was supposed to be off sick. Chris Almond, 15, shot a 74 to reach the final of a Florida schools tournament and was then disqualified after being spotted taking a sip of his father's beer. An Italian-born businessman, Catello D'Auria, claimed damages from the St George's Golf Club, Weybridge, Surrey after a ball smashed through his car window. His lawyer said that it had happened on the first day of the Gulf War and his client thought it was a bomb. The Duke of Westminster closed the private golf club at Eaton Hall, his stately home in Cheshire, because of fears of terrorism.

Sean Connery joined the £100,000 a year Lake Sherwood Golf Club near Los Angeles; he was allocated locker 007. Pat Nolan of New Zealand beat an 18-strong field to win the annual Scott Base-McMurdo tournament in Antarctica. Seal holes and snow tunnels act as bunkers and water hazards on the eight-hole course; local rules allow free drops if the ball is attacked by a skua or lands unplayably in petrified husky droppings. Faisal Qureshi of Pakistan drove from the 10th tee during the All-India Open at Meerut straight into the pocket of Maqbool Singh, who was playing a bunker shot at the fourth. Prince William, 8, the next King but one, suffered a fractured skull after being hit on the head by a schoolmate swinging a club; a doctor wrote in the *British Medical Journal* that golf was more dangerous for children than skateboarding or horse riding.

Ling Hong-Ling, professor of physical education at the North-west Normal University in Lanxhou, China, said golf was invented in China at least 500 years before it was heard of in Scotland. Professor Ling said golf descended from the Chinese game of chiuwan, first referred to in 943 AD. "It's a hoax," said the R and A's historian Bobby Burnet. Residents living near the Valley View course in Freemont, Nebraska complained that nude and nearly nude women walked the course four times a year in tournaments

THE LITTLE MASTER

"For me to win a major has become a necessity. I used to think it would be nice to have a championship but now I realise that to get real recognition I've got to win one......I'd love to stuff it right up 'em."
Ian Woosnam, two days before the Masters

"You dream about holing a putt like that on the last green to win the Masters. I'd been standing there looking and I just had to tell myself "This is the time to go to work.""
Woosnam, after winning

"Play a chorus of God Save the Queen and raise a glass of Britain's best stout to Wee Woosie"
Art Spander, San Francisco Examiner.

"I just stand there and hit it."
Woosnam on technique

"It should be perfectly clear by now that the Brits are still trying to get even with us for whipping them in the Revolutionary War."
Morris Siegel, Washington Times

"I smoke. I drink. I like a bit of fun. I want to be the best. But I'll do it me own little way."
Woosnam

"Now I have my own aircraft, paying for it is a big motivation these days. It puts pressure on me."
Woosnam, after winning the Monte Carlo Open

Question: Why do the Europeans keep winning?
Tom Watson: "I guess they're better."

1991

THE MAJORS

US MASTERS

Augusta, Georgia, Apr 11-14
All players US unless stated

1	IAN WOOSNAM (GB)	72	66	67	72	277
2	José Maria Olazabal (Spa)	68	71	69	70	278
3	Lanny Wadkins	67	71	70	71	279
	Steve Pate	72	73	69	65	279
	Ben Crenshaw	70	73	68	68	279
	Tom Watson	68	68	70	73	279
7	Ian Baker-Finch (Aus)	71	70	69	70	280
	Andrew Magee	70	72	68	70	280
	Jodie Mudd	70	70	71	69	280
10	Tommy Nakajima (Jap)	74	71	67	69	281
	Hale Irwin	70	70	75	66	281
12	Billy Mayfair	72	72	72	66	282
	Mark Calcavecchia	70	68	77	67	282
	Fuzzy Zoeller	70	70	75	67	282
	Craig Stadler	70	72	71	69	282
	Nick Faldo (GB)	72	73	67	70	282
17	Peter Jacobsen	73	70	68	72	283
	Ray Floyd	71	68	71	73	283
	Larry Mize	72	71	66	74	283
	Jim Gallagher jnr	67	74	71	71	283
	Mark McCumber	67	71	73	72	283
22	Scott Simpson	69	73	69	73	284
	Rocco Mediate	72	69	71	72	284
	Corey Pavin	73	70	69	72	284
	Seve Ballesteros (Spa)	75	70	69	70	284
	Steve Elkington (Aus)	72	69	74	69	284
27	Mark O'Meara	74	68	72	71	285
	Jay Don Blake	74	72	68	71	285
29	Jeff Sluman	71	71	72	72	286
	Morris Hatalsky	71	72	70	73	286
	John Huston	73	72	71	70	286
32	David Frost (SAf)	71	73	71	72	287
	Bernhard Langer (Ger)	71	68	74	74	287
	Wayne Levi	69	73	70	75	287
35	Jumbo Ozaki (Jap)	68	77	69	74	288
	Jack Nicklaus	68	72	72	76	288
	Ken Green	70	74	71	73	288
	Fred Couples	68	73	72	75	288
	Mark Brooks	69	72	74	73	288
	Scott Hoch	72	70	73	73	288
	Mark McNulty (Zim)	72	74	75	67	288
42	Donnie Hammond	72	73	73	71	289
	Davis Love III	72	71	74	72	289
	Curtis Strange	72	74	72	71	289
	Billy Ray Brown	74	65	77	73	289
46	Phil Mickelson *	69	73	74	74	290
	Don Pooley	72	71	69	78	290
	Joey Sindelaar	72	70	70	78	290
49	Nick Price (Zim)	72	73	72	74	291
	Lee Trevino	71	72	77	71	291
	Tommy Aaron	70	74	73	74	291
52	Paul Azinger	72	73	67	80	292
53	Brian Tennyson	78	67	75	73	293
	Nolan Henke	73	71	72	77	293
55	Larry Nelson	74	69	76	75	294
56	Tom Kite	71	75	78	71	295
57	Manny Zerman *	71	71	77	80	299

* Denotes amateur

Leaders:
Round 1: 67 Lanny Wadkins, Jim Gallagher jnr, Mark McCumber
Round 2: 136 Tom Watson
Round 3: 205 Ian Woosnam
Notables who failed to make the cut:
Ronan Rafferty, Billy Casper, Sandy Lyle, Greg Norman, Arnold Palmer, Gary Player

US OPEN

Hazletine, Chaska, Minnesota, Jun 13-17
All players US unless stated

1	PAYNE STEWART	67	70	73	72	282
2	Scott Simpson	70	68	72	72	282

(Play off: Stewart 75, Simpson 77)

3	Larry Nelson	73	72	72	68	285
	Fred Couples	70	70	75	70	285
5	Fuzzy Zoeller	72	73	74	67	286
6	Scott Hoch	69	71	74	73	287
7	Nolan Henke	67	71	77	73	288
8	Raymond Floyd	73	72	76	68	289
	José Maria Olazabal (Spa)	73	71	75	70	289
	Corey Pavin	71	67	79	72	289
11	D A Weibring	76	71	75	68	290
	Davis Love III	70	76	73	71	290
	Jim Gallagher jnr	70	72	75	73	290
	Craig Parry (Aus)	70	73	73	74	290
	Hale Irwin	71	75	70	74	290
16	Tom Watson	73	71	77	70	291
	Nick Faldo (GB)	72	74	73	72	291
	Sandy Lyle (GB)	72	70	74	75	291
19	Billy Ray Brown	73	71	77	71	292
	Peter Persons	70	75	75	72	292
	Mark Brooks	73	73	73	73	292
	Tom Sieckmann	74	70	74	74	292
	John Cook	76	70	72	74	292
	Craig Stadler	71	69	77	75	292
	Nick Price (Zim)	74	69	71	78	292
26	Tim Simpson	73	72	76	72	293
	Mike Reid	74	72	74	73	293
	Bob Tway	75	69	75	74	293
	Jodie Mudd	71	70	77	75	293
	Rick Fehr	74	69	73	77	293
31	David Rummells	72	73	77	72	294
	Ed Hemnik	72	70	78	74	294
	Chris Perry	72	73	75	74	294
	Peter Jacobsen	72	73	74	75	294
	Lance Ten Broeck	72	73	74	75	294
	Brian Kamm	69	73	73	79	294
37	Mark Calcavecchia	69	74	78	74	295
	Tom Purtzer	77	68	77	73	295
	Billy Mayfair	72	73	76	74	295
	Keith Clearwater	70	76	74	75	295
	Tom Kite	71	75	74	75	295
	Buddy Gardner	74	72	74	75	295
	Andy North	71	71	77	76	295
44	Ian Baker-Finch (Aus)	77	70	75	74	296
	Jim Hallet	72	74	73	77	296
46	Rodger Davis (Aus)	74	68	81	74	297
	Jack Nicklaus	70	76	77	74	297
	Blaine McCallister	72	72	76	77	297
49	Steve Pate	72	75	77	74	298
	Mike Harwood (Aus)	71	74	77	76	298
	Wayne Levi	72	72	76	78	298
	Loren Roberts	75	70	74	79	298
53	Larry Rinker	72	72	77	78	299
	John Inman	72	72	77	78	299
55	Phil Mickelson *	73	72	80	75	300
	Larry Mize	73	73	79	75	300
	Steve Gotsche	72	75	76	77	300
	Steve Elkington (Aus)	77	69	76	78	300
	Ian Woosnam (GB)	73	68	79	80	300
60	David Graham (Aus)	74	71	80	77	302
61	Stan Utley	73	71	81	78	303
62	John Adams	72	75	78	79	304
63	Terry Snodgrass	74	73	80	78	305
	Lanny Wadkins	76	70	80	79	305
	Wayne Grady (Aus)	73	74	78	80	305

* Denotes amateur

Leaders:
Round 1: 67 Nolan Henke, Payne Stewart
Round 2: 137 Payne Stewart
Round 3: 210 Scott Simpson, Payne Stewart
Notables who failed to make the cut:
Greg Norman, Curtis Strange, Lee Trevino, Bernhard
Langer, Seve Ballesteros

THE 120TH OPEN CHAMPIONSHIP
Royal Birkdale, Jul 18-21
All British unless stated

1	IAN BAKER-FINCH (Aus)	71	71	64	66	272
2	Mike Harwood (Aus)	68	70	69	67	274
3	Mark O'Meara (US)	71	68	67	69	275
	Fred Couples (US)	72	69	70	64	275
5	Bob Tway (US)	75	66	70	66	277
	Eamonn Darcy (Ire)	73	68	66	70	277
	Jodie Mudd (US)	72	70	72	63	277
8	Craig Parry (Aus)	71	70	69	68	278
9	Seve Ballesteros (Spa)	66	73	69	71	279
	Greg Norman (Aus)	74	68	71	66	279
	Bernhard Langer (Ger)	71	71	70	67	279
12	Magnus Sunesson (Swe)	72	73	68	67	280
	David Williams	74	71	68	67	280
	Rodger Davis (Aus)	70	71	73	66	280
	Vijay Singh (Fij)	71	69	69	71	280
	Roger Chapman	74	66	71	69	280
17	Barry Lane	68	72	71	70	281
	Ian Woosnam	70	72	69	70	281
	Andrew Sherbourne	73	70	68	70	281
	Mark Mouland	68	74	68	71	281
	Chip Beck (US)	67	78	70	66	281
	Lee Trevino (US)	71	72	71	67	281
	Nick Faldo	68	75	70	68	281
	Peter Senior (Aus)	74	67	71	69	281
	Paul Broadhurst	71	73	68	69	281
26	Wayne Grady (Aus)	69	70	73	70	282
	Tom Watson (US)	69	72	72	69	282
	Mike Reid (US)	68	71	70	73	282
	Colin Montgomerie	71	69	71	71	282
	Eduardo Romero (Arg)	70	73	68	71	282
	Mark James	72	68	70	72	282
32	Gary Hallberg (US)	68	70	73	72	283
	Mike Miller	73	74	67	69	283
	Gordon Brand jnr	72	72	69	71	283
	Christy O'Connor jnr (Ire)	72	71	71	69	283
	Steven Richardson	74	70	72	67	283
	Payne Stewart (US)	72	72	71	68	283
38	Anders Forsbrand (Swe)	71	72	73	68	284
	Peter O'Malley (Aus)	72	71	70	71	284
	Curtis Strange (US)	70	73	69	72	284
	Jim Payne *	72	72	70	70	284
	Nolan Henke (US)	77	71	66	70	284
	Martin Poxon	71	72	67	74	284
44	Donnie Hammond (US)	70	75	67	73	285
	Costantino Rocca (Ita)	68	73	70	74	285
	Jack Nicklaus (US)	70	75	69	71	285
	Davis Love III (US)	71	72	69	73	285
	Fulton Allem (SAf)	70	72	71	72	285
	Jamie Spence	70	73	70	72	285
	Tom Kite (US)	77	71	68	69	285
	Steve Elkington (Aus)	71	68	76	70	285
	Robert Gamez (US)	71	72	72	70	285
	Nick Price (Zim)	69	72	73	71	285
	Graham Marsh (Aus)	69	73	72	71	285
	Sam Torrance	72	76	70	67	285
	Des Smyth	71	73	73	68	285
57	Hale Irwin (US)	74	70	73	69	286
	Gavin Levenson (SAf)	72	73	73	68	286
	Gary Player (SAf)	75	71	69	71	286
	José Rivero (Spa)	74	73	68	71	286
	Tim Simpson (US)	72	72	72	70	286
	Scott Simpson (US)	74	72	70	70	286
	Andrew Magee (US)	71	74	69	72	286

64	Darren Clarke	79	67	68	73	287
	Andrew Oldcorn	71	67	77	72	287
	Gil Morgan (US)	74	74	74	67	287
	Jay Don Blake (US)	75	73	72	67	287
	Steve Pate (US)	73	72	74	68	287
	Michael McLean	71	75	72	69	287
	Steve Jones (US)	70	77	71	69	287
	Miguel Martin (Spa)	71	75	71	70	287
	Mark McNulty (Zim)	76	71	70	70	287
73	Phil Mickelson (US) *	77	67	73	71	288
	Lanny Wadkins (US)	71	75	71	71	288
	Frank Nobilo (NZ)	74	74	71	69	288
	Martin Gates	67	75	73	73	288
	Peter Jacobsen (US)	75	72	68	73	288
	Tony Johnstone (Zim)	69	74	71	74	288
	Brett Ogle (Aus)	73	75	66	74	288
80	Howard Clark	71	69	73	76	289
	David Gilford	72	67	73	77	289
	Santiago Luna (Spa)	67	77	72	73	289
	José-Maria Olazabal (Spa)	74	67	74	74	289
	Miguel Jimenez (Spa)	74	74	72	69	289
	Fuzzy Zoeller (US)	72	72	75	70	289
	Daniel Silva (Por)	73	71	75	70	289
	Malcolm Mackenzie	71	73	74	71	289
	Ben Crenshaw (US)	71	75	72	71	289
	John Bland (SAf)	71	76	71	71	289
	Martin Brooks (US)	73	74	70	72	289
	Danny Mijovic (Can)	70	72	74	73	289
92	Rick Gibson (Can)	73	75	70	72	290
	Brian Marchbank	72	73	75	70	290
	Peter Teravainen (US)	71	72	72	75	290
95	Patrick Hall	77	71	72	71	291
96	Alastair Webster	73	74	73	72	292
	John Hoskison	74	73	74	71	292
	Peter Allan	70	71	75	76	292
	Peter Hedblom (Swe)	74	74	73	71	292
	Carl Sunesson	69	77	69	77	292
101	Chris Moody	74	71	78	71	294
	Magnus Persson (Swe)	77	71	74	72	294
	Craig Stadler (US)	77	71	74	72	294
	John Morse (US)	73	71	77	73	294
	Tom Weiskopf (US)	74	74	73	73	294
	Jeff Sluman (US)	71	71	75	77	294
107	Stephen McAllister	79	69	70	77	295
108	Robin Mann	73	74	75	75	297
	Eoghan O'Connell (Ire)	74	74	74	75	297
110	Paul Mayo	71	74	71	83	299
	John Oates	77	71	76	75	299
112	Neal Briggs	73	74	77	76	300

Leaders:
Round 1: 66 Seve Ballesteros
Round 2: 138 Mike Harwood, Andrew Oldcorn, Gary
Hallberg
Round 3: 206 Mark O'Meara, Ian Baker-Finch
Notables who failed to make the cut:
Arnold Palmer, Tom Kite, Tom Watson, Lanny Wadkins,
Gary Player, Curtis Strange, Mark Calcavecchia, Tom
Weiskopf, Bob Charles, Isao Aoki, Rodger Davis, Craig
Stadler, Sandy Lyle
*Sandy Lyle, having taken 79 on the first day, tore up his
card on the second day after his tee shot at the 18th went
out of bounds. Richard Boxall suffered a stress fracture of
his right leg after hitting his tee shot at the 9th in the third
round. He was only three strokes off the lead at the time.
Five US pros, Billy Ray Brown, Andy Bean, Ken Green,
Mark McCumber and Jim Hallet failed to turn up for the
qualifying tournament. "We take a very dim view of this,"
said George Wilson of the R and A. Two more, John
Huston and Keith Clearwater, failed to complete
qualifying. Huston described himself as: "Freezing cold,
underpaid, fed up and desperate to go home."*

TOWARDS A MILLION
Open Championship prize money

	Total	First prize
1860	nil	nil
1910	£125	£50
1930	£400	£100
1946	£1000	£150
1960	£7000	£1250
1970	£40,000	£5,250
1980	£200,000	£25,000
1990	£825,000	£85,000
1991	£900,000	£90,000

63 IN THE OPEN

Mark Hayes (US), Turnberry 1977
Isao Aoki (Jap), Muirfield 1980
Greg Norman (Aus), Turnberry 1986
Paul Broadhurst (GB), St Andrews 1990
Jodie Mudd (US), Royal Birkdale 1991

US PGA CHAMPIONSHIP
Crooked Stick, Carmel, Indiana, Aug 8-11
All players US unless stated

1	JOHN DALY	66	67	69	71	276
2	Bruce Lietzke	68	69	72	70	279
3	Jim Gallagher jnr	70	72	72	67	281
4	Kenny Knox	67	71	70	74	282
5	Bob Gilder	73	70	67	73	283
	Steven Richardson (GB)	70	72	72	69	283
7	Raymond Floyd	69	74	72	69	284
	Steve Pate	70	75	70	69	284
	David Feherty (GB)	71	74	71	68	284
	Hal Sutton	74	67	72	71	284
	John Huston	70	72	70	72	284
	Craig Stadler	68	71	69	76	284
13	Andrew Magee	69	73	68	75	285
	Jay Don Blake	75	70	72	68	285
	Payne Stewart	74	70	71	70	285
16	Rocco Mediate	71	71	73	71	286
	Gil Morgan	70	71	74	71	286
	Howard Twitty	70	71	75	70	286
	Wayne Levi	73	71	72	70	286
	Sandy Lyle (GB)	68	75	71	72	286
	Ken Green	68	73	71	74	286
	Nick Faldo (GB)	70	69	71	76	286
23	Seve Ballesteros (Spa)	71	72	71	73	287
	Jack Nicklaus	71	72	73	71	287
	Mike Hulbert	72	72	73	70	287
	Chip Beck	73	73	70	71	287
27	Mark McNulty (Zim)	75	71	69	73	288
	Rick Fehr	70	73	71	74	288
	Fred Couples	74	67	76	71	288
	Loren Roberts	72	74	72	70	288
	Jim Hallet	69	74	73	72	288
32	Steve Elkington (Aus)	74	68	74	73	289
	Greg Norman (Aus)	70	74	72	73	289
	Tom Purtzer	69	76	71	73	289
	Corey Pavin	72	73	71	73	289
	Davis Love III	72	72	72	73	289
	David Edwards	71	75	71	72	289
	Mark Calcavecchia	70	74	73	72	289
	Doug Tewell	75	72	74	68	289
	Jodie Mudd	74	71	74	70	289
	Dan Forsman	73	74	68	74	289
	Billy Andrade	73	74	68	74	289
43	Craig Parry (Aus)	73	70	76	71	290
	Scott Hoch	71	75	72	72	290

	Lanny Wadkins	71	74	72	73	290
	Ed Dougherty	75	70	69	76	290
	Wayne Grady (Aus)	72	70	71	77	290
48	Brad Faxon	72	71	76	72	291
	David Frost (SAf)	74	70	75	72	291
	Keith Clearwater	72	72	76	71	291
	Ian Woosnam (GB)	67	72	76	76	291
52	Tom Sieckmann	68	76	74	74	292
	Tom Kite	73	72	75	72	292
	Eduardo Romero (Arg)	72	75	73	72	292
	David Graham (Aus)	72	73	73	74	292
	Mark McCumber	74	72	71	75	292
57	Nolan Henke	74	70	75	74	293
	Blaine McCallister	71	76	77	69	293
	Lindy Miller	72	72	77	72	293
	Fred Funk	71	69	72	81	293
61	Dave Barr	75	72	76	71	294
	Jeff Sluman	73	73	74	74	294
63	Gene Sauers	75	71	70	79	295
	Bob Wolcott	73	71	79	72	295
	Joey Sindelaar	74	73	71	77	295
66	Mark Wiebe	72	73	73	78	296
	Dillard Pruitt	72	75	73	76	296
	Bob Tway	73	71	78	74	296
	Scott Williams	70	77	76	73	296
70	David Peoples	74	73	75	75	297
	Denny Helper	71	75	75	76	297
	Lonnie Nielsen	74	71	74	78	297
73	Billy Ray Brown	69	75	79	75	298
	Hale Irwin	70	76	74	78	298
	Phil Blackmar	73	72	82	71	298
	Don Pooley	72	74	72	80	298
77	Kenny Perry	72	73	79	76	300

Leaders:
Round 1: 67 Kenny Knox, Ian Woosnam
Round 2: 136 John Daly
Round 3: 205 John Daly
Notables who failed to make the cut:
Fuzzy Zoeller, Tom Watson, Larry Mize, Bernhard
Langer, José-Maria Olazabal, Ian Baker-Finch, Scott
Simpson, Hubert Green, Sam Torrance, Larry Nelson,
Mark O'Meara, Arnold Palmer, Ben Crenshaw, Curtis
Strange. *Fred Couples, Jodie Mudd and Nick Faldo were
the only players to finish under par for 288 holes in the
four majors. Ten other players made the cut in all four*

RYDER CUP

Kiawah Island, South Carolina, Sep 27-29

DAY ONE

Foursomes

(US players first)

Paul Azinger & Chip Beck lost to SEVE BALLESTEROS & JOSE-MARIA OLAZABAL 2&1; RAYMOND FLOYD & FRED COUPLES beat Bernhard Langer & Mark James 2&1; LANNY WADKINS & HALE IRWIN beat David Gilford & Colin Montgomerie 4&2; PAYNE STEWART & MARK CALCAVECCHIA beat Nick Faldo & Ian Woosnam 1 hole

Fourballs

Lanny Wadkins & Mark O'Meara halved with Sam Torrance & David Feherty; Paul Azinger & Chip Beck lost to SEVE BALLESTEROS & JOSE-MARIA OLAZABAL 2&1; Corey Pavin & Mark Calcavecchia lost to STEVEN RICHARDSON & MARK JAMES 5&4; RAYMOND FLOYD & FRED COUPLES beat Nick Faldo & Ian Woosnam 5&3

Day One Score: United States 4 ½ Europe 3 ½

DAY TWO

Foursomes

LANNY WADKINS & HALE IRWIN beat David Feherty & Sam Torrance 4 & 2; MARK CALCAVECCHIA & PAYNE STEWART beat Mark James & Steven Richardson 1 hole; PAUL AZINGER & MARK O'MEARA beat Nick Faldo & David Gilford 7&6; Raymond Floyd & Fred Couples lost to SEVE BALLESTEROS & JOSE-MARIA OLAZABAL 3&2

Fourballs

Paul Azinger & Hale Irwin lost to IAN WOOSNAM & PAUL BROADHURST 2 & 1; Corey Pavin & Steve Pate lost to BERNHARD LANGER & COLIN MONTGOMERIE 2&1; Lanny Wadkins & Wayne Levi lost to MARK JAMES & STEVEN RICHARDSON 3 &1; Payne Stewart & Fred Couples halved with Seve Ballesteros & José-Maria Olazabal

Day Two Score: United States 8 Europe 8

DAY THREE

Singles

Steve Pate and David Gilford halved (after Pate withdrew injured); Raymond Floyd lost to NICK FALDO 2 up; Payne Stewart lost to DAVID FEHERTY 2 & 1; Mark Calcavecchia and Colin Montgomerie halved; PAUL AZINGER beat José-Maria Olazabal 2 up; COREY PAVIN beat Steven Richardson 2&1; Wayne Levi lost to SEVE BALLESTEROS 3 & 2; CHIP BECK beat Ian Woosnam 3 & 1; Mark O'Meara lost to PAUL BROADHURST 3 & 1; FRED COUPLES beat Sam Torrance 3 & 2; LANNY WADKINS beat Mark James 3 & 2; Hale Irwin and Bernhard Langer halved

Final Score: United States 14 ½ Europe 13 ½

THE LEADING INDIVIDUALS

	P	W	H	L
Seve Ballesteros (Eur)	5	4	1	0
Fred Couples (US)	5	4	1	0
José-Maria Olazabal (Eur)	5	3	1	1
Lanny Wadkins (US)	5	3	1	1
Mark Calcavecchia (US)	4	2	1	1
Hale Irwin (US)	4	2	1	1
Payne Stewart (US)	4	2	1	1

Azinger, Floyd and Broadhurst also each won two matches

RYDER CUP RECORDS

Most Appearances

10 Christy O'Connor Snr (GB) 1955-73; **9** Dai Rees (GB) 1937-61; **8** Peter Alliss (GB) 1953-69; **8** Bernard Hunt (GB) 1953-69; **8** Billy Casper (US) 1961-75; **8** Neil Coles (GB) 1961-77; **8** Bernard Gallacher 1969-83; Nick Faldo (GB/Eur) 1977-91.

Most Matches Played

40 Neil Coles (GB); **37** Billy Casper (US); **36** Christy O'Connor Snr (GB); **35** Tony Jacklin (GB/Eur); **32** Arnold Palmer (US); **31** Nick Faldo (GB/Eur), Bernhard Gallacher (GB/Eur)

Most Wins

22 Arnold Palmer (US); **20** Billy Casper (US); **18** Lanny Wadkins (US); **17** Jack Nicklaus (US), Lee Trevino (US), Nick Faldo (GB/Eur), Severiano Ballesteros (Eur).

❝There's more pressure here than you can ever imagine."

Fred Couples

"When I heard the chants of 'USA, USA, USA' I couldn't breathe ... The sphincter factor is high."

Hale Irwin

"I saw two spike marks on my line. It looked a left, a left putt. I talked to my caddie. He said 'Hit it left centre and firm to avoid the spike marks.' That's what I tried to do. It did not go in."

Bernhard Langer

"No one in the world can make that putt. It is too much pressure for anyone. Not even Jack Nicklaus in his prime can make that putt."

Seve Ballesteros on Langer's miss

"I don't think I could have brought myself to hit it."

Michael Bonallack, secretary of the R & A

"America's pride is back. We went over there and thumped the Iraqis. Now we've got the Ryder Cup back."

Paul Azinger

"Next week, we'll still have the best players in the world.❞

Bernard Gallacher

US PGA TOUR 1991
All players US unless otherwise stated

Infiniti Tournament of Champions
Carslbad, California: Jan 3-6
272 TOM KITE; 273 Lanny Wadkins; 276 Fred Couples, Chip Beck, Wayne Levi

Northern Telecom Tucson Open
Tucson, Jan 10-13
272 PHIL MICKELSON; 273 Bob Tway, Tom Purtzer; 275 Craig Stadler
Mickelson became the first amateur to win on US Tour since Scott Verplank in the 1985 Western Open

---

AMATEUR WINNERS ON THE US TOUR (Since 1950)

Gene Littler, 1954 San Diego Open
Doug Sanders, 1956 Canadian Open
Scott Verplank, 1985 Western Open
Phil Mickelson, 1991 Tucson Open

United Hawaiian Open
Honolulu, Jan 17-20
270 LANNY WADKINS; 274 John Cook; 275 Ed Dougherty

Phoenix Open
Phoenix, Jan 24-27
268 NOLAN HENKE; 269 Curtis Strange, Tom Watson, Gil Morgan

AT&T National Pro-Am
Pebble Beach, California, Jan 31-Feb 3
274 PAUL AZINGER: 278 Corey Pavin, Brian Claar; 279 Mike Smith, Rocco Mediate, Davis Love III

Bob Hope Chrysler Classic
Palm Springs, California, Feb 7-10
331 COREY PAVIN, Mark O'Meara; 332 Tim Simpson; 333 Raymond Floyd; 334 Fred Couples
Pavin won play-off at first extra hole

Shearson Lehman Bros Open
Torrey Pines, Utah, Feb 14-17
268 JAY DON BLAKE; 270 Bill Sander; 271 Dan Forsman

Nissan Los Angeles Open
Riviera, Los Angeles, Feb 21-24
272 TED SCHULZ; 273 Jeff Sluman; 274 Craig Stadler, Bruce Lietzke, Davis Love III

Doral Ryder Open
Miami, Feb 28-Mar 3
276 ROCCO MEDIATE, Curtis Strange; 277 Andy Bean, Russ Cochran
Mediate won play-off at first extra hole

"This is a typical American set-up. We never see courses like this. If you don't hit the fairways and the greens you're finished. Golf was never meant to be played like that. It takes away the skill, the flair, the touch, the feel. It is designed for a machine, a robotic golfer, somebody like Scott Simpson. You wind him up and let him go."
Severiano Ballesteros on the USPGA course at Crooked Stick

"There's no imagination required, no invention. If it's 180 yards to the flag, it's a four iron, nothing more, nothing less. In the tougher weather conditions of Europe 180 yards can be anything from an eight iron to a wood and the greens on no two courses are the same. If ever they are, the Europeans will run into the same trouble as we have done."
Jack Nicklaus

"If you ever get a tee time in hell, there will be two certainties: 1. You will be playing behind Bernhard Langer and 2. The course will include Hazeltine's 16th."
Rick Reilly, Sports Illustrated

"Frankly, I can't stand it, all this buggering about that goes on around the greens. How can they take so much time?"
Max Faulkner, 1951 Open champion, on modern players

"Heaven forbid if I ever start putting well. Then I'll start thinking I'm going to street these guys by 10 or 12 shots."
Greg Norman

"I am not one who says it, but there are players who say he has the heart of a grape seed."
Johnny Miller on Greg Norman

"Sometimes I think he needs a good kick up the backside. People are too nice to him."
Jolande Lyle on her husband

"I made, in my career, what the third man in the Order of Merit made last year. But the point is, it was enough."
Tommy Horton, retired golfer

"How many does José-Maria Olazabal put through the gates - 10 to 15 people? If anyone should get appearance money, it should be me."
Brian Barnes

"We are talking about a bloody leisure centre, a golferama, something that will entirely spoil the valley. Just imagine it - corporate dinners, blazing lights, cars everywhere and a bloody indoor swimming pool."
David Astor, Oxfordshire farmer, fighting plans to build a golf course at Lyneham

"This is the classic scene of a lot of selfish people looking out for themselves."
Dudley Carpenter, Lyneham developer

"I've yet to see a well-constructed golf course ruin the look of any piece of land."
Peter Alliss, Golf World

Honda Classic
Coral Springs, Florida, Mar 7-10
279 STEVE PATE; 282 Dan Halldorson, Paul Azinger;
283 Billy Andrade, John Daly, Bruce Lietzke

Nestlé Invitational
Orlando, Florida, Mar 14-17
203 ANDREW MAGEE; 205 Tom Sieckmann; 206 Mark
Calcavecchia, Steve Pate
Play curtailed to three rounds due to bad weather

USF&G Classic
New Orleans, Mar 21-24
275 IAN WOOSNAM (GB); Jim Hallet; 277 Tom
Sieckmann; 278 John Huston
*Woosnam's first win on the US Tour, achieved on second
play-off hole*

Deposit Guarantee Golf Classic
Hattiesburg, Mississippi, Apr 11-14
266 LARRY SILVEIRA; Russ Cochran, Mike Nicolette
Silveira won play-off at first extra hole

MCI Heritage Classic
Hilton Head Island, South Carolina, Apr 18-21
271 DAVIS LOVE III; 273 Ian Baker-Finch (Aus); 274
Lanny Wadkins, Payne Stewart, Hale Irwin

K-Mart Greater Greensboro Open
Greensboro, North Carolina, Apr 25-28
275 MARK BROOKS, Gene Sauers; 276 John Huston,
Bob Wolcott
Brooks won play-off at third extra hole

GTE Byron Nelson Classic
Irving, Texas, May 2-5
270 NICK PRICE (Zim); 271 Craig Stadler; 272 Scott
Simpson, Corey Pavin, Hal Sutton, Raymond Floyd

Bell South Atlanta Classic
Marietta, Georgia, May 9-12
272 COREY PAVIN, Steve Pate; 273 Hale Irwin, Tom
Kite, Mike Springer
Pavin won play-off at second extra hole

Memorial Tournament
Dublin, Ohio, May 17-20
273 KENNY PERRY, Hale Irwin; 275 Corey Pavin; 279
Craig Stadler, Mike Hulbert
Perry won play-off at first extra hole

Southwestern Bell Colonial Tournament
Fort Worth, Texas, May 23-26
267 TOM PURTZER; 270 Scott Hoch, Dave Edwards,
Bob Lohr

PGA Kemper Open
Potomac, Maryland, May 30-Jun 2
263 BILLY ANDRADE, Jeff Sluman; 266 Bill Britton,
Mark Brooks, Greg Norman (Aus), Hal Sutton
Andrade won play-off at first extra hole

Buick Open
Westchester, New York, Jun 6-9
273 BILLY ANDRADE; 275 Bob Bryant; 276 Nolan
Henke, Hale Irwin

Anheuser-Busch Classic
Williamsburg, Pennsylvania, Jun 20-23
266 MIKE HULBERT, Kenny Knox; 267 Fuzzy Zoeller,
Ian Baker-Finch (Aus)
Hulbert won play-off at first extra hole

St Jude Classic
Memphis, Tennessee, Jun 23-30
269 FRED COUPLES; 272 Rick Fehr; 273 Jay Haas,
David Canipe

PGA Western Open
Lemont, Illinois, Jul 4-7
275 RUSS COCHRAN; 277 Greg Norman, 278 Fred
Couples, 282 Bob Gilder
*Cochran is the only regular member of the US Tour who
plays left-handed*

New England Classic
Sutton, Massachusetts, Jul 11-14
268 BRUCE FLEISHER, Ian Baker-Finch (Aus); 269
Gene Sauers; 272 Ted Schulz
*Fleisher won play-off at seventh extra hole. It was the
longest play-off on the US tour since Bob Gilder won at
Phoenix in 1983*

Chattanooga Classic
Chattanooga, Tennessee, Jul 18-21
260 DILLARD PRUITT; 262 Lance Ten Broeck; 264
Dave Rummells, John Daly, Steve Lowery, Jim Gallagher
jnr

Greater Hartford Open
Cromwell, Connecticut, Jul 25-28
271 BILLY RAY BROWN, Rick Fehr, Corey Pavin; 272
Loren Roberts, Billy Andrade, Jim Gallagher
Brown won play-off at first extra hole

Buick Open
Grand Blanc, Michigan, Aug 1-4
271 BRAD FAXON, Chip Beck; 272 John Cook, Steve
Pate
Faxon won play-off at first extra hole

The International
Castle Rock, Colorado, Aug 15-18
10pts JOSÉ-MARIA OLAZABAL (Spa); 7pts Ian Baker-
Finch (Aus), Bob Lohr, Scott Gump

NEC World Series of Golf
Akron, Ohio, Aug 22-25
279 TOM PURTZER, Jim Gallagher, Davis Love III; 280
Mark Brooks, Fred Couples
Purtzer won play-off at second extra hole

Greater Milwaukee Open
Franklin, Wisconsin, Aug 29-Sep 1
270 MARK BROOKS; 271 Robert Gamez; 273 Steve
Jones

Canadian Open
Oakville, Ontario, Sep 5-8
274 NICK PRICE (Zim); 274 Dave Edwards; 275 Fred
Couples, Ken Green

Hardee's Classic
Coral Valley, Illinois, Sep 12-15
267 DA WEIBRING; 268 Peter Jacobsen, Paul Azinger

VOLVO EUROPEAN TOUR 1991
All winners from Great Britain & Northern Ireland unless otherwise stated

Girona Open
Pals, Spain, Feb 21-24
272 STEVEN RICHARDSON; 274 Miguel Jiminez (Spa); 275 José Rivero (Spa)

Fujitzu Mediterranean Open
Nice, Feb 28-Mar 3
279 IAN WOOSNAM; 280 Michael McLean; 282 José-Maria Olazabal (Spa), Miguel Martin (Spa)
There were five holes-in-one: Eamonn Darcy had two of them to become the first man in 17 years to register two in one European PGA tournament.

TWO HOLES IN ONE IN ONE EUROPEAN TOUR EVENT

John Hudson, *1977 Martini International Peter Wilcock, 1974 Penfold Tournament Eamonn Darcy, 1991 Mediterranean Open * Hudson's were at successive holes.

Balearic Open
Santa Ponsa, Mallorca, Mar 7-10
282 GARY LEVENSON (SAf); 283 Steven Richardson; 284 José-Maria Olazabal (Spa)

Catalan Open
Tarragona, Spain, Mar 14-17
271 JOSÉ-MARIA OLAZABAL (Spa); 277 David Feherty; 278 Mike McLean

Portuguese Open
Estela, Mar 21-24
283 STEVEN RICHARDSON; 286 Vicente Fernandez (Arg); 287 Jimmy Heggarty

Volvo Florence Open
Ugolino, Mar 28-31
274 ANDERS FORSBRAND (Swe); 275 Barry Lane, Mark Roe, Sam Torrance; 278 Mats Lanner (Swe)

Jersey European Airways Open
La Moye, Jersey, Apr 11-14
279 SAM TORRANCE; 280 Mark Davis; 282 Mats Lanner (Swe), Jeff Hawkes (SAf), Anders Sorensen (Den)

Benson & Hedges International
St Mellion, Cornwall, Apr 18-21
286 BERNHARD LANGER (Ger); 288 Vijay Singh (Fij); 289 José Rivero (Spa), Phillip Walton
Ian Woosnam missed the cut with two 82s the week after winning the Masters

Madrid Open
Puerto de Hierro, Apr 25-28
272 ANDREW SHERBOURNE; 273 Miguel Martin (Spa); 275 Mark James; 276 Vijay Singh (Fij)

Credit Lyonnaise Cannes Open
Cannes, May 2-5
275 DAVID FEHERTY; 278 Craig Parry (Aus); 279 Mark McNulty (Zim)

Spanish Open
Club de Campo, Madrid, May 9-12
275 EDUARDO ROMERO (Arg), Seve Ballesteros (Spa); 280 Vijay Singh (Fij)
Romero won at seventh extra play-off hole, the second longest play-off in European PGA Tour history

Lancia-Martini Italian Open
Castelconturbia, Italy, May 16-19
279 CRAIG PARRY (Aus); 280 Ian Woosnam; 282 Costantino Rocca (Ita)

Volvo PGA Championship
Wentworth, May 24-27
271 SEVE BALLESTEROS (Spa), Colin Montgomerie; 272 Eamonn Darcy; 273 Bernhard Langer (Ger)
Ballesteros won play-off at first extra hole

Dunhill British Masters
Woburn, May 30-June2
275 SEVE BALLESTEROS (Spa); 278 Tony Johnstone (Zim), Sam Torrance, Keith Waters, David Gilford, Eamonn Darcy (Ire)

Murphy's Cup
Fulford, York, Jun 6-9
40 pts TONY JOHNSTONE (Zim), Eamonn Darcy (Ire); 38 pts Peter O'Malley (Aus), Stephen Field
Johnstone won play-off at second extra hole

Renault Belgian Open
Brussels, Jun 13-16
276 PER-ULRIK JOHANSSON (Swe), Paul Broadhurst; 277 Chris Williams; 278 Jorge Berendt (Arg)
Johansson won play-off at first extra hole

Carroll's Irish Open
Killarney, Jun 20-23
283 NICK FALDO; 286 Colin Montgomerie; 287 Carl Mason, Frank Nobilo (NZ)

Peugeot French Open
Paris, Jun 27-30
281 EDUARDO ROMERO (Arg); 283 Sam Torrance, José-Maria Olazabal (Spa); 284 Nick Faldo

Torras Monte Carlo Open
Mont Agel, Jul 3-6
261 IAN WOOSNAM; 265 Anders Forsbrand (Swe); 266 Mats Lanner (Swe), Peter Mitchell, Rodger Davis (Aus), Vijay Singh (Fij)

Bell's Scottish Open
Gleneagles, Jul 10-13
268 CRAIG PARRY (Aus); 269 Mark McNulty (Zim); 271 David Gilford

Heineken Dutch Open
Noordwijk, Jul 25-28
267 PAYNE STEWART (US); 276 Per-Ulrik Johansson (Swe); Bernhard Langer (Ger)

Scandinavian Masters
Drottningholm, nr.Stockholm, Aug 1-4
270 COLIN MONTGOMERIE; 271 Seve Ballesteros (Spa); 272 Ian Woosnam, Robert Karlsson (Swe)

European Pro-Celebrity
Royal Liverpool, Hoylake, Aug 8-11
272 PAUL BROADHURST; 279 Ronan Rafferty; 280 Keith Waters, Christy O'Connor jnr (Ire)

NM English Open
The Belfry, Aug 15-18
278 DAVID GILFORD; 280 Roger Chapman; 282 Steven Richardson, Seve Ballesteros (Spa)

Volvo German Open
Hubbelrath, Dusseldorf, Aug 22-25
273 MARK McNULTY (Zim), Paul Broadhurst; 277 David Russell, Sam Torrance
McNulty won play-off at first extra hole

GA European Open
Walton Heath, Surrey, Aug 29-Sep 1
277 MIKE HARWOOD (Aus); 279 Sandy Lyle; 280 John Bland (SAf), Payne Stewart (US), Seve Ballesteros (Spa)

Canon European Masters - Swiss Open
Crans-sur-Sierre, Sep 5-8
268 JEFF HAWKES (SAf); 269 Seve Ballesteros (Spa); 270 Peter Teravainen (US)

Lancome Trophy
St. Nom la Breteche, Paris, Sep 12-15
267 FRANK NOBILO (NZ); 268 David Gilford, Peter Fowler (Aus), Jamie Spence, Ian Baker-Finch (Aus)

SONY WORLD RANKINGS
(as at September 8 1991)
Figures in brackets are positions in September 1990
1 (4) Ian Woosnam (GB); 2 (3) José-Maria Olazabal (Spa); 3 (1) Nick Faldo (GB); 4 (2) Greg Norman (Aus); 5 (8) Severiano Ballesteros (Spa); 6 (5) Payne Stewart (US); 7 (9) Paul Azinger (US); 8 (10) Fred Couples (US); 9 (18) Bernhard Langer (Ger); 10 (12) Mark McNulty (Zim); 11 (47) Ian Baker-Finch (Aus); 12 (16) Hale Irwin (US); 13 (7) Tom Kite; 14 (20) Lanny Wadkins (US); 15 (30) Mark O'Meara (US); 16 (61) Corey Pavin (US); 17 (14) Larry Mize (US); 18 (44) Craig Parry (Aus); 19 (22) Rodger Davis (Aus); 20 (6) Mark Calcavecchia (US)
Positions of other players in the top 20 in September 1990: 21 (15) Chip Beck (US); 22 (13) Masashi Ozaki (Jap); 24 (11) Curtis Strange (US); 28 (19) Tim Simpson (US); 42 (17) Ronan Rafferty (GB)

OTHER EVENTS 1991

Walker Cup
Portmarnock, Sep 5-7
(Great Britain and Ireland names first)
Day One
Foursomes
James Milligan and Garry Hay lost to PHIL MICKELSON and BOB MAY 5 & 3; Jim Payne and Gary Evans lost to DAVID DUVAL and MIKE SPOSA 1 hole; Garth McGimpsey and Ricky Willison lost to MITCH VOGES and DAVID EGER 1 hole; Paul McGinley and Padraig Harrington lost to JAY SIGEL and ALLEN DOYLE 2 & 1
Singles
Andrew Colthart lost to MICKELSON 4 & 3; PAYNE beat Franklyn Langham 2 & 1; EVANS beat Duval 2 & 1; Willison lost to MAY 2 & 1; McGIMPSEY beat Sposa 1 hole; McGinley lost to DOYLE 6 & 4; HAY beat Thomas Scherrer 1 hole; Liam White lost to SIGEL 4 & 3
Day Two
Foursomes
MILLIGAN and McGIMPSEY beat Voges and David Eger 2 & 1; EVANS and COLTHART beat Langham and Scherrer 4 & 3; Payne and Willison lost to DUVAL and SPOSA 1 hole; WHIT and McGINLEY beat Mickelson and May 1 hole
Singles
Milligan lost to MICKELSON 1 hole; PAYNE beat Doyle 3 & 1; Evans lost to LANGHAM 4 & 2; COLTHART beat Sigel 1 hole; WILLISON beat Scherrer 3 & 2; Harrington lost to EGER 3 & 2; McGimpsey lost to MAY 4 & 3; Hay lost to VOGES 3 & 1
UNITED STATES WON CUP 14-10

President's Putter
Semi-finals
RICHARD HALL beat Chris Nevill 2 & 1; BRIAN INGLEBY beat Jamie Warman 3 & 2
Final
Rye, Jan 6
Ingleby beat Hall 3 & 2
First all-undergraduate final since 1954

Halford Hewitt Cup
Deal, Apr 14
Final
SHREWSBURY 3 ½ Lancing 1 ½

US PGA Seniors' Championship
Palm Beach Gardens, Florida, Apr 18-21
271 JACK NICKLAUS; 277 Bruce Crampton (Aus), 282 Bob Charles (NZ), 283 Homero Blancas; 284 George Archer

Brabazon Trophy
(English Amateur Stroke Play)
Hunstanton May 17-19
284 GARY EVANS (Worthing) & MARK PULLAN (Sand Moor) shared title; 286 Jim Payne (Sandilands)
Evans also shared the title in 1990

TOP 10 GOLF COURSES IN THE BRITISH ISLES
as ranked by Golf World (Nov 90)

1 Muirfield
2 Royal Birkdale
3 Ballybunion (Old)
4 Turnberry (Ailsa)
5 St Andrews (Old)
6 Portmarnock
7 Sunningdale (Old)
8 Woodhall Spa
9 Royal County Down
10 Royal Dornoch

Forte PGA Seniors' Championship
Wollaton Park, Nottingham, Jun 13-16
277 BRIAN WAITES (Notts); 280 Neil Coles (unattached); 281 Peter Butler (RAC)

Volvo Seniors' British Open
Royal Lytham, Jul 11-14
285 BOBBY VERWEY (SAf); 286 Bob Charles (NZ), Tommy Horton (Eng), Charles Green (Sco); 290 Gary Player (SAf)

English Amateur Championship
Formby, Jul 29-Aug 3
Final
RICKY WILLISON (Ealing) beat Mark Pullan (Sand Moor) 10 & 8

US Amateur Championship
Chattanooga, Tennessee, Aug 22-25
Final
MITCH VOGES beat Manny Zerman 7 & 6

WOMEN'S GOLF: THE MAJORS

Nabisco Dinah Shore
Rancho Mirage, California, Mar 28-31
273 AMY ALCOTT; 281 Dottie Mochrie; 282 Pat
Bradley, Patty Sheehan; 284 Lori Garbacz

Mazda LPGA Championship
Bethesda, Maryland, Jun 27-30
274 MEG MALLON; 275 Pat Bradley, Ayako Okamoto
(Jap); 278 Beth Daniel

US Open
Fort Worth, Texas, Jul 11-14
283 MEG MALLON; 285 Pat Bradley; 286 Amy Alcott;
287 Laurel Kean; 288 Dottie Mochrie, Chris Johnson

Du Maurier Classic
Coquitlam, British Colombia, Sep 12-15
279 NANCY SCRANTON; 282 Debbie Massey, 284
Laura Davies (GB), Trish Johnson, Pam Wright

OTHER WOMEN'S EVENTS
British Amateur Championship
Pannal, Jun 11-15
Final
VALERIE MICHAUD (Fra) beat Wendy Doolan (Aus) 3
& 2
*Michaud was the first French winner of the title since
Catherine Lacoste in 1969*

Weetabix British Open
Woburn, Aug 1-4
284 PENNY GRICE WHITTAKER; 287 Helen
Alfredsson (Swe); Diane Barnard; 288 S Groce (Ita) Laura
Davies

──────1990──────

US PGA TOUR
BC Open
Endicott, New York, Sep 20-23
268 NOLAN HENKE; 271 Mark Wiebe; 272 Doug
Tewell, Brian Tennyson, Jim Benepe, Barry Jaeckel

Southern Open
Columbus, Georgia, Sep 27-30
265 KENNY KNOX, Jim Hallet; 268 Jim Booros
Knox won play-off at 2nd extra hole

Texas Open
San Antonio, Oct 4-7
261 MARK O'MEARA; 262 Gary Hallberg; 263 Nick
Price (Zim)

Las Vegas Invitational
Las Vegas, Oct 10-14
334 BOB TWAY, John Cook; 337 Corey Pavin, Phil
Blackmar
Tway won play-off at first extra hole

Walt Disney World/Oldsmobile Classic
Lake Buena Vista, Florida, Oct 18-21
264 TIM SIMPSON; 265 John Mahaffey; 266 Davis Love
III; 267 Gene Sauers

Nabisco Championship
Houston, Texas, Oct 25-28
273 JODIE MUDD; Billy Mayfair; 276 Wayne Levi, Ian
Baker-Finch (Aus); 277 Nick Price (Zim)
Mudd won play-off at first extra hole

Isuzu Kapalua International
Kapalua, Hawaii, Nov 7-10
264 DAVID PEOPLES; 269 Davis Love III; 270 Nick
Price (Zim)

FINAL MONEY LEADERS
All from US unless otherwise stated
1 (4) Greg Norman (Aus)
2 (16) Wayne Levi
3 (2) Payne Stewart
4 (3) Paul Azinger
5 (26) Jodie Mudd
6 (93) Hale Irwin
7 (5) Mark Calcavecchia
8 (6) Tim Simpson
9 (11) Fred Couples
10 (13) Mark O'Meara
1989 position in brackets

EUROPEAN PGA TOUR
The Equity & Law Challenge
Royal Mid-Surrey, Sep 24-25
22 pts BRIAN MARCHBANK; 21 pts Peter Teravainen
(US), Derrick Cooper; 19 pts Brett Ogle (Aus)

Epson Grand Prix of Europe
St Pierre, Chepstow, Sep 27-30
271 IAN WOOSNAM; 274 José-Maria Olazabal (Spa),
Mark McNulty (Zim)

Mercedes German Masters
Stuttgart, Oct 4-7
272 SAM TORRANCE; 275 Bernhard Langer (Ger), Ian
Woosnam; 277 José-Maria Olazabal (Spa), Mike Harwood
(Aus)

Dunhill Cup
St Andrews, Oct 11-14
Semi-finals
ENGLAND 2 Japan 1; IRELAND 2 ½ New Zealand ½
Third Place Play-off
NEW ZEALAND 2 Japan 1
Final
IRELAND 3 ½ England 2 ½

Austrian Open
Salzburg, Oct 11-14
271 BERNHARD LANGER (Ger), Lanny Wadkins (US);
273 Des Smyth (Ire); 275 Miguel Martin (Spa), Manuel
Moreno (Spa)
Langer won play-off at third extra hole

Portuguese Open
Quinto do Lago, Oct 18-21
274 MICHAEL McLEAN; 275 Mike Harwood (Aus),
Gordon Brand jnr; 276 Mark James, Paul Broadhurst

Volvo Masters
Sotogrande, Spain, Oct 25-28
286 MIKE HARWOOD (Aus); 287 Sam Torrance, Steven
Richardson

VOLVO ORDER OF MERIT 1990
Final Standings
1 (6) Ian Woosnam (Wal)   £574,166
2 (9) Mark McNulty (Zim)   £507,540
3 (2) José-Maria Olazabal (Spa)   £434,765
4 (7) Bernhard Langer (Ger)   £320,449
5 (1) Ronan Rafferty (NI)   £309,851
6 (14) Mike Harwood (Aus)   £280,084

7 (11) Sam Torrance (Sco) £248,203
8 (10) David Feherty (NI) £237,830
9 (44) Rodger Davis (Aus) £233,841
10 (5) Mark James (Eng) £229,742
1989 position in brackets

OTHER 1990 EVENTS

Women's World Team Championship
Christchurch, New Zealand, Oct 18-21
Team
585 UNITED STATES; 597 New Zealand; 605 Great
Britain & Ireland; 607 Japan; 609 Australia
Individual
291 VICKI GOETZE (US); 295 Jan Higgins (NZ), Jae
Soon-Won (SKo)

Men's World Amateur Team Championship (Eisenhower Trophy)
Christchurch, New Zealand, Oct 25-28
Team
879 SWEDEN; 892 New Zealand; 903 Canada; 906 Italy;
908 Australia; 910 Great Britain & Ireland
Individual
286 MATHIAS GRONBERG (Swe); 292 Gabriel
Hjerstedt (Swe); 294 M Long (NZ), S Maruyama (Jap)

Asahi Glass Four Tours World Championship
Tokyo, Nov 1-4
1st: AUSTRALIA/NEW ZEALAND PGA TOUR (Wayne
Grady, Peter Senior, Craig Parry, Rodger Davis, Ian
Baker-Finch, Brian Jones); 2nd: US PGA Tour; 3rd: PGA
European Tour; 4th: PGA Tour of Japan

World Cup
Orlando, Florida, Nov 22-25
Team
556 GERMANY (Bernhard Langer & Torsten Giedeon);
559 England (Mark James & Richard Boxall); 559 Ireland
(Ronan Rafferty & David Feherty); 561 Wales (Ian
Woosnam & Mark Mouland)
Individual
271 PAYNE STEWART (US); 273 Anders Sorensen
(Den); 276 Ian Woosnam (Wal), David Feherty (Ire)

Skins Game
La Quinta, California, Nov 24-25
1 CURTIS STRANGE $220,000; 2 Greg Norman (Aus)
$90,000; 3 Nick Faldo (GB) $70,000, Jack Nicklaus
$70,000

Australian Open
Sydney, Nov 29-Dec 2
283 JOHN MORSE (US), Craig Parry; 286 Greg Norman,
Wayne Riley
*Morse won play-off at first extra hole. He had failed five
times to get his US Tour card.*

Million Dollar Challenge
Bophuthatswana, Sun City, Dec 6-9
284 DAVID FROST (SAf); 285 José-Maria Olazabal
(Spa); 286 Bernhard Langer (FRG), Steve Elkington (Aus)

CHAMPIONS

BRITISH OPEN

Year	Winner	Score	Venue	Runner(s)-up/Score
1860	Willie Park, Snr	174	Prestwick	Tom Morris Snr 176
1861	Tom Morris, Snr	163	Prestwick	Willie Park 167
1862	Tom Morris, Snr	163	Prestwick	Willie Park 176
1863	Willie Park, Snr	168	Prestwick	Tom Morris Snr 170
1864	Tom Morris, Snr	167	Prestwick	Andrew Strath 169
1865	Andrew Strath	162	Prestwick	Willie Park 164
1866	Willie Park, Snr	169	Prestwick	David Park 171
1867	Tom Morris, Snr	170	Prestwick	Willie Park 172
1868	Tom Morris, Jnr	157	Prestwick	Bob Andrew 159
1869	Tom Morris, Jnr	154	Prestwick	Tom Morris Snr 157
1870	Tom Morris, Jnr	149	Prestwick	Bob Kirk, David Strath 161
1872	Tom Morris, Jnr	166	Prestwick	David Strath 169
1873	Tom Kidd	179	St Andrews	Jamie Anderson 180
1874	Mungo Park	159	Musselburgh	Tom Morris Jnr 161
1875	Willie Park, Snr	166	Prestwick	Bob Martin 168
1876	Bob Martin	176	St Andrews	David Strath 176
(Martin awarded title as Strath refused play-off)				
1877	Jamie Anderson	160	Musselburgh	Bob Pingle 162
1878	Jamie Anderson	157	Prestwick	Bob Kirk 157
1879	Jamie Anderson	170*	St Andrews	Andrew Kirkaldy 170
1880	Robert Ferguson	162	Musselburgh	Peter Paxton 167
1881	Robert Ferguson	170	Prestwick	Jamie Anderson 173
1882	Robert Ferguson	171	St Andrews	Willie Fernie 174
1883	Willie Fernie	159*	Musselburgh	Bob Ferguson 159
1884	Jack Simpson	160	Prestwick	William Fernie, Doublas Rolland 164
1885	Bob Martin	171	St Andrews	Archie Simpson, David Ayton 172
1886	David Brown	157	Musselburgh	Willie Campbell 159
1887	Willie Park, Jnr	161	Prestwick	Bob Martin 162
1888	Jack Burns	171	St Andrews	David Anderson, Ben Sayers 172
1889	Willie Park, Jnr	155*	Musselburgh	Andrew Kirkaldy 155
1890	John Ball	164	Prestwick	Willie Fernie, Archie Simpson 167

Year	Winner	Score	Venue	Runner(s)-up/Score
1891	Hugh Kirkaldy	166	St Andrews	Willie Fern, Andrew Kirkaldy 168
1892	Harold H. Hilton	305	Muirfield	John Ball Jnr, James Kirkaldy, Sandy Herd 308
1893	Willie Auchterlonie	322	Prestwick	Johnny Laidlay 324
1894	John H. Taylor	326	Sandwich	Douglas Rolland 331
1895	John H.Taylor	322	St Andrews	Sandy Herd 326
1896	Harry Vardon	316*	Muirfield	John H Taylor 316
1897	Harold H.Hilton	314	Hoylake	James Braid 315
1898	Harry Vardon	307	Prestwick	Willie park 308
1899	Harry Vardon	310	Sandwich	Jack White 315
1900	John H Taylor	309	St Andrews	Harry Vardon 317
1901	James Braid	309	Muirfield	Harry Vardon 312
1902	Sandy Herd	307	Hoylake	Harry Vardon, James Braid 308
1903	Harry Vardon	300	Prestwick	Tom Vardon 306
1904	Jack White	296	Sandwich	James Braid, John H Taylor 297
1905	James Braid	318	St Andrews	John H Taylor, R Jones 323
1906	James Braid	300	Muirfield	John H Taylor 304
1907	Arnaud Massy (Fra)	312	Hoylake	John H Taylor 314
1908	James Braid	291	Prestwick	Tom Ball 299
1909	John H Taylor	295	Deal	James Braid 299
1910	James Braid	299	St Andrews	Sandy Herd 303
1911	Harry Vardon	303*	Sandwich	Arnaud Massy 303
1912	Ted Ray	295	Muirfield	Harry Vardon 299
1913	John H Taylor	304	Hoylake	Ted Ray 312
1914	Harry Vardon	306	Prestwick	John H Taylor 309
1920	George Duncan	303	Deal	Sandy Herd 305
1921	Jock Hutchison (US)	296*	St Andrews	Roger H Wethered 296
1922	Walter Hagen (US)	300	Sandwich	George Duncan, Jim Barnes (US) 301
1923	Arthur Havers	295	Troon	Walter Hagen (US) 296
1924	Walter Hagen (US)	301	Hoylake	Ernest R Whitcombe 302
1925	Jim Barnes (US)	300	Prestwick	Archie Compston 301
1926	Bobby Jones (US)	291	Royal Lytham	Al Watrous (US) 293
1927	Bobby Jones (US)	285	St Andrews	Aubrey Boomer, Fred Robson 291
1928	Walter Hagen (US)	292	Sandwich	Gene Sarazen (US) 294
1929	Walter Hagen (US)	292	Muirfield	John Farrell (US) 298
1930	Bobby Jones (US)	291	Hoylake	Leo Deigel (US), Macdonald Smith (US) 293
1931	Tommy Armour (US)	296	Carnoustie	Jose Jurado (Arg) 297
1932	Gene Sarazen (US)	283	Prince's	Macdonald Smith (US) 288
1933	Densmore Shute (US)	292*	St Andrews	Craig Wood (US) 292
1934	Henry Cotton	283	Sandwich	Sid F Brews (SAf) 288
1935	Alfred Perry	283	Muirfield	Alfred Padgham 287
1936	Alfred Padgham	287	Hoylake	Jimmy Adams 288
1937	Henry Cotton	290	Carnoustie	Reg Whitcombe 292
1938	Reg Whitcombe	295	Sandwich	Jimmy Adams 297
1939	Dick Burton	290	St Andrews	Johnny Bulla (US) 292
1946	Sam Snead (US)	290	St Andrews	Bobby Locke (SAf), Johnny Bulla (US) 294
1947	Fred Daly	293	Hoylake	Reg Horne, Frank Stranahan (US) 294
1948	Henry Cotton	284	Muirfield	Fred Daly 289
1949	Bobby Locke (SAf)	283*	Sandwich	Harry Bradshaw 283
1950	Bobby Locke (SAf)	279	Troon	Roberto de Vicenzo (Arg) 281
1951	Max Faulkner	285	Portrush	Tony Cerda (Arg) 287
1952	Bobby Locke (SAf)	287	Royal Lytham	Peter Thomson (Aus) 288
1953	Ben Hogan (US)	282	Carnoustie	Frank Stranahan (US) 286
1954	Peter Thomson (Aus)	283	Royal Birkdale	Sid Scott, Dai Rees, Bobby Locke (SAf) 284
1955	Peter Thomson (Aus)	281	St.Andrews	Johnny Fallon 283
1956	Peter Thomson (Aus)	286	Hoylake	Flory van Donck (Bel) 289
1957	Bobby Locke (SAf)	279	St Andrews	Peter Thomson (Aus) 282
1958	Peter Thomson (Aus)	278*	Royal Lytham	David Thomas 278
1959	Gary Player (SAf)	284	Muirfield	Flory van Donck (Bel), Fred Bullock 286
1960	Kel Nagle (Aus)	278	St Andrews	Arnold Palmer (US) 279
1961	Arnold Palmer (US)	284	Royal Birkdale	Dai Rees 285
1962	Arnold Palmer (US)	276	Troon	Kel Nagle (Aus) 282
1963	Bob Charles (NZ)	277*	Royal Lytham	Phil Rodgers (US) 277
1964	Tony Lema (US)	279	St Andrews	Jack Nicklaus (US) 284
1965	Peter Thomson (Aus)	285	Royal Birkdale	Christy O'Connor, Brian Huggett 287
1966	Jack Nicklaus (US)	282	Muirfield	David Thomas, Doug Sanders (US) 283
1967	Roberto de Vicenzo (Arg)	278	Hoylake	Jack Nicklaus (US) 280
1968	Gary Player (SAf)	289	Carnoustie	Jack Nicklaus (US), Bob Charles (NZ) 291
1969	Tony Jacklin	280	Royal Lytham	Bob Charles (NZ) 282
1970	Jack Nicklaus (US)	283*	St Andrews	Doug Sanders (US) 283
1971	Lee Trevino (US)	278	Royal Birkdale	Lu Liang Huan (Tai) 279
1972	Lee Trevino (US)	278	Muirfield	Jack Nicklaus (US) 279
1973	Tom Weiskopf (US)	276	Troon	Neil Coles 279
1974	Gary Player (SAf)	282	Royal Lytham	Peter Oosterhuis 286

Year	Winner	Score	Venue	Runner(s)-up/Score
1975	Tom Watson (US)	279*	Carnoustie	Jack Newton (Aus) 279
1976	Johnny Miller (US)	279	Royal Birkdale	Jack Nicklaus (US), Seve Ballesteros (Spa) 285
1977	Tom Watson (US)	268	Turnberry	Jack Nicklaus (US) 269
1978	Jack Nicklaus (US)	281	St.Andrews	Simon Owen (NZ), Ben Crenshaw (US), Ray Floyd (US), Tom Kite (US) 283
1979	Seve Ballesteros (Spa)	283	Royal Lytham	Jack Nicklaus (US), Ben Crenshaw (US) 286
1980	Tom Watson (US)	271	Muirfield	Lee Trevino (US) 275
1981	Bill Rogers (US)	276	Sandwich	Bernhard Langer (FRG) 280
1982	Tom Watson (US)	284	Royal Troon	Peter Oosterhuis, Nick Price (SAf) 285
1983	Tom Watson (US)	275	Royal Birkdale	Hale Irwin (US), Andy Bean (US) 276
1984	Seve Ballesteros (Spa)	276	St Andrews	Bernhard Langer (FRG), Tom Watson (US) 278
1985	Sandy Lyle	282	Sandwich	Payne Stewart (US) 283
1986	Greg Norman (Aus)	280	Turnberry	Gordon Brand jnr 285
1987	Nick Faldo	279	Muirfield	Paul Azinger (US), Rodger Davis (Aus) 280
1988	Seve Ballesteros (Spa)	273	Royal Lytham	Nick Price (Zim) 275
1989	Mark Calcavecchia (US)	275*	Royal Troon	Greg Norman (Aus), Wayne Grady (Aus) 275
1090	Nick Faldo	270	St Andrews	Mark McNulty (Zim), Payne Stewart (US) 275
1991	Ian Baker-Finch (Aus)	272	Royal Birkdale	Mike Harwood (Aus) 274

*denotes won after play-off

British Open Records
Most wins

6 Harry Vardon; **5** James Braid, John H.Taylor, Peter Thomson, Tom Watson, **4** Willie Park, Tom Morris, Snr, Tom Morris, Jnr, Walter Hagen, Bobby Locke *Lowest 72 hole total:* 268 Tom Watson, Turnberry 1977
Lowest 18 hole total: 63 Mark Hayes, Turnberry 1977; Isao Aoki, Muirfield 1980; Greg Norman, Turnberry 1986; Paul Broadhurst, St Andrews, 1990; Jodie Mudd, Birkdale, 1991
Oldest winner: 46y 99d Tom Morris, Snr, 1867
Youngest Winner: 17y 161d Tom Morris, Jnr, 1868

THE OTHER MAJORS

	US OPEN		US PGA		US MASTERS	
1895	Horace Rawlins	173	–		–	
1896	James Foulis	152	–		–	
1897	Joe Lloyd	162	–		–	
1898	Fred Herd	328	–		–	
1899	Willie Smith	315	–		–	
1900	Harry Vardon	313	–		–	
1901	Willie Anderson	331*	–		–	
1902	Laurie Auchterlonie	307	–		–	
1903	Willie Anderson	307*	–		–	
1904	Willie Anderson	303	–		–	
1905	Willie Anderson	314	–		–	
1906	Alex Smith	295	–		–	
1907	Alex Ross	302	–		–	
1908	Fred McLeod	322*	–		–	
1909	George Sargent	290	–		–	
1910	Alex Smith	298*	–		–	
1911	John McDermott	307*	–		–	
1912	John McDermott	294	–		–	
1913	Francis Ouimet	304*	–		–	
1914	Walter Hagen	290	–		–	
1915	Jerome Travers	297	–		–	
1916	Charles Evans Jnr	286	Jim Barnes	1 up	–	
1919	Walter Hagen	301*	Jim Barnes	6 & 5	–	
1920	Ted Ray (GB)	295	Jock Hutchison	1 up	–	
1921	Jim Barnes	289	Walter Hagen	3 & 2	–	
1922	Gene Sarazen	288	Gene Sarazen	4 & 3	–	
1923	Bobby Jones	296*	Gene Sarazen	1 up	–	
1924	Cyril Walker	297	Walter Hagen	2 up	–	
1925	Willie Macfarlane	291*	Walter Hagen	6 & 5	–	
1926	Bobby Jones	293	Walter Hagen	5 & 3	–	
1927	Tommy Armour	301*	Walter Hagen	1 up	–	
1928	Johnny Farrell	294*	Leo Diegel	6 & 5	–	
1929	Bobby Jones	294*	Leo Diegel	6 & 4	–	
1930	Bobby Jones	287	Tommy Armour	1 up	–	
1931	Billy Burke	292*	Tom Creavy	2 & 1	–	
1932	Gene Sarazen	286	Olin Dutra	4 & 3	–	
1933	Johnny Goodman	287	Gene Sarazen	5 & 4	–	
1934	Olin Dutra	293	Paul Runyan	1 up	Horton Smith	284
1935	Sam Parks Jnr	299	Johnny Revolta	5 & 4	Gene Sarazen	282*
1936	Tony Manero	282	Densmore Shute	3 & 2	Horton Smith	285
1937	Ralph Guldahl	281	Densmore Shute	1 up	Byron Nelson	283

	US OPEN		US PGA		US MASTERS	
1938	Ralph Guldahl	284	Paul Runyan	8 & 7	Henry Picard	285
1939	Byron Nelson	284*	Henry Picard	1 up	Ralph Guldahl	279
1940	Lawson Little	287	Byron Nelson	1 up	Jimmy Demaret	280
1941	Craig Wood	284	Vic Ghezzi	1 up	Craig Wood	280
1942	–		Sam Snead	2 & 1	Byron Nelson	280*
1944	–		Bob Hamilton	1 up	–	
1945	–		Byron Nelson	4 & 3	–	
1946	Lloyd Mangrum	284*	Ben Hogan	6 & 4	Herman Keiser	282
1947	Lew Worsham	282*	Jim Ferrier	2 & 1	Jimmy Demaret	281
1948	Ben Hogan	276	Ben Hogan	7 & 6	Claude Harmon	279
1949	Cary Middlecoff	286	Sam Snead	3 & 2	Sam Snead	282
1950	Ben Hogan	287*	Chandler Harper	4 & 3	Jimmy Demaret	283
1951	Ben Hogan	287	Sam Snead	7 & 6	Ben Hogan	280
1952	Julius Boros	281	Jim Turnesa	1 up	Sam Snead	286
1953	Ben Hogan	283	Walter Burkemo	2 & 1	Ben Hogan	274
1954	Ed Furgol	284	Chick Harbert	4 & 3	Sam Snead	289*
1955	Jack Fleck	287	Doug Ford	4 & 3	Cary Middlecoff	279
1956	Cary Middlecoff	281	Jack Burke	3 & 2	Jack Burke Jnr	289
1957	Dick Mayer	282	Lionel Hebert	2 & 1	Doug Ford	282
1958	Tommy Bolt	283	Dow Finsterwald	276	Arnold Palmer	284
1959	Billy Casper	282	Bob Rosburg	277	Art Wall Jnr	284
1960	Arnold Palmer	280	Jay Hebert	281	Arnold Palmer	282
1961	Gene Littler	281	Jerry Barber	277*	Gary Player (SA)	280
1962	Jack Nicklaus	283*	Gary Player (SA)	278	Arnold Palmer	280*
1963	Julius Boros	293*	Jack Nicklaus	279	Jack Nicklaus	286
1964	Ken Venturi	278	Bobby Nichols	271	Arnold Palmer	276
1965	Gary Player (SA)	282*	Dave Marr	280	Jack Nicklaus	271
1966	Billy Casper	278*	Al Geiberger	280	Jack Nicklaus	288*
1967	Jack Nicklaus	275	Don January	281*	Gay Brewer	280
1968	Lee Trevino	275	Julius Boros	281	Bob Goalby	277
1969	Orville Moody	281	Ray Floyd	276	George Archer	281
1970	Tony Jacklin (GB)	281	Dave Stockton	279	Billy Casper	279*
1971	Lee Trevino	280*	Jack Nicklaus	281	Charles Coody	279
1972	Jack Nicklaus	290	Gary Player (SA)	281	Jack Nicklaus	286
1973	Johnny Miller	279	Jack Nicklaus	277	Tommy Aaron	283
1974	Hale Irwin	287	Lee Trevino	276	Gary Player (SA)	278
1975	Lou Graham	287*	Jack Nicklaus	276	Jack Nicklaus	276
1976	Jerry Pate	277	Dave Stockton	281	Ray Floyd	271
1977	Hubert Green	278	Lanny Wadkins	282*	Tom Watson	276
1978	Andy North	285	John Mahaffey	276*	Gary Player (SA)	277
1979	Hale Irwin	284	David Graham (Aus)	272*	Fuzzy Zoeller	280*
1980	Jack Nicklaus	272	Jack Nicklaus	274	Seve Ballesteros (Spa)	275
1981	David Graham (Aus)	273	Larry Nelson	273	Tom Watson	280
1982	Tom Watson	282	Ray Floyd	272	Craig Stadler	284*
1983	Larry Nelson	280	Hal Sutton	274	Seve Ballesteros (Spa)	280
1984	Fuzzy Zoeller	276*	Lee Trevino	273	Ben Crenshaw	277
1985	Andy North	279	Hubert Green	278	Bernhard Langer (FRG)	282
1986	Ray Floyd	279	Bob Tway	276	Jack Nicklaus	279
1987	Scott Simpson	277	Larry Nelson	287	Larry Mize	285*
1988	Curtis Strange	278	Jeff Sluman	272	Sandy Lyle (GB)	281
1989	Curtis Strange	278	Payne Stewart	276	Nick Faldo (GB)	283*
1990	Hale Irwin	280*	Wayne Grady (Aus)	282	Nick Faldo (GB)	278*
1991	Payne Stewart	282*	John Daly	276	Ian Woosnam (GB)	277

* denotes won after a play-off

Most Majors

18 Jack Nicklaus (6 Masters; 5 US PGA; 4 US Open; 3 British Open)
11 Walter Hagen (5 US PGA; 4 British Open; 2 US Open)
9 Ben Hogan (4 US Open; 2 Masters; 2 US PGA, 1 British Open)
9 Gary Player (3 British Open; 3 Masters; 2 US PGA; 1 US Open)
8 Tom Watson (5 British Open; 2 Masters; 1 US Open)

MOST MAJORS 1982-91

4 Nick Faldo (GB) (US); 3 Tom Watson (US); 3 Seve Ballesteros (Spa); 2 Larry Nelson (US); 2 Raymond Floyd (US); 2 Sandy Lyle (GB); 2 Curtis Strange (US); 2 Payne Stewart (US)
Nations
26 United States, 7 Great Britain, 3 Spain, Australia, 1 West Germany

RYDER CUP

United States versus Great Britain 1927-71; Great Britain and Ireland 1973-77;
Europe 1979- . Since 1963 played over three days.

	Venue	Day 1	Day 2	Day 3	GB/Europe	United States
		GB US	**GB US**			
1927	Worcester, Massachusetts	1 – 3	2¹/₂ – 9¹/₂	–	Ted Ray	Walter Hagen
1929	Moortown, Yorks	1¹/₂ – 2¹/₂	7 - 5	–	George Duncan	Walter Hagen
1931	Scioto, Ohio	1 – 3	3 – 9	–	Charles Whitcombe	Walter Hagen
1933	Southport and Ainsdale	2¹/₂ – 1¹/₂	6¹/₂ – 5¹/₂	–	John H Taylor	Walter Hagen
1935	Ridgewood, New Jersey	1 – 3	3 – 9	–	Charles Whitcombe	Walter Hagen
1937	Southport and Ainsdale	1¹/₂ – 2¹/₂	4 – 8	–	Charles Whitcombe	Walter Hagen*
1947	Portland, Oregon	0 – 4	1 – 11	–	Henry Cotton	Ben Hogan
1949	Ganton, Yorks	3 – 1	5 – 7	–	Charles Whitcombe*	Ben Hogan*
1951	Pinehurst, North Carolina	1 – 3	2¹/₂ – 9¹/₂	–	Arthur Lacey*	Sam Snead
1953	Wentworth, Surrey	1 – 3	5¹/₂ – 6¹/₂	–	Henry Cotton*	Lloyd Mangrum
1955	Thunderbird, Calif.	1 – 3	4 – 8	–	Dai Rees	Chick Harbert
1957	Lindrick Club, Yorks	1 – 3	7¹/₂ – 4¹/₂	–	Dai Rees	Jack Burke
1959	Elorado CC, California	1¹/₂ – 2¹/₂	3¹/₂ – 8¹/₂	–	Dai Rees	Sam Snead
1961	Royal Lytham & St Annes	2 – 6	9¹/₂ – 14¹/₂	–	Dai Rees	Jerry Barber
1963	Atlanta, Georgia	2 – 6	4 – 23	9 – 23	Johnny Fallon*	Arnold Palmer
1965	Royal Birkdale, Southport	4 – 4	7 – 9	12¹/₂ – 19¹/₂	Harry Weetman*	Byron Nelson*
1967	Houston, Texas	2¹/₂ – 5¹/₂	3 – 13	8¹/₂ – 23¹/₂	Dai Rees*	Ben Hogan*
1969	Royal Birkdale, Southport	4¹/₂ – 3¹/₂	8 – 7¹/₂	16 – 16	Eric Brown*	Sam Snead*
1971	St Louis, Missouri	4¹/₂ – 3¹/₂	6 – 12¹/₂	13¹/₂ – 18¹/₂	Eric Brown*	Jay Hebert*
1973	Muirfield, Scotland	5¹/₂ – 2¹/₂	8 – 8	13 – 19	Bernard Hunt*	Jack Burke*
1975	Laurel Valley, Pennsylvania	1¹/₂ – 6¹/₂	3¹/₂ – 12¹/₂	11 – 21	Bernard Hunt*	Arnold Palmer*
1977	Royal Lytham & St Annes	1¹/₂ – 3¹/₂	2¹/₂ – 7¹/₂	7¹/₂ – 12¹/₂	Brian Huggett*	Dow Finsterwald*
		Eur US	**Eur US**	**Eur US**		
1979	Greenbrier, West Virginia	2¹/₂ – 5¹/₂	7¹/₂ – 8¹/₂	11 – 17	John Jacobs*	Billy Casper*
1981	Walton Heath GC, Surrey	4¹/₂ – 3¹/₂	5¹/₂ – 10¹/₂	9¹/₂ – 18¹/₂	John Jacobs*	Dave Marr*
1983	PGA National GC, Florida	4¹/₂ – 3¹/₂	8 – 8	13¹/₂ – 14¹/₂	Tony Jacklin*	Jack Nicklaus*
1985	The Belfry, Sutton Coldfield	3¹/₂ – 4¹/₂	9 – 7	16¹/₂ – 11¹/₂	Tony Jacklin*	Lee Trevino*
1987	Muirfield Village, Columbus	6 – 2	10¹/₂ – 5¹/₂	15 – 13	Tony Jacklin*	Jack Nicklaus*
1989	The Belfry, Sutton Coldfield	5 – 3	9 – 7	14 – 14	Tony Jacklin*	Raymond Floyd*
1991	Kiawah Island, South Carolina	4 ¹/₂ –3 ¹/₂	8-8	13 ¹/₂ - 14 ¹/₂	Bernard Gallacher*	Dave Stockton*
1993	The Belfry, Sutton Coldfield					
1995	Oak Hill, New York					

Score: US **22**, Great Britain/Europe **5**, Halved **2**

*Denotes non-playing captain

WORLD MATCH-PLAY CHAMPIONSHIP

Sponsors: Piccadilly 1964-76, Colgate 1977-8, Suntory 1979-

1964	Arnold Palmer (US) beat Neil Coles (GB) 2 & 1
1965	Gary Player (SA) beat Peter Thomson (Aus) 3 & 2
1966	Gary Player (SA) beat Jack Nicklaus (US) 6 & 4
1967	Arnold Palmer (US) beat Peter Thomson (Aus) 1 up
1968	Gary Player (SA) beat Bob Charles (NZ) 1 up
1969	Bob Charles (NZ) beat Gene Littler (US) 37th
1970	Jack Nicklaus (US) beat Lee Trevino (US) 2 & 1
1971	Gary Player (SA) beat Jack Nicklaus (US) 5 & 4
1972	Tom Weiskopf (US) beat Lee Trevino (US) 4 & 3
1973	Gary Player (SA) beat Graham Marsh (Aus) 40th
1974	Hale Irwin (US) beat Gary Player (SA) 3 & 1
1975	Hale Irwin (US) beat Al Geiberger (US) 4 & 2
1976	David Graham (Aus) beat Hale Irwin (US) 38th

1977	Graham Marsh (Aus) beat Ray Floyd (US) 5 & 3
1978	Isoa Aoki (Jap) beat Simon Owen (NZ) 3 & 2
1979	Bill Rogers (US) beat Isao Aoki (Jap) 1 up
1980	Greg Norman (Aus) beat Sandy Lyle (GB) 1 up
1981	Seve Ballesteros (Spa) beat Ben Crenshaw (US) 1 up
1982	Seve Ballesteros (Spa) beat Sandy Lyle (GB) 37th
1983	Greg Norman (Aus) beat Nick Faldo (GB) 3 & 2
1984	Seve Ballesteros (Spa) beat Bernhard Langer (FRG) 2 & 1
1985	Seve Ballesteros (Spa) beat Bernhard Langer (FRG) 6 & 5
1986	Greg Norman (Aus) beat Sandy Lyle (GB) 2 & 1
1987	Ian Woosnam (GB) beat Sandy Lyle (GB) 1 up
1988	Sandy Lyle (GB) beat Nick Faldo (GB) 2 & 1
1989	Nick Faldo (GB) beat Ian Woosnam (GB) 1 up
1990	Ian Woosnam (GB) beat Mark McNulty 4 & 2

Most wins
5 Gary Player; **4** Severiano Ballesteros; **3** Greg Norman; **2** Arnold Palmer, Hale Irwin

TOP MONEY WINNERS OF THE 1980s

	UNITED STATES	$	*EUROPE*	£
1982	**Craig Stadler**	**446,462**	**Sandy Lyle**	**86,141**
1983	**Hal Sutton**	**426,668**	**Nick Faldo**	**140,761**
1984	**Tom Watson**	**476,260**	**Bernhard Langer**	**160,883**
1985	**Curtis Strange**	**542,321**	**Sandy Lyle**	**199,020**
1986	**Greg Norman**	**653,296**	**Seve Ballesteros**	**259,275**
1987	**Curtis Strange**	**925,941**	**Ian Woosnam**	**439,075**
1988	**Curtis Strange**	**1,147,644**	**Seve Ballesteros**	**502,000**
1989	**Tom Kite**	**1,395,278**	**Ronan Rafferty**	**400,311**
1990	**Greg Norman (Aus)**	**1,165,477**	**Ian Woosnam**	**574,166**

WORLD CUP
(Formerly the Canada Cup)

1953	Argentina	1972	Taiwan
1954	Australia	1973	United States
1955	United States	1974	South Africa
1956	United States	1975	United States
1957	Japan	1976	Spain
1958	Ireland	1977	Spain
1959	Australia	1978	United States
1960	United States	1979	United States
1961	United States	1980	Canada
1962	United States	1981	Not held
1963	United States	1982	Spain
1964	United States	1983	United States
1965	South Africa	1984	Spain
1966	United States	1985	Canada
1967	United States	1986	Not held
1968	Canada	1987	Wales
1969	U n :d States	1988	United States
1970	Australia	1989	Australia
1971	United States	1990	Germany

Most wins
Team: **17** United States; **4** Spain; **3** Australia, Canada;
2 South Africa
Played on winning Teams: **6** Jack Nicklaus, Arnold Palmer; **4** Sam Snead
Individual title: **3** Jack Nicklaus (US) 1963-64, 1971; **2** Stan Leonard (Can) 1954, 1959; Roberto de Vicenzo (Arg) 1962, 1970; Johnny Miller (US) 1973, 1975, Gary Player (SA) 1965, 1977

DUNHILL CUP

1985	Australia	1988	Ireland
1986	Australia	1989	United States
1987	England	1990	Ireland

WALKER CUP

Year	Venue	Winners	Score
1922	Long Island, New York	US	8 – 4
1923	St Andrews, Scotland	US	6½ – 5½
1924	Garden City, New York	US	9 – 3
1926	St Andrews, Scotland	US	6½ – 5½
1928	Chicago GC, Illinois	US	11 – 1
1930	Royal St George's, England	US	10 – 2
1932	Brookline, Massachusetts	US	9½ – 2½
1934	St Andrews, Scotland	US	9½ – 2½
1936	Pine Valley, New Jersey	US	10½ – 1½
1938	St Andrews, Scotland	GB	7½ – 4½
1947	St Andrews, Scotland	US	8 – 4
1949	Winged Foot, New York	US	10 – 2
1951	Royal Birkdale, England	US	7½ – 4½
1953	Kittansett, Massachusetts	US	9 – 3
1955	St Andrews, Scotland	US	10 – 2
1957	Minikhada, Minnesota	US	8½ – 3½
1959	Muirfield, Scotland	US	9 – 3
1961	Seattle, Washington	US	11 – 1
1963	Turnberry, Scotland	US	14 – 10
1965	Baltimore, Maryland	Drawn	12 – 12
1967	Royal St George's, England	US	15 – 9
1969	Milwaukee, Wisconsin	US	13 – 11
1971	St Andrews, Scotland	GB	13 – 11
1973	Brookline, Massachusetts	US	14 – 10
1975	St Andrews, Scotland	US	15½ – 8½
1977	Shinnecock Hills, New York	US	16 – 8
1979	Muirfield, Scotland	US	15½ – 8½
1981	Cypress Point, California	US	15 – 9
1983	Royal Liverpool, England	US	13½ – 10½
1985	Pine Valley, Philadelphia	US	13 – 11
1987	Sunningdale, England	US	16½ – 7½
1989	Peachtree, Georgia	GB	12½ – 11½
1991	Portmarnock, Ireland	US	14-10

Wins
29 United States; **3** Great Britain; **1** Drawn

AMATEUR CHAMPIONSHIP
Winners since 1982. All British unless otherwise stated

1982	Martin Thompson
1983	Andrew Parkin
1984	José-Maria Olazabal (Spa)
1985	Garth McGimpsey
1986	David Curry
1987	Paul Mayo
1988	Christian Hardin (Swe)
1989	Stephen Dodd
1990	Rolf Muntz (Hol)
1991	Ricky Willison

US AMATEUR CHAMPIONSHIP
Winners (all US) since 1982

1982	Jay Sigel
1983	Jay Sigel
1984	Scott Verplank
1985	Sam Randolph
1986	Buddy Alexander
1987	Billy Mayfair
1988	Eric Meeks
1989	Chris Patton
1990	Phil Mickelson
1991	Mitch Voges

WOMEN'S MAJORS
Winners since 1980

	US Open	US LPGA	du Maurier	Nabisco Dinah Shaw
1980	Amy Alcott	Sally Little	Pat Bradley	–
1981	Pat Bradley	Donna Caponi	Jan Stephenson	–
1982	Janet Alex	Jan Stephenson	Sandra Haynie	–
1983	Jan Stephenson (Aus)	Patty Sheehan	Hollis Stacey	Amy Alcott
1984	Hollis Stacey	Patty Sheehan	Julie Inkster	Julie Inkster
1985	Kathy Baker	Nancy Lopez	Pat Bradley	Alice Miller
1986	Jane Geddes	Pat Bradley	Pat Bradley	Pat Bradley
1987	Laura Davies (GB)	Jane Geddes	Jody Rosenthal	Betsy King
1988	Liselotte Nuemann (Swe)	Sherri Turner	Sally Little	Amy Alcott
1989	Betsy King	Nancy Lopez	Tammie Green	Julie Inkster
1990	Betsy King	Beth Daniel	Cathy Johnston	Betsy King
1991	Meg Mallon	Meg Mallon	Nancy Scranton	Amy Allcott

BRITISH WOMEN'S OPEN CHAMPIONSHIP
Winners since 1980

1980	Debbie Massey (US)
1981	Debbie Massey (US)
1982	Marta Figueras-Dotti (Spa)
1983	–
1984	Ayako Okamoto (Jap)
1985	Betsy King (US)
1986	Laura Davies (GB)
1987	Alison Nicholas (GB)
1988	Corinne Dibnah (Aus)
1989	Jane Geddes (US)
1990	Helen Alfredsson (Swe)
1991	Penny Grice-Whittaker

——— 1992 ———

THE MAJORS
Apr 9-12: US Masters (Augusta,); Jun 5-6: Curtis Cup (Royal Liverpool); Jun 18-21 US Open (Pebble Beach, California); Jul 16-19 OPEN CHAMPIONSHIP (Muirfield); Aug 13-16 US PGA Championship (Bellerive, Missouri).

GREYHOUND RACING

reyhound racing had one of its most exciting stories in recent years when Ravage Again came tantalisingly close to breaking Ballyregan Bob's sequence of 32 races without defeat. His run reached 29 before he was beaten into fifth place at Powderhall in January.

There was not much encouragement for the sport otherwise. Tote turnover fell in 1990 from £47.8m to £43.6m despite an increase in races; the figure was said to be below that of the late 40s. The *Daily Mail* alleged that 100 greyhounds a week were put down because their owners no longer wanted them; greyhound officials put the figure at 500 a year. The *Mail* also said dogs were being exported to Spain or Morocco, caged in Squalor and raced in scorching heat.

1991

DAILY MIRROR GREYHOUND DERBY
Wimbledon, Jun 22
480 metres

1	Ballinderry Ash	5-1	(Trap 5)
2	Itsallovernow	5-1	(Trap 6)
3	Dempsey Duke	6-1	(Trap 1)
4	Fearless Mustang	Evens f	(Trap 3)
5	Summer Hill Super	6-1	(Trap 4)
6	Dunmurry Brandy	14-1	(Trap 2)

Time: 28.78s
Trainer: Patsy Byrne
The winning owner, Mrs Helen Roche, missed the race: she was on a pilgrimage to Lourdes

GRAND NATIONAL
Hall Green, Apr 3
474 Metres

1	Ideal Man 3-1jf		(Trap 1)
1	Ballycarney Dell 14-1		(Trap 3)

Dead-heat for first place

3	Run on King 7-2		(Trap 2)

Time: 29.81s

CHAMPIONS

GREYHOUND DERBY
At White City 1927-84, except 1940 at Harringay; at Wimbledon 1985 - Raced over 500yd 1927, 525yd 1928-74, 500m 1975-85, 480m 1986

		Price	Trap	Time
1927	Entry Badge	1-4f	5	29.01s
1928	Doher Ash	5-1	1	30.48s
1929	Mick the Miller	4-7f	4	29.96s
1930	Mick the Miller	4-9f	1	30.24s
1931	Seldom Lad	7-2	4	30.04s
1932	Wild Woolley	5-2	6	29.72s
1933	Future Cutlet	6-1	3	29.80s
1934	Davesland	3-1	4	29.81s
1935	Greta Ranee	4-1	3	30.18s
1936	Fine Jubilee	10-11f	3	29.48s
1937	Wattle Bark	5-2	6	29.26s
1938	Lone Keel	9-4	3	29.62s
1939	Highland Rum	2-1jf	6	29.35s
1940	G.R. Archduke	100-7	1	29.66s
1945	Ballyhennessy Seal	Evens f	1	29.56s
1946	Mondays News	5-1	3	29.24s
1947	Trev's Perfection	4-1	2	28.95s
1948	Priceless Border	1-2f	1	28.78s
1949	Narrogar Ann	5-1	2	28.95s
1950	Ballymac Ball	7-2	4	28.72s
1951	Ballylanigan Tanist	11-4	1	28.62s
1952	Endless Gossip	Evens f	6	28.50s
1953	Daws Dancer	10-1	5	29.20s
1954	Paul's Fun	8-15f	3	28.84s
1955	Rushton Mack	5-1	2	28.97s
1956	Dunmore King	7-2	3	29.22s
1957	Ford Spartan	Evens f	1	28.84s
1958	Pigalle Wonder	4-5f	1	28.65s
1959	Mile Bush Pride	Evens f	4	28.76s
1960	Duleek Dandy	25-1	4	29.15s
1961	Palm's Printer	2-1	1	28.84s
1962	The Grand Canal	2-1f	5	29.09s
1963	Lucky Boy Boy	Evens f	1	29.00s
1964	Hack Up Chieftain	20-1	1	28.92s
1965	Chittering Clapton	5-2	6	28.82s
1966	Faithful Hope	8-1	3	28.52s
1967	Tric-Trac	9-2	1	29.00s
1968	Camira Flash	100-8	4	28.89s
1969	Sand Star	5-4f	4	28.76s
1970	John Silver	11-4	2	29.01s
1971	Dolores Rocket	11-4	2	28.74s
1972	Patricia's Hope	7-1	5	28.55s
1973	Patricia's Hope	7-2	5	28.68s
1974	Jimsun	20-1	2	28.76s
1975	Tartan Khan	25-1	2	29.57s
1976	Mutts Silver	6-1	4	29.38s
1977	Balliniska Band	Evens f	5	29.16s
1978	Lacca Champion	6-4f	3	29.42s
1979	Sarah's Bunny	3-1	6	29.53s
1980	Indian Joe	13-8jf	6	29.68s
1981	Parkdown Jet	4-5f	6	29.57s
1982	Laurie's Panther	6-4f	1	29.60s
1983	I'm Slippy	6-1	4	29.40s
1984	Whisper Wishes	7-4f	4	29.43s
1985	Pagan Swallow	9-1	5	29.04s
1986	Tico	6-4jf	5	28.69s
1987	Signal Spark	14-1	4	28.83s
1988	Hit the Lid	3-1	6	28.53s
1989	Lartigue Note	Evens f	2	28.79s
1990	Slippy Blue	8-1	4	28.70s
1991	Ballinderry Ash	5-1	5	28.78s

BBC TELEVISION TROPHY
First Run 1956. Raced at various tracks and distances
Winners since 1981:

	Venue	Winner
1981	Perry Barr	Decoy Boom
1982	Belle Vue	Alfa My Son
1983	Walthamstow	Sandy Lane
1984	Wimbledon	Weston Prelude
1985	Wolverhampton	Scurlogue Champ
1986	Brough Park	Scurlogue Champ
1987	Oxford	Glenowen Queen
1988	Hall Green	Minnie's Siren
1989	Catford	Proud To Run
1990	Walthamstow	Shropshire Lass

Most wins: 2 Scurlogue Champ

GYMNASTICS

A new and particularly improbable nymphette captured the imagination of the sport at the world championships in Indianapolis. Kim Gwang Suk, 15 years old, 4ft 4in, 4 st 7lbs, and from the last hermetic redoubt of Communism, North Korea, enthralled the American audience with a perfect-10 performance on the uneven bars that recalled the glorious flowering of Olga Korbut in Munich in 1972.

An American, Kim Zmeskal, surprisingly won the individual combined championship, dethroning Svetlana Boginskaya of the Soviet Union. Boginskaya said the scoring had been biased against her and that she would have won had the championships been in Europe. Boginskaya refused to shake Zmeskal's hand after the balance beam competition two days later.

The Soviet Union won the team titles as usual but there was considerable concern over the future of Soviet gymnastics. The six-strong men's team came from five different republics and its future was uncertain. Yuri Titov, the president of the International Federation, said the end of government support for gymnastics meant that the number of children practising the sport in the Soviet Union had dropped from about 700,000 four years ago to about half that. South Africa competed for the first time in 25 years but failed to qualify as a team for the 1992 Olympics. By finishing 12th, the British men did qualify, by a fraction of a point.

1991

WORLD CHAMPIONSHIPS
Indianapolis, Sep 6-15
Men
Team
1 Soviet Union 584.425 pts
2 China 577.050 pts
3 Germany 576.125 pts
All-round Individual
1 Vitaly Scherbo (USSR) 117.175 pts
2 Grigori Misutin (USSR) 116.900 pts
3 Valeriy Lyukin (USSR) 116.825 pts
Floor
1 Igor Korobchinski (USSR) 9.875 pts
2 Vitaliy Scherbo (USSR) 9.800 pts
3 Daisuke Nishikawa (Jap) 9.787 pts
Pommel Horse
1 Valeri Beleniki (USSR) 9.912 pts
2 Linyao Guo (Chn) 9.887 pts
3 Jing Li (Chn) 9.875 pts
Ring
1 Grigori Misutin (USSR) 9.875 pts
2 Andreas Wecker (Ger) 9.862 pts
3 Yuri Chechi (Ita) 9.837 pts
Vault
1 Yu Ok-yul (SKo) 9.700 pts
2 Vitaly Scherbo (USSR) 9.699 pts
3 Yutaka Aihara (Jap) 9.631
Parallel Bars
1 Li Jing (Chn) 9.862 pts
2 Igor Korobchinski (USSR) 9.825 pts
3 Linyao Guo (Chn) 9.812 pts
High Bar
1 Li Chunyang (Chn) & Ralf Beuchner (Ger) 9.787 pts
3 Vitaliy Scherbo (USSR) 9.775 pts

Women
Team
1 Soviet Union 396.055 pts
2 United States 394.116 pts
3 Romania 393.841 pts

All-round Individual
1 Kim Zmeskal (US) 39.848 pts
2 Svetlana Boginskaya (USSR) 39.736 pts
3 Cristine Bontas (Rom) 39.711 pts
Beam
1 Svetlana Boginskaya (USSR) 9.962 pts
2 Tatyana Gutsu (USSR) 9.950 pts
3 Elizabeth Okino (US) & Lavinia Milosivici (Rom) 9.900 pts
Floor
1 Cristina Bontas (Rom) & Oksana Tchusovitina (USSR) 9.962 pts
3 Kim Zmeskal (US) 9.950 pts
Vault
1 Lavinia Milosovici (Rom) 9.949 pts
2 Oksana Tchusovitiana (USSR) & Henrietta Onodi (Hun) 9.918 pts
Asymmetrical Bars
1 Kim Gwang Suk (NKo) 10.000 pts
2 Tatyana Gusu (USSR) & Shannon Miller (US) 9.950 pts

BRITISH WOMEN'S CHAMPIONSHIPS
Crawley, Mar 8-10
1 Laura Timmins (Park Wrekin)
2 Rebecca Haynes (Trafford School)
3 Louise Redding (Park Wrekin)

BRITISH MEN'S CHAMPIONSHIPS
Gateshead Mar 16-17
1 Paul Bowler (Manchester)
2 James May (Bristol Hawkes)
3 David Cox (Liverpool School)

BRITISH WOMEN'S RHYTHMIC CHAMPIONSHIPS
Bletchley, Jan 26-27
Individual
1 Viva Seifert (Hillingdon)
2 Alitia Sands (Coventry)
3 Michele Smith (Northampton)

CHAMPIONS

WORLD CHAMPIONSHIPS
(First held 1903)

Men
Team
1983	China
1985	USSR
1987	USSR
1989	USSR
1991	USSR

Combined
(post-war winners)
1950	Walter Lehmann (Swi)
1954	Vikton Chukarin (USSR)
1958	Boris Shakhlin (USSR)
1962	Yuriy Titov (USSR)
1966	Mikhail Voronin (USSR)
1970	Eizo Kenmotsu (Jap)
1974	Shigeru Kasamatsu (Jap)
1978	Nikolay Andrianov (USSR)
1979	Aleksandr Ditiatin (USSR)
1981	Yuriy Korolev (USSR)
1983	Dmitri Belozerchev (USSR)
1985	Yuriy Korolev (USSR)
1987	Dmitri Belozerchev (USSR)
1989	Igor Korobchinski (USSR)
1991	Vitaly Scherbo (USSR)

Individual Disciplines
Winners since 1983

Floor
1983	Tong Fei (Chn)
1985	Tong Fei (Chn)
1987	Lou Yun (Chn)
1989	Igor Korobchinski (USSR)
1991	Igor Korobchinski (USSR)

Vault
1983	Artur Akopian (USSR)
1985	Yuriy Korolev (USSR)
1987	Slvio Kroll (GDR) & Lou Yun (Chn)
1989	Jorg Behrendt (GDR)
1991	Yu Ok-Yul (SKo)

Rings
1983	Dmitriy Belozerchev (USSR) & Koji Gushiken (Jap)
1985	Li Ning (Chn) & Yuriy Korolev (USSR)
1987	Yuriy Korolev (USSR)
1989	Andreas Aguilar (FRG)
1991	Grigori Misutin (USSR)

Pommel Horse
1983	Dmitriy Belozerchev (USSR)
1985	Valentin Mogilnyi (USSR)
1987	Dmitri Belozerchev (USSR) & Zsolt Borkai (Hun)
1989	Valentin Mognilny (USSR)
1991	Valeri Beleniki (USSR)

High Bar
1983	Dmitri Belozerchev (USSR)
1985	Tong Fei (Chn)
1987	Dmitri Belozerchev (USSR)
1989	Li Chunyang (Chn)
1991	Li Chunyang (Chn) & Ralf Beuchuner (Ger)

Parallel Bars
1983	Vladimir Artemov (USSR) & Lou Yun (Chn)
1985	Silvio Kroll (GDR) & Valentin Mogilnyi (USSR)
1987	Vladimir Artemov (USSR)
1989	Vladimir Artemov (USSR) & Li Jing (Chn)
1991	Li Jing (Chn)

Women
Team
1983	USSR
1985	USSR
1987	Romania
1989	USSR
1991	USSR

Combined
(post-war winners)
1950	Helena Rakoczy (Pol)
1954	Galina Roudiko (USSR)
1958	Larissa Latynina (USSR)
1962	Larissa Latynina (USSR)
1966	Vera Cáslavská (Cze)
1970	Lyudmila Tourischeva (USSR)
1974	Lyudmila Tourischeva (USSR)
1978	Yelena Mukhina (USSR)
1979	Nelli Kim (USSR)
1981	Olga Bicherova (USSR)
1983	Natalya Yurchenko (USSR)
1985	Oksana Omelianchuk (USSR) & Yelena Shoushounova (USSR)
1987	Aurelia Dobre (Rom)
1989	Svetlana Boginskaya (USSR)
1991	Kim Zmeskal (US)

Individual Disciplines
Winners since 1983

Vault
1983	Boriana Stoyanova (Bul)
1985	Yelena Shoushounova (USSR)
1987	Yelena Shoushounova (USSR)
1989	Olessia Dudnik (USSR)
1991	Lavinia Milosovici (Rom)

Beam
1983	Olga Mostepanova (USSR)
1985	Daniela Silivas (Rom)
1987	Aurelia Dobre (Rom)
1989	Daniela Silivas (Rom)
1991	Svetlana Boginskaya (USSR)

Floor
1983	Ecaterina Szabo (Rom)
1985	Oksana Omeliantchuk (USSR)
1987	Yelena Shoushounova (USSR) & Daniela Silivas (Rom)
1989	Daniela Silivas (Rom) & Svetlana Boginskaya (USSR.)
1991	Cristina Bontas (Rom) & Oksana Tchusovitina (USSR)

Asymmetrical Bars
1983	Maxi Gnauck (GDR)
1985	Gabriela Fahnrich (GDR)
1987	Daniela Silivas (Rom) & Doerte Thumler (GDR)
1989	Fan Di (Chn) & Daniela Silivas (Rom)
1991	Kim Gwang Suk (NKo)

HOCKEY

1990-91

Men
EUROPEAN INDOOR CLUBS CHAMPIONSHIP
Amiens, Feb 17

SEMI-FINALS
RUSSELSHEIMER 12 Amiens 4; IPSWICH 2 Glasgow Western 1

FINAL
RUSSELSHEIMER 5 Ipswich 2

EUROPEAN INDOOR CHAMPIONSHIP
Birmingham, Feb 23-24

SEMI-FINALS
GERMANY 5 Poland 2; ENGLAND 7 Scotland 3

FINAL
GERMANY 7 England 3

NATIONWIDE ANGLIA CUP FINAL
Luton, Apr 7
HOUNSLOW 3 Havant 2

POUNDSTRETCHER NATIONAL LEAGUE
First Division

			P	W	D	L	F	A	Pts
1	(3)	Havant	15	11	3	1	45	18	36
2	(11)	Indian Gymkhana	15	9	3	3	23	16	30
3	(1)	Hounslow	15	8	4	3	44	19	28
4	(2)	E Grinstead	15	8	3	4	30	16	27
5	(5)	Southgate	15	8	1	6	39	27	25
6	(13)	Old Loughtonians	15	7	4	4	32	22	25
7	(4)	Slough	15	7	3	5	28	24	24
8	(7)	Teddington	15	7	3	5	22	27	24
9	(6)	Stourport	15	6	4	5	31	29	22
10	(10)	Bromley	15	6	3	6	24	25	21
11	(P)	St Albans	15	6	3	6	34	36	21
12	(12)	Cannock	15	5	3	7	19	29	18
13	(P)	Neston	15	3	4	8	20	34	13
14	(8)	Welton	15	3	2	10	18	28	11
15	(9)	Isca	15	2	0	13	17	39	6
16	(14)	Wakefield	15	1	3	11	12	49	6

DIVISION ONE RESULTS

	Brom	Can	Eg	Hav	Hou	IG	Isca	Nes	OL	St A	Sl	Sou	Sto	Ted	Wak	Wel
Bromley	*	1-1	*	*	0-2	*	*	2-2	2-1	*	1-2	*	1-0	1-3	4-1	*
Cannock	*	*	0-1	1-2	*	2-1	0-1	*	*	*	3-1	*	1-0	*	*	2-1
East Grinstead	0-2	*	*	0-4	*	0-0	4-1	*	*	1-0	*	0-1	*	*	*	1-0
Havant	2-2	*	*	*	*	*	*	2-2	1-1	2-1	7-2	3-2	3-1	*	4-1	*
Hounslow	*	5-1	1-1	1-3	*	3-1	3-1	*	*	*	*	*	*	1-1	*	1-1
Indian Gym	2-0	*	*	1-0	*	*	1-0	*	2-0	2-1	3-4	2-1	3-2	*	*	*
Isca	1-2	*	*	0-4	*	*	*	*	2-3	1-2	1-4	0-4	0-2	*	4-1	*
Neston	*	1-1	0-3	*	1-8	0-1	5-3	*	*	*	1-2	*	*	0-1	*	2-1
Old Loughtonians	*	5-0	4-1	*	2-2	*	*	3-1	*	*	1-2	*	*	3-1	3-1	1-1
St Albans	3-2	4-4	*	*	4-3	*	*	4-3	0-1	*	1-1	*	4-4	*	5-2	*
Slough	*	3-0	1-1	*	1-1	*	*	0-1	*	*	*	*	2-0	2-0	2-0
Southgate	4-2	*	*	*	2-1	*	*	3-1	2-3	4-0	3-2	*	4-4	*	6-1	*
Stourport	*	3-1	2-4	*	1-3	*	*	2-1	3-3	*	1-0	*	*	3-0	1-1	*
Teddington	*	*	0-7	1-3	*	3-3	2-1	*	*	4-2	*	2-1	*	*	*	3-1
Wakefield	*	0-2	0-6	*	0-8	0-1	*	0-0	*	*	*	*	*	0-0	*	1-3
Welton	1-2	*	*	2-5	*	0-0	2-1	*	*	2-3	*	3-1	1-2	*	*	*

COUNTY CHAMPIONSHIP FINAL
Plymouth, May 18
MIDDLESEX 4 Kent 3
Middlesex's fourth successive title

EUROPEAN CHAMPIONS' CUP
The Hague, May 20
UHLENHORST (Ger) 4 AtleticoTerrassa (Spa) 2

POUNDSTRETCHER LEAGUE CUP FINALS
Luton, May 26
Division One
HOUNSLOW 4 Havant 1
Division Two
FIREBRANDS 1 Bournville 0

Women
HOME COUNTRIES CHAMPIONSHIP
Durham, Mar 3
Final placings:
1 SCOTLAND; 2 England; 3 Ireland; 4 Wales

TY-PHOO NATIONAL LEAGUE
Leading Positions

		P	W	D	L	F	A	Pts
1	Slough	9	7	1	1	20	8	22
2	Leicester	9	5	4	0	15	5	19
3	Sutton Coldfield	9	4	4	1	20	9	16
4	Ipswich	9	4	3	2	16	13	15
5	Hightown	9	5	0	4	9	6	15

NATIONAL CLUB CHAMPIONSHIP
Ashford, Apr 20-21
SUTTON COLDFIELD 1 Leicester 1
(Sutton won 4-3 on pens)

EUROPEAN CUP
Brussels, May 12

Final
ENGLAND 2 Germany 1
Final Standings: 1 England; 2 Germany; 3 Soviet Union; 4 Holland; 5 Scotland; 6 Spain; 7 Belgium; 8 Ireland; 9 Wales; 10 France; 11 Italy; 12 Austria

EUROPEAN CUP-WINNERS' CUP FINAL
The Hague, May 19
RYTHM GRODNO (USSR) 1 Sutton Coldfield 1 (*Grodno won 4-3 on penalties*)

EUROPEAN CHAMPIONS' CUP
The Hague, May 20
HGC WASSENAAR (Hol) 2 Glasgow Western (Sco) 1

NATIONAL CLUBS' INDOOR CHAMPIONSHIP
Sheffield, Jun 2
HIGHTOWN 5 Slough 3

——————— 1990 ———————

Men

12TH CHAMPIONS TROPHY
Melbourne, Nov 24

FINAL STANDINGS

	P	W	D	L	F	A	Pts
1 Australia	5	4	0	1	14	6	8
2 Holland	5	3	1	1	14	8	7
3 Germany	5	3	1	1	14	12	7
4 Pakistan	5	2	0	3	12	11	4
5 Soviet Union	5	1	0	4	4	11	2
6 Great Britain	5	1	0	4	3	13	2

——————— CHAMPIONS ———————

WORLD CUP
Men
1971	Pakistan
1973	Holland
1975	India
1978	Pakistan
1982	Pakistan
1986	Australia
1990	Holland

Women
1974	Holland
1976	West Germany
1978	Holland
1981	West Germany
1983	Holland
1986	Holland
1990	Holland

WOMEN'S WORLD CHAMPIONSHIP
| 1975 | England |
| 1979 | Holland |

EUROPEAN CHAMPIONS' CUP
Men
1971	Frankfurt 1880 (FRG)
1972	Frankfurt 1880 (FRG)
1973	Frankfurt 1880 (FRG)
1974	Frankfurt 1880 (FRG)
1975	Frankfurt 1880 (FRG)
1976	Southgate (Eng)
1977	Southgate (Eng)
1978	Southgate (Eng)
1979	Klein Zwitserland (Hol)
1980	Slough (Eng)
1981	Klein Zwitserland (Hol)
1982	Dinamo Alma-Ata (USSR)
1983	Dinamo Alma-Ata (USSR)
1984	TG 1846 Frankental (FRG)

1985	Atletico Terrassa (Spa)
1986	Kampong Utrecht (Hol)
1987	Bloemendaal (Hol)
1988	Uhlenhorst (FRG)
1989	Uhlenhorst (FRG)
1990	Uhlenhorst (FRG)
1991	Uhlenhorst (Ger)

Women
1974	Harvestehuder Hamburg (FRG)
1975	Amsterdam (Hol)
1976	Amsterdam (Hol)
1977	Amsterdam (Hol)
1978	Amsterdam (Hol)
1979	Amsterdam (Hol)
1980	Amsterdam (Hol)
1981	Amsterdam (Hol)
1982	Amsterdam (Hol)
1983	HGC Wassenaar (Hol)
1984	HGC Wassenaar (Hol)
1985	HGC Wassenaar (Hol)
1986	HGC Wassenaar (Hol)
1987	HGC Wassenaar (Hol)
1988	Amsterdam (Hol)
1989	Amsterdam (Hol)
1990	Amsterdam (Hol)
1991	HGC Wassenaar (Hol)

ENGLISH LEAGUE CHAMPIONS
(*Known as National League from 1989*)
Men
1975	Bedfordshire Eagles
1976	Slough
1977	Southgate
1978	Southgate
1979	Isca
1980	Slough
1981	Slough
1982	Slough
1983	Slough
1984	Neston
1985	East Grinstead
1986	East Grinstead
1987	Slough
1988	Southgate
1989	Southgate
1990	Hounslow
1991	Havant

Women
1979	Chelmsford	1986	Slough
1980	Norton	1987	Ealing
1981	Sutton Coldfield	1988	Ealing
1982	Slough	1989	Ealing
1983	Slough	1990	Sutton Coldfield
1984	Sheffield	1991	Slough
1985	Ipswich		

HOCKEY ASSOCIATION (HA) CUP
Men
1972	Hounslow	1985	Southgate
1973	Hounslow	1986	Southgate
1974	Southgate	1987	Southgate
1975	Southgate	1988	Southgate
1976	Nottingham	1989	Hounslow
1977	Slough	1990	Havant
1978	Guildford	1991	Hounslow
1979	Slough		
1980	Slough		
1981	Slough		
1982	Southgate		
1983	Neston		
1984	East Grinstead		

HORSE RACING

HARD TIMES AND GENEROSITY

British flat racing acquired a much-needed equine star in 1991. Generous, a chestnut colt who looked like Grundy, won the Derby by a stunning five lengths and went on to put his stamp on the rest of the season. Generous, trained by Paul Cole, beat the French Derby winner Suave Dancer to win the Irish Derby and took the King George with brilliant acceleration to be acclaimed as the best colt since Shergar in 1981. He still was not good enough to win the Arc, finishing unplaced behind Suave Dancer and continuing the melancholy record of Epsom winners at Longchamp. But he was certainly the best best-horse-since-Shergar for at least two seasons.

Generous's jockey Alan Munro, 24, had landed the job as first rider to Prince Fahd Salman only a month before the Derby and immediately impressed everyone with his confidence in the saddle and his cockiness out of it. However, Munro had enough humility to approach the right people for advice and spent the eve of the race studying videos of Lester Piggott's nine Derby winners at the maestro's house and riding a mechanical rocking horse to practise his style. Munro, 24, was the youngest jockey in the race; Generous, foaled in February 1988, was the oldest horse. John Dunlop, trainer of the runner-up Marju, had some consolation next day when he won the Any Other Breeds section of the cattle class at the South of England Show, with a Beef Shorthorn bull.

It was, in most respects, another dispiriting Derby - cold, damp and hit by the recession with only 13 runners and an official attendance figure of 23,600. No one even trotted out the usual statistic of half a million people being on the Downs; there may have been barely enough to fill Wembley. The following day, only 5,000 people attended the Coronation Cup; and there were more people at Sandown at the same time for a packaging and handling exhibition. The Jockey Club reinstated yearling entry for the 1993 Derby in an attempt to rescue the race's dwindling status but deferred a scheme to switch the race back to Saturday.

The only link with the great days at Epsom was Piggott - who had come out of retirement the previous October - wheeling and dealing for a mount and eventually getting one on Hokusai, which was promptly backed down, as of old, to 25-1, but was nowhere near good enough and came seventh. The name L Piggott on a racecard, which caused such a sensation at first, soon seemed as natural as ever even if he was 55, and he certainly chased winners with all his old demonic energy: all over Britain, of course, and

---

IT'S THAT MAN AGAIN

❝It's still the same. One leg each side.❞
Lester Piggott on technique

"Every ride he takes deprives a young jockey of the chance to make a few pounds. Turn it in, Lester."
Letter to the Daily Mirror

"He must be the fittest man of his age I have ever come across."
Michael Allen, Jockey Club doctor

"When I came back I didn't really know whether anyone would give me a ride."
Lester Piggott after winning the Breeders' Cup Mile

"He only arrived half-an-hour ago, has never been here before and yet he looks like he's been here all his life. And it's not an easy track. Extraordinary."
Ernesto Tasende, Italian jockey, on Piggott's riding at Livorno

"I think he's really happy again. He's smiling more than he used to."
Pat Eddery on Piggott

"His career is over, he's 55 and that's far too old to be rushing up and down the country trying to get rides."
Willie Carson on Piggott

"We have got used to, almost blasé, about the miracle. But cast your mind back a twelvemonth and what would have been the betting on Lester padding across the paddock and touching his cap to H Cecil this afternoon? You could have taken a shorter price on Tutankhamen."
Brough Scott, Racing Post

"How sad and ironic that on Derby Day Lester Piggott, who was jailed for tax evasion, should be cold-shouldered by the Queen, who does not pay tax at all. I'm disgusted.❞❞
Letter to the Daily Mirror

to Belmont Park, where he won the Breeders' Cup Mile; to Bombay, where he had his first ride in India for 22 years; to Berlin, where he helped attract 36,000 to the first post-reunification meeting; to Ballinrobe and Killarney in the west of Ireland, which both had their biggest crowds ever; and even to the all-weather track at Southwell. He won the Derby too; alas, it was only the Swedish Derby.

CAN'T PAY? WON'T PAY!

But even the return of Lester could not brighten up the prevailing bleakness of British racing. Betting turnover fell sharply and the Levy Board was forced to announce huge cuts in prize money, from £12,891,000 to £9,420,000; the fixture list for 1992, with 40 meetings dropped, was produced only after intense wrangling between the Board and the Jockey Club. A firm of economic consultants had already shown that owners of Flat horses were paying out £200 million and getting back only £22 million in prize money. Accusing fingers were pointed at the big bookmakers, a view supported by the House of Commons Home Affairs Committee which, after long discussion, said they should put far more money into the sport. The bookmakers disagreed. So did the Government, which rejected this and the committee's other main recommendations of Sunday racing and evening opening of betting shops.

A whole succession of trainers were forced to quit the sport although they found it as impossible to sell their yards as to make them pay; there was a special shock when the successful Yorkshire trainer Lynda Ramsden joined the list. Many owners departed more quietly. The Hanson group, sponsors of the Derby, was reported to have lost £7.72 million in four years owning racehorses; even the Queen decided to cut her string from 36 to 25.

Another leading owner vanished for a very different reason. The Aga Khan removed his 90 horses from Newmarket and announced that he was boycotting British racing when his filly Aliysa was finally disqualified from the 1989 Oaks by the Jockey Club almost 18 months after the race. The disqualification came after the prohibited substance hydroxycamphor had been found in her bloodstream and a £2 million enquiry had been held into how it got there. The Aga Khan's lawyers insisted the weight of scientific evidence was that it must have come from carrots or alfalfa hay. The Horseracing Forensic Laboratory said that was indeed possible if Aliysa had eaten 40 tonnes of alfalfa hay, two tonnes of carrots or a lorry load of woodshavings. Snow Bride was awarded the race.

Among those who remained, the few success stories shone out like beacons: in 1990 Jack Berry trained 127 winners, breaking the previous record of 124 for a northern trainer set by William Elsey in 1905; and in 1991 he smashed into more general records scoring the fastest 50 and fastest 100 of all time, reaching his century when Our Fan won at Hamilton on July 17, six days earlier than Henry Cecil in 1987.

In the saddle, Pat Eddery maintained his dominance. In 1990 he became the first Flat jockey since Sir Gordon Richards (in 1952) to ride 200 winners and in 1991 he became the fifth man to ride 3,000 winners in Britain. It took him 22 years 3 months, quicker than the other four: Sir Gordon, Piggott, Willie Carson and Doug Smith.

Alex Greaves, who made her name riding winners on the all-weather at Southwell,

THE 3,000 CLUB				THE 200 CLUB			
Jockeys who have ridden 3,000 winners in their career				*Jockeys who have ridden 200 winners in a season*			
	First winner	3,000th	Total	No of times		Best	
Sir Gordon Richards	1921	1945	4870	12	Sir Gordon Richards	269	(1947)
Lester Piggott	1948	1975	4397+	8	Fred Archer	246	(1885)
Willie Carson	1962	1990	3286+	1	Tommy Loates	222	(1893)
Doug Smith	1932	1965	3111	1	Peter Scudamore NH	221	(1988-89)
Pat Eddery	1969	1991	3059+	1	Pat Eddery	209	(1990)

Figures for current jockeys correct to Sep 3 1991
World record: 8833 by Bill Shoemaker, US

World record: 598 by Kent Desormeaux, US, 1989

became the first woman to win a major handicap when she took the Lincoln on Amenable. Four days later she rode God's Solution, the 10-year-old grey sprinter trained by David Barron, to his sixth victory in the race now named after him at Catterick. Alan Munro rode six winners in a day (out of ten rides) at Lingfield and Catterick. Gary Carter became the second jockey in Britain (after Paul Cook in 1981) to ride winners at three courses on the same day: Luvly Jubly in the 1.30 at Southwell, Romany Rye in the 4.40 at York and Able Susan in the 8.15 at Doncaster. The feat was matched in the US by Mark Salvaggio, at Philadelphia Park, Delaware Park and Penn National.

The Hull City AFC handicap at Beverley was declared void because it was started one minute 18 seconds early. Trainer George Moore, who lost an 11-1 winner, said the starter should have been shot.

FORTIFIED GARRISON

Garrison Savannah, ridden by Mark Pitman, came to the last fence at Aintree looking certain to be the first horse to do the Gold Cup-Grand National double in the same season since Golden Miller in 1934. He was thwarted on the long run-in, by the soft ground as much as anything, in a defeat reminiscent of the one suffered by Pitman's father Richard on Crisp in 1973. The winner was Seagram, namesake of the race sponsors. However, their delight was tempered by the fact that the Seagram company chairman Ivan Straker twice refused the chance to buy the horse. The winner belonged to a Liverpool haulage firm which chose the name to try and tempt his namesakes into buying him. For 1992, the sponsors changed the race's name to the Martell Grand National. The start of the National was delayed for eight minutes because of a protest by a dozen animal rights protesters in front of the start carrying a banner reading "Stop the Carnage". In the event, no horses were killed; Ballyhane died of a ruptured blood vessel after finishing 11th.

Garrison Savannah's Cheltenham win came after he had run only once all season and had torn a shoulder muscle doing that. His closest rivals were The Fellow (only the second French-trained horse to be placed in the Gold Cup, after Garde Toi in 1950) and Desert Orchid, third for the second year running. The grand old grey had started the season with two indifferent runs and was widely written off. However, his trainer David Elsworth maintained all along that Dessie would be right for Boxing Day and was

DESERT ORCHID AT CHELTENHAM	
1984 Champion Hurdle	Unplaced
1985 Champion Hurdle	Pulled up
1986 Arkle Challenge Trophy	3rd
1987 Queen Mother Champion Chase	3rd
1988 Queen Mother Champion Chase	2nd
1989 Cheltenham Gold Cup	Won
1990 Cheltenham Gold Cup	3rd
1991 Cheltenham Gold Cup	3rd

MARTIN PIPE'S SCHEDULE				
	50th winner	100th	150th	200th
1988-89 (208)	Oct 29	Dec 29	Mar 1	May 19
1989-90 (224)	Oct 26	Dec 14	Mar 3	May 7
1990-91 (230)	Nov 15	Jan 21	Mar 19	May 2

Total number of winners for each season in brackets

proved spectacularly right when his horse won the King George VI Chase for a fourth time, beating the record he shared with Wayward Lad. A brilliant win at Sandown followed but nothing else. "He still has the fight," said his owner Richard Burridge after Cheltenham, "but no longer the talent." After four years, Dessie lost the title of Racegoers' Club champion jumper to the Champion Hurdle winner Morley Street.

Peter Scudamore became National Hunt champion jockey once again but with his total much reduced, to 141. In a way, this represented his most phenomenal achievement yet: he broke his left leg falling off a horse called Black Humour at Market Rasen and was out of the saddle for 2½ months. Richard Dunwoody had a lead of 20 by the time Scudamore returned but the champion slowly whittled it back and his success was finally sealed when Dunwoody was banned for five days for careless riding at Wincanton on April 25. Scudamore finished 14 clear, having had only 423 rides against his rival's 646. Three leading jump jockeys retired: Richard Rowe, to train, Kevin Mooney to become

Barry Hills' assistant and Ron Hyett, to run an edible snail farm. Mogamed Tokov won the Maxwell Motors Glasnost Handicap Hurdle at Kelso to become the first Soviet jockey to win in Britain.

Scudamore was helped by another astonishing year's training by his ally Martin Pipe, who improved his total for the season for the 13th consecutive year, this time to a once-unthinkable 230. Pipe had the 1000th winner of his career at Kempton on December 7 and became the first NH trainer to top £1 million in prize money during a season: £1,203,014. The owner with most winners was Pipe Scudamore Racing plc which had 36 and Pipe's 20-year-old protégé Martin Foster, 20, was the top conditional jockey with 35. The only setback came on the ITV programme The Cook Report, which accused Pipe of running his horses more often than others and risking them on firm ground. Cook said 71 per cent of his horses did not come back into training, whereas other trainers had a wastage rate of 37 per cent. Pipe called the programme "total rubbish" and, after years of whispered suspicions, racing rallied round and indignantly defended him. The empire was even extended to the Flat: a former Pipe horse, Eurolink the Lad, won the Royal Hunt Cup and a current one, Tamarpour, won the Northumberland Plate.

SMALL EARTHQUAKE AT KELSO

Equinoctial, owned and trained by the permit-holder Norman Miller and ridden by Andrew Heywood, became the longest-priced winner ever in British racing, winning the Grant's Whisky Novices Handicap Hurdle at Kelso at 250-1. This beat the 200-1 offered against Theodore, the winner of the 1822 St Leger. The Tote paid only £64.70 to a £1 stake. "I fancied him to run into a place," said Miller. The world record is held by Anntelle, 500-1 winner of the Norman Ross Handicap at Canterbury, Sydney in 1982.

HONEST JOE

❝How would you feel if you saw your teenaged daughter introduced to Count Dracula?"
New York racing official asked whether he favoured the introduction of British bookmakers

"Sports betting reflects poor judgment on the part of the participants and can only inflict criticism of our organisation."
Internal memo to employees of the New York City Off-Track Betting Corporation

"If there is unfair trading in Europe and we think there is, it is in the UK. It is done every day, and it is done to owners, trainers, breeders, jockeys and the lads....Your bookmakers are getting away with daylight robbery."
Louis Romanet, head of the French Jockey Club, on British bookmakers

"When he talks about the French system, the only person he doesn't mention is the customer. He's always conspicuous by his absence."
Peter George, Ladbrokes

"The bookmaker's liability to duty and levy is on his total turnover and it is his liability, not the punter's. To call the deductions 'tax' is at the least disingenuous, at worst less than honest."
Commons Select Committee report on racing

"It is only because of bookmakers that the money comes near racing in the first place. The expertise that goes into marketing racing is never recognised."
Stephen Little, bookmaker

"I applaud the Sporting Life's decision to make free copies available to our troops in the Gulf...isn't it a pity that we can't send some bookmakers along too?"
Letter to the Sporting Life from Graham Swindon of New Malden

"If the Tote were a race horse it would be shot. Or pensioned off to pull a milk float."
Leader in Daily Star after the Tote paid less than 16-1 on the 50-1 Oaks winner

"Does anyone remember how the shops used to be? How there used to be long periods of sepulchral silence broken only by the rustling of paper, the striking of the odd match and, if you listened very carefully, the clanking of some extremely odd brains...Now the punter has to put up with so many split screens, so many interruptions for the latest shows from obscure dog meetings, so many different kinds of nonsense coming at him over the autobabble that the pleasure of an afternoon in the bookies has all but gone.❞
Paul Haigh, Racing Post

There were seven 6-1 co-favourites for the ten-runner Law Society Legal Handicap Hurdle at Hexham on April 29; six of them filled the first six places. This equalled the record set at Haydock in 1975 when there were seven co-favourites at 8-1.

Northern Dancer, the most successful stallion ever, died in Maryland aged 29, three years after his stud career ended. He fathered 605 foals, including the winners of 99 European pattern races. Alydar, probably the most successful stallion at the time, died in Kentucky aged 15, thus hastening the downfall of his owners Calumet Farms - once the dominant force in American bloodstock - which filed for bankruptcy in July, listing liabilities of more than $118 million. On the other hand, *The Sun* reported that Shergar was alive and well in the Channel Islands, eight years after his kidnap and presumed death; the story was universally disregarded and the *Daily Telegraph* correspondent on Alderney refuted it on the grounds that he knew every horse on the island personally.

Racing returned to the famous track at Hialeah, Florida after a two-year gap and trotting was held on the old Kendal Racecourse in Westmorland, last used before the war. Lincoln Racecourse, officially closed in 1964, finally shut down when the three local hunts which staged their point-to-points there fell out with the city's Labour council, which wanted racing to continue only if the profits did not go to hunting. A third, less demanding course opened at Cheltenham to try to get bigger fields in the autumn. A survey of racegoers showed that 60% were satisfied with the value for money and 34% were satisfied with the catering; no one seemed to know anyone who might be in the 34%. Several of Ascot's bowler-hatted jobsworth marshals were reported to have been sacked for fiddling.

A horse called Biganard slipped past the Jockey Club name police and started running in novice chases. Specialist horse-catchers were introduced at Newton Abbot on Boxing Day. Doncaster Racecourse finally introduced soft toilet paper in the stable lads' hostel. All the races at Southwell on March 1 were named after *Sun* readers who won a competition: Brian Hurd, Susan Bolton, Amelia Barry, Jeffrey Butler, David Scoble and Peter Davies.

Lord Hesketh, owner of Towcester, invited 200 local clergymen to the races to celebrate the 450th anniversary of Peterborough Diocese. About 60 turned up and the Bishop, looking rather like a bookie in his trilby and shades, presented his own wine to the winner of each race. Barry Yates, a lorry-driver from Middlesex, won £50 on a £2 treble and rushed out to celebrate, forgetting to put the phone down on the 44p a minute commentary phone line. The bill came to £500. The Duke of Roxburghe, recently divorced, was blackballed by the Jockey Club.

OVERSEAS NEWS

In America, Bill Shoemaker, 59, who hardly had a serious injury in nearly 40 years of riding, suffered a broken neck and almost total paralysis after a car crash in California. Police said he fell asleep at the wheel while over the legal blood alcohol limit. Willie Clark, 69, believed to be America's oldest active jockey, was banned for 30 days at Charles Town, West Virginia, for rough tactics. George 'Jeep' Ryan came out of retirement to ride at River Downs, Ohio aged 63. Betting shops in New York stopped handing out free pencils to save money; 75 of the 98 state-run "betting parlors" were said to be making a loss. All three Triple Crown races in the US attracted their lowest TV ratings ever.

In Japan, however, almost $20 billion was reported to have been spent on legal betting in 1989, with about five times that much on illegal betting; a third of the population were reported to take part, with young women being especially enthusiastic. Racing started in Dubai, the Maktoum family's fiefdom, and resumed in Beirut after five years; 25,000 people packed the bullet-scarred stands at the Palace of Peace. The sport was halted in Baghdad from January 15 until April, owing to extraneous circumstances.

Two Irishmen found at Heathrow with £77 million in allegedly stolen financial documents claimed they were going to the US to buy a racehorse. Sylvester Carmouche, the jockey who waited in the fog to overtake his rivals and win a race at Delta Downs,

Louisiana, was jailed for 30 days. Susan Tracy from Britain was arrested at Ribera, Italy for organising a clandestine horse race and blocking the road. Naples police seized the private racecourse owned by a jailed Mafia boss.

Julie Cecil, estranged wife of the trainer Henry Cecil, said men would get more work done if they were castrated. A survey asking people to name the oddest place they had made love brought the answer: "The water jump at Wolverhampton racecourse." It was not clear whether the respondent meant by the water jump, on it or in it.

1991

THE CLASSICS
General Accident 1000 Guineas
Newmarket, May 2, 1 mile

1	SHADAYID	Willie Carson	4-6 f
2	Kooyonga	Lester Piggott	14-1
3	Crystal Gazing	Frankie Dettori	6-1
4	Once in My Life	Cash Asmussen	20-1
5	Only Yours	Bruce Raymond	50-1
6	Dartrey	Steve Cauthen	9-1
7	Zigaura	Ray Cochrane	16-1
8	Lee Artiste	Tommy Quinn	66-1
9	Positive Acclaim	David Nicholls	150-1
10	Cloche D'Or	Michael Roberts	66-1
11	Tetradonna	John Reid	18-1
12	Gentle Aria	Walter Swinburn	100-1
13	Silver Braid	John Williams	20-1
14	Miranda Jay	Pat Eddery	33-1

Trainer: John Dunlop, Arundel
Owner: Hamdan Al-Maktoum
Time: 1m 38.18s
Distance: 2 lengths
Carson was the first jockey to ride the winner twice running since Charlie Elliott in 1931-32

General Accident 2000 Guineas
Newmarket, May 4, 1 mile

1	MYSTIKO	Michael Roberts	13-2
2	Lysius	Steve Cauthen	16-1
3	Ganges	Freddy Head	16-1
4	Generous	Tommy Quinn	11-1
5	Mukaddemah	Frankie Dettori	14-1
6	Desert Sun	Pat Eddery	7-1
7	Flying Brave	John Reid	66-1
8	Hokusai	Michael Kinane	16-1
9	Malvernico	Christy Roche	66-1
10	Shalford	Bruce Raymond	100-1
11	Marju	Willie Carson	6-4f
12	Bog Trotter	Lester Piggott	11-1
13	Mujaazif	Walter Swinburn	20-1
14	Junk Bond	Eddie Maple	100-1

Trainer: Clive Brittain, Newmarket
Owner: Lady Beaverbrook
Time: 1m 37.83s
Distance: head
Mystiko was the first grey to win since Palestine in 1950. It was only the third time that greys had won both Guineas.

Ever Ready Derby
Epsom, Jun 5, 1 mile 4f

1	GENEROUS	Alan Munro	9-1
2	Marju	Willie Carson	14-1
3	Star of Gdansk	Christy Roche	14-1
4	Hector Protector	Freddy Head	6-1
5	Hundra	Bruce Raymond	66-1
6	Corrupt	Cash Asmussen	4-1jf
7	Hokusai	Lester Piggott	25-1
8	Hailsham	Steve Cauthen	28-1
9	Toulon	Pat Eddery	4-1jf
10	Mystiko	Michael Roberts	5-1

11	Environment Friend	George Duffield	11-1
12	Arokat	Paul Eddery	250-1
13	Mujaazif	Walter Swinburn	33-1

Trainer: Paul Cole, Whatcombe
Owner: Fahd Salman
Time: 2m 34.00s
Distance: 5 lengths
Generous was the fifth Derby winner out of the last six to be drawn in stall 10

Gold Seal Oaks
Epsom, Jun 8, 1 mile 4f

1	JET SKI LADY	Christy Roche	50-1
2	Shamshir	Frankie Dettori	6-1
3	Shadayid	Willie Carson	Evens f
4	Jaffa Line	Michael Roberts	14-1
5	Magnificent Star	Tony Cruz	16-1
6	Dartrey	Steve Cauthen	7-1
7	Ausherra	Alan Munro	12-1
8	Peplum	Pat Eddery	12-1
9	Fragrant Hill	Ray Cochrane	20-1

Trainer: Jim Bolger, Ireland
Owner: Maktoum Al-Maktoum
Time: 2m 37.30s
Distance: 10 lengths
Jet Ski Lady won at the longest price ever, equalled only by Vespa in 1833. The winning margin has been beaten only once in the race (1983) and equalled twice (1868 and 1963). It was the fifth year running a member of the Maktoum family has owned the winner.

Coalite St Leger
Doncaster, Sep 14, 1 mile 6f 127yd

1	TOULON	Pat Eddery	5-2f
2	Saddlers' Hall	John Reid	13-2
3	Micheletti	Lester Piggott	6-1
4	Luchiroverte	Michael Roberts	12-1
5	Fly Away Soon	Tommy Quinn	7-1
6	Corrupt	Frankie Dettori	13-2
7	Jendali	Tony Cruz	15-1
8	Arcadian Heights	Walter Swinburn	12-1
9	Libk	Richard Hills	25-1
10	Jahafil	Willie Carson	11-1

Trainer: André Fabre, France
Owner: Khalid Abdulla
Time: 3m 03.12s
Distance: 1½ lengths

PRIX DE L'ARC DE TRIOMPHE
Longchamp, Oct 6, 2400 metres

1 Suave Dancer	Cash Asmussen	37-10
2 Magic Night	Alain Badel	102-10
3 Pistolet Bleu	Dominic Boeuf	68-10

Trainer: John Hammond, France

SUMMERTIME BLUES

❝ Indifference, together with concrete dust, was in the air...The Derby has become a soulless experience.❞
Michael Calvin, Daily Telegraph

"The empty balconies resembled a rain-swept Spanish time-share complex in December."
William Cash, The Spectator

"Stuff your fairground, Gypsy Rose and whatever; give us a good view and decent toilets."
Letter to The Guardian from Frank Morris of Brighton

"That's my business."
Alan Munro, Derby-winning jockey, repeatedly during victory press conference

"...If charm were weight he could ride lighter than the youngest entrant in a Pony Club gymkhana."
Hugh McIlvanney, The Observer

"It's probably good that I know I gave the impression of behaving like a spoilt little brat...Maybe I can have a look at myself and change it."
Munro

"I have seen every King George VI and Queen Elizabeth Stakes since Supreme Court won the initial running (1951)...In all those years there has been nothing to equal the acceleration unleashed when Alan Munro set sail for home two furlongs out."
Richard Baerlein, The Guardian, on Generous's win

"Is it possible to back winners when you are wearing the sort of clothes we are required to wear on Ladies Day?...When the shoes must be kept shiny, top hat requires scrutiny in passing mirrors to ensure straightness AND you have to tweak the Hermes neckwear a bit and shoot your cuff, it is just too easy to miss the fact that a horse needs a left-hand track, faster ground and longer distance."
Sir Clement Freud, Sporting Life

"Will you two gentlemen please put on your hats. Gentlemen in morning suits are supposed to wear hats. We have had some complaints."
Steward at Ascot to reporters

"All right, all right, all right. I thought everyone's supposed to be broke. ❞❞
Harassed barmaid in Champagne Bar at Ascot

IRISH CLASSICS

Airlie/Coolmore 2000 Guineas
The Curragh, May 18, 1 mile

1 Fourstars Allstar	Mike Smith	9-1
2 Star of Gdansk	Christy Roche	16-1
3 Lycius	Steve Cauthen	Evens f

Trainer: Leo O'Brien, US
Fourstars Allstar was the first US-trained runner in an Irish Classic; his trainer, Leo O'Brien was born in Ireland.

Goff's 1000 Guineas
The Curragh, May 25, 1 mile

1 Kooyonga	Warren O'Connor	4-1
2 Julie La Rousse	John Murtagh	16-1
3 Umniyatee	Willie Carson	6-1

Trainer: Michael Kauntze, Ireland

Budweiser Derby
The Curragh, Jun 30, 1 mile 4f

1 Generous	Alan Munro	Evens f
2 Suave Dancer	Walter Swinburn	9-4
3 Star of Gdansk	Christy Roche	12-1

Trainer: Paul Cole, Whatcombe

Kildangan Stud Oaks
The Curragh, Jul 13, 1 mile 4f

1 Possessive Dancer	Steve Cauthen	8-1
2 Jet Ski Lady	Christy Roche	7-4f
3 Eileen Jenny	John Murtagh	12-1

Trainer: Alex Scott, Newmarket

Jefferson Smurfit Memorial St Leger
The Curragh, Sep 21, 1mile 6f

1 Turgeon	Tony Cruz	3-1
2 Patricia	Steve Cauthen	15-8f
3 Zafodola	John Murtagh	9-1

Trainer: Jonathan Pease, France

FRENCH CLASSICS

Poule d'Essai des Poulains (2000 Guineas)
Longchamp, May 5, 1600 metres

1 Hector Protector	Freddy Head
2 Acteur Francais	Alain Lequeux
3 Sapieha	Walter Swinburn

Trainer: François Boutin, France

Poule d'Essai des Pouliches (1000 Guineas)
Longchamp, May 12, 1600 metres

1 Danseuse du Soir	Dominic Boeuf
2 Sha Tha	Steve Cauthen
3 Caerlina	Lester Piggott

Trainer: E Lellouche, France

Prix du Jockey Club Lancia (Derby)
Chantilly, Jun 2, 2400 metres

1 Suave Dancer	Cash Asmussen
2 Subotica	Thierry Jarnet
3 Cudas	Freddy Head

Trainer: John Hammond, France
Hammond, a 30-year-old Englishman, had never trained the winner of a Group One race before. Suave Dancer started at 1-5 on the pari-mutuel.

Prix de Diane Hermes (Oaks)
Chantilly, Jun 9, 2400 metres

1 Caerlina	Eric Legrix
2 Magic Night	Alain Badel
3 Louve Romaine	Dominic Boeuf

Trainer: Jean de Roualle, France

US TRIPLE CROWN
Kentucky Derby
Churchill Downs, May 4, 1 mile 2f
1 Strike the Gold   Chris Antley
2 Best Pal   Gary Stevens
3 Mane Minister   Alex Solis
Trainer: Nick Zito

Preakness Stakes
Pimlico, Maryland, May 18, 1mile 110y
1 Hansel   Jerry Bailey
2 Corporate Report   Pat Day
3 Mane Minister   Alex Solis
Trainer: Frankie Brothers

Belmont Stakes
Belmont Park, New York, Jun 8, 1mile 4f
1 Hansel   Jerry Bailey
2 Strike the Gold   Chris Antley
3 Mane Minister   Alex Solis
Trainer: Frankie Brothers

THE BIG HANDICAPS

Venue/Date/Distance	*Winner*	*Trainer*	*Jockey*	*Price*
Doncaster, Mar 23, 1 mile 110y				
William Hill LINCOLN HANDICAP	AMENABLE	David Barron	Alex Greaves	22-1
Kempton Park, May 6, 1 mile				
JUBILEE HANDICAP STAKES	ST NINIAN	Peter Easterby	Lester Piggott	9-4f
Chester, May 8, 2 miles 2f 97yds				
Ladbroke CHESTER CUP	STAR PLAYER	John Baker	Frankie Dettori	9-2
Royal Ascot, Jun 19, 1 mile				
ROYAL HUNT CUP	EUROLINK THE LAD	John Dunlop	John Reid	25-1
Royal Ascot, Jun 21, 6f				
WOKINGHAM STAKES	AMIGO MENOR	David Murray-Smith	Colin Rutter	14-1
Newcastle, Jun 29, 2 miles 19yds				
Newcastle Brown Ale NORTHUMBERLAND PLATE	TAMARPOUR	Martin Pipe	Ernie Johnson	10-1
York, Jul 13, 1 mile 2f 85yds				
John Smith's MAGNET CUP	HALKOPOUS	Mark Tompkins	Francis Norton	7-2jf
Goodwood, Jul 30, 6f				
William Hill STEWARDS CUP	NOTELY	Richard Hannon	Richard Perham	14-1
Goodwood, Aug 1, 1 mile				
Schweppes GOLDEN MILE	SKY CLOUD	Reg Akehurst	Tommy Quinn	20-1
Ripon, Aug 18, 6f				
Tote GREAT ST WILFRED HANDICAP	PREMIER TOUCH	David Barron	Alex Greaves	8-1
York, Aug 21, 1mile 5f 194yds				
Tote EBOR HANDICAP	DEPOSKI	Michael Stoute	Francis Norton	12-1
Ayr, Sep 20, 6f				
Ladbroke AYR GOLD CUP	SARCITA	David Elsworth	Brett Doyle	14-1
Ascot, Sep 28, 1 mile 4f				
Krug HANDICAP STAKES	TIDEMARK	Luca Cumani	Frankie Dettori	10-1
Newmarket, Oct 5, 1 mile 1f				
William Hill CAMBRIDGESHIRE	MELLOTTIE	Mary Reveley	John Lowe	10-1

TWO-YEAR-OLD RACES

Venue/Date/Distance	*Winner*	*Trainer*	*Jockey*	*Price*
Royal Ascot, Jun 18, 6f				
COVENTRY STAKES	DILUM	Paul Cole	Alan Munro	11-10f
Royal Ascot, Jun 19, 5f (fillies)				
QUEEN MARY STAKES	MARLING	Geoff Wragg	Gary Carter	11-4f
Royal Ascot, Jun 20, 5f				
NORFOLK STAKES	MAGIC RING	Paul Cole	Alan Munro	7-4f
Salisbury, Jun 27, 6f				
Veuve Cliquot CHAMPAGNE STAKES	CAMBRIAN HILLS	Peter Chapple-Hyam	Paul Eddery	2-1
Newmarket, Jul 9, 6f (fillies)				
Hillsdown CHERRY HINTON STAKES	MUSICALE	Henry Cecil	Steve Cauthen	9-2
Newmarket, Jul 10, 6f				
Anglia Television JULY STAKES	SHOWBROOK	Richard Hannon	Bruce Raymond	13-8jf
Goodwood, Jul 31, 6f				
Scottish Equitable RICHMOND STAKES	DILUM	Paul Cole	Alan Munro	2-7f
York, Aug 21, 6f				
Scottish Equitable GIMCRACK STAKES	RIVER FALLS	Richard Hannon	Bruce Raymond	9-4
York, Aug 22, 6f				
LOWTHER STAKES	CULTURE VULTURE	Paul Cole	Tommy Quinn	85-40f
Doncaster, Sep 11, 1 mile				
May Hill STAKES	MIDNIGHT AIR	Henry Cecil	Pat Eddery	3-1
Doncaster, Sep 13, 7f				
Laurent-Perrier CHAMPAGNE STAKES	RODRIGO DE TRIANO	Peter Chapple-Hyam	Willie Carson	11-8f
Doncaster, Sep 14, 5f				
FLYING CHILDERS STAKES	PARIS HOUSE	Jack Berry	John Carroll	4-6f
Ascot, Sep 28, 1 mile				
ROYAL LODGE William Hill STAKES	MADE OF GOLD	Mohammed Moubarak	Tony Cruz	4-1
Ascot, Sep 28, 1 mile				
Brent Walker FILLIES MILE	CULTURE VULTURE	Paul Cole	Tommy Quinn	5-2f

THREE-YEAR-OLD RACES

Venue/Date/Distance	Winner	Trainer	Jockey	Price
Newmarket, Apr 16, 7f				
Shadwell Stud NELL GWYN STAKES	CRYSTAL GAZING	Luca Cumani	Frankie Dettori	6-4f
Newmarket, Apr 17, 7f				
Ladbroke EUROPEAN FREE HANDICAP	MYSTIKO	Clive Brittain	Michael Roberts	11-1
Newmarket, Apr 18, 1 mile				
Charles Heidsieck CRAVEN STAKES	MARJU	John Dunlop	Willie Carson	11-2
Newbury, Apr 19, 7f 60yds				
Gainsborough FRED DARLING STAKES	SHADAYID	John Dunlop	Willie Carson	8-11f
Newbury, Apr 20, f				
S & F GREENHAM STAKES	BOG TROTTER	Willie Haggas	Lester Piggott	4-11f
Sandown Park , Apr 27, 1 mile 2f				
Thresher CLASSIC TRIAL	HAILSHAM	Clive Brittain	Michael Roberts	3-1
Chester, May 7, 1 mile 4f 65yds				
Dallam CHESTER VASE	TOULON	André Fabre	Pat Eddery	9-4
Lingfield Park, May 11, 1 mile 3f 106yds				
Maxim's Club DERBY TRIAL STAKES	CORRUPT	Neville Callaghan	Cash Asmussen	9-2
Lingfield Park, May 11, 1 mile 3f 106yds				
Marley Roof Tile OAKS TRIAL STAKES	AUSHERRA	Paul Cole	Alan Munro	5-1
York, May 14, 1 mile 2f 110yds				
Tattersalls MUSIDORA STAKES	GUSSY MARLOWE	Clive Brittain	Michael Roberts	7-1
York, May 15, 1 mile 2f 110yds				
William Hill DANTE STAKES	ENVIRONMENT FRIEND	James Fanshawe	George Duffield	20-1
Goodwood, May 21, 1 mile 2f				
A R Dennis PREDOMINATE STAKES	MAN FROM ELDORADO	Guy Harwood	Ray Cochrane	10-1
York, Jun 15, 6f				
William Hill GOLDEN SPURS TROPHY	SHEIKH ALBADOU	Alex Scott	Pat Eddery	9-4f
Royal Ascot, Jun 18, 1 mile 4f				
KING EDWARD VII STAKES	SADDLERS' HALL	Michael Stoute	Lester Piggott	7-1
Royal Ascot, Jun 18, 1 mile				

AT THE STABLE DOOR

"Horses are not machines. They're flesh and blood and muscle and they have minds like everybody else has, and the intensity of it all can blow 'em, blow the minds, certainly blow the bodies."
Ginger McCain, trainer, on Martin Pipe's methods

"The welfare and the care of our horses is always uppermost in our minds."
Martin Pipe

"I run what I believe, and my vets believe, is the best, the most professional yard in the country. I get results and some people in the game don't like that. I've taken the guesswork out of training."
Pipe

"What drives our nation to hit out at its great achievers?"
Carl Bain, one of Pipe's owners

"All this hard ground has thrown the National Hunt game in the direction of greedy bastards who exploit their horses. People who do it for different reasons have been conspicuously less successful. So you have less runners, less winners, less promotion. And everyone calls you a prat and says you can't train racehorses."
Jim Old, trainer

"I have no burn-out in me. I get up at 3.30 a.m. every day and, no matter where I am, I'm down at the track. In 14 years, I've missed only one day at the barn. The closest thing I come to a vacation is the Keeneland Sales but that's hard work, extremely hard, because we look at every horse."
D Wayne Lukas, US trainer

"I'll sell a dentist a yearling and train it for nothing if he can fix my teeth. I've got five sets of dentures and none of them is any good."
Mick Easterby, trainer

"No way I'm leaving this island...I've waited 25 years for a bunch of two-year-olds like this lot."
Bahrain-based trainer, before the Gulf War

"I'm a decent buyer of yearlings - the best I know. But when you are not training for the Arab gentlemen, you are an outsider. Perhaps they should be paying us to provide the opposition."
Paul Kelleway, trainer

"I get the feeling I have done the right thing when I hear other trainers. All of them say 'you must feel a better man' and I have yet to meet one who has said 'don't you wish you were still training?' That suggests to me they are all struggling."
Kim Brassey, insurance company employee, former trainer

"The Government says racing should help itself. I'm just helping myself."
Barney Curley, trainer and gambler, after a late switch of jockey helped him land a coup at Sandown

ST JAMES'S PALACE STAKES	MARJU	John Dunlop	Willie Carson	7-4f
Royal Ascot, Jun 19, 1 mile				
CORONATION STAKES	KOOYONGA	Michael Kauntze	Warren O'Connor	3-1
Royal Ascot, Jun 19, 7f				
JERSEY STAKES	SATIN FLOWER	John Gosden	Steve Cauthen	12-1
Royal Ascot, Jun 19, 2 miles 45yds				
QUEEN'S VASE	JENDALI	Henry Cecil	Steve Cauthen	15-2
Royal Ascot, Jun 20, 1 mile 4f				
RIBBLESDALE STAKES	THIRD WATCH	John Dunlop	John Reid	20-1
Haydock Park, Jul 6, 1 mile 4f				
LANCASHIRE OAKS	PATRICIA	Henry Cecil	Gary Carter	11-1
Goodwood, Jul 30, 1 mile 4f				
GORDON STAKES	STYLISH SENOR	James Fanshawe	George Duffield	11-4
Goodwood, Aug 2, 1mile 2f				
Leslie & Godwin SPITFIRE HANDICAP	GREEN DANUBE	Lord Huntingdon	Alan Munro	25-1
York, Aug 20, 1 mile 3f 195yds				
GRAT VOLTIGEUR STAKES	CORRUPT	Neville Callaghan	Pat Eddery	5-1
York, Aug 21, 1 mile 3f 195yds				
Aston Upthorpe YORKSHIRE OAKS	MAGNIFICENT STAR	Mohammed Moubarak	Tony Cruz	16-1
Doncaster, Sep 11, 1 mile 6f 132yds				
AF Budge PARK HILL STAKES	PATRICIA	Henry Cecil	Steve Cauthen	11-8f

OTHER MAJOR BRITISH RACES

Venue/Date/Distance	*Winner*	*Trainer*	*Jockey*	*Price*
Newmarket, Apr 17, 1 mile 1f				
Earl of Sefton EBF STAKES	TERMON	Clive Brittain	Michael Roberts	7-2f
Newbury, Apr 20, 1 mile 4f				
Lane End JOHN PORTER EBF STAKES	ROCK HOPPER	Michael Stoute	Pat Eddery	3-1
Sandown Park, Apr 26, 1 mile				
Trusthouse Forte MILE	IN THE GROOVE	David Elsworth	Steve Cauthen	15-8
Newmarket, May 3, 1 mile 4f				
General Accident JOCKEY CLUB STAKES	ROCK HOPPER	Michael Stoute	Pat Eddery	8-11f
Newmarket, May 4, 5f				
PALACE HOUSE STAKES	ELBIO	Peter Makin	Steve Cauthen	9-4f
Chester, May 9, 1 mile 5f 88yds				
ORMONDE STAKES	PER QUOD	Ben Hanbury	Bruce Raymond	5-1
York, May 16, 1 mile 6f				
Polo Mints YORKSHIRE CUP	ARZANNI	Luca Cumani	Frankie Dettori	5-1
Newbury, May 17, 1 mile				
Juddmonte LOCKINGE STAKES	POLAR FALCON	John Hammond	Lester Piggott	3-1
Sandown Park, May 27, 2 miles				
Cementone Beaver HENRY II EBF STAKES	TOP OF THE WORLD	Clive Brittain	Michael Roberts	33-1
Epsom, Jun 6, 1 mile 4f				
Hanson CORONATION CUP	IN THE GROOVE	David Elsworth	Steve Cauthen	7-2
Royal Ascot, Jun 18, 1 mile 2f				
PRINCE OF WALES'S STAKES	STAGECRAFT	Michael Stoute	Willie Carson	6-4f
Royal Ascot, Jun 20, 2 miles 4f				
GOLD CUP	INDIAN QUEEN	Lord Huntingdon	Walter Swinburn	25-1

Indian Queen was the first female to win the Gold Cup since 1958 and the first since 1894 to do so while pregnant

Royal Ascot, Jun 20, 6f				
CORK & ORRERY STAKES	POLISH PATRIOT	Guy Harwood	Ray Cochrane	5-1jf
Royal Ascot, Jun 21, 5f				
KING'S STAND STAKES	ELBIO	Peter Makin	Steve Cauthen	13-8f
Royal Ascot, Jun 21, 1 mile 4f				
HARDWICKE STAKES	ROCK HOPPER	Michael Stoute	Pat Eddery	5-6f
Sandown Park, Jul 6, 1 mile 2f				
Coral ECLIPSE STAKES	ENVIRONMENT FRIEND	James Fanshawe	George Duffield	28-1
Newmarket, Jul 9, 1 mile 4f				

TOP BETTING RACES
Ladbrokes' list of the races which attracted the highest turnover in 1990

1	**Grand National (Aintree)**
2	**Derby (Epsom)**
3	**Cheltenham Gold Cup**
4	**2,000 Guineas (Newmarket)**
5	**King George and Queen Elizabeth (Ascot)**
6	**Champion Hurdle (Cheltenham)**
7	**Lincoln Handicap (Doncaster)**
8	**1,000 Guineas (Newmarket)**
9	**Triumph Hurdle (Cheltenham)**
10	**Oaks (Epsom)**

Source: Ladbrokes/Racing Post

PRINCESS OF WALES'S STAKES	ROCK HOPPER	Michael Stoute	Pat Eddery	4-6f
Newmarket, Jul 10, 1 mile				
CHILD STAKES	ONLY YOURS	Richard Hannon	Michael Roberts	10-1
Newmarket, Jul 11, 6f				
Carroll Foundation JULY CUP	POLISH PATRIOT	Guy Harwood	Ray Cochrane	6-1
Chepstow, Jul 11, 1 mile 4f 23yds				
Welsh Brewers PREMIER STAKES	KIMBERS	Charlie Nelson	John Reid	16-1
Ascot, Jul 27, 1mile 4f				
KING GEORGE VI & QUEEN ELIZABETH DIAMOND STAKES	GENEROUS	Paul Cole	Alan Munro	4-6f
Goodwood, Jul 31, 1 mile				
SUSSEX STAKES	SECOND SET	Luca Cumani	Frankie Dettori	5-1
Goodwood, Aug 1, 2 miles				
Dickins & Jones GOODWOOD CUP	FURTHER FLIGHT	Barry Hills	Michael Hills	9-2
Goodwood, Aug 3, 1 mile 2f				
Vodafone NASSAU STAKES	RUBY TIGER	Paul Cole	Tommy Quinn	11-4
Newbury, Aug 16, 7f 64yds				
Forte HUNGERFORD STAKES	ONLY YOURS	Richard Hannon	Michael Roberts	11-2
Newbury, Aug 17, 1 mile 5f 61yds				
Ibn Bey GEOFFREY FREER STAKES	DRUM TAPS	Lord Huntingdon	Frankie Dettori	15-2
York, Aug 20, 1 mile 2f 85yds				
Juddmonte INTERNATIONAL STAKES	TERIMON	Clive Brittain	Michael Roberts	16-1
York, Aug 22, 5f				
Keeneland NUNTHORPE STAKES	SHEIKH ALBADOU	Alex Scott	Pat Eddery	6-1
Haydock, Sep 7, 6f				
Ladbroke SPRINT CUP	POLAR FALCON	John Hammond	Cash Asmussen	13-2
Kempton Park, Sep 7, 1 mile 3f 30yds				
Bonus Print SEPTEMBER STAKES	YOUNG BUSTER	Geoff Wragg	Walter Swinburn	11-4
Doncaster, Sep 12, 2 miles 2f				
DONCASTER CUP	GREAT MARQUESS	Henry Cecil	Pat Eddery	5-1
Ascot, Sep 28, 1 mile				
QUEEN ELIZABETH II STAKES	SELKIRK	Ian Balding	Ray Cochrane	10-1
Ascot, Sep 28, 6f				
Krug DIADEM STAKES	SHALFORD	Richard Hannon	Tony Cruz	4-1

OVERSEAS RACES

Venue/Date/Distance	*Winner*	*Trainer*	*Jockey*	*Price*
Maisons-Laffitte, Jul 21, 5f 110yds				
PRIX ROBERT PAPIN	ARAZI	François Boutin	Gerard Mosse	4-5f
Leopardstown, Aug 11, 6f				
Heinz 57 PHOENIX STAKES	BRADAWN BREEVER	Kevin Prendergast	Rod Griffiths	14-1
Deauville, Aug 18, 6f				
PRIX MORNAY	ARAZI	François Boutin	Gerard Mosse	4-6f
Arlington, Illinois, Sep 1, 1 mile 2f				
ARLINGTON MILLION	TIGHT SPOT	Ron McAnally	Laffit Pincay	18-10f
Longchamp, Sep 8, 1 mile				
PRIX DU MOULIN	PRIOLO	François Boutin	Gerard Mosse	100-30
Longchamp, Sep 8, 7f				
PRIX DE LA SALAMANDRE	ARAZI	François Boutin	Gerard Mosse	1-5f
Longchamp, Sep 15, 1 mile 4f				
PRIX VERMEILLE	MAGIC NIGHT	Philippe Demercastel	Alain Badel	3-1
Longchamp, Oct 6, 5f				
PRIX DE L'ABBAYE	KEEN HUNTER	John Gosden	Steve Cauthen	115-10

1990-91

NATIONAL HUNT RACING

Smurfit Champion Hurdle
Cheltenham, Mar 12, 2 miles

1 MORLEY STREET	Jimmy Frost	4-1f
2 Nomadic Way	Richard Dunwoody	9-1
3 Ruling	Peter Niven	50-1
4 Mole Board	Carl Llewellyn	66-1
5 Voyage Sans Retour	John Lower	33-1
6 Bradbury Star	Eamonn Murphy	66-1
7 Wonder Man	Ben de Haan	50-1
8 Beech Road	Richard Guest	8-1
9 Royal Derbi	Tommy Carmody	66-1
10 Deep Sensation	Declan Murphy	50-1
11 Jinxy Jack	Neale Doughty	16-1
12 Athy Spirit	Tom Taaffe	10-1
13 Rare Holiday	Brendan Sheridan	50-1
14 Vayrua	Mark Perrett	33-1
15 Philosophos	Nigel Coleman	250-1
16 Riverhead	Paul Holley	50-1
17 Danny Harrold	Mark Pitman	16-1
18 Vestris Abu	Charlie Swan	33-1
19 Major Inquiry	Graham Bradley	66-1
20 Sondrio	Peter Scudamore	10-1
21 The Illiad	Pat McWilliams	11-2
f Black Humour	Jamie Osborne	20-1
ur Fidway	Steve Smith Eccles	15-2
pu Sybillin	Mark Dwyer	20-1

Trainer: Toby Balding, Weyhill
Owner: Michael Jackson
Distance: 1½ lengths
Time: 3m 54.6s

Tote Cheltenham Gold Cup

Cheltenham, Mar 14, 3 miles 2f

1 GARRISON SAVANNAH	Mark Pitman	16-1
2 The Fellow	Adam Kondrat	28-1
3 Desert Orchid	Richard Dunwoody	4-1
4 Cool Ground	Luke Harvey	7-1
5 Kildimo	Robert Stronge	66-1
6 Nick the Brief	Robbie Supple	12-1
7 Celtic Shot	Peter Scudamore	5-2f
8 Yahoo	Norman Williamson	100-1
f Norton's Coin	Graham McCourt	16-1
pu Arctic Call	Jamie Osborne	10-1
pu Carrick Hill Lad	Mark Dwyer	11-1
pu Twin Oaks	Neale Doughty	11-1
pu Party Politics	Andy Adams	33-1
pu Martin d'Or	Jean-Noel Joly	250-1

Trainer: Jenny Pitman, Upper Lambourn
Owner: Autofour Engineering
Distance: Short head
Time: 6m 49.8s
*Closest finish in race since 1973 when The Dikler beat
Pendil, also by a short head*

Seagram Grand National

Aintree, Apr 6, 4 miles 4f

1 SEAGRAM	Nigel Hawke	12-1
2 Garrison Savannah	Mark Pitman	7-1
3 Auntie Dot	Mark Dwyer	50-1
4 Over the Road	Robbie Supple	50-1
5 Bonanza Boy	Peter Scudamore	13-2f
6 Durham Edition	Chris Grant	25-1
7 Golden Minstrel	Tom Grantham	50-1
8 Old Applejack	Tim Reed	66-1
9 Leagaune	Mark Richards	200-1
10 Foyle Fisherman	Eamonn Murphy	40-1
11 Ballyhane	Declan Murphy	22-1

12 Harley	Ger Lyons	150-1
13 Mick's Star	Charlie Swan	100-1
14 Ten of Spades	John White	15-1
15 Forest Ranger	David Tegg	100-1
16 Yahoo	Norman Williamson	33-1
17 Golden Freeze	Michael Bowlby	40-1

Non-finishers

f 1st Docklands Express	Anthony Tory	20-1
f 2nd Run and Skip	Derek Byrne	66-1
pu 5th Envopak Token	Mark Perrett	28-1
f 7th Southernair	José Simo	100-1
f 12th Joint Sovereignty	Liam O'Hara	100-1
f 15th Crammer	Mr John Durkan	28-1
pu 17th Fraze	Vaclav Chaloupka	100-1
pu 18th Abba Lad	Dean Gallagher	250-1
pu 19th Master Bob	Jamie Osborne	20-1
ur 19th The Langholm Dyer	Graham McCourt	100-1
r 19th Team Challenge	Ben de Haan	50-1
f 20th Rinus	Neale Doughty	7-1
pu 21st Solidasarock	Graham Bradley	50-1
pu 21st Bumbles Folly	Jimmy Frost	150-1
pu 21st Mister Christian	Simon Earle	100-1
pu 22nd Hotplate	Peter Niven	80-1
ur 22nd Blue Dart	Hywel Davies	80-1
pu 22nd Mister Frisk	Marcus Armytage	25-1
ur 23rd New Halen	Seamus O'Neill	50-1
pu 24th Oklaoma II	Roland Kleparski	66-1
pu 25th Huntworth	Mr Alan Walter	50-1
pu 25th Bigsun	Richard Dunwoody	9-1
pu 27th General Chandos	Mr John Bradburne	150-1

*f= fell; pu = pulled up; ur = unseated rider;
r = refused*
Trainer: David Barons, Kingsbridge
Owner: Sir Eric Parker
Distance: 5 lengths
Time: 9m 29.9s

OTHER BIG JUMP RACES

STEEPLECHASES

Venue/Date/Distance	Winner	Trainer	Jockey	Price
Cheltenham, Nov 10, 2 miles 4f				
Mackeson GOLD CUP	MULTUM IN PARVO	John Edwards	Norman Williamson	12-1
Newbury, Nov 24, 3 miles 2f 82yds				
Hennessy Cognac GOLD CUP	ARCTIC CALL	Oliver Sherwood	Jamie Osborne	5-1
Kempton Park, Dec 26, 3 miles				
KING GEORGE VI Rank CHASE	DESERT ORCHID	David Elsworth	Richard Dunwoody	9-4f
Desert Orchid became the first horse to win the race four times				
Sandown Park, Jan 5, 3 miles 5f 18yds				
ANTHONY MILDMAY HANDICAP CHASE	COOL GROUND	Reg Akehurst	Luke Harvey	6-4
Doncaster, Jan 26, 3 miles 122yds				
William Hill GOLDEN SPURS HANDICAP	DALKEY SOUND	Mary Reveley	Peter Niven	9-1
Kempton Park, Feb 23, 3 miles				
Racing Post HANDICAP CHASE	DOCKLANDS EXPRESS	Kim Bailey	Anthony Tory	7-2
Haydock Park, Mar 2, 3 miles 4f				
Grenall's GOLD CUP HANDICAP	TWIN OAKS	Gordon Richards	Neale Doughty	7-4f
Cheltenham, Mar 12, 2 miles				
Waterford Crystal ARKLE CHALLENGE TROPHY CHASE	REMITTANCE MAN	Nicky Henderson	Richard Dunwoody	85-40
Cheltenham, Mar 13, 3 miles				
Sun Alliance CHASE	ROLLING BALL	Martin Pipe	Peter Scudamore	7-2f
Cheltenham, Mar 13, 2 miles				
QUEEN MOTHER CHAMPION CHASE	KATABATIC	Andy Turnell	Simon McNeil	9-1
Fairyhouse, Apr 1, 3 miles				
Jameson IRISH GRAND NATIONAL	OMERTA	Martin Pipe	Mr Adrian Maguire	6-1f
Chepstow, Apr 2, 2 miles				
WELSH NOVICE CHAMPIONSHIP CHASE	HIGH KNOWL	Martin Pipe	Peter Scudamore	11-8
Aintree, Apr 4, 3 miles 1f				
Martell CUP CHASE	AQUILIFER	Martin Pipe	Richard Dunwoody	11-2
Ayr, Apr 20, 4 miles 120yds				
William Hill SCOTTISH NATIONAL	KILLONE ABBEY	Arthur Stephenson	Mr Kenny Johnson	40-1
Sandown Park, Apr 27, 3 miles 5f 18yds				
Whitbread GOLD CUP	DOCKLANDS EXPRESS	Kim Bailey	Anthony Tory	4-1jf

> **"A woman jockey could jump the race backwards and still survive. In the old days it was tough but now they've become powder-puff fences."**
> *Josh Gifford, trainer, on the Grand National*

"I've rarely heard so much nonsense spoken. Since 1961 there have been no modifications to the fences at Aintree."
John Parrett, clerk of the course

"The jump jockeys aren't wild any more. It's a very serious game now. It gets more like the Flat every day. I don't think it's a good thing and I think that's to do with the money involved."
Ron Hyett, jockey, on retiring

"Desert Orchid and I have a lot in common. We are both greys; vast sums of money are riding on our performance; the Opposition hopes we will fall at the first fence; and we are both carrying too much weight."
Norman Lamont, chancellor of the exchequer, in his Budget

"...It is also true to say both are overhyped, past their best and have no balls."
Letter to Racing Post *from CH Williams of London SW9*

"Only the Jockey Club could approve a list of prohibited substances for horses which includes hay and water...All they have done is name every system in a horse's constitution and declare that any substance that acts on it is prohibited - whether it is supposed to be acting on the nervous system, the cardiovascular system, the respiratory system etc etc. About the only system they have not named is the one that involves the doubling the stakes on losing favourites."
Monty Court, Sporting Life

"Don't bore me with Wordsworth's ridiculous daffodils. The sublime spectacle of encroaching spring is Cheltenham Racecourse and a host of golden bookies swaying between Red Alert and Blue Funk."
Ian Wooldridge, Daily Mail

"Hector Protector must be one of the best post-war milers."
Freddie Head, after his horse won at Deauville

"...I trust he is referring to the Gulf War."
Letter to Racing Post *from Michael Doughty of Hillingdon*

"I approach betting on horses the same way I approach a military campaign. I do a great deal of studying, I look at all the horses in the race, analyse the post positions, consider the weather, gather all the empirical evidence, then I turn to my wife Brenda and ask 'Who should we bet on?' She usually says she likes one horse's name and that's who we bet on."
General Norman Schwarzkopf

HURDLES

Venue/Date/Distance	Winner	Trainer	Jockey	Price
Kempton Park, Jan 19, 2 miles Bic Razor LANZAROTE HANDICAP	STAR SEASON	Richard Holder	Nick Mann	11-2
Wincanton, Feb 21, 2 miles KINGWELL HURDLE	WELSH BARD	Charlie Brooks	Peter Scudamore	11-1
Sandown Park, Mar 9, 2 miles IMPERIAL CUP HANDICAP HURDLE	PRECIOUS BOY	Mike O'Neill	Lorcan Wyer	16-1
Cheltenham, Mar 12, 3 miles 1f Bonusprint STAYERS' HURDLE	KING'S CURATE	Stan Mellor	Mark Perrett	5-2f
Cheltenham, Mar 12, 2 miles Trafalgar House SUPREME NOVICES HURDLE	DESTRIERO	Andrew Geraghty	Pat McWilliams	6-1
Cheltenham, Mar 13, 2 miles 4f Sun Alliance NOVICE HURDLE	CRYSTAL SPIRIT	Ian Balding	Jimmy Frost	2-1f
Cheltenham, Mar 14, 2 miles Daily Express TRIUMPH HURDLE	OH SO RISKY	David Elsworth	Paul Holley	14-1
Aintree, Apr 6, 2 miles 4f Sandeman AINTREE HURDLE	MORLEY STREET	Toby Balding	Jimmy Frost	11-8f
Haydock Park, May 6, 2 miles Swinton Insurance TROPHY HANDICAP	WINNIE THE WITCH	Ken Bridgwater	David Bridgwater	8-1

NATIONAL HUNT TABLES 1990-91

Jockeys	Mounts	Wins
1 Peter Scudamore	423	141
2 Richard Dunwoody	646	127
3 Neale Doughty	349	96
4 Peter Niven	423	86
5 Graham McCourt	435	83
6 Mark Dwyer	380	81

Trainers	Wins	Prizemoney £
1 Martin Pipe	230	1,203,014
2 Gordon Richards	118	524,591
3 Arthur Stephenson	83	458,927
4 Jenny Pitman	43	437,959
5 Toby Balding	48	379,035
6 Oliver Sherwood	56	373,375

TOP 10 SEASONS IN NATIONAL HUNT RACING

	Jockeys				*Trainers*	
221	Peter Scudamore	1988-89		230	Martin Pipe	1990-91
170	Peter Scudamore	1989-90		224	Martin Pipe	1989-90
149	Jonjo O'Neill	1977-78		208	Martin Pipe	1988-89
141	Peter Scudamore	1990-91		129	Martin Pipe	1987-88
132	Peter Scudamore	1987-88		120	Michael Dickinson	1982-83
131	John Francome	1983-84		118	Gordon Richards	1990-91
127	Richard Dunwoody	1990-91		116	Arthur Stephenson	1989-90
125	Ron Barry	1972-73		114	Arthur Stephenson	1969-70
124	Peter Scudamore	1986-87		113	Arthur Stephenson	1971-72
122	Josh Gifford	1966-67		110	Arthur Stephenson	1972-73

1990

BREEDERS' CUP
Belmont Park, Oct 27

Sprint (6f)
1 Safely Kept   Craig Perret
2 Dayjur   Willie Carson
3 Black Tie Affair   Laffit Pincay

Juvenile Fillies (1m 110yd)
1 Meadow Star   Jose Santos
2 Private Treasure   Jerry Bailey
3 Dance Smartly   Sandy Hawley

Distaff (1m 1f)
1 Bayakoa   Laffit Pincay
2 Colonial Waters   Jose Santos
3 Valay Maid   Marco Castaneda

Mile
1 Royal Academy   Lester Piggott
2 Itsallgreektome   Corey Nakatani
3 Priolo   Cash Asmussen

Juvenile (1m 110yd)
1 Fly So Free   Jose Santos
2 Take Me Out   Mike Smith
3 Lost Mountain   Chris McCarron

Turf (1m 4f)
1 In The Wings   Gary Stevens
2 With Approval   Craig Perret
3 El Senor   Angel Cordero

Classic (1m 2f)
1 Unbridled   Pat Day
2 Ibn Bey   Tommy Quinn
3 Thirty Six Red   Mike Smith

MELBOURNE CUP
Flemington Park, Nov 6, 2 miles
1 Kingston Rule   Darren Beadman   7-1jf
2 The Phantom   Grant Cooksley   7-1jf
3 Mr. Brooker   Greg Childs   15-1
*Winner trained by Bart Cummings; it was his eighth
success in the race*

JAPAN CUP
Tokyo, Nov 25, 1 mile 4f
1 Better Loosen Up   Michael Clarke   52-10
2 Ode   Dominic Boeuf   14-1
3 Cacoethes   Ray Cochrane   63-10
*Winner trained by David Hayes of Australia who had been
training for only two months*

FINAL FLAT RACING STATISTICS 1990

Leading Jockeys	*Mounts*	*1st*	*2nd*	*3rd*
1 Pat Eddery	890	209	133	90
2 Willie Carson	906	187	13	103
3 Steve Cauthen	625	142	78	72
4 Frankie Dettori	699	141	83	73
5 Michael Roberts	858	127	114	117
6 Walter Swinburn	736	111	120	108
7 Ray Cochrane	825	109	100	98
8 Alan Munro	632	95	59	59
9 Tommy Quinn	632	86	90	80
10 Dean McKeown	765	84	92	66

Trainers	*Wins*	*Prizemoney (£)*
1 Henry Cecil	111	1,520,121
2 Luca Cumani	108	1,006,038
3 Michael Stoute	78	803,680
4 David Elsworth	41	780,889
5 Barry Hills	110	758,971

Owners	*Wins*	*Prizemoney (£)*
1 Hamdan Al-Maktoum	127	1,536,821
2 Sheikh Mohammed	176	1,498,207
3 Khalid Abdulla	61	690,997
4 B Cooper	3	459,117
5 Robert Sangster	41	347,755

WINNERS OF OTHER LEADING BRITISH RACES
Oct & Nov 1990

Race	Horse	Jockey	Price
Tattersalls CHEVELEY PARK STAKES	CAPRICCIOSA	John Reid	7-1
Tattersalls MIDDLE PARK STAKES	LYCIUS	Cash Asmussen	13-8f
Cheveley Park Stud SUN CHARIOT STAKES	KARTAJANA	Walter Swinburn	11-10f
William Hill CAMBRIDGESHIRE HANDICAP	RISEN MOON	Steve Cauthen	7-1f
JOCKEY CLUB CUP	GREAT MARQUESS	Frankie Dettori	5-1
Three Chimneys DEWHURST STAKES	GENEROUS	Tommy Quinn	50-1
Dubai CHAMPION STAKES	IN THE GROOVE	Steve Cauthen	9-2
Tote CESAREWITCH HANDICAP	TRAINGLOT	Willie Carson	13-2
Vodafone HORRIS HILL STAKES	SAPIEHA	Walter Swinburn	5-2f
ST SIMON STAKES	DOWN THE FLAG	Bruce Raymond	5-1
Racing Post TROPHY	PETER DAVIES	Steve Cauthen	3-1jf
William Hill NOVEMBER HANDICAP	AZAAM	Willie Carson	7-1

AWARDS

Jockeys' Association Awards
London, Mar 24
1990 Jockey of the Year: Pat Eddery
Flat Jockey of the Year: Pat Eddery
Jump Jockey of the Year: Richard Dunwoody
Lady Jockey of the Year: Alex Greaves
Apprentice of the Year: Jimmy Fortune
Conditional Jockey of the Year: Derek Byrne
Sports Person of the Year: Lester Piggott
Special Award: Paul Cook

NEVER MIND THE WEATHER...

All-weather race meetings were called off by:

Fog	**Southwell**	**Nov 14 1989**
Storm damage	**Lingfield**	**Jan 26 1990**
Waterlogging	**Southwell**	**Feb 8 1990**
Gales	**Southwell**	**Feb 27 1990**
Frost	**Southwell**	**Jan 14/16 1991**
Blocked roads	**Lingfield**	**Feb 7 1991**
Blocked roads	**Southwell**	**Feb 8 1991**

Source: *Racing Post*

CHAMPIONS

THE ENGLISH CLASSICS

	1000 Guineas	2000 Guineas	Derby	Oaks	St Leger
1776	-	-	-	-	Allabaculia
1777	-	-	-	-	Bourbon
1778	-	-	-	-	Hollandaise
1779	-	-	-	Bridget	Tommy
1780	-	-	Diomed	Tetoum	Ruler
1781	-	-	Young Eclipse	Faith	Serina
1782	-	-	Assassin	Ceres	Imperatrix
1783	-	-	Saltram	Maid of the Oaks	Phenomenon
1784	-	-	Sergeant	Stella	Omphale
1785	-	-	Aimwell	Trifle	Cowslip
1786	-	-	Noble	Yellow Filly	Paragon
1787	-	-	Sir Peter Teazle	Annette	Spadille
1788	-	-	Sir Thomas	Nightshade	Young Flora
1789	-	-	Skyscraper	Tag	Pewett
1790	-	-	Rhadamanthus	Hippolyta	Ambidexter
1791	-	-	Eager	Portia	Young Traveller
1792	-	-	John Bull	Volante	Tartar
1793	-	-	Waxy	Caelia	Ninety-Three
1794	-	-	Daedalus	Hermione	Beningbrough
1795	-	-	Spread Eagle	Platina	Hambletonian
1796	-	-	Didelot	Pasiot	Ambrosio
1797	-	-	(unnamed colt)	Nike	Lounger
1798	-	-	Sir Harry	Bellissima	Symmetry
1799	-	-	Archduke	Bellina	Cockfighter
1800	-	-	Champion	Ephemera	Champion
1801	-	-	Eleanor	Eleanor	Quiz
1802	-	-	Tyrant	Scotia	Orville
1803	-	-	Ditto	Theophania	Remembrancer
1804	-	-	Hannibal	Pelisse	Sancho
1805	-	-	Cardinal Beaufort	Meteora	Staveley
1806	-	-	Paris	Bronze	Fyldener
1807	-	-	Election	Briseis	Paulina

	1000 Guineas	2000 Guineas	Derby	Oaks	St Leger
1808	-	-	Pan	Morel	Petronius
1809	-	Wizard	Pope	Maid of Orleans	Ashton
1810	-	Hephestion	Whalebone	Oriana	Octavian
1811	-	Trophonius	Phantom	Sorcery	Soothsayer
1812	-	Cwrw	Octavius	Manuella	Otterington
1813	-	Smolensko	Smolensko	Music	Altisidora
1814	Charlotte	Olive	Blucher	Medora	William
1815	Unnamed filly	Tigris	Whisker	Minuet	Fihlo da Puta
1816	Rhoda	Nectar	Prince Leopold	Landscape	The Duchess
1817	Neva	Manfred	Azor	Neva	Ebor
1818	Corinne	Interpreter	Sam	Corinne	Reveller
1819	Catgut	Antar	Tiresias	Shoveler	Antonio
1820	Rowena	Pindarrie	Sailor	Caroline	St Patrick
1821	Zeal	Reginald	Gustavus	Augusta	Jack Spigot
1822	Whizgig	Pastille	Moses	Pastille	Theodore
1823	Zinc	Nicolo	Emilius	Zinc	Barefoot
1824	Cobweb	Schahriar	Cedric	Cobweb	Jerry
1825	Tontine	Enamel	Middleton	Wings	Memnon
1826	Problem	Devise	Lapdog	Lilias	Tarrare
1827	Arab	Turcoman	Mameluke	Gulnare	Matilda
1828	Zoe	Cadland	Cadland	Turquoise	The Colonel
1829	Young Mouse	Patron	Frederick	Green Mantle	Rowton
1830	Charlotte West	Augustus	Priam	Variation	Birmingham
1831	Galantine	Riddlesworth	Spaniel	Oxygen	Chorister
1832	Galata	Archibald	St.Giles	Galata	Margrave
1833	Tarantella	Clearwell	Dangerous	Vespa	Rockingham
1834	May-Day	Glencoe	Plenipotentiary	Pussy	Touchstone
1835	Preserve	Ibrahim	Mundig	Queen of Trumps	Queen of Trumps
1836	Destiny	Bay Middleton	Bay Middleton	Cyprian	Elis
1837	Chapeau D'Espange	Achmet	Phosphorus	Miss Letty	Mango
1838	Barcarolle	Grey Momus	Amato	Industry	Don John
1839	Cara	The Corsair	Bloomsbury	Deception	Charles the Twelth
1840	Crucifix	Crucifix	Little Wonder	Crucifix	Launcelot
1841	Potentia	Ralph	Coronation	Ghunznee	Satirist
1842	Firebrand	Meteor	Attila	Our Nell	The Blue Bonnet
1843	Extempore	Cotherstone	Cotherstone	Poison	Nutwith
1844	Sorella	The Ugly Buck	Orlando	The Princess	Foig a Ballagh
1845	Picnic	Idas	The Merry Monarch	Refraction	The Baron
1846	Mendicant	Sir Tatton Sykes	Pyrrhus the First	Mendicant	Sir Tatton Sykes
1847	Clementina	Conyngham	Cossack	Miami	VanTromp
1848	Canezou	Flatcatcher	Surplice	Cymba	Surplice
1849	The Flea	Nunnykirk	The Flying Dutchman	Lady Evelyn	The Flying Dutchman
1850	Lady Orford	Pitsford	Voltigeur	Rhedycina	Voltigeur
1851	Aphrodite	Hernandez	Teddington	Iris	Newminster
1852	Kate	Stockwell	Daniel O'Rourke	Songstress	Stockwell
1853	Mentmore Lass	West Australian	West Australian	Catherine Hayes	West Australian
1854	Virage	The Hermit	Andover	Mincemeat	Knight of St George
1855	Habena	Lord of the Isles	Wild Dayrell	Marchioness	Saucebox
1856	Manganese	Fazzoletto	Ellington	Mincepie	Warlock
1857	Imperieuse	Vedette	Blink Bonny	Blink Bonny	Imperieuse
1858	Governess	Fitzroland	Beadsman	Governess	Sunbeam
1859	Mayonaise	Promised Land	Musjid	Summerside	Gamester
1860	Sagitta	The Wizard	Thormanby	Butterfly	St Albans
1861	Nemesis	Diophantus	Kettledrum	Brown Duchess	Caller Ou
1862	Hurricane	The Marquis	Caractacus	Fue de Joie	The Marquis
1863	Lady Augusta	Marconi	Marconi	Queen Bertha	Lord Clifden
1864	Tomato	General Peel	Blair Athol	Fille de L'Air	Blair Athol
1865	Siberia	Gladiateur	Gladiateur	Regalia	Gladiateur
1866	Repulse	Lord Lyon	Lord Lyon	Tormentor	Lord Lyon
1867	Achievement	Vauban	Hermit	Hippia	Achievement
1868	Formosa	Moslem} Formosa} (dead heat)	Blue Gown	Formosa	Formosa
1869	Scottish Queen	Pretender	Pretender	Brigantine	Pero Gomez
1870	Hester	Macgregor	Kingcraft	Gamos	Hawthornden
1871	Hannah	Bothwell	Favonius	Hannah	Hannah
1872	Reine	Prince Charlie	Cremorne	Reine	Wenlock
1873	Cecilia	Gang Forward	Doncaster	Marie Stuart	Marie Stuart
1874	Apology	Atlantic	George Frederick	Apology	Apology
1875	Spinaway	Camballo	Galopin	Spinaway	Craig Millar
1876	Camelia	Petrarch	Kisber	Enguerrande} Camelia} dead heat	Petrarch
1877	Belpheobe	Chamant	Silvio	Placida	Silvio

	1000 Guineas	2000 Guineas	Derby	Oaks	St Leger
1878	Pilgrimage	Pilgrimage	Sefton	Jannette	Jannette
1879	Wheel of Fortune	Charibert	Sir Bevys	Wheel of Fortune	Rayon d'Or
1880	Elizabeth	Petronel	Bend Or	Jenny Howlet	Robert the Devil
1881	Thebais	Peregrine	Iroquois	Thebais	Iroquois
1882	St Marguerite	Shotover	Shotover	Geheimniss	Dutch Oven
1883	Hauteur	Galliard	St Blaise	Bonny Jean	Ossian
1884	Busybody	Scot Free	St Gatien }	Busybody	The Lambkin
			Harvester } dead heat		
1885	Farewell	Paradox	Melton	Lonely	Melton
1886	Miss Jummy	Ormonde	Ormonde	Miss Jummy	Ormonde
1887	Reve d'Or	Enterprise	Merry Hampton	Reve d'Or	Kilwarlin
1888	Briarroot	Ayrshire	Ayrshire	Seabreeze	Seabreeze
1889	Minthe	Enthusiast	Donovan	L'Abbesse de Jouarre	Donovan
1890	Semolina	Surefoot	Sainfoin	Memoir	Memoir
1891	Mimi	Common	Common	Mimi	Common
1892	La Fleche	Bona Vista	Sir Hugo	La Fleche	La Fleche
1893	Siffleuse	Isinglass	Isinglass	Mrs Butterwick	Isinglass
1894	Amiable	Ladas	Ladas	Amiable	Throstle
1895	Galeottia	Kirkconnel	Sir Visto	La Sagesse	Sir Visto
1896	Thais	St Frusquin	Persimmon	Canterbury Pilgrim	Persimmon
1897	Chelandry	Galtee More	Galtee More	Limasol	Galtee More
1898	Nun Nicer	Disraeli	Jeddah	Airs and Graces	Wildfowler
1899	Sibola	Flying Fox	Flying Fox	Musa	Flying Fox
1900	Winifreda	Diamond Jubilee	Diamond Jubilee	La Roche	Diamond Jubilee
1901	Aida	Handicapper	Volodyovski	Caps and Bells II	Doricles
1902	Sceptre	Sceptre	Ard Patrick	Sceptre	Sceptre
1903	Quintessence	Rock Sand	Rock Sand	Our Lassie	Rock Sand
1904	Pretty Polly	St Amant	St Amant	Pretty Polly	Pretty Polly
1905	Cherry Lass	Vedas	Cicero	Cherry Lass	Challacombe
1906	Flair	Gorgos	Spearmint	Keystone II	Troutbeck
1907	Witch Elm	Slieve Gallion	Orby	Glass Doll	Wool Winder
1908	Rhodora	Norman III	Signorinetta	Signorinetta	Your Majesty
1909	Electra	Minoru	Minoru	Perola	Bayardo
1910	Winkipop	Neil Gow	Lemberg	Rosedrop	Swynford
1911	Atmah	Sunstar	Sunstar	Cherimoya	Prince Palatine
1912	Tagalie	Sweeper II	Tagalie	Mirska	Tracery
1913	Jest	Louvis	Aboyeur	Jest	Night Hawk
1914	Princess Dorrie	Kennymore	Durbar II	Princess Dorrie	Black Jester
1915	Vaucluse	Pommern	Pommern	Snow Marten	Pommern
1916	Canyon	Clarissimus	Fifinella	Fifinella	Hurry On
1917	Diadem	Gay Crusader	Gay Crusader	Sunny Jane	Gay Crusader
1918	Ferry	Gainsborough	Gainsborough	My Dear	Gainsborough
1919	Roseway	The Panther	Grand Parade	Bayuda	Keysoe
1920	Cinna	Tetratema	Spion Kop	Charlebelle	Caligula
1921	Bettina	Criag an Eran	Humorist	Love in Idleness	Polemarch
1922	Silver Urn	St Louis	Captain Cuttle	Pogrom	Royal Lancer
1923	Tranquil	Ellangowan	Papyrus	Brownhylda	Tranquil
1924	Plack	Diophon	Sansovino	Straitlace	Salmon-Trout
1925	Saucy Sue	Manna	Manna	Saucy Sue	Solario
1926	Pillion	Colorado	Coronach	Short Story	Coronach
1927	Cresta Run	Adam's Apple	Call Boy	Beam	Book Law
1928	Scuttle	Flamingo	Fellstead	Toboggan	Fairway
1929	Taj Mah	Mr Jinks	Trigo	Pennycomequick	Trigo
1930	Fair Isle	Diolite	Blenheim	Rose of England	Singapore
1931	Four Course	Cameronian	Cameronian	Brulette	Sandwich
1932	Kandy	Orwell	April the Fifth	Udaipur	Firdaussi
1933	Bety Brown	Rodosto	Hyperion	Chatelaine	Hyperion
1934	Campanula	Colombo	Windsor Lad	Light Brocade	Windsor Lad
1935	Mesa	Bahram	Bahram	Quashed	Bahram
1936	Tide-Way	Pay Up	Mahmoud	Lovely Rosa	Boswell
1937	Exhibitionist	Le Ksar	Mid-day Sun	Exhibitionist	Chulmleigh
1938	Rockfel	Pasch	Bois Roussel	Rockfel	Scottish Union
1939	Galatea II	Blue Peter	Blue Peter	Galatea II	
1940	Godiva	Djebel	Pont l'Eveque	Godiva	Turkham
1941	Dancing Time	Lambert Simnel	Owen Tudor	Commotion	Sun Castle
1942	Sun Chariot	Big Game	Watling Street	Sun Chariot	Sun Chariot
1943	Herringbone	Kingsway	Straight Deal	Why Hurry	Herringbone
1944	Picture Play	Garden Path	Ocean Swell	Hycilla	Tehran
1945	Sun Stream	Court Martial	Dante	Sun Stream	Chamossaire
1946	Hypericum	Happy Knight	Airborne	Steady Aim	Airborne
1947	Imprudence	Tudor Minstel	Pearl Diver	Imprudence	Sayajirao
1948	Queenpot	My Babu	My Love	Masaka	Black Tarquin

	1000 Guineas	2000 Guineas	Derby	Oaks	St Leger
1949	Musidora	Nimbus	Nimbus	Musidora	Ridge Wood
1950	Camaree	Palestine	Galcador	Asmena	Scratch II
1951	Belle of All	Ki Ming	Arctic Prince	Neasham Belle	Talma II
1952	Zabara	Thunderhead II	Tulyar	Frieze	Tulyar
1953	Happy Laughter	Nearula	Pinza	Ambiguity	Premonition
1954	Festoon	Darius	Never Say Die	Sun Cap	Never Say Die
1955	Meld	Our Babu	Phil Drake	Meld	Meld
1956	Honeylight	Gilles de Retz	Lavandin	Sicarelle	Cambremer
1957	Rose Royale II	Crepello	Crepello	Carrozza	Ballymoss
1958	Bella Paola	Pall Mall	Hard Ridden	Bella Paola	Alcide
1959	Petite Etoile	Taboun	Parthia	Petite Etoile	Cantelo
1960	Never Too Late	Martial	St. Paddy	Never Too Late	St Paddy
1961	Sweet Solera	Rockavon	Psidium	Sweet Solera	Aurelius
1962	Abermaid	Privy Councillor	Larkspur	Monade	Hethersett
1963	Hula Dancer	Only for Life	Relko	Noblesse	Ragusa
1964	Pourparler	Baldric II	Santa Claus	Homeward Bound	Indiana
1965	Night Off	Niksar	Sea Bird II	Long Look	Provoke
1966	Glad Rags	Kashmir II	Charlottown	Valoris	Sodium
1967	Fleet	Royal Palace	Royal Palace	Pia	Ribocco
1968	Caergwrle	Sir Ivor	Sir Ivor	La Lagune	Ribero
1969	Full Dress II	Right Tack	Blakeney	Sleeping Partner	Intermezzo
1970	Humble Duty	Nijinsky	Nijinsky	Lupe	Nijinsky
1971	Altesse Royale	Brigadier Gerard	Mill Reef	Altesse Royale	Athens Wood
1972	Waterloo	High Top	Roberto	Ginevra	Boucher
1973	Mysterious	Mon Fils	Morston	Mysterious	Peleid
1974	Highclere	Nonoalco	Snow Knight	Polygamy	Bustino
1975	Nocturnal Spree	Bolkonski	Grundy	Juliette Marny	Bruni
1976	Flying Water	Wollow	Empery	Pawneese	Crow
1977	Mrs McArdy	Nebbiolo	The Minstrel	Dunfermline	Dunfermline
1978	Enstone Spark	Roland Gardens	Shirley Heights	Fari Salinia	Julio Mariner
1979	One in a Million	Tap On Wood	Troy	Scintillate	Son of Love
1980	Quick as Lightning	Known Fact	Henbit	Bireme	Light Cavalry
1981	Fairy Footsteps	To-Agori-Mou	Shergar	Blue Wind	Cut Above
1982	On the House	Zino	Golden Fleece	Time Charter	Touching Wood
1983	Ma Biche	Lomond	Teenoso	Sun Princess	Sun Princess
1984	Pebbles	El Gran Senor	Secreto	Circus Plume	Commanche Run
1985	Oh So Sharp	Shaheed	Slip Anchor	Oh So Sharp	Oh So Sharp
1986	Midway Lady	Dancing Brave	Shahrastani	Midway Lady	Moon Madness
1987	Miesque	Don't Forget Me	Reference Point	Unite	Reference Point
1988	Ravinella	Doyoun	Kahyasi	Diminuendo	Minster Son
1989	Musical Bliss	Nashwan	Nashwan	Snow Bride	Michelozzo
1990	Salsabil	Tirol	Quest for Fame	Salsabil	Snurge
1991	Shadayid	Mystiko	Generous	Jet Ski Lady	Toulon

Horses underlined won more than one classic

FASTEST TIMES FOR THE ENGLISH CLASSICS

Derby:	2m 33.80s Mahmoud (1936) HT
	2m 33.84s Kahyasi (1988) ET
Oaks:	2m 34.21s Time Charter (1982) ET
1000 Guineas:	1m 36.85s Oh So Sharp (1985) ET
	1m 35.80s My Babu (1948) HT
2000 Guineas:	1m 35.84s Tirol (1990) ET
St Leger:	3m 01.60s Coronach (1926) HT
	3m 01.60s Windsor Lad (1934) HT

HT=Hand Timed, ET=Electronically Timed

THE TRIPLE CROWN: 2,000 GUINEAS, DERBY AND ST LEGER

Horse	Year	Jockey(s)
West Australian	1853	Frank Butler
Gladiateur	1865	Harry Grimshaw
Lord Lyon	1866	Harry Custance 2, R. Thomas 1
Ormonde	1886	Fred Archer 2, George Barrett 1
Common	1891	George Barrett
Isinglass	1893	Tommy Loates
Galtee More	1897	Charlie Wood
Flying Fox	1899	Morny Cannon
Diamond Jubilee	1900	Herbert Jones
Rock Sand	1903	Danny Maher 2, J Martin 1
Pommern	1915	Steve Donoghue
Gay Crusader	1917	Steve Donoghue
Gainsborough	1918	Joe Childs
Bahram	1935	Freddie Fox 2, Charlie Smirke 1
Nijinsky	1970	Lester Piggott

CLASSIC WINNERS DISQUALIFIED

Zanga	St Leger	1789	"In consequence of a jostle"
Running Rein	Derby	1844	Horse was really a four-year-old called Maccabeus
Craganour	Derby	1913	Interference
Stony Ford	Oaks	1918	Interference
Nureyev	2,000 Gns	1980	Interference
Aliysa	Oaks	1989	Failed drugs test. Disqualified Nov 1990

Source: John Randall/*Racing Post*

GRAND NATIONAL WINNERS (1836-1919)

1836 The Duke	1857 Emigrant	1878 Shifnal	1899 Manifesto
1837 The Duke	1858 Little Charley	1879 The Liberator	1900 Ambush II
1838 Sir William	1859 Half Caste	1800 Empress	1901 Grudon
1839 Lottery	1860 Anatis	1881 Woodbrook	1902 Shannon Lass
1840 Jerry	1861 Jealousy	1882 Seaman	1903 Drumcree
1841 Charity	1862 Huntsman	1883 Zoedone	1904 Moifaa
1842 Gay Lad	1863 Emblem	1884 Voluptuary	1905 Kirkland
1843 Vanguard	1864 Emblematic	1885 Roquefort	1906 Ascetic's Silver
1844 Discount	1865 Alcibiade	1886 Old Joe	1907 Eremon
1845 Cureall	1866 Salamander	1887 Gamecock	1908 Rubio
1846 Pioneer	1867 Cortolvin	1888 Playfair	1909 Lutteur III
1847 Matthew	1868 The Lamb	1889 Frigate	1910 Jenkinstown
1848 Chandler	1869 The Colonel	1890 Ilex	1911 Glenside
1849 Peter Simple	1870 The Colonel	1891 Come Away	1912 Jerry M
1850 Abd-el-Kader	1871 The Lamb	1892 Father O'Flynn	1913 Covetcoat
1851 Abd-el-Kader	1872 Casse Tete	1893 Cloister	1914 Sunloch
1852 Miss Mowbray	1873 Disturbance	1894 Why Not	1915 Ally Sloper
1853 Peter Simple	1874 Reugny	1895 Wild Man from Borneo	1916 Vermouth
1854 Bourton	1875 Pathfinder	1896 Soarer	1917 Ballymacad
1855 Wanderer	1876 Regal	1897 Manifesto	1918 Poethlyn
1856 Freetrader	1877 Austerlitz	1898 Drogheda	1919 Poethlyn

GRAND NATIONAL AND OTHER BIG RACE WINNERS SINCE 1920

Grand National	Cheltenham Gold Cup	Champion Hurdle	Arc de Triomphe	Irish Derby
1920 Troytown	-	-	Comrade	He Goes
1921 Shaun Spadah	-	-	Ksar	Ballyheron
1922 Music Hall	-	-	Ksar	Spike Island
1923 Sergeant Murphy	-	-	Parth	Waygood
1924 Master Robert	Red Splash	-	Massine	Zodiac/Haine
1925 Double Chance	Balinode	-	Priori	Zionist
1926 Jack Horner	Koko	-	Biribi	Embargo
1927 Sprig	Thrown In	Blaris	Mon Talisman	Knight of the Grail
1928 Tipperary Tim	Patron Saint	Brown Jack	Kantar	Baytown
1929 Gregalach	Easter Hero	Royal Falcon	Ortello	Kopi
1930 Shaun Goilin	Easter Hero	Brown Tony	Motrico	Rock Star
1931 Grakle	-	-	Pearl Cap	Sea Serpent
1932 Forbra	Golden Miller	-	Motrico	Dastur
1933 Kellsboro' Jack	Golden Miller	Insurance	Crapom	Harinero
1934 Golden Miller	Golden Miller	Chenango	Brantome	Primero/Patriot King
1935 Reynoldstown	Golden Miller	Lion Courage	Samos	Museum
1936 Reynoldstown	Golden Miller	Victor Norman	Corrida	Raeburn
1937 Royal Mail	-	Free Fare	Corrida	Phidias
1938 Battleship	Morse Code	Our Hope	Eclair au Chocolat	Rosewell
1939 Workman	Brendan's Cottage	Africa Sister	Corrida	Mondragon
1940 Bogskar	Roman Hackle	Solford	-	Turkhan
1941 -	Poet Prince	Seneca	La Pacha	Sol Oriens
1942 -	Medoc II	Forestation	Djebel	Windsor Slipper
1943 -	-	-	Verso II	The Phoenix
1944 -	-	-	Ardan	Slide On
1945 -	Red Rower	Brains Trust	Nikellora	Piccadilly
1946 Lovely Cottage	Prince Regent	Distel	Caracella	Bright News
1947 Caughoo	Fortina	National Spirit	Le Paillon	Sayajirao
1948 Sheila's Cottage	Cottage Rake	National Spirit	Migoli	Nathoo
1949 Russian Hero	Cottage Rake	Hatton's Grace	Coronation	Hindostan
1950 Freebooter	Cottage Rake	Hatton's Grace	Tantieme	Dark Warrior
1951 Nickel Coin	Silver Fame	Hatton's Grace	Tantieme	Fraise du Bois II
1952 Teal	Mont Tremblant	Sir Ken	Nuccio	Thirteen of Diamonds
1953 Early Mist	Knock Hard	Sir Ken	La Sorellina	Chamier
1954 Royal Tan	Four Ten	Sir Ken	Sica Boy	Zarathustra
1955 Quare Times	Gay Donald	Clair Soleil	Ribot	Panaslipper
1956 E.S.B.	Limber Hill	Doorknocker	Ribot	Talgo
1957 Sundew	Linwell	Merry Deal	Oreso	Ballymoss
1958 Mr What	Kerstin	Bandalore	Ballymoss	Sindon
1959 Oxo	Roddy Owen	Fare Time	Saint Crespin	Fidalgo
1960 Merryman II	Pas Seul	Another Flash	Pussaint Chef	Chamour
1961 Nicolaus Silver	Saffron Tartan	Ebornezeer	Molvedo	Your Highness
1962 Kilmore	Mandarin	Anzio	Soltikoff	Tambourine II
1963 Ayala	Mill House	Winning Fair	Exbury	Ragusa
1964 Team Spirit	Arkle	Magic Court	Prince Royal II	Santa Claus
1965 Jay Trump	Arkle	Kirriemuir	Sea Bird II	Meadow Court

Grand National	Cheltenham Gold Cup	Champion Hurdle	Arc de Triomphe	Irish Derby
1966 Anglo	Arkle	Salmon Spray	Bon Mot	Sodium
1967 Foinavon	Woodland Venture	Saucy Kit	Topyo	Ribocco
1968 Reg Alligator	Fort Leney	Persian War	Vaguely Noble	Ribero
1969 Highland Wedding	What a Myth	Persian War	Levmoss	Prince Regent
1970 Gay Trip	L'Escargot	Persian War	Sassafras	Nijinsky
1971 Specify	L'Escargot	Bula	Mill Reef	Irish Ball
1972 Well To Do	Glencaraig Lady	Bula	San San	Steel Pulse
1973 Red Rum	The Dikler	Comedy of Errors	Rheingold	Weaver's Hall
1974 Red Rum	Captain Christy	Lanzarote	Allez France	English Prince
1975 L'Escargot	Ten Up	Comedy of Errors	Star Appeal	Grundy
1976 Rag Trade	Royal Frolic	Night Nurse	Ivanjica	Malacate
1977 Red Rum	Davy Lad	Night Nurse	Alleged	The Minstrel
1978 Lucius	Midnight Court	Monksfield	Alleged	Shirley Heights
1979 Rubstic	Alverton	Monksfield	Three Troikas	Troy
1980 Ben Nevis	Master Smudge	Sea Pigeon	Detroit	Tyrnavos
1981 Aldaniti	Little Owl	Sea Pigeon	Gold River	Shergar
1982 Grittar	Silver Buck	For Auction	Akiyda	Assert
1983 Corbiere	Bregawn	Gaye Brief	All Along	Shareef Dancer
1984 Hallo Dandy	Burrough Hill Lad	Dawn Run	Sagace	El Gran Senor
1985 Last Suspect	Forgive N'Forget	See You Then	Rainbow Quest	Law Society
1986 West Tip	Dawn Run	See You Then	Dancing Brave	Shahrastani
1987 Maori Venture	The Thinker	See You Then	Trempolino	Sir Harry Lewis
1988 Rhyme N'Reason	Charter Party	Celtic Shot	Tony Bin	Kahyasi
1989 Little Polveir	Desert Orchid	Beech Road	Carroll House	Old Vic
1990 Mr Frisk	Norton's Coin	Kribensis	Saumarez	Salsabil
1991 Seagram	Garrison Savannah	Morley Street	Suave Dancer	Generous

DERBY WINNERS SINCE 1982

		Jockey	Price	Distance	Time	Trainer	Owner
1982	Golden Fleece	Pat Eddery	3-1	3l	2m 34.27s	Vincent O'Brien	Robert Sangster
1983	Teenoso	Lester Piggott	9-2	3l	2m 49.07s	Geoffrey Wragg	Eric Moller
1984	Secreto	Christy Roche	14-1	sh	2m 39.12s	David O'Brien	Luigi Miglietti
1985	Slip Anchor	Steve Cauthen	9-4	7l	2m 36.23s	Henry Cecil	Lord H de Walden
1986	Shahrastani	Walter Swinburn	11-2	1/2 l	2m 37.13s	Michael Stoute	HH Aga Khan
1987	Reference Point	Steve Cauthen	6-4	1 1/2 l	2m 33.90s	Henry Cecil	Louise Freedman
1988	Kahyasi	Ray Cochrane	11-1	1 1/2 l	2m 33.84s	Luca Cumani	HH Aga Khan
1989	Nashwan	Willie Carson	5-4	5l	2m 34.90s	Dick Hern	Hamdan al Maktoum
1990	Quest for Fame	Pat Eddery	7-1	3l	2m 37.60s	Roger Charlton	Khalid Abdullah
1991	Generous	Alan Munro	9-1	5l	2m 34.00s	Paul Cole	Fahd Salman

GRAND NATIONAL WINNERS SINCE 1982

	Horse	Age/Weight	Jockey	Price	Trainer	Owner
1982	Grittar	9-11-5	Mr Dick Saunders	7-1	Frank Gilman	Frank Gilman
1983	Corbiere	8-11-4	Ben De Haan	13-1	Mrs Jenny Pitman	Brian Burroughs
1984	Hallo Dandy	10-10-2	Neale Doughty	13-1	Gordon Richards	Richard Shaw
1985	Last Suspect	11-10-5	Hywel Davies	50-1	Tim Forster	Duchess of Westminster
1986	West Tip	9-10-11	Richard Dunwoody	15-2	Michael Oliver	Peter Luff
1987	Maori Venture	11-10-13	Steve Knight	28-1	Andy Turnell	Jim Joel
1988	Rhyme n' Reason	9-10-11	Brendon Powell	10-1	David Elsworth	Juliet Reed
1989	Little Polveir	12-10-3	Jimmy Frost	28-1	Toby Balding	Edward Harvey
1990	Mr Frisk	11-10-6	Marcus Armytage	16-1	Kim Bailey	Lois Duffy
1991	Seagram	11-10-6	Nigel Hawke	12-1	David Barons	Sir Eric Parker

CHAMPION FLAT RACE JOCKEYS 1840-1945

1840	Elnathan Flatman	50	1875	Fred Archer	172		1912	Frank Wootton	118
1841	Elnathan Flatman	68	1876	Fred Archer	207		1913	Danny Maher	115
1842	Elnathan Flatman	42	1877	Fred Archer	218		1914	Steve Donoghue	129
1843	Elnathan Flatman	60	1878	Fred Archer	229		1915	Steve Donoghue	62
1844	Elnathan Flatman	64	1879	Fred Archer	197		1916	Steve Donoghue	43
1845	Elnathan Flatman	81	1880	Fred Archer	120		1917	Steve Donoghue	42
1846	Elnathan Flatman	81	1881	Fred Archer	220		1918	Steve Donoghue	66
1847	Elnathan Flatman	89	1882	Fred Archer	210		1919	Steve Donoghue	129
1848	Elnathan Flatman	104	1883	Fred Archer	232		1920	Steve Donoghue	143
1849	Elnathan Flatman	94	1884	Fred Archer	241		1921	Steve Donoghue	141
1850	Elnathan Flatman	88	1885	Fred Archer	246		1922	Steve Donoghue	102
1851	Elnathan Flatman	78	1886	Fred Archer	170		1923	Steve Donoghue &	
1852	Elnathan Flatman	92	1887	Charlie Wood	151			Charlie Elliott	89
1853	John Wells	86	1888	Fred Barrett	108		1924	Charlie Elliott	106
1854	John Wells	82	1889	Tommy Loates	167		1925	Gordon Richards	118
1855	George Fordham	70	1890	Tommy Loates	147		1926	Tommy Weston	95
1856	George Fordham	108	1891	Morny Cannon	137		1927	Gordon Richards	164
1857	George Fordham	84	1892	Morny Cannon	182		1928	Gordon Richards	148
1858	George Fordham	91	1893	Tommy Loates	222		1929	Gordon Richards	135
1859	George Fordham	118	1894	Morny Cannon	167		1930	Freddy Fox	129

1860	George Fordham	146		1895	Morny Cannon	184		1931	Gordon Richards	145
1861	George Fordham	106		1896	Morny Cannon	164		1932	Gordon Richards	190
1862	George Fordham	166		1897	Morny Cannon	145		1933	Gordon Richards	259
1863	George Fordham	103		1898	Otto Madden	161		1934	Gordon Richards	212
1864	Harry Grimshaw	164		1899	Sam Loates	160		1935	Gordon Richards	217
1865	George Fordham	142		1900	Lester Reiff	143		1936	Gordon Richards	174
1866	S Kenyon	123		1901	Otto Madden	130		1937	Gordon Richards	216
1867	George Fordham	143		1902	Willie Lane	170		1938	Gordon Richards	200
1868	George Fordham	110		1903	Otto Madden	154		1939	Gordon Richards	155
1869	George Fordham	95		1904	Otto Madden	161		1940	Gordon Richards	68
1870	W Gray &			1905	Elijah Wheatley	124		1941	Harry Wragg	71
	Charlie Maidment	76		1906	Billy Higgs	149		1942	Gordon Richards	67
1871	George Fordham &			1907	Billy Higgs	146		1943	Gordon Richards	65
	Charlie Maidment	86		1908	Danny Maher	139		1944	Gordon Richards	88
1872	Tommy Cannon	87		1909	Frank Wootton	165		1945	Gordon Richards	104
1873	Harry Constable	110		1910	Frank Wootton	137				
1874	Fred Archer	147		1911	Frank Wootton	187				

CHAMPION FLAT RACE JOCKEYS, TRAINERS AND OWNERS 1946-90

	Jockey		*Apprentice*		*Trainer*	*£*	*Owner*	*£*
1946	Gordon Richards	212	Joe Sime	40	Frank Butters	56,140	HH Aga Khan	24,118
1947	Gordon Richards	269	Dennis Buckle	20	Fred Darling	65,313	HH Aga Khan	44,020
1948	Gordon Richards	224	Dennis Buckle	25	Noel Murless	66,542	HH Aga Khan	46,393
1949	Gordon Richards	261	Willie Snaith	31	Frank Butters	71,721	HH Aga Khan	68,916
1950	Gordon Richards	201	Lester Piggott	52	Charles Semblat	57,044	Marcel Boussac	57,044
1951	Gordon Richards	227	Lester Piggott	51	Jack Jarvis	56,397	Marcel Boussac	39,339
1952	Gordon Richards	231	Joe Mercer	26	Marcus Marsh	92,093	HH Aga Khan	92,518
1953	Gordon Richards	191	Joe Mercer	61	Jack Jarvis	71,546	Victor Sassoon	58,579
1954	Doug Smith	129	Eddie Hide	53	Cecil Boyd-Rochfort	65,326	HM The Queen	40,993
1955	Doug Smith	168	Peter Robinson	46	Cecil Boyd-Rochfort	74,424	Lady Zia Wernher	46,345
1956	Doug Smith	155	Eddie Hide	75	Charles Elsey	61,621	Maj L Holliday	39,327
1957	Scobie Breasley	173	Greville Starkey	45	Noel Murless	116,898	H M The Queen	62,211
1958	Doug Smith	165	Peter Boothman	37	Cecil Boyd-Rochfort	84,186	John McShain	63,264
1959	Doug Smith	157	Bobby Elliott	27	Noel Murless	145,727	H H Aly Khan	100,668
1960	Lester Piggott	170	Bobby Elliott	39	Noel Murless	118,327	Victor Sassoon	90,069
1961	Scobie Breasley	171	Brian Lee	52	Noel Murless	95,972	Maj L Holliday	39,227
1962	Scobie Breasley	179	Bruce Raymond	13	Dick Hern	70,206	Maj L Holliday	70,206
1963	Scobie Breasley	176	David Yates	24	Paddy Prendergast	125,294	Jim Mullion	68,882
1964	Lester Piggott	140	Paul Cook	46	Paddy Prendergast	128,102	Mrs H Jackson	98,270
1965	Lester Piggott	166	Paul Cook	62	Paddy Prendergast	75,323	Jean Ternynck	65,301
1966	Lester Piggott	191	Sandy Barclay	71	Vincent O'Brien	123,848	Lady Zia Wernher	78,075
1967	Lester Piggott	117	Ernie Johnson	39	Noel Murless	256,899	Jim Joel	120,925
1968	Lester Piggott	139	David Coates & Richard Dicey	40	Noel Murless	141,508	Raymond Guest	97,075
1969	Lester Piggott	163	Clive Eccleston	41	Arthur Budgett	105,349	David Robinson	92,553
1970	Lester Piggott	162	Phillip Waldron	59	Noel Murless	199,524	Chas Engelhard	182,059
1971	Lester Piggott	162	Pat Eddery	71	Ian Balding	157,488	Paul Mellon	138,786
1972	Willie Carson	132	R Edmondson	42	Dick Hern	206,767	Mrs Jean Hislop	155,190
1973	Willie Carson	163	Steve Perks	41	Noel Murless	132,984	Nelson B Hunt	124,771
1974	Pat Eddery	148	Alan Bond	40	Peter Walwyn	206,445	Nelson B Hunt	147,244
1975	Pat Eddery	164	Alan Bond	66	Peter Walwyn	382,527	Carlo Vittadini	209,492
1976	Pat Eddery	162	David Dineley	54	Henry Cecil	261,301	Dan Wildenstein	244,500
1977	Pat Eddery	176	Jimmy Bleasdale	67	Vincent O'Brien	439,124	Robert Sangster	348,023
1978	Willie Carson	182	Kevin Darley	70	Henry Cecil	382,812	Robert Sangster	160,405
1979	Joe Mercer	164	Philip Robinson	51	Henry Cecil	683,971	Michael Sobell	339,751
1980	Willie Carson	165	Philip Robinson	59	Dick Hern	831,964	Simon Weinstock	236,332
1981	Lester Piggott	179	Bryn Crossley	45	Michael Stoute	723,786	HH Aga Khan	441,654
1982	Lester Piggott	188	Billy Newnes	57	Henry Cecil	872,614	Robert Sangster	397,749
1983	Willie Carson	159	Michael Hills	39	Dick Hern	549,598	Robert Sangster	461,488
1984	Steve Cauthen	130	Tommy Quinn	62	Henry Cecil	551,939	Robert Sangster	395,901
1985	Steve Cauthen	195	Gary Carter & Willie Ryan	37	Henry Cecil	1,148,206	Shk Mohammed	1,082,502
1986	Pat Eddery	177	Gary Carter	34	Michael Stoute	1,266,807	Shk Mohammed	830,121
1987	Steve Cauthen	197	Gary Bardwell	27	Henry Cecil	1,882,116	Shk Mohammed	1,232,240
1988	Pat Eddery	183	Gary Bardwell	39	Henry Cecil	1,186,122	Shk Mohammed	1,143,343
1989	Pat Eddery	171	Lanfranco Dettori	75	Michael Stoute	1,999,664	Shk Mohammed	1,295,148
1990	Pat Eddery	209	Jimmy Fortune	47	Henry Cecil	1,520,125	H Al-Maktoum	1,536,821

CHAMPION NATIONAL HUNT JOCKEYS & TRAINERS SINCE 1946

Jockey		Trainer	£
1946 Fred Rimell	54	Tom Rayson	9,933
1947 Jack Dowdeswell	58	Fulke Walwyn	11,115
1948 Bryan Marshall	66	Fulke Walwyn	16,790
1949 Tim Molony	60	Fulke Walwyn	15,563
1950 Tim Molony	95	Peter Cazalet	18,427
1951 Tim Molony	83	Fred Rimell	18,381
1952 Tim Molony	99	Neville Crump	19,377
1953 Fred Winter	121	Vincent O'Brien	15,515
1954 Dick Francis	76	Vincent O'Brien	14,274
1955 Tim Molony	67	Ryan Price	13,888
1956 Fred Winter	74	Charlie Hall	15,807
1957 Fred Winter	80	Neville Crump	18,495
1958 Fred Winter	82	Fulke Walwyn	23,013
1959 Tim Brookshaw	83	Ryan Price	26,550
1960 Stan Mellor	68	Peter Cazalet	22,270
1961 Stan Mellor	118	Fred Rimell	34,811
1962 Stan Mellor	80	Ryan Price	40,950
1963 Josh Gifford	70	Keith Piggott	23,091
1964 Josh Gifford	94	Fulke Walwyn	67,129
1965 Terry Biddlecombe	114	Peter Cazalet	36,153
1966 Terry Biddlecombe	102	Ryan Price	42,267
1967 Josh Gifford	122	Ryan Price	41,222
1968 Josh Gifford	82	Denys Smith	37,944
1969 Bob Davies &	77	Fred Rimell	38,344
Terry Biddlecombe	77		
1970 Bob Davies	91	Fred Rimell	61,864
1971 Graham Thorner	74	Fred Winter	60,739
1972 Bob Davies	89	Fred Winter	62,396
1973 Ron Barry	125	Fred Winter	79,066
1974 Ron Barry	94	Fred Winter	101,782
1975 Tommy Stack	82	Fred Winter	74,205
1976 John Francome	96	Fred Rimell	111,740
1977 Tommy Stack	97	Fred Winter	85,202
1978 Jonjo O'Neill	149	Fred Winter	145,915
1979 John Francome	95	Peter Easterby	150,746
1980 Jonjo O'Neill	115	Peter Easterby	218,258
1981 John Francome	105	Peter Easterby	236,867
1982 John Francome &	120	Michael Dickinson	296,028
Peter Scudamore	120		
1983 John Francome	106	Michael Dickinson	358,837
1984 John Francome	131	Michael Dickinson	266,146
1985 John Francome	101	Fred Winter	218,978
1986 Peter Scudamore	91	Nicky Henderson	162,234
1987 Peter Scudamore	123	Nicky Henderson	162,234
1988 Peter Scudamore	132	David Elsworth	344,210
1989 Peter Scudamore	221	Martin Pipe	589,460
1990 Peter Scudamore	170	Martin Pipe	792,544
1991 Peter Scudamore	141	Martin Pipe	956,894

US RACING
Triple Crown
The following horses have all won the Triple Crown:

Horse	Year	Jockey
Sir Barton	1919	John Loftus
Gallant Fox	1930	Earl Sande
Omaha	1935	W Saunders
War Admiral	1937	C Kurtsinger
Whirlaway	1941	Eddie Arcaro
Count Fleet	1943	Johnny Longden
Assault	1946	W Mehrtens
Citation	1948	Eddie Arcaro
Secretariat	1973	Ron Turcotte
Seattle Slew	1977	Jean Cruguet
Affirmed	1978	Steve Cauthen

Breeders' Cup

	Sprint	Mile	Juvenile	Juvenile Fillies
1984	Ellio	Royal Heroine	Chief's Crown	Outstandingly
1985	Precisionist	Cozzene	Tasso	Twilight Ridge
1986	Smile	Last Tycoon	Capote	Brave Raj
1987	Very Subtle	Miesque	Success Express	Epitome
1988	Gulch	Miesque	Is It True?	Open Mind
1989	Dancing Spree	Steinlen	Rhythm	Go for Wand
1990	Safely Kept	Royal Academy	Fly So Free	Meadow Star

	Distaff	Classic	Turf
1984	Princess Rooney	Wild Again	Lashkari
1985	Life's Magic	Proud Truth	Pebbles
1986	Lady's Secret	Skywalker	Manila
1987	Sacahuista	Ferdinand	Theatrical
1988	Personal Ensign	Alysheba	Great Communicator
1989	Bayakoa	Sunday Silence	Prized
1990	Bayakoa	Unbridled	In the Wings

AUSTRALIAN RACING
Melbourne Cup
(Winners since 1981)

1981	Just a Dash
1982	Gurner's Lane
1983	Kiwi
1984	Black Night
1985	What a Nuisance
1986	At Talaq
1987	Kensei
1988	Empire Rose
1989	Tawrrific
1990	Kingston Rule

1992

BIG RACE DATES

Mar 10	Champion Hurdle (Cheltenham)
Mar 12	Cheltenham Gold Cup
Mar 19	Turf Flat season starts (Doncaster)
Apr 4	Grand National (Aintree)
Apr 14-16	Newmarket Craven meeting
Apr 30	1000 Guineas (Newmarket)
May 2	2000 Guineas (Newmarket)
Jun 3	The Derby (Epsom)
Jun 6	The Oaks (Epsom)
Jun 16-19	Royal Ascot
Jul 4	Eclipse Stakes (Sandown)
Jul 7-9	Newmarket July meeting
Jul 25	King George and Queen Elizabeth Stakes (Ascot)
Jul 28-Aug 1	Glorious Goodwood
Aug 18-20	Ebor meeting (York)
Sep 12	St Leger (Doncaster)
Sep 18	Ayr Gold Cup
Sep 26	Festival of British Racing (Ascot)
Oct 3	The Cambridgeshire (Newmarket)
Oct 17	The Cesarewitch (Newmarket)
Dec 26	King George VI Chase (Kempton)

FULL RACING FIXTURES 1992

TURF MEETINGS

JANUARY

1 Catterick, Cheltenham, Devon & Exeter, Leicester, Windsor
2 Ayr, Nottingham
3 Edinburgh, Newton Abbot
4 Haydock, Market Rasen, Sandown
6 Lingfield, Wolverhampton
7 Chepstow, Leicester, Wolverhampton
8 Kelso, Plumpton
9 Edinburgh, Wincanton
10 Ascot, Wetherby
11 Ascot, Market Rasen, Newcastle, Warwick
13 Carlisle, Fontwell
14 Folkestone, Sedgefield
15 Ludlow, Windsor
16 Taunton
17 Catterick, Kempton, Towcester
18 Catterick, Kempton, Haydock, Warwick
20 Leicester, Lingfield
21 Chepstow, Nottingham
22 Sedgefield, Wolverhampton
23 Huntingdon, Newton Abbot
24 Wincanton, Uttoxeter
25 Ayr, Cheltenham, Doncaster
27 Plumpton
28 Leicester, Sedgefield
29 Nottingham, Windsor
30 Edinburgh, Towcester
31 Kelso, Lingfield

FEBRUARY

1 Chepstow, Sandown, Stratford, Wetherby
3 Fontwell, Wolverhampton
4 Carlisle, Warwick
5 Ascot, Ludlow
6 Huntingdon, Wincanton
7 Bangor-on-Dee, Newbury, Sedgefield
8 Ayr, Catterick, Newbury, Uttoxeter
10 Hereford, Plumpton
11 Newton Abbot, Towcester
12 Folkestone, Worcester
13 Leicester, Sandown
14 Edinburgh, Fakenham, Sandown
15 Chepstow, Newcastle, Nottingham, Windsor
17 Fontwell, Woverhampton
18 Huntingdon, Sedgefield
19 Folkestone, Warwick
20 Catterick, Wincanton
21 Kelso, Kempton
22 Doncaster, Edinburgh, Kempton, Stratford
24 Doncaster, Leicester
25 Nottingham
26 Plumpton, Wetherby, Worcester
27 Ludlow
28 Haydock, Newbury
29 Haydock, Hereford, Market Rasen, Newbury

MARCH

2 Leicester, Windsor
3 Sedgefield, Warwick
4 Bangor-on-Dee, Catterick, Folkestone
5 Stratford, Wincanton
6 Carlisle, Market Rasen, Sandown
7 Ayr, Chepstow, Doncaster, Sandown
9 Plumpton, Taunton
10 Cheltenham, Sedgefield
11 Cheltenham, Newton Abbot
12 Cheltenham, Hexham
13 Fakenham, Lingfield, Wolverhampton
14 Chepstow, Lingfield, Newcastle, Uttoxeter
16 Newcastle, Wolverhampton

17 Fontwell, Nottingham
18 Kelso, Worcester
19 DONCASTER, Devon & Exeter, Towcester
20 DONCASTER, Ludlow, Newbury
21 DONCASTER, Bangor-on-Dee, Hexham, Newbury
23 FOLKESTONE, Hexham
24 LEICESTER, Sandown
25 CATTERICK, Worcester
26 BRIGHTON, WOLVERHAMPTON, Taunton
27 BEVERLEY, Plumpton, Wincanton
28 BEVERLEY, WARWICK, Ascot, Southwell
30 FOLKESTONE, NEWCASTLE
31 LEICESTER, Sedgefield

APRIL

1 HAMILTON, Worcester
2 BRIGHTON, Liverpool
3 KEMPTON, Liverpool, Devon & Exeter
4 Hereford, Liverpool
6 WOLVERHAMPTON
7 PONTEFRACT, Southwell
8 RIPON, Ascot, Ludlow
9 HAMILTON, Taunton
10 NEWBURY, THIRSK, Ayr
11 NEWBURY, THIRSK, Ayr, Bangor-on-Dee, Stratford
13 BRIGHTON, EDINBURGH, NOTTINGHAM, Huntingdon
14 NEWMARKET, Fontwell, Sedgefield
15 NEWMARKET, PONTEFRACT, Cheltenham
16 NEWMARKET, RIPON, Cheltenham
18 HAYDOCK, KEMPTON, NEWCASTLE, Newton Abbot, Plumpton, Southwell, Towcester
20 KEMPTON, NEWCASTLE, NOTTINGHAM, WARWICK, Carlisle, Chepstow, Fakenham, Hereford, Huntingdon, Market Rasen, Newton Abbot, Plumpton, Towcester, Uttoxeter, Wetherby, Wincanton
21 WARWICK, Chepstow, Uttoxeter, Wetherby
22 CATTERICK, FOLKESTONE, +Ludlow, Perth
23 BEVERLEY, Perth
24 CARLISLE, SANDOWN, Perth, +Taunton
25 LEICESTER, RIPON, SANDOWN (MIXED), Hexham, Market Rasen, Worcester
27 PONTEFRACT, WOLVERHAMPTON, +WINDSOR, +Hexham
28 BATH, NOTTINGHAM, +Ascot, +Sedgefield
29 ASCOT, +Chelthenham, Kelso
30 REDCAR, NEWMARKET, SALISBURY

MAY

1 HAMILTON, NEWMARKET, +Bangor-on-Dee, Newton Abbot
2 HAYDOCK, NEWMARKET, THIRSK, +Hexham, + Hereford, Uttoxeter
4 DONCASTER, HAYDOCK (mixed), KEMPTON, WARWICK, Devon & Exeter, Fontwell, Ludlow, Newcastle, Southwell, Towcester
5 CHESTER, +SANDOWN, Chepstow, +Sedgefield
6 CHESTER, SALISBURY, +Wetherby, +Worcester
7 BRIGHTON, CARLISLE, CHESTER, +Uttoxeter
8 BEVERLEY, CARLISLE, LINGFIELD, +Stratford, +Wincanton
9 BEVERLEY, BATH, LINGFIELD, Bangor-on-Dee, +Market Rasen, + Newcastle, Warwick
11 HAMILTON, +WINDSOR, WOLVERHAMPTON
12 YORK, +Folkestone, Newton Abbot, +Towcester
13 +KEMPTON, YORK, Hereford, +Newton Abbot, +Perth
14 YORK, +Huntingdon, Perth
15 NEWBURY, NEWMARKET, THIRSK, +Stratford
16 + HAMILTON, NEWBURY, NEWMARKET, THIRSK, +SOUTHWELL, +LINGFIELD, + Warwick
18 BATH, EDINBURGH
19 BEVERLEY, GOODWOOD

20 GODWOOD, +Perth, Worcester
21 GOODWOOD, CATTERICK
22 HAYDOCK, SALISBURY, +PONTEFRACT, Towcester
23 DONCASTER, HAYDOCK, KEMPTON, +LINGFIELD, +SOUTHWELL, +WARWICK, Hexham, Cartmel
25 CHEPSTOW, DONCASTER, LEICESTER, REDCAR, SANDOWN, Cartmel, Hereford, +Hexham, Huntingdon, Fakenham, Fontwell, Uttoxeter, Wetherby
26 LEICESTER, REDCAR, +SANDOWN, +Uttoxeter
27 BRIGHTON, RIPON, Cartmel
28 BRIGHTON, CARLISLE
29 +GOODWOOD, HAMILTON, NEWCASTLE, NOTTINGHAM, +Stratford
30 EDINBURGH, LINGFIELD, + Market Rasen, Stratford

JUNE

1 LEICESTER, REDCAR
2 FOLKESTONE, +NEWBURY, YARMOUTH
3 +BEVERLEY, EPSOM, YARMOUTH
4 BEVERLEY, EPSOM
5 CATTERICK, EPSOM, +GOODWOOD +HAYDOCK, SOUTHWELL
6 +CARLISLE, CATTERICK, EPSOM, HAYDOCK, +LEICESTER
8 NOTTINGHAM, PONTEFRACT
9 SALISBURY, PONTEFRACT
10 BEVERLEY, +HAMILTON, +KEMPTON, SOUTHWELL
11 CHEPSTOW, HAMILTON, NEWBURY
12 +DONCASTER, +GOODWOOD, SANDOWN, SOUTHWELL, YORK
13 BATH, +LINGFELD, +NOTTINGHAM, SANDOWN, YORK, +WOLVERHAMPTON
15 BRIGHTON, EDINBURGH, +WINDSOR
16 ROYAL ASCOT, THIRSK
17 ROYAL ASCOT, RIPON,
18 ROYAL ASCOT, RIPON
19 ROYAL ASCOT, AYR, REDCAR, +NEWMARKET
20 ASCOT, AYR, +LINGFIELD, REDCAR, +SOUTHWELL, +WARWICK
22 EDINBURGH, NOTTINGHAM, +WINDSOR, +WOLVERHAMPTON
23 BRIGHTON, +NEWBURY, YARMOUTH
24 CARLISLE, +CHESTER, +KEMPTON, SALISBURY
25 CARLISLE, SALISBURY
26 +BATH, DONCASTER, +GOODWOOD, +NEWCASTLE, NEWMARKET, LINGFIELD
27 CHEPSTOW, +DONCASTER, +LINGFIELD, NEWCASTLE, NEWMARKET, +WARWICK
28 HAMILTON, PONTEFRACT, +WINDSOR, WOLVERHAMPTON
30 CHEPSTOW, FOLKESTONE

JULY

1 +CATTERICK, +EPSOM, WARWICK, YARMOUTH
2 +BRIGHTON, CATTERICK, HAYDOCK, YARMOUTH
3 +BEVERLEY, HAYDOCK, SOUTHWELL, SANDOWN
4 BATH, BEVERLEY, HAYDOCK, +NOTTINGHAM, +SANDOWN
5 EDINBURGH, LEICESTER, +RIPON, +WINDSOR
7 NEWMARKET, PONTEFRACT
8 BATH, +KEMPTON, NEWMARKET, +REDCAR
9 +CHEPSTOW, NEMARKET, REDCAR
10 +CHESTER, LINGFELD, WARWICK, YORK
11 CHESTER, LINGFIELD, SALISBURY, +SOUTHWELL, YORK
13 +BEVERLEY, EDINBURGH, +WINDSOR, WOLVERHAMPTON
14 BEVERLEY, FOLKESTONE,+LEICESTER
15 CATTERICK, +SANDOWN, +YARMOUTH

16 CATTERICK, +CHEPSTOW,+HAMILTON, SANDOWN
17+HAMILTON, NEWBURY, +NEWMARKET, SOUTHWELL, THIRSK
18 AYR, +LINGFIELD, NEWMARKET, NEWBURY, RIPON, +WOLVERHAMPTON
20 BATH, AYR, +NOTTINGHAM, +WINDSOR
21 AYR, FOLKESTONE
22 DONCASTER, +HAMILTON, +REDCAR, +SANDOWN
YARMOUTH
23 BRIGHTON, +DONCASTER, +HAMILTON, YARMOUTH
24 ASCOT, +AYR, CARLSILE, +PONTEFRACT, YARMOUTH
25 AYR, ASCOT, NEWCASTLE+WARWICK, +SOUTHWELL
27 NEWCASTLE, LINGFIELD, +WINDSOR, +WOLVERHAMPTON
28 BEVERLEY, +LEICESTER, GOODWOOD
29 CATTERICK, +EPSOM, +SOUTHWELL, GOODWOOD
30 GOODWOOD, +SALISBURY, YARMOUTH
31+EDINBURGH, THIRSK, +NEWMARKET, GOODWOOD, Bangor-on-Dee

AUGUST

1 THIRSK, +WINDSOR, NEWMARKET, GOODWOOD, Newton Abbot, +Market Rasen
3 RIPON, +NOTTINGHAM, Newton Abbot
4 REDCAR, BRIGHTON, NOTTINGHAM
5 PONTEFRACT, BRIGHTON, +KEMPTON, Devon &Exeter
6 PONTEFRACT, BRIGHTON,
7+HAYDOCK, +NEWMARKET, REDCAR, WOLVERHAMPTON, Plumpton
8 +LINGFIELD, NEWMARKET, HAYDOCK, REDCAR, +SOUTHWELL, +Worcester
10 +THIRSK, +LEICESTER, WINDSOR, Worcester
11 BATH, YARMOUTH, +CATTERICK, +Fontwell
12 BEVERLEY,SALISBURY
13 BEVERLEY, SALISBURY, Newton Abbot
14 FOLKESTONE, SOUTHWELL, NEWBURY, +HAYDOCK
15 RIPON, NEWBURY, +WOLVERHAMPTON, +LINGFIELD, Bangor-on-Dee, +Market Rasen
17 HAMILTON, WINDSOR
18 FOLKESTONE, YORK
19 YARMOUTH, YORK, +KEMPTON
20 +SALISBURY, YARMOUTH, YORK
21 CHESTER, SANDOWN, Perth
22 CHESTER, RIPON, SANDOWN, +Hereford, Perth
24 NOTTINGHAM, Hexham
25 BRIGHTON, PONTEFRACT
26 REDCAR, BRIGHTON, Devon &Exeter
27 LINGFIELD, Worcester
28 EDINBURGH, GOODWOOD, NEWMARKET, THIRSK
29 GOODWOOD, NEWCASTLE, NEWMARKET, +WINDSOR, Cartmel, + Hereford
31 CHEPSTOW, EPSOM, NEWCASTLE, RIPON, WARWICK, WOLVERHAMPTON, Cartmel, Huntingdon, Newton Abbot, Plumpton, Southwell

SEPTEMBER

1 EPSOM, RIPON, Newton Abbot
2 YORK, Fontwell, Newton Abbot
3 YORK, SALISBURY
4 HAYDOCK, KEMPTON, THIRSK, Stratford
5 HAYDOCK, KEMPTON, THIRSK, Stratford
7 HAMILTON, WOLVERHAMPTON
8 CARLISLE, LEICESTER, LINGFIELD
9 DONCASTER, Devon & Exeter
10 DONCASTER, FOLKESTEONE, Newton Abbot
11 DONCASTER, GOODWOOD, Worcester

12 CHEPSTOW, DONCASTER, GOODWOOD, Bangor-on-Dee, Worcester
14 BATH, LEICESTER, Plumpton
15 SANDOWN, YARMOUTH, Sedgefield
16 AYR, BEVERLEY, SANDOWN, YARMOUTH, Devon &Exeter
17 AYR, BEVERLEY, LINGFIELD, YARMOUTH, Uttoxeter
18 AYR, NEWBURY, SOUTHWELL, Huntingdon
19 AYR, CATTERICK, NEWBURY, Market Rasen, Worcester
21 EDINBURGH, FOLKESTONE, NOTTINGHAM, PONTEFRACT
22 KEMPTON, NOTTINGHAM
23 BRIGHTON, Perth, Southwell
24 ASCOT, Perth, Taunton
25 ASCOT, HAYDOCK, REDCAR, Hereford
26 ASCOT, HAYDOCK, REDCAR, Carlisle, Market Rasen, Straford
28 BATH, HAMILTON, WOLVERHAMPTON, Carlisle, Fontwell
29 BRIGHTON, NEWCASTLE, Devon &Exeter
30 NEWMARKET, SALISBURY, Cheltenham , Sedgefield

OCTOBER

1 LINGFIELD, NEWMARKET, Cheltenham
2 GOODWOOD, NEWMARKET, Hexham
3 GOODWOOD, NEWMARKET, Chepstow, Kelso, Uttoxeter
5 PONTEFRACT, WARWICK, Southwell
6 FOLKESTONE, REDCAR, WARWICK, Newton Abbot
7 HAYDOCK, YORK, Towcester
8 HAYDOCK, YORK, Ludlow, Wincanton
9 ASCOT, Carlisle, Market Rasen
10 ASCOT, YORK, Ayr, Bangor-on-Dee, Southwell, Worcester
12 LEICESTER, Fontwell
13 CHEPSTOW, LEICESTER, Devon & Exeter, Sedgefield
14 REDCAR, Cheltenham, Wetherby
15 NWMARKET, Hexham, Taunton, Uttoxeter
16 CATTERICK, NEWMARKET, Ludlow
17 CATTERICK, NEWMARKET, Kelso, Kempton, Southwell, Stratford
19 EDINBURGH, FOLKESTONE, NOTTINGHAM, Fakenham
20 CHEPSTOW, CHESTER, Plumpton
21 CHESTER, Ascot, Newcastle
22 NEWBURY, PONTEFRACT, Wincanton
23 DONCASTER, Devon & Exeter, Hereford, Newbury
24 DONCASTER, NEWBURY, Catterick, Huntingdon, Worcester
26 LEICESTER, LINGFIELD
27 LEICESTER, REDCAR
28 YARMOUTH, Fontwell, Sedgefield
29 NOTTINGHAM, Kempton, Stratford
30 NEWMARKET, Bangor-on-Dee, WETHERBY
31 NEWMARKET, Sandown, Warwick, Wetherby

NOVEMBER

2 NEWCASTLE, Plumpton, Wolverhampton
3 HAMILTON, Devon & Exeter, Hereford
4 Newbury, Kelso
5 EDINBURGH, Uttoxeter, Wincanton
6 DONCASTER, Hexham, Market Rasen
7 DONCASTER, Chepstow, Newcastle, Windsor
9 Carlisle, Folkestone, Wolverhampton
10 Sedgefield
11 Haydock, Worcester
12 Kelso, Taunton, Towcester
13 Ayr, Cheltenham, Huntingdon
14 Ayr, Cheltenham, Nottingham
16 Leicester, Windsor
17 Newton Abbot, Warwick, Wetherby

18 Haydock, Kempton
19 Haydock, Ludlow, Wincanton
20 Ascot, Leicester, Sedgefield
21 Ascot, Catterick, Market Rasen, Towcester
23 Catterick, Folkestone, Wolverhampton
24 Devon & Exeter, Huntingdon, Stratford
25 Hereford, Hexham,Plumpton
26 Carlisle, Nottingham, Taunton
27 Bangor-on-Dee, Newbury
28 Newbury, Newcastle, Warwick
30 Kelso, Worcester

DECEMBER

1 Fontwell, Newcastle
2 Catterick, Huntingdon, Ludlow
3 Windsor, Uttoxtere
4 Devon &Exeter, Hereford, Nottingham, Sandown
5 Chepstow, Sandown, Towcester, Wetherby
7 Edinburgh, Warwick.
8 Plumpton, Sedgefield
9 Haydock, Worcester
10 Haydock, Taunton
11 Cheltenham, Doncaster, Hexham
12 Cheltenham, Doncaster, Edinburgh, Lingfield
14 Ludlow, Newton Abbot
15 Folkestone
16 Bangor-on-Dee
17 Kelso, Towcester
18 Catterick, Fakenham, Uttoxeter
19 Ascot, Newcastle, Nottingham, Uttoxeter
21 Edinburgh, Lingfield
22 Hereford,
26 Huntingdon, Kempton, Market Rasen, Newton Abbot, Sedgefield, Wetherby, Wincanton, Wolverhampton
28 Chepstow, Kempton, Wetherby, Wolverhampton
29 Plumpton, Stratford
30 Carlisle, Fontwell, Taunton, Warwick
31 Catterick, Cheltenham, Folkestone, Leicester

ALL-WEATHER MEETINGS

LINGFIELD-FLAT
Jan 4, 11, 18, 21, 15
Feb 1,4, 8, 15, 18, 22, 29
Mar 3, 5, 7, 10, 21
Apr 4
Nov 5, 14, 28
Dec 3, 16, 19, 22, 31

LINGFIELD - JUMPING
Jan 2, 7, 9, 14, 23, 28, 30
Feb 6, 11, 13, 20, 25

SOUTHWELL - FLAT
Jan 1, 3, 10, 15, 17, 24, 29, 31
Feb 7, 12, 14, 21, 26, 28
Mar 6, 14, 18
Nov 10, 17, 27
Dec 2, 10, 15, 28

SOUTHWELL- JUMPING
Jan 6, 8, 13, 20, 22, 27
Feb 3, 5, 10, 17, 19, 24
Mar 2, 3, 9

FLAT MEETINGS IN CAPITALS
Other meetings are National Hunt
+ = Evening meetings

(c) The Jockey Club 1991

ICE HOCKEY

For the first time in eight years a US club wrested the Stanley Cup from Canada - but only by courtesy of their resident Canadian. The Pittsburgh Penguins, led by Mario Lemieux, beat the Minnesota North Stars by four games to two, winning the final game by a crushing 8-0.

Lemieux finished the play-offs with 44 points, three short of Wayne Gretzky's record, despite missing the third game against Minnesota, which Pittsburgh lost, with a serious back injury. He had already missed the first 50 games of the season for the same reason and the state of Lemieux's back was the city's major bar-room topic for much of the year. Lemieux was given credit not just for winning the Cup but for saving the club, which once had its gates padlocked by tax officials.

He was supposed to miss the fourth Stanley Cup game as well but the injury went into remission and the Penguins went 3-0 up inside two minutes on the way to levelling the series. Some people talked about Lemieux rivalling Wayne Gretzky's greatness though the Penguins' coach Bob Johnson reserved special praise for Tom Barrasso, his goalie. Barrasso, at least, is an American. It was the Penguins' first championship in their 24-year history.

Two further teams, the Ottawa Senators and Tampa Bay Lightning, were chosen to join the NHL in 1992, bringing the number of teams up to 24; the San Jose Sharks started in 1991. Brett Hull of the St Louis Blues became the fifth player to score 50 goals in the first 50 games of the season. He finished with 86 and followed his father Bobby in winning the Hart Memorial Trophy as the League's Most Valuable Player. Ken Baumgartner of the New York Islanders accidentally punched a linesman during a fight with a Hartford player; he then scooped up seven cents and two bags of sweets that had been thrown on to the ice and gave them to the linesman by way of apology. Pete Taglianetti of the Penguins used peanut butter in a plastic bag to protect a bruise above his ankle.

Durham Wasps emulated the defunct Dundee Rockets (1984) by winning the British Grand Slam of the three main titles, beating the surprise team Peterborough Pirates 7-4 in the Heineken Championship final. The game between Solihull Barons and the Wasps was abandoned after 11 players out of the 12 were involved in a brawl. The Canadian author Lawrence Martin said that there was documentary evidence that the Russians were playing hockey on frozen ponds in St Petersburg in the mid-19th century, thus disproving the myth that the game originated with British soldiers in Ontario.

1990-91

WORLD CHAMPIONSHIP ('A' Group)
Finland, Apr 14-May 5
ROUND ROBIN RESULTS
FINLAND 2 Czechoslovakia 0; SOVIET UNION 3
Switzerland 1; CANADA 4 United States 3; SWEDEN 8
Germany 1; CANADA 3 Switzerland 0; SOVIET UNION
7 Germany 3; Finland 4 Sweden 4; UNITED STATES 4
Czechoslovakia 1; CANADA 3 Germany 2;
CZECHOSLOVAKIA 4 Switzerland 1; SOVIET UNION
3 Finland 0; Sweden 4 United States 4;
CZECHOSLOVAKIA 7 Germany 1; SWEDEN 4
Switzerland 3; CANADA 5 Finland 3; SOVIET UNION
12 United States 2; UNITED STATES 2 Finland 1; Soviet
Union 5 Sweden 5; SWITZERLAND 5 Germany 2;
CZECHOSLOVAKIA 4 Canada 3; Canada 3 Sweden 3;
United States 4 Germany 4; SOVIET UNION 6
Czechoslovakia 2; FINLAND 6 Switzerland 1; SOVIET
UNION 5 Canada 3; SWEDEN 2 Czechoslovakia 1;
FINLAND 6 Germany 0; UNITED STATES 4 Switzerland 2

STANDINGS

	P	W	L	D	F	A	Pts
1 Soviet Union	7	6	0	1	41	16	13
2 Sweden	7	3	0	4	30	21	10
3 Canada	7	4	2	1	24	20	9
4 United States	7	3	3	2	23	28	8
5 Finland	7	3	3	1	22	15	7
6 Czechoslovakia	7	3	4	0	19	19	6
7 Switzerland	7	1	6	0	13	26	2
8 Germany	7	0	6	1	13	40	1

Top four qualified for medal round

MEDAL ROUND
SOVIET UNION 6 United States 4; Sweden 3 Canada 3;
SWEDEN 8 United States 4; Canada 3 Soviet Union 3;
CANADA 9 United States 4; SWEDEN 2 Soviet Union 1

FINAL POSITIONS

	P	W	L	D	F	A	Pts
1 Sweden	3	2	0	1	13	8	5
2 Canada	3	1	0	2	15	10	4
3 Soviet Union	3	1	1	1	10	9	3
4 United States	3	0	3	0	12	23	0

*Germany finished bottom of the relegation group and will
play in 'B' Group in 1992*

NATIONAL HOCKEY LEAGUE (NHL)
Final Standings
(last year's positions in brackets)

Wales Conference
Patrick Division

		P	W	L	T	Pts	GF	GA
1	(5)	Pittsburgh	80	41	33	6	88	342	305
2	(1)	NY Rangers	80	36	31	13	85	297	265
3	(3)	Washington	80	37	36	7	81	258	258
4	(2)	New Jersey	80	32	33	15	79	272	264
5	(6)	Philadelphia	80	33	37	10	76	252	267
6	(4)	NY Islanders	80	25	45	10	60	223	290

Play-offs
PITTSBURGH PENGUINS 4 New Jersey Islanders 3;
WASHINGTON CAPITALS 4 New York Rangers 2
Divisional Final
PITTSBURGH 4 Washington 1

Adams Division

		P	W	L	T	Pts	GF	GA
1	(1)	Boston	80	44	24	12	100	299	264
2	(3)	Montreal	80	39	30	11	89	273	249
3	(2)	Buffalo	80	31	30	19	81	292	278
4	(4)	Hartford	80	31	38	11	73	238	276
5	(5)	Quebec	80	16	50	14	46	236	354

Play-offs
BOSTON BRUINS 4 Hartford Whalers 2; MONTREAL
CANADIENS 4 Buffalo Sabres 2
Divisional Final
BOSTON 4 Montreal 3
Wales Conference Final
PITTSBURGH 4 Boston 2

Campbell Conference
Norris Division

		P	W	L	T	Pts	GF	GA
1	(1)	Chicago	80	49	23	8	106	284	211
2	(2)	St Louis	80	47	22	11	105	310	250
3	(5)	Detroit	80	34	38	8	76	273	298
4	(4)	Minnesota	80	27	39	14	68	256	266
5	(3)	Toronto	80	23	46	11	57	241	318

Play-offs
MINNESOTA NORTH STARS 4 Chicago Blackhawks 2;
ST LOUIS BLUES 4 Detroit Red Wings 3
Divisional Final
MINNESOTA 4 St Louis 2
Smythe Division

		P	W	L	T	Pts	GF	GA
1	(4)	Los Angeles	80	46	24	10	102	340	254
2	(1)	Calgary	80	46	26	8	100	344	263
3	(2)	Edmonton	80	37	37	6	80	272	272
4	(5)	Vancouver	80	28	43	9	65	243	315
5	(3)	Winnipeg	80	26	43	11	63	260	288

Play-offs
LOS ANGELES KINGS 4 Vancouver Canucks 2;
EDMONTON OILERS 4 Calgary Flames 3
Divisional Final
EDMONTON 4 Los Angeles 2
Campbell Conference Final
MINNESOTA 4 Edmonton 1

STANLEY CUP
Game 1: Pittsburgh 4 MINNESOTA 5
Game 2: PITTSBURGH 4 Minnesota 1
Game 3: MINNESOTA 3 Pittsburgh 1
Game 4: Minnesota 3 PITTSBURGH 5
Game 5: PITTSBURGH 6 Minnesota 4
Game 6: Minnesota 0 PITTSBURGH 8
Pittsburgh won best-of-seven series 4-2
Conn Smythe Trophy for MVP in play-offs: Mario
Lemieux (Pittsburgh)
Hart Trophy for NHL MVP: Brett Hull (St Louis)

LEADING SCORERS
1990-91 Regular Season
Most Goals: 86 Brett Hull (St Louis)
(Record : 92 Wayne Gretzky, Edmonton, 1981-82)
Most Assists: 122 Wayne Gretzky (Los Angeles)
(Record : 163 Wayne Gretzky, Edmonton, 1985-86)
Most Points: 163 Wayne Gretzky (Los Angeles)
(Record : 215 Wayne Gretzky, Edmonton, 1985-86)

HEINEKEN LEAGUE
Premier Division
Last season's positions in brackets

			P	W	L	D	F	A	Pts
1	(3)	Durham	36	28	5	3	324	187	59
2	(1)	Cardiff	36	21	13	2	274	237	44
3	(8)	Peterborough	36	19	13	4	287	241	42
4	(2)	Murrayfield	36	19	15	2	264	236	40
5	(7)	Ayr	36	18	15	3	243	243	39
6	(6)	Nottingham	36	16	16	4	200	202	36
7	(9)	Whitley	36	13	19	4	269	292	30
8	(4)	Solihull	36	13	22	1	255	340	27
9	(-)	Cleveland	36	9	22	5	198	246	23
10	(5)	Fife	36	8	24	4	216	306	20

HEINEKEN BRITISH CHAMPIONSHIP
Wembley, Apr 26-28
SEMI-FINAL
PETERBOROUGH PIRATES 7 Cardiff Devils 4;
DURHAM WASPS 11 Murrayfield Racers 6
FINAL
DURHAM 7 Peterborough 4
Att: 9,000

———— CHAMPIONS ————

WORLD CHAMPIONSHIPS

1920 Canada	1965 USSR
1924 Canada	1966 USSR
1928 Canada	1967 USSR
1930 Canada	1968 USSR
1931 Canada	1970 USSR
1932 Canada	1971 USSR
1933 United States	1972 Czechoslovakia
1934 Canada	1973 USSR
1935 Canada	1974 USSR
1936 Great Britain	1975 USSR
1937 Canada	1976 Czechoslovakia
1938 Canada	1977 Czechoslovakia
1939 Canada	1978 USSR
1947 Czechoslovakia	1979 USSR
1948 Canada	1980 United States
1949 Czechoslovakia	1981 USSR
1950 Canada	1982 USSR
1951 Canada	1983 USSR
1952 Canada	1984 USSR
1953 Sweden	1985 Czechoslovakia
1954 USSR	1986 USSR
1955 Canada	1987 Sweden
1956 USSR	1988 USSR
1957 Sweden	1989 USSR
1958 Canada	1990 USSR
1959 Canada	1991 Sweden
1960 United States	**Most wins:**
1961 Canada	**24** USSR; **19** Canada
1962 Sweden	
1963 USSR	
1964 USSR	

STANLEY CUP
(First contested 1893)
Post-war winners

1945-46	Montreal Canadiens
1946-47	Toronto Maple Leafs
1947-48	Toronto Maple Leafs
1948-49	Toronto Maple Leafs
1949-50	Detroit Red Wings
1950-51	Toronto Maple Leafs
1951-52	Detroit Red Wings
1952-53	Montreal Canadiens
1953-54	Detroit Red Wings
1954-55	Detroit Red Wings
1955-56	Montreal Canadiens
1956-57	Montreal Canadiens
1957-58	Montreal Canadiens
1958-59	Montreal Canadiens
1959-60	Montreal Canadiens
1960-61	Chicago Blackhawks
1961-62	Toronto Maple Leafs
1962-63	Toronto Maple Leafs
1963-64	Toronto Maple Leafs
1964-65	Montreal Canadiens
1965-66	Montreal Canadiens
1966-67	Toronto Maple Leafs
1967-68	Montreal Canadiens
1968-69	Montreal Canadiens
1969-70	Boston Bruins
1970-71	Montreal Canadiens
1971-72	Boston Bruins
1972-73	Montreal Canadiens
1973-74	Philadelphia Flyers
1974-75	Philadelphia Flyers
1975-76	Montreal Canadiens
1976-77	Montreal Canadiens
1977-78	Montreal Canadiens
1978-79	Montreal Canadiens
1979-80	New York Islanders
1980-81	New York Islanders
1981-82	New York Islanders
1982-83	New York Islanders
1983-84	Edmonton Oilers
1984-85	Edmonton Oilers
1985-86	Montreal Canadiens
1986-87	Edmonton Oilers
1987-88	Edmonton Oilers
1988-89	Calgary Flames
1989-90	Edmonton Oilers
1990-91	Pittsburgh Pirates

Most Wins:
23 Montreal Canadiens; 11 Toronto Maple Leafs; 7 Detroit
Red Wings; 6 Ottawa Senators; 5 Montreal Victorias;
Boston Bruins; Edmonton Oilers

HEINEKEN BRITISH CHAMPIONSHIP
1982	Dundee Rockets
1983	Dundee Rockets
1984	Dundee Rockets
1985	Fife Flyers
1986	Murrayfield Racers
1987	Durham Wasps
1988	Durham Wasps
1989	Nottingham Panthers
1990	Cardiff Devils
1991	Durham Wasps

JUDO

1991

WORLD CHAMPIONSHIPS
Barcelona, Jul 25-28

Men

Open
1 Naoya Ogawa (Jap)
2 D Khakaleshvili (USSR)
3 Imre Csosz (Hun)
  Georges Mathonnet (Fra)
Heavyweight/over 95kg
1 Sergey Kosorotow (USSR)
2 Garcia Moreno (Cub)
3 Naoya Ogawa (Jap
  Kim Kun-Soo(SKo)
Half-heavyweight/under 95kg
1 Stephane Traineau (Fra)
2 Pavel Nastula (Pol)
3 Marc Meiling (Ger)
  Jiri Sosnar (Cze)
Middleweight/under 86kg
1 Hirotaka Okada (Jap)
2 Joe Wanag (USA)
3 Waldemir Legian (Pol)
  Giorgio Vismara (Ita)
Half-middleweight/under 78kg
1 Daniel Lascau (Ger)
2 Johan Laats (Bel)
3 Bashir Varayev (USSR)
  Hidehiko Yoshida (Jap)
Lightweight/under 71kg
1 Toshihiko Koga (Jap)
2 Joaquin Ruiz (Spa)
3 Hoon Chung (SKo)
  Vladimir Dguebovaze (USSR)
Featherweight/under 65kg
1 Udo Quellmolz (Ger)
2 Nasahiko Okuma (Jap)
3 James Pedro (US)
  S Kosmynin (USSR)
Bantamweight/under 60kg
1 Tadanori Koshino (Jap)
2 Hyun Yoon (SKo)
3 Philippe Pradayrol (Fra)
  Nazim Guseinow (USSR)

Women

Open
1 Yiaoyan Zhuang (Chn)
2 Villanueva Rodriguez (Cub)
3 Claudia Weber (Ger)
  Natalia Lupino (Fra)
Heavyweight/over 72kg
1 Moon Ji-Yoon (SKo)
2 Ying Zhang (Chn)
3 Monique van de Lee (Hol)
  Beata Maksymov (Pol)
Half-heavyweight/under 72kg
1 Kim Mi-Jeong (SKo)
2 Yoko Tanabe (Jap)
3 Marion van Dorssen (Hol)
  Laetitia Meignan (Fra)
Middleweight/under 66kg
1 Emanuela Pierantozzi (Ita)
2 Odalys Rivjiminez (Cub)
3 Ryoko Fujimoto (Jap)
  Kate Howey (GB)

Half-middleweight/under 61kg
1 Frauke Eickhoff (Ger)
2 Diane Bell (GB)
3 Yael Arad (Isr)
  Catherine Fleury (Fra)
Lightweight/under 56kg
1 Miriam Blasco (Spa)
2 Nicole Flagothier (Bel)
3 Nicola Fairbrother (GB)
  Zhong Yun Li (Chn)
Featherweight/under 52kg
1 Alessandra Giungi (Ita)
2 Sharon Rendle (GB)
3 Maritza Cardenas Perez (Cub)
Bantamweight/under 48kg
1 Cecille Nowak (Fra)
2 Karen Briggs (GB)
3 Ryoko Tamura (Jap)
  Rodriguez Verdecia (Cub)

EUROPEAN CHAMPIONSHIPS
Prague, May 18-19
Winners
Men

Open	I Bereznitski (USSR)
Heavyweight/over 95kg	Henry Stöhr (Ger)
Light-heavyweight/under 95kg	Theo Meijer (Hol)
Middleweight/under 86kg	Axel Lobenstein (Ger)
Light-middleweight/under78kg	A Wurth (Hol)
Lightweight/under 71kg	S Dott (Ger)
Featherweight/under 65kg	Eric Born (Swi)
Bantamweight/under 60kg	Philippe Pradayrol (Fra)

Women

Open	Monique van de Lee (Hol)
Heavyweight/over 72kg	Beata Maksymov (Pol)
Light-heavyweight/under 72kg	Laetitia Meignan (Fra)
Middleweight/under 66kg	I Beauruelle (Fra)
Light-middleweight/under 61kg	Z Nagy (Hun)
Lightweight/under 56kg	Miriam Blasco (Spa)
Featherweight/under 52kg	Jesica Gal (Hol)
Bantamweight/under 48kg	Cecille Nowak (Fra)

BRITISH OPEN CHAMPIONSHIPS
Crystal Palace, Apr 14
Winners
Men

Heavyweight/over 95kg	Elvis Gordon (GB)
Light-heavyweight/Under 95kg	Marc Meiling (Ger)
Middleweight/Under 86 kg	Léon Villar (Spa)
Light-middleweight/Under 78kg	Daniel Duquesnoy (Fra)
Lightweight/Under 71kg	Eric Zymna (Ger)
Featherweight/Under 65kg	Jerome Henric (Fra)
Bantamweight/Under 60kg	Nigel Donohue (GB)

Women

Heavyweight/over 72kg	Karin Kutz (Ger)
Light-heavyweight/under 72kg	Irene de Kok (Hol)
Middleweight/under 66kg	Kate Howey (GB)
Light-middleweight/under 61kg	Diane Bell (GB)
Lightweight/under 56kg	Nicole Flagothier (Bel)
Featherweight/under 52 kg	Heidi Goossens (Bel)
Bantamweight/under 48kg	Sylvie Meloux (Fra)

> **It's like the 1800s out there. They haven't got a clue about modern training methods.**
>
> *Tony MacConnell, British coach, after visiting the Japanese dojos*

---------- **1990** ----------

EUROPEAN TEAM CHAMPIONSHIPS
Dubrovnik, Oct 27-28
Men
1 USSR
2 France
3 Great Britain & Holland
Women
1 Great Britain
2 France
3 Italy & Holland

---------- **CHAMPIONS** ----------

WORLD CHAMPIONSHIPS
Winners in past 10 years
Men
Open
1983   Hitoshi Saito (Jap)
1985   Yoshimi Masaki (Jap)
1987   Naoya Ogawa (Jap)
1989   Naoya Ogawa (Jap)
1991   Naoya Ogawa (Jap)
Heavyweight/Over 95kg
1983   Yasuhiro Yamashita (Jap)
1985   Yong-Chul Cho (SKo)
1987   Grigori Vertichev (USSR)
1989   Naoya Ogawa (Jap)
1991   Sergey Kosorotow (USSR)
Half-heavyweight/Under 95kg
1983   Valerily Divisenko (USSR)
1985   Hitoshi Sugai (Jap)
1987   Hitoshi Sugai (Jap)
1989   Koba Kurtanidze (USSR)
1991   Stephane Traineau (Fra)
Middleweight/Under 86kg
1983   Detlef Ultsch (GDR)
1985   Peter Seisenbacher (Aut)
1987   Fabian Canu (Fra)
1989   Fabian Canu (Fra)
1991   Hirotaka Okada (Jap)
Half-middleweight/Under 78kg
1983   Nobutoshi Hikage (Jap)
1985   Nobutoshi Hikage (Jap)
1987   Hirotaka Okada (Jap)
1989   Byung-Ju Kim (SKo)
1991   Daniel Lascau (Ger)
Lightweight/Under 71kg
1983   Hidetoshi Nakanishi (Jap)
1985   Byeong-Kuen Ahn (SKo)
1987   Mike Swain (US)
1989   Toshihiko Koga (Jap)
1991   Toshihiko Koga (Jap)
Featherweight/Under 65kg
1983   Nikolai Soludukhin (USSR)
1985   Yuriy Sokolov (USSR)
1987   Yosuke Yamamoto (Jap)
1989   Drago Becanovic (Yug)
1991   Udo Quellmolz (Ger)
Bantamweight/Under 60kg
1983   Khazret Tletseri (USSR)
1985   Shinji Hosokawa (Jap)
1987   Kim Jae-Yup (SKo)
1989   Amiran Totikashvilli (USSR)
1991   Tadanori Koshino (Jap)

Women
Open
1984   Ingrid Berghmans (Bel)
1986   Fenglian Gao (Chn)
1987   Ingrid Berghmans (Bel)
1989   Estela Rodriguez (Cub)
1991   Yiaoyan Zhuang (Chn)
Heavyweight/Over 72kg
1984   Maria-Teresa Motta (Ita)
1986   Fenglian Gao (Chn)
1987   Fenglian Gao (Chn)
1989   Fenglian Gao (Chn)
1991   Moon Ji-Yoon (SKo)
Half-heavyweight/Under 72kg
1984   Ingrid Berghmans (Bel)
1986   Irene de Kok (Hol)
1987   Irene de Kok (Hol)
1989   Ingrid Berghmans (Bel)
1991   Kim Mi-Jeong (SKo)
Middleweight/under 66kg
1984   Brigitte Deydier (Fra)
1986   Brigitte Deydier (Fra)
1987   Alexandra Schreiber (FRG)
1989   Emanuela Pierantozzi (Ita)
1991   Emanuela Pierantozzi (Ita)
Half-middleweight/Under 61kg
1984   Natasha Hernandez (Ven)
1986   Diane Bell (GB)
1987   Diane Bell (GB)
1989   Catherine Fleury (Fra)
1991   Frauke Eickhoff (Ger)
Lightweight/Under 56kg
1984   Ann-Maria Burns (US)
1986   Ann Hughs (GB)
1987   Catherine Arnaud (Fra)
1989   Catherine Arnaud (Fra)
1991   Miriam Blasco (Spa)
Featherweight/Under 52kg
1984   Kaori Yamaguchi (Jap)
1986   Dominique Brun (Fra)
1987   Sharon Rendle (GB)
1989   Sharon Rendle (GB)
1991   Alessandra Giungi (Ita)
Bantamweight/Under 48kg
1984   Karen Briggs (GB)
1986   Karen Briggs (GB)
1987   Zhang Li (Chn)
1989   Karen Briggs (GB)
1991   Cecille Nowak (Fra)

LACROSSE

Men
BRINE NORTHERN LEAGUE
1st CHEADLE; 2nd Stockport

NORTHERN SENIOR FLAGS
Urmston, Apr 28
CHEADLE 10 Stockport 9 (aet)

SOUTHERN SENIOR FLAGS
Motspur Park, London, Apr 13
HAMPSTEAD 10 Bath 9

ENGLISH CLUB CHAMPIONSHIP
(Iroquois Cup)
Cheadle, Sep 22
CHEADLE 18 Hampstead 5

Women
ALL-ENGLAND CLUB & COLLEGES TROPHY
Cobham, Surrey, Apr 28
CENTAURS 3 Pendley 0

HATTERSLEY SALVER
Reading University, Apr 6-7
Final Placings:
1 WEST; 2 South; 3 East; 4 North; 5 Combined Universities; 6 Midlands

━━━━━━━━ CHAMPIONS ━━━━━━━━

WORLD CHAMPIONSHIPS

Men		Women	
(First held 1967)		(First held 1982)	
1967	United States	1982	United States
1974	United States	1986	Australia
1978	Canada	1989	United States
1982	United States		
1986	United States		
1990	United States		

IROQUOIS CUP
(First held 1890)
Winners since 1982

1982	Sheffield University	1987	Stockport
1983	Sheffield University	1988	Mellor
1984	Cheadle	1989	Stockport
1985	Cheadle	1990	Cheadle
1986	Heaton Mersey	1991	Cheadle

Most wins:
17 Stockport; 11 South Manchester; 10 Old Hulmeians, Mellor; 7 Cheadle, Old Waconians; 6 Heaton Mersey

MODERN PENTATHLON

WORLD MEN'S CHAMPIONSHIP
San Antonio, Texas, Aug 21-23
Individual
1 Arkad Skrzypaszek (Pol) 5,498 pts
2 Peter Steinmann (Swi) 5,476 pts
3 Adam Madaras (Hun) 5,467 pts
Team
1 Soviet Union 16,047 pts
2 Poland 16,037 pts
3 Hungary 15,867 pts

BRITISH MEN'S CHAMPIONSHIP
Corby, Jul 12-14
1 Richard Phelps (Spartan) 5,457 pts
2 Graham Brookhouse (Spartan) 5,402 pts
3 Dominic Mahoney (Army) 5,307 pts
Team: Spartan

BRITISH WOMEN'S CHAMPIONSHIP
Knutsford, Sep 20-22
1 Helen Nicholas (Knutsford) 5,093 pts
2 Rachel McFadden (Edinburgh Univ) 5,051 pts
3 Kath Young (Gloucester) 5,037 pts
Team: Spartan

━━━━━━━━ CHAMPIONS ━━━━━━━━

WORLD CHAMPIONSHIPS
(Not held in Olympic years)

Men	Individual	Team
1981	Janusz Pyciak-Peciak (Pol)	Poland
1982	Daniele Masala (Ita)	USSR
1983	Anatoliy Starostin (USSR)	USSR
1985	Attila Mizser (Hun)	USSR
1986	Carlo Massullo (Ita)	Italy
1987	Joel Bouzou (Fra)	Hungary
1989	Laszlo Fabian (Hun)	Hungary
1990	Gianluca Tiberti (Ita)	USSR
1991	Arkad Skrzypaszek (Pol)	USSR
Women	**Individual**	**Team**
1981	Anne Ahlgren (Swe)	Britain
1982	Wendy Norman (GB)	Britain
1983	Lynn Chernobrywy (Can)	Britain
1984	Svetlana Jakovleva (USSR)	USSR
1985	Barbara Kotowska (Pol)	Poland
1986	Irina Kisselyeva (USSR)	Poland
1987	Irina Kisselyeva (USSR)	USSR
1988	Dorota Idzi (Pol)	Poland
1989	Lori Norwood (US)	Poland
1990	Eva Fjellerup (Den)	Poland

MOTOR CYCLING

T he American Wayne Rainey, the 1990 world 500cc champion, retained his title in 1991 after a tight battle with the Australian Mick Doohan, who was only out of the first three once in the 15 grands prix. Rainey, however, had six wins against Doohan's three.

At the halfway stage of the season Rainey crucially overtook his rival on the track at Jarama on the second lap of the European Grand Prix. Shortly afterwards, he overtook him in the points table as well. Rainey rode a particularly well-judged race to win the French Grand Prix and when the riders returned for a race at Le Mans, he made mathematically sure.

The inconsistent Kevin Schwantz had one of his brilliant days again at Donington Park when he won the British Grand Prix for the third year running, beating Rainey by 0.8 of a second. Before the race at Hockenheim, Doohan threw himself on the ground to ward off the evil spirits that are supposed to attend new leathers; he crashed 30 minutes later. FIM, the sport's ruling body, announced that the universally employed two-stroke engine would be banned from 1993 and four-stroke engines used instead. "They want to see the world championship reduced to the level of club racing," said Paul Butler, spokesman for the teams. Four riders - Ian Young, Petr Hlavatka from Czechoslovakia, a father of three, Frank Duffy and Roy Anderson - were killed during the Isle of Man TT, taking the total killed on the course since 1911 to 160. "The place is starting to frighten

═══ 1991 ═══

WORLD CHAMPIONSHIP GRANDS PRIX
500cc
Japanese GP
Suzuka, Mar 24
1 Kevin Schwantz (US) Suzuki
  Avge.Speed: 98.67mph/158.80kph
2 Michael Doohan (Aus) Honda
3 Wayne Rainey (US) Yamaha
Australian GP
Eastern Creek, Sydney, Apr 7
1 Wayne Rainey (US) Yamaha
  Avge.Speed: 94.59mph/152.23kph
2 Michael Doohan (Aus) Honda
3 John Kocinski (US) Yamaha
United States GP
Laguna Seca, California, Apr 20-21
1 Wayne Rainey (US) Yamaha
  Avge.Speed: 89.86mph/144.62kph
2 Michael Doohan (Aus) Honda
3 Kevin Schwantz (US) Suzuki
Spanish GP
Jerez, May 12
1 Michael Doohan (Aus) Honda
  Avge.Speed: 86.52 mph/139.24kph
2 John Kocinski (US) Yamaha
3 Wayne Rainey (US) Yamaha
Italian GP
Misano, May 19
1 Michael Doohan (Aus) Honda
  Avge.Speed: 100.72mph/162.01kph
2 John Kocinski (US) Yamaha
3 Eddie Lawson (US) Cagiva
German GP
Hockenheim, May 25
1 Kevin Schwantz (US) Suzuki
  Avge.Speed: 125.34mph/201.72kph
2 Wayne Rainey (US) Yamaha

3 Michael Doohan (Aus) Honda
Austrian GP
Salzburgring, Jun 9
1 Michael Doohan (Aus) Honda
  Avge.Speed: 120.52mph/193.96kph
2 Wayne Rainey (US) Yamaha
3 Kevin Schwantz (US) Suzuki
European GP
Jarama, Spain, Jun 16
1 Wayne Rainey (US) Yamaha
  Avge.Speed: 89.97mph/144.79kph
2 Michael Doohan (Aus) Honda
3 Wayne Gardner (Aus) Honda
Dutch TT
Assen ,Jun 29
1 Kevin Schwantz (US) Suzuki
  Avge.Speed: 108.91mph/175.27kph
2 Wayne Rainey (US) Yamaha
3 Wayne Gardner (Aus) Honda
French GP
Paul Ricard, Jul 21
1 Wayne Rainey (US) Yamaha
  Avge.Speed: 102.88mph/165.567kph
2 Michael Doohan (Aus) Honda
3 Eddie Lawson (US) Cagivia
British GP
Donington Park, Aug 4
1 Kevin Schwantz (US) Suzuki
  Avge.Speed: 95.19mph/153.19kph
2 Wayne Rainey (US) Yamaha
3 Michael Doohan (Aus) Honda
San Marino GP
Mugello, Italy, Aug 18
1 Wayne Rainey (US) Yamaha
  Avge. Speed: 101.71mph/163.69kph
2 Kevin Schwantz (US) Suzuki
3 Michael Doohan (Aus) Honda

Czechoslovak GP
Brno, Aug 25
1 Wayne Rainey (US) Yamaha
  Avge. Speed: 97.24mph/156.49kph
2 Michael Doohan (Aus) Honda
3 John Kocinski (US) Honda

Grand Prix Du Mans
Le Mans, France, Sep 8
1 Kevin Schwantz (US) Suzuki
  Avge. Speed: 97.09mph/156.26kph
2 Michael Doohan (Aus) Honda
3 Wayne Rainey (US) Yamaha

Malaysian GP
Shah Alam, Sep 22
1 John Kocinski (US) Yamaha
  Avge. Speed: 93.09 mph/149.81 kph
2 Wayne Gardner (Aus) Honda
3 Michael Doohan (Aus) Honda

FINAL CHAMPIONSHIP STANDINGS
1 Wayne Rainey (US) Yamaha 233 pts
2 Michael Doohan (Aus) Honda 224 pts
3 Kevin Schwantz (US) Suzuki 204 pts
4 John Kocinski (US) Yamaha 161 pts
5 Wayne Gardner (Aus) Honda 161 pts
6 Eddie Lawson (US) Cagiva 126 pts

THE OTHER WORLD CHAMPIONS
250cc
1 Luca Cadalora (Ita) Honda 237 pts
2 Helmut Bradl (Ger) Honda 220 pts
3 Carlos Cardus (Spa) Honda 205 pts

125cc
1 Loris Capirossi (Ita) Honda 200 pts
2 Fausto Gresini (Ita) Honda 181 pts
3 Ralf Waldmann (Ger) Honda 141 pts

Sidecar
1 Steve Webster & Gavin Simmons (GB) LCR 181 pts
2 Rolf Biland & Kurt Waltisperg (Swi) LCR 168 pts
3 Egbert Streur (Hol) & Peter Brown (GB) LCR 134 pts

ISLE OF MAN TT RACES
Isle of Man, Jun 1-7

TT Formula One
1 Steve Hislop (Honda) 121.00mph/194.73kph
2 Carl Fogarty (Honda)
3 Trevor Nation (Norton)
*Hislop set an outright Island lap record of
123.48mph/198.72kph*

Sidecar Race A
1 Mick Boddice & Dave Wells (Honda)
  99.26mph/159.74kph
2 Neil Smith & Steven Mace (Yamaha)
3 Artie Oakes & J.Pitts (Kawasaki)

125cc
1 Robert Dunlop (Honda) 103.68mph/166.86kph
2 Joey Dunlop (Honda)
3 Bob Heath (Honda)
*Robert Dunlop stopped his brother Joey from winning his
14th TT, equalling Mike Hailwood's record*

Supersport 400
1 Dave Leach (Yamaha) 105.49mph/169.77kph
2 Steve Hislop (Honda)
3 Jim Moodie (Yamaha)

Sidecar Race B
1 Mick Boddice & Dave Wells (Honda)
  99.27mph/159.76kph
2 Geoff Bell & Keith Cornbill (Yamaha)

3 Dave Molyneux & Karl Ellison (Kawasaki)

Junior TT
1 Robert Dunlop (Honda) 114.89mph/184.90kph
2 Phil McCallen (Honda)
3 Steve Hazlett (Yamaha)

Supersport 600
1 Steve Hislop (Honda) 114.28mph/189.92kph
2 Steve Cull (Yamaha)
3 Bob Jackson (Honda)

Senior TT
1 Steve Hislop (Honda) 121.09 mph/194.88kph
2 Joey Dunlop (Honda)
3 Phil McCallen (Honda)
*Hislop's eighth TT. This was the second time he had won
three races in one week, a feat previously achieved by
Mike Hailwood and Joey Dunlop*

MOTO CROSS WORLD CHAMPIONS
500cc
1 Georges Jobé (Bel) 296 pts
2 Jacky Martens (Bel) 230 pts
3 Dirk Geukens (Bel) 181 pts

250cc
1 Trampas Parker (US) 242pts
2 Mike Healey (US) 238pts
3 Alessandro Puzar (Ita) 232pts

Team (Moto Cross des Nations)
Valkenswaard, Holland, Sep 15
1 United States 10 pts
2 Belgium 13 pts
3 Holland 13 pts

———— CHAMPIONS ————

WORLD CHAMPIONS

1949		
125cc	Nello Pagani (Ita)	Mondial
250cc	Bruno Ruffo (Ita)	Guzzi
350cc	Freddie Frith (GB)	Velocette
500cc	Leslie Graham (GB)	AJS
Sidecar	Eric Oliver (GB)	Norton

1950		
125cc	Bruno Ruffo (Ita)	Mondial
250cc	Dario Ambrosini (Ita)	Benelli
350cc	Bob Foster (GB)	Velocette
500cc	Umberto Masetti (Ita)	Gilera
Sidecar	Eric Oliver (GB)	Norton

1951		
125cc	Carlo Ubbiali (Ita)	Mondial
250cc	Bruno Ruffo (Ita)	Guzzi
350cc	Geoff Duke (GB)	Norton
500cc	Geoff Duke (GB)	Norton
Sidecar	Eric Oliver (GB)	Norton

1952		
125cc	Cecil Sandford (GB)	MV
250cc	Enrico Lorensetti (Ita)	Guzzi
350cc	Geoff Duke (UK)	Norton
500cc	Umberto Masetti (Ita)	Gilera
Sidecar	Cyril Smith (GB)	Norton

1953		
125cc	Werner Haas (FRG)	NSU
250cc	Werner Haas (FRG)	NSU
350cc	Fergus Anderson (GB)	Guzzi
500cc	Geoff Duke (GB)	Gilera

Sidecar	Eric Oliver (GB)	Norton
1954		
125cc	Rupert Hollaus (Aut)	NSU
250cc	Werner Haas (FRG)	NSU
350cc	Fergus Anderson (GB)	Guzzi
500cc	Geoff Duke (GB)	Gilera
Sidecar	Wilhelm Noll (FRG)	BMW
1955		
125cc	Carlo Ubbiali (Ita)	MV
250cc	Herman Muller (FRG)	NSU
350cc	Bill Lomas (GB)	Guzzi
500cc	Geoff Duke (GB)	Gilera
Sidecar	Wilhelm Faust (FRG)	BMW
1956		
125cc	Carlo Ubbiali (Ita)	MV
250cc	Carlo Ubbiali (Ita)	MV
350cc	Bill Lomas (GB)	Guzzi
500cc	John Surtees (GB)	MV
Sidecar	Wilhelm Noll (FRG)	BMW
1957		
125cc	Tarquinio Provini (Ita)	Mondial
250cc	Cecil Sandford (GB)	Mondial
350cc	Keith Campbell (Aus)	Guzzi
500cc	Libero Liberati (Ita)	Gilera
Sidecar	Fritz Hillebrand (FRG)	BMW
1958		
125cc	Carlo Ubbiali (Ita)	MV
250cc	Tarquinio Provini (Ita)	MV
350cc	John Surtees (GB)	MV
500cc	John Surtees (GB)	MV
Sidecar	Walter Schneider (FRG)	BMW
1959		
125cc	Carlo Ubbiali (Ita)	MV
250cc	Carlo Ubbiali (Ita)	MV
350cc	John Surtees (GB)	MV
500cc	John Surtees (GB)	MV
Sidecar	Walter Schneider (FRG)	BMW
1960		
125cc	Carlo Ubbiali (Ita)	MV
250cc	Carlo Ubbiali (Ita)	MV
350cc	John Surtees (GB)	MV
500cc	John Surtees (GB)	MV
Sidecar	Helmut Fath (FRG)	BMW
1961		
125cc	Tom Phillis (Aus)	Honda
250cc	Mike Hailwood (GB)	Honda
350cc	Gary Hocking (Rho)	MV
500cc	Gary Hocking (Rho)	MV
Sidecar	Max Deubel (FRG)	BMW
1962		
50cc	Ernst Degner (FRG)	Suzuki
125cc	Luigi Taveri (Swi)	Honda
250cc	Jim Redman (Rho)	Honda
350cc	Jim Redman (Rho)	Honda
500cc	Mike Hailwood (GB)	MV
Sidecar	Max Deubel (FRG)	BMW
1963		
50cc	Hugh Anderson (NZ)	Suzuki
100cc	Hugh Anderson (NZ)	Suzuki
125cc	Hugh Anderson (NZ)	Suzuki
250cc	Jim Redman (Rho)	Honda
350cc	Jim Redman (Rho)	Honda

500cc	Mike Hailwood (GB)	MV
Sidecar	Max Deubel (FRG)	BMW
1964		
50cc	Hugh Anderson (NZ)	Suzuki
125cc	Luigi Taveri (Swi)	Honda
250cc	Phil Read (GB)	Yamaha
350cc	Jim Redman (Rho)	Honda
500cc	Mike Hailwood (GB)	MV
Sidecar	Max Deubel (FRG)	BMW
1965		
50cc	Ralph Bryans (Ire)	Honda
125cc	Hugh Anderson (NZ)	Suzuki
250cc	Phil Read (GB)	Yamaha
350cc	Jim Redman (Rho)	Honda
500cc	Mike Hailwood (GB)	MV
Sidecar	Fritz Scheidegger (Swi)	BMW
1966		
50cc	Hans-Georg Anscheidt (FRG)	Suzuki
125cc	Luigi Taveri (Swi)	Honda
250cc	Mike Hailwood (GB)	Honda
350cc	Mike Hailwood (GB)	Honda
500cc	Giacomo Agostini (Ita)	MV
Sidecar	Fritz Scheidegger (Swi)	BMW
1967		
50cc	Hans-Georg Anscheidt(FRG)	Suzuki
125cc	Bill Ivy (GB)	Yamaha
250cc	Mike Hailwood (GB)	Honda
350cc	Mike Hailwood (GB)	Honda
500cc	Giacomo Agostini (Ita)	MV
Sidecar	Klaus Enders (FRG)	BMW
1968		
50cc	Hans-Georg Anscheidt (FRG)	Suzuki
125cc	Phil Read (GB)	Yamaha
250cc	Phil Read (GB)	Yamaha
350cc	Giacomo Agostini (Ita)	MV
500cc	Giacomo Agostini (Ita)	MV
Sidecar	Helmut Fath (FRG)	URS
1969		
50cc	Angel Nieto (Spa)	Derbi
125cc	Dave Simmonds (GB)	Kawasaki
250cc	Kel Carruthers (Aus)	Benelli
350cc	Giacomo Agostini (Ita)	MV
500cc	Giacomo Agostini (Ita)	MV
Sidecar	Klaus Enders (FRG)	BMW
1970		
50cc	Angel Nieto (Spa)	Derbi
125cc	Dieter Braun (FRG)	Suzuki
250cc	Rod Gould (GB)	Yamaha
350cc	Giacomo Agostini (Ita)	MV
500cc	Giacomo Agostini (Ita)	MV
Sidecar	Klaus Enders (FRG)	BMW
1971		
50cc	Jan de Vries (Hol)	Kreidler
125cc	Angel Nieto (Spa)	Derbi
250cc	Phil Read (GB)	Yamaha
350cc	Giacomo Agostini (Ita)	MV
500cc	Giacomo Agostini (Ita)	MV
Sidecar	Horst Owesle (FRG)	Munch
1972		
50cc	Angel Nieto (Spa)	Derbi
125cc	Angel Nieto (Spa)	Derbi
250cc	Jarno Saarinen (Fin)	Yamaha

350cc	Giacomo Agostini (Ita)	MV
500cc	Giacomo Agostini (Ita)	MV
Sidecar	Klaus Enders (FRG)	BMW

1973

50cc	Jan de Vries (Hol)	Kreidler
125cc	Kent Andersson (Swe)	Yamaha
250cc	Dieter Braun (FRG)	Yamaha
350cc	Giacomo Agostini (Ita)	MV
500cc	Phil Read (GB)	MV
Sidecar	Klaus Enders (FRG)	BMW

1974

50cc	Henk van Kessell (Hol)	Kreidler
125cc	Kent Andersson (Swe)	Yamaha
250cc	Walter Villa (Ita)	H-Davidson
350cc	Giacomo Agostini (Ita)	Yamaha
500cc	Phil Read (GB)	MV
Sidecar	Klaus Enders (FRG)	Busch BMW

1975

50cc	Angel Nieto (Spa)	Kreidler
125cc	Paolo Pileri (Ita)	Morbidelli
250cc	Walter Villa (Ita)	H-Davidson
350cc	Johnny Cecotto (Ven)	Yamaha
500cc	Giacomo Agostini (Ita)	Yamaha
Sidecar	Rolf Steinhausen (FRG)	Konig

1976

50cc	Angel Nieto (Spa)	Bultaco
125cc	Pier-Paolo Bianchi (Ita)	Morbidelli
250cc	Walter Villa (Ita)	H-Davidson
350cc	Walter Villa (Ita)	H-Davidson
500cc	Barry Sheene (GB)	Suzuki
Sidecar	Rolf Steinhausen (FRG)	Busch Konig

1977

50cc	Angel Nieto (Spa)	Bultaco
125cc	Pier-Paolo Bianchi (Ita)	Morbidelli
250cc	Mario Lega (Ita)	Morbidelli
350cc	Takazumi Katayama (Jap)	Yamaha
500cc	Barry Sheene (GB)	Suzuki
750cc	Steve Baker (US)	Yamaha
F1	Phil Read (GB)	Honda
Sidecar	George O'Dell (GB)	Yamaha

1978

50cc	Ricardo Tormo (Spa)	Bultaco
125cc	Eugenio Lazzarini (Ita)	MBA
250cc	Kork Ballington (SAf)	Kawasaki
350cc	Kork Ballington (SAf)	Kawasaki
500cc	Kenny Roberts (US)	Yamaha
750cc	Johnny Cecotto (Ven)	Yamaha
F1	Mike Hailwood (GB)	Ducati
Sidecar	Rolf Biland (Swi)	Yamaha

1979

50cc	Eugenio Lazzarini (Ita)	Kreidler
125cc	Angel Nieto (Spa)	Morbidelli
250cc	Kork Ballington (SAf)	Kawasaki
350cc	Kork Ballington (SAf)	Kawasaki
500cc	Kenny Roberts (US)	Yamaha
750cc	Patrick Pons (Fra)	Yamaha
F1	Ron Haslam (GB)	Honda
Sidecar	Rolf Biland (Swi)	Yamaha

1980

50cc	Eugenio Lazzarini (Ita)	Kreidler
125cc	Pier-Paolo Bianchi (Ita)	MBA
250cc	Anton Mang (FRG)	Kawasaki
350cc	John Ekerold (SAf)	Yamaha

500cc	Kenny Roberts (US)	Yamaha
F1	Graeme Crosby (NZ)	Suzuki
Sidecar	Jock Taylor (GB)	Yamaha

1981

50cc	Ricardo Tormo (Spa)	Bultaco
125cc	Angel Nieto (Spa)	Minarelli
250cc	Anton Mang (FRG)	Kawasaki
350cc	Anton Mang (FRG)	Kawasaki
500cc	Marco Lucchinelli (Ita)	Suzuki
F1	Graeme Crosby (NZ)	Suzuki
Sidecar	Rolf Biland (Swi)	Yamaha

1982

50cc	Stefan Dorflinger (Swi)	MBA
125cc	Angel Nieto (Spa)	Garelli
250cc	Jean-Louis Tournadre (Fra)	Yamaha
350cc	Anton Mang (FRG)	Kawasaki
500cc	Franco Uncini (Ita)	Suzuki
F1	Joey Dunlop (Ire)	Honda
Sidecar	Werner Schwarzel (FRG)	Yamaha

1983

50cc	Stefan Dorflinger (Swi)	Kreidler
125cc	Angel Nieto (Spa)	Garelli
250cc	Carlos Lavado (Ven)	Yamaha
500cc	Freddie Spencer (US)	Honda
F1	Joey Dunlop (Ire)	Honda
Sidecar	Rolf Biland (Swi)	Yamaha

1984

80cc	Stefan Dorflinger (Swi)	Zundapp
125cc	Angel Nieto (Spa)	Garelli
250cc	Christain Sarron (Fra)	Yamaha
500cc	Eddie Lawson (US)	Yamaha
F1	Joey Dunlop (Ire)	Honda
Sidecar	Egbert Streuer (Hol)	Yamaha

1985

80cc	Stefan Dorflinger (Swi)	Krauser
125cc	Fausto Gresini (Ita)	Garelli
250cc	Freddie Spencer (US)	Honda
500cc	Freddie Spencer (US)	Honda
F1	Joey Dunlop (Ire)	Honda
Sidecar	Egbert Streuer (Hol)	Yamaha

1986

80cc	Jorge Martinez (Spa)	Derbi
125cc	Luca Cadalora (Ita)	Garelli
250cc	Carlos Lavado (Ven)	Yamaha
500cc	Eddie Lawson (US)	Yamaha
F1	Joey Dunlop (Ire)	Honda
Sidecar	Egbert Streuer (Hol)	Yamaha

1987

80cc	Jorge Martinez (Spa)	Derbi
125cc	Fausto Gresini (Ita)	Garelli
250cc	Anton Mang (FRG)	Honda
500cc	Wayne Gardner (Aus)	Honda
F1	Virginio Ferrari (Ita)	Yamaha
Sidecar	Steve Webster (GB)	LCR Krauser

1988

80cc	Jorge Martinez (Spa)	Derbi
125cc	Jorge Martinez (Spa)	Derbi
250cc	Sito Pons (Spa)	Honda
500cc	Eddie Lawson (US)	Yamaha
F1	Carl Fogarty (GB)	Honda
Sidecar	Steve Webster (GB)	LCR Krauser

1989
80cc	Champi Herreros (Spa)	Derbi
125cc	Alex Crivelle (Spa)	Cobas
250cc	Sito Pons (Spa)	Honda
500cc	Eddie Lawson (US)	Honda
Sidecar	Steve Webster (GB)	Krauser

1990
125cc	Loris Capirossi (Ita)	Honda
250cc	John Kocinski (US)	Yamaha
500cc	Wayne Rainey (US)	Yamaha
Sidecar	Alain Michel (Fra)	Krauser

1991
125cc	Loris Capirossi(Ita)	Honda
250cc	Luca Cadalora (US)	Honda
500cc	Wayne Rainey (US)	Yamaha
Sidecar	Steve Webster (GB)	LCR

ISLE OF MAN - SENIOR TT WINNERS
All winners British Isles unless stated

1911	Oliver Godfrey, Indian 47.63mph
1912	Frank Applebee, Scott 48.69mph
1913	Tim Wood, Scott 48.27mph
1914	Cyril Pullin, Rudge 49.49mph
1915-19	Not held
1920	Tommy De La Hay, Sunbeam 51.48mph
1921	Howard Davies, AJS 54.50mph
1922	Alec Bennett, Sunbeam 58.31mph
1923	Tom Sheard, Douglas 55.55mph
1924	Alec Bennett, Norton 61.64mph
1925	Howard Davies, HRD 66.13mph
1926	Stanley Woods, Norton 67.54mph
1927	Alec Bennett, Norton 68.41mph
1928	Charlie Dodson, Sunbeam 62.98mph
1929	Charlie Dodson, Sunbeam 72.05mph
1930	Wal Handley, Rudge Whitworth 74.24mph
1931	Tim Hunt, Norton 77.90mph
1932	Stanley Woods, Norton 79.38mph
1933	Stanley Woods, Norton 77.16mph
1934	Jimmy Guthrie, Norton 78.01mph
1935	Stanley Woods, Moto Guzzi 84.68mph
1936	Jimmy Guthrie, Norton 85.80mph
1937	Freddie Frith, Norton 88.21mph
1938	Harold Daniell, Norton 89.11mph
1939	Georg Meir (Ger), BMW 89.38mph
1940-46	Not held
1947	Harold Daniell, Norton 82.81mph
1948	Artie Bell, Norton 84.97mph
1949	Harold Daniell, Norton 86.93mph
1950	Geoff Duke, Norton 92.27mph
1951	Geoff Duke, Norton 93.83mph
1952	Reg Armstrong, Norton 92.97mph
1953	Ray Amm (SRho), Norton 93.85mph
1954	Ray Amm (SRho), Norton 88.12mph
1955	Geoff Duke, Gilara 97.93mph
1956	John Surtees, MV Agusta 96.57mph
1957	Bob McIntyre, Gilera 98.99mph
1958	John Surtees, MV Agusta 98.63mph
1959	John Surtees, MV Agusta 87.94mph
1960	John Surtees, MV Agusta 102.44mph
1961	Mike Hailwood, Norton 100.60mph
1962	Gary Hockling (SRho), MV Agusta 103.51mph
1963	Mike Hailwood, MV Agusta 104.64mph
1964	Mike Hailwood, MV Agusta 100.95mph
1965	Mike Hailwood, MV Agusta 91.69mph
1966	Mike Hailwood, Honda 103.11mph
1967	Mike Hailwood, Honda 105.62mph
1968	Giacomo Agostini (Ita), MV Agusta 101.63mph
1969	Giacomo Agostini (Ita), MV Agusta 104.75mph
1970	Giacomo Agostini (Ita), MV Agusta 101.52mph
1971	Giacomo Agostini (Ita), MV Agusta 102.59mph
1972	Giacomo Agostini (Ita), MV Agusta 104.02mph
1973	Jack Findlay (Aus), Suzuki 101.55mph
1974	Phil Carpenter, Yamaha 96.99mph
1975	Mick Grant, Kawasaki 100.27mph
1976	Tom Herron, Yamaha 105.16mph
1977	Phil Read, Suzuki 106.98mph
1978	Tom Herron, Suzuki 111.74mph
1979	Mike Hailwood, Suzuki 111.75mph
1980	Graeme Crosby (NZ), Suzuki 109.65mph
1981	Mick Grant, Suzuki 106.14mph
1982	Norman Brown, Suzuki 110.98mph
1983	Not held
1984	Rob McElnea, Suzuki 115.66mph
1985	Joey Dunlop, Honda 113.69mph
1986	Roger Burnett, Honda 113.98mph
1987	Joey Dunlop, Honda 99.85mph
1988	Joey Dunlop, Honda 117.38mph
1989	Steve Hislop, Honda 118.23mph
1990	Carl Fogarty, Honda 110.95mph
1991	Steve Hislop, Honda 121.09mph

Most wins:
7 Mike Hailwood; 5 Giacomo Agostini (Ita); 4 Stanley Woods, John Surtees; 3 Alec Bennett, Harold Daniell, Geoff Duke, Joey Dunlop
Outright lap record: 123.48mph/198.72kph Steve Hislop, Honda, 1991

1992

GRANDS PRIX
(all dates provisional)

Mar 29	Japanese (Suzuka);
Apr 12	Australian (Eastern Creek);
Apr 26	US (Laguna Seca);
May 17	Spanish (Cataluna);
May 24	Italian (Mugello);
May 31	German (Nurburgring)
Jun 14	Austrian (Salzburgring);
Jun 27	Dutch (Assen);
Jul 5	Belgian (Spa-Francorchamps);
Jul 19	French (tba);
Aug 2	BRITISH (Donington Park);
Aug 9	Swedish (Anderstorp);
Aug 23	Czechoslovak (Brno);
Sep 13	Brazilian (Interlagos);
Sep 27	Malaysian (Johore)
Jun 6-12	Isle of Man TT

MOTOR RACING & RALLYING

MANSELL'S CHASE

After making the most sensational start ever to a Formula One championship, Ayrton Senna found himself harried to the finishing line by the unexpected figure of Nigel Mansell, who a year earlier had insisted he was giving up the sport forever.

Senna won the first four races of the year, an unprecedented sequence and led for 283 of the season's first 291 laps. However, before the season began, there was a feeling that the McLaren cars no longer possessed the huge technical advantage that had previously given Senna the edge. And as the year wore on, the proof came.

Mansell should have won the next race, in Canada, but broke down with engine trouble less than half a mile from an easy victory: he could almost have walked to the line and still won. Mansell said this was the worst of his many disappointments. Then his luck changed. He drove brilliantly in Mexico, driving a reserve car, when he was narrowly beaten by his Williams team-mate Riccardo Patrese. Then he won three in a row: in France, Britain and Germany. At Silverstone, he was roared to victory by a delighted crowd which could almost be heard above the engine noise and, although he was still behind in the table, he had what seemed like unstoppable momentum.

Senna now was the man with troubles. Before the Mexican race he gashed his head in a jet-ski accident and overturned in practice; at Hockenheim he repeatedly turned his car over at 190mph. He suffered only whiplash injuries. What bothered Senna more was his engine, whose high fuel consumption was turning into a handicap. Even after he hit back and won in Belgium and Italy he was insisting that Williams now had the faster car.

But Mansell also still had his inimitable ability to snatch defeat from the jaws of victory. Leading in Portugal, he stopped for a tyre change which his team botched; he then slowed down so they could make a second attempt in a section of the pits reserved for accelerating. Under Rule 133, he was disqualified and Williams did not even bother to protest. The championship seemed to be over but Mansell kept it alive by winning the following week in Spain.

Senna's long feud with Alain Prost, which reached a head during the bitter climax to the 1990 Championship, flared up again at Hockenheim where Senna failed to finish. He blamed Prost's tactics; FISA agreed and imposed a suspended one-race ban. Subsequently, the two men had 90 minutes of peace talks: "It's just a beginning," said Senna.

The Formula One driver Alessandro Nannini had his right forearm severed in a helicopter crash near his parents' home in Siena. Another, Bertrand Gachot of France, was jailed for 18 months by a London court for spraying CS gas in a taxi driver's face; he was lying 11th in the championship at the time. Paul Warwick, 22, younger brother of Derek, was killed at Oulton Park while leading the Gold Cup Formula 3000 race. He was posthumously awarded his fifth successive win.

Juan Manuel Fangio, just short of his 80th birthday, was reported to have spun his Mercedes off the road near his home in Argentina at over 100mph to avoid an oncoming truck. His passengers reported that Fangio just smiled and carried on. Juan Fangio II, the great man's nephew, won the Intercontinental Challenge, immediately after the British Grand Prix. Most of Brooklands, Britain's first circuit, was cleared of weeds as the opening phase in a restoration project. Another nostalgic British name, BRM, announced plans to return to the sport after 14 years' absence. Tomonori Tsuramaki, an art collector and entrepreneur, built a new track in a remote Japanese valley to try to wrest the country's Grand Prix from Suzuka. His £40 million Picasso, *Les Noces de Pierrette*, was housed next to the pits. It was worked out that if Emerson Fittipaldi's Indy 500 engine were put in the average lawn mower, it would cut half an acre in 5.6 seconds.

═══════════════ 1991 ═══════════════

FORMULA ONE WORLD CHAMPIONSHIP
United States GP
Phoenix, Arizona, Mar 10

1 Ayrton Senna (Bra)	McLaren
93.02mph/149.84kph	
2 Alain Prost (Fra)	Ferrari
3 Nelson Piquet (Bra)	Benetton
4 Stefano Modena (Ita)	Tyrrell
5 Satoru Nakajima (Jap)	Tyrrell
6 Aguri Suzuki (Jap)	Lola

Pole Position: Senna
Fastest lap: Jean Alesi (Fra) Ferrari, 95.94mph/154.40kph
Championship leaders:
1 Senna 10 pts; 2 Prost 6; 3 Piquet 4

Brazilian GP
Sao Paulo, Mar 24

1 Ayrton Senna (Bra)	McLaren
116.27mph/187.11kph	
2 Riccardo Patrese (Ita)	Williams
3 Gerhard Berger (Aut)	McLaren
4 Alain Prost (Fra)	Ferrari
5 Nelson Piquet (Bra)	Benetton
6 Jean Alesi (Fra)	Ferrari

This was the first time Senna had won his home grand prix
Pole Position: Senna
Fastest lap: Nigel Mansell (GB) Williams 120.28mph/193.58kph
Championship leaders:
1 Senna 20 pts; 2 Prost 9; 3 Piquet, Patrese 6

San Marino GP
San Marino, Apr 28

1 Ayrton Senna (Bra)	McLaren
120.34 mph/193.67kph	
2 Gerhard Berger (Aut)	McLaren
3 J J Lehto (Fin)	Dallara
4 Pierluigi Martini (Ita)	Minardi
5 Mika Hakkinen (Fin)	Lotus
6 Julian Bailey (GB)	Lotus

First time since Fangio in 1954 that any driver has won first three races of the season
Pole Position: Senna
Fastest Lap: Berger 130.29mph/209.69kph
Championship Leaders:
1 Senna 30 pts; 2 Berger 10; 3 Prost 9

Monaco GP
Monte Carlo, May 12

1 Ayrton Senna (Bra)	McLaren
85.62mph/137.79kph	
2 Nigel Mansell (GB)	Williams
3 Jean Alesi (Fra)	Ferrari
4 Roberto Moreno (Bra)	Benetton
5 Alain Prost (Fra)	Ferrari
6 Emannuelle Pirro (Ita)	Dalara

Senna became the first man to win the opening four races of a season
Pole Position: Senna
Fastest Lap: Prost, 88.24mph/142.01kph
Championship Leaders:
1 Senna 40 pts; 2 Prost 11; 3 Berger 10

Canadian GP
Montreal, Jun 2

1 Nelson Piquet (Bra)	Benetton
113.41mph/186.52kph	
2 Stefano Modena (Ita)	Tyrrell
3 Riccardo Patrese (Ita)	Williams
4 Andrea de Cesaris (Ita)	Jordan
5 Bertrand Gachot (Bel)	Jordan
6 Nigel Mansell (GB)	Williams

Mansell had race won but his car ground to a halt on the last lap with the chequered flag in sight
Pole Position: Patrese
Fastest Lap: Mansell, 120.29mph/193.58kph
Championship Leaders:
1 Senna 40 pts; 2 Piquet 16; 3 Prost 11

Mexican GP
Mexico City, Jun 16

1 Riccardo Patrese (Ita)	Williams
123.60mph/198.91kph	
2 Nigel Mansell (GB)	Williams
3 Ayrton Senna (Bra)	McLaren
4 Andrea de Cesaris (Ita)	Jordan
5 Roberto Moreno (Bra)	Benetton
6 Eric Bernard (Fra)	Lola

Patrese's fourth win in a record 214 grands prix
Pole Position: Patrese
Fastest Lap: Mansell 128.80mph/207.27kph
Championship Leaders: 1 Senna 44pts; 2 Patrese 20; 3 Piquet 16

French GP
Magny Cours, Jul 7

1 Nigel Mansell (GB)	Williams
116.99mph/188.27kph	
2 Alain Prost (Fra)	Ferrari
3 Ayrton Senna (Bra)	McLaren
4 Jean Alesi (Fra)	Ferrari
5 Riccardo Patrese (Ita)	Williams
6 Andrea de Cesaris (Ita)	Jordan

Mansell's 17th win of his career which took him past Stirling Moss as the most successful English driver of all time
Pole position: Patrese
Fastest lap: Mansell 120.68mph/194.22kph
Championship leaders:
1 Senna 48pts; 2 Mansell 23; 3 Patrese 22

British GP
Silverstone, Jul 14

1 Nigel Mansell (GB)	Williams
131.23mph/211.19kph	
2 Gerhard Berger (Aut)	McLaren
3 Alain Prost (Fra)	Ferrari
4 Ayrton Senna (Bra)	McLaren
5 Nelson Piquet (Bra)	Benetton
6 Bertrand Gachot (Bel)	Jordan

Pole Position: Mansell
Fastest Lap: Mansell, 135.33mph/217.84kph
Championship Leaders:
1 Senna 51 pts; 2 Mansell 33; 3 Patrese 22

West German GP
Hockenheim, Jul 28

1 Nigel Mansell (GB) 143.58mph/231.07kph	Williams
2 Riccado Patrese (Ita)	Williams
3 Jean Alesi (Fra)	Ferrari
4 Gerhard Berger (Aut)	McLaren
5 Andrea de Cesaris (Ita)	Jordan
6 Bertrand Gachot (Bel)	Jordan

Pole Position: Mansell
Fastest Lap: Patrese 146.92mph/236.4kph
Championship Leaders:
1 Senna 51pts; 2 Mansell 43; 3 Patrese 28

Hungarian GP
Hungaroring, Budapest, Aug 11

1 Ayrton Senna (Bra) 104.91mph/168.84kph	McLaren
2 Nigel Mansell (GB)	Williams
3 Riccardo Patrese (Ita)	Williams
4 Gerhard Berger (Aut)	Benetton
5 Jean Alesi (Fra)	Ferrari
6 Ivan Capelli (Ita)	Leyton House

Pole Position: Senna
Fastest Lap: Bertrand Gachot (Bel) Jordan 109.48mph/176.20kph
Championship Leaders:
1 Senna 61pts; 2 Mansell 49; 3 Patrese 32

Belgian GP
Spa, Aug 25

1 Ayrton Senna (Bra) 130.42mph/209.89kph	McLaren
2 Gerhard Berger (Aut)	McLaren
3 Nelson Piquet (Bra)	Benetton
4 Roberto Moreno (Bra)	Benetton
5 Riccardo Patrese (Ita)	Williams
6 Mark Blundell (GB)	Brabham

Pole Position: Senna
Fastest Lap: Moreno 134.81mph/216.95kph
Championship Leaders:
1 Senna 71 pts; 2 Mansell 49; 3 Patrese 34

Italian GP
Monza, Sep 8

1 Nigel Mansell (GB)	Williams
2 Ayrton Senna (Bra)	McLaren
3 Alain Prost (Fra)	Ferrari
4 Gerhard Berger(Aut)	McLaren
5 Michael Schumacher (Ger)	Benetton
6 Nelson Piquet (Bra)	Benetton

Pole Position: Senna
Fastest Lap: Senna 150.76mph/241.21kph
Championship Leaders:
1 Senna 77pts; 2 Mansell 59; 3 Patrese 34

Portuguese GP
Estoril, Sep 22

1 Riccardo Patrese (Ita) 120.31mph/193.63kph	Williams
2 Ayrton Senna (Bra)	McLaren
3 Jean Alesi (Fra)	Ferrari
4 Pierluigi Martini (Ita)	Minardi
5 Nelson Piquet (Bra)	Benetton
6 Michael Schumacher (Ger)	Benetton

Pole Position: Patrese
Fastest Lap: Nigel Mansell (GB) Williams 124.47mph/200.31kph
Championship Leaders:
1 Senna 83pts; 2 Mansell 59; 3 Patrese 44

AYRTON & FRIENDS

❝If everybody wants to drive in this way then the sport is finished. Senna is completely the opposite in character to what he wants people to believe. He is the opposite of honest. Motor racing is sport not war.❞
Alain Prost on the crash at Suzuka which cost him the 1990 Championship

"I don't give a damn what Alain Prost says. He took a chance going into the first corner when he couldn't afford to. He knew that I was going to come down the inside and he closed the door."
Senna, ditto

"There's a different feeling about 1991, a feeling that McLaren and Honda can be beaten."
Frank Williams before the season began

"God gave me this victory. How do you explain that I managed to complete the last seven laps with virtually no tyres left? And how do you explain the fact that it only started raining heavily the second I crossed the finish line?"
Senna, after his win in Brazil

"What are we supposed to do: lose occasionally to keep it interesting?"
Ron Dennis, McLaren-Honda team director, after Senna's fourth consecutive win

"For the first time I would say that Senna is now undoubtedly the best driver in the world rather than merely the fastest. If he had a weakness, it was always impatience - a tendency to make mistakes when he was lapping backmarkers put himself and his victory to unnecessary risk. But this year he seems to have taken care of that."
Jackie Stewart

"Oh, what a brilliant blazing triumph.."
The Sun on Mansell's win in the British Grand Prix

"I missed the light at the start then gave it some welly and went into a wheel spin...I got very panicky over the last 10 laps or so. The box began missing gears, jumping gears and, for a moment, not selecting any gears at all..."
Mansell, ditto

"Losers sound like Mansell did...hard as he tries, he never quite comes across, maybe never will, as the hero he was for thousands."
Ken Jones, The Independent

"I know whatever will be, will be.❞
Mansell, after winning in Spain

Spanish GP
Circuit de Catalunya, Sep 29

1 Nigel Mansell (GB)	Williams
116.56mph/187.59kph	
2 Alain Prost (Fra)	Ferrari
3 Riccardo Patrese (Ita)	Williams
4 Jean Alesi (Fra)	Ferrari
5 Ayrton Senna (Bra)	McLaren
6 Michael Schumacher (Ger)	Benetton

Pole Position: Gerhard Berger (Aut) McLaren
Fastest Lap: Patrese 128.19mph/206.30kph
Championship Leaders:
1 Senna 85pts; 2 Mansell 69; 3 Patrese 48

WORLD SPORTSCAR CHAMPIONSHIP
Round One *Suzuka, Japan, Apr 14*
Mauro Baldi (Ita)/Phillipe Alliot (Fra) Peugeot
Round Two *Monza, Italy, May 5*
Derek Warwick/Martin Brundle (GB) Silk Cut Jaguar
Round Three *Silverstone, May 19*
Teo Fabi (Ita)/Martin Brundle (GB) Silk Cut Jaguar
Round Four *Le Mans, Jun 22-23*
Volker Weidler (Ger)/Johnny Herbert (GB)/Bertrand
Gachot (Bel) Mazda
Round Five *Nurburgring, Aug 18*
Derek Warwick (GB)/David Brabham (Aus) Silk Cut
Jaguar
Round six *Magny-Cours, France Sep 15*
Yannick Dalmas (Fra)/Keke Rosberg (Fin) Peugeot

FIA FORMULA 3000 CHAMPIONSHIP
(Winners only)
Round One *Vallelunga, Italy, Apr 14*
Alessandro Zanardi (Ita) Reynard
Round Two *Pau, France, May 20*
Jean-Marc Gounon (Fra) Ralt
Round Three *Jerez, Spain, Jun 9*
Christian Fittipaldi (Bra) Reynard
Round Four *Mugello, Italy, Jun 23*
Alessandro Zanardi (Ita) Reynard
Round Five *Pergusa, Italy, Jul 7*
Emanuelle Naspetti (Ita) Reynard
Round Six *Hockenheim, Germany, Jul 27*
Emanuelle Naspetti (Ita) Reynard
Round Seven *Brands Hatch, Aug 18*
Emanuelle Naspetti (Ita) Reynard
Round Eight *Spa, Belgium, Aug 24*
Emanuelle Naspetti (Ita) Reynard
Round Nine *Le Mans, France, Sep 22*
Antonio Tamburini (Ita) Reynard
Round Ten *Nogaro, France, Oct 6*
Christian Fittipaldi (Bra) Reynard
Champion: Fittipaldi

OTHER MAJOR RESULTS
Daytona 24 Hours
Daytona, Feb 2-3
1 Frank Jelinski (Ger)/John Winter (Ger)/Henri Pescarolo
(Fra)/Hurley Haywood (US) Porsche 106.63mph/
171.13kph
2 Geoff Brabham (Aus)/Chip Robinson (US)/Derek Daly
(Ire)/Bob Earl (US) Nissan
3 John Hotchkis/Jim Adams/Chris Cord (all US) Porsche

Daytona 500
Daytona, Feb 17
1 Ernie Irvan (US) Chevrolet Lumina
148.15mph/238.42kph
2 Sterling Marlin (US) Ford Thunderbird
3 Joe Ruttman (US) Oldsmobile Cutlass

Indianapolis 500
May 27
1 Rick Mears (US) Penske-Chevrolet 176.46 mph/
283.98kph
2 Michael Andretti (US) Lola-Chevrolet
3 Arie Luyendyk (Hol) Lola-Chevrolet

Le Mans 24-Hour Race
Le Mans, Jun 22-23
1 Volker Weidler (Ger)/Johnny Herbert (GB)/Bertrand
Gachot (Bel) Mazda 362 laps 128.33mph/206.53kph
2 Davy Jones (USA)/Raul Boesel (Bra)/Michel Ferte (Fra)
Jaguar 360 laps
3 Bob Wollek (Fra)/Ken Acheson (Ire)/Teo Fabi (Ita)
Jaguar 358 laps

RALLYING
PARIS-DAKAR RALLY
Dec 29-Jan 16
1 Ari Vattanen (Fin) Citroen 32h 20m 50s
2 Pierre Lartigue (Fra) Mitsubishi 35h 03m 17s
3 Jean-Pierre Fontenay (Fra) Mitsubishi 35h 44m 56s
Vattanen's fourth victory

MONTE CARLO RALLY
Jan 24-31
1 Carlos Sainz (Spa) Toyota 6h 57m 21s
2 Miki Biasion (Ita) Lancia 7h 02m 20s
3 Francois Delacour (Fra) Ford 7h 03m 33s

SWEDISH RALLY
Feb 16-18
1 Kenneth Eriksson (Swe) Mitsubishi 4h 56m 16s
2 Mats Jonsson (Swe) Toyota 4h 56m 36s
3 Markku Alén (Fin) Subaru 4h 57m 20s

SAFARI RALLY
Mar 27-Apr 1
1 Juha Kankkunen (Fin) Lancia 2h 07m 10s
2 Mikael Ericsson (Swe) Toyota 2h 33m 34s
3 Jorge Recalde (Arg) Lancia 2h 46m 13s

ACROPOLIS RALLY
Jun 2-5
1 Juha Kankkunen (Fin) Lancia 7h 20m 05s
2 Carlos Sainz (Spa) Toyota 7h 21m 06s
3 Miki Biasion (Ita) Lancia 7h 23m 35s

NEW ZEALAND RALLY
Jun 25-30
1 Carlos Sainz (Spa) Toyota, 6h 57m 18s
2 Juha Kankkunen (Fin) Lancia, 6h 58m 33s
3 Didier Auriol (Fra) Lancia, 6h 59m 36s

ARGENTINA RALLY
Jul 23-27
1 Carlos Sainz (Spa) Toyota 6h 37m 31s
2 Massimo Biasion (Ita) Lancia 6h 37m 39s
3 Didier Auriol (Fra) Lancia 6h 38m 36s

1000 LAKES RALLY
Finland, Aug 20-26
1 Juha Kankkunen (Fin) Lancia 4h 36m 52s
2 Didier Auriol (Fra) Lancia 4h 37m 48s
3 Timo Salonen (Fin) Mitsubishi 4h 38m 59s

AUSTRALIAN RALLY
Sep 23-30
1 Juha Kankkunen (Fin) Lancia 5h 48m 48s
2 Kenneth Eriksson (Swe) Mitsubishi 5h 50m 1s
3 Armin Schwarz (Ger) Toyota 5h 54m 42s

1990

FORMULA ONE GRAND PRIX
Japanese GP
Suzuka, Oct 21
1 Nelson Piquet (Bra) Benetton
  123.08mph/198.08kph
2 Roberto Moreno (Bra) Benetton
3 Aguri Suzuki (Jap) Lola

Australian GP
Adelaide, Nov 4
1 Nelson Piquet (Bra) Benetton
  104.02mph/167.40kph
2 Nigel Mansell (GB) Ferrari
3 Alain Prost (Fra) Ferrari

FINAL STANDINGS
Leading Positions
Drivers
1 Ayrton Senna (Bra) 78 pts
2 Alain Prost (Fra) 71 pts
3 Nelson Piquet (Bra) 43 pts
4 Gerhard Berger (Aut) 43 pts
5 Nigel Mansell (GB) 37 pts
6 Thierry Boutsen (Bel) 34 pts
Constructors
1 McLaren 121 pts
2 Ferrari 110 pts
3 Benetton 71 pts
4 Williams 57 pts
5 Tyrrell 16 pts

CHAMPIONS

FORMULA ONE WORLD CHAMPIONSHIP
Drivers

Year	Winner	Car	Runner-up	Third
1950	Giuseppe Farina (Ita)	Alfa Romeo	Juan Manuel Fangio (Arg)	Luigi Fagioli (Ita)
1951	Juan Manuel Fangio (Arg)	Alfa Romeo	Alberto Ascari (Ita)	Jose Gonzalez (Arg)
1952	Alberto Ascari (Ita)	Ferrari	Giuseppe Farina (Ita)	Piero Taruffi (Ita)
1953	Alberto Ascari (Ita)	Ferrari	Juan Manuel Fangio (Arg)	Giuseppe Farina (Ita)
1954	Juan Manuel Fangio (Arg)	Maserati/Mercedes	Jose Gonzalez (Arg)	Mike Hawthorn (GB)
1955	Juan Manuel Fangio (Arg)	Mercedes-Benz	Stirling Moss (GB)	Eugenio Castellotti (Ita)
1956	Juan Manuel Fangio (Arg)	Lancia-Ferrari	Stirling Moss (GB)	Peter Collins (GB)
1957	Juan Manuel Fangio (Arg)	Maserati	Stirling Moss (GB)	Luigi Musso (Ita)
1958	Mike Hawthorn (GB)	Ferrari	Stirling Moss (GB)	Tony Brooks (GB)
1959	Jack Brabham (Aus)	Cooper-Climax	Tony Brooks (GB)	Stirling Moss (GB)
1960	Jack Brabham (Aus)	Cooper-Climax	Bruce McLaren (NZ)	Stirling Moss (GB)
1961	Phil Hill (US)	Ferrari	Wolfgang von Trips (FRG)	Stirling Moss (GB)
1962	Graham Hill (GB)	BRM	Jim Clark (GB)	Bruce McLaren (NZ)
1963	Jim Clark (GB)	Lotus-Climax	Graham Hill (GB)	Richie Ginther (US)
1964	John Surtees (GB)	Ferrari	Graham Hill (GB)	Jim Clark (GB)
1965	Jim Clark (GB)	Lotus-Climax	Graham Hill (GB)	Jackie Stewart (GB)
1966	Jack Brabham (Aus)	Brabham-Repco	John Surtees (GB)	Jochen Rindt (Aut)
1967	Denny Hulme (NZ)	Brabham-Repco	Jack Brabham (Aus)	Jim Clark (GB)
1968	Graham Hill (GB)	Lotus-Ford	Jackie Stewart (GB)	Denny Hulme (NZ)
1969	Jackie Stewart (GB)	Matra-Ford	Jacky Ickx (Bel)	Bruce McLaren (NZ)
1970	Jochen Rindt (Aut)	Lotus-Ford	Jacky Ickx (Bel)	Clay Regazzoni (Swi)
1971	Jackie Stewart (GB)	Tyrrell-Ford	Ronnie Peterson (Swe)	Francois Cevert (Fra)
1972	Emerson Fittipaldi (Bra)	Lotus-Ford	Jackie Stewart (GB)	Denny Hulme (NZ)
1973	Jackie Stewart (GB)	Tyrrell-Ford	Emerson Fittipaldi (Bra)	Ronnie Peterson (Swe)
1974	Emerson Fittipaldi (Bra)	McLaren-Ford	Clay Regazzoni (Swi)	Jody Scheckter (SA)
1975	Niki Lauda (Aut)	Ferrari	Emerson Fittipaldi (Bra)	Carlos Reutemann (Arg)
1976	James Hunt (GB)	McLaren-Ford	Niki Lauda (Aut)	Jody Scheckter (SA)
1977	Niki Lauda (Aut)	Ferrari	Jody Scheckter (SA)	Mario Andretti (US)
1978	Mario Andretti (US)	Lotus-Ford	Ronnie Peterson (Swe)	Carlos Reutemann (Arg)
1979	Jody Scheckter (SA)	Ferrari	Gilles Villeneuve (Can)	Alan Jones (Aus)
1980	Alan Jones (Aus)	Williams-Ford	Nelson Piquet (Bra)	Carlos Reutemann (Arg)
1981	Nelson Piquet (Bra)	Brabham-Ford	Carlos Reutemann (Arg)	Alan Jones (Aus)
1982	Keke Rosberg (Fin)	Williams-Ford	Didier Pironi (Fra) and John Watson (GB)	
1983	Nelson Piquet (Bra)	Brabham-BMW	Alain Prost (Fra)	Rene Arnoux (Fra)
1984	Niki Lauda (Aut)	McLaren-TAG	Alain Prost (Fra)	Elio de Angelis (Ita)
1985	Alain Prost (Fra)	McLaren-TAG	Michele Alboreto (Ita)	Keke Rosberg (Fin)
1986	Alain Prost (Fra)	McLaren-TAG	Nigel Mansell (GB)	Nelson Piquet (Bra)
1987	Nelson Piquet (Bra)	Williams-Honda	Nigel Mansell (GB)	Ayrton Senna (Bra)

1988	Ayrton Senna (Bra)	McLaren-Honda	Alain Prost (Fra)	Gerhard Berger (Aut)
1989	Alain Prost (Fra)	McLaren-Honda	Ayrton Senna (Bra)	Riccardo Patrese (Ita)
1990	Ayrton Senna (Bra)	McLaren-Honda	Alain Prost (Fra)	Nelson Piquet (Bra)

Most titles: 5 Fangio; **3** Brabham, Stewart, Lauda, Piquet, Prost; **2** Clark, Ascari, Graham Hill, Fittipaldi, Senna

Constructors' Cup

1958 Vanwall	1959 Cooper-Climax	1960 Cooper-Climax	1961 Ferrari	1962 BRM
1963 Lotus-Climax	1964 Ferrari	1965 Lotus-Climax	1966 Brabham-Repco	1967 Brabham-Repco
1968 Lotus-Ford	1969 Matra-Ford	1970 Lotus-Ford	1971 Tyrrell-Ford	1972 Lotus-Ford
1973 Lotus-Ford	1974 McLaren-Ford	1975 Ferrari	1976 Ferrari	1977 Ferrari
1978 Lotus-Ford	1979 Ferrari	1980 Williams-Ford	1981 Williams-Ford	1982 Ferrari
1983 Ferrari	1984 McLaren-Porsche	1985 McLaren-TAG	1986 Williams-Honda	1987 Williams-Honda
1988 McLaren-Honda	1989 McLaren-Honda	1990 McLaren-Honda		

Most titles: 8 Ferrari; **7** Lotus (5 Lotus-Ford; 2 Lotus-Climax); **6** McLaren (1 McLaren-TAG; 1 McLaren-Ford; **3** McLaren-Honda; 1 McLaren-Porsche); **4** Williams (2 Williams-Ford; 2 Williams-Honda)

THE RACE WINNERS
(up to and including Sep 1991)

ALBORETO, Michele (5)
1982 Las Vegas; 1983 Detroit (both Tyrrell); 1984 Belgian; 1985 Canadian, German (all Ferrari)

ANDRETTI, Mario (12)
1971 South African (Ferrari); 1976 Japanese; 1977 United States (West), Spanish, French, Italian; 1978 Argentine, Belgian, Spanish, French, German, Dutch (all Lotus)

ARNOUX, Rene (7)
1980 Brazilian, South African; 1982 French, Italian (all Renault); 1983 Canadian, German, Dutch (all Ferrari)

ASCARI, Alberto (13)
1951 German, Italian; 1952 Belgian, French, British, German, Dutch, Italian; 1953 Argentine, Dutch, Belgian, British, Swiss (all Ferrari)

BAGHETTI, Giancarlo (1)
1961 French (Ferrari)

BANDINI, Lorenzo (1)
1964 Austrian (Ferrari)

BELTOISE, Jean-Pierre (1)
1972 Monaco (BRM)

BERGER, Gerhard (5)
1986 Mexican (Benetton); 1987 Japanese, Australian; 1988 Italian; 1989 Portuguese (all Ferrari)

BONNIER, Jo (1)
1959 Dutch (BRM)

BOUTSEN, Thierry (2)
1989 Canadian, Australian (both Williams)

BRABHAM, Jack (14)
1959 Monaco, British; 1960 Dutch, Belgian, French, British, Portuguese (all Cooper); 1966 French, British, Dutch, German; 1967 French, Canadian; 1970 South African (all Brabham)

BRAMBILLA, Vittorio (1)
1975 Austrian (March)

BROOKS, Tony (6)
1957 British*; 1958 Belgian, German, Italian (all Vanwall); 1959 French, German (both Ferrari)

CEVERT, Francois (1)
1971 United States (Tyrrell)

CLARK, Jim (25)
1962 Belgian, British, United States; 1963 Belgian, Dutch, French, British, Italian, Mexican, South African; 1964 Dutch, Belgian, British; 1965 South African, Belgian, French, British, Dutch, German; 1966 United States; 1967 Dutch, British, United States, Mexican; 1968 South African (all Lotus)

COLLINS, Peter (3)
1956 Belgian, French (both Lancia-Ferrari); 1968 British (Ferrari)

DE ANGELIS, Elio (2)
1982 Austrian; 1985 San Marino (both Lotus)

DEPAILLER, Patrick (2)
1978 Monaco (Tyrrell); 1979 Spanish (Ligier)

FAGIOLI, Luigi (1)
1951 French* (Alfa Romeo)

FANGIO, Juan Manuel (24)
1950 Monaco, Belgian, French; 1951 Swiss, French, Spanish (all Alfa Romeo); 1953 Italian (Maserati); 1954 Argentine, Belgian (both Maserati), French, German, Swiss, Italian; 1955 Argentine, Belgian, Dutch, Italian (all Mercedes-Benz); 1956 Argentine*, British, German (all Lancia-Ferrari); 1957 Argentine, Monaco, French, German (all Maserati)

FARINA, Giuseppe (5)
1950 British, Swiss, Italian; 1951 Belgian (all Alfa Romeo); 1953 German (Ferrari)

FITTIPALDI, Emerson (14)
1970 United States; 1972 Spanish, Belgian, British, Austrian, Italian; 1973 Argentine, Brazilian, Spanish (all Lotus); 1974 Brazilian, Belgian, Canadian; 1975 Argentine, British (all McLaren)

GETHIN, Peter (1)
1971 Italian (BRM)

GINTHER, Richie (1)
1965 Mexican (Honda)

GONZALEZ, Jose Froilan (2)
1951 British; 1954 British (both Ferrari)

GURNEY, Dan (4)
1962 French (Porsche); 1964 French, Mexican (both Brabham); 1967 Belgian (Eagle)

HAWTHORN, Mike (3)
1953 French; 1954 Spanish; 1958 French (all Ferrari)

HILL, Graham (14)
1962 Dutch, German, Italian, South African; 1963 Monaco, United States; 1964 Monaco, United States; 1965 Monaco, United States (all BRM); 1968 Spanish, Monaco, Mexican; 1969 Monaco (all Lotus)

HILL, Phil (3)
1960 Italian; 1961 Belgian, Italian (all Ferrari)

HULME, Denny (8)
1967 Monaco, German (both Brabham); 1968 Italian, Canadian; 1969 Mexico; 1972 South African; 1973 Swedish; 1974 Argentine (all McLaren)

HUNT, James (10)
1975 Dutch (Hesketh); 1976 Spanish, French, German, Dutch, Canadian, United States; 1977 British, United States; Japanese (all McLaren)

ICKX, Jacky (8)
1968 French (Ferrari); 1969 German, Canadian (both Brabham); 1970 Austrian, Canadian, Mexican; 1971 Dutch; 1972 German (all Ferrari)

IRELAND, Innes (1)
1961 United States (Lotus)

JABOUILLE, Jean-Pierre (2)
1979 French; 1980 Austrian (both Renault)

JONES, Alan (12)
1977 Austrian (Shadow); 1979 German, Austrian, Dutch, Canadian; 1980 Argentine, French, British, Canadian,

United States; 1981 United States (West), Las Vegas (all Williams)

LAFFITE, Jacques (6)
1977 Swedish; 1979 Argentine, Brazilian; 1980 German (all Ligier); 1981 Austrian, Canadian (both Talbot-Ligier)

LAUDA, Niki (25)
1974 Spanish, Dutch; 1975 Monaco, Belgian, Swedish, French, United States; 1976 Brazilian, South African, Belgian, Monaco, British; 1977 South African, German, Dutch (all Ferrari); 1978 Swedish, Italian (both Brabham); 1982 United States (West), British; 1984 South African, French, British, Austrian, Italian; 1985 Dutch (all McLaren)

McLAREN, Bruce (4)
1959 United States; 1960 Argentine; 1962 Monaco (all Cooper); 1968 Belgian (McLaren)

MANSELL, Nigel (21)
1985 European, South African; 1986 Belgian, Canadian, French, British, Portuguese; 1987 San Marino, French, British, Austrian, Spanish, Mexican (all Williams); 1989 Brazilian, Hungarian; 1990 Portuguese (all Ferrari); 1991 French, British, German, Italian, Spanish (all Williams)

MASS, Jochen (1)
1975 Spanish (McLaren)

MOSS, Stirling (16)
1955 British (Mercedes-Benz); 1956 Monaco, Italian (both Maserati); 1957 British*, Pescara, Italian (all Vanwall); 1958 Argentine (Cooper), Dutch, Portuguese, Moroccan (all Vanwall); 1959 Portuguese, Italian (Cooper); 1960 Monaco, United States; 1961 Monaco, German (all Lotus)

MUSSO, Luigi (1)
1956 Argentine* (Lancia-Ferrari)

NANNINI, Alessandro (1)
1989 Japanese (Benetton)

NILSON, Gunnar (1)
1977 Belgian (Lotus)

PACE, Carlos (1)
1975 Brazilian (Brabham)

PATRESE, Riccardo (5)
1982 Monaco; 1983 South African (both Brabham) 1990 San Marino ;1991 Mexican, Portuguese (all Williams)

PETERSON, Ronnie (10)
1973 French, Austrian, Italian, United States; 1974 Monaco, French, Italian (all Lotus); 1976 Italian (March); 1978 South African, Austrian (both Lotus)

PIRONI, Didier (3)
1980 Belgian (Ligier); 1982 San Marino, Dutch (both Ferrari)

PIQUET, Nelson (23)
1980 United States (West), Dutch, Italian; 1981 Argentine, San Marino, German; 1982 Canadian; 1983 Brazilian, Italian, European; 1984 Canadian, Detroit; 1985 French (all Brabham); 1986 Brazilian, German, Hungarian, Italian; 1987 German, Hungarian, Italian (all Williams); 1990 Japanese, Australian; 1991 Canadian (all Benetton)

PROST, Alain (44)
1981 French, Dutch, Italian; 1982 South African, Brazilian; 1983 French, Belgian, British, Austrian (all Renault); 1984 Brazilian, San Marino, Monaco, German, Dutch, European, Portuguese; 1985 Brazilian, Monaco, British, Austrian, Italian; 1986 San Marino, Monaco, Austrian, Australian; 1987 Brazilian, Belgian, Portuguese;1988 Brazilian, Monaco, Mexican, French, Portuguese, Spanish, Australian; 1989 United States, French, British, Italian (all McLaren); 1990 Brazilian, Mexican, French, British, Spanish (all Ferrari)

REGAZZONI, Clay (5)
1970 Italian; 1974 German; 1975 Italian; 1976 United States (West) (all Ferrari); 1979 British (Williams)

REUTEMANN, Carlos (12)
1974 South African, Austrian, United States; 1975 German

(all Brabham); 1977 Brazilian; 1978 Brazilian, United States (West), British, United States (all Ferrari); 1980 Monaco; 1981 Brazilian, Belgian (all Williams)

REVSON, Peter (2)
1973 British, Canadian (both McLaren)

RINDT, Jochen (6)
1969 United States; 1970 Monaco, Dutch, French, British, German (all Lotus)

RODRIGUEZ, Pedro (2)
1967 South African (Cooper); 1970 Belgian (BRM)

ROSBERG, Keke (5)
1982 Swiss; 1983 Monaco; 1984 Dallas; 1985 Detroit, Australian (all Williams)

SCARFIOTTI, Ludovico (1)
1966 Italian (Ferrari)

SCHECKTER, Jody (10)
1974 Swedish, British; 1975 South African; 1976 Swedish (all Tyrrell); 1977 Argentine, Monaco, Canadian (all Wolf); 1979 Belgian, Monaco, Italian (all Ferrari)

SENNA, Ayrton (31)
1985 Portuguese, Belgian; 1986 Spanish, Detroit; 1987 Monaco, United States (all Lotus); 1988 San Marino, Canadian, United States, British, German, Hungarian, Belgian, Japanese; 1989 San Marino, Monaco, Mexican, German, Belgian; 1990 United States, Monaco, Canadian, German, Belgian, Italian; 1991 United States, Brazilian, San Marino, Monaco, Hungary, Belgian (all McLaren)

SIFFERT, Jo (2)
1968 British (Lotus); 1971 Austrian (BRM)

STEWART, Jackie (27)
1965 Italian; 1966 Monaco (both BRM); 1968 Dutch, German, United States; 1969 South African, Spanish, Dutch, French, British, Italian (all Matra); 1970 Spanish (March); 1971 Spanish, Monaco, French, British, German, Canadian; 1972 Argentine, French, Canadian, United States; 1973 South African, Belgian, Monaco, Dutch, German (all Tyrrell)

SURTEES, John (6)
1963 German; 1964 German, Italian; 1966 Belgian (all Ferrari), Mexican (Cooper); 1967 Italian (Honda)

TAMBAY, Patrick (2)
1982 German; 1983 San Marino (both Ferrari)

TARUFFI, Piero (1)
1952 Swiss (Ferrari)

TRINTIGNANT, Maurice (2)
1955 Monaco (Ferrari); 1958 Monaco (Cooper)

VILLENEUVE, Gilles (6)
1978 Canadian; 1979 South African, United States (West), United States; 1981 Monaco, Spanish (all Ferrari)

VON TRIPS, Wolfgang (2)
1961 Dutch, British (both Ferrari)

WATSON, John (5)
1976 Austrian (Penske); 1981 British; 1982 Belgian, Detroit; 1983 United States West (all McLaren)

* denotes shared drive
     only half points awarded

Figures in brackets () indicate total wins

Most wins in a season
8 Ayrton Senna (Bra) 1988; 7 Jim Clark (GB) 1963, Alain Prost (Fra) 1984, 1988; 6 Alberto Ascari (Ita) 1952, Juan Manuel Fangio (Arg) 1954, Jim Clark (GB) 1965, Jackie Stewart (GB) 1969, 1971, James Hunt (GB) 1976, Mario Andretti (US) 1978, Nigel Mansell (GB) 1987, Ayrton Senna (Bra) 1990 , 1991

Most successive wins
9 Alberto Ascari (Ita) 1952-3; 5 Jack Brabham (Aus) 1960, Jim Clark (GB) 1965

Most pole positions
59 Ayrton Senna (Bra); 33 Jim Clark (GB); 29 Juan Manuel Fangio (Arg); 24 Niki Lauda (Aut), Nelson Piquet (Bra)

CARS
Race Wins
103 Ferrari 1951-90; **93** McLaren 1968-91; **79** Lotus 1960-87; **51** Williams 1979-91; **35** Brabham 1964-85; **23** Tyrrell 1971-83; **17** BRM 1959-72; **16** Cooper 1958-67; **15** Renault 1979-83; **10** Alfa Romeo 1950-51; **9** Mercedes-Benz 1954-55; Maserati 1953-57; Vanwall 1957-58; Matra 1968-69; **8** Ligier 1977-81; **3** Wolf 1970-76; **3** March 1970-76; **3** Benetton 1986-91; **2** Honda 1965-67; **1** Porsche 1962; Eagle 1967; Hesketh 1975; Penske 1976; Shadow 1977

Most wins in a season
15 McLaren-Honda 1988; **12** McLaren-Porsche 1984; **10** McLaren-Honda 1989; **9** Williams-Honda 1986, 1987; **8** Lotus-Ford 1978; **7** Ferrari 1952,1953; Lotus-Climax 1963; Tyrrell-Ford 1971; Lotus-Ford 1973; Williams 1991

Most successive wins
14 Ferrari 1952-3; **11** McLaren-Honda 1988; **9** Alfa Romeo 1950-51; **8** McLaren-TAG 1984-85

ENGINES
Wins
156 Ford; **103** Ferrari; **64** Honda; **40** Climax; **31** Renault; **26** Porsche/TAG; **18** BRM; **12** Alfa Romeo; **11** Maserati, Offenhauser; **9** BMW, Mercedes-Benz, Vanwall; **8** Repco; **3** Matra; **1** Westlake

BRITISH GRAND PRIX WINNERS
1950-54, 1956, 1958, 1960, 1963, 1965, 1967, 1969, 1971, 1973, 1975, 1977, 1979, 1981, 1983, 1985, 1987-91 at Silverstone; 1955, 1957, 1959, 1961-62 at Aintree; 1964, 1966, 1968, 1970, 1972, 1974, 1976, 1978, 1980, 1982, 1984, 1986 at Brands Hatch

1950	Giuseppe Farina (Ita)	Alfa Romeo
1951	Jose Froilan Gonzalez (Arg)	Ferrari
1952	Alberto Ascari (Ita)	Ferrari
1953	Alberto Ascari (Ita)	Ferrari
1954	Jose Froilan Gonzalez (Arg)	Ferrari
1955	Stirling Moss (GB)	Mercedes-Benz
1956	Juan Manuel Fangio (Arg)	Lancia-Ferrari
1957	Stirling Moss (GB) & Tony Brooks (GB)	Vanwall
1958	Peter Collins (GB)	Ferrari
1959	Jack Brabham (Aus)	Cooper-Climax
1960	Jack Brabham (Aus)	Cooper-Climax
1961	Wolfgang Von Trips (FRG)	Ferrari
1962	Jim Clark (GB)	Lotus-Climax
1963	Jim Clark (GB)	Lotus-Climax
1964	Jim Clark (GB)	Lotus-Climax
1965	Jim Clark (GB)	Lotus-Climax
1966	Jack Brabham (Aus)	Brabham-Repco
1967	Jim Clark (GB)	Lotus-Ford
1968	Jo Siffert (Swi)	Lotus-Ford
1969	Jackie Stewart (GB)	Matra-Ford
1970	Jochen Rindt (Aut)	Lotus-Ford
1971	Jackie Stewart (GB)	Tyrrell-Ford
1972	Emerson Fittipaldi (Bra)	Lotus-Ford
1973	Peter Revson (US)	McLaren-Ford
1974	Jody Scheckter (SA)	Tyrrell-Ford
1975	Emerson Fittipaldi (Bra)	McLaren-Ford
1976	Niki Lauda (Aut)	Ferrari

---

ff It was a full month before I knew I'd crashed."
Martin Donnelly, terribly injured in Spain in 1990

"We are in the depths of a recession yet, for reasons I have difficulty in understanding, we still had 11 cars coming to this race that failed to qualify. I just don't know where people find the money."
Ken Tyrrell at the Monaco Grand Prix

"It's got global exposure, total global hospitality, total media coverage and 600 million people watching every fortnight. It's become the technocrat's Colosseum. It's macho, it's exciting, it's colour, it's international, it's glamour."
Barry Gill, sponsorship consultant, on motor racing

"Seventy-five per cent of it is the car and the team around it. Only 25 per cent is the driver, and much of that is to do with luck."
Juan Manuel Fangio

"There was a place for the playboy in my father's day - the men with the Spitfire pilot image. Today the pressures are so immense, and the money at stake so great, maybe only those with a single-minded intensity of purpose can succeed. JJ
Damon Hill, son of Graham

Highest Placed Britons in the Formula One World Championship

1976	James Hunt	1st
1977	James Hunt	5th
1978	John Watson	6th
1979	John Watson	9th
1980	John Watson	jt. 10th
1981	John Watson	6th
1982	John Watson	jt. 2nd
1983	John Watson	jt. 6th
1984	Derek Warwick	7th
1985	Nigel Mansell	6th
1986	Nigel Mansell	2nd
1987	Nigel Mansell	2nd
1988	Derek Warwick	jt. 7th
1989	Nigel Mansell	4th
1990	Nigel Mansell	5th
1991	Nigel Mansell	

1977	James Hunt (GB)	McLaren-Ford
1978	Carlos Reutemann (Arg)	Ferrari
1979	Clay Regazzoni (Swi)	Williams-Ford
1980	Alan Jones (Aus)	Williams-Ford
1981	John Watson (GB)	McLaren-Ford
1982	Niki Lauda (Aut)	McLaren-Ford
1983	Alain Prost (Fra)	Renault
1984	Niki Lauda (Aut)	McLaren-TAG
1985	Alain Prost (Fra)	McLaren-TAG
1986	Nigel Mansell (GB)	Williams-Honda
1987	Nigel Mansell (GB)	Williams-Honda
1988	Ayrton Senna (Bra)	McLaren-Honda
1989	Alain Prost (Fra)	McLaren-Honda
1990	Alain Prost (Fra)	Ferrari
1991	Nigel Mansell (GB)	Williams-Renault

WORLD SPORTSCAR CHAMPIONS
Inaugurated for types in 1953. A drivers' championship was introduced in 1981

Drivers
1981	Bob Garretson (US) Porsche	
1982	Jacky Ickx (Bel) Porsche	
1983	Jacky Ickx (Bel) Porsche	
1984	Stefan Bellof (FRG) Porsche	
1985	Derek Bell (GB) & Hans Stuck (FRG) Porsche	
1986	Derek Bell (GB) & Hans Stuck (FRG) Porsche	
1987	Raul Boesel (Bra) Jaguar	
1988	Martin Brundle (GB) Jaguar	
1989	Jean-Louis Schlesser (Fra) Mercedes	
1990	Jean-Louis Schlesser (Fra) Mercedes	

Cars
1953	Ferrari	1975	Alfa Romeo
1954	Ferrari	1976	Porsche
1955	Mercedes-Benz	1977	Porsche
1956	Ferrari	1978	Porsche
1957	Ferrari	1979	Porsche
1958	Ferrari	1980	Lancia
1959	Aston Martin	1981	Porsche
1960	Ferrari	1982	Porsche
1961	Ferrari	1983	Porsche
1962-67	Not held	1984	Porsche
1968	Gord	1985	Rothmans-Porsche
1969	Porsche	1986	Brun Motorsport
1970	Porsche	1987	Silk Cut Jaguar
1971	Porsche	1988	Silk Cut Jaguar
1972	Ferrari	1989	Sauber-Mercedes
1973	Matra-Simca	1990	Sauber-Mercedes
1974	Matra-Simca	1991	Silk Cut Jaguar

FIA FORMULA 3000 INTERNATIONAL CHAMPIONSHIP
Inaugurated 1985
1985	Christian Danner (FRG) March-Smith
1986	Ivan Capelli (Ita) March-Mader
1987	Stefano Modena (Ita) March-Cosworth
1988	Roberto Moreno (Bra) Reynard-Nicholson
1989	Jean Alesi (Fra) Reynard-Mugen
1990	Erik Comas (Fra) Lola
1991	Christian Fittipaldi (Bra) Reynard

LE MANS 24-HOUR RACE
First held 1923
Winners since 1982
1982	Derek Bell (GB)/Jacky Ickx (Bel) Porsche
1983	Hurley Haywood/Al Holbert (both US)/Vern Schuppan (Aut) Porsche
1984	Klaus Ludwig (FRG)/Henri Pescarolo (Fra) Porsche
1985	Paulo Barilla (Ita)/Klaus Ludwig/John Winter (both FRG) Porsche
1986	Derek Bell (GB)/Al Holbert (US)/Hans Stuck (FRG) Porsche
1987	Derek Bell (GB)/Al Holbert (US)/ Hans Stuck (FRG) Porsche
1988	Jan Lammers (Hol)/Johnny Dumfries/Andy Wallace (both GB) Jaguar
1989	Stanley Dickens (Swe)/Jochen Mass/Manuel Reuter (both FRG) Mercedes
1990	John Nielsen (Den)/Price Cobb (US)/Martin Brundle (GB) Jaguar
1991	Volker Weidler (Ger)/Johnny Herbert (GB) / Bertrand Gachot (Bel) Mazda

Most wins
6 Jacky Ickx 1969, 1975-77, 1981-82; 5 Derek Bell 1975, 1981-82, 1986-87; 4 Olivier Gendebien (Bel) 1958, 1960-62, Henri Pescarolo 1972-74, 1984

INDIANAPOLIS 500
First held 1911
Winners since 1982. US unless otherwise stated
1982	Gordon Johncock	Wildcat
1983	Tom Sneva	March
1984	Rick Mears	March
1985	Danny Sullivan	March
1986	Bobby Rahal	March
1987	Al Unser	March
1988	Rick Mears	Penske
1989	Emerson Fittipaldi (Bra)	Penske
1990	Arie Luyendyk (Hol)	Chevrolet
1991	Rick Mears	Penske-Chevrolet

Most wins
4 A J Foyt 1961, 1964, 1967, 1977; Al Unser 1970-71, 1978, 1987; Rick Mears 1979, 1984, 1988, 1991

RALLYING

MONTE CARLO RALLY
Inaugurated 1911
Winners since 1982
1982	Walter Rohrl (FRG)	Opel
1983	Walter Rohrl (FRG)	Opel
1984	Walter Rohrl (FRG)	Audi
1985	Ari Vatanen (Fin)	Peugeot
1986	Henri Toivonen (Fin)	Lancia
1987	Miki Biasion (Ita)	Lancia
1988	Bruno Saby (Fra)	Lancia
1989	Miki Biasion (Ita)	Lancia
1990	Didier Auriol (Fra)	Lancia
1991	Carlos Sainz (Spa)	Toyota

Most wins
4 Sandro Munari (Ita) 1972, 1975-77; Walter Rohrl (FRG); 3 Jean Trevoux (Fra) 1939, 1949, 1951

LOMBARD RAC RALLY
Inaugurated 1951
Winners since 1982
1982	Hannu Mikkola (Fin)	Audi
1983	Stig Blomqvist (Swe)	Audi
1984	Ari Vatanen (Fin)	Peugeot
1985	Henri Toivonen (Fin)	Lancia
1986	Timo Salonen (Fin)	Peugeot
1987	Juha Kankkunen (Fin)	Lancia
1988	Markku Alen (Fin)	Lancia
1989	Pentti Arikkala (Fin)	Mitsubishi
1991	Carlos Sainz (Spa)	Toyota

Most wins
4 Hannu Mikola (Fin) 1978-79, 1981-82; 3 Erik Carlsson (Swe) 1960-62, Timo Makinen (Fin) 1973-75

SAFARI RALLY
Inaugurated 1953
Winners since 1982
1982	Shekhar Mehta (Ken)	Datsun
1983	Ari Vatanen (Fin)	Opel
1984	Bjorn Waldegaard (Swe)	Toyota
1985	Juha Kankkunen (Fin)	Toyota
1986	Bjorn Waldegard (Swe)	Toyota
1987	Hannu Mikkola (Fin)	Audi
1988	Miki Biasion (Ita)	Lancia
1989	Miki Biasion (Ita)	Lancia
1990	Bjorn Waldegaard (Swe)	Toyota
1991	Juha Kankkunen (Fin)	Lancia

Most wins
5 Shekhar Mehta; 4 Bjorn Waldegaard 1977, 1984, 1986, 1990; 3 Joginder Singh 1965, 1974, 1974, 1976

WORLD RALLY CHAMPIONS
Drivers
1977	Sandro Munari (Ita)
1978	Markku Alen (Fin)
1979	Bjorn Waldegaard (Swe)
1980	Walter Rohrl (FRG)
1981	Ari Vatanen (Fin)
1982	Walter Rohrl (FRG)
1983	Hannu Mikkola (Fin)
1984	Stig Blomqvist (Swe)
1985	Timo Salonen (Fin)
1986	Juha Kankkunen (Fin)
1987	Juha Kankunnen (Fin)
1988	Miki Biasion (Ita)
1989	Miki Baision (Ita)
1990	*Men:* Carlos Sainz (Spa)
	Women: Louise Aitken-Walker (GB)

━━━━━━ 1992 ━━━━━━

FORMULA ONE SCHEDULE

(all dates to be confirmed)
Mar 1 South African Grand Prix (Kyalami); Mar 22
Mexican (Mexico City); Apr 5 Brazilian (Interlagoa); May
3 Spanish (Barcelona); May 17 San Marino (Imola); May
31 Monaco (Monte Carlo); Jun 14 Canadian (Montreal);
Jul 5 French (Magny-Cours); Jul 12 BRITISH GRAND
PRIX (Silverstone); Jul 26 German (Hockenheim); Aug 16
Hungarian (Budapest); Aug 30 Belgian (Spa); Sep 13
Italian (Monza); Sep 27 Portuguese (Estoril); Oct 4
European (Jerez, Spain); Oct 25 Japanese (Suzuka); Nov 8
Australian (Adelaide)

NETBALL

1991

WORLD CHAMPIONSHIP
Sydney, Australia, Jul 14

Third Place Play-off
JAMAICA 63 England 54

Final
AUSTRALIA 53 New Zealand 52

P.E.S. ENGLISH COUNTIES LEAGUE

First Division		P	W	D	L	F	A	Pts
1(3)	Surrey	7	6	0	1	436	319	31
2(5)	Middlesex	7	5	1	1	300	274	29
3(4)	Birmingham	7	4	1	2	378	361	25
4(2)	Essex Met	7	3	1	3	328	291	21
5(1)	Bedfordshire	7	3	0	4	353	321	19
6(6)	Cheshire	7	3	0	4	281	323	18
7(P)	Kent	7	1	3	3	265	289	17
8(P)	South Yorkshire	7	0	0	7	250	413	4
Second Division		P	W	D	L	F	A	Pts
1(R)	Hampshire North	7	5	1	1	318	251	29
2(P)	Humberside	7	5	0	2	333	301	27
3(R)	Hertfordshire	7	5	0	2	324	300	27
4(6)	Northamptonshire	7	4	1	2	270	277	25
5(P)	West Yorkshire	7	3	2	2	255	249	23
6(4)	East Essex	7	2	0	5	290	271	15
7(5)	Gloucestershire	7	2	0	5	262	293	15
8(3)	Warwickshire	7	0	0	7	207	317	7

Last season's positions in brackets

EVIAN INTER COUNTIES CHAMPIONSHIP
Anerley, London, Apr 20-21

Final
SURREY 21 Birmingham 17

NATIONAL CLUBS KNOCKOUT COMPETITION
Basildon, May 11

HARBORNE (Birmingham) 53 Linden (Birmingham) 49

CHAMPIONS

WORLD CHAMPIONS
First held 1963

1963	Australia
1967	New Zealand
1971	Australia
1975	Australia
1979	Australia, New Zealand, Trinidad & Tobago
	(all shared the title)
1983	Australia
1987	New Zealand
1991	Australia

ENGLISH COUNTIES LEAGUE
(Formerly the National League)
Inaugurated 1985

1985	Birmingham
1986	Birmingham
1987	Birmingham
1988	Surrey
1989	Birmingham
1990	Bedfordshire
1991	Surrey

EVIAN INTER COUNTIES CHAMPIONSHIP
1949-64 Surrey (*16 consecutive years*)

1965	Middlesex
1966	Surrey
1967	Kent
1968	Middlesex
1969	Kent & Surrey
1970	Kent
1971	Kent
1972	Kent
1973	Kent
1974	Kent
1975	Essex
1976	Essex
1977	Essex Metropolitan
1978	Essex Metropolitan
1979	Essex Metropolitan
1980	Essex Metropolitan
1981	Surrey
1982	Essex Metropolitan
1983	Hertfordshire
1984	Hertfordshire
1985	Birmingham
1986	Hertfordshire & Surrey
1987	Kent
1988	Essex Metropolitan/East Essex
1989	Birmingham
1990	Middlesex
1991	Surrey

OLYMPIC GAMES

1992

The XXV Olympics will take place in Barcelona from July 25 to August 9. There are 24 medal sports. The complete schedule for athletics and swimming and the finals in the other sports are listed below. ALL TIMINGS ARE PROVISIONAL AND SUBJECT TO CHANGE. The times are given in BST; Barcelona time is one hour later.

ARCHERY

Vall d'Hebron

4 gold medals (2 men, 2 women)
Jul 31, Aug 1, 2, 3, 4

Mon Aug 3 1400	Men's and Women's Individual Finals
Tue Aug 4 1400	Men's and Women's Team Finals

ASSOCIATION FOOTBALL

Barcelona (Nou Camp), Real Deportivo, Sabadell, Zaragoza, Valencia

1 gold medal (16 men's teams)
Jul 24, 26-30, Aug 1, 2, 5, 7, 8

Sat Aug 8 1900	Final (Nou Camp)

ATHLETICS

Montjuic Olympic Stadium

43 gold medals (24 men, 19 women)
Jul 31, Aug 1, 2, 3, 5, 6, 7, 8, 9

FRI JULY 31

8.30	100m	W	Heat
9.00	Shot	M	Qualifying
9.30	100m	M	Heat
10.30	800m	W	Heat
17.00	Javelin	W	Qualifying
17.05	High jump	M	Qualifying
17.15	100m	W	Quarter-final
17.30	Marathon	W	
17.45	100m	M	Quarter-final
18.00	Shot	M	Final
18.15	800m	M	Heat
18.30	Javelin	W	Qualifying
19.00	3,000m	W	Heat
20.15	10,000m	M	Heat

SAT AUG 1

8.30	Heptathlon (100m hurdles)	W	
9.00	400m	M	Heat
9.30	Heptathlon (high jump)	W	
10.00	400m hurdles	W	Heat
10.30	Hammer	M	Qualifying
12.00	Hammer	M	Qualifying
16.30	Heptathlon (shot)	W	
17.00	100m	W	Semi-final
17.20	100m	M	Semi-final
17.25	Triple jump	M	Qualifying
17.40	800m	M	Quarter-final
18.10	800m	W	Semi-final
18.15	20 Km walk	M	Final
18.20	Javelin	W	Final

18.30	100m	W	Final
18.45	100m	M	Final
19.00	Heptathlon (200m)	W	
19.50	10,000m	W	Heat

SUN AUG 2

9.00	110m hurdles	M	Heat
9.05	Heptathlon (long jump)	W	
9.30	Discus	W	Qualifying
10.00	400m	W	Heat
10.30	Discus	W	Qualifying
15.30	Hammer	M	Final
17.00	High jump	M	Final
17.25	Heptathlon (javelin)	W	Group 1
17.30	110m hurdles	M	Quarter-final
18.15	400m	M	Quarter-final
18.50	400m hurdles	W	Semi-final
19.00	Heptathlon (javelin)	W	Group 2
19.20	800m	M	Semi-final
19.45	800m	W	Final
20.00	3,000m	W	Final
20.30	Heptathlon (800m)	W	

MON AUG 3

8.30	Discus	M	Qualifying
8.35	200m	W	Heat
9.20	200m	M	Heat
10.00	Discus	M	Qualifying
10.15	1500m	M	Heat
11.15	400m hurdles	M	Heat
17.00	110m hurdles	M	Semi-finals
17.20	200m	W	Quarter-final
17.45	200m	M	Quarter-final
17.50	Discus	W	Final
18.10	400m	M	Quarter-final
18.30	Triple jump	M	Final
18.35	400m	M	Semi-final
18.50	10 Km walk	W	Final
19.05	110m hurdles	M	Final
19.45	3,000m S/chse	M	Heat
20.30	400m hurdles	W	Final
20.45	10,000m	M	Final

WED AUG 5

8.00	Decathlon (100m)	M	
8.30	Pole vault	M	Qualifying
9.00	1500m	W	Heat
9.05	Decathlon (long jump)	M	
9.45	100m hurdles	W	Heat
10.45	Decathlon (shot)	M	
16.30	Shot	W	Qualifying
16.35	Decathlon (high jump)	M	

17.00	100m hurdles	W	Quarter-finals
17.35	200m	W	Semi-final
17.35	Long jump	M	Qualifying
17.50	200m	M	Semi-final
18.15	400m hurdles	M	Semi-final
18.30	Discus	M	Final
18.35	400m	W	Semi-final
18.50	3,000m S/chse	M	Semi-final
19.20	400m	M	Final
19.35	200m	W	Final
19.50	200m	M	Final
20.05	800m	M	Final
20.20	Decathlon (400m)	M	
20.45	5,000m	M	Heat

THUR AUG 6

8.00	Decathlon (110m hurdles)	M	
8.30	High jump	W	Qualifying
9.00	Decathlon (discus)	M	Group 1
9.05	Long jump	W	Qualifying
10.30	Decathlon (discus)	M	Group 2
12.00	Decathlon (pole vault)	M	
16.30	Decathlon (javelin)	M	Group 1
17.00	100m hurdles	W	Semi-final
17.30	400m	W	Final
17.45	Decathlon (javelin)	M	Group 2
17.50	Long jump	M	Final
18.00	400m hurdles	M	Final
18.20	1500m	W	Semi-final
18.45	1500m	M	Semi-final
19.10	100m hurdles	W	Final
19.30	5,000m	M	Semi-final
20.15	Decathlon (1500m)	M	

FRI AUG 7

6.30	50 Km walk	M	Final
8.30	4x100m relay	M	Heat
8.35	Javelin	M	Qualifying
9.00	4x100m relay	W	Heat
9.30	4x100m relay	M	Heat
9.45	Javelin	M	Qualifying
16.00	Pole vault	M	Final
17.55	Shot	W	Final
18.00	4x100m relay	W	Semi-final
18.15	Long jump	W	Final
18.30	4x100m relay	M	Semi-final
19.00	4x400m relay	W	Heat
19.30	4x400m relay	M	Semi-final
20.00	3,000m S/chse	M	Final
20.20	10,000m	W	Final

SAT AUG 8

17.30	High jump	W	Final
17.55	Javelin	M	Final
18.00	4x100m relay	W	Final
18.20	4x100m relay	M	Final
18.50	1,500m	W	Final
19.15	1,500m	M	Final
19.40	5,000m	M	Final
20.15	4x400m relay	W	Final
20.40	4x400m relay	M	Final

SUN AUG 9

17.10	Marathon	M	

BADMINTON

La Mar Bella
4 gold medals (2 men, 2 women)
Jul 28, 29, 30, 31, Aug 1, 2, 3, 4
Tue Aug 4 10.00   Men's and Women's
singles and doubles finals

BASEBALL

L'Hospitalet and Viladecans
1 gold medal
(men's tournament for eight teams)
Jul 26, 27, 28, 29, 31, Aug 1, 2, 4, 5
Wed Aug 5 20.00   Final

BASKETBALL

Municipal Sports Hall
2 gold medals
(men's tournament for 12 teams, women's tournament for eight)
Jul 26-Aug 8 (rest day Jul 28)
Fri Aug 7 21.00   Women's final
Sat Aug 8 21.00   Men's final

BOXING

Badalona Club Joventut Pavilion
12 gold medals
Jul 26-Aug 9 (rest day Aug 5)
Sat Aug 8 9.00   Finals
Sun Aug 9 9.00   Finals

CANOEING

El Segre/Castelldefels
16 gold medals (12 men, 4 women)
Aug 1-8
Sat Aug 1 8.00   Wild Water finals
Sun Aug 2 8.00   Wild Water finals
Fri Aug 7 8.00   Flat Water finals
Sat Aug 8 8.00   Flat Water finals

CYCLING

Horta Municipal Velodrome
10 gold medals (7 men, 3 women)
Jul 26-31 and Aug 2

Sun Jul 26	8.00	Men's 100km team time trial (road)
	16.30	Women's individual time trial (road)
Mon Jul 27	19.00	Men's 1km time trial
Wed Jul 29		Men's individual pursuit final
Fri Jul 31	18.20	Men's sprint final
	18.25	Women's sprint final
	19.00	Men's team pursuit final
	19.30	Women's individual pursuit final
	20.00	Men's points race (50km)
Sun Aug 2	7.30	Men's road race

EQUESTRIANISM

Polo Club
6 gold medals (all open)
Jul 27-30, Aug 2-5, 7 and 9

Thu Jul 30	16.00	Three-day event (team and individual) ends
Mon Aug 3	15.00	Team dressage final
Tue Aug 4	14.00	Team show jumping final
Wed Aug 5	8.00	Individual dressage final
Sun Aug 9	8.00/12.30	Individual show jumping final

FENCING

Metallurgy Hall
8 gold medals (6 men, 2 women)
Jul 30 - Aug 7

Thu Jul 30	19.00	Women's foil final
Fri Jul 31	19.00	Men's foil final
Sat Aug 1	19.00	Men's epee final
Sun Aug 2	19.00	Men's sabre final
Tue Aug 4	19.00	Women's team foil final
Wed Aug 5	19.00	Men's team foil final
Thu Aug 6	19.00	Men's team epee final
Fri Aug 7	19.00	Men's team sabre final

GYMNASTICS

Sant Jordi Sports Hall
15 gold medals (8 men, 7 women)
Jul 26 - Aug 2, 6-8

Tue Jul 28	19.00	Women's team optional exercises
Wed Jul 29	19.00	Men's team optional exercises
Thu Jul 30	19.00	Women's multiple individual competition
Fri Jul 31	19.00	Men's multiple individual competition
Sat Aug 1	19.00	Women's apparatus finals (4)
Sun Aug 2	19.00	Men's apparatus finals (6)
Sat Aug 8	15.00	Women's rhythmic finals

HANDBALL

Sant Jordi Sports Hall
2 gold medals
(men's tournament for 12 teams, women's tournament for eight)
Jul 27, 29 - Aug 4, Aug 6-8

Sat Aug 8	11.00	Women's final
	16.00	Men's final

HOCKEY

L'Abat Marcel Sports Complex, Terrassa
2 gold medals
(men's tournament for 12 teams, women's for eight)
Jul 26-30, Aug 1-8

Fri Aug 7	18.30	Women's final
Sat Aug 8	18.30	Men's final

JUDO

Blaugrana Hall
14 gold medals (7 men, 7 women)
Jul 27 - Aug 2

Mon Jul 27	21.18	Women's heavyweight final
	21.23	Men's heavyweight final
Tue Jul 28	21.18	Women's light-heavyweight final
	21.23	Men's light-heavyweight final
Wed Jul 29	21.18	Women's middleweight final
	21.23	Men's middleweight final
Thu Jul 30	21.18	Women's light-middleweight final
	21.23	Men's light-middleweight final
Fri Jul 31	21.18	Women's lightweight final
	21.23	Men's lightweight final
Sat Aug 1	21.18	Women's featherweight final
	21.23	Men's featherweight final
Sun Aug 2	21.18	Women's bantamweight final
	21.23	Men's bantamweight final

MODERN PENTATHLON

Metallurgy Hall/Bernat Piconell Pool/Mollet de Valles/Parc del Migdia/Polo Club
2 gold medals (men's team and individual)
Jul 26-29

Mon Jul 26	8.00	Fencing
Tue Jul 27	11.00	Swimming
	15.30	Shooting
Wed Jul 28	10.00	Cross-country
Thu Jul 29	9.00 and 16.00	Riding

ROWING

Banyoles Lake
14 gold medals (8 men, 6 women)
Jul 27 - Aug 2

Sat Aug 1	8.10	Women's coxless fours final
	8.20	Women's double sculls final
	8.40	Women's coxless pairs final
	9.00	Men's coxed fours final
	9.20	Men's double sculls final
	9.40	Men's coxless pairs final
	10.00	Men's single sculls final
Sun Aug 2	8.10	Women's single sculls final
	8.20	Women's quadruple sculls final
	8.40	Women's coxed eight final
	9.00	Men's coxed pairs final
	9.20	Men's coxless fours final
	9.40	Men's quadruple sculls final
	10.00	Men's coxed eights final

SHOOTING

Mollet de Valles
13 gold medals (7 men, 4 women, 2 open)
Jul 26 - Aug 2

Sun Jul 26	9.30	Women's air rifle final
	14.00	Men's free pistol final
Mon Jul 27	11.30	Men's air rifle final
	13.00	Women's rapid fire pistol final
Tue Jul 28	11.30	Men's air pistol final
	13.00	Open skeet final
Wed Jul 29	11.30	Men's smallbore rifle final

Thu Jul 30	11.30	Women's three positions final
	13.00	Men's rapid fire pistol final
Fri Jul 31	14.30	Men's three positions final
Sat Aug 1	11.00	Women's air pistol final
	13.30	Men's running target final
Sun Aug 2	13.00	Open trap final

SWIMMING

Bernat Piconell Pools
31 gold medals (16 men, 15 women)
Jul 26-31

SUN JUL 26
9.00	100m freestyle	W	Heats
	100m breaststroke	M	Heats
	400m medley	W	Heats
	200m freestyle	M	Heats
17.00	100m freestyle	W	Final
	100m breaststroke	M	Final
	400m medley	W	Final
	200m freestyle	M	Final

MON JUL 27
8.30	100m butterfly	M	Heats
	200m freestyle	W	Heats
	400m medley	M	Heats
	200m breaststroke	W	Heats
	4x200m freestyle	M	Heats
17.00	100m butterfly	M	Final
	200m freestyle	W	Final
	400m medley	M	Final
	200m breaststroke	W	Final
	4x200m freestyle	M	Final

TUE JUL 28
10.00	400m freestyle	W	Heats
	100m freestyle	M	Heats
	100m backstroke	W	Heats
	200m backstroke	M	Heats
	4x100m freestyle	W	Heats
17.00	400m freestyle	W	Final
	100m freestyle	M	Final
	100m backstroke	W	Final
	200m backstroke	M	Final
	4x100m freestyle	W	Final

WED JUL 29
9.00	400m freestyle	M	Heats
	100m butterfly	W	Heats
	200m breaststroke	M	Heats
	100m breaststroke	W	Heats
	4x100m freestyle	M	Heats
	800m freestyle	W	Heats
17.00	400m freestyle	M	Final
	100m butterfly	W	Final
	200m breaststroke	M	Final
	100m breaststroke	W	Final
	4x100m freestyle	M	Final

THU JUL 30
9.00	200m butterfly	M	Heats
	200m medley	W	Heats
	100m backstroke	M	Heats
	4x100m medley relay	W	Heats
	50m freestyle	M	Heats
	1500m freestyle	M	Heats
17.00	200m butterfly	M	Final
	200m medley	W	Final
	50m freestyle	M	Final

	800m freestyle	W	Final
	100m backstroke	M	Final
	4x100m medley	W	Final

FRI JUL 31
9.00	200m butterfly	W	Heats
	200m medley	M	Heats
	200m backstroke	W	Heats
	4x100m medley	M	Heats
	50m freestyle	W	Heats
17.00	200m butterfly	W	Final
	200m medley	M	Final
	50m freestyle	W	Final
	1500m freestyle	M	Final
	200m backstroke	W	Final
	4x100m medley	M	Final

DIVING
Montjuic Pools
4 gold medals (2 men, 2 women)
Jul 26-29, Aug 1-4
Mon Jul 27	14.00	Women's platform final
Wed Jul 29	14.00	Men's springboard final
Mon Aug 3	13.30	Women's springboard final
Tue Aug 4	14.00	Men's platform final

SYNCHRONISED SWIMMING
Bernat Piconell Pools
2 gold medals (women)
Aug 2, 3, 5-7
| Thu Aug 6 | 14.00 | Solo final |
| Fri Aug 7 | 14.00 | Duet final |

WATER POLO
Bernat Piconell Pools
1 gold medal (men)
Aug 1-3, 5, 6, 8, 9
| Sun Aug 9 | 13.00 | Final |

TABLE TENNIS

Estacio del Nord
4 gold medals (2 men, 2 women)
Jul 28 - Aug 6
Mon Aug 3	11.00	Women's doubles final
Tue Aug 4	11.00	Men's doubles final
Wed Aug 5	11.00	Women's singles final
Thu Aug 6	11.00	Men's singles final

TENNIS

Vall d'Hebron
4 gold medals (2 men, 2 women)
Jul 28 - Aug 8
Fri Aug 7	14.00	Men' doubles final
		Women's singles final
Sun Aug 8	14.00	Women's doubles final
		Men's singles final

VOLLEYBALL

Sant Jordi Sports Hall
2 gold medals
(men's tournament for 12 teams, women's tournament for eight)
Jul 26, 27, 29 - Aug 7, 9
Fri Aug 7   20.30   Women's final
Sun Aug 9   12.00   Men's final

WEIGHTLIFTING

Espana Industrial Municipal Pavilion
10 gold medals (men)
Jul 26 - Aug 4
Sun Jul 26   17.30   Up to 52kg final
Mon Jul 27   17.30   Up to 56kg final
Tue Jul 28   17.30   Up to 60kg final
Wed Jul 29   17.30   Up to 67.5kg final
Thu Jul 30   17.30   Up to 75kg final
Fri Jul 31   17.30   Up to 82.5kg final
Sat Aug 1   17.30   Up to 90kg final
Sun Aug 2   17.30   Up to 100kg final
Mon Aug 3   17.30   Up to 110kg final
Tue Aug 4   17.30   Over 110kg final

WRESTLING

Catalan National Institute of Physical Education
20 gold medals (all men, 10 Greco-Roman, 10 Freestyle)
Jul 26-30, Aug 3-7
GRECO-ROMAN
Tue Jul 28   16.00   52, 68, 100 kg finals
Wed Jul 29   16.00   48, 74, 130 kg finals
Thu Jul 30   16.00   57, 62, 82, 90 kg finals
FREESTYLE
Wed Aug 5   16.00   52, 68, 100 kg finals
Thu Aug 6   16.00   48, 74, 130 kg finals
Fri Aug 7   16.00   57, 62, 82, 90 kg finals

YACHTING

Barcelona Olympic Harbour
10 gold medals (3 men, 3 women, 4 open)
Jul 27-30, Aug 1-4 (Jul 31, Aug 5, 6 reserve days)
Sun Aug 2   12.00   Lechner A390, men and women
Mon Aug 3   12.00   Final races: Men's Finn, Women's Europe, Men's 470, Women's 470, Flying Dutchman, Star and Tornado
Tue Aug 4   12.00   Soling match race final
Pelota, roller hockey and tackwando will be demonstration sports

LEADING MEDAL WINNERS

ARCHERY

	G	S	B	Total
United States	12	8	7	27
France	6	9	6	21
Belgium	10	7	2	19
South Korea	4	2	2	8
Soviet Union	1	3	3	7
Britain	2	2	2	6

Britain's two golds were won in 1908 by Queenie Newall and William Dod

ASSOCIATION FOOTBALL

	G	S	B	Total
Hungary	3	1	1	5
Soviet Union	2	0	3	5
Yugoslavia	1	3	1	5
Denmark	0	3	1	4

Britain's three golds are their only medals

ATHLETICS

	G	S	B	Total
United States	273	199	163	635
Soviet Union	64	55	74	193
Britain	44	74	50	168
(West) Germany	22	48	49	119
Finland	47	35	28	110

East Germany	38	36	35	109
Sweden	17	24	43	84
Australia	16	17	22	55
France	10	21	22	53
Canada	11	14	22	47

BASKETBALL

	G	S	B	Total
United States	11	2	1	14
Soviet Union	4	4	4	12
Yugoslavia	1	4	2	7
Brazil	0	0	3	3
Bulgaria	0	1	1	2
Uruguay	0	0	2	2

Britain: no medals

BOXING

	G	S	B	Total
United States	46	19	28	93
Soviet Union	14	19	17	50
Britain	12	10	20	42
Poland	8	9	25	42
Italy	14	12	13	39

Richard Woodhall (light-middleweight, bronze) in 1988 was Britain's last medallist

CANOEING

	G	S	B	Total
Soviet Union	29	13	9	51
Hungary	7	20	16	43
West Germany	8	14	10	32
East Germany	14	7	9	30
Romania	9	9	11	29

Britain: no medals

CYCLING

	G	S	B	Total
France	27	15	20	62
Italy	26	14	6	46
Britain	8	21	14	43
(West) Germany	6	12	13	31
Soviet Union	11	4	9	24
Holland	9	11	4	24

Britain's last medal was a bronze in the 4,000 metres team pursuit in 1976, an event in which the British have won eight bronze medals including six in succession between 1928-56

EQUESTRIANISM

	G	S	B	Total
(West) Germany	24	15	18	57
Sweden	17	8	14	39
France	11	12	9	32
United States	8	15	9	32
Italy	7	9	7	23
Great Britain	5	7	9	21

FENCING

	G	S	B	Total
France	34	32	26	92
Italy	32	34	22	88
Hungary	31	17	24	72
Soviet Union	18	14	16	48
(West) Germany	11	13	6	30

Britain has won one gold and nine silvers. The last medallist was Bill Hoskins (épée silver) in 1964

GYMNASTICS

	G	S	B	Total
Soviet Union	71	68	43	182
Japan	27	27	28	82
United States	23	18	23	64
Switzerland	15	19	13	47
Hungary	12	10	14	36

*Britain **has** won three gymnastics medals: a silver by S W Tysal in the men's combined event in 1908, and bronzes in the men's team competition in 1912 and the women's team event in 1928.*

HANDBALL

	G	S	B	Total
Soviet Union	4	1	1	6
Yugoslavia	3	1	1	5
Romania	0	1	3	4
East Germany	1	1	1	3
South Korea	1	2	0	3

Britain: no medals

HOCKEY

	G	S	B	Total
India	8	1	2	11
Britain	3	2	4	9
Pakistan	3	3	1	7
(West) Germany	1	3	2	6
Holland	0	2	4	6

Four of Britain's nine medals came in 1908 when England, Ireland, Scotland and Wales entered separate teams. Great Britain was also represented by the England team in 1920

JUDO

	G	S	B	Total
Soviet Union	5	5	14	24
Japan	14	2	6	22
South Korea	4	4	5	13
France	3	2	8	13
Great Britain	0	4	7	11

Britain's four silver medallists have been: Dave Starbrook (1972), Keith Remfry (1976), Neil Adams (1980 & 1984)

MODERN PENTATHLON

	G	S	B	Total
Sweden	9	7	5	21
Hungary	8	6	3	17
Soviet Union	5	5	5	15
United States	0	5	3	8
Italy	2	2	2	6

In addition to the gold medal in 1976, Britain has won one other medal, a bronze, also in the team event, in 1988

ROWING

	G	S	B	Total
United States	30	20	15	65
East Germany	33	7	8	48
Soviet Union	12	20	11	43
(West) Germany	17	12	12	41
Britain	16	15	6	37

SHOOTING

	G	S	B	Total
United States	43	24	19	86
Sweden	13	23	18	54
Soviet Union	17	16	19	52
Britain	13	14	19	46
France	12	15	13	40

SWIMMING

	G	S	B	Total
United States	201	154	126	481
Australia	38	31	36	105
East Germany	40	34	25	99
(West) Germany	21	28	34	83
Soviet Union	18	27	34	79
Britain	18	22	28	68

Included in these figures is Britain's tally of one silver and four bronzes in the diving events. The silver was won by Eileen Armstrong in the highboard event in 1928

WATER POLO

	G	S	B	Total
Hungary	6	3	3	12
United States	1	3	4	8
Yugoslavia	3	4	0	7
Soviet Union	2	2	3	7
Belgium	0	4	2	6

Great Britain's four golds are their only medals

TABLE TENNIS

	G	S	B	Total
China	2	2	1	5
South Korea	2	1	1	4
Yugoslavia	0	1	1	2

Great Britain: no medals

TENNIS

	G	S	B	Total
Britain	16	13	15	44
United States	9	5	3	17
France	5	6	6	17
(West) Germany	3	2	2	7
Sweden	0	2	5	7

VOLLEYBALL

	G	S	B	Total
Soviet Union	7	4	1	12
Japan	3	3	2	8
United States	2	1	0	3
Poland	1	0	2	3

Great Britain: no medals

WEIGHTLIFTING

	G	S	B	Total	
Soviet Union	39	21	2	62	
United States	15	16	10	41	
Bulgaria		9	11	4	24
Poland	4	2	16	22	
(West) Germany	5	4	10	19	

Great Britain's medal tally is one gold, three silvers and three bronzes. David Mercer (bronze, 1984) was Britain's last medallist, while the last silver medallist was Louis Martin in 1964.

WRESTLING

Freestyle	G	S	B	Total
United States	38	31	19	88
Soviet Union	27	14	14	55
Japan	16	9	6	31
Turkey	15	10	5	30
Greco-Roman	G	S	B	Total
Soviet Union	34	19	10	63
Finland	19	19	18	56
Sweden	19	15	17	51
Hungary	13	9	11	33

Great Britain: no Greco-Roman medals, but three golds, four silvers and ten bronzes in the freestyle competition. The last British medallist was Noel Loban (bronze, 1984).

YACHTING

	G	S	B	Total
United States	15	13	11	39
Britain	15	8	8	31
Sweden	9	11	9	29
Norway	14	11	2	27
France	9	6	9	24

DEFUNCT SPORTS

The following sports have all been included in the Olympic programme at some time or other, but are no longer part of the Games:

CRICKET
1900 Great Britain

CROQUET
Singles
1900 Aumoitte (Fra)
2-Ball Singles
1900 Waydelick (Fra)
Doubles
1900 Aumoitte & Johin (Fra)
France won every medal available

GOLF
Men
1900 Charles Sands (US)
1904 George Lyon (Can)
Women
1904 Margaret Abbott (US)
Men's Team
1904 United States
Walter Rutherford (silver) and David Robertson (bronze) in the 1900 men's singles were Britain's only medallists

JEU DE PAUME
1908 Jay Gould (US)
Britons, Eustace Miles and Neville Lytton, won the silver and bronze medals behind Gould

LACROSSE
1904 Canada
1908 Canada
Britain won silver in 1908

MOTOR BOATING
Open Class
1908 Émile Thubron (Fra)
8-Metre Class
1908 Bernard Redwood & Thomas Thorneycroft (GB)
Under-60 foot Class
1908 Bernard Redwood & Thomas Thorneycroft (GB)
The above were the only medal winners because there was only one finisher in each class

POLO
1900 Great Britain/United States
1908 Great Britain
1920 Great Britain
1924 Argentina
1936 Argentina

Leading Medal Winners

	G	S	B	Total
Great Britain	3	3	2	8
United States	1	0	2	3
Argentina	2	0	0	2

RACKETS

Men's Singles
1908 Evan Noel (GB)

Men's Doubles
1908 John Astor & Vane Pennel (GB)
Britain won all medals on offer: two golds, two silvers and two bronzes

ROQUE
1904 Charles Jacobus (US)
The only competitors were from the United States

RUGBY UNION
1900 France
1908 Australia
1920 United States
1924 United States

Leading Medal Winners

	G	S	B	Total
France	1	2	0	3
United States	2	0	0	2
Great Britain	0	1	1	2

TUG OF WAR
1900 Denmark/Sweden
1904 United States
1908 Great Britain
1912 Sweden
1920 Great Britain

Leading Medal Winners

	G	S	B	Total
Great Britain	2	2	1	5
United States	1	2	1	4
Sweden	2	0	1	3

RECORDS

Year	Venue	Leading Gold Medal Winners		
1896	Athens	11 United States	10 Greece	7 Germany
1900	Paris	27 France	19 United States	17 Britain
1904	St Louis	70 United States	5 Cuba	4 Canada, Germany
1906	Athens*	15 France	12 United States	8 Britain, Greece
1908	London	57 Britain	23 United States	8 Sweden
1912	Stockholm	25 United States	24 Sweden	10 Britain
1920	Antwerp	41 United States	19 Sweden	15 Finland, Britain
1924	Paris	45 United States	14 Finland	13 France
1928	Amsterdam	22 United States	10 Germany	8 Finland
1932	Los Angeles	41 United States	12 Italy	10 France
1936	Berlin	33 Germany	24 United States	10 Hungary
1948	London	38 United States	16 Sweden	10 France, Hungary
1952	Helsinki	40 United States	22 Soviet Union	16 Hungary
1956	Melbourne	37 Soviet Union	32 United States	13 Australia
1960	Rome	43 Soviet Union	34 United States	13 Italy
1964	Tokyo	36 United States	30 Soviet Union	16 Japan
1968	Mexico City	45 United States	29 Soviet Union	11 Japan
1972	Munich	50 United States	33 United States	20 East Germany
1976	Montreal	49 Soviet Union	40 East Germany	34 United States
1980	Moscow	80 Soviet Union	47 East Germany	8 Bulgaria, Cuba, Italy
1984	Los Angeles	83 United States	20 Romania	17 West Germany
1988	Seoul	55 Soviet Union	37 East Germany	36 United States
1992	Barcelona			

* Intercalated Games to celebrate ten years of the Modern Olympics

1996 ATLANTA
2000 SYDNEY
2004 ATHENS
2008 PEKING
2012 LONDON

LEADING MEDAL-WINNING NATIONS
(Summer Games Only)

Total	Country	G	S	B
1781	United States	746	560	475
1017	Soviet Union	395	323	299
608	Britain	174	224	210
571	West Germany (t)	157	207	207
497	France	153	167	177
439	Sweden	131	139	169

(t) Incl. Germany

Britain's Totals at each Games
(Summer Games Only)

	G	S	B
1896	3	3	1
1900	17	8	12
1904	1	1	-
1906	8	11	6
1908	57	50	40
1912	10	15	16
1920	15	15	13
1924	9	13	12
1928	3	10	7
1932	4	7	5
1936	4	7	3
1948	3	14	6
1952	1	2	8
1956	6	7	11
1960	2	6	12
1964	4	12	2
1968	5	5	3
1972	4	5	9
1976	3	5	5
1980	5	7	9
1984	5	11	21
1988	5	10	9

BRITISH GOLD MEDALS SINCE 1928
1928 **3** Lord Burghley (400 metres hurdles); Douglas Lowe (800 metres); John Lander, Michael Warriner, Richard Beesly, Edward Bevan - all Trinity College, Cambridge (coxless fours)
1932 **4** Thomas Green (50km walk); Tom Hampson (800 metres); Lewis Clive/Arthur Edwards (coxless pairs); John Badcock, Hugh Edwards, Jack Beresford, Rowland George (coxless fours)
1936 **3** Fred Wolff, Godfrey Rampling, William Roberts, Arthur Brown (4x400 metres relay); Harold Whitlock (50km walk); Jack Beresford/Leslie Southwood (double sculls); Charles Leaf, Christopher Boardman, Miles Belville, Russell Harmer, Leonard Martin (6-metre yachting)
1948 **3** Richard Burnell/Herbert Bushnell (double sculls); George Laurie/John Wilson (coxless pairs); Stewart Morris, David Bond (Swallow yachting)
1952 **1** Wilfred White, Douglas Stewart, Harry Llewellyn (Show jumping, team)
1956 **6** Chris Brasher (3,000m steeplechase); Dick McTaggart (lightweight boxing); Gillian Sheen (women's foil); Terry Spinks (flyweight boxing); Frank Weldon, Laurence Rook, Albert Hill (three-day event team); Judy Grinham (women's 100 metres backstroke)
1960 **2** Anita Lonsbrough (200 metres breaststroke); Don Thompson (50km walk)
1964 **4** Lynn Davies (long jump); Ken Matthews (20km walk); Ann Packer (women's 800 metres); Mary Rand (women's long jump)
1968 **5** Derek Allhusen, Richard Meade, Ben Jones (three-day event, team); Chris Finnegan (middleweight

boxing); David Hemery (400 metres hurdles); Rodney Pattisson/Iain McDonald-Smith (Flying Dutchman yachting); Bob Braithwaite (trap shooting)
1972 **4** Richard Meade (three-day event); Richard Meade, Mary Gordon-Watson, Bridget Parker (three-day event, team); Mary Peters (women's pentathlon); Rodney Pattisson/Christopher Davies (Flying Dutchman yachting)
1976 **3** Adrian Parker, Robert Nightingale, Jeremy Fox (modern pentathlon, team); David Wilkie (200 metres breaststroke); John Osborn/Reg White (Tornado yachting)
1980 **5** Allan Wells (100 metres); Sebastian Coe (1500 metres); Steve Ovett (800 metres); Daley Thompson (decathlon); Duncan Goodhew (100 metres breaststroke)
1984 **5** Sebastian Coe (1500 metres); Tessa Sanderson (women's javelin); Daley Thompson (decathlon); Malcolm Cooper (small-bore rifle shooting); Martin Cross, Richard Budgett, Andrew Holmes, Steven Redgrave, Adrian Ellison (coxed fours)
1988 **5** Men's hockey team; Andrew Holmes/Steven Redgrave (coxless pairs); Adrian Moorhouse (100 metres breaststroke); Mike McIntyre/Bryn Vaile (Star yachting); Malcolm Cooper (small-bore rifle shooting)

Most Individual Gold Medals
10 Ray Ewry (US) Athletics, 1900-08

Most Individual Medals (all colours)
18 Larissa Latynina (USSR) Gymnastics, 1956-64

THE YEAR EACH SPORT ENTERED THE GAMES
1896 Athletics, Cycling, Fencing, Gymnastics, Lawn Tennis, Shooting, Swimming, Weightlifting, Wrestling (Greco-Roman)
1900 Archery, Cricket, Croquet, Equestrianism, Golf, Polo, Rowing, Rugby Union, Soccer, Tug of War, Yachting
1904 Boxing, Lacrosse, Roque, Wrestling (Freestyle)
1908 Hockey, Jeu de Paume, Motor Boating, Rackets
1912 Modern Pentathlon
1936 Basketball, Canoeing, Handball
1964 Judo, Volleyball
1988 Table Tennis
1992 Badminton, Baseball

CHAMPIONS

ARCHERY

Men	Individual	Team	Women	Individual	Team
1972	John Williams (US)	-	1972	Doreen Wilber (US)	-
1976	Darrell Pace (US)	-	1976	Luann Ryan (US)	-
1980	Tomi Poikolainen (Fin)	-	1980	Keto Lossaberidze (USSR)	-
1984	Darrell Pace (US)	-	1984	Seo Hyang-Soon (SKo)	-
1988	Jay Barrs (US)	South Korea	1988	Soo Nyang-Kim (SKo)	South Korea

ASSOCIATION FOOTBALL

1900	Great Britain	1956	Soviet Union
1904	Canada	1960	Yugoslavia
1908	Great Britain	1964	Hungary
1912	Great Britain	1968	Hungary
1920	Belgium	1972	Poland
1924	Uruguay	1976	East Germany
1928	Uruguay	1980	Czechoslovakia
1936	Italy	1984	France
1948	Sweden	1988	Soviet Union
1952	Hungary		

ATHLETICS

Men

100 Metres

1896	Thomas Burke (US)	12.0s
1900	Francis Jarvis (US)	11.0s
1904	Archie Hahn (US)	11.0s
1908	Reginald Walker (SAf)	10.8s
1912	Ralph Craig (US)	10.8s
1920	Charles Paddock (US)	10.8s
1924	Harold Abrahams (GB)	10.6s
1928	Percy Williams (Can)	10.8s
1932	Eddie Tolan (US)	10.38s
1936	Jesse Owens (US)	10.3s
1948	Harrison Dillard (US)	10.3s
1952	Lindy Remigino (US)	10.79s
1956	Bobby Morrow (US)	10.62s
1960	Armin Hary (Ger)	10.32s
1964	Robert Hayes (US)	10.06s
1968	James Hines (US)	9.95s
1972	Valeriy Borzov (USSR)	10.14s
1976	Hasely Crawford (Tri)	10.06s
1980	Allan Wells (GB)	10.25s
1984	Carl Lewis (US)	9.99s
1988	Carl Lewis (US)	9.92s

200 Metres

1900	Walter Tewksbury (US)	22.2s
1904	Archie Hahn (US)	21.6s
1908	Robert Kerr (Can)	22.6s
1912	Ralph Craig (US)	21.7s
1920	Allen Woodring (US)	22.0s
1924	Jackson Scholz (US)	21.6s
1928	Percy Williams (Can)	21.8s
1932	Eddie Tolan (US)	21.12s
1936	Jesse Owens (US)	20.7s
1948	Melvin Patton (US)	21.1s
1952	Andrew Stanfield (US)	20.81s
1956	Bobby Morrow (US)	20.75s
1960	Livio Berrutti (Ita)	20.62s
1964	Henry Carr (US)	20.36s
1968	Tommie Smith (US)	19.83s
1972	Valeriy Borzov (USSR)	20.00s
1976	Donald Quarrie (Jam)	20.22s
1980	Pietro Mennea (Ita)	20.19s
1984	Carl Lewis (US)	19.80s
1988	Joe DeLoach (US)	19.75s

400 Metres

1896	Thomas Burke (US)	54.2s
1900	Maxie Long (US)	49.4s
1904	Harry Hillman (US)	49.2s
1908	Wyndham Halswelle (GB)	50.0s
1912	Charles Reidpath (US)	48.2s
1920	Bevil Rudd (SAf)	49.6s
1924	Eric Liddell (GB)	47.6s
1928	Ray Barbuti (US)	47.8s
1932	Bill Carr (US)	46.28s
1936	Archie Williams (US)	46.66s
1948	Arthur Wint (Jam)	46.2s
1952	George Rhoden (Jam)	46.09s
1956	Charles Jenkins (US)	46.86s
1960	Otis Davis (US)	45.07s
1964	Michael Larrabee (US)	45.15s
1968	Lee Evans (US)	43.86s
1972	Vincent Matthews (US)	44.66s
1976	Alberto Juantorena (Cub)	44.26s
1980	Viktor Markin (USSR)	44.60s
1984	Alonzo Babers (US)	44.27s
1988	Steve Lewis (US)	43.87s

800 Metres

1896	Edwin Flack (Aus)	2m 11.0s
1900	Alfred Tysoe (GB)	2m 01.2s
1904	James Lightbody (US)	1m 56.0s
1908	Mel Sheppard (US)	1m 52.8s
1912	James Meredith (US)	1m 51.9s
1920	Albert Hill (GB)	1m 53.4s
1924	Douglas Lowe (GB)	1m 52.4s
1928	Douglas Lowe (GB)	1m 51.8s
1932	Tom Hampson (GB)	1m 49.70s
1936	John Woodruff (US)	1m 52.9s
1948	Malvin Whitfield (US)	1m 49.2s
1952	Malvin Whitfield (US)	1m 49.34s

1956	Thomas Courtney (US) 1m 47.75s
1960	Peter Snell (NZ) 1m 46.48s
1964	Peter Snell (NZ) 1m 45.1s
1968	Ralph Doubell (Aus) 1m 44.40s
1972	David Wottle (US) 1m 45.86s
1976	Alberto Juantorena (Cub) 1m 43.50s
1980	Steve Ovett (GB) 1m 45.40s
1984	Joaquim Cruz (Bra) 1m 43.00s
1988	Paul Ereng (Ken) 1m 44.06s

1500 Metres

1896	Edwin Flack (Aus) 4m 33.2s
1900	Charles Bennett (GB) 4m 06.2s
1904	James Lightbody (US) 4m 05.4s
1908	Mel Sheppard (US) 4m 03.4s
1912	Arnold Jackson (GB) 3m 56.8s
1920	Albert Hill (GB) 4m 01.8s
1924	Paavo Nurmi (Fin) 3m 53.6s
1928	Harri Larva (Fin) 3m 53.2s
1932	Luigi Beccali (Ita) 3m 51.20s
1936	Jack Lovelock (NZ) 3m 47.8s
1948	Henry Eriksson (Swe) 3m 49.8s
1952	Josef Barthel (Lux) 3m 45.28s
1956	Ron Delany (Ire) 3m 41.49s
1960	Herb Elliott (Aus) 3m 35.6s
1964	Peter Snell (NZ) 3m 38.1s
1968	Kipchoge Keino (Ken) 3m 34.91s
1972	Pekka Vasala (Fin) 3m 36.33s
1976	John Walker (NZ) 3m 39.17s
1980	Sebastian Coe (GB) 3m 38.40s
1984	Sebastian Coe (GB) 3m 32.53s
1988	Peter Rono (Ken) 3m 36.21s

5,000 Metres

1912	Hannes Kolehmainen (Fin) 14m 36.6s
1920	Joseph Guillemot (Fra) 14m 55.6s
1924	Paavo Nurmi (Fin) 14m 31.2s
1928	Ville Ritola (Fin) 14m 38.0s
1932	Lauri Lehtinen (Fin) 14m 30.0s
1936	Gunnar Hockert (Fin) 14m 22.2s
1948	Gaston Reiff (Bel) 14m 17.6s
1952	Emil Zatopek (Cze) 14m 06.72s
1956	Vladimir Kuts (USSR) 13m 39.86s
1960	Murray Halberg (NZ) 13m 43.4s
1964	Robert Schul (US) 13m 48.8s
1968	Mohamed Gammoudi (Tun) 14m 05.0s
1972	Lasse Viren (Fin) 13m 26.42s
1976	Lasse Viren (Fin) 13m 24.76s
1980	Miruts Yifter (Eth) 13m 20.91s
1984	Said Aouita (Mor) 13m 05.59s
1988	John Ngugi (Ken) 13m 11.70s

10,000 Metres

1912	Hannes Kolehmainen (Fin) 31m 20.8s
1920	Paavo Nurmi (Fin) 31m 45.8s
1924	Ville Ritola (Fin) 30m 23.2s
1928	Paavo Nurmi (Fin) 30m 18.8s
1932	Janusz Kushocinski (Pol) 30m 11.4s
1936	Ilmari Salminen (Fin) 30m 15.4s
1948	Emil Zatopek (Cze) 29m 59.6s
1952	Emil Zatopek (Cze) 29m 17.0s
1956	Vladimir Kuts (USSR) 28m 45.60s
1960	Pyotr Bolotnikov (USSR) 28m 32.18s
1964	William Mills (US) 28m 24.4s
1968	Naftali Temu (Ken) 29m 27.4s
1972	Lasse Viren (Fin) 27m 38.35s
1976	Lasse Viren (Fin) 27m 40.38s
1980	Miruts Yifter (Eth) 27m 42.69s
1984	Alberto Cova (Ita) 27m 47.54s
1988	Moulay Brahim Boutaib (Mor) 27m 21.46s

Marathon

1896	Spyridon Louis (Gre) 2h 58m 50.0s
1900	Michel Theato (Fra) 2h 59m 45.0s
1904	Thomas Hicks (US) 3h 28m 35.0s

1908	John Hayes (US) 2h 55m 18.4s
1912	Kenneth McArthur (SAf) 2h 36m 54.8s
1920	Hannes Kolehmainen (Fin) 2h 32m 35.8s
1924	Albin Stenroos (Fin) 2h 41m 22.6s
1928	Mohamed El Ouafi (Fra) 2h 32m 57.0s
1932	Juan Zabala (Arg) 2h 31m 36.0s
1936	Kitei Son (Jap) 2h 29m 19.2s
1948	Delfo Cabrera (Arg) 2h 34m 51.6s
1952	Emil Zatopek (Cze) 2h 23m 03.2s
1956	Alain Mimoun (Fra) 2h 25m 00.0s
1960	Abebe Bikila (Eth) 2h 15m 16.2s
1964	Abebe Bikila (Eth) 2h 12m 11.2s
1968	Mamo Wolde (Eth) 2h 20m 26.4s
1972	Frank Shorter (US) 2h 12m 19.8s
1976	Waldemar Cierpinski (GDR) 2h 09m 55s
1980	Waldemar Cierpinski (GDR) 2h 11m 03s
1984	Carlos Lopes (Por) 2h 09m 21s
1988	Gelindo Bordin (Ita) 2h 10m 32s

110 Metres Hurdles

1896	Thomas Curtis (US) 17.6s
1900	Alvin Kraenzlein (US) 15.4s
1904	Fred Schule (US) 16.0s
1908	Forrest Smithson (US) 15.0s
1912	Fred Kelly (US) 15.1s
1920	Earl Thomson (Can) 14.8s
1924	Daniel Kinsey (US) 15.0s
1928	Sydney Atkinson (SAf) 14.8s
1932	George Saling (US) 14.56s
1936	Forrest Towns (US) 14.2s
1948	William Porter (US) 13.9s
1952	Harrison Dillard (US) 13.91s
1956	Lee Calhoun (US) 13.70s
1960	Lee Calhoun (US) 13.98s
1964	Hayes Jones (US) 13.67s
1968	Willie Davenport (US) 13.33s
1972	Rodney Milburn (US) 13.24s
1976	Guy Drut (Fra) 13.30s
1980	Thomas Munkelt (GDR) 13.39s
1984	Roger Kingdom (US) 13.20s
1988	Roger Kingdom (US) 12.98s

400 Metres Hurdles

1900	Walter Tewksbury (US) 57.6s
1904	Harry Hillman (US) 53.0s
1908	Charles Bacon (US) 55.0s
1920	Frank Loomis (US) 54.0s
1924	Morgan Taylor (US) 52.6s
1928	Lord Burghley (GB) 53.4s
1932	Robert Tisdall (Ire) 51.67s
1936	Glenn Hardin (US) 52.4s
1948	Roy Cochran (US) 51.1s
1952	Charles Moore (US) 51.06s
1956	Glenn Davis (US) 50.29s
1960	Glenn Davis (US) 49.51s
1964	Rex Cawley (US) 49.69s
1968	David Hemery (GB) 48.12s
1972	John Akii-Bua (Uga) 47.82s
1976	Edwin Moses (US) 47.63s
1980	Volker Beck (GDR) 48.70s
1984	Edwin Moses (US) 47.75s
1988	Andre Phillips (US) 47.19s

3,000 Metres Steeplechase

1920	Percy Hodge (GB) 10m 00.4s
1924	Ville Ritola (Fin) 9m 33.6s
1928	Toivo Loukola (Fin) 9m 21.8s
1932	Volmari Iso-Hollo (Fin) 10m 33.4s*
1936	Volmari Iso-Hollo (Fin) 9m 03.8s
1948	Tore Sjöstrand (Swe) 9m 04.6s
1952	Horace Ashenfelter (US) 8m 45.68s
1956	Christopher Brasher (GB) 8m 41.35s
1960	Zdzislaw Kryszkowiak (Pol) 8m 34.31s

1964	Gaston Roelants (Bel) 8m 30.8s
1968	Amos Biwott (Ken) 8m 51.0s
1972	Kipchoge Keino (Ken) 8m 23.64s
1976	Anders Gärderud (Swe) 8m 08.02s
1980	Bronislaw Malinowski (Pol) 8m 09.70s
1984	Julius Korir (Ken) 8m 11.80s
1988	Julius Kariuki (Ken) 8m 05.51s

* Competitors ran an extra lap in error.

20,000 Metres Walk

1956	Leonid Spirin (USSR) 1h 31m 27.4s
1960	Vladimir Golubnichiy (USSR) 1h 34m 07.2s
1964	Kenneth Matthews (GB) 1h 29m 34.0s
1968	Vladimir Golubnichiy (USSR) 1h 33m 58.4s
1972	Peter Frenkel (GDR) 1h 26m 42.4s
1976	Daniel Bautista (Mex) 1h 24m 40.6s
1980	Maurizio Damilano (Ita) 1h 23m 35.5s
1984	Ernesto Canto (Mex) 1h 23m 13s
1988	Jozef Pribilinec (Cze) 1h 19m 57s

50,000 Metres Walk

1932	Thomas Green (GB) 4h 50m 10.0s
1936	Harold Whitlock (GB) 4h 30m 41.1s
1948	John Ljunggren (Swe) 4h 41m 52.0s
1952	Giuseppe Dordoni (Ita) 4h 28m 07.8s
1956	Norman Read (NZ) 4h 30m 42.8s
1960	Don Thompson (GB) 4h 25m 30.0s
1964	Abdon Pamich (Ita) 4h 11m 12.4s
1968	Christophe Höhne (GDR) 4h 20m 13.6s
1972	Bernd Kannenberg (GDR) 3h 56m 11.6s
1980	Hartwig Gauder (GDR) 3h 49m 24s
1984	Raul Gonzales (Mex) 3h 47m 26s
1988	Viacheslav Ivanenko (USSR) 3h 38m 29s

4 x 100 Metres Relay

1912	Great Britain 42.4s
1920	United States 42.2s
1924	United States 41.0s
1928	United States 41.0s
1932	United States 40.0s
1936	United States 39.8s
1948	United States 40.6s
1952	United States 40.26s
1956	United States 39.59s
1960	West Germany 39.66s
1964	United States 39.06s
1968	United States 38.23s
1972	United States 38.19s
1976	United States 38.83s
1980	USSR 38.26s
1984	United States 37.83s
1988	USSR 38.19s

4 x 400 Metres Relay

1912	United States 3m 16.6s
1920	Great Britain 3m 22.2s
1924	United States 3m 16.0s
1928	United States 3m 14.2s
1932	United States 3m 08.2s
1936	Great Britain 3m 09.0s
1948	United States 3m 10.4s
1952	Jamaica 3m 04.04s
1956	United States 3m 04.80s
1960	United States 3m 02.37s
1964	United States 3m 00.71s
1968	United States 2m 56.16s
1972	Kenya 2m 59.83s
1976	United States 2m 58.66s
1980	USSR 3m 01.08s
1984	United States 2m 57.91s
1988	United States 2m 56.16s

High Jump

1896	Ellery Clark (US) 1.81m
1900	Irving Baxter (US) 1.90m
1904	Samuel Jones (US) 1.80m
1908	Harry Porter (US) 1.90m
1912	Alma Richards (US) 1.93m
1920	Richard Landon (US) 1.94m
1924	Harold Osborn (US) 1.98m
1928	Robert King (US) 1.94m
1932	Duncan McNaughton (Can) 1.97m
1936	Cornelius Johnson (US) 2.03m
1948	John Winter (Aus) 1.98m
1952	Walter Davis (US) 2.04m
1956	Charles Dumas (US) 2.12m
1960	Robert Shavlakadze (USSR) 2.16m
1964	Valeriy Brumel (USSR) 2.18m
1968	Dick Fosbury (US) 2.24m
1972	Yuriy Tarmak (USSR) 2.23m
1976	Jacek Wszola (Pol) 2.25m
1980	Gerd Wessig (GDR) 2.36m
1984	Dietmar Mögenburg (FRG) 2.35m
1988	Gennady Avdeyenko (USSR) 2.38m

Pole Vault

1896	William Hoyt (US) 3.30m
1900	Irving Baxter (US) 3.30m
1904	Charles Dvorak (US) 3.50m
1908	Edward Cooke & Alfred Gilbert (US) 3.71m
1912	Harry Babcock (US) 3.95m
1920	Frank Foss (US) 4.09m
1924	Lee Barnes (US) 3.95m
1928	Sabin Carr (US) 4.20m
1932	Bill Miller (US) 4.31m
1936	Earle Meadows (US) 4.35m
1948	Guinn Smith (US) 4.30m
1952	Robert Richards (US) 4.55m
1956	Robert Richards (US) 4.56m
1960	Dinald Bragg (US) 4.70m
1964	Frederick Hansen (US) 5.10m
1968	Bob Seagren (US) 5.40m
1972	Wolfgang Nordwig (GDR) 5.50m
1976	Tadeusz Slusarski (Pol) 5.50m
1980	Wladyslaw Kozakiewicz (Pol) 5.78m
1984	Pierre Quinon (Fra) 5.75m
1988	Sergey Bubka (USSR) 5.90m

Long Jump

1896	Ellery Clark (US) 6.35m
1900	Alvin Kraenzlein (US) 7.18m
1904	Myer Prinstein (US) 7.34m
1908	Francis Irons (US) 7.48m
1912	Albert Gutterson (US) 7.60m
1920	William Pettersson (Swe) 7.15m
1924	William De Hart Hubbard (US) 7.44m
1928	Edward Hamm (US) 7.73m
1932	Edward Gordon (US) 7.64m
1936	Jesse Owens (US) 8.06m
1948	William Steele (US) 7.82m
1952	Jerome Biffle (US) 7.57m
1956	Gregory Bell (US) 7.83m
1960	Ralph Boston (US) 8.12m
1964	Lynn Davies (GB) 8.07m
1968	Bob Beamon (US) 8.90m
1972	Randy Williams (US) 8.24m
1976	Arnie Robinson (US) 8.35m
1980	Lutz Dombrowski (GDR) 8.54m
1984	Carl Lewis (US) 8.54m
1988	Carl Lewis (US) 8.72m

Triple Jump

1896	James Connolly (US) 13.71m
1900	Myer Prinstein (US) 14.47m
1904	Myer Prinstein (US) 14.35m
1908	Tim Ahearne (GB) 14.91m
1912	Gustaf Lindblom (Swe) 14.76m

1920	Vilho Tuulos (Fin) 14.50m
1924	Anthony Winter (Aus) 15.52m
1928	Mikio Oda (Jap) 15.21m
1932	Chuhei Nambu (Jap) 15.72m
1936	Naoto Tajima (Jap) 16.00m
1948	Arne Ahman (Swe) 15.40m
1952	Adhemar Ferreira da Silva (Bra) 16.22m
1956	Adhemar Ferreira da Silva (Bra) 16.35m
1960	Jozef Schmidt (Pol) 16.81m
1964	Jozef Schmidt (Pol) 16.85m
1968	Viktor Saneyev (USSR) 17.39m
1972	Viktor Saneyev (USSR) 17.35m
1976	Viktor Saneyev (USSR) 17.29m
1980	Jaak Uudmae (USSR) 17.35m
1984	Al Joyner (US) 17.26m
1988	Hristo Markov (Bul) 17.61m

Shot

1896	Robert Garrett (US) 11.22m
1900	Richard Sheldon (US) 14.10m
1904	Ralph Rose (US) 14.80m
1908	Ralph Rose (US) 14.21m
1912	Patrick McDonald (US) 15.34m
1920	Ville Porhola (Fin) 14.81m
1924	Clarence Houser (US) 14.99m
1928	John Kuck (US) 15.87m
1932	Leo Sexton (US) 16.00m
1936	Hans Woellke (Ger) 16.20m
1948	Wilbur Thompson (US) 17.12m
1952	Parry O'Brien (US) 17.41m
1956	Parry O'Brien (US) 18.57m
1960	William Nieder (US) 19.68m
1964	Dallas Long (US) 20.33m
1968	Randy Matson (US) 20.54m
1972	Wladyslaw Komar (Pol) 21.18m
1976	Udo Beyer (GDR) 21.05m
1980	Vladimir Kiselyov (USSR) 21.35m
1984	Alessandro Andrei (Ita) 21.26m
1988	Ulf Timmermann (GDR) 22.47m

Discus

1896	Robert Garrett (US) 29.15m
1900	Rudolf Bauer (Hun) 36.04m
1904	Martin Sheridan (US) 39.28m
1908	Martin Sheridan (US) 40.89m
1912	Armas Taipale (Fin) 45.21m
1920	Elmer Niklander (Fin) 44.68m
1924	Clarence Houser (US) 46.15m
1928	Clarence Houser (US) 47.32m
1932	John Anderson (US) 49.49m
1936	Ken Carpenter (US) 50.48m
1948	Adolfo Consolini (Ita) 52.78m
1952	Sim Iness (US) 55.03m
1956	Al Oerter (US) 56.36m
1960	Al Oerter (US) 59.18m
1964	Al Oerter (US) 61.00m
1968	Al Oerter (US) 64.78m
1972	Ludvik Danek (Cze) 64.40m
1976	Mac Wilkins (US) 67.50m
1980	Viktor Rashchupkin (USSR) 66.64m
1984	Rolf Danneberg (FRG) 66.60m
1988	Jürgen Schult (GDR) 68.82m

Javelin

1908	Erik Lemming (Swe) 54.82m
1912	Erik Lemming (Swe) 60.64m
1920	Jonni Myyrä (Fin) 65.78m
1924	Jonni Myyrä (Fin) 62.96m
1928	Erik Lundkvist (Swe) 66.60m
1932	Matti Järvinen (Fin) 72.71m
1936	Gerhard Stöck (Ger) 71.84m
1948	Tapio Rautavaara (Fin) 69.77m

1952	Cyrus Young (US) 73.78m
1956	Egil Danielsen (Nor) 85.71
1960	Viktor Tsibulenko (USSR) 84.64m
1964	Pauli Nevala (Fin) 82.66m
1968	Janis Lusis (USSR) 90.10m
1972	Klaus Wolfermann (FRG) 90.48m
1976	Miklos Nemeth (Hun) 94.58m
1980	Dainis Kula (USSR) 91.20m
1984	Arto Harkönen (Fin) 86.76m
1988	Tapio Korjus (Fin) 84.28m

Hammer

1900	John Flanagan (US) 49.73m
1904	John Flanagan (US) 51.23m
1908	John Flanagan (US) 51.92m
1912	Matt McGrath (US) 54.74m
1920	Patrick Ryan (US) 52.87m
1924	Fred Tootell (US) 53.29m
1928	Patrick O'Callaghan (Ire) 51.39m
1932	Patrick O'Callaghan (Ire) 53.92m
1936	Karl Hein (Ger) 56.49m
1948	Imre Nemeth (Hun) 56.07m
1952	Jozsef Csermak (Hun) 60.34m
1956	Harold Connolly (US) 63.19m
1960	Vasiliy Rudenkov (USSR) 67.10m
1964	Romuald Klim (USSR) 69.74m
1968	Gyula Zsivotzky (Hun) 73.36m
1972	Anatoliy Bondarchuk (USSR) 75.50m
1976	Yuriy Sedykh (USSR) 77.52m
1980	Yuriy Sedykh (USSR) 81.80m
1984	Juha Tiainen (Fin) 78.08m
1988	Sergey Litvinov (USSR) 84.80m

Decathlon

Points converted to 1984 tables.

1904	Thomas Kiely (Ire) 6036pts
1912	Jim Thorpe (US) 6564pts†
1920	Helge Løvland (Nor) 5804pts
1924	Harold Osborn (US) 6476pts
1928	Paavo Yrjola (Fin) 6607pts
1932	James Bausch (US) 6735pts
1936	Glenn Morris (US) 7254pts
1948	Robert Mathias (US) 6628pts
1952	Robert Mathias (US) 7580pts
1956	Milton Campbell (US) 7565 pts
1960	Rafer Johnson (US) 7901pts
1964	Willi Holdorf (Ger) 7726pts est
1968	Bill Toomey (US) 8158pts
1972	Nikolai Avilov (USSR) 8466pts
1976	Bruce Jenner (US) 8634pts
1980	Daley Thompson (GB) 8522pts
1984	Daley Thompson (GB) 8847pts
1988	Christian Schenk (GDR) 8488pts

† *Thorpe disqualified for professionalism, and gold medal awarded to Hugo Weislander (Swe). Thorpe was posthumously re-instated in 1982.*

Women
100 Metres

1928	Elizabeth Robinson (US) 12.2s
1932	Stanislawa Walasiewicz (Pol) 11.9s
1936	Helen Stephens (US) 11.5s
1948	Fanny Blankers-Koen (Hol) 11.9s
1952	Marjorie Jackson (Aus) 11.65s
1956	Betty Cuthbert (Aus) 11.82s
1960	Wilma Rudolph (US) 11.08s
1964	Wyomia Tyus (US) 11.49s
1968	Wyomia Tyus (US) 11.08s
1972	Renate Stecher (GDR) 11.07s
1976	Annegret Richter (FRG) 11.08s
1980	Lyudmila Kondratyeva (USSR) 11.06s
1984	Evelyn Ashford (US) 10.97s

1988 Florence Griffith-Joyner (US) 10.54s

200 Metres
1948 Fanny Blankers-Koen (Hol) 24.4s
1952 Marjorie Jackson (Aus) 23.89s
1956 Betty Cuthbert (Aus) 23.55s
1960 Wilma Rudoph (US) 24.03s
1964 Edith Maguire (US) 23.05s
1968 Irena Szewinska (Pol) 22.58s
1972 Renate Stecher (GDR) 22.40s
1976 Barbel Eckert (GDR) 22.37s
1980 Barbel Wockel (née Eckert) (GDR) 22.03s
1984 Valerie Brisco-Hooks (US) 21.81s
1988 Florence Griffith-Joyner (US) 21.34s

400 Metres
1964 Betty Cuthbert (Aus) 52.01s
1968 Colette Besson (Fra) 52.03s
1972 Monika Zehrt (GDR) 51.08s
1976 Irena Szewinska (Pol) 49.29s
1980 Marita Koch (GDR) 48.88s
1984 Valerie Brisco-Hooks (US) 48.83s
1988 Olga Bryzgina (USSR) 48.65s

800 Metres
1928 Lina Radke (Ger) 2m 16.8s
1960 Lyudmila Shevtsova (USSR) 2m 04.50s
1964 Ann Packer (GB) 2m 01.1s
1968 Madeline Manning (US) 2m 00.92s
1972 Hildegard Falck (FRG) 1m 58.55s
1976 Tatyana Kazankina (USSR) 1m 54.94s
1980 Nadezhda Olizarenko (USSR) 1m 53.43s
1984 Doina Melinte (Rom) 1m 57.60s
1988 Sigrun Wodars (GDR) 1m 56.10s

1500 Metres
1972 Lyudmila Bragina (USSR) 4m 01.38s
1976 Tatyana Kazankina (USSR) 4m 05.48s
1980 Tatyana Kazankina (USSR) 3m 56.56s
1984 Gabriella Doria (Ita) 4m 03.25s
1988 Paula Ivan (Rom) 3m 53.96s

3,000 Metres
1984 Maricica Puica (Rom) 8m 35.96s
1988 Tatyana Samolenko (USSR) 8m 26.53s

10,000 Metres
1988 Olga Bondarenko (USSR) 31m 05.21s

Marathon
1984 Joan Benoit (US) 2h 24m 52s
1988 Rosa Mota (Por) 2h 25m 40s

100 Metres Hurdles
(80 metres 1936-68)
1932 Mildred Didrikson (US) 11.7s
1936 Trebisonda Valla (Ita) 11.74s
1948 Fanny Blankers-Koen (Hol) 11.2s
1952 Shirley Strickland (Aus) 11.03s
1956 Shirley Strickland (Aus) 10.96s
1960 Irina Press (USSR) 10.94s
1964 Karin Balzar (Ger) 10.54s
1968 Maureen Caird (Aus) 10.39s
1972 Annelie Ehrhardt (GDR) 12.59s
1976 Johanna Schaller (GDR) 12.77s
1980 Vera Komisova (USSR) 12.56s
1984 Benita Fitzgerald-Brown (US) 12.84s
1988 Jordanka Donkova (Bul) 12.38s

400 Metres Hurdles
1984 Nawal el Moutawakil (Mor) 54.61s
1988 Debbie Flintoff-King (Aus) 53.17s

4 x 100 Metres Relay
1928 Canada 48.4s
1932 United States 47.0s
1936 United States 46.9s
1948 Netherlands 47.5s

1952 United States 46.14s
1956 Australia 44.65s
1960 United States 44.72s
1964 Poland 43.69s
1968 United States 42.87s
1972 West Germany 42.81s
1976 East Germany 42.55s
1980 East Germany 41.60s
1984 United States 41.65s
1988 United States 41.98s

4 x 400 Metres Relay
1972 East Germany 3m 22.95s
1976 East Germany 3m 19.23s
1980 USSR 3m 20.12s
1984 United States 3m 18.29s
1988 USSR 3m 15.18s

High Jump
1928 Ethel Catherwood (Can) 1.59m
1932 Jean Shiley (US) 1.6 m
1936 Ibolya Csak (Hun) 1.60m
1948 Alice Coachman (US) 1.68m
1952 Esther Brand (SA) 1.67m
1956 Mildred McDaniel (US) 1.76m
1960 Iolanda Balas (Rom) 1.85m
1964 Iolanda Balas (Rom) 1.90m
1968 Miloslava Rezkova (Cze) 1.82m
1972 Ulrike Meyfarth (FRG) 1.92m
1976 Rosi Ackermann (GDR) 1.93m
1980 Sara Simeoni (Ita) 1.97m
1984 Ulrike Meyfarth (FRG) 2.02m
1988 Louise Ritter (US) 2.03m

Long Jump
1948 Olga Gyarmati (Hun) 5.69m
1952 Yvette Williams (NZ) 6.24m
1956 Elzbieta Krzesinska (Pol) 6.35m
1960 Vyera Krepkina (USSR) 6.37m
1964 Mary Rand (GB) 6.76m
1968 Viorica Viscopoleanu (Rom) 6.82m
1972 Heide Rosendahl (FRG) 6.78m
1976 Angela Voigt (GDR) 6.72m
1980 Tatyana Kolpakova (USSR) 7.06m
1984 Anisora Stanciu (Rom) 6.96m
1988 Jackie Joyner-Kersee (US) 7.40m

Shot
1948 Micheline Ostermeyer (Fra) 13.75m
1952 Galina Zybina (USSR) 15.28m
1956 Tamara Tishkyevich (USSR) 16.59m
1960 Tamara Press (USSR) 17.32m
1964 Tamara Press (USSR) 18.14m
1968 Margitta Gummel (GDR) 19.61m
1972 Nadezhda Chizhova (USSR) 21.03m
1976 Ivanka Khristova (Bul) 21.16m
1980 Ilona Slupianek (GDR) 22.41m
1984 Claudia Losch (FRG) 20.48m
1988 Natalya Lisovskaya (USSR) 22.24m

Discus
1928 Helena Konopacka (Pol) 39.62m
1932 Lillian Copeland (US) 40.58m
1936 Gisela Mauermayer (Ger) 47.63m
1948 Micheline Ostermeyer (Fra) 41.92m
1952 Nina Ponomaryeva (USSR) 51.42m
1956 Olga Fikotova (Cze) 53.69m
1960 Nina Ponomaryeva (USSR) 55.10m
1964 Tamara Press (USSR) 57.27m
1968 Lia Manoliu (Rom) 58.28m
1972 Faina Melnik (USSR) 66.62m
1976 Evelin Schlaak (GDR) 69.00m
1980 Evelin Jahl (née Schlaak) (GDR) 69.96m
1984 Ria Stalmach (Hol) 65.36m

1988	Martina Hellman (GDR) 72.30m

Javelin
1932	Mildred Didrikson (US) 43.68m
1936	Tilly Fleischer (Ger) 45.18m
1948	Herma Bauma (Aut) 45.57m
1952	Dana Zatopkova (Cze) 50.47m
1956	Inese Jaunzeme (USSR) 53.86m
1960	Elvira Ozolina (USSR) 55.98m
1964	Mihaela Penes (Rom) 60.54m
1968	Angela Nemeth (Hun) 60.36m
1972	Ruth Fuchs (GDR) 63.88m
1976	Ruth Fuchs (GDR) 65.94m
1980	Maria Colon (Cub) 68.40m

1984	Tessa Sanderson (GB) 69.56m
1988	Petra Felke (GDR) 74.68m

Pentathlon
1964	Irina Press (USSR) 5246pts
1968	Ingrid Becker (FRG) 5098pts
1972	Mary Peters (GB) 4801pts
1976	Sigrun Siegl (GDR) 4745pts
1980	Nadezhda Tkachenko (USSR) 5083pts

Heptathlon
1984	Glynis Nunn (Aus) 6390pts
1988	Jackie Joyner-Kersee (US) 7291pts

BASKETBALL

	Men	Women		Men	Women
1936	United States		1968	United States	
1948	United States		1972	USSR	
1952	United States		1976	United States	USSR
1956	United States		1980	Yugoslavia	USSR
1960	United States		1984	United States	United States
1964	United States		1988	USSR	United States

BOXING

Super-heavyweight
1984	Tyrell Biggs (US)
1988	Lennox Lewis (Can)

Heavyweight
1904	Samuel Berger (US)
1908	A.L. Oldham (GB)
1912	Not held
1920	Ronald Rawson (GB)
1924	Otto von Porat (Nor)
1928	Arturo Rodriguez Jurado (Arg)
1932	Santiago Lovell (Arg)
1936	Herbert Runge (Ger)
1948	Rafael Iglesias (Arg)
1952	Edward Sanders (US)
1956	Peter Rademacher (US)
1960	Franco de Piccoli (Ita)
1964	Joe Frazier (US)
1968	George Foreman (US)
1972	Teofilio Stevenson (Cub)
1976	Teofilio Stevenson (Cub)
1980	Teofilio Stevenson (Cub)
1984	Henry Tillman (US)
1988	Ray Mercer (US)

Light-heavyweight
1920	Eddie Eagan (US)
1924	Harry Mitchell (GB)
1928	Victor Avendano (Arg)
1932	David Carstens (SAf)
1936	Roger Michelot (Fra)
1948	George Hunter (SAf)
1952	Norvel Lee (US)
1956	James Boyd (US)
1960	Cassius Clay (US)
1964	Cosimo Pinto (Ita)
1968	Dan Poznyak (USSR)
1972	Mate Parlov (Yug)
1976	Leon Spinks (US)
1980	Slobodan Kacar (Yug)
1984	Anton Jospovic (Yug)
1988	Andrew Maynard (US)

Middleweight
1904	Charles Mayer (US)

1908	John Douglas (GB)
1920	Harry Mallin (GB)
1924	Harry Mallin (GB)
1928	Piero Toscani (Ita)
1932	Carmen Barth (US)
1936	Jean Despeaux (Fra)
1948	Laszlo Papp (Hun)
1952	Floyd Patterson (US)
1956	Genaddy Schatkov (USSR)
1960	Edward Crook (US)
1964	Valery Popenchenko (USSR)
1968	Chris Finnegan (GB)
1972	Vyacheslav Lewechev (USSR)
1976	Michael Spinks (US)
1980	Jose Gomez (Cub)
1984	Sin-Joon Sup (SKo)
1988	Henry Maske (GDR)

Light-middleweight
1952	Laszlo Papp (Hun)
1956	Laszlo Papp (Hun)
1960	Wilbert McClure (US)
1964	Boris Lagutin (USSR)
1968	Boris Lagutin (USSR)
1972	Dieter Kottysch (FRG)
1976	Jerzy Rybicki (Pol)
1980	Armando Martinez (Cub)
1984	Frank Tate (US)
1988	Park Si-Hun (SKo)

Welterweight
1904	Albert Young (US)
1908	not held
1920	Albert Schneider (Can)
1924	Jean Delarge (Bel)
1928	Edward Morgan (NZ)
1932	Edward Flynn (US)
1936	Sten Suvio (Fin)
1948	Julius Torma (Cze)
1952	Zygmunt Chychia (Pol)
1956	Nicolae Linca (Rom)
1960	Giovanni Benvenuti (Ita)
1964	Marian Kasprzyk (Pol)
1968	Manfred Wolke (GDR)

1972	Emilio Correa (Cub)
1976	Jochen Bachfeld (GDR)
1980	Andres Aldama (Cub)
1984	Mark Breland (US)
1988	Robert Wangila (Ken)

Light-welterweight

1952	Charles Adkins (US)
1956	Vladimir Yengibaryan (USSR)
1960	Bohumil Nemecek (Cze)
1964	Jerzy Kulej (Pol)
1968	Jerzy Kulej (Pol)
1972	Ray Seales (US)
1976	Ray Leonard (US)
1980	Patrizio Oliva (Ita)
1984	Jerry Page (US)
1988	Viatcheslav Janovski (USSR)

Lightweight

1904	Harry Spanger (US)
1908	Frederick Grace (GB)
1920	Samuel Mosberg (US)
1924	Hans Neilsen (Den)
1928	Carlo Orlando (Ita)
1932	Lawrence Stevens (SAf)
1936	Imre Harangi (Hun)
1948	Gerald Dreyer (SAf)
1952	Aureliano Bolognesi (Ita)
1956	Dick McTaggart (GB)
1960	Kazimierz Pazdzior (Pol)
1964	Jozef Grudzien (Pol)
1968	Ron Harris (US)
1972	Jan Szczepanski (Pol)
1976	Howard Davis (US)
1980	Angel Herrera (Cub)
1984	Pernell Whitaker (US)
1988	Andreas Zuelow (GDR)

Featherweight

1904	Oliver Kirk (US)
1908	Richard Gunn (GB)
1920	Paul Fritsch (Fra)
1924	John Fields (US)
1928	Lambertus van Klavaren (Hol)
1932	Carmelo Robledo (Arg)
1936	Oscar Casanovas (Arg)
1948	Ernesto Formenti (Ita)
1952	Jan Zachara (Cze)
1956	Vladimir Safronov (USSR)
1960	Francesco Musso (Ita)
1964	Stanislav Stepashkin (USSR)
1968	Antonio Roldan (Mex)
1972	Boris Kousnetsov (USSR)

1976	Angel Herrera (Cub)
1980	Rudi Fink (GDR)
1984	Meldrick Taylor (US)
1988	Giovanni Parisi (Ita)

Bantamweight

1904	Oliver Kirk (US)
1908	Henry Thomas (GB)
1920	Clarence Walker (SAf)
1924	William Smith (SAf)
1928	Vittorio Tamagnini (Ita)
1932	Horace Gwynne (Can)
1936	Ulderico Sergo (Ita)
1948	Tibor Csik (Hun)
1952	Pentti Hamalainen (Fin)
1956	Wolfgang Behrendt (Ger)
1960	Oleg Grigoryev (USSR)
1964	Takao Sakurai (Jap)
1968	Valery Sokolov (USSR)
1972	Orlando Martinez (Cub)
1976	Yung-Jo Gu (NKo)
1980	Juan Hernandez (Cub)
1984	Maurizio Stecca (Ita)
1988	Kennedy McKinney (US)

Flyweight

1904	George Finnegan (US)
1908	not held
1920	Frank Di Gennara (US)
1924	Fidel La Barba (US)
1928	Antal Kocsis (Hun)
1932	Istvan Enekes (Hun)
1936	Willi Kaiser (Ger)
1948	Pascual Perez (Arg)
1952	Nathan Brooks (US)
1956	Terry Spinks (GB)
1960	Gyula Torok (Hun)
1964	Fernando Atzori (Ita)
1968	Ricardo Delgado (Mex)
1972	Georgi Kostadinov (Bul)
1976	Leo Randolph (US)
1980	Peter Lessov (Pul)
1984	Steve McCrory (US)
1988	Kim Kwang-Sun (SKo)

Light-flyweight

1968	Francisco Rodriguez (Ven)
1972	Gyorgy Gedo (Hun)
1976	Jorge Hernandez (Cub)
1980	Shamil Sabyrov (USSR)
1984	Paul Gonzales (US)
1988	Ivalio Hristov (Bul)

CANOEING

Men

500 Metres Kayak Singles

1976	Vasile Diba (Rom)
1980	Vladimir Parfenovich (USSR)
1984	Ian Ferguson (NZ)
1988	Zsolt Gyulay (Hun)

1000 Metres Kayak Singles

1936	Gregor Hradetzky (Aut)
1948	Gert Fredriksson (Swe)
1952	Gert Fredriksson (Swe)
1956	Gert Fredriksson (Swe)
1960	Erik Hansen (Den)
1964	Rolf Peterson (Swe)
1968	Mihaly Hesz (Hun)
1972	Alexandr Shaparenko (USSR)

1976	Rudiger Helm (GDR)
1980	Rudiger Helm (GDR)
1984	Alan Thompson (NZ)
1988	Greg Barton (US)

500 Metres Kayak Pairs

1976	East Germany
1980	USSR
1984	New Zealand
1988	New Zealand

1000 Metres Kayak Pairs

1936	Austria
1948	Sweden
1952	Finland
1956	West Germany
1960	Sweden

1964	Sweden
1968	USSR
1972	USSR
1976	USSR
1980	USSR
1984	Canada
1988	United States

1000 Metres Kayak Fours

1964	USSR
1968	Norway
1972	USSR
1976	USSR
1980	East Germany
1984	New Zealand
1988	Hungary

500 Metres Canadian Singles

1976	Alexandr Rogov (USSR)
1980	Sergey Postrekhin (USSR)
1984	Larry Cain (Can)
1988	Olaf Heukrodt (GDR)

1000 Metres Canadian Singles

1936	Francis Amyot (Can)
1948	Josef Holecek (Cze)
1952	Josef Holecek (Cze)
1956	Leon Rotman (Rom)
1960	Josef Parti (Hun)
1964	Jürgen Eschert (Ger)
1968	Tibor Tatai (Hun)
1972	Ivan Patzaichin (Rom)
1976	Matija Ljubek (Yug)
1980	Lubomir Lubenov (Bul)
1984	Ulrich Eicke (FRG)
1988	Ivan Klementiev (USSR)

500 Metres Canadian Pairs

1976	USSR
1980	Hungary
1984	Yugoslavia
1988	USSR

1000 Metres Canadian Pairs

1936	Czechoslovakia
1948	Czechoslovakia
1952	Denmark
1956	Romania
1960	USSR
1964	USSR
1968	Romania
1972	USSR
1976	USSR
1980	Romania
1984	Romania
1988	USSR

Women

500 Metres Kayak Singles

1948	Karen Hoff (Den)
1952	Sylvi Saimo (Fin)
1956	Elisaveta Dementyeva (USSR)
1960	Anatonina Seredina (USSR)
1964	Lyudmila Khvedosyuk (USSR)
1968	Lyudmila Pinayeva (USSR)
1972	Yulia Ryabchinskaya (USSR)
1976	Carola Zirzow (GDR)
1980	Birgit Fischer (GDR)
1984	Agneta Anderson (Swe)
1988	Vania Guecheva (USSR)

500 Metres Kayak Pairs

1960	USSR
1964	West Germany
1968	West Germany
1972	USSR
1976	USSR
1980	East Germany
1984	Sweden
1988	East Germany

500 Metres Kayak Fours

1984	Romania
1988	East Germany

CYCLING

Men
1000 Metres Sprint

1896	Paul Masson (Fra)
1900	Georges Taillandier (Fra)
1908	No gold medal awarded
1920	Maurice Peeters (Hol)
1924	Lucien Michard (Fra)
1928	René Beaufrand (Fra)
1932	Jacobus van Egmond (Hol)
1936	Toni Merkens (Ger)
1948	Mario Ghella (Ita)
1952	Enzo Sacchi (Ita)
1956	Michel Rousseau (Fra)
1960	Sante Gaiardoni (Ita)
1964	Giovanni Pettenella (Ita)
1968	Daniel Morelon (Fra)
1972	Daniel Morelon (Fra)
1976	Anton Tkac (Cze)
1980	Lutz Hesslich (GDR)
1984	Mark Gorski (US)
1988	Lutz Hesslich (GDR)

1000 Metres Time Trial

1896	Paul Masson (Fra)
1928	Willy Falck-Hansen (Den)
1932	Edgar Gray (Aus)
1936	Arie van Vliet (Hol)
1948	Jacques Dupont (Fra)

1952	Russell Mockridge (Aus)
1956	Leandro Faggin (Ita)
1960	Sante Gaiardoni (Ita)
1964	Patrick Sercu (Bel)
1968	Pierre Trentin (Fra)
1972	Niels-Christian Fredborg (Den)
1976	Klaus-Jürgen Grunke (GDR)
1980	Lothar Thoms (GDR)
1984	Freddy Schmidtke (FRG)
1988	Alexander Kirchenko (USSR)

100 km Team Time Trial

1912	Sweden
1920	France
1924	France
1928	Denmark
1932	Italy
1936	France
1948	Belgium
1952	Belgium
1956	France
1960	Italy
1964	Holland
1968	Holland
1972	USSR
1976	USSR
1980	USSR
1984	Italy
1988	East Germany

4000 Metres Individual Pursuit

1964	Jiri Daler (Cze)
1968	Daniel Rebillard (Fra)
1972	Knut Knudsen (Nor)
1976	Gregor Braun (GDR)
1980	Robert Dill-Bundi (Swi)
1984	Steve Hegg (US)
1988	Giantautus Umarus (USSR)

4000 Metre Team Pursuit

1908	Great Britain
1920	Italy
1924	Italy
1928	Italy
1932	Italy
1936	France
1948	France
1952	Italy
1956	Italy
1960	Italy
1964	Germany
1968	Denmark
1972	West Germany
1976	West Germany
1980	USSR
1984	Australia
1988	USSR

Points Races

1984	Roger Ilegems (Bel)
1988	Dan Frost (Den)

Road Race

1896	Aristidis Konstantinidis (Gre)
1912	Rudolph Lewis (SAf)
1920	Harry Stenqvist (Swe)
1924	Armand Blanchonnet (Fra)
1928	Henry Hansen (Den)
1932	Attilio Pavesi (Ita)
1936	Robert Charpentier (Fra)
1948	José Beyaert (Fra)
1952	André Noyelle (Bel)
1956	Ercole Baldini (Ita)
1960	Viktor Kapitonov (USSR)
1964	Mario Zanin (Ita)
1968	Pierfranco Vianelli (Ita)
1972	Hennie Kuiper (Hol)
1976	Bernt Johansson (Swe)
1980	Sergey Sukhoruchenkov (USSR)
1984	Alexi Grewal (US)
1988	Olaf Ludwig (GDR)

Women

1000 Metres Sprint

1988	Erika Saloumiae (USSR)

Road Race

1984	Connie Carpenter-Phinney (US)
1988	Monique Knol (Hol)

EQUESTRIANISM

Show Jumping
Individual

	Rider	Horse
1900	Aime Haegeman (Bel)	Benton II
1912	Jean Cariou (Fra)	Mignon
1920	Tommaso Lequio (Ita)	Trebecco
1924	Alphonse Gemuseus (Swi)	Lucette
1928	Frantisek Ventura (Cze)	Eliot
1932	Takeichi Nishi (Jap)	Uranus
1936	Kurt Hasse (Ger)	Tora
1948	Humberto Cortes (Mex)	Arete
1952	Pierre d'Oriola (Fra)	Ali Baba
1956	Hans-Gunter Winkler (Ger)	Halla
1960	Raimondo d'Inzeo (Ita)	Posillipo
1964	Pierre d'Oriola (Fra)	Lutteur B
1968	William Steinkraus (US)	Snowbound
1972	Graziano Mancinelli (Ita)	Ambassador
1976	Alwin Schockemohle (FRG)	Warwick Rex
1980	Jan Kowalczyk (Pol)	Artemor
1984	Joe Fargis (US)	Touch of Class
1988	Pierre Durand (Fra)	Jappeloup

Team

1912	Sweden
1920	Sweden
1924	Sweden
1928	Spain
1932	No medals awarded
1936	Germany
1948	Mexico
1952	Britain
1956	Germany
1960	Germany
1964	Germany
1968	Canada
1972	Germany
1976	France
1980	USSR
1984	United States
1988	West Germany

Most gold medals
5 Hans-Gunter Winkler (Team 1956, 1960, 1964, 1972; Individual 1956)

Three-Day Event
Individual

	Rider	Horse
1912	Axel Nordlander (Swe)	Lady Artist
1920	Helmer Morner (Swe)	Germania
1924	Adolph van der Voort van Zijp (Hol)	Silver Piece
1928	Charles P de Mortanges (Hol)	Marcroix
1932	Charles P de Mortanges (Hol)	Marcroix
1936	Ludwig Stubbendorff (Ger)	Nurmi
1948	Bernard Chevallier (Fra)	Aiglonne
1952	Hans von Blixen-Finecke (Swe)	Jubal
1956	Petrus Kastenman (Swe)	Iluster
1960	Lawrence Morgan (US)	Salad Days
1964	Mauro Checcoli (Ita)	Surbean
1968	Jean-Jacques Guyon (Fra)	Pitou
1972	Richard Meade (GB)	Laurieston
1976	Edmund Coffin (US)	Bally-Cor
1980	Federico Roman (Ita)	Rossinan
1984	Mark Todd (NZ)	Charisma
1988	Mark Todd (NZ)	Charisma

Team

1912	Sweden
1920	Sweden
1924	Holland
1928	Holland
1932	United States
1936	Germany
1948	United States
1952	Sweden
1956	Britain
1960	Australia

1964	Italy	
1968	Britain	
1972	Britain	
1976	United States	
1980	USSR	
1984	United States	
1988	West Germany	

Most gold medals
4 Charles Pahud de Mortanges (Team 1924, 1928; Individual 1928, 1932)

Dressage
Individual

	Rider	Horse
1912	Carl Bonde (Swe)	Emperor
1920	Janne Lundblad (Swe)	Uno
1924	Ernst Linder (Swe)	Piccolomini
1928	Carl von Langen (Ger)	Draufganger
1932	Xavier Lesage (Fra)	Taine
1936	Heinz Pollay (Ger)	Kronos
1948	Hans Moser (Swi)	Hummer
1952	Henri St Cyr (Swe)	Master Rufus
1956	Henri St Cyr (Swe)	Juli
1960	Sergey Filatov (USSR)	Absent
1964	Henri Chammartin (Swi)	Woermann

1968	Ivan Kizimov (USSR)	Ichor
1972	Liselott Linsenhoff (FRG)	Piaff
1976	Christine Stuckelberger (Swi)	Granat
1980	Elisabeth Theurer (Aut)	Mon Chérie
1984	Reiner Klimke (FRG)	Ahlerich
1988	Nicole Uphoff (FRG)	Rembrandt
Team		
1928	Germany	
1932	France	
1936	Germany	
1948	France	
1952	Sweden	
1956	Sweden	
1960	Not held	
1964	Germany	
1968	West Germany	
1972	USSR	
1976	West Germany	
1980	USSR	
1984	West Germany	
1988	West Germany	

Most gold medals
4 Henri St Cyr (Team 1952, 1956; Individual 1952, 1956)

FENCING

Men
FOIL

	Individual	Team
1896	Emile Gravelotte (Fra)	-
1900	Emile Coste (Fra)	-
1904	Ramon Fonst (Cub)	Cuba
1908	Not Held	
1912	Nedo Nadi (Ita)	-
1920	Nedo Nadi (Ita)	Italy
1924	Roger Ducret (Fra)	France
1928	Lucien Gaudini (Ita)	Italy
1932	Gustavo Marzi	France
1936	Giulio Gaudini (Ita)	Italy
1948	Jean Buhan (Fra)	France
1952	Christian d'Oriola (Fra)	France
1956	Christian d'Oriola (Fra)	Italy
1960	Viktor Zhadanovich (USSR)	USSR
1964	Egon Franke (Pol)	USSR
1968	Ion Drimba (Rom)	France
1972	Witold Woyda (Pol)	Poland
1976	Fabio Dal Zotto (Ita)	Italy
1980	Vladimir Smirnov (USSR)	USSR
1984	Mauro Numa (Ita)	Italy
1988	Stefano Cerioni (Ita)	USSR

SABRE

	Individual	Team
1896	Jean Georgiadis (Gre)	-
1900	Georges de la Falaise (Fra)	-
1904	Manuel Diaz (Cub)	-
1908	Jeno Fuchs (Hun)	Hungary
1912	Jeno Fuchs (Hun)	Hungary
1920	Nedo Naidi (Ita)	Italy
1924	Sandor Posta (Hun)	Italy
1928	Odon Tersztyanszky (Hun)	Hungary
1932	Gyorgy Piller (Hun)	Hungary
1936	Endre Kabos (Hun)	Hungary
1948	Aldar Gerevich (Hun)	Hungary
1952	Pal Kovacs (Hun)	Hungary
1960	Rudolf Karpati (Hun)	Hungary
1964	Tibor Pezsa (Hun)	USSR
1968	Jerzy Pawlowski (Pol)	USSR
1972	Viktor Sidiak (USSR)	Italy

1976	Viktor Krovopuskov (USSR)	USSR
1980	Viktor Krovopuskov (USSR)	USSR
1984	Jean-François Lamour (Fra)	Italy
1988	Jean-François Lamour (Fra)	Hungary

EPEE

	Individual	Team
1900	Ramon Fonst (Cub)	-
1904	Ramon Fonst (Cub)	-
1908	Gaston Alibert (Fra)	France
1912	Paul Anspach (Bel)	Belgium
1920	Armand Massard (Fra)	Italy
1924	Charles Delport (Bel)	France
1928	Lucien Gaudin (Fra)	Italy
1932	Giancarlo Cornaggia-Medici (Ita)	France
1936	Franco Riccardi (Ita)	Italy
1948	Luigi Cantone (Ita)	France
1952	Edoardo Mangiarotti (Ita)	Italy
1956	Carlo Pavesi (Ita)	Italy
1960	Giuseppe Delfino (Ita)	Italy
1964	Grigoriy Kriss (USSR)	Hungary
1968	Gyozo Kulcsar (Hun)	Hungary
1972	Csaba Fenyvesi (Hun)	Hungary
1976	Alexander Pusch (FRG)	Sweden
1980	Johan Harmenberg (Swe)	France
1984	Philippe Boisse (Fra)	W Germany
1988	Arnd Schmitt (FRG)	France

Women
FOIL (ONLY)

	Individual	Team
1924	Ellen Osiier (Den)	-
1928	Helene Mayer (Ger)	-
1932	Ellen Preis (Aut)	-
1936	Ilona Elek (Hun)	-
1948	Ilona Elek (Hun)	-
1952	Irene Camber (Ita)	-
1956	Gillian Sheen (GB)	-
1960	Heidi Schmid (Ger)	USSR
1964	Ildiko Ujlaki-Rejto (Hun)	Hungary
1968	Yelena Novikova (USSR)	USSR
1972	Antonella Ragno-Lonzi (Ita)	USSR
1976	Ildiko Schwarczenberger (Hun)	USSR
1980	Pascale Trinquet (Fra)	France
1984	Luan Jujie (Chn)	W Germany
1988	Anja Fichtel (FRG)	W Germany

GYMNASTICS

Men
Combined
1900	Gustave Sandras (Fra)
1904	Julius Lenhart (Aut)
1908	Alberto Braglia (Ita)
1912	Alberto Braglia (Ita)
1920	Giorgio Zampori (Ita)
1924	Leon Stukelj (Yug)
1928	Georges Miez (Sui)
1932	Romeo Neri (Ita)
1936	Alfred Schwarzmann (Ger)
1948	Veikko Huhtanen (Fin)
1952	Viktor Chukarin (USSR)
1956	Viktor Chukarin (USSR)
1960	Boris Shakhlin (USSR)
1964	Yukio Endo (Jap)
1968	Sawao Kato (Jap)
1972	Sawao Kato (Jap)
1976	Nikolay Andrianov (USSR)
1980	Aleksandr Ditiatin (USSR)
1984	Koji Gushiken (Jap)
1988	Vladimir Artemov (USSR)

Floor
1932	Istavan Pelle (Hun)
1936	Georges Miez (Swi)
1948	Ferenc Pataki (Hun)
1952	William Thoresson (Swe)
1956	Valentin Muratov (USSR)
1960	Nobuyuki Aihara (Jap)
1964	Franco Menichelli (Ita)
1968	Sawao Kato (Jap)
1972	Nikolay Andrianov (USSR)
1976	Nikolay Andrianov (USSR)
1980	Roland Brückner (GDR)
1984	Li Ning (Chn)
1988	Sergey Kharikov (USSR)

Parallel Bars
1896	Alfred Flatow (Ger)
1904	George Eyser (US)
1908	August Güttinger (Swi)
1928	Ladislav Vacha (Cze)
1932	Romeo Neri (Ita)
1936	Konrad Frey (Ger)
1948	Mickael Reusch (Swi)
1952	Hans Eugster (Swi)
1956	Viktor Chukarin (USSR)
1960	Boris Shakhlin (USSR)
1964	Yukio Endo (Jap)
1968	Akinori Nakayama (Jap)
1972	Sawao Kato (Jap)
1976	Sawao Kato (Jap)
1980	Aleksandr Tkachev (USSR)
1984	Bart Conner (US)
1988	Vladimir Artemov (USSR)

Pommel Horse
1896	Louis Zutter (Swi)
1904	Anton Heida (US)
1924	Josef Wilhelm (Swi)
1928	Hermann Hanggi (Swi)
1932	Istvan Pelle (Hun)
1936	Konrad Frey (Ger)
1948	Paavo Aaltonen (Fin)
	Veikko Huhtanen (Fin) &
	Heikki Savolainen (Fin)
1952	Viktor Chukarin (USSR)
1956	Boris Shakhlin (USSR)
1960	Eugen Ekman (Fin) &
	Boris Shakhlin (USSR)
1964	Miroslav Cerar (Yug)
1968	Miroslav Cerar (Yug)
1972	Viktor Klimenko (USSR)
1976	Zoltán Magyar (Hun)
1980	Zoltán Magyar (Hun)
1984	Li Ning (Chn) &
	Peter Vidmar (US)
1988	Lyubomir Gueraskov (Bul)
	Zsolt Borkai (Hun) &
	Dmitri Belozerchev (USSR)

Rings
1896	Ioannis Mitropoulos (Gre)
1904	Hermann Glass (US)
1924	Francesco Martino (Ita)
1928	Leon Skutelj (Yug)
1932	George Gulack (US)
1936	Alois Hudec (Cze)
1948	Karl Frei (Swi)
1952	Grant Shaginyan (USSR)
1956	Albert Azaryan (USSR)
1960	Albert Azaryan (USSR)
1964	Takuji Hayata (Jap)
1968	Akinori Nakayama (Jap)
1972	Akinori Nakayama (Jap)
1976	Nikolay Andrianov (USSR)
1980	Aleksandr Ditiatin (USSR)
1984	Koji Gushiken (Jap) & Li Ning (Chn)
1988	Holger Behrendt (GDR) & Dmitri Belozerchev (USSR)

Horizontal Bar
1896	Hermann Weingärtner (Ger)
1904	Anton Heida (US) & Edward Hennig (US)
1924	Leon Stukelj (Yug)
1928	Georges Miez (Swi)
1932	Dallas Bixler (US)
1936	Aleksanteri Saavala (Fin)
1948	Josef Stadler (Swi)
1952	Jack Günthard (Swi)
1956	Takashi Ono (Jap)
1960	Takashi Ono (Jap)
1964	Boris Shakhlin (USSR)
1968	Mikhail Voronin (USSR) &
	Akinori Nakayama (Jap)
1972	Mitsuo Tsukahara (Jap)

1976	Mitsuo Tsukahara (Jap)
1980	Stoyan Deltchev (Bul)
1984	Shinji Morisue (Jap)
1988	Vladimir Artemov (USSR) &
	Valeri Lyukine (USSR)

Vault
1896	Carl Schumann (Ger)
1904	Anton Heida (US) George Eyser (US)
1924	Frank Kriz (US)
1928	Eugen Mack (Swi)
1932	Savino Guglielmetti (Ita)
1936	Alfred Schwarzmann (Ger)
1948	Paavo Aaltonen (Fin)
1952	Viktor Chukarin (USSR)
1956	Helmuth Bantz (Ger) & Valentin Muratov (USSR)
1960	Takashi Ono (Jap) & Boris Shakhin (USSR)
1964	Haruhiro Yamashita (Jap)
1968	Mikhail Voronin (USSR)
1972	Klaus Köste (GDR)
1976	Nikolay Andrianov (USSR)
1980	Nikolay Andrianov (USSR)
1984	Lou Yun (Chn)
1988	Lou Yun (Chn)

Team
1904	United States
1908	Sweden
1912	Italy
1920	Italy
1924	Italy
1928	Switzerland
1932	Italy
1936	Germany
1948	Finland
1952	USSR
1956	USSR
1960	Japan
1964	Japan
1968	Japan
1972	Japan
1976	Japan
1980	USSR
1984	United States
1988	USSR

Women
Combined
1952	Maria Gorokhovskaya (USSR)
1956	Larissa Latynina (USSR)
1960	Larissa Latynina (USSR)
1964	Vera Cáslavská (Cze)
1968	Vera Cáslavská (Cze)
1972	Lyudmila Tourischeva (USSR)
1976	Nadia Comaneci (Rom)
1980	Yelena Davydova (USSR)
1984	Mary Lou Retton (US)
1988	Yelena Shoushounova (USSR)

Asymmetrical Bars
1952	Margit Korondi (Hun)
1956	Agnes Keleti (Hun)
1960	Polina Astakhova (USSR)

1964	Polina Astakhova (USSR)
1968	Vera Cáslavská (Cze)
1972	Karin Janz (GDR)
1976	Nadia Comaneci (Rom)
1980	Maxi Gnauck (GDR)
1984	Ma Yanhong (Chn) & Julianne McNamara (US)
1988	Daniela Silivas (Rom)

Beam
1952	Nina Bocharova (USSR)
1956	Agnes Keleti (Hun)
1960	Eva Bosakova (Cze)
1964	Vera Cáslavská (Cze)
1968	Natalya Kuchinskaya (USSR)
1972	Olga Korbut (USSR)
1976	Nadia Comaneci (Rom)
1980	Nadia Comaneci (Rom)
1984	Simona Pauca (Rom) & Ecaterina Szabo (Rom)
1988	Daniela Silivas (Rom)

Floor
1952	Agnes Keleti (Hun)
1956	Larissa Latynina (USSR) & Agnes Keleti (Hun)
1960	Larissa Latynina (USSR)
1964	Larissa Latynina (USSR)
1968	Larissa Petrik (USSR) & Vera Cáslavská (Cze)
1972	Olga Korbut (USSR)
1976	Nelli Kim (USSR)
1980	Nelli Kim (USSR) & Nadia Comaneci (Rom)
1984	Ecaterina Szabo (Rom)
1988	Daniela Silivas (Rom)

Vault
1952	Yekaterina Kalinchuk (USSR)
1956	Larissa Latynina (USSR)
1960	Margarita Nikolayeva (USSR)
1964	Vera Cáslavská (Cze)
1968	Vera Cáslavská (Cze)
1972	Karin Janz (GDR)
1976	Nelli Kim (USSR)
1980	Natalya Shaposhnikova (USSR)
1984	Ecaterina Szabo (Rom)
1988	Svetlana Boginskaya (USSR)

Team
1928	Netherlands
1932	Not held
1936	Germany
1948	Czechoslovakia
1952	USSR
1956	USSR
1960	USSR
1964	USSR
1968	USSR
1972	USSR
1976	USSR
1980	USSR
1984	Romania
1988	USSR

Rhythmic Gymnastics
| 1984 | Fung Lori (Can) |
| 1988 | Marina Lobatch (USSR) |

HANDBALL

Men
1936 Germany
1972 Yugoslavia
1976 Soviet Union
1980 East Germany
1984 Yugoslavia
1988 Soviet Union

Women
1976 Soviet Union
1980 Soviet Union
1984 Yugoslavia
1988 South Korea

HOCKEY

Men

1908	England	1976	New Zealand
1920	Great Britain	1980	India
1928	India	1984	Pakistan
1932	India	1988	Great Britain
1936	India	**Most wins:** 8 India
1948	India	**Women**
1952	India	*First contested 1980*
1956	India	1980	Zimbabwe
1960	Pakistan	1984	Holland
1964	India	1988	Australia
1968	Pakistan		
1972	West Germany		

JUDO

Open
1964 Anton Geesink (Hol)
1972 Willem Ruska (Hol)
1976 Haruki Uemura (Jap)
1980 Dietmar Lorenz (GDR)
1984 Yasuhiro Yamashita (Jap)

Heavyweight/Over 95kg
1964 Isao Inokuma (Jap)
1972 Willem Ruska (Hol)
1976 Sergey Novikov (USSR)
1980 Angelo Parisi (Fra)
1984 Hitoshi Saito (Jap)
1988 Hitoshi Saito (Jap)

Half-heavyweight/Under 95kg
1972 Shota Chochoshvili (USSR)
1976 Kazuhiro Ninomiya (Jap)
1980 Robert Van de Walle (Bel)
1984 Hyeung-Zoo Ha (SKo)
1988 Aurelio Miguel (Bra)

Middleweight/Under 86kg
1964 Isao Okano (Jap)
1972 Shinobu Sekine (Jap)
1976 Isamu Sonoda (Jap)
1980 Jurg Rothlisberger (Swi)
1984 Peter Seisenbacher (Aut)

1988 Peter Seisenbacher (Aut)

Half-middleweight/Under 78kg
1980 Shota Khabareli (USSR)
1984 Frank Weineke (FRG)
1988 Waldemar Legien (Pol)

Lightweight/Under 71kg
1964 Takehide Nakatani (Jap)
1972 Toyokazu Nomura (Jap)
1976 Vladimir Nevzorov (USSR)
1980 Ezio Gamba (Ita)
1984 Byeong-Kuen Ahn (SKo)
1988 Marc Alexandre (Fra)

Half-lightweight/Under 65kg
1972 Takao Kawaguchi (Jap)
1976 Hector Rodriguez (Cub)
1980 Nikoli Soludukhin (USSR)
1984 Yoshiyuki Matsuoda (Jap)
1988 Lee Kuung-Keun (SKo)

Extra-lightweight/Under 60kg
1980 Thierry Rey (Fra)
1984 Shinji Hosokawa (Jap)
1988 Kim Jae-Yup (SKo)

MODERN PENTATHLON

Men Only
Individual

1912	Gosta Lilliehook (Swe)
1920	Gustaf Dryssen (Swe)
1924	Bo Lindman (Swe)
1928	Sven Thofelt (Swe)
1932	Johan Oxenstierna (Swe)
1936	Gotthardt Handrick (Ger)
1948	Willie Grut (Swe)
1952	Lars Hall (Swe)
1956	Lars Hall (Swe)
1960	Ferenc Nemeth (Hun)
1964	Ferenc Torok (Hun)
1968	Bjorn Ferm (Swe)
1972	Andras Balczo (Hun)
1976	Janusz Pyciak-Peciak (Pol)
1980	Anatoly Starostin (USSR)
1984	Daniele Masala (Ita)
1988	Janos Martinek (Hun)

Team

1952	Hungary
1956	USSR
1960	Hungary
1964	USSR
1968	Hungary
1972	USSR
1976	Britain
1980	USSR
1984	Italy
1988	Hungary

ROWING

Men
Single Sculls

1900	Henri Barrelet (Fra)
1904	Frank Greer (US)
1908	Harry Blackstaffe (GB)
1912	William Kinnear (GB)
1920	John Kelly Snr (US)
1924	Jack Beresford Jr (GB)
1928	Henry Pearce (Aus)
1932	Henry Pearce (Aus)
1936	Gustav Schäfer (Ger)
1948	Mervyn Wood (Aus)
1952	Yuriy Tyukalov (USSR)
1956	Vyacheslav Ivanov (USSR)
1960	Vyacheslav Ivanov (USSR)
1964	Vyacheslav Ivanov (USSR)
1968	Henri Jan Wienese (Hol)
1972	Yuriy Malishev (USSR)
1976	Pertti Karppinen (Fin)
1980	Pertti Karppinen (Fin)
1984	Pertti Karppinen (Fin)
1988	Thomas Lange (GDR)

Double Sculls

1904	John Mulcahy/William Varley (US)
1920	Paul Costello/John Kelly (US)
1924	Paul Costello/John Kelly (US)
1928	Paul Costello/Charles McIlvaine (US)
1932	William Garrett Gilmore/Kenneth Myers (US)
1936	Jack Beresford/Leslie Southwood (GB)
1948	Richard Burnell/Herbert Bushnell (GB)
1952	Tranquilo Capozzo/Eduardo Guerrero (Arg)
1956	Aleksandr Berkutov/Yuriy Tyukalov (USSR)
1960	Vaclav Kozak/Pavel Schmidt (Cze)
1964	Boris Dubrovsky/Oleg Tyurin (USSR)
1968	Anatoliy Sass/Aleksandr Timoshinin (USSR)
1972	Gennadiy Korshikov/Aleksandr Timoshinin (USSR)
1976	Alf Hansen/Frank Hansen (Nor)
1980	Joachim Dreifke/Klaus Kroppelien (GDR)
1984	Bradley Lewis/Paul Enquist (US)
1988	Ronald Florjin/Nicolaas Rienks (Hol)

Coxless Pairs

1904	Robert Farnam/Joseph Ryan (US)
1908	John Fenning/Gordon Thomson (GB)
1924	Antonie Beijnen/Wilhelm Rosingh (Hol)
1928	Kurt Moeschter/Bruno Muller (Ger)
1932	Lewis Clive/Arthur Edwards (GB)
1936	Willie Eichorn/Hugo Strauss (Ger)
1948	George Laurie/John Wilson (GB)
1952	Charles Logg/Thomas Price (US)
1956	James Fifer/Duvall Hecht (US)
1960	Valentin Boreyko/Oleg Golovanov (USSR)
1964	George Hungerford/Roger Jackson
1968	Heinz-Jürgen Bothe/Jorg Lucke (GDR)
1972	Siegfried Brietzke/Wolfgang Mager (GDR)
1976	Bernd Landvoigt/Jorg Landvoigt (GDR)
1980	Petru Iosub/Valer Toma (Rom)
1988	Andrew Holmes/Steven Redgrave (GB)

Coxed Pairs

1900	Holland
1906	Italy
1920	Italy
1924	Switzerland
1928	Switzerland
1932	United States
1936	Germany
1948	Denmark
1952	France
1956	United States
1960	Germany
1964	United States
1968	Italy
1972	East Germany
1976	East Germany
1980	East Germany
1984	Italy
1988	Italy

Quadruple Sculls

1976	East Germany
1980	East Germany
1984	West Germany
1988	Italy

Coxless Fours

1904	United States
1908	Great Britain
1924	Great Britain
1928	Great Britain

1932 Great Britain
1936 Germany
1948 Italy
1952 Yugoslavia
1956 Canada
1960 United States
1964 Denmark
1968 East Germany
1972 East Germany
1976 East Germany
1980 East Germany
1984 New Zealand
1988 East Germany

Coxed Fours

1900 Germany
1900† France
1912 Germany
1920 Switzerland
1924 Switzerland
1928 Italy
1932 Germany
1936 Germany
1948 United States
1952 Czechoslovakia
1956 Italy
1960 Germany
1964 Germany
1968 New Zealand
1972 West Germany
1976 USSR
1980 East Germany
1984 Great Britain
1988 East Germany
† There were two finals in 1900

Eights

1900 United States
1904 United States
1908 Great Britain
1912 Great Britain
1920 United States
1924 United States
1928 United States
1932 United States
1936 United States

1948 United States
1952 United States
1956 United States
1960 Germany
1964 United States
1968 West Germany
1972 New Zealand
1976 East Germany
1980 East Germany
1984 Canada
1988 West Germany

Women

Single Sculls

1976 Christine Scheiblich (GDR)
1980 Sanda Toma (Rom)
1984 Valeria Racila (Rom)
1988 Jutta Behrendt (GDR)

Double Sculls

1976 Svetla Otzetova/Zdravka Yordanova (Bul)
1980 Yelena Khlopsteva/Larisa Popova (USSR)
1984 Marioara Popescu/Elisabeta Oleniuc (Rom)
1988 Birgit Peter/Martina Schroeter (GDR)

Coxless Pairs

1976 Stoyanka Grouitcheva/Siika Kelbetcheva (Bul)
1980 Cornelia Klier/Ute Steindorf (GDR)
1984 Rodica Arba/Elena Horvat (Rom)
1988 Rodica Arba/Olga Homeghi (Rom)

Quadruple Sculls

1976 East Germany
1980 East Germany
1984 Romania
1988 East Germany

Coxed Fours

1976 East Germany
1980 East Germany
1984 Romania
1988 East Germany

Eights

1976 East Germany
1980 East Germany
1984 United States
1988 East Germany

SHOOTING

Men

Free Pistol

1896	Sumner Paine (US)
1900	Conrad Roderer (Swi)
1908	Paul von Asbroeck (Bel)
1912	Alfred Lane (US)
1920	Karl Frederick (US)
1936	Torsten Ullmann (Swe)
1948	Edwin Vazquez Cam (Per)
1952	Huelet Benner (US)
1956	Pentti Linnosvuo (Fin)
1960	Aleksey Gushchin (USSR)
1964	Vaino Markkanen (Fin)
1968	Grigory Kossykh (USSR)
1972	Ragner Skanakar (Swe)
1976	Uwe Potteck (GDR)
1980	Aleksandr Melentyev (USSR)
1984	Xu Haifeng (Chn)
1988	Sorin Babii (Rom)

Rapid Fire Pistol

1896	Jean Phrangoudis (Gre)

1900	Maurice Larrouy (Fra)
1912	Alfred Lane (US)
1920	Guilherme Paraense (Bra)
1924	Henry Bailey (US)
1932	Renzo Morigi (Ita)
1936	Cornelius van Oyen (Ger)
1948	Karoly Takacs (Hun)
1952	Karoly Takacs (Hun)
1956	Stefan Petrescu (Rom)
1960	William McMilliam (US)
1964	Pentti Linnosvuo (Fin)
1968	Jozef Zapedzki (Pol)
1972	Jozef Zapedzki (Pol)
1976	Norbert Klaar (GDR)
1980	Corneliu Ion (Rom)
1984	Takeo Kamachi (Jap)
1988	Afanasi Kouzmine (USSR)

Trap

1900	Roger de Barbarian (Fra)
1908	Walter Ewing (Can)
1912	James Graham (US)

1920	Mark Arie (US)
1924	Gyula Halasy (Hun)
1952	George Genereux (Can)
1956	Galliano Rossini (Ita)
1960	Ion Dumitrescu (Rom)
1964	Ennio Mattarelli (Ita)
1968	Bob Braithwaite (GB)
1972	Angelo Scalzone (Ita)
1976	Don Haldeman (US)
1980	Luciano Giovanetti (Ita)
1984	Luciano Giovanetti (Ita)
1988	Dmitri Monakov (USSR)

Running Game Target
1900	Louis Debray (Fra)
1972	Yokov Zheleznial (USSR)
1976	Aleksandr Gazov (USSR)
1980	Igor Sokolov (USSR)
1984	Li Yuwei (Chn)
1988	Tor Heiestad (Nor)

Small Bore Rifle (Prone)
1908	A. A. Carnell (GB)
1912	Frederick Hird (US)
1920	Lawrence Nuesslein (US)
1924	Pierre Coquelin de Lisle (Fra)
1932	Bertil Ronnmark (Swe)
1936	Willy Rogeberg (Nor)
1948	Arther Cook (US)
1952	Iosif Sarbu (Rom)
1956	Gerald Ouellette (Can)
1960	Peter Kohnke (Ger)
1964	Kaszlo Hammerl (Hun)
1968	Jan Kurka (Cze)
1972	Jo-Jun Li (NKo)
1976	Karl_Heinz Smieszek (FRG)
1980	Karoly Varga (Hun)
1984	Edward Etzel (US)
1988	Miroslav Varga (Cze)

Small Bore Rifle (Three Position)
1952	Erling Kongshaug (Nor)

1956	Anatoliy Bogdanov (USSR)
1960	Viktor Shamburkin (USSR)
1964	Lones Wigger (US)
1968	Bernd Klingner (FRG)
1972	John Writer (US)
1976	Lanny Bassham (US)
1980	Viktor Vlasov (USSR)
1984	Malcolm Cooper (GB)
1988	Malcolm Cooper (GB)

Skeet
1968	Yevgeniy Petrov (USSR)
1972	Konrad Wirnhier (FRG)
1976	Josef Panacek (Cze)
1980	Jans Kjeld Rasmussen (Den)
1984	Matthew Dryke (US)
1988	Axel Wegner (GDR)

Air Rifle
1984	Philippe Heberle (Fra)
1988	Goran Maksimovic (Yug)

Air Pistol
1988	Taniou Kiriakov (Bul)

Women
Sport Pistol
1984	Linda Thom (Can)
1988	Non Saluokvadze (USSR)

Small Bore Rifle (Three Position)
1984	Wu Xiaoxuan (Chn)
1988	Silvia Sperber (FRG)

Air Rifle
1984	Pat Spurgin (US)
1988	Irina Chilova (USSR)

Air Pistol
1988	Jasna Sekaric (Yug)

Most Olympic Medals
11 Carl Osburn (US)
8 Konrad Staheli (Swi)
8 Otto Olsen (Nor)

SWIMMING

Men
50 Metres Freestyle
1988	Matt Biondi (US) 22.39s

100 Metres Freestyle
1896	Alfred Hajos (Hun) 1m 22.2s
1904	Zoltan von Halmay (Hun) 1m 22.08s
1908	Charles Daniels (US) 1m 05.6s
1912	Duke Kahanamoku (US) 1m 03.4s
1920	Duke Kahanamoku (US) 1m 01.4s
1924	Johnny Weissmuller (US) 59.0s
1928	Johnny Weissmuller (US) 58.6s
1932	Yasuji Miyazaki (Jap) 58.2s
1936	Ferenc Csik (Hun) 57.6s
1948	Walter Ris (US) 57.3s
1952	Clarke Scholes (US) 57.4s
1956	Jon Henricks (Aus) 55.4s
1960	John Devitt (Aus) 55.2s
1964	Don Schollander (US) 53.4s
1968	Mike Wenden (Aus) 52.2s
1972	Mark Spitz (US) 51.22s
1976	Jim Montgomery (US) 49.99s
1980	Jörg Woithe (GDR) 50.4s
1984	Rowdy Gaines (US) 49.80s
1988	Matt Biondi (US) 48.63s

200 Metres Freestyle
1900	Frederick Lane (Aus) 2m 25.2s

1904	Charles Daniels (US) 2m 44.2s
1968	Mike Wenden (Aus) 1m 55.2s
1972	Mark Spitz (US) 1m 52.78s
1976	Bruce Furniss (US) 1m 50.29s
1980	Sergey Koplyakov (USSR) 1m 49.81s
1984	Michael Gross (FRG) 1m 47.44s
1988	Duncan Armstrong (Aus) 1m 47.25s

400 Metres Freestyle
1896	Paul Neumann (Aut) 8m 12.6s(500m)
1904	Charles Daniels (US) 6m 16.2s
1908	Henry Taylor (GB) 5m 36.8s
1912	George Hodgson (Can) 5m 24.4s
1920	Norman Ross (US) 5m 24.4s
1924	Johnny Weissmuller (US) 5m 04.2s
1928	Alberto Zorilla (Arg) 5m 01.6s
1932	Buster Crabble (US) 4m 48.4s
1936	Jack Medica (US) 4m 44.5s
1948	William Smith (US) 4m 41.0s
1952	Jean Boiteux (Fra) 4m 30.7s
1956	Murray Rose (Aus) 4m 27.3s
1960	Murray Rose (Aus) 4m 18.3s
1964	Don Schollander (US) 4m 12.2s
1968	Mike Burton (US) 4m 09.0s
1972	Brad Cooper (Aus) 4m 00.27s
1976	Brian Goodell (US) 3m 51.93s
1980	Vladimir Salnikov (USSR) 3m 51.31s

| 1984 | George Dicarlo (US) 3m 51.23s |
| 1988 | Uwe Dassler (GDR) 3m 46.95s |

1500 Metres Freestyle

1896	Alfred Hajos (Hun) 18m 22.2s (1200m)
1900	John Jarvis (GB) 13m 40.2s (1000m)
1904	Emil Rausch (Ger) 27m 18.2s (1 Mile)
1908	Henry Taylor (GB) 22m 48.4s
1912	George Hodgson (Can) 22m 00.0s
1920	Norman Ross (US) 22m 23.2s
1924	Andrew Charlton (Aus) 20m 06.6s
1928	Arne Borge (Swe) 19m 51.8s
1932	Kusuo Kitamura (Jap) 19m 12.4s
1936	Noboru Terada (Jap) 19m 13.7s
1948	James McLane (US) 19m 18.5s
1952	Ford Konno (US) 18m 30.0s
1956	Murray Rose (Aus) 17m 58.9s
1960	John Konrads (Aus) 17m 19.6s
1964	Bob Windle (Aus) 17m 01.7s
1968	Mike Burton (US) 16m 38.9s
1972	Mike Burton (US) 15m 52.58s
1976	Brian Goodell (US) 15m 02.40s
1980	Vladimir Salnikov (USSR) 14m 58.27s
1984	Michael O'Brien (US) 15m 05.20s
1988	Vladimir Salnikov (USSR) 15m 00.40s

100 Metres Backstroke

1904	Walter Brack (Ger) 1m 16.8s
1908	Arno Bieberstein (Ger) 1m 24.6s
1912	Harry Hebner (US) 1m 21.2s
1920	Warren Kealoha (US) 1m 15.2s
1924	Warren Kealoha (US) 1m 13.2s
1928	George Kojac (US) 1m 08.2s
1932	Masaji Kiyokawa (Jap) 1m 08.6s
1936	Adolf Kiefer (US) 1m 05.9s
1948	Allen Stack (US) 1m 06.4s
1952	Yoshinobu Oyakawa (US) 1m 05.4s
1956	David Thiele (Aus) 1m 02.2s
1960	David Thiele (Aus) 1m 01.9s
1968	Roland Matthes (GDR) 58.7s
1972	Roland Matthes (GDR) 56.58s
1976	John Naber (US) 55.49s
1980	Bengt Baron (Swe) 56.33s
1984	Rick Carey (US) 55.79s
1988	Daichi Suzuki (Jap) 55.05s

200 Metres Backstroke

1900	Ernst Hoppenberg (Ger) 2m 47.0s
1964	Jed Graef (US) 2m 10.3s
1968	Roland Matthes(GDR) 2m 09.6s
1972	Roland Matthes (GDR) 2m 02.82s
1976	John Naber (US) 1m 59.19s
1980	Sandor Wladar (Hun) 2m 01.93s
1984	Rick Carey (US) 2m 00.23s
1988	Igor Polianski (USSR) 1m 59.37s

100 Metres Breaststroke

1968	Don McKenzie (US) 1m 07.7s
1972	Nobutaka Taguchi (Jap) 1m 04.94s
1976	John Hencken (US) 1m 03.11s
1980	Duncan Goodhew (GB) 1m 03.34s
1984	Steve Lundquist (US) 1m 01.65s
1988	Adrian Moorhouse (GB) 1m 02..04s

200 Metres Breaststroke

1908	Frederick Holman (GB) 3m 01.8s
1912	Walter Bathe (Ger) 3m 01.8s
1920	Haken Malmroth (Swe) 3m 04.4s
1924	Robert Skelton (US) 2m 56.5s
1928	Yoshiyuki Tsuruta (Jap) 2m 48.8s
1932	Yoshiyuki Tsuruta (Jap) 2m 45.4s
1936	Tetsuo Hamuro (Jap) 2m 41.5s
1948	Joseph Verdeur (US) 2m 39.3s
1952	John Davies (Aus) 2m 34.4s

1956	Masaru Furukawa (Jap) 2m 34.7s
1960	William Mulliken (US) 2m 37.4s
1964	Ian O'Brien (Aus) 2m 27.8s
1968	Felipe Munoz (Mex) 2m 28.7s
1972	John Hencken (US) 2m 21.55s
1976	David Wilkie (GB) 2m 15.11s
1980	Robertas Zhulpa (USSR) 2m 15.85s
1984	Victor Davis (Can) 2m 13.34s
1988	Jozef Szabo (Hun) 2m 13.52s

100 Metres Butterfly

1968	Doug Russell (US) 55.9s
1972	Mark Spitz (US) 54.27s
1976	Matt Vogel (US) 54.35s
1980	Pär Arvidsson (Swe) 54.92s
1984	Michael Gross (FRG) 53.08s
1988	Anthony Nesty (Sur) 53.0s

200 Metres Butterfly

1956	William Yorzyk (US) 2m 19.3s
1960	Mike Troy (US) 2m 12.8s
1964	Kevin Berry (Aus) 2m 06.6s
1968	Carl Robie (US) 2m 08.7s
1972	Mark Spitz (US) 2m 00.70s
1976	Mike Bruner (US) 1m 59.76s
1980	Sergey Fesenko (USSR) 1m 59.76s
1984	Jon Sieben (Aus) 1m 57.04s
1988	Michael Gross (FRG) 1m 56.94s

200 Metres Individual Medley

1968	Charles Hickcox (US) 2m 12.0s
1972	Gunnar Larsson (Swe) 2m 07.17s
1984	Alex Baumann (Can) 2m 01.42s
1988	Tamas Darnyi (Hun) 2m 14.75s

400 Metres Individual Medley

1964	Richard Roth (US) 4m 45.4s
1968	Charles Hickcox (US) 4m 48.4s
1972	Gunnar Larsson (Swe) 4m 31.98s
1976	Rod Strachen (US) 4m 23.68s
1980	Aleksandr Sidorenko (USSR) 4m 22.89s
1984	Alex Baumann (Can) 4m 17.41s
1988	Tamas Darnyi (Hun) 4m 14.75s

4 x 100 Metres Freestyle Relay

1964	United States 3m 33.2s
1968	United States 3m 31.7s
1972	United States 3m 26.42s
1984	United States 3m 19.03s
1988	United States 3m 16.53s

4 x 200 Metres Freestyle Relay

1908	Great Britain 10m 55.6s
1912	Australasia 10m 11.6s
1920	United States 10m 04.4s
1924	United States 9m 53.4s
1928	United States 9m 36.2s
1932	Japan 8m 58.4s
1936	Japan 8m 51.5s
1948	United States 8m 46.0s
1952	United States 8m 31.1s
1956	Australia 8m 23.6s
1960	United States 8m 10.2s
1964	United States 7m 52.1s
1968	United States 7m 52.3s
1972	United States 7m 35.78s
1976	United States 7m 23.22s
1980	USSR 7m 23.50s
1984	United States 7m 15.69s
1988	United States 7m 12.51s

4 x 100 Metres Medley Relay

1960	United States 4m 05.4s
1964	United States 3m 58.4s
1968	United States 3m 54.9s
1972	United States 3m 48.16s

1976	United States 3m 42.22s
1980	Australia 3m 45.70s
1984	United States 3m 39.30s
1988	United States 3m 36.93s

Springboard Diving

1908	Albert Zurner (Ger)
1912	Paul Günther (Ger)
1920	Louis Kuehn (US)
1924	Albert White (US)
1928	Peter Desjardin (US)
1932	Michael Galitzen (US)
1936	Richard Degener (US)
1948	Bruce Harlan (US)
1952	David Browning (US)
1956	Robert Clotworthy (US)
1960	Gary Tobian (US)
1964	Kenneth Sitzberger (US)
1968	Bernard Wrightson (US)
1972	Vladimir Vasin (USSR)
1976	Phil Boggs (US)
1980	Aleksandr Portnov (USSR)
1984	Greg Louganis (US)
1988	Greg Louganis (US)

Platform Diving

1904	George Sheldon (US)
1908	Hjalmar Johansson (Swe)
1912	Erik Adlerz (Swe)
1920	Clarence Pinkston (US)
1924	Albert White (US)
1928	Peter Desjardins (US)
1932	Harold Smith (US)
1936	Marshall Wayne (US)
1948	Samuel Lee (US)
1952	Samuel Lee (US)
1956	Joaquin Capilla Perez (Mex)
1960	Robert Webster (US)
1964	Robert Webster (US)
1968	Klaus Dibiasi (Ita)
1972	Klaus Dibiasi (Ita)
1976	Klaus Dibiasi (Ita)
1980	Falk Hoffmann (GDR)
1984	Greg Louganis (US)
1988	Greg Louganis (US)

Women

50 Metres Freestyle

1988	Kristin Otto (GDR) 25.49s

100 Metres Freestyle

1912	Fanny Durack (Aus) 1m 22.2s
1920	Etheleda Bleibtrey (US0 1m 13.6s
1924	Ethel Lackie (US) 1m 12.4s
1928	Albina Osipowich (US) 1m 11.0s
1932	Helene Madison (US) 1m 06.8s
1936	Hendrika Mastenbroek (US) 1m 05.9s
1948	Greta Andersen (Den) 1m 06.3s
1952	Katalin Szöke (Hun) 1m 06.8s
1956	Dawn Fraser (Aus) 1m 02.0s
1960	Dawn Fraser (Aus) 1m 01.2s
1964	Dawn Fraser (Aus) 59.5s
1968	Jan Henne (US) 1m 00.0s
1972	Sandra Neilson (US) 58.59s
1976	Kornelia Ender (GDR) 55.65s
1980	Barbara Krause (GDR) 54.79s
1984	Nancy Hogshead (US) & Carrie Steinseifer (US) 55.92s
1988	Kristin Otto (GDR) 54.93s

200 Metres Freestyle

1968	Debbie Meyer (US) 2m 10.5s
1972	Shane Gould (Aus) 2m 03.56s
1976	Kornelia Ender (GDR) 1m 59.26s

1980	Barbara Krause (GDR) 1m 58.33s
1984	Mary Wayte (US) 1m 59.23s
1988	Heike Freidrich (GDR) 1m 57.65s

400 Metres Freestyle

1920	Ethelda Bleibtrey (US) 4m 34..0s (300m)
1924	Martha Norelius (US) 6m 02..2s
1928	Martha Norelius (US) 5m 42.8s
1932	Helene Madison (US) 5m 28.5s
1936	Hendrika Mastenbroek (Hol) 5m 26.4s
1948	Ann Curtis (US) 5m 17.8s
1952	Valeria Gyenge (Hun) 5m 12.1s
1956	Lorraine Crapp (Aus) 4m 54.6s
1960	Chris von Saltza (US) 4m 50.6s
1964	Virginia Duenkel (US) 4m 43.3s
1968	Debbie Meyer (US) 4m 31.8s
1972	Shane Gould (Aus) 4m 19.04s
1976	Petra Thümer (GDR) 4m 09.89s
1980	Ines Diers (GDR) 4m 08.76s
1984	Tiffany Cohen (US) 4m 07.10s
1988	Janet Evans (US) 4m 03.85s

800 Metres Freestyle

1968	Debbie Mayer (US) 9m 24.0s
1972	Keena Rothhammer (US) 8m 53.68s
1976	Petra Thümer (GDR) 8m 37.14s
1980	Michelle Ford (Aus) 8m 28.90s
1984	Tiffany Cohen (US) 8m 24.95s
1988	Janet Evans (US) 8m 20.20s

100 Metres Backstroke

1924	Sybil Bauer (US) 1m 23.2s
1928	Maria Braun (Hol) 1m 22.0s
1932	Eleanor Holm (US) 1m 19.4s
1936	Nida Senff (Hol) 1m 18.9s
1948	Karen Harup (Den) 1m 14.4s
1952	Joan Harrison (SAf) 1m 14.3s
1956	Judy Grinham (GB) 1m 12.9s
1960	Lynn Burke (US) 1m 09.3s
1964	Cathy Ferguson (US) 1m 07.7s
1968	Kaye Hall (US) 1m 06.2s
1972	Melissa Belote (US) 1m 05.78s
1976	Ulrike Richter (GDR) 1m 01.83s
1980	Rica Reinisch (GDR) 1m 00.86s
1984	Theresa Andrews (US) 1m 02.55s
1988	Kristin Otto (GDR) 1m 00.89s

200 Metres Backstroke

1968	Pokey Watson (US) 2m 24.8s
1972	Melissa Belote (US) 2m 19.19s
1976	Ulrike Richter (GDR) 2m 13.43s
1980	Rica Reinisch (GDR) 2m 11.77s
1984	Jolanda de Rover (Hol) 2m 12.38s
1988	Tania Dangalakova (Bul) 1m 07.95

100 Metres Breaststroke

1968	Djurdica Bjedov (Yug) 1m 15.8s
1972	Catherine Carr (US) 1m 13.58s
1976	Hennelore Anke (GDR) 1m 11.16s
1980	Ute Geweniger (GDR) 1m 10.22s
1984	Petra Van Staveren (Hol) 1m 09.88s
1988	Tania Dangalakova (Bul) 1m 07.95s

200 Metres Breaststroke

1924	Lucy Morton (GB) 3m 33.2s
1928	Hilde Schrader (Ger) 3m 12.6s
1932	Claire Dennis (Aus) 3m 06.3s
1936	Hideko Maehata (Jap) 3m 03.6s
1948	Petronella van Vliet (Hol) 2m 57.2s
1952	Eva Szekely (Hun) 2m 51.7s
1956	Ursula Happe (Ger) 2m 53.1s
1960	Anita Lonsbrough (GB) 2m 49.5s
1964	Galima Prozumenschikova (USSR) 2m 46.4s
1968	Sharon Wichman (US) 2m 44.4s
1972	Beverley Whitfield (Aus) 2m 41.71s

1976	Marina Koshevayua (USSR) 2m 33.35s
1980	Lina Kachushite (USSR) 2m 29.54s
1984	Anne Ottenbrite (Can) 2m 30.38s
1988	Silke Hoerner (GDR) 2m 26.71s

100 Metres Butterfly

1956	Shelley Mann (US) 1m 11.0s
1960	Carolyn Schuler (US) 1m 09.5s
1964	Sharon Stouder (US) 1. 04.7s
1968	Lynette McClements (Aus) 1m 05.0s
1972	Mayumi Aoki (Jap) 1m 03.34s
1976	Kornelia Ender (GDR) 1m 00.13s
1980	Caren Metschuck (GDR) 1m 00.42s
1984	Mary T. Meagher (US) 59.26s
1988	Kristin Otto (GDR) 59.00s

200 Metres Butterfly

1968	Ada Kok (Hol) 2m 24.7s
1972	Karen Moe (US) 2m 15.57s
1976	Andrea Pollack (GDR) 2m 11.41s
1980	Ines Geissler (GDR) 2m 10.44s
1984	Mary T. Meagher (US) 2m 06.90s
1988	Kathleen Nord (GDR) 2m 16.23s

200 Metres Individual Medley

1968	Claudia Kolb (US) 2m 24.7s
1972	Sharon Gould (Aus) 2m 23.07s
1984	Tracy Caulkins (US) 2m 12.64s
1988	Daniela Hunger (GDR) 2m 16.23s

400 Metres Individual Medley

1964	Donna De Varona (US) 5m 18.7s
1968	Claudia Kolb (US) 5m 08.5s
1972	Gail Neall (Aus) 5m 02.97s
1976	Ulrike Tauber (GDR) 4m 42.77s
1980	Petra Schneider (GDR) 4m 36.29s
1984	Tracy Caulkins (US) 4m 39.24s
1988	Janet Evans (US) 4m 37.36s

4 x 100 Metres Freestyle Medley

1912	Great Britain 5m 52.8s
1920	United States 5m 11.6s
1924	United States 4m 58.8s
1928	United States 4m 47.6s
1932	United States 4m 38.0s
1936	Netherlands 4m 36.0s
1948	United States 4m 29.2s
1952	Hungary 4m 24.4s
1956	Australia 4m 17.1s
1960	United States 4m 08.9s
1964	United States 4m 03.8s
1968	United States 4m 02.5s
1972	United States 3m 55.19s
1976	United States 3m 44.82s
1980	East Germany 3m 42. 71s
1984	United States 3m 43. 43s
1988	East Germany 3m 40.63s

4 x 100 Metres Medley Relay

1960	United States 4m 41.1s
1964	United States 4m 33.9s
1968	United States 4m 28.3s
1972	United States 4m 20.75s
1976	East Germany 4m 07.95s
1980	East Germany 4m 06.67s
1984	United States 4m 08.34s
1988	East Germany 4m 03.74s

Springboard Diving

1920	Aileen Riggin (US)
1924	Elizabeth Becker (US)
1928	Helen Meany (US)
1932	Georgia Coleman (US)
1936	Marjorie Gestring (US)
1948	Victoria Draves (US)
1952	Pat McCormick (US)
1956	Pat McCormick (US)
1960	Ingrid Krämer (Ger)
1964	Ingrid Engel (née Krämer) (Ger)
1968	Sue Gossick (US)
1972	Micki King (US)
1976	Jennifer Chandler (US)
1990	Irina Kalinina (USSR)
1984	Sylvie Bernier (Can)
1988	Goa Min (Chn)

Platform Diving

1912	Greta Johansson (Swe)
1920	Stefani Fryland-Clausen (Den)
1924	Caroline Smith (US)
1928	Elizabeth Pinkston (US)
1932	Dorothy Poynton (US)
1936	Dorothy Hill (née Poynton) (US)
1948	Victoria Draves (US)
1952	Pat McCormick (US)
1956	Pat McCormick (US)
1960	Ingrid Krämer (GDR)
1964	Lesley Bush (US)
1968	Milena Duchkova (Cze)
1972	Ulrike Knape (Swe)
1976	Elena Vaytsekhovskaya (USSR)
1980	Martina Jäschke (Ger)
1984	Zhou Jihong (Chn)
1988	Xu Yanmei (Chn)

Synchronised - Solo

1984	Tracie Ruiz (US)
1988	Carolyn Waldo (Can)

Synchronised - Duet

1984	Candy Costie & Tracie Ruiz (US)
1988	Michelle Cameron & Carolyn Waldo (Can)

TABLE TENNIS

First included in 1988

Men's Singles
1988 Yoo Nam-Kyu (Sko)

Women's Singles
1988 Chen Jing (Chn)

Men's Doubles
1988 Chen Longcan/Wei Qingguang (Chn)

Women's Doubles
1988 Hyung Jung-Hwa/Yang Young-Ja (SKo)

TENNIS

Men's Singles
1896 John Boland (GB)
1900 Hugh Doherty (GB)
1904 Beals Wright (US)

1908 Josiah Ritchie (GB)
1908 (*) Arthur Gore (GB)
1912 Charles Winslow (SAf)
1912 (*) André Gobert (Fra)

1920 Louis Raymond (SAf)
1924 Vince Richards (SAf)
1988 Miloslav Mecir (Cze)

Women's Singles
1900 Charlotte Cooper (GB)
Cooper was the first ever female Olympic champion
1908 Dorothea Chambers (GB)
1908 (*) Gwen Eastlake-Smith (GB)
1912 Marguerite Broquedis (Fra)
1912 (*) Edith Hannam (GB)
1920 Suzanne Lenglen (Fra)
1924 Helen Wills (US)
1988 Steffi Graf (FRG)

Men's Doubles
1896 John Boland (Ire) & Fritz Traun (Ger)
1900 Hugh & Reg Doherty (GB)
1904 Edgar Leonard & Beals Wright (US)
1908 Reg Doherty & George Hillyard (GB)

1908 (*) Herbert Roper Barrett & Arthur Gore (GB)
1912 Harold Kitson & Charles Winslow (SAf)
1912 (*) Maurice Germot & André Gobert (Fra)
1920 Oswald Turnbull & Max Woosnam (GB)
1924 Frank Hunter & Vince Richards (GB)
1988 Ken Flach & Robert Seguso (US)

Women's Doubles
1920 Kitty McKane & Winifred McNair (GB)
1924 Hazel Wightman & Helen Wills (US)
1988 Zina Garrison & Pam Shriver (US)

Mixed Doubles
1900 Charlotte Cooper & Reg Doherty (GB)
1912 Dora König & Heinrich Schomburg (Ger)
1912 (*) Edith Hannam & Percy Dixon (GB)
1920 Suzanne Lenglen & Max Decugis (Fra)
1924 Hazel Wightman & Norris Williams (US)
Williams was the only survivor of the Titanic disaster to win an Olympic gold medal

VOLLEYBALL

	Men	Women		Men	Women
1964	USSR	Japan	1980	USSR	USSR
1968	USSR	USSR	1984	United States	China
1972	Japan	USSR	1988	United States	USSR
1976	Poland	Japan			

WATER POLO

1900	Great Britain	1952	Hungary
1904	United States	1956	Hungary
1908	Great Britain	1960	Italy
1912	Great Britain	1964	Hungary
1920	Great Britain	1968	Yugoslavia
1924	France	1972	Soviet Union
1928	Germany	1976	Hungary
1932	Hungary	1980	Soviet Union
1936	Hungary	1984	Yugoslavia
1948	Italy	1988	Yugoslavia

WEIGHTLIFTING

Flyweight (up to 52kg)
1972 Zygmunt Smalacerz (Pol)
1976 Aleksandr Voronin (USSR)
1980 Kanybek Osmonoliev (USSR)
1984 Zeng Guoqiang (Chn)
1988 Sevdalim Marinov (Bul)

Bantamweight (up to 56kg)
1948 Joseph de Pietro (US)
1952 Ivan Udodov (USSR)
1956 Charles Vinci (US)
1960 Charles Vinci (US)
1964 Aleksey Vakhonin (USSR)
1968 Mohammad Nassiri (Irn)
1972 Imre Foldi (Hun)
1976 Norair Nurikyan (Bul)
1980 Daniel Nunez (Cub)
1984 Wu Shude (Chn)
1988 Oleg Mirzoian (USSR)

Featherweight (up to 60kg)
1920 Frans de Haes (Bel)
1924 Pierino Gabetti (Ita)
1928 Franz Andrysek (Aut)
1932 Raymond Suvigny (Fra)
1936 Anthony Terlazzo (US)

1948 Mohmoud Fayad (Egy)
1952 Rafael Chimishkyan (USSR)
1956 Isaac Berger (US)
1960 Yevgeniy Minayev (USSR)
1964 Yoshinobu Miyake (Jap)
1968 Yoshinobu Miyake (Jap)
1972 Norair Nurikyan (Bul)
1976 Nikolai Kolesnikov (USSR)
1980 Viktor Mazin (USSR)
1984 Chen Weiqiang (Chn)
1988 Naim Suleymanoglu (Tur)

Lightweight (up to 67.5kg)
1920 Alfred Neuland (Est)
1924 Edmond Decottignies (Fra)
1928 Kurt Helbig (Ger) &
     Hans Haas (Aut)
1932 René Duverger (Fra)
1936 Anwar M Meshbah (Egy) &
     Robert Fein (Aut)
1948 Ibrahim Shams (Egy)
1952 Tommy Kono (US)
1956 Igor Rybak (USSR)
1960 Viktor Bushuyev (USSR)
1964 Waldemar Baszanowski (Pol)
1968 Waldemar Baszanowski (Pol)

1972	Mukharbi Kirzhinov (USSR)
1976	Pyotr Korol (USSR)
1980	Yanko Rusev (Bul)
1984	Jing Yuan Yao (Chn)
1988	Joachim Kunz (GDR)

Middleweight (up to 75kg)

1920	Henri Gance (Fra)
1924	Carlo Galimberti (Ita)
1928	Roger François (Fra)
1932	Rudolf Ismayr (Ger)
1936	Khadr El Thouni (Egy)
1948	Frank Spellman (US)
1952	Peter George (US)
1956	Fyodor Bogdanovski (USSR)
1960	Aleksandr Kurinov (USSR)
1964	Hans Zdrazila (Cze)
1968	Viktor Kurentsov (USSR)
1972	Yordan Bikov (Bul)
1976	Yordan Bikov (Bul)
1980	Asen Zlatev (Bul)
1984	Karl-Heinz Radschinsky (FRG)
1988	Borislav Guidikov (Bul)

Light-heavyweight (up to 82.5kg)

1920	Ernest Cadine (Fra)
1924	Charles Rigoulot (Fra)
1928	Said Nosseir (Egy)
1932	Louis Hostin (Fra)
1936	Louis Hostin (Fra)
1948	Stanley Stanczyk (US)
1952	Trofim Lomakin (USSR)
1956	Tommy Kono (US)
1960	Ireneusz Palinski (Pol)
1964	Rudolf Plyukfelder (USSR)
1968	Boris Selitsky (USSR)
1972	Leif Jenssen (Nor)
1976	Valeriy Shary (USSR)
1980	Yurik Vardanyan (USSR)
1984	Petre Becheru (Rom)
1988	Israil Arsamakov (USSR)

Middle-heavyweight (up to 90kg)

1952	Norbert Schemansky (US)
1956	Arkadiy Vorobyev (USSR)
1960	Arkadiy Vorobyev (USSR)
1964	Vladimir Golovanov (USSR)
1968	Kaarlo Kangasniemi (Fin)
1972	Andom Nikolov (Bul)
1976	David Rigert (USSR)
1980	Peter Baczako (Hun)
1984	Nicu Vlad (Rom)
1988	Anatoliy Khrapatu (USSR)

Up to 100kg

1980	Ota Zaremba (Cze)
1984	Rolf Milser (FRG)
1988	Pavel Kouznetsov (USSR)

Heavyweight (up to 110kg)

1920	Filippo Bottino (Ita)
1924	Giuseppe Tonani (Ita)
1928	Josef Strassberger (Ger)
1932	Jaroslav Skobla (Cze)
1936	Josef Manger (Aut)
1948	John Davis (US)
1952	John Davis (US)
1956	Paul Anderson (US)
1960	Yuriy Vlasov (USSR)
1964	Leonid Zhabotinsky (USSR)
1968	Leonid Zhabotinsky (USSR)
1972	Jan Talts (USSR)
1976	Yuriy Zaitsev (USSR)
1980	Leonid Taranenko (USSR)
1984	Norberto Oberburger (Ita)
1988	Yuri Zakharevich (USSR)

Super-heavyweight (over 110kg)

1972	Vasiliy Alexeyev (USSR)
1976	Vasiliy Alexeyev (USSR)
1980	Sultan Rakhmanov (USSR)
1984	Dino Lukin (Aus)
1988	Alexander Kurlovich (USSR)

WRESTLING

FREESTYLE

Light-flyweight/Up to 48kg

1904	Robert Curry (US)
1972	Roman Dmitriyev (USSR)
1976	Hassan Issaev (Bul)
1980	Claudio Pollio (Ita)
1984	Robert Weaver (US)
1988	Takashi Kobayashi (Jap)

Flyweight/Up to 52kg

1904	George Mehnert (US)
1948	Lennart Viitala (Fin)
1952	Hasan Gamici (Tur)
1956	Mirian Tsalkalamanidze (USSR)
1960	Ahmet Bilek (Tur)
1964	Yoshikatsu Yoshida (Jap)
1968	Shigeo Nakata (Jap)
1972	Kiyomi Kato (Jap)
1976	Kiyomi Kato (Jap)
1980	Anatoliy Beloglazov (USSR)
1984	Saban Trstena (Yug)
1988	Mitsuru Sato (Jap)

Bantamweight/Up to 57kg

1904	Isidor Niflot (US)
1908	George Mehnert (US)
1924	Kustaa Pihlajamaki (Fin)

1928	Kaarlo Makinen (Fin)
1932	Robert Pearce (US)
1936	Odon Zombori (Hun)
1948	Nasuh Akar (Tur)
1952	Shohachi Ishii (Jap)
1956	Mustafa Dagistanli (Tur)
1960	Terrence McCann (US)
1964	Yojiro Uetake (Jap)
1968	Yojiro Uetake (Jap)
1972	Hideaki Yanagida (Jap)
1976	Vladimir Yumin (USSR)
1980	Sergey Beloglazov (USSR)
1984	Hideaki Tomiyama (Jap)
1988	Sergey Beloglazov (USSR)

Featherweight/Up to 62kg

1904	Benjamin Bradshaw (US)
1908	George Dole (US)
1920	Charles Ackerly (US)
1924	Robin Reed (US)
1928	Allie Morrison (US)
1932	Hermanni Pihlajamaki (Fin)
1936	Kustaa Pihlajamaki (Fin)
1948	Gazanfer Bilge (Tur)
1952	Bayram Sit (Tur)
1956	Shozo Sasahara (Jap)
1960	Mustafa Dagistanli (Tur)

1964	Osamu Watanabe (Jap)
1968	Musaaki Kaneko (Jap)
1972	Zagalav Abdulbekov (USSR)
1976	Jung-Mo Yang (SKo)
1980	Magomedgasan Abushev (USSR)
1984	Randy Lewis (US)
1988	John Smith (US)

Lightweight/Up to 68kg
1904	Otto Roehm (US)
1908	George de Relwyskow (GB)
1920	Kalle Anttila (Fin)
1924	Russell Vis (US)
1928	Osvald Kapp (Est)
1932	Charles Pacome (Fra)
1936	Károly Kárpáti (Hun)
1948	Celál Atik (Tur)
1952	Olle Anderberg (Swe)
1956	Emamali Habibi (Iran)
1960	Shelby Wilson (US)
1964	Enyu Valchev (Bul)
1968	Abdollah Movahed Ardabili (Iran)
1972	Dan Gable (US)
1976	Pavel Pinigin (USSR)
1980	Saipulla Absaidov (USSR)
1984	In-Tak You (SKo)
1988	Arsen Fadzeyev (USSR)

Welterweight/Up to 74kg
1904	Charles Erickson (US)
1924	Hermann Gehri (Swi)
1928	Arvo Haavisto (Fin)
1932	Jack Van Bebber (US)
1936	Frank Lewis (US)
1948	Yasar Dogu (Tur)
1952	William Smith (US)
1956	Mitsuo Ikeda (Jap)
1960	Douglas Blubaugh (US)
1964	Ismail Ogan (Tur)
1968	Mahmut Atalay (Tur)
1972	Wayne Wells (US)
1976	Jiichiro Date (Jap)
1980	Valentin Raitchev (Bul)
1984	David Schulz (US)
1988	Kenneth Monday (US)

Middleweight/Up to 82kg
1908	Stanley Bacon (GB)
1920	Eino Leino (Fin)
1924	Fritz Hagmann (Swi)
1928	Ernst Kyburz (Swi)
1932	Ivar Johansson (Swe)
1936	Emile Poilvé (Fra)
1948	Glen Brand (US)
1952	David Tsimakuridze (USSR)
1956	Nikola Stanchev (Bul)
1960	Hasan Gungor (Tur)
1964	Prodan Gardschev (Bul)
1968	Boris Gurevich (USSR)
1972	Levan Tediashvili (USSR)
1976	John Peterson (US)
1980	Ismail Abilov (Bul)
1984	Mark Schultz (US)
1988	Han Myung-Woo (SKo)

Light-heavyweight/Up to 90kg
1920	Anders Larsson (Swe)
1924	John Spellman (US)
1928	Thure Sjostedt (Swe)
1932	Peter Mehringer (US)
1936	Knut Fridell (Swe)
1948	Henry Wittenberg (US)
1952	Wiking Palm (Swe)

1956	Gholam Takhti Reza (Iran)
1960	Ismet Atli (Tur)
1964	Aleksandr Medved (USSR)
1968	Ahmet Ayik (Tur)
1972	Ben Peterson (US)
1976	Levan Tediashvili (USSR)
1980	Sanasar Oganesyan (USSR)
1984	Ed Banach (US)
1988	Makharbek Khadartsev (USSR)

Mid-heavyweight/Up to 100kg
1904	Bernhuff Hansen (US)
1908	George O'Kelly (GB)
1920	Robert Roth (Swi)
1924	Harry Steel (US)
1928	Johan Richthoff (Swe)
1932	Johan Richthoff (Swe)
1936	Kristjan Palusalu (Est)
1948	Gyula Bóbis (Hun)
1952	Arsen Mekokishvili (USSR)
1956	Hamit Kaplan (Tur)
1960	Wilfried Dietrich (Ger)
1964	Aleksandr Ivanitskiy (USSR)
1968	Aleksandr Medved (USSR)
1972	Ivan Yarygin (USSR)
1976	Ivan Yarygin (USSR)
1980	Ilya Mate (USSR)
1984	Lou Banach (US)
1988	Vasile Puscasu (Rom)

Super-heavyweight/Over 100kg
1972	Aleksandr Medved (USSR)
1976	Soslan Andiyev (USSR)
1980	Soslan Andiyev (USSR)
1984	Bruce Baumgartner (US)
1988	David Gobedzhishvili (USSR)

GRECO ROMAN
Light-flyweight/Up to 48kg
1972	Gheorghe Berceanu (Rom)
1976	Aleksey Schumakov (USSR)
1980	Zaksylik Ushkempirov (USSR)
1984	Vincenzo Maenza (Ita)
1988	Vincenzo Maenza (Ita)

Flyweight/Up to 52kg
1948	Pietro Lombardi (Ita)
1952	Boris Gurevich (USSR)
1956	Nikolay Solovyov (USSR)
1960	Dumitru Pirvulescu (Rom)
1964	Tsutomu Hanahara (Jap)
1968	Peter Kirov (Bul)
1972	Peter Kirov (Bul)
1976	Vitaliy Konstantinov (USSR)
1980	Vakhtang Blagidze (USSR)
1984	Atsuji Miyahara (Jap)
1988	Jon Ronningen (Nor)

Bantamweight/Up to 57kg
1924	Eduard Putsep (Est)
1928	Kurt Leucht (Ger)
1932	Jakob Brendel (Ger)
1936	Màrton Lörincz (Hun)
1948	Kurt Pettersén (Swe)
1952	Imre Hódos (Hun)
1956	Konstantin Vyrupayev (USSR)
1960	Oleg Karaveyev (USSR)
1964	Masamitsu Ichiguchi (Jap)
1968	János Varga (Hun)
1972	Rustem Kazakov (USSR)
1976	Pertti Ukkola (Fin)
1980	Shamil Serikov (USSR)
1984	Pasquale Passarelli (FRG)

1988   Andras Sike (Hun)

Featherweight/Up to 62kg
1912   Kaarlo Koskelo (Fin)
1920   Oskari Friman (Fin)
1924   Kalle Antila (Fin)
1928   Voldemar Väli (Est)
1932   Giovanni Gozzi (Ita)
1936   Yasar Erkan (Tur)
1948   Mehmet Oktav (Tur)
1952   Yakov Punkin (USSR)
1956   Rauno Makinen (Fin)
1960   Müzahir Sille (Tur)
1964   Imre Polyák (Hun)
1968   Roman Rurua (USSR)
1972   Gheorghi Markov (Bul)
1976   Kazimierz Lipién (Pol)
1980   Stylianos Migiakis (Gre)
1984   Weon-Kee Kim (SKo)
1988   Kamadar Madjidov (USSR)

Lightweight/Up to 68kg
1908   Enrico Porro (Ita)
1912   Eemil Väre (Fin)
1920   Eemil Väre (Fin)
1924   Oskari Friman (Fin)
1928   Lajos Keresztes (Hun)
1932   Erik Malmberg (Swe)
1936   Lauri Koskela (Fin)
1948   Gustaf Freij (Swe)
1952   Schazam Safin (USSR)
1956   Kyösti Lehtonen (Fin)
1960   Avtandil Koridze (USSR)
1964   Kazim Ayvaz (Tur)
1968   Munji Mumemura (Jap)
1972   Shamil Khisamutdinov (USSR)
1976   Suren Nalbandyan (USSR)
1980   Stefan Rusu (Rom)
1984   Vlado Lisjak (Yug)
1988   Levon Dzhulfalakyan (USSR)

Welterweight/Up to 74kg
1932   Ivar Johansson (Swe)
1936   Rudolf Svedberg (Swe)
1948   Gösta Andersson (Swe)
1952   Miklós Szelvási (Hun)
1956   Mithat Bayrak (Tur)
1960   Mithat Bayrak (Tur)
1964   Anatoliy Kolesov (USSR)
1968   Rudolf Vesper (GDR)
1970   Vitezslav Mácha (Cze)
1976   Anatoliy Bykov (USSR)
1980   Ferenc Kocsis (Hun)
1984   Jouko Salomaki (Fin)
1988   Kim Young-Nam (SKo)

Middleweight/Up to 82kg
1908   Frithiof Märtensson (Fin)
1912   Claes Johansson (Swe)
1920   Carl Westergren (Swe)
1924   Edvard Westerlund (Fin)
1928   Väinö Kokkinen (Fin)
1932   Väinö Kokkinen (Fin)
1936   Ivar Johansson (Swe)

1948   Axel Grönberg (Swe)
1952   Axel Grönberg (Swe)
1956   Givy Kartoziya (USSR)
1960   Dimiter Dobrev (Bul)
1964   Branislav Simic (Yug)
1968   Lothar Metz (GDR)
1972   Csaba Hegedus (Hun)
1976   Momir Petkovic (Yug)
1980   Gennadiy Korban (USSR)
1984   Ion Draica (Rom)
1988   Mikhail Mamiachvili (USSR)

Light-heavyweight/Up to 90kg
1908   Verner Weckman (Fin)
1912   No winner declared
1920   Claes Johansson (Swe)
1924   Carl Westergren (Swe)
1928   Ibrahim Moustafa (Egy)
1932   Rudolf Svensson (Swe)
1936   Axel Cadier (Swe)
1948   Karl-Eric Nilsson (Swe)
1952   Koelpo Gröndahl (Fin)
1956   Valentin Nikolayev (USSR)
1960   Tevfik Kis (Tur)
1964   Boyan Radev (Bul)
1968   Boyan Radev (Bul)
1972   Valeriy Rezantsev (USSR)
1976   Valeriy Rezantsev (USSR)
1980   Norbert Növényi (Hun)
1984   Steven Fraser (US)
1988   Atanas Komchev (Bul)

Heavyweight/Up to 100kg
1896   Carl Schuhmann (Ger)
1908   Richárd Weisz (Hun)
1912   Yrjö Saarela (Fin)
1920   Adolf Lindfors (Fin)
1924   Henri Deglane (Fra)
1928   Rudolf Svensson (Swe)
1932   Carl Westergren (Swe)
1936   Kristjan Paluslu (Est)
1948   Ahmet Kirecci (Tur)
1952   Johannes Kotkas (USSR)
1956   Anatoliy Parfenov (USSR)
1960   Ivan Bogdan (USSR)
1964   István Kozma (Hun)
1968   István Kozma (Hun)
1972   Nicolae Martinescu (Rom)
1976   Nicolay Balboshin (USSR)
1980   Gheorghi Raikov (Bul)
1984   Vasile Andrei (Rom)
1988   Andrzej Wronski (Pol)

Heavyweight
1972   Anatoliy Roschin (USSR)
1976   Aleksandr Kolchinsky (USSR)
1980   Aleksandr Kolchinsky (USSR)
1984   Jeffrey Blatnick (US)
1988   Alexandr Karelin (USSR)

YACHTING

Champions in current classes

Soling
1972	United States
1976	Denmark
1980	Denmark
1984	United States
1988	East Germany

Star
1932	Gilbert Gray/Andrew Libano Jnr (US)
1936	Peter Bischoff/Hans-Joachim Weise (Ger)
1948	Hilary Smart/Paul Smart (US)
1952	Nicolo Rode/Agostino Strraulino (Ita)
1956	Lawrence Low/Herbert Williams (US)
1960	Timir Pinegin/Fyodor Shukov (USSR)
1964	Cecil Cooke/Durward Knowles (Bah)
1968	Peter Barrett/Lowell North (US)
1972	John Anderson/David Forbes (Aus)
1980	Valentine Mankin/Aleksandr Muzychenko (USSR)
1984	Bill Buchan/Stephen Erickson (US)
1988	Michael McIntyre and Bryn Vaile (GB)

Flying Dutchman
(Previously known as Sharpie class)
1956	John Cropp/Peter Mander (NZ)
1960	Bergvall/Peter Lunde Jur (Nor)
1964	Helmer Pederson/Earle Wells (NZ)
1968	Iain Macdonald-Smith/Rodney Pattisson (GB)
1972	Christopher Davies/Rodney Pattisson (GB)
1976	Eckert Diesch/Jorg Diesch (FRG)
1980	Alejandro Abascal/Miguel Noguer (Spa)
1984	William Carl Buchan/Jonathan McKee (US)
1988	Christian Gronborg/Jorgen Bojsen-Moeller (Den)

Tornado
1976	John Osborn/Reg White (GB)
1980	Lars Bjorkstrom/Alexandre Welter (Bra)
1984	Rex Sellers/Christopher Timms (NZ)

1988	Nicholas Henrad/Jean-Yves Le Deroff (Fra)

Finn
(Formely known as Meulan, International 12-foot, Snowbird, International Olympia and Firefly classes)
1920	Franciscus Hin/Johannes Hin (Hol)
1920	Francis Richards/T Hedberg (GB)
1924	Leon Huybrechts (Bel)
1928	Sven Thorell (Swe)
1932	Jacques Lebrun (Fra)
1936	Daniel Kagchelland (Hol)
1948	Paul Elvstrom (Den)
1952	Paul Elvstrom (Den)
1956	Paul Elvstrom (Den)
1960	Paul Elvstrom (Den)
1964	Willi Kuhweide (Ger)
1968	Valentin Mankin (Fra)
1972	Serge Maury (Fra)
1976	Jochen Schumann (Ger)
1980	Esko Rechardt (Fin)
1984	Russell Coutts (NZ)
1988	Jose-Luis Doreste (Spa)

470 Class
1976	Harro Bode/Frank Hubner (FRG)
1980	Eduardo Pendo/Marcos Soares (Bra)
1984	Jose-Luis Doreste/Roberto Malina (Spa)
1988	Thierry Peponnet/Luc Pillot (Fra)

Boardsailing
1984	Stephen van den Berg (Hol)
1988	Bruce Kendall (NZ)

Women's 470 Class
1988	Lynne Jewell/Alison Jolly (US)

ORIENTEERING

WORLD CHAMPIONSHIPS
Marianske Lazne, Czechoslovakia, Aug 20-25
Men
Individual
1 Jorgen Martensson (Swe) 1h 19m 25s
2 Kent Olsson (Swe) 1h 53m 37s
3 Sixten Sild (USSR) 1 h 53m 48s
Team Relay
1 Switzerland 1h 12m 37s
2 Norway 4h 42m 59s
3 Finland 4h 44m 18s
Switzerland's first ever world title
Women
Individual
1 Katarina Olch (Hun) 1h 19m 52s
2 Kristina Blomquist (Swe) 1h 21m 04s
3 Jana Glaenkova (Cze) 1h 21m 18s
Team Relay
1 Sweden 3h 38m 27s
2 Norway 3h 40m 20s
3 Hungary 3h 51m 15s

TSB BRITISH CHAMPIONSHIPS
Kyloe Forest, Alnwick, Northumberland, May 4-5
Men
1 Stephen Palmer (Walton Chasers) 1h 31m 01s
2 Martin Bagness (Warrior) 1h 31m 06s
3 John Musgrave (Maroc) 1h 31m 37s
Women
1 Yvette Hague (Airienteers) 1h 05m 46s
2 Heather Monro (Cambridge University) 1h 05m 52s
3 Clare Bolland (Edinburgh University) 1h 06m 25s

TSB JAN KJELLSTROM INTERNATIONAL FESTIVAL
Chesterfield, Mar 29-Apr 1
Men
1 Steven Hale (OKTYR) 1h 40m 05s
2 Richard Jones (Clydeside) 1h 45m 26s
3 John Musgrave (Maroc) 1h 46m 37s
Women
1 Yvette Hague (Airienteers) 1h 13m 56s
2 Clare Bolland (Edinburgh University) 1h 15m 29s
3 Heather Monro (Cambridge University) 1h 22m 22s

CHAMPIONS

WORLD CHAMPIONS
Inaugurated 1966. Winners since 1983

Men - Individual		Team
1983	Morten Berglia (Nor)	Norway
1985	Kari Sallinen (Fin)	Norway
1987	Kent Olsson (Swe)	Norway
1989	Peter Thoresen (Nor)	Norway
1991	Jorgen Martensson (Swe)	Switzerland

Most wins: 2 Egil Johansen (Nor), Oynin Thor (Nor).
Team: 7 Norway

Women - Individual		Team
1983	Annichen Kringstad-Svensson (Swe)	Sweden
1985	Annichen Kringstad-Svensson (Swe)	Sweden
1987	Arja Hannus (Swe)	Norway
1989	Marita Skogum (Swe)	Sweden
1991	Katarina Olch (Hun)	Sweden

Most wins: 3 Kringstad-Svensson. **Team 10** Sweden

POLO

CORONATION CUP
Windsor, July 28
England 10 NEW ZEALAND 12

BRITISH OPEN
Cowdray Park, Jun 29-Jul 21
Semi-finals
TRAMONTANA 17 Ellerston Black 5; ELLERSTON WHITE 11 Maple Leafs 10
Final
TRAMONTANA 11 Ellerston White 7

OTHER TOURNAMENTS
Finals
The Queen's Cup:
Guards, May 17-Jun 9
ELLERSTON WHITE 11 Tramontana 5
Ellerston White are owned by Kerry Packer
Prince of Wales Trophy:
Royal Berks, May 17-Jun 8
MUNIPORE 8 Sladmore 6
Warwickshire Cup:
Cirencester, Jun 11-30
BLACK BEARS 13 Munipore 11
Cowdray Park Challenge Cup
Cowdray Park, Jul 29-Aug 4
LOS LOCOS (Rec 2) 15 Windsor Park 8

ROYAL BERKSHIRE INTERNATIONAL WOMEN'S TOURNAMENT
Royal Berks, Aug 12-18
ENGLAND 6 Boston 5½
This was the first major women's international tournament in Britain.

TOP HANDICAP PLAYERS IN BRITAIN
9 goals Howard Hipwood (Royal County of Berkshire); **8 goals** Julian Hipwood (Cowdray Park); **7 goals** Alan Kent (Cowdray Park), Paul Withers (Cowdray Park); **6 goals** Lord Beresford (Royal County of Berkshire), J Horswell (Guards), William Lucas (Cowdray Park)

CHAMPIONS

BRITISH OPEN
Winners since 1982

1982	Southfield
1983	Falcons
1984	Southfield
1985	Maple Leafs
1986	Tramontana
1987	Tramontana
1988	Tramontana
1989	Tramontana
1990	Hildon
1991	Tramontana

RACKETS

1991

LACOSTE WORLD SINGLES CHAMPIONSHIP
Queen's Club, London, Mar 12
JAMES MALE (GB) beat Shannon Hazell (GB) 6-2
(Combined score over two legs)

LACOSTE BRITISH OPEN DOUBLES
Queen's Club, Apr 21
NEIL SMITH & SHANNON HAZELL beat John Prenn &
James Male 15-2 7-15 15-12 13-18 15-4 `12-15 15-12

CHAMPIONS

WORLD CHAMPIONS
*Organised on a challenge basis. All winners British unless
otherwise stated*
Winners

1820	Robert Mackay
1825	Thomas Pittman
1834	John Pittman
1838	John Lamb
1846	L C Mitchell
1860	Francis Erwood
1862	William Hart Dyke
1863	Henry Gray
1866	William Gray
1876	H B Fairs
1878	Joseph Gray
1887	Peter Latham
1903	J Jamsetjhi (Ind)
1911	Charles Williams
1913	Jock Soutar (US)
1929	Charles Williams
1937	David Milford
1947	James Dear
1954	Geoffrey Atkins
1972	William Surtees (US)
1973	Howard Angus
1974	William Surtees (US)
1981	John Prenn
1984	Willie Boone
1986	John Prenn
1988	James Male

REAL TENNIS

1991

HENRY LEAF CUP
Queen's Club, Jan 20
SEMI-FINALS
RADLEY beat Haileybury 6-0 6-2; LANCING beat
Winchester 5-6 6-4 2-5 ret
FINAL
RADLEY beat Lancing 6-0 6-4

BRITISH AMATEUR SINGLES
Lord's, Apr 28
JULIAN SNOW beat Andrew Page 6-1 6-4 6-3

GEORGE WIMPEY BRITISH WOMEN'S OPEN
Seacourt, May 5
PENNY FELLOWS beat Alex Garside 6-0 6-1

GEORGE WIMPEY BRITISH AMATEUR DOUBLES
Seacourt, May 6
JULIAN SNOW & MICHAEL McMURRUGH beat
Andrew Page & Mark Howard 6-5 6-5 6-4

1990

BRITISH PROFESSIONAL SINGLES
Holyport, Maidenhead, May 13
LACHLAN DEUCHAR beat Chris Ronaldson 6-3 6-5 6-4

CHAMPIONS

WORLD CHAMPIONS
Organised on a challenge basis
Men

1740	Clerge (Fra)
1765	Raymond Masson (Fra)
1785	Joseph Barcellon (Fra)
1816	Marchesio (Ita)
1819	Phillip Cox (GB)
1829	Edmond Barre (Fra)
1862	Edmund Tomkins (GB)
1871	George Lambert (GB)
1885	Tom Pettitt (US)
1890	Charles Saunders (GB)
1895	Peter Latham (GB)
1905	Cecil Fairs (GB)
1907	Peter Latham (GB)
1908	Cecil Fairs (GB)
1912	Fred Covey (GB)
1914	Jay Gould (US)
1916	Fred Covey (GB)
1928	Pierre Etchebaster (Fra)
1955	James Dear (GB)
1957	Albert Johnson (GB)
1959	Northrup Knox (US)
1969	Pete Bostwick (US)
1972	Jimmy Bostwick (US)
1976	Howard Angus (GB)
1981	Chris Ronaldson (GB)
1987	Wayne Davies (Aus)

Women
First held 1985, contested biennially

1985	Judy Clarke (Aus)
1987	Judy Clarke (Aus)
1989	Penny Fellows (GB)

ROWING

Britain emerged from the 1991 World Championships in Vienna more successfully than for several years, winning five medals, two of them gold. For the first time, the British won a medal in a women's open-weight event: Fiona Freckleton and Miriam Batten took bronze in the coxless pairs.

British domestic rowing, however, retained its own charming dottiness. Oxford won the Boat Race in 1991 for the 15th year out of 16. Their lightest crew for 10 years won in 16 minutes 59 seconds, the third fastest time in the race's long history. It was also probably the most bitter race ever. One of Oxford's American oarsmen called out "See you later, Max" to a compatriot in the other boat as they passed, Cambridge refused to acknowledge the traditional three cheers from the winners, which were allegedly delivered with some venom, and the Oxford president Rupert Obholzer then appeared to direct an obscene gesture at the Cambridge crew: not the traditional V-sign but the single-digit, which is not merely disgusting but foreign. Guy Pooley, the Cambridge no.4, was in the losing boat for the fourth year running. Richard Young moved from Cambridge to Oxford, suggesting the race was starting to acquire a transfer system. Asked what Cambridge had to do to win, Obholzer replied "Train harder". Cambridge had named their trial eights Iraq and Rest of the World until there were protests; they were changed to Drunk and Disorderly. Both ancient universities were well beaten by London University.

The starting order "Are you ready? Go" was abolished in the Boat Race after 136 years and replaced by "Attention, Set, Go" which is understood better by foreigners. The Henley Royal Regatta, however, decided to retain the old way. "We wouldn't want to be dragged screaming into the 20th century, would we?" said the Regatta chairman Peter Coni. Henley in 1991 had fewer uninterested spectators - there was a 75 per cent drop in the number of corporate hospitality marquees - and fewer Canada geese interfering with the boats, after a fence was erected to keep them away. "They are the yobs of the bird world," said Coni. Competitors were warned by scientists not to fall in the river, because of sewage pollution said to be up to five times European safety limits. Emily Smith, 11, was one of a dozen women denied admission on the opening day because her skirt was too short. "Emily's skirt is no different to the one she wears for school," said her mother. "Stupid," said Emily.

A party held by Hull University Boat Club at Lincoln Castle left the place such a mess, with bras, panties and champagne bottles everywhere, that the staff considered banning student celebrations. "The place has not seen action like this since William the Conqueror," said one castle official.

════ 1991 ════

WORLD CHAMPIONSHIPS
Vienna, Aug 20-25

Men

Single Sculls	Thomas Lange (Ger) 6m 41.29s
Double Sculls	H Zwolle & Nicolaas Rienks (Hol) 6m 06.14s
Quadruple Sculls	Soviet Union 6m 08.39s
Coxless Pairs	Steven Redgrave & Matthew Pinsent (GB) 6m 21.33s
Coxed Pairs	Italy 7m 34.39s
Coxless Fours	Australia 6m 29.69s
Coxed Fours	Germany 5m 58.96s
Eights	Germany 5m 50.87s
Lightweight Single Sculls	Niall O'Toole (Ire) 6m 49.17s
Lightweight Double Sculls	Germany 6m 20.04s
Lightweight Quadruple	
Sculls	Australia 6m 37.02s
Lightweight Coxless Fours	Great Britain 5m 57.50s
Lightweight Eights	Italy 6m 13.21s

Women

Single Sculls	Silke Laumann (Can) 8m 17.58s
Double Sculls	Beate Schramm & Kathrin Boron (Ger) 6m 44.71s
Quadruple Sculls	Germany 6m 55.85s
Coxless Pairs	M McBean & K Heddle (Can) 6m 57.42s
Coxless Fours	Canada 6m 25.47s
Eights	Canada 6m 28.20s
Lightweight Single Sculls	Philippa Baker (NZ) 7m 29.99s
Lightweight Double Sculls	Christiane Weber & Claudia Waldi (Ger) 7m 58.53s
Lightweight Coxless Fours	China 7m 37.06s

LEADING MEDAL WINNERS

	G	S	B	Total
Germany	7	2	3	12
Canada	4	1	0	5
Great Britain	2	1	2	5
Soviet Union	1	3	1	5
United States	0	3	2	5
Romania	0	3	2	5
Italy	2	2	0	4
Holland	1	1	2	4

Britain won silver in the women's lightweight coxless fours and bronzes in the men's eights and women's coxless pairs.

BOAT RACE

Putney to Mortlake, Mar 30
OXFORD UNIVERSITY beat Cambridge University by 4 lengths in a time of 16m 59s, the third fastest time ever.

Oxford

Bow	R W Martin (Durham Johnston & University) 13st 9lb
No.2	J G Michels (La Salle, USA & University) 13st 1lb
No.3	P A J Bridge (Eton & Oriel) 14st 1lb
No.4	H P M Hume (Yale University, USA & Pembroke) 13st 7lb
No.5	C A Maclennan (Camp Hill, Birmingham & Green) 14st 2lb
No.6	M C Pinsent (Eton & St Catherine's) 15st 2lb
No.7	R C Young (Bedford, Downing (Cambridge) & St John's) 12st 12lb
Stroke	R J Obholzer (Hampton & St Catherine's) 13st 10lb
Cox	N Chugani (Hampton & St Catherine's) 7st 13lb

Average weight: 13st 10½ lb
Richard Young became only the second man to compete for both Universities. The first was Bruce Philip who rowed for Cambridge in 1982 and 1983 and then for Oxford in 1985 and 1986.

Cambridge

Bow	R A B Smith (Shrewsbury & Trinity Hall) 12st 10lb
No.2	R J Staite (Prince Henry's, Evesham & St Catharine's) 11st 4lb
No.3	M C J Justicz (Boston University, USA & Sidney Sussex) 13st 8lb
No.4	G R Pooley (Berkhamsted, Imperial College & St John's) 13st 3lb
No.5	K St C Allen (King's, Canterbury & Magdalene) 13st 2lb
No.6	D R Gillard (Bedford Modern & St Catharine's) 14st 6lb
No.7	N J Clarry (John Hampden GS & Jesus) 12st 11lb
Stroke	A J Wright (King Edward VI & Corpus) 13st 6lb
Cox	A J L Bracey (Winchester, University of East Anglia & Magdalene) 7st 12lb

Average weight: 13st 1lb

Reserve Race

GOLDIE (Cambridge) beat Isis (Oxford) by 4 lengths

A GOOD OLD-FASHIONED ROW

"The company has been delighted to be involved with the spirit of courteous rivalry which the Boat Race has represented down the ages."
James Maxwell of Beefeater Gin, the Boat Race sponsors

"Pretty haircuts, shades and poncey clothes... We were very determined to put them in their place. You can't create animosity. There is just something about those guys. If they were at Oxford I'm sure they would still be disliked."
Rupert Obholzer, Oxford president, on the Cambridge crew

"People tend to find Oxford arrogant. They have always behaved like that."
Richard Staite, Cambridge oarsman

"The problem rests with certain personalities in the Oxford boat. Some of them are only at university to row. You need superb academic qualifications to enter Cambridge....It wasn't like this when I first rowed four years ago. We tried to ruin each other's lives and then we had a drink together."
Guy Pooley, Cambridge oarsman

"One can only imagine the shock with which Obholzer's gesture was received by those frail buffers of the Leander Club ... These gracious ancients who shuffle about in plimsolls, wearing absurdly small pink caps and equally under-fitting pink blazers have been the very last sporting redoubt of gentlemanly England. Their elegant fortifications have come tumbling down."
Peter Tory, Daily Express

"It was delivered out of frustration after a heroic performance which necessitated a monumental release of energy. At such times, an athlete's mind does not fully focus on the interpretations of such actions by a number of egotistical journalists."
Steve Royle, Oxford's director of rowing

"Many institutions have an accepted, though unwritten, rule that their good name must not be brought into disrepute. Unfortunately, in its determination to beat Cambridge at any cost, the Oxford University Boat Club seems bent on doing this to the Boat Race."
Letter to The Times from Professor Alistair Cameron of Cambridge

"Cambridge had lost again but with a dignity which gives them command of the moral high water."
Jeff Powell, Daily Mail

WOMEN'S BOAT RACE
Putney to Mortlake, Mar 24
OXFORD beat Cambridge by 3 lengths
Reserve Race
BLONDIE (Cambridge) beat Osiris (Oxford) by 2 lengths

HEAD OF THE RIVER RACE
Mortlake to Putney, Mar 23
1 Leander I 17m 28.14s
2 Molesey I 17m 38.66s
3 University of London I 17m 46.78s

151st HENLEY ROYAL REGATTA
Jul 3-7
Ladies Plate
Leander & Molesey beat University of London by 1 length; 6m 26s
Visitors Cup
Goldie beat University of London by 1¼ lengths; 7m 20s
Thames Cup
University of Pennsylvania 'A' (USA) beat University of London by 1 length; 6m 42s
Prince Philip Cup
Leander & Star beat Dinamo Vilnius, Lithuania by 2¼ lengths; 7m 20s
Wyfold Cup
Nautilus beat Notts County by 2¼ lengths; 7m 21s
Britannia Cup
Notts County beat Nottingham & Union by 5 lengths; 7m 18s
Stewards' Cup
Leander & Molesey beat Leander by 2 lengths; 6m 55s

Henley Steward:
"Sorry, madam, your skirt's too short."
Lady (sailing past):
"Don't be so stupid. It's just that my legs are too long."
Reported exchange

Grand Challenge Cup
Leander & Star beat Dinamo & Soviet Army (USSR) by 2½ lengths; 6m 22s
Princess Elizabeth Cup
Eton beat King's School, Canterbury by 4½ lengths; 6m 59s
Queen Mother Cup
Leander & Tideway Scullers School beat Notts County & London *easily*; 7m 05s
Silver Goblets & Nickalls'
Steven Redgrave & Matthew Pinsent (Leander) beat Josef Robert & Manolo Bermudez (Nautico Banyoles, Spain) *easily*; 7m 38s
Diamond Sculls
Wim van Belleghem (Ghent, Belgium) beat Eric Verdonk (Koru, New Zealand) *not rowed out* 8m 14s
Double Sculls
Bjarne Eltang (Danske Studenters, Denmark) & Henrik Bang (Fana, Norway) beat Robert Luke & Christopher Skuse (Leander) *easily* 7m 32s

---

━━━━ 1990 ━━━━
WORLD CHAMPIONSHIPS
Lake Barrington, Tasmania, Oct 28-Nov 4
Men
Single Sculls	Yuri Janson (USSR) 7m 22.15s
Double Sculls	Austria 6m 56.37s
Coxless Pairs	East Germany 7m 07.91s
Coxed Pairs	Italy 6m 48.30s
Quadruple Sculls	Soviet Union 5m 40.44s
Coxless Fours	Australia 5m 52.20s
Coxed Fours	East Germany 6m 46.73s
Eights	West Germany 5m 26.62s
Lightweight Single Sculls	Frans Gobel (Hol) 7m 21.24s
Lightweight Double Sculls	United States 7m 46.15s
Lightweight Coxless Fours	West Germany 7m 03.68s
Lightweight Quadruple Sculls	Italy 5m 46.38s
Lightweight Eights	Italy 5m 35.03s

Women
Single Sculls	Brigit Peter (GDR) 7m 24.10s
Double Sculls	East Germany 8m 18.63
Coxless Pairs	West Germany 8m 28.37s
Coxed Pairs	Romania 7m 51.68s
Quadruple Sculls	East Germany 6m 14.08s
Eights	Romania 5m 59.26s
Lightweight Single Sculls	Mette Bloch Jansen (Den) 8m 12.64s
Lightweight Double Sculls	Denmark 6m 57.96s
Lightweight Coxless Fours	Canada 6m 38.40s

Leading Medal Winners
	G	S	B	Total
East Germany	5	1	5	11
West Germany	3	3	1	7
Italy	3	0	0	3
Soviet Union	2	3	1	6
Romania	2	0	0	2
Denmark	2	1	1	4
Great Britain	0	0	2	2

Britain's medallists: Steven Redgrave & Matthew Pinsent (coxless pairs); lightweight eight

━━━━ CHAMPIONS ━━━━
WORLD CHAMPIONSHIPS
First held for men 1962, and for women 1974. Not held in Olympic years. Winners in heavyweight classes since 1982:

Men
Single Sculls
1985	Pertti Karppinen (Fin)
1986	Peter-Michael Kolbe (FRG)
1987	Thomas Lange (GDR)
1989	Thomas Lange (GDR)
1990	Yuri Janson (USSR)
1991	Thomas Lange (Ger)

Double Sculls
1985	Thomas Lange/Uwe Heppner (GDR)
1986	Alberto Belgori/Igor Pescialli (Ita)
1987	Danayl Yordanov/Vassil Radev (Bul)
1989	Lars Bjoeness/Rol Bent Thorsen (Nor)
1990	Arnold Junke/Christopher Zerbst (Hol)
1991	Nicolaas Rienks/H Zwolle (Hol)

Coxless Pairs
1985   Nikolay Pimenov/Yuriy Pimenov (USSR)
1986   Nikolay Pimenov/Yuriy Pimenov (USSR)
1987   Andrew Holmes/Steven Redgrave (GB)
1989   Thomas Jung/Uwe Kellner (GDR)
1990   Thomas Jung/Uwe Kellner (GDR)
1991   Steven Redgrave/Matthew Pinsent (GB)

Coxed Pairs
1985   Italy
1986   Great Britain
1987   Italy
1989   Italy
1990   Italy
1991   Italy

Coxless Fours
1985   West Germany
1986   United States
1987   East Germany
1989   East Germany
1990   Australia
1991   Australia

Coxed Fours
1985   USSR
1986   East Germany
1987   East Germany
1989   Romania
1990   East Germany
1991   Germany

Quadruple Sculls
1985   Canada
1986   USSR
1987   USSR
1989   Holland
1990   USSR
1991   USSR

Eights
1985   USSR
1986   Australia
1987   United States
1989   West Germany
1990   West Germany
1991   Germany

Women

Single Sculls
1985   Cornelia Linse (GDR)
1986   Jutta Hampe (GDR)
1987   Magdalena Georgieva (Bul)
1989   Elisabeta Lipa (Rom)
1990   Brigit Peter (GDR)
1991   Silke Laumann (Can)

Double Sculls
1985   Sylvia Schurabe/Martina Schroter (GDR)
1986   Sylvia Schurabe/Beate Schramm (GDR)
1987   Steska Madina/Violeta Ninova (Bul)
1989   Jana Sorgers/Beate Schramm (GDR)
1990   Kathrin Boron/Beate Schramm (GDR)
1991   Beate Schramm/K. Boron (Ger)

Coxless Pairs
1985   Rodica Arba/Elena Florea (Rom)
1986   Rodica Arba/Olga Homeghi (Rom)
1987   Rodica Arba/Olga Homeghi (Rom)
1989   Kathrin Haaker/Judith Zeidler (GDR)
1990   Stephani Worromior/Ingeburg Althoss (FRG)
1991   McBean/K. Heddle (Can)

Quadruple Sculls
1985   East Germany
1986   East Germany
1987   East Germany
1989   East Germany
1990   East Germany
1991   Germany

Coxed Fours
1985   East Germany
1986   Romania
1987   Romania
1990   Romania

Coxless Fours
1986   United States
1987   -
1989   East Germany
1990   Romania
1991   Canada

Eights
1985   USSR
1986   USSR
1987   Romania
1989   Romania
1990   Romania
1991   Canada

UNIVERSITY BOAT RACE
Cambridge wins (69):
1836, 1839-41, 1845-46, 1849, 1856, 1858,1860, 1870-74, 1876, 1879, 1884, 1886-89, 1899-1900, 1902-04, 1906-08, 1914,1920-22,1924-36, 1939, 1947-51, 1953, 1955-58, 1961-62, 1964, 1968-73, 1975, 1986
Oxford wins (67):
1829, 1842, 1849, 1852, 1854, 1857, 1859, 1861-69, 1875, 1878, 1880-83, 1885, 1890-98, 1901, 1905,1 909-13, 1923, 1937-38, 1946, 1952, 1954, 1959-60, 1963, 1965-67, 1974, 1976-85, 1987-91
There was a dead-heat in 1877
Fastest Time: 16 min 45 sec, Oxford (1984)
Biggest winning margin: 20 lengths, Cambridge (1900)
Most winning boats: 6 Boris Rankov (Oxford) 1978-83

Henley Grand Challenge Cup
First held 1839. Winners since 1982
1982   Leander/London RC (GB)
1983   London RC/University of London (GB)
1984   Leander/London RC (GB)
1985   Harvard University (US)
1986   Nautilus (GB)
1987   Soviety Army (USSR)
1988   Leander/University of London (GB)
1989   RC Hansa Dortmund (FRG)
1990   RC Hansa Dortmund (FRG)
1991   Leander &Star
Most wins
32 Leander Club 1840, 1875, 1880, 1891-94, 1896, 1898-1901, 1903-05, 1913, 1922, 1924-26, 1929, 1932, 1934, 1946, 1949, 1952-53, 1975†, 1982†, 1984†, 1988†, 1991†
(† Boat shared with either Thames Tradesmen, London RC; Star or University of London)

1992

Apr 4 Oxford v Cambridge Boat Race (Putney to Mortlake, 2.30pm); Jul 1-5 Henley Royal Regatta; Sep 12-13 FISA Centenary Regatta (Henley)

RUGBY LEAGUE

HANLEY'S HEROICS

One dramatic afternoon at Wembley Stadium gave British rugby league its greatest encouragement for many years. Great Britain beat Australia 19-12 in the First Test, inspiring a surge of interest in the game that went far beyond its traditional boundaries.

Great Britain failed to sustain their success: Australia levelled the series at Old Trafford after another thrilling contest which culminated in a run by Ricky Stuart and a try by Mal Meninga with only 20 seconds to go. Then the Aussies won again at Elland Road, thus continuing the sequence whereby Great Britain have not won a home series against them since 1959.

With the British team starting to age, there was a feeling that a historic opportunity had slipped away. Nonetheless, there was unanimous agreement that the gap between the countries was much narrower and Great Britain later emphasised their confidence with two huge wins over France.

The Wembley triumph was inspired by Ellery Hanley, whose brilliance on the field consistently contrasted with his self-centredness off it: he refused to be interviewed on TV afterwards unless he was paid a fee and refused to speak to any journalists at all, even the editor of the Wigan match programme. But he was playing well enough to be forgiven anything - except signing for Leeds, which he did in September. Before that, his club form had been equally devastating and Wigan again won the League and Cup double.

Wigan steamed up from behind to catch the league leaders in a knackering run-in for the title which included 11 wins out of 12 games in 34 days. In the midst of it, Hanley became the first man to score 200 First Division tries. The decisive victory was a 26-6 win over Widnes on April 9 in front of a full house at Central Park. Almost falling over the line, they beat St Helens 13-8 in a disappointing Cup Final. "The side has been held together by needles and sticking plaster," said the coach John Monie. "I hope no side again has to go through what we've been through." The club announced plans to go full-time in 1991-92.

The other trophies were shared around and Hull won the Premiership, becoming the first Yorkshire team to win a major trophy since Halifax won the Cup in 1987. They beat Widnes who fell apart in the closing weeks and lost their coach, Doug Laughton, to Leeds. The sport's longest-serving coach Roger Millward left Hull Kingston Rovers after 14 years in the job and 25 at the club. Oldham sacked their coach Tony Barrow; he described his former employers as "spineless and despicable".

A Bradford Northern player, Simon Tuffs, failed a dope test for amphetamine and was suspended for two years. He was reinstated after one witness admitted spiking his drink and another said he saw it happen. Rugby League was able to regain its clean record on drugs: more than 500 tests, none positive.

The League agreed a new three-division set-up for 1991-92, based on 14 clubs in the First and Third Divisions but only eight in the Second. Scarborough were admitted to the Third Division. Runcorn Highfield ended a run of 61 defeats, drawing with Carlisle on February 3. A month later, after 854 days, 76 games and five coaches, they beat Dewsbury 9-2 to win their first game since October 30 1988. In the end, they were not even bottom of the League.

A British team comprising Fulham and Ryedale-York players beat the Soviet Union 42-10 in Moscow; five per cent of the £1,180,000 profit generated by the Australian tour was due to go to development of the Soviet game.

Kim Richard Heke, a forward with Browns Plain Bears of Brisbane, was charged with the unlawful killing of Kevin Sharkey of South Sunnybank, who died after a head-high tackle. The Australian federal court rejected a plea by a Western Suburbs player, Robert Cooper, that he was entitled to a tax allowance for food because he had been ordered to keep his weight up. The Australians experimented with unlimited substitutions but after 41 were made in one opening-day game, they were limited to six. It was reported that Wigan's annual Christmas party coincided with a board meeting: Andy Gregory and Joe Lydon left one room for the other, thumped the table and told the chairman they should be taken seriously. Gregory and Lydon were dressed as Donald Duck and Mickey Mouse at the time.

━━━━━━━━ 1990-91 ━━━━━━━━

STONES BITTER CHAMPIONSHIP
Division One

			P	W	D	L	F	A	Pts	Av. Home Attendance	Players Sent Off
1	(1)	**WIGAN**	26	20	2	4	652	313	42	14,493	7
2	(3)	Widnes	26	20	0	6	635	340	40	6,793	2
3	(6)	Hull	26	17	0	9	513	367	34	6,699	1
4	(7)	Castleford	26	17	0	9	578	442	34	6,019	4
5	(2)	Leeds	26	14	2	10	602	448	30	11,102	5
6	(5)	St Helens	26	14	1	11	628	533	29	7,391	1
7	(4)	Bradford	26	13	1	12	434	492	27	5,274	3
8	(10)	Featherstone	26	12	1	13	533	592	25	4,722	1
9	(8)	Warrington	26	10	2	14	404	436	22	5,915	2
10	(9)	Wakefield	26	10	2	14	356	409	22	4,848	2
11	(P)	Hull KR	26	9	3	14	462	615	21	4,952	3
12	(P)	*Oldham*	26	10	0	16	481	562	20	5,094	3
13	(P)	*Sheffield*	26	7	2	17	459	583	16	4,031	2
14	(P)	*Rochdale*	26	1	0	25	317	912	2	2,542	5

Last season's positions in brackets

LEADING SCORERS

Tries	Goals	Points
49 Martin Offiah (Widnes)	177 Steve Kerry (Salford)	423 Steve Kerry
30 Jonathan Davies (Widnes)	126 Frano Botica (Wigan)	342 Jonathan Davies
30 Adrian Hadley (Salford)	119 Paul Eastwood (Hull)	324 Frano Botica
29 Ellery Hanley (Wigan)	112 Jonathan Davies (Widnes)	294 Paul Eastwood
26 Les Quirk (St Helens)	99 Simon Irving (Leeds)	242 Simon Irving
26 Alan Hunte (St Helens)	94 Paul Loughlin (St Helens)	

Results: Division One

	Bradford N	C'ford	Featherstone	Hull	Hull KR	Leeds	Oldham	Rochdale	St.Helens	Sheffield	Wakefield T	Warrington	Widnes	Wigan
BRADFORD	*	24-14	18-34	28-16	26-10	12-21	10-37	23-16	18-16	6-10	12-10	25-16	10-14	31-30
CASTLEFORD	9-0	*	24-19	14-16	30-2	16-14	28-10	42-0	28-4	28-10	42-12	22-18	20-10	18-38
FEATHERSTONE	24-26	6-22	*	14-6	14-14	20-52	28-20	38-8	28-36	25-22	14-8	22-8	22-27	16-24
HULL	34-6	22-6	40-22	*	28-16	34-14	31-4	28-8	20-14	34-6	6-14	17-8	32-6	24-4
HULL KR	12-4	12-16	24-14	20-8	*	16-28	42-14	48-14	26-26	16-16	12-18	20-14	22-20	6-36
LEEDS	26-8	41-16	16-18	22-24	24-18	*	28-12	64-4	23-4	38-16	7-0	20-20	0-38	8-20
OLDHAM	16-18	28-22	18-20	19-14	25-28	32-22	*	18-13	16-20	27-20	26-22	4-2	18-24	4-10
ROCHDALE	19-12	12-76	12-26	18-30	18-32	20-34	12-30	*	18-30	20-24	6-25	10-18	6-60	16-44
ST HELENS	24-20	16-29	54-38	12-10	42-10	22-16	33-22	44-14	*	34-17	36-14	62-16	12-20	15-28
SHEFFIELD	16-36	20-24	24-27	6-16	62-16	6-24	14-24	30-16	18-8	*	34-6	18-20	13-18	4-46
WAKEFIELD	6-16	8-12	8-16	22-6	26-6	14-14	17-12	42-6	8-22	12-4	*	12-12	6-16	14-12
WARRINGTON	12-13	30-12	16-10	2-3	30-12	10-2	22-14	26-9	34-20	30-8	10-18	*	2-6	8-26
WIDNES	32-14	46-4	41-14	28-2	28-18	26-8	24-16	44-20	14-8	14-23	34-6	25-6	*	14-22
WIGAN	18-18	24-4	24-4	34-12	34-4	22-16	38-15	24-2	28-14	18-18	16-8	6-14	26-6	*

Division Two

			P	W	D	L	F	A	Pts	Av. Home Attendance	Players Sent Off
1	(R)	SALFORD	28	26	1	1	856	219	53	2,314	5
2	(5)	Halifax	28	24	2	4	941	311	48	4,458	3
3	(6)	Swinton	28	21	2	5	523	370	44	1,737	1
4	(4)	Ryedale-York	28	20	2	6	559	294	42	1,857	3
5	(R)	Leigh	28	18	1	9	698	372	37	1,719	1
6	(18)	Workington	28	18	1	9	497	323	37	1,426	4
7	(8)	Fulham	28	17	2	9	450	338	36	557	1
8	(17)	Carlisle	28	16	2	10	613	425	34	781	4
9	(9)	Doncaster	28	16	0	12	507	434	32	1,458	4
10	(14)	Hunslet	28	13	2	13	519	438	28	767	6
11	(11)	Huddersfield	28	13	1	14	493	477	27	1,306	1
12	(16)	Whitehaven	28	13	0	15	412	592	26	1,035	3
13	(19)	Keighley	28	12	0	16	456	588	24	985	5
14	(7)	Dewsbury	28	10	1	17	410	455	21	955	5
15	(10)	Trafford	28	10	0	18	508	618	20	638	2
16	(12)	Batley	28	10	0	18	337	466	20	1,188	4
17	(R)	Barrow	28	8	2	18	415	705	18	962	5
18	(15)	Chorley	28	7	1	20	388	721	15	690	7
19	(13)	Bramley	28	7	1	20	379	726	15	805	5
20	(21)	Runcorn	28	3	1	24	351	779	7	632	3
21	(20)	Nottingham	28	2	0	26	284	945	4	255	2

Last season's positions in brackets

Salford were promoted into Division One. The next five clubs and the botttom three from Division One formed the new Division Two. The rest plus Scarborough formed Division Three.

TOP SCORERS
Tries: 47 Greg Austin (Halifax) Goals: 94 Graham Sullivan (Ryedale-York)

WIGAN'S FIVE YEARS OF SUCCESS
League Championship 1987, 1990,1991
Challenge Cup 1988, 1989, 1990, 1991
Premiership 1987
Regal Trophy 1987, 1989, 1990
Lancashire Cup 1987, 1988, 1989
World Club Challenge 1987

SILK CUT CHALLENGE CUP

PRELIMINARY ROUND
Carlisle 8 WORKINGTON 9; Hensingham 7 DEWSBURY 24; Leigh East 12 BRADFORD 24; SALFORD 44 Cutsyke 4; WARRINGTON 20 Huddersfield 4; SHEFFIELD 19 Hull 6

FIRST ROUND
BARROW 13 Hunslet 8; BRADFORD 50 Leigh 4; Bramley 6 OLDHAM 38; Castleford 4 WIGAN 28; Doncaster 4 WIDNES 30; HALIFAX 46 Fulham 6; KEIGHLEY 36 Runcorn 4; LEEDS 40 Dewsbury 20; Nottingham 10 WHITEHAVEN 26; ROCHDALE 14 Chorley 10; Ryedale-York 1 WARRINGTON 8; SALFORD 36 Batley 14; SHEFFIELD 19 Featherstone 12; Swinton 8 ST HELENS 18; WAKEFIELD 18 Trafford 7; WORKINGTON 18 Hull KR 12

SECOND ROUND
Barrow 4 WIDNES 28; BRADFORD 5 Leeds 0; HALIFAX 46 Whitehaven 12; Keighley 10 WARRINGTON 42; Rochdale 4 WIGAN 72; ST HELENS 16 Wakefield 2; Sheffield 16 SALFORD 19; Workington 15 OLDHAM 20

QUARTER-FINALS
Halifax 16 ST HELENS 24; OLDHAM 40 Salford 3; Warrington 14 WIDNES 26; WiGAN 32 Bradford 2

SEMI-FINALS
WIGAN 30 Oldham 16; ST HELENS 19 Widnes 2

FINAL
Wembley Apr 27
WIGAN 13 St Helens 8
Wigan: Hampson; Myers, Iro, Bell, Botica; Edwards, Gregory; Lucas (Clarke), Dermott (Goulding), Platts, Betts, Clarke (Goodway), Hanley
Scorers: *Tries* Myers, Botica; *Goals* Botica (2); Drop Goal Gregory
St Helens: Veivers (Connolly); Hunte, Ropati, Loughlin (Neill, Veivers), Quirk; Griffiths, Bishop; Neill (Groves), Dwyer, Ward, Harrison, Mann, Cooper
Scorers: *Try* Hunte; *Goals* Bishop (2)
Referee: Jim Smith (Halifax)
Attendance: 75,532
Lance Todd Trophy: Dennis Betts
Teams underlined beat opposition from a higher division

WEMBLEY RECORDS 1991
Wigan won for the 11th time in 17 Wembley appearances and fourth year in succession. Ellery Hanley became the first captain to lift the trophy three years in succession, and equalled the records of Derek Turner, Eric Ashton and Alex Murphy as skipper of three winning teams. Andy Gregory appeared in his seventh final at Wembley and collected a sixth winners' medal, equalling the record.

100-POINT TEAMS

LEEDS 102 Coventry 0	League, Apr 12, 1913
HUDDERSFIELD 119 Swinton Park R 2	Challenge Cup, Feb 28, 1914
WIGAN 116 Flimby & Fothergill 0	Challenge Cup, Feb 15, 1925
ST HELENS 112 Carlisle 0	Lancashire Cup, Sep 14, 1986
HULL KR 100 Nottingham City 6	Yorkshire Cup, Aug 19, 1990

WIGAN'S CUP RUN

Since losing to Oldham in the 1st round of the Challenge Cup on Feb 4, 1987, Wigan have won 20 consecutive Challenge Cup ties:

1987-88
Round 1:	Bradford (h)	2-0
Round 2:	Leeds (h)	30-14
Round 3:	Widnes (h)	10-1
Semi-final:	Salford (n)	34-4
Final:	Halifax (n)	32-12

1988-89
Round 1:	Doncaster (a)	38-6
Round 2:	Bradford (a)	17-4
Round 3:	Oldham (a)	12-4
Semi-final:	Warrington (n)	13-6
Final:	St Helens (n)	27-0

1989-90
Round 1:	Hull KR (a)	6-4
Round 2:	Dewsbury (h)	30-6
Round 3:	Wakefield (a)	26-14
Semi-final:	St Helens (n)	20-14
Final:	Warrington (n)	36-14

1990-91
Round 1:	Castleford (a)	28-14
Round 2:	Rochdale (a)	72-4
Round 3:	Bradford (h)	32-2
Semi-final:	Oldham (n)	30-16
Final:	St Helens (n)	13-8

Shaun Edwards is the only player to have appeared in all 20 matches

STONES BITTER PREMIERSHIP
Division One

FIRST ROUND
Castleford 20 LEEDS 24; HULL 28 St Helens 12; WIDNES 46 Bradford 10; Wigan 26 FEATHERSTONE 31

SEMI-FINALS
HULL 10 Leeds 7; WIDNES 42 Featherstone 28

FINAL
Old Trafford, May 12
HULL 14 Widnes 4
Attendance: 42,043
Harry Sunderland Trophy: Greg Mackey (Hull)

Division Two

FIRST ROUND
HALIFAX 42 Fulham 24; Ryedale-York 6 LEIGH 11; SALFORD 26 Carlisle 12; Swinton 12 WORKINGTON 19

SEMI-FINALS
SALFORD 26 Workington 6 (after 9-9 draw); HALIFAX 32 Leigh 8

FINAL
Old Trafford, May 12
SALFORD 27 Halifax 20
Attendance: 42,043

REGAL TROPHY

SEMI-FINALS
Rochdale 2 BRADFORD 13; Widnes 4 WARRINGTON 8

FINAL
Headingley, Jan 12
WARRINGTON 12 Bradford 2
Attendance: 11,154

GRÜNHALLE LANCASHIRE CUP

SEMI-FINALS
WIDNES 20 Warrington 4; SALFORD 16 Leigh 7

FINAL
Central Park, Wigan, Sep 30
WIDNES 24 Salford 18

JOHN SMITH'S YORKSHIRE CUP

SEMI-FINALS
CASTLEFORD 29 Hull KR 6; WAKEFIELD 25 Dewsbury 2

FINAL
Elland Road, Leeds, Sep 23
CASTLEFORD 11 Wakefield 8
Attendance: 11,800

CIS CHARITY SHIELD

Vetch Field, Swansea City FC, Aug 19
WIDNES 24 Wigan 8
Attendance: 11,178

CLUBS SHARING SOCCER GROUNDS

RUGBY CLUB	GROUND	SOCCER CLUB
Chorley	Victory Park	Chorley FC
Highfield	Hoghton Road	St Helens Town FC
Hunslet	Elland Road	Leeds United FC
Scarborough Pirates	Seamer Road	Scarborough FC
Trafford Borough	Moss Lane	Altrincham FC
Rochdale Hornets	Spotland	Rochdale FC

SYDNEY GRAND FINAL
Melbourne, Sep 22
CANBERRA RAIDERS 18 Penrith 14

TEST MATCHES 1990-91
Avignon, Dec 2
France 4 AUSTRALIA 60
Perpignan, Dec 9
France 10 AUSTRALIA 34
Melbourne, Jul 3
Australia 8 NEW ZEALAND 24
Sydney, Jul 24
AUSTRALIA 44 New Zealand 0
Brisbane, Jul 31
AUSTRALIA 40 New Zealand 12
Port Moresby, Jul 7
Papua New Guinea 18 FRANCE 20

AUSTRALIA'S TOUR OF BRITAIN

Date	Opponents	Results	Score	Attendance
Oct 7	St Helens	won	34-4	15,216
Oct 10	Wakefield T	won	36-18	8,000
Oct 14	Wigan	won	34-6	25,101
Oct 17	Cumbria	won	42-10	6,750
(at Workington)				
Oct 21	Leeds	won	22-10	16,037
Oct 27	Great Britain	lost	12-19	54,569
Oct 31	Warrington	won	26-6	10,200
Nov 4	Castleford	won	28-8	9,033
Nov 6	Halifax	won	36-18	8,730
Nov 10	Great Britain	won	14-10	44,615
Nov 14	Hull	won	34-4	13,500
Nov 18	Widnes	won	15-8	14,666
Nov 24	Great Britain	won	14-0	32,000

FIRST TEST
Wembley Stadium, Oct 27

GREAT BRITAIN	19	Australia	12

T: Eastwood 2, Offiah
G: Eastwood 3
DG: Schofield

T: Meninga, McGaw
G: Meninga 2

Great Britain: Hampson; Eastwood, D Powell, Gibson, Offiah; Schofield, A Gregory; Harrison, Jackson, Dixon, Betts, R Powell, Hanley
Australia: Belcher; Hancock, Meninga, McGaw, Ettingshausen; Stuart, Langer; Roach, Kerrod Walters, Bella, Sironen, Cartwright, Lindner
Attendance: 54,569 (British record for a representative match)

SECOND TEST
Old Trafford, Nov 10

Great Britain	10	AUSTRALIA	14

T: Dixon, Loughlin
G: Eastwood

T: Shearer, Lyons Meninga
G: Meninga

Great Britain: Hampson; Eastwood, D Powell, Gibson, Offiah (Loughlin); Schofield, A Gregory; Harrison (Ward), Jackson, Platt, Betts, Dixon, Hanley
Australia: Belcher; Ettingshausen, Meninga, Daley, Shearer; Lyons, Stuart; Roach, Elias, Lazarus, Sironen, Lindner, Mackay
Attendance: 46,615

RULE BRITANNIA (WELL, ALMOST)

❝It just goes to show, a good little 'un will beat a good big 'un every time.❞
Mal Reilly, Great Britain coach, on the win at Wembley

"One of the finest rugby footballers I have seen since the war...in any code."
Terry O'Connor, Daily Mail Rugby Union writer, on Hanley

"Ellery is one hell of a player and I don't think any of us begrudge what he is making, but without being fancy, we should all put something back."
Steve Roach, Australian forward, on Ellery Hanley's refusal to be interviewed.

"Did I run 80 metres? It felt more like 800 metres."
Ricky Stuart, on making the try that tied the series in the Second Test

"If I hadn't dived over the line I'd have probably been through the stand and halfway down the motorway to London."
Mal Meninga, Australian captain, on the same try

"I don't think they quite realise back home that we are taking part in a truly epic series, one for all-time history. That's the measure of the improvement and strength of the British team."
Mal Meninga

"A convert is always the more ferociously committed and I've spent all my career aiming to put one across the Brits."
Bobby Fulton, Australian coach (born Warrington, Lancs)

"Not once on this trip have we come up against a slow, slob forward with his beer belly hanging over his shorts. On the last tour they were ten a penny, certainly in the club matches. Before this tour, whatever happened in the first hour, we knew the Brits would lie down and die in the last 20 minutes. Run out of puff and pride, you would. Not any more."
Peter Frilingos, Sydney RL journalist

"Great Britain's improvement has been there for all to see. They have proved that Test football is alive and well.❞❞
Mal Meninga

THIRD TEST
Elland Road, Leeds, Nov 24

Great Britain   0   AUSTRALIA   14
     T: Ettingshausen, Elias
     Meninga
     G: Meninga

Great Britain: Hampson; Eastwood, D Powell, Gibson (Davies), Offiah; Schofield, A Gregory; Harrison (R Powell), Jackson, Platt, Betts, Dixon (M Gregory), Hanley
Australia: Belcher; Shearer (Alexander), Meninga, Daley, Ettingshausen; Lyons, Stuart; Roach, Elias, Lazarus (Gillespie), Sironen (Sargent), Lindner, Mackay (Hasler)
Attendance: 32,000

GREAT BRITAIN v FRANCE
FIRST TEST
Perpignan, Jan 27

France   10   GREAT BRITAIN   45
T: Auroy, Fraisse   T: Schofield 2, Offiah 2
G: Tisseyre   Edwards 2, Betts, Platt
     G: Eastwood 6
     DG: Schofield

Attendance: 5,500
Ellery Hanley captained Great Britain for the 18th time, beating Alan Prescott's record of 17 in 1955-58.
SECOND TEST; Headingley, Feb 16

GREAT BRITAIN   60   France   4
T: Offiah 5, Schofield 3,   T: Pons
   Eastwood, Edwards,
   Hampson
G: Eastwood 8

Attendance: 5,284
Great Britain's record victory in a full international.
Martin Offiah became the first Great Britain player to score five tries in an international.

AWARDS
Man of Steel: Gary Schofield (Leeds)
First Division Player of the Year: Jonathan Davies (Widnes)
Second Division Player of the Year: Tawere Nickau (Ryedale-York)
Coach of the Year: John Monie (Wigan)
Young Player of the Year: Dennis Betts (Wigan)
Referee of the Year: John Holdsworth (Kippax)

———— CHAMPIONS ————

CHALLENGE CUP
12 Wigan 1924, 1929, 1948, 1951, 1958-59, 1965, 1985, 1988-91; **10** Leeds 1910, 1923, 1932, 1936, 1941-42, 1957, 1968, 1977-78; **7** Widnes 1930, 1937, 1964, 1975, 1979, 1981, 1984; **6** Huddersfield 1913, 1915, 1920, 1933, 1945, 1953; **5** Halifax 1903-4, 1931, 1939, 1987; St Helens 1956, 1961, 1966, 1972, 1976; Wakefield Trinity 1909, 1946, 1960, 1962-63; Warrington 1905, 1907, 1950, 1954, 1974; **4** Bradford Northern 1906, 1944, 1947, 1949; Castleford 1935, 1969-70, 1986; **3** Batley 1897-98, 1901; Featherstone Rovers 1967, 1973, 1983; Oldham 1899, 1925, 1927; Swinton 1900, 1926, 1928; **2** Broughton Rangers 1902, 1911; Dewsbury 1912, 1943; Hull 1914, 1982; Hunslet 1908, 1934; Leigh 1921, 1971; **1** Barrow 1955; Hull KR 1980; Rochdale Hornets 1922; Salford 1938; Workington T 1952

PREMIERSHIP TROPHY
6 Widnes 1980, 1982-83, 1988-90; **3** St Helens 1976-77, 1985; **2** Hull KR 1981, 1984; Leeds 1975, 1979; **1** Bradford Northern 1978; Warrington 1986; Wigan 1987; Hull 1991

DIVISION TWO PREMIERSHIP
2 Oldham 1988, 1990; **1** Swinton 1987, Sheffield E 1989; Salford 1991

CHAMPIONSHIP
(1906-73)
9 Wigan 1909, 1922, 1926, 1934, 1946-47, 1950, 1952, 1960 **7** Huddersfield 1912-13, 1915, 1929-30, 1949, 1962; **6** St Helens 1932, 1953, 1959, 1966, 1970-71; **5** Hull 1920-21, 1936, 1956, 1958; **4** Salford 1914, 1933, 1937, 1939; Swinton 1927-28, 1931, 1935 **3** Leeds 1961, 1969, 1972; Oldham 1910-11, 1957; Warrington 1948, 1954-55 **2** Halifax 1907, 1965; Hull KR 1923, 1925; Hunslet 1908, 1938; Wakefield Trinity 1967-68; **1** Batley 1924, Dewsbury 1973; Leigh 1906; Workington Town 1951
Not Held 1963-64

DIVISION ONE
(1974-91)
3 Hull KR 1979, 1984-85; Widnes 1978, 1988-89; Wigan 1987, 1990-1991; **2** Bradford Northern 1980-81; Salford 1974, 1976; **1** Featherstone Rovers 1977; Halifax 1986; Hull 1983; Leigh 1982; St Helens 1975

DIVISION TWO
(1974-91)
3 Leigh 1978, 1986, 1989 **2** Barrow 1976, 1984; Hull 1977, 1979; Oldham 1982, 1988; **1** Bradford Northern; Featherstone Rovers 1980; Fulham 1983; Huddersfield 1975; Hull KR 1990; Hunslet 1987; Salford 1991; Swinton 1985; York 1981

REGAL TROPHY
(Formerly John Player Special Trophy)
5 Wigan 1983, 1986-87, 1989-90 **4** Warrington 1974, 1978, 1981, 1991; **2** Bradford Northern 1975, 1980; Leeds 1973, 1984; Widnes 1976, 1979 **1** Castleford 1977; Halifax 1972; Hull 1982; Hull KR 1985; St Helens 1988

LANCASHIRE COUNTY CUP
Wins:
20 Wigan 1906, 1909-10, 1913, 1923, 1929, 1939, 1947-52, 1967, 1972, 1974, 1986-89; **10** St Helens 1927, 1954, 1961-65, 1968-69, 1985; **9** Oldham 1908, 1911, 1914, 1920, 1925, 1934, 1957-59; Warrington 1922, 1930, 1933, 1938, 1960, 1966, 1981, 1983, 1990; **7** Widnes 1946, 1975-77, 1979-80, 1991; **5** Salford 1932, 1935-37, 1973; **4** Leigh 1953, 1956, 1971, 1982; Swinton 1926, 1928, 1940, 1970; **3** Rochdale Hornets 1912, 1915, 1919; **2** Barrow 1955, 1984; **1** Workington Town 1978

YORKSHIRE COUNTY CUP
Wins:
17 Leeds 1922, 1929, 1931, 1933, 1935-36, 1938, 1959, 1969, 1971, 1973-74, 1976-77, 1980-81, 1989; **12** Huddersfield 1910, 1912, 1914-15, 1919-20, 1927, 1932, 1939, 1951, 1953, 1958; Bradford Northern 1907, 1941-42, 1944, 1946, 1949-50, 1954, 1966, 1979, 1988, 1990; **9** Wakefield Trinity 1911, 1925, 1947-48, 1952, 1957, 1961-62, 1965; **7** Hull KR 1921, 1930, 1967-68, 1972, 1975, 1986; **5** Halifax 1909, 1945, 1955-56, 1964, Hull 1924, 1970, 1983-85; **4** Castleford 1978, 1982, 1987, 1991; **3** Dewsbury 1926, 1928, 1943; Hunslet 1906, 1908, 1963; York 1923, 1934, 1937; **2** Featherstone Rovers 1940, 1960; **1** Batley 1913
(Years indicate second half of season.)

CHARITY SHIELD
Winners:
1985 Wigan; 1986 Halifax; 1987 Wigan; 1988 Widnes; 1989 Widnes; 1990 Widnes; 1991 Widnes

WORLD CUP
Wins:
6 Australia 1957, 1968, 1970, 1975*, 1977, 1988; **3** Great Britain 1954, 1960, 1972
* Known as The International Championship

SYDNEY PREMIERSHIP
Most Wins:
20 South Sydney 1908-09, 1914, 1918, 1925-29, 1931-32, 1950-51, 1953-55, 1967-68, 1970-71; **15** St George 1941, 1949, 1956-66, 1977, 1979; **11** Balmain 1915-17, 1919-20, 1924, 1939, 1944, 1946-47, 1969; Eastern Suburbs 1911-13, 1923, 1935-37, 1940, 1945, 1974-75

CLUBS WHO HAVE JOINED AND LEFT THE RUGBY LEAGUE SINCE THE WAR
1945	**In** Workington Town
	Out St Helens Recs, Leigh
1946	**In** Leigh
1948	**In** Whitehaven
1951	**In** Cardiff, Doncaster
1952	**Out** Cardiff
1954	**In** Blackpool Borough
1955	**Out** Belle Vue Rangers
1963	**Out** Bradford Northern
1964	**In** Bradford Northern (*)
1980	**In** Fulham
1981	**In** Cardiff City, Carlisle
1983	**In** Kent Invicta
1984	**In** Mansfield Marksmen, Sheffield Eagles
1985	**Out** Southend (formerly Kent Invicta), Bridgend (formerly Cardiff City)
1989	**In** Chorley
1991	**In** Scarborough

(*) Bradford Northern disbanded after 13 matches of the 1963-64 season but were re-formed for the start of the 1964-65 season.

LANCE TODD/HARRY SUNDERLAND WINNERS
(Since 1976)

	Lance Todd*	Harry Sunderland+
1976	Geoff Pimblett *St Helens*	George Nicholls *St Helens*
1977	Steve Pitchford *Leeds*	Geoff Pimblett *St Helens*
1978	George Nicholls *St Helens*	Bob Haigh *Bradford Northern*
1979	Dave Topliss *Wakefield Trinity*	Kevin Dick *Leeds*
1980	Brian Lockwood *Hull Kingston Rovers*	Mal Aspey *Widnes*
1981	Mick Burke *Widnes*	Len Casey *Hull Kingston Rovers*
1982	Eddie Cunningham *Widnes*	Mick Burke *Widnes*
1983	David Hobbs *Featherstone Rovers*	Tony Myler *Widnes*
1984	Joe Lydon *Widnes*	John Dorahy *Hull Kingston Rovers*
1985	Brett Kenny *Wigan*	Harry Pinner *St Helens*

1986	Bob Beardmore *Castleford*	Les Boyd *Warrington*
1987	Graham Eadie *Halifax*	Joe Lydon *Wigan*
1988	Andy Gregory *Wigan*	David Hulme *Widnes*
1989	Ellery Hanley *Wigan*	Alan Tait *Widnes*
1990	Andy Gregory *Wigan*	Alan Tait *Widnes*
1991	Dennis Betts *Wigan*	Greg Mackey *Hull*

* Man of match in Challenge Cup Final
+ Man of match in Premiership Final

MAN OF STEEL
1978	George Nicholls (St Helens)
1979	Doug Laughton (Widnes)
1980	George Fairbairn (Wigan)
1981	Ken Kelly (Warrington)
1982	Mick Morgan (Oldham)
1983	Allan Agar (Featherstone R)
1984	Joe Lydon (Widnes)
1985	Ellery Hanley (Bradford N)
1986	Gavin Miller (Hull KR)
1987	Ellery Hanley (Wigan)

1988   Martin Offiah (Widnes)
1989   Ellery Hanley (Wigan)
1990   Shaun Edwards (Wigan)
1991   Gary Schofield (Leeds)

RECORDS

ALL FIRST-CLASS MATCHES
Single Game Records
Biggest win: 119-2 Huddersfield v Swinton Park Rangers (Challenge Cup) 1914; **Most tries in a match:** 11 George Henry West, Hull Kingston Rovers v Brookland Rovers (Challenge Cup) 1905; **Most goals in a match:** 22 Jim Sullivan, Wigan v Flimby & Fothergill (Challenge Cup, 1925: **Most points in a match:** 53 George Henry West (as above)

Season Records
Most tries: 80 Albert Rosenfeld (Huddersfield) 1913-14; **Most goals:** 221 David Watkins (Salford) 1972-3; **Most points:** 496 (194 goals, 36 tries) Lewis Jones (Leeds) 1956-7

Career Records
Most tries: 796 Brian Bevan (Warrington & Blackpool Borough) 1946-64; **Most goals:** 2,859 Jim Sullivan (Wigan) 1921-46; **Most points:** 6,220 Neil Fox (Wakefield Trinity, Bradford Northern, Hull Kingston Rovers, York, Bramley, Huddersfield) 1956-79; **Most appearances:** 921 Jim Sullivan (Wigan) 1921-46; **Most consecutive club appearances:** 239 Keith Elwell (Widnes) May 1977-Sep 1982; **Most consecutive games scoring points:** 92 David Watkins (Salford) Aug 1972-Apr 1974

INTERNATIONAL MATCHES
Most appearances: 60 Jim Sullivan, Wales, Great Britain & Other Nationalities, 1921-39; **Most tries:** 45 Mick Sullivan, Great Britain & England 1954-63; **Most goals:** 160 Jim Sullivan; **Most points:** 329 Jim Sullivan; **Biggest win:** 70-8 Australia v Papua New Guinea, 1988

ALL-TIME WORST RUGBY LEAGUE RECORDS
(Min qualification 26 matches)

		P	W	D	L	F	A	Pts
1906-07	Liverpool C	30	0	0	30	76	1398	0
1989-90	Runcorn H	28	0	0	28	216	935	0
1912-13	Coventry	27	0	1	26	157	896	1
1914-15	Runcorn	27	0	1	16	84	590	1
1989-90	Barrow	26	1	0	25	201	1133	2
1984-85	Bridgend	28	1	0	27	258	966	2
1976-77	Doncaster	26	1	0	25	243	704	2
1990-91	**Rochdale H**	26	1	0	25	317	912	2

1992

Jan 11 Regal Trophy Final; Jan 25-26 Challenge Cup First Round; Feb 8-9 Challenge Cup Second Round; Feb 16 France v Great Britain, Test match; Feb 22-23 Challenge Cup Third Round; Mar 7 Great Britain v France, Test Match; Mar 14-28 Challenge Cup Semi-finals; May 2 CHALLENGE CUP FINAL (Wembley); May 17 Premiership Final (Old Trafford).

GREAT BRITAIN TOUR
May 24 v Papua New Guinea Selection (Lae); May 27 v Papua New Guinea Selection (Goroka); May 31 v PAPUA NEW GUINEA (Port Moresby); Jun 3 v Queensland Residents (Townsville); Jun 6 v Canberra; Jun 8 v Illawarra (Woolongong); Jun 12 v AUSTRALIA, First Test (Sydney); Jun 16 v New South Wales Country (Parkes); Jun 19 v Parramatta; Jun 23 v Newcastle; Jun 26 v AUSTRALIA, Second Test (Melbourne); Jun 30 v Gold Coast (Tweed Heads); Jul 3 v AUSTRALIA, Third Test (Brisbane); Jul 8 v Auckland; Jul 12 v NEW ZEALAND, First Test (Palmerston North); Jul 15 v Canterbury (Christchurch); Jul 19 v NEW ZEALAND, Second Test (Auckland)

RUGBY UNION

THE RED ROSE RISES

After two years of near-misses, England finally established their dominance over the Five Nations Championship by beating the field in 1991. The significance of this success looked highly questionable a couple of months later when, on the eve of the World Cup, the southern hemisphere teams again proved too good even for the best of the home countries and a different class from the worst.

Nearer home, in the familiar surroundings of a northern winter, England found it easy to believe in winning the World Cup. They began by exorcising the Arms Park ghost - beating Wales away after 28 fruitless years - in spectacular fashion and continued by beating Scotland (methodically), Ireland (rather luckily) and France (thrillingly). France were only beaten 21-19, and were within one kick of winning the Grand Slam themselves and turning Will Carling's team into rugby's perpetual nearly men.

In none of these games did England produce any of the excitement that marked their rugby a year earlier. They set out to avoid errors and managed to stick with the same starting line-up throughout; but the team that was cocky enough to run kickable penalties at Murrayfield in 1990 played with a dour conservatism that produced only five tries all tournament, the lowest-ever by a Grand Slam side and five fewer than winless Ireland. The England-France game will be remembered most for one try by the losers: created for Saint-André by Serge Blanco from an apparently hopeless position.

Most of the excitement around England surrounded their performances off the field. After the Cardiff win, they refused to speak to the press and refused even to say why. However, it seemed unconnected, for once, with anything that had been written and everything to do with the endless negotiations over international rugby's new rules in which the game tried to stay half-virginal, allowing the players to be amateur but rich. Complicated regulations were brought in allowing players to be paid for making speeches and opening supermarkets but not for playing. The English RFU attempted to interpret these regulations far more strictly than other countries. Their England squad, meanwhile, appointed the former England cricket captain Bob Willis as their agent then abruptly sacked him and seemed to spend their weeks in a whirl of intrigue. It was a wonder they found time to play at all.

But theirs were the problems of success. Wales would have loved those. Their efforts in the Five Nations, which culminated in a team with seven changes getting walloped six tries to nil by France, were bad enough. But that was nothing: Wales then had to tour Australia. They lost 71-8 to New South Wales, which was one way of ensuring that the 63-6 defeat in the Test that followed could be construed as an improvement. The Welsh players showed more fight afterwards: there was a punch-up amongst them at the after-match dinner and the captain Paul Thorburn threatened photographers at Heathrow far more vigorously than he had threatened the Wallabies. Thorburn then quit international rugby and was replaced as Captain by Ieuan Evans; Ron Waldron, the coach, was taken ill and forced to stand down. The Baptist Union of Wales condemned the drink trade's domination of the game and the Rev Dr Dafydd Davies of Cardiff said a change of habits would be more effective than a change of coach. Richie Griffiths, a Wales B international, was banned for two years by the Welsh Rugby Union after testing positive for the anabolic steroid Nondrolon, but officials rejected allegations that six unnamed players were also taking steroids; if they were, they were presumably taking them wrong.

England also lost heavily to Australia - 40-15 - at the end of a patchy summer tour. After beating the Emerging Wallabies, England players were invited to a debate in a hotel in Gosford on the subject "Are Pommies whingers?"

THE CRICKET SCORES: WALES 71-8, 63-6 ETC...

"I thought the teletext had gone haywire.**"**
Max Boyce

"Wales were, frankly, nothing. It was sad to see."
Bob Dwyer, Australian coach

"There may not be any coal mines worked in the Valleys now, but Wales are the pits."
Chris Barnett, The Guardian

"We may not be good enough anyway, but what I won't accept is that there aren't Welsh club players who could have done better."
Mike Hall, Welsh centre

"The Welsh Rugby Union should turn to the former stars of the Seventies to help them through this crisis. You must have someone who can command the respect of the players and the public."
JJ Williams, star of the Seventies

"They would struggle to put on a convincing win against sides like the United States and South Korea."
Nick Farr-Jones, Australian captain

"The tour was very enjoyable. Welsh rugby is all right and will survive."
Ron Waldron

"Everything about the game now seems drink-related. I would suggest it is almost impossible for such a culture to produce a team where physical prowess is so necessary."
Rev Dr Dafydd Davies, Welsh Baptist minister

"If the Baptists have any particular influence or divine intervention we would be happy to receive it."
Jonathan Price, WRU official

"If you were looking for indications in recent years of performance-enhancement, I would not think that Welsh rugby was the natural starting point."
Denis Evans, Welsh RU secretary, on allegations of steroid use amongst players

"I haven't felt like this since my uncle's funeral in 1986. We were in the cemetery when somebody got the score from the Arms Park: Wales 15 France 23. It cast a gloom over the whole proceedings.""
Max Boyce

When Australia also beat New Zealand in the opening Bledisloe Cup match, some London bookmakers reacted by making them the new World Cup favourites. The All-Blacks had themselves endured an indifferent tour of France and encountered the first murmurs that their team was over the top. Argentina had an unsuccessful tour of the British Isles and their schoolboy prop Federico Mendez was sent off during the 51-0 defeat against England for punching Paul Ackford and putting him out of the game. Hugo Porta, the long-standing Argentine captain, was dropped before the tour was over and later appointed his country's ambassador to South Africa.

New Zealand protested when the Soviet touring party to visit them included the half-back Alexander Bychkov, who was supposedly permanently banned from the international team for violence on the tour of Australia a year earlier; the Russians insisted the name was their equivalent of John Smith and that this was a different one.

England's success near home even extended to the Welsh Cup final. Two English players - scrum-half Rupert Moon and second-row Tony Copsey - dominated the game, won by Llanelli for the seventh time, with a 24-9 win over Pontypool. Neath won the new Welsh League, leading throughout, although their run of 51 consecutive victories over Welsh clubs was halted by Newport on December 29. Bath regained their control of English League rugby but lost at home in the Cup - to Leicester - for the first time since 1982. Harlequins won the Cup, beating Northampton in extra time. The Edinburgh club Boroughmuir won a tight race for the Scottish League, becoming the first club from outside the Borders to win the title since 1979. The most passionate win of the year was Cornwall's triumph in the County Championship, their first since 1908; a 103-year-old Redruth supporter was among the Cornish hordes present at Twickenham and remembered the previous win. The most improbable victory was that of Widnes over Orrell in the Lancashire Cup; the town is also rumoured to have a Rugby League team.

Oxford University staged a re-run of the great Boat Race dispute when the captain Mark Egan left out two internationals who opposed his leadership, Brian Smith and Troy Coker, but they won the Varsity match anyway. A total of 189 drivers were breathalysed by the police after the game; not one failed.

The RFU working party on injuries called for the crash tackle to be outlawed; its officials stopped pupils at St Joseph's College, Ipswich, playing in helmets. Mark Rice of the Gordano club, Bristol, was jailed for six months for punching an opponent and breaking a bone in his face. Didcot's second team and their opponents, Pennanians from Slough, were sent off for fighting. The referee asked spectators to help break up the fight; they then joined in too.

Graham Dawe, farmer and former England hooker, named his prize bull Mr Chilcott. The United States won the inaugural women's World Cup in Wales. Three of the 5,000 participants (aged between 30 and 84) in the Golden Oldies festival in Perth, Australia died during the event. The International Rugby Board reinstated Ian Williams, a Welsh player who moved to rugby league; he was 76. Cyril Turner was reported to have finally given up playing for Hampshire Heathens; he was 80.

Bridgend supporter Ieuan Jones lost his false teeth while cheering for his team at Newbridge. The Newport Saracens strip went up in flames at a laundrette because the heat from the driers mixed with lingering traces of liniment. Thieves who broke into a player's car in Poole, Dorset ignored the radio and stole his jockstrap.

━━━━1990-91━━━━

INTERNATIONAL CHAMPIONSHIP
National Stadium, Cardiff, Jan 19
Wales 6 ENGLAND 25
Wales: P H Thorburn (capt); I C Evans, M G Ring,I S Gibbs, S P Ford; N R Jenkins, R N Jones (C JBridges); B R Williams, K H Phillips, P Knight,G D Llewellyn, G O Llewellyn, G M George, A JCarter, P Arnold
P: Thorburn, Jenkins
England: S G Hodgkinson; N J Heslop, W D CCarling (Capt), J C Guscott, R Underwood; C RAndrew, R J Hill; J Leonard, B C Moore, J AProbyn, P A Ackford, W A Dooley, M C Teague, P JWinterbottom, D Richards
T: Teague P: Hodgkinson 7
England's first win in Cardiff since 1963. Hodgkinson's seven penalties set a world record for one man in an international between International Board countries

Parc des Princes, Jan 19
FRANCE 15 Scotland 9
France: S Blanco (capt); J-B Lafond, S Mesnel, D Charvet, P Lagisquet; D Camberabero, P Berbizier; G Lascube, P Marocco, P Ondarts, M Tachdjian, O Roumat, X Blond, L Cabannes, M Cecillon
P: Camberabero 2 DG: Camberabero 2, Blanco
Scotland: G Hastings; A Stanger, S Hastings, S Lineen, A Moore; C Chalmers, G Armstrong; D Sole (capt), K Milne, P Burnell, C Gray, D Cronin, D Turnbull, J Jeffrey, D White
P: Chalmers 2 DG: Chalmers
Serge Blanco beat Mike Gibson's record of 81 caps

Murrayfield, Feb 2
SCOTLAND 32 Wales 12
Scotland: G Hastings; A Stanger, S Hastings, S Lineen, A Moore; C Chalmers, G Armstrong; D Sole (capt), J Allan (Milne), P Burnell, C Gray, D Cronin, D Turnbull, J Jeffrey, D White
T: White 2, Armstrong, Chalmers; C: Chalmers, G Hastings; P: G Hastings 2, Chalmers; DG: Chalmers
Wales: P H Thorburn (capt) (Clement); I C Evans, M G Ring, I S Gibbs, S P Ford; N R Jenkins, R N Jones; B R Williams, K H Phillips, P Knight, G D Llewellyn, G O Llewellyn, G M George, A J Carter, P Arnold
T: Ford; C: Thorburn; PG: Thorburn 2
Craig Chalmers became first man since J-P Romeu for France against England in 1974 to score a try, conversion, penalty and dropped goal in an international championship match

Lansdowne Road, Feb 2
Ireland 13 FRANCE 21
Ireland: K J Murphy; S P Geoghegan, B J Mullin, M J Kiernan, K J Hooks; B A Smith, R Saunders (capt); J J Fitzgerald, S J Smith, D C Fitzgerald, M J Galwey, B J Rigney, P M Matthews, G F Hamilton, B F Robinson
T: S J Smith; PG: Kiernan 3
France: S Blanco (capt); J-B Lafond, S Mesnel, D Charvet, P Lagisquet (P Saint-André); D Camberabero, P Berbizier; G Lascube, P Marocco, P Ondarts, O Roumat, M Tachdjian, X Blond, L Cabannes, M Cecillon
T: Lagisquet, Cabannes; C: Camberabero 2; PG: Camberabero 3
Ireland captain Rob Saunders was becamethe first man since Nigel Melville (England) in 1984 to skipper a side on his international debut

Twickenham, Feb 16
ENGLAND 21 Scotland 12
England: S G Hodgkinson; N J Heslop, W D C Carling (capt), J C Guscott, R Underwood; C R Andrew, R J Hill; J Leonard, B C Moore, J A Probyn, P A Ackford, W A Dooley, M C Teague, P J Winterbottom, D Richards
T: Heslop; C: Hodgkinson; PG: Hodgkinson 5
Scotland: G Hastings; A Stanger, S Hastings, S Lineen, A Moore; C Chalmers, G Armstrong; D Sole (capt), K Milne, P Burnell, C Gray, D Cronin, D Turnbull, J Jeffrey, D White
PG: Chalmers 4

National Stadium, Cardiff, Feb 16
Wales 21 Ireland 21
Wales: P H Thorburn (capt); I C Evans, M G Ring, I S Gibbs, S P Ford; N R Jenkins, C J Bridges; M Griffiths, K H Phillips, J D Davies, G D Llewellyn, P Arnold, E W Lewis, M S Morris, P T Davies
T: Arnold, Jenkins; C: Thorburn 2; PG: Thorburn 2; DG: Jenkins
Ireland: J E Staples (K J Murphy); S P Geoghegan, B J Mullin, M J Kiernan, D J Curtis, D M Clarke; B A Smith, R Saunders (capt); J J Fitzgerald, S J Smith, D C Fitzgerald, M J Galwey, B J Rigney, P M Matthews, G F Hamilton, B F Robinson
T: Staples, Mullin, Clarke, Geoghegan; C: B Smith; DG: B Smith

Lansdowne Road, Mar 3
Ireland 7 ENGLAND 16
Ireland: J E Staples; S P Geoghegan, B J Mullin, D J Curtis, K D Crossan; B A Smith, R Saunders (capt); J J Fitzgerald, S J Smith, D C Fitzgerald, B J Rigney, N P J Francis, P M Matthews, G F Hamilton, B F Robinson
T: Geoghegan; P: B Smith
England: S G Hodgkinson; N J Heslop, J C Guscott, W D C Carling (capt), R Underwood; C R Andrew, R J Hill; J Leonard, B C Moore, J A Probyn, P A Ackford, W A Dooley, M C Teague, P J Winterbottom, D Richards
T: Underwood, Teague; C: Hodgkinson; P: Hodgkinson 2
Ireland led until nine minutes from the end

Parc des Princes, Mar 3
FRANCE 36 Wales 3
France: S Blanco (capt); J-B Lafond, S Mesnel, P Sella (E Bonneval), P Saint-André; D Camberabero, P Berbizier; P Ondarts, P Marocco, G Lascube, J-F Gourragne, O Roumat, X Blond, L Cabannes, C Deslandes
T: Sella, Lafond, Mesnel, Roumat, Saint-André, Blanco; C: Camberabero 2, Blanco; P: Camberabero 2
Wales: P H Thorburn (capt); I C Evans, M G Ring, I S Gibbs, A Emyr; N R Jenkins, C J Bridges; M Griffiths, K H Phillips, J D Davies, G D Llewellyn, P Arnold, E W Lewis, M S Morris, P T Davies
P: Thorburn

Twickenham, Mar 16
ENGLAND 21 France 19
England: S G Hodgkinson; N J Heslop, W D C Carling (capt), J C Guscott, R Underwood; C R Andrew, R J Hill; J Leonard, B C Moore, J A Probyn, P A Ackford, W A Dooley, M C Teague, P J Winterbottom, D Richards
T: Underwood; C: Hodgkinson; DG: Andrew; P: Hodgkinson 4
France: S Blanco (capt); J-B Lafond, P Sella, S Mesnel, P Saint-Andre; D Camberabero, P Berbizier; G Lascube, P Marocco, P Ondarts, M Tachdjian (M Cecillon), O Roumat, X Blond, L Cabannes, A Benazzi
T: Saint-André, Camberabero, Mesnel; C: Camberabero 2; P: Camberabero

Murrayfield, Mar 16
SCOTLAND 28 Ireland 25
Scotland: G Hastings; A Stanger, S Hastings, S Lineen, I Tukalo (P Dods); C Chalmers, G Armstrong; D Sole (capt), J Allan, P Burnell, C Gray, D Cronin, D Turnbull, D White, J Jeffrey
T: G Hastings, S Hastings, Stanger; C: Chalmers 2; P: Chalmers 3, G Hastings
Ireland: J E Staples (K J Murphy); S P Geoghegan, B J Mullin, D J Curtis, K D Crossan; B A Smith, R Saunders (capt); J J Fitzgerald, S J Smith, D C Fitzgerald, B J Rigney, N P J Francis, P M Matthews, B F Robinson, G F Hamilton
T: Crossan, Robinson, Geoghegan, Muullin; C: B Smith 3; DG: Smith

FINAL TABLE

	P	W	D	L	F	A	Pts	Tries
England	4	4	0	8	83	44	8	5
France	4	3	0	1	91	46	6	11
Scotland	4	2	0	2	81	73	4	7
Ireland	4	0	1	3	66	86	1	10
Wales	4	0	1	3	42	114	1	3

England's first Grand Slam since 1980
Simon Hodgkinson (England) scored a championship record 60 points, beating the old record of 54 by Jean-Patrick Lescarboura of France in 1984

ENGLAND'S GRAND SLAM YEARS

v.	France	Ireland	Scotland	Wales
1913	20-0 (h)	15-4 (a)	3-0 (h)	12-0 (a)
1914	39-13 (a)	17-12 (h)	16-15 (a)	10-9 (h)
1921	10-6 (a)	15-0 (h)	18-0 (a)	18-3 (h)
1923	12-3 (a)	23-5 (h)	8-6 (a)	7-3 (h)
1924	19-7 (h)	14-3 (a)	19-0 (h)	17-9 (a)
1928	18-8 (h)	7-6 (a)	6-0 (h)	10-8 (a)
1957	9-5 (h)	6-0 (a)	16-3 (h)	3-0 (a)
1980	17-13 (a)	24-9 (h)	30-18 (a)	9-8 (h)
1991	21-19 (h)	16-7 (a)	21-12 (h)	25-6 (a)

MOST PENALTIES IN ONE INTERNATIONAL

8 Mark Wyatt, Canada v Scotland, 1991
7 Hugo Porta, Argentina v France, 1974
7 Simon Hodgkinson, England v Wales1991
6 Don Clarke, New Zealand v Lions, 1959
6 Gerald Bosch, South Africa v France, 1975
6 Gwyn Evans, Wales v France, 1982
6 Ollie Campbell, Ireland v Scotland, 1982
6 Kieran Crowley, New Zealand v England, 1985
6 Ron Andrew, England v Wales, 1986
6 Gavin Hastings, Scotland v France, 1986
6 Michael Lynagh, Australia v France 1986
Crowley and Hastings were both making their international debuts

ENGLAND'S GLORY

❝ It was fabulous. It was Twickenham's loudest and most tumultuous day and a game to rank with any in the history of the Five Nations tournament."
Stephen Jones, Sunday Times, on England v France

"Flippantly, you say this is a dream, but it is more than that. Seven years' hard work and heartache has gone into this...I can't imagine how I would have coped had we lost. It doesn't bear thinking about."
Rob Andrew

"At Murrayfield last year we were a bunch of headless chickens. This time we kept cool. There is more steel in the team."
Rory Underwood

"People haven't exactly been pleased with what they have been doing. But it served a purpose and it's paid off."
Wade Dooley on England's strategy

"LIKE AN OCTOPUS: The English monster got the better of beautiful French tactics. Trapped in the tentacles of the opposing forwards, at least the French were not suffocated."
L'Equipe

"Il est instantané, il est spontané, instinctif. C'est le rugby. Finis."
Serge Blanco, asked if he had planned the great French try at Twickenham

"I am not going to be a cavalier. We cannot play just to please. International sport is not like that."
Will Carling

"I'm the age of Jesus Christ when he was crucified. What better time is there to go?"
Blanco, on retiring

"It may be I only have another year left in me. Everything that is happening around the sport is burning people out. ❞
Will Carling

ARGENTINA IN BRITISH ISLES

Oct 20	Ireland 'B' (Belfast)	lost	12-27
Oct 23	Ireland Students (Cork)	won	23-6
Oct 27	Ireland (Dublin)	lost	18-20
Oct 30	Eastern Counties (Cambridge)	won	28-15
Nov 3	England (Twickenham)	lost	0-51
Nov 6	South of Scotland (Kelso)	won	13-10
Nov 10	Scotland (Edinburgh)	lost	3-49

International Match Details
Landsdowne Road, Oct 27
IRELAND 20 Argentina 18
Ireland: Murphy; Hooks, Mullin (Cunningham), Kiernan, Crossan; Smith, Rolland; Popplewell, McDonald,

D C Fitzgerald, Lenihan, Johns, Mannion, McBride, Lawlor
T: Hooks, Kiernan; P: Kiernan 4
Argentina: Scolni; Ezcurra, Cuseta Silva, Garcia Simon (Arbizu), Jorge; Porta, Crexell; Mendez, le Fort, Cash, Llanes, Sporleder, Garreton, Bertranou, Macome
T: Macombe; C: Porta; P: Porta 4

Twickenham, Nov 3
ENGLAND 51 Argentina 0
England: Hodgkinson; Heslop, Carling, Guscott, Underwood; Andrew, Hill; Leonard, Olver, Probyn, Ackford (Rees), Dooley, Hall, Winterbottom, Richards
T: Underwood 3, Hill, Hall, Guscott 2; C: Hodgkinson 7; P: Hodgkinson 3
Hodgkinson's 23 points broke Douglas Lambert's England record of 22 points in an international set against France at Twickenham in 1911
Argentina: Scolni; Ezcurra, Cuseta Silva, Allen, Jorge; Porta, Camardon; Mendez, le Fort, Cash, Llanes, Sporleder, Garreton, Bertranou, Macome
Murrayfield, Nov 10

SCOTLAND 49 Argentina 3
Scotland: G Hastings; Stanger, S Hastings, Lineen, Moore; Chalmers, Armstrong; Sole, Milne, Burnell, Gray, Weir, Jeffrey, Buchanan-Smith, Marshall
T: Stanger 2, Milne 2, Moore, Armstrong, Gray, G Hastings, Chalmers; C: G Hastings 5; P: G Hastings
Argentina: Angaut; Cuseta Silva, Arbizu, Meson, Allen; Porta (Scolni), Crexell; Aguirre, Cubelli, Cash, Llanes, Sporleder, Garreton, Ezcurra, Bertranou
P: Meson

NEW ZEALAND IN FRANCE
First Test
Nantes, Nov 3
France 3 NEW ZEALAND 24
France: Blanco; Weller, Langlade, Mesnel, Saint-André; Camberabero, Hueber; Ondarts, Armary, Seigne (Marocco), Roumat, Benazzi, Melville, Champ, Rodriguez
P: Camberabero
New Zealand: Crowley; Kirwan, Innes, Little, Wright; Fox, Bachop; McDowell, Fitzpatrick, Lowe, I Jones, G Whetton, A Whetton, M Jones, Brewer (Brooke)
T: Innes, A Whetton; C: Fox 2; P: Fox 3; DG: Fox

Second Test
Paris, Nov 10
France 12 NEW ZEALAND 30
France: Blanco; Lafond, Saint-André, Mesnel, Berty; Camberabero, Sanz; Pujolle, dal Maso, Ondarts, Gourragne, Roumat, Benetton, Benazzi (Cabannes), Deslandes
DG: Camberabero; P: Camberabero 3
New Zealand: Crowley; Kirwan, Innes, Little, Wright; Fox, DG: Camberabero Bachop; McDowell, Fitzpatrick, Lowe, I Jones, G Whetton, A Whetton, M Jones, Brewer
T: Crowley, M Jones; C: Fox 2; P: Fox 6

SCOTLAND IN NORTH AMERICA
Vancouver, May 8

British Columbia	9	SCOTLAND	29
T: Stewart		T: Smith, Stanger, Turnbull,	
C: Graf		Moncrieff, Shiel 2	
PG: Graf		C: P Dods	
		PG: P Dods	

Edmonton, May 11
Alberta 7 SCOTLAND 76
T: Popadynec T: Moncrieff 3, Renwick 2,
PG: L Williams Watt 2, Kirkpatrick 2, Reid,
M Dods 2, Wyllie, Nicol
C: M Dods 10

New York, May 15
USA East 12 SCOTLAND 24
PG: Judge 4 T: Stanger, Nichol, Watt
C: M Dods 3
PG: M Dods 2

Hartford, May 18
United States 12 SCOTLAND 41
PG: Dejong 4 T: Stanger 2, Reid 2,
MacDonald
C: P Dods 3
PG: P Dods 5

Toronto, May 22
Ontario 3 SCOTLAND 44
PG: MacKinnon T: Wylie, M Dods, Nichol
Wilson, Amos, Kirkpatrick
C: P Dods 4
PG: P Dods 4

St John's, May 25
CANADA 24 Scotland 19
PG: Wyatt 8 T: Reid, Stanger
C: P Dods
PG: P Dods 3

FRANCE IN ROMANIA
Only Test
Bucharest, Jun 22
Romania 21 FRANCE 33
T: Dumitras T: Cecillon, Blanco,
C: Nichitean Camberabero, Simon
PG: Nichitean 5 C: Camberabero
PG: Camberabero 5

NEW ZEALAND IN ARGENTINA
First Test
Buenos Aires, Jul 6
Argentina 14 NEW ZEALAND 36
T: Garreton, Carreras T: Earl, Wright
PG: Vidou 2 C: Fox
PG: Fox 5
DG: Crowley

Second Test
Buenos Aires, Jul 13
Argentina 6 NEW ZEALAND 36
PG: Del Castillo 2 T: M Jones, Kirwan, Wright
Brooke
C: Fox 4
PG: Fox 4

WALES IN AUSTRALIA
Perth, Jun 30
Western Australia 6 WALES 22
PG: Johns 2 T: R Jones, D Evans,
A Davies, Lewis
PG: D Evans
DG: A Davies

Brisbane, Jul 7
QUEENSLAND 35 Wales 24
T: Lillicrap 2, T: Webster 2, Ford, Llewellyn
Lynagh, Little, Slattery

C: Lynagh 3 C: Thorburn
PG: Lynagh 3 DG: A Davies 2

Canberra, Jul 10
Australian Capital 3 WALES 7
Territory
PG: Apps T: Legge
PG: Jenkins

Sydney, Jul 14
NEW SOUTH WALES 71 Wales 8
T: Campese 5, Farr-Jones T: Hall, Jones
Gavin, McKenzie, Waugh, Ekert,
Egerton, Roebuck, penalty try
C: Roebuck 8
PG: Roebuck
Wales' biggest ever defeat, surpassing the 54 points conceded against New Zealand in 1988. It was the first time since 1881 they had conceded 13 tries in a match

Rockhampton, Jul 17
Queensland Country XV 7: WALES 35
T: Perrin T: Hall 2, Clement, L Evans 2
PG: Sprecher Penalty try
C: D Evans 4
DG: Davies

Brisbane, Jul 21
AUSTRALIA 63 Wales 6
Australia: Roebuck; Campese, Horan, Little, Egerton;
Lynagh, Farr-Jones (Slattery); Daly, Kearns, McKenzie,
McCall; Eales, Miller, Ofahengaue, Gavin
*T: Horan, Lynagh 2, Ofahengaue, Kearns 2, Roebuck,
Gavin 2, Campese, Egerton, Little; C: Lynagh 6; PG:
Lynagh*
Wales: Thorburn (Clement); I Evans, Gibbs, Hall, Ford, (D
Evans); A Davies, C Bridges; M Davis, Phillips, Williams-
Jones, Arnold, Glyn Llewellyn, Collins, Lewis, P Davies
(Gareth Llewellyn)
PG: Thorburn; DG: A Davies

ENGLAND IN AUSTRALIA AND FIJI
Sydney, Jul 7
NEW SOUTH WALES 21 England 19
T: Toombs, Farr-Jones T: Heslop, Webb,
Underwood
C: Roebuck 2 C: Webb 2
PG: Roebuck 3 PG: Webb

Melbourne, Jul 10
Victoria President's XV 9 ENGLAND 26
T: Sanders T: Hunter, Rees, Hopley
C: Knox Richards, Pears
PG: Knox C: Hodgkinson 3

Brisbane, Jul 14
QUEENSLAND 20 England 14
T: Carozza, Nasser, T: Guscott, Hill, Oti
Scott-Young C: Hodgkinson
C: Lynagh
PG: Lynagh
DG: Lynagh

Lautoka, Jul 16
FIJI 'B' 27 England 13
T: Serevi, Vosanibole, T: Skinner
Tawake PG: Webb 3
C: Serevi 3
PG: Serevi 2
DG: Serevi

Suva, Jul 20

Fiji	12	ENGLAND	28
T: Seru		T: Probyn, Underwood,	
C: Serevi		Andrew	
PG: Serevi		C: Webb 2	
DG: Serevi		PG: Webb 2	
		DG: Andrew 2	

Gosford, New South Wales, Jul 23

Emerging Wallabies	3	ENGLAND	36
PG: Knox		T: Morris 2, Heslop, Hopley,	
		Hunter, Teague	
		C: Hodgkinson 3	
		PG: Hodgkinson	
		DG: Pears	

Sydney, Jul 27

AUSTRALIA	40	England	15

Australia: Roebuck; Campese, Horan, Little, Egerton; Lynagh, Farr-Jones (Slattery); Daly, Kearns, McKenzie, McCall, Eales, Miller, Poidevin, Gavin
T: Campese 2, Ofahengaue 2, Roebuck; C: Lynagh 4; PG: Lynagh 4
England: Webb; Underwood, Guscott, Carling, Oti; Andrew, Hill; Leonard, Moore, Probyn, Ackford, Bayfield, Teague, Winterbottom, Richards
T: Guscott; C: Webb; PG: Webb 3
This was Australia's biggest ever win against England. David Campese increased his world record number of international tries to 40 and Michael Lynagh became the first man to surpass 600 international points

IRELAND IN NAMIBIA

Windhoek, Jul 17

Namibia 'B'	16	IRELAND	45
T: Wentzel 2		T: Wallace 2, Popplewell,	
C: Steenkamp		Smith, D Fitzgerald, Crossan	
PG: Steenkamp 2		PG: Mullin 4, Ahearne 2	
		DG: Mullin	

Windhoek, Jul 20

NAMIBIA	15	Ireland	6
T: Stoop		T: Penalty Try	
C: Coetzee		C: Mullin	
PG: Coetzee 2			
DG: Coetzee			

Clive Norling refereed his, a record 24th international

Keetmanshoop, Jul 23

Namibia South	4	IRELAND	35
T: Van Wielligh		T: Wallace 3, Crossan	
		Galwey	
		C: Ahearne 2, Barry	
		PG: Barry 2, Murphy	

Keetmanshoop, Jul 27

NAMIBIA	26	Ireland	15
T: Stoop, Mans, Maritz,		T: Staples, Cunningham	
Barnard, Coetzee		C: Staples 2	
C: Coetzee 3		DG: Curtis	

REFEREES IN MOST MAJOR INTERNATIONALS

24	C Norling (Wales)
23	K D Kelleher (Ireland)
23	D G Walters (Wales)
22	M Joseph (Wales)
21	R C Williams (Ireland)

MONEY MAKES THE WORLD GO ROUND

There is no British sport - cricket, football, tennis, athletics, boxing - that can look back with credit on administration over the past 30 years, but English rugby is looking particularly silly."
David Miller, The Times

"We, as administrators, are going down a road we are not desperately keen to go down but one we have to go along to some extent."
Mike Pearey, president of the RFU

"We don't want to be seen as money-grabbers. That is not the way we are. Since the Grand Slam no one in the team has mentioned money. I repeat I don't want to be paid to play. It is illogical, though, to deduce that the spirit of the game would be compromised by players profiting from their ability."
Will Carling, England captain

"Am I alone, I wonder, in feeling that the Rugby Football Union and the England team really rather deserve one another?"
Alan Watkins, The Independent

"I acknowledge that if the will to keep the game amateur isn't there it'll go...but it would be a tragedy."
Dudley Wood, secretary of the RFU

"There are committee men putting in a huge amount of time for the good of the game. I think the players should do the same. To pay them would be to degrade them. They would be goods to be bought and sold."
Dudley Wood

"...If earning a living is in some way degrading, there are tens of millions in Britain who should be ashamed of themselves."
Leader in The Sun

"People throughout rugby set Rottweilers on individual players allegedly making tuppence under the counter but then suffer instant and blithe principle-loss when faced with the universal allegations that South Africa have been buying in their rebel and semi-official tours for years."
Stephen Jones, Sunday Times

"You don't own us. You have no God-given right to demand that we speak to you."
Geoff Cooke's press conference after England's triumph in Cardiff

"We refer to Wasps as that famous North London job centre. Rugby League clubs come along with their money but they are honest about it. It is the insidious poaching that comes from outside the north, whether it's money or jobs, which is rather more upsetting. They do things we don't."
Eric Smith, past president of Orrell

PILKINGTON CUP
Third Round
Bath 0 LEICESTER 12; BRISTOL 18 Waterloo 9; Coventry 7 ROSSLYN PARK 21; GLOUCESTER 52 Broughton Park 0; HARLEQUINS 56 Clifton 4; Harrogate 4 NORTHAMPTON 18; High Wycombe 10 MOSELEY 18; LONDON IRISH 20 Sale 16; NEWCASTLE GOSFORTH 19 Blackheath 10 (aet); NOTTINGHAM 10 London Scottish 9; ORRELL 69 Spartans 13; RICHMOND 13 Liverpool St Helens 12; RUGBY 29 London Welsh 3; SARACENS 36 Hartlepool Rovers 0; SHEFFIELD 3 Exeter 0; West Hartlepool 3 WASPS 7

Fourth Round
Bristol 6 MOSELEY 9; Gloucester 13 HARLEQUINS 15; Leicester 13 WASPS 15; LONDON IRISH 22 Rugby 15; NORTHAMPTON 16 Saracens 10; NOTTINGHAM 24 Richmond 6; ORRELL 25 Newcastle Gosforth 9; ROSSLYN PARK 36 Sheffield 0

Quarter-finals
HARLEQUINS 24 Rosslyn Park 12; NORTHAMPTON 10 Moseley 6; NOTTINGHAM 46 London Irish 9; Wasps 9 ORRELL 15

Semi-finals
HARLEQUINS 22 Nottingham 18; NORTHAMPTON 18 Orrell 10
Final
Twickenham, May 4

HARLEQUINS 25	Northampton	13 (aet)
T: Halliday, Harriman	T: Moss	
Glenister, Langhorn	P: Steele 3	
C: Pears 3		
P: Pears		

SCHWEPPES WELSH CUP
Fifth Round
BLACKWOOD 34 Aberavon Q 12; BRIDGEND 36 Abercarn 12; CARDIFF 35 South Wales Police 0; CROSS KEYS 11 Fleur De Lys 9; FELINFOEL 9 St Peter's 4; Glamorgan W 18 TONDU 21; LLANELLI 80 Abertillery 0; MAESTEG 14 Llantrisant 7; Maesteg C 9 BRIDGEND A 12; NEATH 18 Newport 9; NEWBRIDGE 40 Bridgend Sports 8; Pencoed 4 DUNVANT 12; PONTYPOOL 33 Abergavenny 3; Pyle 4 PONTYPRIDD 27; SWANSEA 23 Aberavon 13; Tonyrefail 7 EBBW VALE 15

Sixth Round
BRIDGEND 9 Maesteg 0; CARDIFF 58 Blackwood 3; Dunvant 3 PONTYPOOL 13; NEATH 48 Felinfoel 7; NEWBRIDGE 43 Cross Keys 0; Pontypridd 6 LLANELLI 19; SWANSEA 28 Bridgend A 6; TONDU 12 Ebbw Vale 6

Quarter-finals
Bridgend 10 LLANELLI 16; NEATH 16 Cardiff 13; PONTYPOOL 12 Newbridge 3; SWANSEA 22 Tondu 13

Semi-finals
PONTYPOOL 28 Swansea 10; Neath 10 LLANELLI 22

Final
National Stadium, Cardiff, May 4

LLANELLI	24	Pontypool	9
T: Lewis, I Evans, Jones,		T: V Davies	
Stephens, S Davies		C: Parry	
C: Stephens 2		P: Parry	

ADT COUNTY CHAMPIONSHIP
Semi-finals
CORNWALL 14 Warwickshire 6; YORKSHIRE 14 Middlesex 0

Final
Twickenham, Apr 20
CORNWALL 29 Yorkshire 20 (aet)

Under-21 Final
WARWICKSHIRE 19 Hampshire 18

CATHAY PACIFIC HONG KONG BANK SEVENS
Hong Kong, Mar 23-24

Quarter-finals
FIJI 21 Western Samoa 6; *BARBARIANS* 16 Australia 6; CANADA 24 Scotland 4; *NEW ZEALAND* 30 France 0
Semi-finals
FIJI 22 Barbarians 14; *NEW ZEALAND* 26 Canada 0
Final
FIJI 18 New Zealand 14

SAVE & PROSPER MIDDLESEX SEVENS
Twickenham, May 11
Final
LONDON SCOTTISH 20 Harlequins 16

COMMERCIAL UNION UAU CHAMPIONSHIP
Final
Twickenham, Mar 20
CARDIFF 14 Swansea 3
Only the second ever all-Welsh final. The first was in 1976 when the Institute of Science and Technology (led by Gareth Davies) beat Swansea.

WOMEN'S WORLD CUP
Cardiff, Apr 6-14
Final
UNITED STATES 19 England 6
Inaugural championship

109TH VARSITY MATCH
(Bowring Bowl)
Twickenham, Dec 11
OXFORD 21 Cambridge 12
Under-21 Varsity Match
Stoop Memorial Ground, Dec 11
OXFORD 21 Cambridge 16

COURAGE CLUBS CHAMPIONSHIP

Division One

		P	W	D	L	F	A	Pts	FULL PLAYING RECORD					
									P	W	D	L	F	A
1 (3)	**BATH**	12	11	0	1	280	104	22	34	29	1	4	984	392
2 (1)	Wasps	12	9	1	2	252	151	19	39	21	2	16	987	494
3 (7)	Harlequins	12	8	0	4	267	162	16	31	22	0	9	787	408
4 (5)	Leicester	12	8	0	4	244	140	16	37	28	0	9	926	474
5 (8)	Orrell	12	7	0	5	247	195	14	36	27	1	8	1051	361
6 (2)	Gloucester	12	6	0	6	207	163	12	44	30	1	13	901	676
7 (10)	Rosslyn Park	12	6	0	6	216	174	12	31	19	1	11	594	441
8 (6)	Nottingham	12	6	0	6	138	194	12	35	20	2	13	681	493
9 (P)	Northampton	12	5	1	6	149	254	11	39	20	2	17	795	750
10 (4)	Saracens	12	5	0	7	151	228	10	33	18	1	14	627	474
11 (9)	Bristol	12	4	1	7	135	219	9	39	21	2	16	751	624
12 (11)	*Moseley*	12	1	1	10	113	244	3	42	19	1	22	721	689
13 (P)	*L'pool St Helens*	12	0	0	12	88	349	0	36	12	0	24	495	683

HOW THE LEAD CHANGED HANDS: Oct 13 Leicester; Oct 20 Bath; Oct 27 Harlequins; Nov 11 BATH

━━━ DIVISION ONE RESULTS ━━━

Away team

Home team	Bath	Bristol	Gl'ster	Quins	L'ster	L'pool S.H	Moseley	N'pton	Nottm	Orrell	Rosslyn	Saracens	Wasps
BATH	-	-	-	23-3	-	46-3	11-6	-	-	17-9	45-21	-	15-16
BRISTOL	3-10	-	15-12	-	10-6	-	-	-	6-22	3-36	-	25-6	-
GLOUCESTER	15-17	-	-	38-19	-	-	30-12	-	22-6	9-16	-	21-16	-
HARLEQUINS	-	38-16	-	-	-	41-12	33-6	21-6	-	-	18-6	-	12-18
LEICESTER	3-9	-	18-6	12-15	-	-	-	25-9	15-12	-	29-6	-	
L'POOL ST HELENS	-	6-7	7-26	-	7-28	-	-	13-23	12-13	-	-	3-17	-
MOSELEY	-	9-9	-	-	19-43	20-12	-	10-16	-	-	9-19	-	9-22
NORTHAMPTON	10-16	12-9	6-7	-	18-28	-	-	-	22-15	-	-	15-6	-
NOTTINGHAM	9-22	-	-	6-19	-	-	12-7	-	-	16-12	-	3-28	12-10
ORRELL	-	-	-	12-9	-	38-0	16-0	60-0	-	-	12-3	-	12-14
ROSSLYN PARK	-	16-13	17-12	-	17-15	39-9	-	48-0	9-15	-	-	-	-
SARACENS	6-49	-	-	7-39	-	-	21-6	-	-	19-12	13-11	-	6-15
WASPS	-	46-19	14-9	-	12-22	51-4	-	21-21	-	-	13-10	-	-

Division Two

		P	W	D	L	F	A	Pts	FULL PLAYING RECORD					
									P	W	D	L	F	A
1	(6) **RUGBY**	12	10	0	2	252	146	20	32	25	1	6	801	406
2	(5) **LONDON IRISH**	12	9	1	2	239	192	19	35	19	2	14	626	516
3	(P) Wakefield	12	8	0	4	188	109	16	31	21	0	10	636	439
4	(4) Coventry	12	8	0	4	172	129	16	35	18	0	17	584	603
5	(P) London Scottish	12	7	0	5	240	178	14	27	14	1	12	499	441
6	(12) Newcastle Gosforth	12	6	0	6	169	140	12	34	24	0	10	722	472
7	(9) Sale	12	5	1	6	224	156	11	36	17	3	16	766	509
8	(R) Bedford	12	4	2	6	138	203	10	36	14	2	20	611	824
9	(11) Waterloo	12	4	1	7	154	206	9	31	19	1	11	552	471
10	(10) Blackheath	12	4	0	8	134	169	8	34	15	1	8	471	491
11	(7) Plymouth Albion	12	4	0	8	129	210	8	31	16	1	14	696	447
12	(3) *Richmond*	12	3	1	8	134	245	7	33	10	2	21	451	667
13	(8) *Headingley*	12	3	0	9	125	215	6	32	12	0	20	372	567

HOW THE LEAD CHANGED HANDS: Oct 13 Coventry; Oct 20 Wakefield; Oct 27 Rugby; Nov 17 London Irish; Jan 12 RUGBY

Divison Three

			P	W	D	L	F	A	Pts
1	(3)	WEST HARTLEPOOL	12	9	1	1	282	90	19
2	(P)	MORLEY	12	9	1	1	210	118	19
3	(8)	Fylde	12	7	2	3	183	115	16
4	(6)	Exeter	12	7	2	3	160	139	16
5	(P)	Clifton	12	6	1	5	172	186	13
6	(5)	Askeans	12	4	2	5	141	137	10
7	(10)	Nuneaton	12	5	0	7	180	200	10
8	(P)	Broughton Park	12	5	0	7	109	185	10
9	(7)	Roundhay	12	4	1	7	147	166	9
10	(4)	Sheffield	12	4	1	7	193	222	9
11	(11)	Lydney	12	4	1	7	125	188	9
12	(P)	*Metropolitan Police*	*12*	*4*	*0*	*8*	*130*	*188*	*6*
13	(9)	*Vale of Lune*	12	3	0	9	123	221	3

HOW THE LEAD CHANGED HANDS: Oct 13
Clifton; Oct 20 West Hartlepool
Last season's positions in brackets.
P = Promoted 1989-90: R = Relegated 1989-90

HEINEKEN W.R.U. NATIONAL LEAGUE
Premier Division

		P	W	D	L	F	A	Pts
1	Neath	18	14	0	4	353	218	28
2	Llanelli	18	12	1	5	409	292	25
3	Bridgend	18	10	2	6	288	275	22
4	Cardiff	18	10	1	7	396	261	21
5	Pontypridd	18	9	2	7	353	270	20
6	Pontypool	18	9	1	8	402	293	19
7	Newbridge	18	9	0	9	363	261	18
8	Swansea	18	9	0	9	353	309	18
9	Glamorgan	18	3	0	15	192	496	6
10	Abertillery	18	1	1	16	146	580	3

Inangural Season
OTHER CHAMPIONS
Welsh League
Division One: Newport
Division Two: Dunvant
Division Three: Llandovery
McKewans Scottish League
Division One: Boroughmuir
Division Two: Watsonians
All-Ireland League
Division One: Cork Constitution

ALL THE OTHER CHAMPIONS

Area North	Otley
Area South	Redruth
North Div 1	Aspatria
North Div 2	Stockton
North West Div 1	Northwich
North West Div 2	St Edwards
North East Div 1	Old Cross
North East Div 2	West Park Bramhope
Midlands Div 1	Towcestrians†
Midlands Div 2 (E)	Syston
Midlands Div 2 (W)	Leamington
Staffs/Warwicks	Broad Street
North Midlands	Whitchurch
Notts/Lincs/Derbys	Amber Valley *
East Midlands/Leics	Bedford Athletic
South West Div 1	High Wycombe
South West Div 2	Conderford
Souther Counties	Sherbourne
Western Counties	Coombe Down
Cornwall/Devon	Devon & Cornwall Police
Gloucs/Somerset	Spartans
Berks/Dorset/Wilts	Dorchester
Bucks/Oxon	Olney
London & SE Div 1	Sidcup
London & SE Div 2 (N)	Eton Manor
London & SE Div 2 (S)	Dorking
London & SEt Div 3 (NE)	Harlow
London & SE Div 3 (NW)	Letchworth
London & SE Div 3 (SE)	Old Juddian
London & SE Div 3 (SW)	Old Blues *

* Won division with 100% record; 10 wins out of 10
† Promoted for the third succesive season

FULL PLAYING RECORD

P	W	D	L	F	A
41	31	0	10	880	546
46	35	1	10	1255	688
44	32	2	10	902	566
36	23	1	12	871	518
44	30	2	12	956	557
47	29	1	17	1187	666
47	33	1	13	1211	582
43	29	0	14	994	623
34	14	0	20	503	682
43	13	3	27	504	1069

> **"The most beautiful moment of Easter Day was sitting in a Siop Coffi in Newcastle Emlyn and watching two all-female teams emerge from the Clwb Rygbi. The butchest girl in the red team took it upon herself to massage the neck, and then the elephantine thighs of a bosomy front row forward and they made a beautiful sight, with the Cenarth Falls babbling in the background."**
>
> *A.N. Wilson*, The Spectator

> **"A Kiwi or Aussie will say to his boys before the game 'You've got to go out there and kill. The whole of the rest of your life depends on this one game.' You say that to Fijians and they bust out laughing. How can a GAME matter so much to man?"**
>
> *Tevita Ratevu, Fijian RFU official*

> **"We are asked to point out that the correct name for Bath rugby player Roger Spurrell's business is Balls For You and not as published in the *Evening Post* on Thursday and Friday."** Bristol Evening Post

CHAMPIONS

INTERNATIONAL CHAMPIONS

Year	Winners	Grand Slam	Triple Crown
1883	England	-	England
1884	England	-	England
1885	-	-	-
1886	England	-	-
	Scotland	-	
1887	Scotland	-	-
1888	-	-	-
1889	-	-	-
1890	England	-	-
	Scotland		
1891	Scotland	-	Scotland
1892	England	-	England
1893	Wales	-	Wales
1894	Ireland	-	Ireland
1895	Scotland	-	Scotland
1896	Ireland	-	-
1897	-	-	-
1898	-	-	-
1899	Ireland	-	Ireland
1900	Wales	-	Wales
1901	Scotland	-	Scotland
1902	Wales	-	Wales
1903	Scotland	-	Scotland
1904	Scotland	-	-
1905	Wales	-	Wales
1906	Ireland	-	-
	Wales		
1907	Scotland	-	Scotland
1908	Wales	Wales	Wales
1909	Wales	Wales	Wales
1910	England	-	-
1911	Wales	Wales	Wales
1912	England	-	-
	Ireland		
1913	England	England	England
1914	England	England	England
1920	England	-	-
	Scotland		
	Wales		
1921	England	England	England
1922	Wales	-	-
1923	England	England	England
1924	England	England	England
1925	Scotland	Scotland	Scotland
1926	Scotland	-	-
	Ireland		
1927	Scotland	-	-
	Ireland		
1828	England	England	England
1929	Scotland	-	-
1930	England	-	-
1931	Wales	-	-
1932	England	-	-
	Wales		
	Ireland		
1933	Scotland	-	Scotland
1934	England	-	England
1935	Ireland	-	-
1936	Wales	-	-
1937	England	-	England
1938	Scotland	-	Scotland
1939	England	-	-
	Wales		
	Ireland		
1947	Wales	-	-
	England		

Year	Winners	Grand Slam	Triple Crown
1948	Ireland	Ireland	Ireland
1949	Ireland	-	Ireland
1950	Wales	Wales	Wales
1951	Ireland	-	-
1952	Wales	Wales	Wales
1953	England	-	-
1954	England	-	England
	Wales		
	France		
1955	Wales	-	-
	France		
1956	Wales	-	-
1958	England	-	-
1959	France	-	-
1960	France	-	England
	England		
1961	France	-	-
1962	France	-	-
1963	England	-	-
1964	Scotland	-	-
	Wales		
1965	Wales	-	Wales
1966	Wales	-	-
1967	France	-	-
1968	France	France	-
1969	Wales	-	Wales
1970	Wales	-	-
	France		
1971	Wales	Wales	Wales
1972	-	-	-
1973	Quintuple tie	-	-
1974	Ireland	-	-
1975	Wales	-	-
1976	Wales	Wales	Wales
1977	France	France	Wales
1978	Wales	Wales	Wales
1979	Wales	-	Wales
1980	England	England	England
1981	France	France	-
1982	Ireland	-	Ireland
1983	France	-	-
	Ireland		
1984	Scotland	Scotland	Scotland
1985	Ireland	-	Ireland
1986	France	-	-
	Scotland		
1987	France	France	-
1988	Wales	-	Wales
	France		
1989	France	-	-
1990	Scotland	Scotland	Scotland
1991	England	England	England

WINS

32 Wales	9 England	17 Wales
28 England	8 Wales	16 England
21 Scotland	4 France	10 Scotland
18 Ireland	3 Scotland	6 Ireland
17 France	1 Ireland	

France first played all four home nations in 1910. They withdrew from the Championship because of a dispute over professionalism from 1932 until after the war.

THE INTERNATIONAL CHAMPIONSHIP - THE LAST TEN YEARS:

	ENG v IRE	SCO v ENG	ENG v WAL	IRE v SCO	IRE v WAL
1982	15-16	9-9	17-7	21-12	20-12
1984	12-9	18-6	15-24	9-32	9-18
1986	25-20	33-6	21-18	9-10	12-19
1988	35-3	6-9	3-11	22-18	9-12
1990	23-0	13-7	34-6	10-13	14-8

	IRE v ENG	ENG v SCO	WAL v ENG	SCO v IRE	WAL v IRE
1983	23-15	12-22	13-13	15-18	9-21
1985	13-10	10-7	24-15	15-18	11-15
1987	17-0	21-12	19-12	16-12	11-15
1989	3-16	12-12	12-9	37-21	13-19
1991	7-16	21-12	6-25	28-25	21-21

	WAL v SCO	FRA v ENG	FRA v IRE	SCO v FRA	WAL v FRA
1982	18-34	15-27	22-9	16-7	22-12
1984	9-15	32-18	25-12	21-12	16-21
1986	22-15	29-10	29-9	18-17	15-23
1988	25-20	10-9	25-6	23-12	9-10
1990	9-13	7-26	31-12	21-0	19-29

	SCO v WAL	ENG v FRA	IRE v FRA	FRA v SCO	FRA v WAL
1983	15-19	15-19	22-16	19-15	16-9
1985	21-25	9-9	15-15	11-3	14-3
1987	21-14	15-19	13-19	28-22	16-9
1989	23-7	11-0	21-26	19-3	31-12
1991	32-12	21-19	13-21	15-9	36-3

(a) Wales's last win at home to Ireland was in 1981 (9-8)

(b) Ireland's last win in Paris was in 1972 (14-9), at the Stade Colombes. They have not won at the Parc des Princes since 1914

(c) France's last win at Murrayfield was in 1978 (19-16)

(d) Scotland's last win in Paris was in 1969 (6-3). Their last win at the Parc des Princes was in 1920

(e) Wales's last win in Paris was in 1975 (25-10)

THE FIVE NATIONS AGAINST EACH OTHER

		P	W	D	L	%
ENGLAND v	Ireland	103	59	8	36	61.17
	Scotland	107	51	17	39	55.61
	Wales	96	38	12	46	45.83
	France	66	35	7	24	58.33
SCOTLAND v	England	107	39	17	51	44.39
	Ireland	101	52	4	45	53.47
	Wales	95	41	2	52	44.21
	France	61	29	2	30	49.18
IRELAND v	England	103	36	8	59	38.83
	Scotland	101	45	4	52	46.53
	Wales	93	32	6	55	37.63
	France	64	25	5	34	42.97
WALES v	England	96	46	12	38	54.17
	Ireland	93	55	6	32	62.37
	Scotland	95	52	2	41	55.79
	France	64	36	3	25	58.59
FRANCE v	England	66	24	7	35	41.67
	Ireland	64	34	5	25	57.03
	Scotland	61	30	2	29	50.82
	Wales	64	25	3	36	41.41

Percentage based on wins and draws against matches played. One point allowed for a win and half for a draw.

WORLD CUP
Inaugurated 1987
1987   New Zealand 29 France 9

COUNTY CHAMPIONSHIPS
1889	Yorkshire
1890	Yorkshire
1891	Lancashire
1892	Yorkshire
1893	Yorkshire
1894	Yorkshire
1895	Yorkshire
1896	Yorkshire
1897	Kent
1898	Northumberland
1899	Devon
1900	Durham
1901	Devon
1902	Durham
1903	Durham
1904	Kent
1905	Durham
1906	Devon
1907	Devon & Durham (shared)
1908	Cornwall
1909	Durham
1910	Gloucestershire
1911	Devon
1912	Devon
1913	Gloucestershire
1914	Midlands
1915-19	Not held
1920	Gloucestershire
1921	Gloucestershire
1922	Gloucestershire
1923	Somerset
1924	Cumberland
1925	Leicestershire
1926	Yorkshire
1927	Kent
1928	Yorkshire
1929	Middlesex
1930	Gloucestershire
1931	Gloucestershire
1932	Gloucestershire
1933	Hampshire
1934	East Midlands
1935	Lancashire
1936	Hampshire
1937	Gloucestershire
1938	Lancashire
1939	Warwickshire
1940-46	Not held
1947	Lancashire
1948	Lancashire
1949	Lancashire
1950	Cheshire
1951	East Midlands
1952	Middlesex
1953	Yorkshire
1954	Middlesex
1955	Lancashire
1956	Middlesex
1957	Devon
1958	Warwickshire
1959	Warwickshire
1960	Warwickshire
1961	Cheshire
1962	Warwickshire
1963	Warwickshire
1964	Warwickshire

1965	Warwickshire
1966	Middlesex
1967	Surrey & Durham
1968	Middlesex
1969	Lancashire
1970	Staffordshire
1971	Surrey
1972	Gloucestershire
1973	Lancashire
1974	Gloucestershire
1975	Gloucestershire
1976	Gloucestershire
1977	Lancashire
1978	North Midlands
1979	Middlesex
1980	Lancashire

Finals since 1981

1981	Northumberland			
1982	Lancashire	7	Gloucestershire	6
1983	Gloucestershire	19	Yorkshire	7
1984	Gloucestershire	36	Somerset	18
1985	Middlesex	12	Notts, Lincs, Derbys	9
1986	Warwickshire	16	Kent	6
1987	Yorkshire	22	Middlesex	7
1988	Lancashire	23	Warwickshire	18
1989	Durham	13	Cornwall	9
1990	Lancashire	32	Middlesex	9
1991	Cornwall	29	Yorkshire	20

Most wins: 15 Gloucestershire; **14** Lancashire; **11** Yorkshire; **9** Warwickshire; **8** Durham (including two shared), Middlesex; **7** Devon (including one shared)

PILKINGTON CUP
Formerly John Player Cup

1972	Gloucester	17	Moseley	16
1973	Coventry	27	Bristol	15
1974	Coventry	26	London Scottish	6
1975	Bedford	28	Rosslyn Park	12
1976	Gosforth	27	Rosslyn Park	14
1977	Gosforth	27	Waterloo	11
1978	Gloucester	6	Leicester	3
1979	Leicester	15	Moseley	12
1980	Leicester	21	London Irish	9
1981	Leicester	22	Gosforth	15
1982	Gloucester	12	Moseley	12(shared)
1983	Bristol	28	Leicester	22
1984	Bath	10	Bristol	9
1985	Bath	24	London Welsh	15
1986	Bath	25	Wasps	17
1987	Bath	19	Wasps	12
1988	Harlequins	28	Bristol	22
1989	Bath	10	Leicester	6
1990	Bath	48	Gloucester	6
1991	Harlequins	25	Northampton	13

Most wins: 6 Bath; **3** Leicester, Gloucester (including one shared)

SCHWEPPES WELSH CUP
1972	Neath	15	Llanelli	9
1973	Llanelli	30	Cardiff	7
1974	Llanelli	12	Aberavon	10
1975	Llanelli	15	Aberavon	6
1976	Llanelli	15	Swansea	4
1977	Newport	16	Cardiff	15
1978	Swansea	13	Newport	9
1979	Bridgend	18	Pontypridd	12
1980	Bridgend	15	Swansea	9
1981	Cardiff	14	Bridgend	6
1982	Cardiff*	12	Bridgend	12
1983	Pontypool	18	Swansea	6
1984	Cardiff	24	Neath	19

1985	Llanelli	15	Cardiff	14
1986	Cardiff	28	Newport	21
1987	Cardiff	16	Swansea	15aet
1988	Llanelli	28	Neath	13
1989	Neath	14	Llanelli	13
1990	Neath	16	Bridgend	10
1991	Llanelli	24	Pontypool	9

* Winners on most tries rule
Most wins: 7 Llanelli; **5** Cardiff

COURAGE CLUBS CHAMPIONSHIPS
Formerly National Merit Tables

	League 1	*League 2*	*League 3*
1985-6	Gloucester	Orrell	
1986-7	Bath	Waterloo	Vale of Lane
1987-8	Leicester	Rosslyn Park	Wakefield
1988-9	Bath	Saracens	Plymouth Alb
1989-90	Wasps	Northampton	London Scottish
1990-91	Bath	Rugby	West Hartlepool

UNIVERSITY MATCH
Results since 1981

1981	Cambridge	9	Oxford	9
1982	Cambridge	20	Oxford	13
1983	Cambridge	20	Oxford	9
1984	Cambridge	32	Oxford	6
1985	Oxford	7	Cambridge	6
1986	Oxford	15	Cambrdige	10
1987	Cambridge	15	Oxford	10
1988	Oxford	27	Cambridge	7
1989	Cambridge	22	Oxford	13
1990	Oxford	21	Cambridge	12

Wins: 49 Cambridge; **46** Oxford; **13** Drawn

RECORDS

LEADING INTERNATIONAL SCORERS

	Points	*Appearances*	*Tries*
ENGLAND	240 Dusty Hare	44 Rory Underwood	24 Rory Underwood
IRELAND	317 Michael Kiernan	69 Mike Gibson	15 George Stephenson
SCOTLAND	329 Gavin Hastings	52 Jim Renwick	24 Ian Smith
		52 Colin Deans	
WALES	304 Paul Thorburn	55 J P R Williams	20 Gareth Edwards
			20 Gerald Davies
FRANCE	296 Didier Camberabero	64 Serge Blanco	33 Serge Blanco
AUSTRALIA	607 Michael Lynagh	52 Simon Poidevin	40 David Campese
NEW ZEALAND	467 Grant Fox	55 Colin Meads	26 John Kirwan
SOUTH AFRICA	268 Naas Botha	38 Frik du Preez	15 Danie Gerber
		38 Jan Ellis	

1992

FIVE NATIONS CHAMPIONSHIP

Jan 18	SCOTLAND v ENGLAND (Murrayfield); IRELAND v WALES (Dublin)
Feb 1	ENGLAND v IRELAND (Twickenham); WALES v FRANCE (Cardiff)
Feb 15	FRANCE v ENGLAND (Paris); IRELAND v SCOTLAND (Dublin)
Mar 7	ENGLAND v WALES (Twickenham); SCOTLAND v FRANCE (Murrayfield)
Mar 21	FRANCE v IRELAND (Paris); WALES v SCOTLAND (Cardiff)

OTHER MAJOR FIXTURES

Feb 2	France B v Scotland B
Feb 22	RFU Cup quarter -finals; Welsh cup sixth round
Mar 18	UAU Final (Twickenham)
Apr 4	RFU Cup semi-finals; Welsh Cup quarter-finals
Apr 18	County Championship final (Twickenham)
May 2	RFU Cup final (Twickenham); Welsh Cup semi-finals
May 16	Welsh Cup final (Cardiff)

COURAGE LEAGUE DIVISION ONE

Jan 4 Bristol v Northampton; Gloucester v Rosslyn Park; Harlequins v Bath; Leicester v London Irish; Rugby v Saracens; Wasps v Nottingham

Jan 11 Bath v Leicester; London Irish v Rugby; Northampton v Harlequins; Orrell v Bristol; Rosslyn Park v Wasps; Saracens v Gloucester

Feb 8 Gloucester v London Irish; Harlequins v Orrell; Leicester v Northampton; Nottingham v Rosslyn Park; Rugby v Bath; Wasps v Saracens

Feb 29 Bath v Gloucester; Bristol v Harlequins; London Irish v Wasps; Northampton v Rugby; Orrell v Leicester; Saracens v Nottingham

Mar 14 Gloucester v Northampton; Leicester v Bristol; Nottingham v London Irish; Rosslyn Park v Saracens; Rugby v Orrell; Wasps v Bath

Mar 28 Bath v Nottingham; Bristol v Rugby; Harlequins v Leicester; London Irish v Rosslyn Park; Northampton v Wasps; Orrell v Gloucester

Apr 11 Gloucester v Bristol; Nottingham v Northampton; Rosslyn Park v Bath; Rugby v Harlequins; Saracens v London Irish; Wasps v Orrell

Apr 25 Bath v Saracens; Bristol v Wasps; Harlequins v Gloucester; Leicester v Rugby; Northampton v Rosslyn Park; Orrell v Nottingham

HEINEKEN LEAGUE PREMIER DIVISION

Jan 4 Bridgend v Maesteg; Cardiff v Pontypool; Newbridge v Llanelli; Pontypridd v Neath; Swansea v Newport

Jan 11 Llanelli v Bridgend; Maesteg v Pontypridd; Neath v Cardiff; Newport v Newbridge; Pontypool v Swansea

Feb 8 Cardiff v Swansea; Llanelli v Pontypridd; Neath v Cardiff; Newport v Newbridge; Pontypool v Swansea

Feb 15 Bridgend v Pontypool; Maesteg v Llanelli; Newbridge v Cardiff; Pontypridd v Newport; Swansea v Neath

Feb 29 Cardiff v Bridgend; Llanelli v Neath; Newport v Maesteg; Pontypool v Pontypridd; Swansea v Newbridge

Mar 14 Bridgend v Swansea; Llanelli v Newport; Maesteg v Pontypool; Neath v Newbridge; Pontypridd v Cardiff

Mar 28 Cardiff v Maesteg; Newbridge v Bridgend; Newport v Neath; Pontypool v Llanelli; Swansea v Pontypridd

Apr 11 Llanelli v Cardiff; Maesteg v Swansea; Neath v Bridgend; Newport v Pontypool; Pontypridd v Newbridge

Apr 25 Llanelli v Newbridge; Maesteg v Bridgend; Neath v Pontypridd; Newport v Swansea; Pontypool v Cardiff

May 9 Bridgend v Llanelli; Cardiff v Neath; Newbridge v Newport; Pontypridd v Maesteg; Swansea v Pontypool

SHINTY

SHOOTING

1991

1991

GLENMORANGIE CAMANACHD CUP FINAL
Bught Park, Inverness, Jun 8
KINGUSSIE 3   Fort William 1
Borthwick, Thain, MacNeill (og)   Smith
Attendance: 4,000

122ND NATIONAL RIFLE ASSOCIATION MEETING
Bisley, Jul 15-27

Queen's Prize
1 Chris Fitzpatrick (RAF) 293
2 Colin Brook (City University) 292
3 Anthony Ringer (Uppingham Veterans) 291

Land Rover Grand Aggregate
John Bellinger (Old Epsomians)

Hopton Challenge Cup
Arthur Clark (Army TRC)

Elcho Challenge Shield
England

Ashburton Shield
Epsom

King George V Challenge Cup
Surrey

Daily Telegraph Challenge Cup
James Lewis (Army TRC)

Centenary Overseas Match
Canada

Mackinnon Trophy
England

Save & Prosper St George's Vase
Anthony Ringer (Upton Veterans)

Kolapore Challenge Cup
Great Britain

Vizianagram Trophy
House of Lords 661 House of Commons 645

The Chancellor's Trophy
Cambridge University

Musketeers Trophy
London University 'A'

Families Trophy
The Kents

CHAMPIONS

Camanachd Cup
Started 1896. Winners since the war
1947	Newtonmore
1948	Newtonmore
1949	Oban Celtic
1950	Newtonmore
1951	Newtonmore
1952	Inverness
1953	Lovat
1954	Oban Celtic
1955	Newtonmore
1956	Kyles Athletic
1957	Newtonmore
1958	Newtonmore
1959	Newtonmore
1960	Oban Celtic
1961	Kingussie
1962	Kyles Athletic
1963	Oban Celtic
1964	Kilmallie
1965	Kyles Athletic
1966	Kyles Athletic
1967	Newtonmore
1968	Kyles Athletic
1969	Kyles Athletic
1970	Newtonmore
1971	Newtonmore
1972	Newtonmore
1973	Glasgow Mid Argyll
1974	Kyles Athletic
1975	Newtonmore
1976	Kyles Athletic
1977	Newtonmore
1978	Newtonmore
1979	Newtonmore
1980	Kyles Athletic
1981	Newtonmore
1982	Newtonmore
1983	Kyles Athletic
1984	Kingussie
1985	Newtonmore
1986	Newtonmore
1987	Kingussie
1988	Kingussie
1989	Kingussie
1990	Skye
1991	Kingussie

Most wins
28 Newtonmore; 19 Kyles Athletic; 12 Kingussie; 5 Oban Celtic

National League
1982 Kingussie; 1983 Newtonmore; 1984 Kingussie; 1985 Newtonmore; 1986 Kyles Athletic; 1987-91 Kingussie

CHAMPIONS

QUEEN'S PRIZE
Principal event at the NRA meeting at Bisley every July. Winners since 1982 (All British unless otherwise stated)
1982	Lindsay Peden
1983	Alain Marion (Can)
1984	David Richards
1985	John Bloomfield
1986	Geoffrey Cox
1987	Andrew Tucker
1988	John Pugsley
1989	Jeremy Thompson
1990	John Bloomfield
1991	Chris Fitzpatrick

SNOOKER

PARROTT FASHION

The Liverpudlian John Parrott, the least talked-about of the world's leading players, slipped through the field at the Crucible Theatre to become the 1991 world champion. He took a 7-0 lead in the final against Jimmy White with a brilliant display of potting and held on to win 18-11. It was White's third defeat in a final and his second in a row: "They all play well against me," he moaned.

Parrott gave the credit to his father and the former champion John Spencer, who he said had helped him with his attitude: "John totally changed my thinking." But Spencer could not help Parrott sleep on the Sunday night when he was lying on an 11-5 lead. The following week the new champion paraded his trophy at Anfield, where for once there were no footballing trophies to display.

The 1990 champion Stephen Hendry was beaten in the quarter-finals by Steve James but in the early part of the season he was entirely dominant with a sequence of 36 successive wins in tournament matches. He finished the season with eight major titles, equalling Steve Davis's total in 1987-88. Davis himself mostly struggled - "I'm a bit of an old carthorse at the moment," he admitted at one point - but he reached the final of the UK Open and staged a fantastic showdown with Hendry, eventually losing 16-15 after a match which connoisseurs ranked as second only to the great Dennis Taylor-Davis world final of 1985 on drama and higher than that on quality. Hendry also had an amazing win in the final of the Benson and Hedges Masters, which he was losing 7-0 to Mike Hallett but came back to take 9-8. Hallett's house in Cleethorpes was burgled the same night; an estimated £4,500 worth of valuables was taken.

One former world champion, Ray Reardon, 58, retired from tournament play. Another, Joe Johnson, was advised to retire after suffering a heart attack. An attempt by Barry Hearn to get Alex Higgins, banned for the season, into the £1 million Sky World Masters tournament, was foiled when most of the other leading players threatened to withdraw. Playing in the UK Championship at Preston, Tony Drago was approached by a woman pretending to be an autograph hunter and served with a writ.

1990-91

(All players from British Isles unless otherwise stated. Figures in brackets [ ] indicate world ranking at start of 1990-91 season.)

EMBASSY WORLD PROFESSIONAL CHAMPIONSHIP
Crucible Theatre, Sheffield, Apr 20-May 6

FIRST ROUND
STEPHEN HENDRY [1] beat Warren King (Aus) [39] 10-4; TONY MEO [15] beat Craig Edwards [61] 10-7; ALAIN ROBIDOUX [16] (Can) beat Steve Newbury [20] 10-5; STEVE DAVIS [2] beat Ken Doherty [-] 10-8; TONY KNOWLES [21] beat John Virgo [14] 10-8; STEVE JAMES [9] beat Ian Graham [50] 10-3; NEAL FOULDS [13] beat Eddie Charlton (Aus) [31] 10-7; DENNIS TAYLOR [10] beat Joe Johnson [17] 10-6; JIMMY WHITE [4] beat Nick Dyson [64] 10-3; DEAN REYNOLDS [8] beat Robert Marshall [46] 10-8; TERRY GRIFFITHS [6] beat Barry Pinches [82] 10-3; GARY WILKINSON [19] beat Doug Mountjoy [5] 10-2; MARTIN CLARK [12] beat Mark Bennett [33] 10-6; ALAN McMANUS [-] beat Willie Thorne [11] 10-8; JOHN PARROTT [3] beat Nigel Gilbert [51] 10-6;

TONY JONES [35] beat Mike Hallett [7] 10-4

SECOND ROUND
DAVIS beat Meo 13-6; HENDRY beat Robidoux 13-8; WILKINSON beat Clark 13-9; GRIFFITHS beat McManus 13-12; PARROTT beat Knowles 13-1; WHITE beat Foulds 13-12; TAYLOR beat Jones 13-8; JAMES beat Reynolds 13-12;

QUARTER-FINALS
PARROTT beat Griffiths 13-10; WHITE beat Wilkinson 13-3; JAMES beat Hendry 13-11; DAVIS beat Taylor 13-7

SEMI-FINALS
PARROTT beat Davis 16-10; WHITE beat James 16-9

FINAL
PARROTT beat White 18-11
First Prize: £135,000
Players underlined beat a player of a higher ranking
The 14th frame in the Steve Davis-Tony Meo second-round match lasted 69 minutes and 28 seconds, the longest ever at the Crucible. Davis and Meo took 25 minutes 30 seconds to pot the yellow.

HIGHEST BREAKS
140 Jimmy White; 138 John Parrott, Jimmy White.

OTHER RANKING TOURNAMENTS

ROTHMANS GRAND PRIX
Hexagon Theatre, Reading, Oct 8-21
SEMI-FINALS
NIGEL BOND [38] beat Jimmy White [4] 9-8; STEPHEN HENDRY [1] beat Steve James [9] 9-5
FINAL
HENDRY [1] beat Bond [38] 10-5
Highest break: 140 Jimmy White

555 ASIAN OPEN
Guangzhou, China, Oct 29-Nov 4
SEMI-FINALS
STEPHEN HENDRY [1] beat Mike Hallett [7] 6-1; DENNIS TAYLOR [10] beat Tony Chappel [43] 6-5
FINAL
HENDRY [1] beat Taylor [10] 9-3
Highest break: 121 Steve Newbury

DUBAI DUTY FREE MASTERS
Al Nasr Stadium, Dubai, Nov 5-11
SEMI-FINALS
STEPHEN HENDRY [1] beat Dean Reynolds [8] 6-1; STEVE DAVIS [2] beat Gary Wilkinson [19] 6-4
FINAL
HENDRY [1] beat Davis [2] 9-1
Highest Break: 125 Jim Wych
This was Davis' biggest defeat in a final in 13 years as a professional

STORMSEAL UK OPEN
Preston Guildhall, Nov 16 - Dec 2
SEMI-FINALS
STEVE DAVIS [2] beat John Parrott [3] 9-6; STEPHEN HENDRY [1] beat Alan McManus [-] 9-5
FINAL
HENDRY [1] beat Davis [2] 16-15
Highest Break: 140 John Parrott
In his 9-0 win over Joe O'Boye in the third round, Tony Drago (Malta) established a record for the quickest win in a 17-frame match by winning in 81 minutes.

MERCANTILE CREDIT CLASSIC
Bournemouth, Jan 2-12
SEMI-FINALS
JIMMY WHITE [4] beat Mike Hallett [7] 6-4; STEPHEN HENDRY [1] beat Neal Foulds [13] 6-4
FINAL
WHITE [4] beat Hendry [1] 10-4
Highest break: 131 Ken Doherty

PEARL ASSURANCE BRITISH OPEN
Derby, Feb 17-Mar 2
SEMI-FINALS
GARY WILKINSON [19] beat Jimmy White [4] 9-8; STEPHEN HENDRY [1] beat Steve Davis [2] 9-7
FINAL
HENDRY [1] beat Wilkinson [19] 10-9
Highest break: 139 Gary Wilkinson (twice)
The qualifying match between Bill Werbeniuk and Ian Black at Blackpool on Sep 4, 1990 lasted 5hrs 34min, a record for a 9-frame match.

TULIP EUROPEAN OPEN
Rotterdam, Mar 9-17
SEMI-FINALS
TONY JONES [35] beat Brady Gollan [54] 6-2; MARK

JOHNSTON-ALLEN [59] beat Cliff Thorburn [18] 6-4
FINAL
JONES [35] beat Johnston-Allen [59] 9-7
Highest break: 136 Cliff Thorburn
Stephen Hendry was beaten 5-0 by Mark Johnston-Allen, an ex-public schoolboy from Bristol

---

"I don't know where I found the courage or the concentration to make those two breaks. I amazed myself tonight."
Stephen Hendry, on his win over Steve Davis in the UK Open

"He's like a wounded lion at the moment."
Ian Doyle, Stephen Hendry's manager, after his defeat in the World Championship

"I don't want to be disrespectful to my fellow players but it is a joke how I keep losing to so many mugs."
Jimmy White

"There's absolutely no reason why any man should feel uncomfortable about losing to a girl. There's nothing physical about snooker."
Allison Fisher, professional

"They say the viewing figures are still excellent and the housewives are as crazy about it as ever. Well, I've been a housewife for five years and I'd rather watch peas soak. Barry Hearn found it all so interesting, he's gone into boxing promotion. Once the players had pasts...these new players, the Nigels and Alans and Neals, seem to know only snooker. Their faces stare back at you as hollow and flawless as goldfish bowls. With some of them, there's more expression on their backsides. A few of them are absolutely brilliant, and you don't care a bit."
Julie Welch, The Observer

"He's got a lot more popular. The public perception of winners is that they're inhuman but now Steve is not only not winning, he's a new father who's not winning. That's a double bonus."
Barry Hearn, Steve Davis's manager

"Parrott, like Davis, has no nickname, no bad habits, no soul to bare..He is not the stuff folk heroes are made of. He is just an extremely good player."
Paul Wilson, The Observer

"When a one-legged snooker player from Iceland is drawn against a man who won the world championship three times, there can only be one result: Brynjar Valdimarsson beat John Spencer 6-1."
David Hunn, Sunday Times

OTHER TOURNAMENTS

555 World Series Challenge
JAMES WATTANA (Tha) [32] beat Jimmy White [4] 9-3

Regal Masters
STEPHEN HENDRY [1] beat Terry Griffiths [6] 10-6

Humo Belgian Masters
JOHN PARROTT [3] beat Jimmy White [4] 9-6

International Knockout
DARREN MORGAN [40] beat Mike Hallett [7] 2-1

Norwich Union Grand Prix Final
JOHN PARROTT [3] beat Steve Davis [2] 4-2

Coalite World Match-play Championship
JIMMY WHITE [4] beat Stephen Hendry [2]18-9

European Grand Masters
MARTIN CLARK [12] beat Ray Reardon [73] 4-2

Mita World Masters
Men's Singles
JIMMY WHITE [3] beat Tony Drago (Mal) [30] 10-6
Men's Doubles
STEPHEN HENDRY & MIKE HALLETT beat Jim Wych
& Brady Gollan (Can) 8-5
Women's Singles
KAREN CORR beat Stacey Hillyard 6-2
Women's Doubles
ALLISON FISHER & STACEY HILLYARD beat Ann-
Marie Farren & Karen Corr 5-2
Mixed Doubles
STEVE DAVIS & ALLISON FISHER beat Jimmy White
& Caroline Walch 6-3
Junior (Under-16s)
JOHN HIGGINS beat Mark Williams 6-1

Benson & Hedges Masters
STEPHEN HENDRY [1] beat Mike Hallett [7] 9-8

Benson & Hedges Irish Masters
STEVE DAVIS [2] beat John Parrott [3] 9-5

IBSF World Amateur Championship
STEPHEN O'CONNOR (Ire) beat Steve Lemmens
(Bel) 11-8
*At 18yrs 40days, O'Connor became the youngest world
amateur champion.*

BCE English Amateur Championship
STEVE JUDD (Nottingham) beat Ronnie O'Sullivan
(Ilford) 13-10

Continental Airlines London Masters
STEVE DAVIS [2] beat Stephen Hendry [1] 4-0

Pontins' Professional Championship
NEAL FOULDS [13] beat Mike Hallett [7] 9-6

Trusthouse Forte Matchroom League
1st STEPHEN HENDRY; 2nd Steve Davis
Relegated: Dennis Taylor & Doug Mountjoy
Trusthouse Forte Ladies World Championship
KAREN CORR beat Stacey Hillyard 7-4

WORLD RANKINGS 1991-92

(Last season's positions in brackets)

1	(1)	Stephen Hendry (Scotland)
2	(2)	Steve Davis (England)
3	(4)	Jimmy White (England)
4	(3)	John Parrott (England)
5	(20)	Gary Wilkinson (England)
6	(13)	Neal Foulds (England)
7	(9)	Steve James (England)
8	(7)	Mike Hallett (England)
9	(10)	Dennis Taylor (N.Ireland)
10	(5)	Doug Mountjoy (Wales)
11	(6)	Terry Griffiths (Wales)
12	(8)	Dean Reynolds (England)
13	(16)	Alain Robidoux (Canada)
14	(12)	Martin Clark (England)
15	(36)	Tony Jones (England)
16	(22)	Tony Knowles (England)

Other rankings include:
Eddie Charlton 27; John Virgo 31; Tony Meo 34; Cliff
Thorburn 36; Rex Williams 48; Kirk Stevens 58; David
Taylor 74; John Spencer 85; Graham Miles 101; Alex
Higgins 120; Ray Reardon 126; Fred Davis 131; Bill
Werbeniuk 146

———— CHAMPIONS ————

WORLD PROFESSIONAL CHAMPIONSHIP

(Embassy World Professional Championship since 1976)
All winners British unless otherwise stated

1927	Joe Davis	20-11	Tom Dennis
1928	Joe Davis	16-13	Fred Lawrence
1929	Joe Davis	19-14	Tom Dennis
1930	Joe Davis	25-12	Tom Dennis
1931	Joe Davis	25-21	Tom Dennis
1932	Joe Davis	30-19	Clark McConachy (NZ)
1933	Joe Davis	25-18	Willie Smith
1934	Joe Davis	25-23	Tom Newman
1935	Joe Davis	25-20	Willie Smith
1936	Joe Davis	34-27	Horace Lindrum (Aus)
1937	Joe Davis	32-29	Horace Lindrum (Aus)
1938	Joe Davis	37-24	Sidney Smith
1939	Joe Davis	43-30	Sidney Smith
1940	Joe Davis	37-36	Fred Davis
1946	Joe Davis	78-67	Horace Lindrum (Aus)
1947	Walter Donaldson	82-63	Fred Davis
1948	Fred Davis	84-61	Walter Donaldson
1949	Fred Davis	80-65	Walter Donaldson
1950	Walter Donaldson	51-46	Fred Davis
1951	Fred Davis	58-39	Walter Donaldson
1952	Horace Lindrum	94-49	Clark McConachy (NZ)

Professional Match-Play Championship

1952	Fred Davis	38-35	Walter Donaldson
1953	Fred Davis	37-34	Walter Donaldson
1954	Fred Davis	39-21	Walter Donaldson
1955	Fred Davis	37-34	John Pulman
1956	Fred Davis	38-35	John Pulman
1957	John Pulman	39-34	Jackie Rea

Challenge Matches

1964	John Pulman	19-16	Fred Davis
1964	John Pulman	40-33	Rex Williams
1965	John Pulman	37-36	Fred Davis
1965	John Pulman	25-22	Rex Williams
1965	John Pulman	39-12	Freddie van Rensburg (SAf)
1966	John Pulman	5-2	Fred Davis
1968	John Pulman	39-34	Eddie Charlton (Aus)

Knock-out

1969	John Spencer	37-34	Gary Owen
1970	Ray Reardon	37-33	John Pulman
1971	*John Spencer	37-29	Warren Simpson (Aus)
1972	Alex Higgins	37-32	John Spencer
1973	Ray Reardon	38-32	Eddie Charlton (Aus)
1974	Ray Reardon	22-12	Graham Miles
1975	Ray Reardon	31-30	Eddie Charlton (Aus)
1976	Ray Reardon	27-16	Alex Higgins
1977	John Spencer	25-21	Cliff Thorburn (Can)
1978	Ray Reardon	25-18	Perrie Mans (SAf)
1979	Terry Griffiths	24-16	Dennis Taylor
1980	Cliff Thorburn (Can)	18-16	Alex Higgins
1981	Steve Davis	18-12	Doug Mountjoy
1982	Alex Higgins	18-15	Ray Reardon

1983	Steve Davis	18-6	Cliff Thorburn (Can)
1984	Steve Davis	18-16	Jimmy White
1985	Dennis Taylor	18-17	Steve Davis
1986	Joe Johnson	18-12	Steve Davis
1987	Steve Davis	18-14	Joe Johnson
1988	Steve Davis	18-11	Terry Griffiths
1989	Steve Davis	18-3	John Parrott
1990	Stephen Hendry	18-12	Jimmy White
1991	John Parrott	18-11	Jimmy White

* Played November 1970

RANKING TOURNAMENT WINNERS
BCE International
1981-84 Jameson International; 1985 Goya International; 1986 BCE International; 1987-88 Fidelity Unit Trust International

1982 Tony Knowles
1983 Steve Davis
1984 Steve Davis
1985 Cliff Thorburn (Can)
1986 Neal Foulds
1987 Steve Davis
1988 Steve Davis
1989 Steve Davis
Discontinued 1989

Rothmans Grand Prix
1982-83 Professional Players' Tournament; 1984-Rothmans Grand Prix

1982 Ray Reardon
1983 Tony Knowles
1984 Dennis Taylor
1985 Steve Davis
1986 Jimmy White
1987 Stephen Hendry
1988 Steve Davis
1989 Steve Davis
1990 Stephen Hendry

Mercantile Credit Classic
1984 Lada Classic; 1985-Mercantile Credit Classic

1984 Steve Davis
1985 Willie Thorne
1986 Jimmy White
1987 Steve Davis
1988 Steve Davis
1989 Doug Mountjoy
1990 Steve James
1991 Jimmy White

Stormseal United Kingdom Open
1984-85 Coral UK Open; 1986-88 Tennents UK Open

1984 Steve Davis
1985 Steve Davis
1986 Steve Davis
1987 Steve Davis
1988 Doug Mountjoy
1989 Stephen Hendry
1990 Stephen Hendry
1991 Stephen Hendry

Pearl Assurance British Open
1985-87 Dulux British Open; 1988 MIM Britannia British Open; 1989 Anglian British Open

1985 Silvino Francisco (SAf)
1986 Steve Davis
1987 Jimmy White
1988 Stephen Hendry
1989 Tony Meo
1990 Bob Chaperon (Can)
1991 Stephen Hendry

BCE Canadian Masters
1988 Jimmy White
Discontinued

European Open
1989 John Parrott
1990 John Parrott
1991 Tony Jones

Hong Kong Open
1989 Mike Hallett

555 Asian Open
1989 Stephen Hendry
1990 Stephen Hendry

Dubai Duty Free Masters
1990 Stephen Hendry

RANKING TOURNAMENT WINS
22	**Steve Davis**
11	**Stephen Hendry**
5	**Ray Reardon**
5	**Jimmy White**
3	**John Parrott**
2	**Tony Knowles**
2	**Doug Mountjoy**
2	**Dennis Taylor**
2	**Cliff Thorburn (Can)**
1	**Neal Foulds**
1	**Silvino Francisco (SAf)**
1	**Tony Meo**
1	**Willie Thorne**
1	**John Spencer**
1	**Alex Higgins**
1	**Terry Griffiths**
1	**Joe Johnson**
1	**Mike Hallett**
1	**Steve James**
1	**Bob Chaperon (Can)**
1	**Tony Jones**

OTHER MAJOR TOURNAMENTS
Pot Black
1969 Ray Reardon
1970 John Spencer
1971 John Spencer
1972 Eddie Charlton (Aus)
1973 Eddie Charlton (Aus)
1974 Graham Miles
1975 Graham Miles
1976 John Spencer
1977 Perrie Mans (SAf)
1978 Doug Mountjoy
1979 Ray Reardon
1980 Eddie Charlton (Aus)
1981 Cliff Thorburn (Can)
1982 Steve Davis
1983 Steve Davis
1984 Terry Griffiths
1985 Doug Mountjoy
1986 Jimmy White
(discontinued)

Benson & Hedges Masters
1975 John Spencer
1976 Ray Reardon
1977 Doug Mountjoy
1978 Alex Higgins
1979 Perrie Mans (SAf)
1980 Terry Griffiths
1981 Alex Higgins
1982 Steve Davis
1983 Cliff Thorburn (Can)
1984 Jimmy White
1985 Cliff Thorburn (Can)
1986 Cliff Thorburn (Can)

1987	Dennis Taylor
1988	Steve Davis
1989	Stephen Hendry
1990	Stephen Hendry
1991	Stephen Hendry

World Match-Play Championship

1988	Steve Davis
1989	Jimmy White
1990	Jimmy White

World Amateur Champions

1963	Gary Owen
1966	Gary Owen
1968	David Taylor
1970	Jonathan Barron
1972	Ray Edmonds
1974	Ray Edmonds
1976	Doug Mountjoy
1978	Cliff Wilson
1980	Jimmy White
1982	Terry Parsons
1984	O B (Omprakash) Agrawal (Ind)
1985	Paul Mifsud (Malta)
1986	Paul Mifsud (Malta)
1986	Paul Mifsud (Malta)
1987	Darren Morgan
1988	James Wattana (Tha)
1989	Ken Doherty (Ire)
1990	Stephen O'Connor (Ire)

1992

Jan 1-11 Mercantile Credit Classic (Bournemouth); Jan 12-15 World Masters (Birmingham); Feb 2-9 Masters Tournament (Wembley); Feb 17 - 29 British Open (Derby); Mar 31 - Apr 5 Irish Masters (Kill, Co. Kildare); Apr 18 - May 4 WORLD PROFESSIONAL CHAMPIONSHIP (Crucible Theatre, Sheffield)

SPEEDWAY

1991

WORLD CHAMPIONSHIPS

Individual
Gothenburg, Aug 31
1 Jan Pedersen (Cradley Heath/Den) 15 pts
2 Tony Rickardsson (Ipswich/Swe) 12 pts
3 Hans Nielsen (Oxford/Den) 11 pts
4 Tommy Knudsen (Coventry/Den) 11 pts
5 Paul Thorp (Bradford/Eng) 10 pts
6 Jimmy Nilsen (Berwick/Swe) 10 pts

Pairs
Poznan, Poland, Jul 20
1 Denmark (Hans Nielsen, Jan Pedersen, Tommy Knudsen) 28 pts
2 Sweden (Per Jonsson, Henrik Gustafsson, Jimmy Nilsen) 24 pt
3 Norway (L. Gunestad, Einar Kyllingstad, T-E Hielm) 19 pts

Long Track
Marianske Lazne, Czechoslovakia, Jul 27
1 Gerd Riss (Ger) 24 pts
2 Ales Dryml (Cze) 21 pts
3 Jan Pedersen (Den) 21 pts

Team
Vojens, Denmark, Sep 14
1 Denmark 51 pts
2 Sweden 30 pts
3 United States 28 pts

Wimbledon, champions seven times between 1954 and 1961, closed after 62 years and moved to Eastbourne. Hackney withdrew from the British League leaving London without a speedway track for the first time since the sport began in 1928.

Michael Lee, 32, the 1980 world champion, returned after five years out of the sport to ride for King's Lynn.

1990

DUNLOP BRITISH LEAGUE RIDERS' CHAMPIONSHIP
Belle Vue. Oct 14
1 Hans Nielsen (Oxford) 15 pts
2 Kelly Moran (Belle Vue) 12 pts
3 Ronnie Correy (Wolverhampton) 12 pts
  Marvyn Cox (Bradford) 12 pts
Moran won run-off for second place

SUNBRITE BRITISH LEAGUE

		P	W	D	L	Pts
1(7)	READING	32	19	3	10	54
2(2)	Wolverhampton	32	17	5	10	49
3(4)	Belle Vue	32	19	2	11	47
4(1)	Oxford	32	17	2	13	46
5(8)	Bradford	32	16	1	15	41
6(6)	Swindon	32	15	2	15	41
7(3)	Cradley Heath	32	12	1	19	32
8(5)	Coventry	32	10	3	19	30
9(9)	King's Lynn	32	7	5	20	21

SUNBRITE NATIONAL LEAGUE

		P	W	D	L	Pts
1 (1)	POOLE	32	29	0	3	58
2 (13)	Middlesbrough	32	22	2	8	46
3 (4)	Ipswich	32	22	2	8	46
4 (9)	Glasgow	32	19	0	13	38
5 (6)	Hackney	32	19	0	13	38
6 (3)	Berwick	32	18	1	13	37
7 (2)	Wimbledon	32	16	3	13	35
8 (10)	Stoke	32	16	1	15	33
9 (5)	Exeter	32	15	1	16	31
10(11)	Peterborough	32	15	0	17	30
11(7)	Eastbourne	32	15	0	17	30
12(15)	Newcastle	32	14	0	18	28
13(7)	Edinburgh	32	12	1	19	25
14(12)	Arena Essex	32	12	1	19	25
15(14)	Rye House	32	8	0	24	16
16(17)	Long Eaton	32	7	2	23	16
17(18)	Milton Keynes	32	6	0	26	12

Last season's positions in brackets

CHAMPIONS

BRITISH SPEEDWAY LEAGUE
Champions since formation of two divisions in 1968. Known as British League and National League since 1968.

	British League	National League
1968	Coventry	Belle Vue Colts
1969	Poole	Belle Vue Colts
1970	Belle Vue	Canterbury
1971	Belle Vue	Eastbourne
1972	Belle Vue	Crewe
1973	Reading	Boston
1974	Exeter	Birmingham
1975	Ipswich	Birmingham
1976	Ipswich	Newcastle
1977	White City	Eastbourne
1978	Coventry	Canterbury
1979	Coventry	Mildenhall
1980	Reading	Rye House
1981	Cradley Heath	Middlesbrough
1982	Belle Vue	Newcastle
1983	Cradley Heath	Newcastle
1984	Ipswich	Long Eaton
1985	Oxford	Ellesmere Port
1986	Oxford	Eastbourne
1987	Coventry	Eastbourne
1988	Coventry	Hackney
1989	Oxford	Poole
1990	Reading	Poole

Most Titles
Division One/British League
10 Belle Vue; **8** Wembley; **7** Wimbledon; Coventry

BRITISH LEAGUE RIDERS' CHAMPIONSHIP

1965	Barry Briggs (Swindon)	1978	Ole Olsen (Coventry)
1966	Barry Briggs (Swindon)	1979	John Louis (Ipswich)
1967	Barry Briggs (Swindon)	1980	Les Collins (Leicester)
1968	Barry Briggs (Swindon)	1981	Kenny Carter (Halifax)
1969	Barry Briggs (Swindon)	1982	Kenny Carter (Halifax)
1970	Barry Briggs (Swindon)	1983	Erik Gundersen (Cradley Heath)
1971	Ivan Mauger (Belle Vue)	1984	Chris Morton (Belle Vue)
1972	Ole Olsen (Wolverhampton)	1985	Erik Gundersen (Cradley Heath)
1973	Ivan Mauger (Exeter)	1986	Hans Nielsen (Oxford)
1974	Peter Collins (Belle Vue)	1987	Hans Nielsen (Oxford)
1975	Peter Collins (Belle Vue)	1988	Jan Pedersen (Cradley Heath)
1976	Ole Olsen (Coventry)	1989	Shawn Moran (Belle Vue)
1977	Ole Olsen (Coventry)	1990	Hans Nielsen (Oxford)

WORLD CHAMPIONS

	Individual	*Pairs*	*Team*	*Long Track*
1936	Lionel Van Praag (Aus)	-	-	-
1937	Jack Milne (US)	-	-	-
1938	Bluey Wilkinson (Aus)	-	-	-
1949	Tommy Price (Eng)	-	-	-
1950	Freddie Williams (Wal)	-	-	-
1951	Jack Young (Aus)	-	-	-
1952	Jack Young (Aus)	-	-	-
1953	Freddie Williams (Wal)	-	-	-
1954	Ronnie Moore (NZ)	-	-	-
1955	Peter Craven (Eng)	-	-	-
1956	Ove Fundin (Swe)	-	-	-
1957	Barry Briggs (NZ)	-	-	-
1958	Barry Briggs (NZ)	-	-	-
1959	Ronnie Moore (NZ)	-	-	-
1960	Ove Fundin (Swe)	-	Sweden	-
1961	Ove Fundin (Swe)	-	Poland	-
1962	Peter Craven (Eng)	-	Sweden	-
1963	Ove Fundin (Swe)	-	Sweden	-
1964	Barry Briggs (NZ)	-	Sweden	-
1965	Bjorn Knutsson (Swe)	-	Poland	-
1966	Barry Briggs (NZ)	-	Poland	-
1967	Ove Fundin (Swe)	-	Sweden	-
1968	Ivan Mauger (NZ)	-	Great Britain	-
1969	Ivan Mauger (NZ)	-	Poland	-
1970	Ivan Mauger (NZ)	New Zealand (Moore/Mauger)	Sweden	-
1971	Ole Olsen (Den)	Poland (Szczakiel/Wyglenda)	Great Britain	Ivan Mauger (NZ)
1972	Ivan Mauger (NZ)	England (Wilson/Betts)	Great Britain	Ivan Mauger (NZ)
1973	Jerzy Szczakiel (Pol)	Sweden (Michanek/Jansson)	Great Britain	Ole Olsen (Den)
1974	Anders Michanek (Swe)	Sweden (Michanek/Sjosten)	England	Egon Muller (FRG)
1975	Ole Olsen (Den)	Sweden (Michanek/Jansson)	England	Egon Muller (FRG)
1976	Peter Collins (Eng)	England (Simmons/Louis)	Australia	Egon Muller (FRG)
1977	Ivan Mauger (NZ)	England (Simmons/Collins)	England	Anders Michanek (Swe)
1978	Ole Olsen (Den)	England (Simmons/Kennett)	Denmark	Egon Muller (FRG)
1979	Ivan Mauger (NZ)	Denmark (Olsen/Nielsen)	New Zealand	Alois Weisbock (FRG)
1980	Michael Lee (Eng)	England (Jessup/Collins)	England	Karl Maier (FRG)
1981	Bruce Penhall (US)	United States (Penhall/Schwartz)	Denmark	Michael Lee (Eng)
1982	Bruce Penhall (US)	United States (Sigalos/Schwartz)	United States	Karl Maier (FRG)
1983	Egon Muller (FRG)	England (Carter/Collins)	Denmark	Shawn Moran (US)
1984	Erik Gundersen (Den)	England (Collins/Morton)	Denmark	Erik Gundersen (Den)
1985	Erik Gundersen (Den)	Denmark (Gundersen/Knudsen)	Denmark	Simon Wigg (Eng)
1986	Hans Nielsen (Den)	Denmark (Gundersen/Nielsen)	Denmark	Erik Gundersen (Den)
1987	Hans Nielsen (Den)	Denmark (Gundersen/Nielsen)	Denmark	Karl Maier (FRG)
1988	Erik Gundersen (Den)	Denmark (Gundersen/Nielsen)	Denmark	Karl Maier (FRG)
1989	Hans Nielsen (Den)	Denmark (Gundersen/Nielsen)	England	Simon Wigg (Eng)
1990	Per Jonsson (Swe)	Denmark (Nielsen/Pedersen)	United States	Simon Wigg (Eng)
1991	Jan Pedersen (Den)	Denmark (Nielsen/Pedersen/Knudsen)	Denmark	Gerd Riss (Ger)

Most Wins

Individual 6 Ivan Mauger; 5 Ove Fundin; 4 Barry Briggs; 3 Ole Olsen, Hans Nielsen, Erik Gundersen

Pairs 8 Denmark; 7 England, 3 Sweden
- Ind: 6 Hans Nielsen (Den); 5 Erik Gundersen (Den); 4 Peter Collins (Eng)

Team 9 Denmark; 6 Sweden; 5 England; 4 Britain
- Ind: 8 Hans Nielsen (Den); 7 Erik Gundersen (Den); 6 Ove Fundin (Swe)

Long Track: 4 Egon Muller (FRG), Karl Maier (FRG); 3 Simon Wigg (Eng)

SQUASH

Jahangir Khan of Pakistan overcame lack of form and fitness to beat his compatriot and rival Jansher Khan and win his tenth consecutive British Open title. For much of the season, Jansher had eclipsed him and won the world title when Jahangir was absent and talking of retirement. Lisa Opie became the first home winner of the British Open since 1961 when she won an all-British final against Sue Wright, who had scored a shock win over Susan Devoy, the champion since 1984; the new champion gave the credit to her sports psychologist Graham Jones.

1991

HI-TEC BRITISH OPEN
Wembley Conference Centre, Apr 16-22

Men

QUARTER-FINALS
JANSHER KHAN (Pak) beat Rodney Eyles (Aus) 9-3 9-3 6-9 9-4; CHRIS DITTMAR (Aus) beat Del Harris (GB) 9-1 9-3 9-3; JAHANGIR KHAN (Pak) beat Bryan Beeson (GB) 9-3 9-0 9-0; RODNEY MARTIN (Aus) beat Simon Parke (GB) 9-3 9-3 9-4

SEMI-FINALS
JANSHER KHAN beat Dittmar 9-10 9-1 9-6 9-2; JAHANGIR KHAN beat Martin 9-5 9-2 9-7

FINAL
JAHANGIR KHAN beat Jansher Khan 2-9 9-4 9-4 9-0

Women

QUARTER-FINALS
SUE WRIGHT (GB) beat Susan Devoy (NZ) 4-9 10-9 1-9 9-3 9-2; ROBYN LAMBOURNE (Aus) beat Danielle Drady (Aus) 7-9 9-2 9-7 2-9 9-2; MARTINE LE MOIGNAN (GB) beat Suzanne Horner (GB) 4-9 9-5 9-7 9-3; LISA OPIE (GB) beat Cassie Jackman (GB) 3-9 9-1 9-4 8-10 9-0

SEMI-FINALS
WRIGHT beat Lambourne 7-9 2-9 9-7 9-6 9-2; OPIE beat Le Moignan 4-9 9-4 9-3 9-3

FINAL
OPIE beat Wright 6-9 9-3 9-3 9-4
Opie was the first British winner since Fran Marshall in 1961

EUROPEAN TEAM CHAMPIONSHIPS
Gelsenkirchen, Germany, May 2-5

Men
ENGLAND 5 Finland 0

Women
ENGLAND 3 Holland 0

FIGHT FOR SIGHT NATIONAL CHAMPIONSHIPS
Newcastle, Jan 17-22

Men
SEMI-FINALS
PAUL GREGORY (Surrey) beat Peter Marshall (Leics) scr; SIMON PARKE (Yorks) beat Tony Hands (Essex) 6-9 9-0 9-0 9-1

FINAL
GREGORY beat Parke 9-4 7-9 9-2 9-0

Women
SEMI-FINALS
SUZANNE HORNER (Yorks) beat Sue Wright (Kent) 9-7 9-5 9-3; MARTINE LE MOIGNAN (Hants) beat Lucy Soutter (Gloucs) 9-5 9-2 9-0

FINAL
LE MOIGNAN beat Horner 9-7 9-1 10-8

MEN'S WORLD OPEN CHAMPIONSHIP
Adelaide, Jul 30 - Aug 5

SEMI-FINALS
RODNEY MARTIN (Aus) beat Chris Dittmar (Aus) 5-15 15-13 17-14 15-13; JAHANGIR KHAN (Pak) beat Chris Robertson (Aus) 15-3 14-15 15-6 15-4

FINAL
MARTIN beat Jahangir Khan 14-17 15-9 15-4 15-13

PIMMS PREMIER LEAGUE

Final Table	P	W	L	D	F	A	Pts
1 Cannons	16	12	2	2	48	16	74
2 Wizards	16	10	3	3	41	23	64
3 Lambs	16	10	3	3	40	24	63
4 Allsports	16	7	4	5	37	27	56
5 Stripes	16	5	6	5	32	32	47
6 North Walsham	16	5	7	4	27	37	41
7 Priory	16	3	6	7	28	36	41
8 Surbiton	16	1	11	4	18	46	24
9 Abbeydale	16	0	11	5	17	47	22

1990

WOMEN'S WORLD CHAMPIONSHIP
Sydney, Oct 7-20

Individual

SEMI-FINALS
SUSAN DEVOY (NZ) beat Danielle Drady (Aus) 9-4 9-3 9-2; MARTINE LE MOIGNAN (GB) beat Robyn Lambourne (Aus) 4-9 9-0 5-9 9-5 10-9

THIRD PLACE PLAY-OFF
DRADY beat Lambourne 10-9 9-1 5-9 9-1

FINAL
DEVOY beat Le Moignan 9-4 9-4 9-4

Team

SEMI-FINALS
ENGLAND 3 New Zealand 0; AUSTRALIA 3 Germany 0

FINAL
ENGLAND 2 Australia 1

MEN'S WORLD OPEN CHAMPIONSHIP
Toulouse, France, Nov 7-11

SEMI-FINALS
CHRIS DITTMAR (Aus) beat Tristan Nancarrow (Aus) 15-8 15-3 15-7; JANSHER KHAN (Pak) beat Chris Robertson (Aus) 10-15 15-5 15-13 15-11

FINAL
JANSHER KHAN beat Dittmar 15-8 17-15 13-15 15-5

CHAMPIONS

WORLD OPEN CHAMPIONSHIP -
(Not held 1978)
Men
1976	Geoff Hunt (Aus)
1977	Geoff Hunt (Aus)
1979	Geoff Hunt (Aus)
1980	Geoff Hunt (Aus)
1981	Jahangir Khan (Pak)
1982	Jahangir Khan (Pak)
1983	Jahangir Khan (Pak)
1984	Jahangir Khan (Pak)
1985	Jahangir Khan (Pak)
1986	Ross Norman (NZ)
1987	Jansher Khan (Pak)
1988	Jahangir Khan (Pak)
1989	Jansher Khan (Pak)
1990	Jansher Khan (Pak)
1991	Rodney Martin (Aus)

Women
1976	Heather McKay (Aus)
1979	Heather McKay (Aus)
1981	Rhonda Thorne (Aus)
1983	Vicki Cardwell (Aus)
1985	Susan Devoy (NZ)
1987	Susan Devoy (NZ)
1989	Martine Le Moignan (GB)
1990	Susan Devoy (NZ)

WOMEN'S WORLD TEAM CHAMPIONSHIP
1979	Great Britain
1981	Australia
1983	Australia
1985	England
1987	England
1989	England
1990	England

WORLD AMATEUR/ISRF CHAMPIONSHIP
From 1987 a team competition only
Individual
1967	Geoff Hunt (Aus)
1969	Geoff Hunt (Aus)
1971	Geoff Hunt (Aus)
1973	Cam Nancarrow (Aus)
1975	Kevin Shawcross (Aus)
1977	Maqsood Ahmed (Pak)
1979	Jahangir Khan (Pak)
1981	Steve Bowditch (Aus)
1983	Jahangir Khan (Pak)
1985	Jahangir Khan (Pak)

Team
1967	Australia
1969	Australia
1971	Australia
1973	Australia
1975	Great Britain
1977	Pakistan
1979	Great Britain
1981	Pakistan
1983	Pakistan
1985	Pakistan
1987	Pakistan
1989	Australia

BRITISH OPEN CHAMPIONSHIP
First held in 1922 for women; 1930 for men
Winners since 1971
Men
1971	Jonah Barrington (GB)
1972	Jonah Barrington (GB)
1973	Jonah Barrington (GB)
1974	Geoff Hunt (Aus)
1975	Qamar Zaman (Pak)
1976	Geoff Hunt (Aus)
1977	Geoff Hunt (Aus)
1978	Geoff Hunt (Aus)
1979	Geoff Hunt (Aus)
1980	Geoff Hunt (Aus)
1981	Geoff Hunt (Aus)
1982	Jahangir Khan (Pak)
1983	Jahangir Khan (Pak)
1984	Jahangir Khan (Pak)
1985	Jahangir Khan (Pak)
1986	Jahangir Khan (Pak)
1987	Jahangir Khan (Pak)
1988	Jahangir Khan (Pak)
1989	Jahangir Khan (Pak)
1990	Jahangir Khan (Pak)
1991	Jahangir Khan (Pak)

Most wins
10 Jahangir Khan; **8** Geoff Hunt; **7** Hashim Khan; **6** Abdel Fattah Amr Bey, Jonah Barrington

Women
1971	Heather McKay (Aus)
1972	Heather McKay (Aus)
1973	Heather McKay (Aus)
1974	Heather McKay (Aus)
1975	Heather McKay (Aus)
1976	Heather McKay (Aus)
1977	Heather McKay (Aus)
1978	Susan Newman (Aus)
1979	Barbara Well (Aus)
1980	Vicki Hoffman (Aus)
1981	Vicki Hoffman (Aus)
1982	Vicki Cardwell (née Hoffman) (Aus)
1983	Vicki Cardwell (Aus)
1984	Susan Devoy (NZ)
1985	Susan Devoy (NZ)
1986	Susan Devoy (NZ)
1987	Susan Devoy (NZ)
1988	Susan Devoy (NZ)
1989	Susan Devoy (NZ)
1990	Susan Devoy (NZ)
1991	Lisa Opie (GB)

Most wins
16 Heather McKay; **9** Janet Morgan; **7** Susan Devoy; **6** Margot Lumb.

1992

Apr 3-13 British Open (Lambs and Wembley Conference Centre); Oct World Open, men (Johannesburg)

STUDENT GAMES

Universiade XVI, or the World Student Games, was held in Sheffield and billed as the largest sports and cultural event ever staged in the UK. It was hardly billed at all outside Sheffield. But within the city an extraordinary amount of defensive enthusiasm built up during the fortnight of competition, leading to substantial crowds at improbable occasions and the virtual excommunication of anyone who criticised the project, which had given the city beautiful new sporting facilities and an additional cost projected at a minimum £5 million.

More than 5,500 competitors from 111 countries took part in nine different sports. They were a remarkable collection of people. A lone Danish athlete arrived, although his country was not affiliated, and one competitor arrived from Yemen: he was said to have thought he had entered the soccer. A team from Lebanon arrived unexpectedly: the last letter from the organisers had been returned marked "Return to Sender. Headquarters Bombed". Pedantic officials then refused to let the Lebanese swimmers compete on the grounds of lateness, so the swimmers went into the athletics instead.

At the opening ceremony, Helen Sharman, the cosmonaut, stumbled on her way to light the flame and dropped the torch ("We have lift-off without ignition" said *The Guardian* headline); the gas beacon ignited automatically anyway but it had to be put out 15 minutes later - British Gas refused to sponsor it and said it was an environmental hazard.

This seemed like an ill-omen. But the Universiade acquired the momentum of a more formal Games and had the attendant advantages and disadvantages. On the one hand, 5000 people watched Britain play Poland in the volleyball final and North Korean gymnasts created routines that would have caused TV audiences to go into raptures had they been shown: Bo Sil Hwang finished her programme beautifully, having fallen violently and been concussed. On the other hand, Xinmei Sui of China, winner of the women's shot put, tested positive for anabolic steroids, the first person to do so in the Games's 32-year history.

Britain won more athletics medals than at any Student Games since Tokyo in 1967: the winners included John Mayock in the 5000 metres; he was listed in the media guide as a 20km walker. Five women gymnasts were docked 0.5 of a point for wearing their leotards cut too high; the Uruguayan footballers poured orange juice over their boots so that it would dry stickily and improve their ball control; Ireland complained they were the victims of biased refereeing in the basketball game against Czechoslovakia which they lost 90-63; Cecile Olandez, one of the women's basketball team from Guam, was only five foot tall; three Mozambican athletes took a training run down an invitingly long, wide road: the M1; Iran's soccer team included a player called Coochekisiahkhalehsa; Zimbabwe's women's hockey team played seven matches, scored no goals and conceded 107, including 20 against China. "I'm saving more than are going in and that's a beautiful feeling," said their goalkeeper Janet Chakunda.

Opponents within the city staged two rival events: the Alternative Games ("the second biggest fiasco this century") and the Other Games: this was billed as the smallest sporting event ever organised within walking distance of Endcliffe Park Cafe and cost the organisers £9.60. They lit a 25p candle they had carried from round the corner and staged uphill skiing, swimming on grass and imaginary discus throwing. The winners were awarded foil-wrapped chocolate money.

UNIVERSIADE XVI
Sheffield, Jul 13-24

Athletics
Men

100 Metres	Michael Bates (US) 10.17s	400 Metres	Patrick O'Connor (Jam) 45.52s
200 Metres	Jon Drummond (US) 20.58s	800 Metres	Giuseppe d'Orso (Ita) 1m 46.82s
		1500 Metres	Niall Bruton (Ire) 3m 50.69s
		5000 Metres	John Mayock (GB) 13m 39.25s
		10,000 Metres	Stefan Freigang (Ger) 28m15.84s
		110 Metres Hurdles	Elbert Ellis (US) 13.83s
		400 Metres Hurdles	Derrick Adkins (US) 49.01s

3000 Metres Chase	S Creighton (Aus) 8m 32.30s
20 km Walk	Robert Korzeniowski (Pol) 1h 24m 34s
4 x 100 Metres Relay	United States 39.10s
4 x 400 Metres Relay	Unites States 3m 03.65s
Marathon	Wang Yung-jo (SKo) 2h 12m 40s
High Jump	Hollis Conway (US) 2.37m
Long Jump	A Turner (US) 8.18m
Triple Jump	Brian Wellman (Ber) 17.07m
Pole Vault	Istvan Bagyula (Hun) 5.80m
Javelin	Steve Backley (GB) 87.42m
Shot	Alexandr Kilimenko (USSR) 19.35m
Discus	Adewale Olukoju (Nig) 61.48m
Hammer	Ken Flax (US) 76.46m
Decathlon	S Fritz (US) 8,079 pts

Women

100 Metres	Chryste Gaines (US) 11.27s
200 Metres	Wang Huei-chen (Chn) 23.22s
400 Metres	Maicel Malone (US) 50.65s
800 Metres	Inna Evseyeva (USSR) 1m 59.80s
1500 Metres	Sonia O'Sullivan (Ire) 4m 12.14s
3000 Metres	I Besliu (Rom) 8m 55.42s
10,000 Metres	Anne Marie Letko (US) 32m 36.87s
100 Metres Hurdles	
400 Metres Hurdles	G Tromp (Hol) 55.30s
10 km Walk	Sari Essayah (Fin) 44m 04s
4 x 100 Metres Relay	United States 44.45s
4 x 400 Metres Relay	United States 3m 27.93s
Marathon	Iwai Miyako (Jap) 2h 36m 27s
High Jump	Alison Inverarity (Aus) 1.92m
Long Jump	Inessa Kravetz (USSR) 6.87m
Triple Jump	Uriung Li (Chn) 14.20m
Javelin	Tatyana Shikolenko (USSR) 63.56m
Shot	Svetlana Kriveleva (USSR) 19.62m
Discus	Yanling Xiao (Chn) 64.36m
Heptathlon	Brigit Garius (Ger) 6,419 pts

Basketball

Men	United States
Women	United States

Fencing
Men

Individual Foil	Dmitri Shevchenko (USSR)
Team Foil	Italy
Individual Epée	
Team Epée	Germany
Individual Sabre	Grigory Kirienko (USSR)
Team Sabre	Germany

Women

Individual Foil	Giovanna Trellini (Ita)
Team Foil	Italy
Individual Epée	M Horvath (Hun)
Team Epée	Hungary

Gymnastics
Men

Team	USSR 171.850 pts
Individual All-round	Weng Zong Cheng (Chn) 57.300 pts
Floor	N Racanelli (US) 9.725 pts
Pommel Horse	Dong Huang (Chn) 9.725 pts
Rings	Myong Su-sin (NKo) 9.762 pts
Vault	Hong Chun-yeo (SKo) 9.781 pts
Parallel Bars	A Kan (USSR) 9.762 pts
Horizontal Bar	Pai Gil-su (NKo) 9.800 pts

Women

Team	North Korea 116.500 pts
Individual All-round	Elena Sazonenkova (USSR) 39.150pts
Floor	N Lashonova (USSR) 9.862 pts

Beam	Gyung Hu-choi (NKo) 9.862 pts
Vault	K Seo (Jap) 9.837 pts
Asymmetric Bars	Gyung Hu-choi (NKo) 9.875 pts

Rhythmic

Individual	Gyung Hu-Li (NKo) 36.650pts
Rope	Gyung Hu-Li (NKo) 9.250 pts
Hoop	Suk Yong-Li (NKo) 9.050 pts
Ball	Gyung Hu-Li (NKo) 9.100 pts
Club	Suk Yong-Li (NKo) 9.000 pts

Hockey

Men	Great Britain
Women	Holland

Soccer

Men	South Korea

Swimming
Men
Freestyle

50 Metres	Stephan Caron (Fra) 22.97s
100 Metres	Stephan Caron (Fra) 49.72s
200 Metres	Stephan Caron (Fra) 1m 50.24s
400 Metres	Artur Wojdat (Pol) 3m 52.55s
1500 Metres	Ian Wilson (GB) 15m 15.30s

Backstroke

100 Metres	D Botsford (Can) 56.40s
200 Metres	William Schwenk (US) 2m 00.38s

Butterfly

100 Metres	T Li (Chn) 55.61s
200 Metres	Rick Carey (US) 1m 58.36s

Breaststroke

100 Metres	Brian Pajer (US) 1m 03.21s
200 Metres	Gary O'Toole (Ire) 2m 16.75s

Medley

200 Metres	Greg Burgess (US) 2m 03.90s
400 Metres	Takihiro Fujimoto (Jap) 4m 23.10s

Relay

4 x 100 Free	United States 3m 22.73s
4 x 200 Free	Soviet Union 7m 23.28s
4 x 100 Medley	United States 3m 44.33s

Diving

1m Springboard	Lan Wei (Chn) 377.64 pts
3m Springboard	Li Deliang (Chn) 659.70 pts
10m Platform	Feilong Wu (Chn) 576.90 pts
Water Polo	United States

Women
Freestyle

50 Metres	Yang Wenyi (Chn) 25.92s
100 Metres	Yong Zhuang (Chn) 56.26s
200 Metres	Karen Kraemer (US) 2m 02.23s
400 Metres	Patricia Noall (Can) 4m 16.74s
800 Metres	Francesca Ferrarani (Ita) 8m 43.55s

Backstroke

100 Metres	Barbara Bedford (US) 1m 02.08s
200 Metres	Lin Li (Chi) 2m 15.12s

Butterfly

100 Metres	Xiaohong Wang (Chn) 1m 00.00s
200 Metres	Xiaohong Wang (Chn) 2m 10.76s

Breaststroke

100 Metres	Guylaine Cloutier (Can) 1m 10.93s
200 Metres	Svetlana Kuzmina (USSR) 2m 31.60s

Medley

200 Metres	Lin Li (Chn) 2m 14.22s
400 Metres	Lin Li (Chn) 4m 42.58s

Relay

4 x 100 Free	China 3m 46.41s

| 4 x 200 Free | Soviet Union 8m 14.48s |
| 4 x 100 Medley | United States 4m 11.70s |

Diving

1m Springboard	X Yu (Chn) 270.66 pts
3m Springboard	Gao Min (Chn) 597.48 pts
10m Platform	Kim Chun-ok (NKo) 452.16 pts

Tennis

Men's Singles	Xai Jai Ping (Chn)
Women's Singles	Mana Endo (Jap)
Men's Doubles	Eui Jong-Chan & Jai Seong-Ho (SKo)
Women's Doubles	Kim Il-Soo & Lee Jung-Myung (SKo)
Mixed Doubles	B Hanson & S Gilchrist (US)

Volleyball

| Men | Poland |
| Women | Italy |

LEADING MEDAL WINNERS

	G	S	B	Total
United States	29	23	24	76
China	20	17	11	48
Soviet Union	15	15	21	51
North Korea	11	3	5	19
Italy	6	7	8	21
South Korea	5	1	3	9
Japan	4	15	9	28
Germany	4	8	5	17
Great Britain	4	5	5	14

━━━ RECORDS ━━━

Universiades

I Turin 1959; II Sofia 1961; III Porto Alegre, Brazil 1963; IV Budapest 1965; V Tokyo 1967; VI Turin 1970; VII Moscow 1973; VIII Rome, 1975; IX Sofia 1977; X Mexico City 1979; XI Bucharest, 1981; XII Edmonton, Alberta 1983; XIII Kobe, Japan 1985; XIV Zagreb, Yugoslavia 1987; XV Duisburg, West Germany 1989; XVI Sheffield 1991; XVII Buffalo 1993.

❝This is breathtakingly Gradgrind and grasping.❞
Martin Flannery, Sheffield MP, on British Gas's refusal to sponsor the flame

"There are an awful lot of people in Sheffield struggling to pay their quarterly bills and in the circumstances we did not think it appropriate to burn off £100,000 worth of gas to no practical purpose."
British Gas spokesman

"Sheffield, and all who worked so hard and so long to secure and organise this historic event, can rightly feel proud."
The Star, Sheffield on the opening ceremony

"...rather like being outside the world: thousands of competitors, a buzzing Games village, thousands of spectators, with attendances growing as the Games progressed, some very healthy competition, which touched notable heights on occasions. But few people outside Sheffield knew it was going on and a lot of people in the city were bitter about that. Most of them were local politicians, finding an excuse to cover their original folly, which will leave the city with some magnificent facilities and a heavy debt burden.❞
John Rodda, Athletics Today

SWIMMING

When East Germany died, so did the system that made it one of the great swimming nations. German decline was evident at both the World and European Championships in 1991: the United States dominated the World Championships in Perth, Australia, winning 17 of the 45 medals and the Chinese effectively replaced East Germany, both as the Americans' nearest rivals and as the focus of constant suspicion about how they were doing it.

The Chinese coach Xiong Zhang walked out of a press conference when asked about allegations that his swimmers took steroids: "I can't believe people would speak such things," he said. The former East German star Kristin Otto, asked if the Chinese improvement was due to drugs, replied: "You cannot blame the athletes. The officials, team managers and coaches take the decisions." United Germany won only four golds (compared to 13 for the women alone at the previous championships), as predicted beforehand by Michael Gross who said the old East Germans were now too busy eating junk food. Gross himself, however, took his overall total of Championship medals to 11 with a relay gold.

The other rising power was Hungary, whose 11-strong team won five golds and broke two world records. Norbert Rozsa, 18, snatched both the gold and the record from Britain's 26-year-old Olympic champion Adrian Moorhouse. "I did feel my age," said Moorhouse as he sat at the press conference. "I'm feeling it when I sit next to an 18-year-old who's just beaten me." Silver for Moorhouse and Lorraine Coombes and a bronze for Nick Gillingham were Britain's only successes. "We just aren't good enough," said the team manager Paul Bush. The point was proved again at the European Championships in Athens, where the 17-year-old Hungarian girl Krisztina Egerszegi emerged as the outstanding swimmer.

China's winners included 12-year-old Fu Mingxia, who became the youngest world diving champion when she won the 10-metre platform diving. Her record will presumably never be broken as a lower age limit of 14 for major events came into force two months later. Surprise winners included the Florida-based Dutchman Edwin Jongejens who ended 12 years of US domination of men's diving.

Melvyn Stewart of the US beat Gross in the 200 metres butterfly, setting a formidable new record of 1:55.69, which inhibited his chances of winning a $200,000 sponsors' prize on offer if he beats the record in the US. "If I'd have known I was going so fast, I'd have slowed down." said Stewart. "How am I going to break this now?" The synchronised swimming was won by Sylvie Frechette of Canada who was reported to have revolutionised the sport by abandoning the old jerky movements and exaggerated make-up. She collected seven perfect scores, unprecedented in any major event. Her technique included conducting the spectators in time to the music, using her feet while the rest of her was submerged.

Mark Spitz, winner of seven Olympic golds in 1972, made a hugely-publicised comeback aged 41, losing a succession of races to younger men. He said swimming should quit the Olympics, abolish world records and hold knock-out swim-offs against the clock to attract TV audiences. Ilaria Tocchini wore the first bikini in official competition when she wore a wine-and-black two-piece at the Italian championships; other Italian team members followed her: the suit was considered to have superior hydrodynamic qualities to the traditional one-piece. "It's funny to feel the water on your tummy," said Tocchini. Ted Epstein, a 55-year-old lawyer from Denver, became the first man to swim the 30.5 miles across Lake Baikal in Siberia; it took him 16 hours.

———— 1991 ————

WORLD CHAMPIONSHIPS
Perth, Australia, Jan 5-14

Men
50 Metres Freestyle
1 Tom Jager (US) 22.16s
2 Matt Biondi (US) 22.26s
3 Gennady Prigoda (USSR) 22.62s
100 Metres Freestyle
1 Matt Biondi (US) 49.18s
2 Tommy Werner (Swe) 49.63s
3 Giorgio Lamberti (Ita) 50.04s
200 Metres Freestyle
1 Giorgio Lamberti (Ita) 1m 47.27s
2 Steffen Zesner (Ger) 1m 48.28s
3 Artur Wojdat (Pol) 1m 48.70s
400 Metres Freestyle
1 Joerg Hoffmann (Ger) 3m 48.04s
2 Stefan Pfeiffer (Ger) 3m 48.86s
3 Artur Wojdat (Pol) 3m 49.67s
1500 Metres Freestyle
1 Joerg Hoffmann (Ger) 14m 50.36s
2 Kieren Perkins (Aus) 14m 50.58s
3 Stefan Pfeiffer (Ger) 14m 59.34s
50 Metres Breaststroke
1 Chen Jianhong (Chn) 28.67s
2 Pedro Hernandez (Cub) 28.73s
3 Christian Powziat (Ger) 28.75s
100 Metres Breaststroke
1 Norbert Rosza (Hun) 1m 01.45s
2 Adrian Moorhouse (GB) 1m 01.58s
3 Gianni Minervini (Ita) 1m 01.74s
200 Metres Breaststroke
1 Mike Barrowman (US) 2m 11.23s
2 Norbert Rozsa (Hun) 2m 12.03s
3 Nick Gillingham (GB) 2m 13.12s
50 Metres Butterfly
1 Thilo Haase (Ger) 24.95s
2 Viacheslav Novikov (USSR) 25.03s
3 Milos Milosevic (Yug) 25.05s
100 Metres Butterfly
1 Anthony Nesty (Sur) 53.29s
2 Michael Gross (Ger) 53.31s
3 Viacheslav Kulikov (USSR) 53.74s
200 Metres Butterfly
1 Melvin Stewart (US) 1m 55.69s
2 Michael Gross (Ger) 1m 56.78s
3 Tamas Darnyi (Hun) 1m 58.25s
50 Metres Backstroke
1 Dirk Richter (Ger) 26.44s
2 Mark Tewksbury (Can) 26.57s
3 Vladimir Shemetov (USSR) 26.67s
100 Metres Backstroke
1 Jeff Rouse (US) 55.23s
2 Mark Tewksbury (Can) 55.29s
3 Martin Lopez Zubero (Spa) 55.61s
200 Metres Backstroke
1 Martin Lopez Zubero (Spa) 1m 59.52s
2 Stefano Battistelli (Ita) 1m 59.98s
3 Vladimir Selkov (USSR) 2m 00.33s
200 Metres Individual Medley
1 Tamas Darnyi (Hun) 1m 59.36s
2 Eric Namesnik (US) 2m 01.87s
3 Christian Gessner (Ger) 2m 02.36s
Darnyi became the first man under two minutes
400 Metres Individual Medley
1 Tamas Darnyi (Hun) 4m 12.36s
2 Eric Namesnik (US) 4m 15.21s
3 Stefano Battistelli (Ita) 4m 16.50s

25km Long Distance
Swan River, Perth
1 Chad Hundeby (US) 5h 1m 45.78s
2 Sergio Chariandini (Ita) 5h 03m 18.81s
3 David O'Brien (Aus) 5h 08m 53.35s
4 x 50 Metres Freestyle Relay
1 Germany 1m 30.68s
2 Canada 1m 34.26s
3 Norway 1m 34.97s
4 x 100 Metres Freestyle Relay
1 United States 3m 17.15s
2 Germany 3m 18.88s
3 Soviet Union 3m 18.97s
4 x 200 Metres Freestyle Relay
1 Germany 7m 13.50s
2 United States 7m 14.87s
3 Italy 7m 17.18s
4 x 100 Metres Medley Relay
1 United States 3m 39.66s
2 Soviet Union 3m 40.41s
3 Germany 3m 42.13s
Platform Diving
1 Sun Shuwei (Chn) 626.79 pts
2 Xiong Ni (Chn) 603.81 pts
3 Gyorgy Tchogovadze (USSR) 580.68 pts
1 Metre Springboard Diving
1 Edwin Jongejans (Hol) 588.51 pts
2 M Lenzi (US) 578.22 pts
3 Wang Yijie (Chn) 577.86 pts
3 Metre Springboard Diving
1 Kent Ferguson (US) 650.25 pts
2 Tan Liangde (Chn) 643.95 pts
3 Albin Killat (Ger) 619.77 pts
Water Polo
1 Yugoslavia
2 Spain
3 Hungary
Yugoslavia beat Spain 8-7 in final

Women
50 Metres Freestyle
1 Zhuang Yong (Chn) 25.47s
2 Leigh-Ann Fetter (US) & Catherine Plewinski (Fra) 25.50s
Dead-heat for second place
100 Metres Freestyle
1 Nicola Haislett (US) 55.17s
2 Catherine Plewinski (Fra) 55.31s
3 Zhuang Yong (Chn) 55.65s
200 Metres Freestyle
1 Hayley Lewis (Aus) 2m 00.48s
2 Janet Evans (US) 2m 00.67s
3 Mette Jacobsen (Den) 2m 00.93s
400 Metres Freestyle
1 Janet Evans (US) 4m 08.63s
2 Hayley Lewis (Aus) 4m 09.40s
3 Suzu Chilba (Jap) 4m 11.44s
800 Metres Freestyle
1 Janet Evans (US) 8m 24.05s
2 Grit Mueller (Ger) 8m 30.20s
3 Jana Henke (Ger) 8m 30.31s
50 Metres Breaststroke
1 Yang Wenyi (Chn) 29.58s
2 Sylvia Poll (CR) 30.46s
3 Eva Gysling (Swi) 30.08s
100 Metres Breaststroke
1 Linley Frame (Aus) 1m 08.81s
2 Jana Doerries (Ger) 1m 09.35s
3 Elena Volkova (USSR) 1m 09.66s
200 Metres Breaststroke
1 Elena Volkova (USSR) 2m 29.53s
2 Linley Frame (Aus) 2m 30.02s
3 Jana Doerries (Ger) 2m 30.14s

50 Metres Butterfly
1 Qian Hong (Chn) 27.30s
2 Wang Xiaohong (Chn) 27.70s
3 Sarah Evanetz (Can) 28.06s
100 Metres Butterfly
1 Qian Hong (Chn) 59.68s
2 Wang Xiaohong (Chn) 59.81s
3 Catherine Plewinski (Fra) 59.88s
200 Metres Butterfly
1 Summer Sanders (US) 2m 09.24s
2 Rie Shito (Jap) 2m 11.06s
3 Hayley Lewis (US) 2m 11.09s
50 Metres Backstroke
1 Iulia Landik (USSR) 32.65s
2 Lorraines Coombes (GB) 32.77s
3 Keltie Duggan (Can) 32.83s
100 Metres Backstroke
1 Krisztina Egerszegi (Hun) 1m 01.78s
2 Tunde Szabo (Hun) 1m 01.98s
3 Janie Wagstaff (US) 1m 02.17s

4 x 100 Metres Freestyle Relay
1 United States 3m 43.26s
2 Germany 3m 44.37s
3 Holland 3m 45.05s
4 x 200 Metres Freestyle Relay
1 Germany 8m 02.56s
2 Holland 8m 05.97s
3 Denmark 8m 07.20s
4 x 100 Metres Medley Relay
1 United States 4m 06.51s
2 Australia 4m 08.04s
3 Germany 4m 10.50s
Synchronised Solo
1 Sylvie Frechette (Can) 201.013 pts
2 Kristen Babb (US) 196.314 pts
3 Mikako Kotani (Jap) 195.110 pts

> **"We all took them. In no club in the world were so many pills swallowed."**
> *Raik Hannemann, German swimmer, on the Dynamo Berlin sports club*

> **"I put my head down and then looked around and thought "What's happening? Where is everyone?' "**
> *Hayley Lewis after unexpectedly becoming world 200 metres freestyle champion*

> **"There is no dominating nation any more. Technique is pretty much the same the world over. Everyone knows the methods, and training is based more on knowledge than on gut feeling."**
> *Adrian Moorhouse*

> **"It's sad that some swimmers who do well at distance events would no longer be there, but the sport has to change. I'd like to see knockouts become the main stage. Swimmers would race 200 metres...one swimmer after the next. That way you build up suspense for the audience and swimmers don't feel they have to always be breaking records. Because the distances are short, swimmers could also compete many more times a year, like tennis players."**
> *Mark Spitz outlining his New World Order*

> **"In a worst-case scenario I can always buy a ticket."**
> *Spitz on his prospects of making the 1992 Olympics*

---

200 Metres Backstroke
1 Krisztina Egerszegi (Hun) 2m 09.15s
2 Dagmar Hase (Ger) 2m 12.01s
3 Janie Wagstaff (US) 2m 13.14s
200 Metres Individual Medley
1 Lin Li (Chn) 2m 13.40s
2 Summer Sanders (US) 2m 14.06s
3 Daniela Hunger (Ger) 2m 16.16s
400 Metres Individual Medley
1 Lin Li (Chn) 4m 41.45s
2 Hayley Lewis (Aus) 4m 41.46s
3 Summer Sanders (US) 4m 43.41s
25km Long Distance
Swan River, Perth
1 Shelley Taylor-Smith (Aus) 5h 21m 05.53s
2 Mardia Jahn (US) 5h 25m 16.67s
3 Karen Burton (US) 5h 28m 22.74s
4 x 50 Metres Freestyle Relay
1 Germany 1m 46.8s
2 Canada 1m 46.82s
3 Romania 1m 49.00s

Synchronised Duet
1 Karen & Sarah Josephson (US) 199.762 pts
2 Mikako Kotani & Aki Takayama (Jap) 194.307 pts
3 Kathy Glen & Lisa Alexander (Can) 192.649 pts
Synchronised Team
1 United States 196.144 pts
2 Canada 193.259 pts
3 Japan 189.753 pts
Platform Diving
1 Fu Mingxia (Chn) 426.51 pts
2 Elena Miroshina (USSR) 402.87 pts
3 Wendy Williams (US) 400.23 ptd
1 Metre Springboard Diving
1 Gao Min (Chn) 478.26 pts
2 Wendy Lucero (US) 467.82 pts
3 Heidemarie Bartova (Cze) 449.76 pts
3 Metre Springboard Diving
1 Gao Min (Chn) 539.01 pts
2 Irina Lashko (USSR) 524.70 pts
3 Brita Baldus (Ger) 503. 73 pts

Medal Table

	Total			Men			Women		
	G	S	B	G	S	B	G	S	B
United States	17	11	6	9	5	-	8	6	6
China	11	4	2	2	2	1	9	2	1
Germany	8	9	10	6	5	5	2	4	5
Hungary	5	2	2	3	1	2	2	1	-
Australia	3	5	1	-	1	1	3	4	-
Soviet Union	2	4	7	-	2	6	2	2	1
Canada	1	5	3	-	3	-	1	2	3
Italy	1	2	4	1	2	4	-	-	-
Holland	1	1	1	1	-	-	-	1	1
Spain	1	1	1	1	1	1	-	-	-
Yugoslavia	1	-	1	1	-	1	-	-	-
Surinam	1	-	-	1	-	-	-	-	-
Japan	-	2	3	-	-	-	-	2	3
France	-	2	1	-	-	-	-	2	1
Great Britain	-	2	1	1	1	-	-	1	-
Costa Rica	-	1	-	-	-	-	-	1	-
Cuba	-	1	-	-	1	-	-	-	-
Sweden	-	1	-	-	1	-	-	-	-
Denmark	-	-	2	-	-	-	-	-	2
Poland	-	-	2	-	2	-	-	-	-
Czechoslovakia	-	-	1	-	-	-	-	-	1
Norway	-	-	1	-	1	-	-	-	-
Romania	-	-	1	-	-	-	-	-	1
Switzerland	-	-	1	-	-	-	-	-	1

EUROPEAN CHAMPIONSHIPS
Athens, Aug 18-25

Men
Freestyle
50 metres	Nils Rudolph (Ger) 2.33s
100 metres	Alexander Popov (USSR) 49.18s
200 metres	Artur Wojdat (Pol) 1m 48.10s
400 metres	Evgenyi Sadovyi (USSR) 3m 49.02s
1500 metres	Jorg Hoffmann (Ger) 15m 02.57s

Backstroke
100 metres	Martin Lopez Zubero (Spa) 55.30s
200 metres	Martin Lopez Zubero (Spa) 1m 58.66s

Butterfly
100 metres	Vladislav Kulikov (USSR) 54.22s
200 metres	F Esposito (Fra) 1m 59.59s

Breaststroke
100 metres	Norbert Rozsa (Hun) 1m 01.49s
200 metres	Nick Gillingham (GB) 2m 12.55s

Medley
200 metres	Lars Sorensen (Den) 2m 02.63s
400 metres	Luca Sacchi (Ita) 4m 17.81s

Relay
4x100 Free	Soviet Union 3m 17.11s
4x200m Free	Soviet Union 7m 15.96s
4x100 Medley	Soviet Union 3m 40.68s

Diving
1m Springboard	Andrey Semeniyk (USSR) 395.19 pts
3m Springboard	Albin Killat (Ger) 639.45 pts
Platform	Vladimir Timoshinin (USSR) 606.21 pts
Water Polo	Yugoslavia

Women
Freestyle
50 metres	Simone Osygus (Ger) 25.80s
100 metres	Catherine Plewinski (Fra) 56.20s
200 metres	Mette Jacobsen (Den) 2m 00.29s

Denmark's first gold at the championships since 1950

400 metres	Irene Dalby (Nor) 4m 11.63s
800 metres	Irene Dalby (Nor) 8m 32.08s

Backstroke
100 metres	Krisztina Egerszegi (Hun) 1m 00.31s (WR)
200 metres	Krisztina Egerszegi (Hun) 2m 06.62s (WR)

Butterfly
100 metres	Catherine Plewinski (Fra) 1m 00.32s
200 metres	Mette Jacobsen (Den) 2m 12.87s

Breaststroke
100 metres	Elena Rudkovskaya (USSR) 1m 09.05s
200 metres	Elena Rudkovskaya (USSR) 2m 29.50s

Medley
200 metres	Daniela Hunger (Ger) 2m 15.53s
400 metres	Krisztina Egerszegi (Hun) 4m 39.78s

Relays
4 x 100 Free	Holland 3m 45.36s
4 x 200 Free	Denmark 8m 05.90s
4x100 Medley	Soviet Union 4m 08.55s

Synchronised Swimming
Solo	Olga Sedakova (USSR) 180.286 pts
Team	Soviet Union 178.112 pts

Diving
1m Springboard	Britta Baldus (Ger) 282.54 pts
3m Springboard	Irina Lashko (USSR) 524.97 pts
Platform	Elena Miroshina (USSR) 453.90 pts
Water Polo	Hungary

ASA NATIONAL CHAMPIONSHIPS
Leeds, Aug 1-3

Men
Freestyle
50 metres	Mike Fibbens (Barnet Copthall) 23.21s
100 metres	Mike Fibbens (Barnet Copthall) 51.09s
200 metres	Paul Howe (Brimingham) 1m 51.89s
400 metres	Paul Howe (Birmingham) 3m 57.55s
1500 metres	Ian Wilson (Sunderland) 15m 31.39s

Breaststroke
50 metres	Adrian Moorhouse (Leeds) 29.36s
100 metres	Adrian Moorhouse (Leeds) 1m 03.30s
200 metres	Nick Gillingham (Birmingham) 2m 15.46s

Butterfly
50 metres	Mike Fibbens (Barnet Copthall) 25.48s
100 metres	Mike Fibbens (Barnet Copthall) 56.42s
200 metres	Kevin Crosby (Warrington Warriors) 2m 05.21s

Backstroke
50 metres	Martin Harris (Barnet Copthall) 27.27s

100 metres	Martin Harris (Barnet Copthall) 57.64s
200 metres	Grant Robins (Portsmouth Northsea) 2m 03.80s
Medley	
200 metres	John Davey (Leeds) 2m 06.12s
400 metres	Andy Rolley (Portsmouth Northsea) 4m 26.43s

Women
Freestyle

50 metres	Alison Sheppard (Milngavie & Bearsden) 26.77s
100 metres	Karen Pickering (Ipswich) 57.85
200 metres	Ruth Gilfillan (Dundee) 2m 04.14s
400 metres	Ruth Gilfillan (Dundee) 4m 21.66s
800 metres	Samantha Foggo (Newcastle) 8m 52.65s
Breaststroke	
50 metres	Lorraine Coombes (Southampton) 33.04s
100 metres	Lorraine Coombes (Southampton) 1m 11.98s
200 metres	Jean Hill (Cumbernauld) 2m 38.48s
Butterfly	
50 metres	Nicola Kennedy (Nova Centurion) 28.75s
100 metres	Madelaine Campbell (Portsmouth Northsea) 1m 03.00s
200 metres	Helen Jepson (Kirklees) 2m 16.56s
Backstroke	
50 metres	Kathy Read (Barnet Copthall) 30.39s
100 metres	Kathy Read (Barnet Copthall) 1m 04.39s
200 metres	Kathy Read (Barnet Copthall) 2m 15.68s
Medley	
200 metres	Zara Long (Beckenham) 2m 20.38s
400 metres	Zara Long (Beckenham) 4m 55.39s

Bill Juba Award (outstanding swimmer at the championships): Kathy Read

OPTREX BRITISH CLUB TEAM CHAMPIONSHIPS
Sheffield, Apr 13-14
Men
1 Leeds 232 pts
2 Barnet Copthall 222pts
3 Birmingham 214.5 pts
Women
1 Portsmouth Northsea 224 pts
2 Nova Centurion 219 pts
3 Birmingham 196 pts

WATER POLO
WOMEN'S WORLD CUP
California, Jul 2
Final
HOLLAND 8 Australia 7
Final placings:
1 HOLLAND; 2 Australia; 3 United States; 4 Canada; 5 Italy; 6 Japan; 7 New Zealand; 8 Brazil

MEN'S WORLD CUP
Barcelona, Jul 21
Final
UNITED STATES 7 Yugoslavia 6
Final placings:
1 UNITED STATES; 2 Yugoslavia; 3 Spain; 4 Hungary; 5 Soviet Union; 6 Romania; 7 Australia; 8 Germany

━━ CHAMPIONS ━━
Olympic champions in Olympic Games section.

WORLD CHAMPIONS
Note: 1990 Championships held January 1991

Men
50 Metres Freestyle
1986	Tom Jager (US) 22.49s
1990	Tom Jager (US) 22.16s

100 Metres Freestyle
1973	Jim Montgomery (US) 51.70s
1975	Andrew Coan (US) 51.25s
1978	David McCagg (US) 50.24s
1982	Jorg Woithe (GDR) 50.18s
1986	Matt Biondi (US) 48.94s
1990	Matt Biondi (US) 49.18s

200 Metres Freestyle
1973	Jim Montgomery (US) 1m 53.02s
1975	Tim Shaw (US) 1m 51.04s
1978	William Forrester (US) 1m 51.04s
1982	Michael Gross (FRG) 1m 49.84s
1986	Michael Gross (FRG) 1m 47.92s
1990	Giorgio Lamberti (Ita) 1m 47.27s

400 Metres Freestyle
1973	Rick DeMont (US) 3m 58.18s
1975	Tim Shaw (US) 3m 54.88s
1978	Vladimir Salnikov (USSR) 3m 51.94s
1982	Vladimir Salnikov (USSR) 3m 51.30s
1986	Rainer Henkel (FRG) 3m 50.05s
1990	Joerg Hoffman (Ger) 3m 48.04s

1500 Metres Freestyle
1973	Steve Holland (Aus) 15m 31.85s
1975	Tim Shaw (US) 15m 28.92s
1978	Vladimir Salnikov (USSR) 15m 03.99s
1982	Vladimir Salnikov (USSR) 15m 01.77s
1986	Rainer Henkel (FRG) 15m 05.31s
1990	Joerg Hoffman (Ger)14m 50.36s

50 Metres Backstroke
1990	Dirk Richter (Ger) 26.44s

100 Metres Backstroke
1973	Roland Matthes (GDR) 57.47s
1975	Roland Matthes (GDR) 58.15s
1978	Robert Jackson (US) 56.36s
1982	Dirk Richter (GDR) 55.95s
1986	Igor Polianski (USSR) 55.58s
1990	Jeff Rouse (US) 55.23s

200 Metres Backstroke
1973	Roland Matthes (GDR) 2m 01.87s
1975	Zoltan Verraszto (Hun) 2m 05.05s
1978	Jesse Vassallo (US) 2m 02.16s
1982	Rick Carey (US) 2m 00.82s
1986	Igor Polianski (USSR) 1m 58.78s
1990	Martin Lopez-Zubero (Spa) 1m 59.52s

50 Metres Breaststroke
1990	Chen Jianhong (Chn) 28.67s

100 Metres Breaststroke
1973	John Hencken (US) 1m 04.02s
1975	David Wilkie (GB) 1m 04.26s
1978	Walter Kusch (GDR) 1m 03.56s
1982	Steve Lundquist (US) 1m 02.75s
1986	Victor Davis (Can) 1m 02.71s
1990	Norbert Rozsa (Hun) 1n 01.45s

200 Metres Breaststroke
1973	David Wilkie (GB) 2m 19.28s
1975	David Wilkie (GB) 2m 18.23s
1978	Nick Nevid (US) 2m 18.37s
1982	Victor Davis (Can) 2m 14.77s

1986	Jozsef Szabo (Hun) 2m 14.27s
1990	Mike Barrowman (US) 2m 11.23s

50 Metres Butterfly

1990	Thilo Haase (Ger) 24.95s

100 Metres Butterfly

1973	Bruce Robertson (Can) 55.69s
1975	Greg Jagenburg (US) 55.63s
1978	Joe Bottom (US) 54.30s
1982	Matt Gribble (US) 53.88s
1986	Pablo Morales (US) 53.54s
1990	Anthony Nesty (Sur) 53.29s

200 Metres Butterfly

1973	Robin Backhaus (US) 2m 03.32s
1975	William Forrester (US) 2m 01.95s
1978	Michael Bruner (US) 1m 59.38s
1982	Michael Gross (FRG) 1m 58.85s
1986	Michael Gross (FRG) 1m 56.53s
1990	Melvin Stewart (US) 1m 55.69s

200 Metres Individual Medley

1973	Gunnar Larsson (Swe) 2m 08.36s
1975	Andras Hargitay (Hun) 2m 07.72s
1978	Graham Smith (Can) 2m 03.65s
1982	Aleksey Sidorenko (USSR) 2m 03.30s
1986	Tamas Darnyi (Hun) 2m 01.57s
1990	Tamas Darnyi (Hun) 1m 59.36s

400 Metres Individual Medley

1973	Andras Hargitay (Hun) 4m 31.11s
1975	Andras Hargitay (Hun) 4m 32.57s
1978	Jesse Vassallo (US) 4m 20.05s
1982	Ricardo Prado (Bra) 4m 19.78s
1986	Tamas Darnyi (Hun) 4m 18.98s
1990	Tamas Darnyi (Hun) 4m 12.36s

25km Long Distance

1990	Chad Hundeby (US) 5h 01m 45.78s

4 x 50 Metres Freestyle Relay

1990	Germany 1m 30.68s

4 x 100 Metres Freestyle Relay

1973	United States 3m 27.18s
1975	United States 3m 24.85s
1978	United States 3m 19.74s
1982	United States 3m 19.26s
1986	United States 3m 19.89s
1990	United States 3m 17.15s

4 x 200 Metres Freestyle Relay

1973	United States 7m 33.22s
1975	West Germany 7m 39.44s
1978	United States 7m 20.82s
1982	United States 7m 21.09s
1986	East Germany 7m 15.91s
1990	Germany 7m13.50s

4 x 100 Metres Medley Relay

1973	United States 3m 49.49s
1975	United States 3m 49.0s
1978	United States 3m 44.63s
1982	United States 3m 40.84s
1986	United States 3m 41.25s
1990	United States 3m 39.66s

Springboard Diving

1973	Phil Boggs (US)
1975	Phil Boggs (US)
1978	Phil Boggs (US)
1982	Greg Louganis (US)
1986	Greg Louganis (US)
1990	(1 metre) Edwin Jongejans (Hol)
	(3 metre) Kent Ferguson (US)

Platform Diving

1973	Klaus Dibiasi (Ita)
1975	Klaus Dibiasi (Ita)
1978	Greg Louganis (US)
1982	Greg Louganis (US)
1986	Greg Louganis (US)
1990	Sun Shuwei (Chn)

Women

50 Metres Freestyle

1986	Tamara Costache (Rom) 25.28s
1990	Zhuang Yong (Chn) 25.47s

100 Metres Freestyle

1973	Kornelia Ender (GDR) 57.54s
1975	Kornelia Ender (GDR) 56.50s
1978	Barbara Krause (GDR) 55.68s
1982	Birgit Meineke (GDR) 55.79s
1986	Kristin Otto (GDR) 55.05s
1990	Nicola Haislett (US) 55.17s

200 Metres Freestyle

1973	Keena Rothhammer (US) 2m 04.99s
1975	Shirley Babashoff (US) 2m 02.50s
1978	Cynthia Woodhead (US) 1m 58.53s
1982	Annemarie Verstappen (Hol) 1m 59.53s
1986	Heike Friedrich (GDR) 1m 58.26s
1990	Hayley Lewis (Aus) 2m 00.48s

400 Metres Freestyle

1973	Heather Greenwood (US) 4m 20.28s
1975	Shirley Babashoff (US) 4m 16.87s
1978	Tracey Wickham (Aus) 4m 06.28s
1983	Carmela Schmidt (GDR) 4m 08.98s
1986	Heike Friedrich (GDR) 4m 07.45s
1990	Janet Evans (US) 4m 08.63s

800 Metres Freestyle

1973	Novella Calligaris (Ita) 8m 52.97s
1975	Jenny Turrall (Aus) 8m 44.75s
1978	Tracey Wickham (Aus) 8m 24.94s
1982	Kim Linehan (US) 8m 27.48s
1986	Astrid Strauss (GDR) 8m 28.24s
1990	Janet Evans (US) 8m 24.05s

50 Metres Backstroke

1990	Iulia Landik (USSR) 32.65s

100 Metres Backstroke

1973	Ulrike Richter (GDR) 1m 05.42s
1975	Ulrike Richter (GDR) 1m 03.30s
1978	Linda Jezek (US) 1m 02.55s
1982	Kristin Otto (GDR) 1m 01.30s
1986	Betsy Mitchell (US) 1m 01.74s
1990	Krisztina Egerszegi (Hun) 1m 01.78s

200 Metres Backstroke

1973	Melissa Belote (US) 2m 20.52s
1975	Birgit Treiber (GDR) 2m 15.46s
1978	Linda Jezek (US) 2m 11.93s
1982	Cornelia Sirch (GDR) 2m 09.91s
1986	Cornelia Sirch (GDR) 2m 11.37s
1990	Krisztina Egerszegi (Hun) 2m 09.15s

50 Metres Breaststroke

1990	Yang Wenyi (Chn) 29.58s

100 Metres Breaststroke

1973	Renate Vogel (GDR) 1m 13.74s
1975	Hannalore Anke (GDR) 1m12.72s
1978	Julia Bogdanova (USSR) 1m 10.31s
1982	Ute Geweniger (GDR) 1m 09.14s
1986	Sylvia Gerasch (GDR) 1m 08.11s
1990	Linley Frame (Aus) 1.08.81s

200 Metres Breaststroke

1973	Renate Vogel (GDR) 2m 40.01s
1975	Hannalore Anke (GDR) 2m 37.25s
1978	Lina Kachushite (USSR) 2m 31.42s
1982	Svetlana Varganova (USSR) 2m 28.82s
1986	Silke Hoerner (GDR) 2m 27.40s
1990	Elena Volkova (USSR) 2m 29.53s

50 Metres Butterfly

1990	Qian Hong (Chn) 27.30s

100 Metres Butterfly
1973   Kornelia Ender (GDR) 1m 02.53s
1975   Kornelia Ender (GDR) 1m 01.24s
1978   Mary-Joan Pennington (US) 1m 00.20s
1982   Mary T Meagher (US) 59.41s
1986   Kornelia Gressler (GDR) 59.51s
1990   Quin Hongh (Chn) 59.68s

200 Metres Butterfly
1973   Rosemarie Kother (GDR) 2m 13.76s
1975   Rosemarie Kother (GDR) 2m 13.82s
1978   Tracy Caulkins (US) 2m 09.87s
1982   Ines Geissler (GDR) 2m 08.66s
1986   Mary T Meagher (US) 2m 08.41s
1990   Summer Sanders (US) 2m 09.24s

200 Metres Individual Medley
1973   Angela Hubner (GDR) 2m 20.51s
1975   Kathy Heddy (US) 2m 19.80s
1978   Tracy Caulkins (US) 2m 14.07s
1982   Petra Schneider (GDR) 2m 11.79s
1986   Kristin Otto (GDR) 2m 15.56s
1990   Lin Li (Chn) 2m 13.40s

400 Metres Individual Medley
1973   Gudrun Wegner (GDR) 4m 57.31s
1975   Ulrike Tauber (GDR) 4m 52.76s
1978   Tracy Caulkins (US) 4m 40.83s
1982   Petra Schneider (GDR) 4m 36.10s
1986   Kathleen Nord (GDR) 4m 43.75s
1990   Lin Li (Chn) 4m 41.45s

25km Long Distance
1990   Shelley Taylor-Smith (Aus) 5h 21m 05.53s

4 x 50 Metres Freestyle Relay
1990   Germany 1m 46.80s

4 x 100 Metres Freestyle Relay
1973   East Germany 3m 52.45s
1975   East Germany 3m 49.37s
1978   United ːtates 3m 43.43s
1982   East Germany 3m 43.97s
1986   East Germany 3m 40.57s
1990   United States 3m 43.26s

4 x 200 Metres Freestyle Relay
1986   East Germany 7m 59.33s
1990   Germany 8m 02.56s

4 x 100 Metres Medley Relay
1973   East Germany 4m 16.84s
1975   East Germany 4m 14.74s
1978   United States 4m 08.21s
1982   East Germany 4m 05.88s
1986   East Germany 4m 04.82s
1990   United States 4m 06.51s

Springboard Diving
1973   Christine Kohler (GDR)
1975   Irina Kalinina (USSR)
1978   Irina Kalinina (USSR0
1982   Megan Meyer (US)
1986   Gao Min (Chn)
1990   (1 metre) Gao Min (Chn)
        (3 metre) Gao Min (Chn)

Platform Diving
1973   Ulrike Knape (Swe)
1975   Janet Ely (US)
1978   Irina Kalinina (USSR)
1982   Wendy Wyland (US)
1986   Lin Chen (Chn)
1990   Fu Mingxia (Chn)

Synchronised - Solo
1973   Teresa Andersen (US)
1975   Gail Buzonas (US)
1978   Helen Vanderburg (Can)
1982   Tracie Ruiz (US)
1986   Carolyn Waldo (Can)
1990   Sylvie Frecheltze (Can)

Synchronised - Duet
1973   United States
1975   United States
1978   Canada
1982   Canada
1986   Canada
1990   United States

Synchronised - Team
1973   United States
1975   United States
1978   United States
1982   Canada
1986   Canada
1990   United States

WORLD RECORDS
(September 1991)

Men
50 Metres Freestyle:
21.81s Tom Jager (US) Nashville Tennessee, Mar 24 1990
100 Metres Freestyle:
48.24s Matt Biondi (US) Austin Texas, Aug 10 1988
200 Metres Freestyle:
1m 46.69s Giorgio Lamberti (Ita) Bonn, Aug 15 1989
400 Metres Freestyle:
3m 46.95s Uwe Dassler (GDR) Moscow, Feb 22 1983
800 Metres Freestyle:
7m 50.64s Vladimir Salnikov (USSR) Moscow, Jul 24 1986
1500 Metres Freestyle:
14m 50.36s Joerg Hoffmann (Ger) Perth, Jan 13 1991
100 Metres Backstroke:
53.93s Jeff Rouse (US) Edmonton Canada, Aug 25 1991
100 metres Breaststroke:
1m 01.45s Nobert Rozsa (Hun) Perth, Jan 7 1991, Vasily Ivanov (USSR) Moscow, Jun 12 1991
200 metres Breaststroke:
2m 10.60s Mike Barrowman (US) Fort Lauderdale, Aug 14 1991
100 Metres Butterfly:
52.84s Pablo Morales (US) Orlando Florida, Jun 23 1986
200 Metres Butterfly:
1m 55.69s Melvin Stewart (US) Perth, Jan 12 1991
200 Metres Medley:
1m 59.36s Tamas Darnyi (Hun) Perth, Jan 13 1991
400 Metres Medley:
4m 12.36s Tamas Darnyi (Hun) Perth, Jan 9 1991
4 x 100 Metres Freestyle:
3m 16.53s United States Seoul, Sep 23 1988
4 x 200 Metres Freestyle:
7m 12.51s United States Seoul, Sep 21 1988
4 x 100 Metres Medley:
3m 16.93s United States Seoul, Sep 25 1988

Women
50 Metres Freestyle:
24.98s Yang Wenyi (Chn) Guangzhou China, Apr 11 1988
100 Metres Freestyle:
54.73s Kristin Otto (GDR) Madrid, Aug 19 1986
200 Metres Freestyle:
1m 57.55s Heike Friedrich (GDR) East Berlin, Jun 18 1986
400 Metres Freestyle:
4m 03.85s Janet Evans (US) Seoul, Sep 22 1988
800 Metres Freestyle:
7m 47.85s Kieren Perkins (Aus) Edmonton Canada, Aug 25 1991
1500 Metres Freestyle:
15m 52.10s Janet Evans (US) Orlando Florida, Mar 26 1988

100 Metres Backstroke:
1m 00.31s Krisztina Egerszegi (Hun) Athens, Aug 22 1991
200 Metres Backstroke:
2m 06.62s Krisztina Egerszegi (Hun) Athens, Aug 25 1991
100 Metres Breaststroke:
1m 07.91s Silke Hoerner (GDR) Strasbourg, Aug 21 1987
200 Metres Breaststroke:
2m 26.71s Silke Hoerner (GDR) Seoul, Sep 21 1988
100 Metres Butterfly:
57.93s Mary T Meagher (US) Milwaukee Wisconsin, Aug 16 1981
200 Metres Butterfly:
2m 05.96s Mary T Meagher (US) Milwaukee Wisconsin, Aug 13 1981
200 Metres Medley:
2m 11.73s Ute Geweniger (GDR) East Berlin, Jul 4 1981
400 Metres Medley:
4m 36.10s Petra Schneider (GDR) Guayaquil Ecuador, Aug 1 1982
4 x 100 Metres Freestyle:
3m 40.57s East Germany Madrid, Aug 19 1986
4 x 200 Metres Freestyle:
7m 55.47s East Germany Strasbourg, Aug 18 1987
4 x 100 Metres Medley:
4m 03.69s East Germany Moscow, Aug 24 1984

TABLE TENNIS

1991

WORLD CHAMPIONSHIPS
Tokyo, Apr 30-May 6
Swaythling Cup (Men's Team)
Final
SWEDEN 3 Yugoslavia 2
3rd Czechoslovakia; 4th Belgium
Men's Singles
Semi-finals
JAN-OVE WALDNER (Swe) beat Ma Wenge (Chn) 21-18
18-21 21-7 21-15; JORGEN PERSSON (Swe) beat Kim
Taek Soo (SKo) 21-12 24-22 21-18
Final
PERSSON beat Waldner 21-19 21-18 21-18
Corbillon Cup (Women's Team)
UNITED KOREA 3 China 2
3rd France; 4th Hungary
Women's Singles
Semi-finals
DENG YAPING (Chn) beat Chan Tanlui (HK) 21-16 21-9
21-14; HUI LI-BUN (SKo) beat Qiao Hong (Chn) 24-26
22-20 16-21 22-20
Final
DENG YAPING beat Hui Li-Bun 21-13 21-18 21-14
Men's Doubles
Final
PETER KARLSSON & TOMAS VON SCHEELE (Swe)
beat Wang Tao & Lu Lin (Chn) 16-21 21-16 21-14 18-21
21-18
Women's Doubles
Final
CHEN ZHIE & GAO JUN (Chn) beat Qiao Hong & Deng
Yaping (Chn) 22-20 20-22 21-18 21-17
Mixed Doubles
Final
WANG TAO & LIU WEI (Chn) beat Xie Chaojie & Chen
Zhie (Chn)
21-14 21-19 21-14

EUROPEAN NATIONS CUP
Munich, Jan 18-20
Semi-finals
GERMANY 3 France 1; YUGOSLAVIA 3 Soviet Union 1
Final
GERMANY 3 Yugoslavia 0

ENGLISH NATIONAL CHAMPIONSHIPS
Stourbridge, Mar 9-10
Men's Singles
CARL PREAN (Isle of Wight) beat Desmond Douglas
(Warwickshire) 21-14, 21-18, 21-6
Women's Singles
ANDREA HOLT (Lancashire) beat Lisa Lomas
(Bedfordshire) 10-21, 14-21, 21-16, 21-19, 21-18
Men's Doubles
SKYLET ANDREW (Essex) & NICKY MASON (Surrey)
beat Sean Gibson (Lancashire) & John Holland
(Derbyshire) 21-9, 21-11
Women's Doubles
LISA LOMAS (Bedfordshire) & FIONA ELLIOT
(Staffordshire) beat Alison Gordon (Warwickshire)
Andrea Holt (Lancashire) 21-11, 21-13

COMMONWEALTH CHAMPIONSHIPS
Nairobi, Apr 14-21
Men's Singles
JOHNNY HUANG (Can) beat Kamlesh Mehta (Ind) 21-13
21-12 21-7
Women's Singles
CHAI PO WA (HK) beat Chan Tan Lui (HK) 21-15 21-12
21-7
Men's Doubles
MICHAEL O'DRISCOLL & CHRIS OLDFIELD (Eng)
beat Skylet Andrew & Nicky Mason (Eng) 22-24 21-16
21-18
Women's Doubles
CHAI PO WA & CHAN TAN LUI (HK) beat Alison
Gordon (Eng) & Chan Suk Yuen (HK) 21-5 21-7

1990

WORLD CUP
Chiba, Japan, Nov 14
Semi-finals
JAN-OVE WALDNER (Swe) beat Chen Longcan (Chn)
21-13 21-23 21-19 16-21 21-18; MA WENGE (Chn) beat
Mikael Appelgren (Swe) 21-16 23-21 11-21 19-21 21-9
Final
WALDNER beat Wenge 21-13 13-21 21-19 12-21 21-17

CHAMPIONS

SWAYTHLING CUP
Men's World Team Championship

1927	Hungary
1928	Hungary
1929	Hungary
1930	Hungary
1931	Hungary
1932	Czechoslovakia
1933	Hungary
1934	Hungary
1935	Hungary
1936	Austria
1937	United States
1938	Hungary
1939	Czechoslovakia
1940-46	Not held
1947	Czechoslovakia
1948	Czechoslovakia
1949	Hungary
1950	Czechoslovakia
1951	Czechoslovakia
1952	Hungary
1953	England
1954	Japan
1955	Japan
1956	Japan
1957	Japan
1959	Japan
1961	China
1963	China
1965	China
1967	Japan
1969	Japan
1971	China
1973	Sweden
1975	China
1977	China

1979	Hungary
1981	China
1983	China
1985	China
1987	China
1989	Sweden
1991	Sweden

Most wins
12 Hungary

CORBILLON CUP
Women's World Team Championship

1934	Germany
1935	Czechoslovakia
1936	Czechoslovakia
1937	United States
1938	Czechoslovakia
1939	Germany
1940-46	Not held
1947	England
1948	England
1949	United States
1950	Romania
1951	Romania
1952	Japan
1953	Romania
1954	Japan
1955	Romania
1956	Romania
1957	Japan
1959	Japan
1961	Japan
1963	Japan
1965	China
1967	Japan
1969	USSR
1971	Japan
1973	South Korea
1975	China
1977	China
1979	China
1981	China
1983	China
1985	China
1987	China
1989	China
1991	United Korea

Most wins
9 China

WORLD CHAMPIONSHIPS
Men's Singles

1927	Roland Jacobi (Hun)
1928	Zoltan Mechlovits (Hun)
1929	Fred Perry (Eng)
1930	Victor Barna (Hun)
1931	Miklos Szababos (Hun)
1932	Victor Barna (Hun)
1933	Victor Barna (Hun)
1934	Victor Barna (Hun)
1935	Victor Barna (Hun)
1936	Standa Kolar (Cze)
1937	Richard Bergmann (Aut)
1938	Bohumil Vana (Cze)
1939	Richard Bergmann (Aut)
1940-46	Not held
1947	Bohumil Vana (Cze)
1948	Richard Bergmann (Eng)
1949	Johnny Leach (Eng)
1950	Richard Bergmann (Eng)
1951	Johnny Leach (Eng)
1952	Hiroji Satoh (Jap)
1953	Ferenc Sido (Hun)
1954	Ichiro Ogimura (Jap)

1955	Toshiaki Tanaka (Jap)
1956	Ichiro Ogimura (Jap)
1957	Toshiaki Tanaka (Jap)
1959	Jung Kuo tuan (Chn)
1961	Chuang Tse Tung (Chn)
1963	Chuang Tse Tung (Chn)
1965	Chuang Tse Tung (Chn)
1967	Nobuhiko Hasegawa (Jap)
1969	Shigeo Ito (Jap)
1971	Stellan Bengtsson (Swe)
1973	Hsi En Ting (Chn)
1975	Istvan Jonyere (Hun)
1977	Mitsuru Kohno (Jap)
1979	Seiji Ono (Jap)
1981	Guo Yue Hua (Chn)
1983	Guo Yue Hua (Chn)
1985	Jiang Jialiang (Chn)
1987	Jiang Jialiang (Chn)
1989	Jan-Ove Waldner (Swe)
1991	Jorgen Persson (Swe)

Most wins
5 Victor Barna (Hun)

Women's Singles
Winners since 1961

1961	Chiu Chang Hui (Chn)
1963	Kimiyo Matsuzaki (Jap)
1965	Naoko Fukazu (Jap)
1967	Sachiko Morisawa (Jap)
1969	Toshiko Kowada (Jap)
1971	Lin Hui Ching (Chn)
1973	Hu Yu Lan (Chn)
1975	Pak Yung Sun (NKo)
1977	Pak Yung Sun (NKo)
1979	Ge Hsin Ai (Chn)
1981	Tong Ling (Chn)
1983	Cao Yan Hua (Chn)
1985	Cao Yan Hua (Chn)
1987	He Zhili (Chn)
1989	Qiao Hong (Chn)
1991	Deng Yaping (Chn)

Most wins
6 Angelica Rozeanu (Rom) 1950-55;
5 Maria Mednyanszky (Hun) 1927-31

Men's Doubles
Winners since 1983

1983	Dragutin Surbek/Zoran Kalinic (Yug)
1985	Mikael Appelgren/Ulf Carlsson (Swe)
1987	Chen Longcan/Wei Quingguang (Chn)
1989	Joerg Rosskopf/Steffan Fetzner (FRG)
1991	Peter Karlson/Thomas Von Scheele (Swe)

Most wins
8 Barna (Hun) 1929-35, 1939

Women's Doubles
Winners since 1983

1983	Shen Jianping/Dai Lili (Chn)
1985	Dai Lili/Geng Lijuan (Chn)
1987	Yang Young Ja/Hyun Jung Hua (SKo)
1989	Qiao Hong/Deng Yaping (Chn)
1991	Chen Zhie/Gao Jun (Chn)

Most wins
7 Maria Mednyanszky (Hun) 1928, 1930-35

Mixed Doubles
Winners since 1983

1983	Ni Xialin/Guo Yue Hua (Chn)
1985	Cao Yan Hua/Cai Zhenhua (Chn)
1987	Hui Jun/Geng Lijuan (Chn)
1989	Hyun Jung Hua/Yoo Nam Kyu (SKo)
1991	Wang Tao/Liu Wei (Chn)

Most wins
6 Maria Mednyanszky (Hun) 1927-28, 1930-31, 1933-34

TENNIS

STICH OF DYNAMITE

Everyone spent the first week of Wimbledon 1991 watching the rain and moaning; most people spent the second week wearily forecasting the fourth consecutive final between Stefan Edberg and Boris Becker. But then someone happened; his name was Michael Stich.

Stich, with a dramatic service even by the standards of modern men's tennis, had a fortuitous win over Edberg in the semi-final: Edberg held every single service game but he lost three tie-breaks. So Stich found himself up against Becker in Wimbledon's first all-German final. He served like a rocket and Becker had no answer except to swear to himself in German.

Stich had won only one previous title - at Memphis in 1990 - though he had climbed from 42nd to sixth in the rankings in only six months. This win catapulted him into the forefront of men's tennis which, since he is a humorous and articulate man, he may adorn off the court as well as on it. Overall, the men's game remained even and open. Edberg won the US title and regained his place as no.1 in the world but he failed in the other Grand Slam tournaments: Becker won in Australia and the young American Jim Courier became the third successive shock winner of the French Open.

The players who had most attention won nothing: Wimbledon was graced by the attendance of Andre Agassi who, after three years, finally deigned to accept the All-England Club's dress rules. He showed up and showed off. The speculation about what he would wear reached levels unmatched since Princess Di's wedding. He eventually emerged wearing an all-white outfit, not unlike a maternity smock. For some reason, this publicity stunt captured the heart of the British public, possibly because Agassi went to help a ball girl who had fallen and ricked her ankle.

The fuss increased because it was Thursday before Agassi could appear at all. The first week was appallingly wet, beginning with a total wash-out and continuing with three days that were little better: Becker did not arrive on court until 6pm on Friday. The spectators' disappointment was sharpened by the All-England Club's refusal to give any refunds or make any concession except to allow Monday's spectators to buy (at 1992's increased prices) tickets for the same day the next year. By the Friday the committee found themselves forced to schedule play on the middle Sunday for the first time. With no pre-sold seats or corporate hospitality, a younger, less stuffy, more enthusiastic crowd was let in cheap and created an unprecedented atmosphere: the wave was done on Centre Court and spread to the Royal Box; even the committee was impressed and promised to try and find some way of re-creating the mood in future years.

The All-England Club, negotiating to get more space, raised the possibility of moving to Basingstoke, which caused general hilarity, especially in Basingstoke. Because of the rain, strawberries had to be imported from Belgium. Going down to defeat against Edberg, John McEnroe swore at a linesman six times in ten seconds in an exchange which one paper rendered as follows: "McEnroe, you stupid McEnroe-er. Good McEnroe-ing call, you son of an McEnroe-ing bitch. You McEnroe report me after the match is over and I'll McEnroe ..." The linesman did nothing but an ITN microphone picked it up and McEnroe was fined $10,000, the maximum, but a bargain. The head groundsman Jim Thorn retired after ten championships. He said he was interested in neither tennis nor lawns - he does not have one at home. A man claiming to be President Bush jumped on the scoreboard and briefly interrupted the men's final. "He was completely out to lunch," said a steward.

Only six British men were in the draw, the lowest-ever, all of them by courtesy of wild cards. However, one of the six, 29-year-old Nick Brown, ranked 591 in the world, arrived on his mate's Harley-Davidson and beat Goran Ivanisevic, the 1990 semi-finalist, in the second round before going the way of all British flesh.

Women's tennis in 1991 was entirely dominated by 17-year-old Monica Seles, who won three of the four Grand Slam events and overshadowed the fourth, Wimbledon, by withdrawing three days beforehand and refusing to give an explanation other than that she had "a minor accident". Officials were unable to contact her. In the absence of other information, it was widely assumed - especially by tabloid journalists - that the accident was of a maternal nature.

Eleven days after the final, Seles emerged - in a blaze of Agassi-style hype - to say she had had a stress fracture and that no one had tried to contact her. A spokesman for the International Federation expressed "utter amazement". She seemed to think she was acting like her heroine Madonna; thoughtful observers thought she was acting like a 17-year-old.

Meanwhile Graf regained the championship, winning a tense but terrible final against Gabriela Sabatini. For the first time since 1981, Martina Navratilova failed to reach the final; she was beaten in a classic spring v. autumn quarter-final by the 15-year-old Jennifer Capriati. At the US Open Navratilova came back and beat Graf for the first time in four years, before losing to Seles. At the French Open Arantxa Sanchez Vicario beat Graf 6-0 6-2; it was the first time she had lost a set to love since she was 15. Despite her disappointments, Graf's attempts to liven up her image continued. Wearing a tight black dress, she did an advert in Germany for pasta; the ad agency, however, used a less powerful feminine wrist to serve the food.

MICHAEL WHO?

Q Michael, what will you say to the people who will say 'Who is Michael Stich?'
A Can we get another question, please?
Michael Stich, at press conference after semi-final

"He's not going to realise it now but maybe in a couple of years' time he'll realise how much his life has changed, and will change. But it's up to him how he can cope with it. Now he's a star, but not everything that shines is gold. Some people can handle it, some people can't."
Boris Becker on Stich

"I never expected to see a three-times Wimbledon champion behave like this on Centre Court in the final, I really didn't."
Dan Maskell, BBC TV, on Becker

Q Do you feel old?
A At this stage, I feel very old, yes.
Becker after his defeat

"A time must surely come - and it may be nearer than we think - when the ball is struck so fiercely that if it lands in court it is unplayable...Stich and Becker both served around 100 aces over the fortnight. No one counted the number of nine-stroke rallies in which they became engaged but it was probably fewer than a dozen apiece."
David Irvine, The Guardian

"I'm sure glad it isn't me out there."
Fred Perry, BBC Radio

THE OLD MAN'S GAME

On court, the most thrilling moments were provided at the US Open by Jimmy Connors, once the world no. 1 but lately ranked no. 987, who surged through the tournament with a succession of extraordinary late-night wins under the floodlights. On his 39th birthday, he spent four hours 41 minutes beating Aaron Krickstein. Connors had to be put on an intravenous glucose and saline drip afterwards. He then despatched Paul Haarhuis (who had beaten Becker) and was matched against Courier in the semi-final. By now, Jimbo had all America by the ears and courtside seats were said to be selling for $2000. But it was hopeless: the winner had to play the semi-final and final inside 24 hours to satisfy the TV schedulers. It was too much for Courier: had Connors won, it might have killed him. But it was fun while it lasted. In the French Open, Connors had shown signs of similar form but was forced to withdraw, knackered, at two sets all against Michael Chang. After that, he was reported to be eating more greens and less junk. Becker had his moment of glory during the Australian Open - in which he had never previously progressed beyond the quarter-finals - beating the declining Ivan Lendl in the final. However, he was already showing signs of wearying of the limelight, a mood that grew stronger as the year progressed: Becker left the stadium before the trophy ceremony to go for a run. "I just wanted to be alone," he said. McEnroe reached the semi-finals of the Australian Open as well, but this was the other McEnroe: young,

THE GREATEST COMEBACK ...

"It's a different game now. It's a power game and I'm not sure I like it. Things go too fast."
Jimmy Connors before the US Open

"You son of a bitch. Get out of that chair and get a job. I'm out here playing my butt off at 39 and you're pulling that crap."
Connors to umpire Del Littlewood after a disputed line call

"I've either got to be nuts or else I love the game even more than I thought I did."
Connors, after his four-hour 41-minute win over Aaron Krickstein

"I still have what people love to come and see. I go through every emotion out there, I'm not a robot. I'm sad, I'm happy, I'm angry. I don't mind opening up my chest and showing you my heart."
Connors

"Is it for real? I just don't know. I can't describe it. I've known and loved this tournament for 20 years - now to be able to play like this. There's no describing it. It's going to take me six months to understand what has happened here."
Connors after reaching the semi-finals

"For the last two decades I have been saying that if I had to choose an American to fight for our sovereign's life I would pick James Scott Connors."
Laurie Pignon, Daily Mail

"If your biggest star and your most compelling attraction is an antique who needs to be hooked up to an IV for an electrolyte transfusion after a five-setter, you've got serious trouble. All sports needs dynasties. But Connors was born in the Ming."
Tony Kornheiser, Washington Post

"Getting old is a bitch."
Connors

...AND THE SADDEST

"I have to find the game I used to play ten years ago."
Bjorn Borg

"Ten years ago Borg had played the role of Clint Eastwood on court, now he looked more like Monsieur Hulot."
Ian Ridley, Daily Telegraph

"It was like watching someone take off his underwear in public."
Gene Scott, former US Davis Cup player

"The Bjorn Borg story is not a story at all. It is a picture puzzle whose pieces have been strewn across a few continents, thrown away over years of prosperity, lost over years of waste. Pieces can be found stuck between the cushions of discotheques, clinging on to mirrored surfaces in penthouses, shattered on the floors of various emergency wards. The more pieces one collects, the more baffling and unknowable the puzzle becomes."
Peter Bodo, Tennis

"I was bitterly disappointed by the way I was treated."
Borg

well-mannered Patrick, then ranked 114 in the world. The biggest winner was Pete Sampras, the 1990 US open champion, who won $2 million in the Grand Slam Cup, an overblown tournament even by prevailing standards.

Not every old man found it easy to return. Bjorn Borg (five years younger than Connors) re-appeared at the Monte Carlo Open after his 10-year exile with a wooden racket and lost to Jordi Arrese of Spain 6-2 6-3 amidst squirming embarrassment from everyone except Borg and his 79-year-old fitness aide Ron Thatcher, also known as Tai Honsai, who said Borg could win Wimbledon again. Borg then got rid of Thatcher. The following day Loredana Berte, Borg's wife, attempted suicide. Quietly, plans for Borg to play the French Open and Wimbledon were dropped. Guillermo Vilas, 38, also tried a comeback, starting less ambitiously with an exhibition match against Yannick Noah. "I still have the fire in me," said Vilas. In his other role as a singer and music producer in Argentina, Vilas developed a form of Latin rap.

The connections between tennis and music were everywhere: Mats Wilander took a break from the game to sing and play guitar with his band in Swedish clubs; Pat Cash and John McEnroe made a record to help victims of the Armenian earthquake; Noah's first album "Black and What" was released in France.

British tennis players - Brown's moment of glory aside - made only their usual sort of records: on April 23, when Jeremy Bates dropped to no. 207, there was no British player in the top 200 for the first time since the rankings were invented. After three years, the Australian Warren Jacques was fired as the British men's coach; Richard Lewis was appointed instead. The Russian Olga Morozova was put in charge of Britain's women. Four British children between 12 and 14 went to Moscow to be taught by a leading Soviet coach, Natalie Polschikova. She said they were spoiled. The Lawn Tennis Association announced a deal with Nick Bollettieri's academies to try and unearth a champion somehow. Jeremy and Maria Couch of Leighton Buzzard said they had spent more than £60,000 trying to turn their children, Peter, 14, and Penny, 11, into champions. Andrew Castle was fined £2,400, half the prize money, for carrying an anti-poll tax sign at the National Championship final. The fine was only £1,000 less than the

"Image is everything."
Andre Agassi's line in commercial for Canon

"When Agassi throws his shirts into the crowd and all that stuff, it reminds me of a guy I used to know. That's the sort of shit I used to get up to."
Pat Cash

"Agassi has not yet grasped what his professional duties are. He wears clothes that shock, has an entourage like Michael Jackson and feels that he has to put on an act. He doesn't practise and if the act isn't working he just jumps on the

next plane back to Las Vegas."
Richard Evans, ATP media manager

"I went sightseeing all day and saw a whole bunch of things I don't remember the names of but I enjoyed them."
Agassi at Wimbledon

"Don't know what Wimbledon are playing at. They should have stopped the rot when they had the chance, with McEnroe. They should have insisted Agassi cut his hair, not just wear white."
Peter Coni QC, chairman of Henley Regatta

one levied on McEnroe for swearing at an umpire at the Australian Open and £2,120 more than Castle's poll tax in the London Borough of Merton. When the Federation Cup was staged at Nottingham, Britain's game against New Zealand was put on Court Three which had five park benches, two of them for the players; after protests from British journalists, 264 public seats were hastily put in. Britain did manage to return to the Davis Cup world group by beating Austria.

Members of Queen's Club (entrance fee £850, annual sub: £550) began circulating a petition protesting at being barred from the grass courts for much of the summer because of the Stella Artois tournament and Wimbledon practice. "We are getting a very bad deal," said Angela Buxton, the former Wimbledon doubles champion. "Quite frankly," replied the chairman Sir James Harvie Watt, "I believe subscriptions are too low considering the facilities we have here. If people don't like it they should either shut up or go somewhere else."

Wimbledon officials attended a demonstration during the US Open for a machine that would make all line-calls electronically. A tiny wristband designed to protect against tennis elbow was found to contain enough mercury in each one to pollute 30 million litres of water. Professor Jurgen Weineck, who works with the German Tennis Federation, advocated the abolition of the backhand and suggested youngsters should be taught to play with both hands to prevent them becoming physically unbalanced. This approach was said to have been used by Beverly Baker-Fleitz, a US Wightman Cup player of the 50s; it is thought to be rather tricky at the net. There was more interest in the suggestion by Philippe Chatrier, the outgoing president of the International Tennis Federation, to abolish the second service.

Martina Navratilova was sued for $10 million by her former lover Judy Nelson under the terms of a "nonmarital cohabitation agreement". Two days after losing the US Open final, Martina ran from a courtroom in tears after watching a video of the couple signing the deal at a party in 1986. One reader out of every five surveyed by *World Tennis* answered yes to the question: "Has tennis ever led to an extra-marital relationship?" Another 8% declined to answer. Asked if they thought about sex during tennis, 54% said yes; the magazine did not ask how many thought about tennis during sex.

1991

THE ALL-ENGLAND CHAMPIONSHIPS

Wimbledon, Jun 24-Jul 7
Men's Singles
Third Round
STEFAN EDBERG (Swe) [1] beat Christo van Rensburg (SAf) 6-1 6-3 6-2; JOHN McENROE (US) [16] beat Jean-Phillippe Fleurian (Fra) 6-2 7-6 6-1; THIERRY CHAMPION (Fra) beat Nick Brown (GB) 7-6 1-6 7-5 6-3; JIM COURIER (US) [4] beat Arnaud Boetsch (Fra) 6-2 6-2 6-0; KAREL NOVACEK (Cze) [14] beat Javier Frana (Arg) 6-4 6-4 5-7 6-4; MICHAEL STICH (Ger) [6] beat Omar Camporese (Ita) 7-6 6-2 6-7 6-4; ALEXANDR VOLKOV (USSR) beat Martin Laurendeau (Can) 6-1 6-2 6-1; ANDRE AGASSI (US) [5] beat Richard Krajicek (Hol) 7-6 6-3 7-6; JAN GUNNARSSON (Swe) beat Todd Woodbridge (Aus) 7-6 4-6 6-3 6-4; GUY FORGET (Fra) [7] beat Henri Leconte (Fra) 3-6 4-6 6-1 4-1 rtd; CHRISTIAN BERGSTROM (Swe) beat Brad Gilbert (US) [15] 6-3 6-2 3-6 6-3; TIM MAYOTTE (US) beat Patrick Kuhnen (Ger) 3-6 6-2 7-6 6-4; JACCO ELTINGH (Hol) beat Christian Saceanu (Ger) 6-3 4-6 6-4 7-5; DAVID WHEATON (US) beat Ivan Lendl (Cze) [3] 6-3 3-6 7-6 6-3; DERRICK ROSTAGNO (US) beat Jimmy Connors (US) 7-6 6-1 6-4; BORIS BECKER (Ger) [2] beat Andre Olhovskiy (USSR) 6-1 6-4 3-6 6-3
How the other seeds fell:
First Round: Michael Chang (US) [9] lost to Tim Mayotte (US) 7-6 6-4 1-6 6-7 2-6; Andrei Cherkasov (USSR) [12] lost to Richey Reneberg (US) 4-6 3-6 4-6; Emilio Sanchez (Spa) [11] lost to Patrick McEnroe (US) 3-6 6-7 1-6; *Second Round:* Pete Sampras (US) [8] lost to Derrick Rostagno (US) 4-6 6-3 6-7 4-6; Goran Ivanisevic (Yug) [10] lost to Nick Brown (GB) 6-4 3-6 6-7 3-6; Jakob Hlasek (Swi) [13] lost tc Todd Woodbridge (Aus) 3-6 6-1 5-7 3-6
Brown was the first Briton to beat a seed since John Lloyd put out Eliot Teltscher in 1985
Fourth Round
EDBERG beat McEnroe 7-6 6-1 6-4; CHAMPION beat Rostagno 6-7 6-2 6-1 3-6 6-3; COURIER beat Novacek 6-3 6-4 6-2; STICH beat Volkov 4-6 6-3 7-5 1-6 7-5; AGASSI beat Eltingh 6-3 3-6 6-3 6-4; WHEATON beat Gunnarsson 6-4 6-3 6-1; FORGET beat Mayotte 6-7 7-5 6-2 6-4; BECKER beat Bergstrom 6-4 6-7 6-1 7-6
Quarter-finals
EDBERG beat Champion 6-3 6-2 7-5; STICH beat Courier 6-3 7-6 6-2; WHEATON beat Agassi 6-2 0-6 3-6 7-6 6-2; BECKER beat Forget 6-7 7-6 6-2 7-6

Semi-finals
STICH beat Edberg 4-6 7-6 7-6 7-6; BECKER beat Wheaton 6-4 7-6 7-5
Final
STICH beat Becker 6-4 7-6 6-4

THE MEN'S FINAL

	STICH	BECKER
Points served	100	114
Aces	15	10
Service winners	51	40
Double faults	3	4
Serving points	67	70
Receiving points	44	33

Source: IBM

Women's Singles
Third Round
STEFFI GRAF (Ger) [1] beat Yayuk Basuki (Ina) 6-2 6-3; AMY FRAZIER (US) [14] beat Marianne Werdel (US) 6-2 6-1; ANKE HUBER (Ger) [13] beat Manon Bollegraf (Hol) 6-3 6-7 6-0; ZINA GARRISON (US) [7] beat Maria Strandlund (Swe) 6-3 6-3; ARANTXA SANCHEZ VICARIO (Spa) [4] beat Lori McNeil (US) 6-2 6-4; ANN MINTER (US) beat Gigi Fernandez (US) 6-3 6-3; JUDITH WIESNER (Aut) [16] beat Claudia Kohde-Kilsch (Ger) 3-6 7-5 6-1; MARY JOE FERNANDEZ (US) [5] beat Pam Shriver (US) 6-3 7-5; BRENDA SCHULTZ (Hol) beat Elena Brioukhovets (USSR) 5-7 6-4 7-5; JENNIFER CAPRIATI (US) [9] beat Wiltrud Probst (Ger) 6-3 1-6 6-3; CATARINA LINDQVIST (Swe) beat Elizabeth Smylie (Aus) 6-1 7-6; MARTINA NAVRATILOVA (US) [3] beat Laura Garrone (Ita) 6-2 6-2; KATERINA MALEEVA (Bul) [8] beat Patricia Hy (Can) 6-3 6-4; LAURA GILDEMEISTER (Per) beat Linda Harvey-Wild (US) 2-2 abandoned; NATHALIE TAUZIAK (Fra) [11] beat Linda Ferrando (Ita) 6-1 6-1; GABRIELA SABATINI (Arg) [2] beat Andrea Strnadova (Cze) 6-1 6-3
How the other seeds fell:
First Round: Helena Sukova (Cze) [10] lost to Gigi Fernandez (US) 6-4 1-6 4-6; Sandra Cecchini (Ita) [15] lost to Elizabeth Smylie (Aus) 6-1 6-3; *Second Round:* Jana Novotna (Cze) [6] lost to Brenda Schultz (Hol) 6-4 6-7 4-6; Natalya Zvereva (USSR) [12] lost to Linda Harvey-Wild (US) 4-6 1-6

> **❝Can you please tell me, officer, what time the rain will stop."**
> *Alleged little old lady at Wimbledon*

"The rain which has affected the Wimbledon Championships this year has been laid on by NSBKBT - as a warning. In former times those of us who are uninterested in tennis and repelled by its commercialisation could relieve the tedium by looking forward to the flicking of tennis skirts, dutifully recorded by both press and TV cameramen.

In these socially-engineered days, that small compensation has been taken from us: the TV camera modestly averts its eye from the serve, and the newspaper picture editors censor the merest hint of a frill. We intend to continue to arrange bad weather for Wimbledon until our former pleasures are restored."
Letter to the Sunday Express from Peter J Moore of Birmingham, secretary of the National Society for Bringing Knickers Back to Tennis

"It was frantically crowded and we spent practically all the time queueing. We queued for the bus to take us to the ground, we queued for practically half an hour for admission; spent our time queueing for standing room from which to get a glimpse of the players; queued for ages for a bus to take us to the station & at the station we queued for about 10 mins to discover that we needn't have queued at all."
Benjamin Britten (in his newly-published Letters) describing a visit to Wimbledon in 1933

"They are all insane. I'm insane, the tournament is, everything's insane. The US Open is just more insane."
John McEnroe

"The most ordinary consumer of all has queued, in the wet, to get in; has no refund coming; and can shelter only in the green urinal caverns below the stand or in overflowing catering refuges, consuming strawberries priced, this year, at 16 pence per berry. When that becomes intolerable, one may, with a stamp on one's hand like a Vietnamese in Hong Kong camp, perhaps be allowed outside to sit in a car parked far away across a muddy field. Does officialdom smile? It grunges and growls. Do the men in blazers wafting past manifest concern? They are beings from another planet, head waiters whose eyes can never be caught. Is anybody SORRY? The upper lip is so stiff it would crack if it crinkled.❞**
Leader in The Guardian

Fourth Round

GRAF beat Frazier 6-2 6-1; GARRISON beat Huber 4-6 6-3 6-0; SANCHEZ VICARIO beat Minter 7-5 3-6 6-1; FERNANDEZ beat Wiesner 6-0 7-5; CAPRIATI beat Schultz 3-6 6-1 6-1; NAVRATILOVA beat Lindqvist 6-1 6-3; GILDEMEISTER beat Maleeva 3-6 6-2 6-3; SABATINI beat Tauziat 7-6 6-3

Quarter-finals

GRAF beat Garrison 6-1 6-3; FERNANDEZ beat Sanchez Vicario 6-2 7-5; CAPRIATI beat Navratilova 6-4 7-5; SABATINI beat Gildemeister 6-2 6-1

Semi-finals

GRAF beat Fernandez 6-2 6-4; SABATINI beat Capriati 6-4 6-4

Final

GRAF beat Sabatini 6-4 3-6 8-6

Men's Doubles

John Fitzgerald (Aus) & Anders Jarryd (Swe) [2] beat Javier Frana (Arg) & Leonardo Lavalle (Mex) 6-3 6-4 6-7 6-1

Women's Doubles

Larissa Savchenko & Natalya Zvereva (USSR) [2] beat Gigi Fernandez (US) & Jana Novotna (Cze) [1] 6-4 3-6 6-4

Mixed Doubles

John Fitzgerald & Elizabeth Smylie (Aus) beat Jim Pugh (US) & Natalya Zvereva (USSR) 7-6 6-2

Brenda Schultz and Michiel Schapers won their first-round mixed doubles match 6-3 5-7 29-27. The last set was second-longest ever at Wimbledon, behind the 64-game first set of the men's doubles match between Pancho Segura & Alex Olmedo and Gordon Forbes & Abe Segal in 1968.

THE WOMEN'S FINAL

	GRAF	SABATINI
Points served	97	100
Aces	2	-
Service winners	11	14
Double faults	6	1
Serving points	53	55
Receiving points	48	44

Source: IBM

FASTEST SERVES ON CENTRE COURT

Men	Top speed (mph)	Women	Top speed (mph)
1 Marc Rosset	134	1 Jennifer Capriati	108
2 Michael Stich	126	2 Steffi Graf	107
3 Sandon Stolle	123	3 Radka Zrubakova	102
4 Boris Becker	122	4 Lori McNeil	99
5 Kelly Evernden	121	5 Jana Novotna	98

As recorded by IBM radar gun. Rosset's speed was the fastest ever measured. This table covers singles matches on Centre Court only

WIMBLEDON STATISTICS

Most aces: Boris Becker 99; Michael Stich 97; David Wheaton 82; Tim Mayotte 68

Highest % of first serves in: Javier Sanchez 75%; Jim Courier, Jakob Hlasek, Daniel Orsanic 70%

% first serve points won: Pat Cash 85%; Goran Ivanisevic, Stefan Edberg 84%.

% second serve points won: Gary Muller 65%; Stefan Edberg 63%; Danny Sapsford 60%

% service games won: Stefan Edberg 97%; Gary Muller 94%; Richard Krajicek 93%.

AUSTRALIAN OPEN
Flinders Park, Melbourne, Jan 14-27
Men's Singles
In the third round Boris Becker beat Omar Camporese of Italy 7-6 7-6 0-6 4-6 14-12 in 5 hrs 11 mins. It was the longest match in Australian Open history

Fourth Round
GUY FORGET (Fra) [10] beat Todd Woodbridge (Aus) 6-4 3-6 6-3 6-4; BORIS BECKER (Ger) [2] beat Wayne Ferreira (SAf) 6-4 7-6 6-4; CRISTIANO CARATTI (Ita) beat Richard Krajicek (Hol) 6-3 6-4 6-7 3-6 6-4; PATRICK McENROE (US) beat Mark Woodforde (Aus) 6-2 6-4 6-1; GORAN PRPIC (Yug) beat Jan Siemerink (Hol) 7-6 6-7 6-0 7-6; IVAN LENDL (Cze) [3] beat Aaron Krickstein (US) [13] 6-2 6-2 6-1; STEFAN EDBERG (Swe) [1] beat Jim Courier (US) [16] 4-6 6-0 6-4 5-7 6-2; JAIME YZAGA (Per) beat Mats Wilander (Swe) 7-5 2-6 6-1 3-6 6-1;

Quarter-finals
EDBERG beat Yzaga 6-2 6-3 6-2; LENDL beat Prpic 6-0 7-6 7-6; McENROE beat Caratti 7-6 6-3 4-6 4-6 6-2; BECKER beat Forget 6-2 7-6 6-3

Semi-finals
LENDL beat Edberg 6-4 5-7 3-6 7-6 6-4; BECKER beat McEnroe 6-7 6-4 6-1 6-4

Final
BECKER beat Lendl 1-6 6-4 6-4 6-4

Women's Singles
Fourth Round
ARANTXA SANCHEZ VICARIO (Spa) [6] beat Amy Frazier (US) [13] 6-3 6-2; ANKE HUBER (Ger) beat Natalya Zvereva (USSR) [11] 6-3 6-4; KATERINA MALEEVA (Bul) [5] beat Magdalena Maleeva (Bul) 6-3 6-2; MARY JOE FERNANDEZ (US) [3] beat Sabine Appelmans (Bel) [16] 6-3 6-3; JANA NOVOTNA (Cze) [10] beat Zina Garrison (US) [8] 7-6 6-4; STEFFI GRAF (Ger) [1] beat Karina Habsudova (Cze) 6-0 6-1; GABRIELA SABATINI (Arg) [4] beat Rachel McQuillan (Aus) 6-3 6-1; MONICA SELES (Yug) [2] beat Catherine Tanvier (Fra) 6-2 6-1

Quarter-finals
FERNANDEZ beat Maleeva 6-3 6-2; NOVOTNA beat Graf 5-7 6-4 8-6; SELES beat Huber 6-3 6-1; SANCHEZ VICARIO beat Sabatini 6-1 6-3

Semi-finals
SELES beat Fernandez 6-3 0-6 9-7; NOVOTNA beat

Sanchez Vicario 6-2 6-4
Final
SELES beat Novotna 5-7 6-3 6-1
Seles, aged 17y 1m, became the youngest-ever women's champion

Men's Doubles
SCOTT DAVIS & DAVID PATE (US) [3] beat Patrick McEnroe & David Wheaton (US) [13] 6-7 7-6 6-3 7-5
Women's Doubles
PATTY FENDICK & MARY JOE FERNANDEZ (US) [4] beat Gigi Fernandez (US) and Jana Novotna (Cze) [1] 7-6 6-1
Mixed Doubles
JEREMY BATES & JO DURIE (GB) beat Scott Davis & Robin White (US) 2-6 6-4 6-4

FRENCH OPEN
Roland Garros, Paris, May 27-Jun 9
Men's Singles
Fourth Round
JAKOB HLASEK (Swi) beat Christian Miniussi (Arg) 4-6 6-3 5-7 7-5 6-2; ANDRE AGASSI (US) [4] beat Alberto Mancini (Arg) 6-3 6-3 5-7 6-1; MICHAEL CHANG (US) [10] beat Guy Forget (Fra) [7] 6-1 6-1 4-6 6-3; BORIS BECKER (Ger) [2] beat Francisco Clavet (Spa) 7-6 6-4 6-3; STEFAN EDBERG (Swe) [1] beat Andrei Cherkasov (USSR) 7-6 6-4 6-3; FRANCO DAVIN (Arg) beat Arnaud Boetsch (Fra) 7-6 6-4 6-3 6-1; MICHAEL STICH (Ger) [12] beat Fabrice Santoro (Fra) 6-3 6-1 6-2; JIM COURIER (US) [9] beat Todd Martin (US) 6-2 6-3 6-3

Quarter-finals
AGASSI beat Hlasek 6-3 6-1 6-1; BECKER beat Chang 6-4 6-4 6-2; STICH beat Davin 6-4 6-4 6-4; COURIER beat Edberg 6-4 2-6 6-3 6-4

Semi-finals
AGASSI beat Becker 7-5 6-3 3-6 6-1; COURIER beat Stich 6-2 6-7 6-2 6-4

Final
COURIER beat Agassi 3-6 6-3 2-6 6-1 6-4
First all-US final since Trabert v Larsen in 1954

Women's Singles
Fourth Round
STEFFI GRAF (Ger) [2] beat Sabine Appelmans (Bel) 6-2 6-2; ARANTXA SANCHEZ VICARIO (Spa) [5] beat Tami Whitlinger (US) 6-2 6-1; MARY JOE FERNANDEZ (US) [4] beat Elna Reinach (SAf) 6-4 7-6; JANA NOVOTNA (Cze) [6] beat Leila Meskhi (USSR) [14] 6-0 7-6; NATHALIE TAUZIAT (Fra) [13] beat Naoko Sawamatsu (Jap) 7-5 2-6 12-10; CONCHITA MARTINEZ (Spa) [7] beat Jennifer Capriati (US) [10] 6-3 6-3; MONICA SELES (Yug) [1] beat Sandra Cecchini (Ita) 3-6 6-3 6-0; GABRIELA SABATINI (Arg) [3] beat Rachel McQuillan (Aus) 6-3 6-0

Quarter-finals
SABATINI beat Novotna 5-7 7-6 -0; SANCHEZ VICARIO beat Fernandez 6-3 6-2; GRAF beat Tauziat 6-3 6-2; SELES beat Martinez 6-0 7-5

Semi-finals
SELES beat Sabatini 6-4 6-1; SANCHEZ VICARIO beat Graf 6-0 6-2

Final
SELES beat Sanchez Vicario 6-3 6-4

Men's Doubles
JOHN FITZGERALD (Aus) & ANDERS JARRYD (Swe) [9] beat Rick Leach & Jim Pugh (US) [3] 6-0 7-6
Women's Doubles
GIGI FERNANDEZ (US) & JANA NOVOTNA (Cze) [1] beat Larissa Savchenko & Natalya Zvereva (USSR) [2] 6-4 6-0
Mixed Doubles
HELENA SUKOVA & CYRIL SUK (Cze) beat Caroline Vis & Paul Haarhuis (Hol) 3-6 6-4 6-1

US OPEN
Flushing Meadow, New York, Aug 26-Sep 8
Men's Singles
Fourth Round
IVAN LENDL (Cze) [5] beat Goran Ivanisevic (Yug) 7-5 6-7 6-4 6-2; PETE SAMPRAS (US) [6] beat David Wheaton (US) [11] 3-6 6-2 6-2 6-4; PAUL HAARHUIS (Hol) beat Carl-Uwe Steeb (Ger) 6-2 6-3 6-4; JIMMY CONNORS (US) beat Aaron Krickstein (US) 3-6 7-6 1-6 6-2 7-6; JIM COURIER (US) [4] beat Emilio Sanchez (Spa) [14] 6-4 6-4 6-3; STEFAN EDBERG (Swe) [2] beat Michael Chang (US) 7-6 7-5 6-3; JAVIER SANCHEZ (Spa) beat Gabriel Markus (Arg) 6-4 6-2 6-3; MICHAEL STICH (Ger) [3] beat Derrick Rostagno (US) 6-2 3-6 6-1 7-6
Jimmy Connors' match with Aaron Krickstein lasted a championship record 4 hours 41 minutes; it was on Connors' 39th birthday

Quarter-finals
EDBERG beat Sanchez 6-2 6-2 6-3; COURIER beat Sampras 6-2 7-6 7-6; LENDL beat Stich 6-3 3-6 4-6 7-6 6-1; CONNORS beat Haarhuis 4-6 7-6 6-4 6-2

Semi-finals
EDBERG beat Lendl 6-3 6-3 6-4; COURIER beat Connors 6-3 6-3 6-2

Final
EDBERG beat Courier 6-2 6-4 6-0

Women's Singles
Fourth Round
MARTINA NAVRATILOVA (US) [6] beat Manuela Maleeva-Fragniere (Swi) [10] 7-6 1-6 6-2; ARANTXA SANCHEZ VICARIO (Spa) [4] beat Natalya Zvereva (USSR) 6-3 7-6; CONCHITA MARTINEZ (Spa) [8] beat Zina Garrison (US) [12] 6-4 6-4; STEFFI GRAF (Ger) [1] beat Judith Wiesner (Aut) 7-5 6-4; MONICA SELES (Yug) [2] beat Regina Rajchrtova (Cze) 6-1 6-2; JENNIFER CAPRIATI (US) [7] beat Jo Durie (GB) 6-1 6-2; GABRIELA SABATINI (Arg) [3] beat Jana Novotna (Cze) [9] 6-4 7-6; GIGI FERNANDEZ (US) beat Radka Zrubakova (Cze) 6-2 6-2.

Quarter-finals
SELES beat Fernandez 6-1 6-2; CAPRIATI beat Sabatini 6-3 7-6; GRAF beat Martinez 6-1 6-3; NAVRATILOVA beat Sanchez Vicario 6-7 7-6 6-2

Semi-finals
NAVRATILOVA beat Graf 7-6 6-7 6-4; SELES beat Capriati 6-3 3-6 7-6

Final
SELES beat Navratilova 7-6 6-1

Men's Doubles Final
JOHN FITZGERALD (Aus) & ANDERS JARRYD (Swe) [1] beat Scott Davis & David Pate (US) [2] 6-3 3-6 6-3 6-3

Women's Doubles Final
PAM SHRIVER (US) & NATALYA ZVEREVA (USSR) [6] beat Jana Novotna (Cze) & Larissa Savchenko (USSR) [1] 6-4 4-6 7-6

Mixed Doubles Final
MANON BOLLEGRAF & TOM HIJSSEN (Hol) beat Arantxa Sanchez Vicario & Emilio Sanchez (Spa) 6-2 7-6

OTHER MAJOR EVENTS 1990-91
Men
Bordeaux Tournament *Bordeaux, Sep 9*
GUY FORGET (Fra) beat Goran Ivanisevic (Yug) 6-4 6-3
Swiss Indoor Championship *Basle, Sep 30*
JOHN McENROE (US) beat Goran Ivanisevic (Yug) 6-7 4-6 7-6 6-3 6-4
Australian Indoor Championship *Sydney, Oct 7*
BORIS BECKER (Ger) beat Stefan Edberg (Swe) 7-6 6-4 6-4
Seiko Super Tournament *Tokyo, Oct 14*
IVAN LENDL (Cze) beat Boris Becker (Ger) 4-6 6-3 7-6
European Community Championship *Antwerp, Oct 21*
GORAN IVANISEVIC (Yug) beat Henri Leconte (Fra) 6-2 7-6 4-6 4-6 6-1
Swedish Open *Stockholm, Oct 28*
BORIS BECKER (Ger) beat Stefan Edberg (Swe) 6-4 6-0 6-3
Paris Open *Paris, Nov 4*
STEFAN EDBERG (Swe) beat Boris Becker (Ger) 3-3 rtd.injured
Diet Pepsi Tournament *Wembley, Nov 11*
JAKOB HLASEK (Swi) beat Michael Chang (US) 7-6 6-3
Milan Shootout *Milan, Nov 11*
IVAN LENDL (Cze) beat Jonas Svensson (Swe) 7-5 5-7 6-4
ATP Tour Championship *Frankfurt, Nov 18*
ANDRE AGASSI (US) beat Stefan Edberg (Swe) 5-7 7-6 7-5 6-2
Compaq Grand Slam Cup *Munich, Dec 16*
(Successor to the Grand Prix Masters)
PETE SAMPRAS (US) beat Brad Gilbert (US) 6-3 6-4 6-2
Sampras (19) collected $2 million and gave $200,000 of it away to charity
New South Wales Open *Sydney, Jan 13*
GUY FORGET (Fra) beat Michael Stich (Ger) 6-3 6-4
Milan Indoor Championship *Milan Feb 10*
ALEXANDIR VOLKOV (USSR) beat Cristiano Caratti (Ita) 6-1 7-5
US Pro Indoor Championship *Philadelphia, Feb 2*
IVAN LENDL (Cze) beat Pete Sampras (US) 5-7 6-4 6-4 3-6 6-3
Eurocard Classic *Stuttgart, Feb 24*
STEFAN EDBERG (Swe) beat Jonas Svensson (Swe) 6-2 3-6 7-5 6-2
Volvo Memphis Indoor *Memphis, Feb 24*
IVAN LENDL (Cze) beat Michael Stich (Ger) 7-5 6-3
Volvo Chicago Indoor *Chicago, Mar 3*
JOHN McENROE (US) beat Patrick McEnroe (US) 3-6 6-2 6-4
Champions Cup *Indian Wells, Mar 10*
JIM COURIER (US) beat Guy Forget (Fra) 4-6 6-3 4-6 6-3 7-6
International Players' Championship *Key Biscayne, Mar 24*
JIM COURIER (US) beat David Wheaton (US) 4-6 6-3 6-4
Estoril Open *Lisbon, Apr 7*
SERGI BRUGUERA (Spa) beat Karel Novacek (Cze) 7-6 6-1
Japan Open *Tokyo, Apr 14*
STEFAN EDBERG (Swe) beat Ivan Lendl (Cze) 6-1 7-5 6-0

Nice Open *Nice, Apr 21*
MARTIN JAITE (Arg) beat Goran Prpic (Yug) 3-6 7-6 6-3
AT & T Challenge *Roswell, Georgia, May 5*
ANDRE AGASSI (US) beat David Wheaton (US) 7-6 6-1
German Open *Hamburg, May 12*
KAREL NOVACEK (Cze) beat Magnus Gustafsson (Swe)
6-3 6-3 5-7 0-6 6-1
Italian Open *Rome, May 19*
EMILIO SANCHEZ (Spa) beat Alberto Mancini (Arg)
6-3 6-1 3-0 retired
Stella Artois Championship *Queen's Club, London, Jun 16*
STEFAN EDBERG (Swe) beat David Wheaton (US)
6-2 6-3
Genoa ATP Tournament, *Genoa, Jun 23*
CARL-UWE STEEB (Ger) beat Jordi Arrese (Spa) 6-3 6-4
Swedish Open *Bastaad, Jul 14*
MAGNUS GUSTAFSSON (Swe) beat Alberto Mancini
(Arg) 6-1 6-1
Swiss Open *Gstaad, Jul 14*
EMILIO SANCHEZ (Spa) beat Sergi Bruguera (Spa) 6-1
6-4 6-4
Gunze Indoor Tournament *Osaka, Jul 14*
JIM COURIER (US) beat Michael Chang (US) 6-4 2-6 6-4
Sovran Bank Classic *Washington, Jul 21*
ANDRE AGASSI (US) beat Petr Korda (Cze) 6-3 6-4
Mercedes Cup *Stuttgart, Jul 21*
MICHAEL STICH (Ger) beat Alberto Mancini (Arg) 1-6,
7-6 6-4 6-2
Canadian Open *Montreal, Jul 28*
ANDRE CHESNOKOV (USSR) beat Petr Korda (Cze)
6-3 4-6 6-3
Volvo Los Angeles Tournament *Los Angeles, Aug 4*
PETE SAMPRAS (US) beat Brad Gilbert (US) 6-2 6-7 6-3
Thriftway ATP Championships *Mason, Ohio, Aug 11*
GUY FORGET (Fra) beat Pete Sampras (US) 2-6 7-6 6-4
Volvo International *New Haven, Connecticut, Aug 18*
PETR KORDA (Cze) beat Goran Ivanisevic (Yug) 6-4 6-2

Norstar Bank Hamlet Challenge *Commack,
New York, Aug 25*
IVAN LENDL (Cze) beat Stefan Edberg (Swe) 6-3 6-2

Women
Athens Open *Athens, Sep 16*
CECILIA DAHLMAN (Swe) beat Katia Piccolini (Ita)
7-5 7-5
Bayonne Women's Open *Bayonne, France, Sep 30*
NATHALIE TAUZIAT (Fra) beat Anke Huber (Ger) 6-3 7-6
Soviet Women's Championship *Moscow, Oct 7*
LEILA MESKHI (USSR) beat Elena Brioukhovets
(USSR) 6-4 6-4
European Indoor Championship *Zurich, Oct 14*
STEFFI GRAF (Ger) beat Gabriela Sabatini (Arg) 6-3 6-2
Porsche Tournament *Filderstadt, Germany, Oct 21*
MARY JOE FERNANDEZ (US) beat Barbara Paulus
(Aut) 6-1 6-3
Puerto Rico Open *San Juan, Oct 28*
JENNIFER CAPRIATI (US) beat Zina Garrison (US)
5-7 6-4 6-2
Midland Bank Championships *Brighton, England, Oct 28*
STEFFI GRAF (Ger) beat Helena Sukova (Cze) 7-5 6-3
Virginia Slims of Oakland *Oakland, California, Nov 4*
MONICA SELES (Yug) beat Martina Navratilova (US)
6-3, 7-6
Virginia Slims of New England
Worcester, Massachusetts, Nov 11
STEFFI GRAF (Ger) beat Gabriela Sabatini (Arg) 7-6 6-3
Virginia Slims Championship Finals *New York, Nov 18*
Singles
MONICA SELES (Yug) beat Gabriela Sabatini (Arg) 6-4
5-7 3-6 6-4 6-2
*The first women's five-set match in a major event since the
1901 US Championship doubles*

THE LADIES, BLESS 'EM

❝I don't feel any pressure at all."
*Martina Navratilova before playing Jennifer
Capriati*

"The pressure builds up the older you get."
Martina Navratilova after playing Capriati

**"I did everything for her: the cooking, the
cleaning, cutting and colouring her hair,
picking out her clothes."**
*Judy Nelson, suing her ex-lover Martina
Navratilova*

**"...in the light of what a fright Miss N has
looked for the past seven years - that
chromium yellow hair hacked into the
fetching basin cut, that loathsome
leisurewear worn every hour God sends -
shouldn't it be Miss Navratilova bringing
a suit against Mrs Nelson?"**
Julie Burchill, Mail on Sunday

**"In all ways other than tennis she is,
thankfully, an unremarkable girl. In Paris,
she went to visit Notre Dame assuming it
was a football field. When she was asked
about Napoleon, she referred to him as
'that little dead dude?' That's vintage 15,
all sass and bubbles. I wish her good**

**luck. I just hope that when she's 21,
none of the Capriatis are sorry for the
choices they made."**
Tony Kornheiser, Washington Post

**"Monica's the first one of the new breed to
show the responsibility to the game a top
player should have."**
Chris Evert

"I don't talk to lower-ranked players."
Monica Seles, world no.1

**"It's a drag having to wear socks during
matches because the tan, like, stops at
the ankles. I can never get my skin, like,
colour-coordinated. I guess every sport
has its drawbacks."**
Seles

**"Is Seles just a hurt kid who wanted to get
away from it all? Or is she a savvy
publicity prankster?"**
Sally Jenkins, Sports Illustrated

**"I have so many different personalities.
Maybe I'm still growing up.❞**
Seles

Doubles
KATHY JORDAN (US) and ELIZABETH SMYLIE (Aus)
beat Arantxa Sanchez Vicario (Spa) and Mercedes Paz
(Arg) 7-6 6-4
New South Wales Open *Sydney, Jan 13*
JANA NOVOTNA (Cze) beat Arantxa Sanchez Vicario
(Spa) 6-4 6-2
Women's Shootout *Dallas, Feb 2*
ARANTXA SANCHEZ VICARIO (Spa) beat Jennifer
Capriati (US) 7-4 7-3
Virginia Slims of Chicago *Chicago, Feb 17*
MARTINA NAVRATILOVA (US) beat Zina Garrison
(US) 6-1 6-2
Virginia Slims of Oklahoma *Oklahoma City, Feb 24*
JANA NOVOTNA (Cze) beat Anne Smith (US) 3-6 6-3 6-2
Virginia Slims of Florida *Boca Raton, Mar 10*
GABRIELA SABATINI (Arg) beat Steffi Graf (Ger)
6-4 7-6
International Players' Championship *Key Biscayne, Mar 23*
MONICA SELES (Yug) beat Gabriela Sabatini (Arg)
6-3 7-5
US Women's Hardcourt Championship
San Antonio, Mar 30
STEFFI GRAF (Ger) beat Monica Seles (Yug) 6-4 6-3
Family Circle Magazine Cup *Hilton Head Island, Apr 7*
GABRIELA SABATINI (Arg) beat Leila Meskhi (USSR)
6-1 6-1
Busch & Lomb Championship *Amelia Island,*
Florida, Apr 14
GABRIELA SABATINI (Arg) beat Steffi Graf (Ger)
7-5 7-6
Virginia Slims of Houston *Houston, Apr 21*
MONICA SELES (Yug) beat Mary Joe Fernandez (US)
6-4 6-3
WTA Seat Open *Barcelona, Apr 28*
CONCHITA MARTINEZ (Spa) beat Manuela Maleeva
Fragniere (Swi) 6-4 6-1
German Open *Hamburg, May 6*
STEFFI GRAF (Ger) beat Monica Seles (Yug) 7-5 6-7 6-3
Italian Open *Rome, May 12*
GABRIELA SABATINI (Arg) beat Monica Seles (Yug)
6-3 6-2
Pilkington Open *Eastbourne, England, Jun 23*
MARTINA NAVRATILOVA (US) beat Arantxa Sanchez
Vicario (Spa) 6-4 6-4
Gunze Indoor Tournament *Osaka, Jul 14*
GABRIELA SABATINI (Arg) beat Katerina Maleeva
(Bul) 7-6 6-2
Virginia Slims Hall of Fame *Newport, Rhode Island, Jul 21*
ROSALYN FAIRBANK-NIDEFFER (US) beat Mary Joe
Fernandez (US) 1-6 7-5 6-0
Pathmark Classic *Mahwah, New Jersey, Jul 21*
JENNIFER CAPRIATI (US) beat Monica Seles (Yug)
6-3 7-5
Westchester Ladies Cup *Purchase, New York, Jul 28*
ISABELLE DEMONGEOT (Fra) beat Lori McNeil (US)
6-4 6-4
Mazda Classic *Carlsbad, California, Aug 4*
JENNIFER CAPRIATI (US) beat Monica Seles (Yug)
4-6 6-1 7-6
US Players' Limited Challenge *Toronto, Aug 11*
JENNIFER CAPRIATI (US) beat Katerina Maleeva (Bul)
6-2 6-3
Virginia Slims of Los Angeles *Manhattan Beach,*
California, Aug 18
MONICA SELES (Yug) beat Kimiko Date (Jap) 6-3 6-1
Virginia Slims of Washington *Washington DC, Aug 25*
ARANTXA SANCHEZ VICARIO (Spa) beat Katerina
Maleeva (Bul) 6-2 7-5

DAVIS CUP
World Group
First Round
AUSTRALIA 5 Belgium 0; ARGENTINA 4 New Zealand
1; SPAIN 4 Canada 1; GERMANY 3 Italy 2;
YUGOSLAVIA 4 Sweden 1; CZECHOSLOVAKIA 4
Austria 1; Mexico 2 UNITED STATES 3; FRANCE 5
Israel 0

Quarter-finals
Czechoslovakia 1 YUGOSLAVIA 4; GERMANY 3
Argentina 0; FRANCE 3 Australia 2; UNITED STATES 4
Spain 1
Semi-finals
Sep 20-22
UNITED STATES 3 Germany 2; FRANCE 5 Yugoslavia 0

FEDERATION CUP
Nottingham, Jul 22-28
First Round
BULGARIA 3 Hungary 0; SOVIET UNION 3 Paraguay 0;
INDONESIA 3 Yugoslavia 0; CANADA 2 Denmark 1;
CHINA 3 Brazil 0; FINLAND 3 Romania 0;
AUSTRALIA 2 Japan 1; POLAND 2 France 1; UNITED
STATES 2 Holland 0; GERMANY 3 Greece 0; SPAIN 2
Belgium 0; AUSTRIA 3 Portugal 0; CZECHOSLOVAKIA
2 Sweden 0; GREAT BRITAIN 2 New Zealand 0; ITALY
2 Israel 1; SWITZERLAND 2 Argentina 0

Second Round
UNITED STATES 3 Bulgaria 0; GERMANY 2 Canada 1;
SPAIN 3 Austalia 0; SWITZERLAND 2 China 1;
AUSTRIA 2 Finland 1; CZECHOSLOVAKIA 2 Soviet
Union 1; ITALY 2 Great Britain 0; INDONESIA 2 Poland 1

Quarter-finals
UNITED STATES 2 Austria 1; CZECHOSLOVAKIA 2
Switzerland 1; GERMANY 2 Italy 1; SPAIN 2 Indonesia 0

THE BRITISH CRISIS (continued)

**❝One small word summed up most of the
tennis. Dire.❞**
*David Irvine, The Guardian, on the British
Closed Championships at Telford*

**"One of them earned £300 for losing this
morning, and they won't put in 50p.
Bloody arrogance."**
*Alan Durban, Telford Leisure Centre manager,
on the players' refusal to play snooker with the
light on*

**"We just don't have the talent. I don't think I
did a bad job."**
Warren Jacques on being sacked

**"It's like selecting the England soccer
manager from a club in the Third or
Fourth Division."**
John Lloyd on Richard Lewis's appointment

**"British tennis went wrong after the war. We
had a period of stagnation for two or
three decades.❞❞**
Richard Lewis

Semi-finals
SPAIN 3 Germany 0; UNITED STATES 3 Czechoslovakia 0

Final
SPAIN 2 United States 1
(Spain's names first)
Conchita Martinez lost to JENNIFER CAPRIATI 6-4 6-7 1-6; ARANTXA SANCHEZ VICARIO beat Mary Joe Fernandez 6-3 6-4; MARTINEZ and SANCHEZ VICARIO beat Gigi Fernandez and Zina Garrison 3-6 6-1 6-1
Spain won the title for the first time

WORLD RANKINGS
(as at September 16 1991. Figures in brackets are positions at end of 1990)

Men
1 (1)	Stefan Edberg (Swe)
2 (2)	Boris Becker (Ger)
3 (25)	Jim Courier (US)
4 (3)	Ivan Lendl (Cze)
5 (42)	Michael Stich (Ger)
6 (16)	Guy Forget (Fra)
7 (5)	Pete Sampras (US)
8 (4)	Andre Agassi (US)
9 (34)	Karel Novacek (Cze)
10 (28)	Sergi Bruguera (Spa)
11 (31)	Magnus Gustafsson (Swe)
12 (8)	Emilio Sanchez (Spa)
13 (27)	David Wheaton (US)
14 (38)	Petr Korda (Cze)
15 (9)	Goran Ivanisevic (Yug)
16 (21)	Andrei Cherkasov (USSR)
17 (55)	Goran Prpic (Yug)
18 (18)	Jakob Hlasek (Swi)
19 (47)	Derrick Rostagno (US)
20 (16)	Michael Chang (US)

Becker became No. 1 for the first time after winning the Australian Open on January 28, lost the lead to Edberg on February 18, then regained it after Wimbledon until Edberg's success in the US Open

Women
1 (2)	Monica Seles (Yug)
2 (1)	Steffi Graf (Ger)
3 (5)	Gabriela Sabatini (Arg)
4 (3)	Martina Navratilova (US)
5 (7)	Arantxa Sanchez Vicario (Spa)
6 (8)	Jennifer Capriati (US)
7 (4)	Mary Joe Fernandez (US)
8 (11)	Conchita Martinez (Spa)
9 (13)	Jana Novotna (Cze)
10 (9)	Manuela Maleeva Fragniere (Swi)
11 (6)	Katerina Maleeva (Bul)
12 (10)	Zina Garrison (US)
13 (19)	Leila Meskhi (USSR)
14 (14)	Helena Sukova (Cze)
15 (18)	Nathalie Tauziat (Fra)
16 (17)	Judith Wiesner (Aut)
17 (36)	Gigi Fernandez (US)
18 (34)	Anke Huber (Ger)
19 (15)	Barbara Paulus (Aut)
20 (16)	Amy Frazier (US)

Graf lost her No. 1 ranking to Seles on March 11 after a record 185 weeks. Seles, 17 years 3 months, was the youngest No. 1 ever, 2 months younger than Tracy Austin in April 1980. Graf briefly regained her position in August but lost it again after the US Open

DAVIS CUP FINAL
St Petersburg, Florida, Dec 1-2 1990
UNITED STATES 3 Australia 2
(US names first)
Andre Agassi beat Richard Fromberg 4-6 6-2 4-6 6-2 6-4; MICHAEL CHANG beat Darren Cahill 6-2 7-6 6-0; RICK LEACH & JIM PUGH beat Pat Cash & John Fitzgerald 6-4 6-2 3-6 7-6; Agassi lost to CAHILL 4-6 6-4 *abandoned;* Chang lost to FROMBERG 5-7 6-2 3-6

CHAMPIONS

THE ALL ENGLAND CHAMPIONSHIPS, WIMBLEDON
Men's Singles
(Until 1922 defending champions played only one challenge match against the winners of the open competition)
1877	Spencer Gore (GB) beat W C Marshall (GB) 6-1 6-2 6-4
1878	Frank Hadow (GB) beat Spencer Gore (GB) 7-5 6-1 9-7
1879	Rev John Hartley (GB) beat St L Goold (GB) 6-2 6-4 6-2
1880	Rev John Hartley (GB) beat Herbert Lawford (GB) 6-3 6-2 2-6 6-3
1881	William Renshaw (GB) beat Rev John Hartley (GB) 6-0 6-1 6-1
1882	William Renshaw (GB) beat Ernest Renshaw (GB) 6-1 2-6 4-6 6-2 6-2
1883	William Renshaw (GB) beat Ernest Renshaw (GB) 2-6 6-3 6-3 4-6 6-3
1884	William Renshaw (GB) beat Herbert Lawford (GB) 6-0 6-4 9-7
1885	William Renshaw (GB) beat Herbert Lawford (GB) 7-5 6-2 4-6 7-5
1886	William Renshaw (GB) beat Herbert Lawford (GB) 6-0 5-7 6-3 6-4
1887	Herbert Lawford (GB) beat Ernest Renshaw (GB) 1-6 6-3 3-6 6-4 6-4
1888	Ernest Renshaw (GB) beat Herbert Lawford (GB) 6-3 7-5 6-0
1889	William Renshaw (GB) beat Ernest Renshaw (GB) 6-4 6-1 3-6 6-0
1890	Willoughby Hamilton (GB) beat William Renshaw (GB) 6-8 2-6 3-6 6-1 6-1
1891	Wilfred Baddeley (GB) beat Joshua Pim (GB) 6-4 1-6 7-5 6-0
1892	Wilfred Baddeley (GB) beat Joshua Pim (GB) 4-6 6-3 6-3 6-2
1893	Joshua Pim (GB) beat Wilfred Baddeley (GB) 3-6 6-1 6-3 6-2
1894	Joshua Pim (GB) beat Wilfred Baddeley (GB) 10-8 6-2 8-6
1895	Wilfred Baddeley (GB) beat W V Eaves (GB) 4-6 2-6 8-6 6-2 6-3

POST-WAR BRITISH GRAND SLAM WINNERS

Men's Singles	None		
Women's Singles	Angela Mortimer	1955	French Champs
	Shirley Bloomer	1957	French Champs
	Angela Mortimer	1958	Australian Champs
	Christine Truman	1959	French Champs
	Ann Haydon (later Jones)	1961	French Champs
	Angela Mortimer	1961	Wimbledon
	Ann Jones	1966	French Champs
	Virginia Wade	1968	US Open
	Ann Jones	1969	Wimbledon
	Virginia Wade	1972	Australian Champs
	Sue Barker	1976	French Champs
	Virginia Wade	1977	Wimbledon
Men's Doubles	Roger Taylor (d)	1971	US Open
	Roger Taylor (e)	1972	US Open
Women's Doubles	Angela Mortimer/Anne Shilcock	1955	Wimbledon
	Angela Buxton (a)	1956	French Champs
	Angela Buxton (a)	1956	Wimbledon
	Shirley Bloomer (h)	1957	French Champs
	Christine Truman (m)	1960	Australian Champs
	Ann Jones (i)	1963	French Champs
	Ann Jones (j)	1968	French Champs
	Ann Jones (j)	1969	French Champs
	Virginia Wade (f)	1969	US Open
	Virginia Wade (f)	1973	French Champs
	Virginia Wade (f)	1973	US Open
	Virginia Wade (f)	1973	Australian Champs
	Virginia Wade (f)	1975	US Open
Mixed Doubles	Shirley Bloomer (k)	1958	French Champs
	Billy Knight (l)	1959	French Champs
	Peter Curtis (g)	1968	US Champs
	Ann Jones (b) *	1969	Australian Champs
	Ann Jones (b)	1969	Wimbledon
	John Lloyd (c)	1982	French Champs
	John Lloyd (c)	1983	Wimbledon
	John Lloyd (c)	1984	Wimbledon
	Jeremy Bates/Jo Durie	1987	Wimbledon
	Jeremy Bates/Jo Durie	1991	Australian Champs

* Final not played, title shared beween Jones/Stolle and Marty Riessen and Margaret Court
(a) with Althea Gibson (US) (b) with Fred Stolle (Aus) (c) with Wendy Turnbull (Aus) (d) with John Newcombe (Aus) (e) with Cliff Drysdale (SAf) (f) with Margaret Court (Aus) (g) with Mary-Ann Eisel (US) (h) with Darlene Hard (US) (i) with Renée Schurmann (SAf) (j) with Françoise Durr (Fra) (k) with Nicola Pietrangeli (Ita) (l) with Yola Ramirez (Mex) (m) with Maria Bueno (Bra)

Most Titles:
8 Ann Jones, Virginia Wade; 4 Angela Mortimer 3 Shirley Bloomer, John Lloyd

1896	Harold Mahoney (GB) beat Wilfred Baddeley (GB) 6-2 6-8 5-7 8-6 6-3
1897	Reginald Doherty (GB) beat Harold Mahoney (GB) 6-4 6-4 6-3
1898	Reginald Doherty (GB) beat Lawrence Doherty (GB) 6-3 6-3 2-6 7-5 6-1
1899	Reginald Doherty (GB) beat Arthur Gore (GB)1-6 4-6 6-2 6-3 6-3
1900	Reginald Doherty (GB) beat Sidney Smith (GB) 6-8 6-3 6-1 6-2
1901	Arthur Gore (GB) beat Reginald Doherty (GB) 4-6 7-5 6-4 6-4
1902	Lawrence Doherty (GB) beat Arthur Gore (GB) 6-4 6-3 3-6 6-0
1903	Lawrence Doherty (GB) beat Frank Riseley (GB) 7-5 6-3 6-0
1904	Lawrence Doherty (GB) beat Frank Riseley (GB) 6-1 7-5 8-6
1905	Lawrence Doherty (GB) beat Norman Brookes (Aus) 8-6 6-2 6-4
1906	Lawrence Doherty (GB) beat Frank Riseley (GB) 6-4 6-2 6-3
1907	Norman Brookes (Aus) beat Arthur Gore (GB) 6-4 6-2 6-2
1908	Arthur Gore (GB) beat H Roper Barrett (GB) 6-3 6-2 4-6 3-6 6-4
1909	Arthur Gore (GB) beat Josiah Ritchie (GB) 6-8 1-6 6-2 6-2 6-2
1910	Tony Wilding (NZ) beat Arthur Gore (GB) 6-4 7-5 4-6 6-2
1911	Tony Wilding (NZ) beat H Roper Barrett (GB) 6-4 4-6 2-6 6-2 retired
1912	Tony Wilding (NZ) beat Arthur Gore (GB) 6-4 6-4 4-6 6-4
1913	Tony Wilding (NZ) beat M McLoughlin (US) 8-6 6-3 10-8
1914	Norman Brookes (Aus) beat Tony Wilding (NZ) 6-4 6-4 7-5
1919	Gerald Patterson (Aus) beat Norman Brookes (Aus) 6-3 7-5 7-2

1920	Bill Tilden (US) beat Gerald Patterson (Aus) 2-6 6-3 6-2 6-4
1921	Bill Tilden (US) beat Brian Norton (SAf) 4-6 2-6 6-1 6-0 7-5
1922	Gerald Patterson (Aus) beat Randolph Lycett (GB) 6-3 6-4 6-2
1923	William Johnston (US) beat Frank Hunter (US) 6-0 6-3 6-1
1924	Jean Borotra (Fra) beat René Lacoste (Fra) 6-1 3-6 6-1 3-6 6-4
1925	René Lacoste (Fra) beat Jean Brotra (Fra) 6-3 6-3 4-6 8-6
1926	Jean Borotra (Fra) beat Howard Kinsey (US) 8-6 6-1 6-3
1927	Henri Cochet (Fra) beat Jean Borotra (Fra) 4-6 4-6 6-3 6-4 7-5
1928	René Lacoste (Fra) beat Henri Cochet (Fra) 6-1 4-6 6-4 6-2
1929	Henri Cochet (Fra) beat Jean Borotra (Fra) 6-4 6-3 6-4
1930	Bill Tilden (US) beat William Allison (US) 6-3 9-7 6-4
1931	Sidney Wood (US) beat Frank Shields (US) w.o.
1932	Ellsworth Vines (US) beat Bunny Austin (GB) 6-4 6-2 6-0
1933	Jack Crawford (Aus) beat Ellsworth Vines (US) 4-6 11-9 6-2 2-6 6-4
1934	Fred Perry (GB) beat Jack Crawford (Aus) 6-3 6-0 7-5
1935	Fred Perry (GB) beat Gottfried von Cramm (Ger) 6-2 6-4 6-4
1936	Fred Perry (GB) beat Gottfried von Cramm (Ger) 6-1 6-1 6-0
1937	Donald Budge (US) beat Gottfried von Cramm (Ger) 6-3 6-4 6-2
1938	Donald Budge (US) beat Bunny Austin (GB) 6-1 6-0 6-3
1939	Bobby Riggs (US) beat Ellwood Cooke (US) 2-6 8-6 3-6 6-3 6-2
1946	Yvon Petra (Fra) beat Geoffrey Brown (Aus) 6-2 6-4 7-9 5-7 6-4
1947	Jack Kremer (US) beat Tom Brown (US) 6-1 6-3 6-2
1948	Bob Falkenburg (US) beat John Bromwich (Aus) 7-5 0-6 6-2 3-6 7-5
1949	Ted Schroeder (US) beat Jaroslav Drobny (Cze) 3-6 6-0 6-3 4-6 6-4
1950	Budge Patty (US) beat Frank Sedgman (Aus) 6-1 8-10 6-2 6-3
1951	Dick Savitt (US) beat Ken McGregor (Aus) 6-4 6-4 6-4
1952	Frank Sedgman (Aus) beat Jaroslav Drobny (Egy) 4-6 6-2 6-3 6-2
1953	Vic Seixas (US) beat Kurt Nielsen (Den) 9-7 6-3 6-4
1954	Jaroslav Drobny (Egy) beat Ken Rosewall (Aus) 13-11 4-6 6-2 9-7
1955	Tony Trabert (US) beat Kurt Nielsen (Den) 6-3 7-5 6-1
1956	Lew Hoad (Aus) beat Ken Rosewall (Aus) 6-2 4-6 7-5 6-4
1957	Lew Hoad (Aus) beat Ashley Cooper (Aus) 6-2 6-1 6-2
1958	Ashley Cooper (Aus) beat Neale Fraser (Aus) 3-6 6-3 6-4 13-11
1959	Alex Olmedo (US) beat Rod Laver (Aus) 6-4 6-3 6-4
1960	Neale Fraser (Aus) beat Rod Laver (Aus) 6-4 3-6 9-7 7-5
1961	Rod Laver (Aus) beat Chuck McKinley (US) 6-3 6-1 6-4
1962	Rod Laver (Aus) beat Martin Mulligan (Aus) 6-2 6-2 6-1
1963	Chuck McKinley (US) beat Fred Stolle (Aus) 9-7 6-1 6-4
1964	Roy Emerson (Aus) beat Fred Stolle (Aus) 6-4 12-10 4-6 6-3
1965	Roy Emerson (Aus) beat Fred Stolle (Aus) 6-2 6-4 6-4
1966	Manuel Santana (Spa) beat Dennis Ralston (US) 6-4 11-9 6-4
1967	John Newcombe (Aus) beat Wilhelm Bungert (FRG) 6-3 6-1 6-1
1968	Rod Laver (Aus) beat Tony Roche (Aus) 6-3 6-4 6-2
1969	Rod Laver (Aus) beat John Newcombe (Aus) 6-4 5-7 6-4 6-4
1970	John Newcombe (Aus) beat Ken Rosewall (Aus) 5-7 6-3 6-2 3-6 6-1
1971	John Newcombe (Aus) beat Stan Smith (US) 6-3 5-7 2-6 6-4 6-4
1972	Stan Smith (US) beat Ilie Nastase (Rom) 4-6 6-3 6-3 4-6 7-5
1973	Jan Kodes (Cze) beat Alex Metreveli (USSR) 6-1 9-8 6-3
1974	Jimmy Connors (US) beat Ken Rosewall (Aus) 6-1 6-1 6-4
1975	Arthur Ashe (US) beat Jimmy Connors (US) 6-1 6-1 5-7 6-4
1976	Bjorn Borg (Swe) beat Ilie Nastase (Rom) 6-4 6-2 9-7
1977	Bjorn Borg (Swe) beat Jimmy Connors (US) 3-6 6-2 6-1 5-7 6-4
1978	Bjorn Borg (Swe) beat Jimmy Connors (US) 6-2 6-2 6-3
1979	Bjorn Borg (Swe) beat Roscoe Tanner (US) 6-7 6-1 3-6 6-3 6-4
1980	Bjorn Borg (Swe) beat John McEnroe (US) 1-6 7-5 6-3 6-7 8-6
1981	John McEnroe (US) beat Bjorn Borg (Swe) 4-6 7-6 7-6 6-4
1982	Jimmy Connors (US) beat John McEnroe (US) 3-6 6-3 6-7 7-6 6-4
1983	John McEnroe (US) beat Chris Lewis (NZ) 6-2 6-2 6-2
1984	John McEnroe (US) beat Jimmy Connors (US) 6-1 6-1 6-2
1985	Boris Becker (FRG) beat Kevin Curren (US) 6-3 6-7 7-6 6-4
1986	Boris Becker (FRG) beat Ivan Lendl (Cze) 6-4 6-3 7-5
1987	Pat Cash (Aus) beat Ivan Lendl (Cze) 7-6 6-2 7-5
1988	Stefan Edberg (Swe) beat Boris Becker (FRG) 4-6 7-6 6-4 6-2
1989	Boris Becker (FRG) beat Stefan Edberg (Swe) 6-0 7-6 6-4
1990	Stefan Edberg (Swe) beat Boris Becker (FRG) 6-2 6-2 3-6 3-6 6-4
1991	Michael Stich (Ger) beat Boris Becker (Ger) 6-4 7-6 6-4

Women's Singles

1884	Maud Watson (GB) beat L Watson (GB) 6-8 6-3 6-3
1885	Maud Watson (GB) beat Blanche Bingley (GB) 6-1 7-5
1886	Blanche Bingley (GB) beat Maud Watson (GB) 6-3 6-3

1887	Lottie Dod (GB) beat Blanche Bingley (GB) 6-2 6-0
1888	Lottie Dod (GB) beat Blanche Hillyard (née Bingley) (GB) 6-3 6-3
1889	Blanche Hillyard (GB) beat Helen Rice (GB) 4-6 8-6 6-4
1890	Helen Rice (GB) beat M Jacks (GB) 6-4 6-1
1891	Lottie Dod (GB) beat Blanche Hillyard (GB) 6-2 6-1
1892	Lottie Dod (GB) beat Blanche Hillyard (GB) 6-1 6-1
1893	Lottie Dod (GB) beat Blanche Hillyard (GB) 6-8 6-1 6-4
1894	Blanche Hillyard (GB) beat L Austin (GB) 6-1 6-1
1895	Charlotte Cooper (GB) beat H Jackson (GB) 7-5 8-6
1896	Charlotte Cooper (GB) beat W H Pickering (GB) 6-2 6-3
1897	Blanche Hillyard (GB) beat Charlotte Cooper (GB) 5-7 7-5 6-2
1898	Charlotte Cooper (GB) beat L Martin (GB) 6-4 6-4
1899	Blanche Hillyard (GB) beat Charlotte Cooper (GB) 6-2 6-3
1900	Blanche Hillyard (GB) beat Charlotte Cooper (GB) 4-6 6-4 6-4
1901	Charlotte Sterry (GB) beat Blanche Hillyard (GB) 6-2 6-2
1902	Muriel Robb (GB) beat Charlotte Sterry (GB) 7-5 6-1
1903	Dorothea Douglass (GB) beat E W Thompson (GB) 4-6 6-4 6-2
1904	Dorothea Douglass (GB) beat Charlotte Sterry (GB) 6-0 6-3
1905	May Sutton (US) beat Dorothea Douglass (GB) 6-3 6-4
1906	Dorothea Douglass (GB) beat May Sutton (US) 6-3 9-7
1907	May Sutton (US) beat Dorothea Lambert Chambers (GB) 6-1 6-4
1908	Charlotte Sterry (GB) beat A M Morton (GB) 6-4 6-4
1909	Dora Boothby (GB) beat A M Morton (GB) 6-4 4-6 8-6
1910	Dorothea Lambert Chambers (GB) beat Dora Boothby (GB) 6-2 6-2
1911	Dorothea Lambert Chambers (GB) beat Dora Boothby (GB) 6-0 6-0
1912	Ethel Larcombe (GB) beat Charlotte Sterry (GB) 6-3 6-1
1913	Dorothea Lambert Chambers (GB) beat R J McNair (GB) 6-0 6-4
1914	Dorothea Lambert Chambers (GB) beat Ethel Larcombe (GB) 7-5 6-4
1919	Suzanne Lenglen (Fra) beat Dorothea Lambert Chambers (GB) 10-8 4-6 9-7
1920	Suzanne Lenglen (Fra) beat Dorothea Lambert Chambers (GB) 6-3 6-0
1921	Suzanne Lenglen (Fra) beat Elizabeth Ryan (US) 6-2 6-0
1922	Suzanne Lenglen (Fra) beat Molly Mallory (US) 6-2 6-0
1923	Suzanne Lenglen (Fra) beat Kathleen McKane (GB) 6-2 6-2
1924	Kathleen McKane (GB) beat Helen Wills (US) 4-6 6-4 6-4
1925	Suzanne Lenglen (Fra) beat Joan Fry (GB) 6-2 6-0
1926	Kathleen Godfree (GB) beat Lili d'Alvarez (Spa) 6-2 4-6 6-3
1927	Helen Wills (US) beat Lili d'Alvarez (Spa) 6-2 6-4
1928	Helen Wills (US) beat Lili d'Alvarez (Spa) 6-2 6-3
1929	Helen Wills (US) beat Helen Jacobs (US) 6-1 6-2
1930	Helen Moody (née Wills) (US) beat Elizabeth Ryan (US) 6-2 6-2
1931	Cilly Aussem (Ger) beat Hilda Krahwinkel (Ger) 7-2 7-5
1932	Helen Moody (US) beat Helen Jacobs (US) 6-3 6-1
1933	Helen Moody (US) beat Dorothy Round (GB) 6-4 6-8 6-3
1934	Dorothy Round (GB) beat Helen Jacobs (US) 6-2 5-7 6-3
1935	Helen Moody (US) beat Helen Jacobs (US) 6-3 3-6 7-5
1936	Helen Jacobs (US) beat Hilde Sperling (Ger) 6-2 4-6 7-5
1937	Dorothy Round (GB) beat Jadwiga Jedrzejowska (Pol) 6-2 2-6 7-5
1938	Helen Moody (US) beat Helen Jacobs (US) 6-4 6-0
1939	Alice Marble (US) beat Kay Stammers (GB) 6-2 6-0
1946	Pauline Betz (US) beat Louise Brough (US) 6-2 6-4
1947	Margaret Osborne (US) beat Doris Hart (US) 6-2 6-4
1948	Louise Brough (US) beat Doris Hart (US) 6-3 8-6
1949	Louise Brough (US) beat Margaret du Pont (US) 10-8 1-6 10-8
1950	Louise Brough (US) beat Margaret du Pont (US) 6-1 3-6 6-1
1951	Doris Hart (US) beat Shirley Fry (US) 6-1 6-0
1952	Maureen Connolly (US) beat Louise Brough (US) 7-5 6-3
1953	Maureen Connolly (US) beat Doris Hart (US) 8-6 7-5
1954	Maureen Connolly (US) beat Louise Brough (US) 6-2 7-5
1955	Louise Brough (US) beat Beverly Fleitz (US) 7-5 8-6
1956	Shirley Fry (US) beat Angela Buxton (GB) 6-3 6-1
1957	Althea Gibson (US) beat Darlene Hard (US) 6-3 6-2
1958	Althea Gibson (US) beat Angela Mortimer (GB) 8-6 6-2
1959	Maria Bueno (Bra) beat Darlene Hard (US) 6-2 6-3
1960	Maria Bueno (Bra) beat Sandra Reynolds (SAf) 8-6 6-0
1961	Angela Mortimer (GB) beat Christine Truman (GB) 4-6 6-4 7-5
1962	Karen Susman (US) beat Vera Sukova (Cze) 6-4 6-4
1963	Margaret Smith (Aus) beat Billie Jean Moffitt (US) 6-3 6-4
1964	Maria Bueno (Bra) beat Margaret Smith (Aus) 6-4 7-9 6-3
1965	Margaret Smith (Aus) beat Maria Bueno (Bra) 6-4 7-5
1966	Billie Jean King (Née Moffitt) (US) beat Maria Bueno (Bra) 6-3 3-6 6-1
1967	Billie Jean King (US) beat Ann Jones (GB) 6-3 6-4

1968	Billie Jean King (US) beat Judy Tegart (Aus) 9-7 7-5
1969	Ann Jones (GB) beat Billie Jean King (US) 3-6 6-3 6-2
1970	Margaret Court (née Smith) (Aus) beat Billie Jean King (US) 14-12 11-9
1971	Evonne Goolagong (Aus) beat Margaret Court (Aus) 6-4 6-1
1972	Billie Jean King (US) beat Evonne Goolagong (Aus) 6-3 6-3
1973	Billie Jean King (US) beat Chris Evert Lloyd (US) 6-0 7-5
1974	Chris Evert (US) beat Olga Morozova (USSR) 6-0 6-4
1975	Billie Jean King (US) beat Evonne Cawley (née Goolagong) (Aus) 6-0 6-1
1976	Chris Evert (US) beat Evonne Cawley (Aus) 6-3 4-6 8-6
1977	Virginia Wade (GB) beat Betty Stove (Hol) 4-6 6-3 6-1
1978	Martina Navratilova (Cze) beat Chris Evert- -Lloyd (US) 2-6 6-4 7-5
1979	Martina Navratilova (Cze) beat Chris Evert - Lloyd (US) 6-4 6-4
1980	Evonne Cawley (Aus) beat Chris Evert (US) 6-1 7-6
1981	Chris Evert-Lloyd (US) beat Hana Mandlikova (Cze) 6-2 6-2
1982	Martina Navratilova (US) beat Chris Evert-Lloyd (US) 6-1 3-6 6-2
1983	Martina Navratilova (US) beat Andrea Jaeger (US) 6-0 6-3
1984	Martina Navratilova (US) beat Chris Evert-Lloyd (US) 7-6 6-2
1985	Martina Navratilova (US) beat Chris Evert-Lloyd (US) 4-6 6-3 6-2
1986	Martina Navratilova (US) beat Hana Mandlikova (Cze) 7-6 6-3
1987	Martina Navratilova (US) beat Steffi Graf (FRG) 7-5 6-3
1988	Steffi Graf (FRG) beat Martina Navratilova (US) 5-7 6-2 6-1
1989	Steffi Graf (FRG) beat Martina Navratilova (US) 6-2 6-7 6-1
1990	Martina Navratilova (US) beat Zina Garrison (US) 6-4 6-1
1991	Steffi Graf (Ger) beat Gabriela Sabatini (Arg) 6-4 3-6 8-6

DOUBLES WINNERS
Since 1982
Men's Doubles

1982	Peter Fleming & John McEnroe (US)		1988	Steffi Graf (FRG) & Gabriela Sabatini (Arg)
1983	Peter Fleming & John McEnroe (US)		1989	Jana Novotna & Helena Sukova (Cze)
1984	Peter Fleming & John McEnroe (US)		1990	Jana Novotna & Helena Sukova (Cze)
1985	Heinz Gunthardt (Swi) & Balazs Taroczy (Hun)		1991	Larissa Savchenko & Natalya Zvereva (USSR
1986	Joakim Nylstrom & Mats Wilander (Swe)		**Mixed Doubles**	
1987	Ken Flach & Robert Seguso (US)		1982	Kevin Curren (SA) & Anne Smith (US)
1988	Ken Flach & Robert Seguso (US)		1983	John Lloyd (GB) & Wendy Turnbull (Aus)
1989	John Fitzgerald (Aus) & Anders Jarryd (Swe)		1984	John Lloyd (GB) & Wendy Turnbull (Aus)
1990	Rick Leach & Jim Pugh (US)		1985	Paul McNamee (Aus) & Martina Navratilova (US)
1991	John Fitzgerald (Aus) & Anders Jarryd (Swe)		1986	Ken Flach & Kathy Jordan (US)
Women's Doubles			1987	Jeremy Bates & Jo Durie (GB)
1982	Martina Navratilova & Pam Shriver (US)		1988	Sherwood Stewart & Zina Garrison (US)
1983	Martina Navratilova & Pam Shriver (US)		1989	Jim Pugh (US) & Jana Novotna (Cze)
1984	Martina Navratilova & Pam Shriver (US)		1990	Rick Leach & Zina Garrison (US)
1985	Kathy Jordan (US) & Elizabeth Smylie (Aus)		1991	John Fitzgerald & Elizabeth Smylie (Aus)
1986	Martina Navratilova & Pam Shriver (US)			
1987	Claudia Kohde-Kilsch (FRG) & Helena Sukova (Cze)			

ONE PIECE MISSING

Rod Laver is the only player in the era of Open tennis, starting in 1968, to win all four Grand Slam events. Following Becker's win in the Australian Open and Edberg's win in the US, nine players have now won three titles and missed one:

	Missing title
Arthur Ashe	**French Open**
Boris Becker	**French Open**
Jimmy Connors	**French Open**
Stefan Edberg	**French Open**
Ivan Lendl	**Wimbledon**
John Newcombe	**French Open**
Ken Rosewall	**Wimbledon**
Gullermo Vilas	**Wimbledon**
Mats Wilander	**Wimbledon**

YOUNGEST WINNERS OF GRAND SLAM TITLES

Men

y	m			
17	3	Michael Chang	French Open	1989
17	7	Boris Becker	Wimbledon	1985
17	9	Mats Wilander	French Open	1982
17	*	Rodney Heath	Australian	1905
18		Bjorn Borg	French Open	1974

* exact birthdate unknown

Women

y	m			
15	10	Lottie Dod	Wimbledon	1887
16	6	Monica Seles	French Open	1990
16	9	Tracy Austin	US Open	1979
16	11	Maureen Connolly	US Champs	1951
17	1	Monica Seles	Australian	1991
17	5	Margaret Court	Australian	1960
17	5	Arantxa Sanchez Vicario	French Open	1989
17	9	Monica Seles	French Open	1991
17	10	Monica Seles	US Open	1991
17	10	May Sutton	Wimbledon	1905

> **❝** The commentators don't see what is happening in my heart and from where I get my energy. This is the eroticism I sense between me and the public in a big match. A five-hour match before 20,000 people in the evening atmosphere at Flushing Meadow is for me like an act of love...Spectators don't only want to see you - they want to have you. They want the demonstration of all your power and lust. They want your body and they want your soul. Like in sex, the lust in a big match begins with the foreplay, with the first eye-contact. The moment I come into the stadium the 20,000 spectators have only me in their gaze."
>
> *Boris Becker, October 1990*

> "I still love the game but I don't feel comfortable any more in front of a big crowd. I can feel thousands of eyes drilling holes into me and am not sure how to cope with it all."
>
> *Becker after Wimbledon*

> "Tennis has given me the chance to live like a millionaire without necessarily being one. I question whether today's players have an affection for the game, or for each other."
>
> *Don Budge*

> "As a good Swedish man I was always brought up to believe in equality in household work. Even as a millionaire I think it is important to take responsibility for my own laundry."
>
> *Stefan Edberg*

> "I'm in the entertainment business now. I'm selling tickets and hats and T-shirts and fish sandwiches and sponsorships. If my customers see a lot of tennis players in the process, good."
>
> *Butch Buchholz, promoter of the Lipton Tournament in Florida*

> "The biggest problem we face in tennis is that there is too much money around."
>
> *Philippe Chatrier, retiring head of the ITF*

> "All of a sudden the young players feel like they're doing everyone a favour if they play. Their attitude is horrible."
>
> *John McEnroe on US Davis Cup refuseniks*

> "Tennis is going in the wrong direction and one day it will fail completely. The money is now so great it has to stop and I would not be disappointed if it did. It's obscene. i would rather have played in the days when you played a tennis match and then you showered and went home."
>
> *Becker*

> "Buster Douglas takes $20 million and for that he spends five minutes in the ring. We get whatever the market will bear and I don't take anything away from anybody. **❞**
>
> *Martina Navratilova*

THE OTHER GRAND SLAM SINGLES CHAMPIONS
Post-war winners
MEN'S SINGLES

	Australian Champs	*French Champs*	*US Champs*
1946	John Bromwich (Aus)	Marcel Bernard (Fra)	Jack Kramer (US)
1947	Dinny Pails (Aus)	Jozef Asboth (Hun)	Jack Kramer (US)
1948	Adrian Quist (Aus)	Frank Parker (US)	Ricardo Gonzales (US)
1949	Frank Sedgman (Aus)	Frank Parker (US)	Ricardo Gonzales (US)
1950	Frank Sedgman (Aus)	Budge Patty (US)	Arthur Larsen (US)
1951	Dick Savitt (US)	Jaroslav Drobny (Egy)	Frank Sedgman (US)
1952	Ken McGregor (Aus)	Jaroslav Drobny (Egy)	Frank Sedgman (US)
1953	Ken Rosewall (Aus)	Ken Rosewall (Aus)	Tony Trabert (US)
1954	Mervyn Rose (Aus)	Tony Trabert (US)	Vic Seixas (US)
1955	Ken Rosewall (Aus)	Tony Trabert (US)	Tony Trabert (US)
1956	Lew Hoad (Aus)	Lew Hoad (Aus)	Ken Rosewall (Aus)
1957	Ashley Cooper (Aus)	Sven Davidson (Swe)	Malcolm Anderson (Aus)
1958	Ashley Cooper (Aus)	Mervyn Rose (Aus)	Ashley Cooper (Aus)
1959	Alex Olmedo (US)	Nicola Pietrangeli (Ita)	Neale Fraser (Aus)
1960	Rod Laver (Aus)	Nicola Pietrangeli (Ita)	Neale Fraser (Aus)
1961	Roy Emerson (Aus)	Manuel Santana (Spa)	Roy Emerson (Aus)
1962	Rod Laver (Aus)	Rod Laver (Aus)	Rod Laver (Aus)
1963	Roy Emerson (Aus)	Roy Emerson (Aus)	Raphael Osuna (Mex)
1964	Roy Emerson (Aus)	Manuel Santana (Spa)	Roy Emerson (Aus)
1965	Roy Emerson (Aus)	Fred Stolle (Aus)	Manuel Santana (Spa)
1966	Roy Emerson (Aus)	Tony Roche (Aus)	Fred Stolle (Aus)
1967	Roy Emerson (Aus)	Roy Emerson (Aus)	John Newcombe (Aus)
1968	Bill Bowrey (Aus)	Ken Rosewall (Aus)	Arthur Ashe (US)
Open*			Arthur Ashe (US)
1969	Rod Laver (Aus)	Rod Laver (Aus)	Stan Smith (US)

	Australian Champs	French Champs	US Champs
Open*			Rod Laver(Aus)
1970	Arthur Ashe (US)	Jan Kodes (Cze)	Ken Rosewall (Aus)
1971	Ken Rosewall (Aus)	Jan Kodes (Cze)	Stan Smith (US)
1972	Ken Rosewall (Aus)	Andres Gimeno (Spa)	Ilie Nastase (Rom)
1973	John Newcombe (Aus)	Ilie Nastase (Rom)	John Newcombe (Aus)
1974	Jimmy Connors (US)	Bjorn Borg (Swe)	Jimmy Connors (US)
1975	John Newcombe (Aus)	Bjorn Borg (Swe)	Manuel Orantes (Spa)
1976	Mark Edmondson (Aus)	Adriano Panatta (Ita)	Jimmy Connors (US)
1977	Roscoe Tanner (US) (Jan)	Guillermo Vilas (Arg)	Guillermo Vilas (Arg)
	Vitas Gerulaitis (US) (Dec)	–	-
1978	Guillermo Vilas (Arg)	Bjorn Borg (Swe)	Jimmy Connors (US)
1979	Guillermo Vilas (Arg)	Bjorn Borg (Swe)	John McEnroe (US)
1980	Brian Teacher (US)	Bjorn Borg (Swe)	John McEnroe (US)
1981	Johan Kriek (SA)	Bjorn Borg (Swe)	John McEnroe (US)
1982	Johan Kriek (SA)	Mats Wilander (Swe)	Jimmy Connors (US)
1983	Mats Wilander (Swe)	Yannick Noah (Fra)	Jimmy Connors (US)
1984	Mats Wilander (Swe)	Ivan Lendl (Cze)	John McEnroe (US)
1985	Stefan Edberg (Swe)	Mats Wilander (Swe)	Ivan Lendl (Cze)
1986	–	Ivan Lendl (Cze)	Ivan Lendl (Cze)
1987	Stefan Edberg (Swe)	Ivan Lendl (Cze)	Ivan Lendl (Cze)
1988	Mats Wilander (Swe)	Mats Wilander (Swe)	Mats Wilander (Swe)
1989	Ivan Lendl (Cze)	Michael Chang (US)	Boris Becker (FRG)
1990	Ivan Lendl (Cze)	Andres Gomez (Ecu)	Pete Sampras (US)
1991	Boris Becker (Ger)	Jim Courier (US)	Stefan Edberg (Swe)

WOMEN'S SINGLES

	Australian Champs	French Champs	US Champs
1946	Nancye Bolton (Aus)	Margaret Osborne (US)	Pauline Betz (US)
1947	Nancye Bolton (Aus)	Pat Todd (US)	Louise Brough (US)
1948	Nancye Bolton (Aus)	Nelly Landry (Fra)	Margaret Du Pont (US)
1949	Doris Hart (US)	Margaret Du Pont (US)	Margaret Du Pont (US)
1950	Louise Brough (US)	Doris Hart (US)	Margaret Du Pont (US)
1951	Nancye Bolton (Aus)	Shirley Fry (US)	Maureen Connolly (US)
1952	Thelma Long (US)	Doris Hart (US)	Maureen Connolly (US)
1953	Maureen Connolly (US)	Maureen Connolly (US)	Maureen Connolly (US)
1954	Thelma Long (Aus)	Maureen Connolly (US)	Doris Hart (US)
1955	Beryl Penrose (Aus)	Angela Mortimer (GB)	Doris Hart (US)
1956	Mary Carter (Aus)	Althea Gibson (US)	Shirley Fry (US)
1957	Shirley Fry (US)	Shirley Bloomer (GB)	Althea Gibson (US)
1958	Angela Mortimer (GB)	Zsuzsi Kormoczy (Hun)	Althea Gibson (US)
1959	Mary Reitano (Aus)	Christine Truman (GB)	Maria Bueno (Bra)
1960	Margaret Smith (Aus)	Darlene Hard (US)	Darlene Hard (US)
1961	Margaret Smith (Aus)	Ann Haydon (GB)	Darlene Hard (US)
1962	Margaret Smith (Aus)	Margaret Smith (Aus)	Margaret Smith (Aus)
1963	Margaret Smith (Aus)	Lesley Turner (Aus)	Maria Bueno (Bra)
1964	Margaret Smith (Aus)	Margaret Smith (Aus)	Maria Bueno (Bra)
1965	Margaret smith (Aus)	Lesley Turner (Aus)	Margaret Smith (Aus)
1966	Margaret Smith (Aus)	Ann Jones (GB)	Maria Bueno (Bra)
1967	Nancy Richey (US)	Francoise Durr (Fra)	Billie Jean King (US)
1968	Billie Jean King (US)	Nancy Richey (US)	Margaret Court (Aus)
Open*	–	–	Virginia Wade (GB)
1969	Margaret Court (Aus)	Margaret Court (Aus)	Margaret Court (Aus)
Open*	–	–	Margaret Court (Aus)
1970	Margaret Court (Aus)	Margaret Court (Aus)	Margaret Court (Aus)
1971	Margaret Court (Aus)	Evonne Goolagong (Aus)	Billie Jean King (US)
1972	Virginia Wade (GB)	Billie Jean King (US)	Billie Jean King (US)
1973	Margaret Court (Aus)	Margaret Court (Aus)	Margaret Court (Aus)
1974	Evonne Goolagong (Aus)	Chris Evert (US)	Billie Jean King (US)
1975	Evonne Goolagong (Aus)	Chris Evert (US)	Chris Evert (US)
1976	Evonne Cawley (Aus)	Sue Barker (GB)	Chris Evert (US)
1977	Kerry Reid (Aus) (Jan)	Mimi Jauseovec (Yug)	Chris Evert (US)
	Evonne Cawley (Aus) (Dec)		
1978	Christine O'Neill (Aus)	Virginia Ruzici (Rom)	Chris Evert (US)
1979	Barbara Jordan (US)	Chris Evert-Lloyd (US)	Tracy Austin (US)
1980	Hana Mandlikova (Cze)	Chris Evert-Lloyd (US)	Chris Evert-Lloyd (US)
1981	Martina Navratilova (US)	Hana Mandlikova (Cze)	Tracy Austin (US)
1982	Chris Evert-Lloyd (US)	Martina Navratilova (US)	Ciris Evert-Lloyd (US)
1983	Martina Navratilova (US)	Chris Evert-Lloyd (US)	Martina Navratilova (US)
1984	Chris Evert-Lloyd (US)	Martina Navratilova (US)	Martina Navratilova (US)
1985	Martina Navratilova (US)	Chris Evert-Lloyd (US)	Hana Mandlikova (Cze)

	Australian Champs	*French Champs*	*US Champs*
1986		Chris Evert-Lloyd (US)	Martina Navratilova (US)
1987	Hana Mandlikova (Cze)	Steffi Graf (FRG)	Martina Navratilova (US)
1988	Steffi Graf (FRG)	Steffi Graf (FRG)	Steffi Graf (FRG)
1989	Steffi Graf (FRG)	Arantxa Sanchez Vicario (Spa)	Steffi Graf (FRG)
1990	Steffi Graf (FRG)	Monica Seles (Yug)	Gabriela Sabatini (Arg)
1991	Monica Seles (Yug)	Monica Seles (Yug)	Monica Seles (Yug)

* Two championships held, one for amateurs only

WINNERS OF MOST GRAND SLAM SINGLES TITLES

Wimbledon
Men: 7 William Renshaw
Women: 9 Martina Navratilova

US Championships
Men: 7 Bill Tilden, Dick Sears, Bill Larned
Women: 7 Molla Mallory, Helen Wills-Moody

French Open
Men: 6 Bjorn Borg
Women: 7 Chris Evert-Lloyd

Australian Open
Men: 6 Roy Emerson
Women: 11 Margaret Court (née Smith)

Overall
Men: 12 Roy Emerson
Women: 24 Margaret Court (née Smith)

GRAND SLAM WINNERS
(all four tournaments in one year)
Donald Budge 1938
Rod Laver 1962
Rod Laver 1969
Maureen Connolly 1953
Margaret Court 1970
Steffi Graf 1988

MAIDEN/MARRIED NAMES OF WOMEN PLAYERS

Maiden Name	Married Name
Blanche Bingley	Blanche Hillyard
Evonne Goolagong	Evonne Cawley
Charlotte Cooper	Charlotte Sterry
Dorothea Douglass	Dorothea Lambert Chambers
Chris Evert	Chris Evert-Lloyd
Ann Haydon	Ann Jones
Kathleen McKane	Kathleen Godfree
Margaret Osborne	Margaret Du Pont
Margaret Smith	Margaret Court
Helen Wills	Helen Moody

DAVIS CUP
Challenge system 1900-72

1900	United States	British Isles	3-0
1901	Not Held		
1902	United States	British Isles	3-2
1903	British Isles	United States	4-1
1904	British Isles	Belgium	5-0
1905	British Isles	United States	5-0
1906	British Isles	United States	5-0
1907	Australasia	British Isles	3-2
1908	Australasia	United States	3-2
1909	Australasia	United States	5-0
1910	Not Held		
1911	Australasia	United States	5-0
1912	British Isles	Australasia	3-2

1913	United States	British Isles	3-2
1914	Australasia	United States	3-2
1915-18	Not Held		
1919	Australasia	British Isles	4-1
1920	United States	Australasia	5-0
1921	United States	Japan	5-0
1922	United States	Australasia	4-1
1923	United States	Australasia	4-1
1924	United States	Australasia	5-0
1925	United States	France	5-0
1926	United States	France	4-1
1927	France	United States	3-2
1928	France	United States	4-1
1929	France	United States	3-2
1930	France	United States	4-1
1931	France	Britain	3-2
1932	France	United States	3-2
1933	Great Britain	France	3-2
1934	Great Britain	United States	4-1
1935	Great Britain	United States	5-0
1936	Great Britain	Australia	3-2
1937	United States	Britain	4-1
1938	United States	Australia	3-2
1939	Australia	United States	3-2
1940-45	Not Held		
1946	United States	Australia	5-0
1947	United States	Australia	4-1
1948	United States	Australia	5-0
1949	United States	Australia	4-1
1950	Australia	United States	4-1
1951	Australia	United States	3-2
1952	Australia	United States	4-1
1953	Australia	United States	3-2
1954	United States	Australia	3-2
1955	Australia	United States	5-0
1956	Australia	United States	5-0
1957	Australia	United States	3-2
1958	United States	Australia	3-2
1959	Australia	United States	3-2
1960	Australia	Italy	4-1
1961	Australia	Italy	5-0
1962	Australia	Mexico	5-0
1963	United States	Australia	3-2
1964	Australia	United States	3-2
1965	Australia	Spain	4-1
1966	Australia	India	4-1
1967	Australia	Spain	4-1
1968	United States	Australia	4-1
1969	United States	Romania	5-0
1970	United States	West Germany	5-0
1971	United States	Romania	3-2
1972	United States	Romania	3-2
1973	Australia	United States	5-0
1974	South Africa	India	w.o.
1975	Sweden	Czechoslovakia	3-2
1976	Italy	Chile	4-1
1977	Australia	Italy	3-1
1978	United States	Britain	4-1
1979	United States	Italy	5-0
1980	Czechoslovakia	Italy	4-1

1981	United States	Argentina	3-1
1982	United States	France	4-1
1983	Australia	Sweden	3-2
1984	Sweden	United States	4-1
1985	Sweden	West Germany	3-2
1986	Australia	Sweden	3-2
1987	Sweden	India	5-0
1988	West Germany	Sweden	4-1
1989	West Germany	Sweden	3-2
1990	United States	Australia	3-2

Most wins
29 United States
Since abolition of challenge system: **6** United States; **4** Australia, Sweden

GRAND PRIX MASTERS

1970	1 Stan Smith (US) 2 Rod Laver (Aus) Round Robin series
1971	1 Ilie Nastase (Rom) 2 Stan Smith (US) Round Robin series
1972	Ilie Nastase (Rom) beat Stan Smith (US) 6-3 6-2 3-6 2-6 6-3
1973	Ilie Natase (Rom) beat Tom Okker (Hol) 6-3 7-5 4-6 6-3
1974	Guillermo Vilas (Arg) beat Ilie Nastase (Rom) 7-6 6-2 3-6 3-6 6-4
1975	Ilie Nastase (Rom) beat Bjorn Borg (Swe) 6-2 6-2 6-1
1976	Manuel Orantes (Spa) beat Wojtek Fibak (Pol) 5-7 6-2 0-6 7-6 6-1
1977	(a)
1978	Jimmy Connors (US) beat Bjorn Borg (Swe) 6-4 1-6 6-4
1979	John McEnroe (US) beat Arthur Ashe (US) 6-7 6-3 7-5
1980	Bjorn Borg (Swe) beat Vitas Gerulaitis (US) 6-2 6-2
1981	Bjorn Borg (Swe) beat Ivan Lendl (Cze) 6-4 6-2 6-2

1982	Ivan Lendl (Cze) beat Vitas Gerulaitis (US) 6-7 2-6 7-6 6-2 6-4
1983	Ivan Lendl (Cze) beat John McEnroe (US) 6-4 6-4 6-2
1984	John McEnroe (US) beat Ivan Lendl (Cze) 6-3 6-4 6-4
1985	John McEnroe (US) beat Ivan Lendl (Cze) 7-5 6-0 6-4
1986	Ivan Lendl (Cze) beat Boris Becker (FRG) 6-2 7-6 6-3
1987	Ivan Lendl (Cze) beat Mats Wilander (Swe) 6-2 6-2 6-3
1988	Boris Becker (FRG) beat Ivan Lendl (Cze) 5-7 7-6 3-6 6-2 7-6
1989	Stefan Edberg (Swe) beat Boris Becker (FRG) 4-6 7-6 6-3 6-1
1990	Pete Sampras (US) beat Brad Gilbert (US) 6-3 6-4 6-2

(a) None held in 1977. Moved from late season to early season

---

1992

January 13-26 Australian Open (Melbourne); January 31-Feb 2 Davis Cup First Round; Mar 27-29 Davis Cup Second Round; Apr 20-26 Monte Carlo Open; May 4-10 German Men's Open (Hamburg), Italian Women's Open (Rome); May 11-17 Italian Men's Open (Rome); May 25-Jun 7 French Open (Paris); Jun 8-14 Queen's Club men's tournament, Birmingham women's tournament; Jun 15-20 Manchester men's tournament, Eastbourne women's tournament; Jun 22-Jul 6 WIMBLEDON CHAMPIONSHIPS; Jul 12 Federation Cup (Frankfurt); Aug 31-Sep 13 US Open (New York); Sep 25-27 Davis Cup semi-finals; Oct 19-25 Brighton women's tournament; Dec 4-6 Davis Cup Final; Dec 8-13 Grand Slam Cup (Munich)

VOLLEYBALL

WATER SKIING

— 1991 —

MEN'S EUROPEAN CHAMPIONSHIP
Berlin, Sep 7-15
Semi-finals
ITALY 3 Germany 1; SOVIET UNION 3 Holland 0
Third Place Play-Off
HOLLAND 3 Germany 0
Final
SOVIET UNION 3 Italy 0

ROYAL BANK OF SCOTLAND NATIONAL LEAGUE
Leading Positions
Men's Division One
1 Team Mizuno Mallory 35 pts; 2 Polonia Ealing 24 pts; 3 Reebok Liverpool City 22 pts
Women's Division One
1 Mizuno Britannia 32 pts; 2 Woolwich Brixton Knights 26 pts; 3 Sovereign Leasing Sale 22 pts

ROYAL BANK OF SCOTLAND NATIONAL CUP FINALS
Crystal Palace, Mar 23
Men
POLONIA EALING 3 Reebok Liverpool City 2
Women
MIZUNO BRITANNIA 3 Woolwich Brixton Knights 1

— 1990 —

MEN'S WORLD CHAMPIONSHIP
Rio de Janeiro, Brazil, Oct 17-28
Semi-finals
ITALY 3 Brazil 2; CUBA 3 USSR 1
Final
ITALY 3 Cuba 1
Final Standings
1 Italy; 2 Cuba; 3 USSR; 4 Brazil; 5 Bulgaria; 6 Argentina; 7 Holland; 8 France

— CHAMPIONS —

WORLD CHAMPIONSHIPS

	Men	*Women*
1949	USSR	-
1952	USSR	USSR
1956	Czechoslovakia	USSR
1960	USSR	USSR
1962	USSR	Japan
1966	Czechoslovakia	Japan
1970	East Germany	USSR
1974	Poland	Japan
1978	USSR	Cuba
1982	USSR	China
1986	United States	China
1990	Italy	USSR

— 1991 —

WORLD CHAMPIONSHIPS
Villach, Austria, Sep 6-9
Men

Overall:	Patrice Martin (Fra)
Slalom:	Lucky Lowe (US)
Tricks:	Patrice Martin (Fra)
Jump:	Bruce Neville (Aus)

Women

Overall:	Karen Neville (Aus)
Slalom:	Helen Kjellander (Swe)
Tricks:	Tawn Larsen (US)
Jump:	Sherri Slone (US)

Team   Canada
This was the first time in the history of the championships that the United States did not win the team prize; they finished second instead

EUROPEAN CHAMPIONSHIPS
Poti, Georgia, USSR, Aug 20
Men

Overall:	Andrea Alessi (Ita)
Jump:	Alessi
Slalom:	John Battleday (GB)
Tricks:	Nicolas le Forestier (Fra)

Women

Overall:	Olga Pavlova (USSR)
Jump:	Britta Grebe (Aut)
Slalom:	Phillipa Roberts (GB)
Tricks:	Pavlova

Team   Soviet Union

— CHAMPIONS —

WORLD CHAMPIONS
Last 10 years
Men
Overall

1983	Sammy Duvall (US)
1985	Sammy Duvall (US)
1987	Sammy Duvall (US)
1989	Patrice Martin (Fra)
1991	Patrice Martin (Fra)

Women
Overall

1983	Ana Maria Carrasco (Ven)
1985	Karen Neville (Aus)
1987	Deena Brush (US)
1989	Deena Mapple (nee Brush)(US)
1991	Karen Neville (Aus)

Team
United States won the team title at every world championship since the title was inaugurated in 1957, until Canada won in 1991

WEIGHTLIFTING

1991

WORLD CHAMPIONSHIPS
Donaueschingen, Germany, Sep 27-Oct 3

Up to 52kg
1 Ivan Ivanov (Bul) 272.5kg
2 Sevdalin Minchev (Bul) 257.5kg
3 Ziarong Zhang (Chn) 255.5kg

Up to 56kg
1 Chun Byung-kwan (SKo) 295.0 kg
2 Liu Shoubin (Chn) 292.5 kg
3 Luo Jianming (Chn) 277.5 kg

Up to 60kg
1 Naim Suleymanoglu (Tur) 302.5kg
2 Yurik Sarkissian (USSR) 302.5kg
3 He Yingquinang (Chn) 292.5kg

Up to 67.5kg
1 Yoto Yotov (Bul) 345.0kg
2 Israil Militosian (USSR) 345.0kg
3 Kim Myong-nam (NKo) 340.0kg

Up to 75kg
1 Pablo Lara (Cub) 355.0kg
2 Roman Sevasteyev (USSR) 352.5kg
3 Fjodor Kasadu (USSR) 342.5kg

Up to 82.5kg
1 Ibrahim Samadov (USSR) 367.5kg
2 Alexandr Blychtchyk (USSR) 367.5kg
3 Plamen Bratoichev (Bul) 357.5kg

Up to 90kg
1 Sergey Syrtsov (USSR) 410.0kg
2 Ivan Chakarov (Bul) 387.5kg
3 Kim Byung-chan (SKo) 387.5kg

Up to 100kg
1 Igor Sadyko (USSR) 415.0kg
2 Ivalin Ratchev (Bul) 385.0kg
3 Francis Tournefier (Fra) 382.5kg

Up to 110kg
1 Artur Akoyev (USSR) 427.5kg
2 Ronny Weller (Ger) 420.0kg
3 Ernesto Montoya (Cub) 387.5kg

Over 110kg
1 Alexandr Kurlovich (USSR) 455.0kg
2 Manfred Nerlinger (Ger) 425.0kg
3 Kim Tae-Nyun (SKo) 400.0kg

1990

WORLD CHAMPIONSHIPS
Budapest, Nov 11-18

Flyweight (up to52kg)	Ivan Ivanov (Bul) 265.0kg
Bantamweight (up to 56kg)	Liu Shoubin (Chn) 285.0kg
Featherweight (up to 60kg)	Nikolai Peshalov (Bul) 297.5kg
Lightweight (up to 67.5kg)	Kim Myong-nam (NKo) 342.5kg
Middleweight (up to 75kg)	Fjodor Kasadu (USSR) 360kg
Light-heavyweight (up to 82.5kg)	Alty Orazdurdyev (USSR) 377.5kg
Mid-heavyweight (up to 90kg)	Anatoliy Chrapatyi (USSR) 397.5kg
Up to 100kg	Nicu Vlad (Rom) 412.5kg
Heavyweight (up to 110kg)	Stefan Botev (Bul) 444.0kg
Super-heavyweight (over 110kg)	Leonid Taranenko (USSR) 450kg

RECORDS

WORLD RECORDS
(As at Oct 8 1991)

52kg	Snatch:	120.5kg	Zairong Zhang (Chn) Donaueschingen, Germany, Sep 27, 1991
	Jerk:	155.5kg	Ivan Ivanov (Bul), Donaueschingen, Germany, Sep 27, 1991
	Total:	272.5kg	Ivan Ivanov (Bul), Athens, Greece, Sep 16, 1989; Donaueschingen, Germany, Sep 27, 1991
56kg	Snatch:	135.0kg	Shoubin Liu (Chn), Donaueschingen, Germany, Sep 28, 1991
	Jerk:	171.0kg	Neno Terziiski (Bul), Ostrava, Czechoslovakia, Sep 6, 1987
	Total:	300.0kg	Naim Suleimanov (Bul), Varna, Bulgaria, May 11, 1984
60kg	Snatch:	152.5kg	Naim Suleymanoglu (Tur), Seoul, South Korea, Sep 20, 1988
	Jerk:	190.0kg	Naim Suleymanoglu (Tur), Seoul, South Korea, Sep 20, 1988
	Total:	342.5kg	Naim Suleymanoglu (Tur), Seoul, South Korea, Sep 20, 1988

67.5kg	Snatch:	160.0kg	Israel Militosian (USSR), Athens, Greece, Sep 18, 1989
	Jerk:	200.5kg	Mikhail Petrov (Bul), Ostrava, Czechoslovakia, Sep 9, 1987
	Total:	355.0kg	Mikhail Petrov (Bul), Seoul, South Korea, Dec 5, 1987
75kg	Snatch:	170.0kg	Angel Guenchev (Bul), Miskolc, Hungary, Dec 11, 1987
	Jerk:	215.5kg	Alexander Varbanov (Bul), Seoul, South Korea, Dec 5, 1987
	Total:	382.5kg	Alexander Varbanov (Bul), Plovdiv, Bulgaria, Feb 20, 1988
82.5kg	Snatch:	183.0kg	Asan Zlatev (Bul), Melbourne, Australia, Dec 14, 1986
	Jerk:	225.0kg	Asen Zlatev (Bul), Sofia, Bulgaria, Nov 12, 1986
	Total:	405.0kg	Yuri Vardanian (USSR), Varna, Bulgaria, Sep 14, 1984
90kg	Snatch:	195.5kg	Blagoi Blagoev (Bul), Varna, Bulgaria, May 1, 1983
	Jerk:	235.0kg	Anatoliy Khrapaty (USSR), Cardiff, Wales, Apr 29, 1988
	Total:	422.5kg	Viktor Solodov (USSR), Varna, Bulgaria, Sep 15, 1984
100kg	Snatch:	200.5kg	Nicu Vlad (Rom), Sofia, Bulgaria, Nov 14, 1986
	Jerk:	242.5kg	Alexander Popov (USSR), Tallinn, USSR, Mar 5, 1988
	Total:	440.0kg	Yuri Zacharevich (USSR), Odessa, USSR, Mar 4, 1983
110kg	Snatch:	210.0kg	Yuri Zacharevich (USSR), Seoul, South Korea, Sep 27, 1988
	Jerk:	250.5kg	Yuri Zacharevich (USSR), Cardiff, Wales, Apr 30, 1988
	Total:	455.0kg	Yuri Zacharevich (USSR), Seoul, South Korea, Sep 27, 1988
110+kg	Snatch:	216.0kg	Antonio Krastev (USSR), Ostrava, Czechoslovakia, Sep 13, 1987
	Jerk:	266.0kg	Leonid Taranenko (USSR), Canberra, Australia, Nov 26, 1988
	Total:	475.0kg	Leonid Taranenko (USSR), Canberra, Australia, Nov 26, 1988

WINTER OLYMPICS

1992

Schedule for 1992 Winter Olympics to be held in the French Alps centring on Albertville from February 8 to 23:

OPENING CEREMONY
Feb 8   Albertville

ALPINE SKIING
Feb 9	Men's downhill	Val d'Isere
Feb 10	Men's combined downhill	Val d'Isere
Feb 11	Men's combined slalom	Val d'Isere
Feb 12	Women's combined downhill	Meribel
Feb 13	Women's combined slalom	Meribel
Feb 15	Women's downhill	Meribel
Feb 16	Men's super-G	Val d'Isere
Feb 17	Women's super-G	Meribel
Feb 18	Men's giant slalom	Val d'Isere
Feb 19	Women's giant slalom	Meribe
Feb 20	Women's slalom	Meribel
Feb 22	Men's slalom	Les Menuires

BIATHLON
Les Saises
Feb 11	7.5 km, women
Feb 12	10 km, men
Feb 14	3 x 7.5 km, women
Feb 16	4 x 7.5 km, men
Feb 19	15 km, men
Feb 20	20km, men

BOBSLEIGH
La Plagne
Feb 15	2-man bob
Feb 16	2-man bob
Feb 21	4-man bob
Feb 22	4-man bob

CROSS-COUNTRY SKIING
Les Saises
Feb 9	15 km, women
Feb 10	30 km, men
Feb 13	5 km, women
	15 km, men
Feb 17	4 x 5 km, women
Feb 18	4 x10 km, men
Feb 21	30 km, women
Feb 22	50 km, men

CURLING
Pralognan
Mar 16-22	Tournament

FREESTYLE SKIING
Tignes
Feb 9, 10	Ballet
Feb 11, 12	Moguls
Feb 15, 16	Aerials

ICE HOCKEY
Meribel
Feb 8-23	Tournament

LUGE
La Plagne
Feb 9, 10, 14	Men
Feb 11, 12	Women

NORDIC SKIING
Courchevel
Feb 11	Combined, 90 metres
Feb 12	Combined, 15 km
Feb 17	Combined, 90 metres team
Feb 18	Combined, 3 x 10 km team

SKATING
Albertville
Feb 9, 11, 13-17, 19, 21, 22	Figure skating
Feb 10, 12, 13-18, 20, 22	Speed skating

SKI JUMPING
Courchevel
Feb 9	90 metres
Feb 14	120 metres, team
Feb 16	120 metres

SPEED SKIING
Les Arcs
Feb 18, 19, 21, 22	Competition

CLOSING CEREMONY
Feb 23	Albertville

MEDAL WINNERS

Year	Venue	Leading Gold Nations
1924	Chamonix	4 Finland, Norway, 2 Austria
1928	St Moritz	6 Norway, 2 Finland, United States, Sweden
1932	Lake Placid	6 United States, 3 Norway, 1 Austria, Canada, Finland, France Sweden
1936	Garmisch-Partenkirchen	7 Norway, 3 Germany 2 Sweden
1948	St Moritz	4 Norway, Sweden, 3 Switzerland, United States
1952	Oslo	7 Norway, 4 United States, 3 Finland, Germany
1956	Cortina d'Ampezzo	7 Soviet Union, 4 Austria, 3 Finland, Switzerland
1960	Squaw Valley	7 Soviet Union, 4 Germany, 3 Norway, Sweden, United States
1964	Innsbruck	11 Soviet Union, 4 Austria, 3 Finland, France, Norway, Sweden, Germany
1968	Grenoble	6 Norway, 5 Soviet Union, 4 France, Italy
1972	Sapporo	8 Soviet Union, 4 East Germany, Holland, Switzerland
1976	Innsbruck	13 Soviet Union, 7 East Germany, 3 Norway, United States
1980	Lake Placid	10 Soviet Union, 9 East Germany, 6 United States
1984	Sarajevo	9 East Germany, 6 Soviet Union, 4 Finland, Sweden, United States
1988	Calgary	11 Soviet Union, 9 East Germany, 5 Switzerland

Leading Medal-Winning Nations

Total	Country	G	S	B
195	Soviet Union	79	57	59
168	Norway	54	60	54
123	United States	42	47	34
110	East Germany	39	36	35
110	Finland	33	43	34
98	Austria	28	38	32
(14	Great Britain	6	2	6)

BRITAIN'S MEDALLISTS

1924	Silver:	Ralph Broome, Thomas Arnold, Alexander Richardson, Rodney Soher (four-man bobsleigh)
	Bronze:	Ethel Muckelt (figure skating)
	Bronze:	Ice hockey team
1928	Bronze:	David Northesk (Cresta run)
1936	Gold:	Ice hockey team
	Silver:	Cecilia Colledge (figure skating)
	Bronze:	Frederick McEvoy, James Cardno, Guy Dugdale, Charles Green (four-man bobsleigh)
1948	Bronze:	John Crammond (Cresta Run)
	Bronze:	Jeanette Altwegg (figure skating)
1952	Gold:	Jeanette Altwegg (figure skating)
1964	Gold:	Tony Nash, Robin Dixon (two-man bobsleigh)
1976	Gold:	John Curry (figure skating)
1980	Gold:	Robin Cousins (figure skating)
1984	Gold:	Jayne Torvill & Christopher Dean (ice dancing)

Britain also won one gold (Madge Syers, figure skating), two silvers and three bronzes at winter sports events in the 1908 Olympics and a bronze in the ice hockey in 1920. On both occasions, the winter events formed part of the summer Games

CHAMPIONS

BIATHLON
10km
1980 Frank Ullrich (GDR)
1984 Eirik Kvalfoss (Nor)
1988 Frank-Peter Rotsch (GDR)
20km
1960 Klas Lestander (Swe)
1964 Vladimir Melanin (USSR)
1968 Magnar Solberg (Nor)
1972 Magnar Solberg (Nor)
1976 Nikolai Kruglov (USSR)
1980 Anatoly Alyabiev (USSR)
1984 Peter Angerer (FRG)
1988 Frank-Peter Rotsch (GDR)
4 x 7.5km Relay
1968 Soviet Union
1972 Soviet Union
1976 Soviet Union
1980 Soviet Union
1984 Soviet Union
1988 Soviet Union

BOBSLEIGH AND TOBOGGANING
Men
Two-man Bob
1932　Hubert Stevens/Curtis Stevens (US)
1936　Ivan Brown/Alan Washbond (US)
1948　Felix Endrich/Friedrich Waller (Swi)
1952　Andreas Ostler/Lorenz Nieberl (FRG)
1956　Lamberto Dalla Costa/Giacomo Conti (Ita)

1960 Not held
1964 Tony Nash/Robin Dixon (GB)
1968 Eugenio Monti/Luciano de Paolis (Ita)1972
　　　Wolfgang Zimmerer/Peter Utzschneider (FRG)
1976 Meinhard Nehmer/Bernhard Germeshausen (GDR)
1980 Erich Scharer/Josef Benz (Swi)
1984 Wolfgang Hoppe/Dietmar Schauerhammer (GDR)
1988 Janis Kipours/Vladimir Kozlov (USSR)
Four-man Bob
1924 Switzerland
1928 United States
1932 United States
1936 Switzerland
1948 United States
1952 West Germany
1956 Switzerland
1960 Not held
1964 Canada
1968 Italy
1972 Switzerland
1976 East Germany
1980 East Germany
1984 East Germany
1988 Switzerland
Luge-Single
1964 Thomas Kohler (Ger)
1968 Manfred Schmid (Aut)
1972 Wolfgang Scheidel (GDR)
1976 Dettlef Gunther (GDR)
1980 Bernhard Glass (GDR)

1984 Paul Hildgartner (Ita)
1988 Jens Muller (GDR)

Luge-Double
1964 Josef Feistmantl, Manfred Stengl (Aut)
1968 Klaus Bonsack, Thomas Kohler (GDR)
1972 Horst Hornlein, Reinhard Bredow (GDR)
1976 Hans Rinn, Norbert Hahn (GDR)
1980 Hans Rinn, Norbert Hahn (GDR)
1984 Hans Stanggassinger, Franz Wembacher (FRG)
1988 Jorg Moffmann/Jochen Pietzsch (GDR)

Women
Luge
1964 Ortrun Enderlein (Ger)
1968 Erica Lechner (Ita)
1972 Anna-Maria Muller (GDR)
1976 Margit Schumann (GDR)
1980 Vera Zozulia (USSR)
1984 Steffi Martin (GDR)
1988 Steffi Walter (nee Martin) (GDR)

ICE HOCKEY
1920 Canada
1924 Canada
1928 Canada
1932 Canada
1936 Great Britain
1948 Canada
1952 Canada
1956 Soviet Union
1960 United States
1964 Soviet Union
1968 Soviet Union
1972 Soviet Union
1976 Soviet Union
1980 United States
1984 Soviet Union
1988 Soviet Union

SKATING
Men's Figure
1908 Ulrich Salchow (Swe)
1920 Gillis Grafstrom (Swe)
1924 Gillis Grafstrom (Swe)
1928 Gillis Grafstrom (Swe)
1932 Karl Schafer (Aut)
1936 Karl Schafer (Aut)
1948 Richard Button (US)
1952 Richard Button (US)
1956 Hayes Alan Jenkins (US)
1960 David Jenkins (US)
1964 Manfred Schneldorfer (FRG)
1968 Wolfgang Schwarz (Aut)
1972 Ondrej Napela (Cze)
1976 John Curry (GB)
1980 Robin Cousins (GB)
1984 Scot Hamilton (US)
1988 Brian Boitano (US)

Women's Figure
1908 Madge Syers(GB)
1920 Magda Julin (Swe)
1924 Herma Planck-Szabo (Aut)
1928 Sonja Henie (Nor)
1932 Sonja Henie (Nor)
1936 Sonja Henie (Nor)
1948 Barbara Ann Scott (Can)
1952 Jeanette Altwegg (GB)
1956 Tenley Albright (US)
1960 Carol Heiss (US)
1964 Sjoukje Dijkstra (Hol)

1968 Peggy Fleming (US)
1972 Beatrix Schuba (Aut)
1976 Dorothy Hamill (US)
1980 Anett Potzsch (GDR)
1984 Katarina Witt (GDR
1988 Katarina Witt (GDR)

Pairs
1908 Anna Hubler/Heinrich Burger (Ger)
1920 Ludovika Jakobsson/Walter Jakobsson (Fin)
1924 Helene Engelmann/Alfred Berger (Aut)
1928 Andree Joly/Pierre Brunet (Fra)
1932 Andress Brunet (nee Joly)/Pierre Brunet (Fra)
1936 Maxi Herber/Ernst Baier (Ger)
1948 Micheline Lannoy/Pierre Baugniet (Bel)
1952 Ria Falk/Paul Falk (Ger)
1956 Elisabeth Schwartz/Kurt Oppelt (Aut)
1960 Barbara Wagner/Robert Paul (Can)
1964 Lyudmila Belousova/Oleg Protopopov (USSR)
1968 Lyudmila Belousova/Oleg Protopopov (USSR)
1972 Irina Rodnina/Aleksey Ulanov (USSR)
1976 Irina Rodnina/Aleksandr Zaitsev (USSR)
1980 Irina Rodnina/Aleksandr Zaitsev (USSR)
1984 Yelena Valova/Oleg Vasiliev (USSR)
1988 Yekaterina Gordeyeva/Sergey Grinkov (USSR)

Dance
1976 Lyudmila Pakhomova/Alexsandr Gorshkov (USSR)
1980 Natalya Linitschuck/ Gannadiy Karponosov (USSR)
1984 Jayne Torvill/Christopher Dean (GB)
1988 Natalya Bestemianova/Andre Bukin (USSR)

Speed Skating

Men
500 metres
1924 Charles Jewtraw (US)
1928 Bernt Evensen (Nor)
1932 John Shea (US)
1936 Ivar Ballangrud (Nor)
1948 Finn Helgesen (Nor)
1952 Kenneth Henry (US)
1956 Yevgeny Grishin (USSR)
1960 Yevgeny Grishin (USSR)
1964 Richard "Terry" McDermott (US)
1968 Erhard Keller (Ger)
1972 Erhard Keller (Ger)
1976 Yevgeny Kulikov (USSR)
1980 Eric Heiden (US)
1984 Sergei Fokichev (USSR)
1988 Uwe-Jens Mey (GDR)

1000 metres
1976 Peter Mueller (US)
1980 Eric Heiden (US)
1984 Gaetan Boucher (Can)
1988 Nikolay Gulyayev (USSR)

1500 metres
1924 A. Clas Thunberg (Fin)
1928 A. Clas Thunberg (Fin)
1932 John Shea (US)
1936 Charles Mathisen (Nor)
1948 Sverre Farstad (Nor)
1952 Hjalmar Andersen (Nor)
1956 Yevgeny Grishin (USSR)
1960 Roald Aas (Nor)
1964 Ants Antson (USSR)
1968 Cornelis "Kees" Verkerk (Hol)
1972 Adrianus "Ard" Schenk (Hol)
1976 Jan Egil Storholt (Nor)

1980 Eric Heiden (US)
1984 Gaetan Boucher Can)
1988 Andre Hoffmann (GDR)

5000 metres
1924 A. Claus Thunberg (Fin)
1928 Ivar Ballangrud (Nor)
1932 Irving Jaffee (US)
1936 Ivar Ballangrud (Nor)
1948 Reider Liaklev (Nor)
1952 Hjalmar Andersen (Nor)
1956 Boris Shilkov (USSR)
1960 Viktor Kosichkin (USSR)
1964 Knut Johannesen (Nor)
1968 Fred Anton Maier (Nor)
1972 Adrianus "Ard" Schenk (Hol)
1976 Sten Stensen (Nor)
1980 Eric Heiden (US)
1984 Sven Tomas Gustafson (Swe)
1988 Tomas Gustafsson (Swe)

10000 metres
1924 Julius Skutnabb (Fin)
1928 Irving Jaffee (US)
1932 Irving Jaffee (US)
1936 Ivar Ballangrud (Nor)
1948 Ake Seyffarth (Swe)
1952 Hjalmar Andersen (Nor)
1956 Sigvard Ericsson (Swe)
1960 Knut Johannesen (Nor)
1964 Jonny Nilsson (Swe)
1968 Johnny Hoglin (Swe)
1972 Adrianus "Ard" Schenk (Hol)
1976 Piet Kleine (Hol)
1980 Eric Heiden (US)
1984 Igor Malkov (USSR)
1988 Tomas Gustafsson (Swe)

Women
500 metres
1960 Helga Haase (GDR)
1964 Lydia Skoblikova (USSR)
1968 Lyudmila Titova (USSR)
1972 Anne Henning (US)
1976 Sheila Young (US)
1980 Karin Enke (GDR)
1984 Christa Rothenburger (GDR)
1988 Bonnie Blair (US)

1000 metres
1960 Klara Guseva (USSR)
1964 Lydia Skoblikova (USSR)
1968 Carolina Geijssen (Hol)
1972 Monika Pflug (Ger)
1976 Tatiana Averina (USSR)
1980 Natalia Petruseva (USSR)
1984 Karin Enke (GDR)
1988 Christa Rothenburger (Hol)

1500 metres
1960 Lydia Skoblikova (USSR)
1964 Lydia Skoblikova (USSR)
1968 Kaija Mustonen (Fin)
1972 Dianne Holum (US)
1976 Galina Stepanskaya (USSR)
1980 Annie Borckink (Hol)
1984 Karin Enke (GDR)
1988 Yvonne van Gennip (Hol)

3000 metres
1960 Lydia Skoblikova (USSR)
1964 Lydia Skoblikova (USSR)
1968 Johanna Schut (Hol)
1972 Christina Baas-Kaiser (Hol)
1976 Tatiana Averina (USSR)
1980 Bjorg Eva Jensen (Nor)
1984 Andrea Schone (nee Mitsherlich) (GDR)
1988 Yvonne van Gennip (Hol)

5000 metres
1988 Yvonne van Gennip (Hol)

SKIING - ALPINE
Men
Combined
1936 Franz Pfnur (Ger); 1948 Henri Oreiller (Fra); 1988 Hubert Strolz (Aut)

	Downhill	Slalom	Giant Slalom	Super-Giant Slalom
1948	Henri Oreiller (Fra)	Edy Reinalter (Swi)	-	
1952	Zeno Colo (Ita)	Othmar Schneider (Aut)	Stein Eriksen (Nor)	-
1956	Toni Sailer (Aut)	Toni Sailer (Aut)	Toni Sailer (Aut)	-
1960	Jean Vuarnet (Fra)	Ernst Hinterseer (Aut)	Roger Staub (Swi)	-
1964	Egon Zimmermann (Aut)	Josef Stiegler (Aut)	Francois Boulieu (Fra)	-
1968	Jean-Claude Killy (Fra)	Jean-Claude Killy (Fra)	Jean-Claude Killy (Fra)	-
1972	Bernhard Russi (Swi)	Francisco Fernandez Ochoa (Spa)	Gustavo Thoeni (Ita)	-
1976	Franz Klammer (Aut)	Piero Gros (Ita)	Heini Hemmi (Swe)	-
1980	Leonhard Stock (Aut)	Ingemar Stenmark (Swe)	Ingemar Stenmark (Swe)	-
1984	William Johnson (US)	Phil Mahre (US)	Max Julen (Swi)	-
1988	Pirmin Zurbriggen (Swi)	Alberto Tomba (Ita)	Alberto Tomba (Ita)	Franck Picard (Fra)

Women
Combined
1936 Christel Cranz (Ger); 1948 Trude Beiser (Aut); 1988 Anita Wachter (Aut)

Downhill	Slalom	Giant Slalom
1948 Hedy Schlunegger (Swi)	Gretchen Fraser (US)	-
1952 Trude Jochum (née Beiser)(Aut)	Andrea Mead-Lawrence (US)	Andrea Mead-Lawrence (US)
1956 Madeleine Berthod (Swi)	Renee Colliard (Swi)	Ossi Reichert (FRG)
1960 Heidi Biebi (FRG)	Anne Heggtveit (Can)	Yvonne Ruegg (Swi)
1964 Christl Haas (Aut)	Christine Goitschel (Fra)	Marielle Goitschel (Fra)
1968 Olga Pall (Aut)	Marielle Goitschel (Fra)	Nancy Greene (Can)
1972 Marie-Therese Nadig (Swi)	Barbara Cochran (US)	Marie-Therese Nadig (Swi)
1976 Rosi Mittermaier (FRG)	Rosi Mittermaier (FRG)	Kathy Kreiner (Can)
1980 Annemarie Moser-Proll (Aut)	Hanni Wenzel (Lie)	Hanni Wenzel (Lie)
1984 Michela Figini (Swi)	Paoletta Magoni (Ita)	Debbie Armstrong (USA)
1988 Marina Kiehl (FRG)	Vreni Schneider (Swi)	Vreni Schneider (Swi)

Super-Giant Slalom
(First held 1988)
1988 Sigrid Wolf (Aut)

SKIING-NORDIC
Men
Cross-Country
15km
1924 Thorleif Haug (Nor)
1928 Johan Grottumsbraten (Nor)
1932 Sven Utterstrom (Swe)
1936 Erik-August Larsson (Swe)
1948 Martin Lundstrom (Swe)
1952 Hallgeir Brenden (Nor)
1956 Hallgeir Brenden (Nor)
1960 Hakon Brusveen (Nor)
1964 Eero Mantyranta (Fin)
1968 Harald Gronningen (Nor)
1972 Sven-Ake Lundback (Swe)
1976 Nikolai Bazhukov (USSR)
1980 Thomas Wassberg (Swe)
1984 Gunde Svan (Swe)
1988 Mikhail Devyatyarov (USSR)

30km
1956 Veikko Hakulinen (Fin)
1960 Sixten Jernberg (Swe)
1964 Eero Mantyranta (Fin)
1968 Franco Nones (Ita)
1972 Vyacheslav Vedenine (USSR)
1976 Sergei Saveliev (USSR)
1980 Nikolai Zimyatov (USSR)
1984 Nikolai Zimyatov (USSR)
1988 Alexei Prokurakov (USSR)

50km
1924 Thorleif Haug (Nor)
1928 Per Erik Hedlund (Swe)
1932 Veli Saarinen (Fin)
1936 Elis Wiklund (Swe)
1948 Nils Karlsson (Swe)
1952 Veikko Hakulinen (Fin)
1956 Sixten Jernberg (Swe)
1960 Kalevi Hamalainen (Fin)
1964 Sixten Jernberg (Swe)
1968 Ole Ellefsaeter (Nor)
1972 Pal Tyldum (Nor)
1976 Ivar Formo (Nor)
1980 Nikolai Zimyatov (USSR)
1984 Thomas Wassberg (Swe)
1988 Gunde Kvan (Swe)

4 x 10km Relay
1936 Finland
1948 Sweden
1952 Finland
1956 Soviet Union
1960 Finland
1964 Sweden
1968 Norway
1972 Soviet Union
1976 Finland
1980 Soviet Union
1984 Sweden
1988 Sweden

Combined Individual
1924 Thorleif Haug (Nor)
1928 Johan Grottumsbraten (Nor)
1932 Johan Grottumsbraten (Nor)
1936 Oddbjorn Hagen (Nor)
1948 Heikki Hasu (Fin)
1952 Simon Slattvik (Nor)
1956 Sverre Stenersen (Nor)
1960 Georg Thoma (Ger)
1964 Tormod Knutsen (Nor)
1968 Franz Keller (FRG)
1972 Ulrich Wehling (GDR)
1976 Ulrich Wehling (GDR)
1980 Ulrich Wehling (GDR)
1984 Tom Sandberg (Nor)
1988 Hippolyt Kempf (Swi)

Combined Team
1988 West Germany

Women
Cross-Country
5km
1964 Claudia Boyarskikh (USSR)
1968 Toini Gustafsson (Swe)
1972 Galina Kulakova (USSR)
1976 Helena Takalo (Fin)
1980 Raisa Smetanina (USSR)
1984 Marja-Liisa Hamalainen (Fin)
1988 Marjo Matikainen (Fin)

10km
1952 Lydia Wideman (Fin)
1956 Lyubov Kosyreva (USSR)
1960 Maria Gusakova (USSR)
1964 Claudia Boyarskikh (USSR)
1968 Toini Gustafsson (Swe)
1972 Galina Kulakova (USSR)
1976 Raisa Smetanina (USSR)

1980 Barbara Petzold (GDR)
1984 Marja-Liisa Hamalainen (Fin)
1988 Vida Ventsene (USSR)

20km
1984 Marja-Liisa Hamalainen (Fin)
1988 Tamara Tikmonova (USSR)

4 x 5km Relay
1956 Finland
1960 Sweden
1964 Soviet Union
1968 Norway
1972 Soviet Union
1976 Soviet Union
1980 East Germany
1984 Norway
1988 Finland

SKI JUMPING
70 metres
1988 Matti Nykanen (Fin)

90 metres, individual
1924 Jacob Tullin Thams (Nor)
1928 Alf Andersen (Nor)
1932 Birger Ruud (Nor)
1936 Birger Ruud (Nor)
1948 Petter Hugsted (Nor)
1952 Arnfinn Bergmann (Nor)
1956 Antti Hyvarinen (Fin)
1960 Helmut Recknagel (GDR)
1964 Toralf Engan (Nor)
1968 Vladimir Beloussov (USSR)
1972 Wojciech Fortuna (Pol)
1976 Karl Schnabl (Aut)
1980 Jouko Tormanen (Fin)
1984 Matti Nykanen (Fin)
1988 Matti Nykanen (Fin)

90 metres, team
1988 Finland

——— STEFAN'S SURPRISE ———

Stefan Eberharter of Austria, who had never won a World Cup race, improbably became the only double gold medallist of the 1991 World Championships in Saalbach-Hinterglemm.

The Austrians won 11 medals on their home snow, as many as Switzerland, France and Italy combined. But they had two major disappointments. Franz Heinzer of Switzerland won the race the home crowd wanted most of all, the men's downhill. And the 21-year-old bank clerk Petra Kronberger, the new queen of women's skiing, failed to dominate events in the way everyone expected. She won the downhill all right but fell at the final gate in the next event, the super-G, putting her out of the championship.

Kronberger had already become the first woman to win in all five World Cup disciplines in one season and she dominated competition outside the World Championships. The men's events were more tightly contested but Marc Girardelli was overall champion for the fourth time and finally won his first individual Championship gold, in the slalom.

The Championships were overshadowed by fears of the Gulf War and rumours of a mass pullout - the US team left Europe four days before the start and then came back when events were under way. However, the only defector in the end was the ABC TV network. The US threatened to break away from the entire sport and start their own alternative circuit but were mollified by the promise of new management under a professional commissioner.

World Cup skiing had its first fatal accident for 12 years when the 20-year-old Austrian skier Gernot Reinstadler died in hospital after crashing in a qualifying race at Wengen, Switzerland, having caught a ski tip in protective netting. At the end of a sad season, the world giant slalom champion Rudi Nierlich was killed in a car crash.

The European Parliament appealed for the skiing season to be curtailed because the 100 million tourists were eroding the Alps. The Parliament endorsed a report by a German Green member, Karl Partsch, saying that artificial snow machines, development on glaciers and skiing outside designated slopes should all be banned.

An Austrian company installed TV cameras on the slopes of 18 winter sports areas to relay snow conditions to Austrian viewers every morning. The move came after criticism that it had been difficult to elicit unbiased information during the previous mild winters.

Britain appointed a new coach, the Austrian Hans Anewanter, who had previously coached a more significant skiing country: Liechtenstein. Peter van der Zeil, 46, of Wilmslow, Cheshire built a wooden ramp from the roof of his garden shed to the end of his lawn to practise in his attempt to represent Sri Lanka, where he was born, in bobsleigh in the 1992 Winter Olympics. To overcome the lack of snow, he mounted the bob on a skateboard. "If I pick up too much speed I'll shoot straight through the hedge and out on to the road," he said.

Kareem Abdul-Jabbar, the 7ft 2in basketball star, went to Vail, Colorado to take up skiing; Robert Kjesel, 6ft 10in, was appointed his instructor.

1990-91

ALPINE SKIING
WORLD CHAMPIONSHIPS
Saalbach-Hinterglemm, Austria, Jan 21-Feb 3
Men
Downhill
1 Franz Heinzer (Swi) 1m 54.91s
2 Peter Runggaldier (Ita) 1m 55.16s
3 Daniel Mahrer (Swi) 1m 55.57s
Slalom
1 Marc Girardelli (Lux) 1m 55.38s
2 Thomas Stangassinger (Aut) 1m 55.96s
3 Ole-Christian Furuseth (Nor) 1m 56.00s
Giant Slalom
1 Rudolf Nierlich (Aut) 2m 29.94s
2 Urs Kaelin (Swi) 2m 30.29s
3 Johann Wallner (Swe) 2m 30.73s
Super-Giant Slalom
1 Stefan Eberharter (Aut) 1m 26.73s
2 Kjetil Andre Aamodt (Nor) 1m 28.47s
3 Franck Piccard (Fra) 1m 29.55s
Combined
1 Stefan Eberharter (Aut) 16.28 pts
2 Khristian Ghedina (Ita) 26.41 pts
3 Günter Mader (Aut) 27.54 pts
Women
Downhill
1 Petra Kronberger (Aut) 1m 29.12s
2 Nathalie Bouvier (Fra) 1m 29.56s
3 Svetlana Gladishiva (USSR) 1m 29.63s
Slalom
1 Vreni Schneider (Swi) 1m 25.90s
2 Natasa Bokal (Yug) 1m 26.06s
3 Ingrid Salvenmoser (Aut) 1m 26.56s
Giant Slalom
1 Pernilla Wiberg (Swe) 2m 07.45s
2 Ulrike Maier (Aut) 2m 07.61s
3 Traudi Haecher (Ger) 2m 08.03s
Super-Giant Slalom
1 Ulrike Maier (Aut) 1m 08.72s
2 Carole Merle (Fra) 1m 08.83s
3 Anita Wachter (Aut) 1m 08.85s
Combined
1 Chantal Bournissen (Swi) 26.45 pts
2 Ingrid Stoeckl (Aut) 33.76 pts
3 Vreni Schneider (Swi) 42.13 pts

Medal Table

	G	S	B
Austria	5	3	3
Switzerland	3	1	2
Sweden	1	-	1
Luxembourg	1	-	-
France	-	2	1
Italy	-	2	-
Norway	-	1	1
Yugoslavia	-	1	-
Soviet Union	-	-	1
Germany	-	-	1

Most individual medals
Stefan Eberharter (Aut) 2 gold; Ulrike Maier (Aut) 1 gold,
1 silver; Vreni Schneider (Swi) 1 gold, 1 bronze

WORLD CUP
Men
Overall
1 Marc Girardelli (Lux) 242 pts
2 Alberto Tomba (Ita) 222 pts
3 Rudolf Nierlich (Aut) 201 pts
Downhill
1 Franz Heinzer (Swi) 159 pts
2 Atle Skaardal (Nor) 125 pts
3 Daniel Mahrer (Swi) 81 pts
Slalom
1 Marc Girardelli (Lux) 110 pts
2 Ole-Christian Furuseth (Nor) 102 pts
3 Rudolf Nierlich (Aut) 100 pts
Giant Slalom
1 Alberto Tomba (Ita) 152 pts
2 Rudolf Nierlich (Aut) 101 pts
3 Marc Girardelli (Lux) 84 pts
Super-Giant Slalom
1 Franz Heinzer (Swi) 40 pts
2 Stefan Eberharter (Aut) 33 pts
3 Atle Skaardal (Nor) 28 pts
Women
Overall
1 Petra Kronberger (Aut) 312 pts
2 Sabine Ginther (Aut) 195 pts
3 Vreni Schneider (Swi) 185 pts
Downhill
1 Chantal Bournissen (Swi) 140 pts
2 Sabine Ginther (Aut) 122 pts
3 Petra Kronberger (Aut) 90 pts
Slalom
1 Petra Kronberger (Aut) 83 pts
2 Pernilla Wiberg (Swe) 79 pts
3 Blanca Fernandez-Ochoa (Spa) 76 pts
Giant Slalom
1 Vreni Schneider (Swi) 113 pts
2 Anita Wachter (Aut) 79 pts
3 Pernilla Wiberg (Swe) 61 pts
Super-Giant Slalom
1 Carole Merle (Fra) 88 pts
2 Petra Kronberger (Aut) 70 pts
3 Michaela Gerg (Ger) 44 pts
Nations Cup
1 Austria 2,405 pts
2 Switzerland 1,330 pts
3 Germany 755 pts

NORDIC SKIING
WORLD CHAMPIONSHIPS
Val di Flemme, Italy, Feb 4-11
Men
Individual Combined
1 Fred Borre Lundberg (Nor)
2 Klaus Sulzenbacher (Aut)
3 Klaus Ofner (Aut)
Team - Combined
1 Austria 1h 21m 22.5s
2 France 1h 22m 38.9s
3 Japan 1h 23m 14.4s

Nations Cup
1 Soviet Union 1,056 pts
2 Norway 1,023 pts
3 Sweden 921 pts

> **This is the worst day of my life. To think that on the issue of safety everyone wants to save money. I am disgusted."**
> *Marc Girardelli on the death of Gernot Reinstadler*

"Everything is becoming faster. The courses, the skis, the wax, the preparation. But we have not changed. Our muscles, our bones, our ligaments are the same. I think it's getting dangerous."
Girardelli

"The FIS is old and sleeping. When you have no dreams you have no future."
Serge Lang, deposed World Cup chairman

"If ice dancing ever was truly sport, as opposed to theatre, this year it went beyond the fringe, the chiffon, the taffeta and everything else... Medallists Maia Usova and Alexandr Zhulin of the Soviet Union appeared to open their free dance programme in a woodland, with Zhulin hopping like a rabbit around Usova, who was kneeling like a shrub. What happened next was unclear...No such mistake was made by Isabelle and Paul Duchesnay of France, who issued a press release explaining they would be skating Missing II, a sequel to Missing, last year's ice dancing hit about repression in a South American dictatorship. In Missing II, the dictatorship is over! This must have been terribly good news to the audience, because the Duchesnays received their first standing ovation merely for showing up in tattered garments and looking tortured.
EM Swift, Sports Illustrated, on the world ice dance championships

ICE SKATING
EUROPEAN FIGURE & DANCE CHAMPIONSHIPS
Sofia, Jan 22-27
Men
1 Viktor Petrenko (USSR)
2 Petr Barna (Cze)
3 Viacheslav Zagorodniuk (USSR)
Women
1 Surya Bonsaly (Fra)
2 Evelyn Grossmann (Ger)
3 Marina Kielmann (Ger)
Bonsaly was France's first ever women's champion.
Joanne Conway of Britain was 4th.

Pairs
1 Natalya Mishkutienok & Artur Dmitriev (USSR)
2 Elena Bechke & Denis Petrov (USSR)
3 Evgenia Shishkova & Vadim Naumov (USSR)
Dance
1 Marina Klimova & Sergei Ponomarenko (USSR)
2 Isabelle Duchesnay & Paul Duchesnay (Fra)
3 Maia Usova & Alexandr Zhulin (USSR)

WORLD FIGURE & DANCE CHAMPIONSHIPS
Munich, Mar 11-17
Men
1 Kurt Browning (Can)
2 Viktor Petrenko (USSR)
3 Todd Eldredge (US)
Women
1 Kristi Yamaguchi (US)
2 Tonya Harding (US)
3 Nancy Kerrigan (US)
Pairs
1 Natalya Mishkutienok & Artur Dmitriev (USSR)
2 Isabelle Brasseur & Lloyd Eisler (Can)
3 Natasha Kuchiki & Todd Sand (US)
Dance
1 Maia Usova & Alexandr Zhulin (USSR)
2 Isabelle Duchesnay & Paul Duchesnay (Fra)
3 Marina Klimova & Sergei Ponomarenko (USSR)

SPEED SKATING
MEN'S WORLD CHAMPIONSHIPS
Heerenveen, Holland, Feb 9-10
1 Johann Olav Koss (Nor) 157.396pts
2 Roberto Sighel (Ita) 160.125pts
3 Bart Veldkamp (Hol) 160.391pts
Individual Event Winners:
500m: Peter Adeberg (Ger)
1500m: Koss
5,000m: Koss
10,000m: Koss
WOMEN'S WORLD CHAMPIONSHIPS
Hamar, Norway, Feb 2-3
1 Gunda Kleeman (Ger) 177.263pts
2 Heike Warnicke (Ger) 183.324pts
3 Lia van Schie (Hol) 183.378pts
Individual Event Winners:
500m: Ya Qiaobo (Chn)
1500m: Kleeman
3,000m: Kleeman
5,000m: Kleeman

BOBSLEIGHING
EUROPEAN CHAMPIONSHIPS
Cervinia, Italy, Jan 18-27
Two-man
1 Switzerland I (Gustav Weder & Bruno Gerber) 2m 09.08s
2 Germany II (Volker Dietrich & Peer Hoechel) 2m 09.19s
3 Italy II (Gunther Huber & Stefano Ticci) 2m 09.32s
Four-man
1 Switzerland I 2m 02.99s
2 Germany I 2m 03.47s
3 Germany II 2m 03.55s

WORLD CHAMPIONSHIPS
Altenberg, Germany, Feb 10

Two-man
1 Germany II (Rudi Lochner & Marcus Zimmermann) 3m 49.47s
2 Switzerland I (Gustav Weder & Bruno Gerber) 3m 49.49s
3 Germany I (Wolfgang Hoppe & Rene Hannemann) 3m 50.51s

Four-man
1 Germany II 3m 45.53s
2 Switzerland I 3m 45.65s
3 Germany I 3m 45.67s

CHAMPIONS

ALPINE SKIING
WORLD CUP
Men
Overall Champions
1967 Jean-Claude Killy (Fra); 1968 Jean-Claude Killy (Fra); 1969 Karl Schranz (Aut); 1970 Karl Schranz (Aut); 1971 Gustavo Thoeni (Ita); 1972 Gustavo Thoeni (Ita); 1973 Gustavo Thoeni (Ita); 1974 Piero Gros (Ita); 1975 Gustavo Thoeni (Ita); 1976 Ingemar Stenmark (Swe); 1977 Ingemar Stenmark (Swe); 1978 Ingemar Stenmark (Swe); 1979 Peter Luscher (Swi); 1980 Andreas Wenzel (Lie); 1981 Phil Mahre (US); 1982 Phil Mahre (US); 1983 Phil Mahre (US); 1984 Pirmin Zurbriggen (Swi); 1985 Marc Girardelli (Lux); 1986 Marc Girardelli (Lux); 1987 Pirmin Zurbriggen (Swi); 1988 Pirmin Zurbriggen (Swi); 1989 Marc Girardelli (Lux); 1990 Pirmin Zurbriggen (Swi); 1991 Marc Girardelli (Lux)

	Downhill	Slalom	Giant Slalom	Super-Giant Slalom
1967	Jean-Claude Killy (Fra)	Jean-Claude Killy (Fra)	Jean-Claude Killy (Fra)	-
1968	Gerhard Nenning (Aut)	Dumeng Giovanoli (Swi)	Jean-Claude Killy (Fra)	-
1969	Karl Schranz (Aut)	Alfred Matt (Aut)	Karl Schranz	-
		Alain Penz (Fra)		
		Jean-Noel Augert (Fra)		
		Patrick Russel (Fra)		
1970	Karl Schranz (Aut)	Patrick Russel (Fra)	Gustavo Thoeni (Ita)	-
	Karl Cordin (Aut)	Alain Penz (Fra)		
1971	Bernhard Russi (Swi)	Jean-Noel Augert (Fra)	Gustavo Thoeni (Ita)	-
			Patrick Russell (Fra)	
1972	Bernhard Russi (Swi)	Jean-Noel Augert (Fra)	Gustavo Thoeni (Ita)	-
1973	Roland Collombin (Swi)	Gustavo Thoeni (Ita)	Hans Hinterseer (Aut)	-
1974	Roland Collombin (Swi)	Gustavo Thoeni (Ita)	Piero Gros (Ita)	-
1975	Franz Klammer (Aut)	Ingemar Stenmark (Swe)	Ingemar Stenmark (Swe)	-
1976	Franz Klammer (Aut)	Ingemar Stenmark (Swe)	Ingemar Stenmark (Swe)	-
1977	Franz Klammer (Aut)	Ingemar Stenmark (Swe)	Heini Hemmi (Swi)	-
1978	Franz Klammer (Aut)	Ingemar Stenmark (Swe)	Ingemar Stenmark (Swe)	-
1979	Peter Muller (Swi)	Ingemar Stenmark (Swe)	Ingemar Stenmark (Swe)	-
1980	Peter Muller (Swi)	Ingemar Stenmark (Swe)	Ingemar Stenmark (Swe)	-
1981	Harti Weirather (Aut)	Ingemar Stenmark (Swe)	Ingemar Stenmark (Swe)	-
1982	Steve Podborski (Can)	Phil Mahre (US)	Phil Mahre (US)	-
	Peter Muller (Swi)			
1983	Franz Klammer (Aut)	Ingemar Stenmark (Swe)	Phil Mahre (US)	-
1984	Urs Raber (Swi)	Marc Girardelli (Lux)	Ingemar Stenmark (Swe)	-
1985	Helmet Hoeflehner (Aut)	Marc Girardelli (Lux)	Marc Girardelli (Lux)	-
1986	Peter Wirnsberger (Aut)	Rok Petrovic (Yug)	Joel Gaspoz (Swi)	Markus Wasmeier (FRG)
1987	Pirmin Zurbriggen (Swi)	Bojan Krizaj (Yug)	Pirmin Zurbriggen (Swi)	Pirmin Zurbriggen (Swi)
1988	Pirmin Zurbriggen (Swi)	Alberto Tomba (Ita)	Alberto Tomba (Ita)	Pirmin Zurbriggen (Swi)
1989	Marc Girardelli (Lux)	Armin Bittner (FRG)	Ole Furuseth (Nor)	Pirmin Zurbriggen (Swi)
1990	Helmut Hoehflehner (Aut)	Armin Bittner (FRG)	Ole Furuseth (Nor)	Pirmin Zurbriggen (Swi)
1991	Franz Heinzer (Swi)	Marc Girardelli (Lux)	Alberto Tomba (Ita)	Franz Heinzer (Swi))

Women
Overall Champions
1967 Nancy Greene (Can); 1968 Nancy Greene (Can); 1969 Gertrud Gabl (Aut); 1970 Michele Jacot (Fra); 1971 Annemarie Moser-Proll (Aut); 1972 Annemarie Moser-Proll (Aut); 1973 Annemarie Moser-Proll (Aut); 1974 Annemarie Moser-Proll (Aut); 1976 Rosi Mittermaier (FRG); 1977 Lise-Marie Morerod (Swi); 1978 Hanni Wenzel (Lie); 1979 Annemarie Moser-Proll (Aut); 1980 Hanni Wenzel (Lie); 1981 Marie-Therese Nadig (Swi); 1982 Erika Hess (Swi); 1983 Tamara McKinney (US); 1984 Erika Hess (Swi); 1985 Michela Figini (Swi); 1986 Maria Walliser (Swi); 1987 Maria Walliser (Swi); 1988 Michela Figini (Swi); 1989 Vreni Schneider (Swi); 1990 Petra Kronberger (Aut); 1991 Petra Kronberger (Aut)

	Downhill	Slalom	Giant Slalom
1967	Marielle Goitschel (Fra)	Marielle Goitschel (Fra)	Nancy Greene (Can)
		Annie Famose (Fra)	
1968	Isabelle Mir (Fra)	Annie Famose (Fra)	Nancy Greene (Can)
	Olga Pall (Aut)		

1969	Wiltrud Drexel (Aut)	Gertrud Gabl (Aut)	Marilyn Cochran (US)
1970	Wiltrud Drexel (Aut)	Gertrud Gabl (Aut)	Marilyn Cochran (US)
		Ingrid Laforgue (Fra)	Michele Jacot (Fra)
			Francoise Macchi (Fra)
1971	Annemarie Moser-Proll (Aut)	Britt Laforgue (Fra)	Annemarie Moser-Proll (Aut)
	Betsy Clifford (Can)		
1972	Annemarie Moser-Proll (Aut)	Britt Laforgue (Fra)	Annemarie Moser-Proll (Aut)
1973	Annemarie Moser-Proll (Aut)	Patricia Emonet (Fra)	Monika Kaserer (Aut)
1974	Annemarie Moser-Proll (Aut)	Christa Zechmeister (FRG)	Hanni Wenzel (Lie)
1975	Annemarie Moser-Proll (Aut)	Lise-Marie Morerod (Swi)	Annemarie Moser-Proll (Aut)
1976	Brigette Habersatter-Totschnig (Aut)	Lise-Marie Morerod (Swi)	Lise-Marie Morerod (Swi)
1977	Brigette Habersatter-Totschnig (Aut)	Lise-Marie Morerod (Swi)	Lise-Marie Morerod (Swi)
1978	Annemarie Moser-Proll (Aut)	Hanni Wenzel (Lie)	Lise-Marie Morerod (Swi)
1979	Annemarie Moser-Proll (Aut)	Regina Sackl (Aut)	Christa Kinshoffer (Aut)
1980	Marie-Therese Nadig (Swi)	Perrine Pelen (Fra)	Hanni Wenzel (Lie)
1981	Marie-Therese Nadig (Swi)	Erika Hess (Swi)	Tamara McKinney (US)
1982	Cecile Gros-Gaudenier (Fra)	Erika Hess (Swi)	Irene Epple (FRG)
1983	Doris De Agostini (Swi)	Erika Hess (Swi)	Tamara McKinney (US)
1984	Maria Walliser (Swi)	Tamara McKinney (US)	Erika Hess (Swi)
1985	Michela Figini (Swi)	Erika Hess (Swi)	Michela Figini (Swi)
			Marina Kiehl (FRG)
1986	Maria Walliser (Swi)	Roswitha Steiner (Aut)	Vreni Schneider (Swi)
1987	Michela Figini (Swi)	Corinne Schmidhauser (Swi)	Maria Walliser (Swi)
			Vreni Schneider (Swi)
1988	Michela Figini (Swi)	Roswitha Steiner (Aut)	Mateja Svet (Yug)
1989	Michela Figini (Swi)	Vreni Schneider (Swi)	Vreni Schneider (Swi)
1990	Katrin Gutensohn-Knopf (FRG)	Vreni Schneider (Swi)	Anita Wachter (Aut)
1991	Chantal Bournissen (Swi)	Petra Kronberger (Aut)	Vreni Schneider (Swi)

Super-Giant Slalom
(Instituted 1986)
1986 Marina Kiehl (FRG); 1987 Maria Walliser (Swi); 1988 Michela Figini (Swi); 1989 Carole Merle (Fra); 1990 Carole Merle (Fra); 1991 Carole Merle (Fra)

Most World Cup race wins:
86 Ingemar Stenmark; 62 Annemarie Moser-Proll
Most race wins over season
13 Ingemar Stenmark; 1978-79, Vreni Schneider, 1988-89; Jean-Claude Killy, 1966-67; 11 Annemarie Moser-Proll, 1972-73, Pirmin Zurbriggen 1986-87

NATIONS CUP
(Team prize at World Cup)
1967-68, 1970-72 France; 1969, 1973-82 Austria; 1983-89 Switzerland; 1990-91 Austria

ALPINE SKIING WORLD CHAMPIONSHIPS

(Post-war winners)

Men

Combined
1954 Stein Eriksen (Nor); 1956 Toni Sailer (Aut); 1958 Toni Sailer (Aut); 1960 Guy Perillat (Fra); 1962 Karl Schranz (Aut); 1964 Ludwig Leitner (FRG); 1966 Jean-Claude Killy (Fra); 1968 Jean-Claude Killy (Fra); 1970 Bill Kidd (US); 1972 Gustavo Thoeni (Ita); 1974 Franz Klammer (Aut); 1976 Gustavo Thoeni (Ita); 1978 Andrea Wenzel (Lie); 1980 Phil Mahre (US); 1982 Michel Vion (Fra); 1985 Pirmin Zurbriggen (Swi); 1987 Marc Girardelli (Lux); 1989 Marc Girardelli (Lux); 1991 Stefan Eberharter (Aut)

	Downhill	**Slalom**	**Giant Slalom**	**Super-Giant Slalom**
1950	Zeno Colo (Ita)	Georges Schneider (Swi)	Zeno Colo (Ita)	-
1954	Christian Pravda (Aut)	Stein Eriksen (Nor)	Stein Eriksen (Nor)	-
1958	Toni Sailer (Aut)	Josef Rieder (Aut)	Toni Sailer (Aut)	- .
1962	Karl Schranz	Charles Bozon (Fra)	Egon Zimmermann (Aut)	-
1966	Jean-Claude Killy (Fra)	Carlo Senoner (Ita)	Guy Perillat (Fra)	-
1970	Bernhard Russi (Swi)	Jean-Noel Augert (Fra)	Karl Schranz (Aut)	-
1974	David Zwilling (Aut)	Gustavo Thoeni (Ita)	Gustavo Thoeni (Ita)	-
1978	Josef Walcher (Aut)	Ingemar Stenmark (Swe)	Ingemar Stenmark (Swe)	-
1982	Harti Weirather (Aut)	Ingemar Stenmark (Swe)	Steve Mahre (US)	-
1985	Pirmin Zurbriggen (Swi)	Jonas Nilsson (Swe)	Markus Wasmaier (FRG)	-
1987	Peter Muller (Swi)	Frank Worndl (FRG)	Pirmin Zurbriggen (Swi)	Pirmin Zurbriggen (Swi)
1989	Hansjoerg Tauscher (FRG)	Rudolf Nierlich (Aut)	Rudolf Nierlich (Aut)	Martin Hangl (Swi)
1991	Franz Heinzer (Swi)	Marc Girardelli (Lux)	Rudolf Nierlich (Aut)	Stefan Eberharter (Aut)

Women
Combined

1954 Ida Schopfer (Swi); 1956 Madeleine Berthod (Swi); 1958 Frieda Danzer (Swi); 1960 Anne Heggtveit (Can); 1962 Marielle Goitschel (Fra); 1964 Marielle Goitschel (Fra); 1966 Marielle Goitschel (Fra); 1968 Nancy Greene (Can); 1970 Michele Jacot (Fra); 1972 Annemarie Moser-Proll (Aut); 1974 Fabienne Serrat (Fra); 1976 Rosi Mittermaier (FRG); 1978 Annemarie Moser-Proll (Aut); 1980 Hanni Wenzel (Lie); 1982 Erika Hess (Swi); 1985 Erika Hess (Swi); 1987 Erika Hess (Swi); 1989 Tamara McKinney (US); 1991 Chantal Bournissen (Swi)

	Downhill	Slalom	Giant Slalom
1950	Trude-Beiser-Jochum (Aut)	Dagmar Rom (Aut)	Dagmar Rom (Aut)
1954	Ida Schopfer (Swi)	Trude Klecker (Aut)	Lucienne Schmitt (Fra)
1958	Lucille Wheeler (Can)	Inger Bjornbakken (Nor)	Lucille Wheeler (Can)
1962	Christl Haas (Aut)	Marianne Jahn (Aut)	Marianne Jahn (Aut)
1966	Erika Schinegger (Aut)	Annie Famose (Fra)	Marielle Goitschel (Fra)
1970	Annerosli Zyrd (Swi)	Ingrid Lafforgue (Fra)	Betsy Clifford (Can)
1974	Annemarie Moser-Proll (Aut)	Hanni Wenzel (Lie)	Fabienne Serrat (Fra)
1978	Annemarie Moser-Proll (Aut)	Lea Solkner (Aut)	Maria Epple (FRG)
1982	Gerry Sorensen (Can)	Erika Hess (Swi)	Erika Hess (Swi)
1985	Michela Figini (Swi)	Perrine Pelen (Fra)	Diann Roffe (US)
1987	Maria Walliser (Swi)	Erika Hess (Swi)	Vreni Schneider (Swi)
1989	Maria Walliser (Swi)	Mateja Svet (Yug)	Vreni Schneider (Swi)
1991	Petra Kronberger (Aut)	Vreni Schneider (Swi)	Pernilla Wiberg (Swi)

Super-Giant Slalom
(First held 1987)
1987　Maria Walliser (FRG); 1989 Ulrike Maier (Aut); 1991 Ulrike Maier (Aut)

ICE SKATING
WORLD CHAMPIONSHIPS
Winners since 1982
Men
1982	Scott Hamilton (US)
1983	Scott Hamilton (US)
1984	Scott Hamilton (US)
1985	Alexandre Fadeyev (USSR)
1986	Brian Boitano (US)
1987	Brian Orser (Can)
1988	Brian Boitano (US)
1989	Kurt Browning (Can)
1990	Kurt Browning (Can)
1991	Kurt Browning (Can)

Women
1982	Elaine Zayak (US)
1983	Rosalynn Sumners (US)
1984	Katarina Witt (GDR)
1985	Katarina Witt (GDR)
1986	Debbie Thomas (US)
1987	Katarina Witt (GDR)
1988	Katarina Witt (GDR)
1990	Jill Trenary (US)
1991	Kristi Yamaguchi (US)

Pairs
1982	Sabine Baess/Tassilo Thierbach (GDR)
1983	Yelena Valova/Oleg Vasiliev (USSR)
1984	Barbara Underhill/Paul Martini (Can)
1985	Yelena Valova/Oleg Vasiliev (USSR)
1986	Yekaterina Gordeyeva/Sergey Grinkov (USSR)
1987	Yekaterina Gordeyeva/Sergey Grinkov (USSR)
1988	Yelena Valova/Oleg Vasiliev (USSR)
1989	Yekaterina Gordeyeva/Sergey Grinkov (USSR)
1990	Yakaterina Gordeyeva/Sergey Grinkov (USSR)
1991	Natalya Mishkutienok/Artur Dimitriev (USSR)

Ice Dance
1982	Jayne Torvill/Christopher Dean (GB)
1983	Jayne Torvill/Christopher Dean (GB)
1984	Jayne Torvill/Christopher Dean (GB)
1985	Natalya Bestemianova/Andre Bukin (USSR)
1986	Natalya Bestemianova/Andre Bukin (USSR)
1987	Natalya Bestemianova/Andre Bukin (USSR)
1988	Natalya Bestemianova/Andre Bukin (USSR)
1989	Marina Klimova/Sergey Ponomarenko (USSR)
1990	Marina Klimova/Sergey Ponomarenko (USSR)
1991	Maia Usova/Alexandr Zhulin (USSR)

EUROPEAN CHAMPIONSHIPS
Winners since 1982
Men
1982	Norbert Schramm (GDR)
1983	Norbert Schramm (GDR)
1984	Alexandre Fadeyev (USSR)
1985	Josef Sabovcik (Cze)
1986	Josef Sabovcik (Cze)
1987	Alexandre Fadeyev (USSR)
1988	Alexandre Fadeyev (USSR)
1989	Alexandre Fadeyev (USSR)
1990	Viktor Petrenko (USSR)
1991	Viktor Petrenko (USSR)

Women
1982	Claudia Kristofics-Binder(Aut)
1983	Katarina Witt (GDR)
1984	Katarina Witt (GDR)
1985	Katarina Witt (GDR)
1986	Katarina Witt (GDR)
1987	Katarina Witt (GDR)
1988	Katarina Witt (GDR)
1989	Claudia Leistner (FRG)
1990	Evelyn Grossmann (GDR)
1991	Surya Bosnaly (Fra)

Pairs
1982	Sabine Baess/Tassilo Thierbach (GDR)
1983	Sabine Baess/Tassilo Thierbach (GDR)
1984	Yelena Valova/Oleg Vasiliev (USSR)
1985	Yelena Valova/Oleg Vasiliev (USSR)
1986	Yelena Valova/Oleg Vasiliev (USSR)

1987 Larissa Selezneva/Oleg Makarov (USSR)
1988 Yekaterina Gordeyeva/Sergey Grinkov (USSR)
1989 Larissa Selezneva/Oleg Makarov (USSR)
1990 Yekaterina Gordeyeva/Sergey Grinkov (USSR)
1991 Natalya Mishkutienok/Artur Dimitriev (USSR)

Ice Dance
1982 Jayne Torvill/Christopher Dean (GB)
1983 Natalya Bestemianova/Andre Bukin (USSR)
1984 Jayne Torvill/Christopher Dean (GB)
1985 Natalya Bestemianova/Andre Bukin (USSR)
1986 Natalya Bestemianova/Andre Bukin (USSR)
1987 Natalya Bestemianova/Andre Bukin (USSR)
1988 Natalya Bestemianova/Andre Bukin (USSR)
1989 Marina Klimova/Sergcy Ponomarenko (USSR)
1990 Marina Klimova/Sergey Ponomarenko (USSR)
1991 Marina Klimova/Sergey Ponomarenko (USSR)

BOBSLEIGHING
WORLD CHAMPIONSHIPS
Winners since 1961

Two-man
1961 Eugenio Monti/Sergio Siorpaes (Ita)
1962 Rinaldo Ruatti/Enrico De Lorenzo (Ita)
1963 Eugenio Monti/Sergio Siorpaes (Ita)
1965 Tony Nash/Robin Dixon (GB)
1966 Eugenio Monti/Sergio Siorpaes (Ita)
1967 Erwin Thaler/Reinhold Durnthaler (Aut)
1969 Nevio de Zordo/Adriano Frassinelli (Ita)
1970 Horst Floth/Pepi Bader (FRG)
1971 Gianfranco Gaspari/Mario Armano (Ita)
1973 Wolfgang Zimmerer/Peter Utzschneider (FRG)
1974 Wolfgang Zimmerer/Peter Utzschneider (FRG)
1975 Giorgio Alvero/Franco Perruquet (Ita)
1977 Hans Hilterbrand/Heinz Meier (Swi)
1978 Erich Scharer/Josef Benz (Swi)
1979 Erich Scharer/Josef Benz (Swi)
1981 Bernhard Germeshausen/Hans-Jurgen Gernhardt (GDR)
1982 Erich Scharer/Josef Benz (Swi)
1983 Ralf Pichler/Urs Leuthold (Swi)
1985 Wolfgang Hoppe/Dietmar Schauerhammer (GDR)
1986 Wolfgang Hoppe/Dietmar Schauerhammer (GDR)
1987 Ralf Pichler/Celest Poltera (Swi)
1989 Wolfgang Hoppe/Bogdan Musiol (GDR)
1991 Rudi Lochner/Marcus Zimmermann (Ger)

Four-man
1961 Italy
1962 West Germany
1963 Italy
1965 Canada
1966 Not completed
1967 Not held
1969 West Germany
1970 Italy
1971 Switzerland
1973 Switzerland
1974 West Germany
1975 Switzerland
1977 East Germany
1978 East Germany
1979 West Germany
1981 East Germany
1982 Switzerland
1983 Switzerland
1985 East Germany
1986 Switzerland
1987 Switzerland
1989 Switzerland
1991 Germany

━━━ 1992 ━━━

ALPINE WORLD CUP

Dates in Yugoslavia are provisional

Jan 4-5 Men's slalom and giant slalom (Kranjska Gora, Yugoslavia); Jan 5-6 Women's slalom and giant slalom (Oberstaufen, Germany); Jan 11-12 Men's downhill and super-G (Garmisch-Partenkirchen, Germany), Women's downhill, slalom, combined (Schruns/Tschagguns, Austria); Jan 14 Women's giant slalom (Hinterstoder, Austria); Jan 18-19 Men's downhill, slalom, combined (Kitzbuhel, Austria), Women's slalom and giant slalom (Maribor, Yugoslavia); Jan 21 Men's giant slalom (Adelboden, Switzerland); Jan 25-26 Men's downhill, slalom, combined (Wengen, Switzerland), Women's downhill and super-G (Morzine, France); Feb 1-2 Men's giant slalom and super-G (Megeve/Chamonix, France), Women's downhill, slalom, combined (Grindelwald, Switzerland); Feb 28-29 Women's slalom and giant slalom (Narvik, Norway); Feb 29-Mar 1 Men's downhill and super-G (Morioka/Shizukuishi, Japan); Mar 2 Women's slalom (Sundsvall, Sweden); Mar 7-8 Men's downhill and super-G (Whistler Mountain, Canada), Women's downhill and super-G (Vail, Colorado); Mar 14-15 Men's downhill and super-G (Aspen, Colorado); Mar 17-22 Women's giant slalom, super-G and parallel slalom (Crans-Montana, Switzerland); Mar 18-22 Men's slalom, giant slalom and parallel slalom (Crans-Montana, Switzerland)

SKATING

Jan 17-19 European Speed Championships (Heerenveen, Holland); Jan 21-26 European figure and dance championships (Lausanne); Feb 29 Mar 1 World sprint speed championships (Oslo); Mar 21-22 World Speed Championships (Calgary); Mar 24-29 World figure and dance championships (San Francisco/Oakland, California); Apr 2-4 World short track speed championships (Denver)

WRESTLING

1991

WORLD CHAMPIONSHIPS
Varna, Bulgaria, Sep 27-Oct 6

FREESTYLE

Flyweight (up to 52kg)
1 Zeke Jones (US)
2 Valentin Jordanov (Bul)
3 Vladimir Iogouzou (USSR)

Bantamweight (up to 57kg)
1 Sergey Smal (USSR)
2 Brad Penrith (US)
3 Oveis Mallah (Ira)

Featherweight (up to 62kg)
1 John Smith (US)
2 Giovanni Schillaci (Ita)
3 Gadzhi Rashidov (USSR)

Lightweight (up to 68kg)
1 Arsen Fadzeyev (USSR)
2 Chris Wilson (Can)
3 Valentin Getzov (Bul)

Welterweight (up to 74kg)
1 Amir Khadeem (Ira)
2 Ken Monay (US)
3 Nabir Gadzhihznov (USSR)

Middleweight (up to 82kg)
1 Kevin Jackson (US)
2 Josef Lohyna (Cze)
3 Sebahatin Oztrurk (Tur)

Light-heavyweight (up to 90kg)
1 Makharbek Khadartsev (USSR)
2 Iraklis Desoulidis (Gre)
3 Roberto Limonta (Cub)

Mid-heavyweight (up to 100kg)
1 Levi Khabelov (USSR)
2 Mark Coleman (US)
3 Heiko Balz (Ger)

Super-heavyweight (over 100kg)
1 Andreas Schroder (Ger)
2 Genady Zhiltov (USSR)
3 Jeff Thue (Can)

GRECO-ROMAN

Light-flyweight (up to 48kg)
1 Gooun Duk-Yong (SKo)
2 Reza Simkah (Iran)
3 Sergey Suvorov (USSR)

Flyweight (up to 52kg)
1 Raul Martinez (Cub)
2 Shawn Sheldon (US)
3 Joe Ronningen (Nor)

Bantamweight (up to 57kg)
1 Rifat Yidiz (Ger)
2 Alexandr Ignaenko (USSR)
3 Andras Sike (Hun)

Featherweight (up to 62kg)
1 Sergey Martynov (USSR)
2 Mehmet Akif Prim (Tur)
3 Juan Maren (Cub)

Lightweight (up to 68kg)
1 Islam Doguchiev (USSR)
2 Martin Kornbakk (Swe)
3 Stoyan Dobrev (Bul)

Welterweight (up to 74kg)
1 Mnazakan Iskamdarian (USSR)
2 Jaroslav Zemen (Cze)
3 Yvon Riemer (Fra)

Middleweight (up to 82kg)
1 Peter Farkas (Hun)
2 Todor Angelov Bul)
3 Zoran Kasum (Yug)

Light-heavyweight (up to 90kg)
1 Maik Bullmann (Ger)
2 Renaldo Pena (Cub)
3 Harri Koskela (Fin)

Mid-heavyweight (up to 100kg)
1 Hector Milian (Cub)
2 Jorgen Olsson (Swe)
3 Sergey Demiaschkevich (USSR)

Super-heavyweight (over 100kg)
1 Alexandr Karelin (USSR)
2 Matt Ghaffari (US)
3 Rangel Gerovski (Bul)

CHAMPIONS

WORLD CHAMPIONSHIPS
Since 1985

FREESTYLE

Light-flyweight (up to 48kg)
1985 Kim Chol-Hwan (SKo)
1986 Li Yae-Sik (NKo)
1987 Li Yae-Sik (NKo)
1989 Kim Jong-Shin (SKo)
1990 Aldo Martinez (Cub)

Flyweight (up to 52kg)
1985 Valentin Jordanov (Bul)
1986 Kim Yong-Sik (NKo)
1987 Valentin Jordanov (Bul)
1989 Valentin Jordanov (Bul)
1990 Majid Torkan (Ira)
1991 Zeke Jones (US)

Bantamweight (up to 57kg)
1985 Sergey Beloglazov (USSR)
1986 Sergey Beloglazov (USSR)
1987 Sergey Beloglazov (USSR)
1989 Kim Sik-Seung (NKo)
1990 Alejandro Puerto (Cub)
1991 Sergey Smal (USSR)

Featherweight (up to 62kg)
1985 Viktor Alekseyev (USSR)
1986 Hasar Isayev (USSR)
1987 John Smith (US)
1989 John Smith (US)
1990 John Smith (US)
1991 John Smith (US)

Lightweight (up to 68kg)
1985 Arsen Fadzeyev (USSR)
1986 Arsen Fadzeyev (USSR)
1987 Arsen Fadzeyev (USSR)
1989 Boris Budayev (USSR)
1990 Arsen Fadzeyev (USSR)
1991 Arsen Fadzeyev (USSR)

Welterweight (up to 74kg)
1985 Raul Cascaret (Cub)
1986 Raul Cascaret (Cub)
1987 Adlan Vareyev (USSR)

1989 Ken Monday (US)
1990 Rahmat Sofiyada (Bul)
1991 Amir Khadeem (Ira)

Middleweight (up to 82kg)
1985 Mark Schultz (US)
1986 Vladimir Modosyan (USSR)
1987 Mark Schultz (US)
1989 Elmadi Zhabraylov (USSR)
1990 Josef Lohyna (Cze)
1991 Kevin Jackson (US)

Light-heavyweight (up to 90kg)
1985 Bill Sherr (US)
1986 Markharbek Khadartsev (USSR)
1987 Markharbek Khadartsev (USSR)
1989 Markharbek Khadartsev (USSR)
1990 Markharbek Khadartsev (USSR)
1991 Markharbek Khadartsev (USSR)

Mid-heavyweight (up to 100kg)
1985 Levi Khabelov (USSR)
1986 Aslan Khadartsev (USSR)
1987 Levi Khabelov (USSR)
1989 Akmhed Atanov (USSR)
1990 Levi Khabelov (USSR)
1991 Levi Khabelov (USSR)

Super-heavyweight (over 100kg)
1985 David Gobedzhishvilli (USSR)
1986 Bruce Baumgartner (US)
1987 Aslan Khadartsev (USSR)
1989 Ali Rez Soleimani (Ira)
1990 David Gobedzhishvilli (USSR)
1991 Andreas Schroder (Ger)

GRECO-ROMAN
Light-flyweight (up to 48kg)
1985 Magyatdin Allakhverdyev (USSR)
1986 Magyatdin Allakhverdyev (USSR)
1987 Magyatdin Allakhverdyev (USSR)
1989 Oleg Kucherenko (USSR)
1990 Oleg Kucherenko (USSR)
1991 Gooun Duk-Yong (SKo)

Flyweight (up to 52kg)
1985 Jan Ronningen (Nor)
1986 Sergey Dyudyayev (USSR)
1987 Pedro Roque (Cub)
1989 Alekandr Ignatenko (USSR)
1990 Alexandr Ignatenko (USSR)
1991 Raul Martinez (Cub)

Bantamweight (up to 57kg)
1985 Stojan Balov (Bul)
1986 Emil Ivanov (Bul)
1987 Patrice Mourier (Fra)
1989 Emil Ivanov (Bul)
1990 Rifat Yidiz (Ger)
1991 Rifat Yidiz (Ger)

Featherweight (up to 62kg)
1985 Zhivko Vangelov (Bul)
1986 Kamandar Madzhidov (USSR)
1987 Zhivko Vangelov (Bul)
1989 Kamandar Madzhidov (USSR)
1990 Mario Oliveras (Cub)
1991 Sergey Martynov (USSR)

Lightweight (up to 68kg)
1985 Stefan Negrisan (Rom)
1986 Levon Dzhulfalakyan (USSR)
1987 Aslautdin Abeyev (USSR)
1989 Claudio Passarelli (GDR)
1990 Islam Doguchiev (USSR)
1991 Islam Doguchiev (USSR)

Welterweight (up to 74kg)
1985 Mikhail Mamiashvili (USSR)
1986 Mikhail Mamiashvili (USSR)
1987 Jouko Salomaki (Fin)
1989 Daulet Turlykhanov (USSR)
1990 Mnazakan Iskamdarian (USSR)
1991 Mnazakan Iskamdarian (USSR)

Middleweight (up to 82kg)
1985 Bogdan Daras (Pol)
1986 no medal awarded Bogdan Daras (Pol) and Tibor
     Komaromi (Hun) disqualified
1987 Tibor Komaromi (Hun)
1989 Tibor Komaromi (Hun)
1990 Peter Farkas (Hun)
1991 Peter Farkas (Hun)

Light-heavyweight (up to 90kg)
1985 Michael Houk (US)
1986 Andrzej Malina (Pol)
1987 Vladimir Popov (USSR)
1989 Maik Bullmann (GDR)
1990 Maik Bullmann (Ger)
1991 Maik Bullmann (Ger)

Mid-heavyweight (up to 100kg)
1985 Andrej Dmitrov (Bul)
1986 Tamas Gaspar (Hun)
1987 Guram Gedekhauri (USSR)
1989 Gerhard Himmel (FRG)
1990 Sergey Demiaschkevich (USSR)
1991 Hector Milian (Cub)

Super-heavyweight (over 100kg)
1985 Igor Rostorotskiy (USSR)
1986 Tomas Johansson (Swe)
1987 Igor Rostorotskiy (USSR)
1989 Alexandr Karelin (USSR)
1990 Alexandr Karelin (USSR)
1991 Alexandr Karelin (USSR)

The British challenge for the 1992 America's Cup, to be fought off San Diego, foundered when Peter de Savary, who had scared off the other two British syndicates, said he was withdrawing through lack of sponsorship. There was concern about yachting's other major event of 1992, the Olympics, when competitors in the pre-Games regatta off Barcelona reported serious pollution: British team officials half-filled a bucket with used condoms, sanitary towels and plastic bags in minutes and International Yacht Racing Union officials complained of raw sewage in the water.

Christophe Auguin of France in Groupe Sceta won the BOC Round the World race when his compatriot and rival Alain Gautier ran into strong winds which first split his mainsail, then departed, leaving him becalmed. The one-time leader, John Martin of South Africa, had to be rescued by a fellow-competitor when his yacht sank after hitting an iceberg in the Southern Ocean. The Japanese yachtsmen Yukoh Tada, 60, made it into Sydney on the second leg despite capsizing five times. At various times, Tada was hit by his sewing machine and his saxophone; he also reported that his radio had been broken by bottles of soya bean sauce flying round the cabin.

The 40ft sloop Gypsy Moth III, which Sir Francis Chicester sailed to victory in the first single-handed transatlantic race in 1960, was found in a delapidated state in Gibraltar by two brothers from Nottinghamshire, who said they would restore her. The British maxi-class yacht Rothmans was stripped of line honours in the Sydney-Hobart race after hoisting a spinnaker with the yacht's name on it. By amazing coincidence a tobacco company has the same name.

A British crew sailing in the European Soling Championship off France forcibly repelled two Italian boarders who jumped on to their boat to protest about a collision, unaware that all the British sailors were in the Royal Engineers.

———— 1991 ————

CHAMPAGNE MUMM ADMIRAL'S CUP

Race 1: Solent Race
Aug 1

50ft: Mandrake Krizia (Ita)	John Kolius
Two-ton: Rubin XII (Ger)	Harold Cudmore
One-ton: Brava (Ita)	Francesco de Angelis

Race 2: Channel Race
Aug 3

50ft: Mandrake Krizia (Ita)	John Kolius
Two-ton: Bravura (US)	Steve Benjamin
One-ton: Port Pendennis (GB)	Lawrie Smith

Race 3: Christchurch Bay
Aug 5

50ft: Container (Ger)	Peter Lester
Two-ton: Unibank (Den)	Jens Christensen
One-ton: Vibes (US)	Geoff Stagg

Race 4: Christchurch Bay
Aug 6

50ft: Will (Jap)	Eddie Warden Owen
Two-ton: Unibank (Den)	Jens Christensen
One-ton: Vibes (US)	Geoff Stagg

Race 5: Hayling Bay
Aug 8

50ft: Corum Saphir (Fra)	Pierre Mas
Two-ton: Corum Rubis (Fra)	Philippe Delhumeau
One-ton: Brava (Ita)	Francesco de Angelis

Race 6: Fastnet Race
Aug 10

50ft: Corum Saphir (Fra)	Pierre Mas
Two-ton: Bravura (US)	Steve Benjamin
One-ton: Corum Diamant (Fra)	Xavier Phelipon

Team (Overall)
1 France 138.75pts
2 Italy 138.13pts
3 United States 134.00pts

Individual (50ft)
1 Corum Saphir (Fra) Pierre Mas 56.88pts
2 Will (Jap) Eddie Warden Owen 51.25pts
3 Mandrake Krizia (Ita) John Kolius 42.63pts

Individual (Two-ton)
1 Bravura (US) Steve Benjamin 48pts
2 Larouge (Ita) Lorenzo Bortolotti 44pts
3 Corum Rubis (Fra) Philippe Delhumeau 43.25pts

Individual (One-ton)
1 Brava (Ita) Francesco de Angelis 51.50pts
2 Port Pendennis (GB) Lawrie Smith 47.88pts
3 Vibes (US) Geoff Stagg 47pts

LAND ROVER COWES WEEK
Aug 3-11

Class 1 race winners
Queen's Cup

1 Red Stripe	Don Wood
2 HRG 5	Uli Matheson (Ger)
3 Eagle F1	T Todd

Glazebrook Cup

1 Red Stripe	Don Wood
2 HRG 5	Uli Matheson (Ger)
3 Advocate	John Taylor

Rocking Chair Trophy
1 Advocate	John Taylor
2 HRG 5	Uli Matheson (Ger)
3 Red Stripe	Don Wood

New York YC Trophy
1 HRG 5	Uli Matheson (Ger)
2 Red Stripe	Don Wood
3 Teamwork	David Head

Coronation Bowl
1 Red Stripe	Don Wood
2 Advocate	John Taylor
3 HRG 5	Uli Matheson (Ger)

Royal Corinthian YC Cup
1 Strunje 5	Wolfgang Scäfer (Ger)
2 Red Stripe	Don Wood
3 Advocate	John Taylor

Friendship Cup
1 Advocate	John Taylor
2 HRG 5	Uli Matheson (Ger)
3 10	W Beuton

Sir Walter Preston Cup
1 Strunje 5	Wolfgang Scäfer (Ger)
2 HRG 5	Uli Matheson (Ger)
3 Advocate	John Taylor

BOC CHALLENGE
(Solo Round the World race)
First home reached Newport, Rhode Island on Apr 23

1 Groupe Sceta (Fra)	Christophe Auguin
	120 days, 22 hrs, 36 mins
2 Generali Concorde (Fra)	Alain Gautier
	122 days, 12 hrs, 55 mins
3 Credit Agricole IV (Fra)	Philippe Jeantot
	129 days, 14 hrs, 49 mins

——— CHAMPIONS ———

ADMIRAL'S CUP
Team		Individual (from 1969)	
1957	Britain	1969	Red Rooster (US)
1959	Britain	1971	Ragamuffin (Aus)
1961	United States	1973	Saudale (FRG)
1963	Britain	1975	Noryenna (GB)
1965	Britain	1977	Imp (US)
1967	Australia	1979	Eclipse (GB)
1969	United States	1981	Victory (GB)
1971	Britain	1983	Diva (Fra)
1973	West Germany	1985	Phoenix (GB)
1975	Britain	1987	Propaganda (NZ)
1977	Britain	1989	Jamarella (GB)
1979	Australia	1991	Corum Saphir (Fra)
1981	Britain		
1983	West Germany		
1985	West Germany		
1987	New Zealand		
1989	Britain		
1991	France		

WHITBREAD ROUND THE WORLD RACE
	Winning Skipper/Boat
1973-74	Ramon Carlin (Mex) *Sayula II*
1977-78	Cornelius van Rietschoten (Hol) *Flyer*
1981-82	Cornelius van Rietschoten (Hol) *Flyer II*
1985-86	Pierre Fehlmann (Swi) *UBS Switzerland*
1989-90	Peter Blake (NZ) *Steinlager*

UP FOR THE CUP

❝I think the guys that made up the rule to design these boats are idiots. I think they did it for their own personal benefit and not for the benefit of the guys who have to sail them. I think these boats are incredibly dangerous and very expensive.❞
Bill Koch, America's Cup skipper, on the new class of cup yachts

"They are a fantastic boat to sail, exactly what the America's Cup is all about."
Chris Dickson, America's Cup skipper, ditto

"Life is quite simple. It's no longer the sport of individuals. Costs have escalated. You need sponsorship and, if you haven't got it, you can't do it. But I never lose my enthusiasm."
Peter de Savary, withdrawing from the 1992 cup

"Had de Savary stood aside early, or not been on stage at all, Britain would now have a viable challenge...It is important that what de Savary did - show interest in challenging, secure publicity and then not proceed - does not happen again.❞
Harold Cudmore, former America's Cup skipper

AMERICA'S CUP
	Winning boat	Winning skipper
1870	Magic (US)	Andrew Comstock
1871	Columbia (US)	Nelson Comstock
	& Sappho (US)	Sam Greenwood
1876	Madeleine (US)	Josephus Williams
1881	Mischief (US)	Nathaniel Clock
1885	Puritan (US)	Aubrey Crocker
1886	Mayflower (US)	Martin Stone
1887	Volunteer (US)	Henry Haff
1893	Vigilant (US)	William Hansen
1895	Defender (US)	Henry Haff
1899	Columbia (US)	Charlie Barr
1901	Columbia (US)	Charlie Barr
1903	Reliance (US)	Charlie Barr
1920	Resolute (US)	Charles Adams
1930	Enterprise (US)	Harold Vanderbilt
1934	Rainbow (US)	Harold Vanderbilt
1937	Ranger (US)	Harold Vanderbilt
1958	Columbia (US)	Briggs Cunningham
1962	Weatherly (US)	Emil Mosbacher Jr
1964	Constellation (US)	Bob Bavier Jr
1967	Intrepid (US)	Emil Mosbacher Jr
1970	Intrepid (US)	Bill Ficker
1974	Courageous (US)	Ted Hood
1977	Courageous (US)	Ted Turner
1980	Freedom (US)	Dennis Conner
1983	Australia II (Aus)	John Bertrand
1987	Stars & Stripes (US)	Dennis Conner
1988	Stars & Stripes (US)	Dennis Conner

——— 1992 ———

May 9 America's Cup challenge begins (San Diego, California); Sep 26 British Steel Challenge Round the World race begins (start Southampton, finish May 1993)

MISCELLANY

PANTO TIME

The following improbable people all played in professional pantomimes at Christmas 1990

Ian Botham (cricket): The King, Jack and the Beanstalk, Bradford
Frank Bruno (boxer): The Genie, Aladdin, Nottingham
Geoff Capes (athlete/strongman): The Captain, Dick Whittington, Wolverhampton
Annabel Croft (tennis): Prince Charming, Cinderella, Bristol
Liz Hobbs (water skier): Princess, Jack and the Beanstalk, Bradford
Barry McGuigan (boxer): Odd Job, Snow White, Catford
Tessa Sanderson (athlete): Girl Friday, Robinson Crusoe, Guildford

HONOURS

NEW YEAR'S HONOURS
CBE: Brian Johnston (cricket commentator); Bobby Robson (soccer); Raman Subba Row (cricket).
OBE: Fred Allen (NZ rugby union coach); Bernard Atha (chairman, British Paralympic Association); Peter Blake (yachting); Harry Carpenter (commentator); David Donovan (karate); Graham Gooch (cricket); Nigel Mansell (motor racing); Ron Presley (president, Lawn Tennis Association); Peter Shilton (soccer); Ian Wooldridge (journalist).
MBE: Sue Campbell (director, National Coaching Foundation), George Courtney (soccer referee), Philip Craven (wheelchair basketball); Pauline Edwards (archery); Margaret Johnston (bowls); Les Jones (athletics); John Lyon (amateur boxing); Yvonne Murray (athletics); Wayne Shelford (rugby union).

BIRTHDAY HONOURS
Knighthoods: Bert Millichip (chairman, Football Association); Philip Carter (former president, Football League); Professor Roland Smith (chairman, Manchester United)
CBE: Cyril Washbrook (cricket); Peter O'Sullevan (racing commentator); Ces Blazey (NZ rugby union administrator);
OBE: Brian Clough (football); Mal Reilly (rugby league); Roger Uttley (rugby union); Roy Inman (judo); John Bromley (TV sports administrator);
MBE Kriss Akabusi (athletics); Dennis Andries (boxing); Willie Miller (football); John Whitaker (show jumping);
BEM 'John Egginton (horse racing - clerk of works, United Racecourses)
Carter and Smith were knighted for their non-sporting activities; Clough's wife said his OBE really stood for Old Big 'Ead.

TELEVISION

French TV
Hours each year devoted to each sport by Antenne 2, the French state-run channel

1 Tennis	101	6 Athletics	24
2 Cycling	87	7 Ice skating	8
3 Soccer	58	8 Gymnastics	8
4 Rugby	57	9 Equestrianism	7
5 Basketball	29	10 Golf	4

Protected Events
The following events cannot be shown exclusively on pay-per-view systems in the UK according to new rules announced by the Home Secretary in the Commons on April 17:
Cricket Tests involving England; the Derby; the Grand National; the Olympic Games; the final weekend of Wimbledon; the World Cup finals; the FA Cup Final; (Scotland) the Scottish Cup Final.
The announcement removed the Commonwealth Games, the Boat Race and the first 11 days of Wimbledon from the list.

BETTING

The top 10 non-racing money-spinners at Britain's leading bookmakers

	HILLS	LADBROKES
1	FA Cup	FA Cup
2	Open golf	Open golf
3	Wimbledon	World snooker
4	World snooker	Wimbledon
5	US Masters golf	US Masters golf
6	Ryder Cup	US Open golf
7	World matchplay	Five Nations rugby
8	US Open golf	Ryder Cup
9	Five Nations rugby	British Masters golf
10	US PGA golf	British PGA golf

The chart ignores General Elections and Olympics, not held in the past two years, and irregular events like world title fights

Source: *Racing Post*

WEALTH

WORLD
The Forbes Magazine list of the highest earners in world sport 1991. Figures are in $US million. Last year's position in brackets

		Prize money/Salary	Ancillary	Total
1 (10)	Evander Holyfield	60	5	60.5
2 (1)	Mike Tyson	30	1.5	31.5
3 (8)	Michael Jordan	2.8	13.2	16.0
4 (-)	George Foreman	14	.5	14.5
5 (4)	Ayrton Senna	12	1.0	13.0
6 (5)	Alain Prost	10	1.0	11.0
7 (-)	Razor Ruddock	10	.2	10.2
8 (9)	Arnold Palmer	0.3	9.0	9.3
9 (12)	Nigel Mansell	8.0	1.0	9.0
10 (6)	Jack Nicklaus	0.5	8.0	8.5

The figure for Jordan, the Chicago Bulls basketball star, includes the money he earns advertising Nike, Coca-Cola, McDonald's and Wheaties plus an estimated $2.5m from his videos.
The boxers Buster Douglas and Sugar Ray Leonard, second and third on the 1990 list, are now out of the top 40. Greg Norman, ninth, has dropped to 15th behind Larry Bird, Monica Seles, Joe Montana and Stefan Edberg. Apart from Mansell, Nick Faldo (25th) was the only Briton in the top 40.

Source: Peter Newcomb, *Forbes Magazine*

BRITAIN

The highest earners in British Sport 1990:
Figures are £1,000

	Prize money /Salary	Ancillary	Total
1 Nigel Mansell	4,860	540	5,364
2 Nick Faldo	490	3,000	3,490
3 Ian Woosnam	818	1,200	2,018
4 Pat Eddery	1,039	300	1,339
5 Stephen Hendry	644	650	1,294
6 Willie Carson	997	150	1,147
7 Steve Cauthen	753	150	903
8 Steve Davis	355	500	855
9 Nigel Benn	555	100	655
10 Gary Lineker	414	230	644

Source: John Hopkins, *Financial Times*

AUSTRALIA

Figures are £1,000
The highest earners in Australian sport, 1990:

1 Greg Norman (Golf)	6,000
2 Wayne Gardner (Motor cycling)	1,240
3 Jan Stephenson (Golf)	732
4 Rodger Davis (Golf)	680
5 Ian Baker-Finch (Golf)	640
6 Wayne Grady (Golf)	632
7 Graham Marsh (Golf)	628
8 Michael Doohan (Motor cycling)	600
9 Geoff Brabham (Motor racing)	496
10 Brian Jones (Golf)	460

Allan Border was ranked 28th with an estimated £182,000
Source: Gerard Wright, *Sunday Age*, Melbourne

BOOKS

BEST SELLERS
Best selling books at Sportspages Bookshop, London, Oct 1990 - Sep 1991

1 BOOKABLE OFFENCE - THE WHEN SATURDAY COMES SPECIAL No.2 (When Saturday Comes) £5.95
2 ALL PLAYED OUT - THE FULL STORY OF ITALIA '90 Pete Davies (Heinemann/Mandarin) £14.99/£4.99
3 OFFICIAL F.A. NON-LEAGUE CLUB DIRECTORY Edited by Tony Williams (Daily Mail/Tony Williams) £9.90
4 ROTHMANS FOOTBALL YEARBOOK Edited by Jack Rollin (Queen Anne Press) £17.95/£14.95
5 SPORTSPAGES ALMANAC Matthew Engel & Ian Morrison (Sportspages/Simon & Schuster) £8.95
6 PLAYFAIR CRICKET ANNUAL Edited by Bill Frindall (Queen Anne Press) £2.50
7 GET YOUR WRITS OUT! Edited by Martin Lacey (Juma) £6.95
8 PHYSICAL EDUCATION AND THE STUDY OF SPORT R.J. Davis et al (Wolfe) £14.95
9 THE STORY OF CHARLTON ATHLETIC 1905-1990 Richard Redden (Breedon Books) £16.95
10 A ROUGH RIDE - AN INSIGHT INTO PRO CYCLING Paul Kimmage (Stanley Paul) £12.95/£6.99
11 HAMPDEN BABYLON - SEX AND SCANDAL IN SCOTTISH FOOTBALL Stuart Cosgrove (Canongate) £9.95
12 WISDEN CRICKETERS' ALMANACK Edited by Graeme Wright (John Wisden) £20.00/£16.75
13 THE OFFICIAL RECORD AND FACT BOOK (Partridge Press) £9.99
14 THE GOLF SWING David Leadbetter (Collins Willow) £14.99

15 JACK DOYLE - FIGHTING FOR LOVE Michael Taub (Stanley Paul) £16.99/£7.99

WILLIAM HILL SPORTS BOOK OF THE YEAR AWARD
Winner: A ROUGH RIDE - THE INSIGHT INTO PRO CYCLING Paul Kimmage (Stanley Paul)

The other five books on the short list were:
BASINGSTOKE BOY John Arlott (Harper Collins)
MAIDEN Tracy Edwards and Tim Madge (Simon & Schuster)
SATURDAY'S BOYS Harry Lansdown and Alex Spillius (Harper Collins)
JACK DOYLE - FIGHTING FOR LOVE Michael Taub (Stanley Paul)
RANJI - A GENIUS RICH AND STRANGE Simon Wilde (Heinemann Kingswood)

AWARDS

SPORTS PERSONALITIES
(since 1981)

BRITAIN	*BBC Sports Personality*
1981	Ian Botham
1982	Daley Thompson
1983	Steve Cram
1984	Jayne Torvill & Christopher Dean
1985	Barry McGuigan
1986	Nigel Mansell
1987	Fatima Whitbread
1988	Steve Davis
1989	Nick Faldo
1990	Paul Gascoigne

US	*Sports Illustrated Sportsman of the Year*
1981	Sugar Ray Leonard
1982	Wayne Gretzky
1983	Mary Decker
1984	Mary Lou Retton & Ed Moses
1985	Kareem Abdul-Jabbar
1986	Joe Paterno
1987	*Athletes Who Care*
1988	Orel Hershiser
1989	Greg LeMond
1990	Joe Montana

OBITUARY

Sir Carl AARVOLD, 83, March 17. England rugby centre and captain between 1928 and 1934. Later president of the Lawn Tennis Association and steward of the British Boxing Board of Control. Recorder of London (senior judge at the Old Bailey) 1964-75.

Luke APPLING, 83, January 3. Baseball Hall of Fame player who spent 20 years with the Chicago White Sox and became American League batting champion twice. He hit a home run in an old timers' game aged 75 and retired as a minor league hitting instructor with the Atlanta Braves only two days before he died.

Dame Peggy ASHCROFT, 83, June 14. Actress and cricket fan whose proudest achievements included opening the batting with Cyril Washbrook and scoring 16 (bowled by Len Hutton) in a special game at Stratford in 1963 to celebrate the Wars of the Roses saga. She is said to have kept the RSC cast informed of the Test scores by a small radio in Margaret of Anjou's helmet.

Colin ATKINSON, 59, June 26, after a long illness. Former Somerset captain and headmaster of Millfield.

Pete AXTHELM, 47, February 2, of liver failure. US sports journalist and biographer of Steve Cauthen.

Sammy BALL, 92, June. British scientist who during his 46 years with the Dunlop company became the first man to apply scientific principles to golf-ball manufacture. He discovered that the perfect ball had 332 dimples each .013 of an inch deep and in 1934 evolved the Dunlop 65 ball with Henry Cotton.

Laz BARRERA, 66, April 25. Cuban-born US racehorse trainer who saddled Affirmed to win the 1978 Triple Crown. Leading money-winner five times and winner of the Eclipse Award as outstanding trainer for four successive years, 1976-79.

Jack "Kid" BERG, 81, April 22. Former British lightweight champion who graduated from the Jewish community of the East End ("the Whitechapel Whirlwind") to win 157 out of 192 fights, including the world junior welterweight title (then not recognised in Britain) and defending it nine times in the US in little more than a year.

Brian BEVAN, 66, June 3. Australian-born rugby league winger who scored 796 tries between 1945 and 1964, easily the record - 740 of them in 620 games for Warrington before he ended his career with Blackpool. "Your heart missed a beat whenever he got the ball... bald, no teeth, coughing and spluttering but when he was on the field he was magnificent." - Colin Welland.

P.J. BOATWRIGHT, 63, April 5. Executive director of the US Golf Association 1969-81 and the game's leading expert on the rules.

Harry BRADSHAW, 77, December 1990. Irish golfer who lost the play-off with Bobby Locke at the 1949 Open Championship at Sandwich. He was ahead in the tournament until he hit the ball only a few yards out of the neck of a broken beer bottle.

Freddie BROWN, 80, July 24. Bluff, gruff cricketing all-rounder and captain of Northamptonshire and England whose no-nonsense leadership took England to their first post-war Test win over Australia (Melbourne 1950-51) and turned the weakest county in the Championship into one of the strongest.

Paul BROWN, 82, July 31. Pioneering American football coach: inventor of the playbook and the first man to put a radio transmitter in his quarterback's helmet. He founded the Cleveland Browns (named after him) and coached them to seven Championships before he lost control and started the Cincinnati Bengals instead.

Harold BUTLER, 78, July. Nottinghamshire and England (two Tests in 1947) fast bowler. 919 first-class wickets between 1933 and 1954.

Enrico CAMICI, 78, March 17. Italy's greatest jockey. The rider of 4,801 winners including the double Prix de l'Arc de Triomphe champion Ribot.

Ted CATLIN, 80, November 29 1990. Sheffield Wednesday left-back who played five times for England in 1936-37.

A.B. "Happy" CHANDLER, 92, June 15. Kentucky politician and commissioner of baseball (1945-51) who paved the way for black players to be allowed into the major leagues.

Harold CONRAD, 80, May 18. Journalist, boxing publicist and promoter and all-round American character.

Bill CRAIG, 82, March. Pre-war racing driver who set the lap record, 120 mph, at Brooklands in 1933. Inventor of farming and radar equipment.

Jack CRAWFORD, 83, September 10. Australian tennis player who won a thrilling Wimbledon final in 1933 against Ellsworth Vines and was prevented from winning the Grand Slam only because of a shock defeat by Fred Perry in the US Open final. In a crisis, Crawford would roll up the long sleeves of his cricket shirt; during a long match he would ask for a pot of tea on a tray to drink during changeovers.

John CURRIE, 58, December 8 1990. Bristol, Harlequins and England rugby forward who won 25 caps during England's successful years between 1956 and 1962, usually with David Marques as his second-row partner.

Fred DALY, 79, November 18 1990. The only Irish golfer to win the Open Championship, in 1947 - he finished in the top four of the Open five times in seven years. A Ryder Cup player four times. "Fred was a great ambassador for the game and brought a touch of lightness into it." - Peter Alliss.

Joe DEY, 83, March 4. Executive director US Golf Association 1934-68 and commissioner of the touring division 1969-74. Second American to be named captain of the R & A, in 1975.

Tony DICKINSON, 75, June 25. Northern racehorse trainer and founder of a dynasty which monopolised National Hunt racing for several years in the 70s and 80s.

David EAST, 53, November 1990. Lightweight jockey of the 1960s who rode 94 winners, including several in big handicaps. He weighed under seven stone.

Dorothy ELLIS, 93, January. English bowls administrator. President of the Women's International Bowling Board 1977-81.

Eric EVANS, 69, January 12. Rugby forward for Sale, Lancashire and England (30 caps). He captained England 13 times in the late 50s, led the team to its 1957 Grand Slam and later became a selector.

Margaret EYRE, 99, February 28. Britain's first woman professional tennis coach; England hockey international.

Robin FRIDAY, 38, December 31 1990. Footballer who scored 52 goals in 142 games for Reading and Cardiff in the 1970s.

Keith GEDDES, 72, March 30. Scottish rugby full-back (four caps in 1947) and captain against France when he told the referee, who had ruled against a French try, that the touchdown was fair. The French players presented Geddes with a cigarette case for his sportsmanship. Officials said it would be a breach of amateur rules to accept it.

Les GORE, 77, January 23. Manager of Leyton Orient in six spells - five of them as caretaker - between 1956 and 1966. Chief scout for Charlton.

Harold "Red" GRANGE, 87, January 28. The "Galloping Ghost" who became America's best-known footballer for his achievements as a running back with the University of Illinois in the early 20s and helped popularise the then supposedly murky world of professional football when he signed for the Chicago Bears. Elected to the all-time all-America team in 1950 with the largest number of votes.

> "A streak of fire, a breath of flame,
> Eluding all who reach and clutch.
> A grey ghost thrown into the game
> That rival hands may rarely touch" - Grantland Rice

"Three or four men and a horse rolled into one." - Damon Runyon

John GUISE, 87, June 29. Schoolmaster and cricketer who scored 278 for Winchester against Eton in 1921, a record in public schools cricket. Winchester lost.

Commander Reginald "Wally" HAMMOND, 81, January. Captain of the Royal Navy's cricket, rugby and squash teams and regarded as perhaps the greatest of all Naval sportsmen. Suffered severely from seasickness.

Judge Rowe HARDING, 88, February 10. The oldest Welsh rugby international: 17 caps between 1923 and 1928, four of them as captain.

Sir Cyril HAWKER, 90, February 22. Banker. President of MCC 1970-71.

Howard HEAD, 76, March. American entrepreneur who founded the Head Ski Company in 1948 with $6,000 won at poker and transformed the sport with his lightweight skis. Later took up tennis and introduced the wider, longer racquet pioneered by Pam Shriver.

Viktor HENDRIKSON, 52, April 12, in a helicopter crash. Executive director of the Soviet challenge for the America's Cup.

Arturo HERNANDEZ, 82, November 20 1990. Boxing manager who had charge of 12 Mexican world champions.

Harold HOBBIS, 78, May. Charlton and England (two caps) left-wing of the 1930s. Scored 78 goals in 248 games for Charlton.

Martin HODGSON, 82, July. Former Swinton and Great Britain rugby league forward who holds the record for the longest-ever goal kick: 77 ¼ yards. Last survivor of the Swinton side that won every trophy in 1927-28.

Ken IRVINE, 50, December 1990, of leukaemia. Australian rugby league player - 31 Tests, 33 tries, between 1959 and 1967. One of the fastest wings ever to play the game.

Ryan JARVIS, 77, June 25. Member of one of Newmarket's foremost racing families and a trainer (except for the war) from 1936 until 1980.

Cliff JONES, 76, Welsh rugby fly-half and administrator who made his debut against England as a 19-year-old undergraduate. Injury restricted him to only 13 caps but he acquired a reputation as a great attacking player, became captain in 1938 and chairman of the selectors in the 70s when he was a major influence behind Wales's success.

Peter KANE, 73, July 23. Boxer from Golborne, near Wigan who was world flyweight champion 1938-43 even though he never held the British title. Came back to win the European bantamweight title in 1947 but finally retired in 1948.

Abel KIVIAT, 99, August 24. Former 1,500 metres world record holder (3:55.8) and silver medallist at the 1912 Olympics, when he lost the gold in the final strides to Arnold Jackson of Britain. He ran with the Olympic torch for a kilometre in 1984 when he was 91. Asked about training methods, he said: "They run more in a week today than I did in a year."

Cyril KNOWLES, 47, August 31, after a long illness. Tottenham full-back (401 appearances between 1964 and 1975) who won four England caps and became especially famous as the Cyril of the supporters' song "Nice one, Cyril", which reached no. 14 in the charts in 1973. Subsequently manager of Darlington, Torquay and Hartlepool, who fired him in March when he was already very ill, two months before the club won promotion.

Joe LISTER, 60, January 28. Secretary of Yorkshire County Cricket Club since 1971.

Tommy LOWREY, 79, January 22. Rider of Airborne, winner of the 1946 Derby.

Les McDOWALL, 79, August 19. Member of the Manchester City cup final teams of 1955 and 1956 and later the manager.

Keith MACKENZIE, 69, October 1990, secretary of the Royal and Ancient Golf Club 1966-83 and begetter of the modern Open. "Tennis had boycotts and ballyhoo, thankfully golf had Keith MacKenzie" - *The Guardian*.

Alice MARBLE, 77, December 13 1990. Four-time US tennis champion and winner of Wimbledon in 1939. Female pioneer of the serve-and-volley game. Also a socialite, nightclub singer and US wartime spy.

Farnham "Freddie" MAXWELL, 85, June 2. Racehorse trainer who saddled the winners of three Ascot Gold Cups in the 1960s.

John MAXWELL-HYSLOP, 91, December 10 1990. England's oldest surviving rugby international (three caps in 1922). Sussex prep school head for 40 years.

RJO (Jack) MEYER, 85, March 9. All-round sportsman, educationalist and eccentric who captained Somerset at cricket and founded the sporting forcing-house of Millfield School. He was a triple Cambridge blue (golf, rackets and cricket); he was equally enthusiastic about roulette but less successful, which led to his departure from the school in 1971. He reputedly bowled in his socks at Lord's. "He made my life, it's as simple as that." - Gareth Edwards

George MIDDLETON, 86, December 1990. Manager of the British middleweight Randolph Turpin, who beat Sugar Ray Robinson to win the world championship in 1951.

Stewart MORRIS, 81, February 4. Yachtsman who won Olympic gold for Britain in the Swallow Class at Torquay in 1948. Winner of the Prince of Wales Cup for International 14 class dinghies a record 12 times, the first in 1932, the last in 1965.

Stan MORTENSEN, 69, May 22. Blackpool and England goalscoring star of the post-war years (197 goals in 320 games for Blackpool, 23 in 25 for England including four on his debut against Portugal in 1947). The only player to score a hat-trick in an FA Cup final at Wembley, in the game always known as the Matthews final, after his playing partner for club and country who overshadowed him. "If Stanley Matthews was the magician, then Mortensen was the magician's fire" - David Lacey, *The Guardian*.

Rudi NIERLICH, 25, May, in a car accident. Austrian skier who won three World Championship gold medals.

Colin PAGE, 60, December 14 1990, in a car crash. Kent cricketer and administrator for more than 40 years.

John PASSMORE, 80, September. South African philanthropist and paternalist who worked tirelessly and almost alone over two decades to bring cricket to black children in the Cape.

Jack PETERSEN, 79, November 1990. British and Empire heavyweight champion ("the Henry Cooper of the 1930s") and favourite son of Wales. Later the first former professional to become president of the British Boxing Board of Control and inter-round summariser for BBC radio.

Ron PICKERING, 60, February 13. Athletics coach (notably to the 1964 Olympic long jump champion Lynn Davies), BBC commentator and crusader for fair play in sport on everything from apartheid to drugs.

Bill PONSFORD, 90, April 6. Australian batsman. The only man to reach 400 twice (429 and 437) and the holder of stacks of other batting records including a partnership of 451 with Don Bradman, a world Test record from 1934 until two months before his death. "He was enormously gifted, incredibly undemonstrative and generally as quiet as the proverbial mouse. He was my mate and I am proud of him." - Bill O'Reilly.

Peter POSTON, 77, June. Newmarket racehorse trainer best known for running his horses in Scotland to make use of the travel allowance formerly paid to trainers.

Marie PROVAZNIK, 100, January 11. Director of the Czechoslovak gymnastics team at the 1948 Olympics who then defected to the US.

Idwal REES, 81, August 31. Welsh rugby international. Centre and wing of the 1930s who won 14 caps and played a vital role in the win over the All Blacks in 1935. Later headmaster of Cowbridge Grammar School for 33 years.

Johnny REVOLTA, 79, March 4. US golfer. Winner of the 1935 PGA Championship.

Sir Alec ROSE, 82, January 12. Portsmouth greengrocer who sailed alone round the world in Lively Lady in 1967-68.

Eric SMITH, 67, August. Rugby union player and administrator who was involved with Orrell for 40 years and was largely responsible for guiding the club from junior rugby into the game's top echelon.

Frank SOO, 76, February. Chinese-extraction footballer who played with Matthews at Stoke and won eight wartime caps for England. Later manager of Scunthorpe.

Lt-Col Douglas STEWART, DSO, MC and Bar, 78, July 25. Heroic Army officer (Royal Scots Greys) and horse rider. Member of the show jumping team with Harry Llewellyn and Wilf White that won Britain's only gold of the 1952 Olympics.

Peter TAYLOR, 62, October 4 1990, Brian Clough's assistant manager, right-hand man and resident moderate for many years at Hartlepool, Derby, Brighton and Nottingham Forest until they fell out. Manager in his own right at Brighton and Derby.

Forrest "Spec" TOWNS, 77, April 9. US athlete. Gold medallist in the 110 metres hurdles at the 1936 Olympics. Two weeks later he set a world record in the event (13.7) that stood for 14 years.

Sir Ian TRETHOWAN, 68, December 12 1990. Former director-general of the BBC and chairman of the Horserace Betting Levy Board since 1982.

Bill TUCKER, 87, August. Blackheath and England rugby player (three caps) and pioneering orthopaedic surgeon famous for his treatment of sporting injuries, particularly Denis Compton's knee, the most famous joint in Britain in the late 40s and early 50s.

James VAN ALEN, 88, July 3. Founder of the International Tennis Hall of Fame in Newport, Rhode Island, and inventor (1958) of the tie-break, first used at the US Open in 1970.

Dino VIOLA, 75, January 19. Controversial Italian politician and president of Roma Football Club.

Fulke WALWYN, 80, February 18. Master National Hunt trainer who turned out the winners of 2,170 races including seven Whitbreads, four Gold Cups, two Champion Hurdles and the 1964 Grand National (Team Spirit). "Deep, instinctive sympathy with horses was this great genius's most precious, invisible talent" - John Oaksey

Fred WASHINGTON, 23, December 21 1990, in a car crash. Chicago Bears defensive tackle.

Michael WESTPHAL, 26, June, after two years of illness. West German Davis Cup player.

Alan WIGGINS, 32, January 6, of tuberculosis. Major league baseball player of great promise with San Diego and Baltimore who underwent drug rehabilitation three times and was then banned indefinitely in 1987.

Lew WORSHAM, 73, October 19 1990. US Open golf champion, 1947.

David WORTHY, 37, July 3, after a car crash while covering the Milk Race. Cycling photographer.

Kingsley WRIGHT, 75, September 30 1990. Sports editor of the *Daily Telegraph* 1961-79.

Jim WYNNE, 67, December 21 1990. First world offshore powerboat racing champion and inventor of the outdrive transmission system which revolutionised the sport.

Istvan ZSOLT, 70, May 8. Hungarian referee at three World Cups, four Olympics and more than 3,000 games in all.